T0181737

Lecture Notes in Computer Science 13791

More information about this series at https://link.springer.com/bookseries/558

Shweta Agrawal · Dongdai Lin (Eds.)

Advances in Cryptology – ASIACRYPT 2022

28th International Conference on the Theory
and Application of Cryptology and Information Security
Taipei, Taiwan, December 5–9, 2022
Proceedings, Part I

 Springer

Editors
Shweta Agrawal
Indian Institute of Technology Madras
Chennai, India

Dongdai Lin
Chinese Academy of Sciences
Beijing, China

ISSN 0302-9743   ISSN 1611-3349 (electronic)
Lecture Notes in Computer Science
ISBN 978-3-031-22962-6   ISBN 978-3-031-22963-3 (eBook)
https://doi.org/10.1007/978-3-031-22963-3

This Springer imprint is published by the registered company Springer Nature Switzerland AG
The registered company address is: Gewerbestrasse 11, 6330 Cham, Switzerland

Preface

The 28th Annual International Conference on Theory and Application of Cryptology and Information Security (ASIACRYPT 2022) was held in Taiwan during December 5–9, 2022.

The conference covered all technical aspects of cryptology, and was sponsored by the International Association for Cryptologic Research (IACR).

We received a total of 364 submissions from all over the world, and the Program Committee (PC) selected 98 papers for publication in the proceedings of the conference. The two program chairs were supported by a PC consisting of 79 leading experts in aspects of cryptology. Each submission was reviewed by at least three PC members (or their sub-reviewers). The strong conflict of interest rules imposed by IACR ensure that papers are not handled by PC members with a close working relationship with the authors. The two program chairs were not allowed to submit a paper, and PC members were limited to two submissions each. There were approximately 331 external reviewers, whose input was critical to the selection of papers.

The review process was conducted using double-blind peer review. The conference operated a two-round review system with a rebuttal phase. After the reviews and first-round discussions the PC selected 224 submissions to proceed to the second round and the authors were then invited to participate in an interactive rebuttal phase with the reviewers to clarify questions and concerns. The second round involved extensive discussions by the PC members.

Alongside the presentations of the accepted papers, the program of ASIACRYPT 2022 featured two invited talks by Jian Guo and Damien Stehlé. The conference also featured a rump session which contained short presentations on the latest research results of the field.

The four volumes of the conference proceedings contain the revised versions of the 98 papers that were selected. The final revised versions of papers were not reviewed again and the authors are responsible for their contents.

Using a voting-based process that took into account conflicts of interest, the PC selected the three top papers of the conference: "Full Quantum Equivalence of Group Action DLog and CDH, and More" by Hart Montgomery and Mark Zhandry, "Cryptographic Primitives with Hinting Property" by Navid Alamati and Sikhar Patranabis, and "SwiftEC: Shallue–van de Woestijne Indifferentiable Function to Elliptic Curves" by Jorge Chavez-Saab, Francisco Rodriguez-Henriquez, and Mehdi Tibouchi. The authors of all three papers were invited to submit extended versions of their manuscripts to the Journal of Cryptology.

Many people have contributed to the success of ASIACRYPT 2022. We would like to thank the authors for submitting their research results to the conference. We are very grateful to the PC members and external reviewers for contributing their knowledge and expertise, and for the tremendous amount of work that was done with reading papers and contributing to the discussions. We are greatly indebted to Kai-Min Chung and Bo-Yin Yang, the General Chairs, for their efforts and overall organization. We thank

Bart Preneel, Ron Steinfeld, Mehdi Tibouchi, Jian Guo, and Huaxiong Wang for their valuable suggestions and help. We are extremely grateful to Shuaishuai Li for checking all the LaTeX files and for assembling the files for submission to Springer. We also thank the team at Springer for handling the publication of these conference proceedings.

December 2022   Shweta Agrawal
                                                                          Dongdai Lin

Organization

General Chairs

Kai-Min Chung   Academia Sinica, Taiwan
Bo-Yin Yang   Academia Sinica, Taiwan

Program Committee Chairs

Shweta Agrawal   Indian Institute of Technology, Madras, India
Dongdai Lin   Institute of Information Engineering, Chinese
                                      Academy of Sciences, China

Program Committee

Divesh Aggarwal	National University of Singapore, Singapore
Adi Akavia	University of Haifa, Israel
Martin Albrecht	Royal Holloway, University of London, UK
Ghada Almashaqbeh	University of Connecticut, USA
Benny Applebaum	Tel Aviv University, Israel
Lejla Batina	Radboud University, Netherlands
Carsten Baum	Aarhus University, Denmark
Sonia Belaïd	CryptoExperts, France
Mihir Bellare	University of California, San Diego, USA
Andrej Bogdanov	Chinese University of Hong Kong, China
Christina Boura	Université de Versailles, France
Ran Canetti	Boston University, USA
Jie Chen	East China Normal University, China
Yilei Chen	Tsinghua University, China
Jung Hee Cheon	Seoul National University, South Korea
Ilaria Chillotti	Zama, France
Michele Ciampi	The University of Edinburgh, UK
Craig Costello	Microsoft Research, USA
Itai Dinur	Ben-Gurion University, Israel
Nico Döttling	Helmholtz Center for Information Security (CISPA), Germany
Maria Eichlseder	Graz University of Technology, Austria
Saba Eskandarian	University of North Carolina at Chapel Hill, USA
Marc Fischlin	TU Darmstadt, Germany

Yu Sasaki	NTT Corporation, Japan
Tobias Schneider	NXP Semiconductors, Austria
Dominique Schröder	Friedrich-Alexander-Universität Erlangen-Nürnberg, Germany
abhi shelat	Northeastern University, USA
Mark Simkin	Ethereum Foundation, USA
Ling Song	Jinan University, Guangzhou, China
Fang Song	Portland State University, USA
Pratik Soni	Carnegie Mellon University, USA
Akshayaram Srinivasan	Tata Institute of Fundamental Research, India
Damien Stehlé	ENS de Lyon, France
Ron Steinfeld	Monash University, Australia
Qiang Tang	University of Sydney, Australia
Yiannis Tselekounis	Carnegie Mellon University, USA
Meiqin Wang	Shandong University, China
Xiaoyun Wang	Tsinghua University, China
David Wu	University of Texas at Austin, USA
Wenling Wu	Institute of Software, Chinese Academy of Sciences, China
Shota Yamada	AIST, Japan
Takashi Yamakawa	NTT Corporation, Japan
Jiang Zhang	State Key Laboratory of Cryptology, China

Additional Reviewers

Behzad Abdolmaleki
Calvin Abou Haidar
Damiano Abram
Bar Alon
Pedro Alves
Ravi Anand
Anurag Anshu
Victor Arribas
Thomas Attema
Christian Badertscher
Anubhab Baksi
Zhenzhen Bao
James Bartusek
Christof Beierle
Ritam Bhaumik
Alexander Bienstock
Olivier Blazy
Alex Block
Maxime Bombar

Charlotte Bonte
Carl Bootland
Katharina Boudgoust
Lennart Braun
Marek Broll
Chris Brzuska
BinBin Cai
Matteo Campanelli
Federico Canale
Avik Chakraborti
Suvradip Chakraborty
John Chan
Rohit Chatterjee
Long Chen
Yu Long Chen
Hongyin Chen
Shan Chen
Shiyao Chen
Rongmao Chen

Nai-Hui Chia
Arka Rai Choudhuri
Jiali Choy
Qiaohan Chu
Hien Chu
Eldon Chung
Sandro Coretti-Drayton
Arjan Cornelissen
Maria Corte-Real Santos
Anamaria Costache
Alain Couvreur
Nan Cui
Benjamin R. Curtis
Jan-Pieter D'Anvers
Joan Daemen
Wangchen Dai
Hannah Davis
Luca De Feo
Gabrielle De Micheli

Thomas Debris-Alazard
Amit Deo
Patrick Derbez
Julien Devevey
Siemen Dhooghe
Benjamin Dowling
Leo Ducas
Yen Ling Ee
Jonathan Eriksen
Daniel Escudero
Muhammed F. Esgin
Thomas Espitau
Andre Esser
Hulya Evkan
Jaiden Fairoze
Joël Felderhoff
Hanwen Feng
Joe Fitzsimons
Antonio Flórez-Gutiérrez
Pouyan Forghani
Cody Freitag
Georg Fuchsbauer
Pierre Galissant
Tommaso Gagliardoni
Daniel Gardham
Pierrick Gaudry
Romain Gay
Chunpeng Ge
Rosario Gennaro
Paul Gerhart
Satrajit Ghosh
Ashrujit Ghoshal
Niv Gilboa
Aarushi Goel
Aron Gohr
Jesse Goodman
Mike Graf
Milos Grujic
Aurore Guillevic
Aldo Gunsing
Chun Guo
Hosein Hadipour
Mathias Hall-Andersen
Shuai Han
Helena Handschuh

Lucjan Hanzlik
Yonglin Hao
Keisuke Hara
Patrick Harasser
Jingnan He
Rachelle Heim-Boissier
Minki Hhan
Shoichi Hirose
Seungwan Hong
Akinori Hosoyamada
James Hsin-Yu Chiang
Zhicong Huang
Senyang Huang
Chloé Hébant
Ilia Iliashenko
Laurent Imbert
Joseph Jaeger
Palak Jain
Ashwin Jha
Mingming Jiang
Zhengzhong Jin
Antoine Joux
Eliran Kachlon
Bhavana Kanukurthi
Alexander Karenin
Shuichi Katsumata
Mojtaba Khalili
Hamidreza Khorasgani
Dongwoo Kim
Duhyeong Kim
Young-Sik Kim
Fuyuki Kitagawa
Kamil Kluczniak
Yashvanth Kondi
Rajendra Kumar
Noboru Kunihiro
Fukang Liu
Russell W. F. Lai
Jason LeGrow
Jooyoung Lee
Hyung Tae Lee
Byeonghak Lee
Charlotte Lefevre
Zeyong Li
Yiming Li

Hanjun Li
Shun Li
Xingjian Li
Xiao Liang
Benoît Libert
Damien Ligier
Chao Lin
Chengjun Lin
Yunhao Ling
Eik List
Jiahui Liu
Feng-Hao Liu
Guozhen Liu
Xiangyu Liu
Meicheng Liu
Alex Lombardi
Patrick Longa
Wen-jie Lu
Yuan Lu
Donghang Lu
You Lyu
Reinhard Lüftenegger
Bernardo Magri
Monosij Maitra
Mary Maller
Lenka Mareková
Mark Marson
Takahiro Matsuda
Alireza Mehrdad
Simon-Philipp Merz
Pierre Meyer
Michael Meyer
Peihan Miao
Tarik Moataz
Hart Montgomery
Tomoyuki Morimae
Fabrice Mouhartem
Tamer Mour
Marta Mularczyk
Michael Naehrig
Marcel Nageler
Yusuke Naito
Mridul Nandi
Patrick Neumann
Ruth Ng

Ky Nguyen
Khoa Nguyen
Ngoc Khanh Nguyen
Jianting Ning
Oded Nir
Ryo Nishimaki
Olga Nissenbaum
Semyon Novoselov
Julian Nowakowski
Tabitha Ogilvie
Eran Omri
Hiroshi Onuki
Jean-Baptiste Orfila
Mahak Pancholi
Omer Paneth
Lorenz Panny
Roberto Parisella
Jeongeun Park
Rutvik Patel
Sikhar Patranabis
Alice Pellet-Mary
Hilder Vitor Lima Pereira
Ludovic Perret
Thomas Peyrin
Phuong Pham
Guru Vamsi Policharla
Sihang Pu
Luowen Qian
Chen Qian
Kexin Qiao
Willy Quach
Rahul Rachuri
Srinivasan Raghuraman
Adrian Ranea
Shahram Rasoolzadeh
Christian Rechberger
Krijn Reijnders
Maxime Remaud
Ling Ren
Mahshid Riahinia
Peter Rindal
Mike Rosulek
Adeline Roux-Langlois
Paul Rösler

Yusuke Sakai
Kosei Sakamoto
Amin Sakzad
Simona Samardjiska
Olga Sanina
Roozbeh Sarenche
Santanu Sarker
Tobias Schmalz
Markus Schofnegger
Jacob Schuldt
Sruthi Sekar
Nicolas Sendrier
Akash Shah
Yaobin Shen
Yixin Shen
Yu Shen
Danping Shi
Rentaro Shiba
Kazumasa Shinagawa
Omri Shmueli
Ferdinand Sibleyras
Janno Siim
Siang Meng Sim
Luisa Siniscalchi
Yongsoo Song
Douglas Stebila
Lukas Stennes
Igors Stepanovs
Christoph Striecks
Ling Sun
Siwei Sun
Bing Sun
Shi-Feng Sun
Akira Takahashi
Abdul Rahman Taleb
Chik How Tan
Adrian Thillard
Sri Aravinda Krishnan
    Thyagarajan
Yan Bo Ti
Elmar Tischhauser
Yosuke Todo
Junichi Tomida
Ni Trieu

Monika Trimoska
Yi Tu
Aleksei Udovenko
Rei Ueno
Mayank Varia
Daniele Venturi
Riad Wahby
Roman Walch
Mingyuan Wang
Haoyang Wang
Luping Wang
Xiao Wang
Yuejun Wang
Yuyu Wang
Weiqiang Wen
Chenkai Weng
Benjamin Wesolowski
Yusai Wu
Yu Xia
Zhiye Xie
Shengmin Xu
Guangwu Xu
Sophia Yakoubov
Hailun Yan
Rupeng Yang
Kang Yang
Qianqian Yang
Shao-Jun Yang
Li Yao
Hui Hui Yap
Kan Yasuda
Weijing You
Thomas Zacharias
Yupeng Zhang
Kai Zhang
Lei Zhang
Yunlei Zhao
Yu Zhou
Chenzhi Zhu
Paul Zimmermann
Lukas Zobernig
matthieu rambaud
Hendrik Waldner
Yafei Zheng

Sponsoring Institutions

- Platinum Sponsor: ZAMA
- Gold Sponsor: BTQ, Hackers in Taiwan, Technology Innovation Institute
- Silver Sponsor: Meta (Facebook), Casper Networks, PQShield, NTT Research, WiSECURE
- Bronze Sponsor: Mitsubishi Electric, Algorand Foundation, LatticeX Foundation, Intel, QSancus, IOG (Input/Output Global), IBM

Contents – Part I

Multiparty Computation

Real World Protocols

Blockchains and Cryptocurrencies

Award Papers

Full Quantum Equivalence of Group Action DLog and CDH, and More

Hart Montgomery[1]([⊠])[iD] and Mark Zhandry[2][iD]

[1] Linux Foundation, San Francisco, USA
hart.montgomery@gmail.com
[2] NTT Research and Princeton University, Princeton, USA

Abstract. Cryptographic group actions are a relaxation of standard cryptographic groups that have less structure. This lack of structure allows them to be plausibly quantum resistant despite Shor's algorithm, while still having a number of applications. The most famous example of group actions are built from isogenies on elliptic curves.

Our main result is that CDH for abelian group actions is quantumly *equivalent* to discrete log. Galbraith et al. (Mathematical Cryptology) previously showed *perfectly* solving CDH to be equivalent to discrete log quantumly; our result works for any non-negligible advantage. We also explore several other questions about group action and isogeny protocols.

> *Proving the equivalence of breaking the Diffie-Hellman protocol and computing discrete-log is one of the oldest problems in public key cryptography.*
>
> Boneh and Lipton [BL96]

1 Introduction

Diffie-Hellman key agreement [DH76] is one of the most important protocols in cryptography. Given a generator g of a cyclic group of order p, Alice and Bob choose random $a \leftarrow Z_p$ and $b \leftarrow Z_p$, respectively, and exchange the values g^a and g^b. Their shared key is then $g^{ab} = (g^a)^b = (g^b)^a$.

One way to break Diffie-Hellman is to compute discrete logarithms (DLog): extract a from (g, g^a) and then compute $g^{ab} = (g^b)^a$ from Alice's message. Fortunately, computing discrete logs appears hard, and after decades of cryptanalytic effort the best classical algorithms on certain groups—multiplicative groups of finite fields and elliptic curves—have sub-exponential or exponential complexity.

The security of Diffie-Hellman key exchange, however, is potentially easier than solving DLog. Indeed, computing the shared key is equivalent to solving the computational Diffie-Hellman problem (CDH): computing g^{ab} from (g, g^a, g^b).

A portion of this work was done when the author was employed by Fujitsu Research. The full version of this paper is available at https://eprint.iacr.org/2022/1135.

S. Agrawal and D. Lin (Eds.): ASIACRYPT 2022, LNCS 13791, pp. 3–32, 2022.
https://doi.org/10.1007/978-3-031-22963-3_1

While CDH is clearly no harder than DLog, it is not a priori obvious that the converse should hold. After all, CDH and DLog are very different problems: CDH is in essence computing multiplication $a, b \mapsto a \times b$ homomorphically on the encoded values g^a, g^b, whereas DLog is inverting the encoding. The good news is that there has been classical progress towards proving such an equivalence [den90, Mau94, MW96, BL96]. However, the *polynomial-time* equivalence of DLog and CDH in general groups without any auxiliary information still remains an important fundamental open question. As such, the hardness of CDH must simply be assumed in Diffie-Hellman key exchange, requiring a potentially much stronger assumption than the hardness of DLog.

Quantum Diffie-Hellman. Shor [Sho94] shows that DLog is easy on a quantum computer, meaning the Diffie-Hellman protocol is no longer secure. Numerous proposals have been made for replacement "post-quantum" cryptosystems. One interesting example preserving the spirit of the original Diffie-Hellman protocol is due to Couveignes [Cou06] and Rostovtsev and Stolbunov [RS06]. They propose to replace the group in Diffie-Hellman with a group *action*. Very roughly, the group action allows for a similar operation as discrete exponentiation as in Diffie-Hellman, but does *not* have an analagous operation for multiplying two group elements, as is needed by Shor's attack.

In more detail, a group action consists of a group G and a set X, together with an action $\star : G \times X \to X$ such that for any $a, b \in G$ and $x \in X$, it holds that $(ab) \star x = a \star (b \star x)$. In this setting, DLog is the task of recovering a from $(x, a \star x)$, and CDH is the task of computing $(ab) \star x$ from $(x, a \star x, b \star x)$. If we consider *abelian* and *regular*[1] group actions, we can translate Diffie-Hellman key exchange from groups to group actions by viewing $\mathbf{Z}_p$ as the group acting on the set $\langle g \rangle$ through discrete exponentiation: $a \star x = x^a$. DLog and CDH on the group immediately correspond to DLog and CDH on the group action. However, other group actions that do not correspond to plain groups are possible. The most notable example is isogenies over elliptic curves [CLM+18], one of the leading candidates for post-quantum public key cryptography proposed by Couveignes, Rostovtsev, and Stolbunov[2]. In the full version of the paper, we discuss how other plausibly post-quantum proposals can sometimes also be phrased as group actions.

As in the classical case, the DLog-CDH equivalence is an important fundamental question in the quantum world. It may even be *more* important than the classical equivalence today, as the post-quantum hardness of group actions has so far seen a much smaller cryptanalytic effort than the classical hardness of groups, and therefore our confidence in the post-quantum CDH assumption on group actions is much weaker. An equivalence to DLog would therefore be an

---

[1] A regular group action is a group action that, for every $x_1, x_2 \in X$, there exists a *unique* element $g \in G$ such that $x_1 = g \star x_2$.

[2] A few very recent works [CD22, MM22, Rob22] break a certain isogeny-based protocol called SIDH. SIDH, however, is just one of a number of isogeny protocols, and in particular it is *not* a group action. For a slightly more in depth discussion about different isogeny protocols, see Sect. 2.5.

important step toward improving this confidence. In ordinary groups, the post-quantum equivalence is trivial: they are both easy. In group actions, however, it is less clear: group actions have less exploitable structure for proving such an equivalence, but quantum algorithms are more powerful and can potentially be used to facilitate a reduction.

In a short paper, Galbraith *et al.* [GPSV18] give a promising first step toward proving an equivalence: they show that any *perfect* algorithm for solving CDH in abelian group actions can be converted into a DLog algorithm. The core idea is that a perfect, efficient CDH algorithm essentially turns the set of a group action into a plain group, with $x_1 \times x_2 = \mathsf{CDH}(x_1, x_2)$. One can then apply Shor's DLog algorithm to the derived group. The main difficulty is that solving DLog in the derived group is not exactly identical to DLog in the original group action. Galbraith *et al.* essentially show how to translate one DLog to the other to complete the reduction.

Unfortunately, if the CDH algorithm has even relatively minor correctness error (even, say, 10%), the above algorithm does not work. On the other hand, for cryptographic applications, we want to justify that no efficient algorithm can solve CDH with any *non-negligible* success probability. It could therefore be, for example, that CDH can be broken—and hence also group action key agreement—with probability 0.9, but that DLog is still hard. In plain groups, one can amplify success probability using standard random self-reductions for CDH. However, as pointed out by Galbraith et al., the limited structure of group actions prevents such random self-reductions. They therefore leave the full quantum equivalence of DLog and CDH for group actions as an important open question.

1.1   This Work: Full Quantum Equivalence of DLog and CDH

In this work, we resolve the open question above, showing that DLog and CDH are quantumly equivalent for abelian group actions (Sect. 3). Since the most commonly used group actions in cryptography (from isogenies) are abelian, our results here have wide applicability and can be used directly on isogeny-based cryptosystems such as CSI-FiSh [BKV19][3].

As a secondary result, we also show that the same cannot hold generically for Decisional Diffie-Hellman (DDH), which is equivalent to asking that the shared key not only cannot be predicted by the adversary, but that it is indistinguishable from a random string. In other words, there is no black box quantum equivalence between DLog (or even CDH) and DDH (Sect. 4). We also formally specify a generic model for group actions (Sect. 5), explore relaxations of group actions relevant to certain isogeny protocols (Sect. 6), and discuss the relationship between group actions and the dihedral hidden subgroup problem (Sect. 7).

Our Reduction (Sect. 3). Our DLog-CDH equivalence will use Galbraith et al. to reduce the problem of proving equivalence to that of boosting the success

---

[3] We note that our result does not directly apply to *restricted* effective group actions (REGAs) like CSIDH [CLM+18] and explain this in more detail later.

probability of a CDH algorithm. However, this comes with many challenges, which we now explore. Consider a deterministic algorithm A such that:

$$\Pr_{a,b \leftarrow G}[A(x, a \star x, b \star x) = (ab) \star x] = p \qquad \Pr_{a,b \leftarrow G}[A(x, a \star x, b \star x) = (uab) \star x] = 1 - p$$

for some constant $p \in [0, 1]$ and fixed known group element $u \in G \backslash \{1\}$. This would certainly be a valid CDH adversary with success probability p.

Remark 1. Throughout, we will consider x as being fixed; this is usually how CDH is modeled, and typically makes hardness results for CDH more challenging. It is also possible to consider a variant where x is chosen randomly and A works for a random x. [BMZ19] explore the fixed vs random question for plain groups.

In the plain group setting, the equivalent setup would be that A on input (g, g^a, g^b), outputs g^{ab} with probability p and g^{uab} with probability $1 - p$. An easy random self-reduction for this A would be to run $h \leftarrow A(g, (g^a) \times g^c, (g^b) \times g^d)$ for random choices of c, d. Each trial will run A on random independent inputs, so we know that $h = g^{(a+c)(b+d)}$ with probability p, and $h = g^{u(a+c)(b+d)}$ with probability $1 - p$. We can then compute $h' = h \times (g^a)^{-d}(g^b)^{-c}g^{-cd}$. If $h = g^{(a+c)(b+d)}$, then $h' = g^{ab}$. Meanwhile, if $h = g^{u(a+c)(b+d)}$, then $h' = g^{(u-1)(a+c)(b+d)+ab}$, which is a uniformly random element. Therefore, by repeating this process many times on independent c, d, a p fraction of the elements will be identical to g^{ab}, and the rest will be uniformly random. Taking a majority therefore gives g^{ab} with overwhelming probability. An important feature of this self-reduction is that when A is correct, the self-reduction gives the correct answer, and when A is incorrect, the self-reduction gives a uniformly random answer. The self-reduction can be strengthened to handle arbitrary A, thus giving a generic way to boost success probability.

Unfortunately, the above re-randomization is not possible with group actions, since there is no multiplication analog for set elements. Given $(x, a \star x, b \star x)$, one could try choosing a random c, d and running $(cd)^{-1} \star A(x, c \star (a \star x), d \star (b \star x))$. The result will be $(cd)^{-1} \star [(ac)(bd)] \star x = (ab) \star x$ with probability p and $(uab) \star x$ with probability $1 - p$. This allows us to obtain many samples of each. But unlike the plain group self-reduction, now when A is incorrect we do not output a uniformly random answer, but instead output a fixed incorrect answer $(uab) \star x$. This means we cannot in general take a majority since if $p < 1/2$ this would actually give the incorrect answer. In this case, if we *knew* that $p < 1/2$, we would know to actually take the minority element as output. This would require making non-black box use of A, which is non-standard but acceptable. However, if $p = 1/2$, then the majority or minority element is just a random sample between $(ab) \star x$ and $(uab) \star x$. In this case, even knowing p is not enough to identify the correct answer.

We will now show how to resolve the reduction for this particular class of adversaries. To do so, we consider two cases: $u^2 = 1$, or not. The exponent 2 in $u^2 = 1$ is a result of our algorithm A outputting a random choice amongst two elements, and in more general settings we could consider higher, but still polynomial, exponents. Note that group actions are defined and plausibly hard for non-cyclic or non-prime order groups, so it is reasonable to consider group orders that have small factors. For isogenies, the group order is indeed smooth.

If $u^2 = 1$ and $p = 1/2$, we are basically stuck: A is simply outputting a random sample in the orbit of $(ab) \star x$ under action by u. Nothing we can do will amplify the success probability. Instead, we observe that A can be viewed as essentially solving CDH—with perfect probability!—in the subgroup $G/\langle u \rangle$. We then apply Galbraith et al. to this subgroup to solve DLog relative to $G/\langle u \rangle$. We can then solve for the full DLog in G by brute forcing the $\langle u \rangle$ component. This works regardless of p, but requires u to generate a small group.

If $u^2 \neq 1$ and/or if $p \neq 1/2$, another approach will work. Here, we can first run our re-randomized A several times on $(x, a \star x, b \star x)$ to obtain $y_0 = (ab) \star x$ and $y_1 = (uab) \star x$, but we do not yet know which is which. But in this case, we can use the fact that A is *not* generating uniform outputs in the orbit of $(ab) \star x$ to distinguish the two cases. Concretely, we run the re-randomized A several times on (x, x, y_0) and (x, x, y_1). Since $x = 1 \star x$, we know that (x, x, y_0) will output y_0 with probability p and $u \star y_0 = y_1$ with probability $1 - p$. This distribution of outputs exactly matches the distribution from our original set of trials on $(x, a \star x, b \star x)$. Meanwhile, (x, x, y_1) will output y_1 and $u \star y_1 = (u^2 ab) \star x$ with probabilities p and $1 - p$. This distribution will be different than that from our original set of trials. Thus by comparing the distributions generated from (x, x, y_0) and (x, x, y_1) with the distribution generated from $(x, a \star x, b \star x)$, we can identify which of y_0, y_1 are the correct CDH output.

Our result generalizes the approach above to work with arbitrary adversaries A, and to work without needing any side-information (like the probability p) about the distribution of outputs of A. Essentially, we show that there is always a polynomial-sized subgroup H of G such that we can amplify A to have near-perfect success probability on G/H. We then apply Galbraith et al. to the subgroup, and then brute-force the quotient group.

There are a number of challenges to getting this sketch to work. One issue is to actually identify the subgroup of G. Suppose G has order $n = 2 \times 3 \times 5 \times \dots$. Then the number of subgroups of polynomial-size will be $\lambda^{O \log(\lambda)}$; if G is non-cyclic, the number of small subgroups can even be exponential. So we cannot simply guess the subgroup, and must instead compute it.

Another issue is *thresholding*: we need to make decisions about whether various distributions of elements are close or far. These decisions are made by sampling a number of samples from the distributions, and comparing frequencies. But we can only obtain frequency estimates with inverse-polynomial error. For whatever criteria we use to distinguish distributions, if two distributions are close but not too close, the noise in our estimates will cause the criteria to output just a random bit. The question is then: if the various decisions underlying our algorithm may have random answers, how can we guarantee consistent outputs, as required to achieve a high success probability?

The randomness from thresholding seems impossible to fully overcome. However, we show via careful arguments that the randomness can all be contained within the choice of the subgroup H. Once this subgroup is fixed, we show that we can set our decision-making criteria such that we always make consistent decisions, resulting in consistent CDH solutions.

We note that our main proof assumes the group action is regular, meaning for a fixed x, $a \star x$ is a bijection. This is the most relevant setting to isogeny-based group actions. Nevertheless, we explain in Sect. 3.1 how to extend to arbitrary abelian group actions.

Impossibility of Extending to DDH (Sect. 4). Given the above, one may hope to actually prove that DLog implies DDH, namely that $(ab) \star x$ is indistinguishable from $c \star x$ for a random c, given $x, a \star x, b \star x$.

Unfortunately, we refute this possibility, at least in the composite-order setting that is most relevant to post-quantum cryptosystems. The idea is simple: we start with any group action $\star : G \times X \to X$ where CDH—and maybe even DDH—is hard. We then define a slightly larger group and set $G' = G \times \mathbb{Z}_p$ and $X' = X \times \mathbb{Z}_p$, for some polynomially bounded p. We expand $\star$ to an action of G' on X' by defining $(a, u) \star (x, y) = (a \star x, u + y)$. DLog and CDH easily hold for the expanded group action, but DDH is trivially false just by looking at the $\mathbb{Z}_p$ component, which has no hardness. We note that if G is cyclic, we can make G' cyclic as well by choosing p to be relatively prime to the order of G.

Generic Group Actions (Sect. 5). Next, we propose a generic group action model, analogous to the generic group model of [Sho97]. In this model, the set elements X are just random strings, and the action of G on X is provided by an oracle which can be queried by the adversary. This model is implicit in much of the prior work on group actions, but we are not aware of it being formally written down. We also note that the model trivially extends to the quantum setting, where classical queries are replaced by quantum queries.

On REGAs (Sect. 6). Many isogeny protocols cannot be phrased as clean group actions. Essentially, in some isogeny-based protocols (such as CSIDH [CLM+18]) there is a set of generators $g_1, \ldots, g_\ell \in G$, and it is only known how to efficiently compute the actions of the g_i or g_i^{-1}; one can then compute the action of any $g \in G$ provided one has a representation of $g = \prod_{i=1}^{\ell} g_i^{\alpha_i}$ for polynomially-sized α_i. In general, finding such a representation is believed to be hard. This setting is referred to as a *Restricted Effective Group Action (REGA)*.

Our reduction (as with Galbraith et al.) does not apply to REGAs, since applying Shor's algorithm requires the ability to compute the action of arbitrary group elements g. Formalizing some discussion from Galbraith *et al.*, we show that the reduction works for REGAs if a problem similar to the 1D Short Integer Solution (1D-SIS) problem is easy which we call REGA-SIS.[4] In the case that $G = \mathbb{Z}_p$–which we can assume since we are focused on abelian groups–the problem becomes essentially the one-dimensional version of the inhomogeneous SIS (ISIS) problem [BGLS19]: given a target integer $t \in \mathbb{Z}_p$ and a vector of integers $\mathbf{s} \in \mathbb{Z}_p^\ell$ defined by the REGA description, the problem is to find a vector of integers $\mathbf{v} \in [-\beta, \beta]^\ell$ such that $t = \mathbf{s} \cdot \mathbf{v}$. The only difference between REGA-SIS

---

[4] We defer a formal definition of this problem to the body of the paper. It is shown in [BLP+13] that 1D-SIS, for certain parameter settings, is equivalent to the "standard" LWE problem.

and what a natural definition of "1D-ISIS" would be is that the given vector of integers $\mathbf{s}$ is defined by the REGA rather than sampled randomly.

Essentially, we show that such a REGA-SIS oracle is enough to compute a representation of g in terms of the g_i, which converts the REGA into a standard group action. This shows that in a world where REGA-SIS is easy, our equivalence between DLog and CDH also holds for REGAs. It turns out that the hardness of REGA-SIS is, in fact, inherent in solving DLog on REGAs: we also show that any algorithm which solves DLog on REGAs can be used to solve this REGA-SIS problem. This result is quite interesting since it implies DLog on REGAs is at least as hard as a (not necessarily randomized, and thus maybe not hard) version of a hard lattice problem.

If we could somehow strengthen this to show that a CDH solver on REGAs must also solve REGA-SIS, then we would obtain a full quantum equivalence between DLog and CDH for REGAs. We do not know how to prove such a result, but we give some evidence that *generic* adversaries for CDH on REGAs may have to solve REGA-SIS or, for certain groups, 1D-SIS itself. More precisely, we show a reduction that *generic* adversaries for CDH on REGAs that make *classical* group and group action "queries" can solve REGA-SIS.[5] We leave formally proving this equivalence as an interesting and practically important open problem.

The Dihedral Hidden Subgroup Problem (Sect. 7). Childs et al. [CJS14] apply the Dihedral Hidden Subgroup Problem (DHSP) algorithm of [Kup05] to compute isogenies between elliptic curves. This is a special case of the folklore result that any algorithm for DHSP yields an algorithm for DLog on regular, abelian group actions. We prove this folklore theorem.

The DHSP is the main approach for cryptanalyzing regular, abelian group actions, and no known better general algorithm is known. However, we point out that the two are *not* trivially equivalent: group actions have significant extra structure that could potentially be used for attacks that is not exploited by the reduction to DHSP. We are not aware of this observation being explicitly mentioned previously.

We next conjecture that, nevertheless, DHSP and regular, abelian group actions are *generically* equivalent, meaning any generic algorithm for solving these group actions can be used to solve DHSP generically. We offer some evidence of this conjecture, but leave proving or disproving it as a fascinating open question.

2　Preliminaries

In this section we discuss background material that is used in the rest of the paper. We expect that experienced readers can skip this section. For a more thorough presentation of preliminary material, please see the full version of the paper.

---

[5] The adversary could be quantum but is restricted to classical queries to the group and group action oracles.

2.1   Min-Entropy and Leftover Hash Lemma

Let Z be a discrete random variable Z with sample space Ω. Its *min-entropy* is

$$H_\infty(Z) = \min_{\omega \in \Omega}\{-\log \Pr[Z = \omega]\}.$$

For two random variables Y and Z, we use $H_\infty(Z|Y)$ to denote the min-entropy of Z conditioned on Y. We will use the following lemma, which is a simplified version of the leftover hash lemma [ILL89].

Lemma 1. *Let $\{H_s : \mathcal{Z} \to Y\}_{s \in \mathcal{S}}$ be a family of pairwise independent hash functions, and Z and S be discrete random variables over $\mathcal{Z}$ and $\mathcal{S}$, respectively. If $H_\infty(Z) > \log |Y| + 2\log(\varepsilon^{-1})$ we have $\Delta[(S, H_S(Z)),(S, U)] \le \varepsilon$, where Δ denotes statistical distance and U denotes the uniform distribution over Y.*

We will also use the following corollary of the leftover hash lemma.

Lemma 2.   *Let G be an (additive) finite abelian group such that $|G| = \lambda^{\omega(1)}$. Let $n \in Z$ such that $n > \log |G| + \omega(\log(\lambda))$. If $\mathbf{g} \leftarrow G^n$ and $\mathbf{s} \leftarrow \{0,1\}^n$, then*

$$\left(\mathbf{g}, \sum_{i=1}^{n} s_i \cdot g_i\right) \overset{s}{\approx} (\mathbf{g}, u),$$

where $u \leftarrow G$ is a uniformly chosen element from G.

2.2   1D-SIS Problem

The 1D-SIS problem dates to the original work of Ajtai [Ajt96] and has been used in many cryptographic applications [BV15, BKM17]. These cases use special moduli, but the case for general moduli follows from [BLP+13], where it is shown that the 1D-SIS problem with certain parameters but no special restrictions on the modulus is as hard as standard polynomial modulus LWE.

Definition 1.   *Let m, β, and q be positive integers. In the $1D\text{-}SIS_{m,q,\beta}$ problem, an adversary is given a random vector $\mathbf{v} \leftarrow Z_q^m$ and asked to provide a vector $\mathbf{u} \in Z_q^m$ such that $\|\mathbf{u}\| < \beta$. We say that an adversary efficiently solves the $1d\text{-}SIS_{m,q,\beta}$ problem if it can provide such a vector in PPT time.*

2.3   Cryptographic Group Actions

Here we define cryptographic group actions following Alamati *et al.* [ADMP20], which are based on those of Brassard and Yung [BY91] and Couveignes [Cou06].

Definition 2 (Group Action). *A group G is said to* act *on a set X if there is a map $\star : G \times X \to X$ that satisfies the following two properties:*

1. *Identity: If e is the identity of G, then $\forall x \in X$, we have $e \star x = x$.*
2. *Compatibility: For any $g, h \in G$ and any $x \in X$, we have $(gh) \star x = g \star (h \star x)$.*

We may use the abbreviated notation $(G, X, \star)$ to denote a group action. We extensively consider group actions that are *regular*:

Definition 3. *A group action $(G, X, \star)$ is said to be* regular *if, for every $x_1, x_2 \in X$, there exists a* unique $g \in G$ *such that $x_2 = g \star x_1$.*

We emphasize that most results in group action-based cryptography have focused on regular actions. As emphasized by [ADMP20], if a group action is regular, then for any $x \in X$, the map $f_x : g \mapsto g \star x$ defines a bijection between G and X; in particular, if G (or X) is finite, then we must have $|G| = |X|$.

In this paper, unless we specify otherwise, we will work with *effective* group actions (EGAs). An effective group action $(G, X, \star)$ is, informally speaking, a group action where all of the (well-defined) group operations and group action operations are efficiently computable, there are efficient ways to sample random group elements, and set elements have unique representation. Since the focus of this paper is on abelian group actions in a quantum world, we note that we can efficiently map any abelian group to Z_p for some integer p (see the full version of our paper and our discussion on KEGAs for more details), and all of the less obvious properties needed for EGAs follow automatically. However, the definition of an EGA itself is a little bit tedious (and quite formal so as to properly model isogeny-based constructions in a classical world) so we defer it to the full version of the paper.

2.4   Computational Problems

We next define problems related to group action security that are more semantically similar to typical group-based problems than those that are traditionally used in isogeny literature. We define the formal definitions that are typically used in isogenies (based on [ADMP20] in the full version of the paper, where we also compare them to our (intuitively simpler, but almost equivalent) notions of security defined here. We emphasize that we are defining *problems* here and not *assumptions* because these are easier to use in reductions.

Definition 4 (Group Action Discrete Logarithm). *Given a group action $(G, X, \star)$ and distributions $(\mathcal{D}_X, \mathcal{D}_G)$, the group action discrete logarithm problem is defined as follows: sample $g \leftarrow \mathcal{D}_G$ and $x \leftarrow \mathcal{D}_X$, compute $y = g \star x$, and create the tuple $T = (x, y)$. We say that an adversary solves the group action discrete log problem if, given T and a description of the group action and sampling algorithms, the adversary outputs g.*

Definition 5 (Group Action Computational Diffie-Hellman (CDH)). *Given a group action $(G, X, \star)$ and distributions $(\mathcal{D}_X, \mathcal{D}_G)$, the group action CDH problem is defined as follows: sample $g \leftarrow \mathcal{D}_G$ and $x, x' \leftarrow \mathcal{D}_X$, compute $y = g \star x$, and create the tuple $T = (x, y, x')$. We say that an adversary solves the group action CDH problem if, given T and a description of the group action and sampling algorithms, the adversary outputs $y' = g \star x'$.*

Definition 6 (Group Action Decisional Diffie-Hellman (DDH)). *Given a group action $(G, X, \star)$ and distributions $(\mathcal{D}_X, \mathcal{D}_G)$, the group action DDH problem is defined as follows: sample $g_1, g_2 \leftarrow \mathcal{D}_G$ and $x, z' \leftarrow \mathcal{D}_X$, compute $y_1 = g_1 \star x$, $y_2 = g_2 \star x$, and $z = g_1 g_2 \star x$.*

The group action DDH problem is to distinguish whether a tuple is of the form (x, y_1, y_2, z) or (x, y_1, y_2, z').

Remark 2. The above definitions allow for different distributions $\mathcal{D}_X$ on X. In particular, $\mathcal{D}_X$ could be uniform over X, or it could be a singleton distribution that places all its weight on a single fixed x. Whether x is fixed or uniform potentially changes the nature of these problems (see [BMZ19] for an exploration in the group-based setting). Looking ahead, our reduction between DLog and CDH will preserve x, and therefore it works no matter how x is modeled.

2.5 Instantiations of Cryptographic Group Actions

We next discuss various instantiations of cryptographic group actions and where they fall into our definitions. We start by discussing isogenies. For more details, we refer the reader to [ADMP20], which has an extensive discussion on the classification of various isogeny protocols into group action definitions.

Isogenies that Are EGAs. CSI-FiSh [BKV19] and its derivatives/applications [DM20a] have EGA functionality and are conjectured to even have weak pseudorandomness. However, there have recently been some subexponential attacks on CSI-FiSh [Pei20, BS20] and current cryptosystems built from CSI-FiSh are not particularly efficient. In fact, there are not efficient algorithms to (asymptotically) generate parameter sets for CSI-FiSh. However, if a powerful quantum computer were available, then efficient (quantum) computation of the class group structure could be used to generate arbitrary parameter sets for CSI-FiSh and improve efficiency.

Isogenies that Are *Restricted* EGAs (REGAs). Recall that, in a *REGA*, there is a set of generators $g_1, \ldots, g_\ell \in G$, and it is only known how to efficiently compute the actions of the g_i or g_i^{-1}; one can then compute the action of any $g \in G$ provided one has a representation of $g = \prod_{i=1}^{\ell} g_i^{\alpha_i}$ for polynomial α_i. We define REGAs formally in the full version of the paper. Many of the most commonly used isogeny protocols are based on CSIDH [CLM+18], which is a REGA. These include things like the signature scheme SeaSign [DG19] or OT protocols [LGdSG21].

Isogenies that Are Not GAs. There are many isogeny-based schemes that cannot be modeled as group actions. Examples include SIDH [DJP14] and the recently proposed OSIDH [CK20, Onu21, DDF21]. Most isogeny-based protocols that are not group actions are typically used for key exchange or other very simple cryptographic applications.

Remark 3. A few very recent works [CD22, MM22, Rob22] break SIDH by showing how to solve the discrete log problem. However, the attack crucially exploits certain extra points that are made public in SIDH, and these points are precisely one of the reasons that SIDH is not a group action. In particular, the the attack does not seem to apply to CSI-FISH or CSIDH, the main instantiations of EGAs and REGAs, respectively.

Non-isogeny Group Actions. Currently all instantiations of *abelian* candidate cryptographic group actions that are thought to be secure are isogeny-based [DDF21]. There have been a number of attempts to build key exchange and other basic primitives from nonabelian groups that amount to group actions or have hardness assumptions that can be modeled in some way as group actions [KLC+00, Sti05, SU05a], but the proposed instantiations of these schemes have been completely cryptanalyzed [Shp08, BKT18].

We note that these candidate cryptosystems typically propose an abstract scheme and then attempt to instantiate it with a group. We note that it is not usually the case that the abstract schemes themselves are broken: the cryptanalysis typically works directly on the instantiations, so it is possible that some of these protocols could be implemented securely with different choices of groups.

There have also been some candidate nonabelian cryptographic group actions proposed [JQSY19]. While these are not known to be insecure, they have far fewer applications than abelian group actions.

3   Reducing DLog to CDH Quantumly

Let $(G, X, \star)$ be a regular abelian group action. In Sect. 3.1 we explain how to extend our reduction to non-regular abelian actions. Let $x \in X$ be a fixed set element.

Theorem 1. *If DLog is post-quantum hard in $(G, X, \star)$, then so is CDH. More precisely, there exists an oracle algorithm $R^{\mathcal{A},(G,X,\star)}(\mu, y)$ that runs in time $poly(1/\mu, \log |G|)$ and makes $poly(1/\mu, \log |G|)$ total queries to a supposed CDH adversary $\mathcal{A}$ and group action $(G, X, \star)$, such that the following holds. If $\Pr_{a,b \leftarrow G}[\mathcal{A}(a \star x, b \star x) = (ab) \star x] \geq \mu$, then for any $a \in G$, $\Pr[R^{\mathcal{A},(G,X,\star)}(\mu, a \star x) = a] \geq 0.99$.*

We note that the above means that R is very slightly non-black box, in that its running time and number of calls to $\mathcal{A}$ depend on the success probability μ of $\mathcal{A}$. We note that any amplification of success probability (say, from μ to 0.99) will always come with such a dependence on μ. In our case, amplification is critical to our algorithm, and the dependence on μ would persist even if we only wanted $R^{\mathcal{A}}$ to have very small success probability. The remainder of this section is devoted to proving Theorem 1.

Define CDH to be the function which correctly solves CDH relative to x: $\mathsf{CDH}(a \star x, b \star x) = (ab) \star x$. We will also allow CDH to take as input a vector of elements, behaving as $\mathsf{CDH}(a_1 \star x, \cdots, a_n \star x) = (a_1 \cdots a_n) \star x$. Furthermore, we will allow CDH to take as input distribution(s) over the set X; in this case, CDH will also output a distribution.

Let $a, b \in G$ be group elements, and let $y = a \star x$ and $z = b \star x$. Suppose $\mathcal{A}$ is an efficient (quantum) algorithm such that

$$q := \Pr[\mathcal{A}(y, z) = \mathsf{CDH}(y, z)]$$

is a non-negligible function in the security parameter, where a and b are random elements in G, and the probability is over the randomness of a and b and $\mathcal{A}$.

Our goal is to turn $\mathcal{A}$ into a quantum algorithm for discrete logarithms. As a first step, we introduce a random self-reduction for CDH. In the case of groups (as opposed to group actions), a more powerful random self-reduction allows for amplifying the success probability on any input. The result would be an algorithm for CDH with overwhelming success probability. In our case, due to the restricted nature of group actions, we can only perform a more limited self-reduction. Nevertheless, this self-reduction has useful properties.

The Basic Random Self-reduction. The random self-reduced version of $\mathcal{A}$, denoted $\mathcal{A}_0$, works as follows:

– On input $y = a \star x, z = b \star x$, choose random $a', b' \in G$.
– Let $y' = a' \star y, z' = b' \star z$.
– Run $w' \leftarrow \mathcal{A}(y', z')$.
– Output $w = (a'b')^{-1} \star w'$.

Note that each run of $\mathcal{A}_0$ runs $\mathcal{A}$ exactly once, and uses a constant number of group action operations. This reduction is correct since, if $\mathcal{A}$ is correct, then we output

$$w = (a'b')^{-1} \mathsf{CDH}\left((a'a) \star x, (b'b) \star x\right) = (a'b')^{-1} (aa'bb') \star x = (ab) \star x$$

which is the correct output for CDH. Moreover, the set elements y', z' are uniformly distributed over the possible set elements.

Let $\mathcal{D}$ be the distribution $\mathcal{A}_0(x, x)$. That is, we are feeding the "dummy" distribution to our random self-reduction. While we know what the answer should be $(x = \mathsf{CDH}(x, x))$, we use this distribution to learn more about $\mathcal{A}$'s behavior.

Lemma 3. $\Pr[x \leftarrow \mathcal{D}] = q$.

Proof. Recall that $\mathcal{D}$ is the distribution $\mathcal{A}_0(x, x)$. $\mathcal{A}_0$ on input (x, x) calls $\mathcal{A}(a' \star x, b' \star x)$ for random $a', b' \in G$. With probability q, $\mathcal{A}(a' \star x, b' \star x)$ returns $(a'b') \star x$, and in this case we have $w = x$ as desired.   □

We next generalize our notation. For any $y, z \in X$ where $y = a \star x$ and $z = b \star x$ for some $a, b \in G$, let $D_{y,z}$ be the distribution of outputs of $\mathcal{A}_0(y, z)$.

Lemma 4. *For every $y, z \in X$ such that there exist $a, b \in G$ where $y = a \star x$ and $z = b \star x$, $D_{y,z} = \mathsf{CDH}(y, z, \mathcal{D})$, where $\mathsf{CDH}(\cdot, \cdot, \cdot)$ is the 3-way CDH function. In other words, $\mathcal{A}_0(a \star x, b \star x)$ is identically distributed to $(ab) \star \mathcal{A}_0(x, x)$.*

Proof. Fix $a, b \in G$. Consider the probability that $\mathcal{A}_0(a \star x, b \star x)$ outputs w:

$$
\begin{aligned}
\Pr[\mathcal{A}_0(a \star x, b \star x) = w] &= \Pr_{a', b' \in G}[(a'b')^{-1} \star \mathcal{A}((aa') \star x, (bb') \star x) = w] \\
&= \Pr_{a', b' \in G}[\mathcal{A}((aa') \star x, (bb') \star x) = (a'b') \star w] \\
&= \Pr_{a'', b'' \in G}[\mathcal{A}(a'' \star x, b'' \star x) = (a''b''(ab)^{-1}) \star w] \\
&= \Pr[\mathcal{A}_0(x, x) = (ab)^{-1} \star w]
\end{aligned}
$$

Thus, $\mathcal{A}_0(a \star x, b \star x)$ is just the distribution $\mathcal{A}_0(x, x)$, but shifted by ab.   □

Using this "shift invariance," we can define $\mathcal{D}_w := \mathcal{D}_{w,x} = \mathcal{D}_{x,w} = \mathcal{D}_{y,z}$, if $\mathsf{CDH}(y, z) = w$. Lemma 4 shows that $\mathcal{D}_{y,z}$ outputs $\mathsf{CDH}(y, z)$ with probability q. Thus, by running $\mathcal{A}_0$ many times, the right answer is almost certainly amongst the list of outputs. However, to amplify the success probability, we would need to know which of the list of outputs is the correct answer; we cannot determine this yet.

In the following, we will take steps to remedy this issue. Throughout this section, it is instructive to keep the following examples in mind:

1. Let $g \in G \backslash \{1\}$. $\mathcal{A}(Y, Z)$ outputs $\mathsf{CDH}(y, z)$ with probability $1/3$, and $g \star \mathsf{CDH}(Y, Z)$ with probability $2/3$. Notice that in this case, $\mathcal{A}_0$ has the same distribution of outputs as $\mathcal{A}$. Also notice that taking the majority element will give the wrong answer. Thus, we cannot immediately decide which of the outputs of $\mathcal{A}_0$ is the right answer just by looking at the frequencies.
2. Let $\mathcal{H}$ be a subgroup of G of size $1/q$. Then consider the case where $\mathcal{A}(y, z)$ outputs $c \star \mathsf{CDH}(y, z)$, where $c \leftarrow \mathcal{H}$ is chosen uniformly. Note that $\mathcal{A}$ is still correct with probability q in this case, since $c = 1_{\mathcal{H}}$ with probability q. Similar to Example 1, there is no way to identify the correct output just by looking at frequencies.
3. Suppose $\mathcal{H} = \mathbb{Z}_2^{\log \lambda}$, which we can decompose as a chain of subgroups $\mathcal{H}_i = \mathbb{Z}_2^i$ with $\mathcal{H}_{i-1} \subseteq \mathcal{H}_i$. $\mathcal{A}$ outputs $c \star \mathsf{CDH}(y, z)$, where $c \in \mathcal{H}$. However, c is not uniform. Instead, $i \in [0, \log \lambda]$ is chosen according to some probability distribution, and then c is chosen uniformly from $\mathcal{H}_i$.
4. Suppose $\mathcal{H} = \mathbb{Z}_2^{\log \lambda}$. Again, $\mathcal{A}$ outputs $c \star \mathsf{CDH}(y, z)$, where $c \in \mathcal{H}$ but not uniform. Here, c occurs with probability $1 - \alpha |c|_1$, where $|c|_1$ denotes the Hamming weight of c.

Example 1. It turns out Example 1 can be handled using the shifting property from Lemma 4. Suppose we are given a CDH challenge parameterized by $(y = a \star x, z = b \star x)$. Basically, after repeating many runs of $\mathcal{A}_0(y, z)$, we obtain two elements: $w_0 = (ab) \star x$ and $w_1 = (gab) \star x$. In theory, in this example we could exploit the fact that we know the probabilities with which $\mathcal{A}$ outputs the correct set element and the "g-multiplied" set element, but let's assume that we do not know this. What can we do?

Suppose we feed these outputs back into $\mathcal{A}_0$, running $\mathcal{A}_0(w_0, x)$ and $\mathcal{A}_0(w_1, x)$ several times each. Each of these two runs will output two distinct elements. Since $w_0 = (ab) \star x$, Lemma 4 shows that $\mathcal{A}_0(w_0, x) = \mathcal{D}_{w_0} = \mathcal{D}_{y,z} = \mathcal{A}_0(y, z)$ as distributions. Likewise, since $w_1 = (gab) \star x$, we have $\mathcal{A}_0(w_1, x) = \mathcal{A}_0(g \star y, z)$.

Therefore, because $\mathcal{A}_0(w_0, x)$ is distributed the same as $\mathcal{A}_0(y, z)$ and $\mathcal{A}_0(w_1, x)$ is not, we can effectively distinguish w_0 from w_1 and find the correct CDH output.

Example 2. On the other hand, Example 2 is much harder to handle. Mimicking the above, we first run $\mathcal{A}_0$ several times, obtaining the list of values $c \star \mathsf{CDH}(y, z)$ as c ranges over $\mathcal{H}$, but we don't know c. We can then try, for each $c \star \mathsf{CDH}(y, z)$, running $\mathcal{A}_0(c \star \mathsf{CDH}(y, z), x)$ several times, to obtain tuples of elements. However, this will not give us any useful information: each tuple will be exactly the same list as in the original run of $\mathcal{A}_0$, namely the entire set $\mathcal{H} \star \mathsf{CDH}(y, z)$. The problem is that the output distribution of $\mathcal{A}_0$ is invariant under action by $\mathcal{H}$.

Looking ahead, we cannot improve the CDH algorithm for this example. However, this particular example gives a *perfect* CDH oracle relative to the group $G/\mathcal{H}$ acting on $X/\mathcal{H} := \{\mathcal{H} \star w : w \in X\}$. We will use such an algorithm to solve discrete log in $G/\mathcal{H}$. We can then solve discrete logarithms in $\mathcal{H}$ by brute force, and then piece the two results together to solve discrete logarithms in G.

Examples 3 *and* 4. In general, however, we may not get a perfect CDH oracle for $\mathcal{H}$, and are not even obviously guaranteed that the outputs lie in a small subgroup. In Example 3, consider the distribution over i such that larger subgroups are very unlikely, but not *too* unlikely. For any fixed number of queries, it could be that, with probability $1/2$, all results end up in $\mathcal{H}_i$, but with probability $1/2$ some of the results will end up in $\mathcal{H}_{i+1}$. It might, a priori, not even be possible to identify when you have all the elements from a subgroup, since "chaining" calls to $\mathcal{A}_0$ as we have done above might move us outside a subgroup. So it is unclear if there is a way to always output a consistent complete subgroup, so as to get a near-perfect CDH solver relative to G mod this subgroup.

Next, we will gradually improve our CDH solver to resolve these difficulties.

Restricting to a Small Subgroup. We show how to discard some wrong outputs of $\mathcal{A}_0$ so that the remaining outputs lie in a reasonably-small subgroup of G, while still guaranteeing that we keep $\mathsf{CDH}(y, z)$.

We first give some notation. For any two distributions $\mathcal{D}_0, \mathcal{D}_1$ over X, let $\|\mathcal{D}_0 - \mathcal{D}_1\|_\infty = \max_{w \in X} |\Pr[w \leftarrow \mathcal{D}_0] - \Pr[w \leftarrow \mathcal{D}_1]|$. For a distribution $\mathcal{D}$ over X, consider sampling T elements $w_1, \ldots, w_T$ from $\mathcal{D}$. This vector of w_i gives rise to an "empirical" distribution $\tilde{\mathcal{D}}$, where the probability of any w is just the relative frequency of w amongst the w_i. Note that even though $\tilde{\mathcal{D}}$ has a domain of exponential size, we can represent it by the list $w_1, \ldots, w_T$, which has size T. Also note that there are two distributions here: the empirical distribution $\tilde{\mathcal{D}}$ itself, and the distribution over empirical distributions. We denote the latter as $\tilde{\mathcal{D}} \leftarrow \mathcal{D}^T$.

We are now ready to give our next algorithm, $\mathcal{A}_1(y, z)$:

- Let $T = \lambda/\delta^2$ for some parameter $\delta \in (0, 1)$.

- Run $\tilde{\mathcal{D}}^* \leftarrow \mathcal{A}_0(y, z)^T$
- For each w in the support of $\tilde{\mathcal{D}}^*$, run $\tilde{\mathcal{D}}_w \leftarrow \mathcal{A}_0(w, x)^T$.
- Output L, the set of w in the support of $\tilde{\mathcal{D}}^*$ such that $\|\tilde{\mathcal{D}}_w - \tilde{\mathcal{D}}^*\|_\infty \leq \delta/2$.

We will think of λ being poly$(\log q)$, so that $2^{-\Omega(\lambda)}$ is negligible in $1/q$. Note that $\mathcal{A}_1$ makes at most $T^2 + T = O(\lambda^2/\delta^4)$ evaluations of $\mathcal{A}_1$, and hence $T^2 + T$ evaluations of $\mathcal{A}_0$ and $O(T^2 + T)$ group action operations. In order to analyze the algorithm $\mathcal{A}_1$, we need to give some basic results. First we recall the Dvoretzky-Kiefer-Wolfowitz inequality:

Lemma 5 ([Mas90]). *For any $\zeta > 0$ and distribution $\mathcal{D}$, except with probability $2e^{-2\zeta^2 T}$, $\|\tilde{\mathcal{D}} - \mathcal{D}\|_\infty \leq \zeta$, where $\tilde{\mathcal{D}} \leftarrow \mathcal{D}^T$.*

In other words, the empirical distribution converges to the underlying distribution $\mathcal{D}$ as the number of samples T grows large.

Now consider the distribution $\mathcal{D} = \mathcal{A}_0(x, x)$ from before, and the derived distributions $\mathcal{D}_w = \mathsf{CDH}(w, \mathcal{D})$. Let $d_w = \|\mathcal{D}_w - \mathcal{D}\|_\infty$.

Lemma 6. $\forall y, z \in X$, $\|\mathcal{D}_{\mathsf{CDH}(y,z)} - \mathcal{D}_y\|_\infty = d_z$ and $d_{\mathsf{CDH}(y,z)} \leq d_y + d_z$.

Proof. For the equality, note that $\|\mathcal{D}_{\mathsf{CDH}(y,z)} - \mathcal{D}_y\|_\infty = \|\mathsf{CDH}(y, \mathcal{D}_z) - \mathsf{CDH}(y, \mathcal{D})\|_\infty$. Since $\mathsf{CDH}(y, \cdot)$ simply permutes the elements of X—more precisely, it maps $v \in X$ to $a \star v$ where $y = a \star x$—it does not affect the distance between distributions, and therefore $|\mathsf{CDH}(y, \mathcal{D}_z) - \mathsf{CDH}(y, \mathcal{D})| = |\mathcal{D}_z - \mathcal{D}| = d_z$. For the inequality, we have $d_{\mathsf{CDH}(y,z)} = |\mathcal{D}_{\mathsf{CDH}(y,z)} - \mathcal{D}|_\infty \leq |\mathcal{D}_{\mathsf{CDH}(y,z)} - \mathcal{D}_y|_\infty + |\mathcal{D}_y - \mathcal{D}|_\infty = d_z + d_y$, where we used the equality in the second to last step. □

Now we prove the following general result about abelian groups. Fix an abelian group $\mathcal{H}$ and a set of generators $\mathbf{a} = (a_1, \ldots, a_n)$. For any vector $\mathbf{e} \in \mathbb{N}^n$ of non-negative integers, define $\mathbf{a}^{\mathbf{e}} := \prod_{i=1}^n a_i^{e_i}$. Let $\|\mathbf{e}\|_1 := \sum_{i=1}^n |e_i|$. Then for any $r \in \mathcal{H}$, we define $\|r\| := \min_{\mathbf{e} \in \mathbb{N}^n : r = \mathbf{a}^{\mathbf{e}}} \|\mathbf{e}\|_1$.

Lemma 7. *If $U = \{r \in \mathcal{H} : \|r\| \leq ns\}$ has size at most s, then $U = \mathcal{H}$.*

In other words, if the subset of $\mathcal{H}$ with small $\| \cdot \|$ is not too big, then in fact all of $\mathcal{H}$ has small $\| \cdot \|$.

Proof. Clearly $U \subseteq H$. In the other direction, consider a single a_i. Since U has size at most s, then so does the set $\{a_i^{e_i} : 0 \leq e_i \leq s\} \subseteq U$. As there are $s + 1$ different possibilities for e_i, there must be $e_i' < e_i$ such that $a_i^{e_i} = a_i^{e_i'}$. Then $a_i^{e_i' - e_i} = 1$, and $0 < e_i' - e_i \leq s$. For any $r \in \mathcal{H}$, write $r = \mathbf{a}^{\mathbf{e}}$. Since a_i has order at most s, we can reduce each e_i to an integer smaller than s without changing r. After such a reduction, $\|\mathbf{e}\|_1 \leq ns$, and so $r \in U$. Hence $H \subseteq U$. □

Let $L_\delta \subset G$ be the set of all $a \in G$ such that $d_{a \star x} \leq \delta$, and $\mathcal{H}_\delta$ be the subgroup of G generated by L_δ. We have the following:

Lemma 8. *Let $\epsilon \in (0, 1]$ be a real number. Then if $\delta \leq \epsilon q^4/8$, $|\mathcal{H}_\delta| \leq q^{-1} + \epsilon$.*

Note that ϵ is necessary: $\mathcal{D}$ may output $g \star x$ for a g in a subgroup $\mathcal{H}$ of size n, with q^{-1} negligibly smaller than n. Suppose $\Pr[x \leftarrow \mathcal{D}] = q$ and $\Pr[g \star x \leftarrow \mathcal{D}]$ is slightly less than q for all other g. Then $\mathcal{H}_\delta = \mathcal{H}$ for any non-negligible δ.

Proof. We first prove that $|L_\delta| \leq q^{-1} + \epsilon$. Note that $d_{1_G \star x} = d_x = 0$ and so $1_G \in L_\delta$. From Lemma 3, $\Pr[x \leftarrow \mathcal{D}] = q$. Therefore, for any $a \in L_\delta$,

$$\Pr[a^{-1} \star x \leftarrow \mathcal{D}] = \Pr[x \leftarrow \mathcal{D}_{a \star x}] \geq \Pr[x \leftarrow \mathcal{D}] - \delta = q - \delta,$$

where the inequality follows since $d_{a \star x} \leq \delta$ for $a \in L_\delta$. Then

$$1 = \sum_{a \in G} \Pr[a^{-1} \star x \leftarrow \mathcal{D}] \geq \sum_{a \in L_\delta} \Pr[a^{-1} \star x \leftarrow \mathcal{D}]$$

$$= \Pr[1 \star x \leftarrow \mathcal{D}] + \sum_{a \in L_\delta \setminus \{1\}} \Pr[a^{-1} \star x \leftarrow \mathcal{D}] \geq q + (|L_\delta| - 1)(q - \delta)$$

Solving for $|L_\delta|$ gives $|L_\delta| \leq (1 - \delta)/(q - \delta)$. Setting the right hand side to be $\leq q^{-1} + \epsilon$ gives the desired bound whenever $\delta \leq \epsilon q^2/(1 - q + q\epsilon)$. Note that $(1 - q + q\epsilon) \leq 1$. Therefore, $\delta \leq \epsilon q^4/8$ is only a stronger bound on δ.

We now bound $|\mathcal{H}_\delta|$ by applying Lemma 7 to $\mathcal{H} = \mathcal{H}_\delta$ and $\mathbf{a} = L_\delta$ and $s = 1/q + \epsilon$. Consider some $r = \mathbf{a^e}$ in $\mathcal{H}_\delta$. Then by iteratively applying Lemma 6,

$$d_{r \star x} = d_{\mathsf{CDH}(\underbrace{a_1 \star x, \cdots, a_1 \star x}_{e_1}, \underbrace{a_2 \star x, \cdots, a_2 \star x}_{e_2}, a_3 \star x, \cdots)} \leq \sum_i e_i d_{a_i \star x} \leq \sum_i e_i \delta = |\mathbf{e}|_1 \delta$$

By minimizing over all $\mathbf{e}$, we have that $d_{r \star x} \leq \|r\| \delta$. For U as in Lemma 7, this means that $\Pr[r^{-1} \star x \leftarrow \mathcal{D}] = \Pr[x \leftarrow \mathcal{D}_{r \star x}] \geq q - \|r\| \delta \geq q - ns\delta$. Since the probabilities of each outcome sum to at most 1, we therefore have that $|U| \leq (q - ns\delta)^{-1}$. In order to satisfy the conditions of Lemma 7, we therefore need $1/(q - ns\delta) \leq s$, which is equivalent to $1 \leq s(q - ns\delta)$. Since $n = |L_\delta| \leq 1/q + \epsilon$, we have that this inequality is satisfied whenever $\delta \leq \epsilon q^4/(1 + \epsilon q)^3$. As $1 + \epsilon q \leq 2$, our bound of $\delta \leq \epsilon q^4/8$ is only a stronger bound, showing that $\mathcal{H}_\delta = L_\delta$. Our prior bound on $|L_\delta|$ thus proves Lemma 8.   □

We are finally ready to analyze the algorithm $\mathcal{A}_1$. Let $\mathcal{D}'$ be the distribution $\mathcal{A}_1(x, x)$, and $\mathcal{D}'_{y,z}$ be the distribution $\mathcal{A}_1(y, z)$. The next lemma follows immediately from Lemma 4:

Lemma 9. *For every $y, z \in X$ where $y = a \star x$ and $z = b \star x$ for some $a, b \in G$, $\mathcal{D}'_{y,z} = \mathsf{CDH}(y, z, \mathcal{D}')$.*

Thus, we define $\mathcal{D}'_w := \mathcal{D}'_{w,1} = \mathcal{D}'_{1,w} = \mathcal{D}'_{y,z}$, if $\mathsf{CDH}(y, z) = w$. We now prove:

Lemma 10. *Except with probability $2(T + 1)e^{-\delta^2 T/8} + (1 - q)^T \leq 2^{-\Omega(\lambda)}$ over $L \leftarrow \mathcal{A}_1(x, x)$, we have that $x \in L \subseteq \mathcal{H}_\delta \star x$.*

Proof. Suppose we set $\zeta = \frac{\delta}{4}$. By Lemma 5, we have that $|\tilde{\mathcal{D}}^\star - \mathcal{D}_{\mathsf{CDH}(y,z)}|_\infty \leq \delta/4$ and for each w in the support of $\tilde{\mathcal{D}}^\star$, $|\tilde{\mathcal{D}}_w - \mathcal{D}_w| \leq \delta/4$, each individually except with probability at most $2e^{-\delta^2 T/8}$. We also have that with probability $1-(1-q)^T$, x will be amongst the T samples of $\mathcal{A}_1(x,x)$. By a union bound, all of these happen simultaneously, except with probability $2(T+1)e^{-\delta^2 T/8} + (1-q)^T$.

If all of these happen, then $|\tilde{\mathcal{D}}_x - \tilde{\mathcal{D}}^\star| \leq |\tilde{\mathcal{D}}_x - \mathcal{D}| + |\tilde{\mathcal{D}}^\star - \mathcal{D}| \leq 2\delta/4 = \delta/2$. Thus $x \in L$ assuming the above hold. On the other hand, for any $w \in L$, $d_w = |\mathcal{D}_w - \mathcal{D}| \leq |\tilde{\mathcal{D}}_w - \mathcal{D}_w| + |\tilde{\mathcal{D}}_w - \tilde{\mathcal{D}}^\star| + |\tilde{\mathcal{D}}^\star - \mathcal{D}| \leq \delta$. Hence $w \in L_\delta \star x$ by the definition of the set L_δ, which immediately implies that each $w \in \mathcal{H}_\delta \star x$. $\square$

As a consequence, we have that $\mathcal{D}'$ has negligible support outside of $\mathcal{H}_\delta \star x$. Note that $\mathcal{D}'$ may not be random in $\mathcal{H}_\delta \star x$, as the list L may not include all of $\mathcal{H}_\delta \star x$, and L itself may be randomized. Indeed, in Example 4, α may be such that $\mathcal{D}$ and $\mathcal{D}_{c \star w}$ are sufficiently close for c with small Hamming weight, but $\mathcal{D}_{c \star w}$ is far for c with large Hamming weight. Some c may even be right on the cusp, being included in L with constant probability. The result is that the output may not be a whole subgroup and may have entropy.

We note that by setting ϵ a constant and $\delta = \epsilon q^4/8 = O(q^4)$, we have that $\mathcal{A}_1$ runs in time $O(\lambda q^{-8}) = \tilde{O}(q^{-8})$ and makes $\tilde{O}(q^{-8})$ total queries to $\mathcal{A}$ and the group action operations.

Filling an Entire Subgroup. $\mathcal{A}_1$ outputs a subset of $\mathcal{H}_\delta \star \mathsf{CDH}(y,z)$, and the subset must include $\mathsf{CDH}(y,z)$. We will now devise a new algorithm $\mathcal{A}_2$ which outputs $\mathcal{H} \star \mathsf{CDH}(y,z)$, where $\mathcal{H}$ is a (potentially unknown) subgroup of $\mathcal{H}_\delta$. We split $\mathcal{A}_2(y,z)$ into two phases, $\mathcal{A}_2^0()$, which outputs the set $\mathcal{H} \star x$, and then $\mathcal{A}_2^1(y, z, \mathcal{H} \star x)$, which outputs the set $\mathcal{H} \star \mathsf{CDH}(y,z)$. We first give $\mathcal{A}_2^0()$:

- Initialize list $L = \{x\}$. Let $s = q^{-1} + \epsilon$ be an upper bound on the size of $\mathcal{H}_\delta$.
- Let $T = s\lambda/\tau$, for a parameter $\tau \in (0,1)$ to be chosen later.
- Repeat the following at least T times:
  - For each pair $(w, w') \in L^2$, run $L_{w,w'} \leftarrow \mathcal{A}_1(w, w')$
  - Let $L' = \cup_{w,w'} L_{w,w'}$
  - If $|L'| = |L|$ and the number of iterations so far is $\geq T$, terminate and output L. Otherwise (if the number of iterations is $< T$ or $|L'| \neq |L|$), replace L with L', and continue.

We now analyze the algorithm $L \leftarrow \mathcal{A}_2^0()$.

Lemma 11. *Except with negligible probability $2^{-\Omega(\lambda)}$, all of the following hold:*

- *$L = \mathcal{H} \star x$ for some (potentially unknown) subgroup $\mathcal{H} \subseteq \mathcal{H}_\delta$.*
- *$\mathcal{A}_2^0()$ will terminate in at most $T + s$ steps.*
- *For the resulting $\mathcal{H}$, $\Pr[M \not\subseteq \mathcal{H} : M \leftarrow \mathcal{D}'] < \tau$.*

Proof. Combining Lemmas 9 and 10, we know that except with probability $2^{-\Omega(\lambda)}$, $L_{w,w'}$ will be a list containing $\mathsf{CDH}(w, w')$. Throughout the rest of the proof of Lemma 11, we will therefore assume $\mathsf{CDH}(w, w') \in L_{w,w'}$ for all iterations and for all w, w'.

We first argue that $L \subseteq L'$ in every iteration, except with probability $2^{-\Omega(\lambda)}$. In particular, since L is set to L' at the end of each iteration, this means that L is never decreasing in size, and once an element is added to L it will remain for the rest of the algorithm. Indeed, L initially contains x. By induction, assume L contains x for the first i iterations, and consider computing L' in this iteration. L' is set to $L' = \cup_{w,w'} L_{w,w'}$ where $L_{w,w'} \leftarrow \mathcal{A}_1(w, w')$ as w, w' range over L. In particular, since $x \in L$, L' will contain $L_{w,x} \leftarrow \mathcal{A}_1(w, x)$ for every $w \in L$. Since we assume $L_{w,x}$ contains $\mathsf{CDH}(w, x) = w$, every $w \in L$ will be included in L'.

Therefore, if $|L'| = |L|$, it must mean that $L' = L$. Additionally, once we terminate, we know that $\mathsf{CDH}(w, w') \in L' = L$ for every $w, w' \in L$, meaning L is closed under CDH/multiplication once we terminate. Hence, L forms $\mathcal{H} \star x$ for some subgroup $\mathcal{H}$. By Lemma 10, our algorithm maintains the invariant that $L \subseteq \mathcal{H}_\delta$ at all times, and hence $\mathcal{H} \subseteq \mathcal{H}_\delta$.

Now consider any $w \in \mathcal{H}_\delta$ such that $\Pr[w \in M : M \leftarrow \mathcal{D}'] \geq \tau/s$. Then after T iterations, the probability w never gets added to L is $(1 - \tau/s)^T = (1 - \tau/s)^{s\lambda/\tau} \approx e^{-\lambda}$. Union bounding over at most s such w, we see that all such w get added to L, except with probability at most $2^{-\Omega(\lambda)}$. In this case, a union bound over the w such that $\Pr[w \in M : M \leftarrow \mathcal{D}'] < \tau/s$, of which there are at most s, shows that the probability of sampling any value not in $\mathcal{H}$ is less than τ.   □

We now give the algorithm $\mathcal{A}_2^1(y, z, L)$:

- Initialize $\mathcal{M}$ to be an empty list of unordered sets.
- Repeat the following λ times:
  - Run $M \leftarrow \mathcal{A}_1(y, z)$.
  - For each $w \in M, w' \in L$, run $M_{w,w'} \leftarrow \mathcal{A}_1(w, w')$.
  - Let $M = \cup_{w,w'} M_{w,w'}$. Add M to $\mathcal{M}$ (keeping duplicates).
- Let M^* be the most common element in $\mathcal{M}$.

We now analyze the algorithm $\mathcal{A}_2^1(y, z, L)$.

Lemma 12. *If $\tau \leq 1/4(s^2 + 1)$, then except with probability $2^{-\Omega(\lambda)}$, $L = \mathcal{H} \star x$ for some subgroup $\mathcal{H} \subseteq \mathcal{H}_\delta$, and $M^* = \mathsf{CDH}(y, z, \mathcal{H} \star x)$.*

Proof. Define $w^* = \mathsf{CDH}(y, z)$. We assume the bullets of Lemma 11 hold, which Lemma 11 shows hold with probability $2^{-\Omega(\lambda)}$. Therefore, $L = \mathcal{H} \star x$ for some subgroup $\mathcal{H} \subseteq \mathcal{H}_\delta$. It remains to show that $M^* = \mathsf{CDH}(y, z, \mathcal{H} \star x) = \mathcal{H} \star w^*$. By union-bounding over the $s^2 + 1$ runs of $\mathcal{A}_1$ in each iteration and invoking the last bullet of Lemma 11, the following holds: for each iteration, except with probability at most $\tau \times (s^2 + 1) \leq 1/4$, we have that

- $M_{w,w'} \subseteq \mathcal{H} \star w^*$ for each $w \in M, w' \in L$, and therefore in particular $M \subseteq \mathcal{H} \star w^*$.
- $w^* \in M$.

Provided $M \subseteq \mathcal{H} \star w^*$, except with probability $2^{-\Omega(\lambda)}$, we have $\mathsf{CDH}(w, w') \in M_{w,w'}$, and so $\mathcal{H} \star w^* = \mathsf{CDH}(w^*, \mathcal{H} \star x) \subseteq M$. Therefore, $M = \mathcal{H} \star w^*$ with probability at least $3/4 - 2^{-\Omega(\lambda)} \geq 2/3$. Since each iteration samples independently the distribution over M, by simple concentration bounds $\mathcal{H} \star w^*$ will be the majority element of $\mathcal{M}$, except with probability $2^{-\Omega(\lambda)}$.   □

Note that $\mathcal{A}_2^0$ runs $\mathcal{A}_1$ for $(T+s)|L|^2 = O(|L|^2\lambda/q^3) = \tilde{O}(q^{-5})$ times, giving $\tilde{O}(q^{-13})$ total queries to $\mathcal{A}$ and the group action operation. Meanwhile, $\mathcal{A}_2^1$ runs $\mathcal{A}_1$ for $\lambda|L|^2$ times, giving $\tilde{O}(q^{-10})$ queries to $\mathcal{A}$ and the group operation. From this point on, we fix a single $L \leftarrow \mathcal{A}_2^0()$ once and for all.

Removing Superfluous Information. We will next want to run quantum period-finding algorithms which make queries to $\mathcal{A}_2^1$ on superpositions of inputs. These algorithms, however, assume $\mathcal{A}_2^1$ is a function. Unfortunately, our algorithm generates significant side information, namely all the intermediate computations used to arrive at the final answer. Fortunately, since our algorithm outputs a single answer with overwhelming probability, we can use the standard trick of purifying the execution of $\mathcal{A}_2^1$ and then un-computing all the intermediate values. The result is that $\mathcal{A}_2^1$ is negligibly close to behaving as the function mapping $(y, z) \mapsto \mathcal{H} \star \mathsf{CDH}(y, z)$. From now on, we will therefore assume that $\mathcal{A}_2^1$ is such a function.

Computing $\mathcal{H}$. Given algorithm $\mathcal{A}_2^1$, we can compute the subgroup $\mathcal{H}$ using quantum period-finding [BL95]. Concretely, the function $a \mapsto \mathcal{A}_2^1(a \star x, x, L)$ will output $(a\mathcal{H}) \star x$, which is periodic with set of periods $\mathcal{H}$. Therefore, applying quantum period finding to the procedure $a \mapsto \mathcal{A}_2^1(a\star x, x, L)$ will recover $\mathcal{H}$. This will make $O(\log|G|)$ calls to $\mathcal{A}_2^1(a \star x, x, L)$.

Solving DLog in $G/\mathcal{H}$. Notice that $\mathcal{A}_2^1$ is a (near) perfect CDH-solver, just in the group action corresponding to $G/\mathcal{H}$. Concretely, the group $G/\mathcal{H}$ acts on the set $X/\mathcal{H} := \{\mathcal{H} \star y : y \in X\}$ in the obvious way; the distinguished element of $X/\mathcal{H}$ is $\mathcal{H} \star x$. Our algorithm $\mathcal{A}_2^1$ gives a perfect CDH algorithm for this group action: we compute $\mathsf{CDH}(\mathcal{H}\star y, \mathcal{H}\star z)$ as $\mathcal{A}_2^1(y', z')$ for an arbitrary $y' \in \mathcal{H}\star y, z' \in \mathcal{H}\star z$.

We apply Galbraith et al. [GPSV18] to our CDH adversary for $(G/\mathcal{H}, X/\mathcal{H})$ to obtain a DLog adversary $\mathcal{B}(g\mathcal{H} \star x)$ which computes $g\mathcal{H}$. For completeness, we sketch the idea: Let $\mathbf{a}$ be a set of generators for $G/\mathcal{H}$. Since G is abelian, we can write any g as $\mathbf{a}^{\mathbf{v}}$ for some vector $\mathbf{v} \in \mathbb{Z}_{n_1} \times \cdots \times \mathbb{Z}_{n_k}$ where n_i is the period of a_i. We assume the n_i are fully reduced, so that the choice of $\mathbf{v}$ is unique. Shor's algorithm is used in this step, and we note that Shor's algorithm will not necessarily work if G is not abelian and our group action is not regular, which is why we need this restriction.

The CDH oracle allows, given $h \star (\mathcal{H} \star x)$, to compute $h^y \star (\mathcal{H} \star x)$ in $O(\log y)$ steps using repeated squaring. Given a DLog instance $g \star (\mathcal{H}\star x) = \mathbf{a}^{\mathbf{v}} \star (\mathcal{H}\star x)$, we define the function $(\mathbf{x}, y) \mapsto \mathbf{a}^{\mathbf{x}+y\mathbf{v}} \star (\mathcal{H} \star x)$, which can be computed using the CDH oracle. Then this function is periodic with period $(\mathbf{v}, -1)$. Running quantum period-finding therefore gives $\mathbf{v}$, which can be used to compute h.

Solving DLog in G. We now have an algorithm which solves, with overwhelming probability, DLog in $G/\mathcal{H}$. We now turn this into a full DLog adversary, which works as follows:

- Given $y = c \star x$, first apply the DLog adversary for $G/\mathcal{H}$, which outputs $c\mathcal{H}$.
- For each $a \in c\mathcal{H}$ (which is polynomial sized), test if $y = a \star x$. We output the unique such a.

Overall, assuming q is small relative to $\log|G|$, the running time of the algorithm is dominated by the cost of running $\mathcal{A}_2^0$, namely $\tilde{O}(q^{-13})$ total calls to $\mathcal{A}$ and the group action operations.

Remark 4. The dependence on q in our reduction is not ideal. The cost of our attack, however, is dominated by the cost of determining the subgroup. Typically, however, we expect the possible small-order subgroups to be known, and for there to only be a very limited number of options. In this case, we expect the complexity of our attack could be drastically improved.

3.1   Extending to Non-regular Group Actions

The above assumed a regular group action, which captures all the cryptographic abelian group actions currently known. Here, we briefly sketch how to extend to an arbitrary abelian group action. The idea is that, within any ablelian group action, we can pull out a regular group action, and then apply the reduction above.

Concretely, we first consider restricting $(G, X, \star)$ to the orbit of x under G, namely $G \star x$. Let $S \subseteq G$ the set of a that "stabilizes" x, namely $a \star x = x$. Then S is a subgroup. Moreover, for any $y \in G \star x$, the set of a that stabilize y is also exactly S.

The first step is to compute the (representation of the) subgroup S. Let $f : G \to X$ be defined as $f(a) = a \star x$. Then f is an instance of the abelian hidden subgroup problem with hidden subgroup exactly S. Therefore, we can find S using Shor's quantum algorithm.

Then we can define the new group action $(G/S, G \star x, \star)$, which is a regular abelian group action. CDH in this group action is identical to CDH in the original group action, in that a CDH adversary for one is also a CDH adversary for the other. We can also solve DLog in $(G, X, \star)$ by solving DLog in $(G/S, G \star x, \star)$, and then lifting $a \in G/S$ to $a' = (a, g) \in G$ for an arbitrary $g \in S$.

The main challenge is that our CDH adversary $\mathcal{A}$ may not always output elements in $G \star x$, and it may be infeasible to tell when it outputs an element in $G \star x$ versus a different orbit. Nevertheless, the same reduction as used above applies, and the analysis can be extended straightforwardly but tediously to handle the fact that $\mathcal{A}$ may output elements in different orbits. The rough idea is that L outputted by $\mathcal{A}_1$ may no longer be a subset of $\mathcal{H}_\delta \star x$, as it may have pieces from elements from different orbits. But $L \cap G \star x$ is still a subset of $\mathcal{H}_\delta \star x$, and similar statements hold for $\mathcal{A}_2^0, \mathcal{A}_2^1$ as well. This is enough to ensure that we obtain a near-perfect CDH algorithm on $(G/S)/\mathcal{H}$.

4   On the DDH and CDH (In)Equivalence

A natural question to ask is whether we can show that the group action variants of CDH and DDH are equivalent. In traditional groups, there are a number of ways to argue that CDH and DDH are not equivalent, including by positing the existence of bilinear maps [BF01].

We show that for general group actions, the problems are also *not* equivalent. We do this by providing examples of group actions where "CDH" is hard and "DDH" is easy. In particular, we show that any group action where the group can be written as a non-trivial product group has the potential to be "CDH" hard but not "DDH" hard. This mirrors what we know classically and in the plain group setting, since there we can have groups that are CDH hard but not DDH hard. We state this formally in the following lemma.

Lemma 13.   *Let $(G, X, \star)$ be an effective group action such that no efficient adversary can solve the group action CDH problem (as defined in Definition 5) over it. Then there exists a group action $(G', X', \bigstar)$ where no efficient adversary can solve the CDH problem, but there exists a PPT algorithm for solving the group action DDH problem (as defined in Definition 6).*

Proof. Consider some extra group $\tilde{G}$. We can define a "group action" $\tilde{G} \times \tilde{G} \to \tilde{G}$ where the group action operation is simply group multiplication in $\tilde{G}$. Discrete log is trivial on this group since group inversion is efficient.

From our secure group action $(G, X, \star)$ and our insecure "group action," we construct another group action $(G', X', \bigstar)$ which we define as follows:

$$G' = G \times \tilde{G}$$

$$X' = X \times \tilde{G}$$

$$\bigstar : \left\{ G \times \tilde{G} \right\} \times \left\{ X \times \tilde{G} \right\} \to \left\{ X \times \tilde{G} \right\}$$

For some $g \in G$, $x \in X$, $\tilde{g}_1, \tilde{g}_2 \in \tilde{G}$, we define the action as follows:

$$\{g, \tilde{g}_1\} \bigstar \{x, \tilde{g}_2\} = \{g \star x, \tilde{g}_1 \tilde{g}_2\}$$

Note that this definition meets all of the requirements of the group action. $G \times \tilde{G}$ is a (product) group, and all of the group action axioms hold.

We can immediately build a PPT distinguisher: given a DDH tuple $(x'_1 = (x, \tilde{g}_1), g' \star x'_1 = (g \star x_1, \tilde{g}\tilde{g}_1), x'_2 = (x, \tilde{g}_2), g' \star x'_2 = (g \star x_2, \tilde{g}\tilde{g}_2))$, we can perform the following check:

$$(\tilde{g}\tilde{g}_2)^{-1} (\tilde{g}\tilde{g}_1) = \tilde{g}_2^{-1} \tilde{g}_1$$

This immediately breaks the pseudorandomness of the group action, meaning that the group action DDH problem is not hard over $\left(\tilde{G}, \tilde{X}, \bigstar\right)$. However, any adversary that breaks the group action CDH problem on $\left(\tilde{G}, \tilde{X}, \bigstar\right)$ also breaks it on $(G, X, \star)$, which contradicts our assumption that the CDH problem is hard on this group action. $\square$

In the above example, we used a product group. A nice question is as follows: what happens if we assume that the group must be, say, prime-order cyclic? This case is much harder to show interesting results since we don't have efficiently computable bilinear pairings as in the standard group setting.

5   A Generic Group Action Framework

In this section, we define a generic group action framework. We create two models: one for classical queries, and one which allows quantum queries. Our framework is based on the generic group framework of Shoup [Sho97]. We borrow from Shoup's description in our own explanation below.

Let G be a group of order n, let X be a set that is representable by bit strings of length m, and let $(G, X, \star)$ be a group action. We define additional sets S_G and S_X such that they have cardinality of at least n and 2^m, respectively. We define *encoding functions* of σ_G and σ_X on S_G and S_X, respectively, to be injective maps of the form $\sigma_G : G \to S_G$ and $\sigma_X : X \to S_X$.

A generic algorithm $\mathcal{A}$ for $(G, X, \star)$ on (S_G, S_X) is a probabilistic algorithm that behaves in the following way. It takes as input two *encoding lists* $(\sigma_G(g_1), ..., \sigma_G(g_k))$ and $(\sigma_X(x_1), ..., \sigma_X(x_{k'}))$ where each $g_i \in G$ and $x_i \in X$ and where σ_G and σ_X are encoding functions of G on S_G and X on S_X, respectively. As the algorithm executes, it may consult two oracles, $\mathcal{O}_G$ and $\mathcal{O}_X$.

The oracle $\mathcal{O}_G$ takes as input two strings y, z representing group elements and a sign "$+$" or "$-$", computes $\sigma_G\left(\sigma_G^{-1}(y) \pm \sigma_G^{-1}(z)\right)$. The oracle $\mathcal{O}_X$ takes as input a string y representing a group element and string z representing a set element, and computes $\sigma_X\left(\sigma_G^{-1}(y) \star \sigma_X^{-1}(z)\right)$. As is typical in the literature, we can force all queries to be on either the initial encoding lists or the results of previous queries by making the string length m very long. We typically measure the running time of the algorithm by the number of oracle queries.

We can also extend the generic group action model to the quantum setting, where we allow *quantum* queries to the oracles. We model quantum queries in the usual way: $\mathcal{O}_G \sum_{y,z,\pm,w} \alpha_{y,z,\pm,w} |y, z, \pm, w\rangle = \sum_{y,z,\pm,w} \alpha_{y,z,\pm,w} |y, z, \pm, w \oplus \mathcal{O}_G(y, z, \pm)\rangle$ and $\mathcal{O}_X \sum_{y,z,w} \alpha_{y,z,w} |y, z, w\rangle = \sum_{y,z,w} \alpha_{y,z,w} |y, z, w \oplus \mathcal{O}_X(y, z)\rangle$.

6   On REGAs

Our reductions showing the equivalence of group action DLog and CDH unfortunately only hold for EGAs and not for REGAs. In their work showing an equivalence for a perfect oracle [GPSV18], Galbraith *et al.* suggest that applying the BKZ algorithm [SE94] or other lattice reduction techniques can be used to complete the reduction. In this section, we formalize this idea with a number of results on the relationship between REGAs and lattices, and, in particular, focus on the 1D-SIS problem, which is a lattice problem that is equivalent to the standard form of LWE modulo PPT reductions. Due to space constraints, we only state the relevant lemmas in this section and defer proofs to the full version of the paper. We present the full, unabridged version of this section as well as the formal definitions related to REGAs in full in the full version of the paper.

In this section, we will rely on the fact that, using a generalization of Shor's algorithm [CM01], we can (quantumly) efficiently compute the isomorphism between any abelian group G and a product group over groups of the integers

$$G \cong \mathbb{Z}_1 \times ... \times \mathbb{Z}_m.$$

We additionally note that most of our results here only hold for *regular* group actions. We do not consider this a major drawback since all popular REGAs (e.g. CSIDH and its derivatives) are regular REGAs.

A "1D-SIS Oracle" Completes the DLog/CDH Reduction for REGAs.
We begin by formalizing the argument from Galbraith *et al.* [GPSV18] that efficient lattice reductions could be used to show the discrete log/CDH equivalence of REGAs. While doing this in full would involve completely replicating our earlier proof, we simply point out at which stages using a REGA makes a difference and how we can handle these points.

We first need to ensure that we can randomly sample elements from a REGA. We define a notion of "sampleable REGA" capturing this:

Definition 7.   Sampleable REGA: *Let $(G, X, \star)$ be a REGA with group element vector $\mathbf{g} = (\mathbf{g}_1, ..., \mathbf{g}_m)$ for some m. We say that such a REGA is sampleable if there exists an efficient way to sample a vector $\mathbf{b} \in \{-\gamma, \gamma\}^m$ for some polynomial γ such that the vector $\mathbf{r} = \sum_{i=1}^m \mathbf{b}_i \mathbf{g}_i$ is distributed statistically close to uniform over G.*

This requirement essentially just requires that some form of the leftover hash lemma applies over the group with the action-computable elements as the "base." We note that many cryptosystems build on REGAs (i.e. those using CSIDH) implicitly make this assumption. We need this to rule out cases where the elements of $\mathbf{g}$ are too clustered: for instance, if G is Z_p and all of the $\mathbf{g}_i$ are small integers, we will not be able to effectively compute the group action on randomly distributed group elements. Next, we define a specialized problem we call "REGA-SIS." Note that this is not a standard problem because, among other things, the $\mathbf{g}_i$ distribution comes from the definition of the REGA.

Definition 8.   REGA-SIS: *Let $(G, X, \star)$ be a REGA with group element vector $\mathbf{g} = (\mathbf{g}_1, ..., \mathbf{g}_m)$ for some m. We define $SIS_{REGA,\beta}$ in the following way: given a random element $h \leftarrow G$, the problem is to find some vector $\mathbf{u} \in [-\beta, \beta]^m$ such that $h = \sum_{i=1}^m \mathbf{u}_i \mathbf{g}_i$.*

This problem is parameterized by the REGA and, in particular, by both the group and the computable elements. Furthermore, for $G = \mathsf{Z}_q$ and when each coefficient of $\mathbf{g}$ is distributed uniformly at random, REGA-SIS is exactly the 1D-inhomogeneous SIS (1D-ISIS) problem (which is reducible to standard 1D-SIS with a slight loss in parameters, and 1D-SIS itself is again reducible to and from standard LWE, for appropriate parameter settings). So this problem can be viewed as a slightly unnatural generalization of SIS. We can now state our core lemma on REGAs.

Lemma 14.   *Consider any efficiently sampleable REGA as defined in Definition 7. Then any adversary that can solve the CDH problem on the REGA with advantage ϵ_1 and the $SIS_{REGA,\beta}$ problem for the same REGA and some polynomial β with advantage ϵ_2 can be used to solve the discrete log problem on the same REGA with advantage $\epsilon_1\epsilon_2$.*

Discrete Log on REGAs and 1D-SIS. Recall that a REGA is a group action $(G, X, \star)$ where the action is only computable on a set of group elements defined by a vector $\mathbf{g} = (g_1, \ldots, g_n)$. Suppose that G is an abelian group. We claim that if these group elements are distributed randomly, then any adversary that can solve discrete log on the REGA can be used to solve the 1D-SIS problem for certain parameter settings (which are all reducible to some form of standard LWE). The analysis of most practical REGAs (e.g. CSIDH) assume follow this convention, so this is not an unreasonable assumption to make. We formalize this with the following lemma.

Lemma 15. *Let q and m be integers such that $m \geq 3 \log q$. Let $\mathcal{A}$ be an adversary that can solve the group action DLog problem on regular REGAs of the form $(Z_q, X, \star)$ where the vector of group elements $\mathbf{g} = (g_1, ..., g_m)$ is m elements long and distributed uniformly at random with advantage ϵ. Then $\mathcal{A}$ can be used to solve the 1D-$SIS_{m,q,\beta}$ problem for some polynomial β with advantage ϵ.*

CDH on REGAs. We above showed that an adversary that can solve discrete log on a REGA can solve a variant of the SIS problem, and that any adversary that can solve this SIS variant can also be used to complete the CDH/DLog reduction. Can we tie all of this together to get an unconditional CDH to DLog reduction to work for REGAs?

We give some mild evidence in this direction. We can show that any *generic* adversary that makes only *classical* queries to a generic group action oracle (that may still be able to perform quantum computations) can be used to solve the REGA-SIS problem we defined above in Definition 8. We can then use this to complete the CDH to DLog reduction for generic, classically-querying adversaries. Of course, classically we can prove CDH and DLog are unconditionally hard (this follows from the unconditional hardness of these problems in plain groups), and therefore equivalent. But phrasing the equivalence as a reduction suggests a possible starting point for a quantum equivalence

Lemma 16. *Consider some regular, abelian, and efficiently sampleable REGA $(G, X, \star)$ with computable elements $\mathbf{g} = (\mathbf{g}_1, ..., \mathbf{g}_m)$. Suppose there exists a generic adversary making only classical group and group action queries that can solve the GA-CDH problem on this REGA with advantage ϵ. Then there exists an adversary that can solve REGA-SIS for some polynomial parameter β with advantage $\epsilon/2$.*

Discussion. We have shown three core results on REGAs (stated informally): an adversary for our REGA-SIS problem would complete our CDH/DLog reduction for REGAs, an adversary for DLog on REGAs solves this REGA-SIS problem, and a generic adversary that only makes classical queries that can solve CDH on REGAs can be used to solve REGA-SIS as well. All together, these seemingly tightly bind CDH and DLog on a REGA to a SIS-like problem that appears to be vulnerable to lattice-based cryptanalysis [GPSV18]. We therefore provide some evidence for a quantum DLog-CDH equivalence on REGAs.

7   Hidden Subgroup Problems and GAs

In this section, we discuss some similarities between different kinds of hidden subgroup problems (HSPs) and solving group actions. We particularly focus on the *generalized* dihedral group. We note that, among other things, formalizing a connection between group actions and these kinds of problem would allow us to potentially tie two of the most popular forms of post-quantum cryptosystems (lattices and isogenies) together. Once again, due to space constraints, we just state lemmas here and defer the full presentation to the full version of the paper.

The Generalized Dihedral Hidden Subgroup Problem. We begin by defining the *generalized* dihedral group.

Definition 9.   *Generalized Dihedral Group: Let A be an abelian group. The generalized dihedral group on A, denoted D_A, is the group defined by $\mathbb{Z}_2 \ltimes A$.*

When $A \cong \mathbb{Z}_n$, we get back the standard notion of the dihedral group on $2n$ elements. The dihedral group has a number of nice geometric explanations and properties, but we defer those to others [KLG06]. We next define the general dihedral hidden subgroup problem. However, rather than defining this problem in its traditional sense, we will use an equivalent formulation known as the *abelian hidden shift problem*. These problems are well known to be equivalent [CVD05].

Definition 10.   *Abelian Hidden Shift Problem (equivalent to GDHSP): Consider some functions f, g such that, for some $c \in A$ and for all $b \in \mathbb{Z}_n$, $f(b) = g(b + c)$. We also require that each of the $\|A\|$ output values of f and g are also distinct. We say that an algorithm solves the abelian hidden shift problem if, given descriptions of f and g, it outputs c (which reveals the subgroup in the generalized dihedral hidden subgroup version of the problem).*

The dihedral hidden subgroup problem has strong connections to lattice problems [Reg02], in that if an efficient algorithm for the DHS problem that uses a special type of "coset sampling" exists, then an efficient algorithm for the LWE problem exists as well. The best known algorithms for solving the DHS problem are subexponential and based on Kuperberg's algorithm [Kup05, Reg04, Kup13].

An Algorithm for the AHSP Breaks Regular, Abelian Group Actions. We first show a relatively straightforward result: any algorithm that can solve the abelian hidden shift problem can be used to solve DLog on a regular, abelian group action. This is essentially already folklore since there have been many instances (starting with [CJS14]) using Kuperberg's algorithm or related principles to build attacks against isogenies that can be modelled as EGAs.

Lemma 17.   *Let $(G, X, \star)$ denote a regular, abelian group action. Suppose there exists a PPT algorithm $\mathcal{A}$ for solving the abelian hidden shift problem on A with probability ϵ. Then there exists for solving the GA-DLog problem on $(G, X, \star)$ with probability ϵ.*

Using Group Action Algorithms to Solve the AHSP. What about the other direction? Can we show that an adversary that can break DLog on a group action can solve the AHSP? Unfortunately, this seems difficult: because the AHSP is described so generally–the functions f and g can be anything as long as the functions are injective–so it seems difficult or impossible to prove this for any non-generic algorithm.

But what about generic algorithms? Could we prove that the AHSP is equivalent to generically solving DLog over group actions? This seems like it might be plausible. The most interesting result would show equivalence in a generic group action model with quantum queries. While this may be attainable, unfortunately we do not know how to achieve this result. However, we can show that an adversary that can generically solve group action DLog with classical queries can be used to solve the AHSP, which is seemingly a step in the right direction. We formalize this result below.

Lemma 18. *Let $(G, X, \star)$ be an abelian, regular group action (EGA). Suppose there exists a generic adversary $\mathcal{A}$ that breaks the group action DLog problem (as defined in Definition 4) with advantage ϵ on this group action. Then there exists an algorithm that solves that AHSP on G with advantage ϵ.*

Discussion. Unfortunately, it seems difficult to show a full quantum equivalence between the generalized dihedral hidden subgroup problem and solving DLog on a generic group action. The challenge comes from the fact that it is difficult quantumly to "remember" an adversary's query for later use in the simulation. One possible direction is to use compressed oracles [Zha19], which offer some ability to record quantum queries. However, it appears challenging to adapt the compressed oracle framework to highly structured oracles such as generic group actions. Nevertheless, we close this section with the following conjecture, which we think is very interesting future work:

Conjecture 1. The generalized dihedral hidden subgroup problem on an abelian group A is equivalent to the group action discrete logarithm problem on a regular, abelian group action $(A, X, \star)$ in a quantum generic model.

References

ADMP20. Alamati, N., De Feo, L., Montgomery, H., Patranabis, S.: Cryptographic group actions and applications. In: Moriai, S., Wang, H. (eds.) ASIACRYPT 2020. LNCS, vol. 12492, pp. 411–439. Springer, Cham (2020). https://doi.org/10.1007/978-3-030-64834-3_14

Ajt96. Ajtai, M.: Generating hard instances of lattice problems (extended abstract). In: 28th ACM STOC, pp. 99–108. ACM Press, May 1996

BF01. Boneh, D., Franklin, M.: Identity-based encryption from the weil pairing. In: Kilian, J. (ed.) CRYPTO 2001. LNCS, vol. 2139, pp. 213–229. Springer, Heidelberg (2001). https://doi.org/10.1007/3-540-44647-8_13

BGLS19. Bai, S., Galbraith, S.D., Li, L., Sheffield, D.: Improved combinatorial algorithms for the inhomogeneous short integer solution problem. J. Cryptol. **32**(1), 35–83 (2019)

BKM17. Boneh, D., Kim, S., Montgomery, H.: Private Puncturable PRFs from standard lattice assumptions. In: Coron, J.-S., Nielsen, J.B. (eds.) EUROCRYPT 2017. LNCS, vol. 10210, pp. 415–445. Springer, Cham (2017). https://doi.org/10.1007/978-3-319-56620-7_15

BKT14. Ben-Zvi, A., Kalka, A., Tsaban, B.: Cryptanalysis via algebraic spans. Cryptology ePrint Archive, Report 2014/041 (2014). https://eprint.iacr.org/2014/041

BKT18. Ben-Zvi, A., Kalka, A., Tsaban, B.: Cryptanalysis via algebraic spans. In: Shacham, H., Boldyreva, A. (eds.) CRYPTO 2018. LNCS, vol. 10991, pp. 255–274. Springer, Cham (2018). https://doi.org/10.1007/978-3-319-96884-1_9

BKV19. Beullens, W., Kleinjung, T., Vercauteren, F.: CSI-FiSh: efficient isogeny based signatures through class group computations. In: Galbraith, S.D., Moriai, S. (eds.) ASIACRYPT 2019. LNCS, vol. 11921, pp. 227–247. Springer, Cham (2019). https://doi.org/10.1007/978-3-030-34578-5_9

BL95. Boneh, D., Lipton, R.J.: Quantum cryptanalysis of hidden linear functions. In: Coppersmith, D. (ed.) CRYPTO 1995. LNCS, vol. 963, pp. 424–437. Springer, Heidelberg (1995). https://doi.org/10.1007/3-540-44750-4_34

BL96. Boneh, D., Lipton, R.J.: Algorithms for black-box fields and their application to cryptography. In: Koblitz, N. (ed.) CRYPTO 1996. LNCS, vol. 1109, pp. 283–297. Springer, Heidelberg (1996). https://doi.org/10.1007/3-540-68697-5_22

BLP+13. Brakerski, Z., Langlois, A., Peikert, C., Regev, O., Stehlé, D.: Classical hardness of learning with errors. In: Boneh, D., Roughgarden, T., Feigenbaum, J. (eds.) 45th ACM STOC, pp. 575–584. ACM Press, June 2013

BMZ19. Bartusek, J., Ma, F., Zhandry, M.: The distinction between fixed and random generators in group-based assumptions. In: Boldyreva, A., Micciancio, D. (eds.) CRYPTO 2019. LNCS, vol. 11693, pp. 801–830. Springer, Cham (2019). https://doi.org/10.1007/978-3-030-26951-7_27

BS20. Bonnetain, X., Schrottenloher, A.: Quantum security analysis of CSIDH. In: Canteaut, A., Ishai, Y. (eds.) EUROCRYPT 2020. LNCS, vol. 12106, pp. 493–522. Springer, Cham (2020). https://doi.org/10.1007/978-3-030-45724-2_17

BV15. Brakerski, Z., Vaikuntanathan, V.: Constrained key-homomorphic prfs from standard lattice assumptions. In: Dodis, Y., Nielsen, J.B. (eds.) TCC 2015. LNCS, vol. 9015, pp. 1–30. Springer, Heidelberg (2015). https://doi.org/10.1007/978-3-662-46497-7_1

BY91. Brassard, G., Yung, M.: One-Way Group Actions. In: Menezes, A.J., Vanstone, S.A. (eds.) CRYPTO 1990. LNCS, vol. 537, pp. 94–107. Springer, Heidelberg (1991). https://doi.org/10.1007/3-540-38424-3_7

CD22. Castryck, W., Decru, T.: An efficient key recovery attack on sidh (preliminary version). Cryptology ePrint Archive, Paper 2022/975 (2022). https://eprint.iacr.org/2022/975

CJS14. Childs, A., Jao, D., Soukharev, V.: Constructing elliptic curve isogenies in quantum subexponential time. J. Math. Cryptology **8**(1), 1–29 (2014)

CK20. Colò, L., Kohel, D.: Orienting supersingular isogeny graphs. J. Math. Cryptology **14**(1), 414–437 (2020)

CLM+18. Castryck, W., Lange, T., Martindale, C., Panny, L., Renes, J.: CSIDH: an efficient post-quantum commutative group action. In: Peyrin, T., Galbraith, S. (eds.) ASIACRYPT 2018. LNCS, vol. 11274, pp. 395–427. Springer, Cham (2018). https://doi.org/10.1007/978-3-030-03332-3_15

CM01. Cheung, K.K.H., Mosca, M.: Decomposing finite abelian groups. Quantum Inform. Comput. **1**(3), 26–32 (2001)

Cou06. Jean-Marc Couveignes. Hard homogeneous spaces. Cryptology ePrint Archive, Report 2006/291 (2006). https://eprint.iacr.org/2006/291

CVD05. Childs, A.M., Van Dam, W.: Quantum algorithm for a generalized hidden shift problem. arXiv preprint quant-ph/0507190 (2005)

DDF21. Dartois, P., De Feo, L.: On the security of osidh. Cryptology ePrint Archive (2021)

den90. Boer, B.: Diffie-Hellman is as strong as discrete log for certain primes. In: Goldwasser, S. (ed.) CRYPTO 1988. LNCS, vol. 403, pp. 530–539. Springer, New York (1990). https://doi.org/10.1007/0-387-34799-2_38

DG19. De Feo, L., Galbraith, S.D.: SeaSign: compact isogeny signatures from class group actions. In: Ishai, Y., Rijmen, V. (eds.) EUROCRYPT 2019. Part III, volume 11478 of LNCS, pp. 759–789. Springer, Heidelberg (2019)

DH76. Diffie, W., Hellman, M.E.: New directions in cryptography. IEEE Trans. Inf. Theory **22**(6), 644–654 (1976)

DJP14. De Feo, L., Jao, D., Plût, J.: Towards quantum-resistant cryptosystems from supersingular elliptic curve isogenies. J. Math. Cryptol. **8**(3), 209–247 (2014)

DM20a. De Feo, L., Meyer, M.: Threshold schemes from isogeny assumptions. In: Kiayias, A., Kohlweiss, M., Wallden, P., Zikas, V. (eds.) PKC 2020. LNCS, vol. 12111, pp. 187–212. Springer, Cham (2020). https://doi.org/10.1007/978-3-030-45388-6_7

GPSV18. Galbraith, S., Panny, L., Smith, B., Vercauteren, F.: Quantum equivalence of the DLP and CDHP for group actions. Cryptology ePrint Archive, Report 2018/1199 (2018). https://eprint.iacr.org/2018/1199

ILL89. Impagliazzo, R., Levin, L.A., Luby, M.: Pseudo-random generation from one-way functions (extended abstracts). In: 21st ACM STOC, pp. 12–24. ACM Press, May 1989

JQSY19. Ji, Z., Qiao, Y., Song, F., Yun, A.: General linear group action on tensors: a candidate for post-quantum cryptography. In: Hofheinz, D., Rosen, A. (eds.) TCC 2019. LNCS, vol. 11891, pp. 251–281. Springer, Cham (2019). https://doi.org/10.1007/978-3-030-36030-6_11

KLC+00. Ko, K.H., Lee, S.J., Cheon, J.H., Han, J.W., Kang, J., Park, C.: New public-key cryptosystem using braid groups. In: Bellare, M. (ed.) CRYPTO 2000. LNCS, vol. 1880, pp. 166–183. Springer, Heidelberg (2000). https://doi.org/10.1007/3-540-44598-6_10

KLG06. Kobayashi, H., Le Gall, F.: Dihedral hidden subgroup problem: a survey. Inf. Media Technol. **1**(1), 178–185 (2006)

Kup05. Kuperberg, G.: A subexponential-time quantum algorithm for the dihedral hidden subgroup problem. SIAM J. Comput. **35**(1), 170–188 (2005)

Kup13. Kuperberg, G.: Another subexponential-time quantum algorithm for the dihedral hidden subgroup problem. In: Severini, S., Brandao, F., (eds.) 8th Conference on the Theory of Quantum Computation, Communication and Cryptography (TQC 2013). Leibniz International Proceedings in Informatics (LIPIcs), vol. 22, pp. 20–34, Dagstuhl, Germany, 2013. Schloss Dagstuhl-Leibniz-Zentrum fuer Informatik

LGdSG21. Lai, Y.-F., Galbraith, S.D., Delpech de Saint Guilhem, C.: Compact, efficient and UC-secure isogeny-based oblivious transfer. In: Canteaut, A., Standaert, F.-X. (eds.) EUROCRYPT 2021. LNCS, vol. 12696, pp. 213–241. Springer, Cham (2021). https://doi.org/10.1007/978-3-030-77870-5_8

Mas90. Massart, P.: The tight constant in the Dvoretzky-Kiefer-Wolfowitz inequality. Ann. Probab. **18**(3), 1269–1283 (1990)

Mau94. Maurer, U.M.: Towards the equivalence of breaking the diffie-hellman protocol and computing discrete logarithms. In: Desmedt, Y.G. (ed.) CRYPTO 1994. LNCS, vol. 839, pp. 271–281. Springer, Heidelberg (1994). https://doi.org/10.1007/3-540-48658-5_26

MM22. Maino, L., Martindale, C.: An attack on sidh with arbitrary starting curve. Cryptology ePrint Archive, Paper 2022/1026 (2022). https://eprint.iacr.org/2022/1026

MW96. Maurer, U.M., Wolf, S.: Diffie-Hellman oracles. In: Koblitz, N. (ed.) CRYPTO 1996. LNCS, vol. 1109, pp. 268–282. Springer, Heidelberg (1996). https://doi.org/10.1007/3-540-68697-5_21

Onu21. Onuki, H.: On oriented supersingular elliptic curves. Finite Fields Appl. **69**, 101777 (2021)

Pei20. Peikert, C.: He gives C-sieves on the CSIDH. In: Canteaut, A., Ishai, Y. (eds.) EUROCRYPT 2020. LNCS, vol. 12106, pp. 463–492. Springer, Cham (2020). https://doi.org/10.1007/978-3-030-45724-2_16

Reg02. Regev, O.: Quantum computation and lattice problems. In: 43rd FOCS, pp. 520–529. IEEE Computer Society Press, November 2002

Reg04. Regev, O.: A subexponential time algorithm for the dihedral hidden subgroup problem with polynomial space. arXiv:quant-ph/0406151, June 2004

Rob22. Robert, D.: Breaking sidh in polynomial time. Cryptology ePrint Archive, Paper 2022/1038 (2022). https://eprint.iacr.org/2022/1038

RS06. Rostovtsev, A., Stolbunov, A.: Public-key cryptosystem based on isogenies. cryptology ePrint Archive, Report 2006/145 (2006). https://eprint.iacr.org/2006/145

SE94. Schnorr, C.-P., Euchner, M.: Lattice basis reduction: improved practical algorithms and solving subset sum problems. Math. Program. **66**(1), 181–199 (1994)

Sho94. Shor., P.W.: Algorithms for quantum computation: discrete logarithms and factoring. In: 35th FOCS, pp. 124–134. IEEE Computer Society Press, November 1994

Sho97. Shoup, V.: Lower bounds for discrete logarithms and related problems. In: Fumy, W. (ed.) EUROCRYPT 1997. LNCS, vol. 1233, pp. 256–266. Springer, Heidelberg (1997). https://doi.org/10.1007/3-540-69053-0_18

Shp08. Shpilrain, V.: Cryptanalysis of stickel's key exchange scheme. In: Hirsch, E.A., Razborov, A.A., Semenov, A., Slissenko, A. (eds.) CSR 2008. LNCS, vol. 5010, pp. 283–288. Springer, Heidelberg (2008). https://doi.org/10.1007/978-3-540-79709-8_29

Sti05. Stickel, E.: A new method for exchanging secret keys. In: Third International Conference on Information Technology and Applications (ICITA'05), vol. 2, pp. 426–430. IEEE (2005)

SU05a. Shpilrain, V., Ushakov, A.: A new key exchange protocol based on the decomposition problem. Cryptology ePrint Archive, Report 2005/447 (2005). https://ia.cr/2005/447

SU05b. Shpilrain, V., Ushakov, A.: Thompson's group and public key cryptography. In: Ioannidis, J., Keromytis, A., Yung, M. (eds.) ACNS 2005. LNCS, vol. 3531, pp. 151–163. Springer, Heidelberg (2005). https://doi.org/10.1007/11496137_11

Zha19. Zhandry, M.: How to record quantum queries, and applications to quantum indifferentiability. In: Boldyreva, A., Micciancio, D. (eds.) CRYPTO 2019. LNCS, vol. 11693, pp. 239–268. Springer, Cham (2019). https://doi.org/10.1007/978-3-030-26951-7_9

Cryptographic Primitives with Hinting Property

Navid Alamati[1(⊠)] and Sikhar Patranabis[2]

[1] VISA Research, Palo Alto, USA
nalamati@visa.com
[2] IBM Research India, Bangalore, India

Abstract. A *hinting* PRG is a (potentially) stronger variant of PRG with a "deterministic" form of circular security with respect to the seed of the PRG (Koppula and Waters, CRYPTO 2019). Hinting PRGs enable many cryptographic applications, most notably CCA-secure public-key encryption and trapdoor functions. In this paper, we study cryptographic primitives with the hinting property, yielding the following results:

- We present a novel and conceptually simpler approach for designing hinting PRGs from certain decisional assumptions over cyclic groups or isogeny-based group actions, which enables simpler security proofs as compared to the existing approaches for designing such primitives.
- We introduce *hinting weak PRFs*, a natural extension of the hinting property to weak PRFs, and show how to realize circular/KDM-secure symmetric-key encryption from any hinting weak PRF. We demonstrate that our simple approach for building hinting PRGs can be extended to realize hinting weak PRFs from the same set of decisional assumptions.
- We propose a stronger version of the hinting property, which we call the *functional* hinting property, that guarantees security even in the presence of hints about functions of the secret seed/key. We show how to instantiate functional hinting PRGs and functional hinting weak PRFs for certain (families of) functions by building upon our simple techniques for realizing plain hinting PRGs/weak PRFs. We also demonstrate the applicability of a functional hinting weak PRF with certain algebraic properties in realizing KDM-secure public-key encryption in a black-box manner.
- Finally, we show the first black-box separation between hinting weak PRFs (and hinting PRGs) from public-key encryption using simple realizations of these primitives given only a random oracle.

1 Introduction

A pseudorandom generator (PRG) is one of the most fundamental and widely studied cryptographic primitives. Informally speaking, a PRG is an expanding function with the security guarantee that the output of the PRG on a randomly

---

S. Patranabis—Work done while at VISA Research.

S. Agrawal and D. Lin (Eds.): ASIACRYPT 2022, LNCS 13791, pp. 33–62, 2022.
https://doi.org/10.1007/978-3-031-22963-3_2

chosen input (also called the "seed") is computationally indistinguishable from random. However, a plain PRG does not provide any security guarantees if the adversary has some additional "hint" with respect to the each bit of the seed.

A *hinting* PRG, introduced recently by Koppula and Waters in [KW19], is a (potentially) stronger variant of PRG that provides security even given some hinting information about each bit of the seed. This hinting property can be viewed as a "deterministic" form of circular security with respect to the seed of the PRG. We informally recall the definition of a hinting PRG to provide a more concrete view of what this hinting property actually entails, and how it encapsulates circular security with respect to the seed.

A hinting PRG is a PRG of the form $G : \{0, 1\}^n \to Y^n$ that expands n-bit seed $\mathbf{s} \in \{0, 1\}^n$ into a vector $\mathbf{y} = (y_1, \dots, y_n)$ of n elements from the set Y, such that an $n \times 2$ matrix $\mathbf{Z} = \{z_{i,b}\}_{i \in [n], b \in \{0,1\}}$ distributed as follows:

$$
z_{i,b} = \begin{cases} y_i & \text{if } b = s_i, \\ u_i \leftarrow Y & \text{otherwise,} \end{cases}
$$

is computationally indistinguishable from a truly random matrix $\mathbf{U} \leftarrow Y^{n \times 2}$, where each element is sampled uniformly from the set Y.[1] Note that the matrix $\mathbf{Z}$ not only contains the output of the PRG, but also has some hinting information about each bit s_i of the seed $\mathbf{s}$ encoded into the arrangement of the elements in each row.

Hinting PRGs have been recently used as a key ingredient to construct several cryptographic primitives, such as realizing CCA-secure public-key encryption (PKE) and attribute-based encryption from their CPA-secure counterparts [KW19], trapdoor functions [KMT19a, GHMO21], black-box non-interactive non-malleable commitments [GKLW21], and CCA-compatible public-key infrastructure [KW21]. This wide range of applications motivates: (i) building hinting PRGs from a wide variety of mathematical assumptions, (ii) investigating some natural extensions of the hinting property to other cryptographic primitives, and (iii) studying the complexity of cryptographic primitives with hinting property.

Instantiations of Hinting PRGs. Koppula and Waters [KW19] showed how to realize hinting PRGs from the computational Diffie-Hellman (CDH) and the learning with errors (LWE) assumptions. Their constructions are based on the "missing block" framework that was introduced by Choi *et al.* [CDG+17]. Later, Goyal *et al.* [GVW20] introduced a new accumulation-style framework to build hinting PRGs, and they showed (efficient) constructions of hinting PRGs from the Decisional Diffie-Hellman Inversion (DDHI) and Phi-hiding assumptions. However, despite such considerable progress, it is not known how to realize hinting PRGs from a notable class of plausibly post-quantum secure assumptions, namely isogeny-based assumptions. Note that current techniques to construct

---

[1] The original definition of hinting PRG in [KW19] uses an additional output element $z_0 \in Y$ which has no hint about the seed of the PRG. We omit this element from the definition of hinting PRG here for simplicity of exposition.

hinting PRGs either use groups with infeasible inversion or the missing-block framework, both of which seem to be out of reach based on our understanding of structural properties of isogeny-based assumptions [ADMP20]. This leads to the following question: *can we realize hinting PRGs from isogeny-based assumptions?*

On a related note, a hinting PRG is an ostensibly symmetric-key primitive, and one would expect to achieve it from decisional assumptions (such as the DDH assumption) in a considerably simpler manner than allowed by current constructions and their security proofs. In particular, the closely related notion of symmetric-key circular secure encryption [BRS03] has significantly simpler realizations and security proofs based on decisional assumptions such as the DDH assumption [BHHO08]. This leads to the question: *is there a simple construction of hinting PRGs from decisional assumptions such as DDH?* More concretely, our aim is to achieve constructions and security proofs for hinting PRGs that are simpler than those based on the missing block framework [KW19] or the accumulation framework [GVW20]. Our hope is that a simpler construction of hinting PRGs would be amenable to instantiations from decisonal isogeny-based assumptions, while also naturally enabling extensions of the hinting property to other cryptographic primitives.

Hinting Property for Other Primitives. The authors of [KMT19a] showed that a hinting PRG can be used to construct a *one-time* key-dependent message (KDM) secure symmetric-key encryption (SKE) scheme. This motivates us to ask if there exists a natural extension of hinting PRGs that implies circular/KDM security with respect to *many* encryptions of the secret key, and if so, can such an extension also be realized in a simple manner from decisional assumptions such as DDH or isogeny-based decisional assumptions. Concretely, we ask the following question: *can we instantiate natural extensions of the hinting property to other cryptographic primitives from concrete hardness assumptions?*

Functional Hinting Property. The original definition of hinting PRG, as introduced in [KW19], only considers security in the presence of hints about each bit of the PRG seed itself. A natural extension of this security property would be to guarantee PRG security in the presence of hints about each bit of *some function* of the seed. For example, for a PRG seed $\mathbf{s} = (s_1, \ldots, s_n) \in \{0,1\}^n$, what if the PRG output provides hints about each bit of $f(\mathbf{s}) = (s_i \cdot s_j)_{i,j \in [n]}$, which is an n^2-length vector? This might be particularly challenging to achieve because the adversary now not only gets hints about each bit of $\mathbf{s}$ (via $s_i \cdot s_i = s_i$), but also about the pair-wise product of each bit of $\mathbf{s}$.

This strengthening of the hinting property to its functional counterpart is analogous to the strengthening of circular security to KDM security; in fact, one can view the functional hinting property with respect to a class of functions $\mathcal{F}$ as a "deterministic" form of KDM security with respect to $\mathcal{F}$. Additionally, this property also generalizes to other cryptographic primitives with the hinting property, if such primitives exist. In this paper, we ask the following question: *can we instantiate functional hinting PRG (and natural extensions of the functional hinting property to other cryptographic primitives) in a black-box way from concrete hardness assumptions?*

The Complexity of Primitives with Hinting Property. Another natural direction is to investigate the complexity of a hinting PRG, and its extensions to other cryptographic primitives. Based on the current constructions of hinting PRGs, it is unclear if we necessarily need structured mathematical assumptions to realize hinting PRGs. It is seemingly hard to build a hinting PRG in a generic way from any PRG (or equivalently, any one-way function). On the other hand, a hinting PRG does not immediately entail any "public-key"-style functionalities, and we do not know if it implies PKE. This leads to the following question: *does a hinting PRG (or any of its extensions to other symmetric-key cryptographic primitives) imply PKE in a black-box way?*

Observe that the closely related notion of symmetric-key circular/KDM-secure encryption, in fact, *does not* imply PKE in a black-box way because it can be realized from a random oracle [BRS03]. However, this does not answer the question outlined above because, as the authors of [KMT19a] point out, it is not known if a hinting PRG can be realized from any symmetric-key circular secure encryption scheme in a black-box way.

1.1   Our Contributions

In this paper, we address all of the above questions by showing the following results.

Simpler Constructions of Hinting PRG from DDH or Isogenies. We propose a new approach for realizing hinting PRGs from decisional assumptions. Our approach yields significantly simpler constructions and security proofs for hinting PRGs as compared to the existing constructions and proofs based on the missing block framework [KW19] or the accumulation-style framework [GVW20]. We show how to instantiate our approach based on the DDH assumption, as well as from a recent plausibly post-quantum secure isogeny-based assumption called the linear hidden shift (LHS) assumption [ADMP20] over certain isogeny-based group actions (e.g., variants of CSIDH [CLM+18, BKV19, ADMP20]). To the best of our knowledge, prior to our work, it was not known how to securely realize a hinting PRG from any isogeny-based assumption, including the LHS assumption [ADMP20].

Building upon our technique to realize hinting PRGs from the LHS assumption, we also show a direct construction of trapdoor (one-way) functions (TDFs) from any weak pseudorandom group action (which is a plausibly post-quantum secure analogue of the DDH assumption over isogeny-based group actions, introduced in [ADMP20]) for which the LHS assumption holds. Our construction of TDFs and the corresponding proof of security are significantly simpler as compared to the previously known constructions of TDFs from such isogeny-based assumptions proposed in [ADMP20], which relied on the framework of [KMT19a]. We note that the authors of [GHMO21] proposed a construction of TDFs given any hinting PRG and a PKE scheme with pseudorandom ciphertexts; however, their construction needs the ciphertext space to be a group, which does not hold for any isogeny-based PKE scheme.

Hinting weak PRF and Instantiations. We introduce a natural extension of the hinting property to another symmetric-key primitive, namely a weak pseudorandom function (wPRF). We call the resulting primitive a hinting wPRF, which is a strengthening of a hinting PRG in the sense that it guarantees weak pseudorandomness even in the presence of multiple hints with respect to the key of a weak PRF. We show that a hinting weak PRF can be used to construct a symmetric-key circular-secure encryption scheme (where the circular security guarantee holds with respect to multiple encryptions of the secret key) in a black-box manner (this can be amplified to achieve KDM security, albeit in a non-black-box way using known techniques [App14]). We also show that our approach for constructing hinting PRGs can be leveraged to construct hinting weak PRFs. This yields simple constructions of hinting weak PRFs based on either DDH or the LHS assumption.

Functional Hinting PRG/wPRF and Implications. We introduce functional hinting PRG - a strengthening of hinting PRG that guarantees PRG security in the presence of hints about each bit of *some function* of the seed. We also introduce a natural extension, namely a functional hinting wPRF, that guarantees wPRF security in the presence of hints about each bit of some (adversarially chosen) function of the secret key. We show that a functional hinting weak PRF with respect to a family of functions $\mathcal{F}$ can be used to realize a symmetric-key KDM-secure encryption scheme with respect to the same function family $\mathcal{F}$ in a *black-box* manner. We then build upon our approach of realizing hinting PRGs and hinting weak PRFs to realize simple constructions of functional hinting PRGs and functional weak PRFs for a family of quadratic functions (and functions of higher degree) based on the DDH assumption.

We note that our techniques enable achieving a deterministic form of KDM-security in a black-box manner, which is a different approach as compared to prior works on KDM security [KM19, KMT19b, KM20].

Complexity of Hinting PRG/wPRF. We make progress on understanding the complexity of cryptographic primitives with the hinting property. We show the first black-box separation between hinting PRG and public-key encryption by realizing a hinting PRG given only a random oracle. We then build upon our construction of hinting PRG to also show how to construct a hinting wPRF given only a random oracle. This additionally rules out the possibility of constructing public-key encryption in a black-box manner from any hinting wPRF. In fact, our separation result holds even if we replaced a hinting wPRF with a hinting PRF – a strengthening of a hinting wPRF that satisfies plain/strong PRF security as opposed to weak PRF security in the presence of multiple hints with respect to the secret key.

1.2   Technical Overview

In this section, we provide an overview of our techniques. For simplicity of exposition, we focus primarily on two of our basic results – our construction of hinting PRG from DDH, and our construction of functional hinting PRG from DDH for the quadratic function $f(\mathbf{s} \in \{0,1\}^n) = \mathbf{s} \otimes \mathbf{s} \in \{0,1\}^{n^2}$. For all of our other results, we provide some high-level intuition while referring to the relevant sections in the body of the paper for details.

Hinting PRG from DDH. Let $(\mathbb{G}, g, q)$ be a DDH-hard group of prime order q with generator g. Throughout this paper, we use the notation $[\mathbf{M}]$ to denote $g^{\mathbf{M}}$ (exponentiation being applied componentwise) for any matrix $\mathbf{M} \in \mathbb{Z}_q^{m \times n}$. It was shown in [PW08,FGK+10,AMP19] that for a uniformly sampled matrix $\mathbf{M} \leftarrow \mathbb{Z}_q^{n \times n}$ and a uniformly sampled binary vector $\mathbf{s} \leftarrow \{0,1\}^n$ where n is sufficiently large, we have

$$([\mathbf{M}], [\mathbf{Ms}]) \stackrel{c}{\approx} ([\mathbf{M}], [\mathbf{u}]), \tag{$*$}$$

where $\mathbf{u} \leftarrow \mathbb{Z}_q^n$. Observe that this naturally yields a PRG with public parameter $[\mathbf{M}]$ and seed $\mathbf{s}$ defined as

$$G_{[\mathbf{M}]}(\mathbf{s}) = [\mathbf{Ms}].$$

We now argue that this PRG already satisfies the hinting property. At a high level, our approach is as follows: we reduce the hinting property of G to the pseudorandomness of G, which in turn relies on the DDH assumption. We explain this in more details below.

Suppose we are given a PRG challenge of the form $([\mathbf{M}], [\mathbf{y}])$, where the vector $[\mathbf{y}]$ is either the "real" output of the PRG G, i.e., we have $[\mathbf{y}] = [\mathbf{Ms}]$ for some $\mathbf{s} \leftarrow \{0,1\}^n$, or $[\mathbf{y}]$ is uniformly random, i.e., we have $[\mathbf{y}] \leftarrow \mathbb{G}^n$. We construct a PPT algorithm $\mathcal{B}$ as follows: $\mathcal{B}$ takes as input a PRG challenge of the form $([\mathbf{M}], [\mathbf{y}])$ and outputs $([\mathbf{M}'], [\mathbf{Z}])$ where the matrix $[\mathbf{M}']$ is a uniformly distributed matrix in $\mathbb{G}^{n \times n}$, and $[\mathbf{Z}]$ is an $n \times 2$ matrix of group elements of the form $[\mathbf{Z}] = ([z_{i,b}])_{i \in [n], b \in \{0,1\}}$ such that:

- When $[\mathbf{y}]$ is distributed as the "real" output of the PRG G, $[\mathbf{Z}]$ is distributed as in the "real" hinting PRG game w.r.t. the public parameter $[\mathbf{M}']$.
- On the other hand, when $[\mathbf{y}]$ is uniformly random in $\mathbb{G}^n$, $[\mathbf{Z}]$ is distributed uniformly randomly over $\mathbb{G}^{n \times 2}$.

The main challenge here is that $\mathcal{B}$ needs to produce this output without any knowledge of the seed $\mathbf{s}$ of the PRG G. To do this, given a PRG challenge of the form $([\mathbf{M}], [\mathbf{y}])$, $\mathcal{B}$ "shifts" each diagonal entry $m_{i,i}$ of the matrix $[\mathbf{M}]$ by a random value $d_i \leftarrow \mathbb{Z}_q$ in the exponent of g, i.e., it computes the shifted diagonal element in the exponent as

$$[m'_{i,i}] = [m_{i,i}] + [d_i].$$

Let $[\mathbf{M'}]$ be the corresponding matrix in $\mathbb{G}^{n \times n}$ with the shifted diagonal elements ($[\mathbf{M'}]$ is identical to $[\mathbf{M}]$ in all non-diagonal entries), and define the matrix $[\mathbf{Z}] = ([z_{i,b}])_{i \in [n], b \in \{0,1\}}$ as follows: for each $i \in [n]$ and $b \in \{0,1\}$, set

$$[z_{i,b}] := \begin{cases} [y_i] & \text{if } b = 0, \\ [y_i + d_i] & \text{if } b = 1. \end{cases}$$

Suppose that $[\mathbf{y}] = [\mathbf{Ms}]$, and let $[\mathbf{y'}] = [\mathbf{M's}]$. If $s_i = 0$, we have

$$[z_{i,0}] = [y_i] = [y'_i], \quad [z_{i,1}] = [y'_i + d_i],$$

where the latter is uniformly random. Likewise, if $s_i = 1$, we have

$$[z_{i,1}] = [y_i + d_i] = [y'_i], \quad [z_{i,0}] = [y'_i - d_i],$$

where the latter is again uniformly random. Hence, $[\mathbf{Z}]$ is distributed as in the real hinting PRG game w.r.t. the public parameter $[\mathbf{M'}]$, as desired. On the other hand, when $[\mathbf{y}]$ is uniformly random, so is $[\mathbf{Z}]$. We refer to Sect. 3.1 for a more formal description of our construction and proof.

Translation to Isogeny-Based Group Actions. In the above security proof, the crux of the argument is in introducing a "shift" both in the public parameter $[\mathbf{M}]$ and in the challenge vector $[\mathbf{y}]$ when constructing $([\mathbf{M'}], [\mathbf{Z}])$, without having to solve discrete logs in the group $\mathbb{G}$. It turns out that for certain isogeny-based *effective* group actions (e.g., variants of CSIDH [CLM+18, BKV19, ADMP20]), we can introduce such a "shift" using the algebraic properties of group actions without having to solve a computationally hard problem analogous to discrete log over group actions. This observation allows us to translate our construction and proof technique for hinting PRGs outlined above from DDH-hard groups to group actions satisfying the LHS assumption introduced in [ADMP20]. We refer to Sect. 3.2 for a more formal description.

It turns out that we can extend this technique of publicly computable shifts in the outputs of group action computations to achieve a direct construction of TDFs from any LHS-hard weak pseudorandom effective group action. We refer to Sect. 4 for the detailed construction and proof. We point out that our construction avoids the many layers of generic transformation required by the prior construction of TDFs from such isogeny-based assumption, proposed in [ADMP20] based on the framework of [KMT19a].

Comparison with Prior Works. Our approach for realizing hinting PRGs from DDH-hard groups or LHS-hard effective group actions yields significantly simpler constructions and security proofs as compared to prior constructions and proofs for hinting PRGs based on the missing block framework [KW19] or the accumulation framework [GVW20]. Specifically, the authors of [GVW20] need to prove a new hashing lemma, which is crucial to their proof of security, besides relying on the DDHI assumption, which is a seemingly stronger assumption as compared to DDH. Similarly, the authors of [KW19] propose a construction of hinting PRGs such that proving the hinting property itself requires multiple hybrids, where one of the intermediate hybrids relies on a statistical hashing lemma. On the other hand, in our construction, we directly reduce the hinting property of the PRG to its own pseudorandomness.

We also observe that neither the missing block framework of [KW19] nor the accumulation framework of [GVW20] seems amenable to realizations from isogeny-based assumptions; in particular, their techniques seem incompatible with the algebraic properties of isogeny-based group actions, especially given the long history of failed attempts to integrate standard hashing techniques into the framework of isogeny-based cryptography [BBD+22]. On the other hand, our proposed technique readily extends to the setting of isogeny-based group actions, and enables the first realizations of hinting PRGs from (plausibly post-quantum secure) isogeny-based assumptions.

Hinting wPRF from DDH or LHS. For our hinting PRG construction, we used a simple proof technique that (informally speaking) allows reducing the hinting property of the PRG to its own pseudorandomness. Observe that in this reduction, we rely on the fact that the adversary only sees a single evaluation of the hinting PRG w.r.t. a uniformly sampled seed. To realize hinting wPRF, we use an extension of this technique that allows similarly reducing the hinting property of the wPRF, albeit over *multiple evaluations*, to the weak pseudorandomness of the wPRF. We note that for prior approaches to constructing hinting PRGs (e.g., the construction of hinting PRGs from CDH [KW19]), such an extension to hinting weak PRFs is seemingly hard to achieve.

Our extension is designed to work with both DDH-hard groups as well as any LHS-hard weak pseudorandom effective group action; in particular, we preserve compatibility with the algebraic properties of group actions to enable our isogeny-based constructions of hinting wPRFs. We refer to Sects. 5.1 and 5.2 for the detailed constructions and proofs of hinting wPRFs from DDH and LHS respectively, and to the full version for a simple construction of circular/KDM-secure SKE from any hinting wPRF.

Functional Hinting PRG from DDH. Our simple technique for realizing hinting PRGs from DDH is actually powerful enough to allow constructing functional hinting PRGs, which are strengthenings of hinting PRG that guarantee PRG security in the presence of hints about each bit of *some function* of the seed. For this overview, we show how to construct a functional hinting PRG from DDH, where the function f that we consider is defined as follows: given a seed $\mathbf{s} \in \{0,1\}^n$, $f(\mathbf{s}) = (s_i \cdot s_j)_{i,j \in [n]}$, which is an n^2-length vector.

The starting point of our functional hinting PRG from DDH is a stronger version of the indistinguishability (*) from [PW08,FGK+10] that we prove in this paper based on the DDH assumption: for n^2 uniformly sampled matrices $\left\{\mathbf{M}_i \leftarrow \mathbb{Z}_q^{n \times n}\right\}_{i \in [n^2]}$ and a uniformly sampled binary vector $\mathbf{s} \leftarrow \{0,1\}^n$ (where n is sufficiently large), we have

$$\left([\mathbf{M}_i], [\mathbf{s}^t \mathbf{M}_i \mathbf{s}]\right)_{i \in [n^2]} \stackrel{c}{\approx} \left([\mathbf{M}_i], [u_i]\right)_{i \in [n^2]},$$

where each $u_i \leftarrow \mathbb{Z}_q$. Observe that this naturally yields a PRG with public parameter $([\mathbf{M}_1], \ldots, [\mathbf{M}_{n^2}])$ and seed $\mathbf{s}$ defined as

$$G_{([\mathbf{M}_1], \ldots, [\mathbf{M}_{n^2}])}(\mathbf{s}) = \left([\mathbf{s}^t \mathbf{M}_1 \mathbf{s}], \ldots, [\mathbf{s}^t \mathbf{M}_{n^2} \mathbf{s}]\right).$$

Similar to our technique for proving the security of hinting PRG, even in this case, we can reduce the functional hinting PRG security of the above construction to its own pseudorandomness (which in turn relies on DDH) by introducing shifts on a suitable entry of each matrix $[\mathbf{M}_i]$ in the public parameter. We refer to Sect. 6.1 for the detailed construction and proof of security, and also for extensions of the above construction to achieve functional hinting PRGs w.r.t. functions of higher degree.

Functional Hinting wPRF and Applications. For our functional hinting PRG construction, we use a reduction where we rely on the fact that the adversary only sees a single evaluation of the hinting PRG w.r.t. a uniformly sampled seed, while only getting hints about each bit of a *single function* of the seed. Achieving a functional hinting wPRF is significantly more complicated, since not only can the adversary see multiple evaluations of the wPRF on uniformly random inputs, but also get hints about multiple functions of the secret key, where the function may be chosen adversarially from a fixed function family. In this paper, we show a construction of functional hinting wPRF from DDH w.r.t. the function family $\mathcal{F}$ consisting of (projective) quadratic functions (and functions of higher degree) over the bits of the key. We refer to Sect. 6.2 for the detailed construction and proof of functional hinting wPRFs from DDH.

In the full version, we describe a simple construction of KDM-secure SKE w.r.t. a function family $\mathcal{F}$ from any functional hinting wPRF w.r.t. the same function family $\mathcal{F}$ in a *black-box* manner. We also show a strengthening of this result to obtain a construction of $\mathcal{F}$-KDM secure *public-key* encryption scheme from any $\mathcal{F}$-functional hinting wPRF that additionally satisfies homomorphism between the input and output space – a property that is actually satisfied by our construction of functional hinting weak PRF from DDH.

Note that existing approaches for achieving KDM-secure PKE in a black-box way [BGK11, KMT19b] are somewhat incomparable to ours; in particular, these prior constructions are designed specifically for *arithmetic* function families that inherently require some form of algebraic structure on the secret key space, while the function family that we consider can be viewed as a certain form of boolean function family (e.g., in the case of quadratic functions, an adversary is provided with hints w.r.t. the conjunction/AND of each pair of bits of the secret key). Additionally, the primitive underlying our construction, namely functional hinting weak PRF, provides a deterministic form of KDM-security that has not been considered in prior works to the best of our knowledge.

We note that our construction of (functional) hinting wPRF from DDH/LHS essentially subsumes our construction of hinting PRG from DDH/LHS, while building upon our techniques for the latter construction. More generally, we chose to present our results in a progressive manner, where each result builds upon our techniques used to construct simpler primitives. We do this for ease of exposition, and also for highlighting the simplicity/modularity of our techniques.

Hinting PRF and wPRF in ROM. Let $H : \{0,1\}^n \to Y^{n+1}$ be a truly random function (modeled as a random oracle), where Y is a sufficiently large set. It is easy to see that H is a pseudorandom generator in the random oracle model since for any uniformly random input $\mathbf{s} \leftarrow \{0,1\}^n$, no (computationally unbounded) adversary can distinguish (with non-negligible probability) between $H(\mathbf{s} \leftarrow \{0,1\}^n)$ and $\mathbf{u} \leftarrow Y^{n+1}$ while issuing polynomially many queries to the function H. In the full version, we show that this simple PRG in the ROM actually also satisfies the hinting property via a simple information-theoretic argument. This implies the first black-box separation between hinting PRG and PKE [IR89] to the best of our knowledge.

We then build upon our construction of hinting PRG to also show how to construct a hinting PRF given only a random oracle. As mentioned earlier, a hinting PRF is a strengthening of a hinting wPRF that satisfies plain/strong PRF security as opposed to weak PRF security in the presence of multiple hints with respect to the secret key (i.e., the adversary is allowed to ask for hints with respect to the key of PRF for *arbitrarily* chosen inputs instead of randomly chosen ones). We refer to the full version for the detailed construction and proof. Note that our result also rules out the possibility of constructing PKE in a black-box way from any hinting (weak) PRF [IR89].

2   Preliminaries

Notations. For any positive integer n, we use $[n]$ to denote the set $\{1, \ldots, n\}$. We may use $[a]$ to denote g^a where $a \in \mathbb{Z}_q$ and g is a generator of a cyclic group with order q. However, the difference between $[n]$ and $[a]$ will be clear from context.

We use the notation $\overset{s}{\approx}$ (respectively, $\overset{c}{\approx}$) to denote statistical (respectively, computational) indistinguishability. We denote the security parameter by λ. For a finite set S, we use $s \leftarrow S$ to sample uniformly from the set S.

Definition 1 (Weak PRF). *Let $F : K \times X \to Y$ be a function family, where each set is indexed by the security parameter. We say that F is a weak PRF if for any $Q = \text{poly}(\lambda)$ it holds that*

$$\big\{(x_i, F(k, x_i))\big\}_{i \in [Q]} \overset{c}{\approx} \big\{(x_i, y_i)\big\}_{i \in [Q]},$$

where $k \leftarrow K$, $x_i \leftarrow X$, and $y_i \leftarrow Y$.

Definition 2 (KDM-secure SKE). *Let $\mathcal{F} = \{f_I \mid f_I : \{0,1\}^n \to \{0,1\}^m\}_{I \in \mathcal{I}}$ be a family of boolean functions, and let $\bar{f} \in \mathcal{F}$ where $\bar{f}$ is the constant function $f(\mathbf{x}) = 0^m$. Let $\Pi = (\mathsf{Gen}, \mathsf{Enc}, \mathsf{Enc})$ be a symmetric-key encryption (SKE) scheme with $\mathcal{M} = \{0,1\}^m$ and $\mathcal{K} = \{0,1\}^n$, where $\mathcal{M}$ and $\mathcal{K}$ denote the message space and the key space, respectively. We say that Π is KDM secure with respect to $\mathcal{F}$ if the advantage of any PPT adversary $\mathcal{A}$ in distinguishing the experiments $\mathsf{Exp}_0^{\mathsf{KDM}}$ and $\mathsf{Exp}_1^{\mathsf{KDM}}$ (defined in Fig. 1) is negligible.*

Note that KDM security for public-key encryption with respect to a function family $\mathcal{F}$ is defined similarly, except that the adversary is given public key in the beginning of the experiment.

---

1. The challenger samples a secret key key $\mathsf{sk} \leftarrow \{0,1\}^n$.

2. The adversary queries for a function input $f \in \mathcal{F}$.

3. If $b = 0$, the challenger responds with $\mathsf{Enc}(\mathsf{sk}, 0^m)$.

4. If $b = 1$, the challenger responds with $\mathsf{Enc}(\mathsf{sk}, f(\mathsf{sk}))$.

5. The adversary continues to make input queries as before, and each query is replied by the challenger as described above.

6. Finally, the adversary outputs a bit b'. The advantage of $\mathcal{A}$ is defined to be $\Pr[b = b']$ over all randomness in the experiment.

Fig. 1. Experiment $\mathsf{Exp}_b^{\mathsf{KDM}}$.

We recall the definition of hinting PRG [KW19]. We use a slightly different syntax compared to [KW19] for each block of the output of hinting PRG.[2]

Definition 3 (Hinting PRG). *Let $n = \mathrm{poly}(\lambda)$ be an integer. Let $(\mathsf{Setup}, \mathsf{Eval})$ be a pair of algorithms such that*

- $\mathsf{Setup}(1^\lambda)$ *is a randomized algorithm that outputs some public parameter* pp,
- $\mathsf{Eval}(\mathsf{pp}, \mathbf{s} \in \{0,1\}^n, i \in \{0\} \cup [n])$ *is a deterministic algorithm that outputs (a representation of) some element y in Y, where Y is the codomain of the algorithm and $|Y| = \omega(\log \lambda)$.*

We say that $(\mathsf{Setup}, \mathsf{Eval})$ defines a hinting PRG if for $\mathsf{pp} \leftarrow \mathsf{Setup}(1^\lambda)$ and $\mathbf{s} \leftarrow \{0,1\}^n$ it holds that

$$(\mathsf{pp}, y_0, \mathbf{Y}) \overset{c}{\approx} (\mathsf{pp}, u_0, \mathbf{U}),$$

---

[2] Specifically, the authors of [KW19] use the set $\{0,1\}^\ell$ for each block (where ℓ is fixed during the setup) whereas we use a sufficiently large (efficiently representable) set Y. Our definition allows defining hinting PRG in a setting where Y does not necessarily have a compact representation, i.e., when each element of Y is represented using more than $\log |Y|$ bits (which is the case for isogeny-based group actions). One can obtain a hinting PRG with bit-string blocks by using a suitable (statistical) extractor.

where these terms are distributed as

$$y_0 = \mathsf{Eval}(\mathsf{pp}, \mathbf{s}, 0), \quad y_{i,s_i} = \mathsf{Eval}(\mathsf{pp}, \mathbf{s}, i), \quad y_{i,1-s_i} \leftarrow Y, \quad u_0 \leftarrow Y, \quad \mathbf{U} \leftarrow Y^{n \times 2}.$$

Definition 4 (The DDH Assumption). *Let $\mathbb{G}$ be a group of prime order q with generator g. We say that the DDH assumption holds over $\mathbb{G}$ if for $a \leftarrow \mathbb{Z}_q$, $b \leftarrow \mathbb{Z}_q$, $c \leftarrow \mathbb{Z}_q$ it holds that*

$$(g, g^a, g^b, g^{ab}) \stackrel{c}{\approx} (g, g^a, g^b, g^c).$$

We will use the following special case of leftover hash lemma. We refer to [Reg09] for a proof.

Lemma 1. *Let G be an additively written abelian group such that $|G| = \lambda^{\omega(1)}$, and let $m > \log|G| + \omega(\log \lambda)$ be an integer. If $\mathbf{r} \leftarrow G^m$ and $\mathbf{s} \leftarrow \{0,1\}^m$, it holds that*

$$\left(\mathbf{r}, \sum_{i=1}^{m} s_i r_i\right) \stackrel{s}{\approx} (\mathbf{r}, u),$$

where $u \leftarrow G$ is a uniformly chosen group element.

Definition 5. *An extractor $\mathsf{Ext} : \mathcal{S} \times X \to Y$ is a deterministic function with the seed space $\mathcal{S}$ and domain X such that if $\mathsf{seed} \leftarrow \mathcal{S}$ is sampled uniformly and x is sampled from a distribution over X with min-entropy λ^c (for some constant $0 < c < 1$), then it holds that*

$$(\mathsf{seed}, \mathsf{Ext}(\mathsf{seed}, x)) \stackrel{s}{\approx} (\mathsf{seed}, y),$$

where $y \leftarrow Y$ is sampled uniformly.

2.1 Cryptographic Group Actions

We recall some definitions related to cryptographic group actions from [ADMP20], which provided a framework to construct cryptographic primitives from certain isogeny-based assumptions (e.g., variants of CSIDH [CLM+18, BKV19]).

Notations. We use $(\mathbb{G}, X, \star)$ to denote a group action $\star : \mathbb{G} \times X \to X$. Throughout the paper, we will assume that group actions are abelian and *regular*, i.e., both free and transitive (which is the case for CSIDH-style group actions). Note that for regular group actions, we have $|\mathbb{G}| = |X|$. Thus, if a group action is regular, then for any $x \in X$, the map $f_x : g \mapsto g \star x$ defines a bijection between $\mathbb{G}$ and X.

We always use the additive notation $+$ to denote the group operation in $\mathbb{G}$. Since $\mathbb{G}$ is abelian, it can be viewed as a $\mathbb{Z}$-module and hence for any $z \in \mathbb{Z}$ and $g \in \mathbb{G}$, the term zg is well-defined. This property naturally extends to matrices as well, so for any matrix $\mathbf{M} \in \mathbb{G}^{m \times n}$ and any vector $\mathbf{z} \in \mathbb{Z}^n$, the term $\mathbf{Mz}$ is also well-defined. The group action also extends naturally to the direct product group $\mathbb{G}^n$ for any positive integer n. If $\mathbf{g} \in \mathbb{G}^n$ and $\mathbf{x} \in X^n$, we use $\mathbf{g} \star \mathbf{x}$ to denote a vector of set elements whose ith component is $g_i \star x_i$.

Effective Group Action. We recall the definition of an effective group action (EGA) from [ADMP20]. In a nutshell, an effective group action allows us to do certain computations over $\mathbb{G}$ efficiently (e.g., group operation, inversion, and sampling uniformly), and there is an efficient procedure to compute the action of any group element on any set element. As pointed out by [ADMP20], the CSIDH-style assumption in [BKV19] (called "CSI-FiSh") is an instance of effective group action. We refer to [CLM+18, BKV19, ADMP20] for more details on distributional properties of such group actions.

Definition 6 (Effective Group Action). *A group action* $(\mathbb{G}, X, \star)$ *is* effective *if it satisfies the following properties:*

1. *The group* $\mathbb{G}$ *is finite and there exist efficient (PPT) algorithms for:*
   (a) *Membership testing (deciding whether a binary string represents a group element).*
   (b) *Equality testing and sampling uniformly in* $\mathbb{G}$.
   (c) *Group operation and computing inverse of any element in* $\mathbb{G}$.
2. *The set* X *is finite and there exist efficient algorithms for:*
   (a) *Membership testing (to check if a string represents a valid set element),*
   (b) *Unique representation (there is a canonical representation for any set element* $x \in X$).
3. *There exists a distinguished element* $x_0 \in X$ *with known representation.*
4. *There exists an efficient algorithm that given any* $g \in \mathbb{G}$ *and any* $x \in X$, *outputs* $g \star x$.

Definition 7 (Weak Pseudorandom EGA). *An effective group action* $(\mathbb{G}, X, \star)$ *is said to be a weak pseudorandom EGA (wPR-EGA) if it holds that*

$$(x, y, t \star x, t \star y) \stackrel{c}{\approx} (x, y, u, u'),$$

where $x \leftarrow X$, $y \leftarrow X$, $t \leftarrow \mathbb{G}$, $u \leftarrow X$, *and* $u' \leftarrow X$.

Definition 8 (Linear Hidden Shift assumption [ADMP20]). *Let* $(\mathbb{G}, X, \star)$ *be an effective group action (EGA), and let* $n > \log |\mathbb{G}| + \omega(\log \lambda)$ *be an integer. We say that liner hidden shift (LHS) assumption holds over* $(\mathbb{G}, X, \star)$ *if for any* $\ell = \mathrm{poly}(\lambda)$ *the following holds:*

$$(\mathbf{x}, \mathbf{M}, \mathbf{Ms} \star \mathbf{x}) \stackrel{c}{\approx} (\mathbf{x}, \mathbf{M}, \mathbf{u}),$$

where $\mathbf{x} \leftarrow X^\ell$, $\mathbf{M} \leftarrow \mathbb{G}^{\ell \times n}$, $\mathbf{s} \leftarrow \{0, 1\}^n$, *and* $\mathbf{u} \leftarrow X^\ell$.

3 Hinting PRG from DDH or LHS

In this section, we show how to construct a hinting PRG from either any DDH-hard group or any LHS-hard effective group action.

3.1 Hinting PRG from DDH

We begin by describing our construction of hinting PRG from any DDH-hard group.

Construction. Let $(\mathbb{G}, g, q)$ be a DDH-hard group, and fix some integer n such that $n > \log |\mathbb{G}| + \omega(\log \lambda)$. Given a cyclic group $\mathbb{G}$ with generator g, we use the notation $[a] = g^a$ and $[\mathbf{M}] = g^{\mathbf{M}}$ (exponentiation being applied componentwise) where $a \in \mathbb{Z}_q$ and $\mathbf{M} \in \mathbb{Z}_q^{m \times n}$ for any positive integer m and n. We use the notation $\langle \mathbf{a}, \mathbf{b} \rangle$ to denote the "dot" product of $\mathbf{a} \in \mathbb{Z}_q^n$ and $\mathbf{b} \in \mathbb{Z}_q^n$ modulo q. Our construction of hinting PRG from DDH assumption is as follows:

- Setup(1^λ): Sample $[\mathbf{M}] \leftarrow \mathbb{G}^{(n+1) \times n}$ and publish $\mathsf{pp} = [\mathbf{M}]$.
- Eval($\mathsf{pp} = [\mathbf{M}], \mathbf{s} \in \{0, 1\}^n, i \in \{0\} \cup [n]$): Let $[\mathbf{m}_i]$ denote the ith[3] row of $[\mathbf{M}]$. Output $[\langle \mathbf{m}_i, \mathbf{s} \rangle]$.[4] Note that stacking up evaluation of the PRG on all indices $i \in \{0\} \cup [n]$ can simply be viewed as $[\mathbf{Ms}]$.

Security. We prove the security of the construction via the following theorem.

Theorem 1. *If $(\mathbb{G}, g, q)$ is a DDH-hard group then the construction above yields a hinting PRG.*

Proof. Observe that by Lemma 2 (proved below) we have $([\mathbf{M}], [\mathbf{Ms}]) \overset{c}{\approx} ([\mathbf{M}], [\mathbf{u}])$ (where $[\mathbf{u}] \leftarrow \mathbb{G}^{n+1}$) and hence the pseudorandomness of the output in the plain PRG game follows from Lemma 2. Let $[\mathbf{m}_0] \in \mathbb{G}^n$ be the 0th row of $[\mathbf{M}]$, and let $[\bar{\mathbf{M}}]$ be all but the 0th row of $[\mathbf{M}]$ (i.e., bottom square matrix). To establish the security of the construction in the hinting PRG game, it is enough to show that

$$([\mathbf{m}_0], [\langle \mathbf{m}_0, \mathbf{s} \rangle], [\bar{\mathbf{M}}], [\mathbf{Y}]) \overset{c}{\approx} ([\mathbf{m}_0], [u], [\bar{\mathbf{M}}], [\mathbf{U}]), \qquad (*)$$

where $[u] \leftarrow \mathbb{G}$ and $[\mathbf{U}] \leftarrow \mathbb{G}^{n \times 2}$ are sampled uniformly and $[\mathbf{Y}] \in \mathbb{G}^{n \times 2}$ is distributed as follows

$$[y_{j,s_j}] = [\langle \mathbf{m}_j, \mathbf{s} \rangle], \quad [y_{j,1-s_j}] \leftarrow \mathbb{G}, \quad j \in [n].$$

We prove $(*)$ via a hybrid argument. Let H_0 and H_1 be the hybrids that correspond to the left-hand side and right-hand side of $(*)$, respectively (i.e., "real" game and "ideal" game). We now argue that $H_0 \overset{c}{\approx} H_1$.

Let $\mathcal{A}$ be an adversary that distinguishes H_0 from H_1. We construct an adversary $\mathcal{A}'$ that distinguishes H_0' from H_1' where[5]

$$H_0' := ([\mathbf{m}_0], [\langle \mathbf{m}_0, \mathbf{s} \rangle], [\bar{\mathbf{M}}], [\bar{\mathbf{M}}\mathbf{s}]), \quad H_1' := ([\mathbf{m}_0], [u_0], [\bar{\mathbf{M}}], [\mathbf{u}]),$$

---

[3] For any matrix with $n + 1$ rows, we number rows from 0 to n.
[4] Note that given any vector of group elements $[\mathbf{v}] \in \mathbb{G}^n$ and any vector $\mathbf{s} \in \{0, 1\}^n$, one can efficiently compute $[\langle \mathbf{v}, \mathbf{s} \rangle]$ without the need to solve the discrete log problem.
[5] This is simply Lemma 2 with $k = n + 1$, where we wrote the first row separately.

and by Lemma 2 it follows that the advantage of $\mathcal{A}$ should also be negligible.

Given a tuple $H_b' = ([\mathbf{m}_0], [z_0], [\bar{\mathbf{M}}], [\mathbf{z}])$, where H_b' is either distributed as H_0' or H_1', the external adversary $\mathcal{A}'$ samples a random $[\mathbf{d}] \leftarrow \mathbb{G}^n$. Let $[\mathbf{D}] \in \mathbb{G}^{n \times n}$ be a *diagonal* matrix whose diagonal is $[\mathbf{d}]$, i.e., ijth entry of $\mathbf{D}$ is 0 for any $i \neq j$. In the next step, $\mathcal{A}'$ runs $\mathcal{A}$ on the following tuple

$$([\mathbf{m}_0], [z_0], [\mathbf{M}'] := [\bar{\mathbf{M}} + \mathbf{D}], [\mathbf{Y}]),$$

where $[\mathbf{Y}]$ is an n by 2 matrix whose first and second columns are $[\mathbf{z}]$ and $[\mathbf{z} + \mathbf{d}]$ respectively. We define the output of $\mathcal{A}'$ to be the same as the output of $\mathcal{A}$.

Observe that (in the view of $\mathcal{A}$) the terms $[\mathbf{m}_0]$ and $[\mathbf{M}']$ are distributed uniformly. Moreover, if $[\mathbf{z}]$ is uniform then $[\mathbf{Y}]$ will be distributed uniformly as well. Therefore, $\mathcal{A}'$ perfectly simulates the "ideal" hybrid H_1. On the other hand, if $[\mathbf{z}] = [\bar{\mathbf{M}}\mathbf{s}]$ then from the view of $\mathcal{A}$ the matrix $[\mathbf{Y}]$ is distributed as

$$[y_{j,s_j}] = [\langle \mathbf{m}_j', \mathbf{s} \rangle], \quad [y_{j,1-s_j}] = [(-1)^{s_j} \cdot d_j + \langle \mathbf{m}_j', \mathbf{s} \rangle], \quad j \in [n].$$

To see why the relations above hold, notice that $[\langle \mathbf{m}_j', \mathbf{s} \rangle] = [\langle \bar{\mathbf{m}}_j, \mathbf{s} \rangle + s_j \cdot d_j]$ where $\mathbf{m}_j'$ and $\bar{\mathbf{m}}_j$ denote the jth row of $\mathbf{M}'$ and $\bar{\mathbf{M}}$, respectively. Because $[\mathbf{d}]$ is distributed uniformly and independently from $[\mathbf{M}']$ (in the view of $\mathcal{A}$), it follows that in the view of $\mathcal{A}$ we have

$$\left([\mathbf{M}'], \{[y_{j,s_j}]\}_{j \in n}, [y_{j,1-s_j}]\}_{j \in n}\right) \stackrel{s}{\approx} \left([\mathbf{M}'], \{[y_{j,s_j}]\}_{j \in n}, [\mathbf{u}]\right),$$

where $[\mathbf{u}] \leftarrow \mathbb{G}^n$, and hence $\mathcal{A}'$ properly simulates the "real" hybrid H_0, as required.

A generic version of the following lemma has been proved in [AMP19] for the output group of any key-homomorphic weak PRF. Below, we provide a short proof for any DDH-hard group $\mathbb{G}$.

Lemma 2. *Let $(\mathbb{G}, g, q)$ be a DDH-hard group, and fix some integer ℓ and n such that $n > \log |\mathbb{G}| + \omega(\log \lambda)$ and $\ell = \text{poly}(\lambda)$. If $[\mathbf{M}] \leftarrow \mathbb{G}^{\ell \times n}$ and $\mathbf{s} \leftarrow \{0,1\}^n$, then $([\mathbf{M}], [\mathbf{Ms}]) \stackrel{c}{\approx} ([\mathbf{M}], [\mathbf{u}])$, where $[\mathbf{u}] \leftarrow \mathbb{G}^\ell$ is sampled uniformly.*

Proof. Let $[\bar{\mathbf{M}}] \in \mathbb{G}^{\ell \times n}$ be a matrix of group elements whose (i, j) entry is $[a_i \cdot b_j]$ where $a_i \leftarrow \mathbb{Z}_q, b_j \leftarrow \mathbb{Z}_q$ (for $i \in [\ell], j \in [n]$). By the leftover hash lemma, it follows that given $[\bar{\mathbf{M}}]$, the term $[\bar{\mathbf{M}}\mathbf{s}]$ is statistically indistinguishable from a fresh DDH tuple, i.e., given $[\bar{\mathbf{M}}]$ it holds that

$$[\bar{\mathbf{M}}\mathbf{s}] = \begin{pmatrix} [a_1 \cdot \langle \mathbf{b}, \mathbf{s} \rangle] \\ [a_2 \cdot \langle \mathbf{b}, \mathbf{s} \rangle] \\ \vdots \\ [a_\ell \cdot \langle \mathbf{b}, \mathbf{s} \rangle] \end{pmatrix} \stackrel{s}{\approx} \begin{pmatrix} [a_1 \cdot b^*] \\ [a_2 \cdot b^*] \\ \vdots \\ [a_\ell \cdot b^*] \end{pmatrix},$$

where $b^* \leftarrow \mathbb{Z}_q$ is chosen randomly. By a standard hybrid argument, it follows from the DDH assumption that $([\bar{\mathbf{M}}], [\bar{\mathbf{M}}\mathbf{s}]) \stackrel{c}{\approx} ([\bar{\mathbf{M}}], [\mathbf{u}])$. Moreover, by the DDH assumption we have $[\bar{\mathbf{M}}] \stackrel{c}{\approx} [\mathbf{M}]$. Therefore, it follows from a simple hybrid argument that $([\mathbf{M}], [\mathbf{Ms}]) \stackrel{c}{\approx} ([\mathbf{M}], [\mathbf{u}])$, as desired.

3.2   Hinting PRG from LHS

We now show how to construct a hinting PRG from any LHS-hard EGA. The construction is similar to our DDH-based construction of hinting PRG, with suitable modifications to translate our techniques to the setting of EGA.

Construction. Let $(\mathbb{G}, X, \star)$ be an EGA such that LHS assumption holds. Let n be the secret dimension of the LHS assumption. We describe a construction of hinting PRG from the LHS assumption as follows. In the construction below, note that the group $\mathbb{G}$ is written additively (viewed as a $\mathbb{Z}$-module).

- Setup(1^λ): Sample $\mathbf{M} \leftarrow \mathbb{G}^{(n+1)\times n}$ and $\mathbf{x} = (x_0, x_1, \ldots, x_n) \leftarrow X^{n+1}$, and publish $\mathsf{pp} = (\mathbf{M}, \mathbf{x})$.

- Eval($\mathsf{pp} = \mathbf{M}, \mathbf{s} \in \{0,1\}^n, i \in \{0\} \cup [n]$): Let $\mathbf{m}_i$ denote the ith[6] row of $\mathbf{M}$. Output $\langle \mathbf{m}_i, \mathbf{s}\rangle \star x_i$.
  Note that similar to the DDH-based construction, concatenating evaluation of the PRG on all indices $i \in \{0\} \cup [n]$ can be viewed as a larger instance of LHS assumption, i.e., $\mathbf{Ms} \star \mathbf{x}$.

Security. We argue the security of the construction above based on the LHS assumption as follows.

Theorem 2. Let $(\mathbb{G}, X, \star)$ be an EGA. If LHS assumption holds over $(\mathbb{G}, X, \star)$ then the construction above yields a hinting PRG.

Proof. Pseudorandomness of the output in the plain PRG game follows directly from the LHS assumption. Let $\mathbf{m}_0 \in \mathbb{G}^n$ be the 0th row of $\mathbf{M}$, and let $\bar{\mathbf{M}}$ be all but the 0th row of $\mathbf{M}$ (i.e., bottom square matrix). It suffices to show that

$$H_0 := (\mathbf{x}, \mathbf{m}_0, \langle \mathbf{m}_0, \mathbf{s}\rangle \star x_0, \bar{\mathbf{M}}, \mathbf{Y}) \stackrel{c}{\approx} (\mathbf{x}, \mathbf{m}_0, u, \bar{\mathbf{M}}, \mathbf{U}) := H_1, \qquad (**)$$

where $u \leftarrow X$ and $\mathbf{U} \leftarrow X^{n\times 2}$ are uniform and $\mathbf{Y} \in X^{n\times 2}$ is distributed as

$$y_{j,s_j} = \langle \bar{\mathbf{m}}_j, \mathbf{s}\rangle \star x_j, \quad y_{j,1-s_j} \leftarrow X, \quad j \in [n].$$

Let H_0 and H_1 be the hybrids that correspond to the left-hand side and right-hand side of $(**)$, respectively. We now argue that $H_0 \stackrel{c}{\approx} H_1$.

Let $\mathcal{A}$ be an adversary that distinguishes H_0 from H_1, we construct another adversary $\mathcal{A}'$ that distinguishes between the following tuples

$$H_0' := (\mathbf{x}, \mathbf{m}_0, \langle \mathbf{m}_0, \mathbf{s}\rangle \star x_0, \bar{\mathbf{M}}, \bar{\mathbf{M}}\mathbf{s} \star \bar{\mathbf{x}}), \quad H_1' := (\mathbf{x}, \mathbf{m}_0, u_0, \bar{\mathbf{M}}, \mathbf{u}),$$

where $u_0 \leftarrow X$ and $\mathbf{u} \leftarrow X^n$ are sampled uniformly, and $\bar{\mathbf{x}} = (x_1, \ldots, x_n)$ is the last n components of $\mathbf{x}$. Indistinguishability of H_0' and H_1' follows directly from the LHS assumption. Given a tuple of the form $H_b' = (\mathbf{x}, \mathbf{m}_0, z_0, \bar{\mathbf{M}}, \mathbf{z})$, where H_b'

---

[6] As before, we number rows from 0 to n.

is either distributed as H_0' or H_1', the external adversary $\mathcal{A}'$ samples a random $\mathbf{d} \leftarrow \mathbb{G}^n$. Let $\mathbf{D} \in \mathbb{G}^{n \times n}$ be a *diagonal* matrix whose diagonal is $\mathbf{d}$, i.e., ijth entry of $\mathbf{D}$ is the identity element of $\mathbb{G}$ for any $i \neq j$. In the next step, $\mathcal{A}'$ runs $\mathcal{A}$ on the following tuple

$$(\mathbf{x}, \mathbf{m}_0, z_0, \mathbf{M}' := \bar{\mathbf{M}} + \mathbf{D}, \mathbf{Y}),$$

where $\mathbf{Y} \in X^{n \times 2}$ is a matrix whose first and second rows are $\mathbf{z}$ and $\mathbf{d} \star \mathbf{z}$ respectively. Finally, $\mathcal{A}'$ outputs whatever $\mathcal{A}$ outputs.

It follows by inspection that $\mathcal{A}'$ perfectly simulates the "ideal" hybrid, i.e., it maps H_1' to H_1. On the other hand, if $\mathbf{z} = \bar{\mathbf{M}} \mathbf{s} \star \bar{\mathbf{x}}$ then from the view of $\mathcal{A}'$ the matrix $\mathbf{Y}$ is distributed as

$$y_{j,s_j} = \langle \mathbf{m}_j', \mathbf{s} \rangle \star x_j, \quad y_{j,1-s_j} = \left((-1)^{s_j} \cdot d_j \right) \star \left(\langle \mathbf{m}_j', \mathbf{s} \rangle \star x_j \right), \quad j \in [n].$$

Because $\mathbf{d}$ is distributed uniformly and independently from $\bar{\mathbf{M}}$ (in the view of $\mathcal{A}$), it follows that $\{y_{j,1-s_j}\}_{j \in [n]}$ is distributed uniformly in the view of $\mathcal{A}$ as well, and hence $\mathcal{A}'$ properly simulates the "real" hybrid H_0, as required.

4   Trapdoor Functions from LHS-Hard wPR-EGA

In this section, we extend our technique of publicly computable shifts in the outputs of group action computations used in our construction of hinting PRG from LHS-hard EGA to achieve a direct construction of TDFs from any LHS-hard weak pseudorandom EGA. Our construction avoids the many layers of generic transformation required by the prior construction of TDFs from such isogeny-based assumption, proposed in [ADMP20] based on the framework of [KMT19a].

Construction. Let $(\mathbb{G}, X, \star)$ be a wPR-EGA such that LHS assumptions holds over $(\mathbb{G}, X, \star)$. We now describe a construction of TDF from such EGA. Let $\mathsf{Ext} : \mathcal{S} \times X \to G$ be a (statistical) extractor where $\mathcal{S}$ denotes the seed space.[7]

- Gen(1^λ): Sample $\mathbf{M} \leftarrow \mathbb{G}^{n \times n}$ where $n = n(\lambda)$ is the secret dimension of the LHS assumption. Sample $\bar{\mathbf{x}} \leftarrow X^n$, $\mathbf{x} \leftarrow X^n$, $\mathbf{t} \leftarrow \mathbb{G}^n$, seed $\leftarrow \mathcal{S}$, and let $\mathbf{y} = \mathbf{t} \star \mathbf{x}$ where the action is applied componentwise. Output the tuple $\mathsf{ek} = (\mathsf{seed}, \mathbf{M}, \bar{\mathbf{x}}, \mathbf{x}, \mathbf{y})$ as evaluation key and $\mathbf{t}$ as trapdoor.
- Eval($\mathsf{ek} = (\mathsf{seed}, \mathbf{M}, \bar{\mathbf{x}}, \mathbf{x}, \mathbf{y}), (\mathbf{s} \in \{0,1\}^n, \mathbf{r} \in X^n, \mathbf{r}' \in X^n)$): To evaluate the function on the input $(\mathbf{s}, \mathbf{r}, \mathbf{r}')$, output $(\mathbf{V} \in X^{n \times 2}, \mathbf{Z} \in X^{n \times 2})$ where[8]

$$\begin{aligned} v_{i,s_i} &= \mathsf{Ext}\big(\mathsf{seed}, \langle \mathbf{m}_i, \mathbf{s} \rangle \star \bar{x}_i\big) \star x_i, & v_{i,1-s_i} &= r_i, \\ z_{i,s_i} &= \mathsf{Ext}\big(\mathsf{seed}, \langle \mathbf{m}_i, \mathbf{s} \rangle \star \bar{x}_i\big) \star y_i, & z_{i,1-s_i} &= r_i', & i \in [n]. \end{aligned}$$

---

[7] Note that we cannot use the bit representation of an element of X to generate a group element G without using extractor, because for some EGAs (and in particular for isogeny-based group actions), elements of X do *not* have compact represenation.

[8] $\mathbf{m}_i$ denotes the i row of $\mathbf{M}$.

- Invert$(\mathbf{t}, (\mathbf{V}, \mathbf{Z}))$: To invert on the input $(\mathbf{V}, \mathbf{Z})$ using the trapdoor $\mathbf{t}$, first compute $\mathbf{s}$ as follows:

$$s_i = \begin{cases} 0 & t_i \star v_{i,0} = z_{i,0}, \\ 1 & t_i \star v_{i,1} = z_{i,1}. \end{cases}$$

Let $\mathbf{r}$ and $\mathbf{r}'$ be two vectors such that $r_i = v_{i,1-s_i}$ and $r'_i = z_{i,1-s_i}$ for $i \in [n]$. Output $(\mathbf{s}, \mathbf{r}, \mathbf{r}')$.

Correctness of the inversion algorithm follows by inspection. We prove the one-wayness of the scheme via the following theorem.

Theorem 3. *If $(\mathbb{G}, X, \star)$ is an LHS-hard wPR-EGA then the construction above satisfies one-wayness.*

Proof. To prove the one-wayness it suffices to show that

$$H_0 := (\mathsf{ek}, \mathbf{V}, \mathbf{Z}) \stackrel{c}{\approx} (\mathsf{ek}, \mathbf{U}, \mathbf{U}') := H_3,$$

where ek, $\mathbf{V}$, $\mathbf{Z}$ are distributed as in the construction above, and $\mathbf{U}$, $\mathbf{U}'$ are two random matrices of set elements. We do the proof via a hybrid argument.

- H_0: This is the "real" game and H_0 corresponds to the tuple $(\mathsf{ek}, \mathbf{V}, \mathbf{Z})$ where ek, $\mathbf{V}$, $\mathbf{Z}$ are distributed as in the construction.
- H_1: In this hybrid we change the way two matrices are generated. Specifically, this hybrid corresponds to the tuple $(\mathsf{ek}, \mathbf{V}^{(1)}, \mathbf{Z}^{(1)})$ where $\mathbf{V}^{(1)}$ and $\mathbf{Z}^{(1)}$ are distributed as follows.

$$v^{(1)}_{i,s_i} = \mathsf{Ext}\big(\mathsf{seed}, \langle \mathbf{m}_i, \mathbf{s} \rangle \star \bar{x}_i\big) \star x_i, \qquad v^{(1)}_{i,1-s_i} = \rho_i \star x_i, \quad \rho_i \leftarrow \mathbb{G},$$
$$z^{(1)}_{i,s_i} = \mathsf{Ext}\big(\mathsf{seed}, \langle \mathbf{m}_i, \mathbf{s} \rangle \star \bar{x}_i\big) \star y_i, \qquad z^{(1)}_{i,1-s_i} = \rho_i \star y_i, \qquad i \in [n].$$

- H_2: In this hybrid we use randomly chosen group elements instead of using the vector $\mathbf{s}$ to generate the output matrices. This hybrid corresponds to the tuple $(\mathsf{ek}, \mathbf{V}^{(2)}, \mathbf{Z}^{(2)})$ where $\mathbf{V}^{(2)}$ and $\mathbf{Z}^{(2)}$ are distributed as follows.

$$v^{(2)}_{i,s_i} = \sigma_i \star x_i, \qquad v^{(2)}_{i,1-s_i} = \rho_i \star x_i, \quad (\sigma_i, \rho_i) \leftarrow \mathbb{G}^2,$$
$$z^{(2)}_{i,s_i} = \sigma_i \star y_i, \qquad z^{(2)}_{i,1-s_i} = \rho_i \star y_i, \qquad i \in [n].$$

- H_3: This hybrid corresponds to the tuple $(\mathsf{ek}, \mathbf{U}, \mathbf{U}')$ where two matrices $\mathbf{U}$ and $\mathbf{U}'$ are generated randomly.

We argue the indistinguishability of consecutive hybrids as follows:

- $H_0 \stackrel{c}{\approx} H_1$: This follows from the weak pseudorandomness of the group action. Given a challenge tuple $(\mathbf{x}, \mathbf{y}, \mathbf{x}', \mathbf{y}')$ where $(\mathbf{x}', \mathbf{y}')$ is either uniform and independent of $(\mathbf{x}, \mathbf{y})$ or $x'_i = \rho_i \star x_i$, $y'_i = \rho_i \star y_i$ for $i \in [n]$, the reduction samples

$$\mathsf{seed} \leftarrow \mathcal{S}, \quad \mathbf{M} \leftarrow \mathbb{G}^{n \times n}, \quad \mathbf{s} \leftarrow \{0,1\}^n, \quad \bar{\mathbf{x}} \leftarrow X^n,$$

and outputs $(\mathsf{ek} = (\mathsf{seed}, \mathbf{M}, \bar{\mathbf{x}}, \mathbf{x}, \mathbf{y}), \bar{\mathbf{V}}, \bar{\mathbf{Z}})$, where $\bar{\mathbf{V}}$ and $\bar{\mathbf{Z}}$ are computed as

$$\bar{v}_{i,s_i} = \mathsf{Ext}\big(\mathsf{seed}, \langle \mathbf{m}_i, \mathbf{s} \rangle \star \bar{x}_i\big) \star x_i, \qquad \bar{v}_{i,1-s_i} = x'_i,$$

$$\bar{z}_{i,s_i} = \mathsf{Ext}\big(\mathsf{seed}, \langle \mathbf{m}_i, \mathbf{s} \rangle \star \bar{x}_i\big) \star y_i, \qquad \bar{z}_{i,1-s_i} = y'_i, \qquad i \in [n].$$

It follows by inspection that the reduction maps a totally random tuple to H_0 and a pseudorandom tuple to H_1. Thus, the hybrid H_0 is computationally indistinguishable from H_1 based on the weak pseudorandomness of EGA.

- $H_1 \overset{c}{\approx} H_2$: This follows from the security of the underlying hinting PRG. By Theorem 2 we know that $(\mathbf{M}, \bar{\mathbf{x}}, \mathbf{W}) \overset{c}{\approx} (\mathbf{M}, \bar{\mathbf{x}}, \mathbf{U})$, where $\mathbf{U} \leftarrow X^{n \times 2}$, $w_{i,s_i} = \langle \mathbf{m}_i, \mathbf{s} \rangle \star \bar{x}_i$, and $w_{i,1-s_i} \leftarrow X$ for $i \in [n]$. Given a challenge tuple of the form $(\mathbf{M}, \bar{\mathbf{x}}, \bar{\mathbf{W}})$ such that $\bar{\mathbf{W}}$ is either distributed as $\mathbf{W}$ or $\mathbf{U}$, the reduction samples $\mathsf{seed} \leftarrow \mathcal{S}$, $\mathbf{x} \leftarrow X^n$ and $\mathbf{y} \leftarrow X^n$, and outputs

$$(\mathsf{ek} = (\mathsf{seed}, \mathbf{M}, \bar{\mathbf{x}}, \mathbf{x}, \mathbf{y}), \bar{\mathbf{V}}, \bar{\mathbf{Z}}),$$

where $\bar{\mathbf{V}}$ and $\bar{\mathbf{Z}}$ are computed as

$$\bar{v}_{i,0} = \mathsf{Ext}\big(\mathsf{seed}, \bar{w}_{i,0}\big) \star x_i, \qquad \bar{v}_{i,1} = \mathsf{Ext}\big(\mathsf{seed}, \bar{w}_{i,1}\big) \star x_i,$$

$$\bar{z}_{i,0} = \mathsf{Ext}\big(\mathsf{seed}, \bar{w}_{i,0}\big) \star y_i, \qquad \bar{z}_{i,1} = \mathsf{Ext}\big(\mathsf{seed}, \bar{w}_{i,1}\big) \star y_i, \qquad i \in [n].$$

Observe that the reduction maps "hinting" samples ($\mathbf{W}$) to H_1, and it maps random samples ($\mathbf{U}$) to H_2. Thus, H_1 is computationally indistinguishable from H_2 based on the LHS assumption.

- $H_2 \overset{c}{\approx} H_3$: This follows from the weak pseudorandomness of the group action. The proof is similar to the proof of $H_0 \overset{c}{\approx} H_1$ and hence we omit the details.

5   Hinting Weak PRF: Instantiations and Implications

In this section, we define hinting weak PRF and we show instantiations of this primitive based on DDH or LHS assumption. Informally, a hinting weak PRF can be viewed as an extended version of hinting PRG, where polynomially many hints of the secret key can be provided (as opposed to only one hint in hinting PRG security game).

Definition 9. *Let* $F : K \times X \to \bar{Y}$ *be a weak PRF where* $K = \{0,1\}^n$ *and* $\bar{Y} = Y^n$ *for some efficiently samplable set* Y. *We say that* F *is a hinting weak PRF if for any* $Q = \mathrm{poly}(\lambda)$ *it holds that*

$$\big(x_i, \mathsf{S}(\mathbf{y}^{(i)}, \mathbf{r}^{(i)})\big)_{i \in [Q]} \overset{c}{\approx} \big(x_i, \mathbf{U}_i\big)_{i \in [Q]},$$

where $\mathbf{k} \leftarrow K$, $x_i \leftarrow X$, $\mathbf{r}^{(i)} \leftarrow Y^n$, $\mathbf{U}_i \leftarrow Y^{n \times 2}$, $\mathbf{y}^{(i)} = F(\mathbf{k}, x_i)$, *and* $\mathsf{S}(\mathbf{y}^{(i)}, \mathbf{r}^{(i)})$ *is an* n *by* 2 *"selector" matrix (with respect to* $\mathbf{k}$*) defined as follows:*

$$\mathsf{S}_{j,k_j}(\mathbf{y}^{(i)}, \mathbf{r}^{(i)}) = y_j^{(i)}, \quad \mathsf{S}_{j,1-k_j}(\mathbf{y}^{(i)}, \mathbf{r}^{(i)}) = r_j^{(i)}, \quad j \in [n].$$

To clarify the notation, $\mathsf{S}_{j,b}$ denotes the (j,b)th entry, k_j is the jth bit of $\mathbf{k}$, and $y_j^{(i)}$ (respectively, $r_j^{(i)}$) denotes the jth entry of the vector $\mathbf{y}^{(i)}$ (respectively, $\mathbf{r}^{(i)}$).

5.1   Hinting Weak PRF from DDH

We begin by showing how to construct a hinting weak PRF from any DDH-hard group.

Construction. Let $(\mathbb{G}, g, q)$ be a DDH-hard group, and fix some integer n such that $n > \log |\mathbb{G}| + \omega(\log \lambda)$. We use the notation from Sect. 3.1 to describe a construction of hinting weak PRF from DDH assumption. Our DDH-based hinting weak PRF is a function of the form $F : \{0,1\}^n \times \mathbb{G}^{n \times n} \to \mathbb{G}^n$. Thus, for any input, one group element is published per each bit of the secret key.

- Gen(1^λ): To generate a key, sample $\mathbf{k} \leftarrow \{0,1\}^n$.
- $F(\mathbf{k} = \{0,1\}^n, [\mathbf{M}] \in \mathbb{G}^{n \times n})$: To evaluate the function, output $[\mathbf{Mk}]$.

Security. We argue the security of the hinting weak PRF above based on the DDH assumption as follows.

Theorem 4. *If $(\mathbb{G}, g, q)$ is a DDH-hard group then the construction above yields a hinting weak PRF.*

Proof. Note that weak pseudorandomness of F (in the weak PRF game) follows from Lemma 2. To argue the hinting security property we need to show that

$$H_0 := \left([\mathbf{M}_i], \mathsf{S}([\mathbf{y}^{(i)}], [\mathbf{r}^{(i)}])\right)_{i \in [Q]} \stackrel{c}{\approx} \left([\mathbf{M}_i], [\mathbf{U}_i]\right)_{i \in [Q]} =: H_1, \qquad (\diamondsuit)$$

where $[\mathbf{M}_i] \leftarrow \mathbb{G}^{n \times n}$, $\mathbf{k} \leftarrow \{0,1\}^n$, $[\mathbf{r}^{(i)}] \leftarrow \mathbb{G}^n$, $[\mathbf{U}_i] \leftarrow \mathbb{G}^{n \times 2}$, $[\mathbf{y}^{(i)}] = [\mathbf{M}_i \mathbf{k}]$, and

$$\mathsf{S}_{j,k_j}\left([\mathbf{y}^{(i)}], [\mathbf{r}^{(i)}]\right) = [y_j^{(i)}], \quad \mathsf{S}_{j,1-k_j}\left([\mathbf{y}^{(i)}], [\mathbf{r}^{(i)}]\right) = [r_j^{(i)}], \quad j \in [n].$$

To show that $(\diamondsuit)$ holds, we extend the proof of DDH-based hinting PRG to multiple instances. By Lemma 2 for $Q = \mathrm{poly}(\lambda)$ we have

$$H_0' := \left([\mathbf{M}_i], ([\mathbf{M}_i \mathbf{k}])_{i \in [Q]}\right) \stackrel{c}{\approx} \left([\mathbf{M}_i], [\mathbf{u}_i]\right)_{i \in [Q]} =: H_1'.$$

Let $\mathcal{A}$ be an adversary that distinguishes H_0 from H_1. We construct an adversary $\mathcal{A}'$ to distinguish H_0' from H_1'. Given $H_b' = ([\mathbf{M}_i], [\mathbf{z}^{(i)}])_{i \in [Q]}$ (where H_b' is distributed as either H_0' or H_1'), the adversary $\mathcal{A}'$ samples Q uniform vectors $([\mathbf{d}^{(i)}] \leftarrow \mathbb{G}^n)_{i \in [Q]}$, and it sets $[\mathbf{M}_i'] := [\mathbf{M}_i + \mathbf{D}_i]$ where $\mathbf{D}_i$ is a diagonal matrix whose diagonal is $\mathbf{d}^{(i)}$. It then runs $\mathcal{A}$ on $([\mathbf{M}_i'], [\mathbf{Y}_i])_{i \in [Q]}$ where $[\mathbf{Y}_i]$ is an n by 2 matrix whose first (respectively, second) row is $[\mathbf{z}^{(i)}]$ (respectively, $[\mathbf{z}^{(i)} + \mathbf{d}^{(i)}]$). The output of $\mathcal{A}'$ is defined to be the same as the output of $\mathcal{A}$. It is immediate to see that $\mathcal{A}'$ maps H_1' to H_1. On the other hand, $\{[\mathbf{M}_i'], [\mathbf{d}^{(i)}]\}_{i \in [Q]}$ are uniform in the view of $\mathcal{A}$ and hence if $H_b' \equiv H_0'$ then an argument similar to the proof of DDH-based hinting PRG implies that

$$\left([\mathbf{M}_i'], [\mathbf{Y}_i]\right)_{i \in [Q]} \stackrel{s}{\approx} \left([\mathbf{M}_i'], \mathsf{S}([\mathbf{z}^{(i)}], [\mathbf{r}^{(i)}])\right)_{i \in [Q]}.$$

where $[\mathbf{r}^{(i)}] \leftarrow \mathbb{G}^n$ for each i. Thus, $\mathcal{A}'$ properly maps H_0' to (a hybrid that is statistically indistinguishable from) H_0, and the proof is complete.

5.2   Hinting Weak PRF from LHS

We now show how to construct a hinting weak PRF from any LHS-hard EGA. Our construction is similar to our DDH-based construction of hinting weak PRF, with suitable modifications to translate our techniques to the setting of EGA.

Construction. Let $(\mathbb{G}, X, \star)$ be an EGA such that LHS assumption holds. Let n be the secret dimension of the LHS assumption. Building upon the notation from Sect. 3.2, we describe a hinting weak PRF $F : \{0, 1\}^n \times (\mathbb{G}^{n \times n} \times X^n) \to X^n$.

- Gen(1^λ): To generate a key, sample $\mathbf{k} \leftarrow \{0, 1\}^n$.
- $F(\mathbf{k} = \{0, 1\}^n, (\mathbf{M} \in \mathbb{G}^{n \times n}, \mathbf{x} \in X^n))$: Output $\mathbf{Mk} \star \mathbf{x}$.

Security. We establish the security of the hinting weak PRF above based on the LHS assumption as follows.

Theorem 5. *Let $(\mathbb{G}, X, \star)$ be an EGA. If LHS assumption holds over $(\mathbb{G}, X, \star)$ then F (defined above) is a hinting weak PRF.*

Proof. Weak pseudorandomness of F directly follows from the LHS assumption. To prove hinting security property, it suffices to show that

$$H_0 := \left(\mathbf{x}_i, \mathbf{M}_i, \mathsf{S}(\mathbf{y}^{(i)}, \mathbf{r}^{(i)})\right)_{i \in [Q]} \overset{c}{\approx} \left(\mathbf{x}_i, \mathbf{M}_i, \mathbf{U}_i\right)_{i \in [Q]} =: H_1, \qquad (\Diamond\Diamond)$$

where $\mathbf{M}_i \leftarrow \mathbb{G}^{n \times n}$, $\mathbf{k} \leftarrow \{0, 1\}^n$, $\mathbf{r}^{(i)} \leftarrow X^n$, $\mathbf{U}_i \leftarrow X^{n \times 2}$, $\mathbf{y}^{(i)} = \mathbf{M}_i \mathbf{k} \star \mathbf{x}_i$, and

$$\mathsf{S}_{j,k_j}\left(\mathbf{y}^{(i)}, \mathbf{r}^{(i)}\right) = y_j^{(i)}, \quad \mathsf{S}_{j,1-k_j}\left(\mathbf{y}^{(i)}, \mathbf{r}^{(i)}\right) = r_j^{(i)}, \quad j \in [n].$$

In the next step, we show a reduction from the LHS assumption to $(\Diamond\Diamond)$. First, by the LHS assumption we have

$$H_0' := \left(\mathbf{x}_i, \mathbf{M}_i, \mathbf{M}_i \mathbf{k} \star \mathbf{x}_i\right)_{i \in [Q]} \overset{c}{\approx} \left(\mathbf{x}_i, \mathbf{M}_i, \mathbf{u}_i\right)_{i \in [Q]} =: H_1'.$$

Given an adversary $\mathcal{A}$ that distinguishes H_0 from H_1, we construct another adversary $\mathcal{A}'$ against the LHS assumption. Given an LHS challenge of the form $H_b' = (\mathbf{x}_i, \mathbf{M}_i, \mathbf{z}^{(i)})_{i \in [Q]}$ (where H_b' is identical to either H_0' or H_1'), the adversary $\mathcal{A}'$ samples Q uniform vectors $(\mathbf{d}^{(i)} \leftarrow \mathbb{G}^n)_{i \in [Q]}$ and it sets $\mathbf{M}_i' := \mathbf{M}_i + \mathbf{D}_i$, where $\mathbf{D}_i$ is a diagonal matrix whose diagonal is $\mathbf{d}^{(i)}$. We define the output of $\mathcal{A}'$ to be the output of $\mathcal{A}$ on $(\mathbf{x}_i, \mathbf{M}_i', \mathbf{Y}_i)_{i \in [Q]}$ where $\mathbf{Y}_i \in X^{n \times 2}$ is the matrix whose first and second rows are $\mathbf{z}^{(i)}$ and $\mathbf{d}^{(i)} \star \mathbf{z}^{(i)}$, respectively. Clearly, $\mathcal{A}'$ maps H_1' to H_1. Moreover, $(\mathbf{M}_i', \mathbf{d}^{(i)})_{i \in [Q]}$ are uniform in the view of $\mathcal{A}$ and hence if $H_b' \equiv H_0'$ then an argument similar to the proof of LHS-based hinting PRG implies that

$$\left(\mathbf{x}_i, \mathbf{M}_i', \mathbf{Y}_i\right)_{i \in [Q]} \overset{s}{\approx} \left(\mathbf{x}_i, \mathbf{M}_i', \mathsf{S}(\mathbf{z}^{(i)}, \mathbf{u}^{(i)})\right)_{i \in [Q]},$$

and so $\mathcal{A}'$ properly maps H_0' to (a hybrid that is statistically close to) H_0.

6 Primitives with Functional Hinting Property

In this section, we introduce functional hinting PRG - a strengthening of hinting PRG that guarantees PRG security in the presence of hints about each bit of *some function* of the seed. We also introduce a natural extension, namely a functional hinting wPRF, that guarantees wPRF security in the presence of multiple hints about each bit of some (adversarially chosen) function of the secret key. We show that a functional hinting weak PRF with respect to a family of functions $\mathcal{F}$ can be used to realize a symmetric-key KDM-secure encryption scheme with respect to the same function family $\mathcal{F}$ in a *black-box* manner. We then build upon our approach of realizing hinting PRGs and hinting weak PRFs to realize simple constructions of functional hinting PRGs and functional weak PRFs for the family of projective quadratic functions (and functions of higher degree) based on the DDH assumption.

6.1 Functional Hinting PRG

We first define functional hinting PRG – a generalized version of hinting PRG for which the security game is defined in terms of a *function* of the seed of PRG, rather the seed itself. A plain hinting PRG can be simply viewed as a functional hinting PRG with respect to the identity function.

Definition 10. *Let $f : \{0,1\}^n \to \{0,1\}^m$ be an efficiently computable function. A functional hinting PRG $G_{pp} : \{0,1\}^n \to \bar{Y} = Y^{m+1}$ with respect to f is defined by two algorithms (Setup, Eval) as follows:*

- Setup$(1^\lambda, 1^n, 1^m)$: *A randomized algorithm that takes the seed length n and the number of hinting blocks m, and it outputs pp as the public parameter.*
- Eval$(pp, i \in \{0\} \cup [m], \mathbf{s} \in \{0,1\}^n)$: *A deterministic algorithm that on pp and an index i, it outputs $y_i \in Y$. By stacking the outputs for all $\in \{0\} \cup [m]$, we can view the output as an element of Y^{m+1}, i.e., $G_{pp}(\mathbf{s}) \in Y^{m+1}$.*

We say that G_{pp} (defined by the algorithms above) is a functional hinting PRG with respect to $f : \{0,1\}^n \to \{0,1\}^m$, if for pp $\leftarrow$ Setup$(1^\lambda, 1^n, 1^m)$ and randomly chosen seed $\mathbf{s} \leftarrow \{0,1\}^n$ it holds that

$$\left(y_0, (y_{j,b})_{j\in[m], b\in\{0,1\}}\right) \stackrel{c}{\approx} \left(u_0, (u_{j,b})_{j\in[m], b\in\{0,1\}}\right),$$

where

$$\mathbf{v} := f(\mathbf{s}) \in \{0,1\}^m, \quad (y_0, y_{1,v_1}, \ldots, y_{m,v_m}) = G_{pp}(\mathbf{s}) \in Y^{m+1},$$

and all other elements generated uniformly from Y, i.e.,

$$\{y_{j,1-v_j} \leftarrow Y\}_{j\in[m]}, \quad u_0 \leftarrow Y, \quad \{u_{j,b} \leftarrow Y\}_{j\in[m], b\in\{0,1\}}.$$

In the next part, we describe a construction of functional hinting PRG for the quadratic function of the seed (where the seed is viewed a vector of bits) from the DDH assumption, i.e., it is possible to (securely) provide a hint with respect to $f(\mathbf{s})$ where $f : \{0,1\}^n \to \{0,1\}^{n^2}$ defined as $f(\mathbf{s}) = \mathbf{s} \otimes \mathbf{s}$, which can be viewed as a vectorized form of $\mathbf{ss}^t \in \{0,1\}^{n\times n}$.

Functional Hinting PRG for Quadratic Function from DDH. Let $(\mathbb{G}, g, q)$ be a DDH-hard group, and let n be an integer such that $n > 2 \log |\mathbb{G}| + \omega(\log \lambda)$. We use the notation from Sect. 3.1 to show a construction of functional hinting PRG for the quadratic function based on the DDH assumption. Our construction of functional hinting PRG $G_{pp} : \{0, 1\}^n \to \mathbb{G}^{n^2+1}$ from DDH is as follows:

- Setup($1^\lambda, 1^n, 1^{n^2}$): For each $j \in \{0\} \cup [n^2]$, sample $[\mathbf{M}_j] \leftarrow \mathbb{G}^{n \times n}$ and publish $pp = ([\mathbf{M}_j])_{j \in \{0\} \cup [n^2]}$.
- Eval(pp, $\mathbf{s} \in \{0, 1\}^n, i \in \{0\} \cup [n^2]$): Let $[\mathbf{M}_i]$ denote the ith matrix from pp. Output $[\mathbf{s}^t \mathbf{M}_i \mathbf{s}]$.[9]

Security. We prove the security of the construction via the following theorem.

Theorem 6. *If $(\mathbb{G}, g, q)$ is a DDH-hard group then the construction above yields a functional hinting PRG for the quadratic function from DDH.*

Proof. First, observe that by Lemma 3 (proved below) for $Q = n^2 + 1$ samples we have

$$([\mathbf{M}_j], [\mathbf{s}^t \mathbf{M}_j \mathbf{s}])_{j \in [n^2+1]} \stackrel{c}{\approx} ([\mathbf{M}_j], [u_j])_{j \in [n^2+1]}$$

(where $[u_j] \leftarrow \mathbb{G}$ for each $j \in [n^2 + 1]$) and hence the pseudorandomness of the output in the plain PRG game follows from Lemma 3. Let $\alpha : [n^2] \to [n]$ and $\beta : [n^2] \to [n]$ be two simple index mapping functions that map any index $i \in [n^2]$ to $(\alpha(i) = \lceil i/n \rceil, \beta(i) = i \bmod n)$. Note that α and β simply provide a way to write a vector with n^2 elements as an $n \times n$ matrix.

To establish the security of the construction in the functional hinting PRG game, it is enough to show that

$$([\mathbf{M}_0], [\mathbf{s}^t \mathbf{M}_0 \mathbf{s}], ([\mathbf{M}_i])_{i \in [n^2]}, [\mathbf{Y}]) \stackrel{c}{\approx} ([\mathbf{M}_0], [u], [\bar{\mathbf{M}}], [\mathbf{U}]), \quad (\Box)$$

where $[u] \leftarrow \mathbb{G}$ and $[\mathbf{U}] \leftarrow \mathbb{G}^{n^2 \times 2}$ are sampled uniformly and $[\mathbf{Y}] \in \mathbb{G}^{n^2 \times 2}$ is distributed as follows

$$\sigma(i) = s_{\alpha(i)} \cdot s_{\beta(i)}, \quad [y_{i,\sigma(i)}] = [\mathbf{s}^t \mathbf{M}_i \mathbf{s}], \quad [y_{i,1-\sigma(i)}] \leftarrow \mathbb{G}, \quad i \in [n^2].$$

Note that $\sigma(i)$ outputs the $(\alpha(i), \beta(i))$ entry of $\mathbf{s}\mathbf{s}^t \in \{0, 1\}^{n \times n}$ for any index $i \in [n^2]$. We prove ($\Box$) via a hybrid argument. Let H_0 and H_1 be the hybrids that correspond to the left-hand side and right-hand side of ($\Box$), respectively.

Let $\mathcal{A}$ be an adversary that distinguishes H_0 from H_1. We construct an adversary $\mathcal{A}'$ that distinguishes H_0' from H_1' defined as[10]

$$H_0' := ([\mathbf{M}_0], [\mathbf{s}^t \mathbf{M}_0 \mathbf{s}], ([\mathbf{M}_i])_{i \in [n^2]}, \mathbf{y}), \quad H_1' := ([\mathbf{M}_0], [u], ([\mathbf{M}_i])_{i \in [n^2]}, \mathbf{u}),$$

---

[9] Note that given any matrix of group elements $[\mathbf{M}] \in \mathbb{G}^{n \times n}$ and any binary vector $\mathbf{s} \in \{0, 1\}^n$, one can efficiently compute $[\mathbf{s}^t \mathbf{M} \mathbf{s}]$.

[10] Note that this is simply Lemma 3 with $n^2 + 1$ samples.

where $[y_i] = [\mathbf{s}^t \mathbf{M}_i \mathbf{s}]$ for each $i \in [n^2]$, and by Lemma 3 it follows that the advantage of $\mathcal{A}$ should also be negligible.

Given a tuple $H'_b = ([\mathbf{m}_0], [z_0], ([\mathbf{M}_i])_{i \in [n^2]}, [\mathbf{z}])$, where H'_b is distributed as either H'_0 or H'_1, the external adversary $\mathcal{A}'$ forms n^2 matrices $[\mathbf{P}_{jk}] \in \mathbb{G}^{n \times n}$ (for $j \in [n], k \in [n]$) where $[\mathbf{P}_{jk}]$ is a matrix whose all but one entry is the identity element of the group and the remaining one entry at the position (j,k) is sampled uniformly from $\mathbb{G}$. Concretely, $\mathcal{A}'$ samples a shift vector $[\mathbf{d}] \in \mathbb{G}^{n^2}$, and it sets the $(\alpha(i), \beta(i))$ entry of $[\mathbf{P}_{\alpha(i),\beta(i)}]$ as $[d_i]$ for each $i \in [n^2]$. In the next step, $\mathcal{A}'$ runs $\mathcal{A}$ on the following tuple

$$([\mathbf{m}_0], [z_0], [\mathbf{M}'_i] := [\mathbf{M}_i + \mathbf{P}_{\alpha(i),\beta(i)}], [\mathbf{Y}]),$$

where $[\mathbf{Y}]$ is an n^2 by 2 matrix whose first and second columns are $[\mathbf{z}]$ and $[\mathbf{z}+\mathbf{d}]$ respectively. We define the output of $\mathcal{A}'$ to be the same as the output of $\mathcal{A}$.

Observe that (in the view of the adversary $\mathcal{A}$) $[\mathbf{M}_0]$ and $([\mathbf{M}'_i])_{i \in [n^2]}$ are distributed uniformly. Moreover, if $[\mathbf{z}]$ is uniform then $[\mathbf{Y}]$ will be distributed uniformly as well. Thus, $\mathcal{A}'$ perfectly simulates the "ideal" hybrid H_1. On the other hand, if $[z_i] = [\mathbf{s}^t \mathbf{M}_i \mathbf{s}]$ (for each $i \in [n^2]$) then from the view of $\mathcal{A}'$ the matrix $[\mathbf{Y}]$ is distributed as

$$\sigma(i) = s_{\alpha(i)} \cdot s_{\beta(i)}, \ [y_{i,\sigma(i)}] = [\mathbf{s}^t \mathbf{M}'_i \mathbf{s}], \ [y_{i,1-\sigma(i)}] = [(-1)^{\sigma(i)} \cdot d_i + \mathbf{s}^t \mathbf{M}'_i \mathbf{s}], \quad i \in [n^2].$$

Note that the relations above hold because

$$[\mathbf{s}^t \mathbf{M}'_i \mathbf{s}] = [\mathbf{s}^t \mathbf{M}_i \mathbf{s} + s_{\alpha(i)} \cdot s_{\beta(i)} \cdot d_i], \quad i \in [n^2].$$

Since $[\mathbf{d}]$ is distributed uniformly and independently from $[\mathbf{M}']$ (in the view of $\mathcal{A}$), it follows that in the view of $\mathcal{A}$ we have

$$(([\mathbf{M}'_i])_{i \in [n^2]}, \mathbf{Y}) \overset{s}{\approx} (([\mathbf{M}'_i])_{i \in [n^2]}, \mathbf{U}),$$

where $[\mathbf{U}] \leftarrow \mathbb{G}^{n^2 \times 2}$, and hence $\mathcal{A}'$ properly maps the hybrid H'_0 to (a hybrid that is statistically indistinguishable from) H_0, as required.

Lemma 3. *Let $(\mathbb{G}, g, q)$ be a DDH-hard group, and fix some integer ℓ and n such that $n > 2 \log |\mathbb{G}| + \omega(\log \lambda)$ and $\ell = \mathrm{poly}(\lambda)$. If $\{[\mathbf{M}_i] \leftarrow \mathbb{G}^{n \times n}\}_{i \in [\ell]}$ and $\mathbf{s} \leftarrow \{0,1\}^n$, then*

$$([\mathbf{M}_i], [\mathbf{s}^t \mathbf{M}_i \mathbf{s}])_{i \in [\ell]} \overset{c}{\approx} ([\mathbf{M}_i], [u_i])_{i \in [\ell]},$$

where $[u_i] \leftarrow \mathbb{G}$ is sampled uniformly for each $i \in [\ell]$.

Proof. Let $\bar{\mathbf{M}} \in \mathbb{G}^{n \times n}$ be a matrix of group elements whose (j,k) entry is $[a_j \cdot b_k]$ where $a_j \leftarrow \mathbb{Z}_q, b_k \leftarrow \mathbb{Z}_q$ (for $j \in [\ell], k \in [n]$). In addition, let $([\hat{\mathbf{M}}_i])_{i \in [\ell]}$ be ℓ matrices of group elements defined as

$$[\hat{\mathbf{M}}_i] = [r_i \cdot \bar{\mathbf{M}}], \quad r_i \leftarrow \mathbb{Z}_q, \quad i \in [\ell].$$

By applying the leftover hash lemma to the group $\mathbb{G}^2$, it follows that

$$([\bar{\mathbf{M}}], [\mathbf{s}^t \bar{\mathbf{M}} \mathbf{s}]) \stackrel{s}{\approx} ([\bar{\mathbf{M}}], [u']),$$

where $[u'] \leftarrow \mathbb{G}$, which in turn implies that

$$\left([\hat{\mathbf{M}}_i], [\mathbf{s}^t \hat{\mathbf{M}}_i \mathbf{s}]\right)_{i \in [\ell]} \stackrel{s}{\approx} \left([\hat{\mathbf{M}}_i], [r_i \cdot u']\right)_{i \in [\ell]} \stackrel{c}{\approx} \left([\hat{\mathbf{M}}_i], [u_i]\right)_{i \in [\ell]},$$

and the computational indistinguishability follows from the DDH assumption. On the other hand, by the DDH assumption we have

$$\left([\mathbf{M}_i]\right)_{i \in [\ell]} \stackrel{c}{\approx} \left([\hat{\mathbf{M}}_i]\right)_{i \in [\ell]},$$

and hence a standard hybrid argument implies that

$$\left([\mathbf{M}_i], [\mathbf{s}^t \mathbf{M}_i \mathbf{s}]\right)_{i \in [\ell]} \stackrel{c}{\approx} \left([\mathbf{M}_i], [u_i]\right)_{i \in [\ell]},$$

as required.

Functional Hinting PRG for Higher Degree Functions. The above construction of functional hinting PRG allows us to publish a hint with respect to the function $g(\mathbf{s}) = \mathbf{s} \otimes \mathbf{s} \in \{0,1\}^{n^2}$. Here we describe a way to obtain functional hinting PRG for functions of higher degree. One can generalize the construction above for functions of higher degree $k > 2$ by using n^k many k-dimensional array/tensor of uniformly chosen group elements as the public parameter, and the evaluation will be shrinking down each array in the public parameter to only one group element by computing a $\mathbb{G}$-linear function across each dimension using the seed $\mathbf{s}$. For instance, given n^k many k-dimensional array of uniformly chosen group elements one can construct a functional hinting PRG for degree k functions where each of n^k blocks provides a hint with respect to $s_{i_1} s_{i_2} \cdots s_{i_k}$, for $(i_1, \ldots, i_k) \in [n]^k$. The construction and proof will be similar to the quadratic case, and hence we omit the details.

6.2   Functional Hinting Weak PRF

Similar to the case of hinting PRG, we define a generalized version of hinting weak PRF for which the security game is defined in terms of function(s) of the secret key, rather the key itself. Our notion of hinting weak PRF can be viewed as a functional hinting weak PRF with respect to the identity function. There are two approaches to define a functional hinting weak PRF; one approach is to guarantee security in the presence of multiple hints of a *fixed* function of the secret key (corresponding to different inputs), and another approach is to provide security in the presence of multiple hints of *different* functions of the secret key. We provide a formal definition of the latter in this section, and later we provide an instantiation based on DDH for certain family of functions.

Definition 11. *Let $\mathcal{F} = \{f_I \mid f_I : \{0,1\}^n \to \{0,1\}^m\}_{I \in \mathcal{I}}$ be a family of boolean functions, and let $F : K \times X \to \bar{Y}$ be a weak PRF where $K = \{0,1\}^n$ and $\bar{Y} = Y^m$ for some efficiently samplable set Y. We say that F is a functional hinting weak PRF with respect to $\mathcal{F}$ if the advantage of any PPT attacker in distinguishing between the experiments $\mathsf{Exp}_0^{\mathsf{FHwPRF}}$ and $\mathsf{Exp}_1^{\mathsf{FHwPRF}}$ (described in Fig. 2) is negligible.*

---

1. The challenger samples a weak PRF key $\mathbf{k} \leftarrow \{0,1\}^n$.

2. The adversary chooses a function $f_i \in \mathcal{F}$ (corresponding to the ith query) and sends it to the challenger.

3. The challenger samples $x_i \leftarrow X$, $\mathbf{r}^{(i)} \leftarrow Y^m$, $\mathbf{U}_i \leftarrow Y^{m \times 2}$ uniformly. It then sets $\mathbf{y}^{(i)} = F(\mathbf{k}, x_i)$. Let $\mathsf{S}(f_i, \mathbf{y}^{(i)}, \mathbf{r}^{(i)})$ be an m by 2 "selector" matrix with respect to $f_i(\mathbf{k})$ defined as follows:

$$\mathbf{v}^{(i)} = f_i(\mathbf{k}), \quad \mathsf{S}_{j,v_j^{(i)}}(f_i, \mathbf{y}^{(i)}, \mathbf{r}^{(i)}) = y_j^{(i)}, \quad \mathsf{S}_{j,1-v_j^{(i)}}(f_i, \mathbf{y}^{(i)}, \mathbf{r}^{(i)}) = r_j^{(i)}, \quad j \in [m].$$

4. If $b = 0$, the challenger responds to the ith query with $\left(x_i, \mathsf{S}(f_i, \mathbf{y}^{(i)}, \mathbf{r}^{(i)})\right)$.

5. If $b = 1$, the challenger responds to the ith query with $(x_i, \mathbf{U}_i)$.

6. The adversary continues to make function queries as before, and each query is replied by the challenger as described above.

Fig. 2. Experiment $\mathsf{Exp}_b^{\mathsf{FHwPRF}}$ with respect to $\mathcal{F}$.

For a (boolean) function $g : \{0,1\}^n \to \{0,1\}^m$ we define the projective function family $\mathcal{F}_g$ as follows:

$$\mathcal{F}_g = \{f : \{0,1\}^n \to \{0,1\}^m \mid \exists \mathbf{b} \in \{0,1\}^m : f(\mathbf{x}) = (b_1 \cdot g_1(\mathbf{x}), \ldots, b_m \cdot g_m(\mathbf{x}))\},$$

where $g_i(\mathbf{x})$ denotes the ith bit of $g(\mathbf{x})$ and the condition holds for all $\mathbf{x} \in \{0,1\}^n$. We may drop the subscript g for the sake of simplicity when the function is clear from context. Informally, $\mathcal{F}$ contains all of the functions whose ith bit of the output (on any input) is either 0 or the ith output bit of g (on the same input). Note that given the function g, each function in $\mathcal{F}$ can be described by a binary vector $\mathbf{b}$. For instance, the function g itself corresponds to all-one vector $\mathbf{1}$.

In the next part of this section, we show a construction of functional hinting weak PRF for the family of projective quadratic functions based on the DDH assumption. Later, we describe how we can generalize this construction to the family of projective functions of higher degree. We note that a functional hinting weak PRF for the family of projective quadratic functions can be viewed as an extended version of a functional hinting PRG for the quadratic function $g(\mathbf{s}) = \mathbf{s} \otimes \mathbf{s}$, with an additional property that an adversary can adaptively "fix" the hint for arbitrary positions. Below, we describe a construction of functional hinting weak PRF for the family of projective quadratic functions $\mathcal{F}_g$ (as defined above) based on the DDH assumption.

Functional Hinting Weak PRF for Projective Quadratic Functions. Let $(\mathbb{G}, g, q)$ be a DDH-hard group, and let $n > 2 \log |\mathbb{G}| + \omega(\log \lambda)$ be an integer. We use the notation from Sect. 3.1 to show a construction of functional hinting weak PRF. Consider the weak PRF $F : \{0,1\}^n \times (\mathbb{G}^{n \times n})^{n^2} \to \mathbb{G}^{n^2}$ defined as follows:

- $\mathsf{Gen}(1^\lambda)$: To generate a key, sample $\mathbf{k} \leftarrow \{0,1\}^n$.
- $F(\mathbf{k} = \{0,1\}^n, ([\mathbf{M}_i])_{i \in [n^2]} \in (\mathbb{G}^{n \times n})^{n^2})$: Output $([\mathbf{k}^t \mathbf{M}_i \mathbf{k}])_{i \in [n^2]}$.

Security. We prove the security of the construction via the following theorem.

Theorem 7. *If $(\mathbb{G}, g, q)$ is a DDH-hard group then the construction above yields a functional hinting weak PRF for the projective quadratic function family $\mathcal{F}_g$ from DDH.*

Proof. Weak pseudorandomness of F (in the plain weak PRF game) follows from Lemma 3. To establish the functional hinting security (with respect to $\mathcal{F}_g$) we need to prove that $\mathsf{Exp}_0^{\mathsf{FHwPRF}} \overset{c}{\approx} \mathsf{Exp}_1^{\mathsf{FHwPRF}}$. To show this, we extend the proof of DDH-based functional hinting PRG for quadratic function to multiple instances by keeping track of each function f_i (determined by $\mathbf{b}_i$). As mentioned before, a binary vector $\mathbf{b}_i \in \{0,1\}^{n^2}$ can be used to describe any function $f_i \in \mathcal{F}_g$ (along with g). First, by Lemma 3 for any $Q = \mathrm{poly}(\lambda)$ we have[11]

$$H_0 := \left(([\mathbf{M}_i^{(\ell)}])_{\ell \in [n^2]}, ([\mathbf{k}^t \mathbf{M}_i^{(\ell)} \mathbf{k}])_{\ell \in [n^2]} \right)_{i \in [Q]} \overset{c}{\approx}$$

$$H_1 := \left(([\mathbf{M}_i^{(\ell)}])_{\ell \in [n^2]}, [\mathbf{u}_i] \right)_{i \in [Q]},$$

where $[\mathbf{u}_i] \leftarrow \mathbb{G}^{n^2}$.

Let $\mathcal{A}$ be an adversary that distinguishes $\mathsf{Exp}_0^{\mathsf{FHwPRF}}$ from $\mathsf{Exp}_1^{\mathsf{FHwPRF}}$, and let Q be the total of queries made by $\mathcal{A}$. We construct an adversary $\mathcal{A}'$ to distinguish H_0 from H_1. Given samples of the form

$$H_b := \left(([\mathbf{M}_i^{(\ell)}])_{\ell \in [n^2]}, [\mathbf{z}_i] \right)_{i \in [Q]}$$

where H_b is distributed as either H_0 or H_1, the adversary $\mathcal{A}'$ runs $\mathcal{A}$. Whenever $\mathcal{A}$ makes its ith query for a function $f_i \in \mathcal{F}_g$ determined by a binary vector $\mathbf{b}_i \in \{0,1\}^{n^2}$, the adversary $\mathcal{A}'$ responds the ith query as follows. $\mathcal{A}'$ samples $[\mathbf{d}_i] \leftarrow \mathbb{G}^{n^2}$. Let α and β be the index mapping functions from the proof of Theorem 6. For $\ell \in [n^2]$, the adversary $\mathcal{A}'$ sets

$$[\bar{\mathbf{M}}_i^{(\ell)}] := [\mathbf{M}_i^{(\ell)}] + [b_i^{(\ell)} \cdot d_i^{(\ell)} \cdot \mathbf{E}_{\alpha(\ell), \beta(\ell)}],$$

---

[11] Note that we are using Lemma 3 with $Q \cdot n^2 = \mathrm{poly}(\lambda)$ samples.

where $\mathbf{E}_{\alpha(\ell),\beta(\ell)}$ is an $n \times n$ matrix whose $(\alpha(\ell), \beta(\ell))$ entry is 1, and all other entries are 0. (Note that $\bar{b}_i^{(\ell)}$ and $d_i^{(\ell)}$ denote the ℓth component of $\mathbf{b}_i$ and $\mathbf{d}_i$, respectively.)

$\mathcal{A}'$ sends $(([\bar{\mathbf{M}}_i^{(\ell)}])_{\ell\in[n^2]}, [\mathbf{Y}_i])$ to $\mathcal{A}$ as the response for the ith query, where $[\mathbf{Y}_i] \in \mathbb{G}^{n^2 \times 2}$ is the matrix whose first and columns are $[\mathbf{z}^{(i)}]$ and $[\mathbf{d}^{(i)} + \mathbf{z}^{(i)}]$.

We now argue that $\mathcal{A}'$ properly maps H_b to $\mathsf{Exp}_b^{\mathsf{FHwPRF}}$ for $b \in \{0,1\}$. First, we consider the simpler case $b = 1$. Observe that the matrices $(([\bar{\mathbf{M}}_i^{(\ell)}])_{\ell\in[n^2],i\in[Q]}$ are uniformly distributed in the view of $\mathcal{A}$. Moreover, if $([\mathbf{z}_i])_{i\in[Q]}$ are distributed uniformly and independently (which happens when $b = 1$), then $([\mathbf{Y}_i])_{i\in[Q]}$ will be uniformly distributed as well and hence $\mathcal{A}'$ properly maps H_1 to $\mathsf{Exp}_1^{\mathsf{FHwPRF}}$.

If $b = 0$, based on an argument similar to the proof of DDH-based hinting PRG for the quadratic function, it can be verified that for each $i \in [Q]$ we have

$$[\mathbf{Y}_i] = \mathsf{S}(f_i, [\mathbf{y}^{(i)}], [\mathbf{u}^{(i)}]),$$

where S is the "selector" mapping (as defined in the experiment) and

$$\mathbf{v}^{(i)} := f_i(\mathbf{k}) = \mathbf{b}_i \odot g(\mathbf{k}) = \mathbf{b}_i \odot (\mathbf{k} \otimes \mathbf{k}),$$

$$[\mathbf{y}^{(i)}] := ([\mathbf{k}^t \bar{\mathbf{M}}_i^{(\ell)} \mathbf{k}])_{\ell\in[n^2]}, \quad [\mathbf{u}^{(i)}] := [(-1)^{\mathbf{v}^{(i)}} \odot \mathbf{d}^{(i)} + \mathbf{y}^{(i)}],$$

$$\mathsf{S}_{j,v_j^{(i)}}(f_i, [\mathbf{y}^{(i)}], [\mathbf{u}^{(i)}]) = y_j^{(i)}, \quad \mathsf{S}_{j,1-v_j^{(i)}}(f_i, [\mathbf{y}^{(i)}], [\mathbf{u}^{(i)}]) = u_j^{(i)}, \quad j \in [n^2],$$

where $\odot$ denotes the component-wise/Hadamard product and $(-1)^{\mathbf{v}^{(i)}}$ is the vector obtained by component-wise exponentiation. It follows that in the view of the adversary $\mathcal{A}$

$$(([\bar{\mathbf{M}}_i^{(\ell)}])_{\ell\in[n^2]}, [\mathbf{Y}_i])_{i\in[Q]} \overset{s}{\approx} \mathsf{S}(f_i, [\mathbf{y}^{(i)}], [\mathbf{r}^{(i)}])_{i\in[Q]},$$

where $[\mathbf{r}_i] \leftarrow \mathbb{G}^{n^2}$. Therefore, $\mathcal{A}'$ properly maps the hybrid H_0 to (a hybrid that is statistically indistinguishable from) $\mathsf{Exp}_0^{\mathsf{FHwPRF}}$, as required.

Functional Hinting Weak PRF for Higher Degree Function Families. The construction above allows (securely) publishing many hints with respect to the projective function family $\mathcal{F}_g$ where $g(\mathbf{s}) = \mathbf{s} \otimes \mathbf{s} \in \{0,1\}^{n^2}$. Similar to the case of hinting PRG, we briefly describe how to construct functional hinting weak PRF for the projective function family $\mathcal{F}_h$ (where h is degree k function for some $k > 2$), which enables publishing a hint in each block with respect to a projective function of $s_{i_1} s_{i_2} \cdots s_{i_k}$, for $(i_1, \ldots, i_k) \in [n]^k$. Similar to the case of functional hinting PRG, a generalized version of the construction above can be obtained using n^k many k-dimensional array/tensor of uniformly chosen group elements for each input, and the output of F is obtained by computing a $\mathbb{G}$-linear function across each dimension using the weak PRF key $\mathbf{k}$.

References

[ADMP20] Alamati, N., De Feo, L., Montgomery, H., Patranabis, S.: Cryptographic group actions and applications. In: Moriai, S., Wang, H. (eds.) ASIACRYPT 2020, Part II. LNCS, vol. 12492, pp. 411–439. Springer, Cham (2020). https://doi.org/10.1007/978-3-030-64834-3_14

[AMP19] Alamati, N., Montgomery, H., Patranabis, S.: Symmetric primitives with structured secrets. In: Boldyreva, A., Micciancio, D. (eds.) CRYPTO 2019, Part I. LNCS, vol. 11692, pp. 650–679. Springer, Cham (2019). https://doi.org/10.1007/978-3-030-26948-7_23

[App14] Applebaum, B.: Key-dependent message security: generic amplification and completeness. J. Cryptol. **27**(3), 429–451 (2014)

[BBD+22] Booher, J., et al.: Failing to hash into supersingular isogeny graphs. IACR Cryptol. ePrint Arch., p. 518 (2022)

[BGK11] Brakerski, Z., Goldwasser, S., Kalai, Y.T.: Black-box circular-secure encryption beyond affine functions. In: Ishai, Y. (ed.) TCC 2011. LNCS, vol. 6597, pp. 201–218. Springer, Heidelberg (2011)

[BHHO08] Boneh, D., Halevi, S., Hamburg, M., Ostrovsky, R.: Circular-secure encryption from decision Diffie-Hellman. In: Wagner, D. (ed.) CRYPTO 2008. LNCS, vol. 5157, pp. 108–125. Springer, Heidelberg (2008). https://doi.org/10.1007/978-3-540-85174-5_7

[BKV19] Beullens, W., Kleinjung, T., Vercauteren, F.: CSI-FiSh: efficient isogeny based signatures through class group computations. In: Galbraith, S.D., Moriai, S. (eds.) ASIACRYPT 2019, Part I. LNCS, vol. 11921, pp. 227–247. Springer, Cham (2019). https://doi.org/10.1007/978-3-030-34578-5_9

[BRS03] Black, J., Rogaway, P., Shrimpton, T.: Encryption-scheme security in the presence of key-dependent messages. In: Nyberg, K., Heys, H. (eds.) SAC 2002. LNCS, vol. 2595, pp. 62–75. Springer, Heidelberg (2003). https://doi.org/10.1007/3-540-36492-7_6

[CDG+17] Cho, C., Döttling, N., Garg, S., Gupta, D., Miao, P., Polychroniadou, A.: Laconic oblivious transfer and its applications. In: Katz, J., Shacham, H. (eds.) CRYPTO 2017, Part II. LNCS, vol. 10402, pp. 33–65. Springer, Cham (2017). https://doi.org/10.1007/978-3-319-63715-0_2

[CLM+18] Castryck, W., Lange, T., Martindale, C., Panny, L., Renes, J.: CSIDH: an efficient post-quantum commutative group action. In: Peyrin, T., Galbraith, S. (eds.) ASIACRYPT 2018, Part III. LNCS, vol. 11274, pp. 395–427. Springer, Cham (2018). https://doi.org/10.1007/978-3-030-03332-3_15

[FGK+10] Freeman, D.M., Goldreich, O., Kiltz, E., Rosen, A., Segev, G.: More constructions of lossy and correlation-secure trapdoor functions. In: Nguyen, P.Q., Pointcheval, D. (eds.) PKC 2010. LNCS, vol. 6056, pp. 279–295. Springer, Heidelberg (2010). https://doi.org/10.1007/978-3-642-13013-7_17

[GHMO21] Garg, S., Hajiabadi, M., Malavolta, G., Ostrovsky, R.: How to build a trapdoor function from an encryption scheme. In: Tibouchi, M., Wang, H. (eds.) ASIACRYPT 2021. LNCS, vol. 13092, pp. 220–249. Springer, Cham (2021). https://doi.org/10.1007/978-3-030-92078-4_8

[GKLW21] Garg, R., Khurana, D., Lu, G., Waters, B.: Black-box non-interactive non-malleable commitments. In: Canteaut, A., Standaert, F.-X. (eds.) EUROCRYPT 2021. LNCS, vol. 12698, pp. 159–185. Springer, Cham (2021). https://doi.org/10.1007/978-3-030-77883-5_6

[GVW20] Goyal, R., Vusirikala, S., Waters, B.: New constructions of hinting PRGs, OWFs with encryption, and more. In: Micciancio, D., Ristenpart, T. (eds.) CRYPTO 2020, Part I. LNCS, vol. 12170, pp. 527–558. Springer, Cham (2020). https://doi.org/10.1007/978-3-030-56784-2_18

[IR89] Impagliazzo, R., Rudich, S.: Limits on the provable consequences of one-way permutations. In: 21st ACM STOC, pp. 44–61. ACM Press, May 1989

[KM19] Kitagawa, F., Matsuda, T.: CPA-to-CCA transformation for KDM security. In: Hofheinz, D., Rosen, A. (eds.) TCC 2019, Part II. LNCS, vol. 11892, pp. 118–148. Springer, Cham (2019). https://doi.org/10.1007/978-3-030-36033-7_5

[KM20] Kitagawa, F., Matsuda, T.: Circular security is complete for KDM security. In: Moriai, S., Wang, H. (eds.) ASIACRYPT 2020, Part I. LNCS, vol. 12491, pp. 253–285. Springer, Cham (2020). https://doi.org/10.1007/978-3-030-64837-4_9

[KMT19a] Kitagawa, F., Matsuda, T., Tanaka, K.: CCA security and trapdoor functions via key-dependent-message security. In: Boldyreva, A., Micciancio, D. (eds.) CRYPTO 2019, Part III. LNCS, vol. 11694, pp. 33–64. Springer, Cham (2019). https://doi.org/10.1007/978-3-030-26954-8_2

[KMT19b] Kitagawa, F., Matsuda, T., Tanaka, K.: Simple and efficient KDM-CCA secure public key encryption. In: Galbraith, S.D., Moriai, S. (eds.) ASIACRYPT 2019, Part III. LNCS, vol. 11923, pp. 97–127. Springer, Cham (2019). https://doi.org/10.1007/978-3-030-34618-8_4

[KW19] Koppula, V., Waters, B.: Realizing chosen ciphertext security generically in attribute-based encryption and predicate encryption. In: Boldyreva, A., Micciancio, D. (eds.) CRYPTO 2019, Part II. LNCS, vol. 11693, pp. 671–700. Springer, Cham (2019). https://doi.org/10.1007/978-3-030-26951-7_23

[KW21] Khurana, D., Waters, B.: On the CCA compatibility of public-key infrastructure. In: Garay, J.A. (ed.) PKC 2021. LNCS, vol. 12711, pp. 235–260. Springer, Cham (2021). https://doi.org/10.1007/978-3-030-75248-4_9

[PW08] Peikert, C., Waters, B.: Lossy trapdoor functions and their applications. In: Ladner, R.E., Dwork, C. (eds.) 40th ACM STOC, pp. 187–196. ACM Press, May 2008

[Reg09] Regev, O.: On lattices, learning with errors, random linear codes, and cryptography. J. ACM 56(6), 1–40 (2009). Preliminary version in STOC 2005

SwiftEC: Shallue-van de Woestijne Indifferentiable Function to Elliptic Curves
Faster Indifferentiable Hashing to Elliptic Curves

Jorge Chavez-Saab[1,2], Francisco Rodríguez-Henríquez[1,2], and Mehdi Tibouchi[3(✉)]

[1] Computer Science Department, Cinvestav IPN, Mexico City, Mexico
[2] Cryptography Research Centre, Technology Innovation Institute, Abu Dhabi, United Arab Emirates
jorgechavezsaab@gmail.com
[3] NTT Social Informatics Laboratories, Tokyo, Japan
mehdi.tibouchi.br@hco.ntt.co.jp

Abstract. Hashing arbitrary values to points on an elliptic curve is a required step in many cryptographic constructions, and a number of techniques have been proposed to do so over the years. One of the first ones was due to Shallue and van de Woestijne (ANTS-VII), and it had the interesting property of applying to essentially all elliptic curves over finite fields. It did not, however, have the desirable property of being *indifferentiable from a random oracle* when composed with a random oracle to the base field.

Various approaches have since been considered to overcome this limitation, starting with the foundational work of Brier et al. (CRYPTO 2011). For example, if $f\colon \mathbb{F}_q \to E(\mathbb{F}_q)$ is the Shallue–van de Woestijne (SW) map and $\mathfrak{h}_1, \mathfrak{h}_2$ are *two* independent random oracles to $\mathbb{F}_q$, we now know that $m \mapsto f(\mathfrak{h}_1(m)) + f(\mathfrak{h}_2(m))$ is indifferentiable from a random oracle. Unfortunately, this approach has the drawback of being twice as expensive to compute than the straightforward, but not indifferentiable, $m \mapsto f(\mathfrak{h}_1(m))$. Most other solutions so far have had the same issue: they are at least as costly as two base field exponentiations, whereas plain encoding maps like f cost only one exponentiation. Recently, Koshelev (DCC 2022) provided the first construction of indifferentiable hashing at the cost of one exponentiation, but only for a very specific class of curves (some of those with j-invariant 0), and using techniques that are unlikely to apply more broadly.

In this work, we revisit this long-standing open problem, and observe that the SW map actually fits in a one-parameter family $(f_u)_{u \in \mathbb{F}_q}$ of encodings, such that for independent random oracles $\mathfrak{h}_1, \mathfrak{h}_2$ to $\mathbb{F}_q$, $F\colon m \mapsto f_{\mathfrak{h}_2(m)}(\mathfrak{h}_1(m))$ is indifferentiable. Moreover, on a very large class of curves (essentially those that are either of odd order or of order divisible by 4), the one-parameter family admits a rational parametrization, which lets us compute F at almost the same cost as small f, and finally achieve indifferentiable hashing to most curves with a single exponentiation. Our new approach also yields an improved variant of the Elligator Squared technique of Tibouchi (FC 2014) that represents points of arbitrary elliptic curves as close-to-uniform random strings.

© International Association for Cryptologic Research 2022
S. Agrawal and D. Lin (Eds.): ASIACRYPT 2022, LNCS 13791, pp. 63–92, 2022.
https://doi.org/10.1007/978-3-031-22963-3_3

Keywords: Elliptic curve cryptography · Hashing to curves ·
Indifferentiability · Elligator · Algebraic geometry

1   Introduction

Indifferentiable Hashing to Elliptic Curves. Numerous cryptographic
primitives and protocols constructed over elliptic curve groups involve *hashing*
to an elliptic curve: they assume the existence of a public function $\mathfrak{H}$ mapping
arbitrary bit strings to elliptic curve points/group elements. Moreover, the function $\mathfrak{H}$ is supposed to behave "like a random oracle". Such a functionality is
required for example for many password-authenticated key exchange protocols,
identity-based encryption schemes, short signature schemes, verifiable random
functions, oblivious PRFs and more. It is therefore important to understand how
it can be efficiently instantiated in practice, and moreover with constant-time
implementations, since the data that is hashed to the curve is often sensitive
and can thus be compromised by timing side-channel attacks. This problem is in
fact currently the subject of an IETF standardization effort within the Crypto
Forum Research Group [FHSS+22].

It became an active research topic about a decade ago, particularly after the
work of Brier et al. [BCI+10], which applied Maurer et al.'s *indifferentiability*
framework [MRH04] to properly formalize what it meant for $\mathfrak{H}$ to "behave like a
random oracle", and proposed several constructions satisfying the required properties. The design paradigm that emerged at the time as the main approach to
hashing to elliptic curve groups combines so-called *encoding functions* to the elliptic curve, which are algebraic (or piecewise algebraic) maps from the base field to
the group of points on the curve, with random oracles to the base field and other
sets that are "easy to hash to", as well as simple arithmetic operations on the curve.

More precisely, consider for instance[1] the problem of hashing to the subgroup
$\mathbb{G}$ of cofactor h in $E(\mathbb{F}_q)$, where E is an elliptic curve defined over the finite field
$\mathbb{F}_q$ and such that $E(\mathbb{F}_q)$ is cyclic of order n with generator P. Then Brier et al.
[BCI+10] showed that the following construction:

$$\mathfrak{H}_{\text{slow}}(m) = [h] \cdot \Big(f\big(\mathfrak{h}_1(m)\big) + [\mathfrak{h}_2(m)]P \Big) \tag{1}$$

is *indifferentiable from a random oracle* when $\mathfrak{h}_1$ and $\mathfrak{h}_2$ are modeled as independent random oracles to $\mathbb{F}_q$ and $\mathbb{Z}/n\mathbb{Z}$ respectively (which are easy to realize,
heuristically, using bitstring-valued hash functions) and $f\colon \mathbb{F}_q \to E(\mathbb{F}_q)$ is a
mapping (the encoding function) satisfying mild conditions. This means that
whenever[2] a cryptographic scheme or protocol is proved secure in the random
oracle model with respect to a $\mathbb{G}$-valued random oracle $\mathfrak{H}$, that random oracle
can be instantiated securely with the construction $\mathfrak{H}_{\text{slow}}$.

---

[1] The general case of a non-cyclic $E(\mathbb{F}_q)$ can be treated similarly. We refer to Brier et al. [BCI+10] for details.

[2] Technically, this holds in the case of *single-stage* security games, as clarified by Ristenpart et al. [RSS11]. This limitation is rarely of concern in our context.

As we have mentioned, the construction above requires a suitable *encoding function* $f: \mathbb{F}_q \rightarrow E(\mathbb{F}_q)$. A number of candidates were known at the time for various classes of elliptic curves, such as those of Shallue and van de Woestijne [SvdW06], Ulas [Ula07] or Icart [Ica09], and many more have been proposed since [KLR10,FT10,Far11,FT12,FJT13,BHKL13,WB19]. All of them can be computed in constant time at the cost of one full size exponentiation in $\mathbb{F}_q$ (typically a square root or cube root computation), which dominates the complexity, plus a few other less costly operations in the field, like multiplications, inversions and Jacobi symbol computations.

In contrast, the second term of $\mathfrak{H}_{\text{slow}}$ is a full-size *scalar multiplication* over the curve, which typically exceeds the computationally cost of a field exponentiation by a factor of 10 or more depending on base field size and curve arithmetic. This makes $\mathfrak{H}_{\text{slow}}$ a fairly inefficient construction.

To alleviate this issue, Brier et al. also proved that the following construction is also indifferentiable from a random oracle:

$$\mathfrak{H}_{\text{square}}(m) = [h] \cdot \left(f\big(\mathfrak{h}_1(m)\big) + f\big(\mathfrak{h}_2(m)\big) \right) \tag{2}$$

when $\mathfrak{h}_1$ and $\mathfrak{h}_2$ are modeled as independent random oracles to $\mathbb{F}_q$, and when f is specifically Icart's function. The result was later extended by Farashahi et al. [FFS+13], who showed that basically all of the known encoding functions f could also be plugged into that construction. This provides indifferentiable hashing to arbitrary elliptic curves at the cost of essentially *two* base fields exponentiations.

On the other hand, in certain primitives and protocols proved secure with respect to a $\mathbb{G}$-valued random oracle $\mathfrak{H}$, one can show that $\mathfrak{H}$ can be securely instantiated using the following simpler construction:

$$\mathfrak{H}_{\text{non-unif}}(m) = [h] \cdot f\big(\mathfrak{h}(m)\big) \tag{3}$$

where $\mathfrak{h}$ is modeled as a random oracle to $\mathbb{F}_q$. This construction is not nearly as well-behaved as (2). In fact, f usually only reaches a fraction of the points on $E(\mathbb{F}_q)$, and induces a non-uniform distribution over its image, so that $\mathfrak{H}_{\text{non-unif}}$ can typically be efficiently distinguished from a random oracle, and in particular it is *not* indifferentiable in the sense discussed so far. Nevertheless, certain primitives and protocols do not require the full strength of indifferentiability, and $\mathfrak{H}_{\text{non-unif}}$ is sometimes sufficient to let their security proofs go through.

A rough idea of why this happens is that, in a random oracle proof of security, the simulator generally wants to program the random oracle by setting the hash of some message m to a value Q, but that point Q itself can usually be anything depending on some randomness. So assuming that $h = 1$, the simulator might typically want to set $\mathfrak{H}(m)$ to $Q = [r] \cdot P$ for some random r, say. Now if $\mathfrak{H}$ is defined in the protocol using a construction like (3), the simulator would pick a random r and set $\mathfrak{h}(m)$ to one of the preimages $u \in f^{-1}(P)$ if $P \in f(\mathbb{F}_q)$. If however P is not in the image of f, the simulator would pick another random r and try again.

Therefore, construction (3), while less general and well-behaved than (2), is sometimes good enough for security at half the computational cost. This is a substantial difference in terms of efficiency that practitioners may be sensitive to, so much so that *both* of these constructions are in fact proposed in the current IETF draft [FHSS+22]. Construction (3), however, comes with the caveats that applications using it "SHOULD carefully analyze the security implications of nonuniformity", and that "cryptographic protocols whose security analysis relies on a random oracle that outputs points with a uniform distribution MUST NOT" use it. This results in the somewhat unfortunate situation that implementers have to choose between two approaches for implementing hashing to elliptic curves: one which is secure in all cases but slower, and one which is faster but requires a careful analysis to ascertain that it does not fully compromise the security of the scheme.

The Quest for Fast Indifferentiable Hashing. Ideally, one would prefer to have the best of both worlds: indifferentiable hashing at the cost of a single exponentiation in the base field instead of two. Obtaining this for general elliptic curves is a long-standing open problem.

In special cases, solutions exist: this is particularly the case for supersingular curves of j-invariant 0 and 1728, for which it has long been known [BF01,FT10] that an "almost bijective" encoding function f exists; it is then easy to check that plugging that f into construction (3) does achieve indifferentiability. Unfortunately, those types of supersingular curves, which were popular to reach the 80-bit security level in pairing applications in the early 2000s, are no longer used today due to exceedingly large parameters at higher security levels. Moreover, there are strong reasons to believe that almost bijective encodings cannot exist for general elliptic curves [Tib14b].

Progress towards addressing the general open problem was made by Tibouchi and Kim [TK17], who extended the statistical results of Farashahi et al., and established in particular that, asymptotically, it was possible to achieve indifferentiable hashing at a cost of less than two exponentiations by tweaking construction (1) with a random oracle $\mathfrak{h}_2$ mapping to a short interval. That result is mostly of theoretical significance, however, since it requires very large base fields to provide meaningful error bounds.

Recently, Koshelev [Kos22] made a practically significant advance, by showing that indifferentiable hashing at the cost of a single exponentiation was possible for certain *ordinary* curves of j-invariant 0 over suitable base fields. This is still a negligible fraction of all elliptic curves, but it is practically relevant since it includes pairing-friendly curves like some of the BLS curves [BLS03] used today. Koshelev's approach is also the first one considered in the last decade or so that substantially departs from the framework of constructions (1)–(3) above. While those earlier techniques reduce the problem of indifferentiable hashing to the encoding function $f: \mathbb{F}_q \to E(\mathbb{F}_q)$, which is defined over a one-dimensional domain, Koshelev bases his construction on a map $F: \mathbb{F}_q^2 \to E(\mathbb{F}_q)$ with a two-dimensional range. Looking back at Brier et al.'s original proof for the indifferentiability of construction (2) using Icart's encoding function, this is fairly natural (since that proof was constructed around a two-dimensional argument), but it is an important shift in perspective.

In this paper, we use a similar idea (albeit very different techniques) to settle the open problem for a large class of elliptic curves: for essentially all curves over fields $\mathbb{F}_q$ with $q \equiv 1 \pmod 3$ with either odd order or order divisible by 4 (this includes almost all elliptic curves in current use), we are able to construct a new indifferentiable hashing, which we call SwiftEC, at the cost of a single exponentiation in the base field.

Representing Points as Uniform Random Strings. A very different question, but which has been tackled using similar techniques, was introduced in Bernstein et al.'s *Elligator* paper [BHKL13]: how can one represent a uniform point on $E(\mathbb{F}_q)$ in a public way as a close to uniform random bit string? The stated goal was to achieve a form of steganography for censorship circumvention. Indeed, network traffic containing points on a certain elliptic curve (e.g. public keys for encryption or signature) represented in usual ways (either as full coordinates (x, y), in compressed form $(x, \operatorname{sgn} y)$ or in x-only form) can be easily distinguished from random, which may lead to automated traffic interruption or targeted surveillance.

As a countermeasure, Bernstein et al. suggested to use an encoding function $f: \mathbb{F}_q \to E(\mathbb{F}_q)$ with the property that it maps an interval $I \subset \mathbb{F}_q$ of length $\approx q/2$ *injectively* into $E(\mathbb{F}_q)$. Then, any point in $f(I)$ can be represented by its unique preimage under f in I. In particular, if q is close to a power of two, this readily gives a simple representation of random elements in $f(I) \subset E(\mathbb{F}_q)$ as uniform random bit strings (and when q is far from a power of two, it suffices to represent elements of I as uniform random bit strings, which can be easily done by expanding the representation and introducing randomness).

This approach has two drawbacks. First, suitable encodings f that are injective over a large interval are hard to construct, and only known for limited families of elliptic curves [Far11, FJT13, BHKL13], all of order divisible by 3 or 4 (and hence not including curves of prime order, for example). Second, one needs to address the issue of points falling outside $f(I)$. Since the goal is to represent *random* points on $E(\mathbb{F}_q)$ as bit strings, the assumption is that in the cryptographic protocol under consideration, the point to represent is obtained by some sort of random process, and it is possible to use rejection sampling until reaching $f(I)$. Since the image size covers roughly half of all points on the curve, this will require about two iterations on average, often an acceptable cost. However, if the process generating the point is expensive, rejecting may be less than ideal.

Tibouchi's Elligator Squared paper [Tib14a] addressed these shortcomings by, in essence, applied construction (2) above "in reverse". One of the key properties that makes construction (2) an indifferentiable hash function is the fact that, for an encoding function $f: \mathbb{F}_q \to E(\mathbb{F}_q)$, the following map:

$$\begin{aligned} f^{\otimes 2}: \mathbb{F}_q^2 &\to E(\mathbb{F}_q) \\ (u, v) &\mapsto f(u) + f(v) \end{aligned} \tag{4}$$

induces a close-to-uniform distribution on its image. In particular, a uniformly random preimage of a uniformly random point in $E(\mathbb{F}_q)$ is close to uniform in $\mathbb{F}_q^2$.

This provides a simple solution to the point representation problem that works for general elliptic curves and can represent all points, avoiding the need for rejection sampling inside the protocol to reach a particular subset of the curve. However, representation size is about twice as large as Elligator (a drawback partially addressed in subsequent work [TK17]) and the representation function, computing uniformly random preimages under $f^{\otimes 2}$, is also somewhat more complicated and costly than that of Elligator.

Basically, to compute a random preimage of $P \in E(\mathbb{F}_q)$, one picks a uniform $v \in \mathbb{F}_q$ and computes u as a preimage of $P - f(v)$. However, rejection sampling is necessary to ensure the uniformity of the distribution, which requires multiple iterations, each of them evaluating the function f (at a cost of a field exponentiation each).

In this paper, as a by-product of our new SWIFTEC construction, we also obtain ELLIGATORSWIFT, a much faster variant of Elligator Squared over all the curves over which SWIFTEC is defined. The idea is that fully computing the underlying encoding in the forward direction becomes unnecessary, saving many field exponentiations in the process.

Contributions and Technical Overview. The starting point of our work is to revisit the first construction of an encoding function to general elliptic curves, originally due to Shallue and van de Woestijne [SvdW06]. We observe that construction actually had a number of interesting properties that have not been considered so far, and that we manage to build upon with suitable additional analysis. To describe them, we need to first recall a few facts about the Shallue–van de Woestijne encoding itself.

Given an elliptic curve $E \colon y^2 = g(x) = x^3 + ax + b$ over a finite field $\mathbb{F}_q$ of characteristic ≥ 5, Shallue and van de Woestijne construct a certain algebraic surface S in the affine space over $\mathbb{F}_q$ together with three rational functions x_1, x_2, x_3 such that the product $g(x_1)g(x_2)g(x_3)$ is a square. This means in particular that, when evaluated at any point P of $S(\mathbb{F}_q)$ (outside of the locus of poles), at least one of $x_1(P)$, $x_2(P)$ or $x_3(P)$ must be the x-coordinate of a point in $E(\mathbb{F}_q)$. Indeed, the product $g\big(x_1(P)\big)g\big(x_2(P)\big)g\big(x_3(P)\big)$ is a square in $\mathbb{F}_q$, and since the product of three nonsquares in $\mathbb{F}_q$ is a nonsquare, at least one of the factors must be square, yielding the x-coordinate of a point in $E(\mathbb{F}_q)$. Based on that, we can define an encoding function from $S(\mathbb{F}_q)$ to $E(\mathbb{F}_q)$ simply by mapping a point P to one of the points of x-coordinate $x_i(P)$ that works (selecting the index i and the sign of the y-coordinate in a predetermined way).

The second step of the construction is to note that the specific surface S under consideration can in fact be seen as a one-parameter family of conics over $\mathbb{F}_q$. Based on that, Shallue and van de Woestijne fix the value of the parameter, obtain a single non-degenerate conic over $\mathbb{F}_q$, and use the fact that such a conic always admits a rational parametrization to obtain a map $\mathbb{F}_q \to S(\mathbb{F}_q)$ to the chosen conic. Composing with the previous map finally gives an encoding $\mathbb{F}_q \to E(\mathbb{F}_q)$ as desired, which can be used in constructions (1)–(3) above for hashing, and in the Elligator Squared framework: this is what is usually known as the Shallue–van de Woestijne encoding.

Our contributions rely on two novel observations regarding that original construction:

- first, for a large class of elliptic curves E which we characterize in detail, the surface S regarded as a family of conics actually admits a global, two-parameter parametrization over $\mathbb{F}_q$. This means that one can effectively construct a rational map $\mathbb{F}_q^2 \to S(\mathbb{F}_q)$ that is essentially a bijection. This result is obtained using techniques due to van Hoeij and Cremona [vHC06] classifying conics over function fields;
- second, unlike each of the maps defined by individual conics, the map from $S(\mathbb{F}_q)$ as a whole to the set $X_{E,\mathbb{F}_q}$ of elements of $\mathbb{F}_q$ which are x-coordinates on $E(\mathbb{F}_q)$ is *admissible*: it satisfies the sufficient conditions of Brier et al. [BCI+10] to construct indifferentiable hashing. The most important of those conditions is regularity: the image of a uniform point in $S(\mathbb{F}_q)$ is close to uniform in $X_{E,\mathbb{F}_q}$. We are able to establish that property by giving a precise description of the preimage of an $x \in X_{E,\mathbb{F}_q}$: it consists of the union of one algebraic curve drawn on S (the set of points P such that $x_1(P) = x$, say) and two halves of two other curves (the subset of the curves given by $x_2(P) = x$ and $x_3(P) = x$ respectively, with the condition that $g(x_1(P))$ is a nonsquare). By counting points on those curves and curve subsets, we are able to establish the required statistical properties, and deduce that $S(\mathbb{F}_q) \to X_{E,\mathbb{F}_q}$ is admissible.

Combining those two observations, we obtain, for a large, explicit class of elliptic curves E (including almost all curves in practical use), an admissible encoding $\mathbb{F}_q^2 \to X_{E,\mathbb{F}_q}$. Adding a sign bit to choose the y-coordinate on E yields an admissible encoding $F \colon \mathbb{F}_q^2 \times \{0,1\} \to E(\mathbb{F}_q)$ as well, which can be computed at the cost of a single exponentiation in $\mathbb{F}_q$ (namely, the square root computation needed to derive the y-coordinate). This has the two consequences mentioned above, over the elliptic curves E of interest:

- given a hash function $\mathfrak{h}$ modeled as a random oracle with values in $\mathbb{F}_q^2 \times \{0,1\}$ (which is easy to heuristically instantiate), the map $m \mapsto F\big(\mathfrak{h}(m)\big)$ is indifferentiable from a random oracle, and can be computed at the cost of a single exponentiation. This is the SwiftEC construction;
- given a uniform point on the curve, we can efficiently sample a uniform preimage of it under F, and this becomes a close-to-uniformly distributed element of $\mathbb{F}_q^2 \times \{0,1\}$. Since such an element is easy to represent as a uniform bit string, we thus obtain an Elligator Square-like representation technique which is much faster than Elligator Square itself, as it requires far fewer field exponentiations on average. This is the ElligatorSwift construction.

In addition, we also get indifferentiable hashing to the set $X_{E,\mathbb{F}_q}$ without any field exponentiation at all. This even faster construction, XSwiftEC, is particularly interesting in context where x-only arithmetic is feasible, such as for example BLS signatures [BLS01].

2 Preliminaries

2.1 Quadratic Residuosity

Throughout this paper, $\mathbb{F}_q$ denotes the finite field with q elements. We only consider finite fields of characteristic $\neq 2, 3$. The *quadratic character* $\chi_2 \colon \mathbb{F}_q \to \{-1, 0, 1\}$ is the map that sends 0 to 0, nonzero squares to 1 and nonzero nonsquares to -1. It is well-defined, multiplicative, and extends the unique nontrivial multicative group morphism $\mathbb{F}_q^\times \to \{-1, 1\}$. A related map is IsSquare, which sends all squares to 1 and nonsquares to 0.

When q is prime, the quadratic character coincides with the Legendre symbol, and can be computed efficiently by repeated applications of quadratic reciprocity. This can be implemented in fast constant time [Por20, Ham21, AG21], similar to the constant-time binary GCD technique of Bernstein–Yang for field inversion [BY19]. Similarly, the quadratic character over extension fields can be computed fast by descending to the prime field, and IsSquare can be trivially computed from χ_2.

We also fix an efficiently computable map sgn: $\mathbb{F}_q \to \{-1, 0, 1\}$ called the "sign", with the property that $\mathrm{sgn}\, 0 = 0$, $\mathrm{sgn}\, x \neq 0$ for $x \neq 0$, and $\mathrm{sgn}(-x) = -\,\mathrm{sgn}\, x$. The choice is arbitrary, but for example over prime fields, it is customary to use the sign of an integer representative in the interval $(-q/2, q/2)$ (over extension fields, one might choose the sign of the first nonzero coefficient in some basis over the prime field).

An element $x \in \mathbb{F}_q$ which is a square has exactly two square roots (except 0 which has just one), exactly one of which is of nonnegative sign. We denote it by $\sqrt{x}$; it typically requires a single base field exponentiation to compute (although slightly faster approaches may exist over extension fields).

2.2 Elliptic Curves and Isogenies

An *elliptic curve* is a smooth projective curve of genus 1 endowed with a distinguished rational point. Such curves admit the definition of a point addition law, which gives the curve a structure as group variety, with the distinguished point playing the role of the group identity. Over $\mathbb{F}_q$, any elliptic curve can be written up to isomorphism in the *short Weierstrass form*:

$$E \colon y^2 = x^3 + ax + b,$$

for some $a, b \in \mathbb{F}_q$ such that the discriminant $\Delta_E := -16(4a^3 + 27b^2)$ is nonzero. On such a curve, group inverses are defined by $-(x, y) = (x, -y)$ and the points of order 2 are those with $y = 0$. When Δ_E is a square there are either zero or three points of order 2. Otherwise, there is exactly one.

We denote by $E(\mathbb{F}_q)$ the group of $\mathbb{F}_q$-rational points of E. The cardinality of this group is always $\#E(\mathbb{F}_q) = q - t + 1$ for some t bounded by $|t| \leq 2\sqrt{q}$. We say that the curve is *supersingular* if t is a multiple of the field characteristic, and otherwise the curve is *ordinary*. We focus on the case of ordinary elliptic curves, where finding adequate and efficient encodings has long been a greater challenge.

An *isogeny* is any non-constant rational map between elliptic curves that is also a group homomorphism. Up to an isomorphism, a separable isogeny is uniquely determined by its kernel and its degree as a rational map is equal to the size of the kernel. Any isogeny $\phi\colon E \to E'$ has a dual isogeny $\hat{\phi}\colon E' \to E$ such that the composition $\hat{\phi}\circ\phi$ equals the multiplication-by-d map, where $d = \deg(\phi)$. Two curves over a finite field are isogenous if and only if they have exactly the same number of points.

2.3   Point Counting and Character Sums

A generalization of the result above on the number of rational points of an elliptic curve is that any (absolutely irreducible) smooth curve of bounded genus over $\mathbb{F}_q$ has a number of points over $\mathbb{F}_q$ close to q. More precisely, the following celebrated result holds:

Lemma 1 (Hasse–Weil bound). *For any smooth projective absolutely irreducible curve $X/\mathbb{F}_q$ of genus g, we have:*

$$\left| \#X(\mathbb{F}_q) - (q+1) \right| \leq 2g\sqrt{q}.$$

For curves of bounded degree, the number of points at infinity is also bounded, and we thus get a bound of the form $\#X^{\mathrm{aff}}(\mathbb{F}_q) = q + c\sqrt{q} + O(1)$ ($|c| \leq 2g$) on the number of affine points on X.

A related result concerns character sums on such curves. Let χ be a multiplicative character of $\mathbb{F}_q$ (a group homomorphism $\mathbb{F}_q^\times \to \mathbb{C}^\times$ extended by 0 at 0), and $f \in \mathbb{F}_q(X)$ a rational function on the curve X. We consider the following character sum:

$$W(X,\chi,f) = \sum_{\substack{P \in X(\mathbb{F}_q) \\ f(P) \neq \infty}} \chi\bigl(f(P)\bigr).$$

Using the Bombieri–Weil methodology, Perret [Per91] proves the following bound. See also [CM00, TK17].

Lemma 2 (Perret). *Let X be a smooth projective absolutely irreducible curve of genus g over $\mathbb{F}_q$, χ a nontrivial multiplicative character of order $m | q-1$, and $f \in \mathbb{F}_q(X)$ a rational function which is not a perfect m-th power in $\bar{\mathbb{F}}_q(X)$. The character sum $W(X,\chi,f)$ can be bounded as:*

$$\left| W(X,\chi,f) \right| \leq (2g - 2 + 2\deg f)\sqrt{q}.$$

2.4   Quadratic Residuosity over Function Fields

Many results of classical arithmetic over $\mathbb{Q}$ and number fields have analogues over function fields. This is in particular the case for quadratic reciprocity. We recall some of the relevant results below. An exhaustive treatment is provided in Rosen's textbook [Ros02, pp. 23-31].

For a fixed monic irreducible polynomial $f \in \mathbb{F}_q[t]$, we define the quadratic residue symbol $\left(\frac{g}{f}\right)_2$ for any $g \in \mathbb{F}_q[t]$ as the image of g under the quadratic character of the finite field $\mathbb{F}_q[t]/(f)$. In other words:

$$\left(\frac{g}{f}\right)_2 = \begin{cases} 0 & \text{if } f \text{ divides } g; \\ 1 & \text{if } g \text{ is coprime to } f \text{ and a square modulo } f; \\ -1 & \text{if } g \text{ is coprime to } f \text{ and a nonsquare modulo } f. \end{cases}$$

We then extend this symbol to not necessarily irreducible f's by multiplicativity, similarly to how the Jacobi symbol extends the Legendre symbol. If $f = \alpha f_1^{e_1} \cdots f_n^{e_n}$ with $\alpha \in \mathbb{F}_q^{\times}$ and the f_i irreducible, we let:

$$\left(\frac{g}{f}\right)_2 = \prod_{i=1}^{n} \left(\frac{g}{f_i}\right)_2.$$

Note that the symbol does not depend on the leading coefficient $\mathrm{lc}(f) = \alpha$ of f.

Lemma 3. *The quadratic residue symbol has the following properties.*

- *If $g_1 \equiv g_2 \pmod{f}$, $\left(\frac{g_1}{f}\right)_2 = \left(\frac{g_2}{f}\right)_2$.*
- *$\left(\frac{g_1 g_1}{f}\right)_2 = \left(\frac{g_1}{f}\right)_2 \left(\frac{g_2}{f}\right)_2$.*
- *$\left(\frac{g}{f_1 f_2}\right)_2 = \left(\frac{g}{f_1}\right)_2 \left(\frac{g}{f_2}\right)_2$.*
- *$\left(\frac{g}{f}\right)_2 \neq 0$ if and only if f and g are coprime.*
- *If g is a nonzero square modulo f, then $\left(\frac{g}{f}\right)_2 = 1$ (but the converse does not need to hold).*

Furthermore, it satisfies the following law of quadratic reciprocity. For $f, g \in \mathbb{F}_q[t]$ coprime and nonzero, it holds that:

$$\left(\frac{g}{f}\right)_2 \left(\frac{f}{g}\right)_2 = (-1)^{\frac{q-1}{2} \deg f \deg g} \mathrm{lc}(f)^{\frac{q-1}{2} \deg g} \mathrm{lc}(g)^{\frac{q-1}{2} \deg f}.$$

2.5   Statistical Notions

For $\mathscr{D}$ a probability distribution on a finite set S, we write $\Pr[s \leftarrow \mathscr{D}]$ for the probability assigned to the singleton $\{s\} \subset S$ by $\mathscr{D}$. The uniform distribution on S is denoted by $\mathscr{U}_S$ (or just $\mathscr{U}$ if the context is clear).

Definition 1 (Statistical distance). *Let $\mathscr{D}$ and $\mathscr{D}'$ be two probability distributions on a finite set S. The statistical distance between them is defined as the ℓ_1 norm:*

$$\Delta_1(\mathscr{D}, \mathscr{D}') = \frac{1}{2} \sum_{s \in S} \left| \Pr[s \leftarrow \mathscr{D}] - \Pr[s \leftarrow \mathscr{D}'] \right|.$$

We simply denote by $\Delta_1(\mathscr{D})$ the statistical distance between $\mathscr{D}$ and $\mathscr{U}_S$:

$$\Delta_1(\mathscr{D}) = \frac{1}{2} \sum_{s \in S} \left| \Pr[s \leftarrow \mathscr{D}] - \frac{1}{\#S} \right|,$$

and say that $\mathscr{D}$ is ε-statistically close to uniform when $\Delta_1(\mathscr{D}) \leq \varepsilon$. When $\Delta_1(\mathscr{D})$ is negligible, we simply say than $\mathscr{D}$ is statistically close to uniform.

Definition 2 (Pushforward). *Let S, T be two finite sets and F any mapping from S to T. For any probability distribution $\mathscr{D}_S$ on S, we can define the pushforward $F_*\mathscr{D}_S$ of $\mathscr{D}_S$ by F as the probability distribution on T such that sampling from $F_*\mathscr{D}_S$ is equivalent to sampling a value $s \leftarrow \mathscr{D}_S$ and returning $F(s)$. In other words:*

$$\Pr\left[t \leftarrow F_*\mathscr{D}_S\right] = \Pr\left[s \leftarrow \mathscr{D}_S; \ t = F(s)\right] = \mu_S\left(F^{-1}(t)\right) = \sum_{s \in F^{-1}(t)} \Pr[s \leftarrow \mathscr{D}_S],$$

where μ_S is the probability measure defined by $\mathscr{D}_S$.

Definition 3 (Regularity). *Let S, T be two finite sets and F any mapping from S to T. We say that F is ε-regular when $F_*\mathscr{U}_S$ is ε-close to the uniform distribution. We may omit ε if it is negligible.*

2.6 Admissible Encodings

In their work on the construction of indifferentiable hashing to elliptic curves, Brier et al. [BCI+10] define the notion of an *admissible* map $F: S \to R$ between two sets. The definition, which generalizes an early notion introduced by Boneh and Franklin [BF01], is as follows.

Definition 4 (Admissible encoding). *A function $F: S \to R$ between finite sets is an ε-admissible encoding if it satisfies the following properties:*

Computable: *F is computable in deterministic polynomial time.*
Regular: *F is ε-regular (in the sense of the previous section).*
Samplable: *there is an efficient randomized algorithm $\mathscr{I}: R \to S \sqcup \{\bot\}$ such that for any $r \in R$, $\mathscr{I}(r)$ induces a distribution that is ε-statistically close to the uniform distribution in $F^{-1}(r)$.*

F is an admissible encoding if it is ε-admissible for some negligible ε.

That notion satisfies the suitable properties such that, given an S-valued random oracle $\mathfrak{h}$, the composition $F \circ \mathfrak{h}$ is indifferentiable from a R-valued random oracle.

Moreover a similar results holds for arbitrary compositions of admissible functions (even though admissibility need not be preserved under composition). Namely, if $F_i: S_i \to S_{i-1}$ are admissible encodings for $i = 1, \ldots, n$, then it also holds that, given an S_n-valued random oracle $\mathfrak{h}$, the composition $F_1 \circ \cdots \circ F_n \circ \mathfrak{h}$ is indifferentiable from a S_0-valued random oracle (even though it does not always hold that $F_1 \circ \cdots \circ F_n$ is admissible).

3 The SW Encoding Family

In their seminal ANTS–VII paper [SvdW06], Shallue and van de Woestijne constructed the first encoding function to arbitrary elliptic curves. In this section, we give a description of that construction (restricted for simplicity to base fields of characteristic ≥ 5) that is slightly different but essentially equivalent to the original one, and then we state new properties of that construction.

In the entire section, we fix an elliptic curve $E\colon y^2 = x^3 + ax + b$ over the finite field $\mathbb{F}_q$ (q prime power not divisible by 2 or 3), and denote by $X_{E,\mathbb{F}_q}$ the subset of $\mathbb{F}_q$ consisting of x-coordinates of points in $E(\mathbb{F}_q)$; in other words:

$$X_{E,\mathbb{F}_q} = \left\{ x \in \mathbb{F}_q \ ; \ \exists y, \ (x,y) \in E(\mathbb{F}_q) \right\}.$$

3.1 Construction of the Shallue–van de Woestijne Encoding

Let g and h be the polynomials over $\mathbb{F}_q$ defined by:

$$g(u) = u^3 + au + b \quad \text{and} \quad h(u) = 3u^2 + 4a.$$

The starting point of the Shallue–van de Woestijne construction is the construction of a rational map $\psi\colon S \to V$ from the following quasi-affine surface in the (x,y,u) affine space:

$$S\colon x^2 + h(u)y^2 = -g(u), \quad y \neq 0 \tag{5}$$

to the following threefold in the (x_1, x_2, x_3, z) affine 4-dimensional space:

$$V\colon z^2 = g(x_1)g(x_2)g(x_3).$$

The rational map ψ is given by the following explicit equations and clearly defined everywhere on S:

$$x_1 = \frac{x}{2y} - \frac{u}{2} \qquad x_2 = -\frac{x}{2y} - \frac{u}{2}$$

$$x_3 = u + 4y^2 \qquad z = \frac{g(u + y^2)}{y} \cdot R\left(u, \frac{x}{2y} - \frac{u}{2}\right) \tag{6}$$

where $R(u,v) = u^2 + uv + v^2 + a$. When referring to a point P on S, we will denote by $x_1(P)$, $x_2(P)$, $x_3(P)$ and $z(P)$ the corresponding coordinates of $\psi(P)$ in V. In particular, this defines x_1, x_2, x_3 and z as rational functions on the surface.

A remarkable property of the threefold V is that for any point $(x_1, x_2, x_3, z) \in V(\mathbb{F}_q)$, at least one of the three values x_1, x_2, x_3 must be in $X_{E,\mathbb{F}_q}$. Indeed, $g(x_1)g(x_2)g(x_3)$ is a square in $\mathbb{F}_q$, so by multiplicativity of the quadratic character, they cannot be all nonsquares (and in fact, there must be exactly one or three squares among them, except possibly when $z = 0$).

As a result, one can therefore map points on $S(\mathbb{F}_q)$ to $X_{E,\mathbb{F}_q}$ by first mapping to $V(\mathbb{F}_q)$ with ψ, and then selecting one of the coordinates x_1, x_2, x_3 in a prescribed order. For example, in this paper we will consider the following map:

$$F_0 \colon S(\mathbb{F}_q) \to X_{E,\mathbb{F}_q}$$

$$P \mapsto \begin{cases} x_3(P) & \text{if } g\big(x_3(P)\big) \text{ is a square;} \\ x_2(P) & \text{if } g\big(x_3(P)\big) \text{ is not a square but } g\big(x_2(P)\big) \text{ is;} \\ x_1(P) & \text{if neither } g\big(x_3(P)\big) \text{ nor } g\big(x_2(P)\big) \text{ are squares.} \end{cases} \tag{7}$$

Note that $F_0(P)$ is very efficient to compute from the coordinates (x, y, u) of P using the formulas of (6) and a few quadratic character computations. In particular, it requires no field exponentiation.

Of course, once we have an element $\bar{x} \in X_{E,\mathbb{F}_q}$, it is easy to deduce a point in $E(\mathbb{F}_q)$: simply compute a square root of $g(\bar{x})$ to get the y-coordinate up to sign. Since we prefer to select the sign separately, we define the following extended map to $E(\mathbb{F}_q)$ which takes an additional input bit b:

$$F_0^+ \colon S(\mathbb{F}_q) \times \{0, 1\} \to E(\mathbb{F}_q)$$

$$(P, b) \mapsto \left(F_0(P), \; (-1)^b \sqrt{g\big(F_0(P)\big)} \right). \tag{8}$$

The construction offers a way to map to $E(\mathbb{F}_q)$ provided that one can construct rational points on the surface S itself, which may not be a priori obvious. Fortunately, as seen from Eq. (5), each of the curves S_{u_0} on S obtained by fixing u to some $u_0 \in \mathbb{F}_q$ are simply conics over $\mathbb{F}_q$, with equations:

$$x^2 + h(u_0)y^2 = -g(u_0), \quad y \neq 0.$$

Now, a conic over $\mathbb{F}_q$ always admits a rational parametrization. Therefore, we can construct a map $\mathbb{F}_q \to S_{u_0}(\mathbb{F}_q)$ that can then be composed with F_0^+ to obtain an encoding function $F_{0,u_0} \colon \mathbb{F}_q \to X_{E,\mathbb{F}_q}$ (and similarly to $E(\mathbb{F}_q)$). This is basically the approach taken in the original paper of Shallue and van de Woestijne [SvdW06].

Note that obtaining the parametrization of the conic S_{u_0} for a fixed u_0 requires an a priori costly precomputation (it requires finding a point on the conic, typically by trial-and-error: this costs a square root, and a number of quadratic character computations that is hard to bound uniformly). Therefore, while it may be tempting to try and define a two-parameter map $\mathbb{F}_q^2 \to X_{E,\mathbb{F}_q}$ by $(t, u) \mapsto F_{0,u}(t)$, this is not usually workable for hashing purposes, since a new parametrization would have to be computed for any new input u.

Nevertheless, we show in the remainder of this section that the maps F_0 and F_0^+ on the surface $S(\mathbb{F}_q)$ as a whole have nice statistical properties, and it would therefore be beneficial to overcome the difficulty of efficiently parametrizing it. That problem will then be addressed, at least for a large class of elliptic curves E, in Sect. 4 below.

3.2   Geometry of the SW Family

For a fixed element $\bar{x} \in X_{E,\mathbb{F}_q}$, we now want to describe the set of points in $S(\mathbb{F}_q)$ that map to $\bar{x}$ under the encoding F_0 of (7). By the previous description of the encoding, this is the union of three disjoint sets:

$$F_0^{-1}(\bar{x}) = C_{\bar{x}}^{(3)}(\mathbb{F}_q) \sqcup C_{\bar{x}}^{(2)}(\mathbb{F}_q)^+ \sqcup C_{\bar{x}}^{(1)}(\mathbb{F}_q)^+,$$

where $C_{\bar{x}}^{(i)}$ are algebraic curves on S defined by the condition that $x_i = \bar{x}$ ($i \in \{1, 2, 3\}$) and $C_{\bar{x}}^{(i)}(\mathbb{F}_q)^+$ is the subset of $C_{\bar{x}}^{(i)}(\mathbb{F}_q)$ under the condition that $g(x_j(P))$ is not a square for $j \neq i$. Note that since there are always exactly only 1 or 3 squares, it suffices to define

$$C_{\bar{x}}^{(1)}(\mathbb{F}_q)^+ := \{P \in C_{\bar{x}}^{(1)}(\mathbb{F}_q); \ x_2(P) \text{ not a square}\}$$

$$C_{\bar{x}}^{(2)}(\mathbb{F}_q)^+ := \{P \in C_{\bar{x}}^{(2)}(\mathbb{F}_q); \ x_1(P) \text{ not a square}\}$$

We would like to count the number of points in each of these sets. The first step is to understand the geometry of the curves $C_{\bar{x}}^{(i)}$. It is easy to see that, for a generic $\bar{x}$, they are hyperelliptic curves of genus 2.

Consider for example $C_{\bar{x}}^{(3)}$. It is given by the equations (*cf.* (6)):

$$u + 4y^2 = \bar{x} \quad \text{and} \quad x^2 + h(u)y^2 = -g(u).$$

Eliminating $u = \bar{x} - 4y^2$ between those two equations, we see that $C_{\bar{x}}^{(3)}$ is isomorphic to the curve in the (y, x) affine plane given by the equation:

$$x^2 = -g(\bar{x} - 4y^2) - h(\bar{x} - 4y^2)y^2.$$

The right-hand side is a polynomial of degree 6 in y, namely:

$$16y^6 - 24\bar{x}y^4 + 9\bar{x}^2y^2 - g(\bar{x}),$$

whose discriminant is a polynomial of degree exactly 11 in $\bar{x}$ (or exactly 9 if $a = 0$). We thus get that $C_{\bar{x}}^{(3)}$ is a hyperelliptic curve of genus 2, except for at most 11 points $\bar{x}$. Other than for those exceptional points, we have:

$$\#C_{\bar{x}}^{(3)}(\mathbb{F}_q) = q + c_3\sqrt{q} + O(1), \quad \text{for some } c_3 \text{ such that } |c_3| \leq 4.$$

by the Hasse–Weil bound. Note that the $O(1)$ term comes from the fact that we consider the affine situation rather than the projective one, and we could easily provide an explicit bound for it, but this is typically not of interest for cryptographic applications.

By a similar analysis, we find that both $C_{\bar{x}}^{(1)}$ and $C_{\bar{x}}^{(2)}$ are isomorphic to the curve in the (u, v) affine plane (where $v = y[(u + 2\bar{x})^2 + h(u)]$) of equation:

$$v^2 = -g(u) \cdot [(u + 2\bar{x})^2 + h(u)].$$

The right-hand side is a polynomial of degree 5 in u, namely:

$$-4\big(u^5 + \bar{x}u^4 + (\bar{x}^2 + 2a)u^3 + (a\bar{x} + b)u^2 + (a\bar{x}^2 + b\bar{x} + a^2)u + b(\bar{x}^2 + a)\big),$$

and its discriminant is always of degree 14 in $\bar{x}$ (the degree 14 coefficient is $2^{16} \cdot 3 \cdot (4a^3 + 27b^2) \neq 0$). Thus, $C_{\bar{x}}^{(1)}$ and $C_{\bar{x}}^{(2)}$ are hyperelliptic curves of genus 2, except for at most 14 points $\bar{x}$. Other than for those exceptional points, we therefore have:

$$\#C_{\bar{x}}^{(1)}(\mathbb{F}_q) = q + c_1\sqrt{q} + O(1) \quad \text{for some } c_1 \text{ such that } |c_1| \leq 4$$

$$\#C_{\bar{x}}^{(2)}(\mathbb{F}_q) = q + c_2\sqrt{q} + O(1) \quad \text{for some } c_2 \text{ such that } |c_2| \leq 4$$

by the Hasse–Weil bound.

It remains to evaluate the cardinality of the subsets $C_{\bar{x}}^{(i)}(\mathbb{F}_q)^+ \subset C_{\bar{x}}^{(i)}(\mathbb{F}_q)$ for $i \in \{1, 2\}$. One can do so in various ways, but the simplest is probably to relate them to character sums. Consider for example the following character sum on $C_{\bar{x}}^{(1)}$:

$$W_1 := W\big(C_{\bar{x}}^{(1)}, \chi_2, g \circ x_2\big) = \sum_{P \in C_{\bar{x}}^{(1)}(\mathbb{F}_q)} \chi_2\Big(g\big(x_2(P)\big)\Big),$$

where χ_2 is the quadratic multiplicative character of $\mathbb{F}_q$. The term $\chi_2\Big(g\big(x_2(P)\big)\Big)$ is equal to -1 if $g\big(x_2(P)\big)$ is not a square in $\mathbb{F}_q$, which is exactly when $P \in C_{\bar{x}}^{(1)}(\mathbb{F}_q)^+$. Moreover, it is otherwise equal to 1 (for points outside $C_{\bar{x}}^{(1)}(\mathbb{F}_q)^+$ such that $x_2(P) \neq 0$) or 0 (for points outside $C_{\bar{x}}^{(1)}(\mathbb{F}_q)^+$ such that $x_2(P) = 0$). As a result, we have:

$$W_1 = (-1) \cdot \#C_{\bar{x}}^{(1)}(\mathbb{F}_q)^+ + 1 \cdot (\#C_{\bar{x}}^{(1)}(\mathbb{F}_q) - \#C_{\bar{x}}^{(1)}(\mathbb{F}_q)^+ - N_0) + 0 \cdot N_0$$
$$= \#C_{\bar{x}}^{(1)}(\mathbb{F}_q) - 2 \cdot \#C_{\bar{x}}^{(1)}(\mathbb{F}_q)^+ - N_0,$$

where $N_0 = O(1)$ is the number of points in $C_{\bar{x}}^{(1)}(\mathbb{F}_q)$ such that $x_2(P) = 0$. This gives:

$$\#C_{\bar{x}}^{(1)}(\mathbb{F}_q)^+ = \frac{1}{2}\#C_{\bar{x}}^{(1)}(\mathbb{F}_q) - \frac{W_1}{2} + O(1) = \frac{q}{2} + \frac{c_1}{2}\sqrt{q} - \frac{W_1}{2} + O(1),$$

where the $O(1)$ term accounts both for N_0 and for the fact that we consider an affine situation instead of a projective one.

Then, by the character sum estimate of Lemma 2, we have:

$$|W_1| \leq \big(4 - 2 + 2\deg(g \circ x_2)\big)\sqrt{q} + O(1) = (2 + 2 \cdot 3 \cdot 2)\sqrt{q} + O(1) = 14\sqrt{q} + O(1)$$

since $x_2 = -u - \bar{x}$ on $C_{\bar{x}}^{(1)}$ is a rational function of degree 2. It then follows that:

$$\#C_{\bar{x}}^{(1)}(\mathbb{F}_q)^+ = \frac{q}{2} + c_1^+\sqrt{q} + O(1) \quad \text{for some } c_1^+ \text{ such that } |c_1^+| \leq \frac{4 + 14}{2} = 9.$$

Obviously, the exact same argument applies to $C_{\bar{x}}^{(2)}$, yielding:

$$\#C_{\bar{x}}^{(2)}(\mathbb{F}_q)^+ = \frac{q}{2} + c_2^+ \sqrt{q} + O(1) \quad \text{for some } c_2^+ \text{ such that } |c_2^+| \leq 9.$$

Combining all the previous estimates, we finally obtain the following result.

Theorem 1. *For all* $\bar{x} \in X_{E,\mathbb{F}_q}$ *except at most 39 of them, the number of preimages of* $\bar{x}$ *under the* F_0 *map of Eq. (7) is close to* $2q$, *and the difference is bounded as:*

$$\left| \#F_0^{-1}(\bar{x}) - 2q \right| \leq 22\sqrt{q} + O(1).$$

Proof. Indeed, except for the at most $11 + 14 + 14 = 39$ exceptional points mentioned above, we have:

$$\#F_0^{-1}(\bar{x}) = \left(1 + \frac{1}{2} + \frac{1}{2}\right)q + \left(c_1^+ + c_2^+ + c_3\right)\sqrt{q} + O(1)$$

and since $|c_1^+ + c_2^+ + c_3| \leq 4 + 9 + 9 = 22$, the result follows.

3.3   The SW Family Is Admissible

Using Theorem 1, we are now in a position to prove that the encoding function F_0 is *admissible* in the sense of Sect. 2.6. The main step in doing so is to prove that it is *regular*.

Lemma 4. *The map* $F_0 \colon S(\mathbb{F}_q) \to X_{E,\mathbb{F}_q}$ *of Eq. (7) is* ε-regular for $\varepsilon = \left(6 + o(1)\right)q^{-1/2}$.

Proof. Let $\Delta = \Delta_1\left((F_0)_* \mathscr{U}_{S(\mathbb{F}_q)}\right)$ be the statistical distance between the distribution induced by F_0 on $X_{E,\mathbb{F}_q}$ and the uniform distribution. By definition, we have:

$$\Delta = \frac{1}{2} \sum_{\bar{x} \in X_{E,\mathbb{F}_q}} \left| \frac{\#F^{-1}(\bar{x})}{\#S(\mathbb{F}_q)} - \frac{1}{\#X_{E,\mathbb{F}_q}} \right|.$$

Now for each element $\bar{x} \in X_{E,\mathbb{F}_q}$, there are exactly two points of $E(\mathbb{F}_q)$ with x-coordinate equal to $\bar{x}$, except if $g(\bar{x}) = 0$, in which case there is exactly one (and this happens for at most three values of $\bar{x}$). Taking the point at infinity into account, we therefore get:

$$\#X_{E,\mathbb{F}_q} = \frac{1}{2}\#E(\mathbb{F}_q) + O(1) = \frac{q}{2} + c_E\sqrt{q} + O(1) \quad \text{for some } c_E \text{ with } |c_E| \leq 1$$

by yet another application of the Hasse–Weil bound. Up to sign, the constant c_E is half the normalized Frobenius trace of E.

Moreover, $S(\mathbb{F}_q)$ is the disjoint union of the various affine conics $\{x^2 + h(u_0)y^2 = -g(u_0), \ u = u_0\}$ for all $u_0 \in \mathbb{F}_q$. Those conics are nondegenerate whenever $g(u_0)h(u_0) \neq 0$, in which case they have $q + O(1)$ points. In remaining exceptional cases, they have at most $2q$ points. As a result, we get:

$$\#S(\mathbb{F}_q) = \left(q - O(1)\right) \cdot \left(q + O(1)\right) + O(1) \cdot O(q) = q^2 + O(q).$$

As for the number of preimages of F, we know by Theorem 1 that for each $\bar{x} \in X_{E,\mathbb{F}_q} \setminus X_{\text{bad}}$, where X_{bad} is a set of 39 points, there exists $c_{0,\bar{x}} \in [-22, 22]$ such that:

$$\#F^{-1}(\bar{x}) = 2q + c_{0,\bar{x}}\sqrt{q} + O(1) \qquad \forall \bar{x} \in X_{E,\mathbb{F}_q} \setminus X_{\text{bad}}$$

For $\bar{x} \in X_{\text{bad}}$, we can still obtain a less strict but simpler bound: note that for any fixed $u = u_0 \in \mathbb{F}_q$ the equations $\bar{x} = x_1(x, y, u_0)$, $\bar{x} = x_2(x, y, u_0)$ and $\bar{x} = x_3(x, y, u_0)$ have at most 2, 2, and 4 solutions in S, respectively (these solutions are given explicitly in Sect. 6). Hence, any point can have at most 8 preimages for any fixed u_0 and at most $8q$ preimages in all.

We can now bound Δ as follows:

$$2\Delta = \sum_{\bar{x} \in X_{E,\mathbb{F}_q} \setminus X_{\text{bad}}} \left| \frac{\#F^{-1}(\bar{x})}{\#S(\mathbb{F}_q)} - \frac{1}{\#X_{E,\mathbb{F}_q}} \right| + \sum_{\bar{x} \in X_{\text{bad}}} \left| \frac{\#F^{-1}(\bar{x})}{\#S(\mathbb{F}_q)} - \frac{1}{\#X_{E,\mathbb{F}_q}} \right|$$

$$= \sum_{\bar{x} \in X_{E,\mathbb{F}_q} \setminus X_{\text{bad}}} \left| \frac{2q + c_{0,\bar{x}}\sqrt{q} + O(1)}{q^2 + O(q)} - \frac{1}{q/2 + c_E\sqrt{q} + O(1)} \right|$$

$$+ \sum_{\bar{x} \in X_{\text{bad}}} \left| \frac{c_{\text{bad},\bar{x}}q}{q^2 + O(q)} - \frac{1}{q/2 + c_E\sqrt{q} + O(1)} \right|$$

$$= \sum_{\bar{x} \in X_{E,\mathbb{F}_q} \setminus X_{\text{bad}}} \frac{1}{q} \left| \left(2 + c_{0,\bar{x}}q^{-1/2} + O(q^{-1}) \right) - \left(2 - c_E q^{-1/2} + O(q^{-1}) \right) \right|$$

$$+ \sum_{\bar{x} \in X_{\text{bad}}} \frac{1}{q} \left| \left(c_{\text{bad},\bar{x}} + O(q^{-3}) \right) - \left(2 - c_E q^{-1/2} + O(q^{-1}) \right) \right|$$

$$= \sum_{\bar{x} \in X_{E,\mathbb{F}_q} \setminus X_{\text{bad}}} \frac{1}{q} \left| \left(c_{0,\bar{x}} + c_E \right)q^{-1/2} + O(q^{-1}) \right| + \sum_{\bar{x} \in X_{\text{bad}}} \frac{1}{q} \left| c_{\text{bad},\bar{x}} - 2 + O(q^{-1/2}) \right|$$

where each of the constants $c_{0,\bar{x}}$ is in $[-22, 22]$ and each of the constants $c_{\text{bad},\bar{x}}$ is in $[0, 8]$. In particular, $|c_{0,\bar{x}} + c_E| \leq 23$ and $|c_{\text{bad},\bar{x}} - 2| \leq 6$ for all $\bar{x}$, and we have:

$$2\Delta \leq \frac{\#\left(X_{E,\mathbb{F}_q} \setminus X_{\text{bad}}\right)}{q} \cdot \left(23q^{-1/2} + O(q^{-1}) \right) + \frac{\#X_{\text{bad}}}{q} \cdot \left(6 + O(q^{-1/2}) \right)$$

$$= \frac{\frac{1}{2}q + O(\sqrt{q})}{q} \cdot (23 + o(1))q^{-1/2} + \frac{39}{q} \cdot \left(6 + o(1) \right)$$

$$= \left(\frac{23}{2} + o(1) \right)q^{-1/2} \leq 2 \cdot \left(6 + o(1) \right)q^{-1/2}$$

as required.

As an easy consequence, we obtain the following theorem.

Theorem 2. *The map $F_0 \colon S(\mathbb{F}_q) \to X_{E,\mathbb{F}_q}$ of Eq. (7) is ε-admissible for $\varepsilon = (6+o(1))q^{-1/2}$. In particular, if $\mathfrak{h}$ is a random oracle with values in $S(\mathbb{F}_q)$, $F_0 \circ \mathfrak{h}$ is indifferentiable from an $X_{E,\mathbb{F}_q}$ random oracle.*

Moreover, the same results hold for $F_0^+ \colon S(\mathbb{F}_q) \times \{0, 1\} \to E(\mathbb{F}_q)$.

Proof. By definition, we need to prove that F_0 is efficiently computatable, ε-regular and ε-samplable. Computability is obvious. Regularity is the result of Lemma 4. And 0-samplablity is obtained using the preimage sampling algorithm discussed in Sect. 6 below. To fix ideas, we sketch its construction.

Fix $\bar{x} \in X_{E,\mathbb{F}_q}$. As previously mentioned, for any fixed $u_0 \in \mathbb{F}_q$, there are at most 8 preimages $(x, y, u) \in F^{-1}(\bar{x})$ such that $u = u_0$ (at most two coming from each of x_1 and x_2 and four coming from x_3). We can efficiently compute all those preimages and in particular count them. Therefore, the following simple rejection sampling algorithm has an output distribution uniform in $F^{-1}(\bar{x})$: pick u_0 uniformly at random, compute the list L_{u_0} of preimages with $u = u_0$, restart with probability $1 - \#L_{u_0}/8$ and otherwise return a random element of L_{u_0}.

Finally, the extension to F_0^+ is straightforward.

4   Parametrizing the SW Conic

4.1   Parametrizability Conditions

In the previous section, we have seen how the Shallue–van de Woestijne construction could be leveraged to construct admissible encodings $F_0 \colon S(\mathbb{F}_q) \to X_{E,\mathbb{F}_q}$ and $F_0^+ \colon S(\mathbb{F}_q) \times \{0, 1\} \to E(\mathbb{F}_q)$. However, we have also seen that mapping to $\mathbb{F}_q$-points on the surface S efficiently (without base field exponentiations) is a priori not straightforward, since the most naive approach involves finding points on new conics for all inputs.

Fortunately, the surface S has a fairly simple description: it can be seen as a *one-parameter family* of conics (the conics S_u; this is also called a relative conic over the u-line, or a fibration in conics, etc.). In any case, finding a global, two-parameter parametrization of S is thus a function field analogue of the classical problem, studied by Legendre, of finding rational points on conic over $\mathbb{Q}$.

In their paper [vHC06], van Hoeij and Cremona show that Legendre's original approach can be directly adapted to the function field case. They provide necessary and sufficient conditions for the existence of solutions, as well as an effective algorithm to compute the parametrization if it exists.

A special case of their main result in as follows.

Lemma 5 (van Hoeij–Cremona). *Let r, s be polynomials in $\mathbb{F}_q[u]$ that are coprime, squarefree, and such that at least one of them is of odd degree. Then, the following projective conic over $\mathbb{F}_q(t)$:*

$$X^2 + rY^2 + sZ^2 = 0$$

admits rational points over $\mathbb{F}_q(u)$ (i.e., a global rational parametrization) if and only if the following two conditions hold:

1. $-r$ is a square in $\mathbb{F}_q[u]/(s)$.
2. $-s$ is a square in $\mathbb{F}_q[u]/(r)$.

Moreover, if this is the case, there is an efficient algorithm to compute those points.

Proof. This is a special case of [vHC06, Th. 1]. More precisely, the assumptions ensure that the conic is in reduced form and in "case 1", in the terminology of van Hoeij and Cremona, and the squareness conditions are equivalent to the existence of a "solubility certificate".

The proof presented by van Hoeij and Cremona is constructive in that it yields an explicit algorithm for finding the rational parametrization. Our case of interest, corresponding to the surface S, is $r = h(u) = 3u^2 + 4a$ and $s = g(u) = u^3 + au + b$ (except when $a = 0$, in which case a slight adjustment is necessary to meet the assumptions of the theorem). In that case, if a parametrization exists, it can be put in the form where $Z = 1$, and X, Y are polynomials of degree 2 and 1 in u respectively, as will be shown below. These polynomials depend only on the parameters a, b of the target elliptic curve, so the polynomial coefficients can be precomputed while their evaluation at a given u is done at runtime.

4.2   Curves with a Parametrizable SW Conic

Due to the conditions in Lemma 5, the SwiftEC encoding is not applicable to every ordinary elliptic curve. We present a different characterization of these conditions from the point of view of the target curve's geometric properties.

Theorem 3. *The surface S, as a one-parameter family of conics, admits a global two-parameter parametrization if and only if the following three conditions are satisfied.*

1. *The size of the field satisfies $q \equiv 1 \mod 3$ (i.e., -3 is a square in $\mathbb{F}_q$).*
2. *The discriminant $\Delta_E = -16(4a^3 + 27b^2)$ is a square in $\mathbb{F}_q$ (i.e. E has either zero or three points of order 2).*
3. *At least one of the constants $\nu_\pm = \frac{1}{2}(-b \pm \sqrt{-3\Delta_E}/36)$ is a square in $\mathbb{F}_q$.*

Proof. As a first observation, note that if we let $r = h(u)$ and $s = g(u)$, then r and s are indeed coprime (their resultant is $4a^3 + 27b^2 = -\Delta_E/16 \neq 0$) and s is of odd degree and squarefree. Moreover, r is squarefree if and only if $a \neq 0$. For now, we assume that $a \neq 0$, so that Lemma 5 applies directly. We will treat the special case of $a = 0$ at the end.

Let us first assume that $-h$ is a square in $\mathbb{F}_q[u]/(g)$ and $-g$ is a square in $\mathbb{F}_q[u]/(h)$. Note that h and g are coprime since their resultant is $4a^3 + 27b^2 = -\Delta_E/16 \neq 0$, so the law of quadratic reciprocity over function fields gives

$$\left(\frac{-h}{g}\right)_2 \left(\frac{g}{-h}\right)_2 = (-1)^{\frac{q-1}{2}\deg g \deg h} \chi_2(1)^{\deg h} \chi_2(-3)^{\deg g}$$

$$1 \cdot \left(\frac{g}{-h}\right)_2 = 1 \cdot 1 \cdot \chi_2(-3), \tag{9}$$

where $\left(\frac{\cdot}{f}\right)_2$ and $\chi_2(\cdot)$ denote quadratic residue symbols over $\mathbb{F}_q[u]/(f)$ and $\mathbb{F}_q$, respectively.

On the other hand, we have

$$1 = \left(\frac{-g}{h}\right)_2 = \left(\frac{-1}{h}\right)_2 \left(\frac{-g}{h}\right)_2 = \chi_2(-1)^2 \left(\frac{g}{-h}\right)_2 = \left(\frac{g}{-h}\right)_2,$$

so (9) reduces to $\chi_2(-3) = 1$, which shows the necessity of condition 1.

Next, since $-g$ is a square in $\mathbb{F}_q[u]/(h)$, there exists $\alpha, \beta \in \mathbb{F}_q$ such that:

$$-g \equiv (\alpha u + \beta)^2 \pmod{h}$$

$$-u^3 - au - b \equiv \alpha^2 u^2 + 2\alpha\beta u + \beta^2 \pmod{3u^2 + 4a}$$

$$\frac{4a}{3} u - au - b \equiv -\frac{4a}{3}\alpha^2 + 2\alpha\beta u + \beta^2 \pmod{3u^2 + 4a}$$

$$\frac{a}{3} u - b = 2\alpha\beta u + \left(-\frac{4a}{3}\alpha^2 + \beta^2\right).$$

It follows that the constants α, β satisfy

$$\frac{a}{3} = 2\alpha\beta \tag{10}$$

$$b = \frac{4a}{3}\alpha^2 - \beta^2. \tag{11}$$

Recalling that $a \neq 0$, it follows from (10) that $\alpha, \beta \neq 0$ and we can substitute $\beta = a/(6\alpha)$ into (11) to obtain

$$48a\alpha^4 - 36b\alpha^2 - a^2 = 0, \tag{12}$$

which is a quadratic equation on α^2 whose discriminant is $36^2 b^2 + 192a^3 = -3\Delta_E$. Since -3 is a square, it follows that Δ_E must also be a square for α^2 to exist, showing the necessity of condition 2. The solution to (12) is then given by

$$\alpha^2 = \frac{36b \pm \sqrt{-3\Delta_E}}{96a} = \frac{-3}{4a}\nu_\pm. \tag{13}$$

If a is a square this means that at least one of $\nu_\pm$ must be a square for α to exist. On the other hand, if a is not a square then the same condition always holds since the product $\nu_+\nu_- = -a^3/27$ is a non-square.

The proof of the converse is similar: if conditions 2 and 3 are met then there exists $\alpha, \beta \in \mathbb{F}_q$ that are solutions to (10) and (11), which shows that $-g$ has a square root mod h, and then condition 1 together with (9) shows that $-h$ is a square mod g.

Finally, consider the special case $a = 0$. In that case, since $h(u) = 3u^2$, we can apply the change of variables $Y' = uY$ to reduce to the case of the conic:

$$X^2 + 3Y^2 + gZ^2 = 0,$$

i.e., $r = 3$ and $s = g$. It is then clear that r and s are coprime, squarefree, and one of them is of odd degree. Moreover, the condition that $-s$ is a square modulo r is vacuous, and the condition that $-r$ is a square modulo s simply says that

-3 is a square in $\mathbb{F}_q[u]/(g)$; since that etale algebra admits either $\mathbb{F}_q$ or $\mathbb{F}_{q^3}$ as a factor, this is equivalent to -3 being a square in $\mathbb{F}_q$, namely $q \equiv 1 \pmod 3$ as required. This shows that in this case, condition 1 is necessary and sufficient. The result still holds, however, because conditions 2 and 3 become vacuous: the discriminant $\Delta_E = -16(27b^2) = -3 \cdot 12^2 b^2$ is always a square, and one of $\nu_\pm$ is always zero.

Out of the three conditions in Theorem 3, condition 1 is the most restrictive discarding half of the prime fields. Condition 3 only fails about $1/4$ of the time, whereas condition 2 fails half of the time. However, conditions 2 and 3 are not isogeny-invariant and so they may be circumvented under certain conditions by finding a small-degree isogeny and mapping to the isogenous curve instead, as discussed in the next section.

Notable curves that satisfy the conditions for SwiftEC include the NIST P-256 curve, the curve secp256k1 used in Bitcoin [SEC10] and the pairing-friendly curve BLS12-381 [Bow17] as well as all BN curves [BN06] and BLS curves [BLS03] over any field with $q \equiv 1 \mod 3$. On the other hand, curves such as the Ed448-Goldilocks curve [Ham15] and the NIST P-384 curve are incompatible due to the field cardinality alone.

4.3 Reaching More Curves with Isogenies

While Theorem 3 discards the possibility of applying SwiftEC directly to curves with a non-square discriminant, here we present a small modification that can work around this condition, at least some of the time. The condition that the discriminant be a square is invariant under isomorphisms, but not under isogenies. Hence, we may hope that there is an isogenous curve that satisfies the condition and compose the SwiftEC encoding to this curve with the isogeny to obtain a map to the original curve. Curves with a non-square discriminant always contain exactly one point of order 2, so one may be tempted to exploit the small 2-isogeny that is available. The following result shows that this intuition is correct, and indicates exactly when this is possible.

Theorem 4. *Let $E/\mathbb{F}_q$ be an elliptic curve with non-square discriminant. There exists a curve E' with square discriminant isogenous to E over $\mathbb{F}_q$ if and only if $E(\mathbb{F}_q)$ has a point of order 4. In this case, the isogeny can always be taken to be of degree 2.*

Proof. First suppose we have a point $P_4 \in E(\mathbb{F}_q)$ of order 4, and let $P_2 = 2P_4$ be the unique point of order 2 in $E(\mathbb{F}_q)$. If $\phi : E \to E'$ is the isogeny with kernel $< P_2 >$, then $\phi(P_4)$ is a point of order 2 in E'. There must also exist a point $P_2' \in E'(\mathbb{F}_q)$ of order 2 generating the dual isogeny $\hat{\phi}$, and we cannot have $\phi(P_4) = P_2'$ because $\hat{\phi}(P_2') = 0$ but $\hat{\phi}(\phi(P_4)) = 2P_4 \neq 0$. This means we have two distinct points of order 2 in E', and their addition yields a third point of order 2, so E' must have a square discriminant as desired.

Conversely, if E has no point of order 4 then the group order is divisible by 2 exactly once, so any isogenous curve will also have exactly one point of order 2 and hence have a non-square discriminant.

Note that the application of the 2-isogeny is a 2-to-1 map that would make the distribution easily distinguishable from uniform. However, in essentially all cases of interest, one needs to sample points only in a specific subgroup orthogonal to the 2-torsion subgroup. For instance, consider `Curve25519` [Ber06] which is non-compatible with our construction because it does not have a square discriminant. The curve is given by

$$E_{25519} : y^2 = x^3 + 486662x^2 + x$$

over the prime field of size $p = 2^{255} - 19$. The group order for this curve is $\#E_{25519} = 8\ell$ where ℓ is a large prime, and points in the ℓ-torsion subgroup are used in the ECDH scheme. We can use SwiftEC to map onto the 2-isogenous curve

$$E' : y^2 = x^3 - 102314837774592x + 39834194856773654937 6$$

which does satisfy all conditions of Theorem 3. By composing with the 2-isogeny generated by $P_2' = (-11679888, 0)$ and the multiplication-by-4 map, we are able to hash into the ℓ-torsion subgroup of Curve25519 at the cost of only an additional 20 field multiplications, 7 squarings and 11 additions. This is to our knowledge the only currently known way of hashing deterministically and indistinguishably into this subgroup using a single square root.

Likewise, condition 3 may also be circumvented with isogenies and in this case we are not limited to degree 2 only. For instance, the curve `secp521r1` also known as NIST `P-521` already has a square discriminant but fails condition 3. However, it is 5-isogenous to the curve

$$E'' : y^2 = x^3 + ax + b,$$

a=0x149a4e89bde4ad2e72c830cc3df36200e03c1abb6403f3a50cc56be41b0bd98f6a2bb16b7...

...5027c89a68174a7c458a0333ff283225259b57414a2e04a0681ca279a0

b=0x49d903da04fb382a8daec077738d7f3f5a2ca21e053847fb43c4740c39eaf3d2727a9898...

...d710bdcfa306450d7102a03bf9164294ee1a849928687cc8b343a3ed24

which satisfies all the conditions for SwiftEC, so we can map onto `secp521r1` by using our construction on E'' and then composing with a 5-isogeny at negligible overhead. Since the group order is coprime to 5, the isogeny is already a bijection.

In this way, one can always expect to find some isogeny of arbitrary degree that will work, so condition 3 can in principle always be circumvented, although an isogeny of small degree is more desirable for efficiency reasons. On the other hand, Theorem 4 shows that condition 2 fails irremediably if and only if the group order is divisible by 2 exactly once, so overall we heuristically expect SwiftEC to be adaptable to a fraction 3/4 of all elliptic curves over fields with $q \equiv 1 \mod 3$.

5 The SwiftEC Encoding

5.1 Efficient Computation

As a proof of principle, we have prepared a Sage implementation of SwiftEC that allows adding new compatible curves in a simple way. This implementation makes explicit the number of field operations needed and uses a constant number of them, but is non-constant time to the degree that the built-in field operations are. Our implementation is freely available at https://github.com/Jchavezsaab/SwiftEC.

For curves with $a \neq 0$, the implementation makes use of the polynomials $X_0(u), Y_0(u)$ that evaluate a point in S_u as discussed in Sect. 4. Since these polynomials only depend on the curve coefficients a, b, they are precomputed and stored in the form of five field elements, with explicit formulas provided in the extended version of this work [CRT22]. On input u, t, the initial point $(X_0(u), Y_0(u)) \in S_u$ is evaluated and then a second point $(X, Y) \in S_u$ is obtained from the parametrization

$$X(u,t) = \frac{g(u) + h(u)(Y_0(u) - tX_0(u))^2}{X_0(u)(1 + t^2 h(u))}, \tag{14}$$

$$Y(u,t) = Y_0(u) + t(X - X_0(u)).$$

In the case where $a = 0$, we have simply $g(u) = u^3 + b$ and $h(u) = 3u^2$. In this case the van Hoeij-Cremona algorithm described in Sect. 4 always yields the point at infinity $(X_0 : Y_0 : Z_0) = (\sqrt{-3} : 1 : 0)$, so the formulas for the parametrization have to be adjusted. We can skip the computation of $X_0(u), Y_0(u)$ altogether and apply the following formulas directly:

$$X(u,t) = \frac{u^3 + b - t^2}{2t}, \tag{15}$$

$$Y(u,t) = \frac{X(u,t) + t}{u\sqrt{-3}}.$$

Finally, we apply the map ψ from (6) to get a point $(x_1, x_2, x_3, z) \in V(\mathbb{F}_q)$. It is not actually necessary to compute the z-coordinate of this point, and the x_i coordinates are computed projectively so that what we actually obtain is a projective triplet $(x_1 : x_2 : x_3 : \lambda)$. Note that this introduces a small bias towards the point at infinity: if any of the x_i are infinite then we have to set $\lambda = 0$ and all three points will be interpreted as being infinite. However, we neglect this since the bias is negligible and dealing with this case explicitly would produce a non-constant-time implementation.

We must then find which of the x_i is the x-coordinate of a point in $E(\mathbb{F}_q)$, choosing one arbitrarily but deterministically if all three are. This can be implemented in constant time as shown in Algorithm 1 which prioritizes x_3.

Finally, we use a single inverse to compute the affine x-coordinate and a square root computation (the only one throughout the whole program) to recover the y-coordinate. Note that there is a free choice for the sign of y in the end, which we integrate as an additional input bit.

Algorithm 1. x-picking algorithm.

Input: The projective x_i coordinates $(x_1 : x_2 : x_3 : \lambda)$ of a point in $V(\mathbb{F}_q)$
Output: One of the x_i which is the x-coordinate of a point in $E(\mathbb{F}_q)$.

1: $s_2 \leftarrow x_2^3 \lambda + ax_2 \lambda^3 + b\lambda^4$
2: $s_3 \leftarrow x_3^3 \lambda + ax_3 \lambda^3 + b\lambda^4$
3: $c_2 \leftarrow IsSquare(s_2)$
4: $c_3 \leftarrow IsSquare(s_3)$
5: $cswap(c_2, x_1, x_2)$
6: $cswap(c_3, x_1, x_3)$
7: **return** $(x_1 : \lambda)$

5.2 XSwiftEC: x-Only Computation Without Exponentiation

Note that the only inverse and square root needed for SwiftEC are at the very end when the affine x, y coordinates are computed. However, there are many applications where obtaining an output in x-only projective coordinates is acceptable, and these operations can be omitted. The resulting XSwiftEC algorithm requires no inversions, square roots or exponentiations of any kind, but only two Jacobi symbol computations that are considerably cheaper and other elementary field operations.

This is particularly useful for the cases when SwiftEC is composed with a 2-isogeny as described in Sect. 4.3: even if an affine x, y output is desired, we are better off using XSwiftEC and recovering the affine coordinates after applying the projective x-only 2-isogeny formulas.

Although the output $(x : \lambda)$ that is obtained is indistinguishable from uniform as a projective pair, the individual values of x and λ are not and may leak information about the input. This can be easily circumvented by multiplying both coordinates by a random field element, or it may be ignored to avoid relying on randomness in applications where this leakage is not a concern.

5.3 Implementation Results

We summarize in Table 1 the cost in operations for each version of SwiftEC. The most noteworthy feature is the requirement of only one square root computation (and none when the y coordinate is not required), which is an improvement on previous admissible encodings to ordinary elliptic curves. Moreover, the square-root and the inversion can be performed simultaneously for further savings as described by Hamburg [Ham12].

The results shown are for the $a \neq 0$ implementation. The implementations for $a = 0$ always save exactly 7 additions and 6 multiplications due to the simpler formulas in (15).

6   SwiftEC For Point Representation: ElligatorSwift

In this section we describe an algorithm to efficiently compute a uniformly random preimage of any point under SwiftEC. The existence of this algorithm is

Table 1. Cost in operations of our implementations of SWIFTEC for field additions, squarings, multiplications, Jacobi symbol computations, inversions, and square roots.

	Add	Sqr	Mul	Jac	Inv	Sqrt
SWIFTEC	25	7	18	2	1	1
SWIFTEC with isogeny	36	14	38	2	1	1
XSWIFTEC	22	9	23	2	0	0
XSWIFTEC with isogeny	33	14	35	2	0	0

required for the encoding to be *admissible*, which is crucial for using SWIFTEC as part of a cryptographically secure hash function as described in Sect. 2. Moreover, it is important in practice because it allows us to encode points in an elliptic curve as uniform bitstrings, as is done in Elligator [BHKL13] and Elligator Squared [Tib14a].

Compared to Elligator Squared, our ELLIGATORSWIFT construction has the advantage that it does not need to compute any encodings in the forward direction. Indeed, all we need is to sample a random $u \in \mathbb{F}_q$ and then find an inverse $F_{0,u}^{-1}(P)$ of the SW encoding.

We first focus on inverting the map Ψ and note that under a change of variables $v = x/2y - u/2$ and $w = 2y$, the image in (6) becomes

$$x_1 = v, \qquad x_2 = -u - v, \qquad x_3 = u + w^2,$$

while the equation for the conic becomes

$$w^2(u^2 + uv + v^2 + a) = -(u^3 + au + b). \tag{16}$$

This yields up to four possible preimages for a given point $(x, y) \in E(F)$, namely:

1. $v = x$ and w^2 derived from (16), if x was drawn from x_1
2. $v = -u - x$ and w^2 derived from (16), if x was drawn from x_2
3,4. $w^2 = x - u$ and v derived from (16), if x was drawn from x_3,

where the last case actually contains two preimages since (16) is a quadratic equation for v with solutions

$$v = \frac{-u}{2} \pm \frac{\sqrt{-w^2(4u^3 + 4au + 4b + 3w^2u^2 + 4aw^2)}}{2w^2}.$$

Moreover, all cases have a duplicity from choosing the sign of $w = \sqrt{w^2}$, so there are up to 8 preimages in total per elliptic curve x coordinate. Note that flipping the sign of w produces a new point in S that maps to the same x coordinate, so in cases where we need to distinguish between the choice of sign for the elliptic curve y coordinate this can be encoded into w by always choosing $\mathrm{sgn}(w) = \mathrm{sgn}(y)$. This choice gives up to 4 preimages for each pair of coordinates (x, y), and allows the decoder to recover the correct choice of $\mathrm{sgn}(y)$ when computing SWIFTEC in the forward direction.

Of course, some of the square roots needed may not exist and so different values of u will yield a different number of preimages of a given point (including possibly none). On top of this, if the preimage comes from cases 1 or 2 but results in values where all three x_i yield points in $E(\mathbb{F}_q)$, then the preimage will be invalid even if the square root is well-defined since Algorithm 1 in the forward encoding would have prioritized x_3 over the intended one. Care must therefore be taken to check for the existence of the various square roots and restart the

---

Algorithm 2. ELLIGATORSWIFT.

Input: $(x, y) \in E(\mathbb{F}_q)$

Output: $u, t, b \xleftarrow{\$} \text{SwiftEC}^{-1}(x, y)$

1: $u \xleftarrow{\$} \mathbb{F}_q$
2: $case \xleftarrow{\$} \{1, 2, 3, 4\}$
3: **if** $case == 1$ **then**
4:     $v \leftarrow x$
5:     **if** IsSquare$((-v - u)^3 + a(-v - u) + b)$ **then**
6:         go to 1
7:     **end if**
8:     $w^2 \leftarrow -(u^3 + au + b)/(u^2 + uv + v^2 + a)$
9: **else if** $case == 2$ **then**
10:     $v \leftarrow -x - u$
11:     **if** IsSquare$(v^3 + av + b)$ **then**
12:         go to 1
13:     **end if**
14:     $w^2 \leftarrow -(u^3 + au + b)/(u^2 + uv + v^2 + a)$
15: **else**
16:     $w^2 \leftarrow x - u$
17:     $r \leftarrow \sqrt{-w^2(4u^3 + 4au + 4b + 3w^2u^2 + 4aw^2)}$
18:     **if** $r == Null$ **then**
19:         go to 1
20:     **end if**
21:     $v \leftarrow -u/2 + r/2w^2$
22: **end if**
23: $w \leftarrow \sqrt{w^2}$
24: **if** $w == Null$ **then**
25:     go to 1
26: **end if**
27: **if** $\text{sgn}(w) \neq \text{sgn}(y)$ **then**
28:     $w \leftarrow -w$
29: **end if**
30: $Y \leftarrow 2w/2$
31: $X \leftarrow 2Y(v + u/2)$
32: Evaluate $X_0(u)$ and $Y_0(u)$ from precomputed polynomials
33: $t \leftarrow (Y - Y_0)/(X - X_0)$
34: **return** u, t

---

procedure when appropriate, as shown in Algorithm 2. This makes the algorithm run in non-constant time but ensures that the preimage is uniformly sampled.

What remains is just to switch back to x, y coordinates and invert the parametrization (14) to recover the parameter t.

Remark: For implementations with $a = 0$ we must take into account the different parametrization formulas in (15). In this case, lines 29 and 30 of Algorithm 2 can be replaced by simply $t \leftarrow Yu\sqrt{-3} - X$, where the constant $\sqrt{-3}$ is part of the precomputed parameters.

We assume that the square root function returns $Null$ for non-squares. It is easy to see that the output of Algorithm 2 is uniformly distributed since each u is attempted with a random choice of one of the 4 cases, so the probability of each u being successful is proportional to how many preimages exist under it.

The main cost of Algorithm 2 is an average of 1.5 square root computations per iteration. Since most points have roughly $2q$ preimages as per Theorem 1, we can expect each choice of u to contain on average 2 valid preimages out of the 8 possible ones, and so the expected number of iterations is 4. Notice however that a failed iteration can be aborted before computing any square roots by first computing the corresponding Jacobi symbols, which can be done much more efficiently with constant-time efficient implementations such as [Por20, Ham21, AG21] (by a factor of around 10× for most commonly-used primes). The cost of ELLIGATOR-SWIFT is therefore always exactly 1 or 2 square root computations, and 6 Jacobi symbol computations on average. This is a considerable improvement over Elligator Squared, with an average cost of 6.5 square roots.

As for curves where we need to compose SwiftEC with an isogeny, we can obtain a corresponding variant of ELLIGATORSWIFT by composing with the dual isogeny, but this has the side effect of introducing a multiplication by the isogeny degree in the round trip. This can be circumvented by adding a point division before applying ELLIGATORSWIFT, which is important for demonstrating that the encoding with the isogeny trick is still admissible. However, the resulting ELLIGATORSWIFT construction would be unappealing in terms of efficiency.

7   Conclusion

In this paper we presented SwiftEC, which is the first admissible and constant-time encoding using a single square root that is applicable to a large class of ordinary elliptic curves. This construction can lead to considerable performance speedup compared to previously known methods. For instance, an efficient implementation of SwiftEC and ELLIGATORSWIFT for `secp256k1` benchmarked suggest computational savings of more than 50% when compared to their Elligator Squared counterparts [Wui22]. On the other hand, in applications such as hashing into BLS curves where we ultimately aim to map to points belonging to the elliptic curve subgroups $\mathbb{G}_1$ and $\mathbb{G}_2$, the dominant cost might not be the square-root computation associated to SwiftEC's savings, but rather the clearing of a per-curve fixed cofactor (typically, this cofactor is relatively small for $\mathbb{G}_1$ but much larger for $\mathbb{G}_2$).

While some curves remain incompatible with SwiftEC, our construction applies to roughly $3/4$ of all curves over fields with $q \equiv 1 \mod 3$. The inverse encoding also results in an Elligator-like encoding that is significantly more efficient than previous constructions, using more than four times less square roots on average than Elligator Squared, while retaining the same data transmission size of two field elements.

It is still an open problem to determine if there are any workarounds that could extend this encoding to more of the non-compatible curves, or even to find a single-square root admissible encoding that could be applied to all ordinary elliptic curves.

Acknowledgement. We thank Pieter Wuille for several insights regarding small optimizations and special cases of ElligatorSwift, as well as sharing with us preliminary benchmarks of his optimized SwiftEC and ElligatorSwift implementations. We also thank Diego Aranha for extensive discussions on the efficiency of the Jacobi symbol versus square-root computations.

References

[AG21] Aranha, D.F., Gouvêa, C.P.L.: RELIC is an Efficient LIbrary for Cryptography (2021). https://github.com/relic-toolkit/relic/blob/symbol-asm/src/fp/relic_fp_smb.c

[BCI+10] Brier, E., Coron, J.-S., Icart, T., Madore, D., Randriam, H., Tibouchi, M.: Efficient indifferentiable hashing into ordinary elliptic curves. In: Rabin, T. (ed.) CRYPTO 2010. LNCS, vol. 6223, pp. 237–254. Springer, Heidelberg (2010). https://doi.org/10.1007/978-3-642-14623-7_13

[Ber06] Bernstein, D.J.: Curve25519: new diffie-hellman speed records. In: Yung, M., Dodis, Y., Kiayias, A., Malkin, T. (eds.) PKC 2006. LNCS, vol. 3958, pp. 207–228. Springer, Heidelberg (2006). https://doi.org/10.1007/11745853_14

[BF01] Boneh, D., Franklin, M.: Identity-based encryption from the weil pairing. In: Kilian, J. (ed.) CRYPTO 2001. LNCS, vol. 2139, pp. 213–229. Springer, Heidelberg (2001). https://doi.org/10.1007/3-540-44647-8_13

[BHKL13] Bernstein, D.J., Hamburg, M., Krasnova, A., Lange., T.D.: Elligator: elliptic-curve points indistinguishable from uniform random strings. In: Sadeghi, A.-R., Gligor, V.D., Yung, M., (eds.) ACM CCS 2013, pp. 967–980. ACM Press, November 2013

[BLS01] Boneh, D., Lynn, B., Shacham, H.: Short signatures from the weil pairing. In: Boyd, C. (ed.) ASIACRYPT 2001. LNCS, vol. 2248, pp. 514–532. Springer, Heidelberg (2001). https://doi.org/10.1007/3-540-45682-1_30

[BLS03] Barreto, P.S.L.M., Lynn, B., Scott, M.: Constructing elliptic curves with prescribed embedding degrees. In: Cimato, S., Persiano, G., Galdi, C. (eds.) SCN 2002. LNCS, vol. 2576, pp. 257–267. Springer, Heidelberg (2003). https://doi.org/10.1007/3-540-36413-7_19

[BN06] Barreto, P.S.L.M., Naehrig, M.: Pairing-friendly elliptic curves of prime order. In: Preneel, B., Tavares, S. (eds.) SAC 2005. LNCS, vol. 3897, pp. 319–331. Springer, Heidelberg (2006). https://doi.org/10.1007/11693383_22

[Bow17]   Sean Bowe. BLS12-381: New zk-SNARK elliptic curve construction (2017). https://electriccoin.co/blog/new-snark-curve/

[BY19]   Bernstein, D.J., Yang, B.-Y.: Fast constant-time gcd computation and modular inversion. IACR TCHES, 2019(3), 340–398 (2019). https://tches.iacr.org/index.php/TCHES/article/view/8298

[CM00]   Castro, F.N., Moreno, C.J.: Mixed exponential sums over finite fields. Proc. Amer. Math. Soc. **128**(9), 2529–2537 (2000)

[CRT22]   Chavez-Saab, J., Rodríguez-Henríquez, F., Tibouchi, M.: SwiftEC: Shallue-van de Woestijne indifferentiable function to elliptic curves. Cryptology ePrint Archive, Paper 2022/759 (2022). https://eprint.iacr.org/2022/759

[Far11]   Farashahi, R.R.: Hashing into hessian curves. In: Nitaj, A., Pointcheval, D. (eds.) AFRICACRYPT 2011. LNCS, vol. 6737, pp. 278–289. Springer, Heidelberg (2011). https://doi.org/10.1007/978-3-642-21969-6_17

[FFS+13] Rezaeian Farashahi, R., Fouque, P.-A., Shparlinski, I.E., Tibouchi, M., Felipe Voloch, J.: Indifferentiable deterministic hashing to elliptic and hyperelliptic curves. Math. Comput. **82**(281):491–512 (2013)

[FHSS+22] Faz-Hernandez, A., Scott, S., Sullivan, N., Wahby, R.S., Wood, C.A.: Hashing to elliptic curves. http://www.tools.ietf.org/id/draft-irtf-cfrg-hash-to-curve-14.html, February 2022

[FJT13]   Fouque, P.-A., Joux, A., Tibouchi, M.: Injective encodings to elliptic curves. In: Boyd, C., Simpson, L. (eds.) ACISP 2013. LNCS, vol. 7959, pp. 203–218. Springer, Heidelberg (2013). https://doi.org/10.1007/978-3-642-39059-3_14

[FT10]   Fouque, P.-A., Tibouchi, M.: Deterministic encoding and hashing to odd hyperelliptic curves. In: Joye, M., Miyaji, A., Otsuka, A. (eds.) Pairing 2010. LNCS, vol. 6487, pp. 265–277. Springer, Heidelberg (2010). https://doi.org/10.1007/978-3-642-17455-1_17

[FT12]   Fouque, P.-A., Tibouchi, M.: Indifferentiable hashing to barreto–naehrig curves. In: Hevia, A., Neven, G. (eds.) LATINCRYPT 2012. LNCS, vol. 7533, pp. 1–17. Springer, Heidelberg (2012). https://doi.org/10.1007/978-3-642-33481-8_1

[Ham12]   Hamburg, M.: Fast and compact elliptic-curve cryptography. Cryptology ePrint Archive, Report 2012/309 (2012). https://eprint.iacr.org/2012/309

[Ham15]   Hamburg, M.: Ed448-goldilocks, a new elliptic curve. Cryptology ePrint Archive, Report 2015/625 (2015). https://eprint.iacr.org/2015/625

[Ham21]   Hamburg, M.: Computing the Jacobi symbol using Bernstein-Yang. Cryptology ePrint Archive, Paper 2021/1271 (2021). https://eprint.iacr.org/2021/1271

[Ica09]   Icart, T.: How to hash into elliptic curves. In: Halevi, S. (ed.) CRYPTO 2009. LNCS, vol. 5677, pp. 303–316. Springer, Heidelberg (2009). https://doi.org/10.1007/978-3-642-03356-8_18

[KLR10]   Kammerer, J.-G., Lercier, R., Renault, G.: Encoding points on hyperelliptic curves over finite fields in deterministic polynomial time. In: Joye, M., Miyaji, A., Otsuka, A. (eds.) Pairing 2010. LNCS, vol. 6487, pp. 278–297. Springer, Heidelberg (2010). https://doi.org/10.1007/978-3-642-17455-1_18

[Kos22]   Koshelev, D.: Indifferentiable hashing to ordinary elliptic $\mathbb{F}_q$-curves of $j = 0$ with the cost of one exponentiation in $\mathbb{F}_q$. Des. Codes Cryptogr. **90**(3), 801–812 (2022)

[MRH04] Maurer, U., Renner, R., Holenstein, C.: Indifferentiability, impossibility results on reductions, and applications to the random oracle methodology. In: Naor, M. (ed.) TCC 2004. LNCS, vol. 2951, pp. 21–39. Springer, Heidelberg (2004). https://doi.org/10.1007/978-3-540-24638-1_2

[Per91] Perret, M.: Multiplicative character sums and kummer coverings. Acta Arith **59**, 279–290 (1991)

[Por20] Thomas Pornin. Faster modular inversion and Legendre symbol, and an X25519 speed record. https://research.nccgroup.com/2020/09/28/faster-modular-inversion-and-legendre-symbol-and-an-x25519-speed-record/, September 2020

[Ros02] Rosen, M.: Number Theory in Function Fields. Springer, New York, NY (2002)

[RSS11] Ristenpart, T., Shacham, H., Shrimpton, T.: Careful with composition: limitations of the indifferentiability framework. In: Paterson, K.G. (ed.) EUROCRYPT 2011. LNCS, vol. 6632, pp. 487–506. Springer, Heidelberg (2011). https://doi.org/10.1007/978-3-642-20465-4_27

[SEC10] Certicom research, standards for efficient cryptography 2: Recommended elliptic curve domain parameters, January 2010

[SvdW06] Shallue, A., van de Woestijne, C.E.: Construction of Rational Points on Elliptic Curves over Finite Fields. In: Hess, F., Pauli, S., Pohst, M. (eds.) ANTS 2006. LNCS, vol. 4076, pp. 510–524. Springer, Heidelberg (2006). https://doi.org/10.1007/11792086_36

[Tib14a] Tibouchi, M.: Elligator squared: uniform points on elliptic curves of prime order as uniform random strings. In: Christin, N., Safavi-Naini, R. (eds.) FC 2014. LNCS, vol. 8437, pp. 139–156. Springer, Heidelberg (2014). https://doi.org/10.1007/978-3-662-45472-5_10

[Tib14b] Tibouchi, M.: Impossibility of surjective icart-like encodings. In: Chow, S.S.M., Liu, J.K., Hui, L.C.K., Yiu, S.M. (eds.) ProvSec 2014. LNCS, vol. 8782, pp. 29–39. Springer, Cham (2014). https://doi.org/10.1007/978-3-319-12475-9_3

[TK17] Tibouchi, M., Kim, T.: Improved elliptic curve hashing and point representation. Des. Codes Cryptogr. **82**(1–2), 161–177 (2017)

[Ula07] Ulas, M.: Rational points on certain hyperelliptic curves over finite fields. Bull. Pol. Acad. Sci. Math. **55**(2), 97–104 (2007)

[vHC06] van Hoeij, M., Cremona, J.: Solving conics over function fields. Journal de Théorie des Nombres de Bordeaux **18**(3), 595–606 (2006)

[WB19] Wahby, R.S., Boneh, D.: Fast and simple constant-time hashing to the BLS12-381 elliptic curve. IACR TCHES, 2019(4), 154–179, 2019. https://tches.iacr.org/index.php/TCHES/article/view/8348

[Wui22] Wuille, P.: Efficient software implementation of SwiftEC and Elligator-Swift. Personal communication, June 2022

Functional and Witness Encryption

Multi-Client Functional Encryption with Fine-Grained Access Control

Ky Nguyen[1]([✉])(ID), Duong Hieu Phan[2](ID), and David Pointcheval[1](ID)

[1] DIENS, École normale supérieure, CNRS, Inria, PSL University, Paris, France
ky.nguyen@ens.psl.eu
[2] LTCI, Telecom Paris, Institut Polytechnique de Paris, Palaiseau, France

Abstract. Multi-Client Functional Encryption (MCFE) and Multi-Input Functional Encryption (MIFE) are very interesting extensions of Functional Encryption for practical purpose. They allow to compute joint function over data from multiple parties. Both primitives are aimed at applications in multi-user settings where decryption can be correctly output for users with appropriate functional decryption keys only. While the definitions for a single user or multiple users were quite general and can be realized for general classes of functions as expressive as Turing machines or all circuits, efficient schemes have been proposed so far for concrete classes of functions: either only for access control, *i.e.* the identity function under some conditions, or linear/quadratic functions under no condition.

In this paper, we target classes of functions that explicitly combine some evaluation functions independent of the decrypting user under the condition of some access control. More precisely, we introduce a framework for MCFE with fine-grained access control and propose constructions for both single-client and multi-client settings, for inner-product evaluation and access control via Linear Secret Sharing Schemes (LSSS), with selective and adaptive security. The only known work that combines functional encryption in multi-user setting with access control was proposed by Abdalla *et al.* (Asiacrypt '20), which relies on a generic transformation from the single-client schemes to obtain MIFE schemes that suffer a quadratic factor of n (where n denotes the number of clients) in the ciphertext size. We follow a different path, via MCFE: we present a *duplicate-and-compress* technique to transform the single-client scheme and obtain a MCFE with fine-grained access control scheme with only a linear factor of n in the ciphertext size. Our final scheme thus outperforms the Abdalla *et al.*'s scheme by a factor n, as one can obtain MIFE from MCFE by making all the labels in MCFE a fixed public constant. The concrete constructions are secure under the SXDH assumption, in the random oracle model for the MCFE scheme, but in the standard model for the MIFE improvement.

1 Introduction

Encryption enables people to securely communicate and share sensitive data in an *all-or-nothing* fashion: once the recipients have the secret key then they will

© International Association for Cryptologic Research 2022
S. Agrawal and D. Lin (Eds.): ASIACRYPT 2022, LNCS 13791, pp. 95–125, 2022.
https://doi.org/10.1007/978-3-031-22963-3_4

recover the original data, otherwise the recipients have no information about the plaintext data. Functional Encryption (FE) [17,40], introduced by Boneh, Sahai and Waters, overcomes this all-or-nothing limitation of PKE by allowing recipients to recover encrypted data in a more fine-grained manner: instead of revealing the whole original encrypted data, recipients can get the result of evaluation of some function on the data, according to the function associated to the decryption key, called *functional decryption key*. By allowing computation of partial data, one can aim at getting both: the utility of analysis on large data while preserving personal information private.

FE received large interest from the cryptographic community, first as a generalization of Identity-Based Encryption (IBE) [15,16,23,42] and Attribute-Based Encryption (ABE) [9,29,37,38,40], which are unfortunately only access control, with all-or-nothing decryption as a result. Abdalla *et al.* [2] proposed the first construction for evaluating a concrete function: the inner product between a vector in the ciphertext and a vector in the functional decryption key, hence coined IPFE. The interest in FE then increased, especially in the multi-user setting in which the inputs come from different users, possibly in competition, and the output characterizes a joint function on the inputs [20,32]. Applications are then numerous, and the encryptors can even be the final recipients of aggregated results. Then, this might look similar to multi-party computation (MPC), where several players privately provide their inputs to allow computations on them. But the main difference is that functional encryption is expected as a non-interactive process, and thus quite more interesting in practice. While FE with a single encryptor might be of theoretical interest, in real-life, the number of really useful functions may be limited. When this number of functions is small, any PKE can be converted into FE by additionally encrypting the evaluations by the various functions under specific keys. This approach is impossible for multiple users, even when a unique fixed function is considered.

In the multi-user case, Goldwasser *et al.* [27,28] introduced the notion of Multi-Input Functional Encryption (MIFE) and Multi-Client Functional Encryption (MCFE) where the single input x to the encryption procedure is broken down into an input vector $(x_1, \ldots, x_n)$ with independent components. An index i for each client and, in the case of MCFE, a (typically time-based) tag tag are used for every encryption: $(c_1 = \mathsf{Enc}(1, x_1, \mathsf{tag}), \ldots, c_n = \mathsf{Enc}(n, x_n, \mathsf{tag}))$. Anyone owning a functional decryption key dk_f, for an n-ary function f and multiple ciphertexts (for the same tag tag, in the case of MCFE) can compute $f(x_1, \ldots, x_n)$ but nothing else about the individual x_i's. Implicitly, clients have to be able to coordinate together on the tags, and different usability in practice. In particular, in MCFE, the combination of ciphertexts generated for different tags does not give a valid global ciphertext and the adversary learns nothing from it. This leads to more versatility since encrypting x_i under tag has a different meaning from encrypting x_i under $\mathsf{tag}' \neq \mathsf{tag}$. On the other hand, MIFE does not use tags and once a ciphertext of x_i is computed, it can be reused for different combinations. However, in both situations, encryption must require a private key, otherwise anybody could complete the vector initiated by a user in many ways, and then obtain many various evaluations from a unique functional decryption key. But then, since encryption needs a private key per user, for each component c_i, some of these keys might get corrupted. Therefore, there are two main distinguishing aspects regarding MCFE that have to be dealt with: the role of tags in construction and the danger of corruption for security.

Another classical issue with encryption is the decryption key, even if legitimately obtained: once delivered, it can be used forever. One may expect revocation, or access control with more fine-grained authentication. This has been extensively studied with broadcast encryption, revocation systems and more generally, with attribute-based encryption (ABE) [44]. Finally, as already explained, FE is a generalization of IBE and ABE, and after having been illustrated with IBE and ABE, linear evaluations [3,6,14,18] and quadratic evaluations [8,10,26,33] have been proposed. However, there are still very few works that combine function evaluation and access control with concrete schemes. This could provide FE, with concrete function evaluation for some target users, or revocation (of users or functions). Abdalla *et al.* [4] have been the first to address this problem, for enhancing FE and MIFE with access control. In addition, they informally argue that from an ABE for MIFE one can lift it for free to get MCFE, thus solving both problems at the same time. Precisely, they mentioned *"by resorting for instance, to the notion of multi-client IPFE, where ciphertexts are associated with time-stamps, and only ciphertext with matching time-stamps can be combined (e.g.. [20]) we believe that our proposed primitive provides a more general and versatile solution to the problem"*. Their idea can be interpreted as: tags can be used as specific attributes, and tags can be embedded in policies to automatically obtain multi-client settings. This argument seems formally valid when considering the general form of MIFE and MCFE. However, when considering concrete classes of functions, which is our main focus in this paper, it is unlikely to be efficiently feasible and we will explain the reason in the technical overview in Sect. 3. We underline that the principal difference between MCFE and MIFE is the presence of tags for producing the ciphertext components, which can be jointly decrypted only if all tags are equal. Thus, we can retrieve an MIFE from MCFE by fixing and publishing one tag, which retains the *same* ciphertext's size from the MCFE scheme to the new MIFE one. Moreover, since the combination of ciphertext components in MCFE is restrained by the tags, its security model is far less restrictive than the security model of MIFE that has to deal with arbitrary combination of ciphertext components. For these reasons, our main objective becomes constructing an MCFE having smaller ciphertext size while permitting access control over decryption keys.

We take a completely different approach than in [4] to answer this question. Borrowing the terminology from ABE, our work will focus on *key-policy* (KP) constructions, where the policy is defined at the moment of key extraction and a ciphertext associated with certain attributes can be decrypted only if those attributes satisfy the policy. The dual notion of *ciphertext-policy* (CP) constructions is already studied in [4]. We concentrate solely on particular functionality classes whose description contains two separate parts: a description of functions exclusively for evaluation and a binary relation exclusively for modeling access control. Although this conceptual point of view does *not* take us out of the FE realm and thus can be captured by the general FE notion, it suits perfectly our purpose to compute inner-products along with fine-grained access control provided by Linear Secret Sharing Schemes (LSSS) in this paper. Then, we start from single-client IPFE schemes with LSSS access control and leverage them to get an MCFE scheme, where only tags are needed for hashing during encryption, and the hash function is modeled as a random oracle. Removing labels by fixing a public tag for all ciphertexts leads to an MIFE scheme in the standard model that is more efficient than the one from [4].

1.1 Related Work

Recently, [30] improves upon the single-client construction based on Learning with Errors (LWE) from [4], for IPFE with access control expressed by bounded depth boolean circuits, achieving better security along with smaller ciphertexts. In another work, [39] also studies LWE-based single client constructions for IPFE with access control expressed by general boolean functions but under selective challenge attributes. The single-client LWE-based construction in [39] is later lifted to an MIFE using the generic transformation from [4].

Also in the single-client setting, another line of works attempts to construct FE for a general uniform functionality class such as Turing machines (TMFE), which naturally captures inner-product evaluation under LSSS access control. The work of Agrawal *et al.* [7] provided a non-adaptively simulation-based secure construction for TMFE in the *dynamic bounded collusion* model under subexponential LWE. The construction is later improved in [5] to achieve adaptive security under polynomial LWE, DDH or bilinear decisional Diffie-Hellman in specific groups, or quadratic residuosity. Towards this goal, both works of [5,7] additionally gave constructions of FE for circuits of *unbounded* size and depth, which can also encompass inner-product computation under LSSS access control, based on various standard assumptions such as computational Diffie-Hellman, factoring, or polynomial LWE. All single-client constructions from [5,7] use a wide range of cryptographic primitives in a generic manner, which deviates from our goal to give explicit constructions in the multi-user setting.

1.2 Our Contributions

Single-client Setting. We propose new single-client schemes whose selectively-secure version is almost as efficient as the selectively-secure version in [4] and the adaptively-secure version is nearly three times as efficient as the adaptively-secure version in [4]. More importantly, our schemes can be extended to multi-client settings. Our constructions exploit the *Dual Pairing Vector Spaces* proposed by Okamoto-Takashima [35,37].

Multi-client Setting. Our main contribution is an extension from single-client to multi-client without linearly increasing the complexity in the number n of

Table 1. We compare our constructions with existing works, in terms of the number of group elements in the ciphertext (column $|\mathsf{ct}|$), the largest predicate class that can be handled (column $\mathcal{P}$), the function class (column $\mathcal{F}$), security (column **Security**). We denote by d the number of attributes needed by the policy in a ciphertext. All our schemes are defined for the functionality class $\mathcal{F}^{\mathsf{IP,poly}}_{n,q,\mathsf{LSSS}} = \mathcal{F}^{\mathsf{IP}} \times \mathsf{LSSS}$ constituted by $\mathcal{F}^{\mathsf{IP}} = \{F_{\mathbf{y}} : \mathbb{Z}^n_q \rightarrow \mathbb{Z}_q; \mathbf{x} \mapsto \langle \mathbf{x}, \mathbf{y} \rangle \in \mathcal{R}(\mathbb{Z}_q)\}$ and LSSS of Linear Secret Sharing Schemes over attributes in $\mathbb{Z}_q$, where $n, q \in \mathbb{N}$, q is prime and $|\mathcal{R}(\mathbb{Z}_q)| = \mathsf{poly}(\log q)$. The schemes from [4] are constructed for $\mathcal{F}^{\mathsf{IP}} \times \mathsf{MSP}$ and $\mathcal{F}^{\mathsf{IP}} \times \mathsf{roMSP}$, where $\mathsf{MSP}, \mathsf{roMSP}$ are classes of *monotone span programs*, *read-once monotone span programs* over attributes in $\mathbb{Z}_q$. The shorthands $(\mathsf{mc}, \mathsf{mi}, \mathsf{sel}, \mathsf{ad}, \mathsf{ind}, \mathsf{sim})$ denote multi-client setting, multi-input setting, selective security, adaptive security, indistinguishability-based, simulation-based.

Scheme	$\mathcal{P}$	$\mathcal{F}$	$|\mathsf{ct}|$	Security
[4, Sect. 3.1]	MSP; CP	$\mathcal{F}^{\mathsf{IP,poly}}_{n,q,\mathsf{MSP}}$	$n + 2d + 2$	sel-sim
[4, Sect. 3.2]	roMSP; CP	$\mathcal{F}^{\mathsf{IP,poly}}_{n,q,\mathsf{roMSP}}$	$3nd + 3d + 2$	ad-ind
Sect. 4, Fig. 1	LSSS; KP	$\mathcal{F}^{\mathsf{IP,poly}}_{n,q,\mathsf{LSSS}}$	$n + 8d + 4$	sel-ind
	LSSS; KP		$nd + 2n + 7d + 3$	ad-ind
[4, Sect. 6.2] applied to [4, Sect. 3.1]	MSP; CP	$\mathcal{F}^{\mathsf{IP,poly}}_{n,q,\mathsf{MSP}}$	$n^2 + 2nd + 2n$	mi-ad-ind
Sect. 5.2	LSSS; KP	$\mathcal{F}^{\mathsf{IP,poly}}_{n,q,\mathsf{LSSS}}$	$8nd + 5n$	mc-ad-ind

clients. The generic transformation proposed by Abdalla *et al.* [4, Theorem 6.3] results in a degradation of factor n in both construction and security reduction. As previously stated, Abdalla *et al.*'s generic transformation can only help to achieve a multi-input scheme and is unlikely to be generalized to a multi-client scheme without further seriously degrading efficiency. On the other hand, because MIFE can be defined as MCFE with a fixed public constant tag, our construction yields a much more efficient MIFE with access control than the Abdalla *et al.*'s scheme (in fact, n times more efficient). More concretely, the total communication among n clients in our MCFE construction is a linear function in n and does not suffer a quadratic blow-up of n^2 group elements as in [4].

Comparisons. Our concrete constructions focus on the functionality class whose member's description contains inner-product evaluation functions and binary relations to describe access control. In the pairing-based setting, we give comparisons with existing works in Table 1. Recall that in MCFE, n can be a large number of clients, while d is the number of attributes, generally small, used in a policy. Concretely, we can consider identity-based functional encryption, as outlined in [4], where $d = 1$, whatever the size of n: our ciphertext's size is linear instead of quadratic in n as in [4].

Organization. We first give the necessary preliminaries in Sect. 2, then we present the high-level ideas and intuitions of our results in Sect. 3, before going into purely technical details in Sect. 4 for the single-client schemes and in Sect. 5 for the multi-client schemes.

2   Preliminaries

We write $[n]$ to denote the set $\{1, 2, \ldots, n\}$ for an integer n. For any $q \geq 2$, we let $\mathbb{Z}_q$ denote the ring of integers with addition and multiplication modulo q. For a prime q and an integer N, we denote by $GL_N(\mathbb{Z}_q)$ the general linear group of of degree N over $\mathbb{Z}_q$. We write vectors as row-vectors, unless stated otherwise. For a vector $\mathbf{x}$ of dimension n, the notation $\mathbf{x}[i]$ indicates the i-th coordinate of $\mathbf{x}$, for $i \in [n]$. We will follow the implicit notation in [25] and use $[\![a]\!]$ to denote g^a in a cyclic group $\mathbb{G}$ of prime order q generated by g, given $a \in \mathbb{Z}_q$. This implicit notation extends to matrices and vectors having entries in $\mathbb{Z}_q$. We use the shorthand ppt for "probabilistic polynomial time". In the security proofs, whenever we use an ordered sequence of games $(\mathsf{G}_0, \mathsf{G}_1, \ldots, \mathsf{G}_i, \ldots, \mathsf{G}_L)$ indexed by $i \in \{0, 1, \ldots, L\}$, we refer to the predecessor of G_j by G_{j-1}, for $j \in [L]$.

2.1   Hardness Assumptions

We state the assumptions needed for our constructions.

Definition 1. *In a cyclic group* $\mathbb{G}$ *of prime order* q, *the* **Decisional Diffie-Hellman** (DDH) *problem is to distinguish the distributions*

$$D_0 = \{([\![1]\!], [\![a]\!], [\![b]\!], [\![ab]\!])\} \qquad D_1 = \{([\![1]\!], [\![a]\!], [\![b]\!], [\![c]\!])\}.$$

for $a, b, c \xleftarrow{\$} \mathbb{Z}_q$. *The* DDH *assumption in* $\mathbb{G}$ *assumes that no* ppt *adversary can solve the* DDH *problem with non-negligible probability.*

Definition 2. *In the bilinear setting* $(\mathbb{G}_1, \mathbb{G}_2, \mathbb{G}_t, g_1, g_2, g_t, \mathbf{e}, q)$, *the* **Symmetric eXternal Diffie-Hellman** (SXDH) *assumption makes the* DDH *assumption in both* $\mathbb{G}_1$ *and* $\mathbb{G}_2$.

2.2   Dual Pairing Vector Spaces

Our constructions rely on the *Dual Pairing Vector Spaces* (DPVS) framework in prime-order bilinear group setting $(\mathbb{G}_1, \mathbb{G}_2, \mathbb{G}_t, g_1, g_2, g_t, \mathbf{e}, q)$ and $\mathbb{G}_1, \mathbb{G}_2, \mathbb{G}_t$ are all written additively. The DPVS technique dates back to the seminal work by Okamoto-Takashima [35–37] aiming at adaptive security for ABE as well as IBE, together with the *dual system methodology* introduced by Waters [43]. In [31], the setting for dual systems is composite-order bilinear groups. Continuing on this line of works, Chen *et al.* [19] used prime-order bilinear groups under the SXDH assumption. Let us fix $N \in \mathbb{N}$ and consider $\mathbb{G}_1^N$ having N copies of $\mathbb{G}_1$. Any $\mathbf{x} = [\![(x_1, \ldots, x_N)]\!]_1 \in \mathbb{G}_1^N$ is identified as the vector $(x_1, \ldots, x_N) \in \mathbb{Z}_q^N$.

There is no ambiguity because $\mathbb{G}_1$ is a cyclic group of order q prime. The **0**-vector is $\mathbf{0} = [\![(0,\ldots,0)]\!]_1$. The addition of two vectors in $\mathbb{G}_1^N$ is defined by coordinate-wise addition. The scalar multiplication of a vector is defined by $t \cdot \mathbf{x} := [\![t \cdot (x_1,\ldots,x_N)]\!]_1$, where $t \in \mathbb{Z}_q$ and $\mathbf{x} = [\![(x_1,\ldots,x_N)]\!]_1$. The additive inverse of $\mathbf{x} \in \mathbb{G}_1^N$ is defined to be $-\mathbf{x} := [\![(-x_1,\ldots,-x_N)]\!]_1$. Viewing $\mathbb{Z}_q^N$ as a vector space of dimension N over $\mathbb{Z}_q$ with the notions of bases, we can obtain naturally a similar notion of bases for $\mathbb{G}_1^N$. More specifically, any invertible matrix $B \in GL_N(\mathbb{Z}_q)$ identifies a basis $\mathbf{B}$ of $\mathbb{G}_1^N$, whose i-th row $\mathbf{b}_i$ is $[\![B^{(i)}]\!]_1$, where $B^{(i)}$ is the i-th row of B. The canonical basis $\mathbf{A}$ of $\mathbb{G}_1^N$ consists of $\mathbf{a}_1 := [\![(1,0\ldots,0)]\!]_1, \mathbf{a}_2 := [\![(0,1,0\ldots,0)]\!]_1,\ldots,\mathbf{a}_N := [\![(0,\ldots,0,1)]\!]_1$. It is straightforward that we can write $\mathbf{B} = B \cdot \mathbf{A}$ for any basis $\mathbf{B}$ of $\mathbb{G}_1^N$ corresponding to an invertible matrix $B \in GL_N(\mathbb{Z}_q)$. We write $\mathbf{x} = (x_1,\ldots,x_N)_{\mathbf{B}}$ to indicate the representation of $\mathbf{x}$ in the basis $\mathbf{B}$, i.e. $\mathbf{x} = \sum_{i=1}^N x_i \cdot \mathbf{b}_i$. By convention the writing $\mathbf{x} = (x_1,\ldots,x_N)$ concerns the canonical basis $\mathbf{A}$.

Treating $\mathbb{G}_2^N$ similarly, we can furthermore define a product of two vectors $\mathbf{x} = [\![(x_1,\ldots,x_N)]\!]_1 \in \mathbb{G}_1^N, \mathbf{y} = [\![(y_1,\ldots,y_N)]\!]_2 \in \mathbb{G}_2^N$ by $\mathbf{x} \times \mathbf{y} := \prod_{i=1}^N \mathbf{e}(\mathbf{x}[i], \mathbf{y}[i]) = [\![\langle(x_1,\ldots,x_N),(y_1,\ldots,y_N)\rangle]\!]_t$. Given a basis $\mathbf{B} = (\mathbf{b}_i)_{i\in[N]}$ of $\mathbb{G}_1^N$, we define $\mathbf{B}^*$ to be a basis of $\mathbb{G}_2^N$ by first defining $B' := (B^{-1})^\top$ and the i-th row $\mathbf{b}_i^*$ of $\mathbf{B}^*$ is $[\![B'^{(i)}]\!]_2$. It holds that $B \cdot (B')^\top = I_N$ the identity matrix and $\mathbf{b}_i \times \mathbf{b}_j^* = [\![\delta_{i,j}]\!]_t$ for every $i,j \in [N]$, where $\delta_{i,j} = 1$ if and only if $i = j$. We call the pair $(\mathbf{B}, \mathbf{B}^*)$ a *pair of dual orthogonal bases* of $(\mathbb{G}_1^N, \mathbb{G}_2^N)$. If $\mathbf{B}$ is constructed by a random invertible matrix $B \xleftarrow{\$} GL_N(\mathbb{Z}_q)$, we call the resulting $(\mathbf{B}, \mathbf{B}^*)$ a pair of random dual bases. A DPVS is a bilinear group setting $(\mathbb{G}_1, \mathbb{G}_2, \mathbb{G}_t, g_1, g_2, g_t, \mathbf{e}, q, N)$ with dual orthogonal bases. In this work, we also use extensively *basis changes* over dual orthogonal bases of a DPVS to argue the steps of switching key as well as ciphertext vectors to semi-functional mode in our proofs. The details of such basis changes are recalled in the full version [34].

2.3   Access Structure and Linear Secret Sharing Schemes

We recall below the vocabularies of access structures and linear secret sharing schemes that will be used in this work. Let $\mathsf{Att} = \{\mathsf{att}_1, \mathsf{att}_2, \ldots, \mathsf{att}_m\}$ be a finite universe of attributes. An *access structure* over Att is a family $\mathbb{A} \subseteq 2^{\mathsf{Att}} \setminus \{\varnothing\}$. A set in $\mathbb{A}$ is said to be *authorized*; otherwise it is *unauthorized*. An access structure $\mathbb{A}$ is *monotone* if $\mathsf{S}_1 \subseteq \mathsf{S}_2 \subseteq \mathsf{Att}$ and $\mathsf{S}_1 \in \mathbb{A}$ imply $\mathsf{S}_2 \in \mathbb{A}$. Given a set of attributes $\mathsf{S} \subseteq \mathsf{Att}$, we write $\mathbb{A}(\mathsf{S}) = 1$ if and only if there exists $A \subseteq \mathsf{S}$ such that A is authorized. A secret sharing scheme for an access structure $\mathbb{A}$ over the attributes $\mathsf{Att} = \{\mathsf{att}_1, \mathsf{att}_2, \ldots, \mathsf{att}_m\}$ allows sharing a secret s among the m attributes att_j for $1 \leq j \leq m$, such that: (1) Any authorized set in $\mathbb{A}$ can be used to reconstruct s from the shares of its elements; (2) Given any unauthorized set and its shares, the secret s is statistically identical to a uniform random value. We will use *linear secret sharing schemes* (LSSS), which is recalled below:

Definition 3 (LSSS [11]). *Let K be a field, $d, f \in \mathbb{N}$, and Att be a finite universe of attributes. A* Linear Secret Sharing Scheme LSSS *over K for an access structure $\mathbb{A}$ over Att is specified by a share-generating matrix $\mathbf{A} \in K^{d \times f}$ such that for* *any $I \subset [d]$, there exists a vector $\mathbf{c} \in K^d$ with support I and $\mathbf{c} \cdot \mathbf{A} = (1, 0, \ldots, 0)$ if and only if $\{\mathsf{att}_i \mid i \in I\} \in \mathbb{A}$.*

In order to share s using an LSSS over K, one first picks uniformly random values $v_2, v_3, \ldots, v_f \xleftarrow{\$} K$ and the share for an attribute att_i is the i-th coordinate $\mathbf{s}[i]$ of the share vector $\mathbf{s} := (s, v_2, v_3, \ldots, v_f) \cdot \mathbf{A}^\top$. Then, only an authorized set $\{\mathsf{att}_i \mid i \in I\} \in \mathbb{A}$ for some $I \subseteq [d]$ can recover $\mathbf{c}$ to reconstruct s from the shares by: $\mathbf{c} \cdot \mathbf{s}^\top = \mathbf{c} \cdot (\mathbf{A} \cdot (s, v_2, v_3, \ldots, v_f)^\top) = s$. Some canonical examples of LSSS include Shamir's secret sharing scheme for any f-out-of-d threshold gate [41] or Benaloh and Leichter's scheme for any monotone formula [13]. An access structure $\mathbb{A}$ is said to be LSSS-*realizable* if there exists a linear secret sharing scheme implementing $\mathbb{A}$.

Let $y \in \mathbb{Z}_q$ where q is prime and for the sake of simplicity, let $\mathsf{Att} \subset \mathbb{Z}_q$ be a set of attributes. Let $\mathbb{A}$ be a monotone access structure over Att realizable by an LSSS over $\mathbb{Z}_q$. A *random labeling* procedure $\Lambda_y(\mathbb{A})$ is a secret sharing of y using LSSS:

$$\Lambda_y(\mathbb{A}) := (y, v_2, v_3, \ldots, v_f) \cdot \mathbf{A}^\top \in \mathbb{Z}_q^d \tag{1}$$

where $\mathbf{A} \in \mathbb{Z}_q^{d \times f}$ is the share-generating matrix and $v_2, v_3, \ldots, v_f \xleftarrow{\$} \mathbb{Z}_q$.

2.4 The Masking Lemma

We state a technical lemma that is employed throughout our proofs. A detailed proof can be found in the full version [34]. The general purposes of the variables τ, x, y, z_j in the lemma are discussed in the technical overview in Sect. 3.2.

Lemma 4 (Adapted from [24,35–37]). *Let $\mathbb{A}$ be an LSSS-realizable over a set of attributes $\mathsf{Att} \subseteq \mathbb{Z}_q$. We denote by $\mathsf{List-Att}(\mathbb{A})$ the list of attributes appearing in $\mathbb{A}$ and by P the cardinality of $\mathsf{List-Att}(\mathbb{A})$. Let $\mathsf{S} \subseteq \mathsf{Att}$ be a set of attributes. Let $(\mathbf{H}, \mathbf{H}^*)$ and $(\mathbf{F}, \mathbf{F}^*)$ be two random dual bases of $(\mathbb{G}_1^2, \mathbb{G}_2^2)$ and $(\mathbb{G}_1^8, \mathbb{G}_2^8)$, respectively. The vectors $(\mathbf{h}_1, \mathbf{f}_1, \mathbf{f}_2, \mathbf{f}_3)$ are public, while all other vectors are secret. Suppose we have two random labelings $(a_j)_{j \in \mathsf{List-Att}(\mathbb{A})} \leftarrow \Lambda_{a_0}(\mathbb{A})$ and $(a'_j)_j \leftarrow \Lambda_{a'_0}(\mathbb{A})$ for $a_0, a'_0 \xleftarrow{\$} \mathbb{Z}_q$. Then, under the SXDH assumption in $(\mathbb{G}_1, \mathbb{G}_2)$, the following two distributions are computationally indistinguishable:*

$$D_1 := \begin{cases} x, y & \\ \forall j \in \mathsf{S}: \mathbf{c}_j & = (\sigma_j \cdot (1, -j),\ \psi,\ 0,\ 0,\ 0,\ 0,\ 0)_{\mathbf{F}} \\ \forall j \in \mathsf{List-Att}(\mathbb{A}): \mathbf{k}_j^* & = (\pi_j \cdot (j, 1),\ a_j \cdot z,\ 0,\ 0,\ 0,\ 0,\ 0)_{\mathbf{F}^*} \\ \mathbf{c}_{\mathsf{root}} & = (\psi,\ 0)_{\mathbf{H}} \\ \mathbf{k}_{\mathsf{root}}^* & = (a_0 \cdot z,\ 0)_{\mathbf{H}^*} \end{cases}$$

and

$$D_2 := \begin{cases} x, y \\ \forall\, j \in \mathsf{S}: \ \mathbf{c}_j & = (\sigma_j \cdot (1, -j),\ \psi,\ 0,\ 0,\ \boxed{\tau z_j \cdot x},\ 0,\ 0)_{\mathbf{F}} \\ \forall\, j \in \mathsf{List-Att}(\mathbb{A}): \ \mathbf{k}_j^* = (\pi_j \cdot (j, 1),\ a_j \cdot z,\ 0,\ 0,\ \boxed{a_j' \cdot y/z_j},\ 0,\ 0)_{\mathbf{F}^*} \\ \mathbf{c}_{\mathsf{root}} & = (\psi,\ \boxed{\tau \cdot x})_{\mathbf{H}} \\ \mathbf{k}_{\mathsf{root}}^* & = (a_0 \cdot z,\ \boxed{a_0' \cdot y})_{\mathbf{H}^*} \end{cases}$$

for any $x, y \in \mathbb{Z}_q$ and $z_j, \sigma_j, \pi_j, \psi, \tau, z, r_0' \xleftarrow{\$} \mathbb{Z}_q$.

2.5 Functional Encryption with Fine-Grained Access Control

We first present the syntax of functional encryption with a fine-grained access control following the works in [4,30,39]. The functionality class is $\mathcal{F} \times \mathsf{AC-K}$. The evaluation functions is taken from $\mathcal{F} := \{F_\lambda : \mathcal{D}_\lambda \to \mathcal{R}_\lambda\}_\lambda$ is a family of functions indexed by security parameters $\lambda \in \mathbb{N}$. When $F_\lambda, \mathcal{D}_\lambda$, and $\mathcal{R}_\lambda$ are clear from context, we drop the subscript λ and use the shorthands $F, \mathcal{D}$, and $\mathcal{R}$ respectively. The access control is captured by a relation $\mathsf{Rel} : \mathsf{AC-K} \times \mathsf{AC-Ct} \to \{0, 1\}$, for some sets $\mathsf{AC-Ct}$ and $\mathsf{AC-K}$. A plaintext consists of $(\mathsf{ac-ct}, x) \in \mathsf{AC-Ct} \times \mathcal{D}_\lambda$, whose corresponding ciphertext can be decrypted to $F_\lambda(x)$ using the functional key $\mathsf{sk}_{F_\lambda, \mathsf{ac-k}}$ for $\mathsf{ac-k} \in \mathsf{AC-K}$ if and only if $\mathsf{Rel}(\mathsf{ac-k}, \mathsf{ac-ct}) = 1$. The syntax of such functional encryption schemes is given below:

Definition 5 (Functional encryption with fine-grained access control).
A functional encryption scheme with fine-grained access control for $\mathcal{F} \times \mathsf{AC-K}$ consists of four algorithms (Setup, Extract, Enc, Dec):

Setup(1^λ): *Given as input a security parameter λ, output a pair* (pk, msk).
Extract(msk, F_λ, ac$-$k): *Given* ac$-$k $\in$ AC$-$K, *a function description $F_\lambda \in \mathcal{F}$, and the master secret key* msk, *output a secret key* $\mathsf{sk}_{F_\lambda, \mathsf{ac-k}}$.
Enc(pk, x, ac$-$ct): *Given as inputs* ac$-$ct $\in$ AC$-$Ct, *the public key* pk, *and a message $x \in \mathcal{D}_\lambda$, output a ciphertext* ct.
Dec($\mathsf{sk}_{F_\lambda, \mathsf{ac-k}}$, ct): *Given the functional secret key* $\mathsf{sk}_{F_\lambda, \mathsf{ac-k}}$, *and a ciphertext* ct, *output an element in $\mathcal{R}_\lambda$ or an invalid symbol $\bot$.*

Correctness. For sufficiently large $\lambda \in \mathbb{N}$, for all $(F_\lambda, \mathsf{ac-k}) \in \mathcal{F} \times \mathsf{AC-K}$ and (msk, pk) $\leftarrow$ Setup(1^λ), $\mathsf{sk}_{F_\lambda, \mathsf{ac-k}} \leftarrow$ Extract(msk, F_λ, ac$-$k) for all ac$-$ct satisfying $\mathsf{Rel}(\mathsf{ac-k}, \mathsf{ac-ct}) = 1$, it holds with overwhelming probability that

$$\mathsf{Dec}(\mathsf{sk}_{F_\lambda, \mathsf{ac-k}}, \mathsf{Enc}(\mathsf{pk}, x, \mathsf{ac-ct})) = F_\lambda(x) \text{ whenever } F_\lambda(x) \neq \bot,$$

where the probability is taken over the random coins of the algorithms[1].

---

[1] See [1,12] for discussions about this relaxation. The general reason is that some functionality might contain $\bot$ in its range and if $F_\lambda(x) = \bot$ we do not impose $\mathsf{Dec}(\mathsf{sk}_{F_\lambda, \mathsf{ac-k}}, \mathsf{Enc}(\mathsf{pk}, x, \mathsf{ac-ct})) = F_\lambda(x)$, neither do we disallow it..

Security. We recall in the full version [34] the notion of *indistinguishability-based security against chosen-plaintext attacks (IND-CPA)* in the same manner as in [2], taking into account the attribute-based control using policies, as well as a *simulation-based* notion in a selective setting as in [4].

Remark 6. In Sects. 4 and 5, our concrete constructions instantiate $\mathsf{AC-K}$ as a class of policies and $\mathsf{AC-Ct}$ as a superset over an attribute space, while the relation is the natural evaluation $\mathsf{Rel}(\mathbb{A} \in \mathsf{AC-K}, \mathsf{S} \in \mathsf{AC-Ct}) := \mathbb{A}(\mathsf{S})$. Following the terminology of ABE schemes, our constructions are *key-policy* (KP). By treating $\mathsf{AC-K}$ as a superset over an attribute space and $\mathsf{AC-Ct}$ as a class of policies, we will obtain *ciphertext-policy* (CP) schemes. The KP and CP notions are symmetric in terms of how we determine the support $\mathsf{AC-K} \times \mathsf{AC-Ct}$ of Rel.

3   Technical Overview

3.1   Formalizing Access Control in Functional Encryption

First of all, we discuss how we formalize access control in the notion of functional encryption, which will affect our formal definitions in both single-client setting (Definition 5) and multi-client setting (Definition 8). On the one hand, accompanying an encryption scheme with access control over decryption keys is already expressed by ABE, which in itself is a special case of FE. Thus, FE schemes with fine-grained access control can be described by the general FE notion for any class of functions that can handle the desired access control along with the required computation.

On the other hand, when working with concrete functionality, we usually find ourselves in the context where the evaluation *cannot* express the access control and they cannot be described abstractly using a single functionality. Therefore, in this paper we consider FE with access control as FE schemes for *particular* functionality class whose description can be separated into two parts $\mathcal{F} \times \mathsf{AC-K}$: (1) a first part $F \in \mathcal{F}$ for evaluation, (2) and a second part for access control captured by a binary relation $\mathsf{Rel} : \mathsf{AC-K} \times \mathsf{AC-Ct} \to \{0, 1\}$, for some sets $\mathsf{AC-K}, \mathsf{AC-Ct}$. The key extraction is done with respect to $(\mathsf{ac-k} \in \mathsf{AC-K}, F)$, meanwhile the encryption procedure will receive $(\mathsf{ac-ct} \in \mathsf{AC-Ct}, x)$. A key $\mathsf{sk}_{\mathsf{ac-k},F}$ can decrypt a ciphertext $\mathsf{ct}_{\mathsf{ac-ct}}(x)$ to $F(x)$ if and only if $\mathsf{Rel}(\mathsf{ac-k}, \mathsf{ac-ct}) = 1$. We stress that this way of formulation does not take us out of the FE regime, as it is still captured by the general FE notion.

We show how the above formalization is used in a concrete case. In the following discussion we will distinguish the $\boxed{\text{input}}$ during encryption from the $\overline{\text{parameters}}$ during key extraction. In this paper we focus on $F \in \mathcal{F}^{\mathsf{IP}} = \{F_{\mathbf{y}} : \mathbb{Z}_q^n \to \mathbb{Z}_q\}$ for computing inner products over $\mathbb{Z}_q^n$ for some prime q and $n \in \mathbb{N}$, where $F_{\mathbf{y}}(\mathbf{x}) := \langle \mathbf{x}, \mathbf{y} \rangle$. The simplest non-trivial example for access control is identity-based control, i.e. $\mathsf{AC-K} = \mathsf{AC-Ct} = \mathsf{ID}$ for some identity space ID and $\mathsf{Rel}_{\mathsf{ibe}}(\mathsf{id-k}, \mathsf{id-ct}) = \left(\mathsf{id-k} \stackrel{?}{=} \mathsf{id-ct}\right)$. The functional keys are extracted using $\overline{(\mathsf{id-k}, \mathbf{y})}$ and the ciphertexts are encrypted using $\boxed{(\mathsf{id-ct}, \mathbf{x})}$. First of all, it is *not* immediate how $\mathcal{F}^{\mathsf{IP}}$ can be used to implement the check $\tau z \cdot (\boxed{\mathsf{id\text{-}k}} - \boxed{\mathsf{id\text{-}ct}})$ for the identity-based control, where τ and z are random values generated for encryption and key extraction, respectively, together acting as a mask of the decryption value. Notably, the value z *cannot* be specified as part of the inner-product evaluation function, because the inner-product evaluation itself must be independent of users at the time of generating functional keys, *nor* as part of the ciphertext. It thus seems indispensable to treat the functionality as $\mathcal{F}^{\mathsf{IP}} \times \mathsf{ID}$: the functional key is generated w.r.t $F_{\boxed{\mathbf{y}}} \in \mathcal{F}^{\mathsf{IP}}$ and $\boxed{\mathsf{id\text{-}k}} \in \mathsf{ID}$, while the ciphertext is encrypted w.r.t $\boxed{(\mathsf{id\text{-}ct} \in \mathsf{ID}, \mathbf{x} \in \mathbb{Z}_q^n)}$. During decryption for obtaining $\langle \boxed{\mathbf{x}}, \boxed{\mathbf{y}} \rangle + \tau z \cdot (\boxed{\mathsf{id\text{-}k}} - \boxed{\mathsf{id\text{-}ct}})$, the ID-part of the functional key will implement the control $\tau z \cdot (\boxed{\mathsf{id\text{-}k}} - \boxed{\mathsf{id\text{-}ct}})$ whilst the $\mathcal{F}^{\mathsf{IP}}$-part will compute $\langle \boxed{\mathbf{x}}, \boxed{\mathbf{y}} \rangle$.

Treatment of Tags in MCFE with Access Control. As mentioned in the introduction, our current objective is constructing MCFE schemes with access control having smaller ciphertexts. We use the functionality $\mathcal{F}^{\mathsf{IP}} \times \mathsf{ID}$ as a running example. The input $\boxed{\mathbf{x}}$ for inner-product calculation is broken down into n components for the entries x_i of $\boxed{\mathbf{x}}$. The encryption procedure takes $\boxed{(x_i, \mathsf{id\text{-}ct}_i, \mathsf{tag}_i)}$ and outputs a ciphertext component ct_i, for some identity $\boxed{\mathsf{id\text{-}ct}_i}$ and a tag $\boxed{\mathsf{tag}_i}$. The decryption procedure receives a functional key, which is derived from $F_{\boxed{\mathbf{y}}} \in \mathcal{F}^{\mathsf{IP}}$ and $\boxed{\mathsf{id\text{-}k}} \in \mathsf{ID}$, and the n ciphertext components $(\mathsf{ct}_i)_{i=1}^n$. The decrypted result is $\langle \boxed{\mathbf{x}}, \boxed{\mathbf{y}} \rangle$ if $\boxed{\mathsf{id\text{-}ct}_i} = \boxed{\mathsf{id\text{-}k}}$ for all i and $\boxed{\mathsf{tag}_i} = \boxed{\mathsf{tag}_j}$ for all i, j. In the setting that the identities and tags can be public, if the identity control does not pass or if the tags are not the same, a totally random value is returned by the decryption procedure. We now face the same problem of checking equality among $\boxed{\mathsf{tag}_i}$ in the same manner that has to be done for identities from ID.

First of all, it is unlikely that we want to embed the checks $\boxed{\mathsf{tag}_i} \overset{?}{=} \boxed{\mathsf{tag}_j}$ in the $\mathcal{F}^{\mathsf{IP}}$-part. More specifically, we would have to make the decryption compute $(\sum_{i=1}^n \boxed{x_i} \cdot \boxed{y_i}) + \tau z \cdot (\boxed{\mathsf{id\text{-}k}} - \boxed{\mathsf{id\text{-}ct}_i}) + \sum_{i=1}^{n-1} z_i (\boxed{\mathsf{tag}_i} - \boxed{\mathsf{tag}_{i+1}})$ from n ciphertext components ct_i of $\boxed{(x_i, \mathsf{id\text{-}ct}_i)}$, for some random values $z, z_i \overset{\$}{\leftarrow} \mathbb{Z}_q$ and $\boxed{\mathbf{y} = (y_1, ..., y_n)}$. It is worth noting that the check $z_i (\boxed{\mathsf{tag}_i} - \boxed{\mathsf{tag}_{i+1}})$ needs two values defined at encryption time and not key extraction time. Therefore, in order for the functional key to "perform" the n required checks, all n tags $\boxed{(\mathsf{tag}_1, ..., \mathsf{tag}_n)}$ must be encrypted in an IBE-style in ct_i. Roughly speaking, this makes each ct_i of size linear in n, due to the number of group elements required for encrypting the n tags, in addition to a constant number of group elements for encrypting $\boxed{(x_i, \mathsf{id\text{-}ct}_i)}$. Thus the total communication increases to quadratic in n over all n components ct_i, which is exactly what we are trying to avoid.

Furthermore, it might be tempting to embed the equality checks in the access control but because $\boxed{\mathsf{tag}_i, \mathsf{tag}_j}$ are defined only at encryption time, they are unknown to the key extraction for the ID-part. More generally, in a setting that permits a *different*[2] attribute set $\boxed{\mathsf{S}_i}$ in each individual ciphertext, one can try to regard $\boxed{\mathsf{tag}_i}$ as an attribute in $\boxed{\mathsf{S}_i}$. The correctness insists on the condition $\ulcorner\mathbb{A}\urcorner(\boxed{\mathsf{S}_i}) = 1$ for all i and the equality checks $\boxed{\mathsf{tag}_i} \overset{?}{=} \boxed{\mathsf{tag}_j}$ must somehow be done by $\ulcorner\mathbb{A}\urcorner(\boxed{\mathsf{S}_i})$, which is not possible due to the fact that $\boxed{\mathsf{tag}_j}$ is independent of both $\ulcorner\mathbb{A}\urcorner$ and $\boxed{\mathsf{S}_i}$. Consequently, we have to cope with the tags independently from the functionality's description. As a final remark, this also demonstrates the gap between MIFE and MCFE for the concrete functionality to compute inner products under access control by access structures, even though the general notion of MIFE can describe MCFE, provided that the evaluation functions of the underlying functionality class can test equality between $\boxed{\mathsf{tag}_i}$.

3.2   Adaptively Secure Single-Client Construction

Our construction for functional encryption schemes with fine-grained access control is using *Dual Pairing Vector Spaces* (DPVSes). We highlight our main ideas to achieve adaptive security. We refer to Sect. 2.2 for background on DPVSes. Our schemes are key-policy, such that the access structure $\mathbb{A}$ is expressed in the key using vectors $\{(\mathbf{k}_j^*)_{j\in\mathsf{List-Att}(\mathbb{A})}, \mathbf{k}_{\mathsf{root}}\}$ over $\mathbb{G}_2$ and a set S of attributes are embedded in the ciphertext using vectors $\{(\mathbf{c}_j)_{j\in\mathsf{S}}, \mathbf{c}_{\mathsf{root}}\}$ over $\mathbb{G}_1$, where $\mathsf{List-Att}(\mathbb{A})$ is the list of attributes appearing in the access structure $\mathbb{A}$. We use a linear secret sharing scheme based on $\mathbb{A}$ to create the shares $(a_j)_{j\in\mathsf{List-Att}(\mathbb{A})}$ of $a_0 \overset{\$}{\leftarrow} \mathbb{Z}_q$. The shares will then be embedded in the functional secret key components $(\mathbf{k}_j^*)_{j\in\mathsf{List-Att}(\mathbb{A})}$. When all the components corresponding to an authorized set in $\mathbb{A}$ are present, the shares can be combined to reconstruct the secret value a_0, which is now embedded in a key component $\mathbf{k}_{\mathsf{root}}^*$. In all vectors $(\mathbf{c}_j)_j$ and $\mathbf{c}_{\mathsf{root}}$, we put a random value ψ. Intuitively, $[\![\psi a_0]\!]_t$ is masking the IPFE-related ciphertext of Agrawal *et al.*'s type [6]. The vectors $((\mathbf{k}_j^*)_{j\in\mathsf{List-Att}(\mathbb{A})}, \mathbf{k}_{\mathsf{root}}^*)$ and $((\mathbf{c}_j)_{j\in\mathsf{S}}, \mathbf{c}_{\mathsf{root}})$ lie in the dual orthogonal bases. Performing the products $\mathbf{c}_j \times \mathbf{k}_j^*$ and combining over $j \in \mathsf{S}$, where S is an authorized set, will permit recovering $[\![\psi a_0]\!]_t$ that can be used to cancel out $[\![\psi a_0]\!]_t$ in $\mathbf{c}_{\mathsf{root}} \times \mathbf{k}_{\mathsf{root}}$:

$$
\begin{aligned}
\mathbf{c}_j \; (\; \cdots \; | \; \psi \; | \; 0 \; | \; \cdots \;)_{\mathbf{F}} \; &; \quad \mathbf{c}_{\mathsf{root}} \; (\; \cdots \; | \; \psi \; | \; 0 \; | \; \cdots \;)_{\mathbf{H}} \\
\mathbf{k}_j^* \; (\; \cdots \; | \; a_j \; | \; 0 \; | \; \cdots \;)_{\mathbf{F}^*} \; &; \quad \mathbf{k}_{\mathsf{root}}^* \; (\; \cdots \; | \; a_0 \; | \; 0 \; | \; \cdots \;)_{\mathbf{H}^*}
\end{aligned}
$$

We use the techniques for adaptively-secure ABE introduced in the original work of Okamoto and Takashima [35–37] in the ensuing steps. In vein of the *dual-system methodology*, there are two modes of operation for keys and ciphertexts: a normal mode and a *semi-functional* mode. A normal key can decrypt any ciphertext, a semi-functional key can decrypt only normal ciphertexts, and decrypting semi-functional ciphertexts using semi-functional keys gives totally

---

[2] If all clients must use the *same* set of attributes $\boxed{\mathsf{S}}$, we can treat $\boxed{\mathsf{tag}_i}$ as a virtual attribute in S, while enforcing the same $\boxed{\mathsf{S}}$ for all i. This implies that all $\boxed{\mathsf{tag}_i}$ must be the same. However, this approach requires a consensus among all n clients on S, which general might be more complicated than agreeing on tag.

random values. The dual-system method proves security by a sequence of indistinguishable changes to make the challenge ciphertext semi-functional, then to make the keys semi-functional and in the end the challenge message will be perfectly hidden from the adversary. Interestingly, there is a twist stemming from the security model when integrating this technique into our security proofs for FE with access control: an adversary can additionally query for keys that work with the challenge ciphertext, i.e. the key's policy is satisfied. So as to achieve adaptive security, we have to be much more careful about which key to turn semi-functional, because the keys whose policies are satisfied should be capable of decrypting the (semi-functional) challenge ciphertext.

Our goal is to mask the value a_0 in $\mathbf{k}^*_{\mathsf{root}}$ by introducing a random mask $a'_0 y$ in the coordinate of *hidden* basis vectors, i.e. those that are not used at all in real life and are defined only for the proof, while the facing coordinate in $\mathbf{c}_{\mathsf{root}}$ is also changed to τx so as to mask ψ:

$$\mathbf{c}_j \ (\ \cdots\ |\ \psi\ |\ \boxed{\tau x z_j}\ |\ \cdots\ )_{\mathbf{F}}\ ; \quad \mathbf{c}_{\mathsf{root}}\ (\ \cdots\ |\ \psi\ |\ \boxed{\tau x}\ |\ \cdots\ )_{\mathbf{H}}$$
$$\mathbf{k}^*_j \ (\ \cdots\ |\ a_j\ |\ \boxed{a'_j y / z_j}\ |\ \cdots\ )_{\mathbf{F}^*}\ ; \quad \mathbf{k}^*_{\mathsf{root}}\ (\ \cdots\ |\ a_0\ |\ \boxed{a'_0 y}\ |\ \cdots\ )_{\mathbf{H}^*}\ .$$

The values x, y are known constants, $\tau, a'_0, (z_j)_j \xleftarrow{\$} \mathbb{Z}_q$, and $(a'_j)_{j \in \mathsf{List-Att}(\mathbb{A})}$ is another ensemble of secret shares for a'_0. Consequently, this will introduce a value $[\![\tau a'_0 x y]\!]_{\mathsf{t}}$ masking $[\![\psi a_0]\!]_{\mathsf{t}}$ when performing the product $\mathbf{c}_{\mathsf{root}} \times \mathbf{k}_{\mathsf{root}}$. We note that the value a'_0 is related to $(a'_j / z_j)_j$ by $a'_0 = \sum_{j \in \mathsf{S}'} z_j \cdot (a'_j / z_j)$ for any S' such that $\mathbb{A}(\mathsf{S}') = 1$. In the end, if $\mathbb{A}(\mathsf{S}) = 1$, from $\mathbf{c}_j$ and $\mathbf{k}_j$ it is possible to reconstruct $[\![\tau a'_0 x y]\!]_{\mathsf{t}}$ and recover $[\![\psi a_0]\!]_{\mathsf{t}}$. Otherwise, the entropy of a'_0 is preserved thanks to the randomness provided by $z_j \xleftarrow{\$} \mathbb{Z}_q$ for randomizing $(a'_j)_j$ to $(a'_j / z_j)_j$ in the components $(\mathbf{c}_j)_j$ of the *unique* challenge ciphertext[3], as well as the fact that $\mathbb{A}(\mathsf{S}) = 0$ means there will be some a'_j / z_j missing in the components $(\mathbf{k}^*_j)_j$ and the value z_j is information-theoretically hidden. Hence, if $\mathbb{A}(\mathsf{S}) = 0$ we will be able to change a'_0 to an independent and uniformly random value $r_0 \xleftarrow{\$} \mathbb{Z}^*_q$. It is obligatory that we apply this argument *key by key*, while considering the key's capability to decrypt the challenge ciphertext, because two different keys might mutually leak information about the same z_j and our statistical argument no longer holds. After a sequence of hybrids on the functional key queries, we can mask all the keys as desired so that the key and the challenge ciphertext will become readily semi-functional for later steps in the proof.

However, only for functional keys whose policy is not satisfied can we perform such a change from a'_0 to r_0, and we can decide the satisfiability only when the adversary adaptively queries for functional keys. Our idea is to introduce r_0 in *all* key components and at the same time use a mechanism to "cancel out" the masks $((a'_j / z_j)_j, r_0)$ in $((\mathbf{k}^*_j)_{j \in \mathsf{List-Att}(\mathbb{A})}, \mathbf{k}^*_{\mathsf{root}})$ if $\mathbb{A}(\mathsf{S}) = 1$. It is indispensable to have this mechanism because otherwise, as soon as we change a'_0 to r_0, even the reconstruction $\sum_{j \in \mathsf{S}'} z_j \cdot (a'_j / z_j) = a'_0$ is not able to remove r_0 for a correct decryption. In our particular setting for computing inner-products, we observe

---

[3] Since our single-client scheme is public-key, we can obtain multi-challenge security using a standard hybrid argument.

that if $\mathbb{A}(S) = 1$, then $\langle \Delta \mathbf{x}, \mathbf{y} \rangle = 0$ for the sake of avoiding trivial attacks, where $\Delta \mathbf{x} := \mathbf{x}_1^* - \mathbf{x}_0^*$ is the difference of the two left-or-right challenge messages and $\mathbf{y}$ is specified the functional key. In the selective setting where $\Delta \mathbf{x}$ is known in advance, the key and ciphertext components can simply be masked using the constants $(x, y) := (1, \langle \Delta \mathbf{x}, \mathbf{y} \rangle)$. However, for the goal of adaptive security where $\Delta \mathbf{x}$ is unknown at the time of key extraction, we have to make a trade-off and use DPVSes of dimensions linear in the dimension n of vectors for inner-products and mask the key and ciphertext components as follows:

$$
\begin{array}{llllll}
\mathbf{c}_j & (\cdots & \psi & \boxed{\tau z_j \Delta \mathbf{x}[1]} & \cdots & \boxed{\tau z_j \Delta \mathbf{x}[n]} & \cdots)_{\mathbf{F}} \\
\mathbf{k}_j^* & (\cdots & a_j & \boxed{a_j' \mathbf{y}[1]/z_j} & \cdots & \boxed{a_j' \mathbf{y}[n]/z_j} & \cdots)_{\mathbf{F}^*} \\
\mathbf{c}_{\text{root}} & (\cdots & \psi & \boxed{\tau \Delta \mathbf{x}[1]} & \cdots & \boxed{\tau \Delta \mathbf{x}[n]} & \cdots)_{\mathbf{H}} \\
\mathbf{k}_{\text{root}}^* & (\cdots & a_0 & \boxed{r_0 \mathbf{y}[1]} & \cdots & \boxed{r_0 \mathbf{y}[n]} & \cdots)_{\mathbf{H}^*}
\end{array}
$$

where each i-th pair of constants (x, y) is set to $(\Delta \mathbf{x}[i], \mathbf{y}[i])$ for all $i \in [n]$. Our arguments resort to a slight variant of the technique in [35–37], stated as a technical lemma (see Lemma 4) in Sect. 2.4. The lemma will use some auxiliary hidden vectors (which we do not show here) during the masking process and so as to economize the dimensions of our DPVSes, we apply the lemma n times in a sequence of hybrids to introduce $(\tau \Delta \mathbf{x}[i], r_0 \mathbf{y}[i])_i$ while reusing and cleaning those auxiliary hidden vectors after each application. After successfully laying $(r_0 \mathbf{y}[i])_i$ in place, the rest of the proof will use r_0 as a source of randomness to completely hide the challenge message. Our single-client constructions are presented in Sect. 4.

3.3 The "Duplicate-and-Compress" Technique

We give a glimpse of our main technical method to obtain a multi-client construction from our single-client construction, while maintaining the total ciphertext's size of order linear in n. The intriguing point we observe is as long as each client uses an independent DPVS, the technique we use to take care of the ciphertext/key vectors in the single-client case can be carried out in a *parallel* manner, to some extent. Therefore, in the security proof, we can distribute and accumulate in parallel the necessary information in small-dimension vectors rather than centralizing such information in few vectors of big dimension. Our treatment for the multi-client setting is twofold and we give below the main technical ideas.

The More Restrictive MCFE. Firstly, Sect. 5.2 presents a construction that enforces the same $S_1 = \cdots = S_n = S$ for all clients, by hashing it using a full-domain hash function modeled as a random oracle (RO), along with the tag at the time of encryption. Indeed, we will use an argument resembling what we do in the single-client construction and perform a masking procedure key by key, where the functional key query for $(\mathbb{A}, \mathbf{y}^{(\ell)})$ is indexed by ℓ. For each $i \in [n]$, we mask $(\mathbf{k}_{i,j}^*)_j = (..., a_{i,j}^{(\ell)}, a_{i,j}'^{(\ell)} y/z_j, ...)_j, \mathbf{k}_{i,\text{root}}^* = (..., a_{i,0}^{(\ell)}, a_{i,0}'^{(\ell)} y, ...)$ and $(\mathbf{c}_{i,j})_j = (..., \psi_i, \tau x z_j, ...)_j, \mathbf{c}_{i,\text{root}} = (..., \psi_i, \tau x, ...)$, where $(a_{i,j}^{(\ell)})_j, (a_{i,j}'^{(\ell)})_j$ are secret shares of $a_{i,0}^{(\ell)}, a_{i,0}'^{(\ell)}$ respectively. In this more restrictive case of Sect. 5.2 where all

n clients use the same S, it entails all clients $i \in [n]$ using the same $a_0^{(\ell)}, a_0'^{(\ell)}$ with their secret shares $(a_j^{(\ell)})_j, (a_j'^{(\ell)})_j$ in $(\mathbf{k}_{i,j}^*)_j = (..., a_j^{(\ell)}, a_j'^{(\ell)} y / z_j, ...)_j$ and $\mathbf{k}_{i,\text{root}}^* = (..., a_0^{(\ell)}, a_0'^{(\ell)} y, ...)$. Afterwards, we want to replace $a_0'^{(\ell)}$ by an independent and uniformly random value $r_0^{(\ell)} \overset{\$}{\leftarrow} \mathbb{Z}_q^*$ if $\mathbb{A}(S_i) = 0$ and clearing the masks otherwise. As our first observation, the reasoning is still based crucially on the fact that in S there will lack some j whose corresponding z_j permits recovering $a_0'^{(\ell)} = \sum_j z_j (a_j'^{(\ell)} / z_j)$ if $\mathbb{A}(S) = 0$. It gets clear that as long as $\mathbb{A}(S) = 0$, for all i independently, the same argument will hold because all i use the same set S of attributes. This observation leads to a *compression* of all $(\mathbf{c}_{i,j})_j, (\mathbf{k}_{i,j}^*)_j$ into one pair of dual bases $(\mathbf{F}, \mathbf{F}^*)$ instead of n separate pairs for each $i \in [n]$. As a second observation, when $\mathbb{A}(S) = 1$, all ciphertext components must be combined together for a correct decryption. As a result, to program the canceling mechanism, instead of naively embedding n pairs of constants $(\Delta \mathbf{x}[k], \mathbf{y}^{(\ell)}[k])_{k=1}^n$ in $(\mathbf{c}_{i,\text{root}}, (\mathbf{c}_{i,j})_j, \mathbf{k}_{i,\text{root}}^*, (\mathbf{k}_{i,j}^*)_j)$ for *each* i, we only need to embed $(\Delta \mathbf{x}[i], \mathbf{y}^{(\ell)}[i])$ in $(\mathbf{c}_{i,\text{root}}, (\mathbf{c}_{i,j})_j, \mathbf{k}_{i,\text{root}}^*, (\mathbf{k}_{i,j}^*)_j)$. The grouping by i of the products $\mathbf{c}_{i,\text{root}} \times \mathbf{k}_{i,\text{root}}^*$ as well as $\sum_j \mathbf{c}_{i,j} \times \mathbf{k}_{i,j}^*$ will retrieve $[\![\tau r_0^{(\ell)} \langle \Delta \mathbf{x}, \mathbf{y}^{(\ell)} \rangle]\!]_{\mathrm{t}}$ and we proceed the remaining as in the single-client proof. We point out that in the multi-client setting, it might be the case that some i are corrupted and the retrieval of $[\![\tau r_0^{(\ell)} \langle \Delta \mathbf{x}, \mathbf{y}^{(\ell)} \rangle]\!]_{\mathrm{t}}$ is more complicated when regrouping over i. However, by carefully defining (see Definition 9) and considering only *admissible* adversaries, i.e. they cannot win by trivial attacks[4], it remains the case. This individual insertion of $(\Delta \mathbf{x}[i], \mathbf{y}^{(\ell)}[i])$ for each i leads to a *duplication* of one pair of dual bases $(\mathbf{H}_i, \mathbf{H}_i^*)$ for each $(\mathbf{c}_{i,\text{root}}, \mathbf{k}_{i,\text{root}}^*)$, while all $(\mathbf{c}_{i,j})_j, (\mathbf{k}_{i,j}^*)_j$ are readily put in the same basis following our first observation:

(Compressing) for all $i \in [n]$	$\mathbf{c}_{i,j}$	$(\cdots$	ψ	$\tau \Delta \mathbf{x}[i] z_j$	$\cdots)_{\mathbf{F}}$
	$\mathbf{k}_{i,j}^*$	$(\cdots$	$a_j^{(\ell)}$	$a_j'^{(\ell)} \mathbf{y}^{(\ell)}[i] / z_j$	$\cdots)_{\mathbf{F}^*}$
(Duplicating) for each $i \in [n]$	$\mathbf{c}_{i,\text{root}}$	$(\cdots$	ψ	$\tau \Delta \mathbf{x}[i]$	$\cdots)_{\mathbf{H}_i}$
	$\mathbf{k}_{i,\text{root}}^*$	$(\cdots$	$a_0^{(\ell)}$	$a_0'^{(\ell)} \mathbf{y}^{(\ell)}[i]$	$\cdots)_{\mathbf{H}_i^*}$

We emphasize that this parallel process is feasible thanks to a conveniently smooth control, as low as the level of the vectors' coordinates in DPVSes. This potential of parallelization helps us spread the necessary information for answering adaptive key queries, which accounts for the linearly large dimension, into n collections $\{(\mathbf{k}_{i,j}^*)_{j \in \mathsf{List-Att}(\mathbb{A})}, \mathbf{k}_{i,\text{root}}^*\}_{i \in [n]}$. On the one hand, we change the vectors $(\mathbf{k}_{i,j}^*, \mathbf{c}_{i,j})_{i,j}$ in parallel for all i, while these vectors are written in bases $(\mathbf{F}, \mathbf{F}^*)$. On the other hand, we change the vectors $(\mathbf{k}_{i,\text{root}}^*, \mathbf{c}_{i,\text{root}})_i$ independently for each client i, using the fact that each pair $(\mathbf{k}_{i,\text{root}}^*, \mathbf{c}_{i,\text{root}})$ belong to a separate pair of dual bases $(\mathbf{H}_i, \mathbf{H}_i^*)$. In the end, instead of using n bases of dimension n, we can use n bases of *constant* dimension for $(\mathbf{k}_{i,\text{root}}^*)_i$ along with one *constant-dimension* basis for all $\{(\mathbf{k}_{i,j}^*)_{j \in \mathsf{List-Att}(\mathbb{A})}\}_i$, saving a factor n in the ciphertext's size.

---

[4] For instance, the adversary might corrupt i^*, query a left-or-right challenge $(\mathbf{x}_0, \mathbf{x}_1)$ where $\Delta \mathbf{x}[i^*] := \mathbf{x}_0[i^*] - \mathbf{x}_1[i^*] \neq 0$ and $\Delta \mathbf{x}[i] = 0$ for $i \neq i^*$, then decrypt the challenge ciphertext with a satisfied key for $\mathbf{y}^{(\ell)}$ whose i^*-th entry is non-zero.

The More Flexible MCFE. Section 5.4 discusses an extension of the above MCFE construction where we do not impose the same set of attributes among n clients. Each client i can now encrypt using a different S_i and the decryption can decrypt the inner-product if and only if $\mathbb{A}(S_i) = 1$ for all i. Unsurprisingly, our argument as it is from the previous construction, for masking and for replacing $a'^{(\ell)}_{i,0}$ by an independent and uniformly random value, does not hold anymore because there might be two keys corresponding to $\mathbb{A}^{(\ell)}$ and $\mathbb{A}^{(\ell')}$ such that $\mathbb{A}^{(\ell)}(S_i) \neq \mathbb{A}^{(\ell')}(S_i)$ and the adversary might try to use key components of the ℓ'-th query to recover $a'^{(\ell)}_{i,0}$ in the ℓ-th query. We thus make use of another layer of random secret shares $(d_{\ell,i})_{i=1}^{n}$ over n components of each ℓ-th functional key, facing θ_i in the ciphertext components such that $\sum_{i=1}^{n} \theta_i d_{\ell,i} = 0$. The values $(\theta_i)_i$ are generated as part of the master secret key but $(d_{\ell,i})_{i=1}^{n}$ are chosen independently for each key. A fully working key can be obtain only if all the n components corresponding to $(d_{\ell,i})_{i=1}^{n}$ are combined. That will prevent the adversary from trying to mix components between two different keys, i.e. if $\mathbb{A}^{(\ell)}(S_i) = 0$ we can be sure that $a'^{(\ell)}_{i,0}$ retains its entropy and stays hidden. After a similar masking step using the secret shares $(a'^{(\ell)}_{i,j})_j$ of $a'^{(\ell)}_{i,0}$ independently generated for each i, the randomness provided by $(d_{\ell,i})_{i=1}^{n}$ allows us to tweak $a'^{(\ell)}_{i,0}$ with a uniformly random value $r_0^{(\ell)}$:

(Compressing) for all $i \in [n]$	$\mathbf{c}_{i,j}$	$(\cdots$	ψ	$\tau \Delta \mathbf{x}[i] z_j$	$\cdots$	$\cdots)_{\mathbf{F}}$
	$\mathbf{k}_{i,j}^*$	$(\cdots$	$a_j^{(\ell)}$	$a'^{(\ell)}_{i,j} \mathbf{y}^{(\ell)}[i]/z_j$	$\cdots$	$\cdots)_{\mathbf{F}^*}$
(Duplicating) for each $i \in [n]$	$\mathbf{c}_{i,\text{root}}$	$(\cdots$	ψ	$\tau \Delta \mathbf{x}[i]$	θ_i	$\cdots)_{\mathbf{H}_i}$
	$\mathbf{k}_{i,\text{root}}^*$	$(\cdots$	$a_0^{(\ell)}$	$(a'^{(\ell)}_{i,0} + r_0^{(\ell)}) \mathbf{y}^{(\ell)}[i]$	$d_{\ell,i}$	$\cdots)_{\mathbf{H}_i^*}$

It is of the utmost importance that we rely on $(d_{\ell,i})_{i=1}^{n}$, which is particular for each ℓ-th key, to carry out this change from $a'^{(\ell)}_{i,0}$ to $a'^{(\ell)}_{i,0} + r_0^{(\ell)}$. Or else, the adversary can mix and match the ℓ-th and ℓ'-th keys to remove $a'^{(\ell)}_{i,0}$ and distinguish the adding of $r_0^{(\ell)}$, regardless whether S_i is authorized or not. The argument is now computational, in contrast to the information-theoretical indistinguishability when changing from $a_0'^{(\ell)}$ to $r_0^{(\ell)}$ in the more restrictive MCFE. We now perform an unmasking by going backwards to remove the sharing $(a'^{(\ell)}_{i,j})_j$ and $a'^{(\ell)}_{i,0}$ in the key. This transition is completely symmetric. If $\mathbb{A}(S_i) = 1$ for all i, then the admissibility requires $\langle \Delta \mathbf{x}, \mathbf{y}^{(\ell)} \rangle = 0$ and the noise $\tau r_0^{(\ell)}$ can be removed. Otherwise, in case $\langle \Delta \mathbf{x}, \mathbf{y}^{(\ell)} \rangle \neq 0$, the mask $\tau r_0^{(\ell)}$ persists but the admissibility implies there exists i such that $\mathbb{A}(S_i) = 0$ and the functional key cannot decrypt the challenge ciphertext. We emphasize that the incapability of the key when $\mathbb{A}(S_i) = 0$ is ensured by $(d_{\ell,i})_{i=1}^{n}$. After introducing $r_0^{(\ell)}$, the remaining steps resemble the proof of the less flexible construction in Sect. 5.2. A desirable byproduct of this more flexible construction is that the hash function, which is modeled as a random oracle (RO), is now applied only on the tag. Therefore, we can obtain an MIFE in the standard model that is comparable to the work in [4] by fixing the hash value of a tag for all ciphertexts and publishing it as a parameter of the scheme.

4 Single-Client Functional Encryption for Inner-product with Fine-Grained Access Control via LSSS

We present constructions of FE for the inner-product functionality with attribute-based control expressed using linear secret sharing schemes, starting with the simpler single-client setting. We are in the bilinear group $(\mathbb{G}_1, \mathbb{G}_2, \mathbb{G}_t, g_1, g_2, g_t, \mathbf{e}, q)$ and $\mathbb{G}_1, \mathbb{G}_2, \mathbb{G}_t$ are written additively. The function class of interests is $\mathcal{F}^{\mathsf{IP}} \times \mathsf{LSSS}$ where $\mathcal{F}^{\mathsf{IP}}$ contains $F_{\mathbf{y}} : \left(\mathbb{Z}_q^*\right)^n \to \mathbb{Z}_q$ defined as $F_{\mathbf{y}}(\mathbf{x}) := \langle \mathbf{x}, \mathbf{y} \rangle$. The access control is given by $\mathsf{Rel} : \mathsf{LSSS} \times 2^{\mathsf{Att}} \to \{0, 1\}$, where $\mathsf{Rel}(\mathbb{A}, \mathsf{S}) = \mathbb{A}(\mathsf{S})$, the class LSSS contains Linear Secret Sharing Schemes over Att, and 2^{Att} denotes the superset of an attribute space $\mathsf{Att} \subseteq \mathbb{Z}_q$. Our constructions are key-policy, where $\mathbb{A}$ is embedded in the key and S is specified in the ciphertext. In order to facilitate the understanding and the motivation of our later multi-client constructions in Sect. 5, we present both selectively-secure and adaptively-secure single-client constructions in Fig. 1. We leverage the selectively-secure scheme to obtain the adaptively-secure one by replacing certain elements in the former by $\boxed{\text{the corresponding boxed components}}$ for the latter.

The main difference between the adaptive version and the selectively-secure version is the increase in the dimension of dual bases, from constant dimensions to dimensions linear in n. The details can be found in Fig. 1. The computation for encrypting and decrypting stays essentially the same. We refer to the technical overview in Sect. 3 for the main ideas why using bigger DPVSes allows us to achieve the stronger adaptive notion. The *correctness* can be verified in a straightforward manner. Theorem 7 proves the adaptive IND-security for the construction corresponding to $\boxed{\text{boxed components}}$ in Fig. 1, where the adversary can query a unique challenge ciphertext and multiple functional keys. Using a standard hybrid argument and recalling that our scheme is public-key provide us with adaptive security against multiple challenge ciphertexts. The easier selective security can be proved using similar techniques. Full details can be found in the full version [34].

Theorem 7. *Let $\mathcal{E} = (\mathsf{Setup}, \mathsf{Extract}, \mathsf{Enc}, \mathsf{Dec})$ be an IPFE scheme with fine-grained access control via LSSS presented in Fig. 1 in a bilinear group setting $(\mathbb{G}_1, \mathbb{G}_2, \mathbb{G}_t, g_1, g_2, g_t, \mathbf{e}, q)$, for the functionality class $\mathcal{F}^{\mathsf{IP}} \times \mathsf{LSSS}$. Then, $\mathcal{E}$ is secure against chosen-plaintext attacks, adaptively in the attributes and the challenge messages, if the SXDH assumption holds for $\mathbb{G}_1$ and $\mathbb{G}_2$. More precisely, for $\lambda \in \mathbb{N}$ and for any ppt adversary $\mathcal{A}$, let n be the dimension of vectors for inner-product computation, K denote the total number of functional key queries, and P denote the total number of attributes used by the adversary. We have the following bound:*

$$\mathsf{Adv}^{\mathsf{ind\text{-}cpa}}_{\mathcal{E}, \mathcal{F}^{\mathsf{IP}}, \mathsf{LSSS}, \mathcal{A}}(1^\lambda) \le (2nK \cdot (P(6P + 3) + 2) + 5) \cdot \mathsf{Adv}^{\mathsf{SXDH}}_{\mathbb{G}_1, \mathbb{G}_2}(1^\lambda)$$

where $\mathsf{Adv}^{\mathsf{SXDH}}_{\mathbb{G}_1, \mathbb{G}_2}(1^\lambda)$ denotes the maximum advantage over ppt adversaries against the SXDH problem in $(\mathbb{G}_1, \mathbb{G}_2)$ set up with parameter λ.

Setup(1^λ): Choose two pairs of dual orthogonal bases $(\mathbf{F}, \mathbf{F}^*)$ and $(\mathbf{H}, \mathbf{H}^*)$ where $(\mathbf{H}, \mathbf{H}^*)$ is a pair of bases of the dual pairing vector spaces $(\mathbb{G}_1^4, \mathbb{G}_2^4)$ $\boxed{(\mathbb{G}_1^{n+3}, \mathbb{G}_2^{n+3})}$, and $(\mathbf{F}, \mathbf{F}^*)$ are dual bases of $(\mathbb{G}_1^8, \mathbb{G}_2^8)$ $\boxed{(\mathbb{G}_1^{n+7}, \mathbb{G}_2^{n+7})}$. We write

$$\mathbf{H} = (\mathbf{h}_1, \mathbf{h}_2, \mathbf{h}_3, \mathbf{h}_4) \qquad\qquad \mathbf{H}^* = (\mathbf{h}_1^*, \mathbf{h}_2^*, \mathbf{h}_3^*, \mathbf{h}_4^*)$$

$$\boxed{\mathbf{H} = (\mathbf{h}_1, \mathbf{h}_2, \mathbf{h}_3, \mathbf{h}_4, \ldots, \mathbf{h}_{n+3})} \qquad \boxed{\mathbf{H}^* = (\mathbf{h}_1^*, \mathbf{h}_2^*, \mathbf{h}_3^*, \mathbf{h}_4^*, \ldots, \mathbf{h}_{n+3}^*)}$$

$$\mathbf{F} = (\mathbf{f}_1, \mathbf{f}_2, \mathbf{f}_3, \mathbf{f}_4, \mathbf{f}_5, \mathbf{f}_6, \mathbf{f}_7, \mathbf{f}_8) \qquad \mathbf{F}^* = (\mathbf{f}_1^*, \mathbf{f}_2^*, \mathbf{f}_3^*, \mathbf{f}_4^*, \mathbf{f}_5^*, \mathbf{f}_6^*, \mathbf{f}_7^*, \mathbf{f}_8^*)$$

$$\boxed{\mathbf{F} = (\mathbf{f}_1, \mathbf{f}_2, \mathbf{f}_3, \mathbf{f}_4, \ldots, \mathbf{f}_{n+5}, \mathbf{f}_{n+6}, \mathbf{f}_{n+7})} \quad \boxed{\mathbf{F}^* = (\mathbf{f}_1^*, \mathbf{f}_2^*, \mathbf{f}_3^*, \mathbf{f}_4^*, \ldots, \mathbf{f}_{n+5}^*, \mathbf{f}_{n+6}^*, \mathbf{f}_{n+7}^*)}$$

and sample $\mu, z \xleftarrow{\$} \mathbb{Z}_q^*, S, U \xleftarrow{\$} (\mathbb{Z}_q^*)^n$ and write $S = (s_1, \ldots, s_n)$, $U = (u_1, \ldots, u_n)$. Output the public key and the master secret key as

$$\begin{cases} \mathsf{pk} := (\mathbf{h}_1 + \mu \mathbf{h}_2, \ \mathbf{h}_3, \ (\mathbf{f}_i)_{i \in [3]}, \ ([\![s_i + \mu \cdot u_i]\!]_1)_{i \in [n]}) \\ \mathsf{msk} := (z, \ S, \ U, \ (\mathbf{f}_i^*)_{i \in [3]}, \ (\mathbf{h}_i^*)_{i \in [3]}) \ . \end{cases}$$

Extract($\mathsf{msk}, \mathbb{A}, \mathbf{y} \in \mathbb{Z}_q^n$): Let $\mathbb{A}$ be an LSSS-realizable monotone access structure over a set of attributes $\mathsf{Att} \subseteq \mathbb{Z}_q$. First, sample $a_0 \xleftarrow{\$} \mathbb{Z}_q$ and run the labeling algorithm $\Lambda_{a_0}(\mathbb{A})$ (see (1)) to obtain the labels $(a_j)_j$ where j runs over the attributes in Att. In the end, it holds that $a_0 = \sum_{j \in A} c_j \cdot a_j$ where j runs over an authorized set $A \in \mathbb{A}$ and $\mathbf{c}_A = (c_j)_{j \in A}$ is the reconstruction vector from LSSS w.r.t A. We denote by $\mathsf{List\text{-}Att}(\mathbb{A})$ the list of attributes appearing in $\mathbb{A}$, with possible repetitions. Parse $\mathsf{msk} = (z, S, U, (\mathbf{f}_i^*)_{i \in [3]}, (\mathbf{h}_i^*)_{i \in [3]})$. Compute:

$$\mathbf{k}_j^* := (\pi_j \cdot (j, 1), \ a_j \cdot z, \ 0, \ 0, \ 0, \ 0, \ 0)_{\mathbf{F}^*} \text{ for } j \in \mathsf{List\text{-}Att}(\mathbb{A})$$

$$\boxed{\mathbf{k}_j^* := (\pi_j \cdot (j, 1), \ a_j \cdot z, \overbrace{0, \ldots, 0}^{n \text{ times}}, \ 0, \ 0, \ 0, \ 0)_{\mathbf{F}^*} \text{ for } j \in \mathsf{List\text{-}Att}(\mathbb{A})}$$

$$\mathbf{m}_i^* := [\![\mathbf{y}[i]]\!]_2 \text{ for } i \in [n]$$

$$\mathbf{k}_{\mathsf{ipfe}}^* := (\langle S, \mathbf{y} \rangle, \langle U, \mathbf{y} \rangle, \ a_0 \cdot z, \ 0)_{\mathbf{H}^*} \quad \boxed{\mathbf{k}_{\mathsf{ipfe}}^* := (\langle S, \mathbf{y} \rangle, \langle U, \mathbf{y} \rangle, \ a_0 \cdot z, \overbrace{0, \ldots, 0}^{n \text{ times}})_{\mathbf{H}^*}}$$

where $\pi_j \xleftarrow{\$} \mathbb{Z}_q$. Output $\mathsf{sk}_{\mathbb{A}, \mathbf{y}} := \left((\mathbf{k}_j^*)_j, (\mathbf{m}_i^*)_{i \in [n]}, \mathbf{k}_{\mathsf{ipfe}}^* \right)$.

Enc($\mathsf{pk}, \mathbf{x}, \mathsf{S}$): Parse the public key $\mathsf{pk} = (\mathbf{h}_1 + \mu \mathbf{h}_2, \ \mathbf{h}_3, \ (\mathbf{f}_i)_{i \in [3]}, \ ([\![s_i + \mu \cdot u_i]\!]_1)_{i \in [n]})$ and $\mathsf{S} \subseteq \mathsf{Att} \subseteq \mathbb{Z}_q$ as the set of attributes, then sample $\omega, \psi \xleftarrow{\$} \mathbb{Z}_q$. Compute

$$\mathbf{c}_j = \sigma_j \cdot \mathbf{f}_1 - j \cdot \sigma_j \cdot \mathbf{f}_2 + \psi \cdot \mathbf{f}_3 = (\sigma_j \cdot (1, -j), \ \psi, \ 0, \ 0, \ 0, \ 0, \ 0)_{\mathbf{F}} \text{ for each } j \in \mathsf{S}$$

$$\boxed{\mathbf{c}_j = (\sigma_j \cdot (1, -j), \ \psi, \overbrace{0, \ldots, 0}^{n \text{ times}}, 0, \ 0, \ 0, \ 0)_{\mathbf{F}} \text{ for each } j \in \mathsf{S}}$$

where $\sigma_j \xleftarrow{\$} \mathbb{Z}_q$. Finally, compute

$$\mathbf{t}_i = \omega \cdot [\![s_i + \mu \cdot u_i]\!]_1 + [\![\mathbf{x}[i]]\!]_1 = [\![\omega \cdot (s_i + \mu u_i) + \mathbf{x}[i]]\!]_1 \text{ for } i \in [n]$$

$$\mathbf{c}_{\mathsf{ipfe}} = \omega \cdot (\mathbf{h}_1 + \mu \mathbf{h}_2) + \psi \cdot \mathbf{h}_3 = (\omega, \ \mu \omega, \ \psi, \ 0)_{\mathbf{H}} \quad \boxed{\mathbf{c}_{\mathsf{ipfe}} = (\omega, \ \mu \omega, \ \psi, \ \overbrace{0, \ldots, 0}^{n \text{ times}})_{\mathbf{H}}}$$

where $\sigma_i \xleftarrow{\$} \mathbb{Z}_q$ for every $i \in [n]$ and output $\mathsf{ct} := \left((\mathbf{c}_j)_{j \in \mathsf{S}}, (\mathbf{t}_i)_{i \in [n]}, \mathbf{c}_{\mathsf{ipfe}} \right)$.

Dec($\mathsf{sk}_{\mathbb{A}, \mathbf{y}}, \mathsf{ct}$): Parse $\mathsf{ct} = \left((\mathbf{c}_j)_{j \in \mathsf{S}}, (\mathbf{t}_i)_{i \in [n]}, \mathbf{c}_{\mathsf{ipfe}} \right)$ and $\mathsf{sk}_{\mathbb{A}, \mathbf{y}} := \left((\mathbf{k}_j^*)_{j \in \mathsf{List\text{-}Att}(\mathbb{A})}, (\mathbf{m}_i^*)_{i \in [n]}, \mathbf{k}_{\mathsf{ipfe}}^* \right)$. If there exists $A \subseteq \mathsf{S}$ and $A \in \mathbb{A}$, then compute the reconstruction vector $\mathbf{c} = (c_j)_j$ of the LSSS for A and

$$[\![\mathsf{out}]\!]_{\mathsf{t}} = \sum_{j \in A} \mathbf{c}_j \times (c_j \cdot \mathbf{k}_j^*) + \sum_{i=1}^{n} (e(\mathbf{t}_i, \mathbf{m}_i^*)) - \left(\mathbf{c}_{\mathsf{ipfe}} \times \mathbf{k}_{\mathsf{ipfe}}^* \right)$$

Finally, compute the discrete logarithm and output $\mathsf{out} \in \mathbb{Z}_q$. Else, output $\perp$.

Fig. 1. The selectively-secure and $\boxed{\text{adaptively-secure}}$ single-client constructions for IPFE with fine-grained access control via LSSS. The high-level ideas can be found in the technical overview of Sect. 3 and more details are presented in the full version [34].

5   Multi-Client Functional Encryption for Inner-Product with Fine-Grained Access Control via LSSS

First of all, we define and give the model of security for *multi-client functional encryption with fine-grained access control* in Sect. 5.1. We then present our main contribution by extending our FE scheme in Sect. 4 from the single-client setting to the multi-client setting in Sect. 5.2, for the functionality class to evaluate inner-products under access control by linear secret-sharing schemes. Theorem 14 proves its adaptive security. Finally, in Sect. 5.4 we discuss further our construction and revisit the MIFE regime for comparison with [4].

5.1   Definitions

We extend the notion of functional encryption with fine-grained access control to the multi-client setting. The access control is defined via a relation Rel : $\mathsf{AC-K} \times \mathsf{AC-Ct}_1 \times \cdots \times \mathsf{AC-Ct}_n \to \{0, 1\}$, for some sets $\mathsf{AC-Ct}_1, \ldots, \mathsf{AC-Ct}_n$ and $\mathsf{AC-K}$. A plaintext for client i consists of $(\mathsf{ac-ct}_i, x_i) \in \mathsf{AC-Ct}_i \times \mathcal{D}_\lambda$, whose corresponding ciphertext can be decrypted to $F_\lambda(x)$ using the functional key $\mathsf{sk}_{F_\lambda,\mathsf{ac-k}}$ for $\mathsf{ac-k} \in \mathsf{AC-K}$ if and only if $\mathsf{Rel}(\mathsf{ac-k}, (\mathsf{ac-ct}_i)_i) = 1$.

Definition 8 (Multi-client functional encryption with fine-grained access control). *A* multi-client functional encryption (MCFE) *scheme with fine-grained access control for the functionality class* $\mathcal{F} \times \mathsf{AC-K}$ *consists of four algorithms* (Setup, Extract, Enc, Dec)*:*

$\mathsf{Setup}(1^\lambda)$: *Given as input a security parameter* λ, *output a master secret key* msk *and* $n = n(\lambda)$ *encryption keys* $(\mathsf{ek}_i)_{i \in [n]}$ *where* $n : \mathbb{N} \to \mathbb{N}$ *is a function.*

$\mathsf{Extract}(\mathsf{msk}, F_\lambda, \mathsf{ac-k})$: *Given* $\mathsf{ac-k} \in \mathsf{AC-K}$, *a function description* $F_\lambda \in \mathcal{F}$, *and the master secret key* msk, *output a decryption key* $\mathsf{dk}_{F_\lambda,\mathsf{ac-k}}$.

$\mathsf{Enc}(\mathsf{ek}_i, x_i, \mathsf{tag}, \mathsf{ac-ct}_i)$: *Given as inputs* $\mathsf{ac-ct}_i \in \mathsf{AC-Ct}_i$, *an encryption key* ek_i, *a message* $x_i \in \mathcal{D}_\lambda$, *and a tag* tag, *output a ciphertext* $\mathsf{ct}_{\mathsf{tag},i}$.

$\mathsf{Dec}(\mathsf{dk}_{F_\lambda,\mathsf{ac-k}}, \mathbf{c})$: *Given the decryption key* $\mathsf{dk}_{F_\lambda,\mathsf{ac-k}}$ *and a vector of ciphertexts* $\mathbf{c} := (\mathsf{ct}_{\mathsf{tag},i})_i$ *of length* n, *output an element in* $\mathcal{R}_\lambda$ *or an invalid symbol* $\perp$.

Correctness. For sufficiently large $\lambda \in \mathbb{N}$, for all $(\mathsf{msk}, (\mathsf{ek}_i)_{i \in [n]}) \leftarrow \mathsf{Setup}(1^\lambda)$, $(F_\lambda, \mathsf{ac-k}) \in \mathcal{F} \times \mathsf{AC-K}$ and $\mathsf{dk}_{F_\lambda,\mathsf{ac-k}} \leftarrow \mathsf{Extract}(\mathsf{msk}, F_\lambda, \mathsf{ac-k})$, for all tag and $(\mathsf{ac-ct}_i)_i$ satisfying $\mathsf{Rel}(\mathsf{ac-k}, (\mathsf{ac-ct}_i)_i) = 1$, for all $(x_i)_{i \in [n]} \in \mathcal{D}_\lambda^n$, if $F_\lambda(x_1, \ldots, x_n) \neq \perp$, the following holds with overwhelming probability:

$$\mathsf{Dec}\left(\mathsf{dk}_{F_\lambda,\mathsf{ac-k}}, (\mathsf{Enc}(\mathsf{ek}_i, x_i, \mathsf{tag}, \mathsf{ac-ct}_i))_{i \in [n]}\right) = F_\lambda(x_1, \ldots, x_n)$$

where $F_\lambda : \mathcal{D}_\lambda^n \to \mathcal{R}_\lambda$ and the probability is taken over the coins of algorithm.

Security. We define an indistinguishability-based security notion taking into account the attribute-based access control as well as the possibility of collusion among multiple clients. Below we define the *admissibility* of an adversary $\mathcal{A}$ in the security game against $\mathcal{E} = (\mathsf{Setup}, \mathsf{Extract}, \mathsf{Enc}, \mathsf{Dec})$. Intuitively, we consider only admissible adversaries who do not win our security game in a trivial manner as well as other meaningful restrictions in the multi-client setting. The admissibility additionally takes into account the satisfiability of the relation for access control, which also complicates the way we model the security notion. In the plain setting, interested readers can refer to [20] or [32] for more details.

Definition 9 (Admissible adversaries). *Let $\mathcal{A}$ be a* ppt *adversary and let $\mathcal{E} =$ (Setup, Extract, Enc, Dec) be an MCFE scheme with fine-grained access control for the functionality class $\mathcal{F} \times$ AC$-$K. In the security game given in Fig. 2 for $\mathcal{A}$ considering $\mathcal{E}$, let the sets $(\mathcal{C}, \mathcal{Q}, \mathcal{H})$ be the sets of corrupted clients, functional key queries, and honest clients, in that order. We say that $\mathcal{A}$ is* NOT *admissible w.r.t $(\mathcal{C}, \mathcal{Q}, \mathcal{H})$ if any of the following conditions holds:*

1. *There exist two different partial ciphertexts for $x_i^{(b)} \neq x_i^{(b)'}$, for some $b \in \{0, 1\}$, under one challenge tag* tag *that is queried to* **LoR**.
2. *There exist a tag* tag *and $i, j \in \mathcal{H}$ such that $i \neq j$, there exists a query $(i, x_i^{(0)}, x_i^{(1)}, \mathsf{tag}, \mathsf{ac}-\mathsf{ct}_i)$ to* **LoR** *but there exist no query $(j, x_j^{(0)}, x_j^{(1)}, \mathsf{tag}, \mathsf{ac}-\mathsf{ct}_j)$ to* **LoR**.
3. *There exists $(\mathsf{tag}, \mathsf{ac}-\mathsf{ct}_i)$ for $i \in [n]$, a function $F \in \mathcal{F}$, and $\mathsf{ac}-\mathsf{k} \in$ AC$-$K such that*
   - *We have $\mathsf{Rel}(\mathsf{ac}-\mathsf{k}, (\mathsf{ac}-\mathsf{ct}_i)_i) = 1$ and $(F, \mathsf{ac}-\mathsf{k}) \in \mathcal{Q}$.*
   - *For all $i \in \mathcal{H}$, there exists a query $(i, x_i^{(0)}, x_i^{(1)}, \mathsf{tag}, \mathsf{ac}-\mathsf{ct}_i)$ to* **LoR** *for $(x_i^{(0)}, x_i^{(1)})$.*
   - *For all $i \in \mathcal{C}$, it holds that $x_i^{(0)} = x_i^{(1)}$.*

Otherwise, we say that $\mathcal{A}$ is admissible w.r.t $(\mathcal{C}, \mathcal{Q}, \mathcal{H})$.

Remark 10. As in the plain MCFE with no attribute-based access control in [20,32], we will consider security with no repetitions, i.e. the adversary cannot query **Enc** nor **LoR** for multiple ciphertexts under the same $(i, \mathsf{tag}, \mathsf{ac}-\mathsf{ct}_i)$. Moreover, the adversary is not allowed to query the encryption oracle **Enc** for ciphertexts under the challenge tag^* that was previously queried to **LoR**. The intuition of this restriction is to prevent trivial attacks where, by querying for ciphertexts under tag^*, the adversary can combine them with the challenge ciphertext under the same tag^* to learn much more information about the challenge bit b and win the game. In addition, for every honest clients i, there must be a ciphertext query to **LoR** under the challenge $(\mathsf{tag}, \mathsf{ac}-\mathsf{ct}_i)$. That is, we do not take into account the scenario where only partial (in terms of honest clients) challenge ciphertext is queried to **LoR**. We can relax this condition and allow partial challenge ciphertexts by adding a layer of *All-or-Nothing Encapsulation* (AoNE). The AoNE encapsulates the partial components from clients and guarantees that all encapsulated components can be decapsulated if and only if all components are gathered, otherwise the original information remain hidden. The work by Chotard *et al.* [22] presents constructions for AoNE in the prime-order (asymmetric) bilinear groups compatible with our current setting. In the MIFE realm, the work of [4] considers the similar restriction and expects all honest slots $i \in [n]$ are queried to **LoR**.

Remark 11. Our syntax and model of MCFE with fine-grained access control require that in order to combine the ciphertext components, they must be encrypted under the same tag and the same set of attributes. One can aim for a more flexible notion in which each client i can encrypt their ciphertext component under a different $(\mathsf{tag}, \mathsf{ac}-\mathsf{ct}_i)$. However, this creates a much more intricate situation and we have to take into account non-trivial attacks where two different functional keys, whose policies are satisfied by different subsets of clients, may be combined to evaluate the underlying plaintext components of the union of the foregoing subsets. By hashing the tags and attributes during encryption, our concrete constructions enforce the same set of attributes embedded in the ciphertext components. In Sect. 5.4, we discuss how to relax the constraint and achieve the flexible notion where each client i can use a different $(\mathsf{tag}, \mathsf{ac}-\mathsf{ct}_i)$ and hash only tag. As a result, this more flexible MCFE scheme in the RO model can be morphed into an MIFE scheme in the *standard* model by fixing a public tag and publishing its hash.

We are now ready to give the definition for the indistinguishability-based security.

Definition 12 (IND-security for MCFE with fine-grained access control). *An MCFE scheme with fine-grained access control $\mathcal{E} = (\mathsf{Setup}, \mathsf{Extract}, \mathsf{Enc}, \mathsf{Dec})$ for the functionality class $\mathcal{F} \times \mathsf{AC}-\mathsf{K}$ is IND-secure if for all* ppt *adversaries $\mathcal{A}$, and for all sufficiently large $\lambda \in \mathbb{N}$, the following probability is negligible*

$$\mathsf{Adv}^{\mathsf{mc\text{-}ind\text{-}cpa}}_{\mathcal{E},\mathcal{F},\mathsf{AC}-\mathsf{K},\mathcal{A}}(1^\lambda) := \left| \Pr[\mathsf{Expr}^{\mathsf{mc\text{-}ind\text{-}cpa}}_{\mathcal{E},\mathcal{F},\mathsf{AC}-\mathsf{K},\mathcal{A}}(1^\lambda) = 1] - \frac{1}{2} \right| .$$

The game $\mathsf{Expr}^{\mathsf{mc\text{-}ind\text{-}cpa}}_{\mathcal{E},\mathcal{F},\mathsf{AC}-\mathsf{K},\mathcal{A}}(1^\lambda)$ is depicted in Fig. 2. The probability is taken over the random coins of $\mathcal{A}$ and the algorithms.

In a more relaxed notion, the scheme $\mathcal{E}$ is selectively IND-secure if the following probability is negligible

$$\mathsf{Adv}^{\mathsf{mc\text{-}sel\text{-}ind\text{-}cpa}}_{\mathcal{E},\mathcal{F},\mathsf{AC}-\mathsf{K},\mathcal{A}}(1^\lambda) := \left| \Pr[\mathsf{Expr}^{\mathsf{mc\text{-}sel\text{-}ind\text{-}cpa}}_{\mathcal{E},\mathcal{F},\mathsf{AC}-\mathsf{K},\mathcal{A}}(1^\lambda) = 1] - \frac{1}{2} \right| .$$

We also define a notion of security where only one challenge tag tag^* is allowed. That is, the scheme $\mathcal{E}$ is one-time IND-secure if the following probability is negligible

$$\mathsf{Adv}^{\mathsf{mc\text{-}ind\text{-}cpa\text{-}1\text{-}chal}}_{\mathcal{E},\mathcal{F},\mathsf{AC}-\mathsf{K},\mathcal{A}}(1^\lambda) := \left| \Pr[\mathsf{Expr}^{\mathsf{mc\text{-}ind\text{-}cpa\text{-}1\text{-}chal}}_{\mathcal{E},\mathcal{F},\mathsf{AC}-\mathsf{K},\mathcal{A}}(1^\lambda) = 1] - \frac{1}{2} \right| .$$

Lemma 13 allows us to concentrate on the notion of one-time IND-security for our construction. The proof is a standard hybrid argument and we give it in the full version [34] for completeness.

Lemma 13. *Let $\mathcal{E} = (\mathsf{Setup}, \mathsf{Extract}, \mathsf{Enc}, \mathsf{Dec})$ for the function class $\mathcal{F} \times \mathsf{AC}-\mathsf{K}$ be an MCFE scheme with fine-grained access control. If $\mathcal{E}$ is one-time IND-secure, then $\mathcal{E}$ is IND-secure.*

$$\boxed{\begin{array}{ll}
\textbf{Initialise}(1^\lambda) & \textbf{LoR}(i, x_i^{(0)}, x_i^{(1)}, \text{tag}^*, \text{ac-ct}_i^*) \\
\boxed{\textbf{Initialise}(1^\lambda, (x_i^{(0)}, x_i^{(1)})_{i \in [n]})} & \boxed{\textbf{LoR}(i, \text{tag}^*, \text{ac-ct}_i^*)}
\end{array}}$$

Initialise(1^λ)

$\boxed{\textbf{Initialise}(1^\lambda, (x_i^{(0)}, x_i^{(1)})_{i \in [n]})}$

$b \xleftarrow{\$} \{0, 1\}$
$(\text{msk}, (\text{ek}_i)_{i \in [n]}) \leftarrow \text{Setup}(1^\lambda)$
$\mathcal{Q} := \varnothing, \ \mathcal{C} := \varnothing, \ \mathcal{H} := [n]$
Return pk

Enc$(i, x_i, \text{tag}, \text{ac-ct}_i)$

If $(i, \text{tag}, \text{ac-ct}_i)$ appears previously
or $\text{tag} = \text{tag}^*$:
   Ignore
Else: return $\text{Enc}(\text{ek}_i, x_i, \text{tag}, \text{ac-ct}_i)$

Finalise(b')

If $\mathcal{A}$ is NOT admissible w.r.t $(\mathcal{C}, \mathcal{Q}, \mathcal{H})$:
   return 0
Else return $\left(b' \overset{?}{=} b\right)$

LoR$(i, x_i^{(0)}, x_i^{(1)}, \text{tag}^*, \text{ac-ct}_i^*)$

$\boxed{\textbf{LoR}(i, \text{tag}^*, \text{ac-ct}_i^*)}$

If $(i, \text{tag}^*, \text{ac-ct}_i^*)$ appears previously:
   ⌐or another $(i, \text{tag}', \text{ac-ct}_i')$ was queried:¬
   Ignore
Else: $\text{Enc}(\text{ek}_i, x_i^{(b)}, \text{tag}^*, \text{ac-ct}_i^*) \to \text{ct}_{\text{tag}^*, i}^{(b)}$
Return $\text{ct}_{\text{tag}^*, i}^{(b)}$

Corrupt(i)

$\mathcal{C} := \mathcal{C} \cup \{i\}$
$\mathcal{H} := \mathcal{H} \setminus \{i\}$
Return ek_i

Extract$(F, \text{ac-k})$

$\mathcal{Q} := \mathcal{Q} \cup \{(F, \text{ac-k})\}$
$\text{dk}_{F, \text{ac-k}} \leftarrow \text{Extract}(\text{msk}, F, \text{ac-k})$
Return $\text{dk}_{F, \text{ac-k}}$

Fig. 2. The security games $\text{Expr}_{\mathcal{E}, \mathcal{F}, \text{AC-K}, \mathcal{A}}^{\text{mc-ind-cpa}}(1^\lambda)$, $\boxed{\text{Expr}_{\mathcal{E}, \mathcal{F}, \text{AC-K}, \mathcal{A}}^{\text{mc-sel-ind-cpa}}(1^\lambda)}$ and $\overline{\underline{\text{Expr}_{\mathcal{E}, \mathcal{F}, \text{AC-K}, \mathcal{A}}^{\text{mc-ind-cpa-1-chal}}(1^\lambda)}}$ for Definition 12

5.2 Construction

This section presents a multi-client FE scheme with fine-grained access control, as defined in Sect. 5.1. We are in the bilinear group $(\mathbb{G}_1, \mathbb{G}_2, \mathbb{G}_t, g_1, g_2, g_t, \mathbf{e}, q)$ and $\mathbb{G}_1, \mathbb{G}_2, \mathbb{G}_t$ are written additively. In our concrete construction, the functionality class of interests is $\mathcal{F}^{\text{IP}} \times \text{LSSS}$ and $\mathcal{F}^{\text{IP}}$ contains $F_{\mathbf{y}} : (\mathbb{Z}_q^*)^n \to \mathbb{Z}_q$ that is defined as $F_{\mathbf{y}}(\mathbf{x}) := \langle \mathbf{x}, \mathbf{y} \rangle$. The access control is given by $\text{Rel} : \text{LSSS} \times (\prod_{i=1}^n 2^{\text{Att}}) \to \{0, 1\}$, where $\text{Rel}(\mathbb{A}, (\mathsf{S}_i)_i) = \prod_i \mathbb{A}(\mathsf{S}_i)$, the class LSSS contains Linear Secret Sharing Schemes over Att, and 2^{Att} denotes the superset of an attribute space $\text{Att} \subseteq \mathbb{Z}_q$. Our constructions are key-policy, where $\mathbb{A}$ is embedded in the key and S is specified in the ciphertext. The tag space Tag contains the tags that accompany plaintext components at the time of encryption.

We also need a full domain hash function $\mathsf{H} : \text{Tag} \times 2^{\text{Att}} \to \mathbb{G}_1^2$, where Tag denotes the set of tags and 2^{Att} contains the subsets of attributes of Att. The details of our construction is given in Fig. 3. We remark that currently all clients $i \in [n]$ must use the same S for encrypting their inputs x_i, because S is hashed together with tag by H. Section 5.4 presents another construction that relaxes the matching condition on S and H then receives only tag as inputs. We note that the *duplicate-and-compress* technique is used by putting the vectors $\{(\mathbf{c}_{i,j}, \mathbf{k}_{i,j})_j\}$ in the same pair of dual bases $(\mathbf{F}, \mathbf{F}^*)$ for all client $i \in [n]$, meanwhile each pair of vectors $(\mathbf{c}_{i,\text{ipfe}}, \mathbf{k}_{i,\text{ipfe}})$ is put in bases $(\mathbf{H}_i, \mathbf{H}_i^*)$ for each client $i \in [n]$. In the proof of Theorem 14 we detail how the basis changes in Lemma 4 can be done in parallel for $(\mathbf{H}_i, \mathbf{H}_i^*), (\mathbf{F}, \mathbf{F}^*)$ for all $i \in [n]$. The *correctness* of the scheme is verified by:

$$
\begin{aligned}
[\![\text{out}]\!]_{\text{t}} &= \sum_{i=1}^{n} \left(\left(\sum_{j \in A} \mathbf{c}_{i,j} \times (c_j \cdot \mathbf{k}_{i,j}) \right) - (\mathbf{c}_{i,\text{ipfe}} \times \mathbf{k}_{i,\text{ipfe}}) + \mathbf{e}(\mathbf{t}_i, \mathbf{m}_i) \right) \\
&= \sum_{i=1}^{n} \left([\![\psi_i a_0 z]\!]_{\text{t}} - [\![\omega p_i \cdot \langle S, \mathbf{y} \rangle + \omega' p_i \cdot \langle U, \mathbf{y} \rangle + \psi_i a_0 z]\!]_{\text{t}} \right. \\
&\quad \left. + [\![(\omega s_i + \omega' u_i + x_i) y_i]\!]_{\text{t}} \right) = [\![\langle \mathbf{x}, \mathbf{y} \rangle]\!]_{\text{t}} .
\end{aligned}
$$

5.3   Adaptive Security

We now present the main ideas of the adaptive proof for the multi-client construction described in Sect. 5.2, the detailed proof is presented in the full version [34]. A high-level intuition can be revisited in Sect. 3.

Theorem 14. *Let $\mathcal{E} = (\text{Setup}, \text{Extract}, \text{Enc}, \text{Dec})$ be a multi-client IPFE scheme with fine-grained access control via LSSS for the functionality class $\mathcal{F}^{\text{IP}} \times \text{LSSS}$, constructed in Sect. 5.2 in a bilinear group setting $(\mathbb{G}_1, \mathbb{G}_2, \mathbb{G}_t, g_1, g_2, g_t, \mathbf{e}, q)$. Then, $\mathcal{E}$ is one-time IND-secure if the SXDH assumption holds for $\mathbb{G}_1$ and $\mathbb{G}_2$. More specifically, for $\lambda \in \mathbb{Z}$ and for any adversary $\mathcal{A}$, let K denote the total number of functional key queries, P denote the total number of attributes used by $\mathcal{A}$, and Q denote the maximum number of random oracle (RO) queries. We have the following bound:*

$$
\text{Adv}^{\text{mc-ind-cpa-1-chal}}_{\mathcal{E}, \mathcal{F}^{\text{IP}}, \text{LSSS}, \mathcal{A}}(1^\lambda) \leq (2KP \cdot (6P + 3) + 2K + 2Q + 5) \cdot \text{Adv}^{\text{SXDH}}_{\mathbb{G}_1, \mathbb{G}_2}(1^\lambda)
$$

where $\text{Adv}^{\text{SXDH}}_{\mathbb{G}_1, \mathbb{G}_2}(1^\lambda)$ denotes the maximum advantage over ppt adversaries against the SXDH problem in $(\mathbb{G}_1, \mathbb{G}_2)$ set up with parameter λ.

By combining with Lemma 13, we have the following Corollary:

Corollary 15. *Let $\mathcal{E} = (\text{Setup}, \text{Extract}, \text{Enc}, \text{Dec})$ be a multi-client IPFE scheme with fine-grained access control via LSSS, for the functionality class $\mathcal{F}^{\text{IP}} \times \text{LSSS}$, constructed in Sect. 5.2 in a bilinear group setting $(\mathbb{G}_1, \mathbb{G}_2, \mathbb{G}_t, g_1, g_2, g_t, \mathbf{e}, q)$. Then, $\mathcal{E}$ is IND-secure if the SXDH assumption holds for $\mathbb{G}_1$ and $\mathbb{G}_2$.*

Proof (of Theorem 14- Main ideas). Recall that in the security proof for single-client adaptive security (Theorem 7) we switch the ℓ-th functional key to semi-functional by augmenting the dimension of the dual bases so that the challenge ciphertext is masked by $\tau \Delta \mathbf{x}[i]$, facing the mask $r_0^{(\ell)} \mathbf{y}^{(\ell)}[i]$ in the corresponding coordinate of the ℓ-th key and $\tau, r_0^{(\ell)} \xleftarrow{\$} \mathbb{Z}_q$ where $\Delta \mathbf{x} := \mathbf{x}_1^* - \mathbf{x}_0^*$. Afterwards, when doing the product of vectors in the dual bases, there will exist the quantity $\sum_{i=1}^{n} \tau r_0^{(\ell)} \Delta \mathbf{x}[i] \mathbf{y}^{(\ell)}[i] = \tau r_0^{(\ell)} \langle \Delta \mathbf{x}, \mathbf{y}^{(\ell)} \rangle$, which is non-zero when $\langle \Delta \mathbf{x}, \mathbf{y}^{(\ell)} \rangle \neq 0$.

Setup(1^λ): Choose $n+1$ pairs of dual orthogonal bases $(\mathbf{H}_i, \mathbf{H}_i^*)$ for $i \in [n]$ and $(\mathbf{F}, \mathbf{F}^*)$ where $(\mathbf{H}_i, \mathbf{H}_i^*)$ is a pair of dual bases for $(\mathbb{G}_1^4, \mathbb{G}_2^4)$ and $(\mathbf{F}, \mathbf{F}^*)$ is a pair of dual bases for $(\mathbb{G}_1^8, \mathbb{G}_2^8)$. We denote the basis changing matrices for $(\mathbf{F}, \mathbf{F}^*), (\mathbf{H}, \mathbf{H}_i^*)$ as $(F, F' := (F^{-1})^\top), (H_i, H_i' := (H_i^{-1})^\top)$ respectively (see the full version [34] for basis changes in DPVS):

$$(\mathbf{H}_i = H_i \cdot \mathbf{T}; \ \mathbf{H}_i^* = H_i' \cdot \mathbf{T}^*)_{i \in [n]} \quad (\mathbf{F} = F \cdot \mathbf{W}; \ \mathbf{F}^* = F' \cdot \mathbf{W}^*)$$

where $H_i, H_i' \in \mathbb{Z}_q^{4\times 4}, F, F' \in \mathbb{Z}_q^{8\times 8}$ and $(\mathbf{T} = [\![I_4]\!]_1, \mathbf{T}^* = [\![I_4]\!]_2), (\mathbf{W} = [\![I_8]\!]_1, \mathbf{W}^* = [\![I_8]\!]_2)$ are canonical bases of $(\mathbb{G}_1^4, \mathbb{G}_2^4), (\mathbb{G}_1^8, \mathbb{G}_2^8)$ respectively, for identity matrices I_4 and I_8. We recall that in the multi-client setting the scheme must be a private key encryption scheme. For each $i \in [n]$, we write

$$\mathbf{H}_i = (\mathbf{h}_{i,1}, \mathbf{h}_{i,2}, \mathbf{h}_{i,3}, \mathbf{h}_{i,4}) \qquad \mathbf{H}_i^* = (\mathbf{h}_{i,1}^*, \mathbf{h}_{i,2}^*, \mathbf{h}_{i,3}^*, \mathbf{h}_{i,4}^*)$$
$$\mathbf{F} = (\mathbf{f}_1, \mathbf{f}_2, \mathbf{f}_3, \mathbf{f}_4, \mathbf{f}_5, \mathbf{f}_6, \mathbf{f}_7, \mathbf{f}_8) \qquad \mathbf{F}^* = (\mathbf{f}_1^*, \mathbf{f}_2^*, \mathbf{f}_3^*, \mathbf{f}_4^*, \mathbf{f}_5^*, \mathbf{f}_6^*, \mathbf{f}_7^*, \mathbf{f}_8^*)$$

and sample $\mu \xleftarrow{\$} \mathbb{Z}_q^*, S, U \xleftarrow{\$} (\mathbb{Z}_q^*)^n$ and write $S = (s_1, \ldots, s_n), U = (u_1, \ldots, u_n)$. Perform an n-out-of-n secret sharing on 1, that is, choose $p_i \in \mathbb{Z}_q$ such that $1 = p_1 + \cdots + p_n$. Output the master secret key and the encryption keys as

$$\left\{ \begin{array}{l} \mathsf{msk} := (S, U, \mathbf{f}_1^*, \mathbf{f}_2^*, \mathbf{f}_3^*, (\mathbf{h}_{i,1}^*, \mathbf{h}_{i,2}^*, \mathbf{h}_{i,3}^*)_{i \in [n]}) \\ \mathsf{ek}_i := (s_i, u_i, p_i \cdot H_i^{(1)}, p_i \cdot H_i^{(2)}, \mathbf{h}_{i,3}, \mathbf{f}_1, \mathbf{f}_2, \mathbf{f}_3) \text{ for } i \in [n] \end{array} \right.$$

where $H_i^{(k)}$ denotes the k-th row of H_i.

Extract($\mathsf{msk}, \mathbb{A}, \mathbf{y} \in \mathbb{Z}_q^n$): Let $\mathbb{A}$ be an LSSS-realizable monotone access structure over a set of attributes Att $\subseteq \mathbb{Z}_q$. First, sample $a_0 \xleftarrow{\$} \mathbb{Z}_q$ and run the labeling algorithm $\Lambda_{a_0}(\mathbb{A})$ (see Definition 1) to obtain the labels $(a_j)_j$ where j runs over the attributes in Att. In the end, it holds that $a_0 = \sum_{j \in A} c_j \cdot a_j$ where j runs over an authorized set $A \in \mathbb{A}$ and $\mathbf{c} = (c_j)_j$ is the reconstruction vector from LSSS w.r.t A. We denote by List-Att($\mathbb{A}$) the list of attributes appearing in $\mathbb{A}$, with possible repetitions. Parse $\mathsf{msk} = (S, U, \mathbf{f}_1^*, \mathbf{f}_2^*, \mathbf{f}_3^*, (\mathbf{h}_{i,1}^*, \mathbf{h}_{i,2}^*, \mathbf{h}_{i,3}^*)_{i \in [n]})$ and write $\mathbf{y} = (y_1, \ldots, y_n)$. For each $i \in [n]$, compute $\mathbf{m}_i := [\![y_i]\!]_2$ and

$$\mathbf{k}_{i,j} = (\pi_{i,j} \cdot (j, 1), a_j \cdot z, 0, 0, 0, 0, 0)_{\mathbf{F}^*} \text{ for } j \in \mathsf{List\text{-}Att}(\mathbb{A})$$
$$\mathbf{k}_{i,\mathsf{ipfe}} := (\langle S, \mathbf{y} \rangle, \langle U, \mathbf{y} \rangle, a_0 \cdot z, 0)_{\mathbf{H}_i^*}$$

where $z, \pi_{i,j} \xleftarrow{\$} \mathbb{Z}_q$. Output $\mathsf{dk}_{\mathbb{A}, \mathbf{y}} := \left((\mathbf{k}_{i,j})_{i,j}, (\mathbf{m}_i, \mathbf{k}_{i,\mathsf{ipfe}})_{i \in [n]} \right)$.

Enc($\mathsf{ek}_i, x_i, \mathsf{tag}, \mathsf{S}$): Parse $\mathsf{ek}_i := (s_i, u_i, p_i \cdot H_i^{(1)}, p_i \cdot H_i^{(2)}, \mathbf{h}_{i,3}, \mathbf{f}_1, \mathbf{f}_2, \mathbf{f}_3)$ and $\mathsf{S} \subseteq \mathsf{Att} \subseteq \mathbb{Z}_q$ as the set of attributes, compute $\mathsf{H}(\mathsf{tag}, \mathsf{S}) \to ([\![\omega]\!]_1, [\![\omega']\!]_1) \in \mathbb{G}_1^2$ and sample $\psi_i \xleftarrow{\$} \mathbb{Z}_q$. Use $p_i H_i^{(1)}$ and $p_i H_i^{(2)}$ to compute

$$p_i H_i^{(1)} \cdot [\![\omega]\!]_1 + p_i H_i^{(2)} \cdot [\![\omega']\!]_1 = p_i \cdot \left(\omega H_i^{(1)} \cdot g_1 + \omega' H_i^{(2)} \cdot g_1 \right) = p_i \cdot (\omega \mathbf{h}_{i,1} + \omega' \mathbf{h}_{i,2}) \ .$$

For each $j \in \mathsf{S}$, compute

$$\mathbf{c}_{i,j} = \sigma_{i,j} \cdot \mathbf{f}_1 - j \cdot \sigma_{i,j} \cdot \mathbf{f}_2 + \psi_i \cdot \mathbf{f}_3 = (\sigma_{i,j} \cdot (1, -j), \psi_i, 0, 0, 0, 0, 0)_{\mathbf{F}}$$

where $\sigma_{i,j} \xleftarrow{\$} \mathbb{Z}_q$. Finally, compute

$$\mathbf{t}_i = s_i \cdot [\![\omega]\!]_1 + u_i \cdot [\![\omega']\!]_1 + [\![x_i]\!]_1 = [\![\omega \cdot s_i + \omega' \cdot u_i + x_i]\!]_1$$
$$\mathbf{c}_{i,\mathsf{ipfe}} = p_i \cdot (\omega \cdot \mathbf{h}_{i,1} + \omega' \cdot \mathbf{h}_{i,2}) + \psi_i \cdot \mathbf{h}_{i,3} = (\omega p_i, \omega' p_i, \psi_i, 0)_{\mathbf{H}_i}$$

and output $\mathsf{ct}_{\mathsf{tag}, i} := \left((\mathbf{c}_{i,j})_j, \mathbf{t}_i, \mathbf{c}_{i,\mathsf{ipfe}} \right)$.

Dec($\mathsf{dk}_{\mathbb{A}, \mathbf{y}}, \mathbf{c} := (\mathsf{ct}_{\mathsf{tag}, i})$): Parse $\mathsf{ct}_{\mathsf{tag}, i} = ((\mathbf{c}_{i,j})_{j \in \mathsf{S}}, \mathbf{t}_i, \mathbf{c}_{i,\mathsf{ipfe}})$ and $\mathsf{dk}_{\mathbb{A}, \mathbf{y}} := ((\mathbf{k}_{i,j})_{i \in [n], j \in \mathsf{List\text{-}Att}(\mathbb{A})}, (\mathbf{m}_i, \mathbf{k}_{i,\mathsf{ipfe}})_{i \in [n]})$. If there exists $A \subseteq \mathsf{S}$ and $A \in \mathbb{A}$, then compute the reconstruction vector $\mathbf{c} = (c_j)_j$ of the LSSS for A and

$$[\![\mathsf{out}]\!]_t = \sum_{i=1}^n \left(\left(\sum_{j \in A} \mathbf{c}_{i,j} \times (c_j \cdot \mathbf{k}_{i,j}) \right) - (\mathbf{c}_{i,\mathsf{ipfe}} \times \mathbf{k}_{i,\mathsf{ipfe}}) + e(\mathbf{t}_i, \mathbf{m}_i) \right)$$

Finally, compute the discrete logarithm and output the small value out.

Fig. 3. The construction for multi-client IPFE with fine-grained access control via LSSS from Sect. 5.2.

The dual bases now must have dimension at least n in order to accommodate all the n terms $\Delta\mathbf{x}[i]\mathbf{y}[i]$. However, in the multi-client setting, we are already using n different dual basis pairs $(\mathbf{H}_i, \mathbf{H}_i^*)$ for n clients and the correctness of the construction in Sect. 5.2 makes sure that only when gathering all n ciphertext parts can we decrypt to obtain the inner product. Therefore, it suffices to introduce only $\tau_i\Delta\mathbf{x}[i]$ in the component $\mathbf{c}_{i,\mathsf{ipfe}}$ returned from **LoR** of client i and only $r_{i,0}^{(\ell)}\mathbf{y}^{(\ell)}[i]$ in the corresponding key component $\mathbf{k}_{i,\mathsf{ipfe}}^*$, while duplicating the pair of bases $(\mathbf{H}_i, \mathbf{H}_i^*)$ for each $i \in [n]$. Indeed, this is also the best we can do because a client i is not supposed to know other inputs $\mathbf{x}_b^*[j]$ of other clients j, where $b \xleftarrow{\$} \{0,1\}$ is the challenge bit. At the same time, we compress the components of the access control part $(\mathbf{c}_{i,j})_j, (\mathbf{k}_{i,j}^*)_j$ into the same pair of bases $(\mathbf{F}, \mathbf{F}^*)$ for all clients i. We refer to the introduction for more intuition on this duplicate-and-compress process.

There are some further technical tweaks to be done when applying Lemma 4. First of all, we need the factors $\tau_i, r_{i,0}^{(\ell)}$ to be the same, for the grouping later when doing products of vectors in DPVS. This can be done by using the same $\tau_i = \tau$ for all i and during the basis change to mask the ciphertext component there will be a factor $\Delta\mathbf{x}[i]$. Our argument to introduce $r_{i,0}^{(\ell)}$ in fact does not depend on i and therefore we can use the same $r_{i,0}^{(\ell)} = r_0^{(\ell)}$ for all i as well. One might wonder if the dependence of the masks still relies on $\langle\Delta\mathbf{x}, \mathbf{y}^{(\ell)}\rangle$ because the adversary is not supposed to query **LoR** for corrupted clients and we can only introduce the masks in the vector components of honest i. As a result, the product of vectors in the dual bases in the end will have $\sum_{i\in\mathcal{H}}\tau r_0^{(\ell)}\Delta\mathbf{x}[i]\mathbf{y}^{(\ell)}[i]$. However, the security model imposes that for all corrupted i, the challenge message satisfies $\mathbf{x}_0^*[i] = \mathbf{x}_0^*[i]$ and consequently, $\langle\Delta\mathbf{x}, \mathbf{y}^{(\ell)}\rangle = 0$ if and only if $\sum_{i\in\mathcal{H}}\Delta\mathbf{x}[i]\mathbf{y}^{(\ell)}[i] = 0$. This implies that the mask $\tau r_0^{(\ell)}\sum_{i\in\mathcal{H}}\Delta\mathbf{x}[i]\mathbf{y}^{(\ell)}[i]$ persists only when $\langle\Delta\mathbf{x}, \mathbf{y}^{(\ell)}\rangle \neq 0$, which is our goal. The masking of ciphertext and key components results from the application of Lemma 4 as we are in the adaptive setting and not knowing what policy the ciphertext's attributes will satisfy. The lemma will mask all vectors $\mathbf{k}_{i,\mathsf{ipfe}}^{(\ell)}$ with $a_0'^{(\ell)} \xleftarrow{\$} \mathbb{Z}_q$, using which we perform a random labeling, and under the constraint that all clients i use the same S, the mask $a_0'^{(\ell)}$ will either appear for all i or neither. This enables us to replace it with $r_0^{(\ell)}$, similarly to the *all-at-once-changing* step in the adaptive single-client proof. We recall that currently the constraint on using the same S for all i is guaranteed by hashing $(\mathsf{tag}, \mathsf{S})$ together. The more complicated and flexible case with possibly different S_i for each i is discussed in Sect. 5.4. The application of Lemma 4 needs some auxiliary vectors in the dual bases $(\mathbf{F}, \mathbf{F}^*)$, which are not needed in the real usage of the scheme. Following the terminology of Okamoto-Takashima [37], those auxiliary vectors form a *hidden* part of the bases.

The final steps are to change (s_i, u_i) in the challenge ciphertext to (s_i', u_i') so that the ciphertext from **LoR** is encrypting $\mathbf{x}_0^*$ instead of $\mathbf{x}_b^*$ by solving a linear system for $(\Delta S, \Delta U)$ depending on $\mathbf{x}_b^* - \mathbf{x}_0^*$. We stress that the simulation of corrupted keys can still be done using (s_i, u_i) regardless of the order of **LoR** query, under the admissibility from condition 3. in Definition 9 that requires $\Delta\mathbf{x}[i] = \mathbf{x}_1^*[i] - \mathbf{x}_0^*[i] = 0$ if i is corrupted.

In the case of $\langle \Delta \mathbf{x}, \mathbf{y} \rangle \neq 0$, which then implies $\mathbb{A}(\mathsf{S}) \neq 0$, the functional key queries that are simulated using $(\langle S, \mathbf{y} \rangle, \langle U, \mathbf{y} \rangle)$ are computaionally indistinguishable from the ones in correct forms using $(\langle S', \mathbf{y} \rangle, \langle U', \mathbf{y} \rangle)$, under the SXDH assumption. However, the situation is more complicated than the single-client construction because the oracle **Enc** is using (s_i, u_i) as well. In order to be able to perform the correction step on the functional key, we have to program the full-domain hash function, which is modeled as an RO, such that for all queries $(\mathsf{tag}', \mathsf{S}')$ different from the challenge $(\mathsf{tag}, \mathsf{S})$, the value $\mathsf{H}(\mathsf{tag}', \mathsf{S}')$ belongs to $\mathrm{span}(\llbracket (1,\ \mu) \rrbracket_1) \subseteq \mathbb{G}_1^2$, for $\mu \xleftarrow{\$} \mathbb{Z}_q$. For the challenge $(\mathsf{tag}, \mathsf{S})$, the value $\mathsf{H}(\mathsf{tag}, \mathsf{S})$ remains a pair of random group elements. The main reason behind this is that our correction step requires $\mathsf{H}(\mathsf{tag}', \mathsf{S}')$ belongs to $\mathrm{span}(\llbracket (1,\ \mu) \rrbracket_1)$ so that it will not affect the normal ciphertext returned from **Enc**. This implies a linear relation between $\Delta S := S' - S$ and $\Delta U := U' - U$. However, if we put $\mathsf{H}(\mathsf{tag}, \mathsf{S})$ on the line $\mathrm{span}(\llbracket (1,\ \mu) \rrbracket_1)$ as well, then the intention to switch from $\mathbf{x}_0^*$ to $\mathbf{x}_b^*$ in the ciphertext from **LoR** will create another linear relation, which reduces significantly the degree of freedom to choose $(\Delta S, \Delta U)$ in order to make the simulation successful. In the end, the challenge ciphertext no longer depends on b and the advantage becomes 0, concluding the proof. $\qquad \square$

5.4   Revisiting MIFE in the Standard Model

We recall that currently our MCFE scheme from Sect. 5.2 enforces the same $(\mathsf{tag}, \mathsf{S})$ when encrypting for all client $i \in [n]$, by hashing them using the full-domain hash function that is modeled as an RO in the security proof. In practice, this could render a significant cost for synchronisation among clients so as to agree on tag *and* the attributes S at the time of encryption. In addition, by fixing one public tag, one can only obtain an MIFE scheme whose security can be proven in the ROM because we still need the random oracle to process S.

If we allow different $(\mathsf{tag}, \mathsf{S}_i)$ for each client i and during encryption the input for hashing depends only on tag, i.e. $\llbracket (\omega_{\mathsf{tag}}, \omega'_{\mathsf{tag}}) \rrbracket_1 \leftarrow \mathsf{H}(\mathsf{tag})$, there is a mix-and-match attack among functional keys that has to be considered. More precisely, suppose for two clients $\{1, 2\}$ encrypting $\mathbf{x} = (x_1, x_2)$ under different sets $(\mathsf{S}_1, \mathsf{S}_2)$ of attributes, the ℓ-th and ℓ'-th key queries have access structures $\mathbb{A}$ and $\mathbb{A}'$ where $\mathbb{A}(\mathsf{S}_1) = \mathbb{A}'(\mathsf{S}_2) = 1$ and $\mathbb{A}'(\mathsf{S}_1) = \mathbb{A}(\mathsf{S}_2) = 0$, for the same inner-product with $\mathbf{y} = \mathbf{y}' = (y_1, y_2)$. Neither of these keys should decrypt $x_1 y_1 + x_2 y_2$ for the sake of security. However, the construction from Fig. 3 permits an adversary to use the vectors $\{(\mathbf{c}_{1,j})_j, (\mathbf{k}_{1,j})_j, \mathbf{c}_{1,\mathsf{ipfe}}, \mathbf{k}_{1,\mathsf{ipfe}}\}$ to recover $p_1 \omega_{\mathsf{tag}} \langle S, \mathbf{y} \rangle + p_1 \omega'_{\mathsf{tag}} \langle U, \mathbf{y} \rangle$. Similar computation allows the same adversary to obtain $p_2 \omega_{\mathsf{tag}} \langle S, \mathbf{y} \rangle + p_2 \omega'_{\mathsf{tag}} \langle U, \mathbf{y} \rangle$ using $\{(\mathbf{c}_{2,j})_j, (\mathbf{k}_{2,j})_j, \mathbf{c}_{2,\mathsf{ipfe}}, \mathbf{k}_{2,\mathsf{ipfe}}\}$. Finally, observing that $p_1 + p_2 = 1$, exploiting the linear combination $y_1 \cdot \llbracket \omega_{\mathsf{tag}} s_1 + \omega'_{\mathsf{tag}} u_1 + x_1 \rrbracket_1 + y_2 \cdot \llbracket \omega_{\mathsf{tag}} s_2 + \omega'_{\mathsf{tag}} u_2 + x_2 \rrbracket_1$ permits finding $\langle \mathbf{x}, \mathbf{y} \rangle$. This demonstrates the main reason why we put S as part of the input to the hash function H in our current scheme. The core of the above problem is the fact that the construction from Sect. 5.2 does not prohibit combining different "root" vectors $\mathbf{k}_{1,\mathsf{ipfe}}$ and $\mathbf{k}_{2,\mathsf{ipfe}}$ w.r.t different access structure $\mathbb{A}$ and $\mathbb{A}'$.

In this section we present a solution, with minimal modifications to the scheme, to overcome the need for hashing S. Suppose now we are in the more flexible setting where $[\![(\omega_{\mathsf{tag}}, \omega'_{\mathsf{tag}})]\!]_1 \leftarrow \mathsf{H}(\mathsf{tag})$ during encryption. During setup phase, the pair $(\mathbf{H}_i, \mathbf{H}_i^*)$ is a pair of dual bases for $(\mathbb{G}_1^5, \mathbb{G}_2^5)$, with one more dimension compared to our less flexible construction. The master secret key msk stays the same, while the encryption key ek_i now contains furthermore $\theta_i \mathbf{h}_{i,5}$ for some $\theta_i \xleftarrow{\$} \mathbb{Z}_q$. Given an LSSS-realizable monotone access structure $\mathbb{A}$, the key extraction $\mathsf{Extract}(\mathsf{msk}, \mathbb{A}, \mathbf{y} \in \mathbb{Z}_q^n)$ returns $\mathsf{dk}_{\mathbb{A}, \mathbf{y}} := ((\mathbf{k}_{i,j})_{i,j}, (\mathbf{m}_i, \mathbf{k}_{i,\mathsf{ipfe}})_{i \in [n]})$. The encryption $\mathsf{Enc}(\mathsf{ek}_i, x_i, \mathsf{tag}, \mathsf{S}_i)$ returns $\mathsf{ct}_{\mathsf{tag}, i} := ((\mathbf{c}_{i,j})_j, \mathbf{t}_i, \mathbf{c}_{i,\mathsf{ipfe}})$ for each $i \in [n]$. There is a new element $d_{\mathbb{A}, i}$ appearing in the extra coordinate in $\mathbf{k}_{i,\mathsf{ipfe}}$ for every $i \in [n]$, where $(d_{\mathbb{A}, i})_i$ satisfies $\sum_{i=1}^n \theta_i d_{\mathbb{A}, i} = 0$, independently chosen for each functional keys. The vectors are essentially the same as in Fig. 3, except $(\mathbf{c}_{i,\mathsf{ipfe}}, \mathbf{k}_{i,\mathsf{ipfe}})$ for each i as follows:

$$\mathsf{ek}_i := (s_i, \ u_i, \ p_i \cdot H_i^{(1)}, \ p_i \cdot H_i^{(2)}, \ \mathbf{h}_{i,3}, \ \theta_i \mathbf{h}_{i,5}, \ \mathbf{f}_1, \ \mathbf{f}_2, \ \mathbf{f}_3)$$
$$\mathsf{msk} := (S, \ U, \ (\theta_i)_i, \ \mathbf{f}_1^*, \ \mathbf{f}_2^*, \ \mathbf{f}_3^*, \ (\mathbf{h}_{i,1}^*, \mathbf{h}_{i,2}^*, \mathbf{h}_{i,3}^*)_{i \in [n]})$$
$$\mathbf{c}_{i,\mathsf{ipfe}} := (\omega_{\mathsf{tag}} p_i, \ \omega'_{\mathsf{tag}} p_i, \ \psi_i, \ 0, \ \theta_i)_{\mathbf{H}_i}$$
$$\mathbf{k}_{i,\mathsf{ipfe}} := (\langle S, \mathbf{y} \rangle, \ \langle U, \mathbf{y} \rangle, \ a_{i,0} \cdot z, \ 0, \ d_{\mathbb{A}, i})_{\mathbf{H}_i^*}$$

The decryption calculation stays invariant because $\sum_{i=1}^n \theta_i d_{\mathbb{A}, i} = 0$. In retrospection, the mix-and-match attack we gave at the beginning of this section no longer works, because $\mathbb{A} \neq \mathbb{A}'$ and $\theta_1 d_{\mathbb{A}, 1} + \theta_2 d_{\mathbb{A}', 2} = 0$ only with negligible probability over the choices of $\theta_1, \theta_2, d_{\mathbb{A}, 1}, d_{\mathbb{A}', 2} \xleftarrow{\$} \mathbb{Z}_q$, for two independent random families $(d_{\mathbb{A}, i})_{i \in [2]}$ and $(d_{\mathbb{A}', i})_{i \in [2]}$. More formally, the security proof for this modified scheme, where we exploit the one extra 5-th coordinate in $(\mathbf{H}_i, \mathbf{H}_i^*)$, can be obtained with recourse to the proof of theorem 14 in Sect. 5.2 under few changes. We sketch the proof and highlight the main differences compared to the less flexible scheme in the full version [34].

Remark 16. Adding this new layer of masking increases the ciphertext's size by only a factor linear in n. Moreover, given this new construction where the set of attributes does not involve in the computation of the full-domain hashing anymore, we can obtain an MIFE in the standard model by fixing one tag for every ciphertext. The random oracle can be removed by publishing a random fixed value corresponding to $\mathsf{H}(\mathsf{tag})$ for encryption. In the end, we obtain an attribute-based MIFE for inner-products with adaptive security in the standard model, where the adversary can make the challenge query to **LoR** at most once for each slot $i \in [n]$. To achieve security w.r.t multiple queries for same slot, we can apply the technique in [21] to enhance our construction with repetitions. Finally, we can apply a layer of All-or-Nothing Encapsulation to the ciphertext components of construction in Sect. 5.4, so as to remove the tradeoff with respect to partial challenge ciphertexts in case of $(\mathsf{tag}, \mathsf{S}_i)$ for different S_i.

Acknowledgements. This work was supported in part by the European Union Horizon 2020 ERC Programme (Grant Agreement no. 966570 – CryptAnalytics), the Beyond5G project and the French ANR Project ANR-19-CE39-0011 PRESTO.

References

1. Abdalla, M., Bellare, M., Neven, G.: Robust encryption. In: Micciancio, D. (ed.) TCC 2010. LNCS, vol. 5978, pp. 480–497. Springer, Heidelberg (2010). https://doi.org/10.1007/978-3-642-11799-2_28

2. Abdalla, M., Bourse, F., De Caro, A., Pointcheval, D.: Simple functional encryption schemes for inner products. In: Katz, J. (ed.) PKC 2015. LNCS, vol. 9020, pp. 733–751. Springer, Heidelberg (2015). https://doi.org/10.1007/978-3-662-46447-2_33

3. Abdalla, M., Bourse, F., De Caro, A., Pointcheval, D.: Better security for functional encryption for inner product evaluations. Cryptology ePrint Archive, Report 2016/011 (2016). https://eprint.iacr.org/2016/011

4. Abdalla, M., Catalano, D., Gay, R., Ursu, B.: Inner-product functional encryption with fine-grained access control. In: Moriai, S., Wang, H. (eds.) ASIACRYPT 2020, Part III. LNCS, vol. 12493, pp. 467–497. Springer, Heidelberg (2020). https://doi.org/10.1007/978-3-030-64840-4_16

5. Agrawal, S., Kitagawa, F., Modi, A., Nishimaki, R., Yamada, S., Yamakawa, T.: Bounded functional encryption for turing machines: Adaptive security from general assumptions. Cryptology ePrint Archive, Report 2022/316 (2022). https://ia.cr/2022/316

6. Agrawal, S., Libert, B., Stehlé, D.: Fully secure functional encryption for inner products, from standard assumptions. In: Robshaw, M., Katz, J. (eds.) CRYPTO 2016, Part III. LNCS, vol. 9816, pp. 333–362. Springer, Heidelberg (2016). https://doi.org/10.1007/978-3-662-53015-3_12

7. Agrawal, S., Maitra, M., Vempati, N.S., Yamada, S.: Functional encryption for turing machines with dynamic bounded collusion from LWE. In: Malkin, T., Peikert, C. (eds.) CRYPTO 2021, Part IV. LNCS, vol. 12828, pp. 239–269. Springer, Heidelberg, Virtual Event (2021). https://doi.org/10.1007/978-3-030-84259-8_9

8. Ananth, P., Sahai, A.: Projective arithmetic functional encryption and indistinguishability obfuscation from degree-5 multilinear maps. In: Coron, J.S., Nielsen, J.B. (eds.) EUROCRYPT 2017, Part I. LNCS, vol. 10210, pp. 152–181. Springer, Heidelberg (2017). https://doi.org/10.1007/978-3-319-56620-7_6

9. Attrapadung, N., Libert, B., de Panafieu, E.: Expressive key-policy attribute-based encryption with constant-size ciphertexts. In: Catalano, D., Fazio, N., Gennaro, R., Nicolosi, A. (eds.) PKC 2011. LNCS, vol. 6571, pp. 90–108. Springer, Heidelberg (2011). https://doi.org/10.1007/978-3-642-19379-8_6

10. Baltico, C.E.Z., Catalano, D., Fiore, D., Gay, R.: Practical functional encryption for quadratic functions with applications to predicate encryption. In: Katz, J., Shacham, H. (eds.) CRYPTO 2017, Part I. LNCS, vol. 10401, pp. 67–98. Springer, Heidelberg (2017). https://doi.org/10.1007/978-3-319-63688-7_3

11. Beimel, A.: Secure Schemes for Secret Sharing and Key Distribution. Ph.D. thesis, Technion - Israel Institute of Technology, Haifa, Israel (June 1996). https://www.cs.bgu.ac.il/~beimel/Papers/thesis.pdf

12. Bellare, M., O'Neill, A.: Semantically-secure functional encryption: Possibility results, impossibility results and the quest for a general definition. In: Abdalla, M., Nita-Rotaru, C., Dahab, R. (eds.) CANS 13. LNCS, vol. 8257, pp. 218–234. Springer, Heidelberg (2013). https://doi.org/10.1007/978-3-319-02937-5_12

13. Benaloh, J.C., Leichter, J.: Generalized secret sharing and monotone functions. In: Goldwasser, S. (ed.) CRYPTO'88. LNCS, vol. 403, pp. 27–35. Springer, Heidelberg (1990). https://doi.org/10.1007/0-387-34799-2_3

14. Benhamouda, F., Bourse, F., Lipmaa, H.: CCA-secure inner-product functional encryption from projective hash functions. In: Fehr, S. (ed.) PKC 2017, Part II. LNCS, vol. 10175, pp. 36–66. Springer, Heidelberg (2017). https://doi.org/10.1007/978-3-662-54388-7_2

15. Boneh, D., Franklin, M.K.: Identity-based encryption from the Weil pairing. In: Kilian, J. (ed.) CRYPTO 2001. LNCS, vol. 2139, pp. 213–229. Springer, Heidelberg (2001). https://doi.org/10.1007/3-540-44647-8_13

16. Boneh, D., Gentry, C., Hamburg, M.: Space-efficient identity based encryption without pairings. In: 48th FOCS. pp. 647–657. IEEE Computer Society Press (2007). https://doi.org/10.1109/FOCS.2007.64

17. Boneh, D., Sahai, A., Waters, B.: Functional encryption: Definitions and challenges. In: Ishai, Y. (ed.) TCC 2011. LNCS, vol. 6597, pp. 253–273. Springer, Heidelberg (2011). https://doi.org/10.1007/978-3-642-19571-6_16

18. Castagnos, G., Laguillaumie, F., Tucker, I.: Practical fully secure unrestricted inner product functional encryption modulo p. In: Peyrin, T., Galbraith, S. (eds.) ASIACRYPT 2018, Part II. LNCS, vol. 11273, pp. 733–764. Springer, Heidelberg (2018). https://doi.org/10.1007/978-3-030-03329-3_25

19. Chen, J., Lim, H.W., Ling, S., Wang, H., Wee, H.: Shorter IBE and signatures via asymmetric pairings. In: Abdalla, M., Lange, T. (eds.) PAIRING 2012. LNCS, vol. 7708, pp. 122–140. Springer, Heidelberg (2013). https://doi.org/10.1007/978-3-642-36334-4_8

20. Chotard, J., Dufour Sans, E., Gay, R., Phan, D.H., Pointcheval, D.: Decentralized multi-client functional encryption for inner product. In: Peyrin, T., Galbraith, S. (eds.) ASIACRYPT 2018, Part II. LNCS, vol. 11273, pp. 703–732. Springer, Heidelberg (2018). https://doi.org/10.1007/978-3-030-03329-3_24

21. Chotard, J., Dufour Sans, E., Gay, R., Phan, D.H., Pointcheval, D.: Multi-client functional encryption with repetition for inner product. Cryptology ePrint Archive, Report 2018/1021 (2018). https://eprint.iacr.org/2018/1021

22. Chotard, J., Dufour-Sans, E., Gay, R., Phan, D.H., Pointcheval, D.: Dynamic decentralized functional encryption. In: Micciancio, D., Ristenpart, T. (eds.) CRYPTO 2020, Part I. LNCS, vol. 12170, pp. 747–775. Springer, Heidelberg (2020). https://doi.org/10.1007/978-3-030-56784-2_25

23. Cocks, C.: An identity based encryption scheme based on quadratic residues. In: Honary, B. (ed.) Cryptography and Coding 2001. LNCS, vol. 2260, pp. 360–363. Springer, Heidelberg (2001). https://doi.org/10.1007/3-540-45325-3_32

24. Delerablée, C., Gouriou, L., Pointcheval, D.: Key-policy ABE with delegation of rights. Cryptology ePrint Archive, Report 2021/867 (2021). https://ia.cr/2021/867

25. Escala, A., Herold, G., Kiltz, E., Ràfols, C., Villar, J.: An algebraic framework for Diffie-Hellman assumptions. In: Canetti, R., Garay, J.A. (eds.) CRYPTO 2013, Part II. LNCS, vol. 8043, pp. 129–147. Springer, Heidelberg (2013). https://doi.org/10.1007/978-3-642-40084-1_8

26. Gay, R.: A new paradigm for public-key functional encryption for degree-2 polynomials. In: Kiayias, A., Kohlweiss, M., Wallden, P., Zikas, V. (eds.) PKC 2020, Part I. LNCS, vol. 12110, pp. 95–120. Springer, Heidelberg (2020). https://doi.org/10.1007/978-3-030-45374-9_4

27. Goldwasser, S., Gordon, S.D., Goyal, V., Jain, A., Katz, J., Liu, F.H., Sahai, A., Shi, E., Zhou, H.S.: Multi-input functional encryption. In: Nguyen, P.Q., Oswald, E. (eds.) EUROCRYPT 2014. LNCS, vol. 8441, pp. 578–602. Springer, Heidelberg (2014). https://doi.org/10.1007/978-3-642-55220-5_32

28. Gordon, S.D., Katz, J., Liu, F.H., Shi, E., Zhou, H.S.: Multi-input functional encryption. Cryptology ePrint Archive, Report 2013/774 (2013). https://eprint.iacr.org/2013/774

29. Goyal, V., Pandey, O., Sahai, A., Waters, B.: Attribute-based encryption for fine-grained access control of encrypted data. In: Juels, A., Wright, R.N., De Capitani di Vimercati, S. (eds.) ACM CCS 2006. pp. 89–98. ACM Press (2006). https://doi.org/10.1145/1180405.1180418, available as Cryptology ePrint Archive Report 2006/309

30. Lai, Q., Liu, F.H., Wang, Z.: New lattice two-stage sampling technique and its applications to functional encryption - stronger security and smaller ciphertexts. In: Canteaut, A., Standaert, F.X. (eds.) EUROCRYPT 2021, Part I. LNCS, vol. 12696, pp. 498–527. Springer, Heidelberg (2021). https://doi.org/10.1007/978-3-030-77870-5_18

31. Lewko, A.B., Waters, B.: New techniques for dual system encryption and fully secure HIBE with short ciphertexts. In: Micciancio, D. (ed.) TCC 2010. LNCS, vol. 5978, pp. 455–479. Springer, Heidelberg (2010). https://doi.org/10.1007/978-3-642-11799-2_27

32. Libert, B., Titiu, R.: Multi-client functional encryption for linear functions in the standard model from LWE. In: Galbraith, S.D., Moriai, S. (eds.) ASIACRYPT 2019, Part III. LNCS, vol. 11923, pp. 520–551. Springer, Heidelberg (2019). https://doi.org/10.1007/978-3-030-34618-8_18

33. Lin, H.: Indistinguishability obfuscation from SXDH on 5-linear maps and locality-5 PRGs. In: Katz, J., Shacham, H. (eds.) CRYPTO 2017, Part I. LNCS, vol. 10401, pp. 599–629. Springer, Heidelberg (2017). https://doi.org/10.1007/978-3-319-63688-7_20

34. Nguyen, K., Phan, D.H., Pointcheval, D.: Multi-client functional encryption with fine-grained access control. Cryptology ePrint Archive, Report 2022/215 (2022). https://eprint.iacr.org/2022/215

35. Okamoto, T., Takashima, K.: Fully secure functional encryption with general relations from the decisional linear assumption. In: Rabin, T. (ed.) CRYPTO 2010. LNCS, vol. 6223, pp. 191–208. Springer, Heidelberg (2010). https://doi.org/10.1007/978-3-642-14623-7_11

36. Okamoto, T., Takashima, K.: Adaptively attribute-hiding (hierarchical) inner product encryption. In: Pointcheval, D., Johansson, T. (eds.) EUROCRYPT 2012. LNCS, vol. 7237, pp. 591–608. Springer, Heidelberg (2012). https://doi.org/10.1007/978-3-642-29011-4_35

37. Okamoto, T., Takashima, K.: Fully secure unbounded inner-product and attribute-based encryption. In: Wang, X., Sako, K. (eds.) ASIACRYPT 2012. LNCS, vol. 7658, pp. 349–366. Springer, Heidelberg (2012). https://doi.org/10.1007/978-3-642-34961-4_22

38. Ostrovsky, R., Sahai, A., Waters, B.: Attribute-based encryption with non-monotonic access structures. In: Ning, P., De Capitani di Vimercati, S., Syverson, P.F. (eds.) ACM CCS 2007. pp. 195–203. ACM Press (2007). https://doi.org/10.1145/1315245.1315270

39. Pal, T., Dutta, R.: Attribute-based access control for inner product functional encryption from LWE. In: LATIN 2021 (2021)

40. Sahai, A., Waters, B.R.: Fuzzy identity-based encryption. In: Cramer, R. (ed.) EUROCRYPT 2005. LNCS, vol. 3494, pp. 457–473. Springer, Heidelberg (2005). https://doi.org/10.1007/11426639_27

41. Shamir, A.: How to share a secret. Commun. Assoc. Comput. Mach. **22**(11), 612–613 (1979)

42. Shamir, A.: Identity-based cryptosystems and signature schemes. In: Blakley, G.R., Chaum, D. (eds.) CRYPTO'84. LNCS, vol. 196, pp. 47–53. Springer, Heidelberg (1984)

43. Waters, B.: Dual system encryption: realizing fully secure IBE and HIBE under simple assumptions. In: Halevi, S. (ed.) CRYPTO 2009. LNCS, vol. 5677, pp. 619–636. Springer, Heidelberg (2009). https://doi.org/10.1007/978-3-642-03356-8_36

44. Wee, H.: Broadcast encryption with size $N^{1/3}$ and more from k-lin. In: Malkin, T., Peikert, C. (eds.) CRYPTO 2021, Part IV. LNCS, vol. 12828, pp. 155–178. Springer, Heidelberg (2021). https://doi.org/10.1007/978-3-030-84259-8_6

Compact FE for Unbounded Attribute-Weighted Sums for Logspace from SXDH

Pratish Datta[1]([✉])[iD], Tapas Pal[2][iD], and Katsuyuki Takashima[3][iD]

[1] NTT Research, Inc., Sunnyvale, CA 94085, USA
pratish.datta@ntt-research.com
[2] NTT Social Informatics Laboratories, Musashino-shi, Tokyo 180-8585, Japan
tapas.pal.wh@hco.ntt.co.jp
[3] Waseda University, Shinjuku-ku, Tokyo 169-8050, Japan
ktakashima@waseda.jp

Abstract. This paper presents the *first* functional encryption (FE) scheme for the attribute-weighted sum (AWS) functionality that supports the *uniform* model of computation. In such an FE scheme, encryption takes as input a pair of attributes (x, z) where the attribute x is public while the attribute z is private. A secret key corresponds to some weight function f, and decryption recovers the weighted sum $f(x)z$. This is an important functionality with a wide range of potential real life applications, many of which require the attribute lengths to be flexible rather than being fixed at system setup. In the proposed scheme, the public attributes are considered as binary strings while the private attributes are considered as vectors over some finite field, both having arbitrary polynomial lengths that are not fixed at system setup. The weight functions are modelled as Logspace Turing machines.

Prior schemes [Abdalla, Gong, and Wee, CRYPTO 2020 and Datta and Pal, ASIACRYPT 2021] could only support non-uniform Logspace. The proposed scheme is built in asymmetric prime-order bilinear groups and is proven *adaptively simulation* secure under the well-studied symmetric external Diffie-Hellman (SXDH) assumption against an arbitrary polynomial number of secret key queries both before and after the challenge ciphertext. This is the best possible level of security for FE as noted in the literature. As a special case of the proposed FE scheme, we also obtain the first adaptively simulation secure inner-product FE (IPFE) for vectors of arbitrary length that is not fixed at system setup.

On the technical side, our contributions lie in extending the techniques of Lin and Luo [EUROCRYPT 2020] devised for payload hiding attribute-based encryption (ABE) for uniform Logspace access policies avoiding the so-called "one-use" restriction in the indistinguishability-based security model as well as the "three-slot reduction" technique for simulation-secure attribute-hiding FE for non-uniform Logspace devised by Datta and Pal [ASIACRYPT 2021] to the context of simulation-secure attribute-hiding FE for uniform Logspace.

Keywords: Functional encryption · Attribute-weighted sums · Logspace · Turing machines

© International Association for Cryptologic Research 2022
S. Agrawal and D. Lin (Eds.): ASIACRYPT 2022, LNCS 13791, pp. 126–159, 2022.
https://doi.org/10.1007/978-3-031-22963-3_5

1   Introduction

Functional Encryption: *Functional encryption* (FE), formally introduced by Boneh et al. [8] and O'Neill [22], redefines the classical encryption procedure with the motivation to overcome the limitation of the "all-or-nothing" paradigm of decryption. In a traditional encryption system, there is a single secret key such that a user given a ciphertext can either recover the whole message or learns nothing about it, depending on the availability of the secret key. FE in contrast provides fine grained access control over encrypted data by generating artistic secret keys according to the desired functions of the encrypted data to be disclosed. More specifically, in a public-key FE scheme for a function class $\mathcal{F}$, there is a setup authority which produces a master secret key and publishes a master public key. Using the master secret key, the setup authority can derive secret keys or functional decryption keys SK_f associated with functions $f \in \mathcal{F}$. Anyone can encrypt messages msg belonging to a specified message space $\mathsf{msg} \in \mathbb{M}$ using the master public key to produce a ciphertext CT. The ciphertext CT along with a secret key SK_f recovers the function of the message $f(\mathsf{msg})$ at the time of decryption, while unable to extract any other information about msg. More specifically, the security of FE requires *collusion resistance* meaning that any polynomial number of secret keys together cannot gather more information about an encrypted message except the union of what each of the secret keys can learn individually.

FE for Attribute-Weighted Sum: Recently, Abdalla, Gong and Wee [2] and Datta and Pal [13] studied FE schemes for a new class of functionalities termed as "attribute-weighted sums" (AWS). This is a generalization of the inner product functional encryption (IPFE) [1,4]. In such a scheme, an attribute pair (x, z) is encrypted using the master public key of the scheme, where x is a public attribute (e.g., demographic data) and z is a private attribute containing sensitive information (e.g., salary, medical condition, loans, college admission outcomes). A recipient having a secret key corresponding to a weight function f can learn the attribute-weighted sum $f(x)z$. The attribute-weighted sum functionality appears naturally in several real life applications. For instance, as discussed by Abdalla et al. [2] if we consider the weight function f as a boolean predicate, then the attribute-weighted sum functionality $f(x)$ would correspond to the average z over all users whose attribute x satisfies the predicate f. Important practical scenarios include average salaries of minority groups holding a particular job (z = salary) and approval ratings of an election candidate amongst specific demographic groups in a particular state (z = rating).

The works of [2,13] considered a more general case of the notion where the domain and range of the weight functions are vectors, in particular, the attribute pair of public/private attribute vectors $(\boldsymbol{x}, \boldsymbol{z})$, which is encrypted to a ciphertext CT. A secret key SK_f generated for a weight function f allows a recipient to learn $f(\boldsymbol{x})^\top \boldsymbol{z}$ from CT without leaking any information about the private attribute $\boldsymbol{z}$.

The FE schemes of [2,13] support an expressive function class of *arithmetic branching programs* (ABPs) which captures non-uniform Logspace computations. Both schemes were built in asymmetric bilinear groups of prime order and are proven secure in the simulation-based security model, which is known to be the desirable security model for FE [8,22], under the (bilateral) k-Linear (k-Lin)/ (bilateral) *Matrix Diffie-Hellman* (MDDH) assumption. The FE scheme of [2] achieves semi-adaptive security, where the adversary is restricted to making secret key queries only after making the ciphertext queries, whereas the FE scheme of [13] achieves adaptive security, where the adversary is allowed to make secret key queries both before and after the ciphertext queries.

However, as mentioned above, ABP is a non-uniform computational model. As such, in both the FE schemes [2,13], the length of the public and private attribute vectors must be fixed at system setup. This is clearly a bottleneck in several applications of this primitive especially when the computation is done over attributes whose lengths vary widely among ciphertexts and are not fixed at system setup. For instance, suppose a government hires an external audit service to perform a survey on average salary of employees working under different job categories in various companies to resolve salary discrepancy. The companies create salary databases (X, Z) where $X = (x_i)_i$ contains public attributes $x_i = (\text{job title}, \text{department}, \text{company name})$ and $Z = (z_i)_i$ includes private attribute $z_i = \text{salary}$. To facilitate this auditing process without revealing individual salaries (private attribute) to the auditor, the companies encrypt their own database (X, Z) using an FE scheme for AWS. The government provides the auditor a functional secret key SK_f for a function f that takes input a public attribute X and outputs 1 for x_i's for which the "job title" matches with a particular job, say *manager*. The auditor decrypts ciphertexts of the various companies using SK_f and calculates the average salaries of employees working under that job category in those companies. Now, if the existing FE schemes for AWS [2,13] supporting non-uniform computations are employed then to make the system *sustainable* the government would have to fix a probable size (an upper bound) of the number of employees in all the companies. Also, the size of all ciphertexts ever generated would scale with that upper bound even if the number of employees in some companies, at the time of encryption, are much smaller than that upper bound. This motivates us to consider the following problem.

Open Problem. *Can we construct an* FE *scheme for* AWS *in some uniform computational model capable of handling public/private attributes of arbitrary length?*

Our Results. This work resolves the above open problem. For the *first* time in the literature, we formally define and construct a FE scheme for *unbounded* AWS (UAWS) functionality where the setup only depends on the security parameter of the system and the weight functions are modeled as Turing machines. The proposed FE scheme supports both public and private attributes of *arbitrary* lengths. In particular, the public parameters of the system are completely independent of the lengths of attribute pairs. Moreover, the ciphertext size is *compact* meaning that it does not grow with the number of occurrences of a specific attribute in the weight functions which are represented as Logspace Turing machines. The scheme is *adaptively simulation* secure against the release of an unbounded (polynomial) number of secret keys both before and after the challenge ciphertext. As noted in [8,22], simulation security is the best possible and the most desirable model for FE. Moreover, simulation-based security also captures indistinguishability-based security but the converse does not hold in general.

Our FE for UAWS is proven secure in the standard model based on the symmetric external Diffie-Hellman (SXDH) assumption in the asymmetric prime-order pairing groups. Our main result in the paper is summarized as follows.

Theorem 1.1 (Informal). *Assuming the* SXDH *assumption holds in asymmetric pairing groups of prime-order, there exists an adaptively simulation secure* FE *scheme for the attribute weighted sum functionality with the weight functions modeled as Logspace Turing machines such that the lengths of public and private attributes are unbounded and can be chosen at the time of encryption, the ciphertexts are compact with respect to the multiple occurrences of attributes in the weight functions.*

Viewing IPFE as a special case of FE for AWS, we also obtain the *first* adaptively *simulation* secure IPFE scheme for *unbounded* length vectors (UIPFE), i.e., the length of the vectors is not fixed in setup. Observe that all prior simulation secure IPFE [2,3,13,26] could only support *bounded* length vectors, i.e., the lengths must be fixed in the setup. On the other hand, the only known construction of UIPFE [23] is proven secure in the *indistinguishability-based* model.

The proposed FE construction is semi-generic and extends the frameworks of the works of Lin and Luo [18] and Datta and Pal [13]. Lin and Luo [18] develop an adaptively secure attribute-based encryption (ABE) scheme for Logspace Turing machines proven secure in the indistinguishability-based model. Although the input length of their ABE is unbounded, but an ABE is an *"all-or-nothing"* type primitive which fully discloses the message to a secret key generated for accepting policies. Further, the ABE of [18] is only payload hiding secure meaning that the ciphertexts themselves can leak sensitive information about the associated attributes. In contrast, our FE for UAWS provides more fine grained encryption methodologies where the ciphertexts reveal nothing about the private part of associated attributes but their weighted sums. Our FE construction depends on two building blocks, an *arithmetic key garbling scheme* (AKGS) for Logspace Turing machines which is an information-theoretic tool and a function hiding (bounded) slotted IPFE scheme which is a computational primitive. An important motivation of [18] is to achieve compact ciphertexts for ABEs. In other words, they get rid of the so-called *one-use restriction* from prior adaptively secure ABEs [6,9,10,15–17,20,21,25] by replacing the core information-theoretic step with the computational primitive of function hiding slotted IPFE. The FE of [13] is able to accomplish this property for non-uniform computations by developing a three-slot encryption technique. Specifically, three slots are utilized to simulate the label functions obtained from the underlying AKGS garbling for pre-ciphertext secret keys. Note that, the three-slot encryption technique is an extension of dual system encryption methodologies [15,16,24]. In this work, we extend their frameworks [13,18] to avoid the one-use restriction in the case of FE for UAWS that computes weights via Logspace Turing machines. It is non-trivial to implement such three-slot techniques in the uniform model. The main reason behind this fact is that in case of ABPs [13] the garbling randomness can be sampled knowing the size of ABPs, and hence the garbling algorithm is possible to run while generating secret keys. However, in the case of AKGS for Logspace Turing machines, the garbling randomness depends on the size of the Turing machine as well as its input lengths. Consequently, it is not possible to execute the garbling in the key generation or encryption algorithms as the information about the garbling randomness is distributed between these two algorithms. We tackle this by developing a more advanced three-slot encryption technique with *distributed randomness* which enables us to carry out such a sophisticated procedure for Logspace Turing machines.

Our FE for UAWS is a one-slot scheme. This means one pair of public-private attribute can be processed in a single encryption. An unbounded-slot FE for UAWS [2] enables us to encrypt unbounded many such pairs in a single encryption. Abdalla et al. [2] devise a generic transformation for bootstrapping from one-slot to unbounded-slot scheme. However, this transformation only works if the underlying one-slot scheme is semi-adaptively secure [13]. Thus, if we restrict our scheme to semi-adaptive security then using such transformations [2,13] our one-slot FE scheme can be bootstrapped to support unbounded slots.

Organization. We discuss a detailed technical overview of our results in Sect. 2. We provide useful notations, related definitions, and complexity assumptions in Sect. 3. Our construction of a single key and single ciphertext secure FE scheme for UAWS is described in Sect. 4. The simulator and security analysis of the scheme can be found in the full version. Next, we build our full fledge 1-slot FE scheme for UAWS in Sect. 5. The correctness and security analysis of the scheme is available in the full version. For completeness, we present the definition of function-hiding slotted IPFE and the construction of AKGS for Turing machine computations [18] in the full version.

2   Technical Overview

We now present an overview of our techniques for achieving a FE scheme for AWS functionality which supports the uniform model of computations. We consider prime-order bilinear pairing groups $(\mathbb{G}_1, \mathbb{G}_2, \mathbb{G}_T, g_1, g_2, e)$ with a generator $g_T = e(g_1, g_2)$ of $\mathbb{G}_T$ and denote $[\![a]\!]_i$ by an element $g_i^a \in \mathbb{G}_i$ for $i \in \{1, 2, T\}$. For any vector z, the k-th entry is denoted by $z[k]$ and $[n]$ denotes the set $\{1, \ldots, n\}$.

The Unbounded AWS Functionality. In this work, we consider an unbounded FE scheme for the AWS functionality for Logspace Turing machines (or the class of L), in shorthand it is written as $\mathsf{UAWS}^{\mathsf{L}}$. More specifically, the setup only takes input the security parameter of the system and is independent of any other parameter, e.g., the lengths of the public and private attributes. $\mathsf{UAWS}^{\mathsf{L}}$ generates secret keys $\mathsf{SK}_{(M, \mathcal{I}_M)}$ for a tuple of Turing machines denoted by $M = \{M_k\}_{k \in \mathcal{I}_M}$ such that the index set $\mathcal{I}_M$ contains any *arbitrary* number of Turing machines $M_k \in \mathsf{L}$. The ciphertexts are computed for a pair of public-private attributes (x, z) whose lengths are *arbitrary* and are decided at the time of encryption. Precisely, the public attribute $\boldsymbol{x}$ of length N comes with a polynomial time bound $T = \mathsf{poly}(N)$ and a logarithmic space bound S, and the private attribute $\boldsymbol{z}$ is an integer vector of length n. At the time of decryption, if $\mathcal{I}_M \subseteq [n]$ then it reveals an integer value $\sum_{k \in \mathcal{I}_M} M_k(\boldsymbol{x})\boldsymbol{z}[k]$. Since $M_k(\boldsymbol{x})$ is binary, we observe that the summation selects and adds the entries of $\boldsymbol{z}$ for which the corresponding Turing machine accepts the public attribute $\boldsymbol{x}$. An appealing feature of the functionality is that the secret key $\mathsf{SK}_{(M,\mathcal{I}_M)}$ can decrypt ciphertexts of unbounded length attributes in unbounded time/(logarithmic) space bounds. In contrast, existing FE for AWSs [2,13] are designed to handle non-uniform computations that can only handle attributes of bounded lengths and the public parameters grows linearly with the lengths. Next, we describe the formulation of Turing machines in L considered in UAWS^L.

Turing Machines Formulation. We introduce the notations for Logspace Turning machines (TM) over binary alphabets. A Turing machine $M = (Q, \boldsymbol{y}_{\mathsf{acc}}, \delta)$ consists of Q states with the initial state being 1 and a characteristic vector $\boldsymbol{y}_{\mathsf{acc}} \in \{0,1\}^Q$ of accepting states and a transition function δ. When an input $(\boldsymbol{x}, N, T, S)$ with length N and time, space bounds T, S is provided, the computation of $M|_{N,T,S}(\boldsymbol{x})$ is performed in T steps passing through *configurations* $(\boldsymbol{x}, (i, j, \boldsymbol{W}, q))$ where $i \in [N]$ is the input tape pointer, $j \in [S]$ is the work tape pointer, $\boldsymbol{W} \in \{0,1\}^S$ the content of work tape, and $q \in [Q]$ the state under consideration. The initial *internal* configuration is $(1, 1, \boldsymbol{0}_S, 1)$ and the transition function δ determines whether, on input $\boldsymbol{x}$, it is possible to move from one internal configuration $(i, j, \boldsymbol{W}, q)$ to the next $((i', j', \boldsymbol{W}', q'))$, namely if $\delta(q, \boldsymbol{x}[i], \boldsymbol{W}[j]) = (q', w', \Delta i, \Delta j)$. In other words, the transition function δ on input state q, an input bit $\boldsymbol{x}[i]$ and an work tape bit $\boldsymbol{W}[j]$, outputs the next state q', the new bit w' overwriting $w = \boldsymbol{W}[j]$ by $w' = \boldsymbol{W}'[j]$ (keeping $\boldsymbol{W}[j''] = \boldsymbol{W}'[j'']$ for all $j \neq j''$), and the directions $\Delta i, \Delta j \in \{0, \pm 1\}$ to move the input and work tape pointers.

Our construction of adaptively simulation secure UAWS^L depends on two building blocks: AKGS for Logspace Turing machines, an information-theoretic tool and slotted IPFE, a computation tool. We only need a *bounded* slotted IPFE, meaning that the length of vectors of the slotted IPFE is fixed in the setup, and we only require the primitive to satisfy adaptive indistinguishability based security. Hence, our work shows how to (semi-)generically bootstrap a bounded IPFE to an unbounded FE scheme beyond the inner product functionality. Before going to describe the UAWS^L, we briefly discuss about these two building blocks.

AKGS for Logspace Turing Machines. In [18], the authors present an ABE scheme for Logspace Turing machines by constructing an efficient AKGS for sequence of matrix multiplications over $\mathbb{Z}_p$. Thus, their core idea was to represent a Turing machine computation through a sequence of matrix multiplications. An internal configuration $(i, j, \boldsymbol{W}, q)$ is represented as a basis vector $\boldsymbol{e}_{(i,j,\boldsymbol{W},q)}$ of dimension $NS2^SQ$ with a single 1 at the position $(i, j, \boldsymbol{W}, q)$. We define a *transition matrix* given by

$$\mathbf{M}(\boldsymbol{x})[(i,j,\boldsymbol{W},q),(i',j',\boldsymbol{W}',q')] = \begin{cases} 1, & \text{if } \delta(q, \boldsymbol{x}[i], \boldsymbol{W}[j]) = (q', \boldsymbol{W}'[j], i'-i, j'-j) \\ & \text{and } \boldsymbol{W}'[j''] = \boldsymbol{W}[j''] \text{ for all } j'' \neq j; \\ 0, & \text{otherwise}; \end{cases}$$

such that $e_{(i,j,W,q)}^{\top}\mathbf{M}(x) = e_{(i',j',W',q')}^{\top}$. This holds because the $((i,j,W,q),$ $(i',j',W',q'))$-th entry of $\mathbf{M}(x)$ is 1 if and only if there is a valid transition from $(q,x[i],W[j])$ to $(q',W'[j],i'-i,j'-j)$. Therefore, one can write the Turing machine computation by right multiplying the matrix $\mathbf{M}(x)$ for T times with the initial configuration $e_{(1,1,\mathbf{0}_S,1)}^{\top}$ to reach of one of the final configurations $\mathbf{1}_{[N]\times[S]\times\{0,1\}^S} \otimes y_{\text{acc}}$. In other words, the function $M|_{N,T,S}(x)$ is written as

$$M|_{N,T,S}(x) = e_{(1,1,\mathbf{0}_S,1)}^{\top}(\mathbf{M}_{N,S}(x))^T(\mathbf{1}_{[N]\times[S]\times\{0,1\}^S} \otimes y_{\text{acc}}) \tag{2.1}$$

Thus, [18] constructs an AKGS for the sequence of matrix multiplications as in Eq. (2.1). Their AKGS is inspired from the randomized encoding scheme of [5] and homomorphic evaluation procedure of [7]. Given the function $M|_{N,T,S}$ over $\mathbb{Z}_p$ and two secrets z, β, the garbling procedure computes the label functions

$$L_{\text{init}}(x) = \beta + e_{(1,1,\mathbf{0}_S,1)}^{\top}r_0,$$
$$\text{for } t \in [T]: \quad (L_{t,\theta})_\theta = -r_{t-1} + \mathbf{M}_{N,S}(x)r_t,$$
$$(L_{T+1,\theta})_\theta = -r_T + z\mathbf{1}_{[N]\times[S]\times\{0,1\}^S} \otimes y_{\text{acc}}.$$

and outputs the coefficients of these label functions $\ell_{\text{init}}, \boldsymbol{\ell}_t = (\boldsymbol{\ell}_{t,\theta})_\theta$ where $\theta = (i,j,W,q)$ and $r_t \leftarrow \mathbb{Z}_p^{[N]\times[S]\times\{0,1\}^S\times[Q]}$. To compute the functional value for an input x, the evaluation procedure add ℓ_{init} with a telescoping sum $e_{(1,1,\mathbf{0}_S,1)}^{\top} \cdot \sum_{t=1}^{T}(\mathbf{M}_{N,S}(x))^{t-1}\boldsymbol{\ell}_t$ and outputs $zM|_{N,T,S}(x) + \beta$. More precisely, it uses the fact that

$$e_{i_{t+1},j_{t+1},W_{t+1},q_{t+1}}^{\top}r_{t+1} = e_{i_t,j_t,W_t,q_t}^{\top}r_t + e_{i_t,j_t,W_t,q_t}^{\top}\underbrace{(-r_t + \mathbf{M}(x)r_{t+1})}_{\boldsymbol{\ell}_{t+1}}$$

A crucial and essential property that the AKGS have is the *linearity* of evaluation procedure, meaning that the procedure is linear in the label function values ℓs and, hence can be performed even if ℓs are available in the exponent of a group. Lin and Luo identify two important security notions of AKGS, jointly called *piecewise security*. Firstly, ℓ_{init} can be reversely sampled given a functional value and all other label values, which is known as the *reverse sampleability*. Secondly, ℓ_t is random with respect to the subsequent label functions $L_{t',\theta}$ for all $t' > t$ and z, which is called the *marginal randomness*.

Function Hiding Slotted IPFE. A normal IPFE computes inner product between two vectors v and u using a secret key IPFE.SK$_v$ and a ciphertext IPFE.CT$_u$. The IPFE is said to satisfy indistinguishability-based security if an adversary having received many functional secret keys {IPFE.SK$_v$} remains incapable to extract any information about the message vector u except the inner products {$v \cdot u$}. It is easy to observe that if encryption is done publicly then no security can be ensured about v from the secret key IPFE.SK$_v$ [11] due to the linear functionality. However, if the encryption algorithm is private then IPFE.SK$_v$ can be produced in a fashion to hide sensitive information about v. This is termed as *function hiding* security notion for private key IPFE. Slotted

IPFE [19] is a hybrid of public and private IPFE where vectors are divided into public and private slots, and function hiding is only guaranteed for the entries in the private slots. Further, Slotted IPFEs of [18,19] generate secret keys and ciphertexts even when the vectors are given in the exponent of source groups whereas decryption recovers the inner product in the target group.

2.1 From *All-or-Nothing* to *Functional* Encryption

We are all set to describe our approach to extend the framework of [18] from *all-or-nothing* to *functional* encryption for the uniform model of computations. In a previous work of Datta and Pal [13], an adaptively secure FE for AWS functionality was built for the non-uniform model of computations, ABPs to be precise. Their idea was to garble a function $f_k(\boldsymbol{x})z[k] + \beta_k$ during key generation (keeping $z[k]$ and $\boldsymbol{x}$ as variables) and compute IPFE secret keys to encode the m labels, and a ciphertext associated to a tuple $(\boldsymbol{x}, \boldsymbol{z})$ consists of a collection of IPFE ciphertexts which encode the attributes:

$$\mathsf{SK}_f = \{\mathsf{IPFE.SK}_{v_{k,t<m}}, \widetilde{\mathsf{IPFE.SK}}_{\widetilde{v}_{k,m}}\}_{k,m} : \quad \begin{array}{c} v_{k,t<m} = \boldsymbol{\ell}_{k,t}, \widetilde{v}_{k,m} = \boldsymbol{\ell}_{k,m} \text{ where} \\ (\boldsymbol{\ell}_{k,t})_t \leftarrow \mathsf{Garble}(f_k(\boldsymbol{x})z[k] + \beta_k) \text{ s.t. } \sum_k \beta_k = 0 \end{array}$$

$$\mathsf{CT}_{\boldsymbol{x}} = (\mathsf{IPFE.CT}_u, \{\widetilde{\mathsf{IPFE.CT}}_{\widetilde{u}_k}\}_k) : \quad \boldsymbol{u} = (1, \boldsymbol{x}), \ \widetilde{\boldsymbol{u}}_k = (1, z[k])$$

Therefore, using the inner product functionality, decryption computes the actual label values with $\boldsymbol{x}, z[k]$ as inputs and recovers $f_k(\boldsymbol{x})z[k] + \beta_k$ for each k, and hence finally $\sum_k f_k(\boldsymbol{x})z[k]$. However, this approach fails to build UAWS$^\mathsf{L}$ because we can not execute the AKGS garbling for the function $M_k|_{N,T,S}(\boldsymbol{x})z[k] + \beta_k$ at the time of generating keys. More specifically, the garbling randomness depends on parameters N, T, S, n that are unknown to the key generator. Note that, in contrast to the ABE of [18] where z can be viewed as a payload (hence $n = 1$), the UAWS functionality has an additional parameter n (length of $\boldsymbol{z}$) the value of which is chosen at the time of encryption. Moreover, the compactness of UAWS$^\mathsf{L}$ necessitates the secret key size $|\mathsf{SK}_{(M,\mathcal{I}_M)}| = O(|\mathcal{I}_M|Q)$ to be linear in the number of states Q and the ciphertext size $|\mathsf{CT}_{(\boldsymbol{x},T,S)}| = O(nTNS2^S)$ be linear in $TNS2^S$.

The obstacle is circumvented by the randomness distribution technique used in [18]. Instead of computing the AKGS garblings in key generation or encryption phase, the label values are produced by a joint effort of both the secret key and ciphertext. To do so, the garbling is executed under the hood of IPFE using pseudorandomness, instead of true randomness. That is, some part of the garbling randomness is sampled in key generation whereas the rest is sampled in encryption. More specifically, every true random value $r_t[(i, j, \boldsymbol{W}, q)]$ is written as a product $\boldsymbol{r}_{\boldsymbol{x}}[(t, i, j, \boldsymbol{W})]\boldsymbol{r}_{k,f}[q]$ where $\boldsymbol{r}_{\boldsymbol{x}}[(t, i, j, \boldsymbol{W})]$ is used in the ciphertext and $\boldsymbol{r}_{k,f}[q]$ is utilized to encode the transition blocks of M_k in the secret key. To enable this, the transition matrix associated to M_k is represented as follows:

$$\mathbf{M}(\boldsymbol{x})[(i, j, \boldsymbol{W}, q), (i', j', \boldsymbol{W}', q')] = \delta^{(?)}((i, j, \boldsymbol{W}, q), (i', j', \boldsymbol{W}', q'))$$
$$\times \mathbf{M}_{\boldsymbol{x}[i], \boldsymbol{W}[j], \boldsymbol{W}'[j], i'-i, j'-j}[q, q']$$

where $\delta^{(?)}((i,j,\boldsymbol{W},q),(i',j',\boldsymbol{W}',q'))$ is 1 if there is a valid transition from the configuration $(i,j,\boldsymbol{W},q)$ to $(i',j',\boldsymbol{W}',q')$, otherwise 0. Therefore, every block of $\mathbf{M}(\boldsymbol{x})[(i,j,\boldsymbol{W},q),(i',j',\boldsymbol{W}',q')]$ is either a $Q \times Q$ zero matrix or a *transition block* that belongs to a small set

$$\mathcal{T} = \{\mathbf{M}_\tau \mid \tau = (x,w,w',\Delta i, \Delta j) \in \{0,1\}^3 \times \{0,\pm 1\}^2\}$$

The $(i,j,\boldsymbol{W},q)$-th *block row* $\mathbf{M}_\tau = \mathbf{M}_{x,w,w',\Delta i, \Delta j}$ appears at $\mathbf{M}_{N,S}(\boldsymbol{x})$ $[(i,j,\boldsymbol{W},\_),(i',j',\boldsymbol{W}',\_)]$ if $x = \boldsymbol{x}[i]$, $w = \boldsymbol{W}[j]$, $\Delta i = i' - i$, $\Delta j = j' - j$, and $\boldsymbol{W}'$ is $\boldsymbol{W}$ with j-th entry changed to w'. Thus, every label $\ell_{k,t}[\mathsf{i},q]$ with $\mathsf{i} = (i,j,\boldsymbol{W})$ can be *decomposed* as inner product $\boldsymbol{v}_{k,q} \cdot \boldsymbol{u}_{k,t,i,j,\boldsymbol{W}}$. More precisely,

$\ell_{k,t}[\mathsf{i},q] = -\boldsymbol{r}_{t-1}[\mathsf{i},q] + \mathbf{M}_{k,N,S}(\boldsymbol{x})[(\mathsf{i},q),(\_,\_,\_,\_)]\boldsymbol{r}_t$

$\qquad = -\boldsymbol{r}_{t-1}[\mathsf{i},q] + \displaystyle\sum_{w',\Delta i,\Delta j}(\mathbf{M}_{k,\boldsymbol{x}[i],\boldsymbol{W}[j],w',\Delta i,\Delta j}\boldsymbol{r}_t[\mathsf{i}',\_])[q] \quad (\mathsf{i}' = (i+\Delta i, j+\Delta j, \boldsymbol{W}'))$

$\qquad = \boldsymbol{r}_x[t-1,\mathsf{i}]\boldsymbol{r}_{k,f}[q] + \displaystyle\sum_{w',\Delta i,\Delta j}\boldsymbol{r}_x[t,\mathsf{i}'](\mathbf{M}_{k,\boldsymbol{x}[i],\boldsymbol{W}[j],w',\Delta i,\Delta j}\boldsymbol{r}_{k,f})[q]$

$\qquad = \boldsymbol{r}_x[t-1,\mathsf{i}]\boldsymbol{r}_{k,f}[q] + \displaystyle\sum_{w',\Delta i,\Delta j}\boldsymbol{r}_x[t,\mathsf{i}'](\mathbf{M}_{k,\tau}\boldsymbol{r}_{k,f})[q] = \boldsymbol{v}_{k,q} \cdot \boldsymbol{u}_{k,t,i,j,\boldsymbol{W}}$

so that one can set the vectors

$$\boldsymbol{v}_{k,q} = (\quad -\boldsymbol{r}_{k,f}[q],\quad 0,\quad (\mathbf{M}_{k,\tau}\boldsymbol{r}_{k,f})[q]\quad \|\quad \mathbf{0}\ ),$$
$$\boldsymbol{u}_{t,\mathsf{i}} = (\quad \boldsymbol{r}_x[t-1,\mathsf{i}],\quad 0,\quad c_\tau(\boldsymbol{x};\boldsymbol{r}_x)\quad \|\quad \mathbf{0}\ )$$

where $c_\tau(\boldsymbol{x};\boldsymbol{r}_x)$ (a shorthand of the notation $c_\tau(\boldsymbol{x},t,i,j,\boldsymbol{W};\boldsymbol{r}_x)$ [18]) is given by

$$c_\tau(\boldsymbol{x};\boldsymbol{r}_x) = \begin{cases} \boldsymbol{r}_x[t,\mathsf{i}'], & \text{if } x = \boldsymbol{x}[i], w = \boldsymbol{W}[j]; \\ 0, & \text{otherwise.} \end{cases}$$

Similarly, the other labels can be decomposed: $\ell_{k,\text{init}} = (\boldsymbol{r}_{k,f}[1], \beta_k, 0) \cdot (\boldsymbol{r}_x[(0,1,1,\mathbf{0}_S)],1,0) = \beta_k + \boldsymbol{e}_{(1,1,\mathbf{0}_S,1)}^\top \boldsymbol{r}_0$ and $\ell_{k,T+1}[(\mathsf{i},q)] = \widetilde{\boldsymbol{v}}_{k,q} \cdot \widetilde{\boldsymbol{u}}_{k,T+1,i,j,\boldsymbol{W}} = -\boldsymbol{r}_T[(\mathsf{i},q)] + \boldsymbol{z}[k]\boldsymbol{y}_{k,\text{acc}}[q]$ where

$$\widetilde{\boldsymbol{v}}_{k,q} = (\quad -\boldsymbol{r}_{k,f}[q],\quad \boldsymbol{y}_{k,\text{acc}}[q]\quad \|\quad \mathbf{0}\ ),$$
$$\widetilde{\boldsymbol{u}}_{T+1,\mathsf{i}} = (\quad \boldsymbol{r}_x[T,\mathsf{i}],\quad \boldsymbol{z}[k]\quad \|\quad \mathbf{0}\ )$$

A First Attempt. Armed with this, we now present the first candidate UAWS^L construction in the secret key setting and it supports a single key. We consider two independent master keys imsk and $\widetilde{\mathsf{imsk}}$ of IPFE. For simplicity, we assume the length of private attribute $\boldsymbol{z}$ is the same as the number of Turing machines present in $\boldsymbol{M} = (M_k)_{k \in \mathcal{I}_M}$, i.e., $n = |\mathcal{I}_M|$. We also assume that each Turing machine in the secret key share the same set of states.

$$\mathsf{SK}_{M,\mathcal{I}_M} = \{\mathsf{IPFE.SK}_{v_{k,\mathrm{init}}}, \mathsf{IPFE.SK}_{v_{k,q}}, \widetilde{\mathsf{IPFE.SK}}_{\widetilde{v}_{k,q}}\}_{k \in \mathcal{I}_M} :$$

$$[\![v_{k,\mathrm{init}}]\!]_2 = [\![(\ -r_{k,f}[1], \quad \beta_k, \quad\quad 0, \quad\quad \| \ \mathbf{0}\ )]\!]_2,$$
$$[\![v_{k,q}]\!]_2 = [\![(\ -r_{k,f}[q], \quad 0, \quad (\mathbf{M}_{k,\tau}r_{k,f})[q] \ \| \ \mathbf{0}\ )]\!]_2,$$
$$[\![\widetilde{v}_{k,q}]\!]_2 = [\![(\ -r_{k,f}[q], \quad y_{k,\mathrm{acc}}[q] \quad\quad\quad\quad \| \ \mathbf{0}\ )]\!]_2$$

$$\mathsf{CT}_x = (\mathsf{IPFE.CT}_{u_{\mathrm{init}}}, \mathsf{IPFE.CT}_u, \{\widetilde{\mathsf{IPFE.CT}}_{\widetilde{u}_k}\}_k) :$$

$$[\![u_{\mathrm{init}}]\!]_1 = [\![(\ r_x[(0,1,1,\mathbf{0}_S)], \quad 1, \quad\quad 0, \quad\quad \| \ \mathbf{0}\ )]\!]_1,$$
$$[\![u_{t<T,\mathrm{i}}]\!]_1 = [\![(\quad r_x[t-1,\mathrm{i}], \quad 0, \quad c_\tau(x;r_x) \ \| \ \mathbf{0}\ )]\!]_1,$$
$$[\![\widetilde{u}_{k,T+1,\mathrm{i}}]\!]_1 = [\![(\quad r_x[T,\mathrm{i}], \quad z[k] \quad\quad\quad\quad\quad \| \ \mathbf{0}\ )]\!]_1$$

Observe that the inner products between the ciphertext and secret key vectors yield the label values $[\![\ell_{k,\mathrm{init}}]\!]_\mathrm{T}, [\![\ell_{k,t}]\!]_\mathrm{T} = [\![(\ell_{k,t,\theta})_\theta]\!]_\mathrm{T}$ for $\theta = (i,j,\mathbf{W},q)$. Now, the evaluation procedure of AKGS is applied to obtain the partial values $[\![z[k]M_k|_{N,T,S}(x) + \beta_k]\!]_\mathrm{T}$. Combining all this values gives the required attribute weighted sum $\sum_k M_k|_{N,T,S}(x)z[k]$ Since $\sum_k \beta_k = 0$.

However, this scheme is not *fully* unbounded, in particular, the setup needs to know the length of the private attribute. To realise this, let us try to prove the security of the scheme. The main idea of the proof would be to make all the label values $(\ell_{k,t,\theta})_\theta$ truly random and simulated except the initial labels $\ell_{k,\mathrm{init}}$ so that one can reversely sample $\ell_{k,\mathrm{init}}$ hardcoded with a desired functional value. Suppose, for instance, the single secret key is queried before the challenge ciphertext. In this case, the honest label values are first hardwired in the ciphertext vectors and then the labels are transformed into their simulated version. This is because the ciphertext vectors are computed after the secret key. So, the first step is to hardwire the initial label values $\ell_{k,\mathrm{init}}$ into the ciphertext vector u_{init} and hence it indicates that the length of u_{init} must grow with respect to the number of $\ell_{k,\mathrm{init}}$'s. The same situation arises while simulating the other label values through $u_{t,\mathrm{i}}$. In other word, we need to know the size of $\mathcal{I}_M$ or the length of z in setup, which is against our desired functionality.

To tackle this, we increase the number of u_{init} and $u_{t<T,\mathrm{i}}$ in the above system. More specifically, each of these vectors are now computed for all $k \in [n]$, just like $\widetilde{u}_{k,T+1,\mathrm{i}}$. Although this fix the requirement of unboundedness of the system, there is another issue related to the security that must be solved. Note that, in the current structure, there is a possibility of *mix-and-match* attack since, for example, $\widetilde{u}_{k_1,T+1,\mathrm{i}}$ can be paired with $\widetilde{v}_{k_2,q}$ and this results in some *unwanted* attribute weighted sum of the form $\sum_{k \neq k_1,k_2} M_k(x)z[k] + M_{k_1}(x)z[k_2] + M_{k_2}(x)z[k_1]$. We employ the *index encoding* technique used in previous works achieving unbounded ABE or IPFE [21,23] to overcome the attack. In particular, we add two extra dimension $\rho_k(-k,1)$ in the ciphertext and $\pi_k(1,k)$ in the secret key for encoding the index k in each of the vectors of the system. Observe that for each Turing machine M_k an independent randomness π_k is sampled. It ensures that an adversary can only recover the desired attribute weighted sum and whenever vectors from different indices are paired only a garbage value is obtained.

Combining the Ideas. After combining the above ideas, we describe our $\mathsf{UAWS^L}$ supporting a single key as follows.

$$\mathsf{SK}_{M,\mathcal{I}_M} = \{\mathsf{IPFE.SK}_{v_{k,\mathsf{init}}}, \mathsf{IPFE.SK}_{v_{k,q}}, \widetilde{\mathsf{IPFE.SK}}_{\widetilde{v}_{k,q}}\}_{k\in\mathcal{I}_M} :$$

$$[\![v_{k,\mathsf{init}}]\!]_2 = [\![(\ \pi_k(1,k),\ -r_{k,f}[1],\quad \beta_k,\qquad\qquad 0,\qquad\qquad \|\ \mathbf{0}\ )]\!]_2,$$
$$[\![v_{k,q}]\!]_2 = [\![(\ \pi_k(1,k),\ -r_{k,f}[q],\quad 0,\quad (\mathbf{M}_{k,\tau}r_{k,f})[q]\ \|\ \mathbf{0}\ )]\!]_2,$$
$$[\![\widetilde{v}_{k,q}]\!]_2 = [\![(\ \pi_k(1,k),\ -r_{k,f}[q], y_{k,\mathsf{acc}}[q]\qquad\qquad\qquad \|\ \mathbf{0}\ )]\!]_2$$

$$\mathsf{CT}_x = \{\mathsf{IPFE.CT}_{u_{k,\mathsf{init}}}, \mathsf{IPFE.CT}_{u_{k,t<T,i}}, \widetilde{\mathsf{IPFE.CT}}_{\widetilde{u}_{k,T+1,i}}\}_k :$$

$$[\![u_{k,\mathsf{init}}]\!]_1 = [\![(\ \rho_k(-k,1),\ r_x[(0,1,1,\mathbf{0}_S)],\quad 1,\qquad 0,\qquad \|\ \mathbf{0}\ )]\!]_1,$$
$$[\![u_{k,t<T,i}]\!]_1 = [\![(\ \rho_k(-k,1),\qquad r_x[t-1,i],\qquad 0,\quad c_\tau(x;r_x)\ \|\ \mathbf{0}\ )]\!]_1,$$
$$[\![\widetilde{u}_{k,T+1,i}]\!]_1 = [\![(\ \rho_k(-k,1),\qquad r_x[T,i],\qquad z[k]\qquad\qquad \|\ \mathbf{0}\ )]\!]_1$$

Although the above construction satisfies our desired functionality, preserves the compactness of ciphertexts and resists the aforementioned attack, we face multiple challenges in adapting the proof ideas of previous works [13,18,23].

Security Challenges and Solutions. Next, we discuss the challenges in proving the adaptive simulation security of the scheme. Firstly, the unbounded IPFE scheme of Tomida and Takashima [23] is proved in the *indistinguishability-based* model whereas we aim to prove simulation security that is much more challenging. The work closer to ours is the FE for AWS of Datta and Pal [13], but it only supports a *non-uniform* model of computation and the inner product functionality is *bounded*. Moreover, since the garbling randomness is distributed in the secret key and ciphertext vectors, we can not adapt their proof techniques [13,23] in a straightforward manner. Although the ABE scheme of Lin and Luo [18] handles a uniform model of computation, they only consider *all-or-nothing* type encryptions and hence the adversary is allowed to query secret keys which always fail to decrypt the challenge ciphertext. In contrast, we construct a more advanced encryption mechanism which overcomes all the above constraints of prior works, i.e., our $\mathsf{UAWS^L}$ is an adaptively *simulation* secure *functional encryption scheme* that supports *unbounded* inner product functionality with a *uniform* model of computations over the public attributes.

Our proof technique is inspired by that of [13,18]. One of the core technical challenges is involved in the case where the secret key is queried before the challenge ciphertext. Thus, we focus more on "sk queried before ct" in this overview. As noted above, in the security analysis of [18] the adversary $\mathcal{A}$ is not allowed to decrypt the challenge ciphertext and hence they completely randomize the ciphertext in the final game. However, since we are building a FE scheme any secret key queried by $\mathcal{A}$ should be able to decrypt the challenge ciphertext. For this, we use the pre-image sampleability technique from prior works [12,13]. In particular, the reduction samples a dummy vector $d \in \mathbb{Z}_p^n$ satisfying $\sum_k M_k|_{N,T,S}(x)z[k] = \sum_k M_k|_{N,T,S}(x)d[k]$ where $M = (M_k)_k$ is a pre-challenge secret key. To plant the dummy vector into the ciphertext, we first need to make all label values $\{\ell_{k,t,i,q}\}$ truly random depending on the terms

$r_{k,f}[q]r_x[t-1,i]$'s and then turn them into their simulated forms, and finally traverse in the reverse path to get back the original form of the ciphertext with d taking place of the private attribute z. In order to make all these labels truly random, the honest label values are needed to be hardwired into the ciphertext vectors (since these are computed later) so that we can apply the DDH assumption in $\mathbb{G}_1$ to randomize the term $r_{k,f}[q]r_x[t-1,i]$ (hence the label values). However, this step is much more complicated than [18] since there are two independent IPFE systems in our construction and $r_{k,f}[q]$ appears in both $v_{k,q}$ and $\widetilde{v}_{k,q}$ (i.e., in both the IPFE systems). We design a two-level nested loop running over q and t for relocating $r_{k,f}[q]$ from v's and $\widetilde{v}_{k,q}$ to u's and $\widetilde{u}_{k,T+1,i}$. To this end, we note that the case of "sk queried after ct" is simpler where we embed the reversely sampled initial label values into the secret key. Before going to discuss the hybrids, we first present the *simulator* of the ideal world.

$$\mathsf{SK}_{M,\mathcal{I}_M} = \{\mathsf{IPFE.SK}_{v_{k,\text{init}}}, \mathsf{IPFE.SK}_{v_{k,q}}, \widetilde{\mathsf{IPFE.SK}}_{\widetilde{v}_{k,q}}\}_{k\in\mathcal{I}_M} : \text{ (sk queried before ct)}$$
$$[\![v_{k,\text{init}}]\!]_2 = [\![(\ \pi_k(1,k),\ -r_{k,f}[1],\quad \beta_k,\qquad 0 \qquad \|\ \mathbf{0}\ )]\!]_2,$$
$$[\![v_{k,q}]\!]_2 = [\![(\ \pi_k(1,k),\ -r_{k,f}[q],\quad 0,\quad (\mathbf{M}_{k,\tau}r_{k,f})[q]\ \|\ \mathbf{0}\ )]\!]_2,$$
$$[\![\widetilde{v}_{k,q}]\!]_2 = [\![(\ \pi_k(1,k),\ -r_{k,f}[q],\ y_{k,\text{acc}}[q]\qquad\qquad \|\ \mathbf{0}\ )]\!]_2$$

$$\mathsf{CT}_x = \{\mathsf{IPFE.CT}_{u_{k,\text{init}}}, \mathsf{IPFE.CT}_{u_{k,t<T,i}}, \widetilde{\mathsf{IPFE.CT}}_{\widetilde{u}_{k,T+1,i}}\}_k :$$
$$[\![u_{k,\text{init}}]\!]_1 = [\![(\ \rho_k(-k,1),\ r_x[(0,1,1,\mathbf{0}_S)],\quad 1,\qquad 0,\qquad \|\qquad 1,\qquad \mathbf{0}\ )]\!]_1,$$
$$[\![u_{k,t<T,i}]\!]_1 = [\![(\ \rho_k(-k,1),\qquad r_x[t-1,i],\qquad 0,\quad c_\tau(x;r_x)\ \|\qquad s_x[t,i],\qquad \mathbf{0}\ )]\!]_1,$$
$$[\![\widetilde{u}_{k,T+1,i}]\!]_1 = [\![(\ \rho_k(-k,1),\qquad r_x[T,i],\qquad d[k]\qquad\quad \|\quad s_x[T+1,i],\mathbf{0}\ )]\!]_1$$

$$\mathsf{SK}_{M,\mathcal{I}_M} = \{\mathsf{IPFE.SK}_{v_{k,\text{init}}}, \mathsf{IPFE.SK}_{v_{k,q}}, \widetilde{\mathsf{IPFE.SK}}_{\widetilde{v}_{k,q}}\}_{k\in\mathcal{I}_M} : \text{ (sk queried after ct)}$$
$$[\![v_{k,\text{init}}]\!]_2 = [\![(\ \pi_k(1,k),\ 0, 0, 0\ \|\ \ell_{k,\text{init}},\ \mathbf{0}\ )]\!]_2,$$
$$[\![v_{k,q}]\!]_2 = [\![(\ \pi_k(1,k),\ 0, 0, 0\ \|\ s_{k,f}[q],\mathbf{0}\ )]\!]_2,$$
$$[\![\widetilde{v}_{k,q}]\!]_2 = [\![(\ \pi_k(1,k),\ 0, 0\ \|\ s_{k,f}[q],\mathbf{0}\ )]\!]_2$$
where $\ell_{k,\text{init}} \leftarrow \mathsf{RevSamp}((M_k, x, M_k[x]z[k] + \beta_k, \{\ell_{k,t,i,q}\})$ s.t. $\sum_{k\in\mathcal{I}_M} \beta_k = 0$ if $\mathcal{I}_M \subseteq [n]$; otherwise $\beta_k \leftarrow \mathbb{Z}_p$.

Security Analysis. We use a three-step approach and each step consists of a group of hybrid sequence. At a very high level, we discuss the case of "sk queried before ct". In this overview, for simplicity, we assume that the challenger knows the length of z while it generates the secret key.

First group of Hybrids: The reduction starts with the real scheme. In the first step, the label function $\ell_{k,\text{init}}$ is reversely sampled with the value $M_k[x]z[k] + \beta_k$ which is hardwired in $u_{k,\text{init}}$.

$$\boldsymbol{v}_{k,\text{init}} = (\cdots, \boxed{1}, \boxed{0}, \quad 0 \quad \| \quad 0, \quad \boldsymbol{0}),$$
$$\boldsymbol{v}_{k,q} = (\cdots, -\boldsymbol{r}_{k,f}[q], \quad 0, \quad (\mathbf{M}_{k,\tau}\boldsymbol{r}_{k,f})[q] \quad \| \quad \boxed{\boldsymbol{s}_{k,f}[q]}, \boldsymbol{0}),$$
$$\widetilde{\boldsymbol{v}}_{k,q} = (\cdots, -\boldsymbol{r}_{k,f}[q], \boldsymbol{y}_{k,\text{acc}}[q] \quad \| \quad 0, \quad \boldsymbol{0})$$

$$\boldsymbol{u}_{k,\text{init}} = (\cdots, \boxed{\ell_{k,\text{init}}}, \boxed{0}, \quad 0, \quad \| \quad 0, \quad \boldsymbol{0}),$$
$$\boldsymbol{u}_{k,t<T,\text{i}} = (\cdots, \boldsymbol{r}_x[t-1,\text{i}], \quad 0, \quad c_\tau(\boldsymbol{x};\boldsymbol{r}_x) \quad \| \quad 0, \quad \boldsymbol{0}),$$
$$\widetilde{\boldsymbol{u}}_{k,T+1,\text{i}} = (\cdots, \quad \boldsymbol{r}_x[T,\text{i}], \quad z[k] \quad \| \quad \boxed{\boldsymbol{s}_x[T+1,\text{i}]}, \boldsymbol{0})$$

where $\ell_{k,\text{init}} \leftarrow \mathsf{RevSamp}((M_k, \boldsymbol{x}, M_k[\boldsymbol{x}]z[k] + \beta_k, \{\ell_{k,t,\text{i},q}\})$ and $\ell_{k,t,\text{i},q}$'s are computed honestly. Note that, the secret values $\{\beta_k\}$ are sampled depending on whether the queried key is eligible for decryption. More specifically, if $\mathcal{I}_M \subseteq [n]$, then β_k's are sampled as in the original key generation algorithm, i.e., $\sum_k \beta_k = 0$. On the other hand, if $\max \mathcal{I}_M > n$ then β_k's are sampled uniformly at random, i.e., they do not necessarily be secret shares of zero. This can be done by the function hiding property of IPFE which ensures that the distributions $\{\{\mathsf{IPFE.SK}_{v_k^{(\mathfrak{b})}}\}_{k\in[n+1,|\mathcal{I}_M|]}, \{\mathsf{IPFE.CT}_{\boldsymbol{u}_{k'}}\}_{k'\in[n]}\}$ for $\mathfrak{b} \in \{0,1\}$ are indistinguishable where

$$\boldsymbol{v}_k^{(\mathfrak{b})} = (\quad \pi_k, \quad k \cdot \pi_k, \boldsymbol{0}, \beta_k + \mathfrak{b} \cdot r_k, \boldsymbol{0}) \quad \text{for } k \in [n+1, |\mathcal{I}_M|], r_k \leftarrow \mathbb{Z}_p,$$
$$\boldsymbol{u}_{k'} = (-k' \cdot \rho_{k'}, \quad \rho_{k'}, \quad \boldsymbol{0}, \quad 1, \quad \boldsymbol{0}) \quad \text{for } k' \in [n]$$

Thus, the indistinguishability between the group of hybrids can be guaranteed by the piecewise security of AKGS and the function hiding security of IPFE.

Second Group of Hybrids: The second step is a loop. The purpose of the loop is to change all the honest label values $\ell_{k,t,\text{i},q}$ to simulated ones that take the form $\ell_{k,t,\text{i},q} = \boldsymbol{s}_x[t,\text{i}]\boldsymbol{s}_{k,f}[q]$ where $\boldsymbol{s}_x[t,\text{i}]$ is hardwired in $\boldsymbol{u}_{k,t,\text{i}}$ or $\widetilde{\boldsymbol{u}}_{k,T+1,\text{i}}$ and $\boldsymbol{s}_{k,f}[q]$ is hardwired in $\boldsymbol{v}_{k,q}$ or $\widetilde{\boldsymbol{v}}_{k,q}$.

The whole procedure is executed in via a two-level loop with outer loop running over t and inner loop running over q (both in increasing order). In each iteration of the loop, we move all occurrences of $\boldsymbol{r}_{k,f}[q]$ into the $\boldsymbol{u}$'s in one shot and hardwire the honest labels $\ell_{k,t,\text{i},q}$ into $\boldsymbol{u}_{k,t,\text{i}}$ for all i. Below we present two crucial intermediate hybrids of the loop when $t \leq T$.

$$\boldsymbol{v}_{k,q} = (\cdots, -\boxed{\boldsymbol{\times}\boldsymbol{r}_{k,f}[q]} - \| \boxed{0}, \boxed{1}, \boldsymbol{0}),$$
$$\widetilde{\boldsymbol{v}}_{k,q} = (\cdots, \quad -\boxed{0} - \| \quad 0, \boxed{1}, \boldsymbol{0}),$$

$$\boldsymbol{u}_{k,t<T,\text{i}} = (\cdots, -\boxed{\boldsymbol{\checkmark}\boldsymbol{r}_{k,f}[q]} - \| \boxed{\boldsymbol{s}_x[t,\text{i}]}, \boxed{\begin{array}{l}\text{honest } \ell_{k,t,\text{i},q} \\ = -\boldsymbol{r}_x[t-1,\text{i}]\boldsymbol{r}_{k,f}[q] + \cdots\end{array}}, \boldsymbol{0}),$$

$$\widetilde{\boldsymbol{u}}_{k,T+1,\text{i}} = (\cdots, \boldsymbol{r}_x[T,\text{i}], z[k] \| \boldsymbol{s}_x[T+1,\text{i}], \boxed{\begin{array}{l}\text{honest } \ell_{k,T+1,\text{i},q} \\ = -\boldsymbol{r}_x[T,\text{i}]\boldsymbol{r}_{k,f}[q] + \cdots\end{array}}, \boldsymbol{0})$$

where $\boldsymbol{X}r_{k,f}[q]$ and $\boldsymbol{\checkmark}r_{k,f}[q]$ indicate the presence of $r_{k,f}[q]$ in their respective positions. The indistinguishability can be argued using the function hiding security of IPFE. Next, by invoking DDH in $\mathbb{G}_1$, we first make $r_x[t-1,i]r_{k,f}[q]$ truly random for all i and then transform the label values into their simulated form $\ell_{k,i,q} = s_x[t,i]s_{k,f}[q]$ again by using DDH in $\mathbb{G}_1$ for all i. We *emphasize* that the labels $\ell_{k,T+1,i,q}$ are kept as honest and hardwired when the loop runs for $t \leq T$. Finally, the terms $s_{k,f}[q]$ are shifted back to $v_{k,q}$ or $\widetilde{v}_{k,q}$.

$$v_{k,q} = (\cdots , \boxed{-r_{k,f}[q]}, \qquad 0, \qquad \boxed{(\mathbf{M}_{k,\tau}r_{k,f})[q]} \parallel \boxed{s_{k,f}[q]}, \boxed{0}, \mathbf{0}),$$
$$\widetilde{v}_{k,q} = (\cdots , \boxed{-r_{k,f}[q]}, \boxed{y_{k,\mathrm{acc}}[q]} \qquad\qquad \parallel \qquad 0, \qquad \boxed{0}, \mathbf{0}),$$

$$u_{k,t<T,i} = (\cdots , \quad -\boxed{0}- \quad \parallel \quad s_x[t,i], \quad \boxed{0}, \mathbf{0}),$$
$$\widetilde{u}_{k,T+1,i} = (\cdots , r_x[T,i], z[k] \parallel s_x[T+1,i], \boxed{0}, \mathbf{0})$$

After the two-label loop finishes, the reduction run an additional loop over q with t fixed at $T+1$ to make the last few label values $\ell_{k,T+1,i,q}$ simulated. The indistinguishability between the hybrids follows from a similar argument as in the two-level loop.
$$v_{k,q} = (\cdots , -r_{k,f}[q], \qquad 0, \qquad (\mathbf{M}_{k,\tau}r_{k,f})[q] \parallel s_{k,f}[q], 0, \mathbf{0}),$$
$$\widetilde{v}_{k,q} = (\cdots , -r_{k,f}[q], y_{k,\mathrm{acc}}[q] \qquad\qquad \parallel \boxed{s_{k,f}[q]}, 0, \mathbf{0}),$$

$$u_{k,t<T,i} = (\cdots , \quad -0- \quad \parallel \quad s_x[t,i], \quad 0, \mathbf{0}),$$
$$\widetilde{u}_{k,T+1,i} = (\cdots , -\boxed{0}- \parallel s_x[T+1,i], 0, \mathbf{0})$$

Third Group of Hybrids: After all the label values $\ell_{k,t,i,q}$ are simulated, the third step uses a few more hybrids to reversely sample $\ell_{1,\mathrm{init}}$ and $\ell_{k,\mathrm{init}}|_{k>1}$ with the hardcoded values $M(x)^\top z + \beta_1$ and $\beta_k|_{k>1}$ respectively. This can be achieved through a statistical transformation on $\{\beta_k| \sum_k \beta_k = 0\}$. Finally, we are all set to insert the dummy vector d in place of z keeping $\mathcal{A}$'s view identical.

$$v_{k,\mathrm{init}} = (\cdots , 1, 0, 0 \parallel \quad 0, \quad 0, \mathbf{0}),$$
$$v_{k,q} = (\cdots , -\boxed{0}- \parallel s_{k,f}[q], 0, \mathbf{0}),$$
$$\widetilde{v}_{k,q} = (\cdots , -\boxed{0}- \parallel s_{k,f}[q], 0, \mathbf{0}),$$

$$u_{k,\mathrm{init}} = (\cdots , \boxed{\ell_{k,\mathrm{init}}}, 0, 0, \parallel \quad 0, \quad 0, \mathbf{0}),$$
$$u_{k,t<T,i} = (\cdots , \quad -0- \quad \parallel \quad s_x[t,i], \quad 0, \mathbf{0}),$$
$$\widetilde{u}_{k,T+1,i} = (\cdots , \quad -0- \quad \parallel s_x[T+1,i], 0, \mathbf{0})$$

where all the label values $\{\ell_{k,t,i,q}\}$ are simulated and the initial label values are computed as follows

$$\ell_{1,\text{init}} \leftarrow \text{RevSamp}(M_1, \boldsymbol{x}, \boldsymbol{M}(\boldsymbol{x})^\top \boldsymbol{d} + \beta_1, \{\ell_{k,t,i,q}\}),$$
$$\ell_{k,\text{init}} \leftarrow \text{RevSamp}(M_k, \boldsymbol{x}, \beta_k, \{\ell_{k,t,i,q}\}), \quad \text{for all } k > 1$$

From this hybrid we can traverse in the reverse direction all the way to the very first hybrid while keeping the private attribute as $\boldsymbol{d}$. We also rearrange the elements using the security of IPFE so that the distribution of the ciphertext does not change with the occurrence of the secret key whether it comes before or after the ciphertext. This is important for the public key UAWS$^\mathsf{L}$. The formal security is discussed in Theorem 4.1.

From Single Key to Full-Fledge UAWS$^\mathsf{L}$. The next and final goal is to bootstrap the single key, single ciphertext secure UAWS$^\mathsf{L}$ to a public key UAWS$^\mathsf{L}$ scheme that supports releasing many secret keys and ciphertexts. Observe that our secret key UAWS$^\mathsf{L}$ already supports multiple keys and single ciphertext. However, it fails to remain secure if two ciphertexts are published. This is because the piecewise security of AKGS can not be guaranteed if the label functions are reused. Our bootstrapping procedure takes inspiration from prior works [13,18], that is to sample a random multiplier $s \leftarrow \mathbb{Z}_p$ at the time of encryption, which will randomize the label values in the exponent of $\mathbb{G}_2$. In particular, using IPFE security the random multiplier s is moved to the secret key vectors where the DDH assumption ensures that $s\ell_{k,t,i,q}$'s are pseudorandom in the exponent of $\mathbb{G}_2$. To upgrade the scheme into public key setting, we employ the Slotted IPFE that enables encrypting into the public slots using the public key whereas the function hiding security still holds in the private slots. We describe below our public key UAWS$^\mathsf{L}$ scheme.

$$\mathsf{SK}_{M,\mathcal{I}_M} = \{\mathsf{IPFE.SK}_{\boldsymbol{v}_{\text{pad}}}\mathsf{IPFE.SK}_{\boldsymbol{v}_{k,\text{init}}}, \mathsf{IPFE.SK}_{\boldsymbol{v}_{k,q}}, \widetilde{\mathsf{IPFE.SK}}_{\widetilde{\boldsymbol{v}}_{k,q}}\}_{k\in\mathcal{I}_M} : \alpha \leftarrow \mathbb{Z}_p$$
$$[\![\boldsymbol{v}_{k,\text{init}}]\!]_2 = [\![(\quad 0, \quad \alpha, \quad 0, \quad\quad 0, \quad\quad 0, \quad\quad \| \; \boldsymbol{0} \,)]\!]_2,$$
$$[\![\boldsymbol{v}_{k,\text{init}}]\!]_2 = [\![(\; \pi_k(1,k),\, 0,\, -\boldsymbol{r}_{k,f}[1], \quad \beta_k, \quad\quad 0, \quad\quad \| \; \boldsymbol{0} \,)]\!]_2,$$
$$[\![\boldsymbol{v}_{k,q}]\!]_2 = [\![(\; \pi_k(1,k),\, 0,\, -\boldsymbol{r}_{k,f}[q], \quad 0, \quad (\mathbf{M}_{k,\tau}\boldsymbol{r}_{k,f})[q] \;\| \; \boldsymbol{0} \,)]\!]_2,$$
$$[\![\widetilde{\boldsymbol{v}}_{k,q}]\!]_2 = [\![(\; \pi_k(1,k),\, 0,\, -\boldsymbol{r}_{k,f}[q],\, \alpha\boldsymbol{y}_{k,\text{acc}}[q] \quad\quad \| \; \boldsymbol{0} \,)]\!]_2$$

$$\mathsf{CT}_{\boldsymbol{x}} = \{\mathsf{IPFE.CT}_{\boldsymbol{u}_{k,\text{init}}}, \mathsf{IPFE.CT}_{\boldsymbol{u}_{k,t<T,i}}, \widetilde{\mathsf{IPFE.CT}}_{\widetilde{\boldsymbol{u}}_{k,T+1,i}}\}_k : s \leftarrow \mathbb{Z}_p$$
$$[\![\boldsymbol{u}_{\text{pad}}]\!]_1 = [\![(\quad 0, \quad s, \quad 0, \quad\quad 0, \quad\quad 0, \quad\quad \| \perp)]\!]_1,$$
$$[\![\boldsymbol{u}_{k,\text{init}}]\!]_1 = [\![(\; \rho_k(-k,1),\, 0,\, s\cdot\boldsymbol{r}_{\boldsymbol{x}}[(0,1,1,\boldsymbol{0}_S)], \quad s, \quad\quad 0, \quad\quad \| \perp)]\!]_1,$$
$$[\![\boldsymbol{u}_{k,t<T,i}]\!]_1 = [\![(\; \rho_k(-k,1),\, 0, \quad s\cdot\boldsymbol{r}_{\boldsymbol{x}}[t-1,i], \quad 0, \quad s\cdot c_\tau(\boldsymbol{x};\boldsymbol{r}_{\boldsymbol{x}}) \;\| \perp)]\!]_1,$$
$$[\![\widetilde{\boldsymbol{u}}_{k,T+1,i}]\!]_1 = [\![(\; \rho_k(-k,1),\, 0, \quad s\cdot\boldsymbol{r}_{\boldsymbol{x}}[T,i], \quad s\cdot\boldsymbol{z}[k] \quad\quad \| \perp)]\!]_1$$

The slots at the left/right of " $\|$ " are public/private. The ciphertexts are computed using only the public slots and the private slots are utilized only in the security analysis. At a very high level, we utilize the triple-slot encryption technique devised in [13] to simulate the pre-challenge secret keys with a dummy vector encoded into the ciphertext and hardwire the functional value into the post-challenge secret keys. As mentioned earlier that the triple-slot encryption technique [13] was devised for non-uniform model which crucially uses the fact that the garbling randomness can be (fully) sampled in the key generation process. It does not hold in our setting. Thus, we design a more advanced three-slot encryption technique that is compatible with *distributed randomness* of AKGS garbling procedure. More specifically, we add one additional hidden subspace in order to realize such sophisticated mechanism for Logspace Turing machines. This additional subspace enables us to simulate the post-ciphertext secret keys with distributed randomness. However, shuttle technical challenges still remain to be overcome due to the structure of AKGS for Logspace Turing machines. We prove the security of the scheme in Theorem 5.1 and provide detailed security analysis in the full version.

3 Preliminaries

In this section, we provide the necessary definitions and backgrounds that will be used in the sequence.

Notations. We denote by λ the security parameter that belongs to the set of natural number $\mathbb{N}$ and 1^λ denotes its unary representation. We use the notation $s \leftarrow S$ to indicate the fact that s is sampled uniformly at random from the finite set S. For a distribution $\mathcal{X}$, we write $x \leftarrow \mathcal{X}$ to denote that x is sampled at random according to distribution $\mathcal{X}$. A function $\mathsf{negl} : \mathbb{N} \to \mathbb{R}$ is said to be a negligible function of λ, if for every $c \in \mathbb{N}$ there exists a $\lambda_c \in \mathbb{N}$ such that for all $\lambda > \lambda_c$, $|\mathsf{negl}(\lambda)| < \lambda^{-c}$.

Let Expt be an interactive security experiment played between a challenger and an adversary, which always outputs a single bit. We assume that $\mathsf{Expt}_{\mathcal{A}}^{\mathsf{C}}$ is a function of λ and it is parametrized by an adversary $\mathcal{A}$ and a cryptographic protocol C. Let $\mathsf{Expt}_{\mathcal{A}}^{\mathsf{C},0}$ and $\mathsf{Expt}_{\mathcal{A}}^{\mathsf{C},1}$ be two such experiment. The experiments are computationally/statistically indistinguishable if for any PPT/computationally unbounded adversary $\mathcal{A}$ there exists a negligible function negl such that for all $\lambda \in \mathbb{N}$,

$$\mathsf{Adv}_{\mathcal{A}}^{\mathsf{C}}(\lambda) = |\Pr[1 \leftarrow \mathsf{Expt}_{\mathcal{A}}^{\mathsf{C},0}(1^\lambda)] - \Pr[1 \leftarrow \mathsf{Expt}_{\mathcal{A}}^{\mathsf{C},1}(1^\lambda)]| < \mathsf{negl}(\lambda)$$

We write $\mathsf{Expt}_{\mathcal{A}}^{\mathsf{C},0} \overset{c}{\approx} \mathsf{Expt}_{\mathcal{A}}^{\mathsf{C},1}$ if they are *computationally indistinguishable* (or simply *indistinguishable*). Similarly, $\mathsf{Expt}_{\mathcal{A}}^{\mathsf{C},0} \overset{s}{\approx} \mathsf{Expt}_{\mathcal{A}}^{\mathsf{C},1}$ means *statistically indistinguishable* and $\mathsf{Expt}_{\mathcal{A}}^{\mathsf{C},0} \equiv \mathsf{Expt}_{\mathcal{A}}^{\mathsf{C},1}$ means they are *identically* distributed.

Sets and Indexing. For $n \in \mathbb{N}$, we denote $[n]$ the set $\{1, 2, \ldots, n\}$ and for $n, m \in \mathbb{N}$ with $n < m$, we denote $[n, m]$ be the set $\{n, n+1, \ldots, m\}$. We use lowercase boldface, e.g., $\boldsymbol{v}$, to denote column vectors in $\mathbb{Z}_p^n$ and uppercase boldface, e.g., $\mathbf{M}$, to denote matrices in $\mathbb{Z}_p^{n \times m}$ for $p, n, m \in \mathbb{N}$. The i-th component of a vector $\boldsymbol{v} \in \mathbb{Z}_p^n$ is written as $\boldsymbol{v}[i]$ and the (i, j)-th element of a matrix $\mathbf{M} \in \mathbb{Z}_p^{n \times m}$ is denoted by $\mathbf{M}[i, j]$. The transpose of a matrix $\mathbf{M}$ is denoted by $\mathbf{M}^\top$ such that $\mathbf{M}^\top[i, j] = \mathbf{M}[j, i]$. To write a vector of length n with all zero elements, we write $\mathbf{0}_n$ or simply $\mathbf{0}$ when the length is clear from the context. Let $\boldsymbol{u}, \boldsymbol{v} \in \mathbb{Z}_p^n$, then the inner product between the vectors is denoted as $\boldsymbol{u} \cdot \boldsymbol{v} = \boldsymbol{u}^\top \boldsymbol{v} = \sum_{i \in [n]} \boldsymbol{u}[i] \boldsymbol{v}[i] \in \mathbb{Z}_p$. We define *generalized* inner product between two vectors $\boldsymbol{u} \in \mathbb{Z}_p^{\mathcal{I}_1}, \boldsymbol{v} \in \mathbb{Z}_p^{\mathcal{I}_2}$ by $\boldsymbol{u} \cdot \boldsymbol{v} = \sum_{i \in \mathcal{I}_1 \cap \mathcal{I}_2} \boldsymbol{u}[i] \boldsymbol{v}[i]$.

Tensor Products. Let $\boldsymbol{u} \in \mathbb{Z}_p^{\mathcal{I}_1}$ and $\boldsymbol{v} \in \mathbb{Z}_p^{\mathcal{I}_2}$ be two vectors, their tensor product $\boldsymbol{w} = \boldsymbol{u} \otimes \boldsymbol{v}$ is a vector in $\mathbb{Z}_p^{\mathcal{I}_1 \times \mathcal{I}_2}$ with entries defined by $\boldsymbol{w}[(i,j)] = \boldsymbol{u}[i]\boldsymbol{v}[j]$. For two matrices $\mathbf{M}_1 \in \mathbb{Z}_p^{\mathcal{I}_1 \times \mathcal{I}_2}$ and $\mathbf{M}_1 \in \mathbb{Z}_p^{\mathcal{I}_1' \times \mathcal{I}_2'}$, their tensor product $\mathbf{M} = \mathbf{M} = \mathbf{M}_1 \otimes \mathbf{M}_2$ is a matrix in $\mathbb{Z}_p^{(\mathcal{I}_1 \times \mathcal{I}_1') \times \mathcal{I}_2 \times \mathcal{I}_2'}$ with entries defined by $\mathbf{M}[(i_1,i_1'),(i_2,i_2')] = \mathbf{M}_1[i_1,i_2]\mathbf{M}_2[i_1',i_2']$.

Currying. Currying is the product of partially applying a function or specifying part of the indices of a vector/matrices, which yields another function with fewer arguments or another vector/matrix with fewer indices. We use the usual syntax for evaluating a function or indexing into a vector/matrix, except that unspecified variables are represented by "$\lrcorner$". For example, let $\mathbf{M} \in \mathbb{Z}_p^{([\mathcal{I}_1] \times [\mathcal{I}_2]) \times ([\mathcal{J}_1] \times [\mathcal{J}_2])}$ and $i_1 \in \mathcal{I}_1, j_2 \in \mathcal{J}_2$, then $\mathbf{M}[(i_1, \lrcorner),(\lrcorner, j_2)]$ is a matrix $\mathbf{N} \in \mathbb{Z}_p^{[\mathcal{I}_2] \times [\mathcal{J}_2]}$ such that $\mathbf{N}[i_2,j_1] = \mathbf{M}[(i_1,i_2),(j_1,j_2)]$ for all $i_2 \in \mathcal{I}_2, j_1 \in \mathcal{J}_1$.

Coefficient Vector: Let $f : \mathbb{Z}_p^{\mathcal{I}} \to \mathbb{Z}_p$ be an affine function with coefficient vector $\mathbf{f} \in \mathbb{Z}_p^{\mathcal{S}}$ for $\mathcal{S} = \{\text{const}\} \cup \{\text{coef}_i | \ i \in \mathcal{I}\}$. Then for any $\boldsymbol{x} \in \mathbb{Z}_p^{\mathcal{I}}$, we have $f(\boldsymbol{x}) = \mathbf{f}[\text{const}] + \sum_{i \in \mathcal{I}} \mathbf{f}[\text{coef}_i]\boldsymbol{x}[i]$.

3.1 Bilinear Groups and Hardness Assumptions

We use a pairing group generator $\mathcal{G}$ that takes as input 1^λ and outputs a tuple $\mathsf{G} = (\mathbb{G}_1, \mathbb{G}_2, \mathbb{G}_T, g_1, g_2, e)$ where $\mathbb{G}_1, \mathbb{G}_2, \mathbb{G}_T$ are groups of prime order $p = p(\lambda)$ and g_i is a generator of the group $\mathbb{G}_i$ for $i \in \{1, 2\}$. The map $e : \mathbb{G}_1 \times \mathbb{G}_2 \to \mathbb{G}_T$ satisfies the following properties:

- *bilinear*: $e(g_1^a, g_2^b) = e(g_1, g_2)^{ab}$ for all $a, b \in \mathbb{Z}_p$.
- *non-degenerate*: $e(g_1, g_2)$ generates $\mathbb{G}_T$.

The group operations in $\mathbb{G}_i$ for $i \in \{1, 2, T\}$ and the map e are efficiently computable in deterministic polynomial time in the security parameter λ. For a matrix $\mathbf{A}$ and each $i \in \{1, 2, T\}$, we use the notation $[\![\mathbf{A}]\!]_i$ to denote $g_i^{\mathbf{A}}$ where the exponentiation is element-wise. The group operation is written additively while using the bracket notation, i.e. $[\![\mathbf{A} + \mathbf{B}]\!]_i = [\![\mathbf{A}]\!]_i + [\![\mathbf{B}]\!]_i$ for matrices $\mathbf{A}$ and $\mathbf{B}$. Observe that, given $\mathbf{A}$ and $[\![\mathbf{B}]\!]_i$, we can efficiently compute $[\![\mathbf{AB}]\!]_i = \mathbf{A} \cdot [\![\mathbf{B}]\!]_i$. We write the pairing operation multiplicatively, i.e. $e([\![\mathbf{A}]\!]_1, [\![\mathbf{B}]\!]_2) = [\![\mathbf{A}]\!]_1 [\![\mathbf{B}]\!]_2 = [\![\mathbf{AB}]\!]_T$.

Assumption 3.1 (Symmetric External Diffie-Hellman Assumption). We say that the SXDH assumption holds in a pairing group $\mathsf{G} = (\mathbb{G}_1, \mathbb{G}_2, \mathbb{G}_T, g_1, g_2, e)$ of order p, if the DDH assumption holds in $\mathbb{G}_i$, i.e., $\{[\![a]\!]_i, [\![b]\!]_i, [\![ab]\!]_i\} \approx \{[\![a]\!]_i, [\![b]\!]_i, [\![c]\!]_i\}$ for $i \in \{1, 2, T\}$ and $a, b, c \leftarrow \mathbb{Z}_p$.

3.2   Turing Machine Formulation

In this subsection, we describe the main computational model of this work, which is Turing machines with a read-only input and a read-write work tape. This type of Turing machines are used to handle decision problems belonging to space-bounded complexity classes such as Logspace predicates. We define below Turing machines with time complexity T and space complexity S. The Turing machine can either accept or reject an input string within this time/space bound. We also stick to the binary alphabet for the shake of simplicity.

Definition 3.1 (Turing machine with time/space bound computation).
[18] A (deterministic) Turing machine over $\{0,1\}$ is a tuple $M = (Q, \boldsymbol{y}_{\mathsf{acc}}, \delta)$, where $Q \geq 1$ is the number of states (we use $[Q]$ as the set of states and 1 as the initial state), $\boldsymbol{y}_{\mathsf{acc}} \in \{0,1\}^Q$ indicates whether each state is accepting, and

$$\delta : [Q] \times \{0,1\} \times \{0,1\} \to [Q] \times \{0,1\} \times \{0,\pm 1\} \times \{0,\pm 1\},$$
$$(q,x,w) \mapsto (q',w',\Delta i, \Delta j)$$

is the state transition function, which, given the current state q, the symbol x on the input tape under scan, and the symbol w on the work tape under scan, specifies the new state q', the symbol w' overwriting w, the direction Δi to which the input tape pointer moves, and the direction Δj to which the work tape pointer moves. The machine is required to hang (instead of halting) once it reaches on the accepting state, i.e., for all $q \in [Q]$ such that $\boldsymbol{y}_{\mathsf{acc}}[q] = 1$ and all $x, w \in \{0,1\}$, it holds that $\delta(q,x,w) = (q,w,0,0)$.

For input length $N \geq 1$ and space complexity bound $S \geq 1$, the set of *internal configurations* of M is

$$\mathcal{C}_{M,N,S} = [N] \times [S] \times \{0,1\}^S \times [Q],$$

where $(i,j,\boldsymbol{W},q) \in \mathcal{C}_{M,N,S}$ specifies the input tape pointer $i \in [N]$, the work tape pointer $j \in [S]$, the content of the work tape $\boldsymbol{W} \in \{0,1\}^S$ and the machine state $q \in [Q]$.

For any bit-string $\boldsymbol{x} \in \{0,1\}^N$ for $N \geq 1$ and time/space complexity bounds $T, S \geq 1$, the machine M accepts $\boldsymbol{x}$ within time T and space S if there exists a sequence of internal configurations (*computation* path of T steps) $c_0, \ldots, c_T \in \mathcal{C}_{M,N,S}$ with $c_t = (i_t, j_t, \boldsymbol{W}_t, q_t)$ such that

$$i_0 = 1, j_0 = 1, \boldsymbol{W}_0 = \boldsymbol{0}_S, q_0 = 1 (\text{initial configuration}),$$
$$\text{for } 0 \leq t < T \left\{ \begin{array}{c} \delta(q_t, \boldsymbol{x}[i_t], \boldsymbol{W}_t[j_t]) = (q_{t+1}, \boldsymbol{W}_{t+1}[j_t], i_{t+1} - i_t, j_{t+1} - j_t), \\ \boldsymbol{W}_{t+1}[j] = \boldsymbol{W}_t[j] \text{ for all } j \neq j_t \quad (\text{valid transitions}); \\ \boldsymbol{y}_{\mathsf{acc}}[q_T] = 1 \quad (\text{accepting}). \end{array} \right.$$

Denote by $M|_{N,T,S}$ the function $\{0,1\}^N \to \{0,1\}$ mapping $\boldsymbol{x}$ to whether M accepts $\boldsymbol{x}$ in time T and space S. Define $\mathsf{TM} = \{M | M \text{ is a Turing machine}\}$ to be the set of all Turing machines.

Note that, the above definition does not allow the Turing machines moving off the input/work tape. For instance, if δ specifies moving the input pointer to the left/right when it is already at the leftmost/rightmost position, there is no valid next internal configuration. This type of situation can be handled by encoding the input string described in [18]. The problem of moving off the work tape to the left can be managed similarly, however, moving off the work tape to the right is undetectable by the machine, and this is intended due to the space bound. That is, when the space bound is violated, the input is *silently* rejected.

3.3 Functional Encryption for Unbounded Attribute-Weighted Sum for Turing Machines

We formally present the syntax of FE for unbounded attribute-weighted sum (AWS) and define adaptive simulation security of the primitive. We consider the set of all Turing machines $\mathsf{TM} = \{M | \ M \text{ is a Turing machine}\}$ with time bound T and space bound S.

Definition 3.2 (The AWS Functionality for Turing machines). For any $n, N \in \mathbb{N}$, the class of attribute-weighted sum functionalities is defined as

$$
\left\{ ((\boldsymbol{x} \in \{0,1\}^N, 1^T, 1^{2^S}), \boldsymbol{z} \in \mathbb{Z}_p^n) \mapsto M(\boldsymbol{x})^\top \boldsymbol{z} = \sum_{k \in \mathcal{I}_M} \boldsymbol{z}[k] \cdot M_k(\boldsymbol{x}) \ \left| \ \begin{matrix} N, T, S \geq 1, \\ M_k \in \mathsf{TM} \ \forall k \in [n], \\ \mathcal{I}_M \subseteq [n] \text{ with } |\mathcal{I}_M| \geq 1 \end{matrix} \right. \right\}
$$

Definition 3.3 (Functional Encryption for Attribute-Weighted Sum). An unbounded-slot FE for unbounded attribute-weighted sum associated to the set of Turing machines TM and the message space $\mathbb{M}$ consists of four PPT algorithms defined as follows:

Setup(1^λ): The setup algorithm takes as input a security parameter and outputs the master secret-key MSK and the master public-key MPK.

KeyGen(MSK, $(M, \mathcal{I}_M)$): The key generation algorithm takes as input MSK and a tuple of Turing machines $M = (M_k)_{k \in \mathcal{I}_M}$. It outputs a secret-key $\mathsf{SK}_{(M, \mathcal{I}_M)}$ and make $(M, \mathcal{I}_M)$ available publicly.

Enc(MPK, $((x_i, 1^{T_i}, 1^{S_i}), z_i)_{i \in [\mathcal{N}]}$): The encryption algorithm takes as input MPK and a message consisting of $\mathcal{N}$ number of public-private pair of attributes $(x_i, z_i) \in \mathbb{M}$ such that the public attribute $x_i \in \{0,1\}^{N_i}$ for some $N_i \geq 1$ with time and space bounds given by $T_i, S_i \geq 1$, and the private attribute $z_i \in \mathbb{Z}_p^{n_i}$. It outputs a ciphertext $\mathsf{CT}_{(x_i, T_i, S_i)}$ and make $(x_i, T_i, S_i)_{i \in [\mathcal{N}]}$ available publicly.

Dec$((\mathsf{SK}_{(M, \mathcal{I}_M)}, (M, \mathcal{I}_M)), (\mathsf{CT}_{(x_i, T_i, S_i)}, (x_i, T_i, S_i)_{i \in [\mathcal{N}]}))$: The decryption algorithm takes as input $\mathsf{SK}_{(M, \mathcal{I}_M)}$ along with the tuple of Turing machines and index sets $(M, \mathcal{I}_M)$, and a ciphertext $\mathsf{CT}_{(x_i, T_i, S_i)}$ along with a collection of associated public attributes $(x_i, T_i, S_i)_{i \in [\mathcal{N}]}$. It outputs a value in $\mathbb{Z}_p$ or $\bot$.

Correctness: The unbounded-slot FE for unbounded attribute-weighted sum is said to be correct if for all $((x_i \in \{0,1\}^{N_i}, 1^{T_i}, 1^{S_i}), z_i \in \mathbb{Z}_p^{n_i})_{i \in [\mathcal{N}]}$ and for all $(M = (M_k)_{k \in \mathcal{I}_M}, \mathcal{I}_M)$, we get

$$\Pr\left[\begin{array}{c} \mathsf{Dec}((\mathsf{SK}_{(M,\mathcal{I}_M)},(M,\mathcal{I}_M)),(\mathsf{CT}_{(x_i,T_i,S_i)},(x_i,T_i,S_i)_{i\in[\mathcal{N}]})) = \sum_{i\in\mathcal{N}}\sum_{k\in\mathcal{I}_M} M_k(x_i)z_i[k]: \\ (\mathsf{MSK},\mathsf{MPK})\leftarrow\mathsf{Setup}(1^\lambda),\mathsf{SK}_{(M,\mathcal{I}_M)}\leftarrow\mathsf{KeyGen}(\mathsf{MSK},(M,\mathcal{I}_M)), \\ \mathsf{CT}_{(x_i,T_i,S_i)}\leftarrow\mathsf{Enc}(\mathsf{MPK},((x_i,1^{T_i},1^{S_i}),z_i)_{i\in[\mathcal{N}]}),\mathcal{I}_M\subseteq[n_i]\ \forall i\in\mathcal{N} \end{array}\right]=1$$

We now define the adaptively simulation-based security of FE for unbounded attribute-weighted sum for Turing machines.

Definition 3.4 (Adaptive Simulation Security). Let (Setup, KeyGen, Enc, Dec) be an unbounded-slot FE for unbounded attribute-weighted sum for TM and message space $\mathbb{M}$. The scheme is said to be $(\Phi_{\mathsf{pre}},\Phi_{\mathsf{CT}},\Phi_{\mathsf{post}})$-adaptively simulation secure if for any PPT adversary $\mathcal{A}$ making at most Φ_{CT} ciphertext queries and $\Phi_{\mathsf{pre}},\Phi_{\mathsf{post}}$ secret key queries before and after the ciphertext queries respectively, we have $\mathsf{Expt}_{\mathcal{A},\mathsf{real}}^{\mathsf{UAWS}}(1^\lambda)\overset{c}{\approx}\mathsf{Expt}_{\mathcal{A},\mathsf{ideal}}^{\mathsf{UAWS}}(1^\lambda)$, where the experiments are defined as follows. Also, an unbounded-slot FE for attribute-weighted sums is said to be $(\mathsf{poly},\Phi_{\mathsf{CT}},\mathsf{poly})$-adaptively simulation secure if it is $(\Phi_{\mathsf{pre}},\Phi_{\mathsf{CT}},\Phi_{\mathsf{post}})$-adaptively simulation secure as well as Φ_{pre} and Φ_{post} are unbounded polynomials in the security parameter λ.

$\underline{\mathsf{Expt}_{\mathcal{A},\mathsf{real}}^{\mathsf{UAWS}}(1^\lambda)}$

1. $1^{\mathcal{N}}\leftarrow\mathcal{A}(1^\lambda)$;
2. $(\mathsf{MSK},\mathsf{MPK})\leftarrow\mathsf{Setup}(1^\lambda)$;
3. $(((x_i,1^{T_i},1^{S_i}),z_i\in\mathbb{Z}_p^{n_i})_{i\in[\mathcal{N}]})\leftarrow\mathcal{A}^{\mathcal{O}_{\mathsf{KeyGen}(\mathsf{MSK},\cdot)}}(\mathsf{MPK})$;
4. $\mathsf{CT}_{(x_i,T_i,S_i)}\leftarrow\mathsf{Enc}(\mathsf{MPK},((x_i,1^{T_i},1^{S_i}),z_i)_{i\in[\mathcal{N}]})$;
5. return $\mathcal{A}^{\mathcal{O}_{\mathsf{KeyGen}(\mathsf{MSK},\cdot)}}(\mathsf{MPK},\mathsf{CT})$

$\underline{\mathsf{Expt}_{\mathcal{A},\mathsf{ideal}}^{\mathsf{UAWS}}(1^\lambda)}$

1. $1^N\leftarrow\mathcal{A}(1^\lambda)$;
2. $(\mathsf{MSK}^*,\mathsf{MPK})\leftarrow\mathsf{Setup}^*(1^\lambda,1^N)$;
3. $(((x_i,1^{T_i},1^{S_i}),z_i\in\mathbb{Z}_p^{n_i})_{i\in[\mathcal{N}]})\leftarrow\mathcal{A}^{\mathcal{O}_{\mathsf{KeyGen}_0^*(\mathsf{MSK}^*,\cdot)}}(\mathsf{MPK})$
4. $\mathsf{CT}_{(x_i,T_i,S_i)}\leftarrow\mathsf{Enc}^*(\mathsf{MPK},\mathsf{MSK}^*,(x_i,1^{T_i},1^{S_i},n_i)_{i\in[\mathcal{N}]},\mathcal{V})$;
5. return $\mathcal{A}^{\mathcal{O}_{\mathsf{KeyGen}_1^*(\mathsf{MSK}^*,(x_i,1^{T_i},1^{S_i})_{i\in[\mathcal{N}]},\cdot,\cdot)}}(\mathsf{MPK},\mathsf{CT}_{(x_i,T_i,S_i)})$

$\mathcal{O}_{\mathsf{KeyGen}(\mathsf{MSK},\cdot)}$

1. input: $(M,\mathcal{I}_M)$
2. output: $\mathsf{SK}_{(M,\mathcal{I}_M)}$

$\mathcal{O}_{\mathsf{KeyGen}_0^*(\mathsf{MSK}^*,\cdot)}$

1. input: $(M_\phi,\mathcal{I}_{M_\phi})$ for $\phi\in[\Phi_{\mathsf{pre}}]$
2. output: $\mathsf{SK}_{(M_\phi,\mathcal{I}_{M_\phi})}$

$\mathsf{Enc}^*(\mathsf{MPK},\mathsf{MSK}^*,(x_i,1^{T_i},1^{S_i},n_i)_{i\in[\mathcal{N}]},\cdot)$

1. input: $\mathcal{V}=\{(M_\phi,\mathcal{I}_{M_\phi}),\sum_{i\in[\mathcal{N}]}M_\phi(x_i)^\top z_i:\phi\in[\Phi_{\mathsf{pre}}]\}$
2. output: $\mathsf{CT}_{(x_i,T_i,S_i)}$

$\mathcal{O}_{\mathsf{KeyGen}_1^*(\mathsf{MSK}^*,(x_i^*)_{i\in[N]},\cdot,\cdot)}$

1. input: $(M_\phi,\mathcal{I}_{M_\phi}),\sum_{i\in\mathcal{N}}M_\phi(x_i)^\top z_i$ for $\phi\in[\Phi_{\mathsf{post}}]$
2. output: $\mathsf{SK}_{(M_\phi,\mathcal{I}_{M_\phi})}$

3.4 Arithmetic Key Garbling Scheme for Turing Machines

Lin and Luo [18] introduced arithmetic key garbling scheme (AKGS). The notion of AKGS is an information theoretic primitive, inspired by randomized encodings

[5] and partial garbling schemes [14]. It garbles a function $f : \mathbb{Z}_p^n \to \mathbb{Z}_p$ (possibly of size $(m + 1)$) along with two secrets $z, \beta \in \mathbb{Z}_p$ and produces affine label functions $L_1, \ldots, L_{m+1} : \mathbb{Z}_p^n \to \mathbb{Z}_p$. Given f, an input $\boldsymbol{x} \in \mathbb{Z}_p^n$ and the values $L_1(\boldsymbol{x}), \ldots, L_{m+1}(\boldsymbol{x})$, there is an efficient algorithm which computes $zf(\boldsymbol{x}) + \beta$ without revealing any information about z and β. Lin and Luo [18] additionally design AKGS for Turing machines with time/space bounds. Many parts of this section is verbatim to the Sects. 5 and 7.1 of [18]. Thus, the reader familiar with the notion of AKGS for Turing machines can skip this section. We define AKGS for the function class

$$\mathcal{F} = \{M|_{N,T,S} : \mathbb{Z}_p^N \to \mathbb{Z}_p, N, T, S \geq 1, p \text{ prime}\}$$

for the set of all time/space bounded Turing machine computations. We refer to [18] for a detailed discussion on the computation of Turing machines as a sequence of matrix multiplications, and the construction of AKGS for matrix multiplication.

Definition 3.5 (Arithmetic Key Garbling Scheme (AKGS), [18]). An arithmetic garbling scheme (AKGS) for the function class $\mathcal{F}$, consists of two efficient algorithms:

Garble$((M, 1^N, 1^T, 1^S, p), z, \beta)$: The garbling is a randomized algorithm that takes as input a tuple of a function $M|_{N,T,S}$ over $\mathbb{Z}_p$ from $\mathcal{F}$, an input length N, a time bound T, a space bound S with $N, T, S \geq 1$, a prime p, and two secret integers $z, \beta \in \mathbb{Z}_p$. It outputs a set of affine functions $L_{\mathsf{init}}, (L_{t,\theta})_{t \in [T+1], \theta \in \mathcal{C}_{M,N,S}} :$ $\mathbb{Z}_p^N \to \mathbb{Z}_p$ which are called label functions that specifies how an input of length N is encoded as labels. Pragmatically, it outputs the coefficient vectors $\boldsymbol{\ell}_{\mathsf{init}}$, $(\boldsymbol{\ell}_{t,\theta})_{t \in [T+1], \theta \in \mathcal{C}_{M,N,S}}$.

Eval$((M, 1^N, 1^T, 1^S, p), \boldsymbol{x}, \boldsymbol{\ell}_{\mathsf{init}}, (\boldsymbol{\ell}_{t,\theta})_{t \in [T+1], \theta \in \mathcal{C}_{M,N,S}})$: The evaluation is a deterministic algorithm that takes as input a function $M|_{N,T,S}$ over $\mathbb{Z}_p$ from $\mathcal{F}$, an input vector $\boldsymbol{x} \in \mathbb{Z}_p^N$ and the integers $\boldsymbol{\ell}_{\mathsf{init}}, (\boldsymbol{\ell}_{t,\theta})_{t \in [T+1], \theta \in \mathcal{C}_{M,N,S}} \in \mathbb{Z}_p$ which are supposed to be the values of the label functions at $\boldsymbol{x} \in \mathbb{Z}_p^N$. It outputs a value in $\mathbb{Z}_p$.

Correctness: The AKGS is said to be correct if for all tuple $(M, 1^N, 1^T, 1^S, p)$, integers $z, \beta \in \mathbb{Z}_p$ and $\boldsymbol{x} \in \mathbb{Z}_p^N$, we have

$$\Pr\left[\begin{array}{l} \mathsf{Eval}((M, 1^N, 1^T, 1^S, p), \boldsymbol{x}, \boldsymbol{\ell}_{\mathsf{init}}, (\boldsymbol{\ell}_{t,\theta})_{t \in [T+1], \theta \in \mathcal{C}_{M,N,S}}) = zM|_{N,T,S}(\boldsymbol{x}) + \beta : \\ (\boldsymbol{\ell}_{\mathsf{init}}, (\boldsymbol{\ell}_{t,\theta})_{t \in [T+1], \theta \in \mathcal{C}_{M,N,S}}) \leftarrow \mathsf{Garble}((M, 1^N, 1^T, 1^S, p), z, \beta), \text{ where } \boldsymbol{\ell} \leftarrow L(\boldsymbol{x}) \end{array} \right] = 1$$

The scheme have *deterministic shape*, meaning that the number of label functions, $m = 1 + (T+1)NS2^S Q$, is determined solely by the tuple $(M, 1^N, 1^T, 1^S, p)$, independent of z, β and the randomness in Garble. The number of label functions m is called the *garbling size* of $M|_{N,T,S}$ under this scheme. For the shake of simpler representation, let us number the label values (or functions) as $1, \ldots, m$

in the lexicographical order where the first two label values are $\ell_{\text{init}}, \ell_{(1,1,1,\mathbf{0}_S,1)}$ and the last label value is $\ell_{(T+1,N,S,1^S,Q)}$.

Linearity: The AKGS is said to be *linear* if the following conditions hold:

- Garble$((M, 1^N, 1^T, 1^S, p), z, \beta)$ uses a uniformly random vector $\mathbf{r} \leftarrow \mathbb{Z}_p^m$ as its randomness, where m is determined solely by $(M, 1^N, 1^T, 1^S, p)$, independent of z, β.
- The coefficient vectors $\boldsymbol{\ell}_1, \ldots, \boldsymbol{\ell}_m$ produced by Garble$((M, 1^N, 1^T, 1^S, p), z, \beta)$ are linear in $(z, \beta, \mathbf{r})$.
- Eval$((M, 1^N, 1^T, 1^S, p), \mathbf{x}, \boldsymbol{\ell}_1, \ldots, \boldsymbol{\ell}_m)$ is linear in $\boldsymbol{\ell}_1, \ldots, \boldsymbol{\ell}_m$.

For our UAWS, we consider the piecewise security notion of AKGS defined by Lin and Luo [18][1].

Definition 3.6 (Piecewise Security of AKGS, [18]). An AKGS = (Garble, Eval) for the function class $\mathcal{F}$ is *piecewise* secure if the following conditions hold:

- The first label value is *reversely sampleable* from the other labels together with $(M, 1^N, 1^T, 1^S, p)$ and $\mathbf{x}$. This reconstruction is perfect even given all the other label functions. Formally, there exists an efficient algorithm RevSamp such that for all $M|_{N,T,S} \in \mathcal{F}, z, \beta \in \mathbb{Z}_p$ and $\mathbf{x} \in \mathbb{Z}_p^N$, the following distributions are identical:

$$\left\{ (\ell_1, \ell_2, \ldots, \ell_m) : \begin{array}{l} (\boldsymbol{\ell}_1, \ldots, \boldsymbol{\ell}_m) \leftarrow \text{Garble}((M, 1^N, 1^T, 1^S, p), z, \beta), \\ \ell_1 \leftarrow L_1(\mathbf{x}) \end{array} \right\},$$

$$\left\{ (\ell_1, \ell_2, \ldots, \ell_m) : \begin{array}{l} (\boldsymbol{\ell}_1, \ldots, \boldsymbol{\ell}_m) \leftarrow \text{Garble}((M, 1^N, 1^T, 1^S, p), z, \beta), \\ \ell_j \leftarrow L_j(\mathbf{x}) \text{ for } j \in [2, m], \\ \ell_1 \leftarrow \text{RevSamp}((M, 1^N, 1^T, 1^S, p), \mathbf{x}, zM|_{N,T,S}(\mathbf{x}) + \beta, \ell_2, \ldots, \ell_m) \end{array} \right\}$$

- For the other labels, each is *marginally random* even given all the label functions after it. Formally, this means for all $M|_{N,T,S} \in \mathcal{F}, z, \beta \in \mathbb{Z}_p, \mathbf{x} \in \mathbb{Z}_p^n$ and all $j \in [2, m]$, the following distributions are identical:

$$\left\{ (\ell_j, \ell_{j+1}, \ldots, \ell_m) : \begin{array}{l} (\boldsymbol{\ell}_1, \ldots, \boldsymbol{\ell}_m) \leftarrow \text{Garble}((M, 1^N, 1^T, 1^S, p), z, \beta), \\ \ell_j \leftarrow L_j(\mathbf{x}) \end{array} \right\},$$

$$\left\{ (\ell_j, \ell_{j+1}, \ldots, \ell_m) : \begin{array}{l} (\boldsymbol{\ell}_1, \ldots, \boldsymbol{\ell}_m) \leftarrow \text{Garble}((M, 1^N, 1^T, 1^S, p), z, \beta), \\ \ell_j \leftarrow \mathbb{Z}_p \end{array} \right\}$$

We now define special structural properties of AKGS as given in [18], related to the piecewise security of it.

Definition 3.7 (Special Piecewise Security of AKGS, [18]). An AKGS = (Garble, Eval) for a function class $\mathcal{F}$ is *special* piecewise secure if for any $(M, 1^N, 1^T, 1^S, p) \in \mathcal{F}, z, \beta \in \mathbb{Z}_p$ and $\mathbf{x} \in \mathbb{Z}_p^N$, it has the following special form:

---

[1] The usual simulation-based security considered in previous works [13,14] follows from the piecewise security of AKGS.

- The first label value ℓ_1 is always non-zero, i.e., $\mathsf{Eval}((M, 1^N, 1^T, 1^S, p), \boldsymbol{x}, 1, 0, \ldots, 0) \neq 0$ where we take $\ell_1 = 1$ and $\ell_j = 0$ for $1 < j \leq m$.
- Let $\boldsymbol{r} \leftarrow \mathbb{Z}_p^m$ be the randomness used in $\mathsf{Garble}((M, 1^N, 1^T, 1^S, p), z, \beta)$. For all $j \in [2, m]$. the label function L_j produced by $\mathsf{Garble}((M, 1^N, 1^T, 1^S, p), z, \beta; \boldsymbol{r})$ can be written as

$$L_j(\boldsymbol{x}) = k_j \boldsymbol{r}[j-1] + L_j'(\boldsymbol{x}; z, \beta, \boldsymbol{r}[j], \boldsymbol{r}[j+1], \ldots, \boldsymbol{r}[m])$$

where $k_j \in \mathbb{Z}_p$ is a non-zero constant (not depending on $\boldsymbol{x}, z, \beta, \boldsymbol{r}$) and L_j' is an affine function of $\boldsymbol{x}$ whose coefficient vector is linear in $(z, \beta, \boldsymbol{r}[j], \boldsymbol{r}[j+1], \ldots, \boldsymbol{r}[m])$. The component $\boldsymbol{r}[j-1]$ is called the randomizer of L_j and ℓ_j.

Lemma 3.1 ([18]). *A special piecewise secure* $\mathsf{AKGS} = (\mathsf{Garble}, \mathsf{Eval})$ *for a function class* $\mathcal{F}$ *is also piecewise secure. The* $\mathsf{RevSamp}$ *algorithm (required in piecewise security) obtained for a special piecewise secure* AKGS *is linear in* $\gamma, \ell_2, \ldots, \ell_{m+1}$ *and perfectly recovers* ℓ_1 *even if the randomness of* Garble *is not uniformly sampled. More specifically, we have the following:*

$\mathsf{Eval}((M, 1^N, 1^T, 1^S, p), \boldsymbol{x}, \ell_1, \ldots, \ell_m)$

$$= \ell_1 \mathsf{Eval}((M, 1^N, 1^T, 1^S, p), \boldsymbol{x}, 1, 0, \ldots, 0) + \mathsf{Eval}((M, 1^N, 1^T, 1^S, p), \boldsymbol{x}, 0, \ell_2, \ldots, \ell_m) \qquad (3.1)$$

$\mathsf{RevSamp}((M, 1^N, 1^T, 1^S, p), \boldsymbol{x}, \gamma, \ell_2, \ldots, \ell_m)$

$$= (\mathsf{Eval}((M, 1^N, 1^T, 1^S, p), \boldsymbol{x}, 1, 0, \ldots, 0))^{-1}(\gamma - \mathsf{Eval}((M, 1^N, 1^T, 1^S, p), \boldsymbol{x}, 0, \ell_2, \ldots, \ell_m)) \qquad (3.2)$$

Note that, Eq. (3.1) follows from the linearity of Eval and Eq. (3.2) ensures that $\mathsf{RevSamp}$ perfectly computes ℓ_1 (which can be verified by Eq. (3.1) with $\gamma = zM|_{N,T,S}(\boldsymbol{x}) + \beta$).

Lemma 3.2 ([18]). *A piecewise secure* $\mathsf{AKGS} = (\mathsf{Garble}, \mathsf{Eval})$ *is also special piecewise secure after an appropriate change of variable for the randomness used by* Garble.

4   (1-SK, 1-CT, 1-Slot)-FE for Unbounded AWS in L

In this section, we build a *secret-key*, 1-slot FE scheme for the *unbounded* attribute-weighted sum functionality in L. At a high level, the scheme satisfies the following properties:

- The setup is *independent* of any parameters, other than the security parameter λ. Specifically, the *length* of vectors and attributes, *number* of Turing machines and their *sizes* are not fixed a-priori during setup. These parameters are flexible and can be chosen at the time of key generation or encryption.
- A secret key is associated with a tuple $(\boldsymbol{M}, \mathcal{I}_{\boldsymbol{M}})$, where $\boldsymbol{M} = (M_k)_{k \in \mathcal{I}_{\boldsymbol{M}}}$ is a tuple of Turing machines with indices k from an index set $\mathcal{I}_{\boldsymbol{M}}$. For each $k \in \mathcal{I}_{\boldsymbol{M}}$, $M_k \in \mathsf{L}$, i.e., M_k is represented by a deterministic log-space bounded Turing machine (with an arbitrary number of states).
- Each ciphertext encodes a tuple of public-private attributes $(\boldsymbol{x}, \boldsymbol{z})$ of lengths N and n respectively. The runtime T and space bound S for all the machines in $\boldsymbol{M}$ are associated with $\boldsymbol{x}$ which is the input of each machine M_k.

– Finally, decrypting a ciphertext CT_x that encodes (x, z) with a secret key $\mathsf{SK}_{M, \mathcal{I}_M}$ that is tied to $(M, \mathcal{I}_M)$ reveals the value $\sum_{k \in \mathcal{I}_M} z[k] \cdot M_k(x)$ whenever $\mathcal{I}_M \subseteq [n]$.

We build an FE scheme for the functionality sketched above (also described in Definition 3.2) and prove it to be simulation secure against a *single* ciphertext and secret key query, where the key can be asked either before or after the ciphertext query. Accordingly, we denote the scheme as $\mathsf{SK\text{-}UAWS}^{\mathsf{L}}_{(1,1,1)} = (\mathsf{Setup}, \mathsf{KeyGen}, \mathsf{Enc}, \mathsf{Dec})$, where the index $(1, 1, 1)$ represents in order the number of secret keys, ciphertexts and slots supported. Below, we list the ingredients for our scheme.

1. IPFE $=$ (IPFE.Setup, IPFE.KeyGen, IPFE.Enc, IPFE.Dec): a *secret-key, function-hiding* IPFE based on G, where $\mathsf{G} = (\mathbb{G}_1, \mathbb{G}_2, \mathbb{G}_\mathsf{T}, g_1, g_2, e)$ is pairing group tuple of prime order p. We can instantiate this from [18].
2. AKGS = (Garble, Eval): a special piecewise-secure AKGS for the function class $\mathcal{M} = \{M|_{N,T,S} : \mathbb{Z}_p^N \to \mathbb{Z}_p \mid M \in \mathsf{TM}, N, T, S \geq 1, p \text{ prime}\}$ describing the set of time/space bounded Turing machines. In our construction, the Garble algorithm would run implicitly under the hood of IPFE and thus, it is not invoked directly in the scheme.

We are now ready to describe the $\mathsf{SK\text{-}UAWS}^{\mathsf{L}}_{(1,1,1)} = (\mathsf{Setup}, \mathsf{KeyGen}, \mathsf{Enc}, \mathsf{Dec})$.

Setup(1^λ): On input the security parameter, fix a prime integer $p \in \mathbb{N}$ and define the slots for two IPFE master secret keys as follows:

$$\mathcal{S}_{\text{1-UAWS}} = \{\mathsf{index}_1, \mathsf{index}_2, \mathsf{init}, \mathsf{rand}, \mathsf{rand}^{\mathsf{temp}}, \mathsf{rand}^{\mathsf{comp}}, \mathsf{rand}^{\mathsf{temp,comp}}, \mathsf{acc}, \mathsf{sim}, \mathsf{sim}^{\mathsf{temp}}, \mathsf{sim}^{\mathsf{comp}}\}$$
$$\cup \{\mathsf{tb}_\tau, \mathsf{tb}_\tau^{\mathsf{temp}}, \mathsf{tb}_\tau^{\mathsf{comp}}, \mathsf{tb}_\tau^{\mathsf{temp,comp}} \mid \tau \in \mathcal{T}\},$$
$$\widetilde{\mathcal{S}}_{\text{1-UAWS}} = \{\mathsf{index}_1, \mathsf{index}_2, \mathsf{init}, \mathsf{rand}, \mathsf{rand}^{\mathsf{temp}}, \mathsf{rand}^{\mathsf{temp,comp}}, \mathsf{acc}, \mathsf{acc}^{\mathsf{temp}}, \mathsf{sim}, \mathsf{sim}^{\mathsf{temp}}\}$$

Finally, it returns $\mathsf{MSK} = (\mathsf{IPFE.MSK}, \widetilde{\mathsf{IPFE.MSK}})$.

KeyGen$(\mathsf{MSK}, (M, \mathcal{I}_M))$: On input the master secret key $\mathsf{MSK} = (\mathsf{IPFE.MSK}, \widetilde{\mathsf{IPFE.MSK}})$ and a function tuple $M = (M_k)_{k \in \mathcal{I}_M}$ indexed w.r.t. an index set $\mathcal{I}_M \subset \mathbb{N}$ of arbitrary size , parse $M_k = (Q_k, y_k, \delta_k) \in \mathsf{TM} \; \forall k \in \mathcal{I}_M$ and sample the set of elements

$$\left\{ \beta_k \leftarrow \mathbb{Z}_p \mid \sum_k \beta_k = 0 \mod p \right\}_{k \in \mathcal{I}_M}$$

For all $k \in \mathcal{I}_M$, do the following:

1. For $M_k = (Q_k, y_k, \delta_k)$, compute its transition blocks $\mathbf{M}_{k,\tau} \in \{0,1\}^{Q_k \times Q_k}$, $\forall \tau \in \mathcal{T}$.
2. Sample independent random vectors $r_{k,f} \leftarrow \mathbb{Z}_p^{Q_k}$ and a random element $\pi_k \in \mathbb{Z}_p$.
3. For the following vector $v_{k,\mathsf{init}}$, compute a secret key $\mathsf{IPFE.SK}_{k,\mathsf{init}} \leftarrow \mathsf{IPFE.KeyGen}(\mathsf{IPFE.MSK}, [\![v_{k,\mathsf{init}}]\!]_2)$:

vector	index$_1$	index$_2$	init	rand	acc	tb$_\tau$	the other indices
$v_{k,\text{init}}$	π_k	$k \cdot \pi_k$	$r_{k,f}[1]$	0	β_k	0	0

4. For each $q \in [Q_k]$, compute the following secret keys

$$\text{IPFE.SK}_{k,q} \leftarrow \text{IPFE.KeyGen}(\text{IPFE.MSK}, [\![v_{k,q}]\!]_2) \quad \text{and}$$

$$\widetilde{\text{IPFE.SK}}_{k,q} \leftarrow \text{IPFE.KeyGen}(\widetilde{\text{IPFE.MSK}}, [\![\widetilde{v}_{k,q}]\!]_2),$$

where the vectors $v_{k,q}, \widetilde{v}_{k,q}$ are defined as follows:

vector	index$_1$	index$_2$	init	rand	acc	tb$_\tau$	the other indices
$v_{k,q}$	π_k	$k \cdot \pi_k$	0	$-r_{k,f}[q]$	0	$(\mathbf{M}_{k,\tau} r_{k,f})[q]$	0

vector	index$_1$	index$_2$	rand	acc	the other indices
$\widetilde{v}_{k,q}$	π_k	$k \cdot \pi_k$	$-r_{k,f}[q]$	$y_k[q]$	0

Finally, it returns the secret key as

$$\text{SK}_{(M, \mathcal{I}_M)} = \left((M, \mathcal{I}_M), \left\{ \text{IPFE.SK}_{k,\text{init}}, \left\{ \text{IPFE.SK}_{k,q}, \widetilde{\text{IPFE.SK}}_{k,q} \right\}_{q \in [Q_k]} \right\}_{k \in \mathcal{I}_M} \right).$$

Enc$(\text{MSK}, (x, 1^T, 1^{2^S}), z)$: On input the master secret key $\text{MSK} = (\text{IPFE.MSK}, \widetilde{\text{IPFE.MSK}})$, a public attribute $x \in \{0,1\}^N$ for some arbitrary $N \geq 1$ with time and space complexity bounds given by $T, S \geq 1$ (as $1^T, 1^{2^S}$) respectively, and the private attribute $z \in \mathbb{Z}_p^n$ for some arbitrary $n \geq 1$, it does the following:

1. Sample a random vector $r_x \leftarrow \mathbb{Z}_p^{[0,T] \times [N] \times [S] \times \{0,1\}^S}$.
2. For each $k \in [n]$, do the following:
   (a) Sample a random element $\rho_k \leftarrow \mathbb{Z}_p$.
   (b) Compute a ciphertext $\text{IPFE.CT}_{k,\text{init}} \leftarrow \text{IPFE.Enc}(\text{IPFE.MSK}, [\![u_{k,\text{init}}]\!]_1)$ for the vector $u_{k,\text{init}}$:

vector	index$_1$	index$_2$	init	rand	acc	tb$_\tau$	the other indices
$u_{k,\text{init}}$	$-k \cdot \rho_k$	ρ_k	$r_x[(0,1,1,\mathbf{0}_S)]$	0	1	0	0

   (c) For all $t \in [T], i \in [N], j \in [S], W \in \{0,1\}^S$, do the following:
      (i) Compute the transition coefficients $c_\tau(x; t, i, j, W; r_x), \forall \tau \in \mathcal{T}$ using r_x.

(ii) Compute the ciphertext $\mathsf{IPFE.CT}_{k,t,i,j,\boldsymbol{W}} \leftarrow \mathsf{IPFE.Enc}(\mathsf{IPFE.MSK},$ $[\![\boldsymbol{u}_{k,t,i,j,\boldsymbol{W}}]\!]_1)$ for the vector $\boldsymbol{u}_{k,t,i,j,\boldsymbol{W}}$:

vector	index$_1$	index$_2$	init	rand	acc	tb$_\tau$	the other indices
$\boldsymbol{u}_{k,t,i,j,\boldsymbol{W}}$	$-k \cdot \rho_k$	ρ_k	0	$\boldsymbol{r_x}[(t-1,i,j,\boldsymbol{W})]$	0	$c_\tau(\boldsymbol{x};t,i,j,\boldsymbol{W};\boldsymbol{r_x})$	0

(d) For $t = T+1$, compute the ciphertext $\widetilde{\mathsf{IPFE.CT}}_{k,T+1,i,j,\boldsymbol{W}} \leftarrow \widetilde{\mathsf{IPFE.Enc}}$ $(\widetilde{\mathsf{IPFE.MSK}}, [\![\widetilde{\boldsymbol{u}}_{k,T+1,i,j,\boldsymbol{W}}]\!]_1)$ for the vector $\widetilde{\boldsymbol{u}}_{k,T+1,i,j,\boldsymbol{W}}$:

vector	index$_1$	index$_2$	rand	acc	the other indices
$\widetilde{\boldsymbol{u}}_{k,T+1,i,j,\boldsymbol{W}}$	$-k \cdot \rho_k$	ρ_k	$\boldsymbol{r_x}[(T,i,j,\boldsymbol{W})]$	$\boldsymbol{z}[k]$	0

3. Finally, it returns the ciphertext as

$$\mathsf{CT}_{(\boldsymbol{x},T,S)} = \Big((\boldsymbol{x},T,S), \Big\{ \mathsf{IPFE.CT}_{k,\mathsf{init}}, \{\mathsf{IPFE.CT}_{k,t,i,j,\boldsymbol{W}}\}_{t\in[T]}, $$
$$\widetilde{\mathsf{IPFE.CT}}_{k,T+1,i,j,\boldsymbol{W}} \Big\}_{k\in[n],i\in[N],j\in[S],\boldsymbol{W}\in\{0,1\}^S} \Big).$$

Dec$(\mathsf{SK}_{(M,\mathcal{I}_M)}, \mathsf{CT}_{(\boldsymbol{x},T,S)})$: On input a secret key $\mathsf{SK}_{(M,\mathcal{I}_M)}$ and a ciphertext $\mathsf{CT}_{(\boldsymbol{x},T,S)}$, do the following:

1. Parse $\mathsf{SK}_{(M,\mathcal{I}_M)}$ and $\mathsf{CT}_{(\boldsymbol{x},T,S)}$ as follows:

$$\mathsf{SK}_{(M,\mathcal{I}_M)} = \Big(((M_k)_{k\in\mathcal{I}_M}, \mathcal{I}_M), \Big\{ \mathsf{IPFE.SK}_{k,\mathsf{init}}, \{\mathsf{IPFE.SK}_{k,q}, \widetilde{\mathsf{IPFE.SK}}_{k,q}\}_{q\in[Q_k]} \Big\}_{k\in\mathcal{I}_M} \Big),$$
$$M_k = (Q_k, \boldsymbol{y}_k, \delta_k),$$
$$\mathsf{CT}_{(\boldsymbol{x},T,S)} = \Big((\boldsymbol{x},T,S), \Big\{ \mathsf{IPFE.CT}_{k,\mathsf{init}}, \{\mathsf{IPFE.CT}_{k,t,i,j,\boldsymbol{W}}\}_{t\in[T]}, $$
$$\widetilde{\mathsf{IPFE.CT}}_{k,T+1,i,j,\boldsymbol{W}} \Big\}_{k\in[n],i\in[N],j\in[S],\boldsymbol{W}\in\{0,1\}^S} \Big), \boldsymbol{x}\in\{0,1\}^N.$$

2. Output $\bot$, if $\mathcal{I}_M \not\subseteq [n]$. Else, select the sequence of ciphertexts for the indices $k \in \mathcal{I}_M$ as

$$\mathsf{CT}_{(\boldsymbol{x},T,S)} = \Big((\boldsymbol{x},T,S), \Big\{ \mathsf{IPFE.CT}_{k,\mathsf{init}}, \{\mathsf{IPFE.CT}_{k,t,i,j,\boldsymbol{W}}\}_{t\in[T]}, $$
$$\widetilde{\mathsf{IPFE.CT}}_{k,T+1,i,j,\boldsymbol{W}} \Big\}_{k\in\mathcal{I}_M,i\in[N],j\in[S],\boldsymbol{W}\in\{0,1\}^S} \Big)$$

3. Recall that $\forall k \in \mathcal{I}_M, \mathcal{C}_{M_k,N,S} = [N] \times [S] \times \{0,1\}^S \times [Q_k]$, and that we denote any element in it as $\theta_k = (i,j,\boldsymbol{W},q) \in \mathcal{C}_{M_k,N,S}$ where the only component in the tuple θ_k depending on k is $q \in [Q_k]^2$. Invoke the IPFE decryption to compute all label values as:

---

[2] For simplicity of notations, we enumerate the states of each M_k as $1, \ldots, q$, i.e., $[Q_k] = [Q]$ for some $Q \in \mathbb{N}$.

$$\forall k \in \mathcal{I}_M : [\![\ell_{k,\mathrm{init}}]\!]_\mathrm{T} = \mathsf{IPFE.Dec}(\mathsf{IPFE.SK}_{k,\mathrm{init}}, \mathsf{IPFE.CT}_{k,\mathrm{init}})$$

$$\forall k \in \mathcal{I}_M, t \in [T], \theta_k = (i, j, \boldsymbol{W}, q) \in \mathcal{C}_{M_k, N, S} :$$
$$[\![\ell_{k,t,\theta_k}]\!]_\mathrm{T} = \mathsf{IPFE.Dec}(\mathsf{IPFE.SK}_{k,q}, \mathsf{IPFE.CT}_{k,t,i,j,\boldsymbol{W}})$$

$$\forall k \in \mathcal{I}_M, \theta_k = (i, j, \boldsymbol{W}, q) \in \mathcal{C}_{M_k, N, S} :$$
$$[\![\ell_{k,T+1,\theta_k}]\!]_\mathrm{T} = \widetilde{\mathsf{IPFE.Dec}}(\widetilde{\mathsf{IPFE.SK}}_{k,q}, \widetilde{\mathsf{IPFE.CT}}_{k,T+1,i,j,\boldsymbol{W}})$$

4. Next, invoke the AKGS evaluation and obtain the combined value

$$[\![\mu]\!]_\mathrm{T} = \prod_{k \in \mathcal{I}_M} \mathsf{Eval}\left(\left(M_k, 1^N, 1^T, 1^{2^S}, p \right), \boldsymbol{x}, [\![\ell_{k,\mathrm{init}}]\!]_\mathrm{T}, \left\{ [\![\ell_{k,t,\theta_k}]\!]_\mathrm{T} \right\}_{t \in [T+1], \theta_k \in \mathcal{C}_{M_k, N, S}} \right)$$

5. Finally, it returns $\mu = \mathsf{DLog}_{g_\mathrm{T}}([\![\mu]\!]_\mathrm{T})$, where $g_\mathrm{T} = e(g_1, g_2)$. Similar to [2], we assume that the desired attribute-weighted sum lies within a specified polynomial-sized domain so that discrete logarithm can be solved via brute-force.

Correctness: Correctness follows from that of IPFE and AKGS. The first step is to observe that all the AKGS label values are correctly computed as functions of the input $\boldsymbol{x}$. This holds by the correctness of IPFE and AKGS encoding of the iterated matrix-vector product representing any TM computation. The next (and final) correctness follows from the linearity of AKGS.Eval.

In more detail, for all $k \in \mathcal{I}_M, \theta_k = (i, j, \boldsymbol{W}, q) \in \mathcal{C}_{M_k, N, S}$, let $L_{k,\mathrm{init}}, L_{k,t,\theta_k}$ be the label functions corresponding to the AKGS garbling of $M_k = (Q_k, \boldsymbol{y}_k, \delta_k)$. By the definitions of vectors $\boldsymbol{v}_{k,\mathrm{init}}, \boldsymbol{u}_{\mathrm{init}}$ and the correctness of IPFE, we have

$$\ell_{k,\mathrm{init}} = (-k\rho_k\pi_k + k\pi_k\rho_k) + \boldsymbol{r_x}[(0, 1, 1, \boldsymbol{0}_S)]\boldsymbol{r}_{k,f}[1] + \beta_k$$
$$= \boldsymbol{r}_0[(1, 1, \boldsymbol{0}_S, 1)] + \beta_k = \boldsymbol{e}_{(1,1,\boldsymbol{0}_S,1)}^T \boldsymbol{r}_0 + \beta_k = L_{k,\mathrm{init}}(\boldsymbol{x}).$$

Next, $\forall k \in \mathcal{I}_M, t \in [T], q \in [Q_k]$, the structures of $\boldsymbol{v}_{k,q}, \boldsymbol{u}_{t,i,j,\boldsymbol{W}}$ and the correctness of IPFE yields

$$\ell_{k,t,i,j,\boldsymbol{W},q} = (-k\rho_k\pi_k + k\pi_k\rho_k) - \boldsymbol{r_x}[(t-1, i, j, \boldsymbol{W})]\boldsymbol{r}_{k,f}[q] + \sum_{\tau \in T} c_\tau(\boldsymbol{x}; t, i, j, \boldsymbol{W}; \boldsymbol{r_x})(\mathbf{M}_{k,\tau}\boldsymbol{r}_{k,f})[q]$$
$$= -\boldsymbol{r}_{t-1}[(i, j, \boldsymbol{W}, q)] + \sum_{\tau \in T} c_\tau(\boldsymbol{x}; t, i, j, \boldsymbol{W}; \boldsymbol{r_x})(\mathbf{M}_{k,\tau}\boldsymbol{r}_{k,f})[q] = L_{k,t,i,j,\boldsymbol{W},q}(\boldsymbol{x})$$

Finally, $\forall k \in \mathcal{I}_M, q \in [Q_k]$, the vectors $\widetilde{\boldsymbol{v}}_{k,q}, \widetilde{\boldsymbol{u}}_{k,T+1,i,j,\boldsymbol{W}}$ and the $\widetilde{\mathsf{IPFE}}$ correctness again yields

$$\ell_{k,T+1,i,j,\boldsymbol{W},q} = (-k\rho_k\pi_k + k\pi_k\rho_k) - \boldsymbol{r_x}[(T, i, j, \boldsymbol{W})]\boldsymbol{r}_{k,f}[q] + \boldsymbol{z}[k]\boldsymbol{y}_k[q]$$
$$= -\boldsymbol{r}_T[(i, j, \boldsymbol{W}, q)] + \boldsymbol{z}[k]\left(1_{[N] \times [S] \times \{0,1\}^S} \otimes \boldsymbol{y}_k\right)[(i, j, \boldsymbol{W}, q)]$$
$$= L_{k,T+1,i,j,\boldsymbol{W},q}(\boldsymbol{x}).$$

The above label values are computed in the exponent of the target group $\mathbb{G}_\mathrm{T}$. Once all these are generated correctly, the linearity of Eval implies that the garbling can be evaluated in the exponent of $\mathbb{G}_\mathrm{T}$. Thus, this yields

$$\llbracket \mu \rrbracket_T = \prod_{k \in \mathcal{I}_M} \mathsf{Eval}\left(\left(M_k, 1^N, 1^T, 1^{2^S}, p\right), \boldsymbol{x}, \llbracket \ell_{k,\mathsf{init}} \rrbracket_T, \left\{\llbracket \ell_{k,t,\theta_k} \rrbracket_T\right\}_{t \in [T+1], \theta_k \in \mathcal{C}_{M_k, N, S}}\right)$$

$$= \llbracket \sum_{k \in \mathcal{I}_M} \mathsf{Eval}((M_k, 1^N, 1^T, 1^{2^S}, p), \boldsymbol{x}, \ell_{k,\mathsf{init}}, \{\ell_{k,t,\theta_k}\}_{t \in [T+1], \theta_k \in \mathcal{C}_{M_k, N, S}}) \rrbracket_T$$

$$= \llbracket \sum_{k \in \mathcal{I}_M} (\boldsymbol{z}[k] \cdot M_k|_{N,T,S}(\boldsymbol{x}) + \beta_k) \rrbracket_T = \llbracket \sum_{k \in \mathcal{I}_M} \boldsymbol{z}[k] \cdot M_k|_{N,T,S}(\boldsymbol{x}) \rrbracket_T = \llbracket M(\boldsymbol{x})^\top \boldsymbol{z} \rrbracket_T$$

Theorem 4.1. *Assuming the* SXDH *assumption holds in* $\mathcal{G}$ *and the* IPFE *is function hiding secure, the above construction of* $(1\text{-SK}, 1\text{-CT}, 1\text{-}Slot)$*-FE for* UAWS *is adaptively simulation secure.*

The security analysis is provided in the full version.

5   1-Slot FE for Unbounded AWS for L

In this section, we construct a *public key* 1-slot FE scheme for the *unbounded* attribute-weighted sum functionality for L. The scheme satisfies the same properties as of the $\mathsf{SK\text{-}UAWS}^L_{(1,1,1)}$. However, the *public key* scheme supports releasing polynomially many secret keys and a single challenge ciphertext, hence we denote the scheme as $\mathsf{PK\text{-}UAWS}^L_{(\mathsf{poly},1,1)}$.

Along with the AKGS for Logspace Turing machines we require a *function-hiding slotted* IPFE = (IPFE.Setup, IPFE.KeyGen, IPFE.Enc, IPFE.SlotEnc, IPFE. Dec) based on G, where $\mathsf{G} = (\mathbb{G}_1, \mathbb{G}_2, \mathbb{G}_T, g_1, g_2, e)$ is pairing group tuple of prime order p. We now describe the $\mathsf{PK\text{-}UAWS}^L_{(\mathsf{poly},1,1)} = (\mathsf{Setup}, \mathsf{KeyGen}, \mathsf{Enc}, \mathsf{Dec})$.

Setup(1^λ): On input the security parameter, fix a prime integer $p \in \mathbb{N}$ and define the slots for generating two pair of IPFE master keys as follows:

$$\mathcal{S}_{\mathsf{pub}} = \left\{\mathsf{index}_1, \mathsf{index}_2, \mathsf{pad}, \mathsf{init}^{\mathsf{pub}}, \mathsf{rand}^{\mathsf{pub}}, \mathsf{acc}^{\mathsf{pub}}\right\} \cup \{\mathsf{tb}_\tau^{\mathsf{pub}} | \tau \in \mathcal{T}\},$$

$$\mathcal{S}_{\mathsf{copy}} = \{\mathsf{init}^{\mathsf{copy}}, \mathsf{rand}^{\mathsf{copy}}\} \cup \{\mathsf{tb}_\tau^{\mathsf{copy}} | \tau \in \mathcal{T}\},$$

$$\mathcal{S}_{\mathsf{priv}} = \mathcal{S}_{\mathsf{copy}} \cup \mathcal{S}_{\text{1-UAWS}} \cup \{\mathsf{pad}^{\mathsf{copy}}, \mathsf{pad}^{\mathsf{temp}}, \mathsf{acc}^{\mathsf{perm}}, \mathsf{sim}^{\mathsf{copy}}\},$$

$$\widetilde{\mathcal{S}}_{\mathsf{pub}} = \{\mathsf{index}_1, \mathsf{index}_2, \mathsf{rand}^{\mathsf{pub}}, \mathsf{acc}^{\mathsf{pub}}\},$$

$$\widetilde{\mathcal{S}}_{1,\mathsf{copy}} = \{\mathsf{rand}_1^{\mathsf{copy}}, \mathsf{acc}_1^{\mathsf{copy}}\}, \widetilde{\mathcal{S}}_{2,\mathsf{copy}} = \{\mathsf{rand}_2^{\mathsf{copy}}, \mathsf{acc}_2^{\mathsf{copy}}\},$$

$$\widetilde{\mathcal{S}}_{\mathsf{priv}} = \widetilde{\mathcal{S}}_{1,\mathsf{copy}} \cup \widetilde{\mathcal{S}}_{2,\mathsf{copy}} \cup \widetilde{\mathcal{S}}_{\text{1-UAWS}} \cup \{\mathsf{sim}^{\mathsf{copy}}\}$$

It generates (IPFE.MPK, IPFE.MSK) $\leftarrow$ IPFE.Setup$(\mathcal{S}_{\mathsf{pub}}, \mathcal{S}_{\mathsf{priv}})$ and $(\mathsf{IPFE.\widetilde{MPK}}, \mathsf{IPFE.\widetilde{MSK}}) \leftarrow \mathsf{IPFE.Setup}(\widetilde{\mathcal{S}}_{\mathsf{pub}}, \widetilde{\mathcal{S}}_{\mathsf{priv}})$ and returns MSK = $(\mathsf{IPFE.MSK}, \mathsf{IPFE.\widetilde{MSK}})$ and MPK = $(\mathsf{IPFE.MPK}, \mathsf{IPFE.\widetilde{MPK}})$.

KeyGen(MSK, $(M, \mathcal{I}_M)$): On input the master secret key MSK = (IPFE.MSK, $\mathsf{IPFE.\widetilde{MSK}}$) and a function tuple $M = (M_k)_{k \in \mathcal{I}_M}$ indexed w.r.t. an index set

$\mathcal{I}_M \subset \mathbb{N}$ of arbitrary size , it parses $M_k = (Q_k, \boldsymbol{y}_k, \delta_k) \in \mathsf{TM}$ $\forall k \in \mathcal{I}_M$ and samples the set of elements

$$\left\{ \alpha, \beta_k \leftarrow \mathbb{Z}_p \mid k \in \mathcal{I}_M, \sum_k \beta_k = 0 \mod p \right\}.$$

It computes a secret key $\mathsf{IPFE.SK_{pad}} \leftarrow \mathsf{IPFE.KeyGen}(\mathsf{IPFE.MSK}, [\![\boldsymbol{v}_{\mathsf{pad}}]\!]_2)$ for the following vector $\boldsymbol{v}_{\mathsf{pad}}$: For all $k \in \mathcal{I}_M$, do the following:

vector	index$_1$	index$_2$	pad	init^{pub}	rand^{pub}	acc^{pub}	tb$_\tau^{\mathsf{pub}}$	in $\mathcal{S}_{\mathsf{priv}}$
$\boldsymbol{v}_{\mathsf{pad}}$	0	0	α	0	0	0	0	0

1. For $M_k = (Q_k, \boldsymbol{y}_k, \delta_k)$, compute transition blocks $\mathbf{M}_{k,\tau} \in \{0,1\}^{Q_k \times Q_k}$, $\forall \tau \in \mathcal{T}_k$.
2. Sample independent random vector $\boldsymbol{r}_{k,f} \leftarrow \mathbb{Z}_p^{Q_k}$ and a random element $\pi_k \in \mathbb{Z}_p$.
3. For the following vector $\boldsymbol{v}_{k,\mathsf{init}}$, compute a secret key $\mathsf{IPFE.SK}_{k,\mathsf{init}} \leftarrow \mathsf{IPFE.KeyGen}(\mathsf{IPFE.MSK}, [\![\boldsymbol{v}_{k,\mathsf{init}}]\!]_2)$:

vector	index$_1$	index$_2$	pad	init^{pub}	rand^{pub}	acc^{pub}	tb$_\tau^{\mathsf{pub}}$	in $\mathcal{S}_{\mathsf{priv}}$
$\boldsymbol{v}_{k,\mathsf{init}}$	π_k	$k \cdot \pi_k$	0	$\boldsymbol{r}_{k,f}[1]$	0	β_k	0	0

4. For each $q \in [Q_k]$, compute the following secret keys

$$\mathsf{IPFE.SK}_{k,q} \leftarrow \mathsf{IPFE.KeyGen}(\mathsf{IPFE.MSK}, [\![\boldsymbol{v}_{k,q}]\!]_2) \quad \text{and}$$
$$\widetilde{\mathsf{IPFE.SK}}_{k,q} \leftarrow \mathsf{IPFE.KeyGen}(\widetilde{\mathsf{IPFE.MSK}}, [\![\widetilde{\boldsymbol{v}}_{k,q}]\!]_2)$$

where the vectors $\boldsymbol{v}_{k,q}, \widetilde{\boldsymbol{v}}_{k,q}$ are defined as follows:

vector	index$_1$	index$_2$	pad	init^{pub}	rand^{pub}	acc^{pub}	tb$_\tau^{\mathsf{pub}}$		in $\mathcal{S}_{\mathsf{priv}}$
$\boldsymbol{v}_{k,q}$	π_k	$k \cdot \pi_k$	0	0	$-\boldsymbol{r}_{k,f}[q]$	0	$(\mathbf{M}_{k,\tau}\boldsymbol{r}_{k,f})[q]$		0

vector	index$_1$	index$_2$	rand^{pub}	acc^{pub}	in $\widetilde{\mathcal{S}}_{\mathsf{priv}}$
$\widetilde{\boldsymbol{v}}_{k,q}$	k	$k \cdot \pi_k$	$-\boldsymbol{r}_{k,f}[q]$	$\alpha \cdot \boldsymbol{y}_k[q]$	0

Finally, it returns the secret key as

$$\mathsf{SK}_{(M,\mathcal{I}_M)} = \left((M,\mathcal{I}_M), \mathsf{IPFE.SK}_{\mathsf{pad}}, \left\{ \mathsf{IPFE.SK}_{k,\mathsf{init}}, \{ \mathsf{IPFE.SK}_{k,q}, \widetilde{\mathsf{IPFE.SK}}_{k,q} \}_{q \in [Q_k]} \right\}_{k \in \mathcal{I}_M} \right).$$

Enc$(\mathsf{MPK}, (\boldsymbol{x}, 1^T, 1^{2^S}), \boldsymbol{z})$: On input the master public key $\mathsf{MPK} = (\mathsf{IPFE.MPK}, \widetilde{\mathsf{IPFE.MPK}})$, a public attribute $\boldsymbol{x} \in \{0,1\}^N$ for some arbitrary $N \geq 1$ with time and space complexity bounds given by $T, S \geq 1$ (as $1^T, 1^{2^S}$) respectively, and the private attribute $\boldsymbol{z} \in \mathbb{Z}_p^n$ for some arbitrary $n \geq 1$, it samples $s \leftarrow \mathbb{Z}_p$ and compute a ciphertext $\mathsf{IPFE.CT}_{\mathsf{pad}} \leftarrow \mathsf{IPFE.Enc}(\mathsf{IPFE.MPK}, [\![\boldsymbol{u}_{\mathsf{pad}}]\!]_1)$ for the vector $\boldsymbol{u}_{\mathsf{pad}}$:

vector	index$_1$	index$_2$	pad	init^{pub}	rand^{pub}	acc^{pub}	tb$_\tau^{\mathsf{pub}}$	in $\mathcal{S}_{\mathsf{priv}}$
$\boldsymbol{u}_{\mathsf{pad}}$	0	0	s	0	0	0	0	0

Next, it does the following:

1. Sample a random vector $\boldsymbol{r}_{\boldsymbol{x}} \leftarrow \mathbb{Z}_p^{[0,T] \times [N] \times [S] \times \{0,1\}^S}$.
2. For each $k \in [n]$, do the following:
   (a) Sample a random element $\rho_k \leftarrow \mathbb{Z}_p$.
   (b) Compute a ciphertext $\mathsf{IPFE.CT}_{k,\mathsf{init}} \leftarrow \mathsf{IPFE.SlotEnc}(\mathsf{IPFE.MPK}, [\![\boldsymbol{u}_{k,\mathsf{init}}]\!]_1)$ for the vector $\boldsymbol{u}_{k,\mathsf{init}}$:

vector	index$_1$	index$_2$	pad	init^{pub}		rand^{pub}	acc^{pub}	tb$_\tau^{\mathsf{pub}}$	in $\mathcal{S}_{\mathsf{priv}}$
$\boldsymbol{u}_{k,\mathsf{init}}$	$-k \cdot \rho_k$	ρ_k	0	$s \cdot \boldsymbol{r}_{\boldsymbol{x}}[(0,1,1,\boldsymbol{0}_S)]$	0		s	0	$\perp$

   (c) For all $t \in [T], i \in [N], j \in [S], \boldsymbol{W} \in \{0,1\}^S$, do the following:
      (i) Compute the transition coefficients $c_\tau(\boldsymbol{x}; t, i, j, \boldsymbol{W}; \boldsymbol{r}_{\boldsymbol{x}}), \forall \tau \in \mathcal{T}$ using $\boldsymbol{r}_{\boldsymbol{x}}$.
      (ii) Compute $\mathsf{IPFE.CT}_{k,t,i,j,\boldsymbol{W}} \leftarrow \mathsf{IPFE.SlotEnc}(\mathsf{IPFE.MPK}, [\![\boldsymbol{u}_{k,t,i,j,\boldsymbol{W}}]\!]_1)$ for the vector $\boldsymbol{u}_{k,t,i,j,\boldsymbol{W}}$:

vector	index$_1$	index$_2$	pad	init^{pub}	rand^{pub}		acc^{pub}	tb$_\tau^{\mathsf{pub}}$		in $\mathcal{S}_{\mathsf{priv}}$
$\boldsymbol{u}_{k,t,i,j,\boldsymbol{W}}$	$-k \cdot \rho_k$	ρ_k	0	0	$s \cdot \boldsymbol{r}_{\boldsymbol{x}}[(t-1,i,j,\boldsymbol{W})]$	0		$s \cdot c_\tau(\boldsymbol{x}; t, i, j, \boldsymbol{W}; \boldsymbol{r}_{\boldsymbol{x}})$		$\perp$

   (d) For $t = T+1$, and for all $i \in [N], j \in [S], \boldsymbol{W} \in \{0,1\}^S$, compute $\widetilde{\mathsf{IPFE.CT}}_{k,T+1,i,j,\boldsymbol{W}} \leftarrow \mathsf{IPFE.SlotEnc}(\widetilde{\mathsf{IPFE.MPK}}, [\![\widetilde{\boldsymbol{u}}_{k,T+1,i,j,\boldsymbol{W}}]\!]_1)$ for the vector $\widetilde{\boldsymbol{u}}_{k,T+1,i,j,\boldsymbol{W}}$:

vector	index$_1$	index$_2$	rand^{pub}	acc^{pub}	in $\tilde{\mathcal{S}}_{\text{priv}}$
$\tilde{\boldsymbol{u}}_{k,T+1,i,j,\boldsymbol{W}}$	$-k \cdot \rho_k$	ρ_k	$s \cdot \boldsymbol{r_x}[(T,i,j,\boldsymbol{W})]$	$s \cdot \boldsymbol{z}[k]$	$\perp$

3. Finally, it returns the ciphertext as

$$\mathsf{CT}_{(\boldsymbol{x},T,S)} = \Big((\boldsymbol{x},T,S), n, \mathsf{IPFE.CT}_{\text{pad}}, \big\{ \mathsf{IPFE.CT}_{k,\text{init}}, \{\mathsf{IPFE.CT}_{k,t,i,j,\boldsymbol{W}}\}_{t \in [T]},$$
$$\widetilde{\mathsf{IPFE.CT}}_{k,T+1,i,j,\boldsymbol{W}} \big\}_{k \in [n], i \in [N], j \in [S], \boldsymbol{W} \in \{0,1\}^S} \Big).$$

Dec$(\mathsf{SK}_{(M,\mathcal{I}_M)}, \mathsf{CT}_{(\boldsymbol{x},T,S)})$: On input a secret key $\mathsf{SK}_{(M,\mathcal{I}_M)}$ and a ciphertext $\mathsf{CT}_{(\boldsymbol{x},T,S)}$, do the following:

1. Parse $\mathsf{SK}_{(M,\mathcal{I}_M)}$ and $\mathsf{CT}_{(\boldsymbol{x},T,S)}$ as follows:

$$\mathsf{SK}_{(M,\mathcal{I}_M)} = \Big(\big((M_k)_{k \in \mathcal{I}_M}, \mathcal{I}_M \big), \mathsf{IPFE.SK}_{\text{pad}}, \big\{ \mathsf{IPFE.SK}_{k,\text{init}}, $$
$$\big\{ \mathsf{IPFE.SK}_{k,q}, \widetilde{\mathsf{IPFE.SK}}_{k,q} \}_{q \in [Q_k]} \big\}_{k \in \mathcal{I}_M} \Big), M_k = (Q_k, \boldsymbol{y}_k, \delta_k),$$
$$\mathsf{CT}_{(\boldsymbol{x},T,S)} = \Big((\boldsymbol{x},T,S), n, \mathsf{IPFE.CT}_{\text{pad}}, \big\{ \mathsf{IPFE.CT}_{k,\text{init}}, \{\mathsf{IPFE.CT}_{k,t,i,j,\boldsymbol{W}}\}_{t \in [T]},$$
$$\widetilde{\mathsf{IPFE.CT}}_{k,T+1,i,j,\boldsymbol{W}} \big\}_{k \in [n], i \in [N], j \in [S], \boldsymbol{W} \in \{0,1\}^S} \Big).$$

2. Output $\perp$, if $\mathcal{I}_M \not\subset [n]$. Else, select the sequence of ciphertexts for the indices $k \in \mathcal{I}_M$ as

$$\mathsf{CT}_{(\boldsymbol{x},T,S)} = \Big((\boldsymbol{x},T,S), \big\{ \mathsf{IPFE.CT}_{k,\text{init}}, \{\mathsf{IPFE.CT}_{k,t,i,j,\boldsymbol{W}}\}_{t \in [T]},$$
$$\widetilde{\mathsf{IPFE.CT}}_{k,T+1,i,j,\boldsymbol{W}} \big\}_{k \in \mathcal{I}_M, i \in [N], j \in [S], \boldsymbol{W} \in \{0,1\}^S} \Big).$$

3. Use the IPFE decryption to obtain $[\![\mu_{\text{pad}}]\!]_{\text{T}} \leftarrow \mathsf{IPFE.Dec}(\mathsf{IPFE.SK}_{\text{pad}}, \mathsf{IPFE.CT}_{\text{pad}})$.

4. Recall that $\forall k \in \mathcal{I}_M, \mathcal{C}_{M_k,N,S} = [N] \times [S] \times \{0,1\}^S \times [Q_k]$, and that we denote any element in it as $\theta_k = (i,j,\boldsymbol{W},q) \in \mathcal{C}_{M_k,N,S}$ where the only component in the tuple θ_k depending on k is $q \in [Q_k]$. Invoke the IPFE decryption to compute all label values as:

$$\forall k \in \mathcal{I}_M : [\![\ell_{k,\text{init}}]\!]_{\text{T}} = \mathsf{IPFE.Dec}(\mathsf{IPFE.SK}_{k,\text{init}}, \mathsf{IPFE.CT}_{k,\text{init}})$$
$$\forall k \in \mathcal{I}_M, t \in [T], \theta_k = (i,j,\boldsymbol{W},q) \in \mathcal{C}_{M_k,N,S} :$$
$$[\![\ell_{k,t,\theta_k}]\!]_{\text{T}} = \mathsf{IPFE.Dec}(\mathsf{IPFE.SK}_{k,q}, \mathsf{IPFE.CT}_{k,t,i,j,\boldsymbol{W}})$$
$$\forall k \in \mathcal{I}_M, \theta_k = (i,j,\boldsymbol{W},q) \in \mathcal{C}_{M_k,N,S} :$$
$$[\![\ell_{k,T+1,\theta_k}]\!]_{\text{T}} = \mathsf{IPFE.Dec}(\widetilde{\mathsf{IPFE.SK}}_{k,q}, \widetilde{\mathsf{IPFE.CT}}_{k,T+1,i,j,\boldsymbol{W}})$$

5. Next, invoke the AKGS evaluation procedure and obtain the combined value

$$[\![\mu]\!]_{\text{T}} = \prod_{k \in \mathcal{I}_M} \mathsf{Eval}\Big(\big(M_k, 1^N, 1^T, 1^{2^S}, p\big), \boldsymbol{x}, [\![\ell_{k,\text{init}}]\!]_{\text{T}}, \big\{[\![\ell_{k,t,\theta_k}]\!]_{\text{T}}\big\}_{t \in [T+1], \theta_k \in \mathcal{C}_{M_k,N,S}} \Big)$$

6. Finally, it returns μ' such that $[\![\mu]\!]_T = ([\![\mu_{\mathsf{pad}}]\!]_T)^{\mu'}$, where $g_T = e(g_1, g_2)$. Similar to [2], we assume that the desired attribute-weighted sum lies within a specified polynomial-sized domain so that μ' can be searched via brute-force.

The correctness of our $\mathsf{PK\text{-}UAWS}^{\mathsf{L}}_{(\mathsf{poly},1,1)}$ can be shown similarly to our secret key scheme of the previous section. Please see the full version of the paper for details.

Theorem 5.1. *Assuming the* SXDH *assumption holds in* $\mathcal{G}$ *and the* IPFE *is function hiding secure, the above construction of* 1-Slot FE *for* UAWS *is adaptively simulation secure.*

The description of the simulator and the proof of the above theorem is given in the full version.

References

1. Abdalla, M., Bourse, F., De Caro, A., Pointcheval, D.: Simple functional encryption schemes for inner products. In: Katz, J. (ed.) PKC 2015. LNCS, vol. 9020, pp. 733–751. Springer, Heidelberg (2015). https://doi.org/10.1007/978-3-662-46447-2_33
2. Abdalla, M., Gong, J., Wee, H.: Functional encryption for attribute-weighted sums from k-Lin. In: Micciancio, D., Ristenpart, T. (eds.) CRYPTO 2020. LNCS, vol. 12170, pp. 685–716. Springer, Cham (2020). https://doi.org/10.1007/978-3-030-56784-2_23
3. Agrawal, S., Libert, B., Maitra, M., Titiu, R.: Adaptive simulation security for inner product functional encryption. In: Kiayias, A., Kohlweiss, M., Wallden, P., Zikas, V. (eds.) PKC 2020. LNCS, vol. 12110, pp. 34–64. Springer, Cham (2020). https://doi.org/10.1007/978-3-030-45374-9_2
4. Agrawal, S., Libert, B., Stehlé, D.: Fully secure functional encryption for inner products, from standard assumptions. In: Robshaw, M., Katz, J. (eds.) CRYPTO 2016. LNCS, vol. 9816, pp. 333–362. Springer, Heidelberg (2016). https://doi.org/10.1007/978-3-662-53015-3_12
5. Applebaum, B., Ishai, Y., Kushilevitz, E.: How to garble arithmetic circuits. In: FOCS 2011, pp. 120–129. IEEE Computer Society (2011)
6. Attrapadung, N.: Dual system encryption framework in prime-order groups via computational pair encodings. In: Cheon, J.H., Takagi, T. (eds.) ASIACRYPT 2016. LNCS, vol. 10032, pp. 591–623. Springer, Heidelberg (2016). https://doi.org/10.1007/978-3-662-53890-6_20
7. Boneh, D., et al.: Fully key-homomorphic encryption, arithmetic circuit ABE and compact garbled circuits. In: Nguyen, P.Q., Oswald, E. (eds.) EUROCRYPT 2014. LNCS, vol. 8441, pp. 533–556. Springer, Heidelberg (2014). https://doi.org/10.1007/978-3-642-55220-5_30
8. Boneh, D., Sahai, A., Waters, B.: Functional encryption: definitions and challenges. In: Ishai, Y. (ed.) TCC 2011. LNCS, vol. 6597, pp. 253–273. Springer, Heidelberg (2011). https://doi.org/10.1007/978-3-642-19571-6_16
9. Chen, J., Gay, R., Wee, H.: Improved dual system ABE in prime-order groups via predicate encodings. In: Oswald, E., Fischlin, M. (eds.) EUROCRYPT 2015. LNCS, vol. 9057, pp. 595–624. Springer, Heidelberg (2015). https://doi.org/10.1007/978-3-662-46803-6_20

10. Chen, J., Gong, J., Kowalczyk, L., Wee, H.: Unbounded ABE via bilinear entropy expansion, revisited. In: Nielsen, J.B., Rijmen, V. (eds.) EUROCRYPT 2018. LNCS, vol. 10820, pp. 503–534. Springer, Cham (2018). https://doi.org/10.1007/978-3-319-78381-9_19
11. Datta, P., Dutta, R., Mukhopadhyay, S.: Functional encryption for inner product with full function privacy. In: Cheng, C.-M., Chung, K.-M., Persiano, G., Yang, B.-Y. (eds.) PKC 2016. LNCS, vol. 9614, pp. 164–195. Springer, Heidelberg (2016). https://doi.org/10.1007/978-3-662-49384-7_7
12. Datta, P., Okamoto, T., Takashima, K.: Adaptively simulation-secure attribute-hiding predicate encryption. In: Peyrin, T., Galbraith, S. (eds.) ASIACRYPT 2018. LNCS, vol. 11273, pp. 640–672. Springer, Cham (2018). https://doi.org/10.1007/978-3-030-03329-3_22
13. Datta, P., Pal, T.: (Compact) adaptively Secure FE for attribute-weighted sums from k-Lin. In: Tibouchi, M., Wang, H. (eds.) ASIACRYPT 2021. LNCS, vol. 13093, pp. 434–467. Springer, Cham (2021). https://doi.org/10.1007/978-3-030-92068-5_15
14. Ishai, Y., Wee, H.: Partial garbling schemes and their applications. In: Esparza, J., Fraigniaud, P., Husfeldt, T., Koutsoupias, E. (eds.) ICALP 2014. LNCS, vol. 8572, pp. 650–662. Springer, Heidelberg (2014). https://doi.org/10.1007/978-3-662-43948-7_54
15. Lewko, A., Okamoto, T., Sahai, A., Takashima, K., Waters, B.: Fully secure functional encryption: attribute-based encryption and (hierarchical) inner product encryption. In: Gilbert, H. (ed.) EUROCRYPT 2010. LNCS, vol. 6110, pp. 62–91. Springer, Heidelberg (2010). https://doi.org/10.1007/978-3-642-13190-5_4
16. Lewko, A., Waters, B.: New techniques for dual system encryption and fully secure HIBE with short ciphertexts. In: Micciancio, D. (ed.) TCC 2010. LNCS, vol. 5978, pp. 455–479. Springer, Heidelberg (2010). https://doi.org/10.1007/978-3-642-11799-2_27
17. Lewko, A., Waters, B.: Unbounded HIBE and attribute-based encryption. In: Paterson, K.G. (ed.) EUROCRYPT 2011. LNCS, vol. 6632, pp. 547–567. Springer, Heidelberg (2011). https://doi.org/10.1007/978-3-642-20465-4_30
18. Lin, H., Luo, J.: Compact adaptively secure ABE from k-Lin: beyond NC^1 and towards NL. In: Canteaut, A., Ishai, Y. (eds.) EUROCRYPT 2020. LNCS, vol. 12107, pp. 247–277. Springer, Cham (2020). https://doi.org/10.1007/978-3-030-45727-3_9
19. Lin, H., Vaikuntanathan, V.: Indistinguishability obfuscation from DDH-like assumptions on constant-degree graded encodings. In: FOCS 2016, pp. 11–20. IEEE (2016)
20. Okamoto, T., Takashima, K.: Fully secure functional encryption with general relations from the decisional linear assumption. In: Rabin, T. (ed.) CRYPTO 2010. LNCS, vol. 6223, pp. 191–208. Springer, Heidelberg (2010). https://doi.org/10.1007/978-3-642-14623-7_11
21. Okamoto, T., Takashima, K.: Fully secure unbounded inner-product and attribute-based encryption. In: Wang, X., Sako, K. (eds.) ASIACRYPT 2012. LNCS, vol. 7658, pp. 349–366. Springer, Heidelberg (2012). https://doi.org/10.1007/978-3-642-34961-4_22
22. O'Neill, A.: Definitional issues in functional encryption. IACR Cryptology ePrint Archive, Report 2010/556 (2010)
23. Tomida, J., Takashima, K.: Unbounded inner product functional encryption from bilinear maps. Jpn. J. Ind. Appl. Math. **37**(3), 723–779 (2020). https://doi.org/10.1007/s13160-020-00419-x

24. Waters, B.: Dual system encryption: realizing fully secure IBE and HIBE under simple assumptions. In: Halevi, S. (ed.) CRYPTO 2009. LNCS, vol. 5677, pp. 619–636. Springer, Heidelberg (2009). https://doi.org/10.1007/978-3-642-03356-8_36

25. Wee, H.: Dual system encryption via predicate encodings. In: Lindell, Y. (ed.) TCC 2014. LNCS, vol. 8349, pp. 616–637. Springer, Heidelberg (2014). https://doi.org/10.1007/978-3-642-54242-8_26

26. Wee, H.: Attribute-hiding predicate encryption in bilinear groups, revisited. In: Kalai, Y., Reyzin, L. (eds.) TCC 2017. LNCS, vol. 10677, pp. 206–233. Springer, Cham (2017). https://doi.org/10.1007/978-3-319-70500-2_8

Collusion-Resistant Functional
Encryption for RAMs

Prabhanjan Ananth[1(✉)], Kai-Min Chung[2], Xiong Fan[3], and Luowen Qian[4]

[1] UC Santa Barbara, Santa Barbara, CA, USA
prabhanjan@cs.ucsb.edu
[2] Academia Sinica, Taipei, Taiwan
kmchung@iis.sinica.edu.tw
[3] Rutgers University, Piscataway, NJ, USA
xiong.fan@rutgers.edu
[4] Boston University, Boston, MA, USA
luowenq@bu.edu

Abstract. In recent years, functional encryption (FE) has established itself as one of the fundamental primitives in cryptography. The choice of model of computation to represent the functions associated with the functional keys plays a critical role in the complexity of the algorithms of an FE scheme. Historically, the functions are represented as circuits. However, this results in the decryption time of the FE scheme growing proportional to not only the worst case running time of the function but also the size of the input, which in many applications can be quite large.

In this work, we present the first construction of a public-key collusion-resistant FE scheme, where the functions, associated with the keys, are represented as random access machines (RAMs). We base the security of our construction on the existence of: (i) public-key collusion-resistant FE for circuits and, (ii) public-key doubly-efficient private-information retrieval [Boyle et al., Canetti et al., TCC 2017]. Our scheme enjoys many nice efficiency properties, including input-specific decryption time.

We also show how to achieve FE for RAMs in the bounded-key setting with weaker efficiency guarantees from laconic oblivious transfer, which can be based on standard cryptographic assumptions. En route to achieving our result, we present conceptually simpler constructions of succinct garbling for RAMs [Canetti et al., Chen et al., ITCS 2016] from weaker assumptions.

Keywords: Functional Encryption · RAMs

1 Introduction

Functional Encryption. In the recent years, several interesting cryptographic primitives have been proposed in the domain of computing on encrypted data, with one such primitive being *functional encryption* [11,51,52]. This notion allows for an entity to encrypt their input x such that anyone in possession of secret keys associated with functions $f_1, \ldots, f_q$, also referred to as functional

© International Association for Cryptologic Research 2022
S. Agrawal and D. Lin (Eds.): ASIACRYPT 2022, LNCS 13791, pp. 160–194, 2022.
https://doi.org/10.1007/978-3-031-22963-3_6

keys, can decrypt this ciphertext to obtain the values $f_1(x), \ldots, f_q(x)$ and nothing else. The setting where q is not a priori bounded is called the collusion resistant setting and will be the primary focus of this work.

Functional encryption (FE) has proven to be a useful abstraction for many theoretical applications, including constructing indistinguishability obfuscation [5,10], succinct randomized encodings [1,6,34], watermarking schemes [40], proving lower bounds in differential privacy [47], proving hardness of finding a Nash equilibrium [9,32] and many more.

Model of Computation. A vast majority of FE constructions model the functions associated with the functional keys as circuits. While circuits are easy to work with, when compared to other models of computation, they come with many disadvantages. The parameters in the system tend to grow *polynomially in the worst-case time bound* of the function; this includes the decryption time. Even worse, for functions that take sub-linear runtime in the "big data" setting, the decryption time would now take time proportional to the size of the entire data, which could be massive.

Designing FE for Alternate Models of Computation. These drawbacks prompt us to look beyond circuits and construct FE for more general models of computation. One general model of computation that we could hope to support is random access machines (RAMs). There are many advantages to FE for RAMs, we will mention a couple of them now and defer more when we formally define the primitive in the next section: firstly, the parameters of the scheme do not grow with the worst-case time bound and moreover, the decryption time is input-specific.

Despite its utility, the feasibility of collusion-resistant FE for RAMs had not been explored in prior works. Prior works did make partial progress in this direction by either considering weaker models of computation such as finite automata [2], Turing machines [1,6,7,34,45] or in the single-key setting [36][1]. However, the problem of constructing FE for RAMs was unanswered and has been one of the important open problems in this area.

1.1 Contributions

We resolve this open problem; we give the first feasibility result of functional encryption for RAMs. Before stating our result, we first elaborate on the definition of FE for RAMs. A public-key functional encryption for RAMs consists of the following algorithms:

- The setup algorithm Setup that produces a public key pk and a master secret key MSK. The runtime of the setup algorithm is polynomial in λ (security parameter) and grows poly-logarithmically in the worst-case runtime bound T.

---

[1] Note that the work of [36] also construct an FE for RAMs scheme in the bounded-key setting: however, the decryption time of the bounded-key FE scheme grows polynomially in the database size and thus doesn't enjoy the sublinear decryption runtime property that we desire.

- The key generation algorithm KeyGen that takes as input MSK, a RAM program P and outputs a functional key for P, denoted by sk_P. The running time of key generation is only proportional to λ, the description size of P and grows poly-logarithmically in T.
- The encryption procedure Enc takes as input MSK, database D and outputs a ciphertext CT. The running time of the encryption procedure grows polynomially in λ, $|D|$ and poly-logarithmically in T.
- The decryption procedure Dec, modeled as a RAM program, takes as input ciphertext CT, functional key sk_P and produces the output $P^D()$. The runtime of decryption should grow proportional only to t and λ, where t is the time to execute P^D.

The security notion[2] for the above notion can be appropriately defined along the same lines as (collusion-resistant) FE for circuits.

In terms of efficiency, FE for RAMs schemes enjoy better efficiency guarantees than FE for circuits schemes in terms of both the running time of the key generation algorithm as well as the running time of the decryption algorithm. We clarify this in Fig. 1.

	FE for Circuits	**Our work**
RunTime(Setup)	$\mathsf{poly}(\lambda)$	$\mathsf{poly}(\lambda)$
RunTime(KeyGen)	$\mathsf{poly}(\lambda, |P|, |\mathbf{D}|, \mathbf{T})$	$\mathsf{poly}(\lambda, |P|)$
RunTime(Enc)	$\mathsf{poly}(\lambda, |D|)$	$\mathsf{poly}(\lambda, |D|)$
RunTime(Dec)	$\mathsf{poly}(\lambda, |\mathbf{D}|, t)^{\ddagger}$	$\mathsf{poly}(\lambda, t)$

Fig. 1. Comparison of efficiency guarantees of FE for circuits via naively simulating RAM programs (that is, to issue a key for a program P and time bound T, generate a key for a circuit that runs P for T time steps) and our work. We denote P to be the program input to the key generation algorithm, D to be the database input to the encryption algorithm and T to be the worst case running time of P. We denote t to be the running time of P on D. Since, the typical setting of T is 2^{λ}, we omit mentioning the dependence on poly-log factors in T. ($\ddagger$ A well-known technique for decreasing the running time from T to t is to issue $\log T$ decryption keys, with the i-th one running in time at most 2^i.)

Main Result: Collusion-resistant FE for RAMs. We show how to generically transform any (collusion-resistant) FE for circuits scheme into a (collusion-resistant) FE for RAMs scheme. Our transformation additionally assumes the existence of public-key doubly-efficient private information retrieval (PK-DEPIR) scheme, introduced independently by the works of Boyle et al. [16] and Canetti et al. [21].

In more detail, we show the following.

---

[2] The security notion we consider in this work is indistinguishability-based (IND-based) selective security. We delve more on this when we formally define FE for RAMs in the technical sections.

Theorem 1 (Informal). *There exists a collusion-resistant public-key FE scheme for* RAMs *assuming the existence of:*

- *collusion-resistant public-key FE for circuits and,*
- *public-key doubly efficient PIR [16, 21].*

We note that the construction of public-key DEPIR is currently based on security of VBB for specific class of circuits. However, we note that even demonstrating the feasibility of FE for RAMs from *any* cryptographic assumption was wide open. Thus, we believe that our work takes an important step towards establishing the feasibility of FE for RAMs. We point out that a related primitive, FHE for RAMs [41], was also based on the assumption of public-key DEPIR.

Our construction involves a novel combination of pebbling techniques [31], rewindable ORAMs [41], and hybrid functional encryption techniques [3]. We only work in the selective security setting, where the challenge message query needs to be declared by the adversary even before looking at the public key.

Observe that the assumption of FE for circuits is inherent in Theorem 1 since FE for RAMs imply FE for circuits. It is natural to ask whether the assumption of public-key DEPIR is inherent. While we don't answer this question, we still make a useful observation: an FE for RAMs scheme implies a weaker notion, called *secret-key* DEPIR.

Theorem 2 (Informal). *Assuming the existence of unbounded private-key FE for* RAMs, *there exists a construction for unbounded secret-key DEPIR.*

The works of Boyle et al., Canetti et al. [16,21] also proposed constructions for secret-key doubly efficient PIR; while they are based on new cryptographic assumptions, a thorough study of the assumptions was recently conducted by [15].

Intermediate Result: Succinct Garbled RAMs from Falsifiable Assumptions. Towards proving our main result, we obtain a new construction[3] of succinct garbled RAMs [8,19,20,23,46]. A succinct garbling scheme for RAMs consists of the following algorithms: (i) Database encoding algorithm that encodes a database D in time $\mathsf{poly}(\lambda, |D|)$, (ii) RAM garbling algorithm garbles a program P in time $\mathsf{poly}(\lambda, |P|)$ and, (iii) Evaluation algorithm that takes as input garbling of D, garbling of a program P and outputs $P^D()$, in time polynomial in $(\lambda, |P|, |D|, t)$, where t is the running time of $P^D()$.

It has two advantages over prior constructions: (i) first, it is arguably simpler than existing constructions [4,18,19,23] and, (ii) second, it is based on polynomially secure functional encryption scheme for circuits (a falsifiable assumption) as opposed to existing constructions which are based on indistinguishability obfuscation[4] schemes (a non falsifiable assumption).

---

[3] In fact, we define a stronger version called succinct *reusable* garbled RAM; this notion implies succinct garbled RAM.

[4] In the technical sections, we use indistinguishability obfuscation for circuits with logarithmic inputs to construct succinct reusable garbled RAMs. However, it has been shown [49] that iO for logarithmic inputs is equivalent to collusion-resistant functional encryption for circuits.

Formally, we prove the following.

Theorem 3 (Informal). *There exists a succinct garbling scheme for RAMs assuming polynomially secure (collusion-resistant) public-key functional encryption for circuits.*

Bounded-Key FE for RAMs. Our techniques also extend naturally to the bounded-key setting. In this setting, the adversary can only query an a priori bounded number of functions in the security experiment. We show how to construct a bounded-key FE for RAMs from standard assumptions; unfortunately, the resulting FE for RAMs scheme does not enjoy the same efficiency properties as before. In particular, the algorithms run in time polynomial in the worst case time bound. Nonetheless, this still performs better than the bounded key FE for circuits scheme since the decryption time only grows with the worst case time bound and in particular, does not explicitly depend on the size of the database encrypted. Formally,

Theorem 4 (Informal). *Assuming the existence of laconic oblivious transfer [24] and public-key encryption, there exists a bounded-key public-key FE for RAMs scheme satisfying the following efficiency properties:*

- *The time to compute setup is $\mathsf{poly}(\lambda, Q, |P|, T)$, where T is the worst case time bound and Q is the collusion bound.*
- *The time to compute the key generation of a program P is $\mathsf{poly}(\lambda, Q, |P|, T)$.*
- *The time to compute the encryption of a database D is $\mathsf{poly}(\lambda, Q, |P|, |D|, T)$.*
- *The time to compute the decryption of a functional key associated with P and a ciphertext of database D is $\mathsf{poly}(\lambda, Q, |P|, t)$, where t is the runtime of $P^D()$.*

In comparison, a bounded key FE for circuits scheme has similar setup, key generation and encryption runtimes except that the decryption time is polynomial in $(\lambda, Q, |D|, |P|, t)$. When $t \ll |D|$, our bounded key FE for RAMs scheme outperforms bounded key FE for circuits schemes.

The primitive of laconic oblivious transfer can be instantiated using a host of well studied assumptions (for example, computational Diffie-Helman (CDH), learning with errors [17,24]). Thus, we obtain different constructions of bounded-key FE for RAMs based on standard assumptions.

Corollary 5 (Informal). *Assuming $\mathcal{X} \in \{CDH, LWE, Factoring\}$, there exists a bounded-key public-key encryption scheme for RAMs.*

Related Work. Goldreich and Ostrovsky [38] initiated the area of building cryptographic primitives for RAM programs and since then, several works have proposed cryptographic constructions for RAM computations: for example, garbling schemes [4,8,18–20,23,29,30], secure multiparty computation for RAMs [28,43], doubly-efficient private-information retrieval [16,21], private anonymous data access [42] and fully homomorphic encryption for RAMs [41]. Of particular interest to us is the work of Gentry et al. [36] which introduced and constructed (single-input) functional encryption for RAMs in the single-key setting. We view our work as continuing this exciting line of research.

2   Technical Overview

We present an overview of our construction.

Recap: Garbled RAMs. Towards building FE for RAMs, we first start with a weaker but similar notion of FE for RAMs, popularly referred to as garbled RAMs [29,30,35] in the literature. A garbled RAM allows for separately encoding a RAM program-database pair (P, D) such that the encodings only leak the output $P^D()$ (here we assume the program input is hardcoded in the program); computing both the encodings requires a private key that is not revealed to the adversary. Notice that a garbled RAM scheme already implies a *one-time, secret key* FE for RAM scheme; meaning that the adversary only gets to make a single ciphertext query and a single functional key query in the security experiment.

Traditionally, the following two-step approach is employed to construct a garbled RAM scheme:

- First construct a garbled RAM scheme in the UMA (unrestricted memory access) setting; the setting where the memory access pattern is not hidden.
- To hide the access pattern, generically combine any garbled RAM scheme satisfying UMA security with an oblivious RAM scheme [38].

The blueprint employed to construct a garbled RAM scheme in the UMA setting is the following: to garble a RAM program P (associated with a step circuit C), database D, generate T garbled circuits [54], where T is an upper bound on the running time of P. The ith garbled circuit performs the "CPU circuit" which evaluates the ith time step of P. The garbling of P consists of all T garbled circuits.

To evaluate a garbling of P on a suitably encoded database D, perform the following operations for $i = 1, \ldots, T - 1$: evaluate the ith garbled circuit to obtain output encodings of the ith step of execution of P^D. Next, we compute the *recoding step* that converts the output encodings of the ith step into the wire labels for the $(i + 1)^{th}$ garbled circuit; only the recoding step involves the encoded database where we retrieve information and enforce honest evaluation. The resulting wire labels will be used to evaluate the $(i + 1)^{th}$ garbled circuit.

The output of the Tth garbled circuit is the output of execution of P^D.

Recall that in the UMA setting, we do not hide memory access pattern, memory content, or intermediate states. In order to achieve full security, we additionally need to compile the original program with additional protection, usually this involves a specially crafted oblivious RAM scheme to hide the access pattern, and a suitable secret key encryption to hide the rest.

Towards FE for RAMs: Challenges. To leap from a toy case of FE for RAMs, a.k.a. garbled RAMs, to building a full-fledged collusion-resistant public-key FE for RAMs involves many hurdles. We start by highlighting two such challenges.

CHALLENGE: PARALLEL[5] REUSABILITY. Let the adversary receive as input, encryption of a challenge database D^* and functional keys $\mathsf{sk}_{P_1}, \ldots, \mathsf{sk}_{P_q}$ associated with RAM programs $P_1, \ldots, P_q$. We can decrypt the *same* encryption of D^* using the different functional keys $\mathsf{sk}_{P_1}, \ldots, \mathsf{sk}_{P_q}$ to obtain $P_1^{D^*}, \ldots, P_q^{D^*}$.

Typically, in the RAM setting, however, reusability has only been studied in the sequential setting (also called persistent memory setting [35]) where P_1 first acts on D^* to obtain an updated database; P_2 then acts upon the updated database and so on. To construct FE for RAM, the notion of parallel reusability is required, where different programs $P_1, \ldots, P_q$ need to act upon the same initial database D^*.

Prior results show that some of the existing garbled RAMs are insecure in the parallel reusability setting [42][6].

CHALLENGE: SUCCINCTNESS. Recall that we enforce stringent efficiency requirements on FE for RAMs schemes: the parameters should neither grow with the database length nor with the worst-case time bound, the decryption time should only grow proportional to the input-specific running time and so on. Even for simpler primitives such as randomized encodings, achieving succinctness has proven to be very challenging; for instance, the constructions of *succinct* garbled RAMs by [19,23] are quite complex and involve heavy tools.

Moreover, unlike weaker models, generic constructions of FE using succinct garbling do not work in the RAM setting. For instance, in the setting of Turing machines, here is an approach to obtain FE for Turing machines from FE for circuits: use FE for circuits to generate a succinct garbling of the database encrypted and the TM associated with the functional key. Such solutions would necessarily blow up the decryption time proportional to the size of the database encrypted, even if the program only runs in sublinear time.

Known Tools. The above two challenges are not new and have presented themselves in different contexts. We mention some of the relevant contexts below.

SUCCINCT GARBLING FOR RAMs [8,19,20,23]: Succinct garbling schemes for RAMs do solve the problem of succinctness but does not satisfy the parallel reusability property. They either only allow the evaluation of one garbled program, or only allow evaluating several programs sequentially in a stateful manner, while for functional encryption we would like the program evaluation to be stateless.

---

[5] We note that the parallel notion we consider here is also different from the notion considered by the works of constructing garbled parallel RAM [13,23,25,50], in particular, we consider the setting where each agent can compute a different program in parallel, while garbled parallel RAMs consider the setting where multiple CPUs/agents jointly compute a single program to speed up the computation.

[6] To be precise, [42] shows that traditional ORAM schemes are insecure in the parallel reusability setting. This correspondingly means that the garbled RAMs schemes building upon these ORAM schemes would correspondingly be insecure in the parallel setting.

FE FOR CIRCUITS [11,51,52]: As we mention in the introduction, FE schemes for circuits do address the challenge of parallel reusability; functional keys associated with programs $P_1, \ldots, P_Q$ can be used in parallel to decrypt an encryption of x. However they do not achieve succinctness since the decryption time grows with the worst-case runtime of the computation.

REWINDABLE ORAMs [42]: A recently introduced primitive, rewindable ORAM, allows for rewinding the encoded database of the ORAM scheme to an earlier state. The security property states that the access patterns generated even after rewinding the encoded database should not reveal any information about the underlying database. This primitive does address the challenge of parallel reusability, succinctness (only a small amount of secret state needed to perform evaluation) but in itself is not useful since this gives an interactive solution and hence needs to be used in conjunction with other (possibly non-interactive) primitives.

2.1   Our Template

We show how to combine the techniques used to construct the above seemingly unrelated tools to obtain a construction of FE for RAMs. As mentioned earlier, the current known constructions of succinct garbling schemes for RAMs are difficult to work with. We will first simplify (and improve!) these constructions before achieving our main result.

The template for the rest of the overview is as follows:

- We first tackle the challenge of succinctness. We present a new construction of a garbled RAM (GRAM) scheme. This will serve as an alternative to existing schemes which are significantly more complex and additionally assumes sub-exponentially secure FE for circuits. Our scheme is simpler and only assumes polynomially-secure FE for circuits.
- We upgrade this succinct GRAM scheme to satisfy parallel reusability; the same garbled database can be evaluated upon by multiple garbled programs. We call this succinct reusable GRAM. This notion would imply a single-ciphertext collusion-resistant FE for RAMs in the secret-key setting. The adversary can only make a single ciphertext query. One of the important tools we use to achieve parallel reusability is rewindable ORAMs.
  In the technical sections, we present the construction of succinct reusable GRAM directly, instead of first presenting the non-reusable version and then upgrading it to the reusable version. We present the upgrading step in this overview to explain the construction better to the reader.
- Finally, we combine succinct reusable GRAMs with collusion-resistant FE for *circuits* to obtain collusion-resistant FE for RAMs.

2.2   Starting Point: Simpler, Better and Modular Succinct GRAM

Our starting point is the following template introduced by [8] to construct succinct garbled RAMs.

- We start with a *non-succinct* garbled RAM scheme, i.e. the parameters in the scheme could grow proportional to the worst runtime bound T of the computation. However, we still require that the evaluation runs in time proportional to the runtime of the computation and in particular, could be independent of the database length. Such a garbled scheme can be constructed from one-way functions [29–31], and these constructions follow the two-step approach that we have outlined at the beginning of the section.
- To go from a non-succinct to a succinct garbled RAM scheme, we need to reduce the size of the garbled program to be independent of the worst case bound T. We achieve this size reduction using program obfuscation[7]. Specifically, we use obfuscation to delegate the execution of the non-succinct program garbling procedure to the time of evaluation. That is, to garble a program P via a succinct garbling scheme, compute an obfuscated circuit that produces a non-succinct garbling of P.

To make the above high level approach work, we need to nail down the precise properties that we need from the underlying non-succinct garbled RAM scheme. For starters, just obfuscating the non-succinct garbling procedure would not work: the size of the obfuscated circuit will be as large as the size of the non-succinct garbled program and thus, we didn't achieve size reduction.

Thus, we need to start with a non-succinct garbling scheme where the garbled program can be decomposed into many components such that the obfuscated circuit produces one component at time. Even if we do this, arguing proof turns out to be tricky: a naive approach to reduce to the security of the non-succinct garbling scheme involves hardwiring the entire garbled program inside the obfuscated circuit but this again is not possible as it violates succinctness.

LOCAL SIMULATABILITY: These issues are not unique to our setting and have already been encountered while designing succinct garbled RAMs with bounded space [8] or succinct garbled Turing machines [6,33]. They identified two main properties that are necessary for the underlying non-succinct garbling scheme to satisfy.

- The program being garbled can be broken down into small components (say, of size $\mathsf{poly}(\lambda, \log T)$) and each of these components can be garbled independently. This property also helps in proving security of the succinct garbled Turing machine without having to hardwire the entire garbled circuit inside the obfuscated circuit.
- The security proof of the non-succinct scheme should be argued in such a way that only a "small" (say, $\mathsf{poly}(\lambda, \log T)$) subset of the garbled program components need to be changed from one hybrid to the next hybrid.

---

[7] A program obfuscation is a compiler that transforms a program P into a functionally equivalent program that hides all the implementation details of the original program. In the technical sections, we use a specific definition of obfuscation, called indistinguishability obfuscation.

We now revisit the template mentioned above and change the circuit being obfuscated to output the (non-succinct) garbled program, one component at a time. On input i, the obfuscated circuit outputs the ith component of the garbled program, instead of producing the whole garbled program at once. To argue security, we carry out the hybrids of the non-succinct garbling scheme by only hardwiring a small subset of components at a time. By local simulatability, we are guaranteed that in each hybrid, the amount of hardwired information is never too large and therefore we achieve succinctness.

Therefore, we have reduced the problem of constructing succinct GRAM to identify and instantiate an appropriate non-succinct garbling scheme satisfying the above two properties. This is where previous works fall short. Their instantiations yielded succinct garbling schemes only for Turing machines [6,33] or succinct garbled RAMs with bounded space [8].

NON-SUCCINCT GARBLED RAMS WITH LOCAL SIMULATABILITY[8]: To construct (non-succinct) garbled RAM satisfying the local simulatability property, we split the construction into two parts: in the first part we construct a succinct garbled RAM with unprotected memory access (UMA), where we forget about protecting memory contents, access patterns and intermediate CPU states; in the second part, we bootstrap UMA-GRAM to fully secure GRAM.

For the first step, we observe that the UMA-secure adaptive garbled RAM construction of [31] already satisfies the local simulatability property. For the second part, previous schemes usually employ an ORAM to hide the memory access pattern and an encryption scheme to hide the memory content. However, these tools are not quite compatible with the local simulatability property, therefore, their compatible versions of ORAM with strong localized randomness, and timed encryption scheme – originally introduced by the same paper [31] to construct adaptive garbled RAMs – are needed for the proof.

Timed encryption, at a high level, is an encryption scheme that allows issuing encryption/decryption keys with growing power as the evaluation goes on, i.e. a key issued at time t can decrypt anything that was encrypted under time $t' \leq t$, but any message encrypted at a later time remains hidden. Using the tool of timed encryption allows us to use a sequence of hybrids to remove the timed encryption keys one by one (and hence allowing us to simulate each evaluation step *locally*), from the strongest (which is one hardwired in the last step circuit) to the weakest (which is the one hardwired in the first step circuit).

Looking ahead, there is another more subtle issue for constructing succinct GRAM that is not captured by local simulatability: in the succinct garbling scheme, we can only use a very small amount of randomness in the simulator, as otherwise the size of the simulated circuit will blow up and break succinctness. In particular, this means that we cannot simply hardcode the timed encryption of 0. For this issue, we develop timed encryption with *pseudorandom ciphertexts*, which is a timed encryption whose ciphertext is indistinguishable from uniformly random bitstrings; and construct it from one-way functions. Once we have that,

---

[8] The terminology of local simulation is only introduced for the benefit of describing our techniques and will be implicit in our security proof.

we can simply use a PRF to generate all the simulated ciphertexts in a succinct way.

We now move on to hiding access pattern in a local simulatable way. Strong localized randomness property for ORAM, at a high level, simply requires that the randomness used by ORAM is equipped with some structural properties that will allow us to equivocate (and change) the randomness in a *local* way. For now, the ORAM with strong localized randomness constructed in [31] suffices for succinct (non-resuable) garbled RAM.

2.3   Succinct Garbled RAM: Achieving Reusability

Succinct GRAM alone itself is not going to be sufficient to construct FE for RAMs. Instead, it turns out to require the *reusability* property: given an encoding of a database D and multiple garbled programs $\widetilde{P}_1, \ldots, \widetilde{P}_q$, the adversary can recover the outputs $P_1^D(), \ldots, P_q^D()$ and moreover, the database encoding and the garbled programs do not leak any information about D beyond the outputs that can be recovered. We call this notion succinct *reusable* garbled RAM.

Note that this definition is different from the persistent memory setting [35]; the programs *sequentially* evaluate on the databases as against the parallel execution that we desire. In addition, we also require that the reusable GRAM also satisfies succinctness properties as defined in a succinct GRAM scheme.

From Succinct GRAM to Succinct Reusable GRAM. To construct a succinct reusable garbled RAM, again it is helpful to split things into two part: in the first part we construct a succinct *reusable* garbled RAM with unprotected memory access (UMA), and in the second part we use this UMA primitive to construct fully secure succinct *reusable* garbled RAM. Note that in UMA setting, essentially all we are protecting is the program execution, and we do not face much trouble in adapting the scheme above into the reusable setting. Therefore, we focus on the full security setting and highlight the new challenges in the reusability setting.

CHALLENGES IN PROTECTING MEMORY CONTENT: To protect the content of the memory, we need to include the encryption key into our garbled program. However, once we have given out one garbled program, we can no longer invoke the security of the encryption scheme to say that the adversary has no information about the underlying database, as the garbled program contains a hardwired secret key. Indeed, the adversary can simply read from the encrypted database by simply reading the output of the garbled program. Therefore we need to remove the encryption keys in the hybrids very carefully.   In the non-reusable setting, it has been shown in prior work [31] that using timed encryption fixes this issue. On a high level, their idea is to remove the encryption key one by one in each hybrid, in particular, they would remove the encryption key from the last garbled program (and write junk to the database instead) indistinguishably in the first hybrid, and then move forward and remove the encryption key in the second last garbled program, and so on. Essentially, timed encryption allows us to encrypt messages under a different key in each time step, while the decryption key can only decrypt messages before the current timestep but not after, which allows the hybrid argument to go through. However, this security proof does not work in the reusable case: when we try to equivocate the output/database writes and remove the encryption key, the adversary could in principle still be able to distinguish the two distributions as the same timed encryption key still appears in other garbled programs.

In order to tackle this issue, we employ a different time step labeling and also a different hybrid strategy. In particular, instead of the time steps increasing in each garbled program, each garbled program will use a shared global time counter. Note that this also makes sense from the reusability point of view, as the evaluator can in principle evaluate garbled programs on the garbled database in any order that he wishes.

Now suppose we want to remove the strongest encryption key in the last step circuit. We can employ the following hybrid sequence: first, we use the security of UMA-GRAM to change each last step circuit into a dummy circuit that directly outputs the output in *all* garbled programs *in parallel* (to do it more carefully, we replace each garbled program one by one and argue each change is indistinguishable) – this effectively removes all the timed encryption keys that are used in the last time step; this allows us to do the next step which is to change the encrypted CPU states and write data into garbage *in parallel*; finally, we reverse the change of dummy circuit again in parallel. By doing so, we remove the strongest timed encryption key in *all* garbled programs at once. We can repeat this process for each remaining encryption keys until all encryption keys are removed from garbled program, at which point we can replace the database with an empty database and arrive at the simulated distribution.

CHALLENGES IN PROTECTING MEMORY ACCESS PATTERN: Another issue is that we need to protect the database read/write patterns in a way that is compatible with succinct UMA GRAM. Basically, we need to change each database read/write pattern without hardwiring too much additional information, which would blow up the size of the garbled program and break succinctness. This is further complicated by the fact that the adversary can evaluate different programs on the same database *in parallel* and compare the results to acquire additional information.

To resolve both these issues, we design a rewindable ORAM scheme satisfying strong localized randomness property. The starting point of the construction is the plain rewindable ORAM scheme given in [41], which consists of two parts: a read-only rewindable ORAM and a read-write non-rewindable ORAM. The idea of the construction is that the read-write ORAM will act as a read-write cache to the underlying database, which is encoded in the read-only ORAM.

Given this beautiful construction, it is straightforward to construct a rewindable ORAM scheme with strong localized randomness. In particular, we simply instantiate the read-write ORAM with the ORAM with strong localized randomness property. The access pattern in read-only ORAM is by definition locally sampled, and we can simulate the access pattern in read-write ORAM locally by using the strong localized randomness property of the read-write ORAM that we use.

2.4   Bootstrapping Step: From FE for Circuits to FE for RAMs

Once we construct a succinct reusable garbled RAM scheme, we show how to bootstrap a FE for circuits scheme into a FE for RAMs scheme. Our transformation is inspired by a similar transformation described in [26].

- To encrypt a database D, encode D using a succinct reusable GRAM scheme. Denote the output by $(\widetilde{D}, sk)$. Encrypt sk using an FE for circuits scheme; call the resulting ciphertext ct. Output the ciphertext of the FE for RAMs scheme, $\mathsf{CT} = (\widetilde{D}, ct)$.
- To generate a functional key for a program P, generate a FE key for a circuit G that takes as input a secret key sk and produces a garbling of the program P with respect to sk; call the FE key SK_G. Set the functional key for the FE for RAMs scheme to be SK_G.
- The decryption algorithm first recovers the garbled program $\widetilde{P}$ by running the FE decryption algorithm. It then runs the succinct GRAM evaluation of $\widetilde{P}$ on $\widetilde{D}$ to obtain P^D.

To argue security, we can use the hybrid functional encryption technique of [3,22] to first hardwire the garbled programs in the function keys and then invoke the reusable security of the GRAM scheme to prove the indistinguishability security of the FE scheme.

2.5   Organization

We organize the technical sections of our paper as follows:

- In Sect. 3, we introduce our notations and preliminaries, with additional preliminaries described in the full version.
- In Sect. 4, we present a construction of succinct reusable garbled RAM.
  First, we present the definition of succinct reusable garbled RAM in Sect. 5.1. Next, in Sect. 5.2, we present a construction of succinct garbled RAM in the UMA setting. In this step, we use pebbling techniques in conjunction with indistinguishability obfuscation for inputs of logarithmic length (implied by functional encryption). Finally, in Sect. 5.3, we show how to transform UMA-secure garbled RAM to fully secure garbled RAM in the reusability setting. As a result, we obtain the construction of succinct reusable garbled RAM. We use the tool of rewindable ORAM in this step. The missing proofs in Sect. 5 are presented in the full version.
- In Sect. 6, we show how to combine (collusion-resistant) FE for circuits with succinct reusable garbled RAM to achieve (collusion-resistant) FE for RAMs. The missing proofs in Sect. 6 are presented in the full version. At last, we show implication of FE for RAMs to secret-key DEPIR in the full version as well.

3   Preliminaries

We denote λ to be the security parameter. We denote the computational indistinguishability of two distributions D_1 and D_2 by $D_1 \approx D_2$. We use the abbreviation PPT to denote probabilistic polynomial time algorithms. Additional preliminaries are presented in the full version.

RAM Model of Computation. We recall the definition of RAM computations. A RAM computation consists of a RAM program P and a database D. The representation size of P is independent of the length of the database D. The program P has random access to the database D. We denote the output to be P^D In more detail, the computation proceeds as follows.

The RAM program P is represented as a step-circuit C. It takes as input internal state from the previous step, location to be read, value at that location and it outputs the new state, location to be written into, value to be written and the next location to be read. More formally, for every $\tau \in T$, where T is an upper bound on the running time,

$$(\mathsf{st}^\tau, \mathsf{rd}^\tau, \mathsf{wt}^\tau, \mathsf{wb}^\tau) \leftarrow C(\mathsf{st}^{\tau-1}, \mathsf{rd}^{\tau-1}, b^\tau)$$

where we have the following:

- $\mathsf{st}^{\tau-1}$ denotes the state in the $(\tau-1)^{th}$ step and st^τ denotes the state in the τth step.
- $\mathsf{rd}^{\tau-1}$ denotes the location to be read from, as output by the $(\tau-1)^{th}$ step.
- b^τ denotes the bit at the location $\mathsf{rd}^{\tau-1}$.
- rd^τ denotes the location to be read from, in the τth step.
- wt^τ denotes the location to be written into in the τth step.
- wb^τ denotes the value to be written at τ-th step at the location wt^τ.

Remark 1 (Additional Input). In the literature, when defining RAM programs, we also additionally define an input x and the program in addition to having random access to D, takes as input x, and outputs P^D. Without loss of generality, we assume that the input x is part of the database and hence we omit including this as an explicit input to P.

Remark 2 (Outputs). In this work, we only consider RAM programs with boolean outputs. We can suitably extend the schemes we construct to handle multiple outputs at the cost of blowing up the parameters proportional to the output length.

3.1   Puncturable PRF

Puncturable PRFs [12,14,44] are PRFs for which a key can be given out such that, it allows evaluation of the PRF on all inputs, except for any polynomial-size set of inputs. The following definition is adapted from [53].

Definition 1 (Puncturable PRF). A puncturable family of PRFs F mapping is given by a typle of ppt algorithms $(\mathsf{Gen}_F, \mathsf{Eval}_F, \mathsf{Punc}_F)$ and a pair of computable functions $n(\cdot)$ and $m(\cdot)$, satisfying the following conditions:

- **Functionality preserved under puncturing**: For every ppt adversary $\mathcal{A}$ such that $\mathcal{A}(1^\lambda)$ outputs a set $S \subseteq \{0,1\}^{n(\lambda)}$, then for all $x \in \{0,1\}^{n(\lambda)}$ where $x \notin S$, we have that

$$\Pr[\mathsf{Eval}_F(K, x) = \mathsf{Eval}_F(K_S, x) : K \leftarrow \mathsf{Gen}_F(1^\lambda), K_S = \mathsf{Punc}_F(K, S)] = 1$$

- **Pseudorandom at punctured points**: Foe every ppt adversary $(\mathcal{A}_1, \mathcal{A}_2)$ such that $\mathcal{A}_1(1^\lambda)$ outputs a set $S \subseteq \{0,1\}^{n(\lambda)}$ and state σ, consider an experiment where $K \leftarrow \mathsf{Gen}_F(1^\lambda)$ and $K_S = \mathsf{Punc}_F(K, S)$. Then we have

$$\left| \Pr[\mathcal{A}_2(\sigma, K_S, S, \mathsf{Eval}_F(K, S)) = 1] - \Pr[\mathcal{A}_2(\sigma, K_S, S, U_{m(\lambda)\cdot|S|}) = 1] \right| = \mathsf{negl}(\lambda)$$

where $\mathsf{Eval}_F(K, S)$ denotes the the concatenation of $(\mathsf{Eval}_F(K, x_1), \ldots, \mathsf{Eval}_F(K, x_k))$, where $S = \{x_1, \ldots, x_k\}$ is the enumeration of the elements of S in lexicographic order and U_ℓ denotes the uniform distribution over ℓ bits.

The GGM tree-based construction of PRFs [37] from one-way function are easily seen to yield puncturable PRFS, as shown in [12,14,44]. Thus we have:

Theorem 6. *If one-way functions exist, then for all efficiently computable functions $n(\lambda)$ and $m(\lambda)$, there exists a puncturable PRF family that maps $n(\lambda)$ bits to $m(\lambda)$ bits.*

3.2 Indistinguishability Obfuscation

The definition below is from [27].

Definition 2. A uniform ppt machine $i\mathcal{O}$ is called an Indistinguishability obfuscator for a circuit class $\{C_\lambda\}$, if the following conditions are satisfied:

- For all security parameter λ, all circuit $C \in C_\lambda$, all input x, we have that

$$\Pr[C'(x) = C(x) : C' \leftarrow i\mathcal{O}(\lambda, C)] = 1$$

- For all (not necessarily uniform) ppt adversaries $(\mathcal{A}_0, \mathcal{A}_1)$, there exists a negligible function α, such that the following holds: if $\Pr[\forall x, C_0(x) = C_1(x) : (C_0, C_1, \sigma) \leftarrow \mathcal{A}_0(1^\lambda)] > 1 - \alpha(\lambda)$, then we have

$$\left| \Pr[\mathcal{A}_1(\sigma, i\mathcal{O}(\lambda, C_0)) = 1] - \Pr[\mathcal{A}_1(\sigma, i\mathcal{O}(\lambda, C_1)) = 1] \right| \leq \alpha(\lambda)$$

Theorem 7 [48,49]. *For every large enough security parameter λ, assuming $2^n\epsilon$-secure functional encryption, there exists an ϵ-secure indistinguishability obfuscator for circuits with input length n.*

In particular, when $n = \log(\lambda)$ and ϵ is negligible in security parameter, iO for n-length circuits, can be based on polynomially secure compact functional encryption.

3.3 Selective-Database Laconic Oblivious Transfer

The definition of laconic oblivious transfer is proposed in [24,34]. The security notion we need about laconic oblivious transfer is based on work [45].

A laconic oblivious transfer scheme LacOT consists of four algorithms (crsGen, Hash, Send, Receive) with details as follows:

- crsGen(1^λ) takes as input security parameter λ and outputs a common reference string crs.
- Hash(crs, D) is a deterministic algorithm that takes as input the crs as well as a database $D \in \{0,1\}^*$, and outputs a hash value h and a state $\widehat{D}$.
- Send(crs, h, L, m_0, m_1) takes as input the crs, hash value h, a pair of messages (m_0, m_1) and an index $L \in \mathbb{N}$. It outputs a ciphertext c.
- Receive$^{\widehat{D}}$(crs, c, L) is an algorithm with random access to a database $\widehat{D}$ that takes as input the crs, a ciphertext c and an index $L \in \mathbb{N}$. It outputs a message m.

The scheme LacOT satisfies the following correctness and security properties:

Correctness. We say the scheme LacOT is correct, if for all $D \in \{0,1\}^*$ of size $N = \mathsf{poly}(\lambda)$, all $i \in [N]$ and all $(m_0, m_1) \in \{0,1\}^{p(\lambda)}$, it holds that

$$\Pr\left[\mathsf{Receive}^{\widehat{D}}(\mathsf{crs}, c, L) = m_{D[L]}\right] = 1$$

where crs $\leftarrow$ crsGen(1^λ), $(h, \widehat{D}) \leftarrow$ Hash(crs, D) and $c \leftarrow$ Send(crs, h, L, m_0, m_1).

Selective-Database Adaptive-Message Sender Privacy Against Semi-honest Receivers. There exists a ppt simulator Sim that satisfies the following:

$$|\Pr[\mathsf{Expt}_{\mathsf{real}}^{\mathsf{sel}}(1^\lambda) = 1] - \Pr[\mathsf{Expt}_{\mathsf{sim}}^{\mathsf{sel}}(1^\lambda) = 1]| \leq \mathsf{negl}(\lambda)$$

where the experiments $\mathsf{Expt}_{\mathsf{real}}^{\mathsf{sel}}(1^\lambda)$ and $\mathsf{Expt}_{\mathsf{sim}}^{\mathsf{sel}}(1^\lambda)$ are in Fig. 2:

1. $(D, \mathsf{st}) \leftarrow \mathcal{A}(1^\lambda)$	1. $(D, \mathsf{st}) \leftarrow \mathcal{A}(1^\lambda)$
2. crs $\leftarrow$ crsGen(1^λ)	2. crs $\leftarrow$ crsGen(1^λ)
3. $(h, \widehat{D}) \leftarrow$ Hash(crs, D)	3. $(L, m_0, m_1, \mathsf{st}') \leftarrow$
4. $(L, m_0, m_1, \mathsf{st}') \leftarrow \mathcal{A}(\mathsf{st}, \mathsf{crs})$	$\mathcal{A}(\mathsf{st}, \mathsf{crs})$
5. $e \leftarrow$ Send(crs, h, L, m_0, m_1)	4. $e \leftarrow$ Sim(crs, $D, L, m_{D[L]}$)
6. $b' \leftarrow \mathcal{A}(\mathsf{crs}, e, \mathsf{st}')$	5. $b' \leftarrow \mathcal{A}(\mathsf{crs}, e, \mathsf{st}')$
(a) $\mathsf{Expt}_{\mathsf{real}}^{\mathsf{sel}}(1^\lambda)$	(b) $\mathsf{Expt}_{\mathsf{sim}}^{\mathsf{sel}}(1^\lambda)$

Fig. 2. Experiments associated with sender privacy for reads

where $|D| = N = \mathsf{poly}(\lambda)$, $L \in [N]$ and $m_0, m_1 \in \{0,1\}^{p(\lambda)}$.

Efficiency. We require that $|h|$ is bounded by a fixed polynomial in λ, and being independent of $|D|$. The runtime of algorithm Hash is $|D| \cdot \mathsf{poly}(\log |D|, \lambda)$, and the runtime of Send and Receive are $\mathsf{poly}(\log |D|, \lambda)$.

A variant of laconic OT that supports write operation is called updatable laconic OT, defined in the following:

Definition 3 (Updatable laconic OT [24]). A laconic OT scheme LacOT is called updatable if it supports the following two algorithms:

- $e_w \leftarrow \mathsf{SendWrite}\left(\mathsf{crs}, h, L, b, \{m_{j,0}, m_{j,1}\}_{j=1}^{|h|}\right)$: On input the common reference string crs, a hash value h, a location $L \in [N]$, bit $b \in \{0,1\}$ and $|h|$ pairs of messages $\{m_{j,0}, m_{j,1}\}_{j=1}^{|h|}$, it outputs a ciphertext e_w.
- $\{m_j\}_{j=1}^{|h|} \leftarrow \mathsf{ReceiveWrite}^{\widehat{D}}(\mathsf{crs}, L, b, e_w)$: On input the common reference string crs, location L, a bit $b \in \{0,1\}$, a ciphertext e_w and random access to state $\widehat{D}$, it updates the state $\widehat{D}$ (such that $D[L] = b$) and outputs messages $\{m_j\}_{j=1}^{|h|}$.

We require an updatable laconic oblivious transfer to additionally satisfy the following properties:

- **Correctness of Writes**: Let database D be of size at most $N = \mathsf{poly}(\lambda)$. Let D^* be a database that is identical to D except that $D^*[L] = b$ for bit $b \in \{0,1\}$. For any sequence of messages $\{m_{j,0}, m_{j,1}\}_{j \in [\lambda]} \in \{0,1\}^{p(\lambda)}$, it holds that

$$\Pr[m_j' = m_{j,d_j^*}, \forall j \in [|h|] : \{m_j'\}_{j=1}^{|h|} \leftarrow \mathsf{ReceiveWrite}^{\widehat{D}}(\mathsf{crs}, L, b, e_w)] = 1$$

where $\mathsf{crs} \leftarrow \mathsf{crsGen}(1^\lambda)$, $(d, \widehat{D}) \leftarrow \mathsf{Hash}(\mathsf{crs}, D)$, $(d^*, \widehat{D}^*) \leftarrow \mathsf{Hash}(\mathsf{crs}, D^*)$, and we have

$$e_w \leftarrow \mathsf{SendWrite}\left(\mathsf{crs}, h, L, b, \{m_{j,0}, m_{j,1}\}_{j=1}^{|h|}\right)$$

- **Selective-database adaptive-message sender privacy against semi-honest receivers with regard to writes**: There exists a ppt simulator SimWrite satisfies the following

$$\left|\Pr[\mathsf{Expt}_{\mathsf{real}}^{\mathsf{wrt}}(1^\lambda) = 1] - \Pr[\mathsf{Expt}_{\mathsf{ideal}}^{\mathsf{wrt}}(1^\lambda) = 1]\right| = \mathsf{negl}(\lambda)$$

where experiments $\mathsf{Expt}_{\mathsf{real}}^{\mathsf{wrt}}$ and $\mathsf{Expt}_{\mathsf{ideal}}^{\mathsf{wrt}}$ are defined in Fig. 3, where D^* is identical to D except $D^*[L] = b$.
- **Efficiency.** We require that the runtime of algorithms SendWrite and ReceiveWrite are $\mathsf{poly}(\log |D|, \lambda)$.

1. $(D, \mathsf{st}) \leftarrow \mathcal{A}(1^\lambda)$	1. $(D, \mathsf{st}) \leftarrow \mathcal{A}(1^\lambda)$
2. $\mathsf{crs} \leftarrow \mathsf{crsGen}(1^\lambda)$.	2. $\mathsf{crs} \leftarrow \mathsf{crsGen}(1^\lambda)$.
3. $h = \mathsf{Hash}(\mathsf{crs}, D)$	3. $h = \mathsf{Hash}(\mathsf{crs}, D)$
4. $(L, b, \{m_{j,0}, m_{j,1}\}_{j=1}^{\lvert h \rvert}, \mathsf{st}) \leftarrow \mathcal{A}(\mathsf{st}, \mathsf{crs})$	4. $(L, b, \{m_{j,0}, m_{j,1}\}_{j=1}^{\lvert h \rvert}, \mathsf{st}) \leftarrow \mathcal{A}(\mathsf{st}, \mathsf{crs})$
5.	5. $(h^*, \widehat{D}^*) \leftarrow \mathsf{Hash}(\mathsf{crs}, D^*)$
6. $e \quad \leftarrow \quad \mathsf{SendWrite}(\mathsf{crs}, h, L, b, \{m_{j,0},$ $m_{j,1}\}_{j=1}^{\lvert h \rvert})$	6. $e \leftarrow \mathsf{Sim}(\mathsf{crs}, D, L, b, \{m_{j,h_j^*}\}_{j \in [\lvert h \rvert]})$
7. $b' \leftarrow \mathcal{A}(\mathsf{crs}, e, \mathsf{st}')$.	7. $b' \leftarrow \mathcal{A}(\mathsf{crs}, e, \mathsf{st}')$.
(a) $\mathsf{Expt}_{\mathsf{real}}^{\mathsf{wrt}}(1^\lambda)$	(b) $\mathsf{Expt}_{\mathsf{ideal}}^{\mathsf{wrt}}(1^\lambda)$

Fig. 3. Experiments associated with sender privacy for writes

In [45], the authors show that selective-database laconic OT can be constructed from weakly-selectively secure, single-key public-key functional encryption for circuits, i.e.

Theorem 8 [45]. *Assuming the existence of public-key functional encryption for circuits, there exists selective-database laconic OT.*

Theorem 9 [17,24]. *Assuming the existence of laconic OT, there exists public-key encryption.*

4   Functional Encryption for RAMs

We define a public-key functional encryption scheme for RAM programs [36]. A public-key FE for RAM programs consists of the probabilistic polynomial time (ppt) algorithms $\Pi = (\mathsf{Setup}, \mathsf{Enc}, \mathsf{KeyGen}, \mathsf{Dec})$, defined as follows:

- **Setup algorithm.** $\mathsf{Setup}(1^\lambda, T)$: On input security parameter λ, an upper bound T on the running time of the RAM program, the setup algorithm outputs the master secret key MSK and public key pk.
- **Encryption algorithm.** $\mathsf{Enc}(\mathsf{pk}, D)$: On input public key pk and database D, the encryption algorithm outputs the ciphertext CT.
- **Key generation algorithm.** $\mathsf{KeyGen}(\mathsf{MSK}, P)$: On input master secret key MSK, RAM program P, the key generation algorithm outputs the functional key sk_P.
- **Decryption algorithm.** $\mathsf{Dec}^{\mathsf{CT}}(\mathsf{sk}_P)$: On input a functional key sk_P and with random access to ciphertext CT, the decryption algorithm (modeled as a RAM program) outputs the result y.

Definition 4 (Correctness). A public-key functional encryption for RAMs scheme Π is correct, if there exists a negligible $\mathsf{negl}(\cdot)$ such that for any security parameter λ, any database D, for any RAM program P, it holds that

$$\Pr\left[\mathsf{Dec}^{\mathsf{CT}}(\mathsf{sk}_P) = P^D\right] = 1 - \mathsf{negl}(\lambda)$$

where $(\mathsf{pk}, \mathsf{MSK}) \leftarrow \mathsf{Setup}(1^\lambda, T), \mathsf{CT} \leftarrow \mathsf{Enc}(\mathsf{pk}, D), \mathsf{sk}_P \leftarrow \mathsf{KeyGen}(\mathsf{MSK}, P)$ and the probability is taken over the internal randomness of algorithms Setup, Enc and KeyGen.

Succinctness. Unlike the traditional functional encryption for circuits scheme, where the parameters can grow with the worst case runtime of the computation, we require the parameters in the functional encryption for RAMs schemes to have the following efficiency guarantees.

Definition 5 (Succinctness). A public-key functional encryption for RAMs scheme (Setup, Enc, KeyGen, Dec) satisfies succinctness if the following properties hold:

- $\mathsf{Setup}(1^\lambda, T)$ runs in time $\mathsf{poly}(\lambda, \log(T))$.
- $\mathsf{Enc}(\mathsf{pk}, D)$ runs in time $\mathsf{poly}(\lambda, \log(T), |D|)$.
- $\mathsf{KeyGen}(\mathsf{MSK}, P)$ runs in time $\mathsf{poly}(\lambda, \log(T), |P|)$.
- $\mathsf{Dec}^{\mathsf{CT}}(\mathsf{sk}_P)$ runs in time $\mathsf{poly}(\lambda, T)$.

Remark 3 (Input-Specific Runtime). An astute reader would notice that we only require the decryption time to grow with the worst case time bound, and not with input-specific runtime. Luckily, there is a simple generic transformation that shows how to modify a scheme with worst-case time bound into a scheme that has input-specific runtime: we encourage the reader to refer to [39] for a description of this transformation.

Security. Our security notion is modeled along the same lines as FE for circuits. We only focus on selective security in this work.

Definition 6 (Selective security). A public-key FE for RAMs scheme Π is selectively secure if for any ppt adversary $\mathcal{A}$, there exists a negligible function $\mathsf{negl}(\cdot)$ such that

$$\mathsf{Adv}^{\mathsf{pfe}}_{\Pi, \mathcal{A}}(1^\lambda) = \left| \Pr[\mathsf{Expt}^{\mathsf{pfe}}_{\Pi, \mathcal{A}}(1^\lambda, 0) = 1] - \Pr[\mathsf{Expt}^{\mathsf{pfe}}_{\Pi, \mathcal{A}}(1^\lambda, 1) = 1] \right| \leq \mathsf{negl}(\lambda)$$

for any sufficiently large security parameters λ, where $\mathsf{Expt}^{\mathsf{pfe}}_{\Pi, \mathcal{A}}(1^\lambda, b)$ is defined via the following experiment:

1. **Setup phase:** The challenger computes $(\mathsf{pk}, \mathsf{MSK}) \leftarrow \mathsf{Setup}(1^\lambda, T)$.
2. **Challenge phase:** On input 1^λ, the adversary submits (D_0, D_1), and the challenger replies with pk and $\mathsf{CT} \leftarrow \mathsf{Enc}(\mathsf{pk}, D_b)$.
3. **Query phase:** The adversary adaptively queries the challenger with any RAM program P such that $P^{D_0} = P^{D_1}$. The challenger replies with $\mathsf{sk}_P \leftarrow \mathsf{KeyGen}(\mathsf{MSK}, P)$.
4. **Output phase:** The adversary outputs guess b', which is defined as the output of the experiment.

5 Succinct Reusable Garbled RAM

We first start with the definition of succinct reusable garbled RAM. This will be followed by the construction of succinct UMA-secure reusable GRAM. Finally, we give a transformation from UMA security to full security.

5.1 Syntax and Security Definition

A succinct reusable garbled RAM scheme consists of PPT algorithms $\mathsf{GRAM} = (\mathsf{GrbDB}, \mathsf{GProg}, \mathsf{GEval})$, with details as follows:

- $\mathsf{GrbDB}(1^\lambda, D, T, 1^Q)$: On input security parameter λ, time upper bound T, collusion upper bound Q, a database D, output the garbled database encoding $\widehat{D}$ along with secret key sk.
- $\mathsf{GrbProg}(\mathsf{sk}, P)$: On input secret key sk, and a RAM program P, output the garbled program $\widehat{P}$.
- $\mathsf{GEval}^{\widehat{D}}\left(\widehat{P}\right)$: On input garbled program $\widehat{P}$, database encoding $\widehat{D}$, output y.

Correctness. For correctness, we require that for any program P, any database D, we have that

$$\Pr\left[\mathsf{GEval}^{\widehat{D}}\left(\widehat{P}\right) = P^D()\right] = 1$$

where $(\widehat{D}, \mathsf{sk}) \leftarrow \mathsf{GrbDB}(1^\lambda, T, D)$, and $\widehat{P} \leftarrow \mathsf{GrbProg}(\mathsf{sk}, P)$.

Succinctness. We define succinctness property of garbled RAM. In the definition below, we note the dependence of $\log T$ is implicit since $\log T$ is at most the security parameter.

Definition 7 (Weak succinctness). A garbled RAM scheme $\mathsf{GRAM} = (\mathsf{GrbDB}, \mathsf{GrbProg}, \mathsf{GEval})$ satisfies the weak succinctness property if the following holds:

- $\mathsf{GrbDB}(1^\lambda, T, 1^Q, D)$ runs in time $\mathsf{poly}\,(\lambda, \log T, Q, |D|)$.
- $\mathsf{GrbProg}(\mathsf{sk}, P)$ runs in time $\mathsf{poly}(\lambda, T, \log Q, \log |D|, |P|)$.
- $\mathsf{GEval}^{\widehat{D}}\left(\widehat{P}\right)$ runs in time $\mathsf{poly}(\lambda, t, |P|, \log Q, \log |D|)$.

Definition 8 (Succinctness). A garbled RAM scheme $\mathsf{GRAM} = (\mathsf{GrbDB}, \mathsf{GrbProg}, \mathsf{GEval})$ satisfies (full) succinctness property if the following holds:

- It satisfies the weak succinctness;
- $\mathsf{GrbProg}(\mathsf{sk}, P)$ runs in time $\mathsf{poly}(\lambda, \log T, \log Q, \log |D|, |P|)$, instead of T.

Reusable Security. We define a notion of reusable security that will be compatible with the security definition of FE for RAMs.

To define reusable security, we first describe the experiment below.

$\underline{\mathsf{Expt}^{\mathcal{A}}(1^{\lambda}, b)}$:

- $\mathcal{A}$ submits two databases D_0 and D_1, a collusion bound Q (or $\perp$ for unbounded GRAM scheme), and a running time bound encoded in unary 1^T.
- The challenger responds back with database encoding $\widehat{D_b}$.
- Proceeding adaptively, $\mathcal{A}$ submits RAM programs P_0, P_1. The challenger checks that $P_0^{D_0}() = P_1^{D_1}()$ and each program executes for the same number of time steps. It also checks that $|D_0| = |D_1|$. If both the checks fail, it aborts; otherwise, it sends the garbled program $\widehat{P_b}$ and garbled input $\widehat{x_b}$. $\mathcal{A}$ repeats this step for $Q = \mathsf{poly}(\lambda)$ times.
- $\mathcal{A}$ outputs b'. The output of the experiment is b'.

Definition 9 ((Indistinguishability) reusability). *A garbled RAM scheme* $(\mathsf{GrbDB}, \mathsf{GrbProg}, \mathsf{Eval})$ *satisfies (indistinguishability) reusability property if the following holds for every* ppt *adversary* $\mathcal{A}$:

$$\left| \Pr[0 \leftarrow \mathsf{Expt}^{\mathcal{A}}(1^{\lambda}, 0)] - \Pr[0 \leftarrow \mathsf{Expt}^{\mathcal{A}}(1^{\lambda}, 1)] \right| \leq \mathsf{negl}(\lambda)$$

Remark 4. Our construction actually satisfies a stronger security of simulation security, where simulated version of GrbDB only takes as input $(1^{\lambda}, 1^{|D|})$, and the simulated version of $\mathsf{GrbProg}$ only takes as input $(\mathsf{sk}, 1^{|P|}, y)$. Note that for this definition, simulation security is in fact equivalent to indistinguishability security[9].

Unbounded Reusability. Ideally, we would like the garbled database encoding to be reusable by a priori unbounded number of garbled programs. We capture this in the formal definition below.

Definition 10 (Unbounded reusability). *In addition to succinctness, a succinct garbled RAM scheme satisfies unbounded reusability, if the algorithm* GrbDB *takes* $Q = \perp$ *and all algorithms run in time independent of* Q, *for example,* GrbDB *runs in time* $\mathsf{poly}(\lambda, \log T, |D|)$.

5.2 Succinct UMA Reusable GRAM

To construct succinct reusable GRAM, we start by constructing a succinct garbled RAM scheme that only satisfies a weaker notion of reusable security, which we call UMA security.

---

[9] In general these two notions are not equivalent: in our setting, they are equivalent since we only consider programs with boolean outputs.

UMA Security. UMA security is defined similar as the indistinguishability security above, except that the challenger in addition to checking $P_0^{D_0}() = P_1^{D_1}()$, she also checks that $D_0 = D_1$, and every step circuits in $P_0^{D_0}(), P_1^{D_1}()$ at the same time step output the exact same output.

Ingredients. We use the following ingredients in our construction:

- Selective-database updatable laconic oblivious transfer (crsGen, Hash, Send, SendWrite, Receive, ReceiveWrite).
- A puncturable PRF (PRF.Gen, PRF.Eval, PRF.Punc).
- Indistinguishability obfuscation i$\mathcal{O}$ for circuits with log-sized inputs.

Construction. We construct $\Pi = (\mathsf{GrbDB}, \mathsf{GrbProg}, \mathsf{GEval})$ as follows:

- $\mathsf{GrbDB}(1^\lambda, D, 1^Q, T_{\max})$: On input security parameter λ, database D and running time upper bound $T_{\max}$, it does the following:
  1. Sample crs $\leftarrow$ crsGen(1^λ) and compute $(d, \widehat{D}) = \mathsf{Hash}(\mathsf{crs}, D)$
  2. Output $\widehat{D}$ as garbled database and $(d, \mathsf{crs}, Q, T_{\max})$ as the secret key sk.
- $\mathsf{GrbProg}\,(\mathsf{sk}, P)$: On input secret key sk and program P, it does:
  1. Sample a PRF key $K \leftarrow \mathsf{PRF.Gen}(1^\lambda)$.
  2. For each step $\tau \in [2, T], k \in [\lambda + n + 1]$ and $b \in \{0, 1\}$, let $\mathsf{lab}_{k,b}^\tau = \mathsf{PRF}_K(\tau \| k \| b)$.
  3. We use $\{\mathsf{lab}_{k,b}^\tau\}$ to denote $\{\mathsf{lab}_{k,b}^\tau\}_{k \in [\lambda+n+1], b \in \{0,1\}}$.
  4. Output $\widehat{P} = (\mathsf{i}\mathcal{O}(PG[P, \mathsf{crs}, K, d]), \{\mathsf{lab}_{k,d_k}^1\}_{k \in [\lambda]}, \{\mathsf{lab}_{k+\lambda,0}^1\}_{k \in [n+1]})$, where PG is described in Fig. 4.

     Note: we pad the circuit PG such that its size is $|P| \cdot \mathsf{poly}(\lambda, \log|D|, \log T)$ bits. This will become clear later in the security proof.

Program generator circuit PG

Hardwired values: the program P, the CRS string crs, the PRF key K, the initial digest d

Input: step number τ

(a) Compute $C_{\mathsf{CPU}} \leftarrow P(\tau)$. That is, P on input time step τ outputs the step circuit C_{CPU}.

(b) Output $\mathsf{GarbleCkt}\left(1^\lambda, C\left[C_{\mathsf{CPU}}, \mathsf{crs}, \tau, \{\mathsf{lab}_{k,b}^{\tau+1}\}\right], \{\mathsf{lab}_{k,b}^\tau\}; \mathsf{PRF}_K(\tau)\right)$, where the circuit C is described in Figure 5.

Fig. 4. Description of program generator circuit PG

Step circuit C

Hardwired values: A step circuit C_{CPU}, the CRS string crs, the step number τ and a set of labels $\{\mathsf{lab}_{k,b}\}$
Input: A digest d, state st and read value rv.

(a) Compute $(\mathsf{st}', \mathsf{op}, \mathsf{addr}, \mathsf{wb}) = C_{\mathsf{CPU}}(\mathsf{st}, \mathsf{rv})$.
(b) If st' is in abort state, reset $\mathsf{lab}_{k,b} = b$ for $k \in [\lambda+1, \lambda+n]$ and $b \in \{0,1\}$.
(c) If $\mathsf{op} = \mathsf{write}$, compute $e_w \leftarrow \mathsf{SendWrite}\left(\mathsf{crs}, d, \mathsf{addr}, \mathsf{wb}, \{\mathsf{lab}_{k,b}\}_{k\in[\lambda], b\in\{0,1\}}\right)$. Output

$$\left(\mathsf{op}, \mathsf{addr}, e_w, \mathsf{wb}, \{\mathsf{lab}_{k,\mathsf{st}'[k-\lambda]}\}_{i\in[n], k\in[\lambda+1,\lambda+n]}, \mathsf{lab}_{n+\lambda+1,0}\right)$$

(d) Otherwise, compute $e \leftarrow \mathsf{Send}\left(\mathsf{crs}, d, \mathsf{addr}, \{\mathsf{lab}_{\lambda+n+1,b}\}_{b\in\{0,1\}}\right)$. Output

$$\left(\mathsf{op}, \mathsf{addr}, \{\mathsf{lab}_{k,d_k}\}_{k\in[\lambda]}, \{\mathsf{lab}_{k,\mathsf{st}'[k-\lambda]}\}_{k\in[\lambda+1,\lambda+n]}, e\right)$$

Fig. 5. Description of step circuit C

- $\mathsf{GEval}^{\widehat{D}}\left(\widehat{P}\right)$: With random access to $\widehat{D}$ and on input garbled program $\widehat{P}$,

  1. Extract $\widetilde{\mathsf{lab}} \leftarrow \{\mathsf{lab}^1_{k,x_k}\}_{k\in[\lambda+n+1]}$ from the garbled program
  2. For τ from 1 to T,
     - Invoke the $i\mathcal{O}$ program on τ to obtain $\widehat{C}_\tau$.
     - Compute $(\mathsf{op}, \mathsf{addr}, A, \{\mathsf{lab}_k\}_{k\in[\lambda+1,\lambda+n]}, B) = \mathsf{EvalCkt}\left(\widehat{C}_\tau, \widetilde{\mathsf{lab}}\right)$.
     - If the labels corresponding to st are in plain-text, abort the loop
     - If $\mathsf{op} = \mathsf{write}$, parse A as (e_w, wb) and B as $\{\mathsf{lab}_k\}_{k\in[\lambda+1,\lambda+n]}$. Compute $\{\mathsf{lab}_k\}_{k\in[\lambda]} \leftarrow \mathsf{ReceiveWrite}^{\widehat{D}}(\mathsf{crs}, \mathsf{addr}, \mathsf{wb}, e_w)$.
     - Otherwise, parse A as $\{\mathsf{lab}_k\}_{k\in[\lambda+n]}$ and B as e. Compute $\mathsf{lab}_{\lambda+n+1} \leftarrow \mathsf{Receive}^{\widehat{D}}(\mathsf{crs}, \mathsf{addr}, e)$.
     - Let $\widetilde{\mathsf{lab}} \leftarrow \{\mathsf{lab}_{k,x_k}\}_{k\in[\lambda+n+N]}$
  3. Output $\{\mathsf{lab}_k\}_{k\in[\lambda+1,\lambda+n]}$.

Correctness. We can prove the correctnss of our construction using an inductive argument that for each step τ, the state st and databases are updated correctly at the end of execution of step circuit. The base case is $\tau = 0$. For $\tau \neq 0$, observe that if $\mathsf{op} = \mathsf{write}$, then algorithm Eval updates the database D_j and its associated digest, where D_j is the corresponding database for write location addr. Otherwise, if $\mathsf{op} = \mathsf{read}$, the labels recovered in Eval step 2 correspond to the value in the location addr as requested (Fig. 5).

Succinctness

1. By the efficiency of laconic OT, GrbDB runs in time $\mathsf{poly}(\lambda, |D|) + \log Q + \log T_{\max}$.

2. By the efficiency of indistinguishability obfuscation, GrbProg runs in time $\mathsf{poly}(\lambda, \log T, \log |D|, |P|)$.
3. Finally, GEval runs in time $t \cdot \mathsf{poly}(\lambda, \log T, \log |D|, |P|)$, as it will abort execution once the new state is in abort state.

We now prove that the above scheme is secure.

Theorem 10. *Assuming the security of selective-database updatable laconic oblivious transfer, puncturable PRF and iO with log-sized inputs, there exists a succinct (unbounded) reusable garbled RAM scheme satisfying UMA security.*

The crux of the proof is to show that the above construction satisfies reusable security. Consider a PPT adversary $\mathcal{A}$. Let $\mathcal{A}$ submit Q program pairs $(P_{1,0}, P_{1,1}), \ldots, (P_{Q,0}, P_{Q,1})$. We employ a standard hybrid argument.

$\underline{\mathsf{Hyb}_k^{prog}}$: In this hybrid, the challenger generates the database encoding $\widehat{D}$ honestly. For $i \leq k - 1$, it generates the garbled program $\widehat{P_{i,0}}$ and for $i \geq k$, it generates the garbled program to be $\widehat{P_{i,1}}$.

If we show that $\mathsf{Hyb}_k^{prog} \approx_c \mathsf{Hyb}_{k+1}^{prog}$, for any $k \in \{1, \ldots, Q-1\}$ then this implies that $\mathsf{Hyb}_0^{prog} \approx_c \mathsf{Hyb}_{Q+1}^{prog}$; thus proving that the scheme satisfies reusability security. Due to the space limit, we only describe a sketch here. The full proof is presented in the full version.

Instantiation. Combining the above theorem with the FE-based iO construction [48,49] and FE-based laconic OT construction [45], we arrive at the following corollary.

Corollary 11. *Assuming the existence of public-key functional encryption for circuits, there exists a succinct (unbounded) garbled RAM scheme satisfying UMA security.*

Bounded-key setting. For the bounded-key setting, since we only aim for the weak succinctness, we can consider the same construction as before except that we can instantiate iO with an *inefficient* iO scheme, i.e., a scheme that outputs the truth table of the circuit being obfuscated. Note that since we only consider iO for logarithmic inputs, the size of the truth table is still polynomial in λ. As a result, the running time of GrbProg is now $T \cdot \mathsf{poly}(\lambda, \log T, \log |D|, |P|)$. Thus, we have the following theorem.

Theorem 12. *Assuming the existence of selective-database updatable laconic oblivious transfer, there exists a weakly-succinct (unbounded) garbled RAM scheme satisfying UMA security.*

5.3   Succinct Reusable GRAM: From UMA to Full Security

In this section, we will present the construction of (fully) succinct reusable garbled RAM. We present a transformation that converts a succinct reusable garbled RAM with UMA security into a succinct reusable garbled RAM scheme with full security. While such UMA to full security setting have been known in the past, they have not been studied in the (parallel) reusable setting, which is the focus of our work.

One of the main ingredients in our construction is an initial-state rewindable ORAM scheme satisfying strong localized randomness property. We start by presenting a construction of this.

5.3.1 Rewindable ORAM with Strong Localized Randomness

Alternate Formulation of ORAMs. Before we recall the definition of strong localized randomness, we first consider an alternate (equivalent) definition of ORAM schemes. We consider a pair of PPT algorithms (OData, OProg).

Algorithm $\mathsf{OData}(1^\lambda, D)$ takes as input security parameter λ, database $D \in \{0,1\}^N$ and outputs the oblivious database D^* and some client key ck. Algorithm $\mathsf{OProg}(1^\lambda, 1^{\log N}, 1^T, P, \mathsf{ck})$ takes as input security parameter λ, memory size N, runtime T, a RAM program P, and the client key ck, and outputs a compiled program P^*, which is a RAM program that instead operates on D^*.

Strong Localized Randomness. The additional property we need from ORAM is called strong localized property from an ORAM scheme. The definition we use here is based on [31] and is stronger than the original definition.

Let $D \in \{0,1\}^N$ be any database and (P, x) be any program/input pair. Let the step circuits of P^* be indicated by $\{C_{CPU}^\tau\}_{\tau \in [T']}$ and R be the contents of the random tape used in the execution.

Definition 11 (Strong localized randomness). We say that an ORAM scheme has strong localized randomness property if for any sequence of memory accesses of length T, there exists a sequence of efficiently computable values $1 = \tau_1 < \tau_2 < \cdots < \tau_m = T' + 1$, where $\tau_t - \tau_{t-1} \leq \mathsf{poly}(\log N)$ for all $t \in [2, m]$, such that

1. For every $j \in [m-1]$, there exists an interval I_j of size $\mathsf{poly}(\log N, \lambda)$, such that for any $\tau \in [\tau_j, \tau_{j+1}]$, the random tape accessed by C_{CPU}^τ is given by R_{I_j}.
2. For every $j, j' \in [m-1]$ and $j \neq j'$, it holds that $I_j \cap I_{j'} = \emptyset$.
3. There exists a PPT procedure CkSim that takes as input $(\tau_k, \tau_{k+1}, \mathsf{ck})$ and outputs ck'. It has the following guarantee: there exists a PPT algorithm that takes as input τ_i for $i \neq k$, ck', R_{I_i} and outputs the correct (real world) memory access pattern.

   Furthermore, the following security guarantee is satisfied. $\forall j \in [m], \exists k < j$, the following distributions are computationally indistinguishable:
   - $R_{\backslash I_k \cup I_j}$ (where $R_{\backslash I_k \cup I_j}$ denotes the content of random tape except in positions $I_k \cup I_j$), $\mathsf{ck}' := \mathsf{CkSim}(\tau_k, \tau_{k+1}, \mathsf{ck})$, the memory accesses for $\tau \in [\tau_k, \tau_{k+1})^{10}$ and the memory accesses for $\tau \in [\tau_j, \tau_{j+1})$.

---

[10] $[\tau_k, \tau_{k+1})$ denotes the contents of the random tape starting from τ_k^{th} position to $(\tau_{k+1} - 1)^{th}$ position.

- $R_{\setminus I_k \cup I_j}$, $\mathsf{ck}' := \mathsf{CkSim}(\tau_k, \tau_{k+1}, \mathsf{ck})$ and the memory accesses for $\tau \in [\tau_k, \tau_{k+1})$ and uniformly random memory accesses (with the same length as the memory accesses for $\tau \in [\tau_j, \tau_{j+1})$).

Theorem 13 (ORAM with strong localized randomness [31]). *Assuming one-way functions, there exists ORAM with strong localized randomness property.*

We remark that even though the definition of strong localized randomness in [31] does not talk about CkSim, they implicitly constructed such a simulator at the end of Appendix B, and their proof in Appendix D.1 implicitly relied on the fact that such simulation is possible.

Our Construction. We present our construction of ISR-ORAM with strong localized randomness property.

Theorem 14. *Assuming the existence of ORAM with strong localized randomness and (unbounded) PK-DEPIR, there exists unbounded ISR-ORAM with strong localized randomness.*

Proof. The proof is done via two steps. First, we construct an ORAM with initially-empty database and strong localized randomness property, from an ORAM with strong localized randomness property; next, we add the ISR property to the construction via using PK-DEPIR.

From Large Initial DB to Empty Initial DB. To prove the theorem, first we build an ORAM with initially-empty database *and* strong localized randomness from ORAM with only strong localized randomness property. The requirements for ORAM with an initially-empty database are essentially the same as ordinary ORAM, except that we restrict the scheme to having an empty database at the beginning and allow the size of the database to grow as the number of operations increase. (On the other hand, traditional ORAM works on a fixed-size database who is given in its entirety at the beginning.) Furthermore, it needs to be able to achieve this without knowing an upper bound on the number of operations a priori.

The construction is as follows:

1. Initialize an ORAM D of length C; (at the beginning take C to be any constant, say 1)
2. Read/write to the ORAM until ORAM program has performed over C writes;
3. Reinitialize another ORAM D' of length $2C$ and copy data from D to D';
4. Discard D and take D' to be the new D, return to 2.

Despite possibly running in time linear in the size of the entire database for a single write, this construction will only have amortized cost constant times the original read/write amortized cost. This is because every time we are expanding the database from size S to $2S$, while this costs $O(S)$ operations, it means that we have performed $S/2$ operations since the last expansion. Therefore, we can average the cost of this expansion into each operation, and thus on average the cost for each operation is independent of S. On the other hand, strong localized randomness property follows naturally as we are using an ORAM with strong localized randomness as our building block. Finally, since by construction the expansion only depends on the running time/the number of writes, the security properties are preserved.

Generically Achieving Initial-State Rewindable Property. Next, we recall the construction of ISR-ORAM. The idea is that we will have a read-only ORAM instantiated by PK-DEPIR and another read-write (initially-empty) ORAM "cache" instantiated by the actual ORAM. The overall client state will consists of (ck, k), where ck is the client state for the initially-empty ORAM, and k is the (public) key for the PK-DEPIR. Whenever we do a read, we read from both databases and return the cached result if cache read results in a hit. For writes, we simply write directly to the cache.

To construct unbounded ISR-ORAM with SLR, we simply change the construction above to use the initially-empty ORAM with SLR instead of initially-empty ORAM. Note that the construction has the efficiency we desire as argued above.

We now argue that it satisfies the strong localized randomness property. The first two properties follow naturally, as there are only two places where we use randomness; for the ORAM, this follows as we are using an ORAM with strong localized randomness property; for the DEPIR, this follows as the randomness used by DEPIR is freshly sampled for every access and therefore independent of everything else. To argue the third property, CkSim simulates ck by calling the underlying CkSim of ORAM with SLR, and output the public key k for the PK-DEPIR as is. Using SLR of the initially-empty ORAM, the memory access pattern for ISR-ORAM is indistinguishable from random; and by the security of PK-DEPIR (where the distinguisher gets access to the key), the memory access pattern for PK-DEPIR is indistinguishable from random.

Finally, it is apparent that for this construction, if we start with ORAM without SLR instead of ORAM with SLR, and PK-DEPIR instead of B-bounded SK-DEPIR, we will end up with B-bounded ISR-ORAM without SLR property by the same argument.   □

We are now ready to present the construction of succinct reusable GRAM in the full security setting.

Ingredients. We use the following cryptographic tools:

- Unbounded ISR-ORAM scheme $(\mathsf{OData}, \mathsf{OProg})$ with strong localized randomness (Sect. 5.3).
- UMA-secure reusable garbled RAM scheme (Sect. 5.2).
- Puncturable PRF [12, 14, 44] $(\mathsf{PRF.Gen}, \mathsf{PRF.Eval}, \mathsf{PRF.Punc})$.
- Timed encryption scheme [31] $(\mathsf{TE.KeyGen}, \mathsf{TE.Enc}, \mathsf{TE.Dec}, \mathsf{TE.Constrain})$. Let M be the output length of $\mathsf{TE.Enc}$ when encrypting single bit messages.

Construction. We describe the succinct reusable (fully-secure) GRAM $(\mathsf{GrbDB}, \mathsf{GrbProg}, \mathsf{GEval})$ below:

- GrbDB$(1^\lambda, D, 1^Q, T_{\max})$: On input security parameter λ, database D and running time upper bound $T_{\max}$,
  1. Sample $K \leftarrow$ TE.KeyGen(1^λ).
  2. For $i \in [N]$, compute $D'[i] \leftarrow$ TE.Enc$(K, 0^\lambda, D[i])$.
  3. Compute $(D^*, \mathsf{ck}) \leftarrow$ OData$(1^\lambda, D')$.
  4. Run UGRAM.GrbDB$(1^\lambda, D^*, T'(T_{\max}))$ to obtain $(\mathsf{sk}, \widehat{D})$, where $T'(\cdot)$ is a polynomial corresponding to the running time blow-up of using the ORAM scheme.
  5. Output $\widehat{D}$ as garbled memory and $(\mathsf{sk}, K, \mathsf{ck})$ as secret key SK.
- GrbProg(SK, P): On input secret key $\mathsf{SK} = (\mathsf{sk}, K, \mathsf{ck})$ and a program P,
  1. Generate a puncturable PRF key $K' \leftarrow$ PRF.Gen(1^λ).
  2. Compute $P^* \leftarrow$ OProg$(1^\lambda, N, 1^T, P, \mathsf{ck})$, where P^* runs in time T'.
  3. Construct a RAM program P' such that on input $\tau \in [T']$, do
     (a) Compute $K[\tau] \leftarrow$ TE.Constrain(K, τ).
     (b) Let $\tau_1, \ldots, \tau_m$ be the sequence of values guaranteed by the strong localized randomness property of the ORAM scheme.
     (c) Let $j \in [m-1]$ such that $\tau \in [\tau_j, \tau_{j+1})$ and $C_{\mathsf{CPU}}^{P^*} \leftarrow P^*(\tau)$. Output $C_{\mathsf{CPU}}^\tau = \mathsf{SC}_\tau[C_{\mathsf{CPU}}^{P^*}, \tau, K[\tau], I_j, K']$. The circuit SC is described in Fig. 6.
     Note: We need to pad the program P' such that the total size is $|P| \cdot \mathrm{poly}(\lambda, \log D, \log T)$ bits.
  4. Compute and output $\widehat{P} \leftarrow$ UGRAM.GProg(sk, P').

Step circuit SC_τ

Hardwired values: A circuit C_{CPU}, step number τ, constrained key $K[\tau]$, interval I_j, and the key K'.

Input: A Ciphertext c_{CPU} and a encrypted data X.

(a) Compute decryption as $\mathsf{rv} = $ TE.Dec$(K[\tau], X)$ and $\mathsf{st} = $ TE.Dec$(K[\tau], c_{\mathsf{CPU}})$.

(b) Compute $R_{I_j} = $ PRF.Eval(K', I_j).

(c) Compute $(\mathsf{st}', \mathsf{op}, \mathsf{addr}', \mathsf{wb}) = C_{\mathsf{CPU}}(\mathsf{st}, \mathsf{rv}; R_{I_j})$.

(d) If $\tau = T'$, then output $c'_{\mathsf{CPU}} = \mathsf{st}'$. Else, compute $c'_{\mathsf{CPU}} \leftarrow$ TE.Enc$(K[\tau], \mathsf{st}')$.

(e) Else if $\mathsf{op} = $ write, compute $X' \leftarrow$ TE.Enc$(K[\tau], \tau, \mathsf{wb})$. Output $(c'_{\mathsf{CPU}}, \mathsf{op}, \mathsf{addr}, X')$.

(f) Else if $\mathsf{op} = $ read, output $(c'_{\mathsf{CPU}}, \mathsf{op}, \mathsf{addr}, \bot)$

Fig. 6. Description of step circuit $C_{\mathsf{CPU}}^\tau[\tau, I_j, K[\tau], K']$

- GEval$^{\widehat{D}}(\widehat{P})$: With random access to garbled database $\widehat{D}$ and input $\widehat{P}$, it computes and outputs $y = $ UGRAM.GEval$^{\widehat{D}}(\widehat{P})$.

Theorem 15. *Assuming the existence of public-key functional encryption for circuits and unbounded PK-DEPIR, there exists a succinct reusable garbled RAM scheme.*

Due to the space constraints, we present the proof in the full version.

Bounded Setting. We observe that our techniques can be adapted to get bounded reusable garbled RAM albeit satisfying the weaker succinctness property.

Theorem 16. *Assuming the existence of selective-database updatable laconic oblivious transfer, there exists a weakly-succinct bounded reusable garbled RAM scheme.*

Proof. To put our construction to the Q-bounded-key setting, we implement the following changes for the construction above:

1. UGRAM is replaced by the weakly-succinct reusable UMA GRAM we constructed in Theorem 12;
2. Unbounded ISR-ORAM with strong localized randomness property is replaced with $(Q \cdot T_{\max})$-bounded ISR-ORAM without strong localized randomness property, which can be constructed from one way functions, as we show in Theorem 14.

Even though we lose the strong localized randomness property, since we only need weak succinctness, we can get around the issue by hardwiring all the randomness for the program. Furthermore, as we will only generate at most $Q \cdot T_{\max}$ queries to ISR-ORAM, intuitively, we can simply invoke the security proof above to argue security for the new construction. We present the full proof also in the full version. □

6   Collusion-Resistant Public-Key FE: From Circuits to RAMs

In this part, we show how to construct public-key FE for RAMs from public-key FE for circuits. We use the following tools:

- Public-key FE scheme for circuits scheme $\widetilde{\mathsf{FE}}$.
- Succinct reusable garbled RAM scheme GRAM, where the length of randomness used in algorithm GRAM.GrbProg is ℓ_1, the length of garbled program is ℓ_2 and the length of garbling key is λ.
- Pseudorandom function $\mathsf{PRF}_1 : \mathcal{K} \times \{0,1\}^\lambda \to \{0,1\}^{\ell_1}$, and $\mathsf{PRF}_2 : \mathcal{K} \times \{0,1\}^\lambda \to \{0,1\}^{\ell_2}$ where $\mathcal{K}$ is the space of keys of size λ.

We construct public-key functional encryption for RAMs scheme $\mathsf{FE} = (\mathsf{Setup}, \mathsf{Enc}, \mathsf{KeyGen}, \mathsf{Dec})$ as follows:

- $\mathsf{Setup}(1^\lambda, T)$: On input security parameter λ and upper time bound T,
    1. Compute $(\widetilde{\mathsf{FE}}.\mathsf{MSK}, \widetilde{\mathsf{FE}}.\mathsf{pk}) \leftarrow \widetilde{\mathsf{FE}}.\mathsf{Setup}(1^\lambda)$.
    2. Output $\mathsf{MSK} = \widetilde{\mathsf{FE}}.\mathsf{MSK}, \mathsf{pk} = \widetilde{\mathsf{FE}}.\mathsf{pk}$.
- $\mathsf{Enc}(\mathsf{pk}, D)$: On input public key $\mathsf{pk} = \widetilde{\mathsf{FE}}.\mathsf{pk}$ and database D,

1. Run the garbling database algorithm,

$$(\widehat{D}, \mathsf{GRAM.sk}) \leftarrow \mathsf{GRAM.GrbDB}(1^\lambda, D, T)$$

2. Choose a random PRF key K_1 from PRF key space $\mathcal{K}$.
3. Compute $\widetilde{\mathsf{FE}}.\mathsf{CT} \leftarrow \widetilde{\mathsf{FE}}.\mathsf{Enc}\left(\mathsf{pk}, (\mathsf{GRAM.sk}, K_1, 0^\lambda, 0)\right)$.
4. Output ciphertext as $\mathsf{CT} = \left(\widehat{D}, \widetilde{\mathsf{FE}}.\mathsf{CT}\right)$.

- KeyGen(MSK, P): On input master secret key $\mathsf{MSK} = (\widetilde{\mathsf{FE}}.\mathsf{MSK}, T)$, a RAM program P,
  1. Sample random string $\tau \leftarrow \{0,1\}^\lambda$, and $r \leftarrow \{0,1\}^{\ell_2}$.
  2. Compute $\widetilde{\mathsf{FE}}.\mathsf{sk}_P \leftarrow \widetilde{\mathsf{FE}}.\mathsf{KeyGen}(\widetilde{\mathsf{FE}}.\mathsf{MSK}, C[P, r, \tau])$ for circuit $C[P, r, \tau]$ as described in Fig. 7.
  3. Output $\mathsf{sk}_P = \widetilde{\mathsf{FE}}.\mathsf{sk}_P$.

$$C\left[P, r, \tau\right](\mathsf{GRAM.sk}, K_1, K_2, \beta)$$

Hardwired Values: RAM program P, random strings τ and r.
Input: $(\mathsf{GRAM.sk}, K_1, K_2, \tau, \beta)$.
If $\beta = 1$, then output $r \oplus \mathsf{PRF}_2(K_2, \tau)$.
Else $\beta = 0$,
(a) Run $\mathsf{GRAM.GrbProg}(\mathsf{sk}, P; \mathsf{PRF}_1(K_1, \tau))$ to obtain $\widehat{P}$.
(b) Output garbled program $\widehat{P}$.

Fig. 7. Description of circuit $C[P, r, \tau](\mathsf{GRAM.sk}, K_1, K_2, \beta)$

- $\mathsf{Dec}^{\mathsf{CT}}(\mathsf{sk}_P)$: On input secret key sk_P and random access to ciphertext CT, the decryption algorithm does:
  1. Parse the functional key sk_P as $\widetilde{\mathsf{FE}}.\mathsf{sk}_P$.
  2. Parse the ciphertext CT as $(\widehat{D}, \widetilde{\mathsf{FE}}.\mathsf{CT})$.
  3. Compute $\widehat{P} = \widetilde{\mathsf{FE}}.\mathsf{Dec}\left(\widetilde{\mathsf{FE}}.\mathsf{sk}_P, \widetilde{\mathsf{FE}}.\mathsf{CT}\right)$.
  4. Compute and output $y \leftarrow \mathsf{GRAM.GEval}\left(\widehat{P}, \widehat{D}\right)$.

Correctness. For any RAM program P, database D, let $\mathsf{CT} \leftarrow \mathsf{Enc}(\mathsf{pk}, D)$, and $\mathsf{sk}_P \leftarrow \mathsf{KeyGen}(\mathsf{MSK}, P)$, where $(\mathsf{pk}, \mathsf{MSK})$ are generated as above. Parse CT as $(\widehat{D}, \widetilde{\mathsf{FE}}.\mathsf{CT})$, and $\mathsf{sk}_P = \widetilde{\mathsf{FE}}.\mathsf{sk}_P$. The correctness of $\widetilde{\mathsf{FE}}$ guarantees that $\widehat{P} = \mathsf{GRAM.GrbProg}(\mathsf{GRAM.sk}, P; \mathsf{PRF}(K, \tau))$, where $\widehat{P} = \mathsf{Dec}(\mathsf{sk}_P, \mathsf{CT})$. By the correctness of pseudorandom function PRF and FE scheme $\widetilde{\mathsf{FE}}$, it follows that the output of $\mathsf{GEval}\left(\widehat{P}, \widehat{D}\right) = P^D()$.

Succinctness. We analyze the succinctness property of the construction as follows:

- Setup$(1^\lambda, T)$ runs in time poly$(\lambda, \log(T))$: first observe that $\widetilde{\mathsf{FE}}$.Setup(1^λ) runs in time poly$(\lambda, \log(s))$, where s denotes the size of supported circuits. Now we determine an upper bound for s. By the succinctness of GRAM, GrbProg$(\mathsf{sk}, \cdot; \mathsf{PRF}_1(K_1, \tau))$ can be represented by a circuit of size at most poly$(\lambda, \log(T), |P|)$; thus, $|C| = $ poly$(\lambda, \log(T), |P|)$. Thus, $s = $ poly$(\lambda, \log(T), |P|)$.
- Enc(pk, D) runs in time poly$(\lambda, \log(T), |D|)$: we first note that $\widetilde{\mathsf{FE}}$.Enc$(\mathsf{pk}, $ GRAM.sk$)$ runs in time poly$(\lambda, \log(s))$, while GRAM.GrbDB$(1^\lambda, D, T)$ runs in time poly$(\lambda, \log(T), |D|)$.
- KeyGen(MSK, P) runs in time poly$(\lambda, \log(T), |P|)$: $\widetilde{\mathsf{FE}}$.KeyGen$(\widetilde{\mathsf{FE}}$.MSK, $C[P, r, \tau]$ (GRAM.sk, $K_1, K_2, \beta))$ runs in time poly(λ, s) and from the first bullet, $s = $ poly$(\lambda, \log(T), |P|)$.
- Dec$^{\mathsf{CT}}(\mathsf{sk}_P)$ runs in time poly(λ, T): the runtime of $\widetilde{\mathsf{FE}}$.Dec$(\widetilde{\mathsf{FE}}$.sk$_P, \widetilde{\mathsf{FE}}$.CT$)$ is poly$(\lambda, \log(T), |P|)$. Moreover, from the succinctness of GRAM, the runtime of GEval$\left(\widehat{P}, \widehat{D}\right)$ is poly(λ, t), where t is the time taken to execute $P^D()$.

Theorem 17. *If $\widetilde{\mathsf{FE}}$ is a public-key functional encryption for circuits satisfying indistinguishability security, GRAM is a succinct reusable garbled RAM scheme and PRF is a secure pseudorandom function, then the FE for RAMs construction FE described above is selectively secure.*

Proof. We describe the hybrids below; in the first hybrid $\mathsf{Hyb}_{0,b}$, the challenger uses challenge bit $b \xleftarrow{\$} \{0, 1\}$ to generate the ciphertexts and in the final hybrids Hyb_4, all the parameters in the system computationally hide b.

$\mathsf{Hyb}_{0,b}$: This correspondes to the real experiment. The challenger computes the following: (i) $(\mathsf{pk}, \mathsf{MSK}) \leftarrow$ Setup$(1^\lambda, T)$, (ii) $\mathsf{CT}_b \leftarrow$ Enc(MSK, D_b), and (iii) $\{\mathsf{sk}_P \leftarrow$ KeyGen$(\mathsf{MSK}, P)\}$. It sends public key, functional keys and challenge ciphertext to $\mathcal{A}$.

$\mathsf{Hyb}_{1,b}$: In this hybird, we change how the functional keys are generated for each query. The challenger chooses a key K_2 from $\mathcal{K}$ for PRF_2 and computes $(\widehat{D}_b, \mathsf{GRAM.sk}_b) \leftarrow$ GRAM.GrbDB$(1^\lambda, T, D_b)$ at the very beginning, then for each query P_i, where $i \in [Q]$

1. Sample a random string $\tau \leftarrow \{0, 1\}^\lambda$.
2. Compute $\widehat{P} = $ GRAM.GrbProg(GRAM.sk$_b$, P; $\mathsf{PRF}_1(K_1, \tau)$).
3. Set $r = \widehat{P} \oplus \mathsf{PRF}_2(K_2, \tau)$.
4. Compute and output functional key $\mathsf{sk}_P = \widetilde{\mathsf{FE}}$.KeyGen$(\mathsf{MSK}, C[P, r, \tau])$.

The indistinguishability argument of hybrid $\mathsf{Hyb}_{0,b}$ and $\mathsf{Hyb}_{1,b}$ is based on the pseudorandom property of $\mathsf{PRF}_2(K_2, \tau)$, which is not used in any other place, and the randomness of string τ.

$\mathsf{Hyb}_{2,b}$: In this hybrid, we set the $\widetilde{\mathsf{FE}}.\mathsf{CT}$ part in challenge ciphertext as

$$\widetilde{\mathsf{FE}}.\mathsf{Enc}\left(\mathsf{pk}, (0^\lambda, 0^\lambda, K_2, 1)\right)$$

The indistinguishability between hybrid $\mathsf{Hyb}_{1,b}$ and $\mathsf{Hyb}_{2,b}$ is based on the indistinguishability security of FE scheme $\widetilde{\mathsf{FE}}$, since

$$C\left[P, r, \tau\right](\mathsf{GRAM.sk}, K_1, 0^\lambda, 0) = C\left[P, r, \tau\right](0^\lambda, 0^\lambda, K_2, 1)$$

where r, τ are generated as described in hybrid $\mathsf{Hyb}_{2,b}$.

$\mathsf{Hyb}_{3,b}$: In this hybird, we change how the hardwired value τ is generated in each functional key query. Instead of computing $\widehat{P} = \mathsf{GRAM.GrbProg}(\mathsf{sk}, P; \mathsf{PRF}_1(K_1, \tau))$, we compute $\widehat{P} = \mathsf{GRAM.GrbProg}(\mathsf{sk}, P; u)$, where $u \in \{0,1\}^{\ell_1}$ is a random string.

The indistinguishability of $\mathsf{Hyb}_{2,b}$ and $\mathsf{Hyb}_{3,b}$ follows from the security of pseudorandom function PRF_1 using key K_1, which is not used anywhere else except for computing hardwired value τ.

The indistinguishability of $\mathsf{Hyb}_{3,0}$ and $\mathsf{Hyb}_{3,1}$ follows the reusable security of garbled RAM scheme GRAM and query restraint $P^{D_0} = P^{D_1}$ for program P. $\qquad\square$

Acknowledgement. We than Shota Yamada and anonymous ASIACRYPT 2022 reviewers for improving our work. Luowen Qian is supported by DARPA under Agreement No. HR00112020023.

References

1. Agrawal, S., Maitra, M.: FE and iO for turing machines from minimal assumptions. In: Theory of Cryptography Conference, pp. 473–512 (2018)
2. Agrawal, S., Singh, I.P.: Reusable garbled deterministic finite automata from learning with errors. In: ICALP, Schloss Dagstuhl-Leibniz-Zentrum fuer Informatik (2017)
3. Ananth, P., Brakerski, Z., Segev, G., Vaikuntanathan, V.: From selective to adaptive security in functional encryption. In: Annual Cryptology Conference, pp. 657–677 (2015)
4. Ananth, P., Chen, Y.-C., Chung, K.-M., Lin, H., Lin, W.-K.: Delegating RAM computations with adaptive soundness and privacy. In: Hirt, M., Smith, A. (eds.) TCC 2016. LNCS, vol. 9986, pp. 3–30. Springer, Heidelberg (2016). https://doi.org/10.1007/978-3-662-53644-5_1
5. Ananth, P., Jain, A.: Indistinguishability obfuscation from compact functional encryption. In: Annual Cryptology Conference, pp. 308–326 (2015)
6. Prabhanjan Ananth and Alex Lombardi. Succinct garbling schemes from functional encryption through a local simulation paradigm. In: TCC, pp. 455–472 (2018)
7. Ananth, P., Sahai, A.: Functional encryption for Turing machines. In: Theory of Cryptography Conference, pp. 125–153 (2016)

8. Bitansky, N., Garg, S., Lin, H., Pass, R., Telang, S.: Succinct randomized encodings and their applications. In: STOC (2015)
9. Bitansky, N., Paneth, O., Rosen, A.: On the cryptographic hardness of finding a Nash equilibrium. In: FOCS 2015, pp. 1480–1498. IEEE (2015)
10. Bitansky, N., Vaikuntanathan, V.: Indistinguishability obfuscation from functional encryption. J. ACM (JACM) 65(6), 39 (2018)
11. Boneh, D., Sahai, A., Waters, B.: Functional encryption: definitions and challenges. In: Ishai, Y. (ed.) TCC 2011. LNCS, vol. 6597, pp. 253–273. Springer, Heidelberg (2011). https://doi.org/10.1007/978-3-642-19571-6_16
12. Boneh, D., Waters, B.: Constrained pseudorandom functions and their applications. In: Sako, K., Sarkar, P. (eds.) ASIACRYPT 2013. LNCS, vol. 8270, pp. 280–300. Springer, Heidelberg (2013). https://doi.org/10.1007/978-3-642-42045-0_15
13. Boyle, E., Chung, K.-M., Pass, R.: Oblivious parallel RAM and applications. In: Kushilevitz, E., Malkin, T. (eds.) TCC 2016. LNCS, vol. 9563, pp. 175–204. Springer, Heidelberg (2016). https://doi.org/10.1007/978-3-662-49099-0_7
14. Boyle, E., Goldwasser, S., Ivan, I.: Functional signatures and pseudorandom functions. In: Krawczyk, H. (ed.) PKC 2014. LNCS, vol. 8383, pp. 501–519. Springer, Heidelberg (2014). https://doi.org/10.1007/978-3-642-54631-0_29
15. Boyle, E., Holmgren, J., Weiss, M.: Permuted puzzles and cryptographic hardness. In: TCC (2019)
16. Boyle, E., Ishai, Y., Pass, R., Wootters, M.: Can we access a database both locally and privately? In: TCC, pp. 662–693 (2017)
17. Brakerski, Z., Lombardi, A., Segev, G., Vaikuntanathan, V.: Anonymous IBE, leakage resilience and circular security from new assumptions. In: Nielsen, J.B., Rijmen, V. (eds.) EUROCRYPT 2018. LNCS, vol. 10820, pp. 535–564. Springer, Cham (2018). https://doi.org/10.1007/978-3-319-78381-9_20
18. Canetti, R., Chen, Y., Holmgren, J., Raykova, M.: Adaptive succinct garbled RAM or: how to delegate your database. In: Hirt, M., Smith, A. (eds.) TCC 2016. LNCS, vol. 9986, pp. 61–90. Springer, Heidelberg (2016). https://doi.org/10.1007/978-3-662-53644-5_3
19. Canetti, R., Holmgren, J.: Fully succinct garbled RAM. In: ITCS, pp. 169–178. ACM (2016)
20. Canetti, R., Holmgren, J., Jain, A., Vaikuntanathan, V.: Indistinguishability obfuscation of iterated circuits and RAM programs. In: STOC (2015)
21. Canetti, R., Holmgren, J., Richelson, S., Towards doubly efficient private information retrieval. In: TCC, pp. 694–726 (2017)
22. De Caro, A., Iovino, V., Jain, A., O'Neill, A., Paneth, O., Persiano, G.: On the achievability of simulation-based security for functional encryption. Adv. Cryptol. - CRYPTO 2013, 519–535 (2013)
23. Chen, Y.-C., Chow, S.S.M., Chung, K.-M., Lai, R.W.F., Lin, W.-K., Zhou, H.-S.: Cryptography for parallel RAM from indistinguishability obfuscation. In: Sudan, M., (ed.), ITCS, pp. 179–190. ACM (2016)
24. Cho, C., Döttling, N., Garg, S., Gupta, D., Miao, P., Polychroniadou, A.: Laconic oblivious transfer and its applications. In: Annual International Cryptology Conference, pp. 33–65 (2017)
25. Chung, K.-M., Qian, L.: Adaptively secure garbling schemes for parallel computations. In: Hofheinz, D., Rosen, A., (eds.) TCC (2019)
26. Garg, S., Gentry, C., Halevi, S., Raykova, M.: Two-round secure MPC from indistinguishability obfuscation. In: TCC, pp. 74–94 (2014)

27. Garg, S., Gentry, C., Halevi, S., Raykova, M., Sahai, A., Waters, B.: Candidate indistinguishability obfuscation and functional encryption for all circuits. FOCS **2013**, 40–49 (2013)
28. Garg, S., Gupta, D., Miao, P., Pandey, O.: Secure multiparty ram computation in constant rounds. In: TCC, pp. 491–520 (2016)
29. Garg, S., Lu, S., Ostrovsky, R.: Black-box garbled RAM. In: Guruswami, V., (ed.) FOCS, pp. 210–229. IEEE (2015)
30. Garg, S., Lu, S., Ostrovsky, R., Scafuro, A.: Garbled RAM from one-way functions. In: STOC 2015, pp. 449–458. ACM (2015)
31. Garg, S., Ostrovsky, R., Srinivasan, A.: Adaptive garbled RAM from laconic oblivious transfer. In: Shacham, H., Boldyreva, A. (eds.) CRYPTO 2018. LNCS, vol. 10993, pp. 515–544. Springer, Cham (2018). https://doi.org/10.1007/978-3-319-96878-0_18
32. Garg, S., Pandey, O., Srinivasan, A.: Revisiting the cryptographic hardness of finding a Nash equilibrium. In: Annual International Cryptology Conference, pp. 579–604 (2016)
33. Garg, S., Srinivasan, A.: A simple construction of iO for Turing machines. In: TCC, pp. 425–454 (2018)
34. Garg, S., Srinivasan, A.: Adaptively secure garbling with near optimal online complexity. In: Nielsen, J.B., Rijmen, V. (eds.) EUROCRYPT 2018. LNCS, vol. 10821, pp. 535–565. Springer, Cham (2018). https://doi.org/10.1007/978-3-319-78375-8_18
35. Gentry, C., Halevi, S., Lu, S., Ostrovsky, R., Raykova, M., Wichs, D.: Garbled RAM revisited. In: Nguyen, P.Q., Oswald, E. (eds.) EUROCRYPT 2014. LNCS, vol. 8441, pp. 405–422. Springer, Heidelberg (2014). https://doi.org/10.1007/978-3-642-55220-5_23
36. Gentry, C., Halevi, S., Raykova, M., Wichs, D.: Outsourcing private RAM computation. In: FOCS, pp. 404–413 (2014)
37. Goldreich, O., Goldwasser, S., Micali, S.: How to construct random functions. J. ACM (JACM) **33**(4), 792–807 (1986)
38. Goldreich, O., Ostrovsky, R.: Software protection and simulation on oblivious RAMs. J. ACM (JACM) **43**(3), 431–473 (1996)
39. Goldwasser, S., Tauman Kalai, Y., Popa, R.A., Vaikuntanathan, V., Zeldovich, N.: Reusable garbled circuits and succinct functional encryption. In: STOC 2013, pp. 555–564 (2013)
40. Goyal, R., Kim, S., Manohar, N., Waters, B., Wu, D.J.: Watermarking public-key cryptographic primitives. In: Annual International Cryptology Conference, pp. 367–398 (2019)
41. Hamlin, A., Holmgren, J., Weiss, M., Wichs, D.: On the plausibility of fully homomorphic encryption for RAMs. In: Boldyreva, A., Micciancio, D. (eds.) CRYPTO 2019. LNCS, vol. 11692, pp. 589–619. Springer, Cham (2019). https://doi.org/10.1007/978-3-030-26948-7_21
42. Hamlin, A., Ostrovsky, R., Weiss, M., Wichs, D.: Private anonymous data access. In: Ishai, Y., Rijmen, V. (eds.) EUROCRYPT 2019. LNCS, vol. 11477, pp. 244–273. Springer, Cham (2019). https://doi.org/10.1007/978-3-030-17656-3_9
43. Keller, M., Yanai, A.: Efficient maliciously secure multiparty computation for RAM. In: Nielsen, J.B., Rijmen, V. (eds.) EUROCRYPT 2018. LNCS, vol. 10822, pp. 91–124. Springer, Cham (2018). https://doi.org/10.1007/978-3-319-78372-7_4
44. Kiayias, A., Papadopoulos, S., Triandopoulos, N., Zacharias, T.: Delegatable pseudorandom functions and applications. In: Proceedings of the 2013 ACM SIGSAC Conference on Computer & Communications Security, pp. 669–684. ACM (2013)

45. Kitagawa, F., Nishimaki, R., Tanaka, K., Yamakawa, T.: Adaptively secure and succinct functional encryption: improving security and efficiency, simultaneously. In: Boldyreva, A., Micciancio, D. (eds.) CRYPTO 2019. LNCS, vol. 11694, pp. 521–551. Springer, Cham (2019). https://doi.org/10.1007/978-3-030-26954-8_17

46. Koppula, V., Lewko, A.B., Waters, B.: Indistinguishability obfuscation for Turing machines with unbounded memory. In: STOC (2015)

47. Kowalczyk, L., Malkin, T., Ullman, J., Wichs, D.: Hardness of non-interactive differential privacy from one-way functions. In: Annual International Cryptology Conference, pp. 437–466 (2018)

48. Lin, H., Tessaro, S.: Indistinguishability obfuscation from trilinear maps and block-wise local PRGs. In: Katz, J., Shacham, H. (eds.) CRYPTO 2017. LNCS, vol. 10401, pp. 630–660. Springer, Cham (2017). https://doi.org/10.1007/978-3-319-63688-7_21

49. Liu, Q., Zhandry, M.: Decomposable obfuscation: a framework for building applications of obfuscation from polynomial hardness. In: Kalai, Y., Reyzin, L. (eds.) TCC 2017. LNCS, vol. 10677, pp. 138–169. Springer, Cham (2017). https://doi.org/10.1007/978-3-319-70500-2_6

50. Lu, S., Ostrovsky, R.: Black-box parallel garbled RAM. In: Katz, J., Shacham, H. (eds.) CRYPTO 2017. LNCS, vol. 10402, pp. 66–92. Springer, Cham (2017). https://doi.org/10.1007/978-3-319-63715-0_3

51. O'Neill, A.: Definitional issues in functional encryption. IACR Cryptol. ePrint Arch. **2010**, 556 (2010)

52. Sahai, A., Waters, B.: Fuzzy identity-based encryption. In: Cramer, R. (ed.) EUROCRYPT 2005. LNCS, vol. 3494, pp. 457–473. Springer, Heidelberg (2005). https://doi.org/10.1007/11426639_27

53. Sahai, A., Waters, B.: How to use indistinguishability obfuscation: deniable encryption, and more. In: Shmoys, D.B. (ed.) Symposium on Theory of Computing, STOC 2014, New York, NY, USA, May 31–June 03 2014, pp. 475–484. ACM (2014). https://doi.org/10.1145/2591796.2591825

54. Yao, A.C.-C.: How to generate and exchange secrets (extended abstract). In: FOCS, pp. 162–167 (1986)

Witness Encryption and Null-IO from Evasive LWE

Vinod Vaikuntanathan[1(✉)], Hoeteck Wee[2], and Daniel Wichs[2,3]

[1] MIT CSAIL, Cambridge, USA
vinodv@mit.edu
[2] NTT Research, Sunnyvale, USA
[3] Northeastern University, Boston, USA

Abstract. Witness encryption (WE) allows us to use an arbitrary NP statement x as a public key to encrypt a message, and the witness w serves as a decryption key. Security ensures that, when the statement x is false, the encrypted message remains computationally hidden. WE appears to be significantly weaker than indistinguishability obfuscation (iO). Indeed, WE is closely related to a highly restricted form of iO that only guarantees security for null circuits (null iO). However, all current approaches towards constructing WE under nice assumptions go through iO. Such constructions are quite complex and are unlikely to lead to practically instantiable schemes. In this work, we revisit a very simple WE and null iO candidate of Chen, Vaikuntanathan and Wee (CRYPTO 2018). We show how to prove its security under a nice and easy-to-state assumption that we refer to as *evasive LWE* following Wee (EUROCRYPT 2022). Roughly speaking, the evasive LWE assumption says the following: assume we have some joint distributions over matrices $\mathbf{P}, \mathbf{S}$ and auxiliary information aux such that

$$(\mathbf{SB} + \mathbf{E}, \mathbf{SP} + \mathbf{E}', \mathsf{aux}) \approx_c (\mathbf{U}, \mathbf{U}', \mathsf{aux}),$$

for a uniformly random (and secret) matrix $\mathbf{B}$, where $\mathbf{U}, \mathbf{U}'$ are uniformly random matrices, and $\mathbf{E}, \mathbf{E}'$ are chosen from the LWE error distribution with appropriate parameters. Then it must also be the case that:

$$(\mathbf{SB} + \mathbf{E}, \mathbf{B}^{-1}(\mathbf{P}), \mathsf{aux}) \approx_c (\mathbf{U}, \mathbf{B}^{-1}(\mathbf{P}), \mathsf{aux}).$$

Essentially the above says that given $\mathbf{SB} + \mathbf{E}$, getting the additional component $\mathbf{B}^{-1}(\mathbf{P})$ is no more useful than just getting the product $(\mathbf{SB} + \mathbf{E}) \cdot \mathbf{B}^{-1}(\mathbf{P}) \approx \mathbf{SP} + \mathbf{E}'$.

1 Introduction

Witness encryption (WE), a notion introduced by Garg, Gentry, Sahai and Waters [GGSW13], allows us to use an arbitrary NP statement x as a public key to encrypt a message. If x is a true statement then any user who knows the corresponding witness w for x will be able to decrypt the message, but if x is a false statement then the encrypted message is computationally hidden. For

S. Agrawal and D. Lin (Eds.): ASIACRYPT 2022, LNCS 13791, pp. 195–221, 2022.
https://doi.org/10.1007/978-3-031-22963-3_7

example, the Clay Mathematics Institute could encrypt $1M worth of bitcoin reward under the NP statement that corresponds to the Riemann hypothesis. If anyone comes up with such a proof, they can use that as the witness to decrypt the ciphertext and recover the reward.

WE is known to be implied by indistinguishability obfuscation (iO) [BGI+01, GGH+13b]. However, iO appears to be a significantly stronger primitive than WE, and provably so with respect to black-box constructions [GMM17]. On an intuitive level, in WE, we only require functionality (ability to correctly decrypt) in a setting where the statement is true and there are no security guarantees. Conversely, we only require security to hold in a setting where the statement is false and there is no functionality requirement. On the other hand, iO requires us to provide security and functionality simultaneously since the obfuscated program needs to function correctly on all inputs while at the same time hiding the code of the original program. Indeed, modulo the LWE assumption, WE is equivalent to a very weak form of iO, referred to as null-iO, where security (indistinguishability of circuits) only needs to hold for null programs that output 0 on all inputs, while functionality needs to hold for all programs [WZ17, GKW17].

Despite WE being seemingly much weaker than iO, the current state-of-the-art in constructions does not reflect this. In particular, a beautiful series of recent works constructs iO under simple-to-state assumptions [AJL+19, JLMS19, Agr19, GJLS21], culminating in a recent break-through that bases iO on well-studied hardness assumptions [JLS21b, JLS21a]. Another recent line of works obtains lattice-inspired iO candidates [Agr19, CHVW19, AP20, BDGM20a, WW21, GP21, BDGM20b, DQV+21] that avoid the use of pairings and are plausibly post-quantum secure, but requires less well-studied assumptions pertaining to variants of LWE with leakage. Both of these routes to iO also incur high computational complexity due to the use of non-black-box recursion (following [BV15, AJ15]), making it almost unimaginable that they could be implemented even for the simplest of programs. Unfortunately, the only known avenue for constructing WE under similarly nice assumptions goes through iO and inherits all of its corresponding complexity.

In this work, we turn our attention to earlier frameworks for constructing iO and witness encryption [GGH+13b, GGSW13, GLW14]: encode the corresponding program or NP instance, represented as a branching programs[1], using multi-linear encodings [GGH13a, CLT15, GGH15]. The ensuing schemes are remarkably simple, direct, reasonably efficient (e.g., implemented in [HHSS17]), and could even achieve plausible post-quantum security. Unfortunately, we have attacks on the iO schemes for read-c branching programs for $c = O(1)$ [CHL+15, MSZ16, CLLT16, ADGM17, CLLT17, CGH17, Pel18, CVW18, CCH+19]. On the other hand, none of these attacks are applicable to the WE schemes.

Arguably the simplest of these WE schemes is due to Chen, Vaikuntanathan and Wee [CVW18] (henceforth CVW) based on GGH15 multi-linear encodings [GGH15, CC17]. It only relies on LWE-style tools/algebra and is very simple to

---

[1] For iO, we need some additional pre-processing to prevent mixed-input attacks; see Sect. 7.

write down, with complexity similar to the iO candidate for read-once branching programs implemented in [HHSS17]. We do not currently know any attacks on the CVW WE scheme, nor do we know how to base it on any nice assumption, other than just tautologically assuming its security. This motivates the main question of this work:

> Question: Can we prove security of the CVW scheme for WE (or a variant thereof) under a simple assumption?

For the optimist, the assumption would ideally increase our confidence in the security of the CVW scheme and give us a better understanding of the basis of this security. For the skeptic, the assumption would constitute a simpler and easier target for cryptanalysis. More broadly, the assumption could provide new insights into the security and weakness of GGH15 multi-linear encodings, extending the positive results in [CC17, GKW17, WZ17, GKW18, CVW18].

1.1   Our Results

We prove the security of the CVW schemes for WE and null-IO under a variant of Wee's evasive LWE assumption [Wee22], together with LWE with subexponential hardness. We analyze the CVW schemes essentially "as is", with some modifications to the underlying parameters. We proceed to state the assumption and then provide an overview of our security proof.

Evasive LWE. Fix some efficiently samplable distributions $(\mathbf{S}, \mathbf{P}, \mathsf{aux})$ over $\mathbb{Z}_q^{n' \times n} \times \mathbb{Z}_q^{n \times t} \times \{0, 1\}^*$. We would like to assert statements of the form

$$(\boxed{\mathbf{SB} + \mathbf{E}}, \mathbf{B}^{-1}(\mathbf{P}), \mathsf{aux}) \approx_c (\boxed{\mathbf{C}}, \mathbf{B}^{-1}(\mathbf{P}), \mathsf{aux})$$

where $\mathbf{B} \leftarrow \mathbb{Z}_q^{n \times m}, \mathbf{C} \leftarrow \mathbb{Z}_q^{n' \times m}$ are uniformly random. Think of parameters $O(n \log q) \leq m \leq t$, so that $\mathbf{P}$ is wider than $\mathbf{B}$. We have two distinguishing strategies in the literature:

- distinguish $\mathbf{SB} + \mathbf{E}$ from $\mathbf{C}$ given aux;
- compute $(\mathbf{SB} + \mathbf{E}) \cdot \mathbf{B}^{-1}(\mathbf{P}) \approx \mathbf{SP}$ and distinguish the latter from uniform (the afore-mentioned zeroizing attacks on iO fall into this category).

The evasive LWE assumption essentially asserts that these are the only distinguishing attacks. Namely,

$$\text{if} \qquad (\boxed{\mathbf{SB} + \mathbf{E}}, \boxed{\mathbf{SP} + \mathbf{E}'}, \mathsf{aux}) \approx_c (\boxed{\mathbf{C}}, \boxed{\mathbf{C}'}, \mathsf{aux}), \qquad (1)$$

$$\text{then} \qquad (\boxed{\mathbf{SB} + \mathbf{E}}, \mathbf{B}^{-1}(\mathbf{P}), \mathsf{aux}) \approx_c (\boxed{\mathbf{C}}, \mathbf{B}^{-1}(\mathbf{P}), \mathsf{aux}) \qquad (2)$$

where $\mathbf{E}'$ is a fresh noise matrix of sufficiently larger magnitude than $\mathbf{E}$.[2] In [Wee22] (c.f. Sect. 1.3), the assumption is conceptually similar, but the matrix $\mathbf{B}$

---

[2] Note that $(\mathbf{SB} + \mathbf{E}) \cdot \mathbf{B}^{-1}(\mathbf{P})$ has rank at most m and therefore cannot be pseudorandom whenever $n', m < t$. Instead, we merely require that the high-order bits of $(\mathbf{SB} + \mathbf{E}) \cdot \mathbf{B}^{-1}(\mathbf{P}) \approx \mathbf{SP}$ are pseudorandom, as formalized by $\mathbf{SP} + \mathbf{E}'$ being pseudorandom.

is public and $\mathbf{S}$ is secret and uniformly random, while in our case both $\mathbf{B}, \mathbf{S}$ are secret and $\mathbf{S}$ can be chosen from an arbitrary distribution subject to (1) holding.

First, to give some intuition for the assumption, we begin with two quick sanity checks:

- If $\mathbf{P}$ is drawn from the uniform distribution over $\mathbb{Z}_q^{m \times t}$, then the evasive LWE assumption holds unconditionally. In particular, (2) follows unconditionally from (1), since $\mathbf{B}^{-1}(\mathbf{P})$ is distributed like a random Gaussian and hence can be simulated without knowing a trapdoor for $\mathbf{B}$. This is the case even if aux can depend on $\mathbf{P}$, as long as it is efficiently sampleable given $\mathbf{P}$.
- If $\mathbf{P} = \mathbf{0}$ or $\mathbf{P}$ is the gadget matrix, then both the pre- and post-conditions are false, so evasive LWE is vacuously unconditionally true.

We will need to rely on a version of evasive LWE where $\mathbf{P}$ is not uniformly random, but we still manage to ensure that (1) holds. We use the evasive LWE assumption to argue that (2) holds in this case as well.

Unfortunately, we show that the evasive LWE assumption is unlikely to hold in its completely full generality with arbitrary aux. In particular, we cook up a highly contrived auxiliary info aux that contains a carefully crafted obfuscated program (containing a trapdoor for $\mathbf{P}$). Under a heuristic obfuscation assumption, we show that for this choice of aux, the pre-condition holds, while the post-condition is clearly violated. This is similar in spirit to the implausibility of differing-inputs obfuscation (diO) with general auxiliary information, as shown in [GGHW14]. See Sect. 8.2 for details of our counter-example. Nevertheless, analogously to the case of diO, it is still reasonable to assume security with *essentially any* "natural distribution" of aux that is not specifically cooked up to contain a counter-example. This is the route we take in this work. In addition, we also describe in Sect. 8.2 a class of distributions that are sufficient for our proofs and seem to avoid obfuscated-based counter-examples.

We note that evasive LWE is qualitatively different from the LWE with leakage assumptions used in recent lattice-inspired iO candidates. With the latter, a distinguisher can easily obtain equations of the LWE secrets over the *integers* (which in turn allows zeroizing attacks), whereas the pre-condition in evasive LWE essentially rules this out. Indeed, the variants of LWE with leakage used in [GP21, WW21] have since been broken in [HJL21], whereas the ones in [DQV+21, JLMS19] rely on the pseudorandomness of structured low-degree polynomials over the integers which while plausible, still requires further cryptanalysis (e.g. we do not know how to rule out sum-of-squares attacks, even heuristically).

WE and Null-IO via GGH15 Encodings. We consider a read-once branching program (BP) specified by values $\mathbf{u} \in \{0,1\}^w, \{\mathbf{M}_{i,b} \in \{0,1\}^{w \times w}\}_{i \in [h], b \in \{0,1\}}$. On input $\mathbf{x} \in \{0,1\}^h$ we define $\mathbf{M}_\mathbf{x} := \prod_{i=1}^h \mathbf{M}_{i,x_i}$, and the output of the branching program is determined by $\mathbf{u} \mathbf{M}_\mathbf{x} \stackrel{?}{=} \mathbf{0}$. (Note that the matrices $\mathbf{M}_{i,b}$ are not necessarily permutations.) The GGH15 encoding of such a branching program $\mathsf{ggh.encode}^\otimes(\mathbf{u}, \{\mathbf{M}_{i,b}\})$ is given by

$$\left\{(\mathbf{u}\mathbf{M}_{1,b}\otimes\mathbf{S}_{1,b})\mathbf{A}_1, \mathbf{A}_1^{-1}((\mathbf{M}_{2,b}\otimes\mathbf{S}_{2,b})\mathbf{A}_2),\dots,\mathbf{A}_{h-1}^{-1}((\mathbf{M}_{h,b}\otimes\mathbf{S}_{h,b})\mathbf{A}_h)\right\}_{b\in\{0,1\}}$$

where $\mathbf{S}_{i,b}\leftarrow\mathcal{D}_{\mathbb{Z},\chi}^{n\times n}$, $\mathbf{A}_{i,b}\leftarrow\mathbb{Z}_q^{nw\times O(nw\log q)}$ and we use $\mathbf{A}_{i,b}^{-1}(\cdot)$ to denote random Gaussian pre-images, and we use curly underlines in place of noise terms. Given the encoding and any $\mathbf{x}\in\{0,1\}^h$, we can approximate $(\mathbf{u}\mathbf{M}_\mathbf{x}\otimes\mathbf{S}_\mathbf{x})\mathbf{A}_h$ where $\mathbf{M}_\mathbf{x}:=\prod_{i=1}^h\mathbf{M}_{i,x_i}$, $\mathbf{S}_\mathbf{x}:=\prod_{i=1}^h\mathbf{S}_{i,x_i}$, and therefore check if $\mathbf{u}\mathbf{M}_\mathbf{x}\stackrel{?}{=}\mathbf{0}$.

For WE, we can embed a CNF formula and the message into the read-once BP, and $\mathbf{x}$ corresponds to a truth assignment. For null-IO, we can take an arbitrary branching program or a NC1 formula and perform some additional pre-processing on it to convert it into a read-once BP, and $\mathbf{x}$ corresponds to a repetition-encoding of the input to the program/formula. In either case, the way we do this ensures that, if the formula is unsatisfiable or the program is a null program, it will be the case that $\mathbf{u}\mathbf{M}_\mathbf{x}\neq\mathbf{0}$ for all $\mathbf{x}\in\{0,1\}^h$. (In the case of null iO, this will hold even for values $\mathbf{x}$ that are not valid repetition-encodings of any input.) We show what whenever this condition holds, $\mathsf{ggh.encode}^{\otimes}(\mathbf{u},\{\mathbf{M}_{i,b}\})$ is pseudorandom and therefore hides $\mathbf{u},\{\mathbf{M}_{i,b}\}$. The latter immediately implies security of the CVW schemes for WE and null-IO. We sketch the proof of this statement in our technical overview.

Concurrent Independent Work. The concurrent and independent work of Tsabary [Tsa22] gives a similar construction of witness encryption and shows security under a variant of evasive LWE, via a similar proof strategy. See Appendix A for a comparison.

1.2   Technical Overview

The technical core of this work lies proving the following statement:

Theorem 1 (informal). *Suppose subexponential LWE and evasive LWE holds. If $\mathbf{u}\mathbf{M}_\mathbf{x}\neq\mathbf{0}$ for all $\mathbf{x}\in\{0,1\}^h$, then*

$$\mathsf{ggh.encode}^{\otimes}(\mathbf{u},\{\mathbf{M}_{i,b}\})\approx_c\{\mathbf{C}_{1,b},\mathbf{D}_{2,b},\dots,\mathbf{D}_{h,b}\}_{b\in\{0,1\}}$$

where $\mathbf{C}_{1,b}\leftarrow\mathbb{Z}_q^{n\times O(nw\log q)}$, $\mathbf{D}_{i,b}\leftarrow\mathcal{D}_{\mathbb{Z},\chi}^{O(nw\log q)\times O(nw\log q)}$.

As a warm-up, we prove security under a strengthening of evasive LWE where we omit $\mathbf{SB}+\mathbf{E}$ in the pre-condition, namely we assume:

$$\text{if}\qquad\qquad(\mathbf{SP}+\mathbf{E}',\mathsf{aux})\approx_c(\boxed{\mathbf{C}'},\mathsf{aux}),$$

$$\text{then}\qquad(\boxed{\mathbf{SB}+\mathbf{E}},\mathbf{B}^{-1}(\mathbf{P}),\mathsf{aux})\approx_c(\boxed{\mathbf{C}},\mathbf{B}^{-1}(\mathbf{P}),\mathsf{aux})$$

Intuitively, evasive LWE says that to prove pseudorandomness of $(\mathbf{SB}+\mathbf{E},\mathbf{B}^{-1}(\mathbf{P}))$, it suffices to "peel off" $\mathbf{B}$ and prove pseudorandomness of the product $\mathbf{SP}+\mathbf{E}'$. Our proof essentially proceeds in two steps:

- We will use evasive LWE to successively "peel off" $\mathbf{A}_1, \mathbf{A}_2, \ldots, \mathbf{A}_{h-1}$ in our "encoded program", which leaves us with 2^h products $\{(\mathbf{uM_x} \otimes \mathbf{S_x})$ $\mathbf{A}_h\}_{\mathbf{x} \in \{0,1\}^h}$.
- We then show that these 2^h evaluated products are pseudorandom under the LWE assumption, following the BLMR PRF [BLMR13].

We proceed to describe this in more detail.

Proof Idea. Suppose instead of getting the full "encoded program"

$$\left\{(\mathbf{uM}_{1,b} \otimes \mathbf{S}_{1,b})\mathbf{A}_1, \mathbf{A}_1^{-1}((\mathbf{M}_{2,b} \otimes \mathbf{S}_{2,b})\mathbf{A}_2), \ldots, \mathbf{A}_{h-1}^{-1}((\mathbf{M}_{h,b} \otimes \mathbf{S}_{h,b})\mathbf{A}_h)\right\}_{b \in \{0,1\}},$$

we were only given the 2^h "evaluated products" (with fresh independent errors):

$$\left\{(\mathbf{uM_x} \otimes \mathbf{S_x})\mathbf{A}_h\right\}_{\mathbf{x} \in \{0,1\}^h},$$

which is something we could approximate from evaluating the encoded program on all inputs $\mathbf{x} \in \{0,1\}^h$.[3]

First, by the same security analysis as the BLMR PRF [BLMR13], we can rely on (sub-exponential) LWE to show that such "evaluated products" look pseudorandom. In particular, we have

$$(\mathbf{uM_x} \otimes \mathbf{S_x})\mathbf{A}_h \approx \overbrace{(\mathbf{uM_x} \otimes \mathbf{I})}^{\neq \mathbf{0}} \cdot \overbrace{(\mathbf{I} \otimes \mathbf{S_x})\mathbf{A}_h}^{\text{pseudorandom}} .$$

Next, we rely on evasive LWE with $\mathbf{B} = \mathbf{A}_{h-1}$ to show that if we were given

$$\left\{(\mathbf{uM_x} \otimes \mathbf{S_x})\mathbf{A}_{h-1}\right\}_{\mathbf{x} \in \{0,1\}^{h-1}}, \left\{\mathbf{A}_{h-1}^{-1}((\mathbf{M}_{h,b} \otimes \mathbf{S}_{h,b})\mathbf{A}_h)\right\}_{b \in \{0,1\}}$$

corresponding to 2^{h-1} "evaluated products" for all possible choices of the first $h-1$ bits of the input and the last two components of the "encoded program", the 2^{h-1} "evaluated products" would still look pseudorandom.

We repeat the argument with $\mathbf{B} = \mathbf{A}_{h-2}, \ldots, \mathbf{A}_1$ until we show that just the first 2 "evaluated products" $\left\{(\mathbf{uM}_{1,b} \otimes \mathbf{S}_{1,b})\mathbf{A}_1\right\}_{b \in \{0,1\}}$ look pseudorandom even given all the remaining components of the "encoded program".

---

[3] While a polynomial-time adversary cannot evaluate the encoded program on all 2^h inputs, it can still efficiently approximate some linear combination of an exponential number of inputs, e.g. the sum of all 2^h evaluated products, using $((\mathbf{uM}_{1,0} \otimes \mathbf{S}_{1,0})\mathbf{A}_1 + (\mathbf{uM}_{1,1} \otimes \mathbf{S}_{1,1})\mathbf{A}_1) \cdot \prod_{i=2}^h (\mathbf{A}_{i-1}^{-1}((\mathbf{M}_{i,0} \otimes \mathbf{S}_{i,0})\mathbf{A}_i) + \mathbf{A}_{i-1}^{-1}((\mathbf{M}_{i,1} \otimes \mathbf{S}_{i,1})\mathbf{A}_i)$.

But the first 2 "evaluated products" are just the first two components of the "encoded program" and hence we can replace them by uniformly random matrices $\{\mathbf{C}_{1,b}\}_{b\in\{0,1\}}$ At this point, we can invoke an argument from [CVW18] to replace the subsequent components of the encoded program by uniformly random Gaussians to complete the proof.[4]

Example for $h = 3$. In more detail, let's see an example for $h = 3$. In that case, the proof shows:

$$\left\{(\mathbf{uM_x}\otimes\mathbf{S_x})\mathbf{A}_3\right\}_{\mathbf{x}\in\{0,1\}^3} \approx_c \left\{\mathbf{C_x}\leftarrow\mathbb{Z}_q^{n\times O(nw\log q)}\right\}_{\mathbf{x}\in\{0,1\}^3}$$

$$\implies \left\{(\mathbf{uM_{x'}}\otimes\mathbf{S_{x'}})\mathbf{A}_2\right\}_{\mathbf{x'}\in\{0,1\}^2}, \left\{\mathbf{A}_2^{-1}((\mathbf{M}_{3,b}\otimes\mathbf{S}_{3,b})\mathbf{A}_3)\right\}_{b\in\{0,1\}}$$

$$\approx_c \left\{\mathbf{C_{x'}}\leftarrow\mathbb{Z}_q^{n\times O(nw\log q)}\right\}_{\mathbf{x'}\in\{0,1\}^2}, \left\{\mathbf{A}_2^{-1}((\mathbf{M}_{3,b}\otimes\mathbf{S}_{3,b})\mathbf{A}_3)\right\}_{b\in\{0,1\}}$$

$$\implies \left\{(\mathbf{uM}_b\otimes\mathbf{S}_b)\mathbf{A}_1, \mathbf{A}_1^{-1}((\mathbf{M}_{2,b}\otimes\mathbf{S}_{2,b})\mathbf{A}_2), \mathbf{A}_2^{-1}((\mathbf{M}_{3,b}\otimes\mathbf{S}_{3,b})\mathbf{A}_3)\right\}_{b\in\{0,1\}}$$

$$\approx_c \left\{\mathbf{C}_{1,b}, \mathbf{A}_1^{-1}((\mathbf{M}_{2,b}\otimes\mathbf{S}_{2,b})\mathbf{A}_2), \mathbf{A}_2^{-1}((\mathbf{M}_{3,b}\otimes\mathbf{S}_{3,b})\mathbf{A}_3)\right\}_{b\in\{0,1\}}$$

$$\approx_c \left\{\mathbf{C}_{1,b}, \mathbf{D}_{2,b}, \mathbf{D}_{3,b}\right\}_{b\in\{0,1\}}$$

The first statement uses subexponential LWE, and uses security of the BLMR PRF [BLMR13] (as described earlier) asserting pseudorandomness of the set of values $\left\{(\mathbf{I}\otimes\mathbf{S_x})\mathbf{A}_3\right\}_{\mathbf{x}\in\{0,1\}^3}$, together with the condition $\mathbf{uM_x}\neq\mathbf{0}$ for all $\mathbf{x}$. The next two $\implies$ corresponds to invocations of evasive LWE. In particular, for the second $\implies$, we invoke the assumption with:

$$\mathbf{S} = \begin{pmatrix}\mathbf{uM}_{1,0}\otimes\mathbf{S}_{1,0}\\\mathbf{uM}_{1,1}\otimes\mathbf{S}_{1,1}\end{pmatrix}$$

$$\mathbf{P} = [(\mathbf{M}_{2,0}\otimes\mathbf{S}_{2,0})\mathbf{A}_2\|(\mathbf{M}_{2,1}\otimes\mathbf{S}_{2,1})\mathbf{A}_2]$$

$$\mathsf{aux} = \left\{\mathbf{A}_2^{-1}((\mathbf{M}_{3,b}\otimes\mathbf{S}_{3,b})\mathbf{A}_3)\right\}_{b\in\{0,1\}}$$

For this step, we will actually additionally need to use noise flooding to prove the pre-condition. As a result, the noise parameter in $(\mathbf{uM}_{1,b}\otimes\mathbf{S}_{1,b})\mathbf{A}_1$ is going to much be larger than that in $\mathbf{A}_{j-1}^{-1}((\mathbf{M}_{j,b}\otimes\mathbf{S}_{j,b})\mathbf{A}_j), j = 2,\ldots,h$. The final $\approx_c$

---

[4] The above proof strategy forces us to rely on LWE with sub-exponential security for two distinct reasons. Firstly, in the base case, we rely on LWE with 2^h terms. Secondly, we rely on h levels of induction, where each level of the induction incurs a polynomial security loss.

follows from an argument used in [CVW18], repeatedly applying $\mathbf{A}^{-1}(\underset{\sim}{\mathbf{Z}}) \approx_c \mathbf{D}$ (follows from LWE) from "left to right".

Tying up the Loose Ends. More generally, we invoke evasive LWE $h - 1$ times, where each statement contains up to 2^h terms, so the size of the evasive LWE instances are as large as $2^h \cdot \mathrm{poly}(\lambda)$. With each invocation of evasive LWE, we also incur a multiplicative polynomial security loss (in the size of the instance), and therefore our total security loss is $(2^h \cdot \mathrm{poly}(\lambda))^{O(h)}$.

To extend the argument to the setting where $\mathbf{SB} + \mathbf{E}$ is also provided in the pre-condition, we observe that

$$(\mathbf{SB} + \mathbf{E}, \mathbf{S}, \mathsf{aux}) \approx_c (\mathbf{C}, \mathbf{S}, \mathsf{aux}) \ \wedge \ (\mathbf{SP} + \mathbf{E}', \mathbf{S}, \mathsf{aux}) \approx_c (\mathbf{C}', \mathbf{S}, \mathsf{aux})$$
$$\implies (\mathbf{SB} + \mathbf{E}, \mathbf{SP} + \mathbf{E}', \mathbf{S}, \mathsf{aux}) \approx_c (\mathbf{SB} + \mathbf{E}, \mathbf{C}', \mathbf{S}, \mathsf{aux}) \approx_c (\mathbf{C}, \mathbf{C}', \mathbf{S}, \mathsf{aux})$$

This allows us to treat pseudorandomness of $\mathbf{SB} + \mathbf{E}$ and that of $\mathbf{SP} + \mathbf{E}'$ separately, where the former will rely on security of the BLMR PRF (which holds even if the distinguisher gets $\{\mathbf{S}_{i,b}\}_{i \in [h], b \in \{0,1\}}$) and the latter uses the argument as before. This step is important as it captures the fact that the adversary can in fact compute $2^{2h} - 1$ evaluated products $\{(\underset{\sim}{\mathbf{uM}_{\mathbf{x}'} \otimes \mathbf{S}_{\mathbf{x}'}})\mathbf{A}_j\}_{\mathbf{x}' \in \{0,1\}^j, j \in [h]}$ corresponding to all possible prefixes $\mathbf{x}'$ of length at most h.

1.3   Discussion

Comparison with [Wee22]. Wee's evasive LWE assumption in [Wee22] considers distributions over pairs of matrices $(\mathbf{A}', \mathbf{P})$ together with auxiliary input aux and stipulates that

if $(\mathbf{A}', \mathbf{B}, \mathbf{P}, \boxed{\mathbf{sA} + \mathbf{e}'}, \boxed{\mathbf{sB} + \mathbf{e}}, \boxed{\mathbf{sP} + \mathbf{e}''}, \mathsf{aux}) \approx_c (\mathbf{A}', \mathbf{B}, \mathbf{P}, \boxed{\mathbf{c}'}, \boxed{\mathbf{c}}, \boxed{\mathbf{c}''}, \mathsf{aux})$,

then $(\mathbf{A}', \mathbf{B}, \boxed{\mathbf{sA} + \mathbf{e}'}, \boxed{\mathbf{sB} + \mathbf{e}}, \mathbf{B}^{-1}(\mathbf{P}), \mathsf{aux}) \approx_c (\mathbf{A}', \mathbf{B}, \boxed{\mathbf{c}'}, \boxed{\mathbf{c}}, \mathbf{B}^{-1}(\mathbf{P}), \mathsf{aux})$

For the applications in [Wee22], the auxiliary input includes the coin tosses used to sample $\mathbf{A}', \mathbf{P}$, which rules out obfuscation-based counter-examples.

In [Wee22], evasive LWE was used to build ciphertext-policy ABE for circuits and optimal broadcast encryption schemes. The schemes are very different from the ones analyzed and in particular, do not rely on GGH15 encodings. The techniques are also quite different: in [Wee22], evasive LWE is only invoked once, whereas in this work, we invoke evasive LWE h times. For ease of comparison, we reproduce the informal description of the CP-ABE scheme described in [Wee22, Sect. 2.1] below:

$$\mathsf{mpk} := \mathbf{A}_0, \mathbf{B}_0 \leftarrow \mathbb{Z}_q^{n \times m}, \ \mathbf{B}_1 \leftarrow \mathbb{Z}_q^{mn \times m^2}, \ \mathbf{A} \leftarrow \mathbb{Z}_q^{n \times \ell m}$$
$$\mathsf{ct}_f := \mathbf{s}_0 \mathbf{B}_0, \ \underset{\sim}{\mathbf{s}(\mathbf{A}_f \otimes \mathbf{I}_m)} + \mathbf{s}_0 \mathbf{A}_0 + \mu \cdot \mathbf{g}, \ \mathbf{sB}_1, \ \text{where } \mathbf{s} \leftarrow \mathbb{Z}_q^{mn}, \mathbf{s}_0 \leftarrow \mathbb{Z}_q^n$$
$$\mathsf{sk}_{\mathbf{x}} := \mathbf{B}_0^{-1}(\mathbf{A}_0 \mathbf{r}), \mathbf{B}_1^{-1}((\mathbf{A} - \mathbf{x} \otimes \mathbf{G}) \otimes \mathbf{r}), \mathbf{r}, \ \text{where } \mathbf{r} \leftarrow \mathcal{D}_{\mathbb{Z}, \chi}^m$$

WE Proof Strategies. It is instructive to compare our proof strategy with that for WE in [GLW14] (henceforth GLW) based on static assumptions over multi-linear encodings; unfortunately, existing candidate instantiations for these assumptions are broken due to zeroizing attacks. Our proof uses $O(h)$ hybrids and evasive LWE instances of size $2^h \cdot \text{poly}(\lambda)$, whereas the GLW proof, based on the notion of positional WE, uses 2^h hybrids and problem instances of size $\text{poly}(\lambda)$.

Zeroizing Attacks and iO vs WE. What iO and WE have in common is that they require handling an exponential number of possible evaluations for both correctness and security. A key difficulty in constructing post-quantum iO arises from the fact that all known approaches yield schemes in the *zeroizing regime* [CHL+15] wherein an attacker can easily obtain sufficiently many equations in low-norm secret values —low-norm LWE secrets, error vectors, or both— over the integers that information-theoretically determine these secret values.[5] These equations arise naturally from the interaction of the correctness constraints and the security requirements, and could in turn be exploited to yield a *zeroizing attack* on the scheme [MSZ16, CLLT16, ADGM17, CLLT17, CGH17, Pel18, CVW18, CCH+19, HJL21]. In order to rule out zeroizing attacks, current approaches to post-quantum iO rely on some form of pseudorandomness of low-norm values over the integers [AJL+19, Agr19, CHVW19] to argue that the leakages in the *zeroizing regime* do not lend themselves to an attack. As mentioned earlier in the introduction, the evasive LWE assumption is qualitatively different from these assumptions as it does not refer to pseudorandomness of low-norm values.

Weak Multi-linear Map Models. Prior works analyzed security of iO and WE candidates in the so-called weak multi-linear map models, e.g. [GMM+16, BGMZ18, CHVW19]. Most of these models (notably [CVW18, Sect. 11.3] and [CHVW19]) immediately yield a statement similar to Lemma 2 (used in the proof of Theorem 1), whereas our proof of Lemma 2 from evasive LWE requires a careful inductive argument combined with noise flooding.

On Security Losses. The CVW18-type schemes are the most promising (and currently only) approach towards practical witness encryption, which begs the question: are the schemes secure and the underlying design principle sound? Towards answering these questions, we follow the cryptographic tradition of relating the security of the schemes to a simpler assumption. As is often the case, the parameters we achieve in our security reduction are far from practical. Nonetheless, they constitute some evidence that the underlying design is indeed sound, and the first step in a broader research agenda. Indeed, many NIST post-quantum candidates and the sub-field of "tight security" (e.g. for TLS 1.3)

---

[5] As a point of comparison, we have examples such as k-LWE [LPSS14] and inner product functional encryption [ALS16] based on LWE where it is easy to obtain a few such equations, but the equations do *not* information-theoretically determine the secret values.

start with provably secure schemes with poor parameters, and the parameters for practical instantiations are based on the best-known attacks on the scheme and often more aggressive than the parameters given by the security reduction.

Looking Ahead. Looking ahead, we see 4 possible scenarios, starting with the most optimistic and ambitious:

1. In a few years, we have witness encryption based on LWE, as has been the case for several lattice-based schemes where the initial candidates were based on non-standard assumptions (outside the zeroizing regime), such as fully homomorphic encryption and its multi-key variant, attribute-based encryption and predicate encryption, and the Fiat-Shamir heuristic. If so, we hope that the insights and techniques developed in this work play a small role, but even if not, the ensuing witness encryption scheme will almost certainly be substantially more complex than the CVW scheme. This would place us in a world analogous to the state of the art for discrete-log and pairing-based cryptography: while we do have fairly efficient schemes based on standard assumptions like DDH, the most practical schemes as well as the ones being deployed are often the ones for which we only know how to prove security in the generic group model, possibly augmented with random oracles.
2. The evasive LWE assumption survives cryptanalysis: this gives us confidence in the CVW18 WE, and the techniques in this work would likely further enable other cryptographic constructions based on evasive LWE as well as GGH15 multi-linear encodings.
3. The evasive LWE assumption is broken but the CVW18 WE scheme is not. This would require new and valuable cryptanalytic advances beyond the state-of-the-art zeroizing attacks. The current statement of evasive LWE is fairly general, and an attack could guide us towards identifying restricted variants of the assumption that would suffice for our analysis of the CVW18 scheme and more generally yield new insights into GGH15 multi-linear encodings.
4. The CVW18 scheme (and thus evasive LWE) is broken. This would be a fairly exciting result in cryptanalysis, and we hope that our statement of evasive LWE plays an important role as an intermediate and easier target for cryptanalysis.

We believe any of these scenarios would advance our current scientific understanding of lattice-based cryptography and assumptions (hardness and/or attacks).

2   Preliminaries

Notations. We use boldface lower case for row vectors (e.g. $\mathbf{v}$) and boldface upper case for matrices (e.g. $\mathbf{V}$). For integral vectors and matrices (i.e., those over $\mathbb{Z}$), we use the notation $|\mathbf{v}|, |\mathbf{V}|$ to denote the maximum absolute value over all the entries. We use $v \leftarrow \mathcal{D}$ to denote a random sample from a distribution $\mathcal{D}$, as well as $v \leftarrow S$ to denote a uniformly random sample from a set S. We also use $\mathcal{U}(S)$ to denote the uniform distribution over a set S. We use $\approx_s$ and $\approx_c$ as the abbreviation for statistically close and computationally indistinguishable.

Tensor Product. The tensor product (Kronecker product) for matrices $\mathbf{A} = (a_{i,j}) \in \mathbb{Z}^{\ell \times m}$, $\mathbf{B} \in \mathbb{Z}^{n \times p}$ is defined as

$$\mathbf{A} \otimes \mathbf{B} = \begin{bmatrix} a_{1,1}\mathbf{B}, \dots, a_{1,m}\mathbf{B} \\ \dots, \quad \dots, \quad \dots \\ a_{\ell,1}\mathbf{B}, \dots, a_{\ell,m}\mathbf{B} \end{bmatrix} \in \mathbb{Z}^{\ell n \times mp}.$$

The mixed-product property for tensor product says that

$$(\mathbf{A} \otimes \mathbf{B})(\mathbf{C} \otimes \mathbf{D}) = (\mathbf{AC}) \otimes (\mathbf{BD})$$

We adopt the convention that matrix multiplication takes precedence over tensor product, so that we can write $\mathbf{A} \otimes \mathbf{BC}$ to mean $\mathbf{A} \otimes (\mathbf{BC})$.

2.1 Lattices Background

We use $\mathcal{D}_{\mathbb{Z},\chi}$ to denote the discrete Gaussian distribution over $\mathbb{Z}$ with standard deviation χ.

Learning with Errors (LWE). Given $n, m, q, \chi \in \mathbb{N}$, the $\mathsf{LWE}_{n,m,q,\chi}$ assumption states that

$$(\mathbf{A}, \mathbf{sA} + \mathbf{e}) \approx_c (\mathbf{A}, \mathbf{c})$$

where

$$\mathbf{A} \leftarrow \mathbb{Z}_q^{n \times m}, \mathbf{s} \leftarrow \mathbb{Z}_q^n, \mathbf{e} \leftarrow \mathcal{D}_{\mathbb{Z},\chi}^m, \mathbf{c} \leftarrow \mathbb{Z}_q^m$$

We rely on the LWE assumption with sub-exponential hardness (for time, advantage and modulus-to-noise ratio), namely for some $\delta > 0$, indistinguishability holds against adversaries running in time 2^{n^δ} with advantage at most 2^{-n^δ}, as long as $q/\chi \leq 2^{n^\delta}$.

Trapdoor and Preimage Sampling. Given any $\mathbf{Z} \in \mathbb{Z}_q^{n \times n'}$, $\sigma > 0$, we use $\mathbf{B}^{-1}(\mathbf{Z}, \sigma)$ to denote the distribution of a matrix $\mathbf{Y}$ sampled from $\mathcal{D}_{\mathbb{Z}^{m \times n'}, \sigma}$ conditioned on $\mathbf{BY} = \mathbf{Z} \pmod q$. We sometimes suppress σ when the context is clear.

There is a p.p.t. algorithm $\mathsf{TrapGen}(1^n, q)$ that, given the modulus $q \geq 2$ and dimension n, outputs $\mathbf{B} \approx_s U(\mathbb{Z}_q^{n \times 2n \log q})$ with a trapdoor τ. Moreover, there is a p.p.t. algorithm that given $(\mathbf{B}, \tau) \leftarrow \mathsf{TrapGen}(1^n, q)$, $\mathbf{Z} \in \mathbb{Z}_q^{n \times n'}$, and $\sigma \geq 2\sqrt{n \log q}$, outputs a sample from $\mathbf{B}^{-1}(\mathbf{Z}, \sigma)$.

2.2 Matrix Branching Programs

A (matrix) branching program Γ with width w and length h is a set

$$\Gamma = \left\{ \mathbf{u} \in \{0,1\}^{1 \times w}, \left\{ \mathbf{M}_{i,b} \in \{0,1\}^{w \times w} \right\}_{i \in [h], b \in \{0,1\}}, \varpi : \{0,1\}^\ell \to \{0,1\}^h \right\}$$

where w is called width of branching program and ϖ an input-to-index function. We say that a branching program Γ computes a function $f : \{0,1\}^\ell \to \{0,1\}$ if

$$\forall \mathbf{x} \in \{0,1\}^\ell : \quad \mathbf{u} \prod_{i=1}^{h} \mathbf{M}_{i,\varpi(x)} = \mathbf{0} \iff f(\mathbf{x}) = 1$$

For simplicity, we only consider "oblivious" branching programs, where $\varpi : \{0,1\}^\ell \to \{0,1\}^h$ that outputs h/ℓ copies of $\mathbf{x}$, i.e. $\varpi(\mathbf{x}) = \mathbf{x}|\mathbf{x}| \cdots |\mathbf{x}$. We denote $c := h/\ell$ and call this a read-c branching program. For most of the paper, we will focus on read-once branching programs, with $c = 1, \ell = h$ and ϖ being the identity function, and where we write $\mathbf{M_x} := \prod_{i=1}^{h} \mathbf{M}_{i,x_i}$.

3   Evasive LWE

We proceed to provide a formal statement of our evasive LWE assumption, stated informally in Sect. 1.1.

Evasive LWE. Let Samp be a PPT algorithm that on input 1^λ, outputs

$$\mathbf{S} \in \mathbb{Z}_q^{n' \times n}, \mathbf{P} \in \mathbb{Z}_q^{n \times t}, \mathsf{aux} \in \{0,1\}^*$$

We define the following advantage functions:

$$\begin{aligned}
\mathsf{Adv}_{\mathcal{A}_0}^{\mathrm{PRE}}(\lambda) := &\Pr[\mathcal{A}_0(\boxed{\mathbf{SB} + \mathbf{E}}, \boxed{\mathbf{SP} + \mathbf{E}'}, \mathsf{aux}) = 1] \\
&- \Pr[\mathcal{A}_0(\boxed{\mathbf{C}}, \boxed{\mathbf{C}'}, \mathsf{aux}) = 1], \quad (3) \\
\mathsf{Adv}_{\mathcal{A}_1}^{\mathrm{POST}}(\lambda) := &\Pr[\mathcal{A}_1(\boxed{\mathbf{SB} + \mathbf{E}}, \mathbf{D}, \mathsf{aux}) = 1] \\
&- \Pr[\mathcal{A}_1(\boxed{\mathbf{C}}, \mathbf{D}, \mathsf{aux}) = 1] \quad (4)
\end{aligned}$$

where

$$\begin{aligned}
&(\mathbf{S}, \mathbf{P}, \mathsf{aux}) \leftarrow \mathsf{Samp}(1^\lambda), \\
&\mathbf{B} \leftarrow \mathbb{Z}_q^{n \times m}, \mathbf{E} \leftarrow \mathcal{D}_{\mathbb{Z}, \chi}^{n' \times m}, \mathbf{E}' \leftarrow \mathcal{D}_{\mathbb{Z}, \chi'}^{n' \times t}, \\
&\mathbf{C} \leftarrow \mathbb{Z}_q^{n' \times m}, \mathbf{C}' \leftarrow \mathbb{Z}_q^{n' \times t}, \\
&\mathbf{D} \leftarrow \mathbf{B}^{-1}(\mathbf{P}, \chi)
\end{aligned}$$

We say that the *evasive LWE* assumption holds if for every PPT Samp there exists some polynomial $Q(\cdot)$ such that for every PPT $\mathcal{A}_1$, there exists another PPT $\mathcal{A}_0$ such that

$$\mathsf{Adv}_{\mathcal{A}_0}^{\mathrm{PRE}}(\lambda) \geq \mathsf{Adv}_{\mathcal{A}_1}^{\mathrm{POST}}(\lambda)/Q(\lambda) - \mathrm{negl}(\lambda)$$

and $\mathsf{Time}(\mathcal{A}_0) \leq \mathsf{Time}(\mathcal{A}_1) \cdot Q(\lambda)$. We consider parameter settings for which $\chi' \ll \chi$ so that the pre-condition is stronger, which in turn makes evasive LWE weaker. See Sect. 8 for further discussion.

4   GGH15 Encodings

We describe (generalized) GGH15 encodings, following [GGH15, CC17, CVW18]. We find it helpful to break down the description into two separate algorithms ggh.encode and ggh.encode$^{\otimes}$. The former is more general, and refers to matrices $\widehat{\mathbf{S}}_{i,b}$, whereas the latter instantiates $\widehat{\mathbf{S}}_{i,b}$ with $\mathbf{M}_{i,b} \otimes \mathbf{S}_{i,b}$.

Construction 2 (GGH15   Encodings). *The   randomized   algorithm* ggh.encode *takes the following inputs*

- *parameters* 1^{λ}, $h, m, q, \hat{n}_0, \hat{n} \in \mathbb{N}$ *and Gaussian parameters* $\chi, \chi', \chi'', \chi'''$;
- *matrices* $\widehat{\mathbf{S}}_{1,b} \in \mathbb{Z}_q^{\hat{n}_0 \times \hat{n}}, \widehat{\mathbf{S}}_{2,b}, \dots, \widehat{\mathbf{S}}_{h,b} \in \mathbb{Z}_q^{\hat{n} \times \hat{n}}, b \in \{0, 1\}$;

and

- *samples* $\mathbf{A}_i, \tau_{\mathbf{A}_i} \leftarrow \mathsf{TrapGen}(1^{\hat{n}}, q)$ *for* $i = 1, \dots, h$,
- *samples* $\mathbf{E}_{1,b} \leftarrow \mathcal{D}_{\mathbb{Z},\chi}^{\hat{n}_0 \times m}, \mathbf{E}_{2,b}, \dots, \mathbf{E}_{h,b} \leftarrow \mathcal{D}_{\mathbb{Z},\chi'''}^{\hat{n} \times m}$ *for* $b \in \{0, 1\}$,[6]
- *outputs*

$$\left\{ \widehat{\mathbf{S}}_{1,b}\mathbf{A}_1 + \mathbf{E}_{1,b} \right\}_{b \in \{0,1\}}, \left\{ \mathbf{A}_{i-1}^{-1}(\widehat{\mathbf{S}}_{i,b}\mathbf{A}_i + \mathbf{E}_{i,b}) \right\}_{i=2,\dots,h,b \in \{0,1\}}$$

where $\mathbf{A}_{i-1}^{-1}(\cdot)$ *is computed with Gaussian parameter* χ'' *using* $\tau_{\mathbf{A}_{i-1}}$.

Construction 3 ($\otimes$-GGH15   Encodings). *The   randomized   algorithm* ggh.encode$^{\otimes}$ *takes as input*

$$\mathbf{u} \in \{0,1\}^w, \left\{ \mathbf{M}_{i,b} \in \{0,1\}^{w \times w} \right\}_{i \in [h], b \in \{0,1\}}$$

and

- *samples* $\mathbf{S}_{i,b} \leftarrow \mathcal{D}_{\mathbb{Z},O(1)}^{n \times n}$,
- *sets* $\widehat{\mathbf{S}}_{i,b} := \begin{cases} \mathbf{u}\mathbf{M}_{1,b} \otimes \mathbf{S}_{1,b} & \text{if } i = 1 \\ \mathbf{M}_{i,b} \otimes \mathbf{S}_{i,b} & \text{if } i > 1 \end{cases}$
- *outputs* ggh.encode$\left(\left\{ \widehat{\mathbf{S}}_{i,b} \right\}_{i \in [h], b \in \{0,1\}} \right)$ *with* $\hat{n}_0 = n, \hat{n} = wn$, *i.e.,*

$$\left\{ (\mathbf{u}\mathbf{M}_{1,b} \otimes \mathbf{S}_{1,b})\mathbf{A}_1 + \mathbf{E}_{1,b} \right\}_{b \in \{0,1\}}, \left\{ \mathbf{A}_{i-1}^{-1}((\mathbf{M}_{i,b} \otimes \mathbf{S}_{i,b})\mathbf{A}_i + \mathbf{E}_{i,b}) \right\}_{i=2,\dots,h,b \in \{0,1\}}$$

Correctness. The next lemma from [CVW18, Lemma 5.3] (also [GGH15, CC17]) captures the functionality provided by ggh.encode$^{\otimes}$, namely for all $\mathbf{x} = (x_1, \dots, x_h) \in \{0,1\}^h$:

$$\mathbf{C}_{1,x_1} \cdot \mathbf{D}_{2,x_2} \cdots \mathbf{D}_{h,x_h} \approx (\mathbf{u}\mathbf{M}_\mathbf{x} \otimes \mathbf{S}_\mathbf{x}) \cdot \mathbf{A}_h$$

where $\mathbf{M}_\mathbf{x} := \prod_{i=1}^h \mathbf{M}_{i,x_i}, \mathbf{S}_\mathbf{x} := \prod_{i=1}^h \mathbf{S}_{i,x_i}$.

Lemma 1 (Correctness). *We have for all* $\mathbf{x} \in \{0,1\}^h$: *w.h.p. over*

$$(\mathbf{C}_{1,0}, \mathbf{C}_{1,1}, \mathbf{D}_{2,0}, \mathbf{D}_{2,1}, \dots, \mathbf{D}_{h,0}, \mathbf{D}_{h,1}) \leftarrow \text{ggh.encode}^{\otimes}(\mathbf{u}, \{\mathbf{M}_{i,b}\}_{i \in [h], b \in \{0,1\}})$$

we have

$$|\mathbf{C}_{1,x_1} \cdot \mathbf{D}_{2,x_2} \cdots \mathbf{D}_{h,x_h} - (\mathbf{u}\mathbf{M}_\mathbf{x} \otimes \mathbf{S}_\mathbf{x}) \cdot \mathbf{A}_h| \leq h \cdot \chi \cdot (\lambda nw(\chi'' + \chi''') \log q)^h$$

---

[6] Prior works all use $\chi = \chi'''$. Looking ahead, we require $\chi \gg \chi'''$.

5   Pseudorandomness of GGH15 Encodings from Evasive LWE

In this section, we prove Theorem 1 in the introduction, i.e., pseudorandomness of GGH15 encodings under subexponential LWE and evasive LWE.

Theorem 4 (Theorem 1, restated). *Fix* $\{\mathbf{M}_{i,b} \in \{0,1\}^{w \times w}\}_{i \in [h], b \in \{0,1\}}$, $\mathbf{u} \in \{0,1\}^w$, *such that for all* $\mathbf{x} \in \{0,1\}^h$, *we have* $\mathbf{u}\mathbf{M}_{\mathbf{x}} \neq \mathbf{0}$. *Then, by LWE and the evasive LWE assumption, we have*

$$\mathsf{ggh.encode}^{\otimes}(\mathbf{u}, \{\mathbf{M}_{i,b}\}_{i \in [h], b \in \{0,1\}})$$

$$= \left\{(\mathbf{u}\mathbf{M}_{1,b} \otimes \mathbf{S}_{1,b})\mathbf{A}_1 + \mathbf{E}_{1,b}\right\}_{b \in \{0,1\}}, \left\{\mathbf{A}_{i-1}^{-1}((\mathbf{M}_{i,b} \otimes \mathbf{S}_{i,b})\mathbf{A}_i + \mathbf{E}_{i,b})\right\}_{i=2,\dots,h, b \in \{0,1\}}$$

$$\approx_c \left\{\mathcal{U}(\mathbb{Z}_q^{\hat{n}_0 \times m})\right\}_{b \in \{0,1\}}, \left\{\mathcal{D}_{\mathbb{Z},\chi''}^{m \times m}\right\}_{i=2,\dots,h, b \in \{0,1\}}$$

An overview of the proof is given in Sect. 1.2. We proceed to describe the parameter settings, followed by an overview of the proof structure and then the proof.

Remark 1 (Parameter settings.). Here, 1^λ denotes the security parameter and in particular, the running time of the adversary is $\mathrm{poly}(\lambda)$. We rely on 2^{n^δ}-hardness for LWE (i.e., indistinguishability against adversaries running in time 2^{n^δ} and a modulus-to-noise ratio of 2^{n^δ}), and set the parameters so that

$$
\begin{aligned}
2^{n^\delta} &\geq \max\{2^{h^2\lambda}, q/\chi'''\} & &\text{LWE hardness} \\
\chi' &= \lambda^h \cdot \chi''' \cdot \lambda^{\omega(1)} & &\text{noise flooding} \\
\chi &= \chi' \cdot \lambda^{\omega(1)} & &\text{evasive LWE} \\
q &\geq 4h \cdot \chi \cdot (\lambda n w (\chi'' + \chi''') \log q)^h & &\text{correctness} \\
\chi'' &= 2\sqrt{nw \log q} & &\text{trapdoor sampling}
\end{aligned}
$$

The first line comes from the fact that we need to instantiate Lemma 3 with hardness $2^{h^2\lambda} \gg (2^h \cdot \mathrm{poly}(\lambda))^{\omega(1)}$ to accommodate the fact that the instances have size up to $2^h \cdot \mathrm{poly}(\lambda)$ (we think of the corresponding instantiation of evasive LWE as using security parameter $\lambda' = 2^h\lambda$ so that $n' \leq 2^h \cdot \mathrm{poly}(\lambda)$ is bounded by $\mathrm{poly}(\lambda')$), and we iterate the security loss from evasive LWE a total of h times. We can realize the above constraints with

$$n = (h^2\lambda)^{1/\delta}, \quad q = 2^{n^\delta} = 2^{h^2\lambda}, \quad \chi''' = O(n), \quad m = O(\sqrt{nw \log q})$$

The main differences from prior instantiations is that we use $\chi \gg \chi'''$ (whereas prior works use $\chi = \chi'''$) and that n is much larger as a function of h.

Proof Structure. We break down the proof of Theorem 4 into two separate lemmas: Lemmas 2 and 3.

- In the first lemma, we show that if the 2^h "evaluated products" (with fresh independent errors)

$$\left\{ \underbrace{(\mathbf{u}\mathbf{M}_{\mathbf{x}} \otimes \mathbf{S}_{\mathbf{x}})\mathbf{A}_h} \right\}_{\mathbf{x} \in \{0,1\}^h} \tag{5}$$

are pseudorandom, then the "encoded program" $\mathsf{ggh.encode}^{\otimes}(\mathbf{u}, \{\mathbf{M}_{i,b}\}_{i \in [h], b \in \{0,1\}})$ given by

$$\left\{ (\mathbf{u}\mathbf{M}_{1,b} \otimes \mathbf{S}_{1,b})\mathbf{A}_1 + \mathbf{E}_{1,b} \right\}_{b \in \{0,1\}}, \left\{ \mathbf{A}_{i-1}^{-1}((\mathbf{M}_{i,b} \otimes \mathbf{S}_{i,b})\mathbf{A}_i + \mathbf{E}_{i,b}) \right\}_{i=2,\ldots,h,b \in \{0,1\}}$$

is pseudorandom. This step relies on $h-1$ invocations of evasive LWE. In fact, we prove a more general statement that does not depend on properties of the matrices $\{\mathbf{M}_{i,b}\}_{i \in [h], b \in \{0,1\}}$ or the tensor product structure in $\mathbf{M}_{i,b} \otimes \mathbf{S}_{i,b}$. Specifically, the formalization refers to matrices $\hat{\mathbf{S}}_{i,b}$ in place of $\mathbf{M}_{i,b} \otimes \mathbf{S}_{i,b}$.
- In the second lemma, we show that the 2^h evaluated products in (5) are pseudorandom under the (standard) LWE assumption, provided $\mathbf{u}\mathbf{M}_{\mathbf{x}} \neq \mathbf{0}$ for all $\mathbf{x} \in \{0,1\}^h$.

Lemma 2. *Fix some distributions for* $\left\{ \hat{\mathbf{S}}_{i,b} \right\}_{i \in [h], b \in \{0,1\}}$. *Suppose for all* $j \in [h]$, *we have:*

$$\left\{ \boxed{\hat{\mathbf{S}}_{\mathbf{x}'}\mathbf{A}_j + \mathbf{E}_{\mathbf{x}'}} \right\}_{\mathbf{x}' \in \{0,1\}^j}, \left\{ \hat{\mathbf{S}}_{i,b} \right\}_{i \in [h], b \in \{0,1\}} \approx_c \left\{ \boxed{\mathcal{U}(\mathbb{Z}_q^{\hat{n}_0 \times m})} \right\}_{\mathbf{x}' \in \{0,1\}^j}, \left\{ \hat{\mathbf{S}}_{i,b} \right\}_{i \in [h], b \in \{0,1\}} \tag{6}$$

where

$$\mathbf{A}_j \leftarrow \mathbb{Z}_q^{\hat{n} \times m}, \mathbf{E}_{\mathbf{x}'} \leftarrow \mathcal{D}_{\mathbb{Z}, \chi}^{\hat{n}_0 \times m}$$

Then, by the evasive LWE assumption, we have

$$\mathsf{ggh.encode}\left(\left\{ \hat{\mathbf{S}}_{i,b} \right\}_{i \in [h], b \in \{0,1\}} \right)$$
$$= \left\{ \hat{\mathbf{S}}_{1,b}\mathbf{A}_1 + \mathbf{E}_{1,b} \right\}_{b \in \{0,1\}}, \left\{ \mathbf{A}_{i-1}^{-1}(\hat{\mathbf{S}}_{i,b}\mathbf{A}_i + \mathbf{E}_{i,b}) \right\}_{i=2,\ldots,h,b \in \{0,1\}}$$
$$\approx_c \left\{ \mathcal{U}(\mathbb{Z}_q^{\hat{n}_0 \times m}) \right\}_{b \in \{0,1\}}, \left\{ \mathcal{D}_{\mathbb{Z}, \chi''}^{m \times m} \right\}_{i=2,\ldots,h,b \in \{0,1\}}$$

Proof. The proof proceeds in two steps.

Step 1. First, we show that:

$$\left\{ \boxed{\hat{\mathbf{S}}_{1,b}\mathbf{A}_1 + \mathbf{E}_{1,b}} \right\}_{b \in \{0,1\}}, \left\{ \mathbf{A}_{i-1}^{-1}(\hat{\mathbf{S}}_{i,b}\mathbf{A}_i + \mathbf{E}_{i,b}) \right\}_{i=2,\ldots,h,b \in \{0,1\}}$$
$$\approx_c \left\{ \boxed{\mathcal{U}(\mathbb{Z}_q^{\hat{n}_0 \times m})} \right\}_{b \in \{0,1\}}, \left\{ \mathbf{A}_{i-1}^{-1}(\hat{\mathbf{S}}_{i,b}\mathbf{A}_i + \mathbf{E}_{i,b}) \right\}_{i=2,\ldots,h,b \in \{0,1\}}$$

This proceeds via a proof by induction on $j = h, \ldots, 1$ that:

$$\left\{ \boxed{\widehat{\mathbf{S}}_{\mathbf{x}'}\mathbf{A}_j + \mathbf{E}_{\mathbf{x}'}} \right\}_{\mathbf{x}'\in\{0,1\}^j}, \left\{\mathbf{A}_{i-1}^{-1}(\widehat{\mathbf{S}}_{i,b}\mathbf{A}_i + \mathbf{E}_{i,b})\right\}_{i\geq j+1, b\in\{0,1\}}, \left\{\widehat{\mathbf{S}}_{i,b}\right\}_{i\in[h], b\in\{0,1\}}$$

$$\approx_c \left\{ \boxed{\mathcal{U}(\mathbb{Z}_q^{\hat{n}_0 \times m})} \right\}_{\mathbf{x}'\in\{0,1\}^j}, \left\{\mathbf{A}_{i-1}^{-1}(\widehat{\mathbf{S}}_{i,b}\mathbf{A}_i + \mathbf{E}_{i,b})\right\}_{i\geq j+1, b\in\{0,1\}}, \left\{\widehat{\mathbf{S}}_{i,b}\right\}_{i\in[h], b\in\{0,1\}}$$

$$(7)$$

where we have additionally augmented the distinguisher's view with $\left\{\widehat{\mathbf{S}}_{i,b}\right\}_{i\in[h], b\in\{0,1\}}$. The base case $j = h$ corresponds to the pre-condition (6) in the lemma. For the inductive step, suppose (7) holds for some j and we would like to deduce the same statement for $j-1$.

We want to invoke our evasive LWE assumption with

$$n' = 2^{j-1}\hat{n}_0, \quad t = 2m = O(\hat{n}_0 \log q)$$

$$\mathbf{S} = \widehat{\mathbf{S}}_{j-1} := \left\{\widehat{\mathbf{S}}_{\mathbf{x}'}\right\}_{\mathbf{x}'\in\{0,1\}^{j-1}} \in \mathbb{Z}_q^{2^{j-1}\hat{n}_0 \times \hat{n}},$$

$$\mathbf{P} = \widehat{\mathbf{S}}_{j,0}\mathbf{A}_j + \mathbf{E}_{j,0} \| \widehat{\mathbf{S}}_{j,1}\mathbf{A}_j + \mathbf{E}_{j,1} \in \mathbb{Z}_q^{\hat{n} \times 2m}$$

$$\mathsf{aux} = \left\{\mathbf{A}_{i-1}^{-1}(\widehat{\mathbf{S}}_{i,b}\mathbf{A}_i + \mathbf{E}_{i,b})\right\}_{i\geq j+1, b\in\{0,1\}}, \left\{\widehat{\mathbf{S}}_{i,b}\right\}_{i\in[h], b\in\{0,1\}},$$

$$\mathbf{B} = \mathbf{A}_{j-1},$$

$$\mathbf{E} = \mathbf{E}_{j-1} \leftarrow \mathcal{D}_{\mathbb{Z}, \chi}^{2^{j-1}\hat{n}_0 \times m},$$

$$\mathbf{E}' = \mathbf{E}'_{j-1} \leftarrow \mathcal{D}_{\mathbb{Z}, \chi'}^{2^{j-1}\hat{n}_0 \times 2m}$$

where $\{\cdot\}_{\mathbf{x}'\in\{0,1\}^{j-1}}$ denotes stacking the matrices vertically.

First, we verify that the pre-condition of evasive LWE is satisfied. Observe that

$$\widehat{\mathbf{S}}_{j-1}\mathbf{A}_{j-1} + \mathbf{E}_{j-1}, \boxed{\widehat{\mathbf{S}}_{j-1}\mathbf{P} + \mathbf{E}'_{j-1}}, \mathsf{aux}$$

$$\approx_s \widehat{\mathbf{S}}_{j-1}\mathbf{A}_{j-1} + \mathbf{E}_{j-1}, \boxed{[\widehat{\mathbf{S}}_{j-1}\widehat{\mathbf{S}}_{j,0}\mathbf{A}_j \| \widehat{\mathbf{S}}_{j-1}\widehat{\mathbf{S}}_{j,1}\mathbf{A}_j] + \mathbf{E}'_{j-1}}, \mathsf{aux}$$

$$\approx_c \boxed{\widehat{\mathbf{S}}_{j-1}\mathbf{A}_{j-1} + \mathbf{E}_{j-1}}, \mathcal{U}(\mathbb{Z}_q^{2^{j-1}\hat{n}_0 \times 2m}), \mathsf{aux}$$

$$\approx_c \boxed{\mathcal{U}(\mathbb{Z}_q^{2^{j-1}\hat{n}_0 \times m})}, \mathcal{U}(\mathbb{Z}_q^{2^{j-1}\hat{n}_0 \times 2m}), \mathsf{aux}$$

where

- the $\approx_s$ uses noise flooding to deduce that $\mathbf{E}'_{j-1} \approx_s \mathbf{E}'_{j-1} + \widehat{\mathbf{S}}_{j-1} \cdot [\mathbf{E}_{j,0} \| \mathbf{E}_{j,1}]$;
- the first $\approx_c$ follows from the induction hypothesis (7) for j, since we can expand $[\widehat{\mathbf{S}}_{j-1}\widehat{\mathbf{S}}_{j,0}\mathbf{A}_j \| \widehat{\mathbf{S}}_{j-1}\widehat{\mathbf{S}}_{j,1}\mathbf{A}_j] + \mathbf{E}'_{j-1}$ as $\left\{\widehat{\mathbf{S}}_{\mathbf{x}'}\mathbf{A}_j + \mathbf{E}_{\mathbf{x}'}\right\}_{\mathbf{x}'\in\{0,1\}^j}$, together with the observation that given $\left\{\widehat{\mathbf{S}}_{i,b}\right\}_{i\in[h], b\in\{0,1\}}$ in aux, we can sample a random $\mathbf{A}_{j-1}$ and simulate $\widehat{\mathbf{S}}_{j-1}\mathbf{A}_{j-1} + \mathbf{E}_{j-1}$ (note that aux depends on $\mathbf{A}_j, \ldots, \mathbf{A}_h$ but not $\mathbf{A}_{j-1}$);

– the second $\approx_c$ follows from the pre-condition in (6), along with the fact that given $\left\{\widehat{\mathbf{S}}_{i,b}\right\}_{i\in[h],b\in\{0,1\}}$, we can simulate aux by sampling $\mathbf{A}_j,\ldots,\mathbf{A}_h$ along with the respective trapdoors.

Then, it follows from evasive LWE that

$$\boxed{\widehat{\mathbf{S}}_{j-1}\mathbf{A}_{j-1}+\mathbf{E}_{j-1}},\mathbf{A}_{j-1}^{-1}(\mathbf{P}_j),\mathsf{aux}$$

$$\approx_c \mathcal{U}(\mathbb{Z}_q^{2^{j-1}\hat{n}_0\times m}),\mathbf{A}_{j-1}^{-1}(\mathbf{P}_j),\mathsf{aux}$$

which corresponds to the statement in (7) for $j-1$. This completes the proof of the inductive step.

To complete the proof of this step, we need to write down the parameters for evasive LWE. Let $\mathcal{A}_j$ denote an adversary that breaks the statement in (7). Then, evasive LWE with security parameter $\lambda' = 2^j\lambda$ (so that $n' = 2^{j-1}\hat{n}_0$ is bounded by $\mathsf{poly}(\lambda')$) tells us:

$$\mathsf{Adv}(\mathcal{A}_j)\geq\mathsf{Adv}(\mathcal{A}_{j-1})/\mathsf{poly}(2^j\lambda),\quad\mathsf{Time}(\mathcal{A}_j)\leq\mathsf{Time}(\mathcal{A}_{j-1})\cdot\mathsf{poly}(2^j\lambda)$$

which implies:

$$\mathsf{Adv}(\mathcal{A}_h)\geq\mathsf{Adv}(\mathcal{A}_1)/\mathsf{poly}(2^{h^2}\lambda^h),\quad\mathsf{Time}(\mathcal{A}_h)\leq\mathsf{Time}(\mathcal{A}_1)\cdot\mathsf{poly}(2^{h^2}\lambda^h)$$

That is, we will need $\mathsf{poly}(2^{h^2}\lambda^h)$ hardness for the pre-condition in (6). We account for this when setting the final parameters in Remark 1.

Step 2. Next, we show that

$$\left\{\mathbf{A}_{i-1}^{-1}(\widehat{\mathbf{S}}_{i,b}\mathbf{A}_i+\mathbf{E}_{i,b})\right\}_{i=2,\ldots,h,b\in\{0,1\}}\approx_c\left\{\mathcal{D}_{\mathbb{Z},\chi''}^{m\times m}\right\}_{i=2,\ldots,h,b\in\{0,1\}}$$

This proceeds exactly as in the proof of [CVW18, Lemma 5.11]: for $j = 2,\ldots,h$, we replace $\left\{\mathbf{A}_{j-1}^{-1}(\widehat{\mathbf{S}}_{j,b}\mathbf{A}_i+\mathbf{E}_{j,b})\right\}_{b\in\{0,1\}}$ with $\left\{\mathcal{D}_{\mathbb{Z},\chi''}^{m\times m}\right\}_{b\in\{0,1\}}$, using

$$\left\{\mathbf{A}_{j-1}^{-1}(\widehat{\mathbf{S}}_{j,b}\mathbf{A}_j+\mathbf{E}_{j,b})\right\}_{b\in\{0,1\}},\widehat{\mathbf{S}}_{j,0},\widehat{\mathbf{S}}_{j,1},\mathbf{A}_j,\tau_{\mathbf{A}_j}$$

$$\approx_c\left\{\mathcal{D}_{\mathbb{Z},\chi''}^{m\times m}\right\}_{b\in\{0,1\}},\widehat{\mathbf{S}}_{j,0},\widehat{\mathbf{S}}_{j,1},\mathbf{A}_j,\tau_{\mathbf{A}_j}$$

which in turn follows from LWE [CVW18, Lemma 4.4].

Lemma 3. *Fix* $\mathbf{u}\in\{0,1\}^w,\{\mathbf{M}_{i,b}\in\{0,1\}^{w\times w}\}_{i\in[h],b\in\{0,1\}}$ *such that for all* $\mathbf{x}\in\{0,1\}^h$, *we have* $\mathbf{u}\mathbf{M}_{\mathbf{x}}\neq\mathbf{0}$. *Then, by the LWE assumption, for all* $j\in[h]$, *we have:*

$$\left\{\boxed{\left[(\mathbf{u}\mathbf{M}_{\mathbf{x}'}\otimes\mathbf{S}_{\mathbf{x}'})\mathbf{A}_j+\mathbf{E}_{\mathbf{x}'}\right]}_{\mathbf{x}'\in\{0,1\}^j},\left\{\mathbf{S}_{i,b}\right\}_{i\in[h],b\in\{0,1\}}\right\}\approx_c\left\{\boxed{\left\{\mathcal{U}(\mathbb{Z}_q^{n\times m})\right\}}_{\mathbf{x}'\in\{0,1\}^j},\left\{\mathbf{S}_{i,b}\right\}_{i\in[h],b\in\{0,1\}}\right\}$$

where $\mathbf{A}_j\leftarrow\mathbb{Z}_q^{\hat{n}\times m},\mathbf{E}_{\mathbf{x}'}\leftarrow\mathcal{D}_{\mathbb{Z},\chi}^{\hat{n}_0\times m}$.

Similar statements were shown and used in [CVW18, CHVW19] for the special case $j = h$, and where $\{\mathbf{S}_{i,b}\}_{i \in [h], b \in \{0,1\}}$ were not provided to the adversary. The proof is essentially the same as before, since $\mathbf{uM}_\mathbf{x} \neq \mathbf{0}$ for all $\mathbf{x} \in \{0,1\}^h$ implies $\mathbf{uM}_{\mathbf{x}'} \neq \mathbf{0}$ for all $\mathbf{x}' \in \{0,1\}^j$.

Proof. The proof proceeds in three steps:

- First, by the mixed-product property of tensor products and noise flooding, we have

$$(\mathbf{uM}_{\mathbf{x}'} \otimes \mathbf{S}_{\mathbf{x}'})\mathbf{A}_j + \mathbf{E}_{\mathbf{x}'} \approx_s (\mathbf{uM}_{\mathbf{x}'} \otimes \mathbf{I}_n) \cdot (\mathbf{I}_w \otimes \mathbf{S}_{\mathbf{x}'})\mathbf{A}_j + \mathcal{D}_{\mathbb{Z},\chi'}^{nw \times m}) + \mathbf{E}_{\mathbf{x}'}$$

- Next, by the security of the BLMR PRF [BLMR13, BPR12] (also [CVW18, Lemma 7.4]), we have:

$$\left\{ \boxed{(\mathbf{I}_w \otimes \mathbf{S}_{\mathbf{x}'})\mathbf{A}_j + \mathcal{D}_{\mathbb{Z},\chi'}^{nw \times m}} \right\}_{\mathbf{x}' \in \{0,1\}^j}, \{\mathbf{S}_{i,b}\}_{i \in [h], b \in \{0,1\}}$$

$$\approx_c \left\{ \boxed{\mathcal{U}(\mathbb{Z}_q^{nw \times m})} \right\}_{\mathbf{x}' \in \{0,1\}^j}, \{\mathbf{S}_{i,b}\}_{i \in [h], b \in \{0,1\}}$$

where we use $((\mathbf{I}_w \otimes \mathbf{S})\mathbf{A} + \mathbf{E}, \mathbf{S}) \approx_c (\mathcal{U}(\mathbb{Z}_q^{nw \times m}), \mathbf{S})$, which in turn follows from LWE [BLMR13, CC17].
- Finally, for all $\mathbf{x}' \in \{0,1\}^j$, we have $\mathbf{uM}_{\mathbf{x}'} \cdot \mathcal{U}(\mathbb{Z}_q^{nw \times m}) \approx_s \mathcal{U}(\mathbb{Z}_q^{n \times m})$, since $\mathbf{uM}_{\mathbf{x}'} \neq \mathbf{0}$.

This completes the proof.

We proceed to complete the proof of Theorem 4.

Proof (Proof of Theorem 4). We instantiate Lemma 2 with:

$$\widehat{\mathbf{S}}_{i,b} = \begin{cases} \mathbf{uM}_{1,b} \otimes \mathbf{S}_{1,b} & \text{if } i = 1 \\ \mathbf{M}_{i,b} \otimes \mathbf{S}_{i,b} & \text{if } i > 1 \end{cases}$$

The pre-condition in (6) is satisfied, via Lemma 3.

6   Witness Encryption

6.1   Definition

We recall the definition of witness encryption from [GGSW13].

Definition 1 (Witness encryption [GGSW13]). *A witness encryption scheme for an NP language L (with corresponding witness relation R) consists of the following two p.p.t. algorithms:*

Encryption. $\mathsf{Enc}(1^\lambda, \Psi, \mu)$ *takes as input a security parameter* 1^λ, *an instance* $\Psi \in \{0,1\}^{\mathrm{poly}(\lambda)}$, *and a message* $\mu \in \{0,1\}$, *outputs a ciphertext* ct.

Decryption. $\mathsf{Dec}(\mathsf{ct}, x)$ *takes as input a ciphertext* ct *and string* $x \in \{0,1\}^{\mathrm{poly}(\lambda)}$, *outputs a message* μ *or the symbol* $\perp$.

These algorithms satisfy

Correctness. *For any security parameter* λ, *for any* $\mu \in \{0,1\}$, *and for any* $\Psi \in L$ *such that* $R(\Psi, x)$ *holds, we have that*

$$\Pr[\mathsf{Dec}(\mathsf{Enc}(1^\lambda, \Psi, \mu), x) = \mu] \geq 1 - \mathrm{negl}(\lambda).$$

Soundness. *For any p.p.t. adversary* A, *there exists a negligible function* $\mathrm{negl}(\cdot)$ *such that for any* $\Psi \notin L$, *we have*

$$\left| \Pr[A(\mathsf{Enc}(1^\lambda, \Psi, 0)) = 1] - \Pr[A(\mathsf{Enc}(1^\lambda, \Psi, 1)) = 1] \right| \leq \mathrm{negl}(\lambda).$$

6.2   CVW WE Scheme

To build a witness encryption scheme for all of NP, it suffices to build one for the class of CNF formulas. We describe the CVW18 scheme [CVW18, Sect. 10]:

Construction 5 (CVW witness encryption). *We construct a witness encryption scheme for the class of CNF formula as follows:*

Encryption. $\mathsf{Enc}(1^\lambda, \Psi, \mu)$ *proceeds as follows:*

- *Apply [CVW18, Constructions 6.4,10.2] to the CNF* Ψ *(of c clauses and h literals) to obtain a read-once branching program* $\mathbf{u} = (1 \cdots 1) \in \{0,1\}^{c+1}$ *and* $\{ \mathbf{M}_{i,b} \in \{0,1\}^{(c+1) \times (c+1)} \}_{i \in [h], b \in \{0,1\}}$ *such that for all* $\mathbf{x} \in \{0,1\}^h$:

$$\mathbf{u}\mathbf{M}_\mathbf{x} = \begin{cases} (\mathbf{0} \| \mu) & \text{if } \Psi(\mathbf{x}) = 1 \\ (\neq \mathbf{0} \| \mu) & \text{if } \Psi(\mathbf{x}) = 0 \end{cases}.$$

That is, the program computes $\Psi(\mathbf{x}) = 1 \wedge \mu = 0$. *Concretely,*

1. *Initialization: for all* $i \in [\ell], b \in \{0,1\}$, *Let* $\mathbf{M}_{i,b} := \begin{pmatrix} \mathbf{I}_c \\ \mu \end{pmatrix}$.
2. *If* x_i *appears in* ψ_j: *set the* j^{th} *entry on the diagonal of* $\mathbf{M}_{i,1}$ *to be 0.*
3. *If* $\bar{x}_i$ *appears in* ψ_j: *set the* j^{th} *entry on the diagonal of* $\mathbf{M}_{i,0}$ *to be 0.*
- *Output*

$$\mathsf{ct} = \mathsf{ggh.encode}^\otimes (\mathbf{u}, \{ \mathbf{M}_{i,b} \}_{i \in [h], b \in \{0,1\}})$$

Decryption. $\mathsf{Dec}(\mathsf{ct}, \mathbf{x})$ *takes as input* $\mathsf{ct} = \{ \mathbf{C}_{1,b}, \mathbf{D}_{2,b}, \ldots, \mathbf{D}_{h,b} \}_{b \in \{0,1\}}$ *and* $\mathbf{x} \in \{0,1\}^h$, *outputs 0 if* $|\mathbf{C}_{1,x_1} \cdot \mathbf{D}_{2,x_2} \cdots \mathbf{D}_{h,x_h}| \leq B = h \cdot \chi \cdot (\lambda n w (\chi'' + \chi''') \log q)^h$, *and 1 otherwise.*

We will set the parameters as in Remark 1 with $w = c + 1$. Correctness follows readily from that of $\mathsf{ggh.encode}$. Security follows readily from Theorem 4, together with the fact that if Ψ is not satisfiable, then $\mathbf{u}\mathbf{M}_\mathbf{x} \neq \mathbf{0}$ for all $\mathbf{x} \in \{0,1\}^h$.

7   Null iO

We analyze the CVW iO scheme for branching programs in [CVW18, Sect. 11], incorporating simplifications from [CHVW19, Sect. 6]. The same paper presents a $\text{poly}(\lambda)^{O(c)}$ attack on the iO scheme for read-c branching programs, which could be avoided by artificially padding the branching program when c is small. Here, we show that the scheme is secure as a null-iO scheme for any c even without padding, assuming subexponential LWE and evasive LWE.

7.1   Definition

Definition 2. *An obfuscation scheme* Obf *is a null-iO scheme if it satisfies the following properties:*

Correctness: *There is a negligible function ν such that for all circuits*
$C : \{0,1\}^\ell \to \{0,1\}$:

$$\Pr[\forall x \in \{0,1\}^n \ : \ C(x) = \widetilde{C}(x) \mid \widetilde{C} \leftarrow \text{Obf}(1^\lambda, C)] \geq 1 - \nu(\lambda),$$

where the probability is over the coin tosses of Obf.

Security: *Let $C = \{C_\lambda\}, C' = \{C'_\lambda\}$ be two circuit ensembles, such that C, C' have equal input length and circuit size and furthermore are everywhere null, meaning that $\forall x \ : \ C(x) = C'(x) = 0$. Then we require that:* $\text{Obf}(1^\lambda, C_\lambda) \approx_c \text{Obf}(1^\lambda, C'_\lambda)$.

7.2   CVW Null-IO Scheme

Construction 6 (CVW null-IO)

Obfuscation. On input a branching program $\mathbf{u}, \{\mathbf{M}_{i,b}\}_{i\in[h],b\in\{0,1\}}$ computing a function $C : \{0,1\}^\ell \to \{0,1\}$,

- *Following [CHVW19, Sect. 6], we may assume WLOG (at the cost of increasing the width w) that[7]*

$$\forall \mathbf{x}' \in \{0,1\}^h : \mathbf{u}\mathbf{M}_{\mathbf{x}'} = \mathbf{0} \Longleftrightarrow \mathbf{x}' \in \varpi(\{0,1\}^\ell) \wedge C(\varpi^{-1}(\mathbf{x}')) = 1$$

- *Output*

$$\text{ggh.encode}^\otimes(\mathbf{u}, \{\mathbf{M}_{i,b}\}_{i\in[h],b\in\{0,1\}})$$

Evaluation. On input $\{\mathbf{C}_{1,b}, \mathbf{D}_{2,b}, \dots, \mathbf{D}_{h,b}\}_{b\in\{0,1\}}$ and $\mathbf{x} \in \{0,1\}^\ell$, outputs 0 if $|\mathbf{C}_{1,\varpi(x)_1} \cdot \mathbf{D}_{2,\varpi(x)_2} \cdots \mathbf{D}_{h,\varpi(x)_h}| \leq B = h \cdot \chi \cdot (\lambda n w(\chi'' + \chi''') \log q)^h$, and 1 otherwise.

We will set the parameters as in Remark 1. Correctness follows readily from that of ggh.encode. Security follows readily from Theorem 4, together with the fact that if C is the null program, then $\mathbf{u}\mathbf{M}_{\mathbf{x}'} \neq \mathbf{0}$ for all $\mathbf{x}' \in \{0,1\}^h$.

---

[7] This basically follows from the fact that we can compute $\mathbf{x}' \stackrel{?}{\in} \varpi(\{0,1\}^\ell)$ using a read-once matrix branching program.

8   Cryptanalysis of Evasive LWE

8.1   Algorithmic Attacks

The known algorithmic attacks essentially fall into one of two categories:

- Attacks on LWE: namely break pseudorandomness of $\mathbf{SB}+\mathbf{E}$ given aux, which is ruled out via the pre-condition;
- Zero-izing attacks: here, given aux, an attacker is able to compute a short vector $\mathbf{z}$ such that $\mathbf{SPz} \bmod q \approx \mathbf{0}$ has low-norm; these attacks are also ruled out via the pre-condition. But first, observe that such a $\mathbf{z}$ breaks the post-condition, since

$$(\mathbf{SB} + \mathbf{E}) \cdot \mathbf{B}^{-1}(\mathbf{P}) \cdot \mathbf{z} = \mathbf{SPz} + \mathbf{E} \cdot \mathbf{B}^{-1}(\mathbf{P}) \cdot \mathbf{z} \approx \mathbf{0}$$

and therefore an attacker can distinguish $\mathbf{SB} + \mathbf{E}$ from a random $\mathbf{C}$. On the other hand, we also have

$$(\mathbf{SP} + \mathbf{E}') \cdot \mathbf{z} \approx \mathbf{0}$$

and therefore an attacker can also distinguish $\mathbf{SP} + \mathbf{E}'$ from a random $\mathbf{C}'$, which violates the pre-condition.

A Direct Attack Strategy that Fails. It is instructive to consider the following direct attack strategy: Let aux $= \mathbf{P}$. Find any (big) $\mathbf{x}$ via Gaussian elimination such that: $\mathbf{Px} = \mathbf{0}$ and $\mathbf{Kx}$ is small (but non-zero), where $\mathbf{K} = \mathbf{B}^{-1}(\mathbf{P})$. This would yield a distinguisher for the post-condition since $(\mathbf{SB} + \mathbf{E}) \cdot \mathbf{K} \cdot \mathbf{x}$ is small whereas $\mathbf{C} \cdot \mathbf{K} \cdot \mathbf{x}$ is not small. We provide three explanations why this attack does not work:

- The matrix $\binom{\mathbf{P}}{\mathbf{K}}$ is a $(n + m) \times t$ matrix but only has rank at most m. This is because $[\mathbf{I} \mid -\mathbf{B}]\binom{\mathbf{P}}{\mathbf{K}} = \mathbf{0}$ (that is, the top rows are a linear combination of the bottom ones). Therefore, not every system of linear equations $\binom{\mathbf{P}}{\mathbf{K}}\mathbf{x} = \mathbf{z}$ has a solution $\mathbf{x}$.
- Any solution $\mathbf{x}$ for which $\mathbf{Kx}$ is small yields a solution $\mathbf{Kx}$ to SIS with respect to the random matrix $\mathbf{B}$. Therefore, attacks of this type are already ruled out by SIS.
- More generally, the assumption provably holds when $\mathbf{P}$ is uniformly random and aux is an efficient function of $\mathbf{P}$ that is independent of $\mathbf{S}$. Therefore, an attack on the assumption must crucially exploit some properties of $\mathbf{P}$, aux and fundamentally different from the one here.

8.2   Auxiliary Inputs

Next, we describe a (heuristic) auxiliary-input attack on our assumption based on general obfuscation, and describe a restricted class of $(\mathbf{P}, \text{aux})$ that avoid these attack, while still sufficient for our security proofs.

A (Heuristic) Auxiliary-Input Attack. Suppose $\mathbf{S} \leftarrow \mathbb{Z}_q^{2m \times n}, \mathbf{P} \leftarrow \mathbb{Z}_q^{n \times 2m}$ (that is, $n' = t = 2m$). Let aux be an obfuscation of the follow program $\Pi_{\mathbf{P}, \tau}$ which has $\mathbf{P}$ and a corresponding trapdoor τ hard-wired, and on input $\mathbf{C} \in \mathbb{Z}_q^{2m \times m}, \mathbf{D} \in \mathbb{Z}_q^{m \times 2m}$,

– use τ to solve for $\mathbf{S}_0$ such that $|\mathbf{C} \cdot \mathbf{D} - \mathbf{S}_0 \cdot \mathbf{P}|$ is small
– if $|\mathbf{D}|$ is small and such a $\mathbf{S}$ exists, output 1, else output 0.

Observe that $\Pi_{\mathbf{P}, \tau}$ would output 1 on input $(\mathbf{SB} + \mathbf{E}, \mathbf{B}^{-1}(\mathbf{P}))$, and 0 on input $(\mathcal{U}(\mathbb{Z}_q^{n' \times m}), \mathbf{B}^{-1}(\mathbf{P}))$, which yields a distinguisher for the post-condition. On the other hand, by LWE, $(\mathbf{SB} + \mathbf{E}, \mathbf{SP} + \mathbf{E}')$ is pseudorandom. Moreover, given oracle access to $\Pi_{\mathbf{P}, \tau}$, it is statistically hard to find an accepting input. This means that the pre-condition would hold given an ideal obfuscation of $\Pi_{\mathbf{P}, \tau}$.

Restricted Class $(\mathbf{P}, \mathsf{aux})$. We consider $(\mathbf{P}, \mathsf{aux})$ of the form:

$$\mathbf{P} := [\widehat{\mathbf{S}}_{1,0} \mathbf{A}_1 \| \widehat{\mathbf{S}}_{1,1} \mathbf{A}_1] + \mathbf{E}_1$$
$$\mathsf{aux} := (\mathbf{A}_1^{-1}([\widehat{\mathbf{S}}_{2,0} \mathbf{A}_2 \| \widehat{\mathbf{S}}_{2,1} \mathbf{A}_2] + \mathbf{E}_2), \dots, \mathbf{A}_{\ell-1}^{-1}([\widehat{\mathbf{S}}_{\ell,0} \mathbf{A}_\ell \| \widehat{\mathbf{S}}_{\ell,1} \mathbf{A}_\ell] + \mathbf{E}_\ell),$$
$$\widehat{\mathbf{S}}_{1,0}, \widehat{\mathbf{S}}_{1,1}, \dots, \widehat{\mathbf{S}}_{\ell,0}, \widehat{\mathbf{S}}_{\ell,1}, \mathsf{aux}_0)$$

where $\widehat{\mathbf{S}}_{1,0}, \widehat{\mathbf{S}}_{1,1}, \dots, \widehat{\mathbf{S}}_{\ell,0}, \widehat{\mathbf{S}}_{\ell,1}, \mathsf{aux}_0$ are "public-coin" (by requiring that aux also contains the coin tosses used to sample $\widehat{\mathbf{S}}_{i,b}, \mathsf{aux}_0$) and independent of the random matrices $\mathbf{A}_1, \dots, \mathbf{A}_\ell$. Note that

– the private randomness for aux are only used in sampling (i) $\mathbf{A}_1, \dots, \mathbf{A}_\ell$ along with the respective trapdoors, (ii) $\mathbf{E}_1, \dots, \mathbf{E}_\ell$, as well as (iii) $\mathbf{A}_1^{-1}(\cdot), \dots, \mathbf{A}_\ell^{-1}(\cdot)$;
– we only require that the $\widehat{\mathbf{S}}_{i,b}$'s are "public-coin" and do not require that they compute a tensor of the form $\mathbf{M}_{i,b} \otimes \mathbf{S}_{i,b}$;
– this restricted class of $(\mathbf{P}, \mathsf{aux})$ is sufficient for our security reductions in Lemma 2.

Next, we argue that this restricted class do not capture the obfuscation-based aux. The reasons are two-fold:

– The matrices $\widehat{\mathbf{S}}_{i,b}$'s are public-coin and given to the distinguisher as part of aux, so any secret information (e.g. matrix trapdoors τ) embedded into these matrices will also be provided to the distinguisher in the pre-condition "in the clear".
– The matrices $\widehat{\mathbf{S}}_{i,b}$'s are independent of the random matrices $\mathbf{A}_1, \dots, \mathbf{A}_\ell$ and in particular cannot depend on trapdoors for any of these matrices.

8.3   A Special Case

We consider a special case for evasive LWE that is closely related to the WE and null-IO scheme. Suppose $\mathbf{u}_i \mathbf{M} \neq 0$ for all $i \in [N]$. Then, evasive LWE (plus LWE) tells us that the following distribution is pseudorandom:

$$\{\mathbf{S}_{1,i}, (\mathbf{u}_i \otimes \mathbf{S}_{1,i})\mathbf{A}_1 + \mathbf{E}_{1,i}\}_{i \in [N]}, \mathbf{S}_2, \mathbf{A}_1^{-1}((\mathbf{M} \otimes \mathbf{S}_2)\mathbf{A}_2 + \mathbf{E}_2)$$

We observe that for the case $N = 1$, such a statement follows from LWE. In fact, it suffices to prove pseudorandomness of

$$(\mathbf{u} \otimes \mathbf{I})\mathbf{A}_1, \mathbf{S}_2, \mathbf{A}^{-1}((\mathbf{M} \otimes \mathbf{S}_2)\mathbf{A}_2 + \mathbf{E}_2)$$

- First, we apply LWE with secret $\mathbf{A}_2$ to replace $\underset{\sim}{(\mathbf{I} \otimes \mathbf{S}_2)\mathbf{A}_2}$ with a random $\mathbf{P}$.
- Next, by LWE and adapting an argument from [CVW18], we have

$$(\mathbf{u} \otimes \mathbf{I})\mathbf{A}_2, \mathbf{A}_2^{-1}((\mathbf{M} \otimes \mathbf{I})\mathbf{P} + \mathbf{E}) \approx_c (\mathbf{u} \otimes \mathbf{I})\mathbf{A}_2, ((\mathbf{u} \otimes \mathbf{I})\mathbf{A}_2)^{-1}((\mathbf{uM} \otimes \mathbf{I})\mathbf{P} + \mathbf{E}')$$

The idea is to treat the part of $\mathbf{A}_2$ that is perfectly hidden given $(\mathbf{u} \otimes \mathbf{I})\mathbf{A}_2$ as the LWE secret.
- The rest of the proof follows from a statistical argument.

Acknowledgements. We thank the reviewers for helpful and meticulous feedback. VV was supported by DARPA under Agreement No. HR00112020023, a grant from the MIT-IBM Watson AI, a grant from Analog Devices, a Microsoft Trustworthy AI grant, and a DARPA Young Faculty Award. DW was supported by NSF grant CNS-1750795, CNS-2055510, and the Alfred P. Sloan Research Fellowship.

A   Comparison with [Tsa22]

An independent work of Tsabary [Tsa22] (also independent of [Wee22]) presents a new witness encryption scheme under a variant of evasive LWE. We describe some high-level differences between the two works:

- Tsabary [Tsa22] presents a new witness encryption scheme that uses read-many branching programs and does not consider null-IO. We prove security of *existing* candidate WE and null-IO schemes in CVW, where the former uses read-once (matrix) branching programs.
- The formulation of evasive LWE in [Tsa22] allows $(\mathbf{P}, \mathsf{aux})$ to depend on $\mathbf{B}$, whereas ours and that in [Wee22] does not. In particular, our formulation of evasive LWE is more conservative.
- The analysis in [Tsa22] relies on a formulation of evasive LWE with polynomial hardness and oracle access to a possibly exponential number of matrices, whereas we crucially rely on evasive LWE with instances of exponential size 2^h (which in turn requires a careful setting of parameters). In our security reduction, the adversary receives all possible partial evaluated products, whereas the adversary in [Tsa22] only has oracle access to these quantities. Note that in both analysis, the complexity of the adversary could double with each invocation of evasive LWE, so that we would necessarily need to consider adversaries running in time at least 2^h, for which there is no real distinction between receiving and oracle access to all possible partial products.

References

[ADGM17] Apon, D., Döttling, N., Garg, S., Mukherjee, P.: Cryptanalysis of indistinguishability obfuscations of circuits over GGH13. In: Chatzigiannakis, I., Indyk, P., Kuhn, F., Muscholl, A. (eds.) ICALP 2017. LIPIcs, vol. 80, pp. 38:1–38:16. Schloss Dagstuhl (2017)

[Agr19] Agrawal, S.: Indistinguishability obfuscation without multilinear maps: new methods for bootstrapping and instantiation. In: Ishai, Y., Rijmen, V. (eds.) EUROCRYPT 2019, Part I. LNCS, vol. 11476, pp. 191–225. Springer, Cham (2019). https://doi.org/10.1007/978-3-030-17653-2_7

[AJ15] Ananth, P., Jain, A.: Indistinguishability obfuscation from compact functional encryption. In: Gennaro, R., Robshaw, M. (eds.) CRYPTO 2015, Part I. LNCS, vol. 9215, pp. 308–326. Springer, Heidelberg (2015). https://doi.org/10.1007/978-3-662-47989-6_15

[AJL+19] Ananth, P., Jain, A., Lin, H., Matt, C., Sahai, A.: Indistinguishability obfuscation without multilinear maps: new paradigms via low degree weak pseudorandomness and security amplification. In: Boldyreva, A., Micciancio, D. (eds.) CRYPTO 2019, Part III. LNCS, vol. 11694, pp. 284–332. Springer, Cham (2019). https://doi.org/10.1007/978-3-030-26954-8_10

[ALS16] Agrawal, S., Libert, B., Stehlé, D.: Fully secure functional encryption for inner products, from standard assumptions. In: Robshaw, M., Katz, J. (eds.) CRYPTO 2016, Part III. LNCS, vol. 9816, pp. 333–362. Springer, Heidelberg (2016). https://doi.org/10.1007/978-3-662-53015-3_12

[AP20] Agrawal, S., Pellet-Mary, A.: Indistinguishability obfuscation without maps: attacks and fixes for noisy linear FE. In: Canteaut, A., Ishai, Y. (eds.) EUROCRYPT 2020, Part I. LNCS, vol. 12105, pp. 110–140. Springer, Cham (2020). https://doi.org/10.1007/978-3-030-45721-1_5

[BDGM20a] Brakerski, Z., Döttling, N., Garg, S., Malavolta, G.: Candidate iO from homomorphic encryption schemes. In: Canteaut, A., Ishai, Y. (eds.) EUROCRYPT 2020, Part I. LNCS, vol. 12105, pp. 79–109. Springer, Cham (2020). https://doi.org/10.1007/978-3-030-45721-1_4

[BDGM20b] Brakerski, Z., Döttling, N., Garg, S., Malavolta, G.: Factoring and pairings are not necessary for IO: circular-secure LWE suffices. Cryptology ePrint Archive, Report 2020/1024 (2020)

[BGI+01] Barak, B., et al.: On the (im)possibility of obfuscating programs. In: Kilian, J. (ed.) CRYPTO 2001. LNCS, vol. 2139, pp. 1–18. Springer, Heidelberg (2001). https://doi.org/10.1007/3-540-44647-8_1

[BGMZ18] Bartusek, J., Guan, J., Ma, F., Zhandry, M.: Return of GGH15: provable security against zeroizing attacks. In: Beimel, A., Dziembowski, S. (eds.) TCC 2018, Part II. LNCS, vol. 11240, pp. 544–574. Springer, Cham (2018). https://doi.org/10.1007/978-3-030-03810-6_20

[BLMR13] Boneh, D., Lewi, K., Montgomery, H., Raghunathan, A.: Key homomorphic PRFs and their applications. In: Canetti, R., Garay, J.A. (eds.) CRYPTO 2013, Part I. LNCS, vol. 8042, pp. 410–428. Springer, Heidelberg (2013). https://doi.org/10.1007/978-3-642-40041-4_23

[BPR12] Banerjee, A., Peikert, C., Rosen, A.: Pseudorandom functions and lattices. In: Pointcheval, D., Johansson, T. (eds.) EUROCRYPT 2012. LNCS, vol. 7237, pp. 719–737. Springer, Heidelberg (2012). https://doi.org/10.1007/978-3-642-29011-4_42

[BV15]   Bitansky, N., Vaikuntanathan, V.: Indistinguishability obfuscation from functional encryption. In: Guruswami, V. (ed.) 56th FOCS, pp. 171–190. IEEE Computer Society Press (2015)

[CC17]   Canetti, R., Chen, Y.: Constraint-hiding constrained PRFs for NC^1 from LWE. In: Coron, J.-S., Nielsen, J.B. (eds.) EUROCRYPT 2017, Part I. LNCS, vol. 10210, pp. 446–476. Springer, Cham (2017). https://doi.org/10.1007/978-3-319-56620-7_16

[CCH+19] Cheon, J.H., Cho, W., Hhan, M., Kim, J., Lee, C.: Statistical zeroizing attack: cryptanalysis of candidates of BP obfuscation over GGH15 multilinear map. In: Boldyreva, A., Micciancio, D. (eds.) CRYPTO 2019, Part III. LNCS, vol. 11694, pp. 253–283. Springer, Cham (2019). https://doi.org/10.1007/978-3-030-26954-8_9

[CGH17]   Chen, Y., Gentry, C., Halevi, S.: Cryptanalyses of candidate branching program obfuscators. In: Coron, J.-S., Nielsen, J.B. (eds.) EUROCRYPT 2017, Part III. LNCS, vol. 10212, pp. 278–307. Springer, Cham (2017). https://doi.org/10.1007/978-3-319-56617-7_10

[CHL+15] Cheon, J.H., Han, K., Lee, C., Ryu, H., Stehlé, D.: Cryptanalysis of the Multilinear Map over the Integers. In: Oswald, E., Fischlin, M. (eds.) EUROCRYPT 2015, Part I. LNCS, vol. 9056, pp. 3–12. Springer, Heidelberg (2015). https://doi.org/10.1007/978-3-662-46800-5_1

[CHVW19] Chen, Y., Hhan, M., Vaikuntanathan, V., Wee, H.: Matrix PRFs: Constructions, Attacks, and Applications to Obfuscation. In: Hofheinz, D., Rosen, A. (eds.) TCC 2019, Part I. LNCS, vol. 11891, pp. 55–80. Springer, Cham (2019). https://doi.org/10.1007/978-3-030-36030-6_3

[CLLT16]   Coron, J.-S., Lee, M.S., Lepoint, T., Tibouchi, M.: Cryptanalysis of GGH15 multilinear maps. In: Robshaw, M., Katz, J. (eds.) CRYPTO 2016, Part II. LNCS, vol. 9815, pp. 607–628. Springer, Heidelberg (2016). https://doi.org/10.1007/978-3-662-53008-5_21

[CLLT17]   Coron, J.-S., Lee, M.S., Lepoint, T., Tibouchi, M.: Zeroizing attacks on indistinguishability obfuscation over CLT13. In: Fehr, S. (ed.) PKC 2017, Part I. LNCS, vol. 10174, pp. 41–58. Springer, Heidelberg (2017). https://doi.org/10.1007/978-3-662-54365-8_3

[CLT15]   Coron, J.-S., Lepoint, T., Tibouchi, M.: New multilinear maps over the integers. In: Gennaro, R., Robshaw, M. (eds.) CRYPTO 2015, Part I. LNCS, vol. 9215, pp. 267–286. Springer, Heidelberg (2015). https://doi.org/10.1007/978-3-662-47989-6_13

[CVW18]   Chen, Y., Vaikuntanathan, V., Wee, H.: GGH15 beyond permutation branching programs: proofs, attacks, and candidates. In: Shacham, H., Boldyreva, A. (eds.) CRYPTO 2018, Part II. LNCS, vol. 10992, pp. 577–607. Springer, Cham (2018). https://doi.org/10.1007/978-3-319-96881-0_20

[DQV+21] Devadas, L., Quach, W., Vaikuntanathan, V., Wee, H., Wichs, D.: Succinct LWE sampling, random polynomials, and obfuscation. In: Nissim, K., Waters, B. (eds.) TCC 2021. LNCS, vol. 13043, pp. 256–287. Springer, Cham (2021). https://doi.org/10.1007/978-3-030-90453-1_9

[GGH13a] Garg, S., Gentry, C., Halevi, S.: Candidate multilinear maps from ideal lattices. In: Johansson, T., Nguyen, P.Q. (eds.) EUROCRYPT 2013. LNCS, vol. 7881, pp. 1–17. Springer, Heidelberg (2013). https://doi.org/10.1007/978-3-642-38348-9_1

[GGH+13b] Garg, S., Gentry, C., Halevi, S., Raykova, M., Sahai, A., Waters, B.: Candidate indistinguishability obfuscation and functional encryption for all circuits. In: 54th FOCS, pp. 40–49. IEEE Computer Society Press (2013)

[GGH15] Gentry, C., Gorbunov, S., Halevi, S.: Graph-Induced Multilinear Maps from Lattices. In: Dodis, Y., Nielsen, J.B. (eds.) TCC 2015, Part II. LNCS, vol. 9015, pp. 498–527. Springer, Heidelberg (2015). https://doi.org/10.1007/978-3-662-46497-7_20

[GGHW14] Garg, S., Gentry, C., Halevi, S., Wichs, D.: On the implausibility of differing-inputs obfuscation and extractable witness encryption with auxiliary input. In: Garay, J.A., Gennaro, R. (eds.) CRYPTO 2014, Part I. LNCS, vol. 8616, pp. 518–535. Springer, Heidelberg (2014). https://doi.org/10.1007/978-3-662-44371-2_29

[GGSW13] Garg, S., Gentry, C., Sahai, A., Waters, B.: Witness encryption and its applications. In: Boneh, D., Roughgarden, T., Feigenbaum, J. (eds.) 45th ACM STOC, pp. 467–476. ACM Press (2013)

[GJLS21] Gay, R., Jain, A., Lin, H., Sahai, A.: Indistinguishability obfuscation from simple-to-state hard problems: new assumptions, new techniques, and simplification. In: Canteaut, A., Standaert, F.-X. (eds.) EUROCRYPT 2021, Part III. LNCS, vol. 12698, pp. 97–126. Springer, Cham (2021). https://doi.org/10.1007/978-3-030-77883-5_4

[GKW17] Goyal, R., Koppula, V., Waters, B.: Lockable obfuscation. In: Umans, C. (ed.) 58th FOCS, pp. 612–621. IEEE Computer Society Press (2017)

[GKW18] Goyal, R., Koppula, V., Waters, B.: Collusion resistant traitor tracing from learning with errors. In: Diakonikolas, I., Kempe, D., Henzinger, M. (eds.) 50th ACM STOC, pp. 660–670. ACM Press (2018)

[GLW14] Gentry, C., Lewko, A., Waters, B.: Witness Encryption from Instance Independent Assumptions. In: Garay, J.A., Gennaro, R. (eds.) CRYPTO 2014, Part I. LNCS, vol. 8616, pp. 426–443. Springer, Heidelberg (2014). https://doi.org/10.1007/978-3-662-44371-2_24

[GMM+16] Garg, S., Miles, E., Mukherjee, P., Sahai, A., Srinivasan, A., Zhandry, M.: Secure obfuscation in a weak multilinear map model. In: Hirt, M., Smith, A. (eds.) TCC 2016, Part II. LNCS, vol. 9986, pp. 241–268. Springer, Heidelberg (2016). https://doi.org/10.1007/978-3-662-53644-5_10

[GMM17] Garg, S., Mahmoody, M., Mohammed, A.: Lower bounds on obfuscation from all-or-nothing encryption primitives. In: Katz, J., Shacham, H. (eds.) CRYPTO 2017, Part I. LNCS, vol. 10401, pp. 661–695. Springer, Cham (2017). https://doi.org/10.1007/978-3-319-63688-7_22

[GP21] Gay, R., Pass, R.: Indistinguishability obfuscation from circular security. In: STOC (2021)

[HHSS17] Halevi, S., Halevi, T., Shoup, V., Stephens-Davidowitz, N.: Implementing BP-obfuscation using graph-induced encoding. In: Thuraisingham, B.M., Evans, D., Malkin, T., Xu, D., (eds.) ACM CCS 2017, pp. 783–798. ACM Press (2017)

[HJL21] Hopkins, S., Jain, A., Lin, H.: Counterexamples to new circular security assumptions underlying iO. In: Malkin, T., Peikert, C. (eds.) CRYPTO 2021, Part II. LNCS, vol. 12826, pp. 673–700. Springer, Cham (2021). https://doi.org/10.1007/978-3-030-84245-1_23

[JLMS19] Jain, A., Lin, H., Matt, C., Sahai, A.: How to leverage hardness of constant-degree expanding polynomials over $\mathbb{R}$ to build $i\mathcal{O}$. In: Ishai, Y., Rijmen, V. (eds.) EUROCRYPT 2019, Part I. LNCS, vol. 11476, pp. 251–281. Springer, Cham (2019). https://doi.org/10.1007/978-3-030-17653-2_9

[JLS21a] Jain, A., Lin, H., Sahai, A.: Indistinguishability obfuscation from LPN over F_p, DLIN, and PRGS in NC0. IACR Cryptol. ePrint Arch., p. 1334 (2021)

[JLS21b] Jain, A., Lin, H., Sahai, A.: Indistinguishability obfuscation from well-founded assumptions. In: STOC (2021)

[LPSS14] Ling, S., Phan, D.H., Stehlé, D., Steinfeld, R.: Hardness of k-LWE and applications in traitor tracing. In: Garay, J.A., Gennaro, R. (eds.) CRYPTO 2014, Part I. LNCS, vol. 8616, pp. 315–334. Springer, Heidelberg (2014). https://doi.org/10.1007/978-3-662-44371-2_18

[MSZ16] Miles, E., Sahai, A., Zhandry, M.: Annihilation Attacks for Multilinear Maps: Cryptanalysis of Indistinguishability Obfuscation over GGH13. In: Robshaw, M., Katz, J. (eds.) CRYPTO 2016, Part II. LNCS, vol. 9815, pp. 629–658. Springer, Heidelberg (2016). https://doi.org/10.1007/978-3-662-53008-5_22

[Pel18] Pellet-Mary, A.: Quantum attacks against indistinguishablility obfuscators proved secure in the weak multilinear map model. In: Shacham, H., Boldyreva, A. (eds.) CRYPTO 2018, Part III. LNCS, vol. 10993, pp. 153–183. Springer, Cham (2018). https://doi.org/10.1007/978-3-319-96878-0_6

[Tsa22] Tsabary, R.: Candidate witness encryption from lattice techniques. In: Dodis, Y., Shrimpton, T. (eds.) CRYPTO 2022. LNCS, vol. 13507, pp. 535–559. Springer, Cham (2022). https://doi.org/10.1007/978-3-031-15802-5_19

[Wee22] Wee, H.: Optimal broadcast encryption and CP-ABE from evasive lattice assumptions. In: Dunkelman, O., Dziembowski, S. (eds.) EUROCRYPT 2022. LNCS, vol. 13276, pp. 217–241. Springer, Cham (2022). https://doi.org/10.1007/978-3-031-07085-3_8

[WW21] Wee, H., Wichs, D.: Candidate obfuscation via oblivious LWE sampling. In: Canteaut, A., Standaert, F.-X. (eds.) EUROCRYPT 2021, Part III. LNCS, vol. 12698, pp. 127–156. Springer, Cham (2021). https://doi.org/10.1007/978-3-030-77883-5_5

[WZ17] Wichs, D., Zirdelis, G.: Obfuscating compute-and-compare programs under LWE. In: Umans, C. (ed.) 58th FOCS, pp. 600–611. IEEE Computer Society Press (2017)

Symmetric Key Cryptanalysis

Algebraic Meet-in-the-Middle Attack
on LowMC

Fukang Liu[1]([⊠]), Santanu Sarkar[4], Gaoli Wang[5,6], Willi Meier[7],
and Takanori Isobe[1,2,3]

[1] University of Hyogo, Hyogo, Japan
liufukangs@gmail.com, takanori.isobe@ai.u-hyogo.ac.jp
[2] National Institute of Information and Communications Technology, Tokyo, Japan
[3] PRESTO, Japan Science and Technology Agency, Tokyo, Japan
[4] Indian Institute of Technology Madras, Chennai, India
santanu@iitm.ac.in
[5] East China Normal University, Shanghai, China
glwang@sei.ecnu.edu.cn
[6] Key Lab of Cryptologic Technology and Information Security,
Ministry of Education, Shandong University, Jinan, China
[7] FHNW, Windisch, Switzerland

Abstract. By exploiting the feature of partial nonlinear layers, we propose a new technique called algebraic meet-in-the-middle (MITM) attack to analyze the security of LowMC, which can reduce the memory complexity of the simple difference enumeration attack over the state-of-the-art. Moreover, while an efficient algebraic technique to retrieve the full key from a differential trail of LowMC has been proposed at CRYPTO 2021, its time complexity is still exponential in the key size. In this work, we show how to reduce it to constant time when there are a sufficiently large number of active S-boxes in the trail. With the above new techniques, the attacks on LowMC and LowMC-M published at CRYPTO 2021 are further improved, and some LowMC instances could be broken for the first time. Our results seem to indicate that partial nonlinear layers are still not well-understood.

Keywords: LowMC · LowMC-M · Algebraic attack · Linearization ·
Key recovery · Meet-in-the-middle

1 Introduction

Being the first dedicated symmetric-key primitive design for advanced protocols like secure multiparty computation (MPC) and fully homomorphic encryption (FHE), the LowMC block cipher family [7] has attracted lots of attention from the cryptography community. Especially, one of the alternate third-round candidate signature schemes in NIST post-quantum cryptography competition [1] called Picnic [3,16] uses LowMC as the underlying block cipher, whose security is directly related to the difficulty to recover the key of LowMC from a single plaintext-ciphertext pair.

S. Agrawal and D. Lin (Eds.): ASIACRYPT 2022, LNCS 13791, pp. 225–255, 2022.
https://doi.org/10.1007/978-3-031-22963-3_8

Most importantly, the proposal of LowMC directly starts a new trend to design symmetric-key primitives with different metrics, e.g. low AND depth and low AND gates. There is a long line of research focusing on such primitive designs in recent years, like Kreyvrium [15], FLIP [32], Rasta [20], MiMC [6], GMiMC [5], Jarvis [9], Hades [26], Poseidon [25], Vision [8], Rescue [8] and Ciminion [22].

On the other hand, these primitives also raise new challenges for cryptanalysts to evaluate their security. One reason is that some of them are defined over a (large) prime field, which received little attention in symmetric-key cryptanalysis in the past few decades [13,27]. Another important reason is that some of them adopt unusual designs, which make common cryptanalytic techniques difficult to apply. However, these also imply that some fatal errors may be overlooked at the design phase, which is the case of the algebraic attack on full Jarvis [4] and the guess-and-determine attack on the first version of full FLIP [23]. Moreover, due to the lack of tools to evaluate their security, some designs may be too aggressive and will soon turn out to be vulnerable to some novel attacks [13,19,24,28,30,34]. Therefore, developing new cryptanalytic techniques for these new designs becomes an important task due to the fact that the security of a symmetric-key primitive is highly related to the evolution of cryptanalytic techniques.

In this paper, we focus on new attacks on LowMC [7] for its special design strategy of using partial nonlinear layers, which has inspired the designs of Hades and a real-world hash function Poseidon. Moreover, its applications in the Picnic signature scheme and the backdoored cipher LowMC-M [33] proposed at CRYPTO 2020 also make it meaningful to further understand its security.

Cryptanalysis of LowMC. Since its publication, LowMC has been quickly analyzed with the higher-order differential attack [21] and interpolation attack [19], which directly made LowMC move to LowMC v2.

To study its security with low data complexity, e.g. its application in the Picnic signature scheme, the difference enumeration attack [34] was proposed to break several instances of LowMC v2 with 3 or slightly more chosen plaintexts. Consequently, the formula to determine the secure number of rounds of LowMC was updated further [2], and this version is called LowMC v3. For convenience, LowMC simply refers to LowMC v3 in the following.

However, a recent work [28] at CRYPTO 2021 reveals that some important LowMC instances are still insecure and they could be broken with 2 chosen plaintexts only and negligible memory complexity. Devising the attacks with 2 chosen plaintexts is mainly due to the assumption used in the security proof of the Picnic signature scheme, where LowMC with 2 plaintexts is required to be secure [16]. Moreover, the idea to attack LowMC with 2 chosen plaintexts can be simply extended to the attack with a large number of chosen plaintexts, as can be seen from the powerful attacks on LowMC-M in the same paper [28], which has pushed the designers of LowMC-M to increase the number of rounds.

In another direction, the recent LowMC competition to recover the secret key from a single plaintext-ciphertext pair has motivated three teams to develop new attacks [10,11,18,29] on LowMC in this attack scenario. According to the announcement of the third-round results, the attacks with the MITM method [11] and the polynomial method [18] were selected as currently the best attacks. In particular, the polynomial method [18] requires huge memory.

Regarding the memory complexity, we cite the statement in [18]: *There is no consensus among researchers on a model that takes memory complexity into account and the formal security claims of the Picnic (and LowMC) designers only involve time complexity.* Indeed, the memory complexity of an attack may be reduced as new techniques develop. A very recent related example is the algebraic technique in [28], which not only significantly reduces the memory complexity of the original difference enumeration attack [34] on LowMC v2 but also improves the number of attacked rounds.

Our Contributions. We aim to further improve the difference enumeration attack on LowMC. The general idea of this attack is very simple. Given a pair of plaintexts and the corresponding ciphertexts, the input difference and output difference of the cipher are known. The first step is to enumerate all the possible differential trails such that this input difference can reach this output difference, i.e. to recover the possible difference transitions through each round. The second step is to retrieve the full secret key from each possible differential trail and test its correctness via the plaintext-ciphertext pair.

For the first step, the memory complexity of the simple MITM method in [34] is exponential in the number of attacked rounds. Although the algebraic technique [28] can make the memory complexity negligible, the number of attacked rounds is limited. Specifically, the algebraic technique converts the difference enumeration into the problem to solve a linear equation system. However, as the number of attacked rounds increases, the linear equation system will become under-determined, i.e. the number of equations is smaller than the number of variables, which will increase the time complexity to enumerate all the possible differential trails as there are many solutions to the under-determined linear equation system. In addition, it is unclear how to use additional memory to improve this algebraic technique.

Our first contribution is a new method to handle this under-determined linear equation system. This is based on the fact that the variables in this equation system are not independent and there are nonlinear relations inside them. Our first attempt is to convert solving such a linear equation system into solving a linear equation system and a nonlinear equation system based on a new observation on the LowMC S-box. However, it is difficult to bound its time complexity and it seems inefficient as the number of attacked rounds increases. This motivates us to develop a MITM strategy to exploit the nonlinear relations inside these variables to efficiently solve this under-determined linear equation system. This new strategy is shown to outperform both the simple MITM strategy [34] and the simple algebraic technique [28] and is applicable to a wide range of LowMC parameters. Specifically, it can not only reduce the memory complexity of the simple MITM strategy [34] over the state-of-the-art but also improves the number of attacked rounds by using additional memory for the algebraic technique [28]. In a word, the algebraic technique and the MITM strategy are combined in the new strategy and this is why we call it the algebraic MITM attack.

As the number of attacked rounds increases, it is natural that the number of possible differential trails will increase significantly due to the effect of the S-boxes. Hence, it becomes crucial to further optimize the time complexity to retrieve the full key from a random differential trail for the second step. Otherwise, the final time complexity will exceed that of brute force. While a novel and efficient algebraic technique is proposed in [28] to achieve this purpose, i.e. recovering the key by solving a linear equation system, we observe that it is still not extremely optimized due to an inefficient way to deal with the inactive S-boxes in the differential trail. Specifically, the guess-and-determine strategy is still involved in order to process the inactive S-boxes, which makes the time complexity to retrieve the full key from a random differential trail still exponential in the key size. To handle the inactive S-boxes more efficiently, we directly exploit the nonlinear relations in their inputs and outputs. Specifically, by introducing intermediate variables for the inactive S-boxes, we convert the problem to recover the key into solving a linear equation system and a quadratic equation system in terms of more variables, i.e. the key and the intermediate variables. To ensure that the whole equation system can be efficiently solved, we make a compromise that we may fail to recover the correct key with probability of about 0.5. However, as the success probability is sufficiently high. i.e. 0.5, the new technique is useful in practice. In a word, by directly solving a quadratic equation system, the time complexity to retrieve the full key from a random differential trail is reduced to constant time, i.e. almost close to 1.

Due to the significant improvements for both steps, the attacks on LowMC and LowMC-M will naturally be improved. It can be found in Table 4 and Table 5 that the security margins (see the column $R - r$) of LowMC and LowMC-M decrease quickly and some parameters are extremely vulnerable against our new attacks.

Outline of this Paper. In Sect. 2, we introduce the notations and briefly describe LowMC and LowMC-M. Then, an overview of the algebraic MITM attack is given in Sect. 3. Next, in Sect. 4, we revisit the previous difference enumeration attacks on LowMC and discuss the problems to improve the attacks. The details of the new methods to enumerate differential trails and to efficiently recover the full key from a differential trail are explained in Sect. 5 and Sect. 6, respectively. The summary of our new attacks on LowMC and LowMC-M is shown in Sect. 7. The experimental results are reported in Sect. 8. Finally, the paper is concluded in Sect. 9.

2   Preliminaries

2.1   Notation

Because both LowMC [7] and LowMC-M [33] have many parameters, we use n, k, m, R and D to represent the block size in bits, the key size in bits, the number of S-boxes in each round, the total number of rounds and the allowed $\log_2$ data complexity for each key, respectively. In addition,

1. $rank(M)$ represents the rank of the matrix M.
2. $M_0 \| M_1$ represents the composition of two matrices M_0 and M_1 of the same number of rows.
3. $V_0 | V_1$ represents the composition of the two vectors V_0 and V_1.
4. $E_{j \times j}$ represents an identity matrix of size $j \times j$.
5. $(a_1, a_2, \ldots, a_i)^T$ also represents an i-bit vector. To number the elements in a vector V, we start the index from 1, i.e. $V[i]$ represents the i-th element in V and $V[1]$ is the first element.
6. $V[i : j]$ represents a new vector by taking the i-th element to the j-th element from V.

For example, when $V_0 = (0,0)^T$ and $V_1 = (1,1,0)^T$, we have $V_0 | V_1 = (0,0,1,1,0)^T$ and $V_1[2 : 3] = (1,0)^T$. When $M_0 = \left(\begin{smallmatrix} 0 & 0 \\ 1 & 1 \end{smallmatrix} \right)$ and $M_1 = \left(\begin{smallmatrix} 1 & 0 \\ 0 & 1 \end{smallmatrix} \right)$, we have $M_0 \| M_1 = \left(\begin{smallmatrix} 0 & 0 & 1 & 0 \\ 1 & 1 & 0 & 1 \end{smallmatrix} \right)$.

2.2 Description of LowMC

LowMC [7] is a family of SPN block ciphers proposed at EUROCRYPT 2015. A notable feature of LowMC is that each user can independently choose parameters to instantiate it. LowMC follows a common encryption procedure as most block ciphers. Specifically, it starts with a key whitening (WK) and then iterates a round function R times. The round function at the $(i + 1)$-th ($0 \leq i \leq R - 1$) round can be described as follows:

1. SBoxLayer (S): A 3-bit S-box $(z_0, z_1, z_2) = S(x_0, x_1, x_2)$ with $(z_0, z_1, z_2) = (x_0 \oplus x_1 x_2, x_0 \oplus x_1 \oplus x_0 x_2, x_0 \oplus x_1 \oplus x_2 \oplus x_0 x_1)$ is applied to the first $3m$ bits of the state in parallel, while an identity mapping is applied to the remaining $n - 3m$ bits.
2. MatrixLayer (L): A regular matrix $L_i \in \mathbb{F}_2^{n \times n}$ is randomly generated and the n-bit state is multiplied with L_i.
3. ConstantAddition (AC): An n-bit constant $C_i \in \mathbb{F}_2^n$ is randomly generated and is XORed to the n-bit state.
4. KeyAddition (AK): A full-rank $n \times k$ binary matrix U_{i+1} is randomly generated. The n-bit round key K_{i+1} is obtained by multiplying the k-bit master key with U_{i+1}. Then, the n-bit state is XORed with K_{i+1}.

The whitening key is denoted by K_0 and it is also calculated by multiplying the master key with a random full-rank $n \times k$ binary matrix U_0.

LowMC-M [33] is a family of tweakable block ciphers built on LowMC proposed at CRYPTO 2020. The only difference between them is that there is an additional operation AddSubTweak (AT) after AK and WK in LowMC-M, where the sub-tweaks are the output of an extendable-output-function (XOF) function by setting the tweak as the input. A detailed description can be referred to [33]. As both the tweak and XOF are public, we can equivalently view AT as a known-constant addition operation.

As shown below, in the $(i + 1)$-th round, the difference of the input state of S is denoted by Δ_i and the difference of the corresponding output state is denoted by Δ_i^S. The difference of plaintexts is denoted by Δ_p, i.e. $\Delta_p = \Delta_0$. In our attacks, Δ_i and Δ_i^S will be viewed as n-bit vectors.

$$\Delta_p \xrightarrow{WK} \Delta_0 \xrightarrow{S} \Delta_0^S \xrightarrow{AK} \xrightarrow{L} \xrightarrow{AC} \Delta_1 \to \cdots \to \Delta_{R-1} \xrightarrow{S} \Delta_{R-1}^S \xrightarrow{AK} \xrightarrow{L} \xrightarrow{AC} \Delta_R.$$

In addition, the **compact differential trail** is defined as below:

Definition 1 [28]. *A differential trail $\Delta_0 \to \Delta_1 \to \cdots \to \Delta_r$ is called a r-round* **compact differential trail** *when all (Δ_j, Δ_j^S) $(0 \le j \le r - 1)$ and Δ_r are known.*

3   The Trick for Algebraic MITM Attack on LowMC

We use a toy example to explain the trick used in our algebraic MITM attack on LowMC. Consider an underdetermined equation system in $GF(2)$:

$$A \cdot (\nu_1, \nu_2, \ldots, \nu_6)^T = (\mu_1, \mu_2, \mu_3)^T,$$

where $A = \left(\begin{smallmatrix} 1 & 1 & 0 & 1 & 0 & 1 \\ 0 & 1 & 1 & 1 & 1 & 1 \\ 1 & 1 & 1 & 0 & 0 & 1 \end{smallmatrix} \right)$ and $(\nu_1, \nu_2, \nu_3, \nu_4) \in \mathcal{V} = \{(1, 1, 0, 0), (0, 1, 0, 1)\}$. Note that it is constrained that $(\nu_1, \nu_2, \nu_3, \nu_4)$ can only take 2 possible values. The problem is how to efficiently find $(\nu_1, \nu_2, \ldots, \nu_6)$ for an arbitrary given (μ_1, μ_2, μ_3). With Gaussian elimination, we have

$$A' \cdot (\nu_1, \nu_2, \ldots, \nu_6)^T = B' \cdot (\mu_1, \mu_2, \mu_3)^T,$$

where $A' = \left(\begin{smallmatrix} 1 & 0 & 1 & 0 & 1 & 0 \\ 1 & 1 & 0 & 1 & 0 & 1 \\ 0 & 0 & 1 & 1 & 0 & 0 \end{smallmatrix} \right)$ and $B' = \left(\begin{smallmatrix} 1 & 1 & 0 \\ 1 & 0 & 0 \\ 1 & 0 & 1 \end{smallmatrix} \right)$. Hence, we obtain a linear relation only in $(\nu_1, \nu_2, \nu_3, \nu_4, \mu_1, \mu_2, \mu_3)$, which is

$$(0, 0, 1, 1) \cdot (\nu_1, \nu_2, \nu_3, \nu_4)^T = (1, 0, 1) \cdot (\mu_1, \mu_2, \mu_3)^T.$$

Let $\varpi = (1, 0, 1) \cdot (\mu_1, \mu_2, \mu_3)^T$. We can build a table for the tuple $(\varpi, \nu_1, \nu_2, \nu_3, \nu_4)$ at the offline phase, which is $\mathcal{W} = \{(0, 1, 1, 0, 0), (1, 0, 1, 0, 1)\}$. Then, at the online phase, for any given (μ_1, μ_2, μ_3), we compute ϖ and retrieve $(\nu_1, \nu_2, \nu_3, \nu_4)$ from $\mathcal{W}$ based on ϖ. In this way, $(\nu_1, \nu_2, \nu_3, \nu_4)$ is determined and we then compute (ν_5, ν_6) according to the first two rows of A' and B', thus recovering the full information of $(\nu_1, \nu_2, \ldots, \nu_6)$ for any given (μ_1, μ_2, μ_3).

Abstracting the Above Trick. In the above example, an underdetermined linear equation system $F(\nu_1, \nu_2, \ldots, \nu_i) = \mu$ is considered, where $\mu = (\mu_1, \mu_2, \ldots, \mu_j)$ and $F : \mathbb{F}_2^i \to \mathbb{F}_2^j$ is a linear function. Moreover, some variables of $(\nu_1, \nu_2, \ldots, \nu_i)$ can only take values from a constrained space. The generic procedure of our algebraic MITM attack can be described as follows:

Step 1: Determine the constrained space for some variables. Denote these variables by $I = (\nu_{I_0}, \nu_{I_1}, \ldots, \nu_{I_{i_0}})$ and the constrained space by $\mathcal{V}$, i.e. $I \in \mathcal{V}$.

Step 2: Find some linear relations only in I and μ. Denote these linear relations with a linear equation system

$$A' \cdot (\nu_{I_0}, \nu_{I_1}, \ldots, \nu_{I_{i_0}})^T = B' \cdot (\mu_1, \mu_2, \ldots, \mu_j)^T. \tag{1}$$

For convenience, let $\varpi = B' \cdot (\mu_1, \mu_2, \ldots, \mu_j)^T$.

Step 3: At the offline phase, for each element in $\mathcal{V}$, compute the corresponding ϖ based on Eq. 1 and store (ϖ, I). Denote the set of all possible values of (ϖ, I) by $\mathcal{W}$.

Step 4: At the online phase, for each given μ, compute ϖ using

$$\varpi = B' \cdot (\mu_1, \mu_2, \ldots, \mu_j)^T$$

and retrieve the corresponding I from $\mathcal{W}$ with ϖ. Then, we determine the remaining unknown variables in $(\nu_1, \nu_2, \ldots, \nu_i)$ by considering the whole equation system $F(\nu_1, \nu_2, \ldots, \nu_i) = (\mu_1, \mu_2, \ldots, \mu_j)$.

It can be found that the trick is very simple. However, it is surprising that this has never been utilized nor observed in the cryptanalysis of LowMC. Moreover, from the above generic procedure, it can be found that some variables of $(\nu_1, \nu_2, \ldots, \nu_i)$ are computed on-the-fly. This is indeed the core idea to reduce the memory complexity of the simple difference enumeration attack on LowMC [34].

4   Overview of Previous Difference Enumeration Attacks

The most important application of LowMC is the Picnic signature scheme, which is an alternate third-round candidate in NIST post-quantum cryptography competition. Although the security of Picnic is based on the difficulty to recover the secret key of LowMC under 1 plaintext-ciphertext pair, in its security proof, it is also assumed that the LowMC instance should be secure up to 2 plaintext-ciphertext pairs. This has motivated the LowMC team to devise the difference enumeration attack [34] and they succeeded in breaking many LowMC v2 instances with an extremely low data complexity.

To resist this attack, the formula to compute the secure number of rounds of LowMC is further updated. However, a recent improved attack with algebraic techniques proposed at CRYPTO 2021 indicates that some of the latest LowMC parameters are still insecure. In the following, we will briefly describe the above two attacks.

4.1   The Original Attack Framework [34]

The difference enumeration attack [34] is a meet-in-the-middle-style attack, as depicted in Fig. 1. From now on, we call the original difference enumeration attack [34] **Attack-O**. The attack procedure[1] in general consists of two crucial

---

[1] We consider the standard XOR difference for simplicity.

steps. First, recover the compact differential trail for 2 chosen plaintexts with a meet-in-the-middle method, which we call the **difference enumeration phase**. Second, compute the key from this recovered differential trail, which we call the **key-recovery phase**. Since there must exist a correct compact differential trail, by restricting that only on average one trail will survive after the difference enumeration phase, the trail obtained after this phase will be the correct one.

Some Notations Related to the Complexity of the Attack. Throughout this paper, we denote the time complexity of the difference enumeration phase by T_d and the expected time complexity to retrieve the full key from a compact differential trail by T_k. Moreover, we denote the number of potentially correct compact differential trails after the difference enumeration phase by N_d. In this way, the whole time complexity of the attack is $T_d + N_d T_k$.

An important feature of Attack-O [34] is that $N_d \approx 1$, i.e. only one trail will survive after the difference enumeration phase. Hence, the whole time complexity of the attack becomes $T_d + T_k$.

Constraints at the Difference Enumeration Phase. In the following, we will briefly describe the difference enumeration phase of Attack-O. The key-recovery phase will not be detailed as it is inefficient and it has been significantly improved with algebraic techniques in [28].

As shown in Fig. 1, when targeting a r-round attack, we can split the r rounds into three parts: the first r_0 rounds, the middle r_1 rounds and the last r_2 rounds, i.e. $r = r_0 + r_1 + r_2$. The procedure to find the compact differential trails can be summarized as follows:

Step 1. Find an input difference Δ_0 such that there will be no active S-boxes in the first r_0 rounds. In this way, Δ_{r_0} is uniquely determined. Therefore, $r_0 = \lfloor n/(3m) \rfloor$.

Step 2. Enumerate the state differences forwards from Δ_{r_0} for the next r_1 rounds and store the set of state differences $\Delta_{r_0+r_1}$. Denote such a set by D_f and the size of D_f by $|D_f|$.

Step 3. Encrypt a plaintext pair whose XOR difference is Δ_0 for r rounds and obtain the XOR difference Δ_r of the ciphertexts.

Step 4. Enumerate the state differences backwards from Δ_r for r_2 rounds and again obtain the state difference $\Delta_{r_0+r_1}$. If the obtained $\Delta_{r_0+r_1}$ is in D_f, one compact differential trail is found and exit. Otherwise, repeat enumerating $\Delta_{r_0+r_1}$ from Δ_r.

Since on average one differential trail is allowed to survive and the time complexity T_d cannot exceed 2^k, the constraints[2] specified in [34] are

---

[2] The constraints indeed can be improved with $2^{1.86mr_1-3\tau} < 2^k$, $2^{1.86mr_2} < 2^k$ and $2^{1.86m(r_1+r_2)-3\tau} \leq 2^n$, where $\tau = \lfloor (n - 3mr_0)/3 \rfloor$. This is because we can also make τ S-boxes in the $(r_0 + 1)$-th round inactive. This slight improvement can work for $m > 1$. However, it is not used in [34]. One reason we believe is that this is not that useful to improve the number of attacked rounds and the improvement is slight. Hence, to make a fair comparison and to make the analysis simpler, this trivial trick to slightly improve the attack will not be considered in our new techniques.

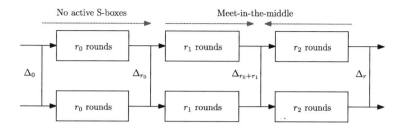

Fig. 1. The original difference enumeration attack framework

$$2^{1.86mr_1} < 2^k, \quad 2^{1.86mr_2} < 2^k, \quad 2^{1.86m(r_1+r_2)} \leq 2^n. \tag{2}$$

For the first two constraints, it is necessary to know the fact that for an input difference of the 3-bit S-box of LowMC, there are on average $29/8 \approx 2^{1.86}$ output differences and vice versa. Hence, the first two constraints mean that the time complexity to construct the set D_f and to enumerate the difference backwards cannot exceed 2^k.

For the last constraint, as the block size is n bits and about $2^{1.86mr_1}$ possible state differences are stored in D_f, the probability to find a match is $2^{-n+1.86mr_1}$. As there are in total $2^{1.86mr_2}$ state differences $\Delta_{r_0+r_1}$ computed backwards, we can expect to find on average $2^{-n+1.86mr_1+1.86mr_2}$ matches, i.e. compact differential trails. To ensure on average one trail survives, we thus have the third constraint $2^{1.86m(r_1+r_2)} \leq 2^n$.

The Drawbacks of Attack-O. The most obvious drawback is the consumption of memory to store D_f, which is directly related to the number r_1, i.e. the memory complexity is $2^{1.86mr_1}$. As r_1 increases, the memory complexity increases exponentially. The second drawback is the strong constraint on N_d, i.e. $N_d \approx 1$ is required. Note that the time complexity of the attack is $T_d + N_d T_k$. Hence, the second drawback can be easily fixed as long as we can make T_k significantly small, which is indeed what the algebraic techniques [28] achieved.

4.2 The Improved Attack Framework

At CRYPTO 2021, Attack-O has been significantly improved with algebraic techniques [28]. The first strategy is to allow many possible r-round compact differential trails to survive after the difference enumeration phase, i.e. N_d can be much larger than 1. The second strategy is to significantly optimize T_k with advanced algebraic techniques. The third strategy is to reduce the memory complexity of the difference enumeration by converting the problem to find a r-round compact trail into the problem to solve a linear equation system, which is inspired by Bar-On et al.'s work [12]. For convenience, we call the improved attack in [28] **Attack-I.**

To avoid the abuse of notation, we still split the r-round LowMC into three parts: the first r_0 rounds, the middle r_1 rounds and the last r_2 rounds, while there will be different constraints for (r_1, r_2) in Attack-I.

The general idea is still the same with Attack-O, i.e. it consists of the difference enumeration phase and the key-recovery phase. As the key-recovery phase will be further optimized in our new attack, its general idea will be explained later and we will mainly focus on the constraints on (r_1, r_2) at the difference enumeration phase in this section.

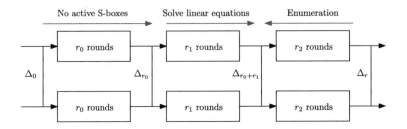

Fig. 2. The improved difference enumeration attack framework

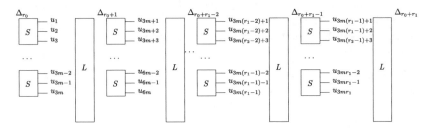

Fig. 3. Introduce variables to represent the output differences of the S-boxes.

As depicted in Fig. 2, the general procedure to find a r-round compact differential trail can be described as follows:

Step 1. It is the same as Step 1 of Attack-O.
Step 2. It is the same as Step 3 of Attack-O.
Step 3. Introduce $3mr_1$ variables $U' = (u_1, u_2, \ldots, u_{3mr_1})^T$ to represent the output difference of the all the mr_1 S-boxes in the middle r_1 rounds, as depicted in Fig. 3. In this way, in the forward direction, $\Delta_{r_0+r_1}$ can be written as linear expressions in these variables, i.e. $\Delta_{r_0+r_1} = H' \cdot U' \oplus c$, where both the coefficient matrix H' and the n-bit constant vector c are fixed.
Step 4. Enumerate the state differences backwards from Δ_r for r_2 rounds and obtain the state difference $\Delta_{r_0+r_1}$. According to $\Delta_{r_0+r_1}$, solve the linear equation system $\Delta_{r_0+r_1} = H' \cdot U' \oplus c$ and get the solutions of $U' = (u_1, u_2, \ldots, u_{3mr_1})^T$. For each solution, the difference transitions

in these r_1 rounds are specified and the correctness can be checked via the differential distribution table (DDT). If it is correct, a potentially correct compact r-round differential trail is found.

The Constraints. Indeed, the variables $(u_{3m(r_1-1)+1}, u_{3m(r_1-1)+2}, \ldots, u_{3mr_1})$ are not necessary. Moreover, based on some properties of the S-box [28], at least $n - 3m + 2m = n - m$ linear equations in terms of $(u_1, u_2, \ldots, u_{3m(r_1-1)})$ can be constructed, i.e. we get at least m linear equations inside $(u_1, u_2, \ldots, u_{3m})$ and we get at least additional m linear equations from the m S-boxes in the $(r_0 + r_1)$–th round. Hence, $T_d = max(2^{1.86mr_2}, 2^{1.86mr_2+(3mr_1-n-2m)})$. To reach the maximal number of attacked rounds, $r_2 = \lfloor k/(1.86m) \rfloor$. In this way, it can be found in [28] that the maximal value of r_1 is either $\lfloor (n+2m)/(3m) \rfloor$ or $\lfloor (n+2m)/(3m) \rfloor + 1$, i.e. $2^{1.86mr_2+(3mr_1-n-2m)} < 2^k$ should hold. Roughly speaking, r_1 is at most $\lfloor n/(3m) \rfloor + 1$.

The Advantages of Attack-I. There is no more a strong constraint $N_d \approx 1$. In other words, $N_d = 2^{1.86m(r_1+r_2)-n}$ can be much larger than 1 as long as $N_d T_k < 2^k$. As T_k is significantly reduced in [28], the upper bound for N_d accordingly increases, which implies that the upper bound for $r_1 + r_2$ increases as well. Moreover, computing a compact differential trail is equivalent to solving a linear equation system in Attack-I and therefore there is no need to use a large amount of memory to store a set of possible values for $\Delta_{r_0+r_1}$ computed forwards, i.e. the memory complexity of Attack-I is negligible.

The Drawbacks of Attack-I. The most obvious drawback of Attack-I is that the constraint on r_1 is too strong, i.e. its maximal value is about $\lfloor n/(3m) \rfloor + 1$, which will directly limit the number of attacked rounds.

4.3   Problems to Improve the Attacks

The maximal values of (r_0, r_2) in both Attack-O and Attack-I are the same, which are specified below:

$$r_0 = \lfloor n/(3m) \rfloor, \quad r_2 = \lfloor k/(1.86m) \rfloor. \tag{3}$$

There seems to be little room to improve the upper bounds for (r_0, r_2).

However, this seems to be not the case for r_1. Assuming T_k can be reduced to 1, the maximal value of $N_d = 2^{1.86m(r_1+r_2)-n}$ will then be slightly smaller than 2^k, i.e. $T_k N_d < 2^k$ has to hold. In this way, with the simple MITM strategy of Attack-O, the maximal value for r_1 is $\lfloor k/(1.86m) \rfloor$ and the memory complexity is $2^{1.86mr_1}$. With the algebraic techniques of Attack-I, the maximal value for r_1 is about $\lfloor n/(3m) \rfloor + 1$ and the memory complexity is negligible.

When n is much larger than k and m is small, e.g. $(n, k, m) = (1024, 128, 1)$, the algebraic technique is more powerful than the simple MITM strategy as the upper bound for r_1 is much larger. Moreover, the memory complexity is negligible. However, it is not difficult to observe that even allowing attackers to use memory in Attack-I, it is unclear how to use it to further increase r_1, i.e. what should we store in advance?

When $n = k$, e.g. $(n, k, m) = (128, 128, 1)$, the simple MITM strategy is more powerful because it is possible to pick an r_1 such that $r_1 > \lfloor n/(3m) \rfloor + 1$ at the cost of using $2^{1.86mr_1}$ memory.

Hence, the to-be-solved problems now become clear, as stated below:

Problem 1. For the case when the simple MITM strategy is more powerful at the cost of using memory, e.g. $n = k$, how to significantly optimize the memory complexity?

Problem 2. For the case when the algebraic technique is more powerful, e.g. $n >> k$, how to further enlarge r_1 by using memory?

5   The Algebraic MITM Attack Framework

In Attack-I, finding a compact differential trail is reduced to solving a linear equation system with the introduction of intermediate variables. An implicit assumption in this attack is that these intermediate variables are independent. Obviously, this is not the fact because we still need to check the validity of the obtained solutions of these variables via DDT. This motivates us to consider whether it is possible to exploit some nonlinear relations in these variables.

5.1   A New Observation on the 3-Bit S-box

Denote the input difference and output difference of the 3-bit LowMC S-box by $(\Delta x_0, \Delta x_1, \Delta x_2)$ and $(\Delta z_0, \Delta z_1, \Delta z_2)$, respectively. We observe that the following 2 cubic equations are sufficient to fully describe its DDT:

$$(1 \oplus \Delta x_0)(1 \oplus \Delta x_1)(1 \oplus \Delta x_2) = (1 \oplus \Delta z_0)(1 \oplus \Delta z_1)(1 \oplus \Delta z_2),$$
$$(1 \oplus \Delta x_0)(1 \oplus \Delta x_1)(1 \oplus \Delta x_2) = \Delta x_0 \Delta z_0 \oplus \Delta x_1 \Delta z_1 \oplus \Delta x_2 \Delta z_2 \oplus 1.$$

Moreover, when $(\Delta x_0, \Delta x_1, \Delta x_2) \neq (0, 0, 0)$ and $(\Delta z_0, \Delta z_1, \Delta z_2) \neq (0, 0, 0)$, all the possible values of $(\Delta x_0, \Delta x_1, \Delta x_2, \Delta z_0, \Delta z_1, \Delta z_2)$ can be fully described with only 1 quadratic equation, while all the invalid values do not satisfy it, as specified below:

$$\Delta x_0 \Delta z_0 \oplus \Delta x_1 \Delta z_1 \oplus \Delta x_2 \Delta z_2 \oplus 1 = 0. \tag{4}$$

This quadratic equation perfectly explains the property used in [28] that for each nonzero input difference, its output differences form an affine space of dimension 2 and vice versa.

Although the above equations are derived by hand, it is also possible to run a simple algorithm to find them. Specifically, we first guess the degree of the equations and then determine the coefficients of the terms in the equations, which can be converted into solving a linear equation system in terms of the to-be-determined coefficients. Each solution of the coefficients will correspond to a possible equation. This is a widely-used method [17]. Using this algorithm, we can simply prove that the DDT of the LowMC S-box cannot be described with only 1 quadratic or cubic equation.

What Does the New Property Imply? With the algebraic technique to find a compact differential trail, it seems possible to enlarge r_1. In particular, if not considering the dependency between the $3m(r_1 - 1)$ variables, we can obtain at least $n - m$ linear equations in these variables. When $n + 2m - 3mr_1 \approx 0$, these variables can be easily solved as in Attack-I. However, when $3mr_1 - n - 2m >> 0$, we may need to enumerate too many solutions to this linear equation system. However, we may reduce the cost to enumerate the solutions by solving nonlinear equations based on the new observations. Specifically, after performing Gaussian elimination on the $n - m$ linear equations, we obtain $3mr_1 - 2m - n$ free variables. Then, by utilizing the nonlinear relations in the input difference and output difference of the 3-bit S-box, equations of degree 3 in these free variables can be constructed because it is unclear which S-box is inactive. In this way, enumerating the solutions is equivalent to solving a multivariate system of degree-3 equations.

As r_1 increases, the number of free variables $3mr_1 - 2m - n$ increases in a very fast way. In addition, it is difficult to bound the time complexity to solve such a system of nonlinear equations. Moreover, when $2^{1.86r_2}$ becomes close to 2^k, it is required to solve such an equation system with time complexity close to 1. One way to remove this constraint is to decrease r_2 and increase r_1 at the cost to solve a system of nonlinear equations in much more variables, which will further make the complexity evaluation difficult. We leave this observation here. In the following, we will describe a different way to utilize these nonlinear relations, which is combining the MITM strategy and the algebraic techniques.

5.2   A New Attack Framework

As mentioned above, it is necessary to develop a new technique to solve an under-determined system of linear equations by utilizing the nonlinear relations in the variables. Moreover, it is expected that the time complexity to solve these variables is 1.

To avoid the abuse of notation, we still split the r-round LowMC into three parts as in Attack-O and Attack-I, i.e. the first r_0 rounds, the middle r_1 rounds and the last r_2 rounds. An overview of the new attack framework is depicted in Fig. 4 and we call it **Attack-N**.

Focus on $(\Delta_{r_0+r_1-1}[1:3e], \Delta^S_{r_0+r_1-1})$, where $\Delta^S_{r_0+r_1-1}$ is computed by performing the inverse of the linear transform on $\Delta_{r_0+r_1}$ and $\Delta_{r_0+r_1-1}[1:3e]$ is obtained by further enumerating the input differences for the first e S-boxes starting from $\Delta^S_{r_0+r_1-1}$. Note that $\Delta^S_{r_0+r_1-1}[3m+1:n] = \Delta_{r_0+r_1-1}[3m+1:n]$ due to the partial nonlinear layer.

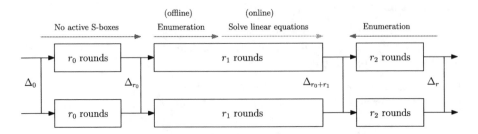

Fig. 4. The new difference enumeration attack framework

Let

$$l = r_1 - 1, \tag{5}$$

$$\gamma = \Delta_{r_0+r_1-1}[1:3e] || \Delta_{r_0+r_1-1}[3m+1:n], \tag{6}$$

i.e. γ is a $(3e + n - 3m)$-bit vector representing the concatenation of the 1st bit to the 3e-th bit and the $(3m + 1)$-th bit to the n-th bit of $\Delta_{r_0+r_1-1}$.

Similarly, we introduce $3ml$ variables $U = (u_1, u_2, \ldots, u_{3ml})$ variables to represent the output differences of the S-boxes in the first $r_1 - 1$ rounds of the middle r_1 rounds. In this way, we have

$$\gamma = M \cdot (u_1, u_2, \ldots, u_{3ml})^T \oplus \alpha, \tag{7}$$

where M is a fixed matrix of size $(n - 3m + 3e) \times 3ml$ and $\alpha \in \mathbb{F}_2^{n-3m+3e}$ is uniquely determined by the fixed state difference Δ_{r_0}.

We now only consider the case when Eq. 7 is under-determined, i.e. $n - 3m + 3e < 3ml$. Our aim is to efficiently solve the variables $U = (u_1, u_2, \ldots, u_{3ml})$ given an arbitrary γ. For this purpose, we adopt a two-phase method, i.e. the offline phase and online phase.

Solving the Under-Determined Linear Equation System. Before moving to the details of the two phases, we need to perform some analysis for this under-determined linear equation system. Our critical observation is that both the coefficient matrix M and the constant vector α are fixed.

Let $M = M_0 || M_1$, where M_0 represents the first q columns of M while M_1 represents the last $3ml - q$ columns of M, i.e. M_0 is of size $(n - 3m + 3e) \times q$ and M_1 is of size $(n - 3m + 3e) \times (3ml - q)$.

First, let

$$Q' = M_1 || E_{(n-3m+3e) \times (n-3m+3e)}.$$

Note that $E_{j \times j}$ represents an identity matrix of size $j \times j$.

Then, we perform the Gaussian elimination on the matrix Q' such that M_1 becomes the reduced row echelon form. Denote the new matrix after Gaussian elimination by $Q = Q_0 || Q_1$, where Q_0 is of size $(n - 3m + 3e) \times (3ml - q)$ and Q_1 is of size $(n - 3m + 3e) \times (n - 3m + 3e)$. In this way, we have

$$Q_0 = Q_1 \cdot M_1$$

and Q_0 is in reduced row echelon form.

Let

$$\omega = n - 3m + 3e - rank(Q_0). \tag{8}$$

Then, the elements in the last ω rows of Q_0 are all zero.

After obtaining the transform matrix Q_1, we apply it to Eq. 7, as shown below:

$$Q_1 \cdot \gamma = Q_1 \cdot M \cdot (u_1, u_2, \ldots, u_{3ml})^T \oplus Q_1 \cdot \alpha.$$

Note that the above new equation system is equivalent to the original equation system Eq. 7.

Let

$$\beta = Q_1 \cdot \gamma, \ \ \epsilon = Q_1 \cdot \alpha, \ \ P = Q_1 \cdot M, \ \ P_0 = Q_1 \cdot M_0. \tag{9}$$

In this way, $P = P_0 \| Q_0$ due to $Q_0 = Q_1 \cdot M_1$ and we can further obtain an equivalent representation of Eq. 7, as specified below:

$$\beta = P_0 \cdot (u_1, u_2, \ldots, u_q)^T \oplus Q_0 \cdot (u_{q+1}, u_{q+2}, \ldots, u_{3ml})^T \oplus \epsilon. \tag{10}$$

Note that Q_0 is in reduced row echelon form.

Analyzing Equation 10. Since the elements in the last ω rows of Q_0 are all zero, we immediately obtain ω linear equations only involving β, ϵ and $(u_1, u_2, \ldots, u_q)$, as shown below:

$$\beta' = P_0' \cdot (u_1, u_2, \ldots, u_q)^T \oplus \epsilon', \tag{11}$$

where P_0' is the submatrix of P_0 representing the last ω rows of P_0, while β' and ϵ' are both an ω-bit vector representing the last ω elements of the bit vectors β and ϵ, respectively. Formally speaking,

$$\beta' = \beta[n - 3m + 3e - \omega + 1 : n - 3m + 3e],$$
$$\epsilon' = \epsilon[n - 3m + 3e - \omega + 1 : n - 3m + 3e]. \tag{12}$$

Suppose that there are N_u possible values of $(u_1, u_2, \ldots, u_q)$, which can be computed independent of $(u_{q+1}, u_{q+2}, \ldots, u_{3ml})$. In this case, for each possible value of $(u_1, u_2, \ldots, u_q)$, we can uniquely determine β' as ϵ' is a constant vector. Therefore, we can precompute N_u possible values for $(u_1, u_2, \ldots, u_q, \beta')$.

As β' represents an ω-bit vector, it can take in total 2^ω values. Hence, for the computed N_u possible values of $(u_1, u_2, \ldots, u_q, \beta')$, we can equivalently say that on average each β' corresponds to $N_u/2^\omega$ solutions of $(u_1, u_2, \ldots, u_q)$.

5.3   The Algebraic MITM Strategy

With the above analysis in mind, it is now easy to explain how to combine the MITM strategy and the algebraic technique. Note that $(u_{3i+1}, u_{3i+2}, u_{3i+3})$

represents the output difference of an S-box. Let us focus on the first $3t$ variables, i.e. the variables $(u_1, u_2, \ldots, u_{3t})$.

The Offline Phase. For such a configuration, we have $q = 3t$. Moreover, there are about $2^{1.86t}$ possible values for $(u_1, u_2, \ldots, u_{3t})$ if we enumerate the state difference Δ_{r_0} in the forward direction, thus resulting in $N_u = 2^{1.86t}$. In other words, on average each β' will correspond to $2^{1.86t}/2^\omega$ solutions of $(u_1, u_2, \ldots, u_{3t})$, which can be computed in advance via Eq. 11. Hence, the offline phase can be described as follows.

Step 1: Enumerate the state difference Δ_{r_0} forwards to obtain all the solutions of $(u_1, u_2, \ldots, u_{3t})$. For each solution, move to step 2. After all solutions are traversed, move to Step 3.

Step 2: Compute β' via Eq. 11 and insert the tuple $(u_1, u_2, \ldots, u_{3t}, \beta')$ into a table denoted by D_u.

Step 3: Sort the table D_u according to β'.

The Online Phase. For each value of $(\Delta_{r_0+r_1-1}[1 : 3e], \Delta^S_{r_0+r_1-1})$ computed backwards, we need to find the solutions of $(u_1, u_2, \ldots, u_{3ml})$. The procedure can be stated as follows:

Step 1: Compute $\gamma = \Delta_{r_0+r_1-1}[1 : 3e] || \Delta^S_{r_0+r_1-1}[3m + 1 : n]$ and $\beta = Q_1 \cdot \gamma$ as well as $\beta' = \beta[n - 3m + 3e - \omega + 1, n - 3m + 3e]$.

Step 2: For the computed β', retrieve from D_u the corresponding values of the tuple $(u_1, u_2, \ldots, u_{3t})$. For each retrieved $(u_1, u_2, \ldots, u_{3t})$, move to Step 3.

Step 3: Only $(u_{3t+1}, u_{3t+2}, \ldots, u_{3ml})$ in Eq. 10 remain unknown, where $q = 3t$. As Q_0 is in reduced row echelon form, there will be in total $2^{(3ml-3t)-rank(Q_0)} = 2^{(3ml-3t)-(n-3m+3e-\omega)} = 2^{3m(l+1)-3t-n-3e+\omega} = 2^{3mr_1-3t-n-3e+\omega}$ solutions of $(u_{3t+1}, u_{3t+2}, \ldots, u_{3ml})$, which can be easily enumerated. For each solution of $(u_1, u_2, \ldots, u_{3ml})$, the difference transitions in the middle r_1 rounds are fully specified and the correctness can be easily verified via DDT. If it passes the verification, a possible r-round compact differential trail is obtained.

Complexity Evaluation. For the offline phase, the time and memory complexity are both $2^{1.86t}$. For the online phase, for each β', there are on average $2^{1.86t}/2^\omega$ solutions of $(u_1, u_2, \ldots, u_{3t})$. For each such solution, there are $2^{3mr_1-3t-n-3e+\omega}$ solutions of $(u_{3t+1}, u_{3t+2}, \ldots, u_{3ml})$. In other word, for each given γ, there will be on average $2^{1.86t-\omega+(3mr_1-3t-n-3e+\omega)} = 2^{3mr_1-n-3e-1.14t}$ full solutions of $(u_1, u_2, \ldots, u_{3ml})$.

5.4 How to Choose Parameters

The time complexity and the memory complexity of the offline phase cannot exceed 2^k and therefore we have

$$2^{1.86t} < 2^k. \tag{13}$$

Second, the total number of potentially correct compact differential trails cannot exceed 2^k. Hence,

$$N_d = 2^{1.86m(r_1+r_2)-n} < 2^k. \tag{14}$$

Finally, the time complexity to enumerate the differences cannot exceed 2^k. Note that as we need to compute $\gamma = \Delta_{r_0+r_1-1}[1:3e]||\Delta^S_{r_0+r_1-1}[3m+1:n]$, it is necessary to enumerate the difference backwards for the last r_2 rounds to compute $\Delta^S_{r_0+r_1-1}[3m+1:n]$ and further enumerate the input differences for the first e S-boxes in the (r_0+r_1)-th round to compute $\Delta_{r_0+r_1-1}[1:3e]$. Therefore, it is equivalent to say that $e+mr_2$ S-boxes are taken into account at the backward difference enumeration phase and the time complexity becomes $2^{1.86(mr_2+e)}$. For each γ computed backwards, we need to perform the online phase to retrieve the full solution of $(u_1, u_2, \ldots, u_{3ml})$. Hence, the time complexity to enumerate the difference is

$$max(2^{1.86(mr_2+e)}, 2^{1.86(mr_2+e)+3mr_1-n-3e-1.14t})$$
$$= max(2^{1.86(mr_2+e)}, 2^{1.86mr_2+3mr_1-n-1.14e-1.14t}), \tag{15}$$

which implies

$$1.86(mr_2+e) < k, \; 1.86mr_2+3mr_1-1.14e-1.14t < k+n. \tag{16}$$

5.5 Maximizing the Attacked Rounds Using Less Memory

To ensure the memory complexity is less than that of the simple MITM strategy, the following additional constraint should be added:

$$2^{1.86t} < 2^{1.86m(r_1-1)} \rightarrow t < m(r_1-1). \tag{17}$$

We should emphasize that $t \leq m(r_1-1)$ holds because we do not care about the S-boxes in the last round of the middle r_1 rounds. Indeed, we can also apply this to the simple MITM strategy, i.e. ignoring the S-boxes in the last round of the middle r_1 rounds. This is why we use the constraint $2^{1.86t} < 2^{1.86m(r_1-1)}$ rather than $2^{1.86t} < 2^{1.86mr_1}$.

With these constraints in mind, it is possible to discuss Problem 1 and Problem 2.

The Parameter $(n, k, m, D) = (128, 128, 1, 1)$. In this case, $n - 3m = 125$. First, choose the maximal values for (r_0, r_2), which are $r_0 = 42$ and $r_2 = 68$ based on $r_0 = \lfloor(n/3m)\rfloor$ and $r_2 = \lfloor(k/1.86m)\rfloor$. Therefore, $e = 0$ according to Eq. 16. Then, according to Eq. 16 and Eq. 17, there will be $1.14t > 3r_1 - 127$ and $t < r_1 - 1$. As the memory complexity of the offline phase is $2^{1.86t}$, we expect that t takes the minimal value, i.e. $t = \lceil(3r_1 - 129.52)/1.14\rceil$. With the constraint $t < r_1 - 1$, the maximal value for r_1 is 68 and $t = 66$. For $r_1 = 68$ and $t = 66$, the memory complexity of our new algebraic MITM strategy is $2^{122.7}$, while it is $2^{124.6}$ for the simple MITM strategy, which shows the advantage of the new technique. When r_1 becomes smaller, the advantage is more clear, as shown in Table 1.

Table 1. Comparison between the memory complexity of the algebraic MITM strategy (M_1) and the simple MITM strategy (M_0) for different r_1.

r_1	≤ 42	43	44	...	61	62	63	64	65	66	67	68
t	0	1	3	...	47	50	53	55	58	61	63	66
$\log_2 M_0$	$1.86(r_1-1)$	78.1	79.9	...	111.6	113.4	115.3	117.1	119.0	120.9	122.7	124.6
$\log_2 M_1$	0	1.8	5.5	...	87.4	93	98.5	102.3	107.8	113.4	117.1	122.7

The Parameter $(n, k, m, D) = (128, 128, 10, 1)$. In this case, $n - 3m = 98$. First, $r_0 = 4$ and $r_2 = 6$ are determined in a similar way. Then, we choose e such that $1.86(mr_2 + e) < k$ and therefore $e = 8$. Finally, we determine r_1 and t according to Eq. 16 and Eq. 17. Similarly, $t = \lceil (3mr_1 - k - n - 1.14e + 1.86mr_2)/1.14 \rceil = \lceil (3mr_1 - 153.52)/1.14 \rceil$ and $t < m(r_1 - 1)$. Hence, the maximal value for r_1 is 7 and $t = 50$. This implies that our attack requires less memory when $r_1 \leq 7$. Specifically, for $r_1 = 7$, the memory complexity of the simple MITM strategy is $2^{111.6}$, while our new technique only requires 2^{93} memory.

The parameter $(n, k, m, D) = (1024, 128, 1, 1)$. For such a parameter, $r_0 = 341$, $r_2 = 68$ and $e = 0$. Based on Eq. 13, the maximal value for t is 68. According to Eq. 16, we have $1.14t > 3mr_1 - k - n - 1.14e + 1.86mr_2 = 3r_1 - 1025.52$. Therefore, the maximal value for r_1 is 367. In other words, by using $2^{1.86t} = 2^{126.48}$ memory, our attack can reach up to $341 + 68 + 367 = 776$ rounds and the claimed secure number of rounds is exactly 776.

Since there must exist one valid compact differential trail and $N_d = 2^{-214.9}$, after the difference enumeration, there will be only 1 valid compact differential trail surviving. Based on the key-recovery technique in [28], we can recover the correct key from this trail with time complexity much smaller than 2^{128}, i.e. $2^{128} >> T_k$. Hence, even without optimizing the key-recovery technique in [28], according to Eq. 15, we have already broken the full rounds of such an instance with time complexity $2^{126.48} + 2^{126.48} = 2^{127.48}$ and memory complexity $2^{126.48}$.

5.6   Advantages of the Algebraic MITM Technique

Based on the above discussions, **Problem** 1 and **Problem** 2 have been successfully addressed. Indeed, the two problems are the same, which is how to reduce the memory complexity of the simple MITM strategy. For example, with the simple MITM strategy, the attack on the parameter $(n, k, m, D) = (1024, 128, 1, 1)$ with $(r_0, r_1, r_2) = (341, 367, 68)$ will require $2^{1.86r_1} = 2^{682.62}$ memory and it soon becomes ineffective. However, our new technique can reduce this to $2^{126.48}$ and an effective attack is immediately obtained.

Compared with the simple MITM strategy to find differential trails, our new MITM technique is applicable to a wide range of parameters, i.e. $n \gg k$. Compared with the algebraic technique, this new technique sheds new insight into how to combine the algebraic technique and the usage of memory to increase r_1. Hence, the algebraic MITM technique is more generic and can optimize the memory complexity of the simple MITM strategy over the state-of-the-art.

6   Recovering the Key by Solving Quadratic Equations

Based on the above algebraic MITM strategy, we can increase r_1 while using less memory. As r_1 increases, there will be much more potentially correct r-round compact differential trails left, i.e. $N_d = 2^{1.86m(r_1+r_2)-n}$. To keep $N_d T_k < 2^k$, it becomes crucial to further optimize T_k.

Our new key-recovery strategy is essentially built on the algebraic technique proposed in [28]. Therefore, we first revisit the technique and then describe how to further optimize it.

6.1   The Algebraic Technique in [28]

The algebraic technique to retrieve the full key from a random r-round compact differential trail is based on the following critical property of the LowMC S-box.

Observation 1 [28]. *For each valid non-zero difference transition $(\Delta x_0, \Delta x_1, \Delta x_2) \rightarrow (\Delta z_0, \Delta z_1, \Delta z_2)$, the inputs conforming to such a difference transition will form an affine space of dimension 1. In addition, (z_0, z_1, z_2) becomes linear in (x_0, x_1, x_2), i.e. the S-box is freely linearized for a valid non-zero difference transition. A similar property also applies to the inverse of the S-box.*

Example. We give an example for better understanding. If $(\Delta x_0, \Delta x_1, \Delta x_2) = (0, 0, 1)$ and $(\Delta z_0, \Delta z_1, \Delta z_2) = (0, 0, 1)$, there will be $x_0 = 0$ and $x_1 = 0$. In addition, the S-box is freely linearized, i.e. we have $z_0 = 0$, $z_1 = 0$ and $z_2 = x_2$.

Based on this simple property, given a random r-round compact differential trail, the procedure to recover the key can be roughly described[3] as follows, which is further illustrated in Fig. 5.

1. Starting from a ciphertext, check the S-boxes in the backward direction round by round and one by one.
   (a) If the S-box is active, write its input as linear expressions in terms of the output and obtain 2 linear equations[4] in terms of the key, i.e. there are two bits conditions on the output to ensure such a difference transition and the S-box is freely linearized based on Observation 1.

---

[3] There are some optimizations, but the general idea is still guess-and-determine.

[4] This is because the output can be written as linear expressions in the key bits. Specifically, each S-box is linearized and the round function can be treated as a linear function. Similar explanations also apply to the inactive S-boxes.

    (b) If the S-box is inactive, guess 2 output bits and write the input as linear expressions in the output. From the 2 guessed bits, we again obtain 2 linear equations in the key bits.

    (c) If more than k linear equations are obtained, move to Step 2.

2. After obtaining more than k linear equations, solve the linear equation system to determine the full key and test its correctness via the plaintext-ciphertext pair. If it is the wrong key, try another guess and repeat the same procedure until all possible guesses are traversed.

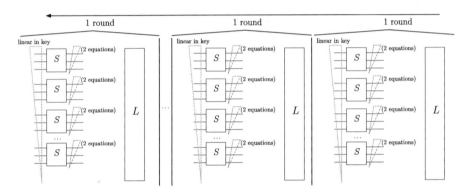

Fig. 5. Illustration of the key-recovery phase in [28]

    Although a novel and efficient way is used to process the active S-boxes in the algebraic technique, processing the inactive S-boxes is rather inefficient. We are thus motivated to consider whether there is a more efficient way to handle them. Although the authors also mentioned to introduce intermediate variables to represent the input of the inactive S-box [28], the collected equations are still from the active S-boxes, which makes the complexity evaluation difficult. Hence, they simply adopted the above guess-and-determine method and provided a loose upper bound for the average time complexity to retrieve the full key from a random r-round compact differential trail. While this bound is sufficient to break some instances, we need to further optimize it because $N_d = 2^{1.86m(r_1+r_2)-n}$ will become very huge in Attack-N due to the increase of r_1.

6.2 A New Method to Handle the Inactive S-boxes

In this part, we show that from a random r-round compact differential trail together with 2 plaintext-ciphertext pairs, it is possible to recover the full key with time complexity 1 and with success rate of about 0.5.

    We still follow the general procedure to recover the key described above, apart from using a new method to process the inactive S-boxes. First, let us discuss a useful property of the LowMC S-box. In [29], it is revealed that there are at most 14 linearly independent quadratic equations to describe the LowMC S-box, as specified below:

$$z_0 = x_0 \oplus x_1 x_2, \; z_1 = x_0 \oplus x_1 \oplus x_0 x_2, \; z_2 = x_0 \oplus x_1 \oplus x_2 \oplus x_0 x_1,$$

$$x_0 = z_0 \oplus z_1 \oplus z_1 z_2, \; x_1 = z_1 \oplus z_0 z_2, \; x_2 = z_0 \oplus z_1 \oplus z_2 \oplus z_0 z_1,$$

$$z_0 x_1 = x_0 x_1 \oplus x_1 x_2, \; z_0 x_2 = x_0 x_2 \oplus x_1 x_2, \; z_1 x_0 = x_0 \oplus x_0 x_1 \oplus x_0 x_2,$$

$$z_1 x_2 = x_1 x_2, \; z_2 x_0 = x_0 \oplus x_0 x_2, \; z_2 x_1 = x_1 \oplus x_1 x_2,$$

$$z_0 x_0 \oplus x_0 = z_1 x_1 \oplus x_0 x_1 \oplus x_1, \; z_1 x_1 \oplus x_0 x_1 \oplus x_1 = z_2 x_2 \oplus x_0 x_2 \oplus x_1 x_2 \oplus x_2.$$

Note that the above 14 equations can also be found with the algorithm in [17].

These quadratic equations are useful to handle the inactive S-boxes. Specifically, instead of only deriving linear equations from the active S-boxes, we can also derive these quadratic equations from the inactive S-boxes. Hence, the attack procedure can be described as follows once we utilize the last h S-boxes in the last $\lceil h/m \rceil \leq r_1 + r_2$ rounds for the key recovery.

Step 1: Choose a threshold a_{min} and initialize two counters a and b as 0.

Step 2: If there are fewer than a_{min} active S-boxes in these h S-boxes[5], exit and return **Failure**. Otherwise, move to Step 3.

Step 3: Starting from a ciphertext, check the S-boxes in the backward direction round by round and one by one.

    (a) If the S-box is active, increase a by 1 and write its input as linear expressions in terms of the output and obtain **2 linear equations** in terms of the key and the intermediate variables, i.e. there are two bits conditions on the output to ensure such a difference transition and the S-box is freely linearized based on Observation 1.

    (b) If the S-box is inactive, increase b by 1 and introduce 3 intermediate variables to represent its input and obtain **14 quadratic equations** in terms of the input bits and output bits.

    (c) If

$$2a \geq k + 3b, \tag{18}$$

    or

$$2a < k + 3b,$$
$$14b \geq (k + 3b - 2a) + (k + 3b - 2a)(k + 3b - 2a - 1)/2, \tag{19}$$

    move to Step 4.

Step 4: At this step, we have collected $2a$ linear equations and $14b$ quadratic equations in terms of $k + 3b$ variables, i.e. the key bits and the intermediate variables. If we reach this step according to Eq. 18, we only need to solve $2a$ linear equations to uniquely determine the k-bit key. If we reach this step according to Eq. 19, we need to first perform the

---

[5] We choose this condition mainly for easily bounding the success probability.

Gaussian elimination on the $2a$ linear equations to obtain $k + 3b - 2a$ free variables. Then, we rewrite the $14b$ quadratic equations in these $k + 3b - 2a$ free variables and perform the Gaussian elimination on it, where each quadratic term is viewed as a new variable[6]. As Eq. 19 holds, we can expect to obtain a unique solution to these $k+3b-2a$ free variables and then compute the remaining variables according to the $2a$ linear equations. For both cases, we obtain a unique solution to the full key and the correctness can be easily verified via a plaintext-ciphertext pair. If it is the correct key, output it and return **Success**.

For better comparison, the new algebraic key-recovery technique is depicted in Fig. 6.

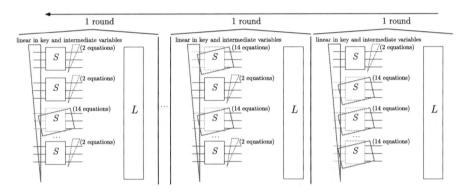

Fig. 6. Illustration of the new key-recovery phase, where the inactive S-boxes are colored in orange (Color figure online)

How to Choose (a_{min}, h). According to the above procedure, we start solving the equation system to recover the key only when (a, b) satisfies some constraints. In addition, before moving to Step 3, we will directly reject some compact differential trails by counting the number of active S-boxes among the last h S-boxes. It is possible that the correct differential trail is the rejected one and our attack will then fail to recover the key. Once moving to Step 3, we expect that either Eq. 18 or Eq. 19 must hold. To achieve a high success probability and to make either Eq. 18 or Eq. 19 hold, we thus add the following constraints on (a_{min}, h):

$$a_{min} = \lceil (7h)/8 \rceil,$$
$$14h - 14a_{min} \geq (k + 3h - 5a_{min}) + (k + 3h - 5a_{min})(k + 3h - 5a_{min} - 1)/2,$$
$$k + 3h - 5a_{min} > 0.$$

Suppose there are a' active S-boxes among the h S-boxes. The first constraint is based on the well-known statistical property that when $a_{min} \approx (7h)/8$, there is $Pr[a' \geq a_{min}] = \sum_{i=a_{min}}^{h} \binom{h}{i} \times (7/8)^i \times (1/8)^{h-i} \approx 0.5$.

---

[6] This is called the linearization technique.

The last two constraints can ensure that when the number of free variables is a positive integer, i.e. there are exactly a_{min} active S-boxes among the last h S-boxes and $(k + 3h - 5a_{min}) > 0$, the quadratic equation system can still be efficiently solved with the linearization technique. Obviously, if $(k + 3h - 5a_{min}) \leq 0 \rightarrow 2a_{min} \geq k + 3(h - a_{min})$, all the unknowns can be directly computed by solving the $2a_{min}$ linear equations. Then, for any a' satisfying $h \geq a' \geq a_{min}$, either Eq. 18 or Eq. 19 must hold if moving to Step 3. Specifically, the key can be directly recovered by solving an equation system.

Therefore, with the above constraints on (a_{min}, h), we can ensure a success probability[7] of about 0.5 to recover the key.

Some concrete choices for (h, a_{min}) for different key sizes are specified in Table 2. For example, the best choice is $(h, a_{min}) = (81, 71)$ for $k = 128$, which will result in $Pr[a' \geq a_{min}] \approx 0.56$. Then, it is required to solve at most 142 linear equations and at most 140 quadratic equations, which corresponds to the worst case when $a' = a_{min} = 71$. We simply estimate the cost to solve these equation systems as $142^3/(rn^2)$ times of LowMC encryptions because each LowMC encryption costs about $2rn^2$ binary operations.

Table 2. Choices for (h, a_{min}) for different k

k	h	a_{min}	Pro.	Linear	Quadratic	Cost (T_k)
128	81	71	0.56	142	140	$142^3/(rn^2)$
192	124	109	0.51	218	210	$218^3/(rn^2)$
256	169	148	0.54	296	294	$296^3/(rn^2)$

Comparison. Compared to the algebraic key-recovery technique in [28], the new method requires no guessing phase and the key is directly computed via solving a quadratic boolean equation system and a linear equation system. This is based on a new way to handle the inactive S-box, i.e. we exploit the nonlinear relations between its input and output rather than linearize it by guessing some input or output bits as in [28]. The only drawback is that this new technique cannot work for an arbitrarily given compact differential trail, i.e. its success rate is about 0.5. However, 0.5 is high enough to claim an effective attack.

6.3   Recovering the Key in the Extended Attack Framework

In the extended framework [28], by using sufficiently many plaintext pairs, i.e. when $D \gg 1$, it is possible to find a pair of plaintext such that there is no active S-box in the last $r_3 = \lfloor (D - 1)/(3m) \rfloor$ rounds either, as depicted in Fig. 7. The time complexity and data complexity of this phase are both 2^{3mr_3+1} because we

---

[7] The computed probability is just a lower bound, which is explained in [31] and is intuitive.

need to try 2^{3mr_3} pairs of plaintexts. As all the S-boxes are inactive in the last r_3 rounds, the constraints on (r_1, r_2) will not change, i.e. we can still choose (r_1, r_2) based on the constraints specified in Sect. 5.4. However, the key-recovery phase will change as the last mr_3 S-boxes are always inactive. Hence, it is required to modify the constraints on (a_{min}, h) in the extended framework in order to efficiently recover the key.

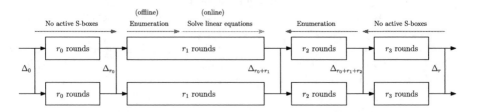

Fig. 7. The extended attack framework [28] embedded with the algebraic MITM strategy

Modifying the constraints is not difficult as we can equivalently consider the case where the last mr_3 S-boxes are always inactive in the last h S-boxes used for key recovery. The modified constraints are specified below:

$$h' = h - mr_3,$$
$$a_{min} = \lceil (7h')/8 \rceil,$$
$$14h - 14a_{min} \geq (k + 3h - 5a_{min}) + (k + 3h - 5a_{min})(k + 3h - 5a_{min} - 1)/2.$$

The success probability is then computed with $\sum_{i=a_{min}}^{h'} \binom{h'}{i} \times (7/8)^i \times (1/8)^{h'-i}$.

Table 3. Choices for (h', a_{min}) for different (mr_3, k)

k	mr_3	h'	a_{min}	Pro.	linear	quadratic	cost (T_k)
128	20	114	100	0.54	228	476	$476^3/(rn^2)$
128	21	116	102	0.51	232	490	$490^3/(rn^2)$
256	20	203	178	0.52	406	630	$630^3/(rn^2)$
256	21	205	180	0.50	410	644	$644^3/(rn^2)$

In Table 3, we provide the accurate values of (h', a_{min}) for some (mr_3, k) that are relevant to our attacks on LowMC-M. The explanation of this table can be referred to that for Table 2. Note that in this framework, $\lceil h'/m \rceil \leq r_1 + r_2$ has to hold.

7 Improved Attacks on LowMC and LowMC-M

With the above new techniques, we could significantly improve the number of attacked rounds for both LowMC and LowMC-M. The correctness of these techniques has been verified by experiments.

The Attacks on LowMC. For the attacks on LowMC, we only consider the parameters where $D = 1$, i.e. the data complexity is 2. When $D \gg 1$, we can trivially use the extended attack framework and we only need to slightly modify the key-recovery phase. Indeed, the attacks on LowMC-M are achieved under the extended attack framework. As already mentioned, the attack consists of two phases: the difference enumeration phase and the key-recovery phase. For an attack on $r = r_0 + r_1 + r_2$ rounds of LowMC (refer to Fig. 4), we first determine r_0 with $r_0 = \lfloor n/(3m) \rfloor$. Then, we determine (r_1, r_2) as well as (t, e) based on the constraints Eq. 13, Eq. 14 and Eq. 16. Examples have already been given in Sect. 5.5.

The time complexity of the difference enumeration phase is

$$2^{1.86t} + max(2^{1.86(mr_2+e)}, 2^{1.86mr_2+3mr_1-n-1.14e-1.14t})$$

and the memory complexity is $2^{1.86t}$. The time complexity of the key-recovery phase is $N_d T_k = 2^{1.86m(r_1+r_2)-n} T_k$, where the accurate estimation of T_k has been explained at Sect. 6.2. The whole time complexity T_w is thus

$$T_w = 2^{1.86m(r_1+r_2)-n} T_k + 2^{1.86t} + max(2^{1.86(mr_2+e)}, 2^{1.86mr_2+3mr_1-n-1.14e-1.14t}).$$

For attacks with success probability of about 0.5, $T_w < 2^{k-1}$ should hold. For our attacks on the parameters where $n \gg k$ in Table 4, the success probability is 1 because we simply use the key-recovery technique in [29]. In this case, $2^{1.86t} + max(2^{1.86(mr_2+e)}, 2^{1.86mr_2+3mr_1-n-1.14e-1.14t})$ dominates T_w because only 1 differential trail will survive after the difference enumeration phase, i.e. $1 \gg 2^{1.86m(r_1+r_2)-n}$. Our results are summarized in Table 4.

The Attacks on LowMC-M. LowMC-M is almost the same as LowMC. The only difference is that after the key addition operation, there is a subtweak addition operation and the subtweak can be derived from a public tweak. It has been studied in [14] that by exploiting the freedom of the tweak, in the difference enumeration attack, r_0 can be increased to $\lfloor (2k+n)/(3m) \rfloor$ by finding a proper tweak pair with time complexity $2^{(3mr_0-n)/2}$, i.e. the first r_0 rounds contain no active S-boxes. A detailed explanation can be referred to [28]. Moreover, $D = 64$ in all the specified parameters for LowMC-M. Hence we utilize the extended difference enumeration attack framework depicted in Fig. 7 where we choose $mr_3 \in \{20, 21\}$ to make full use of the allowed data complexity, i.e. the data complexity of our attacks on LowMC-M is either 2^{61} or 2^{64} and the last r_3 rounds contain no active S-boxes. As for (r_1, r_2), we determine their values and estimate the corresponding time/memory complexity as in the above attacks on LowMC. Due to the costly phase to find a proper tweak pair, the whole time complexity becomes $2^{(3mr_0-n)/2} + T_w$. The improved attacks on LowMC-M are summarized in Table 5. Note we consider the latest version of LowMC-M, which only differs from the original LowMC-M [33] in the number of rounds.

Table 4. Summary of the attacks on LowMC, where D, T, M, Pro. and $R - r$ represent the $\log_2$ data/time/memory complexity, success probability and security margin, respectively. Moreover, $-$ represents negligible memory.

n	k	m	D	R	r_0	r_1	r_2	t	e	r	D	T	M	Pro.	$R-r$	Ref.
128	128	1	1	182	42	43	67	0	0	152	1	124.62	$-$	1	30	[28]
					42	51	59	21	0	152	1	110.8	39.06	0.56	30	This paper
					42	68	67	66	0	177	1	125.38	122.76	0.56	5	This paper
128	128	10	1	20	4	5	6	0	0	15	1	122.8	$-$	1	5	[28]
					4	7	6	53	7	17	1	125.2	98.58	0.56	3	This paper
192	192	1	1	273	64	64	101	0	0	229	1	187.86	$-$	1	44	[28]
					64	101	102	98	0	267	1	189.72	182.28	0.51	6	This paper
192	192	10	1	30	6	7	10	0	0	23	1	186	$-$	1	7	[28]
					6	9	10	67	2	25	1	189.72	124.62	0.51	5	This paper
256	256	1	1	363	85	86	137	0	0	306	1	254.82	$-$	1	57	[28]
					85	136	136	133	0	357	1	253.34	247.38	0.54	9	This paper
256	256	10	1	38	8	9	13	0	0	30	1	241.8	$-$	1	8	[28]
					8	13	13	101	6	34	1	253.82	187.86	0.54	4	This paper
1024	128	1	1	776	341	342	66	0	0	749	1	122.76	$-$	1	27	[28]
					341	367	68	68	0	776	1	127.48	126.48	1	0	This paper
1024	256	1	1	819	341	342	136	0	0	819	1	253	$-$	1	0	[28]
					341	393	136	136	0	870	1	253.96	252.96	1	-51	This paper

8   Experimental Verifications

In our experiments, the concrete LowMC instances are generated with the official reference code [2]. The source code of our experiments is available at https://anonymous.4open.science/r/lowMC_algebraicMITM-3B1C/.

Verifying the Algebraic Difference Enumeration. Considering the cost of the matrix multiplication in the difference enumeration phase, for efficient verifications, we choose the parameters such that the time complexity of this phase is about 2^{25}. Therefore, we choose to perform experiments on the parameter $(n, k, m, r) = (128, 128, 1, 103)$. For such a parameter, we choose $r_0 = 128/3 = 42$, $r_2 = 13$, $r_1 = 48$ and $e = 0$. Then, to keep $2^{1.86r_2+3r_1-n-1.14t-1.14e}$ be about 2^{25}, we choose $t = 13$. Hence, the theoretical memory complexity is $2^{1.86t} = 2^{24.18}$ and the theoretical time complexity to enumerate the differences backwards is

$$max(2^{1.86r_2}, 2^{1.86r_2+3r_1-n-1.14t-1.14e}) = 2^{25.36}.$$

For such a configuration, it is necessary to introduce $3 \times (r_1 - 1) = 141$ variables $(u_1, u_2, \ldots, u_{141})$ to represent the output differences of the S-boxes in the middle $r_1 - 1$ rounds. First, we construct the matrices M, M_1, Q_0, Q_1 and P_0 according to the generated LowMC instance [2], the sizes of which are 125×141, 125×102, 125×102 and 125×125, respectively. It is found that $\omega = n - 3m - rank(Q_0) = 128 - 3 - 102 = 23$ and hence we obtain 23 linear equations only in terms of $(u_1, u_2, \ldots, u_{39})$ and $(\beta_{103}, \beta_{104}, \ldots, \beta_{125})$.

Table 5. Summary of the attacks on LowMC-M

n	k	m	D	R	r_0	r_1	r_2	r_3	t	e	r	D	T	M	Pro.	$R-r$	Ref.
128	128	1	64	294	122	43	64	21	0	0	250	64	120	−	1	44	[28]
					124	66	66	21	60	0	277	64	124.36	111.6	0.51	17	This paper
128	128	2	64	147	61	22	32	10	0	0	125	61	120	−	1	22	[28]
					62	33	33	10	60	0	138	61	124.36	111.6	0.52	9	This paper
128	128	3	64	99	40	15	21	7	0	0	83	64	118.18	−	1	16	[28]
					41	22	22	7	60	0	92	64	124.36	111.6	0.51	7	This paper
128	128	10	64	32	12	5	6	2	0	0	25	61	118	−	1	7	[28]
					12	7	6	2	53	7	27	61	125.2	98.58	0.52	5	This paper
256	256	1	64	555	253	86	136	21	0	0	496	64	252.96	−	1	59	[28]
					253	136	136	21	133	0	546	64	253.34	247.38	0.50	9	This paper
256	256	3	64	186	83	29	45	7	0	0	164	64	250.1	−	1	22	[28]
					84	45	45	7	129	1	181	64	252.96	239.94	0.50	5	This paper
256	256	20	64	30	12	5	6	1	0	0	24	61	232	−	1	6	[28]
					12	7	6	1	115	15	26	61	251.1	213.9	0.52	4	This paper

For the offline phase, according to the experiments, the size of the table D_u is $17134432 \approx 2^{24.03}$, which is almost the same as the expected value $2^{1.86t} = 2^{24.18}$. As β' is a 23-bit value, each β' will correspond to about $2^{1.18}$ different values of $(u_1, u_2, \ldots, u_{39})$ in D_u.

At the online phase, for each computed γ in the backward direction, we first compute β' according to Eq. 9 and Eq. 12. Then, retrieve the corresponding $(u_1, u_2, \ldots, u_{39})$ from D_u according to β'. Finally, determine the remaining unknowns $(u_{40}, u_{41}, \ldots, u_{141})$ by solving Eq. 10, which can be efficiently solved as Q_0 is in reduced row echelon form and $rank(Q_0) = 102$. In this way, the difference transitions in the middle r_1 rounds are fully known and their correctness can be easily verified via DDT. After the online phase, we succeed in recovering all the possible compact differential trails with time complexity of about $2^{25.45}$, which is almost consistent with the theoretical value $2^{24.18+1.18} = 2^{25.36}$.

Verifying the Optimized Key-Recovery Phase. There are two main concerns regarding the optimized key-recovery phase. First, what is the actual success probability? Second, can the key be really efficiently computed via solving an overdefined system of quadratic equations with the linearization technique? To deal with these concerns, we choose to perform experiments on the parameter $(n, k, m, r) = (128, 128, 1, 177)$. In this case, $r_0 = 42$ and $r_1 + r_2 = 135 > 81$.

For the success probability, we randomly choose 10000 plaintext pairs such that there is no difference in the first 42 rounds. For each plaintext pair, we record the corresponding r-round differential trail by tracing the encryption phase and count the number of active S-boxes in the last 81 rounds. Finally, we compute the number of plaintext pairs denoted by N_p such that the number of active S-boxes in the last 81 rounds is not smaller than 71. It is found that $N_p/10000 \approx 0.56$, which means the success probability is correct.

To verify the correctness of the key recovery, for each recorded r-round differential trail where there are at least 71 active S-boxes in the last 81 rounds, we first construct the corresponding overdefined system of quadratic equations and then solve it with the linearization technique. It is found that the key can be correctly recovered, thus demonstrating the correctness of the optimized key-recovery strategy.

9   Conclusion

We propose a simple yet novel technique called algebraic MITM attack to analyze LowMC. This new technique can better capture the feature of partial nonlinear layers. Since using partial nonlinear layers is a relatively new design strategy, developing new techniques to understand its security is both important and meaningful. As a consequence of this new technique and an extremely optimized algebraic key-recovery technique for LowMC, the attacks on LowMC and LowMC-M are significantly improved. Regarding the LowMC S-box, some new algebraic properties are discovered, though they are not exploited in a pure "algebraic" way in this work. It is interesting to investigate whether they can be used to mount another type of algebraic attack on LowMC and whether studying similar equations for DDT is useful for differential attacks on other ciphers.

Acknowledgement. We thank the reviewers of Asiacrypt 2022 for their comments. Fukang Liu is supported by Grant-in-Aid for Research Activity Start-up (Grant No. 22K21282). Takanori Isobe is supported by JST, PRESTO Grant Number JPMJPR2031, Grant-in-Aid for Scientific Research. This research was in part conducted under a contract of "Research and development on new generation cryptography for secure wireless communication services" among "Research and Development for Expansion of Radio Wave Resources (JPJ000254)", which is supported by the Ministry of Internal Affairs and Communications, Japan. These research results were also obtained from the commissioned research(No.05801) by National Institute of Information and Communications Technology (NICT) , Japan. Gaoli Wang is supported by the National Key R&D Program of China (Grant No. 2022YFB2700014), National Natural Science Foundation of China (No. 62072181), NSFC-ISF Joint Scientific Research Program (No. 61961146004), Shanghai Trusted Industry Internet Software Collaborative Innovation Center.

References

1. https://csrc.nist.gov/projects/post-quantum-cryptography
2. Reference Code (2017). https://github.com/LowMC/lowmc
3. The Picnic signature algorithm specification (2019). https://microsoft.github.io/Picnic/

4. Albrecht, M.R., et al.: Algebraic cryptanalysis of STARK-friendly designs: application to MARVELlous and MiMC. In: Galbraith, S.D., Moriai, S. (eds.) ASIACRYPT 2019. LNCS, vol. 11923, pp. 371–397. Springer, Cham (2019). https://doi.org/10.1007/978-3-030-34618-8_13

5. Albrecht, M.R., et al.: Feistel structures for MPC, and More. In: Sako, K., Schneider, S., Ryan, P.Y.A. (eds.) ESORICS 2019. LNCS, vol. 11736, pp. 151–171. Springer, Cham (2019). https://doi.org/10.1007/978-3-030-29962-0_8

6. Albrecht, M., Grassi, L., Rechberger, C., Roy, A., Tiessen, T.: MiMC: efficient encryption and cryptographic hashing with minimal multiplicative complexity. In: Cheon, J.H., Takagi, T. (eds.) ASIACRYPT 2016. LNCS, vol. 10031, pp. 191–219. Springer, Heidelberg (2016). https://doi.org/10.1007/978-3-662-53887-6_7

7. Albrecht, M.R., Rechberger, C., Schneider, T., Tiessen, T., Zohner, M.: Ciphers for MPC and FHE. In: Oswald, E., Fischlin, M. (eds.) EUROCRYPT 2015. LNCS, vol. 9056, pp. 430–454. Springer, Heidelberg (2015). https://doi.org/10.1007/978-3-662-46800-5_17

8. Aly, A., Ashur, T., Ben-Sasson, E., Dhooghe, S., Szepieniec, A.: Design of symmetric-key primitives for advanced cryptographic protocols. IACR Trans. Symm. Cryptol. **2020**(3), 1–45 (2020)

9. Ashur, T., Dhooghe, S.: MARVELlous: a STARK-Friendly Family of Cryptographic Primitives. Cryptology ePrint Archive, Report 2018/1098 (2018). https://eprint.iacr.org/2018/1098

10. Banik, S., Barooti, K., Durak, F.B., Vaudenay, S.: Cryptanalysis of LowMC instances using single plaintext/ciphertext pair. IACR Trans. Symm. Cryptol. **2020**(4), 130–146 (2020)

11. Banik, S., Barooti, K., Vaudenay, S., Yan, H.: New attacks on LowMC instances with a single plaintext/ciphertext pair. In: Tibouchi, M., Wang, H. (eds.) ASIACRYPT 2021. LNCS, vol. 13090, pp. 303–331. Springer, Cham (2021). https://doi.org/10.1007/978-3-030-92062-3_11

12. Bar-On, A., Dinur, I., Dunkelman, O., Lallemand, V., Keller, N., Tsaban, B.: Cryptanalysis of SP networks with partial non-linear layers. In: Oswald, E., Fischlin, M. (eds.) EUROCRYPT 2015. LNCS, vol. 9056, pp. 315–342. Springer, Heidelberg (2015). https://doi.org/10.1007/978-3-662-46800-5_13

13. Beyne, T.: Out of oddity – new cryptanalytic techniques against symmetric primitives optimized for integrity proof systems. In: Micciancio, D., Ristenpart, T. (eds.) CRYPTO 2020. LNCS, vol. 12172, pp. 299–328. Springer, Cham (2020). https://doi.org/10.1007/978-3-030-56877-1_11

14. Beyne, T., Li, C.: Cryptanalysis of the MALICIOUS Framework. Report 2020/1032 (2020). https://ia.cr/2020/1032

15. Canteaut, A., et al.: Stream ciphers: a practical solution for efficient homomorphic-ciphertext compression. J. Cryptol. **31**(3), 885–916 (2018). https://doi.org/10.1007/s00145-017-9273-9

16. Chase, M., et al.: Post-quantum zero-knowledge and signatures from symmetric-key primitives. In: CCS, pp. 1825–1842. ACM (2017)

17. Courtois, N.T., Pieprzyk, J.: Cryptanalysis of block ciphers with overdefined systems of equations. In: Zheng, Y. (ed.) ASIACRYPT 2002. LNCS, vol. 2501, pp. 267–287. Springer, Heidelberg (2002). https://doi.org/10.1007/3-540-36178-2_17

18. Dinur, I.: Cryptanalytic applications of the polynomial method for solving multivariate equation systems over GF(2). In: Canteaut, A., Standaert, F.-X. (eds.) EUROCRYPT 2021. LNCS, vol. 12696, pp. 374–403. Springer, Cham (2021). https://doi.org/10.1007/978-3-030-77870-5_14

19. Dinur, I., Liu, Y., Meier, W., Wang, Q.: Optimized interpolation attacks on LowMC. In: Iwata, T., Cheon, J.H. (eds.) ASIACRYPT 2015. LNCS, vol. 9453, pp. 535–560. Springer, Heidelberg (2015). https://doi.org/10.1007/978-3-662-48800-3_22

20. Dobraunig, C.: Rasta: a cipher with low ANDdepth and few ANDs per bit. In: Shacham, H., Boldyreva, A. (eds.) CRYPTO 2018. LNCS, vol. 10991, pp. 662–692. Springer, Cham (2018). https://doi.org/10.1007/978-3-319-96884-1_22

21. Dobraunig, C., Eichlseder, M., Mendel, F.: Higher-order cryptanalysis of LowMC. In: Kwon, S., Yun, A. (eds.) ICISC 2015. LNCS, vol. 9558, pp. 87–101. Springer, Cham (2016). https://doi.org/10.1007/978-3-319-30840-1_6

22. Dobraunig, C., Grassi, L., Guinet, A., Kuijsters, D.: Ciminion: symmetric encryption based on toffoli-gates over large finite fields. In: Canteaut, A., Standaert, F.-X. (eds.) EUROCRYPT 2021. LNCS, vol. 12697, pp. 3–34. Springer, Cham (2021). https://doi.org/10.1007/978-3-030-77886-6_1

23. Duval, S., Lallemand, V., Rotella, Y.: Cryptanalysis of the FLIP family of stream ciphers. In: Robshaw, M., Katz, J. (eds.) CRYPTO 2016. LNCS, vol. 9814, pp. 457–475. Springer, Heidelberg (2016). https://doi.org/10.1007/978-3-662-53018-4_17

24. Eichlseder, M., et al.: An algebraic attack on ciphers with low-degree round functions: application to full MiMC. In: Moriai, S., Wang, H. (eds.) ASIACRYPT 2020. LNCS, vol. 12491, pp. 477–506. Springer, Cham (2020). https://doi.org/10.1007/978-3-030-64837-4_16

25. Grassi, L., Khovratovich, D., Rechberger, C., Roy, A., Schofnegger, M.: Poseidon: a new hash function for zero-knowledge proof systems. In: USENIX Security Symposium, pp. 519–535. USENIX Association (2021)

26. Grassi, L., Lüftenegger, R., Rechberger, C., Rotaru, D., Schofnegger, M.: On a generalization of substitution-permutation networks: the HADES design strategy. In: Canteaut, A., Ishai, Y. (eds.) EUROCRYPT 2020. LNCS, vol. 12106, pp. 674–704. Springer, Cham (2020). https://doi.org/10.1007/978-3-030-45724-2_23

27. Jakobsen, T., Knudsen, L.R.: The interpolation attack on block ciphers. In: Biham, E. (ed.) FSE 1997. LNCS, vol. 1267, pp. 28–40. Springer, Heidelberg (1997). https://doi.org/10.1007/BFb0052332

28. Liu, F., Isobe, T., Meier, W.: Cryptanalysis of full LowMC and LowMC-M with algebraic techniques. In: Malkin, T., Peikert, C. (eds.) CRYPTO 2021. LNCS, vol. 12827, pp. 368–401. Springer, Cham (2021). https://doi.org/10.1007/978-3-030-84252-9_13

29. Liu, F., Meier, W., Sarkar, S., Isobe, T.: New low-memory algebraic attacks on LowMC in the picnic setting. IACR Trans. Symm. Cryptol. **2022**(3), 102–122 (2022)

30. Liu, F., Sarkar, S., Meier, W., Isobe, T.: Algebraic attacks on rasta and dasta using low-degree equations. In: Tibouchi, M., Wang, H. (eds.) ASIACRYPT 2021. LNCS, vol. 13090, pp. 214–240. Springer, Cham (2021). https://doi.org/10.1007/978-3-030-92062-3_8

31. Liu, F., Sarkar, S., Wang, G., Meier, W., Isobe, T.: Algebraic Meet-in-the-Middle Attack on LowMC. Cryptology ePrint Archive, Paper 2022/019 (2022). https://eprint.iacr.org/2022/019

32. Méaux, P., Journault, A., Standaert, F.-X., Carlet, C.: Towards stream ciphers for efficient FHE with low-noise ciphertexts. In: Fischlin, M., Coron, J.-S. (eds.) EUROCRYPT 2016. LNCS, vol. 9665, pp. 311–343. Springer, Heidelberg (2016). https://doi.org/10.1007/978-3-662-49890-3_13

33. Peyrin, T., Wang, H.: The MALICIOUS framework: embedding backdoors into tweakable block ciphers. In: Micciancio, D., Ristenpart, T. (eds.) CRYPTO 2020. LNCS, vol. 12172, pp. 249–278. Springer, Cham (2020). https://doi.org/10.1007/978-3-030-56877-1_9
34. Rechberger, C., Soleimany, H., Tiessen, T.: Cryptanalysis of low-data instances of full LowMCv2. IACR Trans. Symm. Cryptol. **2018**(3), 163–181 (2018)

Latin Dances Reloaded: Improved Cryptanalysis Against Salsa and ChaCha, and the Proposal of Forró

Murilo Coutinho[1]([✉]), Iago Passos[1], Juan C. Grados Vásquez[2],
Fábio L. L. de Mendonça[1], Rafael Timteo de Sousa Jr.[1], and Fábio Borges[3]

[1] Electrical Engineering Department (ENE), Technology College,
University of Brasília, Brasília, Brazil
`murilo.coutinho@redes.unb.br`
[2] Technology Innovation Institute, Abu Dhabi, UAE
[3] National Laboratory for Scientific Computing, Petrópolis, Brazil

Abstract. In this paper, we present 4 major contributions to ARX ciphers and in particular to the Salsa/ChaCha family of stream ciphers:

(a) We propose an improved differential-linear distinguisher against ChaCha. To do so, we propose a new way to approach the derivation of linear approximations by viewing the algorithm in terms of simpler subrounds. Using this idea we show that it is possible to derive almost all linear approximations from previous works from just 3 simple rules. Furthermore, we show that with one extra rule it is possible to improve the linear approximations proposed by Coutinho and Souza at Eurocrypt 2021 [11].

(b) We propose a technique called Bidirectional Linear Expansions (BLE) to improve attacks against Salsa. While previous works only considered linear expansions moving forward into the rounds, BLE explores the expansion of a single bit in both forward and backward directions. Applying BLE, we propose the first differential-linear distinguishers ranging 7 and 8 rounds of Salsa and we improve PNB key-recovery attacks against 8 rounds of Salsa.

(c) Using all the knowledge acquired studying the cryptanalysis of these ciphers, we propose some modifications in order to provide better diffusion per round and higher resistance to cryptanalysis, leading to a new stream cipher named Forró. We show that Forró has higher security margin, this allows us to reduce the total number of rounds while maintaining the security level, thus creating a faster cipher in many platforms, specially in constrained devices.

(d) Finally, we developed *CryptDances*, a new tool for the cryptanalysis of Salsa, ChaCha, and Forró designed to be used in high performance environments with several GPUs. With *CryptDances* it is possible to compute differential correlations, to derive new linear approximations for ChaCha automatically, to automate the computation of the complexity of PNB attacks, among other features. We make *CryptDances* available for the community at https://github.com/MurCoutinho/cryptDances.

© International Association for Cryptologic Research 2022
S. Agrawal and D. Lin (Eds.): ASIACRYPT 2022, LNCS 13791, pp. 256–286, 2022.
https://doi.org/10.1007/978-3-031-22963-3_9

Keywords: Differential-linear cryptanalysis · ARX · ChaCha · Salsa · Forró

1 Introduction

Cryptography is an indispensable tool used to protect information in computing systems. It is used to protect data at rest and data in motion by billions of people everyday. For example, cryptography is used in financial transactions, mobile messaging applications, blockchain technology, authentication systems, and many other systems and solutions. Among the most important cryptographic primitives, stream ciphers are symmetric algorithms used to encrypt large amounts of data with high performance both in software and in hardware.

In particular, ARX-based design is a major building block of modern ciphers due to its efficiency in software. ARX stands for addition, word-wise rotation and XOR. Indeed, ciphers following this framework are composed of those operations and avoid the computation of smaller S-boxes through look-up tables. ARX-based designs are not only efficient but also provide good security properties. The algebraic degree of ARX ciphers is generally high after only a very few rounds as the carry bit within one modular addition already reaches almost maximal degree. For differential and linear attacks, ARX-based designs show weaknesses for a small number of rounds. However, after some rounds the differential and linear probabilities decrease rapidly. Thus, the probabilities of differentials and the absolute correlations of linear approximations decrease very quickly as we increase the number of rounds.

Salsa [6] is an ARX-based stream cipher designed by Bernstein in 2005 as a candidate for the *eSTREAM* competition [27]. The original proposal was for 20 rounds. The 12-round variant of Salsa - Salsa20/12 - was accepted into the final *eSTREAM* software portfolio. Salsa is especially important and is used in practice in several applications, such as DNS implementations, in the Linux Kernel, Password managers (e.g., KeePassX and MacPass), messaging software (e.g., Viber and Discord), and many other (see [19] for a huge list of applications, protocols and libraries using Salsa).

Later, in 2008, Bernstein proposed some modifications to Salsa in order to provide better diffusion per round and higher resistance to cryptanalysis. These changes created a new stream cipher, a variant named ChaCha [5]. Although Salsa was one of the winners of the eSTREAM competition, ChaCha has received much more attention through the years. Nowadays, we see the usage of this cipher in several projects and applications.

ChaCha, along with Poly1305 [4], is one of the cipher suites of the new TLS 1.3 [21], which has been used by Google on both Chrome and Android. Not only has ChaCha been used in TLS but also in many other protocols such as SSH, Noise and S/MIME 4.0. In addition, the RFC 7634 proposes the use of ChaCha in IKE and IPsec. ChaCha has been used not only for encryption, but also as a pseudo-random number generator in any operating system running Linux kernel 4.8 or newer. Additionally, ChaCha has been used in several applications such as

WireGuard (VPN) (see [18] for a huge list of applications, protocols and libraries using ChaCha).

Related Work. Due to the popularity of both Salsa and ChaCha, it is important to evaluate their security. Indeed, the cryptanalysis of Salsa is well understood and several authors studied its security [8,17,25]. The cryptanalysis of Salsa was introduced by Crowley [13] in 2005. Later, Aumasson et al. at FSE 2008 [2] presented one of the most important works on the cryptanalysis of these ciphers with the introduction of the notion of Probabilistic Neutral Bits (PNBs), showing attacks against Salsa20/7, Salsa20/8, ChaCha20/6 and ChaCha20/7.

After that, several authors proposed small enhancements on the attack of Aumasson et al. For example, the work by Shi et al. [28] introduced the concept of Column Chaining Distinguisher (CCD) to achieve some incremental advancements over [2] Salsa and ChaCha. Maitra, Paul, and Meier [24] studied an interesting observation regarding round reversal of Salsa, but no significant cryptanalytic improvement could be obtained using this method. Maitra [23] used a technique of Chosen IVs to obtain certain improvements over existing results. Dey and Sarkar [15] showed how to choose values for the PNB to further improve the attack.

Then, in a paper presented at FSE 2017, Choudhuri and Maitra [9] significantly improved the attacks by considering the mathematical structure of Salsa and ChaCha to find differential characteristics with much higher correlations. Other types of attacks were also studied, such as, related-cipher attacks [16] and chosen-IV attacks [23].

Recently, several works presented improvements in attack against ChaCha. First, Coutinho and Souza [10] proposed new multi-bit differentials using the mathematical framework of Choudhuri and Maitra. In Crypto 2020, Beierle et al. [3] proposed improvements to the framework of differential-linear cryptanalysis against ARX-based designs and further improved the attacks against ChaCha. At Eurocrypt 2021, Coutinho and Souza [11] developed a new technique to expand linear trails improving the attack against ChaCha even further. However, these new techniques were not used against Salsa. At Eurocrypt 2022 Dey et al. [14] improved the analysis of the PNB construction and key recovery attacks against ChaCha. Finally, in Crypto 2022, rotational-cryptanalysis of ChaCha was improved [26].

Our Contribution. In this work, we present new attacks against ChaCha and Salsa. In the case of ChaCha, we propose a simpler way to derive linear approximations for the cipher. To do so, we view the algorithm in terms of subrounds. With this approach, we are able to derive the results from previous works from just 3 simple rules. As a reference, the methods of Coutinho and Souza [11] at Eurocrypt 2021 encompasses at least 18 different rules to derive linear approximations for ChaCha. Moreover, with our techniques we are able to improve the complexity of the best differential-linear distinguisher against ChaCha, reducing the complexity from 2^{224} to 2^{214}.

To attack Salsa, we introduce a novel technique called Bidirectional Linear Expansions (BLE). While previous works only considered linear expansions moving forward into the rounds, BLE explores the expansion of a single bit in both forward and backward directions. As we show, BLE is specially useful in situations that we do not have enough computational power to compute a differential correlation for the target single bit, but we can do so for each bit derived in backward direction individually, and then combining them using the Piling-up Lemma. Using BLE we were able to improve attacks against Salsa. In particular, we improved key recovery attacks, significantly reducing the complexity from $2^{244.9}$ to 2^{218} for 8 rounds of Salsa. Also, we provide the first differential-linear distinguishers ranging 7 and 8 rounds of Salsa in the literature. Still using BLE, we were able to find several new differential for 3.5 rounds of ChaCha. Unfortunately, we were not able to improve key recovery attacks in this case.

Next, we propose a new modification of Salsa and ChaCha, the stream cipher Forró. We show that Forró has a higher security margin. For comparison, the best distinguishers against 5 rounds of Salsa, ChaCha, and Forró, have complexities of 2^8, 2^{16}, and 2^{130}, respectively. To achieve that we introduce a new design strategy, called Pollination, constructed to speed up confusion and diffusion. Then, we show that Forró can deliver the same security in less time in several platforms, specially in constrained devices. Finally, we present a new tool, called *CryptDances* (https://github.com/MurCoutinho/cryptDances) designed to allow researchers to explore the cryptanalysis of ChaCha, Salsa, and Forró in a high performance environment configured using MPI to distribute the work to several GPUs. We provide a summary of our cryptanalytic results in Table 1.

Organization of the Paper. This paper is organized as follows: in Sect. 2, we review previous works and techniques. In Sect. 3, we propose a new approach to the derivation of linear approximations for ChaCha and present a new and improved differential-linear distinguisher. Then, in Sect. 4, we propose a new technique called Bidirectional Linear Expansions (BLE) and use it to improve attacks against Salsa. Next, in Sect. 5, we present the new stream cipher Forró and in Sect. 6 we give a brief description of the tool CryptDances. Finally, in Sect. 7 we present the conclusions and future works.

2   Specifications and Preliminaries

This section is divided in 5 parts as follows: first in Sects. 2.1 and 2.2 we describe the algorithms Salsa and ChaCha, respectively. Then, in Sect. 2.3 we review the state-of-the-art differential-linear cryptanalysis, and in Sect. 2.4 we review the key recovery attacks using PNBs as used to attack Salsa and ChaCha. Finally, in Sect. 2.5 we review state-of-the-art techniques to create linear approximations for ARX ciphers and in particular to Salsa and ChaCha. To improve readability, we provide a summary of the main notation used throughout the paper in Table 2.

2.1   Salsa

Salsa operates on a state of 64 bytes, organized as a 4×4 matrix with 32-bit integers, initialized with a 256-bit key $k_0, k_1, ..., k_7$, a 64-bit nonce v_0, v_1 and a

Table 1. Time and data complexity for the best attacks against ChaCha, Salsa, and Forró.

Rounds	Algorithm	Type	Time	Data	Reference
3	Forró	Distinguisher	2^{19}	2^{19}	This work
4	ChaCha	Distinguisher	2^6	2^6	[9]
	Forró	Distinguisher	2^{37}	2^{37}	This work
5	Salsa	Distinguisher	2^8	2^8	[9]
	ChaCha	Distinguisher	2^{16}	2^{16}	[9]
	Forró	Key Recovery	2^{158}	2^{57}	This work
	Forró	Distinguisher	2^{130}	2^{130}	This work
6	Salsa	Distinguisher	2^{32}	2^{32}	[9]
	ChaCha	Key Recovery	2^{139}	2^{30}	[2]
	ChaCha	Key Recovery	$2^{127.5}$	$2^{37.5}$	[9]
	ChaCha	Key Recovery	$2^{77.4}$	2^{58}	[3]
	ChaCha	Distinguisher	2^{116}	2^{116}	[9]
	ChaCha	Distinguisher	2^{51}	2^{51}	[11]
7	Salsa	Key Recovery	2^{137}	2^{61}	[9]
	Salsa	Distinguisher	2^{109}	2^{109}	This work
	ChaCha	Key Recovery	2^{248}	2^{27}	[2]
	ChaCha	Key Recovery	$2^{237.7}$	2^{96}	[9]
	ChaCha	Key Recovery	$2^{230.86}$	$2^{48.8}$	[3]
	ChaCha	Key Recovery	$2^{221.95}$	$2^{48.83}$	[14]
	ChaCha	Distinguisher	2^{224}	2^{224}	[11]
	ChaCha	Distinguisher	2^{214}	2^{214}	This work
8	Salsa	Key Recovery	$2^{244.9}$	2^{96}	[9]
	Salsa	Key Recovery	2^{218}	2^{114}	This work
	Salsa	Distinguisher	2^{216}	2^{216}	This work

64-bit counter t_0, t_1 (we may also refer to the nonce and counter words as IV words), and 4 constants $c_0 = \text{0x61707865}$, $c_1 = \text{0x3320646e}$, $c_2 = \text{0x79622d32}$ and $c_3 = \text{0x6b206574}$. For Salsa, we have the following initial state matrix:

$$X^{(0)} = \begin{pmatrix} x_0^{(0)} & x_1^{(0)} & x_2^{(0)} & x_3^{(0)} \\ x_4^{(0)} & x_5^{(0)} & x_6^{(0)} & x_7^{(0)} \\ x_8^{(0)} & x_9^{(0)} & x_{10}^{(0)} & x_{11}^{(0)} \\ x_{12}^{(0)} & x_{13}^{(0)} & x_{14}^{(0)} & x_{15}^{(0)} \end{pmatrix} = \begin{pmatrix} c_0 & k_0 & k_1 & k_2 \\ k_3 & c_1 & v_0 & v_1 \\ t_0 & t_1 & c_2 & k_4 \\ k_5 & k_6 & k_7 & c_3 \end{pmatrix}. \tag{1}$$

The state matrix is modified in each round by a *Quarter Round Function* (QRF), named $QR_{Salsa}(a, b, c, d)$, which receives and updates 4 integers in the following way:

Table 2. Notation

Notation	Description
X	A 4×4 state matrix
$X^{(m)}$	State matrix after application of m rounds
$X^{[s]}$	State matrix after application of s subrounds
Z	Output of Salsa, ChaCha or Forró, i.e., $Z = X + X^{(R)}$
$x_i^{(m)}$	i^{th} word of the state matrix $X^{(m)}$
$x_{i,j}^{(m)}$	j^{th} bit of ith word of the state matrix $X^{(m)}$
$x_i^{(m)}[j_0, j_1, ..., j_t]$	The sum $x_{i,j_0}^{(m)} \oplus x_{i,j_1}^{(m)} \oplus \cdots \oplus x_{i,j_t}^{(m)}$
$x + y$	Addition of x and y modulo 2^{32}
$\Theta(x, y)$	Carry function of the sum $x + y$
$x \oplus y$	Bitwise XOR of x and y
$x \lll n$	Rotation of x by n bits to the left
Δx	XOR difference of x and x'. $\Delta x = x \oplus x'$
$\mathcal{ID}$	Input difference
$\mathcal{OD}$	Output difference

$$\begin{aligned}
x_b^{(m)} &= x_b^{(m-1)} \oplus ((x_d^{(m-1)} + x_a^{(m-1)}) \lll 7) \\
x_c^{(m)} &= x_c^{(m-1)} \oplus ((x_a^{(m-1)} + x_b^{(m)}) \lll 9) \\
x_d^{(m)} &= x_d^{(m-1)} \oplus ((x_c^{(m)} + x_b^{(m)}) \lll 13) \\
x_a^{(m)} &= x_a^{(m-1)} \oplus ((x_d^{(m)} + x_c^{(m)}) \lll 18)
\end{aligned} \tag{2}$$

One round of Salsa is defined as 4 applications of the QRF. There is a difference, however, between odd and even rounds. Thus, for odd rounds, when $m \in \{1, 3, 5, 7, ...\}$, $X^{(m)}$ is defined from $X^{(m-1)}$, from $QR_{Salsa}(a, b, c, d)$ with $(a, b, c, d) = \{(0, 4, 8, 12), (5, 9, 13, 1), (10, 14, 2, 6), (15, 3, 7, 11)\}$, and for even rounds $m \in \{2, 4, 6, ...\}$ from $QR_{Salsa}(a, b, c, d)$ with $(a, b, c, d) = \{(0, 1, 2, 3), (5, 6, 7, 4), (10, 11, 8, 9), (15, 12, 13, 14)\}$.

The output of Salsa20/R is then defined as the sum of the initial state with the state obtained after R rounds of operations $Z = X^{(0)} + X^{(R)}$. One should note that it is possible to parallelize each application of the QRF on each round and that each round is reversible, hence we can compute $X^{(m-1)}$ from $X^{(m)}$. For more information on Salsa, we refer to [6].

2.2 ChaCha

The stream cipher ChaCha was also proposed by Bernstein [5] as an improvement of Salsa. ChaCha consists of a series of ARX (addition, rotation, and XOR) operations on 32-bit words, being highly efficient in software and hardware.

Each round of ChaCha has a total of 16 bitwise XOR, 16 addition modulo 2^{32} and 16 constant-distance rotations.

ChaCha operates on a state of 64 bytes, organized as a 4×4 matrix with 32-bit integers, initialized with a 256-bit key $k_0, k_1, ..., k_7$, a 64-bit nonce v_0, v_1 and a 64-bit counter t_0, t_1 (we may also refer to the nonce and counter words as IV words), and 4 constants $c_0 = 0x61707865$, $c_1 = 0x3320646e$, $c_2 = 0x79622d32$ and $c_3 = 0x6b206574$. For ChaCha, we have the following initial state matrix:

$$X^{(0)} = \begin{pmatrix} x_0^{(0)} & x_1^{(0)} & x_2^{(0)} & x_3^{(0)} \\ x_4^{(0)} & x_5^{(0)} & x_6^{(0)} & x_7^{(0)} \\ x_8^{(0)} & x_9^{(0)} & x_{10}^{(0)} & x_{11}^{(0)} \\ x_{12}^{(0)} & x_{13}^{(0)} & x_{14}^{(0)} & x_{15}^{(0)} \end{pmatrix} = \begin{pmatrix} c_0 & c_1 & c_2 & c_3 \\ k_0 & k_1 & k_2 & k_3 \\ k_4 & k_5 & k_6 & k_7 \\ t_0 & t_1 & v_0 & v_1 \end{pmatrix}. \tag{3}$$

The state matrix is modified in each round by a *Quarter Round Function* (QRF), denoted by $QR_{ChaCha}\left(x_a^{(r-1)}, x_b^{(r-1)}, x_c^{(r-1)}, x_d^{(r-1)}\right)$, which receives and updates 4 integers in the following way:

$$\begin{aligned} x_{a\prime}^{(r-1)} &= x_a^{(r-1)} + x_b^{(r-1)}; & x_{d\prime}^{(r-1)} &= (x_d^{(r-1)} \oplus x_{a\prime}^{(r-1)}) \lll 16; \\ x_{c\prime}^{(r-1)} &= x_c^{(r-1)} + x_{d\prime}^{(r-1)}; & x_{b\prime}^{(r-1)} &= (x_b^{(r-1)} \oplus x_{c\prime}^{(r-1)}) \lll 12; \\ x_a^{(r)} &= x_{a\prime}^{(r-1)} + x_{b\prime}^{(r-1)}; & x_d^{(r)} &= (x_{d\prime}^{(r-1)} \oplus x_a^{(r)}) \lll 8; \\ x_c^{(r)} &= x_{c\prime}^{(r-1)} + x_d^{(r)}; & x_b^{(r)} &= (x_{b\prime}^{(r-1)} \oplus x_c^{(r)}) \lll 7; \end{aligned} \tag{4}$$

One round of ChaCha is defined as 4 applications of the QRF. There is, however, a difference between odd and even rounds. For odd rounds, i.e. $r \in \{1, 3, 5, 7, ...\}$, $X^{(r)}$ is obtained from $X^{(r-1)}$ by applying $QR_{ChaCha}(a, b, c, d)$ with $(a, b, c, d) = \{(0, 4, 8, 12), (1, 5, 9, 13), (2, 6, 10, 14), (3, 7, 11, 15)\}$, and for even rounds $m \in \{2, 4, 6, ...\}$ from $QR_{ChaCha}(a, b, c, d)$ with $(a, b, c, d) = \{(0, 5, 10, 15), (1, 6, 11, 12), (2, 7, 8, 13), (3, 4, 9, 14)\}$.

The output of ChaCha20/R is then defined as the sum of the initial state with the state after R rounds $Z = X^{(0)} + X^{(R)}$. One should note that it is possible to parallelize each application of the QRF on each round and also that each round is reversible. Hence, we can compute $X^{(r-1)}$ from $X^{(r)}$.

Next, we introduce the concept of subrounds for ChaCha which will be very useful in the rest of this paper. First, we define the *Subround Function* (SRF), denoted by

$$\left(x_a^{[s]}, x_b^{[s]}, x_c^{[s]}, x_d^{[s]}\right) = SR_{ChaCha}\left(x_a^{[s-1]}, x_b^{[s-1]}, x_c^{[s-1]}, x_d^{[s-1]}, r_1, r_2\right),$$

which receives and updates 4 integers giving two rotation distances in the following way:

$$\begin{aligned} x_a^{[s]} &= x_a^{[s-1]} + x_b^{[s-1]}; & x_d^{[s]} &= (x_d^{[s-1]} \oplus x_a^{[s]}) \lll r_1; \\ x_c^{[s]} &= x_c^{[s-1]} + x_d^{[s]}; & x_b^{[s]} &= (x_b^{[s-1]} \oplus x_c^{[s]}) \lll r_2; \end{aligned} \tag{5}$$

Note that we can define the QRF in terms of the SRF. More precisely, we have that

$$QR_{ChaCha}(a, b, c, d) = SR_{ChaCha}(SR_{ChaCha}(a, b, c, d, 16, 12), 8, 7). \tag{6}$$

Therefore, it is easy to see that we can redefine ChaCha in terms of the SRF. Note that, giving our notation, for each round of ChaCha we have 2 subrounds being executed. In other words, if $X^{[2s]}$ denotes the state matrix after $2s$ subrounds, then we have that $X^{(s)} = X^{[2s]}$.

2.3   A Review of Differential-Linear Cryptanalysis

In this section, we describe the technique of Differential-Linear cryptanalysis as used to attack ChaCha. Let E be a cipher and suppose we can write $E = E_2 \circ E_1$, where E_1 and E_2 are sub ciphers, covering m and l rounds of the main cipher, respectively. We can apply an input difference $\mathcal{ID}$ $\Delta X^{(0)}$ in the sub cipher E_1 obtaining an output difference $\mathcal{OD}$ $\Delta X^{(m)}$ (see the left side of Fig. 1). The next step is to apply Linear Cryptanalysis to the second sub cipher E_2. Using masks Γ_m and Γ_{out}, we attempt to find good linear approximations covering the remaining l rounds of the cipher E. Applying this technique we can construct a differential-linear distinguisher covering all $m + l$ rounds of the cipher E. This is the main idea in Langford and Hellman's classical approach [20].

Alternatively the cipher E can be represented as the product of three ciphers, as follows: $E = E_3 \circ E_2 \circ E_1$. In this scenario, we can explore properties of the cipher in the first part E_1, and then apply a differential linear attack where we divide the differential part of the attack in two (see the right side of Fig. 1). Here, the $\mathcal{OD}$ from the sub cipher E_1 after r rounds, namely $\Delta X^{(r)}$, is the $\mathcal{ID}$ for the sub cipher E_2 which produces an output difference $\Delta X^{(m)}$. For more information in this regard, see [3].

It is important to understand how to compute the complexity of a differential-linear attack. We denote the differential of the state matrix as $\Delta X^{(r)} = X^{(r)} \oplus X'^{(r)}$ and the differential of individual words as $\Delta x_i^{(r)} = x_i^{(r)} \oplus x_i'^{(r)}$. Let $x_{i,j}^{(r)}$ denote the j-th bit of the i-th word of the state matrix after r rounds and let $\mathcal{J}$ be a set of bits. Also, let σ and σ' be linear combinations of bits in the set $\mathcal{J}$, i.e., $\sigma = \left(\bigoplus_{(i,j) \in \mathcal{J}} x_{i,j}^{(r)} \right), \sigma' = \left(\bigoplus_{(i,j) \in \mathcal{J}} x_{i,j}'^{(r)} \right)$. Then $\Delta\sigma = \left(\bigoplus_{(i,j) \in \mathcal{J}} \Delta x_{i,j}^{(r)} \right)$ is the linear combination of the differentials. We can write $\Pr\left[\Delta\sigma = 0 | \Delta X^{(0)}\right] = \frac{1}{2}(1 + \varepsilon_d)$, where ε_d is the differential correlation.

Using linear cryptanalysis, it is possible to go further and find new relations between the initial state and the state after $R > r$ rounds. To do so, let $\mathcal{L}$ denote another set of bits and define $\rho = \left(\bigoplus_{(i,j) \in \mathcal{L}} x_{i,j}^{(R)} \right), \rho' = \left(\bigoplus_{(i,j) \in \mathcal{L}} x_{i,j}'^{(R)} \right)$. Then, as before, $\Delta\rho = \left(\bigoplus_{(i,j) \in \mathcal{L}} \Delta x_{i,j}^{(R)} \right)$. We can define $\Pr[\sigma = \rho] = \frac{1}{2}(1 + \varepsilon_L)$, where ε_L is the linear correlation. We want to find γ such that $\Pr\left[\Delta\rho = 0 | \Delta X^{(0)}\right] = \frac{1}{2}(1 + \gamma)$. To compute γ, we write (to simplify the notation we make the conditional to $\Delta X^{(0)}$ implicit):

$$\Pr[\Delta\sigma = \Delta\rho] = \Pr[\sigma = \rho] \cdot \Pr\left[\sigma' = \rho'\right] + \Pr[\sigma = \bar{\rho}] \cdot \Pr\left[\sigma' = \overline{\rho'}\right] = \frac{1}{2}\left(1 + \varepsilon_L^2\right).$$

Then, $\Pr[\Delta \rho = 0] = \dfrac{1}{2}\left(1 + \varepsilon_d \cdot \varepsilon_L^2\right)$. Therefore, the differential-linear correlation is given by $\gamma = \varepsilon_d \cdot \varepsilon_L^2$, which defines a distinguisher with complexity $\mathcal{O}(\varepsilon_d^{-2}\varepsilon_L^{-4})$. For further information on differential-linear cryptanalysis we refer to [7].

2.4 Probabilistic Neutral Bits

This section reviews the attack of Aumasson et al. [2]. The attack first identifies good choices of truncated differentials, then it uses probabilistic backwards computation with the notion of Probabilistic Neutral Bits (PNB), and, finally, it estimates the complexity of the attack. In [2], the $\mathcal{ID}$ is defined for a single-bit difference $\Delta x_{i,j}^{(0)} = 1$ and a single-bit $\mathcal{OD}$ after r rounds $\Delta x_{p,q}^{(r)}$, such differential is denoted $(\Delta x_{p,q}^{(r)} | \Delta x_{i,j}^{(0)})$ and it has correlation ε_d.

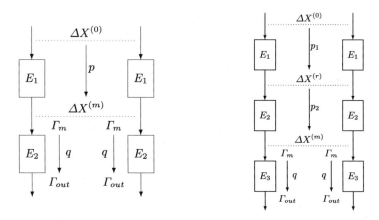

Fig. 1. A classical differential-linear distinguisher (on the left) and a differential-linear distinguisher with experimental evaluation of the correlation p_2 (on the right). E is divided into sub-ciphers $E = E_2 \circ E_1$, or $E = E_3 \circ E_2 \circ E_1$. In the differential part we may apply an $\mathcal{ID}$ $\Delta X^{(0)}$ in the sub cipher E_1 obtaining an $\mathcal{OD}$ $\Delta X^{(m)}$ after m rounds. The next step is to apply Linear Cryptanalysis using masks Γ_m and Γ_{out}. Applying this technique we can construct a differential-linear distinguisher of the cipher E. One way to improve attacks is to explore properties of the cipher in the first part E_1 (on the right), and then apply a differential linear attack where we divide the differential part of the attack in two.

Assume that the differential is fixed, and we observe outputs Z and Z' of $R = l + r$ rounds for nonce v, counter t and unknown key k. If we guess the key k we can invert l rounds of the algorithm to get $X^{(r)}$ and $X'^{(r)}$ and compute $\Delta x_{p,q}^{(r)}$. Then, let f be the function which executes this procedure, i.e., $f(k, v, t, Z, Z') = \Delta x_{p,q}^{(r)}$. Hence, we expect that $f(\hat{k}, v, t, Z, Z')$ has correlation ε_d only if $\hat{k} = k$. Then, if we have several pairs of Z and Z', it is possible to test our guesses for k. Thus, we can search only over a subkey of $m = 256 - n$ bits, provided we can find a function g that approximates f but only uses m key bits as input. Then, let $\bar{k}$ correspond to the subkey of m bits of key k and let f to be correlated to g with correlation ε_a, i.e., $\Pr(f(k, v, t, Z, Z') = g(\bar{k}, v, t, Z, Z')) = \frac{1}{2}(1 + \varepsilon_a)$.

If we denote the correlation of g by ε we can approximate ε by $\varepsilon_d \varepsilon_a$. The problem that remains is how to efficiently find such a function g. In [2], this is done by first identifying key bits that have little influence on the result of $f(k, v, t, Z, Z')$, these are called *probabilistic neutral bits* (PNBs). This is done by defining the *neutrality measure* $\gamma_{i,j}$ of a key bit $k_{i,j}$. After computing $\gamma_{i,j}$ (see [2] for a method of estimation), for all $i = (0, 1, ..., 7)$ and $j = (0, 1, ..., 31)$, we can define the set of significant key bits as $\Psi = \{(i,j) : \gamma_{i,j} \leq \gamma\}$ where γ is a threshold value, and then define our approximation g as $g(k_\Psi, v, t, Z, Z') = f(k^*, v, t, Z, Z')$ where k_Ψ is defined as the subkey with key bits in the set Ψ and k^* is computed from k_Ψ by setting $k_{i,j} = 0$ for all $(i, j) \notin \Psi$.

We refer to [2] for further information about the estimation of the data and time complexity of the attack and for further details on the described technique. We also note that Dey et al. [14] provided new formulas to compute the complexities, correcting some problems with previous formulas.

2.5 Linear Approximations for ARX Ciphers

To attack Salsa and ChaCha, only two simple approximations to the carry function have been used. Let $\Theta(x, y) = x \oplus y \oplus (x + y)$ be the carry function of the sum $x + y$. Define $\Theta_i(x, y)$ as the i-th bit of $\Theta(x, y)$. By definition, we have $\Theta_0(x, y) = 0$. Using Theorem 3 of Wallén [29], we can generate all possible linear approximations with a given correlation. In particular, at Eurocrypt 2021, Coutinho and Souza [11] used the following linear approximations:

$$\Pr(\Theta_i(x, y) = y_{i-1}) = \frac{1}{2}\left(1 + \frac{1}{2}\right), i > 0. \tag{7}$$

$$\Pr(\Theta_i(x, y) \oplus \Theta_{i-1}(x, y) = 0) = \frac{1}{2}\left(1 + \frac{1}{2}\right), i > 0. \tag{8}$$

As Coutinho and Souza explained, by combining Eqs. 7 and 8 when attacking ARX ciphers we can create a strategy to improve linear approximations when considering more rounds. The main idea is that when using Eq. 7 in one round we will create consecutive terms that can be expanded together using Eq. 8.

Next, we review previous linear approximations for Salsa and ChaCha.

Linear Approximations for Salsa. In the following, we review the work of [9] using the notation of Coutinho and Souza [11]. We can write the QRF equations of Salsa (Eq. 2) as

$$x_{b,i}^{(m)} = x_{b,i}^{(m-1)} \oplus x_{a,i-7}^{(m-1)} \oplus x_{d,i-7}^{(m-1)} \oplus \Theta_{i-7}(x_d^{(m-1)}, x_a^{(m-1)}) \tag{9}$$

$$x_{c,i}^{(m)} = x_{c,i}^{(m-1)} \oplus x_{b,i-9}^{(m)} \oplus x_{a,i-9}^{(m-1)} \oplus \Theta_{i-9}(x_a^{(m-1)}, x_b^{(m)}) \tag{10}$$

$$x_{d,i}^{(m)} = x_{d,i}^{(m-1)} \oplus x_{c,i-13}^{(m)} \oplus x_{b,i-13}^{(m)} \oplus \Theta_{i-13}(x_c^{(m)}, x_b^{(m)}) \tag{11}$$

$$x_{a,i}^{(m)} = x_{a,i}^{(m-1)} \oplus x_{d,i-18}^{(m)} \oplus x_{c,i-18}^{(m)} \oplus \Theta_{i-18}(x_d^{(m)}, x_c^{(m)}) \tag{12}$$

Inverting these equations and changing to positive indexes, we get:

$$x_{a,i}^{(m-1)} = \mathcal{L}_{a,i}^{(m)} \oplus \Theta_{i+14}(x_d^{(m)}, x_c^{(m)}) \tag{13}$$

$$x_{d,i}^{(m-1)} = \mathcal{L}_{d,i}^{(m)} \oplus \Theta_{i+19}(x_c^{(m)}, x_b^{(m)}) \tag{14}$$

$$x_{c,i}^{(m-1)} = \mathcal{L}_{c,i}^{(m)} \oplus \Theta_{i+23}(x_a^{(m-1)}, x_b^{(m)}) \oplus \Theta_{i+5}(x_d^{(m)}, x_c^{(m)}) \tag{15}$$

$$x_{b,i}^{(m-1)} = \mathcal{L}_{b,i}^{(m)} \oplus \Theta_{i+25}(x_d^{(m-1)}, x_a^{(m-1)}) \oplus \Theta_{i+7}(x_d^{(m)}, x_c^{(m)}) \oplus \Theta_{i+12}(x_c^{(m)}, x_b^{(m)}) \tag{16}$$

where

$$\mathcal{L}_{a,i}^{(m)} = x_{a,i}^{(m)} \oplus x_{d,i+14}^{(m)} \oplus x_{c,i+14}^{(m)} \tag{17}$$

$$\mathcal{L}_{b,i}^{(m)} = x_{b,i}^{(m)} \oplus x_{a,i+25}^{(m)} \oplus x_{d,i+7}^{(m)} \oplus x_{c,i+7}^{(m)} \oplus x_{d,i+25}^{(m)} \oplus x_{c,i+12}^{(m)} \oplus x_{b,i+12}^{(m)} \tag{18}$$

$$\mathcal{L}_{c,i}^{(m)} = x_{c,i}^{(m)} \oplus x_{b,i+23}^{(m)} \oplus x_{a,i+23}^{(m)} \oplus x_{d,i+5}^{(m)} \oplus x_{c,i+5}^{(m)} \tag{19}$$

$$\mathcal{L}_{d,i}^{(m)} = x_{d,i}^{(m)} \oplus x_{c,i+19}^{(m)} \oplus x_{b,i+19}^{(m)} \tag{20}$$

From Eq. (7) and these equations is possible to derive the following result:

Lemma 1. *For Salsa's QRF, the following linear approximations hold*

Equation	Probability	Condition
$x_{a,18}^{(m-1)} = \mathcal{L}_{a,18}^{(m)}$	1	-
$x_{a,i}^{(m-1)} = \mathcal{L}_{a,i}^{(m)} \oplus x_{c,i+13}^{(m)}$	$\frac{1}{2}(1 + \frac{1}{2})$	$i \neq 18$
$x_{d,13}^{(m-1)} = \mathcal{L}_{d,13}^{(m)}$	1	-
$x_{d,i}^{(m-1)} = \mathcal{L}_{d,i}^{(m)} \oplus x_{b,i+18}^{(m)}$	$\frac{1}{2}(1 + \frac{1}{2})$	$i \neq 13$
$x_{c,9}^{(m-1)} = \mathcal{L}_{c,9}^{(m)} \oplus x_{c,13}^{(m)}$	$\frac{1}{2}(1 + \frac{1}{2})$	-
$x_{c,27}^{(m-1)} = \mathcal{L}_{c,27}^{(m)} \oplus x_{b,17}^{(m)}$	$\frac{1}{2}(1 + \frac{1}{2})$	-
$x_{c,i}^{(m-1)} = \mathcal{L}_{c,i}^{(m)} \oplus x_{a,i+22}^{(m)}$	$\frac{1}{2}(1 - \frac{1}{4})$	$i \neq 9, 27$
$x_{b,7}^{(m-1)} = \mathcal{L}_{b,7}^{(m)} \oplus x_{c,13}^{(m)} \oplus x_{b,18}^{(m)}$	$\frac{1}{2}(1 + \frac{1}{4})$	-
$x_{b,20}^{(m-1)} = \mathcal{L}_{b,20}^{(m)} \oplus x_{a,12}^{(m)}$	$\frac{1}{2}(1 - \frac{1}{4})$	-
$x_{b,25}^{(m-1)} = \mathcal{L}_{b,25}^{(m)} \oplus x_{d,17}^{(m)}$	$\frac{1}{2}(1 - \frac{1}{4})$	-
$x_{b,i}^{(m-1)} = \mathcal{L}_{b,i}^{(m)} \oplus x_{a,i+24}^{(m)} \oplus x_{b,i+11}^{(m)}$	$\frac{1}{2}(1 - \frac{1}{8})$	$i \neq 7, 20, 25$

Proof. See Lemmas 2 and 7 of [9].   □

Linear Approximations for ChaCha. In this section, we review the work presented in [9,10], and in [11]. Since there are many results presented in these papers, here we focus only on the linear approximations that we will need throughout this paper.

Lemma 2. *(Lemma 9 of [9] combined with Lemma 6 of [11]) For one active input bit in round $m-1$ and multiple active output bits in round m, the following holds for $i > 0$.*

$$
\begin{aligned}
x_{b,i}^{(m-1)} &= x_{b,i+19}^{(m)} \oplus x_{c,i}^{(m)} \oplus x_{c,i+12}^{(m)} \oplus x_{d,i}^{(m)} \oplus x_{d,i-1}^{(m)}, && w.p.\ \tfrac{1}{2}\left(1+\tfrac{1}{2}\right) \\
x_{a,i}^{(m-1)} &= x_{a,i}^{(m)} \oplus x_{b,i+7}^{(m)} \oplus x_{b,i+19}^{(m)} \oplus x_{c,i+12}^{(m)} \oplus x_{d,i}^{(m)} \oplus \\
&\quad x_{b,i+6}^{(m)} \oplus x_{b,i+18}^{(m)} \oplus x_{c,i+11}^{(m)} \oplus x_{d,i-1}^{(m)}, && w.p.\ \tfrac{1}{2}\left(1+\tfrac{1}{2^3}\right) \\
x_{c,i}^{(m-1)} &= x_{a,i}^{(m)} \oplus x_{c,i}^{(m)} \oplus x_{d,i}^{(m)} \oplus x_{d,i+8}^{(m)} \oplus x_{a,i-1}^{(m)} \oplus x_{d,i+7}^{(m)} \oplus x_{d,i-1}^{(m)}, && w.p.\ \tfrac{1}{2}\left(1+\tfrac{1}{2^2}\right) \\
x_{d,i}^{(m-1)} &= x_{a,i}^{(m)} \oplus x_{a,i+16}^{(m)} \oplus x_{b,i+7}^{(m)} \oplus x_{c,i}^{(m)} \oplus x_{d,i+24}^{(m)} \oplus x_{c,i-1}^{(m)} \oplus x_{b,i+6}^{(m)}, && w.p.\ \tfrac{1}{2}\left(1+\tfrac{1}{2}\right)
\end{aligned}
$$

Proof. See [9] and [11]. We provide an alternative proof of this lemma in Sect. 3. □

Lemma 3. *(Lemma 10 of [11]) The following linear approximation holds with probability $\tfrac{1}{2}\left(1+\tfrac{1}{2^8}\right)$*

$$
\begin{aligned}
x_{3,0}^{(3)} \oplus x_{4,0}^{(3)} ={}& x_0^{(6)}[0,16] \oplus x_1^{(6)}[0,6,7,11,12,22,23] \oplus x_2^{(6)}[0,6,7,8,16,18, \\
& 19,24] \oplus x_4^{(6)}[7,13,19] \oplus x_5^{(6)}[7] \oplus x_6^{(6)}[7,13,14,19]\oplus \\
& x_7^{(6)}[6,7,14,15,26] \oplus x_8^{(6)}[0,7,8,19,31] \oplus x_9^{(6)}[0,6,12,26]\oplus \\
& x_{10}^{(6)}[0] \oplus x_{11}^{(6)}[6,7] \oplus x_{12}^{(6)}[0,11,12,19,20,30,31]\oplus \\
& x_{13}^{(6)}[0,14,15,24,26,27] \oplus x_{14}^{(6)}[8,25,26] \oplus x_{15}^{(6)}[24].
\end{aligned}
$$

Proof. See [11]. □

3   A More Effective Approach to Derive Linear Approximations for ChaCha

In this section, we propose a new approach to the derivation of linear approximations for ChaCha. To do so, instead of considering the QRF as in previous works, here we will consider the SRF, as defined in Eq. (5). We point out that we used the techniques of this section to implement automatic linear expansions of ChaCha in *CryptDances*.

3.1   New Framework: Linear Approximations to the SRF

From Eq. (5), we can write the SRF equations of ChaCha as

$$
\begin{aligned}
x_{a,i}^{[s]} &= x_{a,i}^{[s-1]} \oplus x_{b,i}^{[s-1]} \oplus \Theta_i(x_a^{[s-1]}, x_b^{[s-1]}); & x_{d,i+r_1}^{[s]} &= x_{d,i}^{[s-1]} \oplus x_{a,i}^{[s]}; \\
x_{c,i}^{[s]} &= x_{c,i}^{[s-1]} \oplus x_{d,i}^{[s]} \oplus \Theta_i(x_c^{[s-1]}, x_d^{[s]}); & x_{b,i+r_2}^{[s]} &= x_{b,i}^{[s-1]} \oplus x_{c,i}^{[s]};
\end{aligned} \tag{21}
$$

Inverting these equations, we get:

$$x_{b,i}^{[s-1]} = x_{b,i+r_2}^{[s]} \oplus x_{c,i}^{[s]} \tag{22}$$

$$x_{c,i}^{[s-1]} = x_{c,i}^{[s]} \oplus x_{d,i}^{[s]} \oplus \Theta_i(x_c^{[s-1]}, x_d^{[s]}) \tag{23}$$

$$x_{d,i}^{[s-1]} = x_{a,i}^{[s]} \oplus x_{d,i+r_1}^{[s]} \tag{24}$$

$$x_{a,i}^{[s-1]} = x_{a,i}^{[s]} \oplus x_{b,i+r_2}^{[s]} \oplus x_{c,i}^{[s]} \oplus \Theta_i(x_a^{[s-1]}, x_b^{[s-1]}) \tag{25}$$

Note that the expansions for $x_{b,i}^{[s-1]}$ and $x_{d,i}^{[s-1]}$ are deterministic. Therefore, we only need to focus on expansions for $x_{a,i}^{[s-1]}$ and $x_{c,i}^{[s-1]}$. To this end, consider the following three lemmas:

Lemma 4. *Consider the SR_{ChaCha} with rotation distances r_1 and r_2. Then we have that $x_{c,0}^{[s-1]} = x_{c,0}^{[s]} \oplus x_{d,0}^{[s]}$ and $x_{a,0}^{[s-1]} = x_{a,0}^{[s]} \oplus x_{b,r_2}^{[s]} \oplus x_{c,0}^{[s]}$.*

Proof. The proof follows from Eqs. (23) and (25) and using $\Theta_0(.) = 0$. $\square$

Lemma 5. *For one active input bit in subround $s - 1$ and multiple output bits in subround s, the following linear approximations hold with probability $\frac{1}{2}(1 + \frac{1}{2})$ for the function SR_{ChaCha} with rotation distances r_1 and r_2 when $i > 0$*

$$x_{c,i}^{[s-1]} = x_{c,i}^{[s]} \oplus x_{d,i}^{[s]} \oplus x_{d,i-1}^{[s]},$$
$$x_{a,i}^{[s-1]} = x_{a,i}^{[s]} \oplus x_{b,i+r_2}^{[s]} \oplus x_{c,i}^{[s]} \oplus x_{b,i+r_2-1}^{[s]} \oplus x_{c,i-1}^{[s]}.$$

Proof. The proof follows directly from the application of Eq. (7) in Eqs. (23) and (25). $\square$

Lemma 6. *For two active input bits in subround $s - 1$ and multiple output bits in subround s, the following linear approximations hold with probability $\frac{1}{2}(1 + \frac{1}{2})$ for the function SR_{ChaCha} with rotation distances r_1 and r_2*

$$x_{c,i}^{[s-1]} \oplus x_{c,i-1}^{[s-1]} = x_{c,i}^{[s]} \oplus x_{d,i}^{[s]} \oplus x_{c,i-1}^{[s]} \oplus x_{d,i-1}^{[s]},$$
$$x_{a,i}^{[s-1]} \oplus x_{a,i-1}^{[s-1]} = x_{a,i}^{[s]} \oplus x_{b,i+r_2}^{[s]} \oplus x_{c,i}^{[s]} \oplus x_{a,i-1}^{[s]} \oplus x_{b,i+r_2-1}^{[s]} \oplus x_{c,i-1}^{[s]}.$$

Proof. The proof follows directly from the application of Eq. (8) after expanding the left side of the equations with Eqs. (23) and (25). $\square$

As we will show, from these three Lemmas it is possible to reproduce previous works. Before that, we show an additional lemma that we use to improve previous results.

Lemma 7. *For two active input bits in subround $s - 1$ and multiple output bits in subround s, the following linear approximations hold with probability $\frac{1}{2}(1 + \frac{1}{2})$ for the function SR_{ChaCha} with rotation distances r_1 and r_2*

$$x_{c,i}^{[s-1]} \oplus x_{c,i-1}^{[s-1]} = x_{c,i}^{[s]} \oplus x_{d,i}^{[s]},$$
$$x_{a,i}^{[s-1]} \oplus x_{a,i-1}^{[s-1]} = x_{a,i}^{[s]} \oplus x_{b,i+r_2}^{[s]} \oplus x_{c,i}^{[s]}.$$

Proof. See the extended version of this paper. $\square$

Strategies. As the reader may have noticed, Lemmas 6 and 7 are actually expanding the same pair of bits. Then we may ask which is the best choice. However, it depends on the situation. As a general rule, we always look for minimizing the number of active bits in the equations. That is because fewer terms means fewer expansions which means a higher correlation (usually). From this assertion, the reader might conclude that Lemma 7 is better. Notice, however, that adjacent bits are always expanded together (due to Lemma 6) and should be counted as one. Therefore, the best rule will be the one that results in other bits being canceled (see the extended version of this paper for a complete example). We conclude that each situation needs to be evaluated individually by considering all options to reach the best possible linear approximation.

3.2 Deriving Linear Approximations of Previous Works Using the New Approach

The new framework proposed in Sect. 3 is simpler to understand and to use when compared with previous works. For example, the methods of Coutinho and Souza [11] encompasses at least 18 different rules to derive linear approximations for ChaCha. Of course, being simpler is not enough, as the proposed framework should also be at least as effective. Our claim is that using Lemmas 4, 5, and 6 is possible to derive most of the linear approximations (if not all) of previous works. Of course, proving that to each one of them individually would be an extremely tedious task. Therefore, here we will just prove this result to Lemma 2 that is the base to generate almost all linear approximations of ChaCha in the literature, we leave the rest as a conjecture.

Proposition 1. *Lemma 2 is a consequence of Lemmas 5 and 6.*

Proof. See the extended version of this paper. □

3.3 Improve Linear Approximations and Differential-Linear Distinguisher for ChaCha

In this section, we improve the best differential-linear distinguisher against ChaCha by improving its linear part by using the framework of Sect. 3.1. We highlight that the improvements are achieved through an intelligent use of Lemma 7. The new result is given by the following lemma.

Lemma 8. *The following linear approximation holds with probability* $\frac{1}{2}\left(1 + \frac{1}{2^{53}}\right)$

$$x_{3,0}^{[6]} \oplus x_{4,0}^{[6]} = x_0^{[14]}[0,3,4,7,8,11,12,14,15,18,20,27,28] \oplus x_1^{[14]}[0,5,7,8,10,14,$$
$$15,16,22,23,24,25,27,30,31] \oplus x_2^{[14]}[7,9,10,16,19,25,26] \oplus x_3^{[14]}[6,7,8,24] \oplus$$
$$x_4^{[14]}[0,2,3,5,18,22,23,27] \oplus x_5^{[14]}[1,2,9,10,13,14,18,21,22,25,29] \oplus x_6^{[14]}[0,2,$$
$$3,7,10,11,13,14,19,22,23,25,27,31] \oplus x_7^{[14]}[1,2,13,25,26,30,31] \oplus x_8^{[14]}[8,11,$$
$$13,20,25,27,28,30,31] \oplus x_9^{[14]}[2,3,6,7,11,14,15,18,23,27] \oplus x_{10}^{[14]}[0,3,4,6,8,$$
$$12,13,14,18,20,23,25,27,28] \oplus x_{11}^{[14]}[6,14,15,18,19,23,24,27] \oplus$$
$$x_{12}^{[14]}[3,4,6,11,13,22,23,24,26,27,30,31] \oplus x_{13}^{[14]}[1,2,6,7,8,13,14,16,$$
$$18,20,22,23,24,25,26] \oplus x_{14}^{[14]}[0,7,13,14,15,16,17,18,23,24] \oplus x_{15}^{[14]}[16,25,26]$$

Proof. We present just a sketch of the proof, for the complete proof see the extended version of this paper. We start from the linear approximation of Lemma 3. Notice that since we are transitioning from round 6 to 7 (subrounds 12 to 14), we have $(a,b,c,d) \in \{(0,4,8,12),(1,5,9,13),(2,6,10,14),(3,7,11,15)\}$. Therefore, we can divide the bits of the equation in 4 distinct groups:

- Group I - $x_0^{[12]}[0,16], x_4^{[12]}[7,13,19], x_8^{[12]}[0,7,8,19,31],\ x_{12}^{[12]}[0,11,12,19,20,$ $30,31]$.
- Group   II   - $x_1^{[12]}[0,6,7,11,12,22,23],\quad x_5^{[12]}[7],\quad x_9^{[12]}[0,6,12,26],$ $x_{13}^{[12]}[0,14,15,24,26,27]$.
- Group   III   - $x_2^{[12]}[0,6,7,8,16,18,19,24], x_6^{[12]}[7,13,14,19],\quad x_{10}^{[12]}[0],$ $x_{14}^{[12]}[8,25,26]$.
- Group IV - $x_7^{[12]}[6,7,14,15,26],\ x_{11}^{[12]}[6,7], x_{15}^{[12]}[24]$.

We divide the proof for each group, and the proof for Group I and Group IV is identical as the one of Lemma 11 of [11], with probabilities $\frac{1}{2}\left(1+\frac{1}{2^{12}}\right)$ and $\frac{1}{2}\left(1+\frac{1}{2^4}\right)$, respectively. For Group II, it is possible to show that

$$x_1^{[12]}[0,6,7,11,12,22,23] \oplus x_5^{[12]}[7] \oplus x_9^{[12]}[0,6,12,26] \oplus$$
$$x_{13}^{[12]}[0,14,15,24,26,27] = x_1^{[14]}[0,5,7,8,10,14,15,16,22,23,24,25,27,$$
$$30,31] \oplus x_5^{[14]}[1,2,9,10,13,14,18,21,22,25,29] \oplus x_9^{[14]}[2,3,6,7,11,14, \quad (26)$$
$$15,18,23,27] \oplus x_{13}^{[14]}[1,2,6,7,8,13,14,16,18,20,22,23,24,25,26],$$

with probability $\frac{1}{2}\left(1+\frac{1}{2^{14}}\right)$. And for Group III, we get

$$x_2^{[12]}[0,6,7,8,16,18,19,24] \oplus x_6^{[12]}[7,13,14,19] \oplus x_{10}^{[12]}[0] \oplus x_{14}^{[12]}[8,25,26] =$$
$$x_2^{[14]}[7,9,10,16,19,25,26] \oplus x_6^{[14]}[0,2,3,7,10,11,13,14,19,22,23,25,27,31] \oplus$$
$$x_{10}^{[14]}[0,3,4,6,8,12,13,14,18,20,23,25,27,28] \oplus$$
$$x_{14}^{[14]}[0,7,13,14,15,16,17,18,23,24],$$

$$(27)$$

with probability $\frac{1}{2}\left(1+\frac{1}{2^{15}}\right)$. Aggregating the correlation via the Piling-up Lemma completes the proof.   □

Computational Result 1. *The linear approximations of Eqs. (26) and (27) hold computationally with $\varepsilon_{L_2} = 0.000201 \approx 2^{-12.31}$ and $\varepsilon_{L_3} = 0.000141 \approx 2^{-12.813}$, respectively. These correlations were verified using 2^{42} random samples.*

Finally, we compute the differential-linear distinguisher. For that, we use the differential correlation $\varepsilon_d = 0.00048$ for $(a, b) = (3, 4)$ described in [10], and the Computational Results 1, 2 and 5 of [11] for linear correlations $\varepsilon_{L_0} = 0.006942$, $\varepsilon_{L_1} = 0.000301$, and $\varepsilon_{L_4} = 0.0625$, respectively. Additionally, we use our Computational Result 1 for the linear correlations ε_{L_2} and ε_{L_3}. From that, we get $\varepsilon_d(\varepsilon_{L_0}\varepsilon_{L_1}\varepsilon_{L_2}\varepsilon_{L_3}\varepsilon_{L_4})^2 \approx 2^{-107}$ which gives us a distinguisher for 7 rounds of ChaCha with complexity approximately 2^{214}.

4 Bidirectional Linear Expansions

In this section, we propose a new technique called Bidirectional Linear Expansions (BLE). This section is divided in three parts: in Sect. 4.1 we present BLE. In Sects. 4.2 and 4.3, we use BLE to study Salsa and ChaCha, respectively.

4.1 Proposed Technique

Previous works on the cryptanalysis of Salsa and ChaCha used an intensive computational approach to find significant correlations for the differential part of the attacks. To do so, authors considered an $\mathcal{ID}$ $\Delta X^{(0)}$ and used several random simulations to estimate a correlation for a single bit $\Delta x_{i,j}^{(m)}$. From this point, this single bit was expanded into several bits using linear approximations, like in the following diagram:

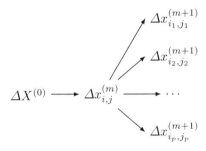

In this work, we propose a different approach. More precisely, we expand a single bit in both forward and backward directions. Therefore, in the differential part we need to find a correlation for a combination of bits instead of just one. This approach leads to the worst differential correlations, however it improves the linear correlations. Since the linear part has a higher weight on the complexity of the attack, the proposed technique leads to better results overall. We illustrate the proposed technique in the following diagram:

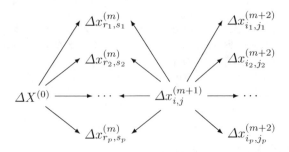

This technique is useful to find differentials that reach more rounds. The reason is that when we try to find differentials experimentally we have two parameters to set: (1) the number of differentials to be tested D; and (2) the number of random samples N to estimate the differential. Since for each differential we need to execute the algorithm two times, then we need $2DN$ executions to try to find successful differential correlations. However, as the number of rounds increases, the correlations decreases, then we have to increase N accordingly. Because of that, the computation quickly becomes infeasible.

Using BLE we can leverage the backward linear approximation to search for correlations in the previous round. For example, suppose that we compute all possible single bit differentials for m rounds of ChaCha and that we have a backward linear approximation $x_{i,j}^{(m+1)} = x_{r_1,s_1}^{(m)} \oplus x_{r_2,s_2}^{(m)} \oplus ... \oplus x_{r_p,s_p}^{(m)}$. Then, we can use the Piling-up Lemma to aggregate the correlation for each single bit from the previous round, achieving a differential correlation for further rounds. Mathematically, if we define $\Pr(\Delta x_{r_k,s_k}^{(m)}|\mathcal{ID}) = \frac{1}{2}(1+\varepsilon_k)$, and $\Pr(\Delta x_{i,j}^{(m+1)}|\mathcal{ID}) = \frac{1}{2}(1+\varepsilon_d)$, then we can estimate $\varepsilon_d = \prod_{k=1}^{p} \varepsilon_k$.

4.2   Applying BLE to Salsa

Next, we use the techniques proposed in Sect. 4.1 to improve the attacks against Salsa. This section is divided in three parts: first we present the first single bit differential reaching 5 rounds of Salsa. Then, we present new linear approximations for Salsa, starting from the proposed differential. Finally, we use these results to improve attacks against Salsa.

Proposed Differential for 5 Rounds of Salsa. In this section, we present a new single bit differential correlation for 5 rounds of Salsa, constructed by applying the technique proposed in the previous section. To do so, first notice from Eq. (9), that we can write $x_{b,7}^{(5)} = x_{b,7}^{(4)} \oplus x_{a,0}^{(4)} \oplus x_{d,0}^{(4)}$, with probability 1, where $(a, b, d) \in \{(0, 4, 12), (5, 13, 1), (10, 2, 6), (15, 7, 11)\}$. Using this relationship, we will find a correlation for a bit in the fifth round $x_{b,7}^{(5)}$ by combining the correlation of three other bits in the fourth round.

To achieve this result, we start from the single bit $\mathcal{ID}$ of $\Delta x_{7,31}^{(0)} = 1$, proposed by Aumasson et al. [2], which is the one that provides the highest correlations presented in the literature. However, instead of relying on computational results only, we expanded the first round theoretically and used the techniques proposed by Beierle et al. [3] (see Sect. 2.3) to find differentials with amplified probabilities. Here, we apply the techniques proposed by Lipmaa and Moriai on efficient algorithms for computing differential properties of addition [22]. In the referred work, the authors define the Differential Probability of Addition (DPA) modulo 2^n as a triplet of two input and one output differences, denoted as $(\alpha, \beta \to \gamma)$, where $\alpha, \beta, \gamma \in \mathbb{F}_2^n$, and is defined as $\mathrm{DP}^+(\delta) = \mathrm{DP}^+(\alpha, \beta \to \gamma) := \Pr_{x,y}[(x + y) \oplus ((x \oplus \alpha) + (y \oplus \beta)) = \gamma]$.

One important question is how to find γ such that $\mathrm{DP}^+(\delta)$ is maximum given α and β. In other words, we want to find $\mathrm{DP}^+_{\max}(\alpha, \beta) := \max_\gamma \mathrm{DP}^+(\alpha, \beta \to \gamma)$. In [22], the authors provide two important algorithms to compute $\mathrm{DP}^+_{\max}(\alpha, \beta)$. Specifically, Algorithm 3 of [22] returns all (α, β)-optimal output differences γ, and Algorithm 4 of [22] finds an (α, β)-optimal γ in log-time.

Thus, starting from the $\mathcal{ID}$ given by $\Delta X^{(0)}$, we propagated the differential using the algorithms from [22] and chose the one that minimized the hamming weight, from this we get (in hexadecimal notation):

$$\Psi = \Delta X^{(1)} = \begin{pmatrix} 0\ 0\ 0 & 0x00000000 \\ 0\ 0\ 0 & 0x80000000 \\ 0\ 0\ 0 & 0x00001000 \\ 0\ 0\ 0 & 0x40020000 \end{pmatrix}.$$

The probability that $\Delta X^{(0)}$ leads to $\Delta X^{(1)}$ is 2^{-1}. To compute this probability, we used Algorithm 2 of [22]. At this point, we used the strategy of Beierle et al. [3] (see Sect. 2.3) to find differentials with amplified probabilities. We may apply this technique because, as with ChaCha, the QRF of Salsa is independently applied to each column in the first round. Therefore, when the output difference of one QRF is restricted, the input of the other three QR functions is trivially independent of the output difference. It implies that we have 96 independent bits, and we can easily amplify the probability of the differential-linear distinguisher.

We summarize the differential part combined with the backward linear expansion of the proposed attacks in the diagram of Fig. 2.

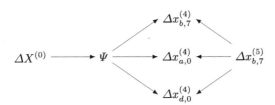

Fig. 2. Differential part of the proposed attack.

Considering Fig. 2, we need to estimate the transition probability from Ψ to $\Delta x_{b,7}^{(5)}$. We performed this task computationally, and we achieved the best results when considering $b = 4$. Thus, consider the following computational result:

Computational Result 2. *The following differentials were found computationally using 2^{45} random samples.*

$\mathcal{ID}$	$\mathcal{OD}$	*Correlation*
$\Delta X^{(1)} = \Psi$	$\Delta x_{0,0}^{(4)}$	-0.00000159
$\Delta X^{(1)} = \Psi$	$\Delta x_{4,7}^{(4)}$	-0.00085
$\Delta X^{(1)} = \Psi$	$\Delta x_{12,0}^{(4)}$	0.000167

From this result, we can use the Piling-Up Lemma to reach a differential correlation from round 1 to round 5 of Salsa. More precisely, we can write

$$\Pr(\Delta x_{4,7}^{(5)} = 0 | \Delta X^{(1)} = \Psi) = \frac{1}{2}(1 + \varepsilon_d), \tag{28}$$

where $\varepsilon_d \approx 2^{-42.01}$. Unfortunately, checking this correlation is computationally infeasible as it would require approximately 2^{84} samples. We note, however, that we tested if the Piling-up Lemma holds using this technique for ChaCha and Salsa for smaller correlations in fewer rounds. In our tests, the observed correlation was always higher than predicted, therefore, our attack using this correlation is probably better than what we report in this paper.

In the next section, we will present the linear expansion for the bit $x_{b,7}^{(5)}$ to complete the differential-linear distinguisher.

New Linear Approximations for Salsa. First, we propose the following Lemma:

Lemma 9. *For two active input bits in round $m - 1$ and multiple active output bits in round m of Salsa, the following holds for $i \notin \mathcal{I}$*

$$x_{\lambda,i}^{(m-1)} \oplus x_{\lambda,i-1}^{(m-1)} = \mathcal{L}_{\lambda,i}^{(m)} \oplus \mathcal{L}_{\lambda,i-1}^{(m)}, \; w.p. \; \frac{1}{2}\left(1 + \frac{1}{2^\sigma}\right),$$

where $(\lambda, \sigma, \mathcal{I}) \in \{(a, 1, \{18\}), (b, 3, \{7, 20, 25\}), (c, 2, \{9, 27\}), (d, 1, \{13\})\}$ and $\mathcal{L}$ is given in Eqs. (17)–(20).

Proof. This proof follows from Eqs. (13)–(16) by noting that always we have pair with the form $\Theta_i(x) \oplus \Theta_{i-1}(x)$. When $i > 1$ we apply the approximation of Eq. (8) to get $\Theta_i(x) \oplus \Theta_{i-1}(x) = 0$ with probability $\frac{1}{2}(1 + \frac{1}{2})$. When $i = 1$ we use the fact that $\Theta_0(x) = 0$ to get $\Theta_1(x) \oplus \Theta_0(x) = \Theta_1(x) = 0$ again with probability $\frac{1}{2}(1 + \frac{1}{2})$. When $i = 0$, $\Theta_i(x) \oplus \Theta_{i-1}(x) \neq 0$, thus we exclude these indexes. All that is left is to use the Piling-Up Lemma to combine the probabilities. □

Next, we consider new linear approximations to the bit $x_{4,7}^{(5)}$.

Lemma 10. *The following linear approximation holds with probability* $\frac{1}{2}\left(1 - \frac{1}{2^6}\right)$

$$x_{4,7}^{(5)} = x_0^{(7)}[0] \oplus x_2^{(7)}[12,13] \oplus x_3^{(7)}[17] \oplus x_4^{(7)}[7,18,19] \oplus x_6^{(7)}[25,26] \oplus x_7^{(7)}[26,31]\oplus$$
$$x_8^{(7)}[13,14,19] \oplus x_{11}^{(7)}[31] \oplus x_{12}^{(7)}[0,14] \oplus x_{14}^{(7)}[12,13] \oplus x_{15}^{(7)}[16,17].$$

Proof. From $x_{4,7}^{(5)}$ we use the expansion for $x_{d,i}$ of Lemma 1 to get $x_{4,7}^{(5)} = x_{4,7}^{(6)} \oplus$ $x_{6,25}^{(6)} \oplus x_{6,26}^{(6)} \oplus x_{7,26}^{(6)}$, with probability $\frac{1}{2}\left(1 + \frac{1}{2}\right)$. Then, we use the expansion for $x_{b,7}$ and $x_{c,i}$ of Lemma 1 to get $x_{4,7}^{(6)} = \mathcal{L}_{4,7}^{(m)} \oplus x_{8,13}^{(m)} \oplus x_{4,18}^{(m)}$ with probability $\frac{1}{2}\left(1 + \frac{1}{4}\right)$, and $x_{7,26}^{(6)} = \mathcal{L}_{7,26}^{(m)} \oplus x_{15,16}^{(m)}$ with probability $\frac{1}{2}\left(1 - \frac{1}{4}\right)$. Additionally, using Lemma 9 we get $x_{6,25}^{(6)} \oplus x_{6,26}^{(6)} = \mathcal{L}_{6,25}^{(7)} \oplus \mathcal{L}_{6,26}^{(7)}$, with probability $\frac{1}{2}\left(1 + \frac{1}{2}\right)$. Finally, using the Piling-Up Lemma to combine the probabilities completes the proof. □

Lemma 11. *The following linear approximation holds with probability* $\frac{1}{2}\left(1 + \frac{1}{2^{34}}\right)$

$$x_{4,7}^{(5)} = x_0^{(8)}[0,3,4] \oplus x_2^{(8)}[4,12,14,17,18] \oplus x_3^{(8)}[14,18] \oplus x_4^{(8)}[0,1,4,7,31]\oplus$$
$$x_5^{(8)}[16,17,18,19,21,22] \oplus x_6^{(8)}[17,22] \oplus x_7^{(8)}[0,1,4]\oplus$$
$$x_8^{(8)}[6,11,13,14,18,24] \oplus x_9^{(8)}[6,18,19] \oplus x_{10}^{(8)}[4,5,9,10,23,24]\oplus$$
$$x_{11}^{(8)}[4,5,11,31] \oplus x_{12}^{(8)}[11,12,14,25,26,30,31] \oplus x_{13}^{(8)}[0,7,12,21,26,30]\oplus$$
$$x_{14}^{(8)}[12,13,21,25,30,31] \oplus x_{15}^{(8)}[6,7,16,17,24,25].$$

Proof. See the extended version of this paper. □

Additionally, we verified the theoretical results of Lemmas 10 and 11 computationally. In particular, for Lemma 11 the experiment is divided in 4 parts leading to the correlations $\varepsilon_{L_1}, \varepsilon_{L_2}, \varepsilon_{L_3}$ and ε_{L_4} (for more details, see the extended version of the paper).

Computational Result 3. *The linear approximation of Lemma 10 holds computationally with* $\varepsilon_{L_0} = -0.015627 \approx -2^{-5.999}$. *This correlation was verified using* 2^{38} *random samples.*

Computational Result 4. *The linear approximations for Lemma 11 hold computationally with correlations* $\varepsilon_{L_1} = 0.083980 \approx 2^{-3.57}$, $\varepsilon_{L_2} = 0.007814 \approx 2^{-6.99}$, $\varepsilon_{L_3} = 0.006368 \approx 2^{-7.29}$, $\varepsilon_{L_4} = 0.002234 \approx 2^{-8.81}$, *respectively. These correlations were verified using* 2^{38} *random samples.*

New Attacks Against Salsa. Using the linear approximations of Lemma 10 and Lemma 11, the differential correlation $\varepsilon_d \approx -2^{-42.01}$ given in Eq. (28), and the estimated correlations from the Computational Results 3 and 4, we get $\varepsilon_d(\varepsilon_{L_0})^2 \approx 2^{-53.99}$ and $\varepsilon_d(\varepsilon_{L_0}\varepsilon_{L_1}\varepsilon_{L_2}\varepsilon_{L_3}\varepsilon_{L_4})^2 \approx 2^{-107.31}$ which gives us a distinguisher for 7 and 8 rounds of Salsa with complexity less than $2^{-107.98}$ and

$2^{-214.62}$, respectively. As in [3], we have to repeat this attack 2 times on average because of the transition probability from $\Delta X^{(0)}$ to $\Delta X^{(1)} = \Psi$. Therefore, we have a distinguisher with data and time complexity of $2^{108.98}$ for Salsa20/7 and $2^{215.62}$ for Salsa20/8.

Additionally, it is straightforward to combine the new differential-linear distinguisher for 5 rounds presented in Eq. 28 with the technique of PNB presented in Sect. 2.4. More precisely, to use the differential correlation for $\Delta x_{4,7}^{(5)}$, we used the variation of PNB attack described by Beierle in [3]. Thus, consider $(x_{4,7}^{(5)}|\Delta X^{(1)} = \Psi)$. To attack 8 rounds, we need to go back 3 rounds to reach the desired differential. In this case, using $\gamma = 0.3$ we found 152 PNBs, and we obtained $\varepsilon_a = 0.000305$. As in [3], we have to repeat this attack 2 times on average because of the transition probability from $\Delta X^{(0)}$ to $\Delta X^{(1)} = \Psi$. Thus, the final attack has data complexity of $2^{113.14}$ and time complexity $2^{217.14}$.

4.3   Applying BLE Against ChaCha

Finding differentials for 3.5 rounds of ChaCha experimentally is very difficult, only a few have been presented in the literature [3,11]. By searching for all possible single bit differentials for 3 rounds of ChaCha we were able to find more than 1000 new differentials using the backward expansion. Unfortunately, we were not able to improve attacks in this case.

5   Forró: a Novel Latin Dance

Although they have a very similar structure, the literature (including this work) suggests that ChaCha is safer than Salsa. Therefore, a natural question that arises is if we can do better with fewer operations, it turns out the answer is yes, and we show how with the design of a new stream cipher named Forró. To do that, in Sect. 5.1 we will introduce a new concept which we call *Pollination*. Then, in Sects. 5.2, 5.3, and 5.4 we present the design, security, and performance of Forró, respectively.

5.1   Pollination

In this section, we propose a new technique that we call *Pollination*. We chose this name as an analogy to the real Pollination in nature: when a bee collects nectar from a flower, the pollen sticks to the hairs of her body. When she visits the next flower, some of this pollen is rubbed off onto the stigma, making fertilization possible. Here, our idea is to use the element that is likely to maximize confusion and diffusion (we call this best element *pollen*) to bring non-linearity and confusion to other elements in the state matrix.

Actually, one of the reasons behind the improved diffusion of ChaCha when compared to Salsa is, in fact, pollination. Since the QRF function updates one element after the other, using the previously updated element as input, then it is a natural consequence that the element updated last $(x_b^{(r)})$ has higher diffusion. In ChaCha, the pattern of application of the QRF actually means that the elements in the second row (which are the parameter $x_b^{(r)}$ for each QRF application), are used to update the first element in the next round. Salsa does not have such a property, hence the improved diffusion of ChaCha.

ChaCha achieves pollination from one round to another, however, it fails to do so within each round because the QRF is applied independently in each column or diagonal. Thus, it is possible to have more diffusion with fewer operations if we create a chain of pollination from one application of the QRF to the other. It can be argued that we will lose parallelism in each round, however, as we will show later, the improved diffusion will allow the same security in fewer rounds, reducing the total number of operations. Also, in Sect. 5.4, we show that there is another way to explore concurrency inside the processor to achieve better performance.

5.2   Design

Forró's Round Function. To deliver pollination from one round to the other we propose to include an extra parameter into the QRF. Nevertheless, we want to maintain (or to decrease) the number of arithmetic operations to achieve competitive performance. Notice that each rotation in Eq. (4) actually makes the same element be updated twice in a row, thus we could update more elements if we had fewer rotations.

Actually, in [6], Bernstein asked the question of whether there should be fewer rotations in the QRF, because rotations account for about $1/3$ of the integer operations in Salsa (and also in ChaCha), he wrote:

"If rotations are simulated by shift-shift-xor (as they are on the Ultra-SPARC and with XMM instructions) then they account for about $1/2$ of the integer operations in Salsa20. Replacing some of the rotations with a comparable number of additions might achieve comparable diffusion in less time."

With those ideas in mind, we define the subround function $X^{[m]} = SR_{forró}(a, b, c, d, e, X^{[m-1]})$ as the following set of operations over indexes a, b, c, d and e

$$
\begin{aligned}
x_d'^{(m-1)} &= x_d^{(m-1)} + x_e^{(m-1)}; & x_c'^{(m-1)} &= x_c^{(m-1)} \oplus x_d'^{(m-1)}; \\
x_b'^{(m-1)} &= \left(x_b^{(m-1)} + x_c'^{(m-1)}\right) \lll r_1; \\
x_a'^{(m-1)} &= x_a^{(m-1)} + x_b'^{(m-1)}; & x_e^{(m)} &= x_e^{(m-1)} \oplus x_a'^{(m-1)}; \\
x_d^{(m)} &= \left(x_d'^{(m-1)} + x_e^{(m)}\right) \lll r_2; \\
x_c^{(m)} &= x_c'^{(m-1)} + x_d^{(m)}; & x_b^{(m)} &= x_b'^{(m-1)} \oplus x_c^{(m)}; \\
x_a^{(m)} &= \left(x_a'^{(m-1)} + x_b^{(m)}\right) \lll r_3;
\end{aligned}
\tag{29}
$$

where $r_1 = 10, r_2 = 27$ and $r_3 = 8$.

Notice that SR_{forro} has a total of 12 operations, just like QR_{ChaCha}, but fewer rotations. Also, notice that SR_{forro} is asymmetric in the sense that of all elements there is one, namely $x_e^{(r)}$ that is updated less frequently than the others. However, this behavior is actually acceptable since $x_e^{(r)}$ is the element used for pollination, thus its job is to provide non-linearity and confusion and not to gain more necessarily. In addition, except in the first subround, $x_e^{(r)}$ is always updated in the previous subround. Finally, notice that as the element $x_a^{(r)}$ is the last to be updated, then it will likely have the more complex boolean functions in comparison to $x_b^{(r)}, x_c^{(r)}, x_d^{(r)}$ and $x_e^{(r)}$, therefore $x_a^{(r)}$ will become the pollen for the next application of SR_{forro}.

We define each round of Forró in terms of its subrounds. More precisely, each round has 4 subrounds, thus we have $X^{(r)} = X^{[4r]}$ (see Sect. 2.2). Then, in an odd round, when $r \in \{1, 3, 5, 7, ...\}$, $X^{(r)}$ is defined from $X^{(r-1)}$ in the following manner

$$X^{[4r-3]} = SR(0, 4, 8, 12, 3, X^{[4r-4]}); \quad X^{[4r-2]} = SR(1, 5, 9, 13, 0, X^{[4r-3]});$$
$$X^{[4r-1]} = SR(2, 6, 10, 14, 1, X^{[4r-2]}); \quad X^{[4r]} = SR(3, 7, 11, 15, 2, X^{[4r-1]});$$
$$(30)$$

and for even rounds $r \in \{2, 4, 6, 8, , ...\}$ from

$$X^{[4r-3]} = SR(0, 5, 10, 15, 3, X^{[4r-4]}); \quad X^{[4r-2]} = SR(1, 6, 11, 12, 0, X^{[4r-3]});$$
$$X^{[4r-1]} = SR(2, 7, 8, 13, 1, X^{[4r-2]}); \quad X^{[4r]} = SR(3, 4, 9, 14, 2, X^{[4r-1]});$$
$$(31)$$

Initialization. To initialize the state matrix we have 16 integers available, being 8 key words, 2 nonce words, 2 counter words and 4 constants. All positions in the state matrix are different in terms of diffusion and whether it is used sooner or later. Forró's initialization matrix is defined by

$$X^{(0)} = \begin{pmatrix} x_0^{(0)} & x_1^{(0)} & x_2^{(0)} & x_3^{(0)} \\ x_4^{(0)} & x_5^{(0)} & x_6^{(0)} & x_7^{(0)} \\ x_8^{(0)} & x_9^{(0)} & x_{10}^{(0)} & x_{11}^{(0)} \\ x_{12}^{(0)} & x_{13}^{(0)} & x_{14}^{(0)} & x_{15}^{(0)} \end{pmatrix} = \begin{pmatrix} k_0 & k_1 & k_2 & k_3 \\ t_0 & t_1 & c_0 & c_1 \\ k_4 & k_5 & k_6 & k_7 \\ v_0 & v_1 & c_2 & c_3 \end{pmatrix}. \quad (32)$$

When comparing Eqs. (3) and (32), one can notice that Forró's initialization is different from ChaCha's. In differential cryptanalysis usually the attacker is allowed to choose arbitrary values to t_0, t_1, v_0 and v_1, thus it is a good idea to update these values as soon as possible allowing the differential to be propagated faster decreasing the probability of a differential characteristic. Thus, we defined the initialization in such a way that t_0, t_1, v_0 and v_1 are used in the first two columns, however, separated by the application of parts of the key.

Rotations. The rotation distances for Forró are set as $r_1 = 10, r_2 = 27$ and $r_3 = 8$. Most authors of ARX algorithms in the literature do not justify the choice of the rotation distances with a numerical argument. It is generally argued that it is difficult to find bad rotation distances for ARX. Therefore, authors tend to choose aligned rotation distances (multiple of 8) because these are much faster than unaligned rotation distances on many non-64-bit architectures. For example, many 8-bit microcontrollers have only 1-bit shifts of bytes, so rotation by 3 bits is particularly expensive. Even 64-bit systems can benefit from alignment, for example, when a sequence of shift-shift-xor can be replaced by SSSE3's pshufb byte-shuffling instruction [1].

On the other hand, it may be possible to improve the security of the algorithm by carefully studying the behavior of the cipher when each combination of rotation distances is evaluated. This approach could allow for a reduced number of rounds to achieve the desired security. Hence, this approach could also improve performance. For example, in [12] authors showed that changing the rotation distances of ChaCha to $(19, 17, 25, 11)$ improved the resistance of ChaCha against known attacks.

Here, the rotation distances were defined following a similar approach as proposed in [12], with some adaptations. First, we define $\mathcal{R}$ as the set of all combinations of rotation distances (note that $|\mathcal{R}| = 32^3$). Next, we define Algorithm 1, which returns the maximum observed differential correlation among all single bit differentials $(\mathcal{ID}, \mathcal{OD})$ for a given combination of rotation distances $\mathbf{r} = (r_1, r_2, r_3) \in \mathcal{R}$ when considering N random trials. Then, to define the optimal rotation distances we executed the following steps:

1. Execute Algorithm 1 for all $\mathbf{r}_i \in \mathcal{R}$, obtaining a list $L = \{\delta_{\mathbf{r}_i}\}$.
2. Compute $\delta_{\min} = \min(L)$.
3. For each $\delta_{\mathbf{r}_i} \in L$, test the hypothesis $H_i : \delta_{\mathbf{r}_i} = \delta_{\min}$. More precisely, we used the standard statistical test to compare two proportions by converting the correlation to a probability $p_{\mathbf{r}_i} = (\delta_{\mathbf{r}_i} + 1)/2$. In addition, since we are dealing with multiple hypothesis tests, we used the Family-Wise Error Rate (FWER) technique to guard against type-I errors.
4. Discard all rotations distances $\mathbf{r}_i \in \mathcal{R}$ that lead to the hypothesis H_i being rejected. Thus, we are left with a subset of rotation distances $\mathcal{R}^* \subset \mathcal{R}$.
5. For each $\mathbf{r}_j \in \mathcal{R}^*$, compute the average neutrality measure $\bar{\gamma}_{\mathbf{r}_j}$ using Algorithm 1 of [2]. In this case, we considered an encryption with 5 rounds of Forró and 3 rounds executed backwards.
6. For each $\mathbf{r}_j \in \mathcal{R}^*$, define the metric $\mu_{\mathbf{r}_j} = \delta_{\mathbf{r}_j} \times \bar{\gamma}_{\mathbf{r}_j}$.
7. Define the rotation distances for Forró as $\arg\min_{\mathbf{r}_j}\{\mu_{\mathbf{r}_j}\}$.

Algorithm 1. Returns the maximum observed differential correlation for all possible single bit differentials.

1: INPUT: rotation distances (r_1, r_2, r_3), the number of trials N.
2: Setup Forró with rotation distances (r_1, r_2, r_3).
3: **for** each single bit input difference $\mathcal{ID}$ **do**
4:     **for** $i \in \{1, 2, ..., N\}$ **do**
5:         Generate random key k, nonce v, and counter t.
6:         Initialize Forró's state matrix X.
7:         Execute 2 rounds of Forró from X, obtaining Y.
8:         Compute $X' = \mathcal{ID} \oplus X$.
9:         Execute 2 rounds of Forró from X', obtaining Y'.
10:        Compute $\mathcal{OD} = Y \oplus Y'$.
11:        Update the differential correlation $\delta_{\mathcal{ID},j}$ for each bit of $\mathcal{OD}$, where $j \in \{0, 1, ..., 512\}$.
12: **return** $\max(|\delta_{\mathcal{ID},j}|)$

We executed these steps using a cluster of 24 *NVIDIA GPUs RTX 2080ti*. This setup allowed us to run Algorithm 1 with $N = 24 \times 2^{20}$, for all $\mathbf{r} \in \mathcal{R}$, in two days of computation. From these, we defined Forró's rotation distances as $(r_1, r_2, r_3) = (10, 27, 8)$. See the extended version of this paper for some interesting patterns that could be observed.

Constants. Since the choice of the constants does not impact security or performance, we decided to go through a cultural route: the constants correspond to the ASCII string *"voltadaasabranca"*, little-endian encoded. *"A volta da asa branca"* is the name of a song of the Brazilian singer Luiz Gonzaga. It is a continuation of the song *"asa branca"*, one of the greatest classics of Brazilian music, composed more than 70 years ago. In *"asa branca"*, Luiz Gonzaga and Humberto Teixeira tell us the story of a man who lost everything due to the drought in the Brazilian northeast region and had to leave his home in search of better living conditions. In *"a volta da asa branca"*, he returns to his home and is reunited with his love with whom he intends to marry.

Number of Rounds. From Table 1, we know that we can attack a maximum of 7 rounds of ChaCha and 5 rounds of Forró. Therefore, we know that we do not need 20 rounds of Forró to achieve the security of ChaCha20 against known attacks. That said, it is not easy to quantify exactly how many rounds would give that security margin. Assuming that for every 7 rounds of ChaCha we can save 2 rounds in Forró, we recommend using Forró with a total of 14 rounds (Forro14) to achieve a security margin comparable with ChaCha20. Also, we recommend Forró with 10 rounds (Forro10) to achieve higher security than ChaCha12.

5.3   Security

In the extended version of this paper, we present a complete analysis of the security of Forró when considering the same techniques that are applied against ChaCha and Salsa. In this version, we only present the main results.

Distinguishers. We constructed distinguishers for Forró by following the best techniques used against ChaCha in the literature [9,11]. More precisely, we looked for single bit differentials ranging 2 and 3 rounds of Forró. To do so, we tested all possible single bit input differences (128 possibilities) combined with every possible single bit output difference (512 possibilities). Hence, we tested a total of 2^{15} differentials. In each case, we estimated the correlation experimentally with a total of 2^{34} random samples. We present some examples in Table 3.

Table 3. Some of the best single bit differentials for 2 rounds of Forró.

$\mathcal{ID}$	$\mathcal{OD}$	Correlation
$\Delta X_5^{(0)} = 2^{18}$	$\Delta X_{15}^{(2)} = 2^7$	−0.00379
$\Delta X_5^{(0)} = 2^{18}$	$\Delta X_{10}^{(2)} = 2^7$	−0.00221
$\Delta X_5^{(0)} = 2^{11}$	$\Delta X_{15}^{(2)} = 1$	−0.00139
$\Delta X_5^{(0)} = 2^{11}$	$\Delta X_{10}^{(2)} = 1$	−0.00053

Next, using *CryptDances* we expanded the linear equations of Forró automatically. Using *CryptDances* functionalities, we also constructed distinguishers against Forró for every single differential that had a statistically significant correlation. From this study, we derived the best distinguisher for 3, 4, 5 and 5.25 rounds of Forró. We could not find any distinguishers against 5.5 rounds of Forró or more. In the following, we present more information about these distinguishers.

Distinguisher Against 3 Rounds of Forró. In this case, consider that single bit differential with $\mathcal{OD} = \Delta X_{15}^{(2)} = 1$ presented in Table 3. Thus, we have $\varepsilon_d = 0.00139$. For the linear part, we have to expand the bit $x_{15,0}^{(2)}$ (or, considering subrounds, $x_{15,0}^{[8]}$), obtaining $x_{15,0}^{[8]} = x_{15,27}^{[12]} \oplus x_{3,8}^{[12]} \oplus x_{7,0}^{[12]}$, with probability 1. Clearly, $\varepsilon_L = 1$, then the complexity of the differential-linear distinguisher for 3 rounds of Forró is $\frac{1}{\varepsilon_d^2} \approx 2^{18.9814}$.

Distinguisher Against 4 Rounds of Forró. In this case, consider that single bit differential with $\mathcal{OD} = \Delta X_{10}^{(2)} = 1$ presented in Table 3. Thus, we have $\varepsilon_d = 0.00053$. For the linear part, we have to expand the bit $x_{10,0}^{(2)} = x_{10,0}^{[8]}$, which results in the following Lemma:

Lemma 12. *The following linear approximation holds with probability* $\frac{1}{2}\left(1 + \frac{1}{2^5}\right)$

$$x_{10,0}^{[8]} = x_1^{[16]}[8] \oplus x_2^{[16]}[16] \oplus x_3^{[16]}[2,3,24] \oplus x_4^{[16]}[0,15,16,26,27] \oplus$$
$$x_7^{[16]}[7,8] \oplus x_9^{[16]}[0] \oplus x_{10}^{[16]}[0] \oplus x_{11}^{[16]}[0] \oplus x_{14}^{[16]}[22,27] \oplus x_{15}^{[16]}[0,27].$$

Proof. See the extended version of this paper. □

Computational Result 5. *The linear approximation of Lemma 12 holds computationally with* $\varepsilon_{L_0} = 0.0476 \approx 2^{-4.39}$. *This correlation was verified using* 2^{38} *random samples.*

We conclude that the complexity of the differential-linear distinguisher for 4 rounds of Forró is $\frac{1}{\varepsilon_d^2 \varepsilon_{L_0}^4} \approx 2^{36.55}$.

Distinguisher Against 5 and 5.25 Rounds of Forró. For these distinguishers, we just keep expanding the equation from Lemma 12. This will lead to differential-linear distinguishers with complexities $2^{129.68}$ and $2^{176.81}$ for 5 and 5.25 rounds of Forró, respectively. See the extended version of this paper for a complete description and proof of these distinguishers.

Attacks Using PNBs. In this section, we use the techniques developed by [2] and later improved by [9] to attack Forró, see Sect. 2.4. We tested several different attacks for different values of γ for all differentials presented in Table 3. With this approach, the best attack we found against 5 rounds of Forró uses 2 rounds forward and 3 rounds backwards. The attack uses the differential $(\Delta_{10,0}^{(2)}|\Delta_{5,11}^{(0)})$, thus, from Table 3 we get $\varepsilon_d = -0.00053$. Using $\gamma = 0.25$ we get a total of 155 PNBs. From that, we estimated $\varepsilon_a = 0.000068$ which leads to an attack with data complexity of 2^{57} and time complexity of 2^{158}.

5.4   Performance

By design, Forró achieves the same security with less operations than ChaCha, the implication being that on embedded devices with limited concurrency capabilities, such as the Raspberry Pi and others used in IoT, Forró naturally has better performance, see Table 4 for measurements. However, in more advanced processors, where speculative execution and out-of-order execution are empowered by large caches, such as modern x86, ChaCha still has an advantage. It is possible, however, to work around this apparent limitation with a clever implementation.

In order to pipeline instructions, the processor detects (or speculates) instructions that don't have dependencies on each others output and are nearby to anticipate them, so while one executes, the other can be fetching, for example. In ChaCha, the QRF is applied independently inside a round, and pipelining occurs without much impediment. In Forró, because of Pollination, every operation in a round has a dependency on the previous output, causing a serial data dependency. Meaning that the processor can't detect independent instructions to pipeline, or if it guesses the instructions are likely to not retire.

However, just like ChaCha, in order to get the next 512 bits of keystream, the algorithm needs to be executed from the start with an increment on the counter. This execution is completely independent of the previous one. Unfortunately, the processor doesn't have the foresight to anticipate that, since the code for it is far into the future, but that can be bypassed. To take full advantage of pipelining, whenever there is a need for more than 512 bits of keystream, we implement it so that the code for the two executions of Forró is in the same scope, a technique that for this specific use case we kindly named, "Xote". This strategy permits that Forró continues to leverage it's better diffusion to produce better performance on such processors, which can be seen in our measurements that are available on Table 4. For reference, the measurements also contain ChaCha with Xote. We make these implementations available at (https://github.com/MurCoutinho/forro_cipher).

Table 4. Performance comparison generating a 4096 bytes keystream between Salsa, ChaCha and Forró on ARMv7, ARMv7 using NEON, ARMv8 (64 bits), Intel x86-64 and Intel x86-64 using SIMD (AVX2 and SSE as available).

	ARMv7	ARMv7 NEON	ARMv8	Intel x86-64	Intel x86-64 SIMD
Algorithm	Cycles	Cycles	Cycles	Cycles	Cycles
Salsa20	83689	-	24622	20542	4418
Chacha20	89495	51914	35100	20118	3934
Chacha20 (Xote)	138284	-	36214	19362	4480
Forro14	73230	49575	46700	34472	6244
Forro14 (Xote)	76236	-	31666	20748	4826

6   CryptDances: A New Tool for Cryptanalysis of ARX Ciphers

The final contribution of this work is a tool to perform cryptanalysis of ChaCha, Salsa and Forró in high performance environments. As a brief summary, in the current version of CryptDances we have:

- Implementation of most attacks from the literature for Salsa and ChaCha, in particular from [2,3,9–11] (attacks for [14] are not yet available).
- It is easy to test any new differential or linear approximation for Salsa, ChaCha or Forró.
- Automatic linear expansions for ChaCha and Forró (Salsa in development).
- Given a differential and linear expansion, CryptDances can compute the complexity of distinguishers and PNB attacks.

CryptDances is available at https://github.com/MurCoutinho/cryptDances.

7   Conclusion

In this work, we provided several contributions for ARX ciphers. In particular, we provided a new way to derive linear approximations for ChaCha, improving the complexity of the best differential-linear distinguisher from 2^{224} to 2^{214}. In addition, using the proposed BLE, we improved attacks against Salsa. More precisely, we presented the first distinguishers against 7 and 8 rounds of Salsa with complexities 2^{109} and 2^{216}, and improved key recovery attacks achieving a complexity of 2^{212} for 8 rounds when the best know attack so far had complexity of $2^{244.9}$.

Another contribution of this work is a new stream cipher called Forró. We showed that Forró can achieve the same security as ChaCha with fewer operations. Because of that, Forró can achieve faster performance in certain platforms, specially in constrained devices. Finally, we developed *CryptDances*, a new tool for the cryptanalysis of Salsa, ChaCha, and Forró designed to be used in high performance environments with several GPUs, making it available for the community at https://github.com/MurCoutinho/cryptDances.

For future works, the techniques developed in this paper may be used to improve cryptanalysis against other ARX primitives, such as Chaskey or the hash function Blake. Also, the security of Forró should be analyzed further, specially against other types of attacks, such as rotational cryptanalysis. Finally, the tool *CryptDances* can be used by researchers to try to improve further attacks against Salsa, ChaCha, and Forró.

Acknowledgements. This work is supported in part by FAPDF - Brazilian Federal District Research Support Foundation, in part by CNPq - Brazilian National Research Council (Grants 312180/2019-5 PQ-2 and 465741/2014-2 INCT on Cybersecurity), in part by the Ministry of Justice and Public Security (Grant MJSP 01/2019), in part by the Administrative Council for Economic Defense (Grant CADE 08700.000047/2019-14), in part by the General Attorney of the Union (Grant AGU 697.935/2019), in part by the National Auditing Department of the Brazilian Health System (Grant DENASUS 23106.118410/2020-85), and in part by the General Attorney's Office for the National Treasure (Grant PGFN 23106.148934/2019-67).

References

1. Aumasson, J.-P., Bernstein, D.J.: SipHash: a fast short-input PRF. In: Galbraith, S., Nandi, M. (eds.) INDOCRYPT 2012. LNCS, vol. 7668, pp. 489–508. Springer, Heidelberg (2012). https://doi.org/10.1007/978-3-642-34931-7_28

2. Aumasson, J.-P., Fischer, S., Khazaei, S., Meier, W., Rechberger, C.: New features of Latin dances: analysis of salsa, ChaCha, and Rumba. In: Nyberg, K. (ed.) FSE 2008. LNCS, vol. 5086, pp. 470–488. Springer, Heidelberg (2008). https://doi.org/10.1007/978-3-540-71039-4_30

3. Beierle, C., Leander, G., Todo, Y.: Improved differential-linear attacks with applications to ARX ciphers. In: Micciancio, D., Ristenpart, T. (eds.) CRYPTO 2020. LNCS, vol. 12172, pp. 329–358. Springer, Cham (2020). https://doi.org/10.1007/978-3-030-56877-1_12

4. Bernstein, D.J.: The poly1305-AES message-authentication code. In: Gilbert, H., Handschuh, H. (eds.) FSE 2005. LNCS, vol. 3557, pp. 32–49. Springer, Heidelberg (2005). https://doi.org/10.1007/11502760_3

5. Bernstein, D.J.: Chacha, a variant of salsa20. In: Workshop Record of SASC, vol. 8, pp. 3–5 (2008)

6. Bernstein, D.J.: The Salsa20 family of stream ciphers. In: Robshaw, M., Billet, O. (eds.) New Stream Cipher Designs. LNCS, vol. 4986, pp. 84–97. Springer, Heidelberg (2008). https://doi.org/10.1007/978-3-540-68351-3_8

7. Blondeau, C., Leander, G., Nyberg, K.: Differential-linear cryptanalysis revisited. J. Cryptol. **30**(3), 859–888 (2017). https://doi.org/10.1007/s00145-016-9237-5

8. Hernandez-Castro, J.C.H., Tapiador, J.M.E., Quisquater, J.-J.: On the Salsa20 core function. In: Nyberg, K. (ed.) FSE 2008. LNCS, vol. 5086, pp. 462–469. Springer, Heidelberg (2008). https://doi.org/10.1007/978-3-540-71039-4_29

9. Choudhuri, A.R., Maitra, S.: Significantly improved multi-bit differentials for reduced round Salsa and ChaCha. IACR Trans. Symmetric Cryptol. **2016**(2), 261–287 (2016). https://doi.org/10.13154/tosc.v2016.i2.261-287

10. Coutinho, M., Neto, T.C.S.: New multi-bit differentials to improve attacks against ChaCha. IACR Cryptology ePrint Archive 2020/350 (2020). https://eprint.iacr.org/2020/350

11. Coutinho, M., Souza Neto, T.C.: Improved linear approximations to ARX ciphers and attacks against ChaCha. In: Canteaut, A., Standaert, F.-X. (eds.) EUROCRYPT 2021. LNCS, vol. 12696, pp. 711–740. Springer, Cham (2021). https://doi.org/10.1007/978-3-030-77870-5_25

12. Coutinho, M., Passos, I., de Sousa Jr, R.T., Borges, F.: Improving the security of ChaCha against differential-linear cryptanalysis (2020)

13. Crowley, P.: Truncated differential cryptanalysis of five rounds of salsa20. IACR Cryptology ePrint Archive 2005/375 (2005). http://eprint.iacr.org/2005/375

14. Dey, S., Garai, H.K., Sarkar, S., Sharma, N.K.: Revamped differential-linear cryptanalysis on reduced round ChaCha. In: Dunkelman, O., Dziembowski, S. (eds.) Advances in Cryptology. LNCS, vol. 13277, pp. 86–114. Springer, Cham (2022). https://doi.org/10.1007/978-3-031-07082-2_4

15. Dey, S., Sarkar, S.: Improved analysis for reduced round salsa and ChaCha. Discret. Appl. Math. **227**, 58–69 (2017). https://doi.org/10.1016/j.dam.2017.04.034

16. Ding, L.: Improved related-cipher attack on salsa20 stream cipher. IEEE Access **7**, 30197–30202 (2019). https://doi.org/10.1109/ACCESS.2019.2892647

17. Fischer, S., Meier, W., Berbain, C., Biasse, J.-F., Robshaw, M.J.B.: Non-randomness in eSTREAM candidates Salsa20 and TSC-4. In: Barua, R., Lange, T. (eds.) INDOCRYPT 2006. LNCS, vol. 4329, pp. 2–16. Springer, Heidelberg (2006). https://doi.org/10.1007/11941378_2

18. IANIX: ChaCha usage & deployment (2020). https://ianix.com/pub/chacha-deployment.html. Accessed 13 Jan 2020

19. IANIX: Salsa20 usage & deployment (2021). https://ianix.com/pub/salsa20-deployment.html. Accessed 02 Feb 2021

20. Langford, S.K., Hellman, M.E.: Differential-linear cryptanalysis. In: Desmedt, Y.G. (ed.) CRYPTO 1994. LNCS, vol. 839, pp. 17–25. Springer, Heidelberg (1994). https://doi.org/10.1007/3-540-48658-5_3

21. Langley, A., Chang, W., Mavrogiannopoulos, N., Strömbergson, J., Josefsson, S.: Chacha20-poly1305 cipher suites for transport layer security (TLS). RFC **7905**, 1–8 (2016). https://doi.org/10.17487/RFC7905

22. Lipmaa, H., Moriai, S.: Efficient algorithms for computing differential properties of addition. In: Matsui, M. (ed.) FSE 2001. LNCS, vol. 2355, pp. 336–350. Springer, Heidelberg (2002). https://doi.org/10.1007/3-540-45473-X_28

23. Maitra, S.: Chosen IV cryptanalysis on reduced round ChaCha and salsa. Discret. Appl. Math. **208**, 88–97 (2016). https://doi.org/10.1016/j.dam.2016.02.020

24. Maitra, S., Paul, G., Meier, W.: Salsa20 cryptanalysis: new moves and revisiting old styles. IACR Cryptology ePrint Archive 2015/217 (2015). http://eprint.iacr.org/2015/217

25. Mouha, N., Preneel, B.: A proof that the ARX cipher salsa20 is secure against differential cryptanalysis. IACR Cryptology ePrint Archive 2013/328 (2013). http://eprint.iacr.org/2013/328

26. Niu, Z., Sun, S., Liu, Y., Li, C.: Rotational differential-linear distinguishers of ARX ciphers with arbitrary output linear masks. Cryptology ePrint Archive (2022)

27. Robshaw, M.J.B., Billet, O. (eds.): New Stream Cipher Designs - The eSTREAM Finalists. LNCS, vol. 4986. Springer, Heidelberg (2008). https://doi.org/10.1007/978-3-540-68351-3

28. Shi, Z., Zhang, B., Feng, D., Wu, W.: Improved key recovery attacks on reduced-round Salsa20 and ChaCha. In: Kwon, T., Lee, M.-K., Kwon, D. (eds.) ICISC 2012. LNCS, vol. 7839, pp. 337–351. Springer, Heidelberg (2013). https://doi.org/10.1007/978-3-642-37682-5_24

29. Wallén, J.: Linear approximations of addition modulo 2^n. In: Johansson, T. (ed.) FSE 2003. LNCS, vol. 2887, pp. 261–273. Springer, Heidelberg (2003). https://doi.org/10.1007/978-3-540-39887-5_20

Mind the TWEAKEY Schedule: Cryptanalysis on SKINNYe-64-256

Lingyue Qin[1,5,6], Xiaoyang Dong[2,5,6(✉)], Anyu Wang[2,4,5,6(✉)],
Jialiang Hua[2(✉)], and Xiaoyun Wang[2,3,4,5,6(✉)]

[1] BNRist, Tsinghua University, Beijing, China
qinly@tsinghua.edu.cn
[2] Institute for Advanced Study, BNRist, Tsinghua University, Beijing, China
{xiaoyangdong,anyuwang,huajl18,xiaoyunwang}@tsinghua.edu.cn
[3] Key Laboratory of Cryptologic Technology and Information Security
(Ministry of Education), School of Cyber Science and Technology,
Shandong University, Qingdao, China
[4] Shangdong Institute of Blockchain, Jinan, China
[5] Zhongguancun Laboratory, Beijing, China
[6] National Financial Cryptography Research Center, Beijing, China

Abstract. Designing symmetric ciphers for particular applications becomes a hot topic. At EUROCRYPT 2020, Naito, Sasaki and Sugawara invented the threshold implementation friendly cipher SKINNYe-64-256 to meet the requirement of the authenticated encryption PFB_Plus. Soon, Thomas Peyrin pointed out that SKINNYe-64-256 may lose the security expectation due the new tweakey schedule. Although the security issue of SKINNYe-64-256 is still unclear, Naito *et al.* decided to introduce SKINNYe-64-256 v2 as a response.

In this paper, we give a formal cryptanalysis on the new tweakey schedule of SKINNYe-64-256 and discover unexpected differential cancellations in the tweakey schedule. For example, we find the number of cancellations can be up to 8 within 30 consecutive rounds, which is significantly larger than the expected 3 cancellations. Moreover, we take our new discoveries into rectangle, MITM and impossible differential attacks, and adapt the corresponding automatic tools with new constraints from our discoveries. Finally, we find a 41-round related-tweakey rectangle attack on SKINNYe-64-256 and leave a security margin of 3 rounds only.

As STK accepts arbitrary tweakey size, but SKINNY and SKINNYe-64-256 v2 only support up to $4n$ tweakey size. We introduce a new design of tweakey schedule for SKINNY-64 to further extend the supported tweakey size. We give a formal proof that our new tweakey schedule inherits the security requirement of STK and SKINNY. We also discuss possible ways to extend the tweakey size for SKINNY-128.

Keywords: SKINNY · TWEAKEY · Rectangle · Meet-in-the-middle · Impossible differential

The full version of the paper is available at https://eprint.iacr.org/2022/789.

S. Agrawal and D. Lin (Eds.): ASIACRYPT 2022, LNCS 13791, pp. 287–317, 2022.
https://doi.org/10.1007/978-3-031-22963-3_10

1   Introduction

The design of symmetric cryptographic constructions for important security goals and practical applications becomes more and more popular. Typical algorithms including LowMC [3], MiMC [2], etc., provide efficient implementation for multi-party secure computing (MPC), fully homomorphic encryption (FHE), and zero-knowledge proofs (ZK). Another important topic is to design symmetric ciphers that can be efficiently implemented against side-channel attacks [12,28,47], especially because NIST lightweight cryptography competition optionally takes into account the security of the cryptographic modules against side-channel attack (SCA). Masking is by far the most common countermeasure against SCA [40,52]. Threshold implementation (TI) introduced by Nikova *et al.* [52] is a masking particularly popular for hardware implementation. Several TI-friendly Sboxes [13,36] are proposed. At TCHES 2020, Naito and Sugawara [51] discovered that for recently ciphers such as SKINNY [9] and GIFT [6], the complexity of TI for the linear key schedule function is significantly smaller than the nonlinear round function. With this asymmetry, Naito and Sugawara [51] proposed a TBC-based scheme PFB which is particularly efficient with TI. To further exploit this asymmetry, at EUROCRYPT 2020, Naito, Sasaki and Sugawara [48] invented tweakable block cipher (TBC) based AE modes PFB_Plus, PFBw, as well as a new TBC, i.e. SKINNYe-64-256, which are very efficient in threshold implementations.

At ASIACRYPT 2014, Jean, Nikolić and Peyrin introduced the TWEAKEY framework [42] with the goal to unify the design of tweakable block ciphers and allow to build a primitive with arbitrary tweak and key sizes. It treats the key input and the tweak input in the same way as the tweakey. Towards simplifying the security analysis when the tweakey size is large, Jean *et al.* identified a subclass of TWEAKEY, named as STK construction, which updates the round tweakey by the use of finite field multiplications on low hamming weight constants. SKINNY [9] is a well-known lightweight block cipher family proposed by Beierle *et al.* at CRYPTO 2016, which follows closely the STK construction [42]. However, instead of using multiplications by non-zero constants in a finite field adopted by STK construction, SKINNY updates the tweakey cells by the cheap 4-bit or 8-bit LFSRs (depending on the size of the cell) to minimize the hardware cost, while maintaining the cancellation behavior required by the STK construction: for a given position, $z - 1$ cancellations can only happen every 15 rounds for TK-z[1].

As a concrete STK-like design, SKINNY only supports TK-1/-2/-3, while for STK construction, the size of tweakey can be of arbitrary length. However, in practical applications, tweakable block ciphers with large tweakeys may be required, such as the TI-friendly AE modes PFB_Plus and PFBw proposed by Naito, Sasaki and Sugawara [48]. Without TK-4 available for SKINNY, Naito *et al.* decided to build the SKINNYe-64-256 to support $zn = 4n$ tweakey with $n = 64$. In order to inherit the numerous cryptanalytic efforts on SKINNY-64 [4,24,30,31,37,46,54], SKINNYe-64-256 does not modify any components to

---

[1] For TK-z, if the size of internal state is n, the size of tweakey will be zn.

realize TK_1, TK_2, and TK_3, and only find a new LFSR for updating TK_4. With the expectation of keeping a similar security margin with 36-round SKINNY-64-128 and 40-round SKINNY-64-192, the authors decided to keep the same rate for increasing the number of rounds, namely 44 rounds for SKINNYe-64-256. However, Thomas Peyrin found that the security claim of SKINNYe-64-256 may not hold due to the tweakey schedule. Although the authors of SKINNYe-64-256 were unclear whether this issue causes some attacks against the whole cipher [50, Section 7], they proposed an updated version of SKINNYe-64-256, named as SKINNYe-64-256 v2 in Eprint 2020/542 [50].

Our Contributions. In this paper, we try to clarify the security issue of SKINNYe-64-256 [48] by delving into its new tweakey schedule. There are some previous works considered the relations of keys, such as the key-bridging technique [26,33]. The relations of subtweakeys for SKINNY and SKINNYe-64-256 are mostly dependent on the $LFSR_m$ updating the cells of the tweakey states. For $LFSR_2$ used for TK_2 and $LFSR_4$ used for TK_4 of SKINNYe-64-256, both of them shift the 4-bit input to the left by 1 bit, while $LFSR_2$ updates 1 output bit with 1 XOR and $LFSR_4$ updates 2 output bits with 3 XORs. Suppose for a given cell of TK_2 and TK_4 with the initial value 0x8, then apply $LFSR_2$ and $LFSR_4$ respectively to the given cell for 14 times and we get two sequences, i.e.,

$$[\underline{0x8}, \underline{0x1}, \underline{0x2}, 0x4, \underline{0x9}, \underline{0x3}, 0x6, 0xd, \underline{0xa}, 0x5, \underline{0xb}, 0x7, 0xf, 0xe, 0xc],$$
$$[\underline{0x8}, \underline{0x1}, \underline{0x2}, 0x5, \underline{0x9}, \underline{0x3}, 0x7, 0xc, \underline{0xa}, 0x4, \underline{0xb}, 0x6, 0xe, 0xf, 0xd].$$

For example, run $LFSR_2$ or $LFSR_4$ on 0x8 for 3 times, we get $LFSR_2^3(0x8)$ = 0x4 and $LFSR_4^3(0x8)$ = 0x5, respectively. Intuitively, the longest common subsequence of the two sequences is [0x8,0x1,0x2,0x9,0x3,0xa,0xb] which is highlighted with underlines. In other words, when the initial values (or differences) for a given cell position of TK_2 and TK_4 are 0x8 and TK_1 and TK_3 are set to 0x0, the difference cancellations can happen 7 times within 15 LFSR applications.

In order to further clarify the cancellation property of the new tweakey schedule, we give a formal analysis of relations of subtweakeys. Since the tweakey schedule of SKINNYe-64-256 is linear, each cell of subtweakeys can be derived via multiplying some cells of the master tweakeys by certain binary matrix A, which is determined by cell updating functions, i.e., LFSRs. The differential cancellation behavior means active input leads to zero output by multiplying A. We analyze the properties of matrix A, especially for the influence of its rank on the cancellations in the differential-like distinguishers, as well as the subtweakey guessing strategy in the key-recovery phase. For the differential cancellation behavior, we find the number of cancellations can be up to 8 within 30 consecutive rounds for SKINNYe-64-256 (a cell is updated by LFSR in every two rounds in SKINNY), which is significantly larger than the expected 3 cancellations. By exploring the properties of A in rectangle attack, meet-in-the-middle (MITM) attack and impossible differential attack, we discover unexpected distinguishers or key-recovery attacks:

– **Related-tweakey rectangle attacks.** The properties can not only extend the rectangle distinguisher significantly, but also improve the key-recovery phase. At EUROCRYPT 2022, Dong *et al.* [30] introduced the attacks on the 25-round SKINNY-64-128 with an 18-round distinguisher as well as the 31-round SKINNY-64-192 with a 22-round distinguisher. With our discoveries on SKINNYe-64-256, we find a 30-round rectangle distinguisher, where the gap between SKINNY-64-192 and SKINNYe-64-256 is significantly increased to $30-22 = 8$ rounds comparing to $22-18 = 4$ rounds between SKINNY-64-128 and SKINNY-64-192. Moreover, in the key-recovery phase, we explore the key relations in detail with the help of matrix A, and finally perform a 41-round key-recovery attack on SKINNYe-64-256.

  In order to find the optimal configurations of the rectangle attack, we tweak Dong *et al.*'s automatic model by applying the properties of the new tweakey schedule into the model. Our attack leaves only a 3-round security margin for SKINNYe-64-256, which is significantly reduced comparing to the 11-round and 9-round security margins for SKINNY-64-128 and SKINNY-64-192.

– **MITM attacks in single-tweakey setting.** Not only the differential cancellation property can be used to improve attacks, but also the non-full rank property of A. The MITM attack explores two independent chunks that overlap in a match point. Suppose A is of non-full rank, we compute the solution space of $Ax = c$ for given vector c. In SKINNYe-64-256, x is the master tweakey bits and c is the subtweakey bits that will XORed into the internal state. Denote solution set as $\{x : Ax = c\}$, if it is not empty, then its size will be $|\{x : Ax = c\}| > 1$ due to non-full rank property of A. In the MITM, those $x \in \{x : Ax = c\}$ will have the same effect on the internal states, i.e., the vector c. When building independent forward and backward chunks in MITM, we may prefix c and c' for these two chunks, then the values in $\{x : Ax = c\}$ and $\{y : A'y = c'\}$ will have independent effects.

  We adapt the automatic tools [7,29] for MITM attacks by taking the non-full rank properties of A into the model. Finally, we find 31-round MITM attack on SKINNYe-64-256, while previous MITM attacks on SKINNY-64-128 and SKINNY-64-192 reach 18 and 23 rounds, respectively. In other words, the gaps of the attacked rounds increase from $23-18 = 5$ rounds between SKINNY-64-128 and SKINNY-64-192 to currently $31-23 = 8$ rounds between SKINNY-64-192 and SKINNYe-64-256.

– **Related-tweakey impossible differential attack.** With the differential cancellation properties, we find a 21-round impossible differential for SKINNYe-64-256 based on a cancellation pattern, while previous impossible differential reaches 16 rounds [46] for SKINNY-64-192 and 15 rounds [56] for SKINNY-64-128, respectively.

Our cryptanalysis proves that SKINNYe-64-256 does not keep a similar security margin to SKINNY-64-128 and SKINNY-64-192 as expected by the designers. The non-trivial properties of the new tweakey schedule can be used to improve the attacks from the distinguishers to key-recovery.

In addition, we also analyze the updated version, i.e., SKINNYe-64-256 v2 [50], and obtain a 37-round related-tweakey rectangle attack, a 27-round MITM attack, as well as an 18-round impossible differential. Comparing to the attacks on SKINNY-64-128 and SKINNY-64-192, the attacked rounds on SKINNYe-64-256 v2 keep the same rate as expected by the designers. We summarize results on SKINNY-64 and SKINNYe-64-256 and its version 2 in Table 1 and Table 2.

Table 1. Rectangle attacks on SKINNY-64 and SKINNYe-64-256 and its version 2

Version	Rounds	Data	Time	Memory	Distinguisher	Setting	Ref.
SKINNY-64-128	23/36	$2^{60.54}$	$2^{120.7}$	$2^{60.9}$	19	RK	[37]
	24/36	$2^{61.67}$	$2^{96.83}$	2^{84}	18	RK	[54]
	25/36	$2^{61.67}$	$2^{118.43}$	$2^{64.26}$	18	RK	[30]
SKINNY-64-192	29/40	$2^{62.92}$	$2^{181.7}$	2^{80}	23	RK	[37]
	30/40	$2^{62.87}$	$2^{163.11}$	$2^{68.05}$	22	RK	[54]
	31/40	$2^{62.78}$	$2^{182.07}$	$2^{62.79}$	22	RK	[30]
SKINNYe-64-256	41/44	$2^{62.24}$	$2^{237.06}$	$2^{62.26}$	30	RK	Sect. 4.3
SKINNYe-64-256 v2	37/44	$2^{62.8}$	$2^{240.03}$	$2^{62.8}$	26	RK	Full Ver. [53]

Table 2. MITM attacks on SKINNY-64 and SKINNYe-64-256 and its version 2

Version	Rounds	Data	Time	Memory	Approach	Setting	Ref.
SKINNY-64-128	18/36	2^{16}	2^{124}	2^4	MITM	SK	[39]
SKINNY-64-192	23/40	2^{52}	2^{188}	2^4	MITM	SK	[29]
SKINNYe-64-256	31/44	2^{52}	2^{254}	2^{52}	MITM	SK	Full Ver. [53]
SKINNYe-64-256 v2	27/44	2^{52}	2^{252}	2^{52}	MITM	SK	Full Ver. [53]

Note that STK construction supports arbitrary length of tweakey, but SKINNY and SKINNYe-64-256 v2 supports upto $4n$-bit tweakey. As stated in [48, Page 5]: "... there is no consensus about the adequate tweak size to support". SKINNY with larger tweakey size may be useful in future applications, such as the TI-friendly AE modes PFB_Plus and PFBw with SKINNYe-64-256 v2. Therefore, as another contribution, we propose a uniformed design strategy for tweakey schedule of SKINNY-n-zn for positive integer $z \leq 14$. Our uniformed tweakey schedule satisfies the security requirements of the STK construction with a formal proof. Interestingly, our schedule will be reduced to SKINNY-64 when $z = 1, 2, 3$, and to SKINNYe-64-256 v2 when $z = 4$. In addition, we also discuss possible ways to extend the tweakey size for SKINNY-128.

2   Preliminaries

2.1   The TWEAKEY Framework

At ASIACRYPT 2014, Jean *et al.* [42] proposed a generic framework for tweakable block ciphers, named as the TWEAKEY framework. They consider the tweak and key inputs in a unified manner, i.e., tweakey, that can be used to design a tweakable block cipher with any key and any tweak sizes. The TWEAKEY framework uses the tweakey scheduling algorithm. The ciphertext is computed from the plaintext by applying the permutation f iteratively. Each round is composed of three parts, a sub-tweakey extraction function g from the tweakey state, an internal update permutation f and a tweakey state update function h. Based on the TWEAKEY framework, many designs of tweakable block ciphers are proposed, including Deoxys [43], SKINNY [9], and CRAFT [11], etc. Moreover, Jean *et al.* identified a subclass of tweakey for AES-like ciphers named as Superposition TWEAKEY (STK) construction shown in Fig. 1. In the STK construction, the n-bit internal state and zn-bit tweakey state (denoted as TK-z) are partitioned into n/c and zn/c c-bit cells respectively. The functions g and h become:

- the function g simply XORs all the z n-bit words of the tweakey state to the internal state (AddRoundTweakey, denoted ART).
- the function h first applies the same cell position permutation function P to each of the z n-bit words of the tweakey state, and then multiply each c-bit cell of the j-th n-bit word by a nonzero coefficient α_j in the finite field $GF(2^c)$ (with $\alpha_i \neq \alpha_j$ for all $1 \leq i \neq j \leq z$).

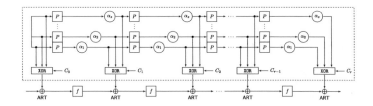

Fig. 1. The STK [42]. (Thanks to https://www.iacr.org/authors/tikz/)

2.2   SKINNY Family and SKINNYe-64-256

SKINNY is a family of lightweight block cipher proposed by Beierle *et al.* at CRYPTO 2016 [9]. Following the TWEAKEY framework and STK construction [42], the round function of SKINNY that replaces the f function of STK in Fig. 1 is given in Fig. 2. There are six main versions SKINNY-n-zn: $n = 64, 128$, $z = 1, 2, 3$. The internal state is viewed as a 4×4 square arrays of cells. The tweakey state is viewed as z 4×4 square arrays of cells, denoted as (TK_1) when $z = 1$,

(TK_1, TK_2) when $z = 2$, and (TK_1, TK_2, TK_3) when $z = 3$. Denote the i-th cell of TK_m as $TK_{m,i}$ $(1 \leq m \leq z, 0 \leq i \leq 15)$. An important difference between the STK construction [42] and SKINNY is that in the tweakey schedule the cells of the tweakey are updated by LFSRs for SKINNY instead of multiplying α_j. As shown in Fig. 2, the round function applies 5 transformations: SubCells (SC), AddConstants (AC), AddRoundTweakey (ART), ShiftRows (SR) and MixColumns (MC). For the details, please refer to [9].

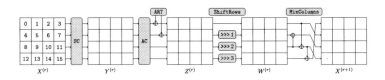

Fig. 2. Round function of SKINNY

For the block size $n = 64$, SKINNY supports the tweakey sizes up to 192 bits. At EUROCRYPT 2020, to support the TI-friendly AE modes PFB_Plus and PFBw, Naito, Sasaki, and Sugawara [48] extended the design of SKINNY-64 to support a 256-bit tweakey and derived SKINNYe-64-256, which applies the same round function of SKINNY but a new tweakey schedule. However, Thomas Peyrin found that the security claim of SKINNYe-64-256 may not hold due to the new tweakey schedule. In response, Naito *et al.* decided to propose an updated version of SKINNYe-64-256, i.e., SKINNYe-64-256 v2 in Eprint 2020/542 [50].

New Tweakey Schedule. The 256-bit tweakey state is viewed as 4 4 × 4 square arrays of nibbles as (TK_1, TK_2, TK_3, TK_4). Denote the tweakey arrays as $TK_1^{(r)}$, $TK_2^{(r)}$, $TK_3^{(r)}$ and $TK_4^{(r)}$ in round r $(r \geq 0)$, where $TK_m^{(0)} = TK_m$ $(1 \leq m \leq 4)$. For $r \geq 1$, $TK_m^{(r)}$ is generated in two steps.

First, apply the permutation $P = [9, 15, 8, 13, 10, 14, 12, 11, 0, 1, 2, 3, 4, 5, 6, 7]$ on each nibble of all tweakey arrays:

$$TK_{m,i}^{(r)} \leftarrow TK_{m,P[i]}^{(r-1)}, \; 1 \leq m \leq 4, \; 0 \leq i \leq 15, r \geq 1. \tag{1}$$

Then, apply LFSR$_m$ to update each nibble of the first and second rows of $TK_m^{(r)}$ with $2 \leq m \leq 4$. The LFSR for $TK_4^{(r)}$ used in SKINNYe-64-256 and SKINNYe-64-256 v2 is different. The LFSRs are given in Table 3.

In the ART operation, only the first two rows of subtweakey $STK^{(r)}$ are xored to the internal state, where

$$STK_i^{(r)} = TK_{1,i}^{(r)} \oplus TK_{2,i}^{(r)} \oplus TK_{3,i}^{(r)} \oplus TK_{4,i}^{(r)}, 0 \leq i \leq 7, \; r \geq 0. \tag{2}$$

Lemma 1. *For any given SKINNY S-box S and any two non-zero differences δ_{in} and δ_{out}, the equation $S_i(y) \oplus S_i(y \oplus \delta_{in}) = \delta_{out}$ has one solution on average.*

Table 3. The LFSRs used in SKINNYe-64-256 and SKINNYe-64-256 v2

TK	LFSRs
TK_2	$(x_3\|x_2\|x_1\|x_0) \rightarrow (x_2\|x_1\|x_0\|x_3 \oplus x_2)$
TK_3	$(x_3\|x_2\|x_1\|x_0) \rightarrow (x_0 \oplus x_3\|x_3\|x_2\|x_1)$
TK_4	$(x_3\|x_2\|x_1\|x_0) \rightarrow (x_2\|x_1\|x_2 \oplus x_0\|x_3 \oplus x_2 \oplus x_1)$
TK_4 v2	$(x_3\|x_2\|x_1\|x_0) \rightarrow (x_1\|x_0\|x_3 \oplus x_2\|x_2 \oplus x_1)$

3 Properties of the Tweakey Schedule of SKINNYe-64-256

In round $r \geq 0$, each of the 64-bit tweakey $TK_m^{(r)}$ ($1 \leq m \leq 4$) of SKINNYe-64-256 can be represented as a 4×16 binary matrix $\boldsymbol{TK}_m^{(r)}$ ($1 \leq m \leq 4$, $r \geq 0$) as

$$\boldsymbol{TK}_m^{(r)} = \begin{pmatrix} x_{m,0}^{(r)} & x_{m,4}^{(r)}, \ldots, x_{m,60}^{(r)} \\ x_{m,1}^{(r)} & x_{m,5}^{(r)}, \ldots, x_{m,61}^{(r)} \\ x_{m,2}^{(r)} & x_{m,6}^{(r)}, \ldots, x_{m,62}^{(r)} \\ x_{m,3}^{(r)} & x_{m,7}^{(r)}, \ldots, x_{m,63}^{(r)} \end{pmatrix},$$

with $x_{m,j}^{(r)} \in \{0,1\}$ ($0 \leq j \leq 63$). Denote $\boldsymbol{TK}_m^{(r)}[*,i]$ as the i-th column of the binary matrix $\boldsymbol{TK}_m^{(r)}$. Then $\boldsymbol{TK}_m^{(r)}[*,i]$ is actually the i-th nibble of $TK_m^{(r)}$, i.e., $TK_{m,i}^{(r)}$ ($0 \leq i \leq 15$), which is denoted as a binary vector $\boldsymbol{tk}_{m,i}^{(r)} \in \mathbb{F}_2^4$,

$$\boldsymbol{tk}_{m,i}^{(r)} = [x_{m,4i}^{(r)}, x_{m,4i+1}^{(r)}, x_{m,4i+2}^{(r)}, x_{m,4i+3}^{(r)}]^T, \ 0 \leq i \leq 15, \ 1 \leq m \leq 4, r \geq 0.$$

Since $TK_m^{(0)} = TK_m$, we also write $\boldsymbol{tk}_{m,i}^{(0)} = [x_{m,4i}, x_{m,4i+1}, x_{m,4i+2}, x_{m,4i+3}]^T$ for simplicity. We can deduce the relations between the subtweakeys transformed from the same nibble of the master tweakey. For TK_1, only the permutation P is applied in each round. Assume P^r means to apply the permutation P for r times. We have $\boldsymbol{tk}_{1,i}^{(r)} = \boldsymbol{tk}_{1,P^r[i]}^{(0)}$, $0 \leq i \leq 15$.

For TK_2, TK_3 and TK_4, after applying the permutation, a LFSR is applied to update each cell of the 1st and 2nd rows in each round, which is equivalent to multiplying the cell by a 4×4 binary matrix. For SKINNYe-64-256 and its version 2, the LFSRs used for TK_2 and TK_3 are the same, whose corresponding matrices are denoted as $\boldsymbol{L}_2$ and $\boldsymbol{L}_3$. The LFSRs used in TK_4 for SKINNYe-64-256 and version 2 are different, which are denoted as $\boldsymbol{L}_4$ and $\tilde{\boldsymbol{L}}_4$. We have

$$\boldsymbol{L}_2 = \begin{pmatrix} 0&1&0&0 \\ 0&0&1&0 \\ 0&0&0&1 \\ 1&1&0&0 \end{pmatrix}, \ \boldsymbol{L}_3 = \begin{pmatrix} 1&0&0&1 \\ 1&0&0&0 \\ 0&1&0&0 \\ 0&0&1&0 \end{pmatrix}, \ \boldsymbol{L}_4 = \begin{pmatrix} 0&1&0&0 \\ 0&0&1&0 \\ 0&1&0&1 \\ 1&1&1&0 \end{pmatrix}, \ \tilde{\boldsymbol{L}}_4 = \begin{pmatrix} 0&0&1&0 \\ 0&0&0&1 \\ 1&1&0&0 \\ 0&1&1&0 \end{pmatrix}.$$

Since only the first two rows of subtweakey are XORed to the internal state, the tweakey cells involved in the r-th round encryption will be involved again in the $(r+2)$-th round according to $P = [9, 15, 8, 13, 10, 14, 12, 11, 0, 1, 2, 3, 4, 5, 6, 7]$. For simplicity, we first consider the formulas of subtweakeys for SKINNYe-64-256, and for version 2, the formulas are different only for TK_4. Assume L_m^i represents the i-th power of matrix L_m in $GF(2)$ and $L_m^0 = I$ ($2 \leq m \leq 4$). Note that the LFSRs for TK_2 and TK_3 in SKINNY and the new LFSR for TK_4 in SKINNYe-64-256 have the same cycle of 15, which lead to $L_m^{15} = I$ ($2 \leq m \leq 4$). For SKINNYe-64-256 v2, although the update function for TK_4 is not a LFSR, it also has a cycle of 15, i.e., $\tilde{L}_4^{15} = I$. In the tweakey schedule, for each nibble of $TK_m^{(r)}$, the LFSR is applied in every two rounds, we deduce: $\forall m \in \{2, 3, 4\}$,

$$
\begin{cases}
tk_{m,i}^{(r)} = L_m^{\lceil r/2 \rceil} \cdot tk_{m, P^r[i]}^{(0)}, \ 0 \leq i \leq 7, \\
tk_{m,i}^{(r)} = L_m^{\lfloor r/2 \rfloor} \cdot tk_{m, P^r[i]}^{(0)}, \ 8 \leq i \leq 15.
\end{cases}
$$

Denote the nibble $STK_i^{(r)}$ ($0 \leq i \leq 7$) as a binary vector $stk_i^{(r)} = (y_{4i}^{(r)}, y_{4i+1}^{(r)}, y_{4i+2}^{(r)}, y_{4i+3}^{(r)})^T$. Then we obtain $stk_i^{(r)} = \bigoplus_{m=1}^{4} tk_{m,i}^{(r)}$ for $0 \leq i \leq 7$. Considering subtweakey cells $stk_i^{(r)}$ derived from master tweakey, we get

$$
stk_i^{(r)} = [I \ L_2^{\lceil r/2 \rceil} \ L_3^{\lceil r/2 \rceil} \ L_4^{\lceil r/2 \rceil}] \cdot \left(tk_{1, P^r[i]}^{(0)}, tk_{2, P^r[i]}^{(0)}, tk_{3, P^r[i]}^{(0)}, tk_{4, P^r[i]}^{(0)} \right)^T . \quad (3)
$$

Without losing generality, we analyze the subtweakeys in the even rounds, which are all transformed from the first two rows of master tweakeys. Let $\bar{P} = [8, 9, 10, 11, \ 12, 13, 14, 15, 2, 0, 4, 7, 6, 3, 5, 1]$ be the inverse permutation of P. For a set $\texttt{Index} = \{r_1, \cdots, r_t\}$ ($|\texttt{Index}| = t$), which corresponding to a set of subtweakeys $\{STK^{(2r_1)}, STK^{(2r_2)} \cdots, STK^{(2r_t)}\}$, we can get a set of linear equations as

$$
\begin{pmatrix} stk_{\bar{P}^{2r_1}[i]}^{(2r_1)} \\ stk_{\bar{P}^{2r_2}[i]}^{(2r_2)} \\ \vdots \\ stk_{\bar{P}^{2r_t}[i]}^{(2r_t)} \end{pmatrix} = \begin{pmatrix} I & L_2^{r_1} & L_3^{r_1} & L_4^{r_1} \\ I & L_2^{r_2} & L_3^{r_2} & L_4^{r_2} \\ \vdots & \vdots & \vdots & \vdots \\ I & L_2^{r_t} & L_3^{r_t} & L_4^{r_t} \end{pmatrix} \cdot \begin{pmatrix} tk_{1,i}^{(0)} \\ tk_{2,i}^{(0)} \\ tk_{3,i}^{(0)} \\ tk_{4,i}^{(0)} \end{pmatrix}, \ 0 \leq i \leq 7. \quad (4)
$$

Because the tweakey schedule only contains the permutation and LFSRs, Eq. (4) is linear equation. Denote coefficient matrix as A and its rank as $rank(A) = a$. The image space of A represents the solution space of $\{STK_{\bar{P}^{2r_1}[i]}^{(2r_1)}, STK_{\bar{P}^{2r_2}[i]}^{(2r_2)} \cdots, STK_{\bar{P}^{2r_t}[i]}^{(2r_t)}\}$ with arbitrary $\{tk_{1,i}^{(0)}, tk_{2,i}^{(0)}, tk_{3,i}^{(0)}, tk_{4,i}^{(0)}\}$, whose size is $|Im(A)| = 2^a$. Let the kernel space of A be $Ker(A) = \{x \in \mathbb{F}_2^{4t} : Ax = 0\}$, then the size of the kernel space is $|Ker(A)| = 2^{16-a}$. For example, assuming $\texttt{Index} = \{0, 1, 2, 3\}$, we can obtain the equations of

$\{STK^{(0)}, STK^{(2)}, STK^{(4)}, STK^{(6)}\}$ as Eq. (4). For $i = 0$, there is

$$
\begin{pmatrix} stk_0^{(0)} \\ stk_2^{(2)} \\ stk_4^{(4)} \\ stk_6^{(6)} \end{pmatrix} = \begin{pmatrix} I & L_2^0 & L_3^0 & L_4^0 \\ I & L_2^1 & L_3^1 & L_4^1 \\ I & L_2^2 & L_3^2 & L_4^2 \\ I & L_2^3 & L_3^3 & L_4^3 \end{pmatrix} \begin{pmatrix} tk_{1,0}^{(0)} \\ tk_{2,0}^{(0)} \\ tk_{3,0}^{(0)} \\ tk_{4,0}^{(0)} \end{pmatrix} = \begin{pmatrix} 1\,0\,0\,0\,1\,0\,0\,0\,1\,0\,0\,0\,1\,0\,0\,0 \\ 0\,1\,0\,0\,0\,1\,0\,0\,0\,1\,0\,0\,0\,1\,0\,0 \\ 0\,0\,1\,0\,0\,0\,1\,0\,0\,0\,1\,0\,0\,0\,1\,0 \\ 0\,0\,0\,1\,0\,0\,0\,1\,0\,0\,0\,1\,0\,0\,0\,1 \\ 1\,0\,0\,0\,1\,0\,0\,1\,0\,0\,1\,0\,0\,1\,0\,0 \\ 0\,1\,0\,0\,0\,1\,0\,1\,0\,0\,0\,0\,0\,0\,1\,0 \\ 0\,0\,1\,0\,0\,0\,0\,1\,0\,1\,0\,0\,0\,1\,0\,1 \\ 0\,0\,0\,1\,1\,1\,0\,0\,0\,0\,1\,0\,1\,1\,1\,0 \\ 1\,0\,0\,0\,0\,0\,1\,0\,1\,0\,1\,1\,0\,0\,1\,0 \\ 0\,1\,0\,0\,0\,0\,1\,1\,0\,0\,1\,0\,1\,0\,1 \\ 0\,0\,1\,0\,1\,1\,0\,0\,1\,0\,0\,0\,1\,1\,0\,0 \\ 0\,0\,0\,1\,0\,1\,1\,0\,0\,1\,0\,0\,0\,0\,1\,1 \\ 1\,0\,0\,0\,0\,0\,0\,1\,1\,1\,1\,1\,0\,1\,0\,1 \\ 0\,1\,0\,0\,1\,1\,0\,0\,1\,0\,1\,1\,1\,1\,0\,0 \\ 0\,0\,1\,0\,0\,1\,1\,0\,1\,0\,0\,1\,0\,1\,1\,0 \\ 0\,0\,0\,1\,0\,0\,1\,1\,1\,0\,0\,0\,1\,0\,1\,1 \end{pmatrix} \begin{pmatrix} x_{1,0} \\ x_{1,1} \\ x_{1,2} \\ x_{1,3} \\ x_{2,0} \\ x_{2,1} \\ x_{2,2} \\ x_{2,3} \\ x_{3,0} \\ x_{3,1} \\ x_{3,2} \\ x_{3,3} \\ x_{4,0} \\ x_{4,1} \\ x_{4,2} \\ x_{4,3} \end{pmatrix}.
$$
(5)

The rank of the coefficient matrix $\boldsymbol{A}$ in Eq. (5) is 14. Therefore, the size of its kernel space and image space is $|Ker(\boldsymbol{A})| = 2^2$ and $|Im(\boldsymbol{A})| = 2^{14}$.

Let $\boldsymbol{A}_{r_j} = [\boldsymbol{I}\ \boldsymbol{L}_2^{r_j}\ \boldsymbol{L}_3^{r_j}\ \boldsymbol{L}_4^{r_j}]$, which is a 4×16 matrix. Then the coefficient matrix of Eq. (4) can be represented as $\boldsymbol{A}_{\{r_1,r_2,\cdots,r_t\}} = [\boldsymbol{A}_{r_1}^T\ \boldsymbol{A}_{r_2}^T\ \cdots\ \boldsymbol{A}_{r_t}^T]^T$, which is a $4t \times 16$ matrix. Since $\boldsymbol{L}_i^{15} = \boldsymbol{I}$ for $2 \le i \le 4$, we can assume that all subscripts of $\boldsymbol{A}_{\{r_1,r_2,\cdots,r_t\}}$ are mod 15. We call $\boldsymbol{A}_{\{r_1,r_2,\cdots,r_t\}}$ a full rank matrix if and only if $rank(\boldsymbol{A}_{\{r_1,r_2,\cdots,r_t\}}) = \min\{4t, 16\}$. We find that when $t \ge 4$, certain sets of Index lead to non-full rank coefficient matrices. Let $\mathcal{K} = \{0, 1, 2, \cdots, 14\}$, for any subset $\{r_1, r_2, \cdots, r_t\} \subset \mathcal{K}$ and $0 \le r' \le 14$, we have

$$
\begin{aligned}
\boldsymbol{A}_{\{r_1+r',r_2+r',\cdots,r_t+r'\}} \\
= \begin{pmatrix} \boldsymbol{I} & \boldsymbol{L}_2^{r_1+r'} & \boldsymbol{L}_3^{r_1+r'} & \boldsymbol{L}_4^{r_1+r'} \\ \boldsymbol{I} & \boldsymbol{L}_2^{r_2+r'} & \boldsymbol{L}_3^{r_2+r'} & \boldsymbol{L}_4^{r_2+r'} \\ \vdots & \vdots & \vdots & \vdots \\ \boldsymbol{I} & \boldsymbol{L}_2^{r_t+r'} & \boldsymbol{L}_3^{r_t+r'} & \boldsymbol{L}_4^{r_t+r'} \end{pmatrix} = \begin{pmatrix} \boldsymbol{I} & \boldsymbol{L}_2^{r_1} & \boldsymbol{L}_3^{r_1} & \boldsymbol{L}_4^{r_1} \\ \boldsymbol{I} & \boldsymbol{L}_2^{r_2} & \boldsymbol{L}_3^{r_2} & \boldsymbol{L}_4^{r_2} \\ \vdots & \vdots & \vdots & \vdots \\ \boldsymbol{I} & \boldsymbol{L}_2^{r_t} & \boldsymbol{L}_3^{r_t} & \boldsymbol{L}_4^{r_t} \end{pmatrix} \cdot \begin{pmatrix} \boldsymbol{I} & & & \\ & \boldsymbol{L}_2^{r'} & & \\ & & \boldsymbol{L}_3^{r'} & \\ & & & \boldsymbol{L}_4^{r'} \end{pmatrix} \\
= \boldsymbol{A}_{\{r_1,r_2,\cdots,r_t\}} \cdot diag(\boldsymbol{I}, \boldsymbol{L}_2^{r'}, \boldsymbol{L}_3^{r'}\ \boldsymbol{L}_4^{r'}).
\end{aligned}
$$
(6)

Since $\boldsymbol{L}_2, \boldsymbol{L}_3$ and $\boldsymbol{L}_4$ are all 4×4 full rank matrices, $D_{r'} = diag(\boldsymbol{I}, \boldsymbol{L}_2^{r'}, \boldsymbol{L}_3^{r'}\ \boldsymbol{L}_4^{r'})$ is a 16×16 full rank matrix. Then we can deduce that

$$
rank(\boldsymbol{A}_{\{r_1+r',r_2+r',\cdots,r_t+r'\}}) = rank(\boldsymbol{A}_{\{r_1,r_2,\cdots,r_t\}}).
$$
(7)

Since the rank of the coefficient matrix is our most concern, we introduce the concept of *rank-equivalent* as follows.

Definition 1 (rank-equivalent). *Given two subsets* $x = \{r_1, r_2, \ldots, r_t\}$, $y = \{r_1', r_2', \ldots, r_t'\} \subset \mathcal{K}$, *we say* x *and* y *are rank-equivalent if there exits an integer* r' *such that*

$$
r_i \equiv r_i' + r' \bmod 15 \text{ for all } 1 \le i \le t.
$$

The rank-equivalence class of the subset x *is defined by*

$$
[x] := \{y \subset \mathcal{K} : x \text{ and } y \text{ are rank-equivalent}\}.
$$

From Eq. (7), $rank(\boldsymbol{A}_x) = rank(\boldsymbol{A}_y)$ holds for any rank-equivalent subsets x and y.

Table 4. Rank-equivalence class of non-full rank coefficient matrix for SKINNYe-64-256

rank	t	Rank-equivalence class $[\{r_1, r_2, \cdots, r_t\}]$
14	4	$[\{0,1,2,3\}],[\{0,1,2,10\}],[\{0,1,3,4\}],[\{0,1,3,7\}],[\{0,1,3,13\}],[\{0,1,4,5\}],[\{0,1,4,12\}],$ $[\{0,1,5,6\}],[\{0,1,5,8\}],[\{0,1,5,11\}],[\{0,1,6,7\}],[\{0,1,6,10\}],[\{0,1,6,12\}],[\{0,1,7,8\}],$ $[\{0,1,7,9\}],[\{0,1,11,13\}],[\{0,2,4,6\}],[\{0,2,5,7\}],[\{0,2,5,12\}],[\{0,2,6,8\}],[\{0,2,6,11\}],$ $[\{0,2,7,9\}],[\{0,2,7,10\}],[\{0,2,7,11\}],[\{0,2,9,12\}],[\{0,3,6,9\}],[\{0,3,7,10\}],[\{0,3,7,11\}]$
15	4	$[\{0,1,2,4\}],[\{0,1,2,5\}],[\{0,1,2,6\}],[\{0,1,2,7\}],[\{0,1,2,8\}],[\{0,1,2,9\}],[\{0,1,2,11\}],$ $[\{0,1,2,12\}],[\{0,1,2,13\}],[\{0,1,3,5\}],[\{0,1,3,6\}],[\{0,1,3,8\}],[\{0,1,3,9\}],[\{0,1,3,10\}],$ $[\{0,1,3,11\}],[\{0,1,3,12\}],[\{0,1,4,6\}],[\{0,1,4,7\}],[\{0,1,4,8\}],[\{0,1,4,9\}],[\{0,1,4,10\}],$ $[\{0,1,4,11\}],[\{0,1,4,13\}],[\{0,1,5,7\}],[\{0,1,5,9\}],[\{0,1,5,10\}],[\{0,1,5,12\}],[\{0,1,5,13\}],$ $[\{0,1,6,8\}],[\{0,1,6,9\}],[\{0,1,6,11\}],[\{0,1,6,13\}],[\{0,1,7,10\}],[\{0,1,7,11\}],[\{0,1,7,12\}],$ $[\{0,1,7,13\}],[\{0,1,8,10\}],[\{0,1,8,11\}],[\{0,1,8,12\}],[\{0,1,8,13\}],[\{0,1,9,11\}],[\{0,1,9,12\}],$ $[\{0,1,9,13\}],[\{0,1,10,12\}],[\{0,1,10,13\}],[\{0,2,4,7\}],[\{0,2,4,8\}],[\{0,2,4,9\}],[\{0,2,4,10\}],$ $[\{0,2,4,11\}],[\{0,2,4,12\}],[\{0,2,5,8\}],[\{0,2,5,9\}],[\{0,2,5,10\}],[\{0,2,5,11\}],[\{0,2,6,9\}],$ $[\{0,2,6,10\}],[\{0,2,6,12\}],[\{0,2,7,12\}],[\{0,2,8,11\}],[\{0,2,8,12\}],[\{0,3,6,10\}],[\{0,3,6,11\}]$
	5	$[\{0,1,2,3,7\}],[\{0,1,2,3,10\}],[\{0,1,2,3,11\}],[\{0,1,2,3,13\}],[\{0,1,2,4,5\}],[\{0,1,2,4,8\}],$ $[\{0,1,2,4,10\}],[\{0,1,2,5,8\}],[\{0,1,2,5,10\}],[\{0,1,2,6,9\}],[\{0,1,2,6,10\}],[\{0,1,2,6,12\}],$ $[\{0,1,2,7,10\}],[\{0,1,2,7,11\}],[\{0,1,2,7,13\}],[\{0,1,2,8,10\}],[\{0,1,2,9,10\}],[\{0,1,2,9,12\}],$ $[\{0,1,2,10,11\}],[\{0,1,2,10,12\}],[\{0,1,2,10,13\}],[\{0,1,2,11,13\}],[\{0,1,3,4,7\}],[\{0,1,3,4,9\}],$ $[\{0,1,3,5,6\}],[\{0,1,3,5,7\}],[\{0,1,3,5,8\}],[\{0,1,3,5,12\}],[\{0,1,3,6,7\}],[\{0,1,3,6,8\}],$ $[\{0,1,3,6,12\}],[\{0,1,3,7,8\}],[\{0,1,3,7,9\}],[\{0,1,3,7,10\}],[\{0,1,3,7,11\}],[\{0,1,3,7,12\}],$ $[\{0,1,3,7,13\}],[\{0,1,3,8,12\}],[\{0,1,3,10,11\}],[\{0,1,3,10,13\}],[\{0,1,3,11,13\}],[\{0,1,4,5,8\}],$ $[\{0,1,4,5,10\}],[\{0,1,4,6,11\}],[\{0,1,4,6,12\}],[\{0,1,4,6,13\}],[\{0,1,4,7,9\}],[\{0,1,4,8,10\}],$ $[\{0,1,4,11,13\}],[\{0,1,5,6,12\}],[\{0,1,5,7,8\}],[\{0,1,5,7,12\}],[\{0,1,5,8,9\}],[\{0,1,5,8,10\}],$ $[\{0,1,5,8,11\}],[\{0,1,5,8,12\}],[\{0,1,5,8,13\}],[\{0,1,5,9,11\}],[\{0,1,5,9,13\}],[\{0,1,5,11,13\}],$ $[\{0,1,6,7,12\}],[\{0,1,6,8,12\}],[\{0,1,6,9,12\}],[\{0,1,6,10,12\}],[\{0,1,6,11,13\}],[\{0,1,7,10,13\}],$ $[\{0,1,7,11,13\}],[\{0,1,8,11,13\}],[\{0,1,9,11,13\}],[\{0,2,4,6,11\}],[\{0,2,4,7,11\}],[\{0,2,4,8,10\}],$ $[\{0,2,4,9,12\}],[\{0,2,5,7,11\}],[\{0,2,5,8,10\}],[\{0,2,5,9,12\}],[\{0,2,6,9,12\}]$
	6	$[\{0,1,2,3,7,10\}],[\{0,1,2,3,7,11\}],[\{0,1,2,3,7,13\}],[\{0,1,2,3,10,11\}],[\{0,1,2,3,10,13\}],$ $[\{0,1,2,3,11,13\}],[\{0,1,2,4,5,8\}],[\{0,1,2,4,5,10\}],[\{0,1,2,4,8,10\}],[\{0,1,2,5,8,10\}],$ $[\{0,1,2,6,9,10\}],[\{0,1,2,6,9,12\}],[\{0,1,2,6,10,12\}],[\{0,1,2,7,10,11\}],[\{0,1,2,7,10,13\}],$ $[\{0,1,2,7,11,13\}],[\{0,1,2,9,10,12\}],[\{0,1,2,10,11,13\}],[\{0,1,3,4,7,9\}],[\{0,1,3,5,6,8\}],$ $[\{0,1,3,5,6,12\}],[\{0,1,3,5,7,8\}],[\{0,1,3,5,7,12\}],[\{0,1,3,5,8,12\}],[\{0,1,3,6,7,12\}],$ $[\{0,1,3,6,8,12\}],[\{0,1,3,7,8,12\}],[\{0,1,3,7,10,11\}],[\{0,1,3,7,10,13\}],[\{0,1,3,7,11,13\}],$ $[\{0,1,4,5,8,10\}],[\{0,1,4,6,11,13\}],[\{0,1,5,7,8,12\}],[\{0,1,5,8,11,13\}],[\{0,1,5,9,11,13\}]$
	7	$[\{0,1,2,3,7,10,11\}],[\{0,1,2,3,7,10,13\}],[\{0,1,2,3,7,11,13\}],[\{0,1,2,3,10,11,13\}],$ $[\{0,1,2,4,5,8,10\}],[\{0,1,2,6,9,10,12\}],[\{0,1,2,7,10,11,13\}],[\{0,1,3,5,6,8,12\}],$ $[\{0,1,3,5,7,8,12\}]$
	8	$[\{0,1,2,3,7,10,11,13\}]$

For SKINNYe-64-256, we compute all the rank-equivalence classes whose corresponding coefficient matrix is non-full rank with Algorithm 1 in Supplementary Material A in our full version paper [53] and list the results in Table 4.

Similarly, for SKINNYe-64-256 v2, we set $\tilde{\boldsymbol{A}}_{r_j} = [\boldsymbol{I} \ \boldsymbol{L}_2^{r_j} \ \boldsymbol{L}_3^{r_j} \ \tilde{\boldsymbol{L}}_4^{r_j}]$, which is also a 4×16 matrix. Then the coefficient matrix of Eq. (4) can be represented as $\tilde{\boldsymbol{A}}_{\{r_1, r_2, \cdots, r_t\}} = [\tilde{\boldsymbol{A}}_{r_1}^T \ \tilde{\boldsymbol{A}}_{r_2}^T \ \cdots \ \tilde{\boldsymbol{A}}_{r_t}^T]^T$, which is a $4t \times 16$ matrix. For arbitrary $\{r_1, r_2, \cdots, r_t\} \subset \mathcal{K}$, the matrix $\tilde{\boldsymbol{A}}_{\{r_1, r_2, \cdots, r_t\}}$ is full rank. That is, when $t \leq 4$, the rank of $\tilde{\boldsymbol{A}}_{\{r_1, r_2, \cdots, r_t\}}$ is $4t$, otherwise the rank is 16.

The Subtweakey Difference Cancellations. For a given active tweakey cell, $z - 1$ subtweakey difference cancellation happens every 30 rounds for SKINNY-n-zn [9] with $z = 2, 3$. However, for SKINNYe-64-256, although $z = 4$, we have more cancellations than $z - 1 = 3$. Since the tweakey schedule is linear, the differences of subtweakeys can be computed by the differences injected in the master tweakey with Eq. (4). Assume that there is at least one $1 \leq m \leq 4$ that $\Delta TK_{m,i} \neq 0$. Set $A_{[\{r_1, r_2, \cdots, r_t\}]} \cdot [tk_{1,i}^{(0)}, tk_{2,i}^{(0)}, tk_{3,i}^{(0)}, tk_{4,i}^{(0)}]^T = \mathbf{0}$, which means the subtweakey difference cancellations happen at $\{STK_{\bar{P}^{2r_1}[i]}^{(2r_1)} \cdots,$ $STK_{\bar{P}^{2r_t}[i]}^{(2r_t)}\}$ if $0 \leq i \leq 7$, or $\{STK_{\bar{P}^{2r_1+1}[i]}^{(2r_1+1)} \cdots, STK_{\bar{P}^{2r_t+1}[i]}^{(2r_t+1)}\}$ if $8 \leq i \leq 15$. When $rank(A_{[\{r_1, r_2, \cdots, r_t\}]}) = 16$, the size of its kernel space is 1. Then $[tk_{1,i}^{(0)}, tk_{2,i}^{(0)}, tk_{3,i}^{(0)}, tk_{4,i}^{(0)}]$ has only one zero solution, which means $\Delta TK_{m,i} = 0$ for all $m = 1, 2, 3, 4$. When $rank(A_{[\{r_1, r_2, \cdots, r_t\}]}) < 16$, we have non-zero solutions for $\Delta TK_{m,i}$, i.e., the subtweakey difference cancellations happen. Obviously, when $t \leq 3$, $rank(A_{[\{r_1, r_2, \cdots, r_t\}]}) = 4t \leq 16$. For $t \geq 4$, we obtain all rank-equivalence classes whose corresponding coefficient matrices are non-full rank from Table 4. So each rank-equivalence class corresponds to a set of positions of the subtweakey difference cancellations. We find several properties of the rank-equivalence classes:

- When $t = 4$, we find the matrix $A_{\{r_1, r_2, r_3, r_4\}}$ with arbitrary $\{r_1, r_2, r_3, r_4\} \subset \mathcal{K}$ is non-full rank. That is, for the given active nibbles in the master key, the subtweakey difference cancellations can happen four times in arbitrary round for every 30 rounds. Especially for $rank(A_{\{0,1,2,3\}}) = 14$ and $|Ker(A_{\{0,1,2,3\}})| = 2^2$, there are 3 non-zero solutions of the difference for the active nibbles of the master tweakey. For SKINNYe-64-256, there can be nine consecutive rounds with fully inactive internal states.

- When $t \geq 5$, for all $[\{r_1, r_2, \cdots, r_t\}]$ in Table 4, $rank(A_{[\{r_1, r_2, \cdots, r_t\}]}) = 15$. For $A_{[\{r_1, r_2, \cdots, r_t\}]} \cdot [tk_{1,i}^{(0)}, tk_{2,i}^{(0)}, tk_{3,i}^{(0)}, tk_{4,i}^{(0)}]^T = \mathbf{0}$, there is only one nonzero solution. We find that for some different rank-equivalence classes, the solutions are the same. For example, for rank-equivalence classes $[\{0, 1, 2, 7, 10\}]$ and $[\{0, 1, 3, 11, 13\}]$, when $0 \leq i \leq 7$ we set

$$A_{[\{0,1,2,7,10\}]} \cdot [tk_{1,i}^{(0)}, tk_{2,i}^{(0)}, tk_{3,i}^{(0)}, tk_{4,i}^{(0)}]^T = \mathbf{0}, \tag{8}$$

$$A_{[\{0,1,3,11,13\}]} \cdot [tk_{1,i}^{(0)}, tk_{2,i}^{(0)}, tk_{3,i}^{(0)}, tk_{4,i}^{(0)}]^T = \mathbf{0}, \tag{9}$$

where the cancellations happen at $\{STK_i^{(0)}, STK_{\bar{P}^2[i]}^{(2)}, STK_{\bar{P}^4[i]}^{(4)}, STK_{\bar{P}^{14}[i]}^{(14)},$ $STK_{\bar{P}^{20}[i]}^{(20)}\}$ for Eq. (8) and $\{STK_i^{(0)}, STK_{\bar{P}^2[i]}^{(2)}, STK_{\bar{P}^6[i]}^{(6)}, STK_{\bar{P}^{22}[i]}^{(22)},$ $STK_{\bar{P}^{26}[i]}^{(26)}\}$ for Eq. (9). The non-zero solutions of both two linear equations are $tk_{1,i}^{(0)} = [0,0,0,1]^T$, $tk_{2,i}^{(0)} = [0,1,1,1]^T$, $tk_{3,i}^{(0)} = [0,0,0,0]^T$, $tk_{4,i}^{(0)} = [0,1,1,0]^T$. Namely, the cancellations happen at $\{STK_i^{(0)}, STK_{\bar{P}^2[i]}^{(2)},$ $STK_{\bar{P}^4[i]}^{(4)}, STK_{\bar{P}^6[i]}^{(6)}, STK_{\bar{P}^{14}[i]}^{(14)}, STK_{\bar{P}^{20}[i]}^{(20)}, STK_{\bar{P}^{22}[i]}^{(22)}, STK_{\bar{P}^{26}[i]}^{(26)}\}$ at the same time, which corresponds to the rank-equivalence class $[\{0, 1, 2, 3, 7, 10,$

$11, 13\}]$. The situation for $8 \leq i \leq 15$ is the same. Further, we find that for arbitrary $\{r_1, r_2, \cdots, r_t\} \subset \{0, 1, 2, 3, 7, 10, 11, 13\}$ $(t \geq 5)$, the solution of $\boldsymbol{A}_{[\{r_1, r_2, \cdots, r_t\}]} \cdot [\boldsymbol{tk}_{1,i}^{(0)}, \boldsymbol{tk}_{2,i}^{(0)}, \boldsymbol{tk}_{3,i}^{(0)}, \boldsymbol{tk}_{4,i}^{(0)}]^T = \boldsymbol{0}$ is the same to $\boldsymbol{A}_{[\{0,1,2,3,7,10,11,13\}]} \cdot [\boldsymbol{tk}_{1,i}^{(0)}, \boldsymbol{tk}_{2,i}^{(0)}, \boldsymbol{tk}_{3,i}^{(0)}, \boldsymbol{tk}_{4,i}^{(0)}]^T = \boldsymbol{0}$, which means that there is only one difference cancellation behaviour for those rank-equivalence classes.

Remark. It is worth noting that there are some rank-equivalence classes $[\{r_1, r_2, \cdots, r_t\}]$ in Table 4, where $\{r_1, r_2, \cdots, r_t\}$ is not directly the sub set of $\{0, 1, 2, 3, 7, 10, 11, 13\}$ but corresponds to the same difference cancellation behaviour. Taking the rank-equivalence class $[\{0, 1, 2, 6, 9\}]$ as an example, we can assume $\boldsymbol{A}_{[\{0,1,2,6,9\}]} \cdot [\boldsymbol{\bar{tk}}_{1,i}^{(0)}, \boldsymbol{\bar{tk}}_{2,i}^{(0)}, \boldsymbol{\bar{tk}}_{3,i}^{(0)}, \boldsymbol{\bar{tk}}_{4,i}^{(0)}]^T = \boldsymbol{0}$, and obtain $\boldsymbol{\bar{tk}}_{1,i}^{(0)} = [0, 0, 0, 1]^T$, $\boldsymbol{\bar{tk}}_{2,i}^{(0)} = [1, 1, 1, 1]^T$, $\boldsymbol{\bar{tk}}_{3,i}^{(0)} = [0, 0, 0, 0]^T$, $\boldsymbol{\bar{tk}}_{4,i}^{(0)} = [1, 1, 1, 0]^T$. Applying the same solution, we can also deduce $\boldsymbol{A}_{[\{0,1,2,6,9,10,12,14\}]} \cdot [\boldsymbol{\bar{tk}}_{1,i}^{(0)}, \boldsymbol{\bar{tk}}_{2,i}^{(0)}, \boldsymbol{\bar{tk}}_{3,i}^{(0)}, \boldsymbol{\bar{tk}}_{4,i}^{(0)}]^T = \boldsymbol{0}$. Similarly, for arbitrary $\{r_1, r_2, \cdots, r_t\} \subset \{0, 1, 2, 6, 9, 10, 12, 14\}$ $(t \geq 5)$, we deduce that there is only one difference cancellation behaviour. Further, due to rank-equivalence class in Definition 1, there is $[\{0, 1, 2, 3, 7, 10, 11, 13\}] = [\{0, 1, 2, 6, 9, 10, 12, 14\}]$. The two sets $\{0, 1, 2, 3, 7, 10, 11, 13\}$ and $\{0, 1, 2, 6, 9, 10, 12, 14\}$ only represent the difference cancellations starting from different rounds every 15 rounds for TK-z, and actually show the same difference cancellation behaviour.

In summary, there are only two kinds of the difference cancellation behaviours:

- For rank-equivalence class $[\{0, 1, 2, 4, 5, 8, 10\}]$, the subtweakey difference cancellations happen 7 times in the fixed positions for the given active nibble of the master key in every 30 rounds. Assuming $\boldsymbol{A}_{[\{0,1,2,4,5,8,10\}]} \cdot [\boldsymbol{tk}_{1,i}^{(0)}, \boldsymbol{tk}_{2,i}^{(0)}, \boldsymbol{tk}_{3,i}^{(0)}, \boldsymbol{tk}_{4,i}^{(0)}]^T = \boldsymbol{0}$, we can compute the only one nonzero solution, where $\boldsymbol{tk}_{1,i}^{(0)} = [0, 0, 0, 0]^T$, $\boldsymbol{tk}_{2,i}^{(0)} = [1, 0, 0, 0]^T$, $\boldsymbol{tk}_{3,i}^{(0)} = [0, 0, 0, 0]^T$, $\boldsymbol{tk}_{4,i}^{(0)} = [1, 0, 0, 0]^T$.

- For rank-equivalence class $[\{0, 1, 2, 3, 7, 10, 11, 13\}]$, the subtweakey difference cancellations happen 8 times in the fixed positions every 30 rounds. Assuming $\boldsymbol{A}_{[\{0,1,2,3,7,10,11,13\}]} \cdot [\boldsymbol{tk}_{1,i}^{(0)}, \boldsymbol{tk}_{2,i}^{(0)}, \boldsymbol{tk}_{3,i}^{(0)}, \boldsymbol{tk}_{4,i}^{(0)}]^T = \boldsymbol{0}$, the nonzero solution is $\boldsymbol{tk}_{1,i}^{(0)} = [0, 0, 0, 1]^T$, $\boldsymbol{tk}_{2,i}^{(0)} = [0, 1, 1, 1]^T$, $\boldsymbol{tk}_{3,i}^{(0)} = [0, 0, 0, 0]^T$, $\boldsymbol{tk}_{4,i}^{(0)} = [0, 1, 1, 0]^T$.

For SKINNYe-64-256 v2, there is $rank(\boldsymbol{\tilde{A}}_{\{r_1, r_2, r_3, r_4\}}) = 16$ for arbitrary $\{r_1, r_2, r_3, r_4\} \subset \mathcal{K}$. That is, at most three difference cancellations can happen every 30 rounds for a given active tweakey nibble and there can be seven rounds of fully inactive internal states at most.

Key Guessing Strategy Based on the Relations of Subtweakeys. In key-recovery attacks, several rounds are added before and after the distinguisher and the involved subtweakeys should be guessed to recover the master tweakey. We can use the relations of subtweakeys to get more accurate

and efficient key guessing strategy following similar idea of the key-bridge technique [26,33]. For example, assume that a set of subtweakeys $\{stk^{(2r_1)}_{\bar{P}^{2r_1}[i]},$ $stk^{(2r_2)}_{\bar{P}^{2r_2}[i]} \cdots , stk^{(2r_t)}_{\bar{P}^{2r_t}[i]}, stk^{(2r_{t+1})}_{\bar{P}^{2r_{t+1}}[i]}\}$ derived from the same i-th $(0 \leq i \leq 7)$ nibble of the master tweakey are involved in the key-recovery phase. Suppose $rank(A_{\{r_1,r_2,\cdots,r_t\}}) = a$ and $rank(A_{\{r_1,r_2,\cdots,r_{t+1}\}}) = b$ $(b > a)$. The number of possible values for $\{stk^{(2r_1)}_{\bar{P}^{2r_1}[i]}, stk^{(2r_2)}_{\bar{P}^{2r_2}[i]} \cdots , stk^{(2r_t)}_{\bar{P}^{2r_t}[i]}\}$ is $|Im(A_{\{r_1,r_2,\cdots,r_t\}})| = 2^a$. After we guessed $\{stk^{(2r_1)}_{\bar{P}^{2r_1}[i]}, stk^{(2r_2)}_{\bar{P}^{2r_2}[i]} \cdots , stk^{(2r_t)}_{\bar{P}^{2r_t}[i]}\} \in Im(A_{\{r_1,r_2,\cdots,r_t\}})$, the number of possible guesses for the last nibble $stk^{(2r_{t+1})}_{\bar{P}^{2r_{t+1}}[i]}$ will be 2^{b-a}.

4   Rectangle Attacks on SKINNYe-64-256 and Its Version 2

4.1   Preliminary for Boomerang and Rectangle Attacks

The boomerang attack proposed by Wagner [63] is a differential-based attack, which uses two short differential characteristics instead of one long characteristic as shown in Fig. 3. The boomerang attack is developed into the amplified boomerang attack [44] and rectangle attack [17], which require only chosen plaintext queries. To clarify the probability of boomerang, Biryukov $et\ al.$ [19] introduced the $boomerang\ switch$ technique, which is generalized by Dunkelman $et\ al.$ [34] as the $sandwich\ attack$. In the attack, the cipher E_d is considered as $\tilde{E}_1 \circ E_m \circ \tilde{E}_0$, where $\tilde{p}$ and $\tilde{q}$ are the probability of the differentials used for the r_0-round $\tilde{E}_0$ and r_1-round $\tilde{E}_1$. The middle part r_m-round E_m handles the dependence of the two short differentials. If the probability of generating a right quartet for E_m is ξ, the probability of the whole rectangle distinguisher is $2^{-n}\tilde{p}^2\tilde{q}^2\xi$. Then, Cid $et\ al.$ [23] introduced the boomerang connectivity table (BCT) to clarify the probability around the boundary of boomerang and compute its probability more accurately. Further, various studies or improvements [21,24,61,64] on BCT technique enrich boomerang attacks.

Related-key boomerang and rectangle attacks were proposed by Biham $et\ al.$ [18]. As shown in Fig. 4, the cipher E is decomposed into $E_f \circ E_d \circ E_b$, where $E_d = E_1 \circ E_0$ is the related-key rectangle distinguisher and E_b and E_f are the extended rounds before and after the distinguisher. Assuming we use a related-key differential $\alpha \to \beta$ over E_0 under a key difference ΔK and $\delta \to \gamma$ over E_1 under a key difference ∇K. If the master key K_1 is known, the other three keys are all determined, where $K_2 = K_1 \oplus \Delta K$, $K_3 = K_1 \oplus \nabla K$, and $K_4 = K_1 \oplus \Delta K \oplus \nabla K$. Denote r_b as the number of unknown bits in the difference α' of plaintexts. Let k_b be the set of subkey bits that involved in E_b while encrypting the plaintext to the known difference α and decrypting to get the corresponding plaintext. Denote the number $m_b = |k_b|$. Similarly, we have r_f and $m_f = |k_f|$ for E_f.

There are several key-recovery frameworks of rectangle attacks [15–17,46] in both single-key setting and related-key setting. As shown by Biham $et\ al.$

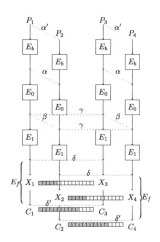

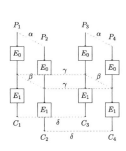

Fig. 3. Boomerang attack   **Fig. 4.** Rectangle attack on E

[15], when the key schedule is linear (e.g. SKINNY), the differences between the subkeys of K_1, K_2, K_3 and K_4 are all determined in each round. Exploring this property, Dong et al. [30] proposed a new related-key rectangle attack for ciphers with linear key schedule (see Supplementary Material B.1 in our full version paper [53]). They try to guess all k_b and part of k_f, denoted as k'_f before generating quartets. Then with partial decryption, they may gain h_f inactive bits (or bits with fixed differences) from the internal state as filters. They also built a uniform automatic tool to search for the entire rectangle key-recovery attack on SKINNY, which is based on a series of automatic tools [24,37,54].

4.2 Automatic Search for Related-Tweakey Rectangle Attacks for SKINNYe-64-256 and Its Version 2

We apply Dong et al.'s automatic tool [30] by modifying the constraints of the subtweakey to include more differential cancellation behaviours studied in Sect. 3. For simplicity, we put Dong et al.'s automatic tool in Supplementary Material B in our full version paper [53], and only list the differences of the modelling here.

In previous automatic models [9,24,37] for SKINNY-n-zn ($z = 1, 2, 3$), for a given cell position in the tweakey schedule, the number of cancellations can only be $z - 1$ within 30 consecutive rounds. The constraints for the cancellations are given by the designers of SKINNY [10, Page 52], e.g., for 0-th nibble of the master tweakey within the 30 consecutive rounds:

$$\text{LANE}_0 - stk_0^{(0)} \geq 0, \ \text{LANE}_0 - stk_{P^{2i}[0]}^{(2i)} \geq 0, \ 1 \leq i \leq 14,$$
$$stk_0^{(0)} + stk_{P^2[0]}^{(2)} + \cdots + stk_{P^{28}[0]}^{(28)} - 15 \cdot \text{LANE}_0 \geq -(z-1), \tag{10}$$

where the binary variable LANE_0 is 0 only if $TK_{m,0} = 0$ for all $1 \le m \le z$, and the binary variable $stk_{Pr[0]}^{(r)}$ is 0 if and only if the nibble $STK_{Pr[0]}^{(r)}$ is inactive. Similar constraints are applied to other nibble positions.

However, for SKINNYe-64-256, although $z = 4$, we have more cancellations than $z - 1 = 3$ according to Sect. 3. The possible number and positions of cancellations are diverse, which needs to be modeled by new constraints for the upper and lower differentials besides Constraint (10). According to Sect. 3, the automatic models are divided into two cases according to different subtweakey difference cancellation behaviours to search for the distinguisher suitable for Dong *et al.*'s rectangle attack framework:

- $t \le 4$: When $t \le 3$, the rank of $\boldsymbol{A}_{\{r_1,\cdots,r_t\}}$ is $4t \le 16$. When $t = 4$, the matrix $\boldsymbol{A}_{\{r_1,r_2,r_3,r_4\}}$ is non-full rank. That is, when $t \le 4$, $rank(\boldsymbol{A}_{\{r_1,\cdots,r_t\}}) < 16$. For a given active nibble in the master key, the subtweakey difference cancellations can happen at most four times in arbitrary 30 rounds. In this case, we only need to modify the last constraint of Eq. (10) to be ($z = 4$):

$$stk_0^{(0)} + stk_{P^2[0]}^{(2)} + \cdots + stk_{P^{28}[0]}^{(28)} - 15 \cdot \text{LANE}_0 \ge -z.$$

- $t > 4$: There are only two kinds of the difference cancellation behaviours in Sect. 3, i.e., $[\{0, 1, 2, 4, 5, 8, 10\}]$ and $[\{0, 1, 2, 3, 7, 10, 11, 13\}]$. For the rank-equivalence class $[\{0, 1, 2, 4, 5, 8, 10\}]$, we fixed the positions of difference cancellations for the i-th active nibble of the master tweakey to build the model. For each $0 \le r' \le 14$, we set the subtweakey differences to 0 in $\{2r', 2(r' + 1) \bmod 30, 2(r' + 2) \bmod 30, 2(r' + 4) \bmod 30, 2(r' + 5) \bmod 30, 2(r' + 8) \bmod 30, 2(r' + 10) \bmod 30\}$ rounds when $0 \le i \le 7$, and in $\{2r' + 1, (2(r' + 1) + 1) \bmod 30, (2(r' + 2) + 1) \bmod 30, (2(r' + 4) + 1) \bmod 30, (2(r'+5)+1) \bmod 30, (2(r'+8)+1) \bmod 30, (2(r'+10)+1) \bmod 30\}$ rounds when $8 \le i \le 15$ to run the model. Similar for case $[\{0, 1, 2, 3, 7, 10, 11, 13\}]$.

Searching with different automatic models, we select a 30-round related-tweakey (RTK) boomerang distinguisher for SKINNYe-64-256 in Table 5, where the difference cancellation behaviour $[\{0, 1, 2, 3, 7, 10, 11, 13\}]$ is used both in the upper and lower differentials. We also experimentally verify the probabilities of the middle part of the distinguishers, and list details of the distinguisher, the experimental results and full figures in Table 12, Table 14 and Figure 12 in Supplementary Material C.1 and I in our full version paper [53]. Our source codes are based on the open source in [24,30], which is provided in https://github.com/skinny64/Skinny64-256.

For SKINNYe-64-256 v2, we find a 26-round related-tweakey boomerang distinguisher in Table 11 and 13 in Supplementary Material C.1 in our full version paper [53].

4.3   Rectangle Attack on 41-round SKINNYe-64-256

We use the 30-round rectangle distinguisher for SKINNYe-64-256 in Table 5, whose probability is $2^{-n}\tilde{p}^2\xi\tilde{q}^2 = 2^{-64-56.47} = 2^{-120.47}$. The attack follows

Table 5. The 30-round RTK boomerang distinguisher for SKINNYe-64-256.

$r_0 = 12$, $r_m = 5$, $r_1 = 13$, $\tilde{p} = 2^{-3.46}$, $\xi = 2^{-30.95}$, $\tilde{q} = 2^{-9.30}$, $\tilde{p}^2\xi\tilde{q}^2 = 2^{-56.47}$
$\Delta TK_1 = $ 0, 0, 0, 0, 0, 0, 0, 0, 1, 0, 0, 0, 0, 0, 0, 0
$\Delta TK_2 = $ 0, 0, 0, 0, 0, 0, 0, 0, 5, 0, 0, 0, 0, 0, 0, 0
$\Delta TK_3 = $ 0, 0, 0, 0, 0, 0, 0, 0, 0, 0, 0, 0, 0, 0, 0, 0
$\Delta TK_4 = $ 0, 0, 0, 0, 0, 0, 0, 0, 4, 0, 0, 0, 0, 0, 0, 0
$\Delta X^{(0)} = $ 0, 0, 0, 0, 0, 0, 0, 0, 0, 0, 0, 0, 0, 0, 0, 4
$\nabla TK_1 = $ 0, 0, 0, 0, 0, 0, 0, 0, 0, 0, 0, 0, 0, 0, 0, 1
$\nabla TK_2 = $ 0, 0, 0, 0, 0, 0, 0, 0, 0, 0, 0, 0, 0, 0, 0, 8
$\nabla TK_3 = $ 0, 0, 0, 0, 0, 0, 0, 0, 0, 0, 0, 0, 0, 0, 0, 0
$\nabla TK_4 = $ 0, 0, 0, 0, 0, 0, 0, 0, 0, 0, 0, 0, 0, 0, 0, 8
$\nabla X^{(30)} = $ 0, 0, 0, 1, 0, 0, 0, 1, 0, 0, 0, 0, 0, 0, 0, 1

the Dong *et al.*'s rectangle attack framework [30], which is also given in Algorithm 2 in Supplementary Material B.1 in our full version paper [53]. Adding 4-round E_b and 7-round E_f, we attack 41-round SKINNYe-64-256, as illustrated in Fig. 5. For simplicity, let $STK_{j_1,j_2}^{(i)}$ be the j_1-th and j_2-th nibble of the i-th round STK. In the first round, we use subtweakey $ETK^{(0)} = \text{MC} \circ \text{SR}(STK^{(0)})$ instead of $STK^{(0)}$, and there is $ETK_i^{(0)} = ETK_{i+4}^{(0)} = ETK_{i+12}^{(0)} = STK_i^{(0)}$ for $0 \leq i \leq 3$, and $ETK_8^{(0)} = STK_7^{(0)}$, $ETK_9^{(0)} = STK_4^{(0)}$, $ETK_{10}^{(0)} = STK_5^{(0)}$, $ETK_{11}^{(0)} = STK_6^{(0)}$. Construct the structures at $\bar{W}^{(0)}$ and $r_b = 12 \cdot 4 = 48$. The cells need to be guessed in E_b are $k_b = \{STK_{0,2,4}^{(2)}, STK_{0-3,5-7}^{(1)}, STK_{0-7}^{(0)}\}$ and $m_b = 18 \cdot 4 = 72$. In E_f, we have $r_f = 16 \cdot 4 = 64$ and $m_f = 45 \cdot 4 = 180$ where $k_f = \{STK_{3,7}^{(34)}, STK_{2-4,7}^{(35)}, STK_{1-7}^{(36)}, STK_{0-7}^{(37)}, STK_{0-7}^{(38)}, STK_{0-7}^{(39)}, STK_{0-7}^{(40)}\}$. The subtweakey cells guessed in advance are marked by red boxes, which are $k_f' = \{STK_{3,6,7}^{(37)}, STK_{0-2,4-7}^{(38)}, STK_{0-7}^{(39)}, STK_{0-7}^{(40)}\}$, and we have $m_f' = 26 \cdot 4 = 104$. Then, we get 7 cells in the internal states (marked by red boxes in $W^{(37)}$ and $W^{(36)}$) as additional filters with the guessed m_f'-bit key, i.e., $h_f = 7 \cdot 4 = 28$ as $\{W_{6,11,15}^{(36)}, W_{5,6,11,12}^{(37)}\}$.

Key Bridges. To further accelerate our attack, we identify some tweakey relations in E_b and E_f according to the analysis in Sect. 3 . We list the subtweakeys transformed from the i-th ($0 \leq i \leq 15$) nibble of the master key $TK_m^{(0)}$ ($1 \leq m \leq 4$) in Table 6. For example in line 0 of Table 6, there are 5 subtweakeys in k_b and k_f transformed from the 0-th nibbles of $TK_m^{(0)}$, where

$$\left(stk_0^{(0)}, stk_2^{(2)}, stk_4^{(36)}, stk_6^{(38)}, stk_5^{(40)}\right)^T = A_{\{0,1,3,4,5\}} \cdot \left(tk_{1,0}^{(0)}, tk_{2,0}^{(0)}, tk_{3,0}^{(0)}, tk_{4,0}^{(0)}\right)^T.$$

Since $rank(A_{\{0,1,3,4,5\}}) = 16$, the number of possible values of $\{ETK_0^{(0)} = STK_0^{(0)}, STK_2^{(2)}, STK_4^{(36)}, STK_6^{(38)}, STK_5^{(40)}\}$ is $|Im(A_{\{0,1,3,4,5\}})| = 2^{16}$.

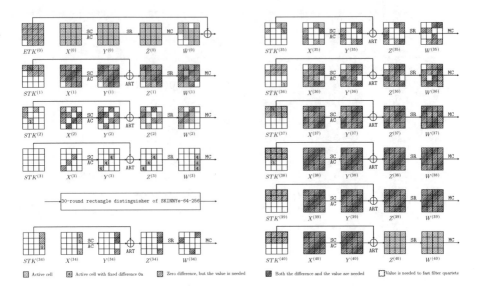

Fig. 5. The 41-round attack against `SKINNYe-64-256`.

Similarly, the number of possible values of $\{ETK_0^{(0)}, STK_2^{(2)}, STK_6^{(38)}, STK_5^{(40)}\} \in k_b \cup k'_f$ is $|Im(A_{\{0,1,4,5\}})| = 2^{14}$. In total, the key size involved in E_b and E_f is only 224-bit due to the key relations although $m_b + m_f = 72 + 180 = 252$, denoted as $|k_b \cup k_f| = 2^{224}$. Similarly, we have $|k_b \cup k'_f| = 2^{170}$ although $m_b + m'_f = 72 + 104 = 176$.

The details of our attack are given as follows:

1. Construct $y = \sqrt{s} \cdot 2^{n/2-r_b}/\sqrt{\tilde{p}^2 \xi \tilde{q}^2} = \sqrt{s} \cdot 2^{12.24}$ structures of $2^{r_b} = 2^{48}$ plaintexts each. For each structure, encrypt the 2^{48} plaintexts under the four related tweakeys K_1, K_2, K_3 and K_4 to get corresponding ciphertexts and store the plaintext-ciphertext pairs in L_1, L_2, L_3 and L_4. The data and memory complexity here is both $\sqrt{s} \cdot 2^{n/2+2}/\sqrt{\tilde{p}^2 \xi \tilde{q}^2} = \sqrt{s} \cdot 2^{62.24}$.

2. Guess 2^x possible values of $k_b \cup k'_f$ ($2^x \le |k_b \cup k'_f|$):
   (a) Initialize $|k_b \cup k_f|/2^x = 2^{224-x}$ counters with memory cost 2^{224-x}.
   (b) Guess all the remaining $|k_b \cup k'_f|/2^x = 2^{170-x}$ possible values in $k_b \cup k'_f$:
      i. For each structure, partially encrypt each plaintext P_1 under the guessed values of k_b to $Y_{6,9,12}^{(3)}$. After xoring the known difference α, partially decrypt it to get the plaintext P_2. Do the same for each P_3 to get P_4. Store the pairs in S_1 and S_2, whose sizes are $y \cdot 2^{r_b} = \sqrt{s} \cdot 2^{60.24}$.
      ii. For each element in S_1, partially decrypt (C_1, C_2) under guessed k'_f to get $W_{6,11,15}^{(36)} \| W_{5,6,11,12}^{(37)}$. Insert the element in S_1 into a hash table H indexed by the $h_f = 28$-bit $W_{6,11,15}^{(36)} \| W_{5,6,11,12}^{(37)}$ of C_1 and $h_f = 28$-bit $\tilde{W}_{6,11,15}^{(36)} \| \tilde{W}_{5,6,11,12}^{(37)}$ of C_2. For each element in S_2, partially decrypt (C_3, C_4) under guessed k'_f to get the $2h_f = 56$ internal state bits,

Table 6. Relations of the subtweakeys involved in the 41-round attack on SKINNYe-64-256, where the subtweakeys marked in bold are among k'_f.

i	k_b	k_f		
0	$ETK_0^{(0)}, STK_2^{(2)}$	$STK_4^{(36)}, \boldsymbol{STK_6^{(38)}}, \boldsymbol{STK_5^{(40)}}$	$\lvert Im(A_{\{0,1,3,4,5\}})\rvert = 2^{16}$	$\lvert Im(A_{\{0,1,4,5\}})\rvert = 2^{14}$
1	$ETK_1^{(0)}, STK_0^{(2)}$	$STK_2^{(36)}, \boldsymbol{STK_4^{(38)}}, \boldsymbol{STK_6^{(40)}}$	$\lvert Im(A_{\{0,1,3,4,5\}})\rvert = 2^{16}$	$\lvert Im(A_{\{0,1,4,5\}})\rvert = 2^{14}$
2	$ETK_2^{(0)}, STK_4^{(2)}$	$STK_6^{(36)}, \boldsymbol{STK_5^{(38)}}, \boldsymbol{STK_3^{(40)}}$	$\lvert Im(A_{\{0,1,3,4,5\}})\rvert = 2^{16}$	$\lvert Im(A_{\{0,1,4,5\}})\rvert = 2^{14}$
3	$ETK_3^{(0)}$	$STK_7^{(34)}, STK_1^{(36)}, \boldsymbol{STK_0^{(38)}}, \boldsymbol{STK_2^{(40)}}$	$\lvert Im(A_{\{0,2,3,4,5\}})\rvert = 2^{15}$	$\lvert Im(A_{\{0,4,5\}})\rvert = 2^{12}$
4	$ETK_9^{(0)}$	$STK_5^{(36)}, STK_3^{(38)}, \boldsymbol{STK_7^{(40)}}$	$\lvert Im(A_{\{0,3,4,5\}})\rvert = 2^{15}$	$\lvert Im(A_{\{0,5\}})\rvert = 2^{8}$
5	$ETK_{10}^{(0)}$	$STK_3^{(34)}, STK_7^{(36)}, \boldsymbol{STK_1^{(38)}}, \boldsymbol{STK_0^{(40)}}$	$\lvert Im(A_{\{0,2,3,4,5\}})\rvert = 2^{15}$	$\lvert Im(A_{\{0,4,5\}})\rvert = 2^{12}$
6	$ETK_{11}^{(0)}$	$STK_3^{(36)}, \boldsymbol{STK_7^{(38)}}, \boldsymbol{STK_1^{(40)}}$	$\lvert Im(A_{\{0,3,4,5\}})\rvert = 2^{15}$	$\lvert Im(A_{\{0,4,5\}})\rvert = 2^{12}$
7	$ETK_8^{(0)}$	$\boldsymbol{STK_2^{(38)}}, \boldsymbol{STK_4^{(40)}}$	$\lvert Im(A_{\{0,4,5\}})\rvert = 2^{12}$	$\lvert Im(A_{\{0,4,5\}})\rvert = 2^{12}$
8	$STK_2^{(1)}$	$STK_4^{(35)}, \boldsymbol{STK_6^{(37)}}, \boldsymbol{STK_5^{(39)}}$	$\lvert Im(A_{\{1,3,4,5\}})\rvert = 2^{15}$	$\lvert Im(A_{\{1,4,5\}})\rvert = 2^{12}$
9	$STK_0^{(1)}$	$STK_2^{(35)}, STK_4^{(37)}, \boldsymbol{STK_6^{(39)}}$	$\lvert Im(A_{\{1,3,4,5\}})\rvert = 2^{15}$	$\lvert Im(A_{\{1,5\}})\rvert = 2^{8}$
10		$STK_5^{(37)}, \boldsymbol{STK_3^{(39)}}$	$\lvert Im(A_{\{4,5\}})\rvert = 2^{8}$	$\lvert Im(A_{\{5\}})\rvert = 2^{4}$
11	$STK_7^{(1)}$	$STK_0^{(37)}, \boldsymbol{STK_2^{(39)}}$	$\lvert Im(A_{\{1,4,5\}})\rvert = 2^{12}$	$\lvert Im(A_{\{1,5\}})\rvert = 2^{8}$
12	$STK_6^{(1)}$	$\boldsymbol{STK_3^{(37)}}, \boldsymbol{STK_1^{(39)}}$	$\lvert Im(A_{\{1,4,5\}})\rvert = 2^{12}$	$\lvert Im(A_{\{1,4,5\}})\rvert = 2^{12}$
13	$STK_3^{(1)}$	$STK_7^{(35)}, STK_1^{(37)}, \boldsymbol{STK_0^{(39)}}$	$\lvert Im(A_{\{1,3,4,5\}})\rvert = 2^{15}$	$\lvert Im(A_{\{1,5\}})\rvert = 2^{8}$
14	$STK_5^{(1)}$	$STK_3^{(35)}, \boldsymbol{STK_7^{(37)}}, \boldsymbol{STK_1^{(39)}}$	$\lvert Im(A_{\{1,3,4,5\}})\rvert = 2^{15}$	$\lvert Im(A_{\{1,4,5\}})\rvert = 2^{12}$
15	$STK_1^{(1)}$	$STK_2^{(37)}, \boldsymbol{STK_4^{(39)}}$	$\lvert Im(A_{\{1,4,5\}})\rvert = 2^{12}$	$\lvert Im(A_{\{1,5\}})\rvert = 2^{8}$
			$\lvert k_b \cup k_f\rvert = 2^{224}$	$\lvert k_b \cup k'_f\rvert = 2^{170}$

and check against H to find the pairs (C_1, C_2), where (C_1, C_3) and (C_2, C_4) collide at the $2h_f = 56$ bits. The time complexity here is $T_1 = \sqrt{s} \cdot 2^{\lvert k_b \cup k'_f\rvert + n/2 + 1} / \sqrt{\tilde{p}^2 \xi \tilde{q}^2} = \sqrt{s} \cdot 2^{170+32+1+28.24} = \sqrt{s} \cdot 2^{231.24}$. We get $s \cdot 2^{\lvert k_b \cup k'_f\rvert - 2h_f - n + 2r_f} / (\tilde{p}^2 \xi \tilde{q}^2) = s \cdot 2^{170-56-64+128+56.47} = s \cdot 2^{234.47}$ quartets.

iii. For each of the $s \cdot 2^{234.47}$ quartets, determine the key candidates step by step, whose time complexity is ε:

A: In round 38, guess 2^4 possible values of $STK_3^{(38)}$. As shown in Table 7, with other guessed k'_f together, we compute $Z_{0,12}^{(37)}$ and deduce $\Delta Y_0^{(37)}$ and $\Delta X_{12}^{(37)}$. For the 1st column of $X^{(37)}$ of (C_1, C_3), we obtain $\Delta X_0^{(37)} = \Delta X_{12}^{(37)}$ by property of MC, and deduce $STK_0^{(37)}$ by Lemma 1. Similarly, we deduce $STK_0'^{(37)}$ for (C_2, C_4). Then the fixed $\Delta STK_0^{(37)} = STK_0^{(37)} \oplus STK_0'^{(37)}$ is a 4-bit filter. $s \cdot 2^{234.47} \cdot 2^4 \cdot 2^{-4} = s \cdot 2^{234.47}$ quartets remain.

B: In round 37, guessing 2^4 possible values of $STK_2^{(37)}$, following Table 7 we compute $Z_{3,15}^{(36)}$ and deduce $\Delta Y_3^{(36)}$ and $\Delta X_{15}^{(36)}$. For the 4-th column of $X^{(36)}$ of (C_1, C_3), we deduce $\Delta X_3^{(36)} = \Delta X_{15}^{(36)}$ by MC and deduce $STK_3^{(36)}$. Since the number of possible values[2] of $STK_3^{(36)}$

---

[2] The number of possible values of $STK_3^{(36)}$ is computed via Table 6. For example, in line 6 of Table 6, $\{ETK_{11}^{(0)}, STK_7^{(38)}, STK_1^{(40)}\} \in k_b \cup k'_f$ derived from the 6-th nibble have already been guessed, so the number of possible values of $STK_3^{(36)}$ is $\lvert Im(A_{\{0,3,4,5\}})\rvert / \lvert Im(A_{\{0,4,5\}})\rvert = 2^{15-12} = 2^3$. Similarly, we compute all the number of possible values for subtweakey cells involved in the guess and filter procedure, which are listed in Table 7.

is only 2^3 as shown in Table 7, which acts as a filter of $2^3/2^4 = 2^{-1}$. Similarly, we deduce $STK_3'^{(36)}$ for (C_2, C_4). Then the fixed $\Delta STK_3^{(36)}$ is a 4-bit filter. $s \cdot 2^{234.47} \cdot 2^4 \cdot 2^{-1} \cdot 2^{-4} = s \cdot 2^{233.47}$ quartets remain.

C: Guessing 2^4 possible values of $STK_4^{(37)}$, we compute $Z_7^{(36)}$ and deduce $\Delta Y_7^{(36)}$. For the 4-th column of $X^{(36)}$ of (C_1, C_3), we can obtain $\Delta X_7^{36} = \Delta X_{15}^{(36)}$ by MC. With the known $\Delta X_{15}^{(36)}$ in **step B**, we deduce $STK_7^{(36)}$. The number of possible values of $STK_7^{(36)}$ is 2^3, which can act as a filter of $2^3/2^4 = 2^{-1}$. Similarly, we deduce $STK_7'^{(36)}$ for (C_2, C_4). Then the fixed $\Delta STK_7^{(36)}$ is a 4-bit filter. $s \cdot 2^{233.47} \cdot 2^4 \cdot 2^{-1} \cdot 2^{-4} = s \cdot 2^{232.47}$ quartets remain.

D: Guessing 2^4 possible values of $STK_1^{(37)}$, we compute $Z_{6,10,14}^{(36)}$. Then $\Delta Y_6^{(36)}$ and $\Delta X_{10,14}^{(36)}$ are deduced. For the 3rd column of $X^{(36)}$ of (C_1, C_3), we can obtain $\Delta X_6^{(36)} = \Delta X_{10}^{(36)} \oplus \Delta X_{14}^{(36)}$ by MC and deduce $STK_6^{(36)}$. The number of possible values of $STK_6^{(36)}$ is 2^2, which acts as a filter of $2^2/2^4 = 2^{-2}$. Similarly, we deduce $STK_6'^{(36)}$ for (C_2, C_4) and $\Delta STK_6^{(36)}$ can act as a 4-bit filter. $s \cdot 2^{232.47} \cdot 2^4 \cdot 2^{-2} \cdot 2^{-4} = s \cdot 2^{230.47}$ quartets remain.

E: In round 36, guessing $2^4 \times 2^2 \times 2^2$ possible values for $(STK_5^{(37)}, STK_2^{(36)}, STK_4^{(36)})$, we compute $Z_{3,7,15}^{(35)}$ and deduce $\Delta Y_{3,7}^{(35)}$ and $\Delta X_{15}^{(35)}$. For the 4-th column of $X^{(35)}$ of (C_1, C_3), we can obtain $\Delta X_3^{(35)} = \Delta X_7^{(35)} = \Delta X_{15}^{(35)}$ by MC and deduce $STK_3^{(35)}$ and $STK_7^{(35)}$. Both the numbers of possible values of $STK_3^{(35)}$ and $STK_7^{(35)}$ are 2^3, which acts as two filters of $2^3/2^4 = 2^{-1}$. Similarly, we deduce $STK_3'^{(35)}$ and $STK_7'^{(35)}$ for (C_2, C_4). Then the fixed $\Delta STK_3^{(35)}$ and $\Delta STK_7^{(35)}$ can act as two 4-bit filters. Thereafter, in round 34, we deduce $Z_3^{(34)}$ from $Z_7^{(35)}$ and $STK_7^{(35)}$. Since $STK_3^{(34)}$ only has one possible value[3], we deduce $X_3^{(34)}$. So $\Delta X_3^{(34)} = $ 0x1 acts a 4-bit filter both for (C_1, C_3) and (C_2, C_4). $s \cdot 2^{230.47} \cdot 2^8 \cdot 2^{-1} \cdot 2^{-1} \cdot 2^{-8} \cdot 2^{-8} = s \cdot 2^{220.47}$ quartets remain.

F: Guessing $2^3 \times 2^3 \times 2^3 \times 2^3$ possible values of $(STK_1^{(36)}, STK_5^{(36)}, STK_2^{(35)}, STK_4^{(35)})$, compute $Z_{7,15}^{(34)}$ and deduce $X_{15}^{(34)}$. Since $STK_7^{(34)}$ only has one possible value, we can deduce $X_7^{(34)}$. $\Delta X_7^{(34)} = $ 0x1 and $\Delta X_{15}^{(34)} = $ 0x1 are two 4-bit filters for both (C_1, C_3) and (C_2, C_4). $s \cdot 2^{220.47} \cdot 2^{12} \cdot 2^{-8} \cdot 2^{-8} = s \cdot 2^{216.47}$ quartets remain.

So for each quartet, $\varepsilon = 2^4 \cdot \frac{4}{41} + 2^4 \cdot \frac{4}{41} + 2^{-1} \cdot 2^4 \cdot \frac{4}{41} + 2^{-2} \cdot 2^4 \cdot \frac{4}{41} + 2^{-4} \cdot 2^8 \cdot \frac{4}{41} + 2^{-14} \cdot 2^{12} \cdot \frac{4}{41} \approx 2^{2.56}$ and $T_2 = s \cdot 2^{234.47} \cdot \varepsilon = s \cdot 2^{237.03}$.

---

[3] As shown in line 5 of Table 6, with $STK_7^{(36)}$ deduced in **step C** and other cells guessed in $k_b \cup k_f'$, the number of possible values is only 1 for $STK_3^{(34)}$.

(c) (Exhaustive search) Select the top $|k_b \cup k_f| \cdot 2^{-x-h} = 2^{224-x-h}$ hits in the counter as the key candidates. Guess the remaining $k - 224 = 32$-bit key to check the full key, and $T_3 = 2^{k-h}$.

Set $s = 1$, $h = 32$ and $x = 168$ ($x \le 170$, $h \le 224 - x$). We have $T_1 = 2^{231.24}$, $T_2 = 2^{237.03}$ and $T_3 = 2^{224}$. The memory complexity is $2^{62.24} + 2^{56} \approx 2^{62.26}$. In total, for the 41-round attack on SKINNYe-64-256, the data complexity is $2^{62.24}$, the memory complexity is $2^{62.26}$, and the time complexity is $2^{237.06}$. The success probability is about 70.6%.

In addition, for SKINNYe-64-256 v2 we give a 37-round related-tweakey rectangle attack (given in the Supplementary Material C.2 in our full version paper [53]) based on a 26-round related-tweakey boomerang distinguisher. The data complexity is $2^{62.8}$, the memory complexity is $2^{62.8}$, and the time complexity is $2^{240.03}$. The success probability is about 66.3%.

Table 7. Tweakey recovery for 41-round SKINNYe-64-256. The red cells are among k_f' or gained in the previous steps. D/G: deduced/guessed subtweakeys.

Step	State	Involved subtweakeys	Number of values
A	$Z_0^{(37)}$	$STK_4^{(38)}, STK_5^{(39)}, STK_{0,6,7}^{(40)}$	G: $STK_3^{(38)}$: 2^4
	$Z_{12}^{(37)}$	$STK_3^{(38)}, STK_{2,7}^{(39)}, STK_{1,4,6}^{(40)}$	D: $STK_0^{(37)}$: 2^4
B	$Z_3^{(36)}$	$STK_7^{(37)}, STK_4^{(38)}, STK_{3,5,6}^{(39)}, STK_{0-2,6,7}^{(40)}$	G: $STK_7^{(37)}$: 2^4
	$Z_{15}^{(36)}$	$STK_2^{(37)}, STK_{1,6}^{(38)}, STK_{0,5,7}^{(39)}, STK_{2-6}^{(40)}$	D: $STK_1^{(36)}$: 2^3
C	$Z_7^{(36)}$	$STK_4^{(37)}, STK_{3,5,6}^{(38)}, STK_{0-2,6,7}^{(39)}, STK_{0-7}^{(40)}$	G: $STK_4^{(37)}$: 2^4
			D: $STK_7^{(36)}$: 2^3
D	$Z_6^{(36)}$	$STK_7^{(37)}, STK_{2,4,5}^{(38)}, STK_{0,1,3,5,6}^{(39)}, STK_{0-7}^{(40)}$	G: $STK_1^{(37)}$: 2^4
	$Z_{10}^{(36)}$	$STK_4^{(37)}, STK_{3,5}^{(38)}, STK_{0,2,6,7}^{(39)}, STK_{1-4,6,7}^{(40)}$	D: $STK_6^{(36)}$: 2^2
	$Z_{14}^{(36)}$	$STK_1^{(37)}, STK_{0,5}^{(38)}, STK_{3,4,6}^{(39)}, STK_{1,2,4,5,7}^{(40)}$	
E	$Z_3^{(35)}$	$STK_7^{(36)}, STK_4^{(37)}, STK_{3,5,6}^{(38)}, STK_{0-2,6,7}^{(39)}, STK_{0-7}^{(40)}$	G: $STK_5^{(37)}$: 2^4
	$Z_7^{(35)}$	$STK_4^{(36)}, STK_{3,5,6}^{(37)}, STK_{0-2,6,7}^{(38)}, STK_{0-7}^{(39)}, STK_{0-7}^{(40)}$	G: $STK_2^{(36)}$: 2^2
	$Z_{15}^{(35)}$	$STK_2^{(36)}, STK_{1,6}^{(37)}, STK_{0,5,7}^{(38)}, STK_{2-6}^{(39)}, STK_{0-7}^{(40)}$	G: $STK_4^{(36)}$: 2^2
	$Z_3^{(34)}$	$STK_7^{(35)}, STK_4^{(36)}, STK_{3,5,6}^{(37)}, STK_{0-2,6,7}^{(38)}, STK_{0-7}^{(39)}, STK_{0-7}^{(40)}$	D: $STK_3^{(35)}$: 2^3
			D: $STK_7^{(35)}$: 2^3
			D: $STK_3^{(34)}$: 2^0
F	$Z_7^{(34)}$	$STK_4^{(35)}, STK_{3,5,6}^{(36)}, STK_{0-2,6,7}^{(37)}, STK_{0-7}^{(38)}, STK_{0-7}^{(39)}, STK_{0-7}^{(40)}$	G: $STK_1^{(36)}$: 2^3
	$Z_{15}^{(34)}$	$STK_2^{(35)}, STK_{1,6}^{(36)}, STK_{0,5,7}^{(37)}, STK_{2-6}^{(38)}, STK_{0-7}^{(39)}, STK_{0-7}^{(40)}$	G: $STK_5^{(36)}$: 2^3
			G: $STK_2^{(35)}$: 2^3
			G: $STK_4^{(35)}$: 2^3
			D: $STK_7^{(34)}$: 2^0

5   MITM and Impossible Differential Attacks on SKINNYe-64-256 and Its Version 2

5.1   The Meet-in-the-Middle Attack

The three-subset meet-in-the-middle attack was proposed by Bogdanov and Rechberger [20] and was summarized by Isobe [41]. Several important techniques significantly enhance and enrich the MITM methodology, including the *splice-and-cut* technique [5], initial structure [58,59], (indirect-)partial matching [58, 59], sieve-in-the-middle [22], match-box technique [35], and dissection [27], etc. Recently, several automatic tools [7,8,25,38,57,60] on MITM attacks are presented. At CRYPTO 2021, Dong *et al.* [29] developed the MILP model for MITM key-recovery attack on SKINNY. Combining Dong *et al.*'s model and our new discoveries on tweakey schedule of SKINNYe-64-256, we develop MITM key-recovery attacks on 31-round SKINNYe-64-256 and 27-round SKINNYe-64-256 v2 in Supplementary Material D in our full version paper [53].

5.2   Related-Tweakey Impossible Differential

The impossible differential attack is proposed by Biham *et al.* [14] and Knudsen [45] independently. It uses a differential with probability zero to act as a distinguisher, named as the impossible differential. With several rounds appended before and after the impossible differential distinguisher, one partially encrypts/decrypts a given pair by a candidate key to the input and output of the distinguisher. The key candidate that leads to the impossible differential will be the wrong one and will be rejected. This technique provides a sieving of the key space and the remaining candidates can be tested by exhaustive search. There are several works analyzed the security of SKINNY family against the impossible differential attacks [4,31,46,56,62], in both single-tweakey and related-tweakey setting. We introduce related-tweakey impossible differentials on 21-round SKINNYe-64-256 and 18-round SKINNYe-64-256 v2 in Supplementary Material E in our full version paper [53].

6   A Proposal for Tweakey Schedule of SKINNY Family

At ASIACRYPT 2014, Jean *et al.* [42] introduced the STK construction as shown in Fig. 1, which absorbs arbitrary length of tweakey. It updates each cell of the tweakey states by multiplying a non-zero α_j. For SKINNY-n-zn, the tweakey cells are updated by dedicated chosen lightweight LFSRs, which guarantees at most $z-1$ cancellations within 30 consecutive rounds. However, SKINNY family [9] only gives instances for $z = 1, 2, 3$. SKINNYe-64-256 [48] extends z to 4, but fails to satisfy its expected security claim[4]. In the updated version SKINNYe-64-256 v2 [50], the designers fixed the issue and claimed that the LFSR for TK_4 is the only one to ensure at most 3 cancellations after exhaustively testing 2^{16} choices. It is not trivial to extend SKINNY to support arbitrary length of tweakey with similar *subtweakey difference cancellation property* to STK construction: for a given cell position, $z - 1$ cancellations can only happen every 15 rounds for TK-z (or every 30 rounds for SKINNY-n-zn).

---

[4] Similar issue happens to Lilliput-AE [1], one of the first-round candidates at the NIST competition, specifies TBCs with up to $z = 7$. However, they also ignored the rationale of the original tweakey framework to ensure the security, and were actually attacked practically [32].

As stated by Naito *et al.* [48, Page 5] that PFB_Plus "... give new insight to TBC designers considering that there is no consensus about the adequate tweak size to support". It is interesting to consider a uniformed tweakey schedule to extend SKINNY to support larger tweakey size, while obeying the property of STK construction, which may have potential application, such as SKINNYe-64-256 v2 in TI-friendly constructions.

For general $z \le 14$, the output nibbles can be represented by linear combinations of the input nibbles as in Eq. (4), i.e.,

$$
\begin{pmatrix}
stk^{(2\times0)}_{\bar{P}^{2\times0}[i]} \\
stk^{(2\times1)}_{\bar{P}^{2\times1}[i]} \\
\vdots \\
stk^{(2\times14)}_{\bar{P}^{2\times14}[i]}
\end{pmatrix}
=
\begin{pmatrix}
I & L_2^0 & \cdots & L_z^0 \\
I & L_2^1 & \cdots & L_z^1 \\
\vdots & \vdots & \ddots & \vdots \\
I & L_2^{14} & \cdots & L_z^{14}
\end{pmatrix}
\cdot
\begin{pmatrix}
tk^{(0)}_{1,i} \\
tk^{(0)}_{2,i} \\
\vdots \\
tk^{(0)}_{z,i}
\end{pmatrix}
, \quad 0 \le i \le 7.
\tag{11}
$$

To satisfy the subtweakey difference cancellation property, the coefficient matrix in (11) must satisfy the 'block-MDS' property [42], i.e.,

$$
\det
\begin{pmatrix}
I & L_2^{r_1} & \cdots & L_z^{r_1} \\
I & L_2^{r_2} & \cdots & L_z^{r_2} \\
\vdots & \vdots & \vdots & \vdots \\
I & L_2^{r_z} & \cdots & L_z^{r_z}
\end{pmatrix}
\ne 0
\tag{12}
$$

for all $0 \le r_1 < r_2 < \cdots < r_z \le 14$. In other words, the goal of our design is to choose L_i's such that the 'block-MDS' property is guaranteed. Although the coefficient matrix in (11) has a block Vandermonde form, there is no simple formula to compute the determinant of its squared sub-matrices for general L_i's. When the L_i's are pairwise commutable, a formula can be deduced for squared block Vandermonde matrices, which we refer to Supplementary Material F in our full version paper [53].

6.1   The Choice of L_i

Our construction can be viewed as an extension of the generator matrices of Reed-Solomon codes to the block matrix form. Specifically, denoting $L_1 = I$, and we choose the L_i's to be consecutive powers of a matrix L, i.e.,

$$
\{L_i\}_{1 \le i \le z} = \{L^{\alpha+1}, \cdots, L^{\alpha+z}\}
\tag{13}
$$

for some integer $\alpha \in [-z, -1]$. Then we can show that the 'block-MDS' property is guaranteed if the matrix L satisfies specific property.

Proposition 1. *Suppose L is a 4×4 matrix over $GF(2)$ such that the characteristic polynomial $p_L(\lambda)$ is a primitive polynomial of degree 4 over $GF(2)$. Then L has cycle 15, and for any integer α,*

$$\det \begin{pmatrix} (\boldsymbol{L}^{\alpha+1})^{r_1} & (\boldsymbol{L}^{\alpha+2})^{r_1} & \cdots & (\boldsymbol{L}^{\alpha+z})^{r_1} \\ (\boldsymbol{L}^{\alpha+1})^{r_2} & (\boldsymbol{L}^{\alpha+2})^{r_2} & \cdots & (\boldsymbol{L}^{\alpha+z})^{r_2} \\ \vdots & \vdots & \ddots & \vdots \\ (\boldsymbol{L}^{\alpha+1})^{r_z} & (\boldsymbol{L}^{\alpha+2})^{r_z} & \cdots & (\boldsymbol{L}^{\alpha+z})^{r_z} \end{pmatrix} \neq 0 \tag{14}$$

for all $0 \le r_1 < r_2 < \cdots < r_z \le 14$.

Proof. Let $\lambda_i, 1 \le i \le 4$, be the eigenvalues of $\boldsymbol{L}$, then λ_i is primitive in $GF(2^4)$ and $\boldsymbol{L}^r$ has eigenvalues $\lambda_i^r, 1 \le i \le 4$. For $1 \le r < 15$, we have $\lambda_i^r \neq 1, 1 \le i \le 4$, and thus $\boldsymbol{L}^r \neq \boldsymbol{I}$. For $r = 15$, note that $p_L(\lambda) \mid (\lambda^{15} - 1)$, and by the Cayley-Hamilton theorem (see Section 9 of [55]) we have $p_L(\boldsymbol{L}) = \boldsymbol{0}$. Then it follows that $\boldsymbol{L}^{15} - \boldsymbol{I} = \boldsymbol{0}$.

To show the determinant is nonzero, we observe that

$$\begin{pmatrix} (\boldsymbol{L}^{\alpha+1})^{r_1} & \cdots & (\boldsymbol{L}^{\alpha+z})^{r_1} \\ (\boldsymbol{L}^{\alpha+1})^{r_2} & \cdots & (\boldsymbol{L}^{\alpha+z})^{r_2} \\ \vdots & \ddots & \vdots \\ (\boldsymbol{L}^{\alpha+1})^{r_z} & \cdots & (\boldsymbol{L}^{\alpha+z})^{r_z} \end{pmatrix} = \begin{pmatrix} \boldsymbol{L}^{\alpha r_1} & & & \\ & \boldsymbol{L}^{\alpha r_2} & & \\ & & \ddots & \\ & & & \boldsymbol{L}^{\alpha r_z} \end{pmatrix} \cdot \begin{pmatrix} \boldsymbol{L}^{r_1} & \cdots & (\boldsymbol{L}^{r_1})^z \\ \boldsymbol{L}^{r_2} & \cdots & (\boldsymbol{L}^{r_2})^z \\ \vdots & \ddots & \vdots \\ \boldsymbol{L}^{r_z} & \cdots & (\boldsymbol{L}^{r_z})^z \end{pmatrix}. \tag{15}$$

Then it suffices to show that $\det\left((\boldsymbol{L}^{r_i})^j\right)_{1 \le i,j \le z} \neq 0$ for all $0 \le r_1 < r_2 < \cdots < r_z \le 14$, which we refer to Supplementary Material F in full version paper [53]. □

Construction of $\boldsymbol{L}$. One simple way to construct $\boldsymbol{L}$ is to take $\boldsymbol{L}$ to be the companion matrix of a primitive polynomial. For example, for the primitive polynomial $\lambda^4 + \lambda + 1$, we can take $\boldsymbol{L}$ to be the companion matrix

$$\boldsymbol{L} = \begin{pmatrix} 0 & 1 & 0 & 0 \\ 0 & 0 & 1 & 0 \\ 0 & 0 & 0 & 1 \\ 1 & 1 & 0 & 0 \end{pmatrix}. \tag{16}$$

It can be readily checked that the characteristic polynomial $p_L(\lambda) = \lambda^4 + \lambda + 1$ and thus the eigenvalues of $\boldsymbol{L}$ are distinct primitive elements in $GF(2^4)$. On the other hand, taking companion matrices of primitive polynomials is not the only way to obtain $\boldsymbol{L}$. In fact, we perform an exhaustive search of all binary 4×4 binary matrices, and find totally 1344 distinct $\boldsymbol{L}$ whose characteristic polynomial is primitive over $GF(2)$.

An Example for $z = 4$. Taking $\alpha = -2$ and $\boldsymbol{L}$ equals to that in (16), then

$$\{\boldsymbol{L}_i\}_{1 \le i \le 4} = \{\boldsymbol{L}^{-1}, \boldsymbol{L}^0, \boldsymbol{L}^1, \boldsymbol{L}^2\}. \tag{17}$$

Without loss of generality, let

$$\boldsymbol{L}_2 = \boldsymbol{L}^1 = \begin{pmatrix} 0 & 1 & 0 & 0 \\ 0 & 0 & 1 & 0 \\ 0 & 0 & 0 & 1 \\ 1 & 1 & 0 & 0 \end{pmatrix}, \boldsymbol{L}_3 = \boldsymbol{L}^{-1} = \begin{pmatrix} 1 & 0 & 0 & 1 \\ 1 & 0 & 0 & 0 \\ 0 & 1 & 0 & 0 \\ 0 & 0 & 1 & 0 \end{pmatrix}, \boldsymbol{L}_4 = \boldsymbol{L}^2 = \begin{pmatrix} 0 & 0 & 1 & 0 \\ 0 & 0 & 0 & 1 \\ 1 & 1 & 0 & 0 \\ 0 & 1 & 1 & 0 \end{pmatrix}. \tag{18}$$

Considering the LFSRs defined by (18), we found that the LFSRs for TK_2 and TK_3 coincide with the original LFSRs in SKINNY, and the LFSRs for TK_4 coincides with that constructed in SKINNYe-64-256 v2. *From this point of view, our construction can be viewed as a natural extension of the original SKINNY-64 and SKINNYe-64-256 v2.*

For general $z \leq 14$, the 'block-MDS' property of our construction guarantees there are at most $z-1$ difference cancellations every 15 rounds for TK-z (or every 30 rounds SKINNY-n-zn). We derive the lower bounds of the number of active S-boxes for SKINNY-n-zn ($z \leq 14$) with our construction of the tweakey schedule (see Supplementary Material G in our full version paper [53]). The results (see Table 17 in our full version paper [53]) show that our new tweakey schedule for TK-z ($z \leq 14$) leads to a natural increase of the bounds compared to TK-1, TK-2 and TK-3 in [9] and TK-4 in [50].

Efficiency Considerations. How to choose L_i's to optimize the implementation efficiency is also an important issue. As pointed in [48], one direction of optimization is to minimize the total number of XORs required by the LFSRs. For $z = 4$, the LFSRs constructed through (18) require only 4 XORs totally, i.e., L_2 and L_3 require only 1 XOR respectively, and L_4 requires 2 XORs. Note that in [48] it was proved that there is no secure LFSRs for TK_4 with only a single XOR, therefore the LFSRs constructed through (18) is optimal with respect to the number of XORs. For all $4 \leq z \leq 7$, we enumerate all possible L and α, and give the optimal number of XORs required in our construction in Table 8.

Table 8. Optimal number of XORs required in our construction.

z	L	$\{L_i\}_{2 \leq i \leq z}$	Number of XORs	Total XORs
4	$\begin{pmatrix} 0&1&0&0 \\ 0&0&1&0 \\ 0&0&0&1 \\ 1&1&0&0 \end{pmatrix}$	$\{L, L^{-1}, L^2\}$	$\{1, 1, 2\}$	4
5	$\begin{pmatrix} 0&1&0&0 \\ 0&0&1&0 \\ 0&0&0&1 \\ 1&1&0&0 \end{pmatrix}$	$\{L, L^{-1}, L^2, L^{-2}\}$	$\{1, 1, 2, 3\}$	7
6	$\begin{pmatrix} 0&1&0&0 \\ 0&0&1&0 \\ 0&0&0&1 \\ 1&1&0&0 \end{pmatrix}$	$\{L, L^{-1}, L^2, L^{-2}, L^3\}$	$\{1, 1, 2, 3, 3\}$	10
7	$\begin{pmatrix} 0&1&0&0 \\ 0&0&1&0 \\ 0&0&0&1 \\ 1&1&0&0 \end{pmatrix}$	$\{L, L^{-1}, L^2, L^{-2}, L^3, L^4\}$	$\{1, 1, 2, 3, 3, 5\}$	15

Another direction of optimization is to minimize the circuit area of the LFSRs. In our construction, all L_i's are powers of a matrix L, therefore a minimal area implementation can be supported by instantiating only one circuit of L and computing each L_i iteratively. For example, for $z = 4$ we take $\alpha = -1$ and $L_2 = L, L_3 = L^2, L_4 = L^3$. Then L_2, L_3 and L_4 can be computed by repeating L in $1, 2$ and 3 times respectively, and the total latency is as 6 times as that of a single L. On the other hand, we propose an area-latency trade-off to reduce the latency by slightly increasing the area. Again we take $z = 4$ and $L_2 = L, L_3 = L^2$ and $L_4 = L^3$ for an example. In this case we instantiate a circuit of L and a circuit of L^2. Then taking $x_2, x_3, x_4 \in GF(2)^4$ as inputs, the output states $L_2 x_2, L_3 x_3, L_4 x_4$ can be computed in two steps, i.e., firstly compute $L x_2$ and $L^2 x_4$, then compute $L(L^2 x_4)$ and $L^2 x_3$. As a result, the total latency is reduced by a third at the cost of double area[5]. In Table 9 we list the area-latency trade-off for our construction for $4 \leq z \leq 7$.

A More Scalable Construction. Our construction can be naturally extended to choose $c \times c$ $(c \geq 4)$ matrices L_i's such that the 'block-MDS' property in (12) is satisfied. The discussion is given in Supplementary Material H in our full version paper [53], where possible ways to extend the tweakey size for SKINNY-128 are introduced. Similar methods can also be applied to Deoxys-BC to extend its tweakey size.

Table 9. The area-latency trade-off for our construction.

z	$\{L_i\}_{2 \leq i \leq z}$	Instantiated circuit	Area	Latency
4	$\{L, L^2, L^3\}$	$\{L\}$	1	6
	$\{L, L^2, L^3\}$	$\{L, L^2\}$	2	2
5	$\{L, L^2, L^3, L^4\}$	$\{L\}$	1	10
	$\{L, L^{-1}, L^2, L^{-2}\}$	$\{L, L^{-1}\}$	2	3
	$\{L, L^2, L^3, L^4\}$	$\{L, L^2, L^3\}$	3	2
6	$\{L, L^2, L^3, L^4, L^5\}$	$\{L\}$	1	15
	$\{L, L^2, L^3, L^4, L^5\}$	$\{L, L^2\}$	2	4
	$\{L, L^2, L^3, L^4, L^5\}$	$\{L, L^2, L^4\}$	3	3
	$\{L, L^2, L^3, L^4, L^5\}$	$\{L, L^2, L^3, L^4\}$	4	2
7	$\{L, L^2, L^3, L^4, L^5, L^6\}$	$\{L\}$	1	21
	$\{L, L^{-1}, L^2, L^{-2}, L^3, L^{-3}\}$	$\{L, L^{-1}\}$	2	6
	$\{L, L^2, L^3, L^4, L^5, L^6\}$	$\{L, L^2, L^4\}$	3	3
	$\{L, L^{-1}, L^2, L^{-2}, L^3, L^{-3}\}$	$\{L, L^{-1}, L^2, L^{-2}\}$	4	2

7   Conclusion

The unexpected cancellations in the new tweakey schedule of SKINNYe-64-256 significantly enhances several attacks on SKINNYe-64-256 when compared to that on SKINNY-64-128 and SKINNY-64-192, and leaves a security margin of 3 rounds in related-tweakey setting. Moreover, we give some cryptanalysis results on the updated version 2, which indicates that the current version satisfies the security claims of the designers. At last, we introduce a uniformed design strategy

---

[5] The area of the trade-off implementation mainly includes the circuit for L and L^2 and two 4-bit registers. In area optimization implementation, the area is the circuit of L and one 4-bit register. Assume the registers bound the area, we can say trade-off method costs double area.

for the tweakey schedule of SKINNY-n-zn ($z \leq 14$), and prove that it satisfies the security requirements of the STK construction.

At CRYPTO 2022, Naito, Sasaki, Sugawara further introduced a new tweakable block cipher SKINNYee [49] based on SKINNYe-64-256 version 2. It supports 128-bit key and a (256+3)-bit tweak with a 64-bit plaintext block. The method to extend the tweakey size is different from what we suggest in Sect. 6. It is an interesting open problem to explore its security margin.

Acknowledgments. We would like to thank the anonymous reviewers from ASIACRYPT 2022 for their valuable comments. This work is supported by National Key R&D Program of China (2018YFA0704701), the Major Program of Guangdong Basic and Applied Research (2019B030302008), Natural Science Foundation of China (62272257, 61902207, 62072270, 62072207), Major Scientific and Technological Innovation Project of Shandong Province, China (2020ZLYS09 and 2019JZZY010133), Natural Science Foundation of Shanghai (19ZR1420000), and Open Foundation of Network and Data Security Key Laboratory of Sichuan Province (University of Electronic Science and Technology of China).

References

1. Adomnicai, A.: Lilliput-AE: a new lightweight tweakable block cipher for authenticated encryption with associated data. Submission to NIST Lightweight Cryptography Project (2019)
2. Albrecht, M., Grassi, L., Rechberger, C., Roy, A., Tiessen, T.: MiMC: efficient encryption and cryptographic hashing with minimal multiplicative complexity. In: Cheon, J.H., Takagi, T. (eds.) ASIACRYPT 2016, Part I. LNCS, vol. 10031, pp. 191–219. Springer, Heidelberg (2016). https://doi.org/10.1007/978-3-662-53887-6_7
3. Albrecht, M.R., Rechberger, C., Schneider, T., Tiessen, T., Zohner, M.: Ciphers for MPC and FHE. In: Oswald, E., Fischlin, M. (eds.) EUROCRYPT 2015, Part I. LNCS, vol. 9056, pp. 430–454. Springer, Heidelberg (2015). https://doi.org/10.1007/978-3-662-46800-5_17
4. Ankele, R., et al.: Related-key impossible-differential attack on reduced-round SKINNY. In: Gollmann, D., Miyaji, A., Kikuchi, H. (eds.) ACNS 2017. LNCS, vol. 10355, pp. 208–228. Springer, Cham (2017). https://doi.org/10.1007/978-3-319-61204-1_11
5. Aoki, K., Sasaki, Yu.: Preimage attacks on one-block MD4, 63-step MD5 and more. In: Avanzi, R.M., Keliher, L., Sica, F. (eds.) SAC 2008. LNCS, vol. 5381, pp. 103–119. Springer, Heidelberg (2009). https://doi.org/10.1007/978-3-642-04159-4_7
6. Banik, S., Pandey, S.K., Peyrin, T., Sasaki, Yu., Sim, S.M., Todo, Y.: GIFT: a small present. In: Fischer, W., Homma, N. (eds.) CHES 2017. LNCS, vol. 10529, pp. 321–345. Springer, Cham (2017). https://doi.org/10.1007/978-3-319-66787-4_16
7. Bao, Z., Dong, X., Guo, J., Li, Z., Shi, D., Sun, S., Wang, X.: Automatic search of meet-in-the-middle preimage attacks on AES-like hashing. In: Canteaut, A., Standaert, F.-X. (eds.) EUROCRYPT 2021. LNCS, vol. 12696, pp. 771–804. Springer, Cham (2021). https://doi.org/10.1007/978-3-030-77870-5_27
8. Bao, Z., Guo, J., Shi, D., Tu, Y.: Superposition meet-in-the-middle attacks: updates on fundamental security of AES-like hashing. In: Dodis, Y., Shrimpton, T. (eds.)

Advances in Cryptology – CRYPTO 2022, CRYPTO 2022, Lecture Notes in Computer Science, vol. 13507, pp. 64–93, Springer, Cham (2022). https://doi.org/10.1007/978-3-031-15802-5_3

9. Beierle, C., et al.: The SKINNY family of block ciphers and its low-latency variant MANTIS. In: Robshaw, M., Katz, J. (eds.) CRYPTO 2016, Part II. LNCS, vol. 9815, pp. 123–153. Springer, Heidelberg (2016). https://doi.org/10.1007/978-3-662-53008-5_5

10. Beierle, C., et al.: The SKINNY family of block ciphers and its low-latency variant MANTIS. Cryptology ePrint Archive, Report 2016/660 (2016)

11. Beierle, C., Leander, G., Moradi, A., Rasoolzadeh, S.: CRAFT: lightweight tweakable block cipher with efficient protection against DFA attacks. IACR Trans. Symmetric Cryptology **2019**(1), 5–45 (2019)

12. Bellizia, D., et al.: Spook: sponge-based leakage-resistant authenticated encryption with a masked tweakable block cipher. IACR Trans. Symmetric Cryptology **2020**(S1), 295–349 (2020)

13. Beyne, T., Bilgin, B.: Uniform first-order threshold implementations. In: Avanzi, R., Heys, H. (eds.) SAC 2016. LNCS, vol. 10532, pp. 79–98. Springer, Cham (2017). https://doi.org/10.1007/978-3-319-69453-5_5

14. Biham, E., Biryukov, A., Shamir, A.: Cryptanalysis of skipjack reduced to 31 rounds using impossible differentials. In: Stern, J. (ed.) EUROCRYPT 1999. LNCS, vol. 1592, pp. 12–23. Springer, Heidelberg (1999). https://doi.org/10.1007/3-540-48910-X_2

15. Biham, E., Dunkelman, O., Keller, N.: New cryptanalytic results on IDEA. In: Lai, X., Chen, K. (eds.) ASIACRYPT 2006. LNCS, vol. 4284, pp. 412–427. Springer, Heidelberg (2006). https://doi.org/10.1007/11935230_27

16. Biham, E., Dunkelman, O., Keller, N.: New results on boomerang and rectangle attacks. In: Daemen, J., Rijmen, V. (eds.) FSE 2002. LNCS, vol. 2365, pp. 1–16. Springer, Heidelberg (2002). https://doi.org/10.1007/3-540-45661-9_1

17. Biham, E., Dunkelman, O., Keller, N.: The rectangle attack — rectangling the serpent. In: Pfitzmann, B. (ed.) EUROCRYPT 2001. LNCS, vol. 2045, pp. 340–357. Springer, Heidelberg (2001). https://doi.org/10.1007/3-540-44987-6_21

18. Biham, E., Dunkelman, O., Keller, N.: Related-key boomerang and rectangle attacks. In: Cramer, R. (ed.) EUROCRYPT 2005. LNCS, vol. 3494, pp. 507–525. Springer, Heidelberg (2005). https://doi.org/10.1007/11426639_30

19. Biryukov, A., Khovratovich, D.: Related-key cryptanalysis of the full AES-192 and AES-256. In: Matsui, M. (ed.) ASIACRYPT 2009. LNCS, vol. 5912, pp. 1–18. Springer, Heidelberg (2009). https://doi.org/10.1007/978-3-642-10366-7_1

20. Bogdanov, A., Rechberger, C.: A 3-subset meet-in-the-middle attack: cryptanalysis of the lightweight block cipher KTANTAN. In: Biryukov, A., Gong, G., Stinson, D.R. (eds.) SAC 2010. LNCS, vol. 6544, pp. 229–240. Springer, Heidelberg (2011). https://doi.org/10.1007/978-3-642-19574-7_16

21. Boura, C., Canteaut, A.: On the boomerang uniformity of cryptographic sboxes. IACR Trans. Symmetric Cryptology **2018**(3), 290–310 (2018)

22. Canteaut, A., Naya-Plasencia, M., Vayssière, B.: Sieve-in-the-middle: improved MITM attacks. In: Canetti, R., Garay, J.A. (eds.) CRYPTO 2013, Part I. LNCS, vol. 8042, pp. 222–240. Springer, Heidelberg (2013). https://doi.org/10.1007/978-3-642-40041-4_13

23. Cid, C., Huang, T., Peyrin, T., Sasaki, Yu., Song, L.: Boomerang connectivity table: a new cryptanalysis tool. In: Nielsen, J.B., Rijmen, V. (eds.) EUROCRYPT 2018, Part II. LNCS, vol. 10821, pp. 683–714. Springer, Cham (2018). https://doi.org/10.1007/978-3-319-78375-8_22

24. Delaune, S., Derbez, P., Vavrille, M.: Catching the fastest boomerangs application to SKINNY. IACR Trans. Symmetric Cryptology **2020**(4), 104–129 (2020)
25. Derbez, P., Fouque, P.-A.: Automatic search of meet-in-the-middle and impossible differential attacks. In: Robshaw, M., Katz, J. (eds.) CRYPTO 2016, Part II. LNCS, vol. 9815, pp. 157–184. Springer, Heidelberg (2016). https://doi.org/10.1007/978-3-662-53008-5_6
26. Derbez, P., Fouque, P.-A., Jean, J.: Improved key recovery attacks on reduced-round , in the single-key setting. In: Johansson, T., Nguyen, P.Q. (eds.) EUROCRYPT 2013. LNCS, vol. 7881, pp. 371–387. Springer, Heidelberg (2013). https://doi.org/10.1007/978-3-642-38348-9_23
27. Dinur, I., Dunkelman, O., Keller, N., Shamir, A.: Efficient dissection of composite problems, with applications to cryptanalysis, knapsacks, and combinatorial search problems. In: Safavi-Naini, R., Canetti, R. (eds.) CRYPTO 2012. LNCS, vol. 7417, pp. 719–740. Springer, Heidelberg (2012). https://doi.org/10.1007/978-3-642-32009-5_42
28. Dobraunig, C., Eichlseder, M., Mangard, S., Mendel, F., Unterluggauer, T.: ISAP - towards side-channel secure authenticated encryption. IACR Trans. Symmetric Cryptology **2017**(1), 80–105 (2017)
29. Dong, X., Hua, J., Sun, S., Li, Z., Wang, X., Hu, L.: Meet-in-the-middle attacks revisited: key-recovery, collision, and preimage attacks. In: Malkin, T., Peikert, C. (eds.) CRYPTO 2021, Part III. LNCS, vol. 12827, pp. 278–308. Springer, Cham (2021). https://doi.org/10.1007/978-3-030-84252-9_10
30. Dong, X., Qin, L., Sun, S., Wang, X.: Key guessing strategies for linear key-schedule algorithms in rectangle attacks. In: EUROCRYPT 2022, Proceedings, Part III, vol. 13277 of LNCS, pp. 3–33 (2022)
31. Dunkelman, O., Huang, S., Lambooij, E., Perle, S.: Single tweakey cryptanalysis of reduced-round SKINNY-64. In: Dolev, S., Kolesnikov, V., Lodha, S., Weiss, G. (eds.) CSCML 2020. LNCS, vol. 12161, pp. 1–17. Springer, Cham (2020). https://doi.org/10.1007/978-3-030-49785-9_1
32. Dunkelman, O., Keller, N., Lambooij, E., Sasaki, Yu.: A practical forgery attack on Lilliput-AE. J. Cryptol. **33**(3), 910–916 (2020)
33. Dunkelman, O., Keller, N., Shamir, A.: Improved single-key attacks on 8-round AES-192 and AES-256. In: Abe, M. (ed.) ASIACRYPT 2010. LNCS, vol. 6477, pp. 158–176. Springer, Heidelberg (2010). https://doi.org/10.1007/978-3-642-17373-8_10
34. Dunkelman, O., Keller, N., Shamir, A.: A practical-time related-key attack on the KASUMI cryptosystem used in GSM and 3G telephony. J. Cryptology **27**(4), 824–849 (2014)
35. Fuhr, T., Minaud, B.: Match box meet-in-the-middle attack against KATAN. In: Cid, C., Rechberger, C. (eds.) FSE 2014. LNCS, vol. 8540, pp. 61–81. Springer, Heidelberg (2015). https://doi.org/10.1007/978-3-662-46706-0_4
36. Gao, S., Roy, A., Oswald, E.: Constructing TI-friendly substitution boxes using shift-invariant permutations. In: Matsui, M. (ed.) CT-RSA 2019. LNCS, vol. 11405, pp. 433–452. Springer, Cham (2019). https://doi.org/10.1007/978-3-030-12612-4_22
37. Hadipour, H., Bagheri, N., Song, L.: Improved rectangle attacks on SKINNY and CRAFT. IACR Trans. Symmetric Cryptology **2**, 140–198 (2021)
38. Hua, J., Dong, X., Sun, S., Zhang, Z., Lei, H., Wang, X.: Improved MITM cryptanalysis on Streebog. IACR Trans. Symmetric Cryptology **2022**(2), 63–91 (2022)
39. Hua, J., Liu, T., Cui, Y., Qin, L., Dong, X., Cui, H.: Low-data cryptanalysis on SKINNY block cipher. Comput. J. (2022)

40. Ishai, Y., Sahai, A., Wagner, D.: Private circuits: securing hardware against prob-
    ing attacks. In: Boneh, D. (ed.) CRYPTO 2003. LNCS, vol. 2729, pp. 463–481.
    Springer, Heidelberg (2003). https://doi.org/10.1007/978-3-540-45146-4_27
41. Isobe, T.: A single-key attack on the full GOST block cipher. In: Joux, A. (ed.)
    FSE 2011. LNCS, vol. 6733, pp. 290–305. Springer, Heidelberg (2011). https://doi.
    org/10.1007/978-3-642-21702-9_17
42. Jean, J., Nikolić, I., Peyrin, T.: Tweaks and keys for block ciphers: the TWEAKEY
    framework. In: Sarkar, P., Iwata, T. (eds.) ASIACRYPT 2014. LNCS, vol. 8874, pp.
    274–288. Springer, Heidelberg (2014). https://doi.org/10.1007/978-3-662-45608-
    8_15
43. Jean, J., Nikolić, I., Peyrin, T., Seurin, Y.: Submission to CAESAR : Deoxys v1.41,
    October 2016
44. Kelsey, J., Kohno, T., Schneier, B.: Amplified boomerang attacks against reduced-
    round MARS and Serpent. FSE **1978**, 75–93 (2000)
45. Knudsen, L.R.: DEAL - a 128-bit block cipher. Complexity **258**(2), 216 (1998)
46. Liu, G., Ghosh, M., Song, L.: Security analysis of SKINNY under related-tweakey
    settings. IACR Trans. Symmetric Cryptology **3**, 37–72 (2017)
47. Mennink, B.: Beyond birthday bound secure fresh rekeying: application to authen-
    ticated encryption. In: Moriai, S., Wang, H. (eds.) ASIACRYPT 2020. LNCS, vol.
    12491, pp. 630–661. Springer, Cham (2020). https://doi.org/10.1007/978-3-030-
    64837-4_21
48. Naito, Y., Sasaki, Yu., Sugawara, T.: Lightweight authenticated encryption mode
    suitable for threshold implementation. In: Canteaut, A., Ishai, Y. (eds.) EURO-
    CRYPT 2020, Part II. LNCS, vol. 12106, pp. 705–735. Springer, Cham (2020).
    https://doi.org/10.1007/978-3-030-45724-2_24
49. Naito, Y., Sasaki, Y., Sugawara, T.: Secret can be public: low-memory AEAD
    mode for high-order masking. In: Dodis, Y., Shrimpton, T. (eds.) Advances in
    Cryptology – CRYPTO 2022, CRYPTO 2022. Lecture Notes in Computer Science,
    vol. 13509, pp. 315–345. Springer, Cham (2022). https://doi.org/10.1007/978-3-
    031-15982-4_11
50. Naito, Y., Sasaki, Y., Sugawara, T.: Lightweight authenticated encryption mode
    suitable for threshold implementation. Cryptol. ePrint Arch. (2020)
51. Naito, Y., Sugawara, T.: Lightweight authenticated encryption mode of operation
    for tweakable block ciphers. IACR Trans. Cryptographic Hardware Embed. Syst.
    2020(1), 66–94 (2020)
52. Nikova, S., Rechberger, C., Rijmen, V.: Threshold implementations against side-
    channel attacks and glitches. In: Ning, P., Qing, S., Li, N. (eds.) ICICS 2006.
    LNCS, vol. 4307, pp. 529–545. Springer, Heidelberg (2006). https://doi.org/10.
    1007/11935308_38
53. Qin, L., Dong, X., Wang, A., Hua, J., Wang, X.: Mind the tweakey schedule:
    cryptanalysis on skinnye-64-256. Cryptology ePrint Archive, Paper 2022/789, 2022.
    https://eprint.iacr.org/2022/789
54. Qin, L., Dong, X., Wang, X., Jia, K., Liu, Y.: Automated search oriented to
    key recovery on ciphers with linear key schedule applications to boomerangs in
    SKINNY and ForkSkinny. IACR Trans. Symmetric Cryptology **2**, 249–291 (2021)
55. Rotman, J.J.: Advanced modern algebra. American Mathematical Soc., (2010)
56. Sadeghi, S., Mohammadi, T., Bagheri, N.: Cryptanalysis of reduced round SKINNY
    block cipher. IACR Trans. Symmetric Cryptology **2018**(3), 124–162 (2018)
57. Sasaki, Yu.: Integer linear programming for three-subset meet-in-the-middle
    attacks: application to GIFT. In: Inomata, A., Yasuda, K. (eds.) IWSEC 2018.

LNCS, vol. 11049, pp. 227–243. Springer, Cham (2018). https://doi.org/10.1007/978-3-319-97916-8_15

58. Sasaki, Yu.: Meet-in-the-middle preimage attacks on AES hashing modes and an application to whirlpool. In: Joux, A. (ed.) FSE 2011. LNCS, vol. 6733, pp. 378–396. Springer, Heidelberg (2011). https://doi.org/10.1007/978-3-642-21702-9_22

59. Sasaki, Yu., Aoki, K.: Finding preimages in full MD5 faster than exhaustive search. In: Joux, A. (ed.) EUROCRYPT 2009. LNCS, vol. 5479, pp. 134–152. Springer, Heidelberg (2009). https://doi.org/10.1007/978-3-642-01001-9_8

60. Schrottenloher, A., Stevens, M.: Simplified MITM modeling for permutations: new (quantum) attacks. In: CRYPTO (2022)

61. Song, L., Qin, X., Hu, L.: Boomerang connectivity table revisited. application to SKINNY and AES. IACR Trans. Symmetric Cryptology **2019**(1), 118–141 (2019)

62. Tolba, M., Abdelkhalek, A., Youssef, A.M.: Impossible differential cryptanalysis of reduced-round SKINNY. In: Joye, M., Nitaj, A. (eds.) AFRICACRYPT 2017. LNCS, vol. 10239, pp. 117–134. Springer, Cham (2017). https://doi.org/10.1007/978-3-319-57339-7_7

63. Wagner, D.: The boomerang attack. In: Knudsen, L. (ed.) FSE 1999. LNCS, vol. 1636, pp. 156–170. Springer, Heidelberg (1999). https://doi.org/10.1007/3-540-48519-8_12

64. Wang, H., Peyrin, T.: Boomerang switch in multiple rounds. application to AES variants and Deoxys. IACR Trans. Symmetric Cryptology **2019**(1), 142–169 (2019)

Enhancing Differential-Neural Cryptanalysis

Zhenzhen Bao[1,2,4(✉)] ⓘ, Jian Guo[2] ⓘ, Meicheng Liu[3] ⓘ, Li Ma[3] ⓘ,
and Yi Tu[2] ⓘ

[1] Institute for Network Sciences and Cyberspace, BNRist, Tsinghua University,
Beijing, China
zzbao@tsinghua.edu.cn
[2] School of Physical and Mathematical Sciences, Nanyang Technological University,
Singapore, Singapore
guojian@ntu.edu.sg, tuyi0002@e.ntu.edu.sg
[3] State Key Laboratory of Information Security, Institute of Information
Engineering, Chinese Academy of Sciences, Beijing, China
liumeicheng@iie.ac.cn
[4] Zhongguancun Laboratory, Beijing, China

Abstract. In CRYPTO 2019, Gohr shows that well-trained neural networks can perform cryptanalytic distinguishing tasks superior to traditional differential distinguishers. Moreover, applying an unorthodox key guessing strategy, an 11-round key-recovery attack on a modern block cipher SPECK32/64 improves upon the published state-of-the-art result. This calls into the next questions. To what extent is the advantage of machine learning (ML) over traditional methods, and whether the advantage generally exists in the cryptanalysis of modern ciphers? To answer the first question, we devised ML-based key-recovery attacks on more extended round-reduced SPECK32/64. We achieved an improved 12-round and the first practical 13-round attacks. The essential for the new results is enhancing a classical component in the ML-based attacks, that is, the neutral bits. To answer the second question, we produced various neural distinguishers on round-reduced SIMON32/64 and provided comparisons with their pure differential-based counterparts.

Keywords: Differential cryptanalysis · Machine learning · SPECK · SIMON · Neural distinguisher · Key recovery · Neutral bits

1 Introduction

Cryptography and machine learning (ML) share many concerns, *e.g.*, distinguishing, classification, decision, searching, and optimization. It has been a long-standing challenge to answer whether computers could "learn to perform cryptanalytic tasks" [25]. These years, ML has made rapid progress in application domains ranging from machine translation, visual recognition, and autonomous vehicles to playing board games at superhuman levels [26]. ML has also been used to construct new types of cryptographic schemes [1] or crack ancient ciphers [14].

© International Association for Cryptologic Research 2022
S. Agrawal and D. Lin (Eds.): ASIACRYPT 2022, LNCS 13791, pp. 318–347, 2022.
https://doi.org/10.1007/978-3-031-22963-3_11

However, whether ML models can learn from scratch and then break modern ciphers at a superior level is still unpredictable. Nevertheless, one can still look forward to the prospect that ML approaches become substantial positive additions to the existing cryptanalysis toolkit, which has already been true in side-channel cryptanalysis [24].

For using ML to assist classical cryptanalysis, there are several questions to explore. That might include the follows:

- Can ML models learn new features with/without prior human cryptanalysis?
- Can ML provide more accurate and efficient measurements of known features?
- Can various ML approaches combined with various cryptanalysis techniques perform cryptanalysis tasks at a superior level to orthodox techniques, then be interpreted, and in turn, help to develop innovative and general cryptanalytic techniques?

In CRYPTO 2019, a remarkable work by Gohr [13] shows that commonly used neural networks could be trained to be superior cryptographic distinguishers. The work shed light on positive answers to the first two questions. It showed that deep neural-network distinguisher could exploit features that strong classical distinguishers fail to capture for SPECK. In [13], neural networks were trained with principles of differential cryptanalysis in mind. They show a remarkable capability in distinguishing attacks. More importantly, combining them with classical differentials and a highly selective key search policy forms a powerful key-recovery attack. Specifically, using the obtained neural distinguishers ($\mathcal{ND}$s) as the main engines, prepending them with a classical differential ($\mathcal{CD}$), applying basic reinforcement learning mechanisms, i.e., the Upper Confidence Bounds (UCB) and Bayesian optimization, an 11-round key-recovery attack on SPECK32/64 can achieve an unparalleled speed. However, to attack more rounds, one has to extend either the classical component, i.e., the prepended $\mathcal{CD}$, or the $\mathcal{ND}$. Both are facing obstacles that have not been overcome since [13].

In EUROCRYPT 2021, Ghor's $\mathcal{ND}$ got a deeper interpretation by Benamira et al. [7]. They were found to have learned not only the differential distribution on the output pairs but also the differential distribution in penultimate and antepenultimate rounds. Still, the other enhanced new component, i.e., the UCB and Bayesian optimization-based key-recovery phase in the superior 11-round attack in [13], has not been fully interpreted and theorized, thus still missing necessary guidance on tuning various parameters and sound theoretical models on analyzing data/time complexity and success probability.

Note that one of the main difficulties in evaluating the scope of applicability of ML algorithms is the lack of a formally specified theoretical model. Strong theoretical models for ML-based cryptanalysis are vital for generalizing the techniques. However, in parallel or even before our community achieve sound theoretical models, devising a sufficient number of successful attacks as positive examples in this new setting is essential. Without providing the best attacks as examples, it might be harder to obtain a theoretical model that produces the most powerful attacks. This work provides strong positive examples and extensive experimental data to support the first steps towards a realistic theoretical model for effective ML-based cryptanalysis.

OUR CONTRIBUTION. The contribution of this work includes the following.

- Practical attacks and rules of thumb
    - The first practical 13-round and an improved 12-round $\mathcal{ND}$-based key-recovery attacks on SPECK32/64 are devised. They have considerable advantages in time complexity over attacks devised using orthodox cryptanalysis. In addition, the first practical 16-round $\mathcal{ND}$-based key-recovery attack on SIMON32/64 is devised, which has a considerable advantage in data complexity. These results are summarized in Table 1.
    - Substantial illustrations unveil previously hidden details of the unorthodox key-recovery phase. Furthermore, observations derived from the illustrations provide rules of thumb for tuning critical parameters.
- Applications of enhanced cryptanalytic techniques
    The improved attacks are achieved by enhancing the classical components in the differential-neural attack scheme in [13], which are the $\mathcal{CD}$'s neutral bits (NBs). NBs and NB sets were first introduced by Biham and Chen in the cryptanalysis of hash function SHA-0 [8]. Later, many extensions and related concepts were proposed and applied in classical cryptanalysis, including message modification [29], tunnels [20], boomerangs [19], probabilistic NBs [4], and free bits [21]. Flipping an NB of a differential's conforming pair, the resulting pair also conforms to the differential. Thus, NBs can be used to derive a batch of data pairs from a single pair, and they conform or do not conform to the differential simultaneously. Single-bit NBs are employed in ML-based attacks in [13] to boost signals from $\mathcal{ND}$s. However, NBs of long $\mathcal{CD}$ are too scarce to boost signals from a weak but long $\mathcal{ND}$, thus inhibiting the ML-based attack from extending more rounds. In this work, we exploit various generalized NBs to make weak $\mathcal{ND}$ usable again. Particularly, we employed conditional simultaneous neutral bit-sets (CSNBS) and switching bit for adjoining differentials (SBfAD), which are essential for achieving efficient 12-round and practical 13-round attacks.
- New observations
    - We note the output difference of the $\mathcal{CD}$ matters to $\mathcal{ND}$, but not the input difference. Hence, more than one $\mathcal{CD}$ can be prepended to $\mathcal{ND}$, as long as they share the same output difference. Some neutral bits can be shared by multiple such differentials. Using such differentials might enable data reuse, thus slightly reducing data complexity.
    - We find that there are additional constraints on subkeys for some differential trails used in the presented attacks as well as the previous best attacks on SPECK32/64 [9,11,27]. Thus, the attacks only work for a subspace of the keys, $i.e.$, weak keys up to half of the keyspace.
- Various $\mathcal{ND}$s and DDT-based distinguishers ($\mathcal{DD}$) for SIMON32/64
    - Besides the Residual Network (ResNet) [16] considered by Gohr in [13], other neural networks that have shown advantages on ResNet in specific tasks, including Dense Network (DenseNet) [18] and the Squeeze-and-Excitation Network (SENet) [17], are investigated. Additionally, various training schemes, including direct training, key-averaging, and staged

training, were attempted. This effort results in various $\mathcal{ND}$s covering up to 11-round SIMON32/64.

- The full distribution of differences induced by the input difference (0x0000, 0x0040) up to 11 rounds are computed for SIMON32/64, which results in various $\mathcal{DD}$s. These $\mathcal{DD}$s provide solid baselines for $\mathcal{ND}$. We note that r-round $\mathcal{ND}$ should be compared with $(r-1)$-round $\mathcal{DD}$ for SIMON (different from SPECK). The results show that r-round $\mathcal{ND}$s achieve similar but weaker classification accuracy than $(r-1)$-round $\mathcal{DD}$s (see Table 5). We conjecture that r-round $\mathcal{ND}$s can learn to "decrypt" one un-keyed round and try to learn the distribution of the $(r-1)$-round differential, but fails to learn more features beyond the distribution of differences.

The source codes of the new attacks and the new $\mathcal{ND}$s can be found via https://github.com/differential-neural-cryptanalysis/speck32_simon32.

Table 1. Summary of key-recovery attacks on SPECK32/64 and SIMON32/64

Target	#R	Time (#Enc)	Data (#CP)	Succ. Rate	Weak keys	Configure	Ref.
SPECK32/64	11	2^{46}	2^{14}	–	2^{64}	1+6+4	[11]
		2^{38*}	$2^{13.6}$	0.52	2^{64}	1+2+7+1	[13]
	12	2^{51}	2^{19}	–	2^{64}	1+7+4	[11]
		$2^{43.40*}$	$2^{22.97}$	0.40	2^{64}	1+2+8+1	[13]
		$2^{44.89*}$	$2^{22.00}$	**0.86**	2^{64}	1+2+8+1	Sect. 4.3
		$\mathbf{2^{42.97*}}$	$\mathbf{2^{18.58}}$	**0.83**	2^{63}	1+3+7+1	Sect. 4.3
	13	2^{57}	2^{25}	–	2^{64}	1+8+4	[11]
		$\mathbf{2^{48.67*+r}}$	2^{29}	**0.82**	2^{63}	1+3+8+1	Sect. 4.2
SIMON32/64	14	$2^{62.47}$	$2^{30.47}$	–	2^{64}	1+9+4	[27]
	16	$2^{26.48}$	$2^{29.48}$	0.62	2^{64}	2+12+2	[3]
		$2^{41.81*+r}$	$\mathbf{2^{21}}$	0.49	2^{64}	1+3+11+1	Sect. E.4 [5]
	18	$2^{46.00}$	$2^{31.2}$	0.63	2^{64}	1+13+4	[2]
	21	$2^{55.25}$	$2^{31.0}$	–	2^{64}	4+13+4	[28]

- Not available.

* Under the assumption that one second equals the time of 2^{28} executions of SPECK32/64 or SIMON32/64 on a CPU.

r : $\log_2(cpu/gpu)$, where cpu and gpu are the CPU and GPU time running an attack, respectively. In our computing systems, $r = 2.4$ (The worse case execution time of the core of the 12-round attack on SPECK32/64 (without guessing the one key bit of k_0) took 6637 and 1265 s on CPU and GPU, respectively).

In the column entitled "Configure", the numbers colored in blue and red are the numbers of round covered by $\mathcal{CD}$s and $\mathcal{ND}$s, respectively.

Please see [5] for the full version of this article.

ORGANIZATION. The rest of the paper is organized as follows. Section 2 gives the preliminary on ML-based differential cryptanalysis and introduces the design of SPECK and SIMON. Section 3 introduces concepts of generalized neutral bits and some new notice on differential trails of SPECK32/64. The framework of the enhanced differential-neural cryptanalysis and its applications to SPECK32/64 and SIMON32/64 are presented in Sect. 4 and Section E of the full version [5]. Section 5 exhibits details of important statistics during the key-recovery phase. Rules of thumb are provided for tuning various parameters for the attacks. Section 6 presents various of $\mathcal{ND}$s and $\mathcal{DD}$s on SIMON32/64 reduced up to 11 rounds.

2   Preliminary

2.1   Brief Description of SPECK32/64 and SIMON32/64

Notations. Denote by n the word size in bits, $2n$ the state size in bits. Denote by (x_r, y_r) the left and right branches of a state after the encryption of r rounds. Denote by $x[i]$ (resp. $y[i]$) the i-th bit of x (resp. y) counted starting from 0; Denote by $[j]$ the index of the j-th bit of the state, *i.e.*, the concatenation of x and y, where $y[0]$ is the 0-th bit, and $x[0]$ is the 16-th bit. Denote by $\oplus$ the bit-wise XOR, $\boxplus$ the addition modulo 2^n, $\&$ the bit-wise AND, $x^{\lll s}$ the bit-wise left rotation by s positions, $x^{\ggg s}$ the bit-wise right rotation by s positions. Denote by F_k (resp. F_k^{-1}) the round function (resp. inverse of the round function) using subkey k of the encryption.

Brief Description of SPECK32/64 and SIMON32/64. SPECK32/64 and SIMON32/64 are small members of the lightweight block cipher families SPECK and SIMON [6] designed by researchers from the National Security Agency (NSA) of the USA. Both SPECK32/64 and SIMON32/64 have a Feistel-like structure[1], a block size and a key size of 32 resp. 64 bits. The round functions use combinations of rotation, XOR, and addition modulo 2^{16} (SPECK) or bit-wise AND (SIMON). SPECK32/64 has 22 rounds, and SIMON32/64 has 32 rounds. The encryption algorithms of SPECK32/64 and SIMON32/64 are listed in Algorithms 1 and 2. The subkeys of 16-bit for each round are generated from a master key of 64-bit by the non-linear key schedule using the same round function (SPECK32/64) or linear functions of simple rotation and XOR (SIMON32/64).

Algorithm 1: Encryption of SPECK32/64	**Algorithm 2:** Encryption of SIMON32/64
Input: $P = (x_0, y_0), \{k_0, \cdots, k_{21}\}$ **Output:** $C = (x_{22}, y_{22})$ **for** $r = 0$ *to* 21 **do** $\quad\mid x_{r+1} \leftarrow x_r^{\ggg 7} \boxplus y_r \oplus k_r$ $\quad\mid y_{r+1} \leftarrow y_r^{\lll 2} \oplus x_{r+1}$ **end**	**Input:** $P = (x_0, y_0), \{k_0, \cdots, k_{31}\}$ **Output:** $C = (x_{32}, y_{32})$ **for** $r = 0$ *to* 31 **do** $\quad\mid x_{r+1} \leftarrow$ $\quad\mid (x_r^{\lll 1} \& x_r^{\lll 8}) \oplus x_r^{\lll 2} \oplus y_r \oplus k_r$ $\quad\mid y_{r+1} \leftarrow x_r$ **end**

---

[1] SPECK can be represented as a composition of two Feistel maps [6].

2.2   Differential-Based Neural Distinguishers

The work in [13] shows that a neural network could be trained to capture the non-randomness of the distribution of values of output pairs when the input pairs to round-reduced SPECK32/64 are of specific difference, and thus play the role of distinguisher in cryptanalysis. This differential-based $\mathcal{ND}$ is the first known machine learning model that successfully performed cryptanalysis tasks on modern ciphers (beyond the applications on side-channel attacks).

In the following, the way of training the differential-based $\mathcal{ND}$ introduced in [13] is briefly recalled.

The Training Data and Input Representation. For a target cipher, the neural network is trained to distinguish between examples of ciphertext pairs corresponding to plaintext pairs with particular difference and those corresponding to random plaintext pairs. Thus, each of the training data is a data pair of the form (C, C') together with a label taking a value 0 or 1, where 0 means the corresponding plaintext pair is generated randomly, and 1 from a particular plaintext difference Δ_I. For SPECK32/64, the Δ_I is chosen to be of a single active bit, $i.e.$, $(\texttt{0x0040}, \texttt{0000})$, which is the intermediate difference lying in a known best differential characteristic.

The state of SPECK32/64 has left and right parts; thus, a pair of data is transformed into a quadruple of words (x, y, x', y') where $C = x\|y$ and $C' = x'\|y'$. The word quadruple is then interpreted into a 4×16-matrix with each word as a row-vector before being fed into the neural network with an input layer consisting of 64 units. Among the training data (and verification data), half are positive and half are negative examples, labeled by 1 and 0, respectively.

Training Schemes. The neural network structure used in [13] is a deep residual network. There are three training schemes proposed in [13]. The first is a basic training scheme that is sufficient for successfully training short-round distinguishers. The second is an improved training scheme for r-round distinguishers that simulate the output of the KEYAVERAGING algorithm used with an $(r-1)$-round distinguisher. Using the second scheme, the best $\mathcal{ND}$ on 7-round SPECK32/64 was achieved in [13]. The third is a staged training method that turns an already trained $(r-1)$-round distinguisher into an r-round distinguisher in several stages. Using the third scheme, the longest $\mathcal{ND}$ on SPECK32/64, which is an 8-round one, was achieved.

2.3   Upper Confidence Bounds and Bayesian Optimization

Besides a basic key-recovery attack, an improved attack using specifics of the targeted cipher ($i.e.$, the wrong key randomization hypothesis does not hold when only one round of trial decryption is performed) and elements from reinforcement learning ($i.e.$, automatic exploitation versus exploration trade-off based on upper confidence bounds) was proposed in [13].

The improved key-recovery attack employs an r-round main and an $(r-1)$-round helper $\mathcal{ND}$ trained with data pairs corresponding to input pairs with difference Δ_I; a short s-round differential, $\Delta_{I'} \to \Delta_I$ with probability denoted by 2^{-p}, is prepended on top of the $\mathcal{ND}$s (refer to Fig. 1 for an illustration of the components of the key-recovery attack.) About $c \cdot 2^p$ (denoted by n_{cts}) data pairs with difference $\Delta_{I'}$ are randomly generated, where c is a small constant; Neutral bits of the s-round differential are used to expand each data pair to a structure of n_b data pairs. The resulting n_{cts} structures of data pairs are decrypted by one round with 0 as the subkey[2] to get plaintext structures. All plaintext structures are queried to obtain the corresponding ciphertext structures.

Each ciphertext structure is to be used to generate candidates of the last subkey by the r-round main $\mathcal{ND}$ (and latter of the second to the last subkey by the $(r-1)$-round helper $\mathcal{ND}$) with a highly selective key search policy based on a variant of Bayesian optimization.

More specifically, the key search policy depends on an important observation that the expected response of the distinguisher upon wrong-key decryption will depend on the bit-wise difference between the trial key and the real key. This *wrong key response profile*, which can be precomputed, is used to recommend new candidate values for the key from previous candidate values by minimizing the weighted Euclidean distance as the criteria in an BAYESIANKEYSEARCH (see Algorithm 4 in the full version [5].) It recommends a set of subkeys and provides their scores without exhaustively performing trail decryptions.

The use of ciphertext structures is also highly selective using a standard exploration-exploitation technique, namely *Upper Confidence Bounds* (UCB). Each ciphertext structure is assigned a priority according to the scores of the subkeys they recommended and how often they were visited.

An important detail in the BAYESIANKEYSEARCH is that the responses $v_{i,k}$ from the $\mathcal{ND}$ on ciphertext pairs in the ciphertext structure (of size n_b) are combined using the Formula 1 and used as the score s_k of the recommended subkey k (refer to Algorithm 4 in the full version [5]). This score is highly decisive for the execution time and success rate of the attack. It will determine whether the recommended subkey will be further treated as its score passes or fails to pass the cutoff and also determine the priority of ciphertext structures to be visited. The number of ciphertext pairs in each structure is decisive when the $\mathcal{ND}$ has low accuracy.

$$s_k := \sum_{i=0}^{n_b-1} \log_2\left(\frac{v_{i,k}}{1 - v_{i,k}}\right) \tag{1}$$

3   Deep Exploring of Neutral Bits

3.1   The Motivation of Neutral Bits

Typically, the more rounds a $\mathcal{ND}$ covers, the lower its accuracy. When the accuracy becomes marginally higher than 0.5, it is hard to be used in a practical key-

---

[2] For SPECK, there is no whitening key and the first subkey is XORed after the first non-linear operation, which makes the first round free in differential attack (see the top of Fig. 3 in [5]).

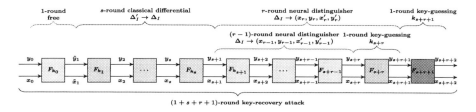

Fig. 1. Components of the key-recovery attacks

recovery attack. Thus, Gohr in [13] used the combined response (Formula 1) of the $\mathcal{ND}$ over large number of samples of the same distribution as a distinguisher (named as combined-response-distinguisher, $\mathcal{CRD}$). By doing so, the signal from the $\mathcal{ND}$ is boosted, and the distinguishability is increased. For a $\mathcal{CRD}$ built on top of a weak $\mathcal{ND}$ to reach its most potential with respect to distinguishability, the number of samples of the same distribution should be sufficiently large (see Sect. C of the full version [5] for a detailed experimental study on the relation between the distinguishability of $\mathcal{CRD}$ and the number of combined samples).

For the hybrid differential distinguisher used in the key-recovery attack in [13], it is not straightforward to aggregate enough samples of the same distribution fed to the $\mathcal{ND}$ due to the prepended $\mathcal{CD}$. To overcome this problem, Gohr in [13] used the neutral bits of the $\mathcal{CD}$, which is a notion first introduced by Biham and Chen for attacking SHA-0 [8]. The neutral bit has many extensions and related concepts, including message modification [29], tunnels [20], boomerangs [19], probabilistic neutral bits [4], and free bits [21]. Changing the values at the neutral bits of an input pair does not change the conformability to the differential. Thus, one can use m neutral bits to derive 2^m data pairs from a single pair such that they conform or do not conform to the differential simultaneously. The more neutral bits there are for the prepended $\mathcal{CD}$, the more the samples of the same distribution that could be generated for the $\mathcal{ND}$. However, generally, the longer the $\mathcal{CD}$, the fewer the neutral bits.

Finding enough neutral bits for prepending a long $\mathcal{CD}$ over a weak $\mathcal{ND}$ becomes a difficult problem for devising a key-recovery to cover more rounds. Thus, the first part of this work focuses on finding various types of neutral bits.

3.2   Neutral Bits and Generalized Neutral Bits

Notations. Let $\delta := \Delta_{in} \to \Delta_{out}$ be a differential of an r-round encryption F^r. Let (P, P') be the input pair and (C, C') be the output pair, where $P \oplus P' = \Delta_{in}$, $C = F^r(P)$, and $C' = F^r(P')$. If $C \oplus C' = \Delta_{out}$, (P, P') is said to *conform* to the differential δ (conforming pairs, or correct pairs of the differential). The primary notion of neutral bits can be interpreted as follows.

Definition 1 (Neutral bits of a differential, NBs [8]). *Let $e_0, e_1, \ldots, e_{n-1}$ be the standard basis of $\mathbb{F}_2^n$. Let i be an index of a bit (starting from 0). The i-th bit is a neutral bit of the differential $\Delta_{in} \to \Delta_{out}$, if for any conforming pair (P, P'), $(P \oplus e_i, P' \oplus e_i)$ is also a conforming pair.*

Let $\{i_1, i_2, \ldots, i_n\}$ be the set of NBs of a differential $\Delta_{in} \to \Delta_{out}$. Denote the subspace of $\mathbb{F}_2^n$ with basis $\{e_{i_1}, e_{i_2}, \ldots, e_{i_n}\}$ by $\mathcal{S}$. Then, from one input pair (P, P') where $P \oplus P' = \Delta_{in}$, one can generate a set $\{(P_i, P_i') \mid P_i \in P \oplus \mathcal{S}, P_i' = P_i \oplus \Delta_{in}\}$ that forms a structure with the same conformability to the differential.

For a differential $\Delta_{in} \to \Delta_{out}$ of F^r, in the view of a system of equations defined on the derivative function of F^r, i.e., $D_{\Delta_{in}} F^r(P) = \Delta_{out}$, a set of neutral bits $\mathcal{NB}$ partitions the solution space of $D_{\Delta_{in}} F^r(x) = \Delta_{out}$ into equivalence classes. It can be seen that the more neutral bits for a differential, the more structured the solution space.

Generalization of Neutral Bits. In general, neutral bits of non-trivial differentials are scarce. In [13], because of the lack of neutral bits for the 2-round differential of SPECK32/64, probabilistic neutral bits (PNBs for short) are exploited. This notion of PNB has already been introduced by Aumasson *et al.* in previous differential cryptanalysis of stream ciphers Salsa20 and Chacha, and compression function Rumba [4]. Formally, it can be defined as follows.

Definition 2 (Probabilistic neutral bits, PNBs [4]). *Let i be an index of a bit. The i-th bit is a p-probabilistic neutral bit of the differential $\Delta_{in} \to \Delta_{out}$, if the event that when (P, P') conforms to the differential then $(P \oplus e_i, P' \oplus e_i)$ also conforms to the differential under the same key, has a probability p (over the choice of P and the key).*

In the sequel attacks, the higher the probability p is, the higher the neutrality quality, and the more useful the neutral bit becomes. For convenience, when $p = 1$, the neutral bits are said to be *deterministic neutral bits*.

In this work, two types of generalized neutral bits are considered beyond the (probabilistic) neutral bits considered in [13]. The first type, named simultaneous-neutral bit-set (SNBSs for short), has already been introduced together with the notion of neutral bit in [8]. That is, for a differential, given a conforming pair, complementing individual bits, the conformability might be changed, but simultaneously complementing a set of bits does not change the conformability of the resulted pair. Formally, it can be defined as follows.

Definition 3 (Simultaneous-neutral bit-sets, SNBSs [8]). *Let $I_s = \{i_1, i_2, \ldots, i_s\}$ be a set of bit indices. Denote $f_{I_s} = \bigoplus_{i \in I_s} e_i$. The bit-set I_s is a simultaneous-neutral bit-set of the differential $\Delta_{in} \to \Delta_{out}$, if for any conforming pair (P, P'), $(P \oplus f_{I_s}, P' \oplus f_{I_s})$ is also a conforming pair, while for any subsets of I_s, the conformability of the resulted pair does not always hold.*

If we view that finding neutral bits is to form a subspace of $\mathbb{F}_2^n$ in which the corresponding data have the same conformability to the differential, the essence of generalizing to SNBS is that, instead of only considering the standard basis corresponding to single-bit NBs, we now consider arbitrary bases.

The second type, which is a natural generalization, is named in this work as conditional (simultaneous-) neutral bit(-set)s (CSNBSs for short), that is, the bits or bit-sets are neutral for input pairs fulfilling specific conditions. Formally, it can be defined as follows.

Definition 4 (Conditional (simultaneous-) neutral bit(-set)s, CSNBSs).
let $I_s = \{i_1, i_2, \ldots, i_s\}$ be a set of bit indices. Denote $f_{I_s} = \bigoplus_{i \in I_s} e_i$. Let $\mathcal{C}$ be a set of constraints on the value of an input P, and $\mathcal{P}_{\mathcal{C}}$ be the set of inputs that fulfill the constraints $\mathcal{C}$. The bit-set I_s is a conditional simultaneous-neutral bit-set of the differential $\Delta_{in} \to \Delta_{out}$, if for any conforming pair (P, P') where $P \in \mathcal{P}_{\mathcal{C}}$, $(P \oplus f_{I_s}, P' \oplus f_{I_s})$ is also a conforming pair.

The most straightforward constraints can be that some bit values of P are fixed. However, the constraints on the values of input P can be a more involved system of linear or non-linear equations.

Remark 1. Interestingly, various 'tunnels' have been used in [20] to speed up the search of MD5 collisions. They are essentially (generalized) neutral bits, including PNBs and CNBs. For consistency, in this paper, we use the extended names of the more well-known concept of 'neutral bits' instead of 'tunnels'.

Remark 2. The neutrality of CSNBSs depends on the values of some particular bits. The selected data is at an intermediate round in our attacks in this work, although the difference does not depend on the round-key, the values do. Thus, using CSNBSs, the attack requires guessing some key bits of the first round.

3.3 Automatic Procedure to Search for CSNBSs

To find CSNBSs, we use an automatic procedure to experimentally evaluate the conditional neutral probability of candidate SNBSs. Concretely, we investigate how the neutrality of each candidate SNBS is influenced by values of bits in some involved and controllable variables (for SPECK32/64, such variables are supposed to be the variables involved in the first modular addition, particularly, they are x_1, y_1, and $x_1^{\ggg 7} \oplus y_1^3$), and search CSNBSs conditioned on bits of these variables with the procedure in Algorithm 3.

3.4 Switching Bits for Adjoining Differentials

One knows that for a differential $\delta_1 = \Delta_{in_1} \to \Delta_{out}$, flipping a *non-neutral* bit of a conforming pair might make the resulting pair not conform to the differential. However, it is interesting that the resulted pair might turn into a conforming pair of another differential $\delta_2 = \Delta_{in_2} \to \Delta_{out}$ (after adjusting the input difference). If flipping this bit turns all conforming pairs of δ_1 into all conforming pairs of δ_2, then δ_2 has the same probability as δ_1. Since δ_1 and δ_2 have the same probability and share the same output difference, which will be the connecting difference in a hybrid distinguisher, the two differential are equally useful. In this case, that non-neutral bit can play the same role as neutral bits for generating structures of pairs simultaneously satisfying the connecting difference in a hybrid distinguisher. Formally, we define such bits that relate two differential as follows.

---

[3] In these considered variables, $(x_1, y_1) = (\tilde{x}_1 \oplus k_0, \tilde{y}_1 \oplus k_0)$ is the real input to the $\mathcal{CD}$ (see Fig. 3 in [5]), where $(\tilde{x}_1, \tilde{y}_1)$ is the chosen data in the key-recovery attack (since, in the key-recovery attack, the $\mathcal{CD}$ will be freely extended one round backward).

Algorithm 3: An automatic procedure to search for CSNBSs

1. Generate N random conforming pairs of the differential, each with a different random key.
2. For each candidate SNBS, denoted by I, for each bit b of a variable x possibly influencing the neutrality, and for $c \in \{0, 1\}$, do the following.
3. Experimentally evaluate the following probabilities over the conforming pairs.
   - $\Pr[I$ is neutral], *i.e.*, the neutral probability of I;
   - $\Pr[b = c]$, *i.e.*, the probability of b taking value c;
   - $\Pr[I$ is neutral and $b = c]$, *i.e.*, the probability of I is neutral and b taking value c for a random conforming pair;
4. Compute $\Pr[I$ is neutral $\mid b = c]$ as $\frac{\Pr[I \text{ is neutral and } b=c]}{\Pr[b=c]}$ (when $\Pr[b = c] = 0$, set $\Pr[I$ is neutral $\mid b = c]$ as 0.
5. If $\Pr[I$ is neutral $\mid b = c] - \Pr[I$ is neutral$] > \tau$ and $\Pr[I$ is neutral $\mid b = c] > \xi$, take I as a useful CSNBS and $b = c$ as its condition, and store in a set $\mathcal{CNB}$.

- In our experiments, N takes 1000. Statistics using 10, 100, 5000 conforming pairs were also made as preliminary tests. The statistical results do not have obvious divergence when using more than 100 conforming pairs, thus 1000 should be sufficient.
- In this procedure, τ and ξ are thresholds which can be adjusted to make trade-offs between the cost of imposing the condition, the number of CNBs, and the quality of CNBs. Typically, set τ be 0.2 and ξ be 0.8 will work well.

Definition 5 (Switching bits for adjoining differentials, SBfADs). *Let i be an index of a bit. The i-th bit is an switching bit of two differentials $\delta_1 = \Delta_{in_1} \to \Delta_{out}$ and $\delta_2 = \Delta_{in_2} \to \Delta_{out}$, if for any conforming pair $(P, P \oplus \Delta_{in_1})$ of δ_1, flipping the i-th bit and adjusting the input difference, the resulted pair $(P \oplus e_i, P \oplus e_i \oplus \Delta_{in_2})$ conforms to δ_2 under the same key. We call δ_1 and δ_2 adjoining differentials.*

Conceivably, such adjoining differentials and switching bit should be rare. However, they do exist. Currently, we found one type for XOR ($\oplus$) differential of addition modulo 2^n ($\boxplus$), and the details can be found in Sect. A of the full version [5]. A concrete example can be found in Sect. 4.1.

3.5   Paired Differentials Sharing the Same Neutral Bits

From the connecting difference between the $\mathcal{CD}$ and the $\mathcal{ND}$ propagating upward, there might be multiple differentials similar to $\mathcal{CD}$ and have equally good probability. These similar differentials are likely to share many neutral bits. When a shared neutral bit happens to be exactly the difference between input differences of two differentials, one can re-group ciphertext pairs within each ciphertext structure corresponding to one differential, and obtain ciphertext structures corresponding to the other differential without additional queries, *i.e.*, doubling the number of ciphertext structures for free. Formally, one has the following.

Definition 6 (Paired Differentials). *Let $\delta_1 = \Delta_{in_1} \to \Delta_{out}$ and $\delta_2 = \Delta_{in_2} \to \Delta_{out}$ be two differentials with the same output difference and with input differences satisfying $\Delta_{in_1} \oplus \Delta_{in_2} = \Delta_{nb_i}$. Suppose nb_i is a NB/SNBS for both δ_1 and*

δ_2. *Then, once a pair of input pair* $\{(P, P \oplus \Delta_{in_1}), (P \oplus \Delta_{nb_i}, P \oplus \Delta_{in_1} \oplus \Delta_{nb_i})\}$ *is generated for differential* δ_1, *one can re-pair the inputs as* $\{(P, P \oplus \Delta_{in_1} \oplus \Delta_{nb_i}), (P \oplus \Delta_{nb_i}, P \oplus \Delta_{in_1})\}$ *and obtain a pair of input pair for differential* δ_2. *Thus, by re-pairing the corresponding ciphertext pairs, the number of ciphertext structures is doubled. Such two differentials are said to be* paired differentials.

Exploiting paired differentials can reduce the data complexity by half, but is only of interest when the two differentials are with almost equally good probability and share enough neutral bits to be used in key-recovery attacks. An example can be found in Sect. 4.1.

Remark 3. Noticeably, the example of paired differentials is exactly the example of adjoining differentials in Sect. 4.1. However, this same example plays different roles when employed as paired differentials or as adjoining differentials. Employing as the former is to reuse data by re-pairing, employing as the latter is to achieve the effect of neutral bits. If a single pair of differentials acts as paired differentials and adjoining differentials simultaneously, the generated data *pairs* will be all different. Thus, two differentials can play both roles at the same time.

Remark 4. Reusing data to form different pairs adds dependencies between the chosen data pairs. However, the influence of such dependencies should not matter. We performed the attacks with and without reusing the data. The results show that as long as the total number of ciphertext structures and their size are the same, the success rates are roughly the same.

Remark 5. There is an implicit relation between neutral bits of a differential and high-order differential. An SNBS I_s of a differential $\Delta_{in} \to \Delta_{out}$ defines a special high-order differential $\Delta_{a_1,a_2} \to 0$, where $a_1 = \Delta_{in}$ and $a_2 = \bigoplus_{i \in I_s} e_i$.
    Besides, there is an interesting relation between neutral bits and the mixture-differential distinguisher of AES [15]. Some neutral bits found for SPECK32/64 and SIMON32/64 in this work can result in some bit-level mixture quadruples.

4   Key Recovery Attack on Round-Reduced SPECK32/64

This section shows that the neural distinguishers have not reached their full potential in the key-recovery attacks in [13]. They could be harnessed to cooperate with classical cryptanalytic tools and perform key-recovery attacks competitive to the attacks devised by orthodox cryptanalysis. In the following, we present key-recovery attacks employing the same neural distinguishers used in the 11-round and 12-round attacks on SPECK32/64 in [13]. The first neural distinguishers based 13-round attack and an improved 12-round attack were obtained.
    The improved attacks follow the framework of the improved key-recovery attacks in [13]. An r-round main and an $(r-1)$-round helper $\mathcal{ND}$s are employed, and an s-round $\mathcal{CD}$ is prepended. The key guessing procedure applies a simple reinforcement learning procedure. The last subkey and the second to last subkey are to be recovered without exhaustively using all candidate values to do one-round decryption. Instead, a Bayesian key search employing the wrong key response profile is to be used.

The prepended $\mathcal{CD}$s to be used in the improved attacks include the same 2-round differential used in the attack in [13] and four new 3-round differentials. The preliminary is to find enough NBs of these differentials to obtain enough samples of the same distribution so that we can use the combined response from the $\mathcal{ND}$s. In the following, the SNBSs, CNBs, and SBfADs introduced in Sect. 3 are to be found and exploited.

4.1   Finding CSNBSs for SPECK32/64

For finding NBs of the differential of round-reduced SPECK32/64, we used an exhaustive search for empirical results because of the complexity brought by the carry of modular addition.

Finding SNBSs for 2-round Differential. For the prepended 2-round $\mathcal{CD}$ on top of the $\mathcal{ND}$s, one can experimentally obtain three deterministic NBs and two SNBSs (simultaneously complementing up to 4 bits) using an exhaustive search. Besides, bits and bit-sets that are (simultaneous-)neutral with high probabilities are also detected. Concretely, for the 2-round differential (0x0211, 0x0a04) → (0x0040, 0x0000), bits and bit-sets that are (probabilistic) (simultaneous-)neutral are summarized in Table 2.

Table 2. (Probabilistic) SNBSs for 2-round differential (0x0211, 0x0a04) → (0x0040, 0x0000) of SPECK32/64. The statistics were performed on 1000 correct pairs, each with a different random key. For comparison, one can find the NBs used by attacks in [13] in Table 9 of the full version [5].

NBs	Pr.	NBs	Pr.	NBs	Pr.	NBs	Pr.	NBs	Pr.	NBs	Pr.	NBs	Pr.
[20]	1	[21]	1	[22]	1	[9, 16]	1	[2, 11, 25]	1	[14]	0.965	[15]	0.938
[6, 29]	0.91	[23]	0.812	[30]	0.809	[7]	0.806	[0]	0.754	[11, 27]	0.736	[8]	0.664

Finding SNBSs for 3-round Differential. The 2-round differential (0x0211, 0x0a04) → (0x0040, 0x0000) can be extended to two optimal (prob. $\approx 2^{-11}$) 3-round differentials, i.e.,

(0x0a20, 0x4205) → (0x0040, 0x0000), (0x0a60, 0x4205) → (0x0040, 0x0000).

However, the NBs/SNBSs of these two optimal differentials are very scarce. There are four sub-optimal 3-round differentials (prob. $\approx 2^{-12}$ when being estimated following Markov model, but are actually 2^{-11} for 2^{63} keys and 0 for another 2^{63} keys, see Sect. D of the full version [5] for more details), i.e.,

(0x8020, 0x4101) → (0x0040, 0x0000), (0x8060, 0x4101) → (0x0040, 0x0000),
(0x8021, 0x4101) → (0x0040, 0x0000), (0x8061, 0x4101) → (0x0040, 0x0000).

For these 3-round differentials, the hamming weights of the input differences are low, and they have more NBs/SNBSs. Still, the numbers of NBs/SNBSs are not enough for appending a weak neural network distinguisher. Thus, conditional ones were searched using the procedure in Algorithm 3. For $\xi = 0.7$, the obtained CSNBSs and their conditions are summarized together with unconditional NBs/SNBSs in Table 4. In the table, the columns titled 'Post.' are finally verified neutral probabilities of the (C)SNBSs when all four conditions are fulfilled.

For each of the four differentials, there are three linear conditions (xy-type) that are necessary for a pair $((x, y), (x', y'))$ to conform to it, which are listed in Table 3 (without coloring in gray). For each linear condition, once it is fulfilled, the probability of the differential increases by a factor of 2^1. In the following key-recovery attacks, the linear conditions can be fulfilled by chosen data once the corresponding bits of k_0 are guessed.

Table 3. Necessary conditions to conform to the 3-round differentials (or the dominant trail in the differential, intermediate differences in the dominant trail are colored in gray, the condition for the trail instead of the differential is colored in gray, where $c = (x^{\ggg 7} \boxplus y) \oplus (x^{\ggg 7} \oplus y)$. Each column corresponds to one differential (trail).)

(0x8020, 0x4101)	(0x8060, 0x4101)	(0x8021, 0x4101)	(0x8061, 0x4101)
(0x0201, 0x0604)	(0x0201, 0x0604)	(0x0201, 0x0604)	(0x0201, 0x0604)
(0x1800, 0x0010)	(0x1800, 0x0010)	(0x1800, 0x0010)	(0x1800, 0x0010)
(0x0040, 0x0000)	(0x0040, 0x0000)	(0x0040, 0x0000)	(0x0040, 0x0000)
$\begin{cases} x[7] = 0, \\ x[5] \oplus y[14] = 1, \\ x[15] \oplus y[8] = 0, \\ x[0] \oplus y[9] = 0. \end{cases}$	$\begin{cases} x[7] = 0, \\ x[5] \oplus y[14] = 0, \\ x[15] \oplus y[8] = 0, \\ x[0] \oplus y[9] = 0. \end{cases}$	$\begin{cases} x[7] = 0, \\ x[5] \oplus y[14] = 1, \\ x[15] \oplus y[8] = 1, \\ y[9] \oplus c[9] = 0. \end{cases}$	$\begin{cases} x[7] = 0, \\ x[5] \oplus y[14] = 0, \\ x[15] \oplus y[8] = 1, \\ y[9] \oplus c[9] = 0. \end{cases}$

Table 4. (C)SNBSs for 3-round differential (0x8020, 0x4101) $\rightarrow$ (0x0040, 0x0000), (0x8060, 0x4101) $\rightarrow$ (0x0040, 0x0000), (0x8021, 0x4101) $\rightarrow$ (0x0040, 0x0000), and (0x8061, 0x4101) $\rightarrow$ (0x0040, 0x0000) of SPECK32/64.

Bit-set	(8020, 4101) Pre.	Post.	(8060, 4101) Pre.	Post.	(8021, 4101) Pre.	Post.	(8061, 4101) Pre.	Post.	Condition
[22]	0.995	1.000	0.995	1.000	0.996	1.000	0.997	1.000	−
[20]	0.986	1.000	0.997	1.000	0.996	1.000	0.995	1.000	−
[13]	0.986	1.000	0.989	1.000	0.988	1.000	0.992	1.000	−
[12, 19]	0.986	1.000	0.995	1.000	0.993	1.000	0.986	1.000	−
[14, 21]	0.855	0.860	0.874	0.871	0.881	0.873	0.881	0.876	−
[6, 29]	0.901	0.902	0.898	0.893	0.721	0.706	0.721	0.723	−
[30]	0.803	0.818	0.818	0.860	0.442	0.442	0.412	0.407	−
[0, 8, 31]	0.855	0.859	0.858	0.881	0.000	0.000	0.000	0.000	−
[5, 28]	0.495	1.000	0.495	1.000	0.481	1.000	0.469	1.000	$x[12] \oplus y[5] = 1$ $y[1] = 0$
[15, 24]	0.482	1.000	0.542	1.000	0.498	1.000	0.496	1.000	−
[4, 27, 29]	0.672	0.916	0.648	0.905	0.535	0.736	0.536	0.718	$x[11] \oplus y[4] = 1$
[6, 11, 12, 18]	0.445	0.903	0.456	0.906	0.333	0.701	0.382	0.726	$x[2] \oplus y[11] = 0$

A condition at the end of a row is specific to the bit-set at the same row. '-' means that there is no condition for the corresponding bit-set.

Pre.: probability obtained using 1000 correct pairs without imposing the conditions.

Post.: probability obtained using 1000 correct pairs and imposing all conditions in the last column.

□: Neutral bit(-set)s used in the 13-round attack $\mathcal{A}^{\text{SPECK13}R}$ on SPECK32/64.

□: Neutral bit(-set)s used in the 12-round attack $\mathcal{A}^{\text{SPECK12}R}$ on SPECK32/64.

Exploiting SBfADs. Among the four 3-round differentials, $(0x8020, 0x4101) \rightarrow (0x0040, 0x0000)$ and $(0x8060, 0x4101) \rightarrow (0x0040, 0x0000)$ are adjoining differentials, and $(0x8021, 0x4101) \rightarrow (0x0040, 0x0000)$ and $(0x8061, 0x4101) \rightarrow (0x0040, 0x0000)$ are adjoining differentials (refer to Sect. 3.4). The bit 5 of x (the bit 21 of $x\|y$) is the SBfAD of both pairs. An SBfAD plays the same role as a deterministic unconditional NB, thus is better to be used than probabilistic and conditional NBs. Specifically, employing SBfAD saves one guessed key bit and reduces both time and data complexity by half compared to employing the CSNBS. In the presented 13-round (resp. 12-round) attacks, this SBfAD is employed, and one CSNBS (resp. PNBS) in Table 4 can be dismissed.

The reasoning on why one can switch between these differentials by bit 5 of x can be found in Sect. A.2 of the full version [5]. Experiments were performed and have verified that this SBfAD plays a better role than a CSNBS or a PNBS.

Exploiting Paired Differentials. The four 3-round differentials share most of the high-probabilistic NBs and the conditions on the NBs. Besides, the neutral bit [22] makes $(0x8020, 0x4101) \rightarrow (0x0040, 0x0000)$ and $(0x8060, 0x4101) \rightarrow (0x0040, 0x0000)$ (resp. $(0x8021, 0x4101) \rightarrow (0x0040, 0x0000)$ and $(0x8061, 0x4101) \rightarrow (0x0040, 0x0000)$) be paired differentials as introduced in Sect 3.5.

Specifically, take the first two differentials for example. They share the neutral bit [22] and all other useful NB. Since $(0x8020, 0x4101) \oplus (0x8060, 0x4101) = (0x0040, 0000)$, while bit [22] corresponds to difference $\Delta_{22} = (0x0040, 0000)$, ciphertext structures for $(0x8060, 0x4101) \rightarrow (0x0040, 0x0000)$ can be directly obtained from that of $(0x8020, 0x4101) \rightarrow (0x0040, 0x0000)$ (refer to Sect. 3.5). Thus, using a paired differentials (as in the following attack $\mathcal{A}^{\text{SPECK}13R}$ on the 13-round SPECK32/64), one can generate half of the required data pairs for free. Accordingly, the data complexity to get one pair of ciphertexts is one instead of two.

Further, the data complexity can be slightly reduced by using both paired differentials when the attack requires no more than six NBs (the number of shared unconditional NBs). For the ease of notation, let us denote $(0x8020, 0x4101)$ as example difference Δ_E^1, and $(0x8021, 0x4101)$ as Δ_E^2. Six queries of a plaintext structure consisting of $(P,\ P \oplus \Delta_E^1,\ P \oplus \Delta_{22},\ P \oplus \Delta_E^1 \oplus \Delta_{22},\ P \oplus \Delta_E^2,\ P \oplus \Delta_E^2 \oplus \Delta_{22})$ result in eight pairs to be used in the upcoming attack $\mathcal{A}^{\text{SPECK}12R}$ on the 12-round SPECK32/64. The eight pairs are two pairs $(P, P \oplus \Delta_E^1)$ and $(P \oplus \Delta_{22}, P \oplus \Delta_E^1 \oplus \Delta_{22})$ following input difference Δ_E^1, two pairs $(P, P \oplus \Delta_E^1 \oplus \Delta_{22})$, $(P \oplus \Delta_{22}, P \oplus \Delta_E^1)$ following input difference $\Delta_E^1 \oplus \Delta_{22}$, two pairs $(P, P \oplus \Delta_E^2)$, $(P \oplus \Delta_{22}, P \oplus \Delta_E^2 \oplus \Delta_{22})$ following input difference Δ_E^2, and two pairs $(P, P \oplus \Delta_E^2 \oplus \Delta_{22})$, $(P \oplus \Delta_{22}, P \oplus \Delta_E^2)$ following input difference $\Delta_E^2 \oplus \Delta_{22}$. In such a way, the average data complexity to get one pair of ciphertexts reduces from 2 to 3/4.

4.2   Key Recovery Attack on 13-Round SPECK32/64

Employing two classical differentials that can simultaneously act as adjoining differentials and paired differentials, and combining them with neural distinguishers, we examine how far a practical attack can go on reduced-round SPECK32/64. A 13-round attack, denoted by $\mathcal{A}^{\mathrm{SPECK}13R}$, is devised as follows.

The preliminary components that capture characteristics of SPECK32/64 for devising the attack $\mathcal{A}^{\mathrm{SPECK}13R}$ are as follows.

1. Two 3-round $\mathcal{CD}$s $(0\mathrm{x}8020, 0\mathrm{x}4101) \to (0\mathrm{x}0040, 0\mathrm{x}0000)$, $(0\mathrm{x}8060, 0\mathrm{x}4101) \to (0\mathrm{x}0040, 0\mathrm{x}0000)$ (refer to the rounds colored in blue in Fig. 3 in the full version [5]), which act as both adjoining differentials and paired differentials (refer to Remark 3), 11 common NBs (including single-bit NBs, SNBSs, CSNBSs), $i.e.$, $\mathcal{NB}$: $\{[22], [13], [20], [5, 28], [15, 24], [12, 19], [6, 29], [4, 27, 29], [14, 21], [0, 8, 31], [30]\}$ (refer to the columns framed by blue lines in Table 4), and a SBfAD [21];
2. An 8-round $\mathcal{ND}$, named $\mathcal{ND}^{\mathrm{SPECK}8R}$, trained with difference $(0\mathrm{x}0040, 0\mathrm{x}0000)$ and its wrong key response profiles $\mathcal{ND}^{\mathrm{SPECK}8R}.\mu$ and $\mathcal{ND}^{\mathrm{SPECK}8R}.\sigma$;
3. A 7-round $\mathcal{ND}$, named $\mathcal{ND}^{\mathrm{SPECK}7R}$, trained with difference $(0\mathrm{x}0040, 0\mathrm{x}0000)$ and its wrong key response profiles $\mathcal{ND}^{\mathrm{SPECK}7R}.\mu$ and $\mathcal{ND}^{\mathrm{SPECK}7R}.\sigma$.

The parameters for recovering the last two subkeys are denoted as follows.

1. n_{kg}: the number of possible values for the few guessed bits of k_0.
2. n_{cts}: the number of ciphertext structures.
3. n_b: the number of ciphertext pairs in each ciphertext structure, $i.e.$, $2^{|\mathcal{NB}|+1}$.
4. n_{it}: the total number of iterations on the ciphertext structures.
5. c_1 and c_2: the cutoffs with respect to the scores of the recommended last subkey and second to last subkey, respectively.
6. n_{byit1}, n_{cand1} and n_{byit2}, n_{cand2}: the number of iterations and number of key candidates within each iteration in the BAYESIANKEYSEARCH procedures (refer to Algorithm 4 in the full version [5] for guessing each of the last and second to last subkeys.

The attack procedure is as follows (refer to Figs. 2 and 3 in [5]).

1. Initialize variables $Gbest_{\mathrm{key}} \leftarrow (\mathrm{None}, \mathrm{None})$, $Gbest_{\mathrm{score}} \leftarrow -\infty$.
2. For each of the n_{kg} values of the 5 key bits $k_0[7]$, $k_0[15] \oplus k_0[8]$, $k_0[12] \oplus k_0[5]$, $k_0[1]$, $k_0[11] \oplus k_0[4]^4$,
   (a) Generate $n_{cts}/2$ random data pairs, $i.e.$, $(\tilde{x}_1 || \tilde{y}_1, \tilde{x}_1' || \tilde{y}_1')$'s, with difference $(0\mathrm{x}8020, 0\mathrm{x}4101)$, and satisfying the conditions for conforming pairs,
   $i.e.,$ $\begin{cases} \tilde{x}_1[7] = k_0[7], \\ \tilde{x}_1[15] \oplus \tilde{y}_1[8] = k_0[15] \oplus k_0[8], \end{cases}$ and the conditions for three CSNBSs
   $i.e.,$ $\begin{cases} \tilde{x}_1[12] \oplus \tilde{y}_1[5] \oplus 1 = k_0[12] \oplus k_0[5], \\ \tilde{y}_1[1] = k_0[1], \\ \tilde{x}_1[11] \oplus \tilde{y}_1[4] \oplus 1 = k_0[11] \oplus k_0[4], \end{cases}$ (refer to Tables 3 and 4).

---

4 Since the first two 3-round $\mathcal{CD}$s are used as paired differentials, the key bit $k_0[5] \oplus k_0[14]$ does not need to be guessed. Besides, since the CSNBS [6, 11, 12, 18] in Table 4 is not used in the attack, the key bit $k_0[2] \oplus k_0[11]$ does not need to be guessed. In total only 5 bits of k_0 are guessed.

(b) From the $n_{cts}/2$ random data pairs, generate $n_{cts}/2$ structures using the NBs in $\mathcal{NB}$, marking the correspondence between old pairs and new pairs that are generated using the NB [22].

(c) Use the SBfAD [21] to double the number of pairs in each of the $n_{cts}/2$ structures. The new pairs are generated by flipping the [21] bit in the original pairs and adjusting the difference to be (0x8060, 0x4101).

(d) Decrypt one round using zero as the subkey for all data in the structures obtained above and obtain $n_{cts}/2$ plaintext structures;

(e) Query for the ciphertexts under 13-round SPECK32/64 of the $n_{cts}/2 \times n_b \times 2$ plaintexts, obtaining $n_{cts}/2$ ciphertext structures.

(f) For each couple of ciphertext pairs, denoted by (c_1, c_1') and (c_2, c_2'), whose corresponding couple of data pairs are related by flipping the neutral bit [22], that is the couple $(\tilde{x}_1 || \tilde{y}_1, \tilde{x}_1 || \tilde{y}_1 \oplus (0x8020, 0x4101))$ and $(\tilde{x}_1 || \tilde{y}_1 \oplus (0x0040, 0000), \tilde{x}_1 || \tilde{y}_1 \oplus (0x8020, 0x4101) \oplus (0x0040, 0000))$, obtain a new couple of ciphertext pairs, that is (c_1, c_2') and (c_2, c_1'). As a result, the new couples generated in this way correspond to couples of plaintext pairs for the second differential (0x8060, 0x4101) and its neutral bit [22]. Thus, additional $n_{cts}/2$ ciphertext structures can be obtained without new queries. In total, n_{cts} ciphertext structures, denoted by $\{\mathcal{C}_1, \ldots, \mathcal{C}_{n_{cts}}\}$, are obtained.

(g) Initialize an array $w_{\max}$ and an array n_{visit} to record the highest scores and the numbers of visits obtained by ciphertext structures.

(h) Initialize variables $best_{score} \leftarrow -\infty$, $best_{key} \leftarrow (None, None)$, $best_{pos} \leftarrow$ None to record the best score, the corresponding best-recommended values for the two subkeys obtained among all ciphertext structures and the index of this ciphertext structure.

(i) For j from 1 to n_{it}:

   i. Compute the priority of each of the ciphertext structures as follows: $s_i = w_{\max i} + \alpha \cdot \sqrt{\log_2(j)/n_{visit i}}$, for $i \in \{1, \ldots, n_{cts}\}$, and $\alpha = \sqrt{n_{cts}}$; This formula of priority is designed according to a general method in reinforcement learning for achieving automatic exploitation versus exploration trade-off based on Upper Confidence Bounds. It is motivated to focus the key search on the most promising ciphertext structures [13].

   ii. Pick the ciphertext structure with the highest priority score for further processing in this j-th iteration, denote it by $\mathcal{C}$, and its index by idx, $n_{visit idx} \leftarrow n_{visit idx} + 1$.

   iii. Run BAYESIANKEYSEARCH with $\mathcal{C}$, the neural distinguisher $\mathcal{ND}^{SPECK8R}$ and its wrong key response profile $\mathcal{ND}^{SPECK8R}.\mu$ and $\mathcal{ND}^{SPECK8R}.\sigma$, n_{cand1}, and n_{byit1} as input parameters; obtain the output, that is a list L_1 of $n_{byit1} \times n_{cand1}$ candidate values for the last subkey and their scores, i.e., $L_1 = \{(g_{1i}, v_{1i}) : i \in \{1, \ldots, n_{byit1} \times n_{cand1}\}\}$.

   iv. Find the maximum $v_{1\max}$ among v_{1i} in L_1, if $v_{1\max} > w_{\max idx}$, $w_{\max idx} \leftarrow v_{1\max}$.

   v. For each recommended last subkey $g_{1i} \in L_1$, if the score $v_{1i} > c_1$,

    A. Decrypt the ciphertexts in $\mathcal{C}$ using the g_{1i} by one round and obtain the ciphertext structure $\mathcal{C}'$ of 12-round SPECK32/64.

    B. Run BAYESIANKEYSEARCH with $\mathcal{C}'$, $\mathcal{ND}^{\mathrm{SPECK7R}}$ and its wrong key response profile $\mathcal{ND}^{\mathrm{SPECK7R}}.\mu$ and $\mathcal{ND}^{\mathrm{SPECK7R}}.\sigma$, n_{cand2}, and n_{byit2} as input parameters; obtain the output, that is a list L_2 of $n_{byit2} \times n_{cand2}$ candidate values for the second to last subkey and their scores, i.e., $L_2 = \{(g_{2i}, v_{2i}) : i \in \{1, \ldots, n_{byit2} \times n_{cand2}\}\}$.

    C. Find the maximum among v_{2i} and the corresponding g_{2i} in L_2, and denote them by $v_{2\mathrm{max}}$ and $g_{2\mathrm{max}}$.

    D. If $v_{2\mathrm{max}} > best_{\mathrm{score}}$, update
$$best_{\mathrm{score}} \leftarrow v_{2\mathrm{max}}, \ best_{\mathrm{key}} \leftarrow (g_{1i}, g_{2\mathrm{max}}), \ best_{\mathrm{pos}} \leftarrow idx.$$

  vi. If $best_{\mathrm{score}} > c_2$, go to Step 2j.

(j) Make a final improvement using VERIFIERSEARCH [12] on the value of $best_{\mathrm{key}}$ by examining whether the scores of a set of keys obtained by changing at most 2 bits on top of the incrementally updated $best_{\mathrm{key}}$ could be improved recursively until no improvement is obtained, update $best_{\mathrm{score}}$ to the best score in the final improvement; If $best_{\mathrm{score}} > Gbest_{\mathrm{score}}$, update $Gbest_{\mathrm{score}} \leftarrow best_{\mathrm{score}}$, $Gbest_{\mathrm{key}} \leftarrow best_{\mathrm{key}}$.

3. Return $Gbest_{\mathrm{key}}$, $Gbest_{\mathrm{score}}$.

Remark 6. In Gohr's implementations of the attack [12], two bits of g_1 are randomly assigned instead of being recommended by minimizing the weighted euclidean distance. This is based on observation of the symmetry of the wrong key response profiles, which indicates that values of the last two bits of the last subkey have almost the same influence on the response, thus hard to be correctly guessed. In our implementations, guessing these two bits in the last subkey is integrated into guessing the second to last subkey, which is done using the stronger helper $\mathcal{ND}$. The wrong key response profile with respect to the helper $\mathcal{ND}$ are thus on 18 key bits. In doing so, these two key bits can be correctly recommended with a higher probability.

In the experimental verification of the attack $\mathcal{A}^{\mathrm{SPECK13R}}$, the 8-round and 7-round neural distinguishers provided in [12] were used. The accuracy of $\mathcal{ND}^{\mathrm{SPECK8R}}$ (resp. $\mathcal{ND}^{\mathrm{SPECK7R}}$) is about 0.514 (resp. 0.616). Concrete parameters and the complexity of $\mathcal{A}^{\mathrm{SPECK13R}}$ are as follows (see Fig. 5 in the full version [5]).

$$n_{kg} = 2^5, \quad n_b = 2^{11+1}, \quad n_{cts} = 2^{12}, \quad\quad n_{it} = 4 \times n_{cts}$$
$$c_1 = 18, \quad\ c_2 = -500, \quad n_{byit1} = n_{byit2} = 5, \quad n_{cand1} = n_{cand2} = 32$$

The data complexity is $n_{kg} \times n_b \times n_{cts}$, that is, $2^{5+11+1+12}$, i.e., 2^{29} plaintexts (because of the use of two matched differentials, data complexity for getting each ciphertext pair is 1 instead of 2.)

To make the experimental verification economic, we tested the core of the attack with the five conditions being fulfilled only. That is, tested whether a particular one of $2^{n_{kg}}$ loops in Step 2 can successfully recover the last two subkeys. In that particular loop, the trialed value of the 5 bits of k_0 is correct. In the other loops, the trialed values deviate from the correct value by at least one bit. The other loops can be expected to obtain worse scores and wrong key guesses than that particular loop. Besides, since the prepended classical differentials are valid to keys fulfilling $k_2[12] \neq k_2[11]$, we tested for these valid keys only, and the presented attack works for 2^{63} keys (refer to Sect. D of the full version [5]).

The core of the attack was examined in 40 trials. We count a key guess as successful if the returned last two subkeys and the real two subkeys have a Hamming distance at most two in total. Among the 40 trials, there are 33 successful trials. Thus, the success rate is $33/40$, which is 0.8250.

The trials were executed using a server with 8 GPUs[5]. The maximum execution time (worst-case run time) among the 40 runs is 14.5 h (which runs all the n_{it}, i.e., 2^{14} iterations). For 2^5 loops in Step 2, the worst situation is that within each loop, all n_{it} iterations are executed. Accordingly, the full attack requires about $2^5 \times 14.5$, i.e., 464 GPU hours, which is equivalent to $2^{48.67+r}$ executions of SPECK32/64[6].

Remark 7. For invalid guesses of the few bits of k_0, worse scores and wrong key guesses for the last two subkeys will be obtained. Invalided guesses of bits of k_0 directly cause all or most ciphertext pairs in all ciphertext structures to be nonconforming pairs (wrong ciphertext structures). For wrong ciphertext structures, the scores of the recommended last and the second to last subkeys will be very low such that fewer last subkeys will pass cutoff c_1, and almost no second to last subkey will pass cutoff c_2. Therefore, under invalid key guesses of k_0, all n_{it} iterations will be used. Using n_{kg} times the worst-case run-time (which is taken by a failed trial using all the n_{it} iterations) of an attack core provides a conservative estimation of the time complexity of a full attack.

4.3   Key Recovery Attack on 12-Round Speck32/64

To devise key-recovery attack on 12-round SPECK32/64, Gohr in [13] used the 2-round classical differential $(0x0211, 0x0a04) \to (0x0040, 0x0000)$ combined with the 8-round and 7-round $\mathcal{ND}$s. For amplifying the weak signal from the 8-round neural distinguisher, 13 single-bit NBs of the prepended 2-round $\mathcal{CD}$ were exploited. However, many of the 13 NBs are neutral with probabilities that are not high (refer to Table 9 in the full version [5]). Besides, 500 ciphertext structures and 2000 iterations were used to achieve a success rate of 0.40. Thus, the data complexity is $500 \times 2^{13} \times 2$, i.e., $2^{22.97}$ plaintexts. The attack takes roughly 12 h on a quad-core PC (as listed in Table 1).

From Table 2, one can see that there are many SNBSs being deterministically neutral or neutral with relatively high probability. Using 13 SNBSs, cutting the required data by nearly half, and using the following parameters, our experiments

---

[5] Tesla V100-SXM2-32GB, computeCapability: 7.0; coreClock: 1.53 GHz; coreCount: 80; deviceMemorySize: 31.72 GB; deviceMemoryBandwidth: 836.37 GB/s).

[6] Under the assumption that one second equals the time of 2^{28} executions of SPECK32/64 on a CPU, and $r = \log_2(cpu/gpu)$, where *cpu* is the CPU time and *gpu* is the GPU time running an attack. In our computing systems, $r = 2.4$.

show that the success rate of the resulting attack can be increased to 0.86 using fewer data (see Fig. 6 in the full version [5]).

$$n_{kg} = 0, \quad n_b = 2^{13}, \quad n_{cts} = 2^8, \quad\quad n_{it} = 2^{10}$$
$$c_1 = 15, \quad c_2 = 500, \quad n_{byit1} = n_{byit2} = 5, \quad n_{cand1} = n_{cand2} = 32$$

However, the data complexity is still bounded by the weakness of the 8-round $\mathcal{ND}$. To further reduce the data requirement, we employ the 3-round $\mathcal{CD}$s and combine them with the stronger 7-round (and 6-round) $\mathcal{ND}$. In this case, unconditional SNBSs are enough for the 7-round $\mathcal{ND}$. Thus, those conditional ones can be dismissed in such a 12-round attack. Besides, since bit [21] is an SBfAD which switches the first two and the last two differentials, it can be used to replace a probabilistic NB. The four 3-round differentials share enough NBs, thus, all can be employed, which makes it possible to obtain one plaintext pair with 3/4 instead of 2 queries (as discussed in Sect. 4.1).

Concretely, the components of the 12-round key-recovery attack, denoted by $\mathcal{A}^{\text{SPECK}12R}$, are as follows.

1. Four 3-round $\mathcal{CD}$s (0x8020, 0x4101) $\rightarrow$ (0x0040, 0x0000), (0x8060, 0x4101) $\rightarrow$ (0x0040, 0x0000), (0x8021, 0x4101) $\rightarrow$ (0x0040, 0x0000), (0x8061, 0x4101) $\rightarrow$ (0x0040, 0x0000), five neutral bit(-set)s $\mathcal{NB}$: {[22], [13], [20], [12, 19], [14, 21]} (refer to the rows framed by green lines in Table 4), one SBfAD [21];
2. A 7-round $\mathcal{ND}$, named $\mathcal{ND}^{\text{SPECK}7R}$, trained with difference (0x0040, 0x0000) and its wrong key response profiles $\mathcal{ND}^{\text{SPECK}7R}.\mu$ and $\mathcal{ND}^{\text{SPECK}7R}.\sigma$;
3. A 6-round $\mathcal{ND}$, named $\mathcal{ND}^{\text{SPECK}6R}$ trained with difference (0x0040, 0x0000) and its wrong key response profiles $\mathcal{ND}^{\text{SPECK}6R}.\mu$ and $\mathcal{ND}^{\text{SPECK}6R}.\sigma$.

The framework of the 12-round attack $\mathcal{A}^{\text{SPECK}12R}$ follows that of $\mathcal{A}^{\text{SPECK}13R}$. The difference is that, in the beginning, we only guess one key bit of k_0, that is $k_0[7]$, because for all four 3-round differentials, there is only one common condition for conforming pairs, i.e., $x_1[7] = 0$ (refer to Table 3). Thus, n_{kg} is 2^1, and there are only 2 outermost loops.

The concrete parameters and complexity of $\mathcal{A}^{\text{SPECK}12R}$ are as follows (see Fig. 7 in [5] for details). The accuracy of $\mathcal{ND}^{\text{SPECK}7R}$ (resp. $\mathcal{ND}^{\text{SPECK}6R}$) is about 0.616 (resp. 0.788).

$$n_{kg} = 2^1, \quad n_b = 2^{5+1}, \quad n_{cts} = 2^{12}, \quad\quad n_{it} = 2^{13}$$
$$c_1 = 8, \quad c_2 = 10, \quad n_{byit1} = n_{byit2} = 5, \quad n_{cand1} = 2 \times n_{cand2} = 64$$

The data complexity is $n_{kg} \times n_{cts} \times n_b \times 3/4$, that is, $2^{18.58}$ plaintexts. To compare with previous attacks, the experiments were done using CPUs. Concretely, 128 trials were done with 32 threads in a CPU server[7]. Within the 128 trials, 2 trials have no correct ciphertext structures. In the remaining 126 trials, there are 107 successful trials (the returned last two subkeys have a Hamming distance to the real subkeys at most two). The success rate is $107/128$, i.e., 0.8359.

---

[7] Equipped with a 32-core Intel Cascade-Lake Xeon(R) Platinum 9221 2.30 GHz, and with 384 GB RAM, on CentOS 7.6.

The maximum execution time among the trials is 4.4 h (which runs all the n_{it}, *i.e.*, 8192 iterations). Repeating 2^1 times, the maximum run time should be about 8.8 CPU hours, which is equivalent to $2^{42.97}$ executions of SPECK32/64.

Trade-off. If accepting a success rate of 0.6016, the data complexity can be further reduced to $2^{17.58}$ (by setting $n_{cts} = 2^{11}, c_1 = 7, n_{cand1} = 32$) (see Fig. 8 in [5] for details).

Comparison. Compared to classical attacks on SPECK32/64 (refer to Table 1), these new attacks commonly employ longer distinguishers consisting of short $\mathcal{CD}$s and $\mathcal{ND}$s, and their key-guessing phase covers fewer rounds. As for complexity, their advantage is considerable in terms of time. Compared to previous ML-based results in [13], for attacking 12-round, the success rate improves considerably using fewer data; most importantly, one more round is covered.

5   Tuning Parameters for the Key Recovery Attacks

The key-recovery attack with UCB and BAYESIANKEYSEARCH has shown its effectiveness in guessing keys in [13] and this work. However, the tuning of the parameters, especially the cutoffs, which determine the execution time and the success rate, is still missing theoretical guidance up to the time of this work. Thus, in this section, we provide detailed experimental data and derived observations to bring some light on tuning important parameters and making better trade-offs.

5.1   Exhibitions of Important Statistics in Various Attacks

It is noticed that $v_{1\max}$ (*i.e.*, $\max(\{v_{1i} \mid v_{1i} \in L_1\})$) in the key-recovery phase is an important variable determining the priority of each ciphertext structure and indicates whether promising sub-keys are discovered in each run of BAYESIANKEYSEARCH. Investigating the distributions of this variable corresponding to correct ciphertext structures (denoted by $\mathcal{D}_r^{v_{1\max}}$) and wrong ciphertext structures (denoted by $\mathcal{D}_w^{v_{1\max}}$) is helpful. These distributions can be used to learn how to tune cutoff c_1 to make trade-offs between time complexity and success rate. Investigating the distributions of $v_{2\max}$ (*i.e.*, $\max(\{v_{2i} \mid v_{2i} \in L_2\})$) could be used to learn how to tune cutoff c_2 (denoted by $\mathcal{D}_r^{v_{2\max}}$ and $\mathcal{D}_w^{v_{2\max}}$ for correct ciphertext structures and wrong structures, respectively). Thus, together with the information on attack configurations, attack complexity, and success rate, histograms are given to show $\mathcal{D}_r^{v_{1\max}}, \mathcal{D}_w^{v_{1\max}}, \mathcal{D}_r^{v_{2\max}}, \mathcal{D}_w^{v_{2\max}}$ for each presented attack ($\mathcal{A}^{\text{SPECK13}R}$ and $\mathcal{A}^{\text{SPECK12}R}$). Concretely, for each attack, details of the following statistics are illustrated in its corresponding figure (*e.g.*, Figs. 5 to 8 in the full version [5]).

- $\mathcal{D}_w^{v_{1\max}}, \mathcal{D}_r^{v_{1\max}}, \mathcal{D}_s^{v_{1\max}}$: indicated using **rand**, **real**, and **succ** in the histograms, respectively; $\mathcal{D}_s^{v_{1\max}}$ is the distribution of $v_{1\max}$ corresponding to the successfully recovered subkeys.

- qct_w, qct_r: percentage of $v_{1\max}$'s corresponding to wrong (resp. correct) ciphertext structures passing cutoff c_1;
- percentage of passing samples if different cutoffs are set, including both the quantile plot with the samples and the plot with the best fitting generalized logistic distribution on the samples;
- similar statistics for $v_{2\max}$ (including $\mathcal{D}_r^{v_{2\max}}$, $\mathcal{D}_w^{v_{2\max}}$, $\mathcal{D}_s^{v_{2\max}}$)[8];
- distribution of Hamming distances between returned and the real subkeys;
- distribution of the used number of iterations in successful attacks.

5.2   Some Rules of Thumb

Apart from substantial illustrations of previously hidden details of the key-recovery phase, the following observations are made to provide some rules of thumb for deciding the number of data required and the cutoff c_1. Before that, we note that compared to c_1, cutoff c_2 is much easier to decide because a successful attack requires the value of c_2 to be 'at the top rank' (compared with a 'threshold' sense of cutoff c_1). Thus, it is safe to select a value for c_2 that is just large enough to be uncovered by $\mathcal{D}_w^{v_{2\max}}$.

Observation 1. *Suppose in the above attack framework, the probability of the prepended differential is p, the number of ciphertext structures is n_{cts}. Denote the attack success probability by P_s.*

Note that $P_s \leq 1 - (1 - p \cdot q)^{n_{cts}}$, where q is the probability for the response $v_{1\max}$ from a correct ciphertext structure pass the cutoff c_1, i.e., $q = \mathrm{Pr}_{\mathcal{C}_r}[v_{1\max} \geq c_1]$, where $\mathcal{C}_r$ is space of correct ciphertext structures.

Thus, the following relation should be fulfilled:

$$n_{cts} \geq \frac{\log_2(1 - P_s)}{\log_2(1 - p \cdot q)}.$$

For given n_{cts}, p, and P_s, the cutoff c_1 should be chosen such that

$$c_1 \leq Q(1 - \frac{1 - (1 - P_s)^{\frac{1}{n_{cts}}}}{p}),$$

where $Q(\cdot)$ is the quantile function of the distribution of $v_{1\max}$ corresponding to correct ciphertext structures, i.e., $\mathcal{D}_r^{v_{1\max}}$.

For example, in the attack configuration in Fig. 5 in the full version [5], after correctly guessing the key bits in k_0, the probability p of the prepended differential is 2^{-9}; suppose c_1 is selected as 18 so that q is 0.31; then, to have a success probability of 0.82, the required number of ciphertext structures, *i.e.*, n_{cts} should satisfy $n_{cts} \geq \log 2(1-0.82)/\log 2(1-2^{-9} \cdot 0.31) \approx 2831.33 \approx 2^{11.4673}$. On the other hand, suppose one selects n_{cts} to be 2^{12}, and aims P_s to be 0.82; since p is 2^{-9}, this requires $c_1 \leq Q(1-(1-(1-0.82)^{2^{-12}})/2^{-9}) = Q(1-0.2143) \approx 20.5$.

---

[8] Some $v_{2\max}$'s corresponding to success cases are lower than cutoff c_2; that is due to the final improvement.

Note that Observation 1 provides an upper bound on the value of the cutoff c_1. As for a lower bound on c_1, we provide the following observations.

The cutoff c_1 seems to be the smaller, the better for having a high success probability. However, a smaller cutoff c_1 is not a better choice for having a good time complexity than a larger one. On the one hand, even using the correct ciphertext structures, if a recommended subkey gets a small score v_1, then, typically, it also has a large Hamming distance towards the real subkeys; thus, it is hard to produce good recommendations for the second to last subkeys. On the other hand, too small cutoff c_1 results in a high percentage of v_1 from the wrong ciphertext structures passing it. As a consequence, a lot of running time will be wasted on the wrong ciphertext structures. Thus, the cutoff c_1 is better to be large enough such that a low percentage of v_1 of bad recommendations of last subkeys (*e.g.*, with more than Hamming distance 3 to the real subkey) from both correct and wrong ciphertext structures is passing it.

The preliminary to use these observations as guidance to tune the parameters is to have a good knowledge of the distribution $\mathcal{D}_r^{v_1\max}$ and $\mathcal{D}_w^{v_1\max}$. Experimental investigations on $\mathcal{D}_r^{v_1\max}$ and $\mathcal{D}_w^{v_1\max}$ can be found in [5, Sect. B.3].

6   Neural Distinguishers on Round-Reduced SIMON32/64

This section presents the neural distinguishers on SIMON32/64 obtained in this work, using which a key-recovery attack covering 16 rounds is devised and presented in [5, Sect. E]. Besides, DDT-based $\mathcal{DD}$s are computed and provide baselines for $\mathcal{ND}$s. Comparisons between $\mathcal{DD}$s and $\mathcal{ND}$s are made accordingly.

6.1   The Choice of the Network Architecture

Considering that several state-of-the-art neural network structures have been developed, a preliminary search for a better network other than the Residual Network (ResNet) [16] used in [13] was conducted. Specifically, Dense Network (DenseNet) [18] shows advantages in parameter efficiency, implicit deep supervision, and feature reuse. Squeeze-and-Excitation Network (SENet) [17] won the first place in the *ImageNet Large Scale Visual Recognition Challenge* (ILSVRC 2017) for classification tasks. SENet can also be combined with existing deep architectures to boost performance at a minimal additional computational cost. One example is the SE-ResNeXt that employs squeeze-and-excitation blocks and uses the ResNeXt as backbone. Thus, these two networks, together with ResNet, were investigated. The results on the performance of distinguishers that cover 7 to 9 rounds SIMON32/64 under the three different network structures are presented in Table 5. From the comparison, for longer rounds, SENet yields distinguishers that are superior to that of the other two. In the following, we only report essential details of the distinguishers trained using the SENet.

6.2   The Training of Neural Distinguishers

The training schemes follow that in [13]. All three schemes are attempted. For short rounds, the basic training scheme already works well. For longer rounds, the KeyAverageing and Staged schemes are necessary to achieve distinguishers with non-marginal advantage. Due to the specific round structure of SIMON, distinguishers fed with partial values combined with partial differences between ciphertext pairs, instead of full values of ciphertext pairs, should be more useful than their counterparts for carrying out key-recovery attacks. Thus, we trained distinguishers accepting data composed partial values and partial differences.

The input difference is $(\texttt{0x0000}, \texttt{0x0040})$. This choice takes into account both the $\mathcal{ND}$ and the prepended $\mathcal{CD}$, whose output difference is this input difference of the $\mathcal{ND}$. The goal is to obtain the best hybrid distinguisher to make the longest key-recovery attack. Therefore, the firstly examined were the intermediate differences in the best 13-round differential trail [9]. All intermediate differences were examined by training $\mathcal{ND}$s. This difference, $(\texttt{0x0000}, \texttt{0x0040})$, yielded the best 7, 8, and 9-round $\mathcal{ND}$s and, at the same time, allows prepending a good $\mathcal{CD}$, thus resulting in the best hybrid distinguisher. Note that since the differentials of SIMON32/64 has a rotational equivalent property along with the 16-bit word, all r-round $\mathcal{ND}$s with input difference $(0, e_i)$ and $(r-1)$-round $\mathcal{ND}$s with input difference $(e_i, 0)$ were found to have similar accuracy, for $0 \le i < 16$.

Training Using the Basic Scheme. Using the basic training scheme and adopting SENet (more precisely, the adopted is the SE-ResNeXt variant), neural distinguishers to recognize output pairs of 7-, 8-, 9-round SIMON32/64 with the input difference $(\texttt{0x0000}, \texttt{0x0040})$ are obtained. That is, given an output pair (x, y) and (x', y') and represented in the form of (x, y, x', y'), they can predict whether the data corresponds to input pairs with difference $(\texttt{0x0000}, \texttt{0x0040})$ of the 7-, 8-, 9-round SIMON32/64. To make a distinction from their counterparts accepting transformed data, i.e., $(x, x', y \oplus y')$, the 7-, 8-, 9-round neural distinguishers presented here are named as $\mathcal{ND}_{\mathbf{VV}}^{\text{SIMON7}R}$, $\mathcal{ND}_{\mathbf{VV}}^{\text{SIMON8}R}$, and $\mathcal{ND}_{\mathbf{VV}}^{\text{SIMON9}R}$, respectively. The 7-round $\mathcal{ND}_{\mathbf{VV}}^{\text{SIMON7}R}$ achieves an accuracy as high as 0.9825, which drops by 0.17 per round to 0.8151 and 0.6325 for $\mathcal{ND}_{\mathbf{VV}}^{\text{SIMON8}R}$ and $\mathcal{ND}_{\mathbf{VV}}^{\text{SIMON9}R}$, respectively.

Training to Simulate KeyAverageing Algorithm. Successful training of the 10-round distinguisher is achieved by adopting the training scheme of simulating a KeyAverageing Algorithm [13] used with the 9-round $\mathcal{ND}_{\mathbf{VV}}^{\text{SIMON9}R}$. Concretely, a size 2^{20} sample set $\mathcal{S}$ of ciphertext pairs for 10-round SIMON32/64 is generated, one half corresponds to plaintext pairs with difference $(\texttt{0x0000}, \texttt{0x0040})$ and the other half corresponds to random plaintext pairs. The labels of these samples are not assigned directly but using the KeyAverageing Algorithm calling the 9-round $\mathcal{ND}_{\mathbf{VV}}^{\text{SIMON9}R}$. That is, each ciphertext pair c_i in the set $\mathcal{S}$ is decrypted by one-round using all possible values of the 10-th round subkey; thus 2^{16} intermediate values $c'_{i,j}$'s for $j \in \{0,1\}^{16}$ are generated; grading the $c'_{i,j}$'s using the 9-round $\mathcal{ND}_{\mathbf{VV}}^{\text{SIMON}9R}$, and combining the 2^{16} scores into a score for the ciphertext pair c_i by transforming the scores into real-vs-random likelihood ratios and averaging. This combined score is then taken as the label of c_i in $\mathcal{S}$. Using the sample set $\mathcal{S}$ with the labels so obtained, a training, which follows the training of the best 7-round neural distinguisher in [13], is performed from a randomly initialized network state. This training procedure results in a 10-round distinguisher, named $\mathcal{ND}_{\mathbf{VV}}^{\text{SIMON}10R}$, with an accuracy of 0.5551.

Training Using the Staged Training Method. The best 10-round and 11-round distinguisher are trained using the staged training method, which was the same method used to train the 8-round distinguisher of SPECK32/64 in [13]. Concretely, for training an 11-round $\mathcal{ND}$, in the first stage, the best 9-round distinguisher $\mathcal{ND}_{\mathbf{VV}}^{\text{SIMON}9R}$ is retained to recognize 8-round SIMON32/64 with the input difference $(0x0440, 0x0100)$. Note that the most likely difference to appear three rounds after the input difference $(0x0000, 0x0040)$ is $(0x0440, 0x0100)$, and the probability is about 2^{-4}. In this first stage, the number of examples for training and for testing are 2^{28} and 2^{26}, respectively. The number of epochs is 10 and the learning rate is 10^{-4}. In the second stage, the resulted network of the first stage is retained to recognize 11-round SIMON32/64 with the input difference $(0x0000, 0x0040)$. For this training, 2^{30} examples are freshly generated and fed, and 2^{28} examples are for verification. One epoch with a learning rate of 10^{-4} is done. In the last stage, the resulting network of the second stage is retained in two epochs with 2^{30} freshly generated data for training and 2^{28} data for verification. The learning rate is 10^{-5}. The resulting distinguisher $\mathcal{ND}_{\mathbf{VV}}^{\text{SIMON}11R}$ achieves an accuracy of 0.5174.

Training using Data of Form $(x, x', y \oplus y')$. Notice that once the output of the r-th round (x_r, x'_r, y_r, y'_r) is known, one can directly compute $(x_{r-1}, x'_{r-1}, y_{r-1} \oplus y'_{r-1})$ without knowing the $(r-1)$-th subkey. Thus, an $(r-1)$-round distinguisher accepting data of the form $(x, x', y \oplus y')$ can be used as an r-round distinguisher in the key-recovery attack. With this consideration, $(r-1)$-round distinguishers accepting data of the form $(x, x', y \oplus y')$ are trained to see whether they are superior to r-round distinguishers accepting data of the form (x, x', y, y'). To make a distinction, let us denote the former by $\mathcal{ND}_{\mathbf{VD}}^{\text{SIMON}(r-1)R}$ and the latter by $\mathcal{ND}_{\mathbf{VV}}^{\text{SIMON}rR}$.

The results show that $\mathcal{ND}_{\mathbf{VD}}^{\text{SIMON}(r-1)R}$ could achieve slightly better accuracy than $\mathcal{ND}_{\mathbf{VV}}^{\text{SIMON}rR}$. Besides, the wrong key response profiles of $\mathcal{ND}_{\mathbf{VD}}^{\text{SIMON}8R}$ and that of $\mathcal{ND}_{\mathbf{VV}}^{\text{SIMON}9R}$ share observable pattern and symmetry. For key values that have little different from the real value, responses from $\mathcal{ND}_{\mathbf{VD}}^{\text{SIMON}8R}$ are higher than responses from $\mathcal{ND}_{\mathbf{VV}}^{\text{SIMON}9R}$. Similar observations can be derived from a comparison between that of $\mathcal{ND}_{\mathbf{VD}}^{\text{SIMON}9R}$ and that of $\mathcal{ND}_{\mathbf{VV}}^{\text{SIMON}10R}$.

Summaries on various distinguishers are presented in Table 5 for detailed accuracy and in Fig. 19 in [5] for their wrong key response profiles.

Table 5. Summary of neural distinguishers on SIMON32/64

#R	Name	Network	Accuracy	True Positive Rate	True Negative Rate
6	$\mathcal{DD}_{\mathbf{DD}}^{\text{SIMON}6R}$	DDT	0.9918	0.9995	0.9841
7		ResNet	$0.9823 \pm 1.2 \times 10^{-4}$	$0.9996 \pm 2.7 \times 10^{-5}$	$0.9650 \pm 2.3 \times 10^{-4}$
	$\mathcal{ND}_{\mathbf{VV}}^{\text{SIMON}7R}$	SENet†	$0.9802 \pm 1.3 \times 10^{-4}$	$0.9987 \pm 4.2 \times 10^{-5}$	$0.9617 \pm 2.4 \times 10^{-4}$
		DenseNet	$0.9244 \pm 2.7 \times 10^{-4}$	$0.9670 \pm 2.2 \times 10^{-4}$	$0.8818 \pm 4.5 \times 10^{-4}$
7	$\mathcal{DD}_{\mathbf{DD}}^{\text{SIMON}7R}$	DDT	0.8465	0.8641	0.8288
8	$\mathcal{ND}_{\mathbf{VV}}^{\text{SIMON}8R}$	SENet†	$0.8150 \pm 4.2 \times 10^{-4}$	$0.8418 \pm 5.5 \times 10^{-4}$	$0.7882 \pm 5.1 \times 10^{-4}$
		ResNet	$0.7912 \pm 4.2 \times 10^{-4}$	$0.8041 \pm 5.5 \times 10^{-4}$	$0.7783 \pm 6.2 \times 10^{-4}$
		DenseNet	$0.7789 \pm 4.4 \times 10^{-4}$	$0.7709 \pm 6.8 \times 10^{-4}$	$0.7868 \pm 5.6 \times 10^{-4}$
8	$\mathcal{DD}_{\mathbf{DD}}^{\text{SIMON}8R}$	DDT	0.6628	0.5781	0.7476
8	$\mathcal{ND}_{\mathbf{VD}}^{\text{SIMON}8R}$	SENet†	$0.6587 \pm 4.8 \times 10^{-4}$	$0.5586 \pm 7.4 \times 10^{-4}$	$0.7588 \pm 5.6 \times 10^{-4}$
9	$\mathcal{ND}_{\mathbf{VV}}^{\text{SIMON}9R}$	SENet†	$0.6515 \pm 5.3 \times 10^{-4}$	$0.5334 \pm 7.0 \times 10^{-4}$	$0.7695 \pm 5.7 \times 10^{-4}$
		ResNet	$0.6296 \pm 4.5 \times 10^{-4}$	$0.5164 \pm 6.3 \times 10^{-4}$	$0.7429 \pm 5.5 \times 10^{-4}$
		DenseNet	$0.6443 \pm 4.1 \times 10^{-4}$	$0.5337 \pm 6.1 \times 10^{-4}$	$0.7550 \pm 5.0 \times 10^{-4}$
9	$\mathcal{DD}_{\mathbf{DD}}^{\text{SIMON}9R}$	DDT	0.5683	0.4691	0.6674
9	$\mathcal{ND}_{\mathbf{VD}}^{\text{SIMON}9R}$	SENet†	$0.5657 \pm 4.9 \times 10^{-4}$	$0.4748 \pm 7.1 \times 10^{-4}$	$0.6565 \pm 6.6 \times 10^{-4}$
10	$\mathcal{ND}_{\mathbf{VV}}^{\text{SIMON}10R}$ +	SENet†	$0.5610 \pm 4.5 \times 10^{-4}$	$0.4761 \pm 6.0 \times 10^{-4}$	$0.6460 \pm 7.2 \times 10^{-4}$
	$\mathcal{ND}_{\mathbf{VV}}^{\text{SIMON}10R}$ *	SENet†	$0.5549 \pm 4.6 \times 10^{-4}$	$0.4605 \pm 6.5 \times 10^{-4}$	$0.6493 \pm 7.7 \times 10^{-4}$
10	$\mathcal{DD}_{\mathbf{DD}}^{\text{SIMON}10R}$	DDT	0.5203	0.5002	0.5404
11	$\mathcal{ND}_{\mathbf{VV}}^{\text{SIMON}11R}$	SENet†	$0.5174 \pm 5.3 \times 10^{-4}$	$0.5041 \pm 7.1 \times 10^{-4}$	$0.5307 \pm 7.9 \times 10^{-4}$
11	$\mathcal{DD}_{\mathbf{DD}}^{\text{SIMON}11R}$	DDT	0.5044	0.4852	0.5236

$\dagger$ More precisely, the adopted is the SE-ResNeXt variant.

- The network structure and parameters for the ResNet follow exactly that used in [12] for training the $\mathcal{ND}$s on SPECK32/64 except for the learning rate. Using a smaller learning rate (*i.e.*, cyclic_lr(10,0.001,0.00001)) instead of the original learning rate (*i.e.*, cyclic_lr(10,0.002,0.0001)) results in a better accuracy (*e.g.*, 0.6296 vs 0.6110 for 9-round) for $\mathcal{ND}$s on SIMON32/64.

* This neural distinguisher is trained using the KEYAVERAGING algorithm.

+ This neural distinguisher is trained using the staged training method.

6.3 Computing $\mathcal{DD}$s and Further Interpretations

To provide baselines for $\mathcal{ND}$s, we calculate the full distribution of differences for SIMON32/64 induced by the input difference 0x0000/0040 up to 11 rounds (see Table 5). This is done using the framework of Gohr's implementation for SPECK32/64 and integrating the algorithm for computing one-round differential probability for SIMON offered by Kölbl *et al.* in [22]. Note that, the fed data to r-round ND are values of ciphertexts, from which, for SIMON, one can directly compute the differences on $(r-1)$-round outputs without knowing the subkey. Thus, $\mathcal{ND}_{\mathbf{VV}}^{\text{SIMON}rR}$ or $\mathcal{ND}_{\mathbf{VD}}^{\text{SIMON}(r-1)R}$ should be compared with $\mathcal{ND}_{\mathbf{DD}}^{\text{SIMON}(r-1)R}$.

Table 6. Comparing $\mathcal{ND}$ and $\mathcal{DD}$ on SIMON32/64 using statistics in a simple key recovery attack on 11-round SIMON32/64. The configuration is 1+8+1+1, *i.e.*, a free prepended invert round, an 8-round distinguisher, a free inverting round, and a key-guessing (last) round. All data are based on 1000 trials of the respective attacks, all measurements of these statistics follow that in [13]: The rank of the real subkey is in the range $[0, 2^{16})$; it is defined as the number of subkeys ranked higher, *i.e.*, rank 0 corresponds to successful key recovery. When several keys were ranked equally, the right key was assumed to be in a random position among the equally ranked keys. The reported error bars around the mean are for a 2σ confidence interval, where σ is calculated based on the observed standard deviation of the key rank. #D indicates the number of chosen plaintexts.

#D	Distinguisher	Mean of key rank	Median key rank	Success rate
32×2	$\mathcal{DD}_{\mathbf{DD}}^{\text{SIMON}_{8R}}$	11.8 ± 3.1	1.0	0.238
	$\mathcal{ND}_{\mathbf{VD}}^{\text{SIMON}_{8R}}$	43.9 ± 21.4	2.0	0.188
64×2	$\mathcal{DD}_{\mathbf{DD}}^{\text{SIMON}_{8R}}$	0.9 ± 0.2	1.0	0.415
	$\mathcal{ND}_{\mathbf{VD}}^{\text{SIMON}_{8R}}$	1.3 ± 0.2	1.0	0.335

The results show that $\mathcal{ND}_{\mathbf{VV}}^{\text{SIMON}_{rR}}$ and $\mathcal{ND}_{\mathbf{VD}}^{\text{SIMON}_{(r-1)R}}$ achieve similar but weaker classification accuracy than $\mathcal{ND}_{\mathbf{DD}}^{\text{SIMON}_{(r-1)R}}$. To further evaluate the gaps between the advantage of $\mathcal{DD}$ over $\mathcal{ND}$, we devised a key ranking task, as done by Gohr for comparing $\mathcal{ND}$s and $\mathcal{DD}$s on SPECK32/64 in [13]. Specifically, a simple key ranking procedure to recover the last subkey on 11-round SIMON32/64 can be performed both by $\mathcal{DD}_{\mathbf{DD}}^{\text{SIMON}_{8R}}$ or $\mathcal{ND}_{\mathbf{VD}}^{\text{SIMON}_{8R}}$ in a configuration of 1+8+2. Table 6 shows the performance of $\mathcal{DD}_{\mathbf{DD}}^{\text{SIMON}_{8R}}$ and $\mathcal{ND}_{\mathbf{VD}}^{\text{SIMON}_{8R}}$ in the ranking for real subkeys among 2^{16} candidate subkeys. It can be seen that they both work well in this task; the data requirement is 64 chosen plaintexts to achieve a success rate of around 20%. However, $\mathcal{ND}_{\mathbf{VD}}^{\text{SIMON}_{8R}}$ is slightly inferior to $\mathcal{DD}_{\mathbf{DD}}^{\text{SIMON}_{8R}}$. To achieve the same success rate, $\mathcal{ND}_{\mathbf{VD}}^{\text{SIMON}_{8R}}$ requires more data than $\mathcal{DD}_{\mathbf{DD}}^{\text{SIMON}_{8R}}$, but the difference is less than twice.

These comparisons suggest that r-round $\mathcal{ND}_{\mathbf{VV}}^{\text{SIMON}_{rR}}$ can "decrypt" one un-keyed round to obtain the $(r-1)$-round difference and learn the differential distribution, which confirms the interpretation in [7], but fails to learn more features beyond the distribution of differences.

Remark 8. This fact for SIMON is different from the corresponding conclusion for SPECK. For SPECK, knowing values of ciphertexts, without knowing the subkey, one can only compute half but not full of the differences on $(r-1)$-round outputs. Thus, the counterpart of r-round $\mathcal{ND}$ is r-round $\mathcal{DD}$. From [13], r-round $\mathcal{ND}$ learns additional features beyond differences and has better classification accuracy than r-round $\mathcal{DD}$. We conjecture that the mean reason is that, for SPECK, pure XOR-difference $\mathcal{DD}$s cannot provide the best baselines for $\mathcal{ND}$s. On the one hand, they are not accurate because of being computed following the Markov assumption. On the other hand, features related to generalized XOR-difference through modular addition and multi-bit constraints [10,23] might be useful to capture the additional features in outputs of SPECK32/64. For examples, Tables 7 and 8 in [5] present generalized constraints beyond XOR-differences on some differential trails, considering which the probability of the trails could be refined. In contrast, for SIMON32/64, the XOR-differences distribution table computed using the Markov model might already be an accurate approximation for the actual differential distribution.

We note that the $\mathcal{N}\mathcal{D}$s on SPECK32/64 might also "decrypt" half of the "unkeyed" last round to retrieve the input values on the right branch y_{r-1}. This interesting fact that the $\mathcal{N}\mathcal{D}$s can "learn to decrypt up to the values not messed up by outer subkey" might be due to the design by Gohr, as explained in [13] as "the use of the initial width-1 convolutional layer is intended to make the learning of simple bit-sliced functions such as bit-wise addition easier". Remarkably, for SIMON32/64, the $\mathcal{N}\mathcal{D}$s seems to have also successfully peeled off the nonlinear bit-wise AND layer in the last round. For deeper look into the $\mathcal{N}\mathcal{D}$s on SIMON32/64, please refer to the full version [5, Sect. G].

7   Conclusions and Future Work

This paper shows practical key-recovery attacks up to 13 rounds of SPECK32/64. This advances state of the art on practical attacks by one round. It shows that the way the underlying neural distinguishers were used in the previous differential-neural attacks is not optimal. Accordingly, the differential-neural cryptanalysis on SPECK32/64 has more potential than it originally exhibited.

The methods developed, particularly those generalized neutral bits, are not intrinsically linked to neural network-based cryptanalysis. They are expected to be useful for the conversion of a wider range of deep weak distinguishers to competitive key recovery attacks in general.

The experiments made on various distinguishers on round-reduced SIMON32/64 indicate that differential-based neural distinguishers should work well in general on modern ciphers. Still, they may not always be superior to their classical counterparts. Their advantages might be easier to show on ciphers whose differential-like properties can not been accurately evaluated using existing tools.

The provided rules of thumb on turning parameters in the UCB and Bayesian optimization-based key-recovery phase are helpful but far from perfect. For this advanced key-recovery strategy to be widely applied, a rigorous theoretical model on the relation between attack parameters, attack complexity, and success probability is missing, and the building of which is left as future work.

Acknowledgments. The authors would like to thank anonymous reviewers for their insightful and helpful comments which helped us improve the manuscript significantly. This research is partially supported by Nanyang Technological University in Singapore under Start-up Grant 04INS000397C230, and Ministry of Education in Singapore under Grants RG91/20 and MOE2019-T2-1-060; Zhenzhen Bao was supported by the Gopalakrishnan – NTU Presidential Postdoctoral Fellowship 2020; the Tsinghua University in China under Start-up Grant 533344001; the National Key R&D Program of China (Grant No. 2018YFA0704701), the Major Program of Guangdong Basic and Applied Research (Grant No. 2019B030302008), the Shandong Province Key R&D Project (Nos. 2020ZLYS09 and 2019JZZY010133). Meicheng Liu was supported by the National Natural Science Foundation of China (Grant Nos. 62122085 and 12231015), and the Youth Innovation Promotion Association of Chinese Academy of Sciences.

References

1. Abadi, M., Andersen, D.G.: Learning to protect communications with adversarial neural cryptography. arXiv preprint arXiv:1610.06918 (2016)
2. Abed, F., List, E., Lucks, S., Wenzel, J.: Differential cryptanalysis of round-reduced SIMON and SPECK. In: Cid, C., Rechberger, C. (eds.) FSE 2014. LNCS, vol. 8540, pp. 525–545. Springer, Heidelberg (2015). https://doi.org/10.1007/978-3-662-46706-0_27
3. Alkhzaimi, H.A., Lauridsen, M.M.: Cryptanalysis of the SIMON family of block ciphers. Cryptology ePrint Archive, Report 2013/543 (2013). https://eprint.iacr.org/2013/543
4. Aumasson, J.-P., Fischer, S., Khazaei, S., Meier, W., Rechberger, C.: New features of Latin dances: analysis of Salsa, ChaCha, and Rumba. In: Nyberg, K. (ed.) FSE 2008. LNCS, vol. 5086, pp. 470–488. Springer, Heidelberg (2008). https://doi.org/10.1007/978-3-540-71039-4_30
5. Bao, Z., Guo, J., Liu, M., Ma, L., Tu, Y.: Enhancing differential-neural cryptanalysis. Cryptology ePrint Archive, Report 2021/719 (2021). https://eprint.iacr.org/2021/719
6. Beaulieu, R., Shors, D., Smith, J., Treatman-Clark, S., Weeks, B., Wingers, L.: The SIMON and SPECK Families of Lightweight Block Ciphers. Cryptology ePrint Archive, Report 2013/404 (2013). https://eprint.iacr.org/2013/404
7. Benamira, A., Gerault, D., Peyrin, T., Tan, Q.Q.: A deeper look at machine learning-based cryptanalysis. In: Canteaut, A., Standaert, F.-X. (eds.) EURO-CRYPT 2021. LNCS, vol. 12696, pp. 805–835. Springer, Cham (2021). https://doi.org/10.1007/978-3-030-77870-5_28
8. Biham, E., Chen, R.: Near-collisions of SHA-0. In: Franklin, M. (ed.) CRYPTO 2004. LNCS, vol. 3152, pp. 290–305. Springer, Heidelberg (2004). https://doi.org/10.1007/978-3-540-28628-8_18
9. Biryukov, A., Roy, A., Velichkov, V.: Differential analysis of block ciphers SIMON and SPECK. In: Cid, C., Rechberger, C. (eds.) FSE 2014. LNCS, vol. 8540, pp. 546–570. Springer, Heidelberg (2015). https://doi.org/10.1007/978-3-662-46706-0_28
10. De Cannière, C., Rechberger, C.: Finding SHA-1 characteristics: general results and applications. In: Lai, X., Chen, K. (eds.) ASIACRYPT 2006. LNCS, vol. 4284, pp. 1–20. Springer, Heidelberg (2006). https://doi.org/10.1007/11935230_1
11. Dinur, I.: Improved differential cryptanalysis of round-reduced speck. In: Joux, A., Youssef, A. (eds.) SAC 2014. LNCS, vol. 8781, pp. 147–164. Springer, Cham (2014). https://doi.org/10.1007/978-3-319-13051-4_9
12. Gohr, A.: Implementation of the Improving Attacks on Round-Reduced Speck32/64 Using Deep Learning. GitHub Repository (2019). https://github.com/agohr/deep_speck
13. Gohr, A.: improving attacks on round-reduced speck32/64 using deep learning. In: Boldyreva, A., Micciancio, D. (eds.) CRYPTO 2019. LNCS, vol. 11693, pp. 150–179. Springer, Cham (2019). https://doi.org/10.1007/978-3-030-26951-7_6

14. Gomez, A.N., Huang, S., Zhang, I., Li, B.M., Osama, M. and Kaiser, L.: Unsupervised cipher cracking using discrete gans. In: 6th International Conference on Learning Representations, ICLR 2018, Vancouver, BC, Canada, 30 April–3 May , 2018, Conference Track Proceedings (2018). OpenReview.net

15. Grassi, L.: Mixture differential cryptanalysis: a new approach to distinguishers and attacks on round-reduced AES. IACR Trans. Symmetric Cryptol. **2018**(2), 133–160 (2018)

16. He, K., Zhang, X., Ren, S., Sun, J.: Deep residual learning for image recognition. In: 2016 IEEE Conference on Computer Vision and Pattern Recognition, CVPR 2016, Las Vegas, NV, USA, 27–30 June 2016, pp. 770–778. IEEE Computer Society (2016)

17. Hu, J., Shen, L., Albanie, S., Sun, G., Wu, E.: Squeeze-and-excitation networks. IEEE Trans. Pattern Anal. Mach. Intell. **42**(8), 2011–2023 (2020)

18. Huang, G., Liu, Z., Van Der Maaten, L., Weinberger, K.Q.: Densely connected convolutional networks. In: 2017 IEEE Conference on Computer Vision and Pattern Recognition, CVPR 2017, Honolulu, HI, USA, 21–26 July 2017, pp. 2261–2269. IEEE Computer Society (2017)

19. Joux, A., Peyrin, T.: Hash functions and the (Amplified) Boomerang attack. In: Menezes, A. (ed.) CRYPTO 2007. LNCS, vol. 4622, pp. 244–263. Springer, Heidelberg (2007). https://doi.org/10.1007/978-3-540-74143-5_14

20. Klima, V.: Tunnels in hash functions: MD5 collisions within a minute. Cryptology ePrint Archive, Report 2006/105 (2006). https://eprint.iacr.org/2006/105

21. Knellwolf, S., Meier, W., Naya-Plasencia, M.: Conditional differential cryptanalysis of NLFSR-based cryptosystems. In: Abe, M. (ed.) ASIACRYPT 2010. LNCS, vol. 6477, pp. 130–145. Springer, Heidelberg (2010). https://doi.org/10.1007/978-3-642-17373-8_8

22. Kölbl, S., Leander, G., Tiessen, T.: Observations on the SIMON block cipher family. In: Gennaro, R., Robshaw, M. (eds.) CRYPTO 2015. LNCS, vol. 9215, pp. 161–185. Springer, Heidelberg (2015). https://doi.org/10.1007/978-3-662-47989-6_8

23. Leurent, G.: Construction of differential characteristics in ARX designs application to skein. In: Canetti, R., Garay, J.A. (eds.) CRYPTO 2013. LNCS, vol. 8042, pp. 241–258. Springer, Heidelberg (2013). https://doi.org/10.1007/978-3-642-40041-4_14

24. Rijsdijk, J., Wu, L., Perin, G., Picek, S.: Reinforcement learning for hyperparameter tuning in deep learning-based side-channel analysis. IACR TCHES **2021**(3), 677–707 (2021). https://tches.iacr.org/index.php/TCHES/article/view/8989

25. Rivest, R.L.: Cryptography and machine learning. In: Imai, H., Rivest, R.L., Matsumoto, T. (eds.) ASIACRYPT 1991. LNCS, vol. 739, pp. 427–439. Springer, Heidelberg (1993). https://doi.org/10.1007/3-540-57332-1_36

26. Silver, D., et al.: A general reinforcement learning algorithm that masters chess, shogi, and go through self-play. Science **362**(6419), 1140–1144 (2018)

27. Song, L., Huang, Z., Yang, Q.: Automatic differential analysis of ARX block ciphers with application to SPECK and LEA. Cryptology ePrint Archive, Report 2016/209 (2016). https://eprint.iacr.org/2016/209

28. Wang, N., Wang, X., Jia, K., Zhao, J.: Differential attacks on reduced SIMON versions with dynamic key-guessing techniques. Cryptology ePrint Archive, Report 2014/448 (2014). https://eprint.iacr.org/2014/448

29. Wang, X., Yu, H.: How to break MD5 and other hash functions. In: Cramer, R. (ed.) EUROCRYPT 2005. LNCS, vol. 3494, pp. 19–35. Springer, Heidelberg (2005). https://doi.org/10.1007/11426639_2

Towards Tight Security Bounds
for **OMAC**, **XCBC** and **TMAC**

Soumya Chattopadhyay[1]([✉]), Ashwin Jha[2]🆔, and Mridul Nandi[1]🆔

[1] Indian Statistical Institute, Kolkata, India
`s.c.2357@gmail.com`
[2] CISPA Helmholtz Center for Information Security, Saarbrücken, Germany
`ashwin.jha@cispa.de`

Abstract. OMAC — a single-keyed variant of CBC-MAC by Iwata and Kurosawa — is a widely used and standardized (NIST FIPS 800-38B, ISO/IEC 29167-10:2017) message authentication code (MAC) algorithm. The best security bound for OMAC is due to Nandi who proved that OMAC's pseudorandom function (PRF) advantage is upper bounded by $O(q^2\ell/2^n)$, where n, q, and ℓ, denote the block size of the underlying block cipher, the number of queries, and the maximum permissible query length (in terms of n-bit blocks), respectively. In contrast, there is no attack with matching lower bound. Indeed, the best known attack on OMAC is the folklore birthday attack achieving a lower bound of $\Omega(q^2/2^n)$. In this work, we close this gap for a large range of message lengths. Specifically, we show that OMAC's PRF security is upper bounded by $O(q^2/2^n + q\ell^2/2^n)$. In practical terms, this means that for a 128-bit block cipher, and message lengths up to 64 GB, OMAC can process up to 2^{64} messages before rekeying (same as the birthday bound). In comparison, the previous bound only allows 2^{48} messages. As a side-effect of our proof technique, we also derive similar tight security bounds for XCBC (by Black and Rogaway) and TMAC (by Kurosawa and Iwata). As a direct consequence of this work, we have established tight security bounds (in a wide range of ℓ) for all the CBC-MAC variants, except for the original CBC-MAC.

Keywords: OMAC · CMAC · XCBC · TMAC · CBC-MAC · PRF · Tight security

1 Introduction

Message Authentication Code (or, MAC) algorithms are symmetric-key primitives which are used for data authenticity and integrity. The sender generates a short tag based on message and a secret key which can be recomputed by any authorized receiver. MACs are commonly designed either based on a hash function or a block cipher. CBC-MAC is a block cipher-based MAC (message

A. Jha carried out this work in the framework of the French-German-Center for Cybersecurity, a collaboration of CISPA and LORIA.

S. Agrawal and D. Lin (Eds.): ASIACRYPT 2022, LNCS 13791, pp. 348–378, 2022.
https://doi.org/10.1007/978-3-031-22963-3_12

authentication code) which is based on the CBC mode of operation invented by Ehrsam et al. [11]. Given an n-bit block cipher E instantiated with a key K, the CBC-MAC construction is defined recursively as follows: for any $x \in \{0,1\}^n$, $\mathsf{CBC}_{E_K}(x) := E_K(x)$. For all $m = (m[1], \ldots, m[\ell]) \in (\{0,1\}^n)^\ell$ where $\ell \geq 2$, we define

$$\mathsf{CBC}_{E_K}(m) := E_K(\mathsf{CBC}_{E_K}(m[1], \ldots, m[\ell-1]) \oplus m[\ell]) \tag{1}$$

It was an international standard, and has been proven secure for fixed-length messages or prefix-free message spaces (i.e., no message is a prefix to another message). Simple length extension attacks prohibit its usage for arbitrary length messages. However, appropriately chosen operations to process the last block can resist these attacks. One such idea was first applied in EMAC [2,4], where the CBC-MAC output was encrypted using an independently keyed block cipher. It worked for all messages with lengths that are divisible by the block size of the underlying block cipher. Black and Rogaway proposed [5] three-keyed constructions, ECBC, FCBC, and XCBC, which are proven to be secure against adversaries querying arbitrary length messages. Later, in back-to-back works, Iwata and Kurosawa proposed two improved constructions (in terms of the key size), namely, TMAC [17] that uses two keys, and OMAC[1] [12] that requires just a single key. Nandi proposed [20] GCBC1 and GCBC2, a slight improvement over OMAC in terms of the number of block cipher calls for multi-block messages.

1.1 Related Works and Motivation

It is well-established [1] that the security of any deterministic MAC can be quantified via the pseudorandom function (or PRF[2]) security. Consequently, most of the works on CBC-MAC variants analyze their PRF security. For constructions like ECBC, FCBC and EMAC, Pietrzak [25] showed a PRF bound of $O(q^2/2^n)$ for $\ell < 2^{n/8}$, where q and ℓ denote the number of messages and the maximum permissible length (no. of n-bit blocks) of the messages. Later, Jha and Nandi [15] discovered a flaw in the proof of the earlier bound and showed a bound of $O(q/2^{n/2})$ up to $\ell < 2^{n/4}$. However, in these constructions an extra (independent) block cipher is called at the end. Considering the number of block cipher calls, XCBC, TMAC and OMAC are better choices. XCBC uses two independent masking keys for the last block which are used depending on whether the last block is padded or not. In case of TMAC, the two masking keys are derived from a single n-bit key. OMAC optimized the key derivation further. Here, both the keys are derived using the underlying block cipher itself. Thus, it is much better in this respect. Classical bound for these constructions was $O(\sigma^2/2^n)$ [5,17], σ being the total number blocks among all the messages. Later, in a series of work [13,19,21,22], the improved bounds for XCBC, TMAC, and OMAC were shown to be in the form of $O(q^2\ell/2^n)$, $O(\sigma^2/2^n)$ and $O(\sigma q/2^n)$. Interestingly, it has also

---

[1] This is same as CMAC [10] — a NIST recommended AES based MAC — for appropriate choice of constants.

[2] A keyed construction is called a PRF if it is computationally infeasible to distinguish it from a random function.

been shown in [14] that if we use a PRF, instead of a block cipher in these constructions, there is an attack with roughly $\Omega(q^2\ell/2^n)$ advantage, which is tight. No such attack is known in the presence of a block cipher. This gives an implicit motivation to study the exact security of these constructions in the presence of block ciphers. In this paper, we aim to show birthday-bound security for these block cipher based MACs for a suitable range of message lengths.

In a different paradigm but with similar motivations, recently Chattopadhyay et al. [8] showed birthday-bound security for another standardized MAC called LightMAC [18]. However, similar result for original PMAC [6] is still an open problem (although a result is available for its variant in [7]). In addition to the improved bound for LightMAC, Chattopadhyay et al. proposed a new proof approach called the reset-sampling method. They also hinted (via a very brief discussion) that this method could be useful for proving better security for OMAC. However, the discussion in [8] is overly simplistic and contains no formal analysis of bad events. Indeed, the reset-sampling is more involved than anticipated in [8], giving rise to some crucial and tricky bad events (see Sect. 4). To their credit, they do say that

> A more formal and rigorous analysis of OMAC using reset-sampling will most probably require handling of several other bad events, and could be an interesting future research topic.

In this paper, we take up this topic and give a complete and rigorous analysis.

1.2   Our Contributions

In Sect. 3, we show that the PRF advantages for OMAC, XCBC and TMAC are upper bounded by $O\left(q^2/2^n\right) + O\left(q\ell^2/2^n\right)$, which is almost tight in terms of the number of queries q while $\ell \ll 2^{n/4}$. This bound is not exactly the birthday bound $O\left(q^2/2^n\right)$, but for any fixed target advantage, in terms of the limit on q it behaves almost like the birthday bound for a fairly good range of ℓ (see the following discussion). The proof of our security bound is given in Sect. 4 and follows the recently introduced reset-sampling approach [8]. These improved bounds, in combination with previous results [15,16] for EMAC, ECBC and FCBC, completely characterize (see Table 1) the security landscape of CBC-MAC variants for message lengths up to $2^{n/4}$ blocks.

A NOTE ON THE TIGHTNESS AND IMPROVEMENT IN BOUNDS: In Fig. 1, we present a graph[3] comparing the best known bound for OMAC [21], i.e., $B_1(\ell, q) = 10q^2\ell/2^n$, the ideal birthday bound, i.e., $B_{id} = q^2/2^n$, and the bound shown in this paper (see Theorem 3.1), i.e., $B_2(\ell, q) \approx \frac{16q^2}{2^n} + \frac{2q\ell^2}{2^n}$ (as the remaining terms are dominated by these two terms). In the graph, we show the trade-off curve for the parameters $X = \log \ell$ and $Y = \log q$, where log denotes "log base 2", for a fixed choice of advantage value, say $\epsilon = 2^{-a}$ for some $a \in \mathbb{N}$. Let $n_a := n - a$. Then, we have

---

[3] Using GeoGebra Classic available at https://www.geogebra.org/classic.

Table 1. Summary of security (PRF advantage) bounds for the CBC-MAC family. Here n, q, ℓ, and σ denote the block size, number of queries, maximum permissible message length, and sum of message lengths of all q queries, respectively.

Scheme	State-of-the-art		This paper	
	Bound	Restriction	Bound	Restriction
CBC-MAC [11]	$O\left(\sigma q/2^n\right)$ [15, 16]	$\ell = o\left(2^{n/3}\right)$	-	-
EMAC [2,4]	$O\left(q^2/2^n + q\ell^2/2^n\right)$ [15, 16]	-	-	-
ECBC,FCBC [5]	$O\left(q^2/2^n + q\ell^2/2^n\right)$ [15, 16]	-	-	-
XCBC [5], TMAC [17]	$O\left(q^2\ell/2^n\right)$ [19][a] $O\left(\sigma^2/2^n\right)$ [13][a]	$\ell = o\left(2^{n/3}\right)$ -	$O\left(q^2/2^n + q\ell^2/2^n\right)$	-
OMAC [12]	$O\left(\sigma q/2^n\right)$ [21]	$\ell = o\left(2^{n/3}\right)$	$O\left(q^2/2^n + q\ell^2/2^n\right)$	-

[a] σ^2 and $q^2\ell$ are incomparable, as they depend on the query length distribution.

$$B_{\mathrm{id}} : Y = \frac{n_a}{2} \quad B_1 : X + 2Y = n_a - \log 10 \quad B_2 : \log(16 \cdot 2^{2Y} + 2 \cdot 2^{2X+Y}) = n_a.$$

Looking at the equation related to the bound B_2 we can see that it is actually a combination of two linear equations: $2Y = n_a - 4$ and $2X + Y = n_a - 1$, the choice depending on whether $16q^2/2^n$ or $2q\ell^2/2^n$ dominates. Precisely, the curve expressing the relation between $\log \ell$ and $\log q$ in B_2 is $\{(X, Y) : X \leq n/4, Y = \min\{(n_a - 4)/2, n_a - 1 - 2X\}\}$. From the above linear equations two important facts about the curve related to B_2 can be noticed:

- It remains very close to the straight line corresponding to B_{id} from $(0, \frac{n_a-4}{2})$ to $(\frac{n_a+2}{4}, \frac{n_a-4}{2})$ and then moves downward.
- At around $(\frac{n_a+1}{3}, \frac{n_a-5}{3})$ it starts to degrade below the curve related to B_1 .

For example, if we take $(n, a) = (128, 32)$, the bound proved in this paper is very close to the birthday bound for $\ell \leq 2^{25}$ and even after degrading, it remains better than the bound in [21] till $\ell \leq 2^{32}$. Moreover, if we take $(n, a) = (128, 64)$, q remains 2^{30} until $\ell \leq 2^{16}$ and degrades below the existing bound only after $\ell \geq 2^{22}$. Thus, if we consider the advantage in general terms, we can always take the minimum among the advantage proved in this paper and that proved in [21].

2   Preliminaries

For $n \in \mathbb{N}$, $[n]$ and $(n]$ denote the sets $\{1, 2, \ldots, n\}$ and $\{0\} \cup [n]$, respectively. The set of all bit strings (including the empty string $\perp$) is denoted $\{0,1\}^*$. The length

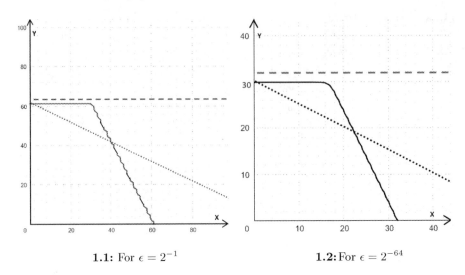

1.1: For $\epsilon = 2^{-1}$ **1.2:** For $\epsilon = 2^{-64}$

Fig. 1. $(\log \ell, \log q)$-Trade-off Graph for the bounds of OMAC. For $n = 128$, and two different choices of the target advantage, $\epsilon = 2^{-1}$ (on the left), and $\epsilon = 2^{-64}$ (on the right), the above graphs show the relation between $X = \log \ell$ and $Y = \log q$. The *dashed*, *dotted* and *continuous* curves represent the equations B_{id}, B_1, and B_2, respectively.

of any bit string $x \in \{0,1\}^*$, denoted $|x|$, is the number of bits in x. For $n \in \mathbb{N}$, $\{0,1\}^n$ denotes the set of all bit strings of length n, and $\{0,1\}^{\leq n} := \bigcup_{i=0}^n \{0,1\}^i$. For $x, y \in \{0,1\}^*$, $z = x\|y$ denotes the concatenation of x and y. Additionally, x (resp. y) is called the *prefix* (resp. *suffix*) of z. For $x, y \in \{0,1\}^*$, let $\mathsf{Prefix}(x, y)$ denote the length of the largest possible common prefix of x and y. For $1 \leq k \leq n$, we define the falling factorial $(n)_k := n!/(n-k)! = n(n-1)\cdots(n-k+1)$. Any pair of q-tuples $\widetilde{x} = (x_1, \ldots, x_q)$ and $\widetilde{y} = (y_1, \ldots, y_q)$, are said to be *permutation compatible*, denoted $\widetilde{x} \leftrightsquigarrow \widetilde{y}$, if $(x_i = x_j) \iff (y_i = y_j)$, for all $i \neq j$. By an abuse of notation, we also use $\widetilde{x}$ to denote the set $\{x_i : i \in [q]\}$ for any $\widetilde{x}$.

2.1 Security Definitions

DISTINGUISHERS: A (q, T)-distinguisher $\mathscr{A}$ is an oracle Turing machine, that makes at most q oracle queries, runs in time at most T, and outputs a single bit. For any oracle $\mathcal{O}$, we write $\mathscr{A}^{\mathcal{O}}$ to denote the output of $\mathscr{A}$ after its interaction with $\mathcal{O}$. By convention, $T = \infty$ denotes computationally unbounded (information-theoretic) and deterministic distinguishers. In this paper, we assume that the distinguisher is non-trivial, i.e., it never makes a duplicate query. Let $\mathbb{A}(q, T)$ be the class of all non-trivial distinguishers limited to q queries and T computations.

Primitives and Their Security: The set of all functions from $\mathcal{X}$ to $\mathcal{Y}$ is denoted $\mathcal{F}(\mathcal{X}, \mathcal{Y})$, and the set of all permutations of $\mathcal{X}$ is denoted $\mathcal{P}(\mathcal{X})$. We simply write $\mathcal{F}(a, b)$ and $\mathcal{P}(a)$, whenever $\mathcal{X} = \{0,1\}^a$ and $\mathcal{Y} = \{0,1\}^b$. For a finite set $\mathcal{X}$, $\mathsf{X} \leftarrow_\$ \mathcal{X}$ denotes the uniform at random sampling of X from $\mathcal{X}$.

PSEUDORANDOM FUNCTION: A $(\mathcal{K}, \mathcal{X}, \mathcal{Y})$-*keyed function* F with key space $\mathcal{K}$, domain $\mathcal{X}$, and range $\mathcal{Y}$ is a function $F : \mathcal{K} \times \mathcal{X} \to \mathcal{Y}$. We write $F_k(x)$ for $F(k, x)$.

The *pseudorandom function* or PRF advantage of any distinguisher $\mathscr{A}$ against a $(\mathcal{K}, \mathcal{X}, \mathcal{Y})$-keyed function F is defined as

$$\mathbf{Adv}_F^{\mathsf{prf}}(\mathscr{A}) = \mathbf{Adv}_{F;\Gamma}(\mathscr{A}) := \left| \Pr_{\mathsf{K} \leftarrow_\$ \mathcal{K}} \left(\mathscr{A}^{F_\mathsf{K}} = 1 \right) - \Pr_{\Gamma \leftarrow_\$ \mathcal{F}(\mathcal{X}, \mathcal{Y})} \left(\mathscr{A}^\Gamma = 1 \right) \right|. \quad (2)$$

The *PRF insecurity* of F against $\mathbb{A}(q, T)$ is defined as

$$\mathbf{Adv}_F^{\mathsf{prf}}(q, T) := \max_{\mathscr{A} \in \mathbb{A}(q, T)} \mathbf{Adv}_F^{\mathsf{prf}}(\mathscr{A}).$$

PSEUDORANDOM PERMUTATION: For some $n \in \mathbb{N}$, a $(\mathcal{K}, \mathcal{B})$-*block cipher* E with key space $\mathcal{K}$ and block space $\mathcal{B} := \{0,1\}^n$ is a $(\mathcal{K}, \mathcal{B}, \mathcal{B})$-keyed function, such that $E(k, \cdot)$ is a permutation over $\mathcal{B}$ for any key $k \in \mathcal{K}$. We write $E_k(x)$ for $E(k, x)$.

The *pseudorandom permutation* or PRP advantage of any distinguisher $\mathscr{A}$ against a $(\mathcal{K}, \mathcal{B})$-block cipher E is defined as

$$\mathbf{Adv}_E^{\mathsf{prp}}(\mathscr{A}) = \mathbf{Adv}_{E;\Pi}(\mathscr{A}) := \left| \Pr_{\mathsf{K} \leftarrow_\$ \mathcal{K}} \left(\mathscr{A}^{E_\mathsf{K}} = 1 \right) - \Pr_{\Pi \leftarrow_\$ \mathcal{P}(n)} \left(\mathscr{A}^\Pi = 1 \right) \right|. \quad (3)$$

The *PRP insecurity* of E against $\mathbb{A}(q, T)$ is defined as

$$\mathbf{Adv}_E^{\mathsf{prp}}(q, T) := \max_{\mathscr{A} \in \mathbb{A}(q, T)} \mathbf{Adv}_E^{\mathsf{prp}}(\mathscr{A}).$$

2.2 H-coefficient Technique

Let $\mathscr{A}$ be a computationally unbounded and deterministic distinguisher that's trying to distinguish the real oracle $\mathcal{O}_1$ from the ideal oracle $\mathcal{O}_0$. The collection of all queries and responses that $\mathscr{A}$ made and received to and from the oracle, is called the *transcript* of $\mathscr{A}$, denoted as ν. Let V_1 and V_0 denote the transcript random variable induced by $\mathscr{A}$'s interaction with $\mathcal{O}_1$ and $\mathcal{O}_0$, respectively. Let $\mathcal{V}$ be the set of all transcripts. A transcript $\nu \in \mathcal{V}$ is said to be *attainable* if $\Pr(\mathsf{V}_0 = \nu) > 0$, i.e., it can be realized by $\mathscr{A}$'s interaction with $\mathcal{O}_0$.

Following these notations, we state the main result of the so-called H-coefficient technique [23,24] in Theorem 2.1. A proof of this result is available in [24].

Theorem 2.1 [H-coefficient]. *For $\epsilon_1, \epsilon_2 \geq 0$, suppose there is a set $\mathcal{V}_{\mathsf{bad}} \subseteq \mathcal{V}$, referred as the set of all bad transcripts, such that the following conditions hold:*

- $\Pr(\mathsf{V}_0 \in \mathcal{V}_{\mathsf{bad}}) \leq \epsilon_1$; *and*
- *For any $\nu \in \mathcal{V} \setminus \mathcal{V}_{\mathsf{bad}}$, ν is attainable and $\dfrac{\Pr(\mathsf{V}_1 = \nu)}{\Pr(\mathsf{V}_0 = \nu)} \geq 1 - \epsilon_2$.*

Then, for any computationally unbounded and deterministic distinguisher $\mathscr{A}$, we have

$$\mathbf{Adv}_{\mathcal{O}_1;\mathcal{O}_0}(\mathscr{A}) \leq \epsilon_1 + \epsilon_2.$$

Reset-Sampling Method: In H-coefficient based proofs, often we release additional information to the adversary in order to make it easy to define the bad transcripts. In such scenarios, one has to define how this additional information is sampled, and naturally the sampling mechanism is construction specific. The reset-sampling method [8] is a sampling philosophy, within this highly mechanized setup of H-coefficient technique, where some of the variables are reset/resampled (hence the name) depending upon the consistency requirement for the overall transcript. We employ this sampling approach in our proof.

3   The **CBC-MAC** Family

Throughout, n denotes the *block size*, $\mathcal{B} := \{0,1\}^n$, and any $x \in \mathcal{B}$ is referred as a *block*. For any non-empty $m \in \{0,1\}^*$, $(m[1], \ldots, m[\ell_m]) \xleftarrow{n} m$ denotes the *block parsing* of m, where $|m[i]| = n$ for all $1 \leq i \leq \ell_m - 1$ and $1 \leq |m[\ell_m]| \leq n$. In addition, we associate a boolean flag δ_m to each $m \in \{0,1\}^*$, which is defined as

$$\delta_m := \begin{cases} -1 & \text{if } |m| = n\ell_m, \\ 0 & \text{otherwise.} \end{cases}$$

For any $m \in \{0,1\}^{\leq n}$, we define

$$\overline{m} := \begin{cases} m \| 10^{n-|m|-1} & \text{if } |m| < n, \\ m & \text{otherwise.} \end{cases}$$

CBC FUNCTION: The CBC function, based on a permutation[4] $\pi \in \mathcal{P}(n)$, takes as input a non-empty message $m \in \mathcal{B}^*$ and computes the output $\mathsf{CBC}_\pi(m) := y_m^\pi[\ell_m]$ inductively as described below:

$y_m^\pi[0] = 0^n$ and for $1 \leq i \leq \ell_m$, we have

$$\begin{aligned} x_m^\pi[i] &:= y_m^\pi[i-1] \oplus m[i], \\ y_m^\pi[i] &:= \pi(x_m^\pi[i]), \end{aligned} \tag{4}$$

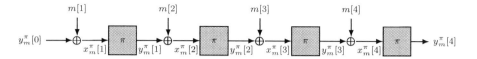

Fig. 2. Evaluation of CBC function over a 4-block message m.

where $(m[1], \ldots, m[\ell_m]) \xleftarrow{n} m$. For empty message, we define the CBC output as the constant 0^n. Figure 2 illustrates the evaluation of CBC function over a 4-block message m.

Given the definition of CBC_π, one can easily define all the variants of CBC-MAC. Here, we define XCBC, TMAC and OMAC— the three constructions that we study in this paper.

XCBC: The XCBC algorithm is a three-key construction, based on a permutation $\pi \in \mathcal{P}(n)$ and keys $(L_{-1}, L_0) \in \mathcal{B}^2$, that takes as input a non-empty message $m \in \{0,1\}^*$, and computes the output

$$\mathsf{XCBC}_{\pi, L_{-1}, L_0}(m) := t = \pi \left(\mathsf{CBC}_\pi (m^*) \oplus \overline{m[\ell_m]} \oplus L_{\delta_m} \right), \tag{5}$$

where $(m[1], \ldots, m[\ell_m]) \xleftarrow{n} m$, and $m^* := m[1]\| \cdots \|m[\ell_m - 1]$.

TMAC: The TMAC algorithm is a two-key construction, based on a permutation $\pi \in \mathcal{P}(n)$ and key $L \in \mathcal{B}$, that takes as input a non-empty message $m \in \{0,1\}^*$, and computes the output

$$\mathsf{TMAC}_{\pi, L}(m) := t = \pi \left(\mathsf{CBC}_\pi (m^*) \oplus \overline{m[\ell_m]} \oplus \mu_{\delta_m} \odot L \right), \tag{6}$$

where $(m[1], \ldots, m[\ell_m]) \xleftarrow{n} m$, $m^* := m[1]\| \cdots \|m[\ell_m - 1]$, μ_{-1} and μ_0 are constants chosen from $\mathrm{GF}(2^n)$ (viewing $\mathcal{B}$ as $\mathrm{GF}(2^n)$), such that $\mu_{-1}, \mu_0, 1 \oplus \mu_{-1}, 1 \oplus \mu_0$ are all distinct and not equal to either 0 or 1, and $\odot$ denotes the field multiplication operation over $\mathrm{GF}(2^n)$ with respect to a fixed primitive polynomial. For the sake of uniformity, we define $L_{\delta_m} := \mu_{\delta_m} \odot L$ in context of TMAC.

OMAC: The OMAC algorithm is a single-keyed construction, based on a permutation $\pi \in \mathcal{P}(n)$, that takes as input a non-empty message $m \in \{0,1\}^*$, and computes the output

$$\mathsf{OMAC}_\pi(m) := t = \pi \left(\mathsf{CBC}_\pi (m^*) \oplus \overline{m[\ell_m]} \oplus \mu_{\delta_m} \odot \pi(0^n) \right), \tag{7}$$

where $(m[1], \ldots, m[\ell_m]) \xleftarrow{n} m$, $m^* := m[1]\| \cdots \|m[\ell_m - 1]$, μ_{-1} and μ_0 are constants chosen analogously as in the case of TMAC. For the sake of uniformity, we define $L_{\delta_m} := \mu_{\delta_m} \odot \pi(0^n)$ in context of OMAC.

---

[4] Instantiated with a block cipher in practical applications.

Input and Output Tuples: In the context of CBC evaluation within OMAC, we refer to $x_m^\pi := (x_m^\pi[1], \ldots, x_m^\pi[\ell_m - 1])$ and $y_m^\pi := (y_m^\pi[0], \ldots, y_m^\pi[\ell_m - 1])$ as the *intermediate input* and *output* tuples, respectively, associated to π and m. We define the final input variable as $x_m^\pi[\ell_m] := y_m^\pi[\ell_m - 1] \oplus \overline{m[\ell_m]} \oplus \mu_{\delta_m} \odot \pi(0^n)$. Clearly, the input and output tuples (including the final input) are well defined for OMAC. Analogous definitions are possible (and useful in proof) for XCBC and TMAC as well. It is worth noting that the intermediate input tuple x_m^π is uniquely determined by the intermediate output tuple y_m^π and the message m, and it is independent of the permutation π. Going forward, we drop π from the notations, whenever it is clear from the context.

3.1   Tight Security Bounds for OMAC, XCBC and TMAC

The main technical result of this paper, given in Theorem 3.1, is a tight security bound for OMAC for a wide range of message lengths. The proof of this theorem is postponed to Sect. 4. In addition, we also provide similar result for XCBC and TMAC in Theorem 3.2. We skip the proof since it is almost identical to the one for Theorem 3.1, and has slightly less relevance given that a more efficient and standardized algorithm OMAC already achieves similar security. In what follows we define

$$\epsilon'(q, \ell) := \frac{16q^2 + q\ell^2}{2^n} + \frac{8q^2\ell^4 + 32q^3\ell^2 + 2q^2\ell^3}{2^{2n}}$$
$$+ \frac{3q^3\ell^5 + 143q^3\ell^6 + 11q^4\ell^3}{2^{3n}} + \frac{17q^4\ell^6 + 5462q^4\ell^8}{2^{4n}}.$$

Theorem 3.1 (OMAC bound). *Let $q, \ell, \sigma, T > 0$. For $q + \sigma \leq 2^{n-1}$, the PRF insecurity of OMAC, based on block cipher E_K, against $\mathbb{A}(q, T)$ is given by*

$$\mathbf{Adv}_{\mathsf{OMAC}_{E_K}}^{\mathsf{prf}}(q, \ell, \sigma, T) \leq \mathbf{Adv}_E^{\mathsf{prp}}(q + \sigma, T') + \frac{4\sigma}{2^n} + \epsilon'(q, \ell), \tag{8}$$

where q denotes the number of queries, ℓ denotes an upper bound on the number of blocks per query, σ denotes the total number of blocks present in all q queries, $T' = T + \sigma O(T_E)$ and T_E denotes the runtime of E.

Theorem 3.2 (XCBC-TMAC bound). *Let $q, \ell, \sigma, T > 0$. For $q + \sigma \leq 2^{n-1}$, the PRF insecurity of XCBC and TMAC, based on block cipher E_K and respective masking keys $(\mathsf{L}, \mathsf{L}_{-1}, \mathsf{L}_0)$, against $\mathbb{A}(q, T)$ is given by*

$$\mathbf{Adv}_{\mathsf{XCBC}_{E_K, \mathsf{L}_{-1}, \mathsf{L}_0}}^{\mathsf{prf}}(q, \ell, \sigma, T) \leq \mathbf{Adv}_E^{\mathsf{prp}}(q + \sigma, T') + \epsilon'(q, \ell) \tag{9}$$

$$\mathbf{Adv}_{\mathsf{TMAC}_{E_K, \mathsf{L}}}^{\mathsf{prf}}(q, \ell, \sigma, T) \leq \mathbf{Adv}_E^{\mathsf{prp}}(q + \sigma, T') + \epsilon'(q, \ell) \tag{10}$$

where q denotes the number of queries, ℓ denotes an upper bound on the number of blocks per query, σ denotes the total number of blocks present in all q queries, $T' = T + \sigma O(T_E)$ and T_E denotes the runtime of E.

Proof of this theorem is almost same as that of Theorem 3.1. The bad event on a collision on zero block input is redundant and hence dropped here. Rest of the proof remains the same and so we skip the details.

Remark 3.1. Note that the actual advantage cannot exceed 1. Let us denote $\frac{q^2}{2^n} = \alpha$ and $\frac{q\ell^2}{2^n} = \beta$. Looking at $\epsilon(q, \ell)$ (where $\epsilon(q, \ell) = \epsilon'(q, \ell) + \frac{4\sigma}{2^n}$ in case of OMAC and $\epsilon(q, \ell) = \epsilon'(q, \ell)$ in case of XCBC, TMAC), we see that any term in the expression is upper bounded by $c \cdot \alpha^s \beta^t$ for some constant c and $s, t \geq 0$ such that at least one of s and t is at least 1. As we can assume both α, β to be less than 1, each $\alpha^s \beta^t$ will be less than or equal to α or β. Thus, the above PRF-advantage expressions for $\mathsf{MAC} \in \{\mathsf{OMAC}, \mathsf{XCBC}, \mathsf{TMAC}\}$ can be written as

$$\mathbf{Adv}^{\mathsf{prf}}_{\mathsf{MAC}}(q, \ell, \sigma) = O\left(\frac{q^2}{2^n}\right) + O\left(\frac{q\ell^2}{2^n}\right).$$

Indeed, under the assumption that $\ell \leq 2^{n/4-0.5}$ and $q \leq 2^{n/2-1}$, one can simplify the above bounds to $20q^2/2^n + 23q\ell^2/2^n$.

A NOTE ON THE PROOF APPROACH: In the analysis of OMAC, XCBC and TMAC, we have to handle the case that the final input collides with some intermediate input, the so-called *full collision* event. In earlier works the probability of this event is shown to be $q^2\ell/2^n$ (as there are less than $q\ell$ many intermediate inputs and q final inputs and any such collision happens with roughly $1/2^n$ probability). So, in a way they avoid handling this tricky event by disallowing it all together. In this work, we allow full collisions as long as the next intermediate input is not colliding with some other input (intermediate or final). Looking ahead momentarily, this is captured in BadW3. We can do this via the application of reset-sampling, resulting in a more amenable $(q^2/2^n + q\ell^2/2^n)$ bound.

4   Proof of Theorem 3.1

First, using the standard hybrid argument, we get

$$\mathbf{Adv}^{\mathsf{prf}}_{\mathsf{OMAC}_{E_K}}(q, \ell, \sigma, T) \leq \mathbf{Adv}^{\mathsf{prp}}_{E}(q + \sigma, T') + \mathbf{Adv}^{\mathsf{prf}}_{\mathsf{OMAC}_{\Pi}}(q, \ell, \sigma, \infty). \quad (11)$$

Now, it is sufficient to bound $\mathbf{Adv}^{\mathsf{prf}}_{\mathsf{OMAC}_{\Pi}}(q, \ell, \sigma, \infty)$, where the corresponding distinguisher $\mathscr{A}$ is computationally unbounded and deterministic. To bound this term, we employ the H-coefficient technique (see Sect. 2.2), and the recently introduced *reset-sampling* method [8]. The remaining steps of the proof are given in the remainder of this section.

4.1   Oracle Description and Corresponding Transcripts

Real Oracle: The real oracle corresponds to OMAC_{Π}. It responds faithfully to all the queries made by $\mathscr{A}$. Once the query-response phase is over, it releases all the intermediate inputs and outputs, as well as the masking keys L_{-1} and L_0 to $\mathscr{A}$. We write $\mathsf{L} = \Pi(0^n)$.

In addition, the real oracle releases three binary variables, namely, FlagT, FlagW and FlagX, all of which are degenerately set to 0. These flags are more of a technical requirement, and their utility will become apparent from the description of ideal oracle. For now, it is sufficient to note that these flags are degenerate in the real world.

Formally, we have $\mathsf{V}_1 := (\widetilde{\mathsf{M}}, \widetilde{\mathsf{T}}, \widetilde{\mathsf{X}}, \widetilde{\mathsf{X}}^*, \widetilde{\mathsf{Y}}, \mathsf{L}_{-1}, \mathsf{L}_0, \mathsf{FlagT}, \mathsf{FlagW}, \mathsf{FlagX})$, where

- $\widetilde{\mathsf{M}} = (\mathsf{M}_1, \ldots, \mathsf{M}_q)$, the q-tuple of queries made by $\mathscr{A}$, where $\mathsf{M}_i \in \{0,1\}^*$ for all $i \in [q]$. In addition, for all $i \in [q]$, let $\ell_i := \left\lceil \frac{|\mathsf{M}_i|}{n} \right\rceil$.
- $\widetilde{\mathsf{T}} = (\mathsf{T}_1, \ldots, \mathsf{T}_q)$, the q-tuple of final outputs received by $\mathscr{A}$, where $\mathsf{T}_i \in \mathcal{B}$.
- $\widetilde{\mathsf{X}} = (\mathsf{X}_1, \ldots, \mathsf{X}_q)$, where X_i denotes the intermediate input tuple for the i-th query.
- $\widetilde{\mathsf{X}}^* = (\mathsf{X}_1[\ell_1], \ldots, \mathsf{X}_q[\ell_q])$, where $\mathsf{X}_i[\ell_i]$ denotes the final input for the i-th query.
- $\widetilde{\mathsf{Y}} = (\mathsf{Y}_1, \ldots, \mathsf{Y}_q)$, where Y_i denotes the intermediate output tuple for the i-th query.
- L_{-1} and L_0 denote the two masking keys. Note that L_{-1} and L_0 are easily derivable from L. So we could have simply released L. The added redundancy is to aid the readers in establishing an analogous connection between this proof and the proof for XCBC and TMAC.
- $\mathsf{FlagT} = \mathsf{FlagW} = \mathsf{FlagX} = 0$.

From the definition of OMAC, we know that $\Pi(\mathsf{X}_i[a]) = \mathsf{Y}_i[a]$ for all $(i, a) \in [q] \times [\ell_i]$. So, *in the real world we always have* $(0^n, \widetilde{\mathsf{X}}, \widetilde{\mathsf{X}}^*) \leftrightsquigarrow (\mathsf{L}, \widetilde{\mathsf{Y}}, \widetilde{\mathsf{T}})$, *i.e.*, $(0^n, \widetilde{\mathsf{X}}, \widetilde{\mathsf{X}}^*)$ *is permutation compatible with* $(\mathsf{L}, \widetilde{\mathsf{Y}}, \widetilde{\mathsf{T}})$. We keep this observation in our mind when we simulate the ideal oracle.

Ideal Oracle: By reusing notations from the real world, we represent the ideal oracle transcript as $\mathsf{V}_0 := (\widetilde{\mathsf{M}}, \widetilde{\mathsf{T}}, \widetilde{\mathsf{X}}, \widetilde{\mathsf{X}}^*, \widetilde{\mathsf{Y}}, \mathsf{L}_{-1}, \mathsf{L}_0, \mathsf{FlagT}, \mathsf{FlagW}, \mathsf{FlagX})$. This should not cause any confusion, as we never consider the random variables V_1 and V_0 jointly, whence the probability distributions of the constituent variables will always be clear from the context.

The ideal oracle transcript is described in three phases, each contingent on some predicates defined over the previous stages. Specifically, the ideal oracle first initializes $\mathsf{FlagT} = \mathsf{FlagW} = \mathsf{FlagX} = 0$, and then follows the sampling mechanism given below:

PHASE I (QUERY-RESPONSE PHASE): In the query-response phase, the ideal oracle faithfully simulates $\Gamma \leftarrow_\$ \mathcal{F}(\{0,1\}^*, \mathcal{B})$. Formally, for $i \in [q]$, at the i-th query $\mathsf{M}_i \in \{0,1\}^*$, the ideal oracle outputs $\mathsf{T}_i \leftarrow_\$ \mathcal{B}$. The partial transcript generated at the end of the query-response phase is given by $(\widetilde{\mathsf{M}}, \widetilde{\mathsf{T}})$, where

- $\widetilde{\mathsf{M}} = (\mathsf{M}_1, \ldots, \mathsf{M}_q)$ and $\widetilde{\mathsf{T}} = (\mathsf{T}_1, \ldots, \mathsf{T}_q)$.

Now, we define a predicate on $\widetilde{\mathsf{T}}$:

$$\mathsf{BadT} : \quad \exists i \neq j \in [q], \text{ such that } \mathsf{T}_i = \mathsf{T}_j.$$

If BadT is true, then FlagT is set to 1, and $\widetilde{X}$, $\widetilde{X}^*$, and $\widetilde{Y}$ are defined degenerately: $X_i[a] = Y_i[b] = 0^n$ for all $i \in [q]$, $a \in [\ell_i]$, $b \in (\ell_i - 1]$. Otherwise, the ideal oracle proceeds to the next phase.

PHASE II (OFFLINE INITIAL SAMPLING PHASE):Onward, we must have $T_i \neq T_j$ whenever $i \neq j$, and FlagT $= 0$, since this phase is only executed when BadT is false. In the offline phase, the ideal oracle's initial goal is to sample the input and output tuples in such a way that the intermediate input and output tuples are permutation compatible. For now we use notations W and Z, respectively, instead of X and Y, to denote the input and output tuples. This is done to avoid any confusions in the next step where we may have to reset some of these variables. To make it explicit, W and Z respectively denote the input and output tuples before resetting, and X and Y denote the input and output tuples after resetting.

Let P be a key-value table representing a partial permutation of $\mathcal{B}$, which is initialized to empty, i.e., the corresponding permutation is undefined on all points. We write P.domain and P.range to denote the set of all keys and values utilized till this point, respectively. The ideal oracle uses this partial permutation P to maintain permutation compatibility between intermediate input and output tuples, in the following manner:

Initial sampling

$L \xleftarrow{\$} \mathcal{B} \setminus \widetilde{T}$

$L_{-1} \leftarrow \mu_{-1} \odot L$

$L_0 \leftarrow \mu_0 \odot L$

$P(0^n) \leftarrow L$

for $i = 1$ **to** q **do**

    $Z_i[0] \leftarrow 0^n$

    for $a = 1$ **to** $\ell_i - 1$ **do**

        $W_i[a] \leftarrow Z_i[a-1] \oplus M_i[a]$

        if $W_i[a] \in$ P.domain

        $Z_i[a] \leftarrow P(W_i[a])$

    else

        $Z_i[a] \xleftarrow{\$} \mathcal{B} \setminus \left(\widetilde{T} \cup \text{P.range}\right)$

        $P(W_i[a]) \leftarrow Z_i[a]$

    $W_i[\ell_i] \leftarrow Z_i[\ell_i - 1] \oplus \overline{M}_i[\ell_i] \oplus L_{\delta_{M_i}}$

At this stage we have $Z_i[a] = Z_j[b]$ if and only if $W_i[a] = W_j[b]$ for all $(i,a) \in [q] \times [\ell_i - 1]$ and $(j,b) \in [q] \times [\ell_j - 1]$. In other words, $(0^n, \widetilde{W}) \leftrightsquigarrow (L, \widetilde{Z})$. But it is obvious to see that the same might not hold between $(0^n, \widetilde{W}, \widetilde{W}^*)$ and $(L, \widetilde{Z}, \widetilde{T})$. In the next stage our goal will be to reset some of the Z variables in such a way that the resulting input tuple is compatible with the resulting output tuple. However, in order to reset, we have to identify and avoid certain contentious input-output tuples.

IDENTIFYING CONTENTIOUS INPUT-OUTPTUT TUPLES: We define several predicates on $(\widetilde{W}, \widetilde{W}^*)$, each of which represents some undesirable property of the sampled input and output tuples.

First, observe that L is chosen outside the set $\widetilde{T}$. This leads to the first predicate:

BadW1 : $\exists (i, a) \in [q] \times [\ell_i]$, such that $(W_i[a] = 0^n)$ and $(\ell_i > 1 \implies a > 1)$.

since, if BadW1 is true, then $(0^n, \widetilde{W}^*)$ is not compatible with $(L, \widetilde{T})$. In fact, $\neg$BadW1 implies that none of the inputs, except the first input which is fully in adversary's control, can possibly be 0^n. This stronger condition will simplify the analysis greatly. The second predicate simply states that the final input tuple is not permutation compatible with the tag tuple, i.e., we have

BadW2 : $\exists i \neq j \in [q]$, such that $W_i[\ell_i] = W_j[\ell_j]$.

At this point, assuming $\neg$(BadW1 $\vee$ BadW2) holds true, the only way we can have permutation incompatibility is if $W_i[a] = W_j[\ell_j]$, for some $i, j \in [q]$ and $a \in [\ell_i - 1]$. A simple solution will be to reset $Z_i[a]$ to T_j, for all such (i, a, j). In order to do this, we need that the following predicates must be false:

BadW3 : $\exists i, j, k \in [q], a \in [\ell_i - 1], b \in [\ell_k]$, such that

$$(W_i[a] = W_j[\ell_j]) \wedge (W_i[a+1] = W_k[b]) \wedge \mathsf{Prefix}(M_i, M_k) < \max\{a+1, b\}.$$

BadW4 : $\exists i, j, k \in [q], a \neq b \in [\ell_i - 1]$, such that

$$(W_i[a] = W_j[\ell_j]) \wedge (W_i[b] = W_k[\ell_k]).$$

BadW5 : $\exists i, j, k \in [q], a \in [\ell_i - 1], b \in [\ell_j - 1]$, such that

$$(W_i[a] = W_j[\ell_j]) \wedge (W_j[b] = W_k[\ell_k]).$$

If BadW3 is true, then once $Z_i[a]$ is reset, we lose the permutation compatibility since, the reset next input, i.e., $X_i[a+1] = W_i[a+1] \oplus Z_i[a] \oplus T_j = M_i[a+1] \oplus T_j \neq W_k[b]$ with high probability, whereas $Z_i[a+1] = Z_k[b]$ with certainty. BadW4 simply represents the scenario where we may have to apply the initial resetting to two indices in a single message. Looking ahead momentarily, this may lead to contradictory *induced* resettings. Avoiding this predicate makes the resetting operation much more manageable. Similarly, avoiding BadW5, is just proactive prevention of contradictory resetting at $Z_i[a]$, since if BadW5 occurs, then we may have a case where $X_j[\ell_j]$ is reset due to induced resetting, leading to the case, $X_i[a] \neq X_j[\ell_j]$ and $Y_i[a] = T_j$, where recall that $Y_i[a]$ is the resetting value of $Z_i[a]$. We write

$$\mathsf{BadW} := \mathsf{BadW1} \vee \mathsf{BadW2} \vee \mathsf{BadW3} \vee \mathsf{BadW4} \vee \mathsf{BadW5}.$$

If BadW is true, then FlagW is set to 1, and $(\widetilde{X}, \widetilde{X}^*, \widetilde{Y})$ is again defined degenerately, as in the case of BadT. Otherwise, the ideal oracle proceeds to the next and the final phase, i.e., the resetting phase.

PHASE III.A INITIAL RESETTING PHASE: At this stage we must have $\neg(\textsf{BadT} \vee \textsf{BadW})$, i.e., $\textsf{FlagW} = \textsf{FlagT} = 0$. We describe the resetting phase in two sub-stages. First, we identify the indices affected by the initial resetting operation.

Definition 4.1 [full collision index]. *Any $(i, a, j) \in [q] \times [\ell_i - 1] \times [q]$ is called a full collision index (FCI) if $\textsf{W}_i[a] = \textsf{W}_j[\ell_j]$. Additionally, let*

$$\textsf{FCI} := \{(i, a, j) : i, j \in [q], a \in [\ell_i - 1], \text{ such that } (i, a, j) \text{ is an } FCI\}$$
$$\widetilde{\textsf{FCI}} := \{(i, a) \in [q] \times [\ell_i - 1] : \exists j \in [q], \text{ such that } (i, a, j) \text{ is an } FCI\}$$

The first sub-stage, executes a resetting for full collision indices in the following manner:

1. For all $(i, a, j) \in \textsf{FCI}$, define $\textsf{Y}_i[a] := \textsf{T}_j$;
2. For all $(i, a, j) \in \textsf{FCI}$, define

$$\boxed{\textsf{X}_i[a+1]} := \textsf{W}_i[a+1] \oplus \textsf{Z}_i[a] \oplus \textsf{Y}_i[a] = \overline{\textsf{M}}_i[a+1] \oplus \textsf{T}_j \oplus 1_{a=\ell_i-1} \odot \textsf{L}_{\delta_{\textsf{M}_i}},$$

where $1_{a=\ell_i-1}$ is an indicator variable that evaluates to 1 when $a = \ell_i - 1$, and 0 otherwise.

Once the initial resetting is executed, it may result in new permutation incompatibilities. This necessitates further resettings, referred as *induced resettings*, which require that the following predicates are false:

BadX1 : $\exists (i, a, j) \in \textsf{FCI}, k \in [q], b \in [\ell_k] \setminus \{1\}$, such that

$$(\boxed{\textsf{X}_i[a+1]} = \textsf{W}_k[b]) \vee (\boxed{\textsf{X}_i[a+1]} = 0^n).$$

BadX2 : $\exists (i, a, j) \in \textsf{FCI}, k \in [q]$, such that

$$(\boxed{\textsf{X}_i[a+1]} = \textsf{M}_k[1]) \wedge (\textsf{M}_i[a+2, \ldots, \ell_i] = \textsf{M}_k[2, \ldots, \ell_k]).$$

BadX3 : $\exists (i, a, j), (k, b, l) \in \textsf{FCI}$, such that $(\boxed{\textsf{X}_i[a+1]} = \textsf{M}_k[1])$.

BadX4 : $\exists (i, a, k), (j, b, l) \in \textsf{FCI}$, such that

$$(\boxed{\textsf{X}_i[a+1]} = \boxed{\textsf{X}_j[b+1]}) \wedge (\textsf{Prefix}(\textsf{M}_i, \textsf{M}_j) < \max\{a+1, b+1\}).$$

Here, the variable highlighted in red denotes the update after initial resetting. Let's review these predicates in slightly more details. First, BadX1, represents the situation where after resetting the next input (highlighted text) collides with some intermediate input or 0^n. This would necessitate induced resetting at $\textsf{Z}_i[a+1]$. In other words, if BadX1 is false then no induced resettings occur, unless the next input collides with some first block input. This case is handled in the next two predicates. BadX2 represents the situation when the next input collides with a first block and the subsequent message blocks are all same. This would induce a chain of resetting going all the way to the final input. As BadT is false, this would immediately result in a permutation incompatibility since tags are distinct. If BadX2 is false, then the chain of induced resetting must end at some point. BadX3 is used to avoid circular or contradictory resettings. It is analogous to BadW5 defined earlier. If it is false, then we know that the k-th message is free from resetting, so the induced resetting will be manageable. Finally, BadX4 represents the situation when two newly reset variables collide. We write

$$\text{BadX1234} := \text{BadX1} \lor \text{BadX2} \lor \text{BadX3} \lor \text{BadX4}$$

If BadX1234 is true, then FlagX is set to 1, and $(\widetilde{X}, \widetilde{X}^*, \widetilde{Y})$ is again defined degenerately, as in the cases of BadT and BadW. Otherwise, the ideal oracle proceeds to the second and the final sub-stage of resetting.

PHASE III.B INDUCED RESETTING PHASE: Here, the goal is to execute the induced resettings necessitated by the initial resetting operation.

First, we define the *index of induced resetting* for each $(i, a) \in \widetilde{\text{FCI}}$, as the smallest index j such that $X_i[a + 1] = M_j[1]$ and

$$\text{Prefix}(M_i[a+2, \ldots, \ell_i], M_j[2, \ldots, \ell_j]) = \max\{\text{Prefix}(M_i[a+2, \ldots, \ell_i], M_{j'}[2, \ldots, \ell_{j'}]) : j' \in [q]\},$$

i.e., $\text{Prefix}(M_i[a + 2, \ldots, \ell_i], M_j[2, \ldots, \ell_j])$ maximizes.

Definition 4.2 [induced collision sequence]. *A sequence of tuples $((i, a + 1, j, 1), \ldots, (i, a + p + 1, j, p + 1))$ is called an induced collision sequence (ICS), if $(i, a) \in \widetilde{\text{FCI}}$, and j is the index of induced resetting for (i, a), where $p := \text{Prefix}(M_i[a + 2, \ldots, \ell_i], M_j[2, \ldots, \ell_j])$. The individual elements of an ICS are referred as induced collision index (ICI). Additionally, we let*

$$\text{ICI} := \{(i, a, j, b) : i, j \in [q], a \in [\ell_i - 1], b \in [\ell_j - 1], \text{ and } (i, a, j, b) \text{ is an ICI.}\}$$

$$\widetilde{\text{ICI}} := \{(i, a) \in [q] \times [\ell_i - 1] : \exists (j, b) \in [q] \times [\ell_j - 1], \text{ and } (i, a, j, b) \text{ is an ICI.}\}$$

Now, as anticipated, in the second sub-stage of resetting, we reset the induced collision indices in the following manner:

1. For all $(i, a, j, b) \in \text{ICI}$, define $Y_i[a] := Z_j[b]$;
2. For all $(i, a, j, b) \in \text{ICI}$, define

$$X_i[a + 1] := W_i[a + 1] \oplus Z_i[a] \oplus Y_i[a] = \overline{M}_i[a + 1] \oplus Z_j[b] \oplus 1_{a = \ell_i - 1} \odot L_{\delta_{M_k}},$$

where $1_{a = \ell_i - 1}$ is an indicator variable that evaluates to 1 when $a = \ell_i - 1$, and 0 otherwise.

Given $\neg$BadX1234, we know that the induced resetting must stop at some point before the final input. Now, it might happen that once the first chain of induced resetting stops, the next input again collides which may result in nested resetting or permutation incompatibility. The predicates BadX5, BadX6, and BadX7 below represent these scenarios.

– BadX5 : $\exists (i, a, k, b) \in \mathsf{ICI}, l \in [q], b \in [\ell_l - 1]$, such that

$$(\boxed{\mathsf{X}_i[a + 2 + p]} = \mathsf{W}_l[b]) \vee (\boxed{\mathsf{X}_i[a + 2 + p]} = 0^n),$$

where $p := \mathsf{Prefix}(\mathsf{M}_i[a + 2, \ldots, \ell_i], \mathsf{M}_k[2, \ldots, \ell_k])$.

– BadX6 : $\exists (i, a) \in \widetilde{\mathsf{FCI}}, (j, b, k, c) \in \mathsf{ICI}$, such that $(\boxed{\mathsf{X}_i[a + 1]} = \boxed{\mathsf{X}_j[b + 2 + p]})$, where $p := \mathsf{Prefix}(\mathsf{M}_j[b + 2, \ldots, \ell_j], \mathsf{M}_k[2, \ldots, \ell_k])$.

– BadX7 : $\exists (i, a, k, c), (j, b, l, d) \in \mathsf{ICI}$, such that

$$(\boxed{\mathsf{X}_i[a + 2 + p]} = \boxed{\mathsf{X}_j[b + 2 + p']}) \wedge (\mathsf{Prefix}(\mathsf{M}_i, \mathsf{M}_j) < \max\{a+2+p, b+2+p'\}),$$

where $p := \mathsf{Prefix}(\mathsf{M}_i[a + 2, \ldots, \ell_i], \mathsf{M}_k[2, \ldots, \ell_k])$, and $p' := \mathsf{Prefix}(\mathsf{M}_j[b + 2, \ldots, \ell_j], \mathsf{M}_l[2, \ldots, \ell_l])$.

Here, the variables highlighted in red and blue denote the update after initial resetting and induced resetting, respectively. These predicates are fairly self-explanatory. First BadX5 represents the situation that the immediate input after induced resetting collides with some intermediate input or 0^n. This may cause permutation incompatibility and would lead to nested induced resetting at $Z_i[a + 2 + p]$. BadX6 handles a similar collision with a full collision resetted variable, and BadX7 handles the only remaining case where the immediate inputs after two different induced resetting collides. Note that, $\neg(\mathsf{BadX5} \vee \mathsf{BadX6} \vee \mathsf{BadX7})$ would imply that for each message resetting stops at some point before the final input, and the next input is fresh.[5] We write

$$\mathsf{BadX} := \mathsf{BadX1} \vee \mathsf{BadX2} \vee \mathsf{BadX3} \vee \mathsf{BadX4} \vee \mathsf{BadX5} \vee \mathsf{BadX6} \vee \mathsf{BadX7}.$$

If BadX is true, then FlagX is set to 1, and $(\widetilde{\mathsf{X}}, \widetilde{\mathsf{X}}^*, \widetilde{\mathsf{Y}})$ is again defined degenerately, as in the case of BadT and BadW. Otherwise, for any remaining index $(i, a) \in [q] \times (\ell_i - 1) \setminus (\widetilde{\mathsf{FCI}} \cup \widetilde{\mathsf{ICI}})$, the ideal oracle resets as follows:

1. define $\mathsf{Y}_i[a] := \mathsf{Z}_i[a]$;
2. define $\mathsf{X}_i[a + 1] := \mathsf{W}_i[a + 1]$.

At this point, the ideal oracle transcript is completely defined. Intuitively, if the ideal oracle is not sampling $(\widetilde{\mathsf{X}}, \widetilde{\mathsf{X}}^*, \widetilde{\mathsf{Y}})$ degenerately at any stage, then we must have $(0^n, \widetilde{\mathsf{X}}, \widetilde{\mathsf{X}}^*) \rightsquigarrow (\mathsf{L}, \widetilde{\mathsf{Y}}, \widetilde{\mathsf{T}})$. The following proposition justifies this intuition.

Proposition 4.1. *For* $\neg(\mathsf{BadT} \vee \mathsf{BadW} \vee \mathsf{BadX})$*, we must have* $(0^n, \widetilde{\mathsf{X}}, \widetilde{\mathsf{X}}^*) \rightsquigarrow (\mathsf{L}, \widetilde{\mathsf{Y}}, \widetilde{\mathsf{T}})$*.*

Proof. Let $\neg(\mathsf{BadT} \vee \mathsf{BadW} \vee \mathsf{BadX})$ hold. Recall that $(0^n, \widetilde{\mathsf{W}}, \widetilde{\mathsf{W}}^*)$ may not be permutation compatible with $(\mathsf{L}, \widetilde{\mathsf{Z}}, \widetilde{\mathsf{T}})$. For any $(i, a) \in \widetilde{\mathsf{FCI}}$, there exists $i' \in [q]$

---

[5] Does not collide with any other input.

such that $W_i[a] = W_{i'}[\ell_{i'}]$ but $Z_i[a] \neq T_{i'}$. We apply the initial resetting to solve this issue. However, as a result of initial resetting, induced resetting takes place. Our goal is to show that the non-occurrence of the bad events assures that the compatibility is attained in the final reset tuples $(0^n, \widetilde{X}, \widetilde{X}^*)$ and $(L, \widetilde{Y}, \widetilde{T})$. We prove all possible cases as follows:

- $X_i[a] = 0^n \iff Y_i[a] = L$: If $a = 1$ and $X_i[a] = 0$, then $(i, a) \notin \widetilde{\mathsf{FCI}}$ due to $\neg\mathsf{BadW1}$. Also, $(i, 1) \notin \widetilde{\mathsf{ICI}}$. Thus, $Y_i[a] = Z_i[a] = L$ and the converse also holds. Otherwise, due to $\neg\mathsf{BadX1}$, $X_i[a]$ can not be equal to 0. Also, due to $\neg\mathsf{BadW1}$, $Y_i[a]$ can not be equal to L.

- $X_i[a] = X_{i'}[\ell_{i'}] \iff Y_i[a] = T_{i'}$: For $(i, a) \in \widetilde{\mathsf{FCI}}$, this equivalence holds. Otherwise, $X_i[a] = X_{i'}[\ell_{i'}]$ can not hold due to $\neg(\mathsf{BadX1} \vee \mathsf{BadX5})$. Also $Y_i[a] = T_{i'}$ can not hold due to definition of $\widetilde{T}$ and $\neg\mathsf{BadX2}$.

- $X_i[a] = X_j[b] \iff Y_i[a] = Y_j[b]$: To prove this part we divide it in the following subcases:

  - $\boxed{(i,a), (i,b) \notin \widetilde{\mathsf{FCI}} \cup \widetilde{\mathsf{ICI}}}$: Since in this case the variables are simply renamed due to definitions of resetting and $\neg\mathsf{BadW3}$, the result follows from $\widetilde{W} \rightsquigarrow \widetilde{Z}$.

  - $\boxed{(i,a), (j,b) \in \widetilde{\mathsf{FCI}}}$: Since $(i, a), (j, b) \in \widetilde{\mathsf{FCI}}$, there exists unique $i', j' \in [q]$, such that $W_i[a] = W_{i'}[\ell_{i'}]$ and $W_j[b] = W_{j'}[\ell_{j'}]$. Now, note that $X_i[a] = W_i[a]$ and $X_j[b] = W_j[b]$ since $\widetilde{\mathsf{FCI}} \cap \widetilde{\mathsf{ICI}} = \emptyset$ due to $\neg\mathsf{BadW4}$; $W_{i'}[\ell_{i'}] = X_{i'}[\ell_{i'}]$ and $W_{j'}[\ell_{j'}] = X_{j'}[\ell_{j'}]$ due to $\neg\mathsf{BadW5}$. Therefore, we must have $X_{j'}[\ell_{j'}] = W_{j'}[\ell_{j'}] = W_j[b] = X_j[b] = X_i[a] = W_i[a] = W_{i'}[\ell_{i'}] = X_{i'}[\ell_{i'}]$, which is possible if and only if $i' = j'$ (since $\neg\mathsf{BadW2}$ holds).

  - $\boxed{(i,a), (j,b) \in \widetilde{\mathsf{ICI}}}$: Since $(i, a), (j, b) \in \widetilde{\mathsf{ICI}}$, there exists $i', j' \in [q]$ and $a' \in [\ell_{i'} - 1], b' \in [\ell_{j'} - 1]$, such that $X_i[a] = W_{i'}[a']$ and $X_j[b] = W_{j'}[b']$. Further, $(i', a'), (j', b') \notin \widetilde{\mathsf{FCI}} \cup \widetilde{\mathsf{ICI}}$ (due to $\neg\mathsf{BadX3}$). If $X_j[b] = X_i[a]$, then we have $W_{j'}[b'] = W_{i'}[a']$. This gives us $Y_j[b] = Z_{j'}[b'] = Z_{i'}[a'] = Y_i[a]$ (due to $\widetilde{W} \rightsquigarrow \widetilde{Z}$). Similarly, $X_i[a] \neq X_j[b]$ implies $Y_i[a] \neq Y_j[b]$.

  - $\boxed{(i,a) \in \widetilde{\mathsf{FCI}} \text{ and } (j,b) \in \widetilde{\mathsf{ICI}}}$: Since $(i, a) \in \widetilde{\mathsf{FCI}}$, there exists a unique $i' \in [q]$, such that $X_i[a] = W_i[a] = W_{i'}[\ell_{i'}] = X_{i'}[\ell_{i'}]$ (the first equality is due to $\neg\mathsf{BadW4}$, the second equality is due to the definition of full collision, the third equality is due to $\neg\mathsf{BadW5}$). Since $(j, b) \in \widetilde{\mathsf{ICI}}$, we also have $X_j[b] = W_{j'}[b']$. If $X_i[a] = X_j[b]$, then $W_{j'}[b'] = W_{i'}[\ell_{i'}]$. Thus, $(j', b') = (i', \ell_{i'})$ due to $\neg\mathsf{BadX3}$. Now, we have $Y_i[a] = T_{i'}$. Also, $Y_j[b] = Y_{j'}[b'] = Y_{i'}[\ell_{i'}] = T_{i'}$. Therefore, $Y_i[a] = Y_j[b]$. Moreover, $X_i[a] \neq X_j[b]$ implies that $Y_i[a] \neq Y_j[b]$ due to similar arguments as above and also $\neg\mathsf{BadT}$.

  - $\boxed{(i,a) \in \widetilde{\mathsf{ICI}} \text{ and } (j,b) \in \widetilde{\mathsf{FCI}}}$: Similar as the above case.

- $(i,a) \in \widetilde{\mathsf{FCI}} \cup \widetilde{\mathsf{ICI}}$ and $(j,b) \notin \widetilde{\mathsf{FCI}} \cup \widetilde{\mathsf{ICI}}$: Since $(j,b) \notin \widetilde{\mathsf{FCI}} \cup \widetilde{\mathsf{ICI}}$, we have $X_j[b] = W_j[b]$ and $Y_j[b] = Z_j[b]$. Suppose, $(i,a) \in \widetilde{\mathsf{FCI}}$. Then $X_i[a] = X_j[b]$ is not possible since it would imply that $(j,b) \in \widetilde{\mathsf{FCI}}$. Also, $Y_i[a] = Y_j[b]$ is not possible since it would contradict the definition of $\widetilde{\mathsf{T}}$. Now, suppose, $(i,a) \in \widetilde{\mathsf{ICI}}$. Therefore, $X_i[a] = W_{i'}[a']$ for some $i' \in [q]$ and $a' \in [\ell_{i'} - 1]$. If $X_i[a] = X_j[b]$, then $W_j[b] = X_j[b] = X_i[a] = W_{i'}[a']$. So, $Y_j[b] = Z_j[b] = Z_{i'}[a'] = Y_i[a]$. Similarly, $X_i[a] \neq X_j[b]$ implies $Y_i[a] \neq Y_j[b]$.

- $(i,a) \notin \widetilde{\mathsf{FCI}} \cup \widetilde{\mathsf{ICI}}$ and $(j,b) \in \widetilde{\mathsf{FCI}} \cup \widetilde{\mathsf{ICI}}$: Similar as the above case.

4.2   Transcript Analysis

SET OF TRANSCRIPTS: Given the description of transcript random variable corresponding to the ideal oracle, we can now define the set of transcripts $\mathcal{V}$ as the set of all tuples $\nu = (\widetilde{m}, \widetilde{t}, \widetilde{x}, \widetilde{x}^*, \widetilde{y}, l_{-1}, l_0, \mathrm{flagT}, \mathrm{flagW}, \mathrm{flagX})$, where

- $\widetilde{m} = (m_1, \ldots, m_q)$, where $m_i \in \{0,1\}^*$ for $i \in [q]$. Let $\ell_i = \left\lceil \frac{|m_i|}{n} \right\rceil$ for $i \in [q]$.
- $\widetilde{t} = (t_1, \ldots, t_q)$, where $t_i \in \mathcal{B}$ for $i \in [q]$.
- $\widetilde{x} = (x_1, \ldots, x_q)$, where $x_i = (x_i[1], \ldots, x_i[\ell_i - 1])$ for $i \in [q]$.
- $\widetilde{x}^* = (x_1[\ell_1], \ldots, x_q[\ell_q])$.
- $\widetilde{y} = (y_1, \ldots, y_q)$, where $y_i = (y_i[0] = 0^n, y_i[1], \ldots, y_i[\ell_i - 1])$ for $i \in [q]$.
- $l_{-1} = \mu_{-1} \odot l, l_0 = \mu_0 \odot l$ where $l \in \mathcal{B}$ and μ_{-1}, μ_0 are constants chosen from $\mathrm{GF}(2^n)$ as defined before.
- $\mathrm{flagT}, \mathrm{flagW}, \mathrm{flagX} \in \{0,1\}$.

Furthermore, the following must always hold:

1. if $\mathrm{flagI} = 1$ for some $I \in \{T, W\}$, then $x_i[a] = y_j[b] = 0^n$ for all $i,j \in [q]$, $a \in [\ell_i]$, and $b \in [\ell_j - 1]$.
2. if $\mathrm{flagT} = 0$, then t_i's are all distinct.
3. if $\mathrm{flagI} = 0$ for all $I \in \{T, W, X\}$, then $x_i[a] = y_i[a - 1] \oplus \overline{m}_i[a]$ and $(0^n, \widetilde{x}, \widetilde{y}^\oplus) \rightsquigarrow (L, \widetilde{y}, \widetilde{t})$.

The first two conditions are obvious from the ideal oracle sampling mechanism. The last condition follows from Proposition 4.1 and the observation that in ideal oracle sampling for any $I \in \{T, Z, X\}$, $\mathrm{FlagI} = 1$ if and only if BadI is true. Note that, condition 3 is vacuously true for real oracle transcripts.

BAD TRANSCRIPT: A transcript $\nu \in \mathcal{V}$ is called *bad* if and only if the following predicate is true:

$$(\mathsf{FlagT} = 1) \vee (\mathsf{FlagW} = 1) \vee (\mathsf{FlagX} = 1).$$

In other words, we term a transcript bad if the ideal oracle sets $(\widetilde{X}, \widetilde{X}^*, \widetilde{Y})$ degenerately. Let

$$\mathcal{V}_{\mathsf{bad}} := \{\nu \in \mathcal{V} : \nu \text{ is bad.}\}.$$

All other transcript $\nu' = (\widetilde{m}, \widetilde{t}, \widetilde{x}, \widetilde{x}^*, \widetilde{y}, l_{-1}, l_0, \mathsf{flagT}, \mathsf{flagW}, \mathsf{flagX}) \in \mathcal{V} \setminus \mathcal{V}_{\mathsf{bad}}$ are called *good*. From the preceding characterization of the set of transcripts, we conclude that for any good transcript ν', we must have $(0^n, \widetilde{x}, \widetilde{x}^*) \rightsquigarrow (L, \widetilde{y}, \widetilde{t})$. Henceforth, we drop flagT, flagW, and flagX for any good transcript with an implicit understanding that $\mathsf{flagT} = \mathsf{flagW} = \mathsf{flagX} = 0$.

Following the H-coefficient mechanism, we have to upper bound the probability $\Pr(\mathsf{V}_0 \in \mathcal{V}_{\mathsf{bad}})$ and lower bound the ratio $\Pr(\mathsf{V}_1 = \nu) / \Pr(\mathsf{V}_0 = \nu)$ for any $\nu \in \mathcal{V} \setminus \mathcal{V}_{\mathsf{bad}}$.

Lemma 4.1 (bad transcript analysis). *For $q + \sigma \leq 2^{n-1}$, we have*

$$
\Pr(\mathsf{V}_0 \in \mathcal{V}_{\mathsf{bad}}) \leq \frac{4\sigma}{2^n} + \frac{16q^2 + q\ell^2}{2^n} + \frac{8q^2\ell^4 + 32q^3\ell^2 + 2q^2\ell^3}{2^{2n}}
$$
$$
+ \frac{3q^3\ell^5 + 143q^3\ell^6 + 11q^4\ell^3}{2^{3n}} + \frac{17q^4\ell^6 + 5462q^4\ell^8}{2^{4n}}.
$$

The proof of this lemma is postponed to Sect. 5.

GOOD TRANSCRIPT: Now, fix a good transcript $\nu = (\widetilde{m}, \widetilde{t}, \widetilde{x}, \widetilde{x}^*, \widetilde{y}, l_{-1}, l_0)$. Let σ be the total number of blocks (and one additional for 0^n) and $\sigma' := |\widetilde{x} \cup \{0^n\}|$. Since, ν is good, we have $(0^n, \widetilde{x}, \widetilde{x}^*) \rightsquigarrow (L, \widetilde{y}, \widetilde{t})$. Then, we must have $|\widetilde{x}^*| = q$. Further, let $|\widetilde{x} \cap \widetilde{x}^*| = r$. Thus, $|\{0^n\} \cup \widetilde{x} \cup \widetilde{x}^*| = q + \sigma' - r$.

Real world: In the real world, the random permutation Π is sampled on exactly $q + \sigma' - r$ distinct points. Thus, we have

$$
\Pr(\mathsf{V}_1 = \nu) = \frac{1}{(2^n)_{q+\sigma'-r}}. \tag{12}
$$

Ideal World: In the ideal world, we employed a two stage sampling. First of all, we have

$$
\Pr\left(\widetilde{\mathsf{T}} = \widetilde{t}, \mathsf{P}(0^n) = L\right) \leq \frac{1}{2^{nq}}, \tag{13}
$$

since each T_i is sampled uniformly from the set $\mathcal{B}$ independent of others. Now, observe that all the full collision and induced collision indices are fully determined from the transcript ν itself. In other words, we can enumerate the set $\widetilde{\mathsf{CI}} := \widetilde{\mathsf{FCI}} \cup \widetilde{\mathsf{ICI}}$. Now, since the transcript is good, we must have $|\widetilde{\mathsf{CI}}| = \sigma - \sigma' + |\widetilde{x} \cap \widetilde{x}^*| = \sigma - \sigma' + r$, and for all indices $(i, a) \notin \widetilde{\mathsf{CI}}$, we have $\mathsf{Y}_i[a] = \mathsf{Z}_i[a]$. Thus, we have

$$
\Pr\left(\mathsf{Y}_i[a] = y_a^i \wedge (i, a) \notin \widetilde{\mathsf{CI}} \mid \widetilde{\mathsf{T}} = \widetilde{t}\right) = \Pr\left(\mathsf{Z}_i[a] = y_a^i \wedge (i, a) \notin \widetilde{\mathsf{CI}} \mid \widetilde{\mathsf{T}} = \widetilde{t}\right)
$$
$$
= \frac{1}{(2^n - q)_{\sigma'-r}}, \tag{14}
$$

where the second equality follows from the fact that truncation[6] of a without replacement sample from a set of size $(2^n - q)$ is still a without replacement sample from the same set. We have

$$\Pr\left(V_0 = \omega\right) = \Pr\left(\widetilde{T} = \hat{t}\right) \times \Pr\left(\widetilde{Y} = \tilde{y} \mid \widetilde{T} = \hat{t}\right)$$

$$\leq \frac{1}{2^{nq}} \times \Pr\left(Y_i[a] = y_i[a] \wedge (i, a) \notin \widetilde{\mathsf{CI}} \mid \widetilde{T} = \hat{t}\right) = \frac{1}{2^{nq}(2^n - q)_{\sigma' - r}}.$$

$$(15)$$

The above discussion on good transcripts can be summarized in shape of the following lemma.

Lemma 4.2 *For any $\nu \in V \setminus V_{\mathsf{bad}}$, we have $\dfrac{\Pr\left(V_1 = \nu\right)}{\Pr\left(V_0 = \nu\right)} \geq 1$.*

Proof The proof follows from dividing (12) by (15).

Using Theorem 2.1, and Lemma 4.1 and 4.2, we get

$$\mathbf{Adv}^{\mathsf{prf}}_{\mathsf{OMAC}_\Pi}(q, \ell, \sigma, \infty) \leq \frac{4\sigma}{2^n} + \frac{16q^2 + q\ell^2}{2^n} + \frac{8q^2\ell^4 + 32q^3\ell^2 + 2q^2\ell^3}{2^{2n}}$$

$$+ \frac{3q^3\ell^5 + 143q^3\ell^6 + 11q^4\ell^3}{2^{3n}} + \frac{17q^4\ell^6 + 5462q^4\ell^8}{2^{4n}}.$$

$$(16)$$

Theorem 3.1 follows from (11) and (16).

5   Proof of Lemma 4.1

Our proof relies on a graph-based combinatorial tool, called structure graphs [3,15]. A concise and complete description of this tool and relevant results are available in the full version of this paper [9, Appendix A]. Our aim will be to bound the probability of bad events only when they occur in conjunction with some "manageable" structure graphs. In all other cases, we upper bound the probability by the probability of realizing an unmanageable structure graph. Formally, we say that the structure graph $\mathcal{G}_{\mathsf{P}}(\widetilde{\mathsf{M}})$ is manageable if and only if:

1. for all $i \in [q]$, we have $\mathsf{Acc}(\mathcal{G}_{\mathsf{P}}(\mathsf{M}_i)) = 0$, i.e., each M_i-walk is a path.
2. for all distinct $i, j \in [q]$, we have $\mathsf{Acc}(\mathcal{G}_{\mathsf{P}}(\mathsf{M}_i, \mathsf{M}_j)) \leq 1$.
3. for all distinct $i, j, k \in [q]$, we have $\mathsf{Acc}(\mathcal{G}_{\mathsf{P}}(\mathsf{M}_i, \mathsf{M}_j, \mathsf{M}_k)) \leq 2$.
4. for all distinct $i, j, k, l \in [q]$, we have $\mathsf{Acc}(\mathcal{G}_{\mathsf{P}}(\mathsf{M}_i, \mathsf{M}_j, \mathsf{M}_k, \mathsf{M}_l)) \leq 3$.

---

[6] Removing some elements from the tuple.

Let unman denote the event that $\mathcal{G}_P(\widetilde{M})$ is unmanageable. Then, using [9, Corollary A.1], we have

$$\Pr(\text{unman}) \leq \Pr(\exists i \in [q] : \text{Acc}(\mathcal{G}_P(M_i)) \geq 1) + \Pr(\exists i < j \in [q] : \text{Acc}(\mathcal{G}_P(M_i, M_j)) \geq 2)$$

$$+ \Pr(\exists i < j < k \in [q] : \text{Acc}(\mathcal{G}_P(M_i, M_j, M_k)) \geq 3)$$

$$+ \Pr(\exists i < j < k < l \in [q] : \text{Acc}(\mathcal{G}_P(M_i, M_j, M_k, M_l)) \geq 4)$$

$$\leq \sum_{i \in [q]} \frac{(\ell_i - 1)^2}{2^n} + \sum_{i < j \in [q]} \frac{(\ell_i + \ell_j - 2)^4}{2^{2n}} + \sum_{i < j < k \in [q]} \frac{(\ell_i + \ell_j + \ell_k - 3)^6}{2^{3n}}$$

$$+ \sum_{i < j < k < l \in [q]} \frac{(\ell_i + \ell_j + \ell_k + \ell_l - 4)^8}{2^{4n}}$$

$$\leq \frac{q\ell^2}{2^n} + \frac{8q^2\ell^4}{2^{2n}} + \frac{121.5q^3\ell^6}{2^{3n}} + \frac{5461.34q^4\ell^8}{2^{4n}}. \tag{17}$$

From now on we only consider manageable graphs. Observe that apart from the fact that a manageable graph is just a union of M_i-paths, there is an added benefit that it has no zero collision. Let $\text{TU} := \neg(\text{BadT} \vee \text{unman})$ and $\text{TUW} := \neg(\text{BadT} \vee \text{unman} \vee \text{BadW})$. Now, we have

$$\Pr(V_0 \in \mathcal{V}_{\text{bad}}) = \Pr((\text{FlagT} = 1) \vee (\text{FlagW} = 1) \vee (\text{FlagX} = 1))$$

$$\overset{1}{\leq} \Pr(\text{BadT} \vee \text{BadW} \vee \text{BadX})$$

$$\leq \Pr(\text{BadT}) + \Pr(\text{BadW}|\neg\text{BadT}) + \Pr(\text{BadX}|\neg(\text{BadT} \vee \text{BadW}))$$

$$\overset{2}{\leq} \Pr(\exists i \neq j : T_i = T_j) + \Pr(\text{BadW}|\neg\text{BadT}) + \Pr(\text{BadX}|\neg(\text{BadT} \vee \text{BadW}))$$

$$\overset{3}{\leq} \frac{q^2}{2^{n+1}} + \Pr(\text{unman}) + \Pr(\text{BadW}|\text{TU}) + \Pr(\text{BadX}|\text{TUW})$$

$$\overset{4}{\leq} \frac{0.5q^2 + q\ell^2}{2^n} + \frac{8q^2\ell^4}{2^{2n}} + \frac{122q^3\ell^6}{2^{3n}} + \frac{5462q^4\ell^8}{2^{4n}}$$

$$+ \Pr(\text{BadW}|\text{TU}) + \Pr(\text{BadX}|\text{TUW}) \tag{18}$$

Here, inequalities 1 and 2 follow by definition; 3 follows from the fact that T_i is chosen uniformly at random from $\mathcal{B}$ for each i; and 4 follows from (17).

BOUNDING $\Pr(\text{BadW}|\neg(\text{BadT} \vee \text{unman}))$: Let $\text{Ei} = \neg(\text{TU} \vee \text{BadW1} \vee \cdots \vee \text{BadWi})$. We have

$$\Pr(\text{BadW}|\text{TU}) \leq \Pr(\text{BadW1}|\text{TU}) + \Pr(\text{BadW2}|\text{E1}) + \Pr(\text{BadW3}|\text{E2})$$

$$+ \Pr(\text{BadW4}|\text{E3}) + \Pr(\text{BadW5}|\text{E4}) \tag{19}$$

We bound the individual terms on the right hand side as follows:

Bounding $\Pr(\text{BadW1}|\text{TU})$: Fix some $(i, a) \in [q] \times [\ell_i]$. The only way we can have $\overline{W_i}[a] = 0^n$, for $1 < a < \ell_i$, is if $Z_i[a-1] = M_i[a]$. This happens with probability at most $(2^n - q)^{-1}$. For $a = \ell_i$, the equation

$$\mu_{\delta_{M_i}} \odot L \oplus Z_i[\ell_i - 1] \oplus \overline{M}_i[\ell_i] = 0^n$$

must hold non-trivially. The probability that this equation holds is bounded by at most $(2^n - q - 1)^{-1}$. Assuming $q + 1 \leq 2^{n-1}$, and using the fact that there can be at most σ choices for (i, a), we have

$$\Pr\left(\texttt{BadW1}|\texttt{TU}\right) \leq \frac{2\sigma}{2^n}. \tag{20}$$

Bounding $\Pr\left(\texttt{BadW2}|\texttt{E1}\right)$: Fix some $i \neq j \in [q]$. Since $\neg\texttt{unman}$ holds, we know that $\mathsf{Acc}(\mathcal{G}_\mathsf{P}(\mathsf{M}_i, \mathsf{M}_j)) \leq 1$. We handle the two resulting cases separately:

(A) $\mathsf{Acc}(\mathcal{G}_\mathsf{P}(\mathsf{M}_i, \mathsf{M}_j)) = 1$: Suppose the collision source of the only accident are (i, a) and (j, b). Then, we have the following system of two equations

$$\mathsf{Z}_i[a] \oplus \mathsf{Z}_j[b] = \mathsf{M}_i[a + 1] \oplus \mathsf{M}_j[b + 1]$$
$$(\mu_{\delta_{\mathsf{M}_i}} \oplus \mu_{\delta_{\mathsf{M}_j}}) \odot \mathsf{L} \oplus \mathsf{Z}_i[\ell_i - 1] \oplus \mathsf{Z}_j[\ell_j - 1] = \overline{\mathsf{M}}_i[\ell_i] \oplus \overline{\mathsf{M}}_j[\ell_j]$$

Suppose $\delta_{\mathsf{M}_i} \neq \delta_{\mathsf{M}_j}$, i.e. $\mu_{\delta_{\mathsf{M}_i}} \oplus \mu_{\delta_{\mathsf{M}_j}} \neq 0^n$. Using the fact that $\neg\texttt{BadW1}$ holds, we infer that $\mathsf{L} \notin \{\mathsf{Z}_i[a], \mathsf{Z}_j[b], \mathsf{Z}_i[\ell_i - 1], \mathsf{Z}_j[\ell_j - 1]\}$. So, the two equations are linearly independent, whence the rank is 2 in this case. Again, using [9, Lemma A.4], and the fact that there are at most $q^2/2$ choices for i and j, and ℓ^2 choices for a and b, we get

$$\Pr\left(\texttt{BadW2} \wedge \text{Case A} \wedge \delta_{\mathsf{M}_i} \neq \delta_{\mathsf{M}_j} \middle| \texttt{E1}\right) \leq \frac{q^2\ell^2}{2(2^n - q - \sigma + 2)^2}.$$

Now, suppose $\delta_{\mathsf{M}_i} = \delta_{\mathsf{M}_j}$, i.e. $\mu_{\delta_{\mathsf{M}_i}} \oplus \mu_{\delta_{\mathsf{M}_j}} = 0^n$. Then, we can rewrite the system as

$$\mathsf{Z}_i[a] \oplus \mathsf{Z}_j[b] = \mathsf{M}_i[a + 1] \oplus \mathsf{M}_j[b + 1]$$
$$\mathsf{Z}_i[\ell_i - 1] \oplus \mathsf{Z}_j[\ell_j - 1] = \overline{\mathsf{M}}_i[\ell_i] \oplus \overline{\mathsf{M}}_j[\ell_j]$$

We can have two types of structure graphs relevant to this case, as illustrated in Fig. 3. For type 1 all variables are distinct. So, the two equations are linearly independent, whence the rank is 2 in this case. Again, using [9, Lemma A.4], we get

$$\Pr\left(\texttt{BadW2} \wedge \text{Case A} \wedge \delta_{\mathsf{M}_i} = \delta_{\mathsf{M}_j} \wedge \text{Type 1} \middle| \texttt{E1}\right) \leq \frac{q^2\ell^2}{2(2^n - q - \sigma + 2)^2}.$$

Type (1)   Type (2)

Fig. 3. Accident-1 manageable graphs for two messages. The solid and dashed lines correspond to edges in $\mathcal{W}_i$ and $\mathcal{W}_j$, respectively. $*$ denotes optional parts in the walk.

For type 2, it is clear that $Z_j[\ell_j - 1] = Z_i[\ell_i - 1]$. So, we can assume that the second equation holds trivially, thereby deriving a system in $Z_i[a]$ and $Z_j[b]$, with rank 1. Further, a and b are uniquely determined as $\ell_i - p$ and $\ell_j - p$, where p is the longest common suffix of M_i and M_j. So we have

$$\Pr\left(\texttt{BadW2} \wedge \text{Case A} \wedge \delta_{M_i} = \delta_{M_j} \wedge \text{Type 2}|\text{E1}\right) \leq \frac{q^2}{2(2^n - q - \sigma + 1)}.$$

(B) $\text{Acc}(\mathcal{G}_P(M_i, M_j)) = 0$: In this case, we only have one equation of the form

$$(\mu_{\delta_{M_i}} \oplus \mu_{\delta_{M_j}}) \odot L \oplus Z_i[\ell_i - 1] \oplus Z_j[\ell_j - 1] = \overline{M}_i[\ell_i] \oplus \overline{M}_j[\ell_j]$$

If $\delta_{M_i} \neq \delta_{M_j}$, we have an equation in three variables, namely L, $Z_i[\ell_i - 1]$, and $Z_j[\ell_j - 1]$; and if $\delta_{M_i} = \delta_{M_j}$, we have an equation in two variables, namely $Z_i[\ell_i - 1]$, and $Z_j[\ell_j - 1]$. In both the cases, the equation can only hold non-trivially, i.e., rank is 1. Using [9, Lemma A.4], we get

$$\Pr\left(\texttt{BadW2} \wedge \text{Case B}|\text{E1}\right) \leq \frac{q^2}{2(2^n - q - \sigma + 1)}.$$

On combining the three cases, we get

$$\Pr\left(\texttt{BadW2}|\text{E1}\right) \leq \frac{q^2}{2^n - q - \sigma + 1} + \frac{q^2 \ell^2}{(2^n - q - \sigma + 2)^2}. \tag{21}$$

Bounding $\Pr\left(\texttt{BadW3}|\text{E2}\right)$: Fix some $i, j, k \in [q]$. Since $\neg\texttt{unman}$ holds, we must have $\text{Acc}(\mathcal{G}_P(M_i, M_j, M_k)) \leq 2$. Accordingly, we have the following three cases:

(A) $\text{Acc}(\mathcal{G}_P(M_i, M_j, M_k)) = 2$: Suppose (α_1, β_1) and (α_2, β_2) are collision source leading to one of the accident, and (α_3, β_3) and (α_4, β_4) are collision source leading to the other accident. Then, considering $W_i[a] = W_j[\ell_j]$, we have the following system of equations

$$Z_{\alpha_1}[\beta_1] \oplus Z_{\alpha_2}[\beta_2] = M_{\alpha_1}[\beta_1 + 1] \oplus M_{\alpha_2}[\beta_2 + 1]$$
$$Z_{\alpha_3}[\beta_3] \oplus Z_{\alpha_4}[\beta_4] = M_{\alpha_3}[\beta_3 + 1] \oplus M_{\alpha_4}[\beta_4 + 1]$$
$$Z_j[a - 1] \oplus \mu_{\delta_{M_j}} \odot L \oplus Z_j[\ell_j - 1] = \overline{M}_j[\ell_j] \oplus M_i[a]$$

The first two equations are independent by definition. Further, using $\neg\texttt{BadW1}$, we can infer that the last equation is also independent of the first two equations. Thus the system has rank 3. There are at most $q^3/6$ choices for (i, j, k), and for each such choice we have 3 choices for $(\alpha_1, \alpha_2, \alpha_3, \alpha_4)$ and at most ℓ^5 choices for $(\beta_1, \beta_2, \beta_3, \beta_4, a)$. Using [9, Lemma A.4], we have

$$\Pr\left(\texttt{BadW3} \wedge \text{Case A}|\text{E2}\right) \leq \frac{q^3 \ell^5}{2(2^n - q - \sigma + 3)^3}.$$

(B) $\mathsf{Acc}(\mathcal{G}_{\mathsf{P}}(\mathsf{M}_i, \mathsf{M}_j, \mathsf{M}_k)) = 1$: Suppose (α_1, β_1) and (α_2, β_2) are collision source leading to the accident. First consider the case $a < \ell_i - 1$ and $b < \ell_k$. In this case, we have the following system of equations

$$Z_{\alpha_1}[\beta_1] \oplus Z_{\alpha_2}[\beta_2] = \mathsf{M}_{\alpha_1}[\beta_1 + 1] \oplus \mathsf{M}_{\alpha_2}[\beta_2 + 1]$$

$$Z_i[a-1] \oplus \mu_{\delta_{\mathsf{M}_j}} \odot \mathsf{L} \oplus Z_j[\ell_j - 1] = \overline{\mathsf{M}}_j[\ell_j] \oplus \mathsf{M}_i[a]$$

$$Z_i[a] \oplus Z_k[b-1] = \mathsf{M}_i[a+1] \dot{\oplus} \mathsf{M}_k[b]$$

The first two equations are clearly independent. Further, since $\mathsf{M}_i \neq \mathsf{M}_k$, the last equation must correspond to a true collision as a consequence of the accident. So, the rank of the above system is 2. Once we fix (i, j, k) and (a, b), we have at most 3 choices for (α_1, α_2), and β_1 and β_2 are uniquely determined as $a + 1 - p$ and $b - p$, where p is the largest common suffix of $\mathsf{M}_i[1, \ldots, a+1]$ and $\mathsf{M}_k[1, \ldots, b]$. So, we have

$$\Pr\left(\mathsf{BadW3} \wedge \text{Case B} \wedge a < \ell_i - 1 \wedge b < \ell_k | \mathsf{E2}\right) \leq \frac{q^3 \ell^2}{2(2^n - q - \sigma + 2)^2}.$$

Now, suppose $a = \ell_i - 1$. Then we can simply consider the first two equations

$$Z_{\alpha_1}[\beta_1] \oplus Z_{\alpha_2}[\beta_2] = \mathsf{M}_{\alpha_1}[\beta_1 + 1] \oplus \mathsf{M}_{\alpha_2}[\beta_2 + 1]$$

$$Z_j[\ell_i - 2] \oplus \mu_{\delta_{\mathsf{M}_j}} \odot \mathsf{L} \oplus Z_j[\ell_j - 1] = \overline{\mathsf{M}}_j[\ell_j] \oplus \mathsf{M}_i[\ell_i - 1]$$

Clearly, the two equations are independent. We have at most q^3 choices for (i, j, k), 3 choices for (α_1, α_2), and ℓ^2 choices for (β_1, β_2). So we have

$$\Pr\left(\mathsf{BadW3} \wedge \text{Case B} \wedge a = \ell_i - 1 | \mathsf{E2}\right) \leq \frac{q^3 \ell^2}{2(2^n - q - \sigma + 2)^2}.$$

The case where $a < \ell_i - 1$ and $b = \ell_k$ can be handled similarly by considering the first and the third equations.

(C) $\mathsf{Acc}(\mathcal{G}_{\mathsf{P}}(\mathsf{M}_i, \mathsf{M}_j, \mathsf{M}_k)) = 0$: In this case, we know that the three paths, $\mathcal{W}_i$, $\mathcal{W}_j$, and $\mathcal{W}_k$ do not collide. This implies that we must have $a = \ell_i - 1$, or $b = \ell_k$ or both, in order for $\mathsf{W}_i[a+1] = \mathsf{W}_k[b]$ to hold. First, suppose both $a = \ell_i - 1$ and $b = \ell_k$. Then, we have the following system of equations:

$$Z_j[\ell_i - 2] \oplus \mu_{\delta_{\mathsf{M}_j}} \odot \mathsf{L} \oplus Z_j[\ell_j - 1] = \overline{\mathsf{M}}_j[\ell_j] \oplus \mathsf{M}_i[\ell_i - 2]$$

$$(\mu_{\delta_{\mathsf{M}_i}} \oplus \mu_{\delta_{\mathsf{M}_k}}) \odot \mathsf{L} \oplus Z_i[\ell_i - 1] \oplus Z_k[\ell_k - 1] = \overline{\mathsf{M}}_i[\ell_i] \oplus \overline{\mathsf{M}}_k[\ell_k]$$

Using the properties of μ_{-1} and μ_0, and $\neg\mathsf{BadW1}$, we can conclude that the above system has rank 2. There are at most $q^3/6$ choices for (i, j, k), and at most ℓ^2 choices for (a, b). So, we have

$$\Pr\left(\mathsf{BadW3} \wedge \text{Case C} \wedge a = \ell_i - 1 \wedge b = \ell_k | \mathsf{E2}\right) \leq \frac{q^3 \ell^2}{6(2^n - q - \sigma + 2)^2}.$$

The remaining two cases are similar. We handle the case $a = \ell_i - 1$ and $b < \ell_k$, and the other case can be handled similarly. We have the following system of equations

$$Z_j[\ell_i - 2] \oplus \mu_{\delta_{M_j}} \odot L \oplus Z_j[\ell_j - 1] = \overline{M}_j[\ell_j] \oplus M_i[\ell_i - 2]$$

$$\mu_{\delta_{M_i}} \odot L \oplus Z_i[\ell_i - 1] \oplus Z_k[b - 1] = \overline{M}_i[\ell_i] \oplus M_k[b]$$

If $\delta_{M_i} \neq \delta_{M_j}$, then using the same argument as above, we can conclude that the system has rank 2, and we get

$$\Pr\left(\texttt{BadW3} \wedge \text{Case C} \wedge a = \ell_i - 1 \wedge b < \ell_k \wedge \delta_{M_i} \neq \delta_{M_j} \mid \texttt{E2}\right) \leq \frac{q^3 \ell^2}{6(2^n - q - \sigma + 2)^2}.$$

So, suppose $\delta_{M_i} = \delta_{M_j}$. Now, in order for the second equation to be a consequence of the first equation, we must have $Z_i[\ell_i - 2] = Z_j[\ell_j - 1]$ and $Z_i[\ell_i - 1] = Z_k[b]$. The only we way this happens trivially is if $M_i[1, \ldots, \ell_i - 1] = M_j[1, \ldots, \ell_j - 1]$ and $M_i[1, \ldots, \ell_i - 1] = M_k[1, \ldots, b]$. But, then we have $b = \ell_i - 1$, and once we fix (i, k) there's a unique choice for j, since $M_j[1, \ldots, \ell_j - 1] = M_i[1, \ldots, \ell_i - 1]$ and $\overline{M}_j[\ell_j] = \overline{M}_i[\ell_i] \oplus M_i[\ell_i - 2] \oplus M_k[b]$. So, we get

$$\Pr\left(\texttt{BadW3} \wedge \text{Case C} \wedge a = \ell_i - 1 \wedge b < \ell_k \wedge \delta_{M_i} = \delta_{M_j} \mid \texttt{E2}\right) \leq \frac{q^2}{2(2^n - q - \sigma + 1)}.$$

By combining all three cases, we have

$$\Pr\left(\texttt{BadW3} \mid \texttt{E2}\right) \leq \frac{q^3 \ell^5}{2(2^n - q - \sigma + 3)^3} + \frac{2q^3 \ell^2}{(2^n - q - \sigma + 2)^2} + \frac{q^2}{2(2^n - q - \sigma + 1)}. \tag{22}$$

Type (1)   Type (2)

Fig. 4. Manageable graphs for case B.1. The solid, dashed and dotted lines correspond to edges in $\mathcal{W}_i$, $\mathcal{W}_j$, and $\mathcal{W}_k$, respectively.

Bounding $\Pr\left(\texttt{BadW4} \mid \texttt{E3}\right)$: Fix some $i, j, k \in [q]$. The analysis in this case is very similar to the one in case of $\texttt{BadW3} \mid \texttt{E2}$. So we will skip detailed argumentation whenever possible. Since $\neg\texttt{unman}$ holds, we must have $\text{Acc}(\mathcal{G}_P(M_i, M_j, M_k)) \leq 2$. Accordingly, we have the following three cases:

(A) $\text{Acc}(\mathcal{G}_P(M_i, M_j, M_k)) = 2$: This can be bounded by using exactly the same argument as used in Case A for $\texttt{BadW3} \mid \texttt{E2}$. So, we have

$$\Pr\left(\texttt{BadW4} \wedge \text{Case A} \mid \texttt{E3}\right) \leq \frac{q^3 \ell^5}{2(2^n - q - \sigma + 3)^3}.$$

(B) $\mathsf{Acc}(\mathcal{G}_{\mathsf{P}}(\mathsf{M}_i, \mathsf{M}_j, \mathsf{M}_k)) = 1$: Suppose (α_1, β_1) and (α_2, β_2) are collision source leading to the accident. Without loss of generality we assume $a < b$. Specifically, $b \le \ell_i - 1$ and $a \le b - 2$ due to $\neg(\mathsf{BadW2} \wedge \mathsf{BadW3})$. First consider the case $b = \ell_i - 1$. In this case, considering $\mathsf{W}_i[b] = \mathsf{W}_k[\ell_k]$, we have the following system of equations

$$\mathsf{Z}_{\alpha_1}[\beta_1] \oplus \mathsf{Z}_{\alpha_2}[\beta_2] = \mathsf{M}_{\alpha_1}[\beta_1 + 1] \oplus \mathsf{M}_{\alpha_2}[\beta_2 + 1]$$

$$\mathsf{Z}_i[b-1] \oplus \mu_{\delta_{\mathsf{M}_k}} \odot \mathsf{L} \oplus \mathsf{Z}_k[\ell_k - 1] = \overline{\mathsf{M}}_k[\ell_k] \oplus \mathsf{M}_i[b]$$

Using a similar argument as used in previous such cases, we establish that the two equations are independent. Now, once we fix (i, j, k), we have exactly one choice for b, at most 3 choices for (α_1, α_2), and ℓ^2 choices for (β_1, β_2). So, we have

$$\Pr\left(\mathsf{BadW4} \wedge \text{Case B} \wedge b = \ell_i - 1 | \mathsf{E3}\right) \le \frac{q^3 \ell^2}{2(2^n - q - \sigma + 2)^2}.$$

Now, suppose $b < \ell_i - 1$. Here we can have two cases:

(B.1) $\mathcal{W}_i$ *is involved in the accident*: Without loss of generality assume that $\alpha_1 = i$ and $\beta_1 \in [\ell_i - 1]$. Then, we have the following system of equations:

$$\mathsf{Z}_i[\beta_1] \oplus \mathsf{Z}_{\alpha_2}[\beta_2] = \mathsf{M}_i[\beta_1 + 1] \oplus \mathsf{M}_{\alpha_2}[\beta_2 + 1]$$

$$\mathsf{Z}_i[a-1] \oplus \mu_{\delta_{\mathsf{M}_j}} \odot \mathsf{L} \oplus \mathsf{Z}_j[\ell_j - 1] = \overline{\mathsf{M}}_j[\ell_j] \oplus \mathsf{M}_i[a]$$

$$\mathsf{Z}_i[b-1] \oplus \mu_{\delta_{\mathsf{M}_k}} \odot \mathsf{L} \oplus \mathsf{Z}_k[\ell_k - 1] = \overline{\mathsf{M}}_k[\ell_k] \oplus \mathsf{M}_i[b]$$

Suppose $\mathsf{Z}_i[\beta_1] = \mathsf{Z}_i[a-1]$. Then, we must have $\beta_1 = a - 1$ as the graph is manageable. In this case, we consider the first two equations. It is easy to see that the two equations are independent, and once we fix i, j, k, there are at most 2 choices for α_2 and ℓ^2 choices for (β_1, β_2), which gives a unique choice for a. So, we have

$$\Pr\left(\mathsf{BadW4} \wedge \text{Case B.1} \wedge \beta_1 = a - 1 | \mathsf{E3}\right) \le \frac{q^3 \ell^2}{2(2^n - q - \sigma + 2)^2}.$$

We get identical bound for the case when $\mathsf{Z}_i[\beta_1] = \mathsf{Z}_i[b-1]$. Suppose $\mathsf{Z}_i[\beta_1] \notin \{\mathsf{Z}_i[a-1], \mathsf{Z}_i[b-1]\}$. Then, using the fact that there is only one accident in the graph and that accident is due to (i, β_1) and (α_2, β_2), we infer that $\mathsf{Z}_{\alpha_2}[\beta_2] \notin \{\mathsf{Z}_i[a-1], \mathsf{Z}_i[b-1]\}$. Now, the only way rank of the above system reduces to 2, is if $\mathsf{Z}_i[a-1] = \mathsf{Z}_k[\ell_k - 1]$ and $\mathsf{Z}_i[b-1] = \mathsf{Z}_j[\ell_j - 1]$ trivially. However, if this happens then a and b are uniquely determined by our choice of $(i, j, k, \beta_1, \alpha_2, \beta_2)$. See Fig. 4 for the two possible structure graphs depending upon the value of α_2. Basically, based on the choice of α_2, $a \in \{\ell_k, \ell_k - \beta_2 + \beta_1\}$. Similarly, $b \in \{\ell_j, \ell_j - \beta_2 + \beta_1\}$. So, using [9, Lemma A.4], we get

$$\Pr\left(\mathsf{BadW4} \wedge \text{Case B.1} \wedge \beta_1 \notin \{a - 1, b - 1\} | \mathsf{E3}\right) \le \frac{2q^3 \ell^2}{3(2^n - q - \sigma + 2)^2}.$$

(B.2) $\mathcal{W}_i$ *is not involved in the accident*: Without loss of generality assume $\alpha_1 = j$ and $\alpha_2 = k$. Then, we have the following system of equations:

$$Z_j[\beta_1] \oplus Z_k[\beta_2] = M_j[\beta_1 + 1] \oplus M_k[\beta_2 + 1]$$

$$Z_i[a-1] \oplus \mu_{\delta_{M_j}} \odot L \oplus Z_j[\ell_j - 1] = \overline{M}_j[\ell_j] \oplus M_i[a]$$

$$Z_i[b-1] \oplus \mu_{\delta_{M_k}} \odot L \oplus Z_k[\ell_k - 1] = \overline{M}_k[\ell_k] \oplus M_i[b]$$

Since the graph is manageable, $\{Z_i[a-1], Z_i[b-1]\} \cap \{Z_j[\ell_j-1], Z_k[\ell_k - 1]\} \neq \emptyset$. Suppose $\{Z_i[a-1], Z_i[b-1]\} = \{Z_j[\ell_j - 1], Z_k[\ell_k - 1]\}$. Without loss of generality, assume $Z_i[a-1] = Z_k[\ell_k - 1]$ and $Z_i[b-1] = Z_j[\ell_j - 1]$. This can only happen if the resulting graph is of Type 2 form in Fig. 4, which clearly shows that we have unique choices for a and b when we fix the other indices. Now, suppose $|\{Z_i[a-1], Z_i[b-1]\} \cap \{Z_j[\ell_j - 1], Z_k[\ell_k - 1]\}| = 1$. Then, we must have $Z_i[a-1] \in \{Z_j[\beta_1], Z_k[\beta_2]\}$ since $a < b$. Without loss of generality we assume that $Z_i[a-1] = Z_k[\beta_2]$ and $Z_i[b-1] = Z_j[\ell_j - 1]$. Using similar argument as before, we conclude that a and b are fixed once we fix all other indices. So using [9, Lemma A.4], we get

$$\Pr(\text{BadW4} \wedge \text{Case B.2}|\text{E3}) \leq \frac{2q^3\ell^2}{3(2^n - q - \sigma + 2)^2}.$$

(C) $\text{Acc}(\mathcal{G}_P(M_i, M_j, M_k)) = 0$: In this case, we know that the three paths, $\mathcal{W}_i$, $\mathcal{W}_j$, and $\mathcal{W}_k$ do not collide. We have the following system of equations:

$$Z_i[a-1] \oplus \mu_{\delta_{M_j}} \odot L \oplus Z_j[\ell_j - 1] = \overline{M}_j[\ell_j] \oplus M_i[a]$$

$$Z_i[b-1] \oplus \mu_{\delta_{M_k}}) \odot L \oplus Z_k[\ell_k - 1] = \overline{M}_i[\ell_k] \oplus M_i[b]$$

Using a similar analysis as in case C of BadW3|E2, we get

$$\Pr(\text{BadW4} \wedge \text{Case C}|\text{E3}) \leq \frac{q^3\ell^2}{6(2^n - q - \sigma + 2)^2} + \frac{q^2}{2(2^n - q - \sigma + 1)}.$$

By combining all three cases, we have

$$\Pr(\text{BadW4}|\text{E3}) \leq \frac{q^3\ell^5}{2(2^n - q - \sigma + 3)^3} + \frac{3q^3\ell^2}{(2^n - q - \sigma + 2)^2} + \frac{q^2}{2(2^n - q - \sigma + 1)}. \tag{23}$$

Bounding $\Pr(\text{BadW5}|\text{E4})$: Fix some $i, j, k \in [q]$. The analysis in this case is again similar to the analysis of BadW3|E2 and BadW4|E3. We have the following three cases:

(A) $\text{Acc}(\mathcal{G}_P(M_i, M_j, M_k)) = 2$: This can be bounded by using exactly the same argument as used in Case A for BadW3|E2. So, we have

$$\Pr(\text{BadW5} \wedge \text{Case A}|\text{E4}) \leq \frac{q^3\ell^5}{2(2^n - q - \sigma + 3)^3}.$$

(B) $\mathsf{Acc}(\mathcal{G}_\mathsf{P}(\mathsf{M}_i, \mathsf{M}_j, \mathsf{M}_k)) = 1$: Suppose (α_1, β_1) and (α_2, β_2) are collision source leading to the accident. In this case, we have the following system of equations

$$Z_{\alpha_1}[\beta_1] \oplus Z_{\alpha_2}[\beta_2] = \mathsf{M}_{\alpha_1}[\beta_1 + 1] \oplus \mathsf{M}_{\alpha_2}[\beta_2 + 1]$$

$$Z_i[a-1] \oplus \mu_{\delta_{\mathsf{M}_j}} \odot \mathsf{L} \oplus Z_j[\ell_j - 1] = \overline{\mathsf{M}}_j[\ell_j] \oplus \mathsf{M}_i[a]$$

$$Z_j[b-1] \oplus \mu_{\delta_{\mathsf{M}_k}} \odot \mathsf{L} \oplus Z_k[\ell_k - 1] = \overline{\mathsf{M}}_k[\ell_k] \oplus \mathsf{M}_j[b]$$

We can have two sub-cases:

(B.1) Suppose the third equation is simply a consequence of the second equation. Then, we must have $\delta_{\mathsf{M}_i} = \delta_{\mathsf{M}_j}$ and $Z_i[a-1] = Z_j[b-1]$ and $Z_j[\ell_j - 1] = Z_k[\ell_k - 1]$ must hold trivially, since the graph is manageable. We claim that $a = b = \mathsf{Prefix}(\mathsf{M}_i[1], \mathsf{M}_j[1]) + 1$. If not, then $\mathsf{M}_i[\ell_i] = \mathsf{M}_j[\ell_j]$ which in conjunction with $Z_j[\ell_j - 1] = Z_k[\ell_k - 1]$ implies that $\mathsf{W}_i[\ell_i] = \mathsf{W}_j[\ell_j]$ which contradicts $\mathsf{BadW2}$. So, using [9, Lemma A.4], we get

$$\Pr(\mathsf{BadW5} \wedge \text{Case B.1}|\mathsf{E4}) \leq \frac{q^3\ell^2}{2(2^n - q - \sigma + 2)^2}.$$

(B.2) The second and third equation are independent. Considering the subsystem consisting of these two equations, and using [9, Lemma A.4], we get

$$\Pr(\mathsf{BadW5} \wedge \text{Case B.2}|\mathsf{E4}) \leq \frac{q^3\ell^2}{6(2^n - q - \sigma + 2)^2}.$$

(C) $\mathsf{Acc}(\mathcal{G}_\mathsf{P}(\mathsf{M}_i, \mathsf{M}_j, \mathsf{M}_k)) = 0$: We have the following system of equations:

$$Z_i[a-1] \oplus \mu_{\delta_{\mathsf{M}_j}} \odot \mathsf{L} \oplus Z_j[\ell_j - 1] = \overline{\mathsf{M}}_j[\ell_j] \oplus \mathsf{M}_i[a]$$

$$Z_i[b-1] \oplus \mu_{\delta_{\mathsf{M}_k}} \odot \mathsf{L} \oplus Z_k[\ell_k - 1] = \overline{\mathsf{M}}_i[\ell_k] \oplus \mathsf{M}_i[b]$$

Let r denote the rank of the above system. Using a similar analysis as in case B.1 above, we conclude that $a = b = \mathsf{Prefix}(\mathsf{M}_i[1], \mathsf{M}_j[1]) + 1$ if $r = 1$. Using [9, Lemma A.4], we get

$$\Pr(\mathsf{BadW5} \wedge \text{Case C} \wedge r = 1|\mathsf{E4}) \leq \frac{q^2}{2(2^n - q - \sigma + 1)}.$$

$$\Pr(\mathsf{BadW5} \wedge \text{Case C} \wedge r = 2|\mathsf{E4}) \leq \frac{q^3\ell^2}{6(2^n - q - \sigma + 2)^2}.$$

By combining all three cases, we have

$$\Pr(\mathsf{BadW5}|\mathsf{E4}) \leq \frac{q^3\ell^5}{2(2^n - q - \sigma + 3)^3} + \frac{5q^3\ell^2}{6(2^n - q - \sigma + 2)^2} + \frac{q^2}{2(2^n - q - \sigma + 1)}. \tag{24}$$

Further, from Eqs. (19)–(24), we have

$$\Pr\left(\mathsf{BadW}|\mathsf{TU}\right) \leq \frac{2\sigma}{2^n} + \frac{5q^2}{2(2^n - q - \sigma + 1)} + \frac{7q^3\ell^2}{(2^n - q - \sigma + 2)^2} + \frac{3q^3\ell^5}{2(2^n - q - \sigma + 3)^3}. \tag{25}$$

BOUNDING $\Pr\left(\mathsf{BadX}|\mathsf{TUW}\right)$: In the full version [9, Appendix B] of this paper, we show that

$$\Pr\left(\mathsf{BadX}|\mathsf{TUW}\right) \leq \frac{2\sigma}{2^n} + \frac{10q^2}{2^n - q - \sigma + 1} + \frac{15q^3\ell^2 + q^2\ell^3}{(2^n - q - \sigma + 2)^2}$$
$$+ \frac{12q^3\ell^6 + 6q^4\ell^3}{(2^n - q - \sigma + 3)^3} + \frac{8q^4\ell^6}{(2^n - q - \sigma + 4)^4} \tag{26}$$

Combining Eqs. (18), (25), and (26), we have

$$\Pr\left(\mathsf{V}_0 \in \mathcal{V}_{\mathsf{bad}}\right) \leq \frac{4\sigma}{2^n} + \frac{16q^2 + q\ell^2}{2^n} + \frac{8q^2\ell^4 + 32q^3\ell^2 + 2q^2\ell^3}{2^{2n}}$$
$$+ \frac{3q^3\ell^5 + 143q^3\ell^6 + 11q^4\ell^3}{2^{3n}} + \frac{17q^4\ell^6 + 5462q^4\ell^8}{2^{4n}}. \tag{27}$$

6   Conclusion

In this paper we proved that OMAC, XCBC and TMAC are secure up to $q \leq 2^{n/2}$ queries, while the message length $\ell \leq 2^{n/4}$. As a consequence, we have proved that OMAC – a single-keyed CBC-MAC variant – achieves the same security level as some of the more elaborate CBC-MAC variants like EMAC and ECBC. This, in combination with the existing results [15,16], shows that the security is tight up to $\ell \leq 2^{n/4}$ for all CBC-MAC variants except for the original CBC-MAC. It could be an interesting future problem to extend our analysis and derive similar bounds for CBC-MAC over prefix-free message space. In order to prove our claims, we employed reset-sampling method by Chattopadhyay et al. [8], which seems to be a promising tool in reducing the length-dependency in single-keyed iterated constructions. Indeed, we believe that this tool might even be useful in obtaining better security bounds for single-keyed variants of many beyond-the-birthday-bound constructions.

References

1. Bellare, M., Goldreich, O., Mityagin, A.: The power of verification queries in message authentication and authenticated encryption. IACR Cryptol. ePrint Arch. **2004**, 309 (2004)
2. Bellare, M., Kilian, J., Rogaway, P.: The security of cipher block chaining. In: Proceedings of Advances in Cryptology - CRYPTO 1994, pp. 341–358 (1994)

3. Bellare, M., Pietrzak, K., Rogaway, P.: Improved security analyses for CBC macs. In: Proceedings of Advances in Cryptology - CRYPTO 2005, pp. 527–545 (2005)
4. Berendschot, A., et al.: Final Report of RACE Integrity Primitives, vol. 1007, LNCS, Springer-Verlag, Berlin (1995). https://doi.org/10.1007/3-540-60640-8
5. Black, J., Rogaway, P.: CBC macs for arbitrary-length messages: the three-key constructions. In: Proceedings of Advances in Cryptology - CRYPTO 2000, pp. 197–215 (2000)
6. Black, J., Rogaway, P.: A block-cipher mode of operation for parallelizable message authentication. In: Proceedings of Advances in Cryptology - EUROCRYPT 2002, pp. 384–397 (2002)
7. Chakraborty, B., Chattopadhyay, S., Jha, A., Nandi, M.: On length independent security bounds for the PMAC family. IACR Trans. Symmet. Cryptol. **2021**(2), 423–445 (2021)
8. Chattopadhyay, S., Jha, A., Nandi, M.: Fine-tuning the ISO/IEC Standard Lightmac. In: Proceedings of Advances in Cryptology - ASIACRYPT 2021, pp. 490–519 (2021)
9. Chattopadhyay, S., Jha, A., Nandi, M.: Towards tight security bounds for OMAC, XCBC and TMAC. IACR Cryptol. ePrint Arch. **2022**, 1234 (2022)
10. Dworkin, M.: Recommendation for block cipher modes of operation: the CMAC mode for authentication. NIST Special Publication 800–38b, National Institute of Standards and Technology, U. S. Department of Commerce (2005)
11. Ehrsam, W.F., Meyer, C.H.W., Smith, J.L., Tuchman, W.L.: Message verification and transmission error detection by block chaining. Patent 4,074,066, USPTO (1976)
12. Iwata, T., Kurosawa, K.: OMAC: One-Key CBC MAC. In: Fast Software Encryption - FSE 2003, Revised Papers, pp. 129–153 (2003)
13. Iwata, T., Kurosawa, K.: Stronger Security Bounds for OMAC, TMAC, and XCBC. In: Proceedings of Progress in Cryptology - INDOCRYPT 2003, pp. 402–415 (2003)
14. Jha, A., Mandal, A., Nandi, M.: On the exact security of message authentication using pseudorandom functions. IACR Trans. Symmetric Cryptol. **2017**(1), 427–448 (2017)
15. Jha, A., Nandi, M.: Revisiting structure graphs: applications to CBC-MAC and EMAC. J. Math. Cryptol. **10**(3–4), 157–180 (2016)
16. Jha, A., Nandi, M.: Revisiting structure graphs: applications to CBC-MAC and EMAC. IACR Cryptol. ePrint Arch. **2016**, 161 (2016)
17. Kurosawa, K., Iwata, T.: TMAC: two-key CBC MAC. In: Proceedings of Topics in Cryptology - CT-RSA 2003, pp. 33–49 (2003)
18. Luykx, A., Preneel, B., Tischhauser, E., Yasuda, K.: A MAC mode for lightweight block ciphers. In: Fast Software Encryption - FSE 2016, Revised Selected Papers, pp. 43–59 (2016)
19. Minematsu, K., Matsushima, T.: New bounds for PMAC, TMAC, and XCBC. In: Fast Software Encryption - FSE 2007, Revised Selected Papers, pp. 434–451 (2007)
20. Nandi, M.: Fast and secure CBC-type MAC algorithms. In: Fast Software Encryption - FSE 2009, Revised Selected Papers, pp. 375–393 (2009)
21. Nandi, M.: Improved security analysis for OMAC as a pseudorandom function. J. Math. Cryptol. **3**(2), 133–148 (2009)
22. Nandi, M., Mandal, A.: Improved security analysis of PMAC. J. Math. Cryptol. **2**(2), 149–162 (2008)

23. Patarin, J.: Etude des Générateurs de Permutations Pseudo-aléatoires Basés sur le Schéma du DES. Ph.D. thesis, Université de Paris (1991)
24. Patarin, J.: The "coefficients H" technique. In: Selected Areas in Cryptography - SAC 2008. Revised Selected Papers, pp. 328–345 (2008)
25. Pietrzak, K.: A tight bound for EMAC. In: Proceedings of Automata, Languages and Programming - ICALP 2006, Part II, pp. 168–179 (2006)

A Modular Approach to the Security Analysis of Two-Permutation Constructions

Yu Long Chen[✉]

imec-COSIC, KU Leuven, Leuven, Belgium
yulong.chen@kuleuven.be

Abstract. Constructions based on two public permutation calls are very common in today's cryptographic community. However, each time a new construction is introduced, a dedicated proof must be carried out to study the security of the construction. In this work, we propose a new tool to analyze the security of these constructions in a modular way. This tool is built on the idea of the classical mirror theory for block cipher based constructions, such that it can be used for security proofs in the ideal permutation model. We present different variants of this public permutation mirror theory such that it is suitable for different security notions.

We also present a framework to use the new techniques, which provides the bad events that need to be excluded in order to apply the public permutation mirror theory. Furthermore, we showcase the new technique on three examples: the Tweakable Even-Mansour cipher by Cogliati et al. (CRYPTO '15), the two permutation variant of the pEDM PRF by Dutta et al. (ToSC '21(2)), and the two permutation variant of the nEHtM$_p$ MAC algorithm by Dutta and Nandi (AFRICACRYPT '20). With this new tool we prove the *multi-user* security of these constructions in a considerably simplified way.

Keywords: Mirror theory · Two permutation calls constructions · Multi-user security · Modular framework

1 Introduction

PERMUTATION-BASED CRYPTO. Following the selection of Keccak as the winner of the SHA-3 competition [2], cryptographic schemes based on public permutations gained a lot of traction in the research community. Nowadays, permutation-based constructions have become a trend in cryptography, and form a successful and full-fledged alternative to block-cipher based designs. Recently, in the first round of the ongoing NIST lightweight competition [1], 24 out of 57 submissions are based on public permutations, and 16 out of 24 permutation-based designs have been selected for the second round. These statistics show without a doubt the wide acceptance of permutation based designs in the community. The long line of research on the design of secret key constructions using public permutations originates with Even and Mansour [23], who designed a secret random

© International Association for Cryptologic Research 2022
S. Agrawal and D. Lin (Eds.): ASIACRYPT 2022, LNCS 13791, pp. 379–409, 2022.
https://doi.org/10.1007/978-3-031-22963-3_13

permutation using a public permutation by xoring random keys to the input and output of this permutation. Later, their work was generalized to the Iterated Even-Mansour construction or the Key Alternating Cipher by [6,9,17,26], which is the backbone of today's block ciphers.

CONSTRUCTIONS BASED ON TWO PERMUTATION CALLS. In recent years, beyond birthday bound security has become a very popular topic in the field of symmetric key cryptography due to the rise of lightweight primitives. Admittedly, the state size of a permutation is typically very large: for example the SHA-3 permutation is of size 1600 bits, and a simple birthday bound secure construction built on SHA-3 would be secure up to an attack complexity of 2^{800}. However, this example permutation is on the extreme end: a big drawback of these big permutations is that they were not designed with lightweight applications in mind, the state of lightweight permutations such as SPONGENT [5] and PHOTON [25] can be as small as 88 and 100 bits, respectively. Hence, birthday bound secure constructions using these types of permutations are inadequate.

Due to the above-mentioned reason, beyond birthday-bound constructions based on two permutations are interesting to investigate. Indeed, it is possible to break any single-permutation construction by finding a collision between the input of the underlying permutation of the given construction and an input to the oracle of the public primitive, which happens with probability $\Omega(qp/2^n)$, where q is the number of queries to the construction and p is the number of queries to the underlying permutation. Constructions using more than two permutation calls can achieve even better security, however these are less efficient and difficult to analyze. On the other hand, constructions based on two permutation calls can achieve a resulting security bound of the form $O(qp^2/2^{2n})$, which is usually sufficient for most practical applications. In the last years, several types of constructions based on two permutation calls were proposed and analyzed. The most notable examples are the 2-round Even-Mansour cipher by Bogdanov et al. [6] and Chen et al. [8], the tweakable block cipher TEM by Cogliati et al. [15] and Dutta [19], the pseudorandom function SoEM by Chen et al. [11] and pEDM by Dutta et al. [22], the FPTP hash function by Chen and Tessaro [12], and the nonce-based MAC algorithm nEHtM$_p$ by Dutta and Nandi [20]. Due to the similarity in the structures, the security proofs of these construction all share some relevance.

SINGLE VS MULTI-USER SECURITY. The security of most of the above constructions has been proven in the single-user setting. In practice, however, commonly used cryptographic constructions are usually deployed in contexts with a large number of users. An obvious question is to what extent the number of users will affect the security bound of these permutation-based constructions, or more specifically, can these constructions still have a security bound of the form $O(qp^2/2^{2n})$ in the multi-user setting? The concept of multi-user security was first introduced by Bellare, Boldyreva and Micali [3] in the context of public key cryptography, and was later extended by Biham [4] to symmetric key cryptanalysis. In the multi-user setting, attackers can adaptively distribute their q construction queries across multiple users with independent keys, and the attackers succeed as long as they can compromise one user key. Unfortunately, research on provable multi-user security for permutation-based constructions has been missing until now. The notable exceptions are the work of key-alternating ciphers by Mouha and Luykx for a single round [31], and Hoang and Tessaro for multiple rounds [26]. These works show that evaluating how security degrades as the number of users grows is a challenging technical problem, even when the security is known in the single-user setting. The generic reduction [7], however, does not help the constructions to maintain beyond birthday-bound security in the multi-user setting. For example, suppose the number of users is u, then simply applying the generic reduction to obtain multi-user security from single-user security introduces an extra factor u in the security bound. If the attacker only asks one query per user, then the security bound becomes

$$\frac{uqp^2}{2^{2n}} \leq \frac{q^2 p^2}{2^{2n}},$$

which is only comparable to the $O(qp/2^n)$ security of one-call constructions.

Therefore, it appears that a dedicated analysis of the multi-user security is needed. Most security proofs in symmetric key cryptography today are based on the H-coefficients technique [9,33]. The idea behind this technique is that only a smaller number of transcripts are significantly more likely to appear in the ideal world than in the real world, namely: the bad transcripts. Usually, such proofs are performed as follows: (1) we first define a set of bad transcripts, (2) then the probability of observing bad transcripts in the ideal world is upper bounded, (3) and finally the ratio of observing good transcripts in the real and the ideal world is lower bounded. Note that points (1) and (3) are completely different problems than point (2). Since upper bounding the probability of the bad transcripts is a purely combinatorial problem and has little to do with cryptography, it relies heavily on the randomness of the generated keys. Defining the bad transcripts and lower bounding the ratio of the good transcripts depend, however, strongly on the way a particular construction is built. Unlike the case of block cipher-based constructions, where single-user security is usually proven in the standard model and multi-user security in the ideal-cipher model. For permutation-based constructions, ideal-permutation model analysis is used for both the single and multi-user settings. This raises the question whether or not it is possible to derive a modular approach that can be applied to constructions based on two permutation calls, which generically find the set of bad transcripts and a tight lower bound for the ratio of the corresponding good transcripts in both the *single* and *multi*-user settings, avoiding the long and involved dedicated analysis.

PATARIN'S MIRROR THEORY. Before we give an answer to this question, we recall Patarin's mirror theory [34], which is a very powerful but currently still unverified technique. Mirror theory is concerned with systems of $q_m \geq 1$ equations with $r \geq q_m$ unknowns of the form $v \oplus y = \lambda$, where v and y are two unknowns, and λ is a known value. The goal is to determine a lower bound on the number of possible solutions to the unknowns such that the solution does not contain collisions. Originally, Patarin derived mirror theory in order to prove the optimal n-bits security of the Xor of two secret Permutations construction (XoP). After the modernization by Mennink and Neves [30], who used mirror theory to prove the pseudorandom function security of EDM, EDMD and EWCDM, the applications of mirror theory seem to be increasing. For example, mirror theory was used to prove the security of the 2-round CLRW tweakable block cipher by Jha and Nandi [27], and to prove the security of the nonce-less MAC algorithms PolyMAC, SUM-ECBC, PMAC-Plus, 3kf9, and LightMAC-Plus by Kim et al. [28]. Datta et al. [18] were first to extend the mirror theory by including a system of $q_a \geq 1$ non-equations of the form $v \oplus y \neq \lambda$, and used it to prove the security of the nonce-based MAC algorithm DWCDM. Later, Dutta et al. [21], and Kim et al. [14] used it to prove the security of the nonce-based MAC algorithm nHEtM.

THE NEW IDEA. The reason why we can apply mirror theory to the above mentioned block cipher based constructions is because all these constructions can be viewed as the xor of two secret permutations. Note that when the permutations become public, the constructions have a structure that follows the Sum of Even-Mansour (SoEM) construction of Chen et al. [11]. Since the proofs of public permutation based constructions are all performed in the ideal permutation model, the attacker also gets access to the underlying permutations. Hence it is necessary to have an xor before the input and after the output of each of the permutation evaluations. Due to this important observation, almost all constructions based on two permutation calls can be viewed as the xor of two public permutations in the middle. This observation leads to the answer to the previous question, and the goal of this paper is to use the idea of mirror theory to build a modular technique that can be applied to all of the above mentioned permutation-based constructions.

1.1 Our Contribution

The goal of this paper is to derive a generic tool that can be used for the security analysis of constructions based on two public permutation calls and for different security notions. In order to do that, there are a few difficulties that we need to resolve. First of all, the traditional mirror theory is only suitable for the prf security, and we cannot simply apply it to the other settings. The second problem is that mirror theory does not consider primitive queries, and we need to include these queries in order to apply the theory for ideal permutation model proofs.

We solve the first problem using the approach proposed by Jha and Nandi [27] (see full version of the paper), and we derive different versions of public permutation mirror theory that are suitable for almost all popular security notions in symmetric key cryptography. On the other hand, since each primitive query defines exactly the input and the output of one permutation evaluation, we can solve the second problem by including a set of uni-variant affine equations of the form $v = \lambda$ and $y = \lambda$. Each uni-variate affine equation defines exactly one primitive query (where the input and output values of these queries are well defined).

With all these in mind, we derive two new theorems for the ideal public permutation model proofs. In Sect. 3.1, we explain the general setting for traditional mirror theory, and our new technique for the ideal permutation model is defined and given in Sect. 3.2. We provide four theorems for different type of settings. Theorem 1 (a) is suitable for security notions such as sprp and tsprp, Theorem 1 (b) is suitable for security notions such as prf, weak prf, and (t)ccr [24], and Theorem 2 (b) is suitable for notions such as mac security (prf with non-equations). Since these three theorems already cover all currently know security notions, Theorem 2 (a) (sprp or tsprp with non-equations) has been added for the sake of completeness, as we are not aware of any notions on which it can be applied and will leave this for future research. We want to emphasize that our aim here is not to fix the proofs in the traditional mirror theory, but rather to focus on a new modular technique for permutation-based constructions. Hence, our technique focuses only on $2n/3$-bit security, since this is a tight security bound (as we will see from the three examples) for constructions based on two permutations due to the presence of the primitive queries.

Another important contribution in this work is to provide a general framework to use the new techniques for the (multi-user) security analysis of constructions based on two independent permutation calls. The framework is given in Sect. 4. In general, to prove the security of constructions based on two permutation calls, one should first turn the query transcript into a system of bi-variate (non-)equations and uni-variate equations. This system of (non-)equations can be used to define the transcript graph (see Sect. 4.2). In our case, we decompose our graph into four subgraphs - the union of the components containing one "colliding vertex" (defined by an uni-variate affine equation), the union of "star" components, the set of isolated edges, and the set of isolated vertices. However, the graph may contain other types of components that prevent us from using the new technique, these components need to be excluded in our analysis. A very important part about this framework is that it provides a set of bad events that need to be considered in the security analysis to exclude these components. It seems, especially when non-equations also need to be considered, the analysis becomes very complex, which increases the chance to miss some bad events (see Sect. 4.3). The probability of these bad events must be upper bounded based on the randomness of the generated keys, sometimes difficult combinatorial techniques are required in the case of limited randomness. After these bad events are excluded, our new theory can be applied to the given system to determine a lower bound on the number of possible solutions to the unknowns, which in its turn defines the ratio of observing good transcripts in the real and the ideal world (see Sect. 4.4). This framework is useful for future designs, such that the future analysis will not miss any necessary bad events.

APPLICATIONS. We illustrate the new techniques by applying them to prove the *multi-user* security of Tweakable Even Mansour (TEM), permutation-based Encrypted Davies-Mayer (pEDM), and permutation-based version of nonce-based Enhance Hash-then-Mask (nEHtM$_p$). These three constructions are chosen because they use three important security notions in symmetric-key cryptography, namely tsprp, prf and mac, allowing us to demonstrate the new technique on different notions. On the other hand, the three constructions are the permutation-based variants of important block cipher-based schemes LRW2 [27], EDM [16], nEHtM [21], which have already received much attention in the field.

Firstly, we consider the 2-round TEM construction that was proposed by Cogliati et al. [15]. They showed that 2-round TEM achieves $2n/3$-bit security in the single-user setting. In Sect. 5, we apply the public permutation mirror theory suitable for tsprp (Theorem 1 (a)) to the TEM construction, and show that TEM also achieves $2n/3$-bit security in the multi-user setting.

Secondly, we consider the pEDM construction that was proposed by Dutta et al. [22]. Again, pEDM was showed to achieve $2n/3$-bit security in the single-user setting. In Sect. 6, we apply the public permutation mirror theory suitable for prf (Theorem 1 (b)) to pEDM construction, and show that pEDM also achieves $2n/3$-bit security in the multi-user setting. In this example we can clearly see that the analysis in the multi-user setting is more complex than the one in the single-user setting.

Thirdly, we consider the nEHtM_p MAC algorithm, proposed by Dutta and Nandi [20]. They showed that nEHtM_p based on a single permutation (using domain separation) achieves $2n/3$-bit security. We first note that the proof of [20] is incomplete since, according to our framework for MAC designs, the authors missed some bad events in their analysis. This observation was also verified by the authors [10]. Some of these additional bad events, however, require involved arguments to bound. In order to solve this problem, we modify the nEHtM_p construction by adding an extra universal hash function call. This modified construction uses more randomness, which in turn enables us to bound the additional bad events easily. We would like to note that our analysis does not imply infeasibility in fixing the proof of nEHtM_p. In Sect. 7, we will prove the *multi-user* security of this modified variant nEHtM_p using our public permutation extended mirror theory (Theorem 2 (b)), and we show that it achieves $2n/3$-bit security in the multi-user setting.

We believe that the techniques have a wide range of applications in the future design of public permutation based schemes. For example, when building nonce-less MAC algorithms and (authenticated) encryption schemes with beyond birthday bound security using public permutations, as done in the case of block cipher-based mirror theory [13,28].

2   Preliminaries

For $n \in \mathbb{N}$, we denote by $[n]$ the shorthand notation for $\{1, \ldots, n\}$, and by $\{0,1\}^n$ the set of bit strings of length n. For two bit strings $X, Y \in \{0,1\}^n$, we denote their bitwise addition as $X \oplus Y$. For a value Z, we denote by $A \leftarrow Z$ the assignment of Z to the variable A. For a finite set $\mathcal{S}$, we denote by $S \xleftarrow{\$} \mathcal{S}$ the uniformly random selection of S from $\mathcal{S}$. We denote by $\text{Func}(m, n)$ the set of all functions that map $\{0,1\}^m$ to $\{0,1\}^n$, and by $\text{Func}(n)$ the set of all functions that maps $\{0,1\}^n$ to $\{0,1\}^n$. We denote by $\text{Perm}(n)$ the set of all permutations on $\{0,1\}^n$, and by $\widetilde{\text{Perm}}(t, n)$ the set of all functions $\tilde{\pi} : \{0,1\}^t \times \{0,1\}^n \to \{0,1\}^n$

such that $\tilde{\pi}(T, \cdot)$ is in $\mathrm{Perm}(n)$ for all $T \in \{0,1\}^t$. For any integers a, b such that $1 \leq b \leq a$, we have $(a)_b = a \cdot (a-1) \ldots (a-b+1)$ and $(a)_0 = 1$.

For $q \in \mathbb{N}$, we denote by x^{*q} the q-tuple $(x_1, \ldots, x_q)$, and by $\hat{x}^{*q}$ the set $\{x_i : i \in [q]\}$. By an abuse of notation we also use x^{*q} to denote the multiset $\{x_i : i \in [q]\}$, and we denote by $\mu(x^{*q}, x')$ the multiplicity of $x' \in x^{*q}$. For two disjoint sets P and Q, we denote their (disjoint) union as $P \sqcup Q$.

2.1   Tweakable Block Ciphers Based on Public Permutations

For $k, n, r, t, u \in \mathbb{N}$, consider a tweakable block cipher $\tilde{E} : \{0,1\}^k \times \{0,1\}^t \times \{0,1\}^n \to \{0,1\}^n$ that is based on $\pi_1, \ldots, \pi_r \xleftarrow{\$} \mathrm{Perm}(n)$, such that for fixed key $K \in \{0,1\}^k$, the function $\tilde{E}_K(T, \cdot) = \tilde{E}(K, T, \cdot)$ is a permutation on $\{0,1\}^n$. We denote its inverse (for fixed key and tweak) by $\tilde{E}_K^{-1}(T, \cdot) = \tilde{E}^{-1}(K, T, \cdot)$, and $\tilde{E}_K^{-1}$ should behave independently for different tweaks. We will consider the multi-user tweakable strong pseudorandom permutation (mu-tsprp) security of $\tilde{E}$, where the distinguisher $\mathcal{D}$ is given two-directional access to either $(\tilde{E}_{K_1}^{\pm}, \ldots, \tilde{E}_{K_u}^{\pm}, \pi_1^{\pm}, \ldots, \pi_r^{\pm})$ for secret keys $K_1, \ldots, K_u \xleftarrow{\$} \{0,1\}^k$, or $(\tilde{\pi}_1^{\pm}, \ldots, \tilde{\pi}_u^{\pm}, \pi_1^{\pm}, \ldots, \pi_r^{\pm})$ for $\tilde{\pi}_1, \ldots, \tilde{\pi}_u \xleftarrow{\$} \widetilde{\mathrm{Perm}}(t, n)$. The goal is to determine which world it interacted with:

$$\mathbf{Adv}_{\tilde{E}}^{\mathrm{mu\text{-}tsprp}}(\mathcal{D}) = \left| \Pr\left[\mathcal{D}^{\tilde{E}_{K_1}^{\pm}, \ldots, \tilde{E}_{K_u}^{\pm}, \pi_1^{\pm}, \ldots, \pi_r^{\pm}} = 1 \right] - \Pr\left[\mathcal{D}^{\tilde{\pi}_1^{\pm}, \ldots, \tilde{\pi}_u^{\pm}, \pi_1^{\pm}, \ldots, \pi_r^{\pm}} = 1 \right] \right|.$$

Here the superscript $\pm$ indicates that the distinguisher has bi-directional access. When $u = 1$, we consider the single-user security of $\tilde{E}$, and we simply denote $\mathcal{D}$'s advantage in distinguishing the real world from random by $\mathbf{Adv}_{\tilde{E}}^{\mathrm{tsprp}}(\mathcal{D})$.

2.2   Pseudorandom Functions Based on Public Permutations

For $k, m, n, r, u \in \mathbb{N}$, consider a pseudorandom function $F \colon \{0,1\}^k \times \{0,1\}^m \to \{0,1\}^n$ that is based on $\pi_1, \ldots, \pi_r \xleftarrow{\$} \mathrm{Perm}(n)$, such that for fixed key $K \in \{0,1\}^k$, $F_K(\cdot) = F(K, \cdot)$ is a function that maps $\{0,1\}^m$ to $\{0,1\}^n$. We will consider the multi-user pseudorandom function (mu-prf) security of F, where the distinguisher $\mathcal{D}$ is given access to either $(F_{K_1}, \ldots, F_{K_u}, \pi_1^{\pm}, \ldots, \pi_r^{\pm})$ for secret keys $K_1, \ldots, K_u \xleftarrow{\$} \{0,1\}^k$, or $(\varphi_1, \ldots, \varphi_u, \pi_1^{\pm}, \ldots, \pi_r^{\pm})$ for $\varphi_1, \ldots, \varphi_u \xleftarrow{\$} \mathrm{Func}(n)$. The goal is to determine which world it interacted with:

$$\mathbf{Adv}_F^{\mathrm{mu\text{-}prf}}(\mathcal{D}) = \left| \Pr\left[\mathcal{D}^{F_{K_1}, \ldots, F_{K_u}, \pi_1^{\pm}, \ldots, \pi_r^{\pm}} = 1 \right] - \Pr\left[\mathcal{D}^{\varphi_1, \ldots, \varphi_u, \pi_1^{\pm}, \ldots, \pi_r^{\pm}} = 1 \right] \right|.$$

Here the superscript $\pm$ for π's indicates that the distinguisher has bi-directional access. When $u = 1$, we consider the single-user security of F, and we simply denote $\mathcal{D}$'s advantage in distinguishing the real world from random by $\mathbf{Adv}_F^{\mathrm{prf}}(\mathcal{D})$.

2.3   Nonce-Based MAC Algorithms Based on Public Permutations

For $k, n, r, t \in \mathbb{N}$, consider a nonce-based message authentication code (MAC) algorithm $F \colon \{0,1\}^k \times \{0,1\}^n \times \{0,1\}^* \to \{0,1\}^t$ that is based on $\pi_1, \ldots, \pi_r \xleftarrow{\$} \mathrm{Perm}(n)$. For any fixed key $K \in \{0,1\}^k$, we write $F_K(\cdot, \cdot) = F(K, \cdot, \cdot)$. We denote by $\mathsf{Ver} \colon \{0,1\}^k \times \{0,1\}^n \times \{0,1\}^* \times \{0,1\}^t \to 1/0$ the verification oracle that is based on $\pi_1, \ldots, \pi_r$, which takes as input a key $K \in \{0,1\}^k$, a nonce $N \in \{0,1\}^n$, a message $M \in \{0,1\}^*$, and tag $T \in \{0,1\}^t$, and outputs 1 if the tag T is correct and 0 otherwise.

For $u \in \mathbb{N}$, the multi-user message authentication code (mu-mac) security of F is measured by considering a distinguisher $\mathcal{D}$ that is given access to $(F_{K_1}, \mathsf{Ver}_{K_1}), \ldots, (F_{K_u}, \mathsf{Ver}_{K_u})$ for secret keys $K_1, \ldots, K_u \xleftarrow{\$} \{0,1\}^k$, and the primitive oracles $\pi_1, \ldots, \pi_r$. For any $j = 1, \ldots, u$, the goal of $\mathcal{D}$ is to fool the verification oracle with a valid but new (j, N, M, T), and its advantage with respect to this task is defined as

$$\mathbf{Adv}_F^{\mathrm{mu\text{-}mac}}(\mathcal{D}) = \Pr\left[K_1, \ldots, K_u \xleftarrow{\$} \{0,1\}^k \colon \right.$$
$$\left. \mathcal{D}^{(F_{K_1}, \mathsf{Ver}_{K_1}), \ldots, (F_{K_u}, \mathsf{Ver}_{K_u}), \pi_1^{\pm}, \ldots, \pi_r^{\pm}} \text{ forges}\right],$$

where "forges" means that the distinguisher enters a tuple (j, N, M, T) such that $\mathsf{Ver}_{K_j}(N, M, T)$ returns 1 and $F_{K_j}(N, M)$ has never been queried.

We call a MAC query to the j-th user (j, N, M) a faulty query if the distinguisher $\mathcal{D}$ has already queried F_{K_j} with the same nonce N and a different message M. The distinguisher $\mathcal{D}$ is allowed to make at most μ faulty MAC queries over u users. We call $\mathcal{D}$ a nonce-respecting adversary if $\mu = 0$, and nonce-misusing if $\mu \geq 1$. We stress that $\mathcal{D}$ may always repeat nonces in its verification queries.

It will be more convenient to express $\mathbf{Adv}_F^{\mathrm{mu\text{-}mac}}(\mathcal{D})$ as a distinguisher's advantage. For $j = 1, \ldots, u$, we define perfectly random oracles $\mathsf{Rand}_j \colon \{0,1\}^n \times \{0,1\}^* \to \{0,1\}^t$, and rejection oracles $\mathsf{Rej}_j \colon \{0,1\}^n \times \{0,1\}^* \times \{0,1\}^t \to 0$.

To obtain an upper bound for the forging advantage of a message authentication code F with respect to the distinguisher $\mathcal{D}$, we consider another distinguisher $\mathcal{D}'$, that is given access to either the real world oracles $\mathcal{O}, \pi_1^{\pm}, \ldots, \pi_r^{\pm}$, or the ideal world oracles $\mathcal{P}, \pi_1^{\pm}, \ldots, \pi_r^{\pm}$. Then, $\mathcal{D}'$'s advantage is upper bounded by:

$$\mathbf{Adv}_F^{\mathrm{mu\text{-}mac}}(\mathcal{D}') \leq \left| \Pr\left[\mathcal{D}'^{\mathcal{O}, \pi_1^{\pm}, \ldots, \pi_r^{\pm}} = 1\right] - \Pr\left[\mathcal{D}'^{\mathcal{P}, \pi_1^{\pm}, \ldots, \pi_r^{\pm}} = 1\right]\right|,$$

with $\mathcal{O} = ((F_{K_1}, \mathsf{Ver}_{K_1}), \ldots, (F_{K_u}, \mathsf{Ver}_{K_u}))$ for secret keys $K_1, \ldots, K_u \xleftarrow{\$} \{0,1\}^k$, and $\mathcal{P} = ((\mathsf{Rand}_1, \mathsf{Rej}_1), \ldots, (\mathsf{Rand}_u, \mathsf{Rej}_u))$.

Here the superscript $\pm$ for the π_i's indicates that the distinguisher has bi-directional access. We call a distinguisher $\mathcal{D}'$ non-trivial if it never makes a query (j, N, M, T) to its j-th verification oracle when a previous query (j, N, M) to its j-th MAC oracle returned T. When $u = 1$, we consider the single-user security of F, and we simply denote $\mathcal{D}'$'s advantage in distinguishing the real world from random by $\mathbf{Adv}_F^{\mathrm{mac}}(\mathcal{D}')$.

2.4   Universal Hash Functions

For $n \in \mathbb{N}$, let $H \colon \mathcal{K}_h \times \mathcal{M} \to \{0,1\}^n$ such that for $K_h \in \mathcal{K}_h$, $H_{K_h}(\cdot) = H(K_h, \cdot)$ is called an ϵ-almost XOR universal (ϵ-AXU) hash function [29] if for all distinct $M, M' \in \mathcal{M}$ and all $C \in \{0,1\}^n$, we have

$$\Pr\left[K_h \xleftarrow{\$} \mathcal{K}_h \colon H_{K_h}(M) \oplus H_{K_h}(M') = C\right] \le \epsilon.$$

For $q \in \mathbb{N}$, fix $M_1, \ldots, M_q \in \mathcal{M}$. For $K_h \in \mathcal{K}_h$, let $X_i = H_{K_h}(M_i)$ for $i = 1, \ldots, q$. We define an equivalence relation $\sim$ on $[q]$ as: $\alpha \sim \beta$ if and only if $X_\alpha = X_\beta$, for $\alpha, \beta \in [q]$. For $r \in \mathbb{N}$, we denote by $\mathcal{P}_1, \ldots, \mathcal{P}_r$ the non-trivial equivalence classes of $[q]$ with respect to $\sim$, and we define $\nu_i = |\mathcal{P}_i| \ge 2$ for $i = 1, \ldots, r$. Jha and Nandi [27] proved the following lemmas, that will be useful in our security proof.

Lemma 1. *Let $\nu_i, i = 1, \ldots, r$, be the random variables as defined above. Then, we have*

$$\boldsymbol{E}\left[\sum_{i=1}^{r} \nu_i\right] \le q^2 \epsilon/2, \qquad \boldsymbol{E}\left[\sum_{i=1}^{r} \nu_i^2\right] \le 2q^2 \epsilon.$$

Lemma 2. *Let $\nu_{\max} = \max\{\nu_i : i \in [r]\}$. Then, for some $a \ge 2$, we have*

$$\Pr[\nu_{\max} \ge a] \le \frac{2q^2 \epsilon}{a^2}.$$

2.5   Expectation Method

In this work, we use the expectation method by Hoang and Tessaro [26], a generalization of Patarin's H-coefficient technique [9,33].

Consider two oracles $\mathcal{O}$ and $\mathcal{P}$, and a deterministic distinguisher $\mathcal{D}$ that has query access to either of these oracles. The distinguisher's goal is to distinguish both worlds, and we denote by

$$\mathbf{Adv}(\mathcal{D}) = \left|\Pr\left[\mathcal{D}^{\mathcal{O}} = 1\right] - \Pr\left[\mathcal{D}^{\mathcal{P}} = 1\right]\right|$$

its advantage. We define a transcript τ which summarizes all query-response tuples learned by $\mathcal{D}$ during its interaction with its oracle $\mathcal{O}$ or $\mathcal{P}$. We denote by $X_{\mathcal{O}}$ and $X_{\mathcal{P}}$ the random variables equal to transcript produced when interacting with $\mathcal{O}$ and $\mathcal{P}$, respectively. We call a transcript $\tau \in \mathcal{T}$ attainable if $\Pr[X_{\mathcal{P}} = \tau] > 0$, or in other words if the transcript τ can be obtained from an interaction with $\mathcal{P}$.

Lemma 3 (expectation method [26]). *Consider a deterministic distinguisher $\mathcal{D}$. Define a partition $\mathcal{T} = \mathcal{T}_{\text{good}} \sqcup \mathcal{T}_{\text{bad}}$, where $\mathcal{T}_{\text{good}}$ is the subset of $\mathcal{T}$ which contains all the "good" transcripts and $\mathcal{T}_{\text{bad}}$ is the subset with all the* *"bad" transcripts. Let $\phi\colon \mathcal{T} \to [0,\infty)$ be a non-negative function mapping any attainable transcript to a non-negative real value, such that for all $\tau \in \mathcal{T}_{\text{good}}$:*

$$\frac{\Pr[X_{\mathcal{O}} = \tau]}{\Pr[X_{\mathcal{P}} = \tau]} \geq 1 - \phi(\tau). \tag{1}$$

Then, we have $\mathbf{Adv}(\mathcal{D}) \leq \mathbf{E}[\phi(X_{\mathcal{P}})] + \Pr[X_{\mathcal{P}} \in \mathcal{T}_{\text{bad}}]$.

The H-coefficients technique can be seen as a simple corollary of the expectation method when ϕ is equal to a constant function. **Preliminary Observations.**

For $\pi \xleftarrow{\$} \text{Perm}(n)$ and a permutation queries transcript τ_π, we say that π extends τ_π, denoted $\pi \vdash \tau_\pi$, if $\pi(u) = v$ for all $(u,v) \in \tau_\pi$. By extension, for $\boldsymbol{\pi} = (\pi_1, \ldots, \pi_r) \xleftarrow{\$} \left(\text{Perm}(n)\right)^r$ and a tuple of permutation queries transcript $\tau_{\boldsymbol{\pi}} = (\tau_{\pi_1}, \ldots, \tau_{\pi_r})$, we say that $\boldsymbol{\pi}$ extends $\tau_{\boldsymbol{\pi}}$, denoted $\boldsymbol{\pi} \vdash \tau_{\boldsymbol{\pi}}$, if $\pi_i \vdash \tau_{\pi_i}$ for $i = 1, \ldots, r$.

Consider an attainable transcript $\tau \in \mathcal{T}_{\text{good}}$, and let $\mathcal{P}$ be an uniformly chosen random oracle. For permutation based constructions, let $\tau = (\tau_0, \tau_{\boldsymbol{\pi}})$, where τ_0 contains queries to the construction oracle $\mathcal{O}$ or $\mathcal{P}$, and $\tau_{\boldsymbol{\pi}}$ contains the queries to the primitive oracles $\boldsymbol{\pi} = (\pi_1, \ldots, \pi_r)$. To compute $\Pr[X_{\mathcal{O}} = \tau]$ and $\Pr[X_{\mathcal{P}} = \tau]$, it suffices to compute the probability of oracles that could result in view τ. We first consider the ideal world oracle $\mathcal{P}$, and obtain

$$\Pr[X_{\mathcal{P}} = \tau] = \frac{1}{|\mathcal{K}|^r} \cdot \left(\frac{1}{(2^n)_p}\right)^r \cdot \Pr[\mathcal{P}\colon \mathcal{P} \vdash \tau_0].$$

The first term corresponds to the number of dummy keys that are drawn uniformly at random; the second term is the probability that $\boldsymbol{\pi}$ extends $\tau_{\boldsymbol{\pi}}$; and the last term is the probability that $\mathcal{P}$ extends τ_0.

Similarly we say that a real world oracle $\mathcal{O}$ extends τ if it extends τ_0 and $\tau_{\boldsymbol{\pi}}$. For $K \xleftarrow{\$} \mathcal{K}^r$, we have

$$\Pr[X_{\mathcal{O}} = \tau] = \frac{1}{|\mathcal{K}|^r} \cdot \left(\frac{1}{(2^n)_p}\right)^r \cdot \Pr\left[\boldsymbol{\pi} \xleftarrow{\$} \left(\text{Perm}(n)\right)^r \colon \mathcal{O}_K^{\boldsymbol{\pi}} \vdash \tau_0 \mid \boldsymbol{\pi} \vdash \tau_{\boldsymbol{\pi}}\right].$$

The first term corresponds to the number of randomly drawn keys that are used in the construction; the second term is the probability that $\boldsymbol{\pi}$ extends $\tau_{\boldsymbol{\pi}}$; and the last term is the probability that $\mathcal{O}_K^{\boldsymbol{\pi}}$ extends τ_0, given that $\boldsymbol{\pi}$ extends $\tau_{\boldsymbol{\pi}}$.

Let $\rho(\tau) = \Pr\left[\boldsymbol{\pi} \xleftarrow{\$} \left(\text{Perm}(n)\right)^r \colon \mathcal{O}_K^{\boldsymbol{\pi}} \vdash \tau_0 \mid \boldsymbol{\pi} \vdash \tau_{\boldsymbol{\pi}}\right]$. Take for instance $r = 2$, and assume that each primitive query transcript contains p queries to the given permutation. Suppose we sample distinct outputs of π_1 (resp., π_2) over for example q_V (resp., q_Y) distinct inputs. Then, it is easy to see that $\rho(\tau) = h_q/(2^n - p)_{q_V - p}(2^n - p)_{q_Y - p}$, where h_q is the number of solutions of distinct outputs of π_1 and π_2. Then we have

$$\frac{\Pr[X_{\mathcal{O}} = \tau]}{\Pr[X_{\mathcal{P}} = \tau]} = \rho(\tau)/\Pr[\mathcal{P}\colon \mathcal{P} \vdash \tau_0] \geq 1 - \varepsilon_1. \tag{2}$$

3 (Extended) Mirror Theory in Ideal Permutation Model

We explain the general settings behind the traditional (extended) mirror theory in Sect. 3.1, which involves only bi-variate affine equations and possible non-equations. In Sect. 3.2, we introduce the new public permutation mirror theory, that takes primitive queries into account by including uni-variate affine equations.

3.1 System of Bi-variate Affine Equations and Non-equations

Let $q_m, q_a, q_V, q_Y \geq 1$. Let $\mathcal{V} = \{v_1, \ldots, v_{q_V}\}$ be a set of q_V unknowns and $\mathcal{Y} = \{y_1, \ldots, y_{q_Y}\}$ be a set of q_Y unknowns. We consider a system $\mathcal{E}_m$ of q_m bi-variate affine equations

$$\mathcal{E}_m = \{v_{I_1} \oplus y_{I_1} = \lambda_1, \ldots, v_{I_{q_m}} \oplus y_{I_{q_m}} = \lambda_{q_m}\}.$$

In some cases (for example mac security), we also need to consider a system $\mathcal{E}_a$ of q_a bi-variate affine non-equations

$$\mathcal{E}_a = \{v'_{J_1} \oplus y'_{J_1} \neq \lambda'_1, \ldots, v'_{J_{q_a}} \oplus y'_{J_{q_a}} \neq \lambda'_{q_a}\},$$

where v_{I_i}'s, y_{I_i}'s, v'_{J_j}'s, and y'_{J_j}'s are unknowns, and λ_i's and λ'_j's are knowns, for $i = 1, \ldots, q_m$ and $j = 1, \ldots, q_a$. We want to state that the sets $\mathcal{V}$ and $\mathcal{Y}$ are disjoint.

We define two surjective index mappings:

$$\varphi_V : \{I_1, \ldots, I_{q_m}, J_1, \ldots, J_{q_a}\} \rightarrow \{1, \ldots, q_V\},$$
$$\varphi_Y : \{I_1, \ldots, I_{q_m}, J_1, \ldots, J_{q_a}\} \rightarrow \{1, \ldots, q_Y\}.$$

such that $q_V, q_Y \leq q_m + q_a$. Note that I_i and J_j are respectively the indices of the unknowns in $\mathcal{E}_m$ and $\mathcal{E}_a$. However, multiple unknowns with different indices can be the same. In that case, these unknown are all mapped to the same value using φ_V or φ_Y. The system $\mathcal{E} = \mathcal{E}_m \sqcup \mathcal{E}_a$ is uniquely determined by $(\varphi'_V, \varphi'_Y, \lambda^{*q_m}, \lambda'^{*q_a})$.

Consider a graph $\mathcal{G}(\mathcal{E}) = (\mathcal{V}, \mathcal{Y}, \mathcal{S} \sqcup \mathcal{S}')$, where the edge set is partitioned into two disjoint sets $\mathcal{S}$ and $\mathcal{S}'$. Here $\mathcal{S}$ and $\mathcal{S}'$ denote the set of λ-labeled edges and the set of λ'-labeled edges, respectively. The graph $\mathcal{G}(\mathcal{E})$ can be seen as a superposition of two subgraphs $\mathcal{G}(\mathcal{E}_m) = (\mathcal{V}, \mathcal{Y}, \mathcal{S})$ and $\mathcal{G}(\mathcal{E}_a) = (\mathcal{V}, \mathcal{Y}, \mathcal{S}')$. Let $\overline{v_s y_t} \in \mathcal{S}$ be an edge for $v_s \in \mathcal{V}$ and $y_t \in \mathcal{Y}$, then $\overline{v_s y_t}$ is labeled with an element in λ^{*q_m}. If the given edge is labeled with λ_i (for $i = 1, \ldots, q_m$), then this edge and the connected vertices v_s and y_t represent the equation $v_s \oplus y_t = \lambda_i$, where $s = \varphi_V(I_i)$ and $t = \varphi_Y(I_i)$. Similarly, let $\overline{v_s y_t} \in \mathcal{S}'$ be an edge for $v_s \in \mathcal{V}$ and $y_t \in \mathcal{Y}$, then $\overline{v_s y_t}$ is labeled with an element in λ'^{*q_a}. If the given edge is labeled with λ'_j (for $j = 1, \ldots, q_a$), then this edge and the connected vertices v_s and y_t represent the non-equation $v_s \oplus y_t \neq \lambda'_j$, where $s = \varphi_V(J_j)$ and $t = \varphi_Y(J_j)$. Here, each equation in $\mathcal{E}_m$ corresponds to a unique λ-labeled edge in $\mathcal{G}(\mathcal{E}_m)$, and each non-equation in $\mathcal{E}_a$ corresponds to a unique λ'-labeled edge in $\mathcal{G}(\mathcal{E}_a)$.

Note that when the system of non-equations $\mathcal{E}_a$ is empty, then the graph $\mathcal{G}(\mathcal{E})$ does not contain isolated vertices, every vertex is incident with at least one λ-labeled edge. Otherwise, the subgraph $\mathcal{G}(\mathcal{E}_m)$ may contain isolated vertices, and these vertices are connected with a λ'-labeled edge in $\mathcal{G}(\mathcal{E}_a)$.

We say two distinct equations in $\mathcal{E}_m$ are in the same component if and only if the corresponding edges (or vertices) in $\mathcal{G}(\mathcal{E}_m)$ are in the same component. Let $\ell > 0$ and a path

$$\mathcal{L} : a_0 \overset{\lambda_1}{-} a_1 \overset{\lambda_2}{-} \ldots \overset{\lambda_\ell}{-} a_\ell$$

in $\mathcal{G}(\mathcal{E}_m)$, for some vertices $a_0, a_1, \ldots, a_\ell \in \mathcal{V} \sqcup \mathcal{Y}$ that are in the same component. The label of $\mathcal{L}$ is defined as

$$\lambda(\mathcal{L}) = \lambda_1 \oplus \lambda_2 \oplus \ldots \oplus \lambda_\ell.$$

In case $\mathcal{E}_a$ is empty, a graph $\mathcal{G}(\mathcal{E})$ is called a *good* graph if its subgraph $\mathcal{G}(\mathcal{E}_m)$ satisfies the following properties.

Definition 1 (acyclic). *There is an unique path $\mathcal{L}$ in the subgraph $\mathcal{G}(\mathcal{E}_m)$ between any two vertices a and b in the same connected component, for $a, b \in \mathcal{V} \sqcup \mathcal{Y}$.*

Definition 2 (non-degeneracy). *For all paths $\mathcal{L}$ of even length at least 2 in the subgraph $\mathcal{G}(\mathcal{E}_m)$, we have $\lambda(\mathcal{L}) \neq 0$.*

Definition 3. (ξ-block-maximality). *For a component $\mathcal{I}$, we denote its size by $\xi(\mathcal{I})$, which is the number of vertices in $\mathcal{I}$. We denote the maximum component size by $\xi_{\max}$ such that $\xi(\mathcal{I}) \leq \xi_{\max}$ for all $\mathcal{I}$ in $\mathcal{G}(\mathcal{E}_m)$.*

In case the system $\mathcal{E}_a$ contains at least one non-equation, a graph $\mathcal{G}(\mathcal{E})$ is called a *good* graph if its subgraph $\mathcal{G}(\mathcal{E}_m)$ satisfies the above three properties, and if $\mathcal{G}(\mathcal{E})$ also satisfies the following property.

Definition 4 (non-zero cycle label (NCL)). *If vertices v and y are connected with a λ'-labeled edge, then they are not connected by a $\lambda(\mathcal{L})$-labeled path in $\mathcal{G}(\mathcal{E}_m)$ such that $\lambda(\mathcal{L}) = \lambda'$, for $v \in \mathcal{V}'$ and $y \in \mathcal{Y}'$.*

In an edge-labeled bipartite graph $\mathcal{G}$, we call a component $\mathcal{I}$ of $\mathcal{G}$ an isolated component if $\mathcal{I}$ only contains a path of length one. So $\mathcal{I}$ only contains an edge (v, y, λ) where both v and y have degree 1. We call a component $\mathcal{I}$ of $\mathcal{G}$ a star component if $\xi(\mathcal{I}) \geq 3$, and if there is an unique vertex in $\mathcal{I}$ with degree $\xi(\mathcal{I}) - 1$. We call this vertex the center of $\mathcal{I}$. Further, we call $\mathcal{I}$ a v-$\star$ (resp., y-$\star$) component if its center lies in v (resp., y).

3.2   System of Bi-variate and Uni-variate Affine Equations and Bi-variate Affine Non-equations

In order to handle the primitive queries, we extend the system of bi-variate affine equations and non-equations with $2p$ uni-variate affine equations. Each uni-variate affine equation defines one primitive queries. Let $q_m, q_a, q_V^p, q_Y^p, p \geq 1$. Let $\mathcal{V}^p = \{v_1, \ldots, v_{q_V^p}\}$ be a set of q_V^p unknowns and $\mathcal{Y}^p = \{y_1, \ldots, y_{q_Y^p}\}$ be a set of q_Y^p unknowns. The new systems are $\mathcal{E}_m^p$, that contains q_m bi-variate affine equations and $2p$ uni-variate affine equations

$$\mathcal{E}_m^p = \{v_{I_1} \oplus y_{I_1} = \lambda_1, \ldots, v_{I_{q_m}} \oplus y_{I_{q_m}} = \lambda_{q_m},$$
$$v_{I_{q_m+1}} = \lambda_{q_m+1}, \ldots, v_{I_{q_m+p}} = \lambda_{q_m+p},$$
$$y_{I_{q_m+1}} = \lambda_{q_m+p+1}, \ldots, y_{I_{q_m+p}} = \lambda_{q_m+2p}\}.$$

In some cases (for example mac security), we also need to consider a system $\mathcal{E}_a$ of q_a bi-variate affine non-equations

$$\mathcal{E}_a = \{v'_{J_1} \oplus y'_{J_1} \neq \lambda'_1, \ldots, v'_{J_{q_a}} \oplus y'_{J_{q_a}} \neq \lambda'_{q_a}\},$$

where v_{I_i}'s, y_{I_i}'s, v'_{J_j}'s, and y'_{J_j}'s are unknowns, and λ_k's and λ'_j's are knowns, for $i = 1, \ldots, q_m + p$, $j = 1, \ldots, q_a$, and $k = 1, \ldots, q_m + 2p$, such that $\lambda_{q_m+1} \neq \cdots \neq \lambda_{q_m+p}$ and $\lambda_{q_m+p+1} \neq \cdots \neq \lambda_{q_m+2p}$. We want to state that the sets $\mathcal{V}^p$ and $\mathcal{Y}^p$ are disjoint.

We define two surjective index mappings:

$$\varphi_V^p : \{I_1, \ldots, I_{q_m+p}, J_1, \ldots, J_{q_a}\} \to \{1, \ldots, q_V^p\},$$
$$\varphi_Y^p : \{I_1, \ldots, I_{q_m+p}, J_1, \ldots, J_{q_a}\} \to \{1, \ldots, q_Y^p\},$$

such that $q_V, q_Y \leq q_m + q_a + p$. The system $\mathcal{E}^p = \mathcal{E}_m^p \sqcup \mathcal{E}_a$ is uniquely determined by $(\varphi_V^p, \varphi_Y^p, \lambda^{*q_m+2p}, \lambda'^{*q_a})$.

Since the last $2p$ uni-variate affine equations define the values of the $2p$ unknowns v_{I_i}'s and y_{I_i}'s exactly, for $i = q_m + 1, \ldots, q_m + p$, we know that exactly p unknowns in $\mathcal{V}^p$ and p unknowns in $\mathcal{Y}^p$ are already well defined by the system $\mathcal{E}_m^p$. We define

$$V_0 = \{v_{\varphi_V^p(I_{q_m+1})}, \ldots, v_{\varphi_V^p(I_{q_m+p})}\}, \qquad Y_0 = \{y_{\varphi_Y^p(I_{q_m+1})}, \ldots, y_{\varphi_Y^p(I_{q_m+p})}\},$$

as the sets that contain these $2p$ unknowns such that $|V_0| = p$ and $|Y_0| = p$. We are particularly interested in the unknowns from the sets $\mathcal{V}^p \setminus V_0$ and $\mathcal{Y}^p \setminus Y_0$, since these are the unknowns that appear in the q_m bi-variate affine equations and q_a bi-variate affine non-equations.

Consider a bipartite edge-labeled graph $\mathcal{G}(\mathcal{E}^p) = (\mathcal{V}^p, \mathcal{Y}^p, \mathcal{S} \sqcup \mathcal{S}')$, the edge set is partitioned into two disjoint sets $\mathcal{S}$ and $\mathcal{S}'$ as before. The graph $\mathcal{G}(\mathcal{E}^p)$ can be seen as a superposition of two subgraphs $\mathcal{G}(\mathcal{E}_m^p) = (\mathcal{V}^p, \mathcal{Y}^p, \mathcal{S})$ and $\mathcal{G}(\mathcal{E}_a) = (\mathcal{V}^p, \mathcal{Y}^p, \mathcal{S}')$. Here, each of the q_m bi-variate affine equations in $\mathcal{E}_m^p$ corresponds to a unique λ-labeled edge in $\mathcal{G}(\mathcal{E}_m^p)$, each non-equation in $\mathcal{E}_a$ corresponds to a unique λ'-labeled edge in $\mathcal{G}(\mathcal{E}_a)$, and each of the $2p$ uni-variate affine equations in $\mathcal{E}_m^p$ corresponds to a vertex with well defined value in $\mathcal{G}(\mathcal{E}^p)$. Note that the subgraph $\mathcal{G}(\mathcal{E}_m^p)$ may contain isolated vertices, and these vertices are either connected with a λ'-labeled edge in $\mathcal{G}(\mathcal{E}_a)$ or they are isolated colliding vertices in $\mathcal{G}(\mathcal{E}^p)$ with a well-defined value. The subgraph $\mathcal{G}(\mathcal{E}_m^p)$ may also contain components that contain vertices with well defined value. We call these components the "colliding components", and the vertices with well defined values the "colliding vertices".

We distinguish two different cases. In the first case, assume that $\mathcal{E}_a$ is empty, hence we will focus on a graph $\mathcal{G}(\mathcal{E}^p)$ where its subgraph $\mathcal{G}(\mathcal{E}_m^p)$ satisfies the (i) acyclic, (ii) non-degeneracy, and (iii) ξ-block-maximality properties (Definition 1–3). In addition, $\mathcal{G}(\mathcal{E}_m^p)$ also needs to satisfy the following property.

Definition 5 (single colliding vertex (SCV)).   *Each component in the graph $\mathcal{G}(\mathcal{E}_m^p)$ contains at most one colliding vertex.*

Note that Definition 5 is necessary in order to give a unique assignment to every vertex in the graph, since if a vertex is assigned with any value, then the labeled edges determine the values of all other vertices in the component containing this vertex. We call any graph that satisfies these four properties a *good* graph. Given a good graph $\mathcal{G}(\mathcal{E}_m^p) = (\mathcal{V}^p, \mathcal{Y}^p, \mathcal{S})$, a solution to $\mathcal{G}(\mathcal{E}_m^p)$ is an assignment of distinct values to the v vertices in $\mathcal{V}^p$ and distinct values to the y vertices in $\mathcal{Y}^p$ satisfying all λ-labeled equations.

We consider a system of bi-variate and uni-variate affine equations $\mathcal{E}_m^p$, such that each component in $\mathcal{G}(\mathcal{E}_m^p)$ is either an isolated edge, a star, or isolated colliding vertex. In order to find the number of solutions to $\mathcal{G}(\mathcal{E}_m^p)$, we first decompose the graph $\mathcal{G}(\mathcal{E}_m^p)$ into its connected components such that $\mathcal{G}(\mathcal{E}_m^p) = \mathcal{I} \sqcup \mathcal{A} \sqcup \mathcal{B} \sqcup \mathcal{C}$, where

$$\mathcal{A} = \mathcal{A}_1 \sqcup \cdots \sqcup \mathcal{A}_{c_1} \sqcup \mathcal{A}_{c_1+1} \sqcup \cdots \sqcup \mathcal{A}_{c_1+c_2},$$
$$\mathcal{B} = \mathcal{B}_1 \sqcup \cdots \sqcup \mathcal{B}_{c_3} \sqcup \mathcal{B}_{c_3+1} \sqcup \cdots \sqcup \mathcal{B}_{c_3+c_4},$$
$$\mathcal{C} = \mathcal{C}_1 \sqcup \cdots \sqcup \mathcal{C}_{c_5},$$

for some $c_1, c_2, c_3, c_4, c_5 \geq 0$. Here $\mathcal{I}$ is the union of isolated colliding vertices. $\mathcal{A}$ is the union of colliding components, where $\mathcal{A}_1 \sqcup \cdots \sqcup \mathcal{A}_{c_1}$ is the union of colliding components with a colliding v vertex; and $\mathcal{A}_{c_1+1} \sqcup \cdots \sqcup \mathcal{A}_{c_1+c_2}$ is the union of colliding components with a colliding y vertex. $\mathcal{B}$ is the union of the remaining star components (that are not colliding components), where $\mathcal{B}_1 \sqcup \cdots \sqcup \mathcal{B}_{c_3}$ is the union of v-$\star$ components, and $\mathcal{B}_{c_3+1} \sqcup \cdots \sqcup \mathcal{B}_{c_3+c_4}$ is the union of y-$\star$ components. $\mathcal{C}$ is the union of the remaining isolated components (that are not colliding components).

Let $q_1, q_2, q_3, q_4,$ and q_5 denote the number of equations (edges) in $\mathcal{A}_1 \sqcup \cdots \sqcup \mathcal{A}_{c_1}$, $\mathcal{A}_{c_1+1} \sqcup \cdots \sqcup \mathcal{A}_{c_1+c_2}$, $\mathcal{B}_1 \sqcup \cdots \sqcup \mathcal{B}_{c_3}$, $\mathcal{B}_{c_3+1} \sqcup \cdots \sqcup \mathcal{B}_{c_3+c_4}$, and $\mathcal{C}$, respectively. Therefore, we have $c_5 = q_5$. Note that the equations in $\mathcal{E}_m^p$ can be arranged in any arbitrary order without affecting the number of solutions. For the sake of simplicity, we fix the ordering in such a way that the union $\mathcal{I}$ comes first, followed by $\mathcal{A}$, $\mathcal{B}$, and $\mathcal{C}$. Now, our goal is to give a lower bound on the number of solutions of $\mathcal{E}_m^p$.

Theorem 1. *For positive integers q_m and p, let $\mathcal{G}(\mathcal{E}_m^p) = (\mathcal{V}^p, \mathcal{Y}^p, \mathcal{S})$ be a good graph as described above such that $|\mathcal{S}| = q_m$. Assume that $p + q_m \leq 2^{n-2}$ and $\xi_{max} \cdot (p + q_m) \leq 2^{n-1}$, let $h(\mathcal{G}(\mathcal{E}_m^p))$ denote the number of solutions to $\mathcal{G}(\mathcal{E}_m^p)$.*

(a) *For settings such as (t)sprp, we have*

$$\frac{h(\mathcal{G}(\mathcal{E}_m^p))\prod_{\lambda' \in \hat{\lambda}^{q_m}}(2^n)_{\mu(\lambda^{*q_m},\lambda')}}{(2^n - p)_{q_2+c_3+q_4+q_5}(2^n - p)_{q_1+q_3+c_4+q_5}} \geq 1 - \frac{\sum_{i=1}^{c_1+c_2}q_m}{2^n} - \frac{3q_m^3}{2^{2n}}$$
$$- \frac{2(p+q_m)^2}{2^{2n}}\left(\eta + q_m\right).$$

(b) *For settings such as prf, weak prf, (t)ccr, we have*

$$\frac{h(\mathcal{G}(\mathcal{E}_m^p))2^{nq_m}}{(2^n - p)_{q_2+c_3+q_4+q_5}(2^n - p)_{q_1+q_3+c_4+q_5}} \geq 1 - \frac{2(p+q_m)^2}{2^{2n}}\left(\eta + q_m\right).$$

where $\eta = \sum_{i=c_1+c_2}^{c_1+c_2+c_3+c_4-1}(\eta_{i+1}^2 + \eta_{i+1})$, $\eta_j = \xi_j - 1$ *and* ξ_j *denotes the size (number of vertices) of the j-th component, for all* $j \in [c_1 + c_2 + c_3 + c_4 + c_5]$.

Proof. The proof is given in the full version of the paper. □

We will illustrate Theorem 1 (a) to tweakable block ciphers in Sect. 5, and Theorem 1 (b) to PRFs in Sect. 6. Looking back at the discussion given towards the end of Sect. 2.5, one can see the motivation behind the difference between the expressions given in Theorem 1 (a) and Theorem 1 (b).

For the second case, the system $\mathcal{E}_a$ contains at least one non-equation. Here we will focus on a graph $\mathcal{G}(\mathcal{E}^p)$ such that its subgraph $\mathcal{G}(\mathcal{E}_m^p)$ satisfies the (i) acyclic, (ii) non-degeneracy, (iii) ξ-block-maximality, (v) NCL, and (iv) SCV properties (Definition 1–5). In addition, $\mathcal{G}(\mathcal{E})$ also need to satisfy the following property.

Definition 6 (non-zero distance label (NDL)). *There are no* λ'*-labeled edges that connect two vertices v and y from two colliding components* $\mathcal{I}_1$ *and* $\mathcal{I}_2$, *where the distance between v and y (defined as* $v \oplus y$*) is* λ', *for* $v \in \mathcal{V}'^p$ *and* $y \in \mathcal{Y}'^p$.

Note that if there is a λ'-labeled non-equations between vertices v and y of two different colliding components, then it means $v \oplus y \neq \lambda'$. However, for any colliding component, the values of all vertices in this component are uniquely defined. If the distance $v \oplus y$ is equal to λ', then we will have a contradiction with the non-equation. Definition 6 actually excludes this situation. We call any graph that satisfies these six properties a *good* graph. Given a good graph $\mathcal{G}(\mathcal{E}^p) = (\mathcal{V}^p, \mathcal{Y}^p, \mathcal{S} \sqcup \mathcal{S}')$, a solution to $\mathcal{G}(\mathcal{E}^p)$ is an assignment of distinct values to the v vertices in $\mathcal{V}^p$ and distinct values to the y vertices in $\mathcal{Y}^p$ satisfying all λ-labeled equations and λ'-labeled non-equations.

We consider a system $\mathcal{E}^p$ with its corresponding graph $\mathcal{G}(\mathcal{E}^p)$ such that each component in the subgraph $\mathcal{G}(\mathcal{E}_m^p)$ is a star, an isolated edge, or an isolated vertex. In order to find the number of solutions to $\mathcal{G}(\mathcal{E}^p)$, we first decompose the subgraph $\mathcal{G}(\mathcal{E}_m^p)$ into its connected components such that $\mathcal{G}(\mathcal{E}_m^p) = \mathcal{I} \sqcup \mathcal{A} \sqcup \mathcal{B} \sqcup \mathcal{C} \sqcup \mathcal{D}$, with $\mathcal{I}, \mathcal{A}, \mathcal{B}$, and $\mathcal{C}$ the union of components defined before. Here, $\mathcal{D}$ is the union of isolated vertices in the subgraph $\mathcal{G}(\mathcal{E}_m^p)$ that are not colliding vertices, note that these vertices are connected with λ'-labeled edges in the subgraph $\mathcal{G}(\mathcal{E}_a)$. Let c_6 be the number of such isolated v vertices, and c_7 be the number of such isolated y vertices. Again, we fix the ordering in such a way that the union $\mathcal{I}$ comes first, followed by $\mathcal{A}, \mathcal{B}, \mathcal{C}$, and $\mathcal{D}$. Now, our goal is to give a lower bound on the number of solutions of $\mathcal{E}^p$.

Theorem 2. *For positive integers q_m, q_a and p, let $\mathcal{G}(\mathcal{E}^p) = (\mathcal{V}'^p, \mathcal{Y}'^p, \mathcal{S} \sqcup \mathcal{S}')$ be a good graph as described above such that $|\mathcal{S}| = q_m$, $|\mathcal{S}'| = q_a$. Assume that $p + q_m \leq 2^{n-2}$ and $\xi_{\max} \cdot (p + q_m) \leq 2^{n-1}$, let $h(\mathcal{G}(\mathcal{E}^p))$ denote the number of solutions to $\mathcal{G}(\mathcal{E}^p)$.*

(a) For settings such as (t)sprp with non-equations, we have

$$\frac{h(\mathcal{G}(\mathcal{E}^p)) \prod_{\lambda' \in \hat{\lambda}^{qm}} (2^n)_{\mu(\lambda^{*qm}, \lambda')}}{(2^n - p)_{q_2 + c_3 + q_4 + q_5 + c_6} (2^n - p)_{q_1 + q_3 + c_4 + q_5 + c_7}} \geq 1 - \frac{\sum_{i=1}^{c_1 + c_2} q_m}{2^n} - \frac{3q_m^3}{2^{2n}}$$
$$- \frac{2(p + q_m)^2}{2^{2n}} \left(\eta + q_m \right) - \frac{2q_a}{2^n}.$$

(b) For settings such as mac (prf with non-equations), we have

$$\frac{h(\mathcal{G}(\mathcal{E}^p)) 2^{nq_m}}{(2^n - p)_{q_2 + c_3 + q_4 + q_5 + c_6} (2^n - p)_{q_1 + q_3 + c_4 + q_5 + c_7}} \geq 1 - \frac{2(p + q_m)^2}{2^{2n}} \left(\eta + q_m \right) - \frac{2q_a}{2^n}.$$

where $\eta = \sum_{i=c_1 + c_2}^{c_1 + c_2 + c_3 + c_4 - 1} (\eta_{i+1}^2 + \eta_{i+1})$, $\eta_j = \xi_j - 1$ and ξ_j denotes the size (number of vertices) of the j-th component, for all $j \in [c_1 + c_2 + c_3 + c_4 + c_5]$.

Proof. The proof is given in the full version of the paper. □

We will illustrate Theorem 2 (b) to nonce-based MAC algorithms in Sect. 7.

4 A Framework for Security Proof Using Public Permutation Mirror Theory

The goal of this section is to establish a general framework for (multi-user) security proof using Theorem 1–2. Note that a framework for specific security notions such as sprp, tsprp, prf, mac, ... can be derived directly from this framework. We consider an algorithm F which is built on two independent public permutations with the following special structure.

Let $n, s, t \in \mathbb{N}$, and let $\pi_1, \pi_2 \xleftarrow{\$} \mathrm{Perm}(n)$. One can consider the generic construction $F^{\pi_1, \pi_2} \colon \mathcal{K} \times \mathcal{I}_1 \times \cdots \times \mathcal{I}_s \to \mathcal{R}_1 \times \cdots \times \mathcal{R}_t$ based on π_1 and π_2, where $\mathcal{K}$ is the key space, $\mathcal{I}_1 \times \cdots \times \mathcal{I}_s$ are the input spaces, and $\mathcal{R}_1 \times \cdots \times \mathcal{R}_t$ are the output spaces. Note that here F can be a tweakable block cipher, a PRF, a MAC algorithm, etc. In this work, we will focus on algorithms that can be viewed as the xor of the public permutations

$$Z = \pi_1(A) \oplus \pi_2(B),$$

for $\pi_1, \pi_2 \xleftarrow{\$} \mathrm{Perm}(n)$. Here A, B, and Z are functions of the secret key K, the inputs $I_1, \ldots, I_s$, and the outputs $R_1, \ldots, R_t$. Although there are no strict restrictions for Z, we do require that the equality patterns of A and B satisfy certain conditions. More precisely, equality pattern of B should not depend on the value of $\pi_1(A)$ and vice versa. This is the condition to use the mirror theory based lower bound as formalized in [32].

4.1 General Setting and Transcripts

Let $u \in \mathbb{N}$, $K_1, \ldots, K_u \xleftarrow{\$} \mathcal{K}$, and $\pi_1, \pi_2 \xleftarrow{\$} \mathrm{Perm}(n)$. Consider any distinguisher $\mathcal{D}$ that has access to the oracles: $(\mathcal{O}_m, \mathcal{O}_a, \pi_1^{\pm}, \pi_2^{\pm})$ in the real world or $(\mathcal{P}_m, \mathcal{P}_a, \pi_1^{\pm}, \pi_2^{\pm})$ in the ideal world. Here we have $\mathcal{O}_m = (F_{K_1}^{\pi_1,\pi_2}, \ldots, F_{K_u}^{\pi_1,\pi_2})$, and $\mathcal{O}_a$ is the possible set of verification oracles (for example the case of mac notion in Sect. 2.3). The oracle $\mathcal{P}_m$ is the idealized version of $(F_{K_1}^{\pi_1,\pi_2}, \ldots, F_{K_u}^{\pi_1,\pi_2})$, which these idealized oracles are depend on the considered security notion (see Sects. 2.1–2.3 for more details), and $\mathcal{P}_a$ is the possible set of rejection oracles. We require that $\mathcal{D}$ is computationally unbounded and deterministic. For user index $j \in \{1, \ldots, u\}$, $\mathcal{D}$ makes q_m queries to $\mathcal{O}_m$ or $\mathcal{P}_m$, and these are summarized in a transcript

$$\tau_m = \{(j^{(1)}, I_1^{(1)}, \ldots, I_s^{(1)}, R_1^{(1)}, \ldots, R_t^{(1)}), \ldots,$$
$$(j^{(q_m)}, I_1^{(q_m)}, \ldots, I_s^{(q_m)}, R_1^{(q_m)}, \ldots, R_t^{(q_m)})\},$$

and q_a queries to $\mathcal{O}_a$ or $\mathcal{P}_a$, these are summarized in a transcript

$$\tau_a = \{(j'^{(1)}, I_1'^{(1)}, \ldots, I_s'^{(1)}, R_1'^{(1)}, \ldots, R_t'^{(1)}, b'^{(1)}), \ldots,$$
$$(j'^{(q_a)}, I_1'^{(q_a)}, \ldots, I_s'^{(q_a)}, R_1'^{(q_a)}, \ldots, R_t'^{(q_a)}, b'^{(q_a)})\}.$$

Note that τ_a is empty for notions where no verification oracles are considered (such as sprp, tsprp, prf, tccr, etc.). $\mathcal{D}$ also makes p primitive queries to $\pi_1^{\pm}$ and p primitive queries to $\pi_2^{\pm}$, and like before, these are respectively summarized in transcripts τ_1 and τ_2. We assume that τ_m, τ_a, τ_1, and τ_2 do not contain duplicate elements. After $\mathcal{D}$'s interaction with the oracles, but before it outputs its decision, we disclose the keys $K_1, \ldots, K_u$ to the distinguisher. In the real world, these are the keys used in the construction. In the ideal world, $K_1, \ldots, K_u$ are dummy keys that are drawn uniformly at random. The complete view is denoted $\tau = (\tau_m, \tau_a, \tau_1, \tau_2, K_1, \ldots, K_u)$.

4.2 Attainable Index Mappings

In the real world, each query $(j^{(i)}, I_1^{(i)}, \ldots, I_s^{(i)}, R_1^{(i)}, \ldots, R_t^{(i)}) \in \tau_m$ corresponds to an evaluation of the $j^{(i)}$-th oracle in $\mathcal{O}_m$, each query $(j'^{(a)}, I_1'^{(a)}, \ldots, I_s'^{(a)}, R_1'^{(a)}, \ldots, R_t'^{(a)}, b'^{(a)}) \in \tau_a$ corresponds to an evaluation of the $j'^{(a)}$-th oracle in $\mathcal{O}_a$, and each primitive query $(u, v) \in \tau_1$ (resp., $(x, y) \in \tau_2$) corresponds to an evaluation of the primitive oracle $\pi_1^{\pm}$ (resp., $\pi_2^{\pm}$). Note that each algorithm F consists of an evaluation of π_1 and an evaluation of π_2. For the queries in τ_m, these are of the form $A^{(i)} \mapsto \pi_1(A^{(i)})$ and $B^{(i)} \mapsto \pi_2(B^{(i)})$ such that $\pi_1(A^{(i)}) \oplus \pi_2(B^{(i)}) = Z^{(i)}$. Likewise, for the queries in τ_a, there are evaluations $A'^{(a)} \mapsto \pi_1(A'^{(a)})$ and $B'^{(a)} \mapsto \pi_2(B'^{(a)})$, such that $\pi_1(A'^{(a)}) \oplus \pi_2(B'^{(a)}) \neq Z'^{(a)}$. The values of $A^{(i)}, B^{(i)}, Z^{(i)}$ and $A'^{(a)}, B'^{(a)}, Z'^{(a)}$ are specific for the particular construction, and can be deduced from τ. Without loss of generality, we assume that all primitive queries are made in the forward direction, then these are of the form $u \mapsto \pi_1(u)$ or $x \mapsto \pi_2(x)$ such that $\pi_1(u) = v$ and $\pi_2(x) = y$. The transcript τ defines $q_m + 2p$ equations and q_a non-equations on the unknowns, and these (non)-equations are

$$
\mathcal{E}_m^p = \begin{cases} \pi_1(A^{(1)}) \oplus \pi_2(B^{(1)}) = Z^{(1)}, \\ \quad\vdots \\ \pi_1(A^{(q_m)}) \oplus \pi_2(B^{(q_m)}) = Z^{(q_m)}, \\ \pi_1(u) = v \quad \text{for } (u,v) \in \tau_1, \\ \pi_2(x) = y \quad \text{for } (x,y) \in \tau_2, \end{cases} \quad \mathcal{E}_a = \begin{cases} \pi_1(A'^{(1)}) \oplus \pi_2(B'^{(1)}) \neq Z'^{(1)}, \\ \quad\vdots \\ \pi_1(A'^{(q_a)}) \oplus \pi_2(B'^{(q_a)}) \neq Z'^{(q_a)}. \end{cases}
$$
(3)

In the above $q_m + 2p$ equations, some of the unknowns may be equal to each other. We have that $\pi_1(A^{(i)}) \neq \pi_1(A^{(k)})$ if and only if $A^{(i)} \neq A^{(k)}$, and $\pi_2(B^{(i)}) \neq \pi_2(B^{(k)})$ if and only if $B^{(i)} \neq B^{(k)}$. No condition holds for $\pi_1(A^{(i)})$ versus $\pi_2(B^{(i)})$, as these are defined by independent permutations. The same holds for verification queries and primitive queries. However, no a priori condition holds for (non-)equality between values $\pi_1(A^{(i)})$ versus $\pi_1(A'^{(a)})$ versus $\pi_1(u)$, and $\pi_2(B^{(i)})$ versus $\pi_2(B'^{(a)})$ versus $\pi_2(x)$.

Thus,

$$
\{\pi_1(A^{(i)})\}_{1 \leq i \leq q_m} \cup \{\pi_1(A'^{(a)})\}_{1 \leq a \leq q_a} \cup \{\pi_1(u)\}_{(u,v) \in \tau_1},
$$
$$
\{\pi_2(B^{(i)})\}_{1 \leq i \leq q_m} \cup \{\pi_2(B'^{(a)})\}_{1 \leq a \leq q_a} \cup \{\pi_2(x)\}_{(x,y) \in \tau_2},
$$

are identified with two sets of unknowns $\mathcal{V}'^p = \{v_1, \ldots, v_{q_{\mathcal{V}'}^p}\}$ and $\mathcal{Y}'^p = \{y_1, \ldots, y_{q_{\mathcal{Y}'}^p}\}$, with $q_{\mathcal{V}'}^p, q_{\mathcal{Y}'}^p \leq q_m + q_a + p$. Since $\mathcal{V}'^p$ and $\mathcal{Y}'^p$ are defined by independent permutations, we know that $\mathcal{V}'^p$ and $\mathcal{Y}'^p$ are disjoint. We also know that

$$
V_0 = \{\pi_1(u) \mid (u,v) \in \tau_1\}, \qquad Y_0 = \{\pi_2(x) \mid (x,y) \in \tau_2\}.
$$

are already well defined by the system. Hence the only unknowns that are left are in the sets $\mathcal{V}'^p \setminus V_0$ and $\mathcal{Y}'^p \setminus Y_0$. For $v_s \in \mathcal{V}'^p$ and $y_t \in \mathcal{Y}'^p$, we connect v_s and y_t with a λ-labeled edge of label $Z^{(i)}$ if $\pi_1(A^{(i)}) = v_s$ and $\pi_2(B^{(i)}) = y_t$ for some $i \in [q_m]$. Similarly, we connect v_s and y_t with a λ'-labeled edge of label $Z'^{(a)}$ if $\pi_1(A'^{(a)}) = v_s$ and $\pi_2(B'^{(a)}) = y_t$ for some $a \in [q_a]$. Finally, v_s (resp., y_t) represents an isolated colliding vertex if it is not connected with an edge, for these vertices we have $\pi_1(u) = v_s$ (resp., $\pi_2(v) = y_t$) for $(u, v_s) \in \tau_1$ and $(x, y_t) \in \tau_2$. In this way, we obtain a graph on $\mathcal{V}'^p \sqcup \mathcal{Y}'^p$, called the transcript graph of τ, and we denote it by $\mathcal{G}_\tau(\mathcal{E}^p)$.

4.3 Bad Transcripts

Informally, bad events are the properties which would make the public permutation extended mirror theory inapplicable. One can only apply the mirror theory if $\mathcal{G}_\tau(\mathcal{E}^p)$ is (1). acyclic, (2). satisfies the non-degeneracy condition, (3). satisfies the NCL condition, (4). satisfies the SCV condition, (5). satisfies the NDL condition, and (6). is $(\xi + 1)$-block-maximal. For some parameter ξ that will be defined later on, we say a system of equations is $(\xi + 1)$-block-maximal if it does not contain a $(\xi + 1)$-block-collision, which means that neither of the two permutations evaluates the same input more than ξ times. As our security analysis will cap on $2n/3$-bit security only, we can keep it simple by introducing an event that excludes all alternating paths of length 3, and events that exclude all $v\text{-}\star$ component with a y-colliding vertex and $y\text{-}\star$ component with a v-colliding vertex. Below, we will give a formal description of the bad events.

For simplicity, we denote by $A^{(i)}$ the i-th input to π_1, $B^{(i)}$ the i-th input to π_2, and $Z^{(i)} = \pi_1(A^{(i)}) \oplus \pi_2(B^{(i)})$ for the MAC queries. Similarly we have $A'^{(a)}$, $B'^{(a)}$ and $Z'^{(a)}$ for the verification queries. Given a parameter $\xi \in \mathbb{N}$, we say that $\tau \in \mathcal{T}_{\text{bad}}$ if and only if one of the following conditions holds:

(i) A component with two colliding vertices.

$$\exists i \in [q_m], (u, v) \in \tau_1, (x, y) \in \tau_2 \text{ such that } A^{(i)} = u \wedge B^{(i)} = x,$$

$$\exists i \in [q_m], (u, v) \in \tau_1, (x, y) \in \tau_2 \text{ such that } A^{(i)} = u \wedge Z^{(i)} = v \oplus y,$$

$$\exists i \in [q_m], (u, v) \in \tau_1, (x, y) \in \tau_2 \text{ such that } Z^{(i)} = v \oplus y \wedge B^{(i)} = x.$$

(ii) An alternating path of length 3.

$$\exists i \neq k, k \neq l \in [q_m] \text{ such that } A^{(i)} = A^{(k)} \wedge B^{(k)} = B^{(l)}.$$

(iii) An alternating path of length 2 such that $\lambda(\mathcal{L}) = 0$.

$$\exists i \neq k \in [q_m] \text{ such that } A^{(i)} = A^{(k)} \wedge Z^{(i)} = Z^{(k)},$$

$$\exists i \neq k \in [q_m] \text{ such that } Z^{(i)} = Z^{(k)} \wedge B^{(i)} = B^{(k)}.$$

(iv) A $v\text{-}\star$ colliding component with y-colliding vertices, or a $y\text{-}\star$ colliding component with v-colliding vertices.

$$\exists i \neq k \in [q_m], (u, v) \in \tau_1 \text{ such that } A^{(i)} = u \wedge B^{(i)} = B^{(k)},$$

$$\exists i \neq k \in [q_m], (x, y) \in \tau_2 \text{ such that } B^{(i)} = x \wedge A^{(i)} = A^{(k)},$$

$$\exists i \neq k \in [q_m], (u, v), (u', v') \in \tau_1 \text{ such that}$$
$$A^{(i)} = u \wedge A^{(k)} = u' \wedge v \oplus Z^{(i)} = v' \oplus Z^{(k)},$$

$$\exists i \neq k \in [q_m], (x, y), (x', y') \in \tau_2 \text{ such that}$$
$$B^{(i)} = x \wedge B^{(k)} = x' \wedge y \oplus Z^{(i)} = y' \oplus Z^{(k)}.$$

(v) A $(\xi+1)$-block-collision.

$$\exists i_1,\ldots,i_{\xi+1} \in \{1,\ldots,q_m\} \text{ such that } A^{(1)} = \cdots = A^{(\xi+1)},$$
$$\exists i_1,\ldots,i_{\xi+1} \in \{1,\ldots,q_m\} \text{ such that } B^{(1)} = \cdots = B^{(\xi+1)}.$$

(vi) An alternating circle of length 2 with a λ'-labeled edge.

$$\exists i \in [q_m], a \in [q_a] \text{ such that } A^{(i)} = A'^{(a)} \wedge B^{(i)} = B'^{(a)} \wedge Z^{(i)} = Z'^{(a)}.$$

(vii) A λ'-labeled edge between two vertices with distance λ'.

$$\exists a \in [q_a], (u,v) \in \tau_1, (x,y) \in \tau_2 \text{ such that}$$
$$A'^{(a)} = u \wedge B'^{(a)} = x \wedge Z'^{(a)} = v \oplus y,$$
$$\exists i \in [q_m], a \in [q_a], (u,v), (u'v') \in \tau_1 \text{ such that}$$
$$A^{(i)} = u \wedge B^{(i)} = B'^{(a)} \wedge A'^{(a)} = u' \wedge Z'^{(a)} = v \oplus Z^{(i)} \oplus v',$$
$$\exists i \in [q_m], a \in [q_a], (x,y), (x',y') \in \tau_2 \text{ such that}$$
$$B^{(i)} = x \wedge A^{(i)} = A'^{(a)} \wedge B'^{(a)} = x' \wedge Z'^{(a)} = y \oplus Z^{(i)} \oplus y',$$
$$\exists i \neq k \in [q_m], a \in [q_a], (u,v) \in \tau_1, (x,y) \in \tau_2 \text{ such that } A^{(i)} = u$$
$$\wedge\, B^{(k)} = x \wedge B^{(i)} = B'^{(a)} \wedge A^{(k)} = A'^{(a)} \wedge Z'^{(a)} = v \oplus Z^{(i)} \oplus y \oplus Z^{(k)}.$$

Note that by (ii) and (iv), we will end up with a graph that contains only isolated and $v\text{-}\star$ colliding components with a v-colliding vertex, isolated and $y\text{-}\star$ colliding components with a y-colliding vertex, $v\text{-}\star$ components, $y\text{-}\star$ components, isolated components, and isolated vertices. The resulting graph is good since it

1. satisfies the SCV condition by conditions (i), (ii), and (iv),
2. acyclic by conditions (ii),
3. satisfies the non-degeneracy condition by conditions (ii) and (iii),
4. is $(\xi+1)$-block-maximal by conditions (ii) and (v),
5. satisfies the NCL condition by conditions (ii) and (vi),
6. satisfies the NDL condition by conditions (ii), (iv), and (vii).

The probability that $\tau \in \mathcal{T}_{\mathrm{bad}}$ happens, is given by the sum of the probabilities that each of the above mentioned bad events happens. When the above mentioned events can be excluded in the transcript, then $\mathcal{G}_\tau$ forms a good transcript graph for $\tau \in \mathcal{T}_{\mathrm{good}}$.

4.4   Ratio for Good Transcripts

Once bad transcripts have been defined, we will show that

$$\Pr[X_{\mathcal{P}} \in \mathcal{T}_{\mathrm{bad}}] \leq \varepsilon_{\mathrm{bad}},$$

for a small $\varepsilon_{\mathrm{bad}} > 0$. Next, we fix a good transcript τ. According to (2), we only have to consider $\rho(\tau)/\Pr[\mathcal{P}_m : \mathcal{P}_m \vdash \tau_m \wedge \mathcal{P}_a \vdash \tau_a]$, with

$$\rho(\tau) = \Pr\left[\pi_1, \pi_2 \xleftarrow{\$} \mathrm{Perm}(n) : \mathcal{O}_m \vdash \tau_m \wedge \mathcal{O}_a \vdash \tau_a \mid \pi_1 \vdash \tau_1 \wedge \pi_2 \vdash \tau_2\right].$$

This is exactly the ratio given by Theorem 1 and 2. From (2), we obtain

$$\frac{\Pr[X_{\mathcal{O}} = \tau]}{\Pr[X_{\mathcal{P}} = \tau]} \geq 1 - \varepsilon_{\text{ratio}},$$

and by Lemma 3, we have

$$\mathbf{Adv}_{\text{MAC}}^{\text{mac}}(\mathcal{D}) \leq \boldsymbol{E}[\varepsilon_{\text{ratio}}] + \varepsilon_{\text{bad}}.$$

5   Multi-user Security of Tweakable Even-Mansour Cipher

In this section we consider the 2-round Tweakable Even-Mansour (TEM) construction that was proposed by Cogliati et al. [15]. They showed that 2-round TEM achieves $2n/3$-bit security in the single-user setting. Here we show that same level of security can be achieved in the *multi-user* setting using the technique proposed in this work.

Let $n \in \mathbb{N}$, let $\pi_1, \pi_2 \xleftarrow{\$} \text{Perm}(n)$, and let $\mathcal{H}$ be an ϵ-AXU function family. One can consider a generic construction TEM: $\mathcal{H}^2 \times \mathcal{T} \times \{0,1\}^n \to \{0,1\}^n$ as

$$\text{TEM}(h_1, h_2, T, M) = \pi_2(\pi_1(M \oplus h_1(T)) \oplus h_1(T) \oplus h_2(T)) \oplus h_2(T). \quad (4)$$

The security of TEM based on π_1 and π_2 is given in the following Theorem.

Theorem 3. *Let $n \in \mathbb{N}$ and let $\mathcal{H}$ be a uniform ϵ-AXU family of functions from $\mathcal{T}$ to $\{0,1\}^n$. We consider TEM: $\mathcal{H}^2 \times \mathcal{T} \times \{0,1\}^n \to \{0,1\}^n$ based on two permutations $\pi_1, \pi_2 \xleftarrow{\$} \text{Perm}(n)$ and u pairs of uniform user hash keys $(h_1^1, h_2^1), \ldots, (h_1^u, h_2^u) \xleftarrow{\$} \mathcal{H}^2$. For any distinguisher $\mathcal{D}$ making at most q construction queries distributed over its u construction oracles, at most p primitive queries to $\pi_1^{\pm}$ and p primitive queries to $\pi_2^{\pm}$, we have*

$$\mathbf{Adv}_{\text{TEM}}^{\text{mu-tsprp}}(\mathcal{D}) \leq 3q^3\epsilon^2 + q^2 p\epsilon^2 + 6\sqrt{q}p\epsilon + \frac{6q^{3/2}}{2^n} + \frac{2q(p+q)^2}{2^{2n}}\left(1 + 13q\epsilon\right).$$

Proof. Let $(h_1^1, h_2^1), \ldots, (h_1^u, h_2^u) \xleftarrow{\$} \mathcal{H}^2$, $\pi_1, \pi_2 \xleftarrow{\$} \text{Perm}(n)$, and $\tilde{\pi}_1, \ldots, \tilde{\pi}_u \xleftarrow{\$} \widetilde{\text{Perm}}(t,n)$. Here, we consider any distinguisher $\mathcal{D}$ that has access to either $(\text{TEM}_{h_1^1,h_2^1}^{\pi_1,\pi_2^{-1}}, \ldots, \text{TEM}_{h_1^u,h_2^u}^{\pi_1,\pi_2^{-1}}, \pi_1, \pi_2)$ in the real world, or $(\tilde{\pi}_1, \ldots, \tilde{\pi}_u, \pi_1, \pi_2)$ in the ideal world. The security proof relies on Theorem 1 (a), although this application is not straightforward. Most importantly, we consider $(\text{TEM}_{h_1^j,h_2^j}^{\pi_1,\pi_2^{-1}})_{j=1}^u$ instead of $(\text{TEM}_{h_1^j,h_2^j}^{\pi_1,\pi_2})_{j=1}^u$. As π_1, π_2 are drawn independently, these two constructions are provably equally secure. We can view an evaluation $C = \text{TEM}_{h_1^j,h_2^j}^{\pi_1,\pi_2^{-1}}(T,M)$ as the xor of two public permutations in the middle of the function, $\pi_1(M \oplus h_1^j(T)) \oplus \pi_2(M \oplus h_2^j(T)) = h_1^j(T) \oplus h_2^j(T)$. Therefore, q evaluations of $\text{TEM}_{h_1^j,h_2^j}^{\pi_1,\pi_2^{-1}}$ can be translated to a system of q bi-variate affine equations. Including $2p$ uni-variate affine equations that are defined by the primitive queries, these equations can be written in the form (3).

$\Pr[X_{\mathcal{P}} \in \mathcal{T}_{\mathbf{bad}}]$. Following the framework given in Sect. 4, we first perform the bad transcripts analysis. By replacing $A = M \oplus h_1^j(T)$, $B = M \oplus h_2^j(T)$, and $Z = h_1^j(T) \oplus h_2^j(T)$ in the framework of Sect. 4.3, we get the following bad events. Given a parameter $\xi \in \mathbb{N}$, we say that $\tau \in \mathcal{T}_{\mathbf{bad}}$ if and only if there exist construction queries $(j, T, M, C), (j', T', M', C'), (j'', T'', M'', C'') \in \tau_m$, primitive queries $(u, v), (u', v') \in \tau_1$ and $(x, y), (x', y') \in \tau_2$ such that one of the following conditions holds:

(i) A component with two colliding vertices.

$$\text{bad}_1 : M \oplus u = h_1^j(T) \wedge C \oplus x = h_2^j(T),$$
$$\text{bad}_2 : M \oplus u = h_1^j(T) \wedge v \oplus y = h_1^j(T) \oplus h_2^j(T),$$
$$\text{bad}_3 : v \oplus y = h_1^j(T) \oplus h_2^j(T) \wedge C \oplus x = h_2^j(T).$$

(ii) An alternating path of length 3.

$$\text{bad}_4 : M \oplus h_1^j(T) = M' \oplus h_1^{j'}(T') \wedge C' \oplus h_2^{j'}(T') = C'' \oplus h_2^{j''}(T'').$$

(iii) An alternating path of length 2 such that $\lambda(\mathcal{L}) = 0$.

$$\text{bad}_5 : M \oplus h_1^j(T) = M' \oplus h_1^{j'}(T') \wedge h_1^j(T) \oplus h_2^j(T) = h_1^{j'}(T') \oplus h_2^{j'}(T'),$$
$$\text{bad}_6 : h_1^j(T) \oplus h_2^j(T) = h_1^{j'}(T') \oplus h_2^{j'}(T') \wedge C \oplus h_2^j(T) = C' \oplus h_2^{j'}(T').$$

(iv) A v-$\star$ colliding component with y-colliding vertices, or a y-$\star$ colliding component with v-colliding vertices .

$$\text{bad}_7 : M \oplus u = h_1^j(T) \wedge C \oplus h_2^j(T) = C' \oplus h_2^{j'}(T),$$
$$\text{bad}_8 : C \oplus x = h_2^j(T) \wedge M \oplus h_1^j(T) = M' \oplus h_1^{j'}(T'),$$
$$\text{bad}_9 : M \oplus u = h_1^j(T) \wedge M' \oplus u' = h_1^{j'}(T')$$
$$\wedge v \oplus h_1^j(T) \oplus h_2^j(T) = v' \oplus h_1^{j'}(T') \oplus h_2^{j'}(T'),$$
$$\text{bad}_{10} : C \oplus x = h_2^j(T) \wedge C' \oplus x' = h_2^{j'}(T)$$
$$\wedge y \oplus h_1^j(T) \oplus h_2^j(T) = y' \oplus h_1^{j'}(T') \oplus h_2^{j'}(T').$$

(v) A $(\xi + 1)$-block-collision.

$$\text{bad}_{11} : \{i_1, \ldots, i_{\xi+1}\} \in [q] \text{ such that } M_{i_1} \oplus h_1^{j_{i_1}}(T_{i_1}) = \cdots = M_{i_{\xi+1}} \oplus h_1^{j_{\xi+1}}(T_{i_{\xi+1}}),$$
$$\text{bad}_{12} : \{i_1, \ldots, i_{\xi+1}\} \in [q] \text{ such that } C_{i_1} \oplus h_2^{j_{i_1}}(T_{i_1}) = \cdots = C_{i_{\xi+1}} \oplus h_2^{j_{\xi+1}}(T_{i_{\xi+1}}).$$

Since there is a $\sum_{i=1}^{c_1+c_2} q/2^n$ term in Theorem 1 (a), and we want to get $2n/3$-bits security, we also need the following two bad events

$$\text{bad}_{c_1} : c_1 = |(j, T, M, C) \in \tau_m : M \oplus h_1^j(T) \in \tau_1| \geq \sqrt{q},$$
$$\text{bad}_{c_2} : c_2 = |(j, T, M, C) \in \tau_m : C \oplus h_2^j(T) \in \tau_2| \geq \sqrt{q}.$$

Lemma 4. *For any integers q and p, one has*

$$\Pr[\tau \in \mathcal{T}_{\text{bad}}] \leq 4qp^2\epsilon^2 + 3q^3\epsilon^2 + q^2 p\epsilon^2 + \frac{q^3}{2^{2n}} + 2\sqrt{q}p\epsilon + \frac{16q^2(p+q)^2\epsilon}{2^{2n}}.$$

The proof of the lemma is given in the full version of the paper.

$\Pr[X_{\mathcal{O}} = \tau]/\Pr[X_{\mathcal{P}} = \tau]$. The next step is the calculate the ratio for good transcripts. Note that by $\neg \text{bad}_{c_1}$ and $\neg \text{bad}_{c_2}$, we have $\sum_{i=1}^{c_1+c_2} q \leq 2q^{3/2}$. We use Theorem 1 (a) to get

$$\epsilon_{\text{ratio}} \leq \frac{2q^{3/2}}{2^n} + \frac{3q^3}{2^{2n}} + \frac{2(p+q)^2 \sum_{i=c_1+c_2}^{c_1+c_2+c_3+c_4-1}(\eta_{i+1}^2 + \eta_{i+1})}{2^{2n}} + \frac{2q(p+q)^2}{2^{2n}}.$$

Let $\sim_1$ (resp., $\sim_2$) be an equivalence relation on $[q]$ as $\alpha \sim_1 \beta$ (resp., $\alpha \sim_2 \beta$) if and only if $A_\alpha = A_\beta$ (resp. $B_\alpha = B_\beta$). Now, each η_i random variable denotes the cardinality of some non-singleton equivalence class of $[q]$ with respect to either $\sim_1$ or $\sim_2$. For $r, s \in \mathbb{N}$, we denote by $\mathcal{P}_1^1, \ldots, \mathcal{P}_r^1$ and $\mathcal{P}_1^2, \ldots, \mathcal{P}_s^2$ the non-singleton equivalence classes of $[q]$ with respect to $\sim_1$ and $\sim_2$, respectively. Further, for $k \in [r]$ and $l \in [s]$, let $\nu_k = |\mathcal{P}_k^1|$ and $\nu_l' = |\mathcal{P}_l^2|$. Then, we have

$$E\left[\sum_{i=c_1+c_2}^{c_1+c_2+c_3+c_4-1}(\eta_{i+1}^2 + \eta_{i+1})\right] \leq E\left[\sum_{k=1}^r \nu_k^2 + \nu_k\right] + E\left[\sum_{l=1}^s \nu_l'^2 + \nu_l'\right]$$

$$\leq 5q^2\epsilon,$$

using Lemma 1 and the fact that $(h_1^1, h_2^1), \ldots, (h_1^u, h_2^u) \xleftarrow{\$} \mathcal{H}^2$.

Finally, Theorem 3 is proven by combining Lemma 4 and ϵ_{ratio} with Lemma 3. □

6 Multi-user Security of pEDM PRF

In this section we consider the permutation based version of Encrypted Davies-Mayer (pEDM) construction, that was proposed by Dutta et al. [22]. They showed that pEDM based on a single permutation achieves $2n/3$-bit security. Here we will prove the *multi-user* security of pEDM based on two independent permutations, and we show that same level of security can be achieved using the technique proposed in this work. In this case, the multi-user security analysis is more complex than the single-user analysis, since the inputs to π_1 do not need to be fresh, this leads to more bad events and a more complex good transcripts ratio analysis when a dedicated proof need to be performed.

Let $n \in \mathbb{N}$, let $\pi_1, \pi_2 \xleftarrow{\$} \text{Perm}(n)$. One can consider a generic construction pEDM: $\{0,1\}^{2n} \times \{0,1\}^n \to \{0,1\}^n$ as

$$\text{pEDM}(K_1, K_2, M) = \pi_2(\pi_1(M \oplus K_1) \oplus M \oplus K_1 \oplus K_2) \oplus K_1. \tag{5}$$

The security of pEDM based on π_1 and π_2 is given in the following Theorem.

Theorem 4. *Let* $n \in \mathbb{N}$ *and* $1 \leq \xi \leq 2^{n-1}/(p+q)$. *We consider* pEDM: $\{0,1\}^{2n} \times \{0,1\}^n \rightarrow \{0,1\}^n$ *based on two permutations* $\pi_1, \pi_2 \xleftarrow{\$}$ Perm(n), *and* u *pairs of uniform user keys* $(K_1^1, K_2^1), \ldots, (K_1^u, K_2^u) \xleftarrow{\$} \{0,1\}^{2n}$. *For any distinguisher* $\mathcal{D}$ *making at most* q *construction queries distributed over its* u *construction oracles, at most* p *primitive queries to* $\pi_1^{\pm}$ *and* p *primitive queries to* $\pi_2^{\pm}$, *we have*

$$\mathbf{Adv}_{\mathrm{pEDM}}^{\mathrm{mu\text{-}prf}}(\mathcal{D}) \leq \frac{2}{2^n} + \frac{4qp^2}{2^{2n}} + \frac{3q^2p}{2^{2n}} + \frac{3p\sqrt{nq}}{2^n} + \frac{2q^3}{2^{2n}}$$

$$+ \frac{p^{3/2}}{2^n} + \frac{(p+q)^2}{2^{2n}}\left(7q + \frac{5u(u-1)}{2^n}\right) + \frac{\binom{q}{\xi+1}}{2^{n\xi}}.$$

Proof. Let $(K_1^1, K_2^1), \ldots, (K_1^u, K_2^u) \xleftarrow{\$} \{0,1\}^{2n}$, $\pi_1, \pi_2 \xleftarrow{\$}$ Perm(n), and $\varphi_1, \ldots, \varphi_u \xleftarrow{\$}$ Func(n). Here, we consider any distinguisher $\mathcal{D}$ that has access to either $(\mathrm{pEDM}_{K_1^1,K_2^1}^{\pi_1,\pi_2}, \ldots, \mathrm{pEDM}_{K_1^u,K_2^u}^{\pi_1,\pi_2}, \pi_1, \pi_2)$ in the real world, or $(\varphi_1, \ldots, \varphi_u, \pi_1, \pi_2)$ in the ideal world. The security proof relies on Theorem 1 (b). As before, we consider $(\mathrm{pEDM}_{K_1^j,K_2^j}^{\pi_1,\pi_2^{-1}})_{j=1}^u$ instead of $(\mathrm{pEDM}_{K_1^j,K_2^j}^{\pi_1,\pi_2})_{j=1}^u$. We can view an evaluation $C = \mathrm{pEDM}_{K_1^j,K_2^j}^{\pi_1,\pi_2^{-1}}(M)$ as the xor of two public permutations in the middle of the function, $\pi_1(M \oplus K_1^j) \oplus \pi_2(C \oplus K_1^j) = M \oplus K_1^j \oplus K_2^j$. Therefore, q evaluations of $\mathrm{pEDM}_{K_1^j,K_2^j}^{\pi_1,\pi_2^{-1}}$ can be translated to a system of q bivariate affine equations. Including $2p$ uni-variate affine equations that are defined by the primitive queries.

$\mathbf{Pr}[X_{\mathcal{P}} \in \mathcal{T}_{\mathbf{bad}}]$. Following the framework given in Sect. 4, we first perform the bad transcripts analysis. By replacing $A = M \oplus K_1^j$, $B = C \oplus K_1^j$, and $Z = M \oplus K_1^j \oplus K_2^j$ in the framework of Sect. 4.3, we get the following bad events. Given a parameter $\xi \in \mathbb{N}$, we say that $\tau \in \mathcal{T}_{\mathrm{bad}}$ if and only if there exist construction queries $(j, M, C), (j', M', C'), (j'', M'', C'') \in \tau_m$, and primitive queries $(u, v), (u', v') \in \tau_1$ and $(x, y), (x', y') \in \tau_2$ such that one of the following conditions holds:

(i) A component with two colliding vertices.

$$\mathrm{bad}_1 : M \oplus u = K_1^j \wedge C \oplus x = K_1^j,$$
$$\mathrm{bad}_2 : M \oplus u = K_1^j \wedge v \oplus y = M \oplus K_1^j \oplus K_2^j,$$
$$\mathrm{bad}_3 : v \oplus y = M \oplus K_1^j \oplus K_2^j \wedge C \oplus x = K_1^j.$$

(ii) Alternating paths of length 3 *across different users.*

$$\mathrm{bad}_4 : M \oplus K_1^j = M' \oplus K_1^{j'} \wedge C' \oplus K_1^{j'} = C'' \oplus K_1^{j''}.$$

(iii) Alternating paths of length 2 such that $\lambda(\mathcal{L}) = 0$ *across different users.*

$$\mathrm{bad}_5 : M \oplus K_1^j = M' \oplus K_1^{j'} \wedge M \oplus K_1^j \oplus K_2^j = M' \oplus K_1^{j'} \oplus K_2^{j'},$$
$$\mathrm{bad}_6 : M \oplus K_1^j \oplus K_2^j = M' \oplus K_1^{j'} \oplus K_2^{j'} \wedge C \oplus K_1^j = C' \oplus K_1^{j'}.$$

(iv) A v-$\star$ colliding component with y-colliding vertices, or a y-$\star$ colliding component with v-colliding vertices.

$$\text{bad}_7: M \oplus u = K_1^j \wedge C \oplus K_1^j = C' \oplus K_1^{j'},$$

$$\text{bad}_8: C \oplus x = K_1^j \wedge M \oplus K_1^j = M' \oplus K_1^{j'},$$

$$\text{bad}_9: M \oplus u = K_1^j \wedge M' \oplus u' = K_1^{j'}$$
$$\wedge\, v \oplus M \oplus K_1^j \oplus K_2^j = v' \oplus M' \oplus K_1^{j'} \oplus K_2^{j'},$$

$$\text{bad}_{10}: C \oplus x = K_1^j \wedge C' \oplus x' = K_1^{j'}$$
$$\wedge\, y \oplus M \oplus K_1^j \oplus K_2^{j'} = y' \oplus M' \oplus K_1^j \oplus K_2^{j'}.$$

(v) A $(\xi+1)$-block-collision.

$$\text{bad}_{11}: \{i_1, \ldots, i_{\xi+1}\} \in [q] \text{ such that } C_{i_1} \oplus K_1^{j_{i_1}} = \cdots = C_{i_{\xi+1}} \oplus K_1^{j_{\xi+1}}.$$

Note that the events bad_4-bad_6 and bad_8 will not appear when the *single user* setting is considered, since in that case the distinguisher is not allow to query the same M to the construction oracle.

Lemma 5. *Let* $1 \leq \xi \leq 2^{n-1}/(p+q)$. *For any integers* q *and* p, *one has*

$$\Pr[\tau \in \mathcal{T}_{\text{bad}}] \leq \frac{2}{2^n} + \frac{4qp^2}{2^{2n}} + \frac{3q^2p}{2^{2n}} + \frac{3p\sqrt{nq}}{2^n} + \frac{2q^3}{2^{2n}} + \frac{p^{3/2}}{2^n} + \frac{\binom{q}{\xi+1}}{2^{n\xi}}.$$

The proof of the lemma is given in the full version of the paper.

$\Pr[X_{\mathcal{O}} = \tau]/\Pr[X_{\mathcal{P}} = \tau]$. The next step is the calculate the ratio for good transcripts. We use Theorem 1 (b) to get

$$\epsilon_{\text{ratio}} \leq \frac{2(p+q)^2 \sum_{i=c_1+c_2}^{c_1+c_2+c_3+c_4-1}(\eta_{i+1}^2 + \eta_{i+1})}{2^{2n}} + \frac{2q(p+q)^2}{2^{2n}}.$$

As before, for $r, s \in \mathbb{N}$, we denote by $\mathcal{P}_1^1, \ldots, \mathcal{P}_r^1$ and $\mathcal{P}_1^2, \ldots, \mathcal{P}_s^2$ the non-singleton equivalence classes of $[q]$ with respect to $\sim_1$ and $\sim_2$, respectively. Further, for $k \in [r]$ and $l \in [s]$, let $\nu_k = |\mathcal{P}_k^1|$ and $\nu_l' = |\mathcal{P}_l^2|$. Then, we have

$$E\left[\sum_{i=c_1+c_2}^{c_1+c_2+c_3+c_4-1}(\eta_{i+1}^2 + \eta_{i+1})\right] \leq E\left[\sum_{k=1}^r \nu_k^2 + \nu_k\right] + E\left[\sum_{l=1}^s \nu_l'^2 + \nu_l'\right]$$

$$\leq \frac{5u(u-1)}{2^{n-1}} + \frac{5q^2}{2^{n-1}}.$$

The non-freshness of π_1 in the multi-user setting leads to the existence of v-$\star$ components ($c_3 \neq 0$). The difficulty introduced by this can easily be handled by our new technique without performing a long and complicated analysis. Note that when $u = 1$, we are back to the single user setting, then there are no v-$\star$ components ($c_3 = 0$), since M is always different. Finally, Theorem 4 is proven by combining Lemma 5 and ϵ_{ratio} with Lemma 3. $\qquad\qquad\square$

7   Multi-user Security of nEHtM$_p$ MAC Algorithm

In this section we consider the public permutation based nonce-based Enhance Hash-then-Mask (nEHtM$_p$) MAC algorithm, that was proposed by Dutta and Nandi [20]. They showed that nEHtM$_p$ based on a single permutation (using domain separation) achieves $2n/3$-bit security when the number of faulty nonces μ is sufficiently smaller than $2^{n/3}$. However, according to the framework given in Sect. 4.3, the authors missed some bad events in their analysis, namely the two last events of (iv) and the three last events of (vii) of Sect. 4.3. Taking into account these missing bad events, the extended mirror theory used in [20] is *not* sufficient for the good transcripts ratio analysis of nEHtM$_p$. As a result, their ratio analysis of the construction is also incomplete. More precisely, non-equations between a colliding component and a normal component were not considered in the ratio analysis of [20]. This observation was also verified by the authors [10].

In this section, we will fix this problem using the techniques proposed in this work without performing a new complicated analysis, since these non-equations are already covered in our public permutation extended mirror theory (Theorem 2). Some of these additional bad events, however, require involved arguments to bound. Since the goal of this work is to illustrate the power of our new modular proof approaches, rather than presenting strong combinatorial results to bound these events. We will modify the design of nEHtM$_p$ by xoring an universal hash evaluation of the input message M using an extra hash key h^* to the output tag. This modified m-nEHtM$_p$ construction uses more randomness, which in turn enables us to bound the additional bad events easily. We would like to note that our analysis of m-nEHtM$_p$ does not imply infeasibility in fixing the proof of nEHtM$_p$. In fact, we believe that the security of the original nEHtM$_p$ construction can also be proven with our new approaches in combination with some strong techniques to bound these bad events. Here we will prove that this m-nEHtM$_p$ construction based on two independent permutations achieves $2n/3$-bit security in the *multi-user* setting using the technique proposed in this work.

Let $n \in \mathbb{N}$, let $\pi_1, \pi_2 \xleftarrow{\$} \text{Perm}(n)$, and let $\mathcal{H}$ be an ϵ-AXU function family. One can consider a generic construction m-nEHtM$_p$: $\{0,1\}^n \times \mathcal{H}^2 \times \{0,1\}^n \times \mathcal{M} \to \{0,1\}^n$ as

$$\text{m-nEHtM}_p(K, h, h^*N, M) = \pi_1(N \oplus K) \oplus \pi_2(N \oplus h(M)) \oplus h^*(M). \qquad (6)$$

The security of m-nEHtM$_p$ based on π_1 and π_2 is given in the following Theorem.

Theorem 5. *Let $n \in \mathbb{N}$, and let $\mathcal{H}$ be a uniform ϵ-AXU family of functions from $\mathcal{M}$ to $\{0,1\}^n$. We consider* m-nEHtM$_p$: $\{0,1\}^n \times \mathcal{H}^2 \times \{0,1\}^n \times \mathcal{M} \to \{0,1\}^n$ *based on two permutations $\pi_1, \pi_2 \xleftarrow{\$} \text{Perm}(n)$, u uniform user keys $K_1, \ldots, K_u \xleftarrow{\$} \{0,1\}^n$ and u pairs of uniform user hash keys $(h_1, h_1^*), \ldots, (h_u, h_u^*) \xleftarrow{\$} \mathcal{H}^2$. Let μ be a fixed parameter. For any distinguisher $\mathcal{D}$ making at most q_m queries with at most μ faulty nonces distributed over its u construction MAC oracles, q_a queries* *distributed over its u construction verification oracles, at most p primitive queries to $\pi_1^{\pm}$ and p primitive queries to $\pi_2^{\pm}$, we have*

$$\mathbf{Adv}^{\mathrm{mu\text{-}mac}}_{\mathrm{m\text{-}nEHtM}_p}(\mathcal{D}) \leq 7\sqrt{q_m}p\epsilon + 2\mu^2\epsilon + 4q_m^3\epsilon^2 + \frac{q_m^2 p\epsilon}{2^n} + 2\mu p\epsilon + q_m^2 q_a \epsilon^2 + \frac{q_a p^2 \epsilon}{2^n}$$

$$+ \frac{3q_m q_a p\epsilon}{2^n} + p\sqrt{q_m q_a}\epsilon^{\frac{3}{2}} + \frac{(p+q_m)^2}{2^{2n}}\left(5\mu^2 + 7q_m + \frac{5u(u-1)}{2^n}\right) + \frac{q_a}{2^n}.$$

Proof. Let $K_1, \ldots, K_u \xleftarrow{\$} \{0,1\}^n$, $(h_1, h_1^*), \ldots, (h_u, h_u^*) \xleftarrow{\$} \mathcal{H}^2$, and $\pi_1, \pi_2 \xleftarrow{\$}$ Perm(n). Here, we consider any distinguisher $\mathcal{D}$ that has access to either $(\mathcal{O}, \pi_1, \pi_2)$ in the real world or $(\mathcal{P}, \pi_1, \pi_2)$ in the ideal world, with $\mathcal{O} = ((\mathrm{m\text{-}nEHtM}^{\pi_1, \pi_2}_{p(K_1, h_1, h_1^*)}, \mathsf{Ver}^{\pi_1, \pi_2}_{(K_1, h_1, h_1^*)}), \ldots, (\mathrm{m\text{-}nEHtM}^{\pi_1, \pi_2}_{p(K_u, h_u, h_u^*)}, \mathsf{Ver}^{\pi_1, \pi_2}_{(K_u, h_u, h_u^*)}))$ and $\mathcal{P} = ((\mathsf{Rand}_1, \mathsf{Rej}_1), \ldots, (\mathsf{Rand}_u, \mathsf{Rej}_u))$. The security proof relies on Theorem 2 (b).

$\mathbf{Pr}[X_{\mathcal{P}} \in \mathcal{T}_{\mathrm{bad}}]$. Following the framework given in Sect. 4, we first perform the bad transcripts analysis. For the notational simplicity, we denote $H_j = h_j(M)$, and By replacing $A = N \oplus K_j$, $B = N \oplus h_j(M)$, and $Z = T \oplus h_j^*(M)$ in Sect. 4.3, we get the following bad events. Given a parameter $\xi \in \mathbb{N}$, we say that $\tau \in \mathcal{T}_{\mathrm{bad}}$ if and only if there exist construction MAC queries $(j, N, M, T), (j', N', M', T'), (j'', N'', M'', T'') \in \tau_m$, a construction verification query $(j^{(a)}, N^{(a)}, M^{(a)}, T^{(a)}, b^{(a)}) \in \tau_a$ and primitive queries $(u, v), (u', v') \in \tau_1$ and $(x, y), (x', y') \in \tau_2$ such that one of the following conditions holds:

(i) A component with two colliding vertices.

$$\mathrm{bad}_1: N \oplus u = K_j \wedge N \oplus x = H_j,$$
$$\mathrm{bad}_2: N \oplus u = K_j \wedge v \oplus y = T \oplus H_j^*,$$
$$\mathrm{bad}_3: v \oplus y = T \oplus H_j^* \wedge N \oplus x = H_j.$$

(ii) An alternating path of length 3.

$$\mathrm{bad}_4: N \oplus K_j = N' \oplus K_{j'} \wedge N' \oplus H_{j'} = N'' \oplus H_{j''}.$$

(iii) An alternating path of length 2 such that $\lambda(\mathcal{L}) = 0$.

$$\mathrm{bad}_5: N \oplus K_j = N' \oplus K_{j'} \wedge T \oplus H_j^* = T' \oplus H_{j'}^*,$$
$$\mathrm{bad}_6: T \oplus H_j^* = T' \oplus H_{j'}^* \wedge N \oplus H_{j'} = N' \oplus H_{j'}.$$

(iv) A v-$\star$ colliding component with y-colliding vertices, or a y-$\star$ colliding component with v-colliding vertices.

$$\mathrm{bad}_7: N \oplus u = K_j \wedge N \oplus H_j = N' \oplus H_{j'},$$
$$\mathrm{bad}_8: N \oplus x = H_j \wedge N \oplus K_j = N' \oplus K_{j'},$$
$$\mathrm{bad}_9: N \oplus u = K_j \wedge N' \oplus u' = K_{j'} \wedge v \oplus T \oplus H_j^* = v' \oplus T' \oplus H_{j'}^*,$$
$$\mathrm{bad}_{10}: N \oplus x = H_j \wedge N' \oplus x' = H_{j'} \wedge y \oplus T \oplus H_j^* = y' \oplus T' \oplus H_{j'}^*.$$

(v) A $(\xi + 1)$-block-collision.

$\quad$ bad_{11}: $\{i_1, \ldots, i_{\xi+1}\} \in [q_m]$ such that $N_{i_1} \oplus H_{j_{i_1}} = \cdots = N_{i_{\xi+1}} \oplus H_{j_{i_{\xi+1}}}$.

(vi) An alternating circle of length 2 with a λ'-labeled edge.

$$\mathrm{bad}_{12}: N \oplus K_j = N^{(a)} \oplus K_{j^{(a)}} \wedge N \oplus H_j = N^{(a)} \oplus H_{j^{(a)}}$$
$$\wedge \; T \oplus H_j^* = T^{(a)} \oplus H_{j^{(a)}}^*.$$

(vii) A λ'-labeled edge between two vertices with distance λ'.

$$\mathrm{bad}_{13}: N^{(a)} \oplus u = K_{j^{(a)}} \wedge N^{(a)} \oplus x = H_{j^{(a)}} \wedge T^{(a)} \oplus H_{j^{(a)}}^* = v \oplus y,$$

$$\mathrm{bad}_{14}: N \oplus u = K_j \wedge N \oplus H_j = N^{(a)} \oplus H_{j^{(a)}} \wedge N^{(a)} \oplus u' = K_{j^{(a)}}$$
$$\wedge \; T^{(a)} \oplus H_{j^{(a)}}^* = v \oplus T \oplus H_j^* \oplus v',$$

$$\mathrm{bad}_{15}: N \oplus x = H_j \wedge N \oplus K_j = N^{(a)} \oplus K_{j^{(a)}} \wedge N^{(a)} \oplus x' = H_{j^{(a)}}$$
$$\wedge \; T^{(a)} \oplus H_{j^{(a)}}^* = y \oplus T \oplus H_j^* \oplus y',$$

$$\mathrm{bad}_{16}: N \oplus u = K_j \wedge N' \oplus x = H_{j'} \wedge N \oplus H_j = N^{(a)} \oplus H_{j^{(a)}} \wedge$$
$$N' \oplus K_{j'} = N^{(a)} \oplus K_{j^{(a)}} \wedge T^{(a)} \oplus H_{j^{(a)}}^* = v \oplus T \oplus H_j^* \oplus y \oplus T' \oplus H_{j'}^*.$$

Note that the events bad_9-bad_{10} and bad_{14}-bad_{16} are the missing events that were not considered by the authors of [20].

Lemma 6. *For any integers q_m, q_a and p, then one has*

$$\Pr[\tau \in \mathcal{T}_{\mathrm{bad}}] \leq 7\sqrt{q_m}p\epsilon + 2\mu^2\epsilon + 4q_m^3\epsilon^2 + \frac{q_m^2 p\epsilon}{2^n} + 2\mu p\epsilon$$
$$+ \frac{8q_m^2(p + q_m)^2\epsilon}{2^{2n}} + q_m^2 q_a\epsilon^2 + \frac{q_a p^2\epsilon}{2^n} + \frac{3q_m q_a p\epsilon}{2^n} + p\sqrt{q_m q_a}\epsilon^{3/2}.$$

The proof of this Lemma is given in the full version of the paper.

$\mathbf{Pr[X_{\mathcal{O}} = \tau]}/\mathbf{Pr[X_{\mathcal{P}} = \tau]}$. The next step is the calculate the ratio for good transcripts. We use Theorem 2 (b) to get

$$\epsilon_{\mathrm{ratio}} \leq \frac{2(p + q_m)^2 \sum_{i=c_1+c_2}^{c_1+c_2+c_3+c_4-1}(\eta_{i+1}^2 + \eta_{i+1})}{2^{2n}} + \frac{2q_m(p + q_m)^2}{2^{2n}} + \frac{2q_a}{2^n}.$$

As before, for $r, s \in \mathbb{N}$, we denote by $\mathcal{P}_1^1, \ldots, \mathcal{P}_r^1$ and $\mathcal{P}_1^2, \ldots, \mathcal{P}_s^2$ the non-singleton equivalence classes of $[q_m]$ with respect to $\sim_1$ and $\sim_2$, respectively. For $k \in [r]$ and $l \in [s]$, let $\nu_k = |\mathcal{P}_k^1|$ and $\nu_l' = |\mathcal{P}_l^2|$. Then, we have

$$E\left[\sum_{i=c_1+c_2}^{c_1+c_2+c_3+c_4-1}(\eta_{i+1}^2 + \eta_{i+1})\right] \leq E\left[\sum_{k=1}^{r}\nu_k^2 + \nu_k\right] + E\left[\sum_{l=1}^{s}\nu_l'^2 + \nu_l'\right]$$
$$\leq \frac{5\mu^2}{2} + \frac{5u(u-1)}{2^{n-1}} + \frac{5q_m^2\epsilon}{2},$$

using Lemma 1 and the fact that $K_1, \ldots, K_u \xleftarrow{\$} \{0,1\}^n$ and $(h_1, h_1^*), \ldots,$ $(h_u, h_u^*) \xleftarrow{\$} \mathcal{H}^2$. Note that when $u = 1$, we are back to the single-user setting, in this case the $v\text{-}\star$ components (collision in the inputs of π_1) can only be formed by queries with repeated nonces, hereby the $5\mu^2/2$ term in the bound. Finally, Theorem 5 is proven by combining Lemma 6 and ϵ_{ratio} with Lemma 3. □

Acknowledgments. This work was supported in part by the Research Council KU Leuven: GOA TENSE (C16/15/058). The author was supported by a Ph.D. Fellowship from the Research Foundation - Flanders (FWO). I want to thank Tim Beyne and the reviewers for their valuable comments and suggestions.

References

1. NIST Lightweight Cryptography. https://csrc.nist.gov/Projects/Lightweight-Cryptography
2. NIST SHA-3 Project. https://csrc.nist.gov/projects/hash-functions/sha-3-project
3. Bellare, M., Boldyreva, A., Micali, S.: Public-Key encryption in a multi-user setting: security proofs and improvements. In: Preneel, B. (ed.) EUROCRYPT 2000. LNCS, vol. 1807, pp. 259–274. Springer, Heidelberg (2000). https://doi.org/10.1007/3-540-45539-6_18
4. Biham, E.: How to decrypt or even substitute des-encrypted messages in 2^{28} steps. Inf. Process. Lett. **84**(3), 117–124 (2002)
5. Bogdanov, A., Knežević, M., Leander, G., Toz, D., Varıcı, K., Verbauwhede, I.: SPONGENT: a lightweight hash function. In: Preneel, B., Takagi, T. (eds.) CHES 2011. LNCS, vol. 6917, pp. 312–325. Springer, Heidelberg (2011). https://doi.org/10.1007/978-3-642-23951-9_21
6. Bogdanov, A., Knudsen, L.R., Leander, G., Standaert, F.-X., Steinberger, J., Tischhauser, E.: Key-alternating ciphers in a provable setting: encryption using a small number of public permutations. In: Pointcheval, D., Johansson, T. (eds.) EUROCRYPT 2012. LNCS, vol. 7237, pp. 45–62. Springer, Heidelberg (2012). https://doi.org/10.1007/978-3-642-29011-4_5
7. Chatterjee, S., Menezes, A., Sarkar, P.: Another look at tightness. In: Miri, A., Vaudenay, S. (eds.) SAC 2011. LNCS, vol. 7118, pp. 293–319. Springer, Heidelberg (2012). https://doi.org/10.1007/978-3-642-28496-0_18
8. Chen, S., Lampe, R., Lee, J., Seurin, Y., Steinberger, J.: Minimizing the two-round even-Mansour cipher. In: Garay, J.A., Gennaro, R. (eds.) CRYPTO 2014. LNCS, vol. 8616, pp. 39–56. Springer, Heidelberg (2014). https://doi.org/10.1007/978-3-662-44371-2_3
9. Chen, S., Steinberger, J.: Tight security bounds for key-alternating ciphers. In: Nguyen, P.Q., Oswald, E. (eds.) EUROCRYPT 2014. LNCS, vol. 8441, pp. 327–350. Springer, Heidelberg (2014). https://doi.org/10.1007/978-3-642-55220-5_19
10. Chen, Y.L., Dutta, A., Nandi, M.: Multi-user BBB security of public permutations based MAC. Cryptogr. Commun. **14**(5), 1145–1177 (2022)
11. Chen, Y.L., Lambooij, E., Mennink, B.: How to build pseudorandom functions from public random permutations. In: Boldyreva, A., Micciancio, D. (eds.) CRYPTO 2019. LNCS, vol. 11692, pp. 266–293. Springer, Cham (2019). https://doi.org/10.1007/978-3-030-26948-7_10

12. Chen, Y.L., Tessaro, S.: Better security-efficiency trade-offs in permutation-based two-party computation. In: Tibouchi, M., Wang, H. (eds.) ASIACRYPT 2021. LNCS, vol. 13091, pp. 275–304. Springer, Cham (2021). https://doi.org/10.1007/978-3-030-92075-3_10

13. Choi, W., Lee, B., Lee, J., Lee, Y.: Toward a fully secure authenticated encryption scheme from a pseudorandom permutation. In: Tibouchi, M., Wang, H. (eds.) ASIACRYPT 2021. LNCS, vol. 13092, pp. 407–434. Springer, Cham (2021). https://doi.org/10.1007/978-3-030-92078-4_14

14. Choi, W., Lee, B., Lee, Y., Lee, J.: Improved security analysis for nonce-based enhanced hash-then-mask MACs. In: Moriai, S., Wang, H. (eds.) ASIACRYPT 2020. LNCS, vol. 12491, pp. 697–723. Springer, Cham (2020). https://doi.org/10.1007/978-3-030-64837-4_23

15. Cogliati, B., Lampe, R., Seurin, Y.: Tweaking even-Mansour ciphers. In: Gennaro, R., Robshaw, M. (eds.) CRYPTO 2015. LNCS, vol. 9215, pp. 189–208. Springer, Heidelberg (2015). https://doi.org/10.1007/978-3-662-47989-6_9

16. Cogliati, B., Seurin, Y.: EWCDM: an efficient, beyond-birthday secure, nonce-misuse resistant MAC. In: Robshaw, M., Katz, J. (eds.) CRYPTO 2016. LNCS, vol. 9814, pp. 121–149. Springer, Heidelberg (2016). https://doi.org/10.1007/978-3-662-53018-4_5

17. Daemen, J., Rijmen, V.: The Design of Rijndael - The Advanced Encryption Standard (AES). Information Security and Cryptography, 2nd edn. Springer, Heidelberg (2020). https://doi.org/10.1007/978-3-662-04722-4

18. Datta, N., Dutta, A., Nandi, M., Yasuda, K.: Encrypt or decrypt? To make a single-key beyond birthday secure nonce-based MAC. In: Shacham, H., Boldyreva, A. (eds.) CRYPTO 2018. LNCS, vol. 10991, pp. 631–661. Springer, Cham (2018). https://doi.org/10.1007/978-3-319-96884-1_21

19. Dutta, A.: Minimizing the two-round tweakable even-Mansour cipher. In: Moriai, S., Wang, H. (eds.) ASIACRYPT 2020. LNCS, vol. 12491, pp. 601–629. Springer, Cham (2020). https://doi.org/10.1007/978-3-030-64837-4_20

20. Dutta, A., Nandi, M.: BBB secure nonce based MAC using public permutations. In: Nitaj, A., Youssef, A. (eds.) AFRICACRYPT 2020. LNCS, vol. 12174, pp. 172–191. Springer, Cham (2020). https://doi.org/10.1007/978-3-030-51938-4_9

21. Dutta, A., Nandi, M., Talnikar, S.: Beyond birthday bound secure MAC in faulty nonce model. In: Ishai, Y., Rijmen, V. (eds.) EUROCRYPT 2019. LNCS, vol. 11476, pp. 437–466. Springer, Cham (2019). https://doi.org/10.1007/978-3-030-17653-2_15

22. Dutta, A., Nandi, M., Talnikar, S.: Permutation based EDM: an inverse free BBB secure PRF. IACR Trans. Symmetric Cryptol. 2, 31–70 (2021)

23. Even, S., Mansour, Y.: A construction of a cipher from a single pseudorandom permutation. In: Imai, H., Rivest, R.L., Matsumoto, T. (eds.) ASIACRYPT 1991. LNCS, vol. 739, pp. 210–224. Springer, Heidelberg (1993). https://doi.org/10.1007/3-540-57332-1_17

24. Guo, C., Katz, J., Wang, X., Yu, Y.: Efficient and secure multiparty computation from fixed-key block ciphers. In: 2020 IEEE Symposium on Security and Privacy, pp. 825–841 (2020)

25. Guo, J., Peyrin, T., Poschmann, A.: The PHOTON family of lightweight hash functions. In: Rogaway, P. (ed.) CRYPTO 2011. LNCS, vol. 6841, pp. 222–239. Springer, Heidelberg (2011). https://doi.org/10.1007/978-3-642-22792-9_13

26. Hoang, V.T., Tessaro, S.: Key-alternating ciphers and key-length extension: exact bounds and multi-user security. In: Robshaw, M., Katz, J. (eds.) CRYPTO 2016. LNCS, vol. 9814, pp. 3–32. Springer, Heidelberg (2016). https://doi.org/10.1007/978-3-662-53018-4_1

27. Jha, A., Nandi, M.: Tight security of cascaded LRW2. J. Cryptol. **33**(3), 1272–1317 (2020)

28. Kim, S., Lee, B., Lee, J.: Tight security bounds for double-block hash-then-sum MACs. In: Canteaut, A., Ishai, Y. (eds.) EUROCRYPT 2020. LNCS, vol. 12105, pp. 435–465. Springer, Cham (2020). https://doi.org/10.1007/978-3-030-45721-1_16

29. Krawczyk, H.: LFSR-based hashing and authentication. In: Desmedt, Y.G. (ed.) CRYPTO 1994. LNCS, vol. 839, pp. 129–139. Springer, Heidelberg (1994). https://doi.org/10.1007/3-540-48658-5_15

30. Mennink, B., Neves, S.: Encrypted davies-meyer and its dual: towards optimal security using mirror theory. In: Katz, J., Shacham, H. (eds.) CRYPTO 2017. LNCS, vol. 10403, pp. 556–583. Springer, Cham (2017). https://doi.org/10.1007/978-3-319-63697-9_19

31. Mouha, N., Luykx, A.: Multi-key security: the even-Mansour construction revisited. In: Gennaro, R., Robshaw, M. (eds.) CRYPTO 2015. LNCS, vol. 9215, pp. 209–223. Springer, Heidelberg (2015). https://doi.org/10.1007/978-3-662-47989-6_10

32. Nandi, M.: Mind the composition: birthday bound attacks on EWCDMD and SoKAC21. In: Canteaut, A., Ishai, Y. (eds.) EUROCRYPT 2020. LNCS, vol. 12105, pp. 203–220. Springer, Cham (2020). https://doi.org/10.1007/978-3-030-45721-1_8

33. Patarin, J.: The "coefficients H" technique (invited talk). In: Avanzi, R.M., Keliher, L., Sica, F. (eds.) SAC 2008. LNCS, vol. 5381, pp. 328–345. Springer, Heidelberg (2009). https://doi.org/10.1007/978-3-642-04159-4_21

34. Patarin, J.: Mirror theory and cryptography. Appl. Algebra Eng. Commun. Comput. **28**(4), 321–338 (2017)

Optimizing Rectangle Attacks: A Unified and Generic Framework for Key Recovery

Ling Song[1,3], Nana Zhang[2,5], Qianqian Yang[2,5(✉)], Danping Shi[2,5], Jiahao Zhao[2,5], Lei Hu[2,5], and Jian Weng[1,3,4]

[1] College of Cyber Security, Jinan University, Guangzhou, China
songling.qs@gmail.com, cryptjweng@gmail.com
[2] State Key Laboratory of Information Security, Institute of Information Engineering, Chinese Academy of Sciences, Beijing, China
{zhangnana,yangqianqian,shidanping,zhaojiahao,hulei}@iie.ac.cn
[3] National Joint Engineering Research Center of Network Security Detection and Protection Technology, Jinan University, Guangzhou, China
[4] Guangdong Key Laboratory of Data Security and Privacy Preserving, Jinan University, Guangzhou, China
[5] School of Cyber Security, University of Chinese Academy of Sciences, Beijing, China

Abstract. The rectangle attack has shown to be a very powerful form of cryptanalysis against block ciphers. Given a rectangle distinguisher, one expects to mount key recovery attacks as efficiently as possible. In the literature, there have been four algorithms for rectangle key recovery attacks. However, their performance vary from case to case. Besides, numerous are the applications where the attacks lack optimality. In this paper, we investigate the rectangle key recovery in depth and propose a unified and generic key recovery algorithm, which supports any possible attacking parameters. Notably, it not only covers the four previous rectangle key recovery algorithms, but also unveils five types of new attacks which were missed previously. Along with the new key recovery algorithm, we propose a framework for automatically finding the best attacking parameters, with which the time complexity of the rectangle attack will be minimized using the new algorithm. To demonstrate the efficiency of the new key recovery algorithm, we apply it to `Serpent`, `CRAFT`, `SKINNY` and `Deoxys-BC-256` based on existing distinguishers and obtain a series of improved rectangle attacks.

Keywords: Boomerang attack · Rectangle attack · Key recovery algorithm · `Serpent` · `CRAFT` · `SKINNY` · `Deoxys-BC`

1 Introduction

Differential cryptanalysis, which was introduced by Biham and Shamir [BS91], is one of the most powerful cryptanalytic approaches for assessing the security of block ciphers. The basic idea is to exploit non-random propagation of input

© International Association for Cryptologic Research 2022
S. Agrawal and D. Lin (Eds.): ASIACRYPT 2022, LNCS 13791, pp. 410–440, 2022.
https://doi.org/10.1007/978-3-031-22963-3_14

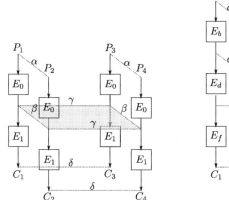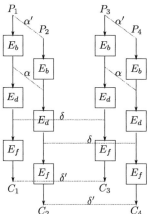

Fig. 1. Basic boomerang attack (left) and the schematic view of the key recovery (right)

difference to output difference, *i.e.*, high-probability differentials. In many cases, it is may be hard to find a long differential of high probability. In 1999, Wagner proposed the boomerang attack [Wag99], which divides a cipher E into two sub-ciphers and utilizes two short differentials of high probability to construct a long one.

Suppose $E = E_1 \circ E_0$, where there are two short differentials $\alpha \to \beta$ and $\gamma \to \delta$ with probability p and q for E_0 and E_1, respectively. The boomerang attack, as depicted in Fig. 1 (left), exploits the high probability of the following differential property:

$$\Pr\left[E^{-1}\left(E(x) \oplus \delta\right) \oplus E^{-1}\left(E(x \oplus \alpha) \oplus \delta\right) = \alpha\right] = p^2 q^2. \tag{1}$$

The basic boomerang attack requires adaptive chosen plaintexts and cipher-texts. Later, Kelsey *et al.* developed a chosen-plaintext variant, named the amplified boomerang attack [KKS00]. However, this transition reduced the probability of the distinguisher to $2^{-n} p^2 q^2$. In [BDK01], Biham *et al.* further converted the amplified boomerang attack into the rectangle attack by considering as many differences as possible in the middle to estimate the probability more accurately. As a result, the probability of a rectangle distinguisher becomes $2^{-n} \hat{p}^2 \hat{q}^2$, where $\hat{p} = \sqrt{\Sigma_i \mathrm{Pr}^2(\alpha \to \beta_i)}$ and $\hat{q} = \sqrt{\Sigma_j \mathrm{Pr}^2(\gamma_j \to \delta)}$. The boomerang and rectangle attack then have been applied to numerous block ciphers, such as Serpent [BDK01], AES [BK09], KASUMI [DKS10b,DKS14], etc.

Since the boomerang attack was proposed, there has been a line of research on estimating the probability of boomerang distinguishers more accurately so as to find better distinguishers. At first, the probability of a boomerang distinguisher was considered as $p^2 q^2$ by simply assuming the two differentials are indepen-dent until the dependency issue between the two differentials came into view. In boomerang or rectangle attacks on concrete ciphers, observations were made that the probability computed via p^2q^2 may be inaccurate in some cases from [BK09,Mur11], where the probability can be higher by using tricks or the two chosen differentials may be even incompatible. Taking the dependency between the two differentials into account, Dunkelman *et al.* suggested the sandwich attack [DKS10b,DKS14] which estimates the probability by p^2q^2r, where r is the exact probability for a middle part. Later, a new tool named boomerang connectivity table (BCT) was proposed to estimate the probability r theoretically [CHP+18,SQH19].

Another line of research on the boomerang and rectangle attack is to mount key recovery attacks as efficiently as possible. Figure 1 (right) displays a schematic view of key recovery attacks based on a distinguisher over the middle part E_d. The first rectangle key recovery algorithm was proposed by Biham *et al.* in [BDK01] along with the proposal of the rectangle attack. This algorithm was applied to 10-round `Serpent` [ABK98] with an 8-round rectangle distinguisher. Shortly after that, in [BDK02] the same authors introduced the second rectangle key recovery algorithm which can improve the result on `Serpent` by reducing the time complexity. There was no improvement until Zhao *et al.* proposed a new rectangle key recovery algorithm in [ZDM+20] which originally works for ciphers with a linear key schedule in the related-key setting, but it can be converted to the single-key setting trivially. Such an algorithm, when applied to `SKINNY` [BJK+16a] outperforms the two previous key recovery algorithms. However, the algorithm presented in a very recent work [DQSW22] makes a step further on improving rectangle attacks on `SKINNY` and some other ciphers.

Motivation. Even though the two recent rectangle key recovery algorithms provide surprisingly good results on `SKINNY`, we carefully check that they do not beat the algorithm in [BDK02] when applied to `Serpent`. On the other hand, the algorithm in [BDK02] is not efficient on `SKINNY` when compared with the two recent ones. Then, the following questions arise.

- Given a rectangle distinguisher of a block cipher, how efficient the key recovery can be?
- Are there any other ways to mount key recovery attacks?

Not only would answers to these questions be of great significance to the cryptanalysis of block ciphers, but also provide a deeper understanding of the key recovery of the rectangle attack.

Our Contributions. In this paper, we investigate the rectangle key recovery in depth and completely answer the above questions. In the previous key recovery algorithms, the involved subkey bits in the rounds added around the distinguisher may or may not be guessed. The four previous algorithms use four different kinds of subkey guessing strategies. Our basic idea is that any possible guessing strategy should be allowed and that there must be a guessing strategy leading to optimal complexities of the key recovery attack. To achieve these, we have to solve two problems. The first is that how the attack proceeds when partial key bits (the extreme cases are full/none of subkey bits) are guessed on both sides of the distinguisher. Note such generalized cases have never been considered before. The second problem is how the attack proceeds so that the time complexity is low.

The starting point of our work is some new insights that the key recovery of the rectangle attack always includes steps of constructing pairs from single messages and quartets from pairs, whereas the number of pairs or quartets that will be constructed is affected by guessed subkey bits. Unlike in the previous works, we do not have to restrain ourselves to only one side and can generate pairs on either side. With this in mind, we come up with a unified and generic rectangle key recovery algorithm which supports any possible attacking parameters, together with a framework to find the best attacking parameters, including the subkey bits to be guessed. Our contributions on the key recovery algorithm are summarized as follows.

- Based on a deeper understanding of the rectangle key recovery, a unified and generic key recovery algorithm is proposed. It supports any number of guessed key bits and covers the four previous rectangle key recovery algorithms, $i.e.$, any of the previous four algorithms is a special case of our algorithm. What's more, it unveils five types of new attacks which were missed previously (see Fig. 4 in Sect. 4 for more information).
- Although our new algorithm supports any set of attacking parameters, it does not tell which is the best on its own. As a complement, we propose a framework for automatically finding the best parameters for the new algorithm. When we feed the parameters returned by this framework to our new key recovery algorithm, the time complexity of the rectangle attack will be minimized.
- We also develop variants of the new key recovery algorithm for related attacks, including the rectangle attack in the related-key setting for ciphers with a linear key schedule and boomerang attacks in both single-key and related-key setting, etc.

Previously, the four mentioned key recovery algorithms are treated as separate ones. Given a rectangle distinguisher, one can compute the complexities for all algorithms and pick the algorithm with the lowest complexity. Now, we can work with the new algorithm only. To demonstrate the efficiency of the new key recovery algorithm, we apply it to four block ciphers using existing distinguishers and obtain a series of improved results.

- We revisit the attack on 10-round Serpent and find better attacks than the one given in [BDK02].
- We revisit the rectangle attacks on round-reduced SKINNY in [DQSW22], which are the best existing attacks on SKINNY in the related-tweakey setting. For the four distinguishers of SKINNY, we find better attacks for three of them, despite the fact that these distinguishers were searched dedicated for the key recovery algorithm in [DQSW22].

- We extend the rectangle attack on CRAFT by one round and give the first 19-round attack, which is the best attack on this cipher so far in the single-key setting.
- On Deoxys-BC-256, we improved the 11-round rectangle attack and extend the boomerang attack by one round in the related-tweakey setting. These are the best attacks on Deoxys-BC-256 so far in terms of time complexity.

These results are summarized in Table 1. According to these applications, we find that the best attacking parameters differ significantly from those which were used in previous works and even the number rounds added around the distinguisher is different. Notably, these new attacking parameters are not covered by the previous key recovery algorithms in many cases. Thus, it is likely that previous rectangle attacks can be improved to some extent using the new key recovery algorithm.

Table 1. Summary of the cryptanalytic results.

Cipher	Rounds	Data	Memory	Time	Approach	Setting	Ref.
Serpent	10	$2^{126.8}$	2^{192}	2^{217}	Rectangle	SK	[BDK01]
		$2^{126.3}$	$2^{126.3}$	$2^{173.8}$	Rectangle	SK	[BDK02]
		$2^{126.3}$	$2^{126.3}$	$2^{159.11}$	Rectangle	SK	Section 5.1
		$2^{124.15}$	$2^{124.15}$	$2^{155.67}$	Rectangle	SK	Section 5.1
CRAFT	18	$2^{60.92}$	2^{84}	$2^{101.7}$	Rectangle	SK	[HBS21]
	19	$2^{60.92}$	2^{72}	$2^{112.61}$	Rectangle	SK	Section 5.2
SKINNY-64-128	25	$2^{61.67}$	$2^{64.26}$	$2^{118.43}$	Rectangle	RK	[DQSW22]
		$2^{61.67}$	$2^{63.67}$	$2^{110.03}$	Rectangle	RK	Section 5.3
SKINNY-128-384	32	$2^{123.54}$	$2^{123.54}$	$2^{354.99}$	Rectangle	RK	[DQSW22]
		$2^{123.54}$	$2^{129.54}$	$2^{344.78}$	Rectangle	RK	Full version
SKINNY-128-256	26	$2^{126.53}$	2^{136}	$2^{254.4}$	Rectangle	RK	[DQSW22]
		$2^{126.53}$	2^{136}	$2^{241.38}$	Rectangle	RK	Full version
Deoxys-BC-256	10	$2^{127.58}$	$2^{127.58}$	2^{204}	Rectangle	RK	[CHP+17]
	11	$2^{122.1}$	$2^{128.2}$	$2^{249.9}$	Rectangle	RK	[ZDJ19]
	11	$2^{126.78}$	2^{128}	$2^{222.49}$	Rectangle	RK	Full version
	10	$2^{98.4}$	2^{88}	$2^{249.9}$	Boomerang	RK	[ZDJ19]
	11	$2^{122.4}$	2^{128}	$2^{218.65}$	Boomerang	RK	Section 5.4

Organization. The rest of the paper is organized as follows. In Sect. 2, we give notations which will be used throughout the paper. In Sect. 3, the new rectangle key recovery algorithm will be introduced as well as the framework for automatically finding the best attacking parameters and extensions of the new algorithm. In Sect. 4, we compare our new rectangle key recovery algorithm with the four previous ones in detail. Section 5 presents applications of the new algorithm to four block ciphers. We conclude this paper in Sect. 6.

2   Notations

In this paper, we focus on the key recovery for a given boomerang distinguisher. For simplicity, we treat a target cipher $E : \{0,1\}^n \times \{0,1\}^k \to \{0,1\}^n$ as $E = E_f \circ E_d \circ E_b$, where there is a boomerang distinguisher over E_d of probability P^2, i.e.,

$$\Pr\left[E_d^{-1}(E_d(P_1) \oplus \delta) \oplus E_d^{-1}(E_d(P_1 \oplus \alpha) \oplus \delta) = \alpha\right] = P^2. \qquad (2)$$

That is, we take the probability of the boomerang distinguisher for P^2 and do not pay attention to whether it is evaluated with p^2q^2r or $\hat{q}^2\hat{q}^2$. Figure 1 (right) depicts the framework of E, where E_b and E_f are added around E_d. The aim of the key recovery is to identify partial subkeys used in E_b and E_f by utilizing the distinguisher over E_d and further to find the master key more efficiently than the exhaustive search.

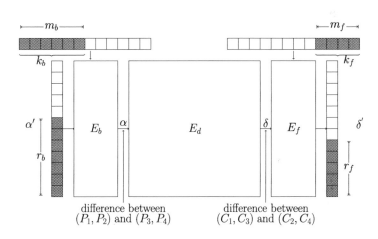

difference between   difference between
(P_1, P_2) and (P_3, P_4) (C_1, C_3) and (C_2, C_4)

Fig. 2. Outline of rectangle key recovery attack

To describe the key recovery, a series of notations are used through out the paper. For convenience, we borrow some notations which are frequently used in the previous works on rectangle attacks, such as [BDK02, LGS17, ZDM+20, DQSW22]. As shown in Fig. 2, the input difference of the distinguisher α propagates back over E_b^{-1} to α'. Let V_b be the space spanned by all possible α' where $r_b = \log_2 |V_b|$. The output difference of the distinguisher δ propagates forward over E_f to δ'. Let V_f be the space spanned by all possible δ' where $r_f = \log_2 |V_f|$. Let k_b be the subset of subkey bits which are employed in E_b and affect the propagation $\alpha' \to \alpha$. Similarly, let k_f be the subset of subkey bits which are used in E_b and affect the propagation $\delta \leftarrow \delta'$. Then let $m_b = |k_b|$ and $m_f = |k_f|$ be the number of bits in k_b and k_f, respectively.

In a specific key recovery algorithm, a part of k_b and k_f, denoted by k_b', k_f', may be guessed at first. Let $m_b' = |k_b'|$ and $m_f' = |k_f'|$. With the guessed subkey bits, the differential propagations $\alpha' \to \alpha$ and $\delta \leftarrow \delta'$ can be partially verified. Suppose under the guessed subkey bits a r_b'-bit condition on the top and a r_f'-bit condition on the bottom can be verified. Finally, let $r_b^* = r_b - r_b'$ and $r_f^* = r_f - r_f'$.

In this paper, we mainly focus on the rectangle key recovery algorithms in the single-key setting and these can be easily converted into the related-key setting for ciphers with linear key schedule.

3   A Unified and Generic Key Recovery Algorithm

In this section, we present our unified and generic key recovery algorithm for the rectangle attack. Before specifying our algorithm, we recall basics of the rectangle attack and provide new insights into the key recovery, which will be the base of our algorithm. Our algorithm is generic and supports any possible key guessing strategy. However, given a specific rectangle distinguisher, which parameters are the best for our algorithm? A framework for automatically finding the best parameters is then introduced afterwards. Finally, we discuss extensions of our algorithm to related cases.

3.1   Basic Ideas and Intuitions

In this subsection, we recall the principles of the rectangle attack and give some new insights on the key recovery which are core ideas behind our new algorithm.

As can be seen from Fig. 1 and Eq. (2), the boomerang distinguisher is built on a nonrandom property of quartets. The rectangle distinguisher is its chosen-plaintext variant. This nonrandom property is then used to extract subkey information in E_b and E_f. As in standard differential cryptanalysis, candidates for subkey k_b and k_f are identified if they are suggested by a sufficiently large number of quartets. Here, k_b and k_f are suggested by a quartet $(P_i, C_i), i = 1, 2, 3, 4$, if

$$E_b(k_b, P_1) \oplus E_b(k_b, P_2) = E_b(k_b, P_3) \oplus E_b(k_b, P_4) = \alpha,$$
$$E_f^{-1}(k_f, C_1) \oplus E_f^{-1}(k_f, C_3) = E_f^{-1}(k_f, C_2) \oplus E_f^{-1}(k_f, C_4) = \delta$$

holds. As shown in Fig. 2, the α difference propagates to α' via E_b^{-1} and $\alpha' \in V_b$. It does not mean every element of V_b is a possible α', whereas any difference outside V_b is impossible for α. The same applies for the bottom side. This means, quartets with plaintext difference outside V_b or ciphertext difference outside V_f will not suggest any subkeys. Therefore, an important step in rectangle key recovery algorithms is to construct quartets which are possible to suggest subkeys and at least satisfy $P_1 \oplus P_2, P_3 \oplus P_4 \in V_b$ and $C_1 \oplus C_3, C_2 \oplus C_4 \in V_f$.

Data Complexity. A commonly-used idea to improve differential cryptanalysis is to employ plaintext structures. A plaintext structure takes all possible values for the r_b bits and chooses a constant for the remaining $n - r_b$ bits. It allows to enjoy the birthday effect. For each structure, there are 2^{2r_b-1} pairs of plaintext with difference in V_b and 2^{r_b-1} of them satisfy α difference by meeting the r_b-bit condition.

Given a boomerang distinguisher with probability P^2, the number of quartets satisfying the input difference α of the distinguisher should be at least $sP^{-2}2^n$ for a rectangle attack, where s is the expected number of right quartets (say $s = 4$). These quartets can be formed from plaintext pairs taken in structures. Suppose the number of structures needed is y. Note y structures can constitute $2 \cdot \binom{y2^{r_b-1}}{2}^1$ quartets that satisfy α difference. Then $y = \sqrt{s}2^{n/2-r_b+1}/P$ and the data complexity is $D = y \cdot 2^{r_b} = \sqrt{s}2^{n/2+1}/P$. This infers that the data complexity is the same with different key recovery algorithms.

Time Complexity. Next, let us investigate the time complexity from a high-level perspective. We stress that the key recovery of the rectangle attack always includes steps of constructing pairs from single messages and quartets from pairs. Therefore, the whole key recovery can be split into the following phases: (1) data collection, (2) pair construction, (3) constructing quartets and processing them to extract subkeys, and last (4) a brute force search for the unique right master key among key candidates. The time complexities of the first and the last phases are easy to estimate, so let us focus on the time complexities of the middle two phases, which we denote by T_2 and T_3, respectively.

T_3 is mainly affected by the number of quartet candidates. From D plaintexts, we can construct $N = D^2 \cdot 2^{2r_b+2r_f-2n-2}$ quartet candidates with plaintext difference in V_b and ciphertext difference in V_f. This seems to be a fixed term like the data complexity. However, the number of quartets to be processed may be reduced when some subkey bits are guessed. Recall that m_b-bit k_b and m_f-bit k_f are involved for the propagation $\alpha' \leftarrow \alpha$ and $\delta \rightarrow \delta'$ and verifying α difference and δ difference for such a quartet takes $2r_b$-bit and $2r_f$-bit conditions (as there are two pairs), respectively. Thus, there will be $N \cdot 2^{m_b+m_f-2r_b-2r_f} = D^2 \cdot 2^{m_b+m_f-2n-2}$ suggestions for k_b and k_f in total. On average, the number of suggestions for a wrong subkey is less than 1 as $D^2 \cdot 2^{-2n-2} < 1$, while it is s for the right subkey. On the one hand, this confirms that the rectangle attack works; on the other hand, it means when the subkey is fixed, most quartets are wrong and thus may likely be filtered out before being constructed. This is what has been done in the first rectangle key recovery algorithm proposed in [BDK01], which guesses the whole k_b and k_f.

However, a full guess of k_b and k_f is not necessary to reduce the number of quartet candidates, as studied in [ZDM+20, DQSW22]. In this paper, we consider the most general situation where a part of k_b, i.e., k_b', and a part of k_f, i.e., k_f' are guessed, with $m_b' = |k_b'|$, $m_f' = |k_f'|$, $0 \leq m_b' \leq m_b$ and $0 \leq m_f' \leq m_f$. To have a better view of this situation, we present a toy example in Fig. 3 to illustrate the parameters. Assume under the guess a r_b'-bit (resp. r_f'-bit) condition can

---

[1] If both (P_1, P_2) and (P_3, P_4) satisfy α difference, then we can form two quartets: (P_1, P_2, P_3, P_4) and (P_1, P_2, P_4, P_3).

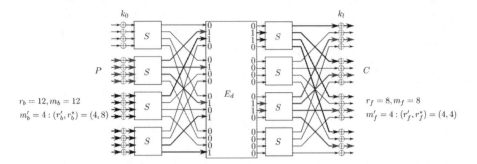

Fig. 3. A toy example to illustrate the parameters of the rectangle key recovery. Both E_b and E_f contain one round. Bold lines stand for active bits, so $r_b = 12$, $r_f = 8$ and the number of involved subkey bits in E_b and E_f are $m_b = 12$ and $m_f = 8$, respectively. The subkey bits corresponding to blue lines are guessed. With the guessed subkey bits, $r_b' = 4$ out of $r_b = 12$ bits of conditions can be ensured. Likewise, $r_f' = 4$ out of $r_f = 8$ bits of conditions can be ensured. (Color figure online)

be verified for a plaintext (resp. ciphertext) pair. Then the number of quartets to be processed is $2^{m_b' + m_f'} \cdot D^2 \cdot 2^{2r_b^* + 2r_f^* - 2n - 2}$, where $r_b^* = r_b - r_b'$ and $r_f^* = r_f - r_f'$. We point out the number of quartet candidates gets smaller as long as $m_b' + m_f' < 2r_b' + 2r_f'$.

Let us come to the time complexity of constructing pairs, i.e., T_2. Note that T_2 is determined by the number of pairs that are used to construct quartets. We emphasize that pairs can be constructed either on the top for plaintexts or on the bottom for ciphertexts. Still assume partial subkey bits are guessed. Then the number of filters for plaintext pairs is $n - r_b^*$ while it is roughly $n - r_f^*$ for ciphertext pairs (we will present the exact number of filters in the next subsection). Since filters for plaintext pairs and filters for ciphertext pairs work on different faces, they can not be taken into account simultaneously in the phase of constructing pairs. *The key principle is to form pairs on the side with more filters so that T_2 is lower.*

Questions. Then, there come two questions:

Question 1: *How does the key recovery algorithm proceed when k_b' and k_f' are guessed, where $m_b' = |k_b'|$, $m_f' = |k_f'|$, $0 \le m_b' \le m_b$ and $0 \le m_f' \le m_f$?*

Question 2: *What is the best choice for (k_b', k_f') so that the overall time complexity is minimized?*

To answer the first question, we propose a detailed algorithm for the rectangle key recovery in the next subsection. Because this algorithm supports any possible (k_b', k_f') and covers all previous key recovery algorithms, we call it a generic and unified algorithm for the rectangle key recovery. For the second question, we present a framework for automatically finding the best (k_b', k_f') in Sect. 3.3. Combining both, we are able to find the most efficient rectangle key recovery attack.

3.2   Generic and Unified Algorithm for the Rectangle Key Recovery Attack

In the following, we describe our algorithm for the rectangle key recovery attack which works for any number of guessed key bits. Like the most key recovery algorithm, our new algorithm also employs the counting method. Namely, we set counters for the involved subkey bits and search for the correct one among the subkey candidates with a large number of suggestions. Suppose m'_b-bit k'_b and m'_f-bit k'_f are to be guessed. For these guessed subkey bits, we may or may not set counters for them. To enjoy such flexibility, we set counters for t bits of the guessed subkey bits, $0 \leq t \leq m'_b + m'_f$.

Then the specific steps of our algorithm are as follows. Note the toy example in Fig. 3 would be helpful for understanding the algorithm.

1. Collect and store y structures of 2^{r_b} plaintexts. Hence, the data complexity is $D = y \cdot 2^{r_b}$. The time and memory complexities of this step are also D.
2. Split $(m'_b + m'_f)$-bit $k'_b \| k'_f$ into two parts: $G_L \| G_R$ where G_L has t bits.
3. Guess G_R:
   (a) Initialized a list of key counters for G_L and the unguessed key bits of k_b, k_f. The memory complexity in this step is $2^{t+m_b+m_f-m'_b-m'_f}$.
   (b) Guess the t-bit G_L:
       i. For each data (P_1, C_1), partially encrypt P_1 and partially decrypt C_1 under the guessed subkey bits. Let $P_1^* = Enc_{k'_b}(P_1)$ and $C_1^* = Dec_{k'_f}(C_1)$. For each structure, we will get $2^{r'_b}$ sub-structures, each of which includes $2^{r_b-r'_b} = 2^{r_b^*}$ plaintexts which take all possible values for the active bits. In other words, there are $y^* = y \cdot 2^{r'_b}$ structures of $2^{r_b^*}$ plaintexts. The time complexity of this step is D.
       ii. Let $2^{-\mu} = D \cdot 2^{-n}$. If $r_b^* \leq r_f^* - \mu^2$, it turns to step (A); else if $r_b^* > r_f^* - \mu$, it turns to step (D).
           A. Insert all the obtained (P_1^*, C_1^*) into a hash table according to $n - r_b^*$ bits of P_1^*. Then construct a set as $S = \{(P_1^*, C_1^*, P_2^*, C_2^*) : P_1^*$ and P_2^* have difference only in r_b^* bits$\}$. The size of S is $y \cdot 2^{r_b} \cdot 2^{2(r_b-r'_b)-1} = D \cdot 2^{r_b^*-1}$. Hence, the time and memory complexities of this step are both $D \cdot 2^{r_b^*-1}$.
           B. Insert S into a hash table by $n - (r_f - r'_f) = n - r_f^*$ inactive bits of C_1^* and $n - (r_f - r'_f) = n - r_f^*$ inactive bits of C_2^*.
           C. For each $2(n-r_f^*)$-bit index, we pick two distinct $(P_1^*, C_1^*, P_2^*, C_2^*)$, $(P_3^*, C_3^*, P_4^*, C_4^*)$ to generate the quartet. We will get

           $$2 \cdot \binom{\frac{|S|}{2^{2(n-r_f^*)}}}{2} \cdot 2^{2(n-r_f^*)} = D^2 \cdot 2^{2r_b^*} \cdot 2^{2r_f^*} \cdot 2^{-2n-2}$$

           quartets. Then go to step (iii).

---

[2] The number of filters for plaintext pairs is $n - r_b^*$ while it is $n - r_f^* + \mu$ for ciphertext pairs.

D. Insert all the obtained (P_1^*, C_1^*) into a hash table according to $n - r_f^*$ bits of C_1^*. Then construct a set as $S = \{(P_1^*, C_1^*, P_3^*, C_3^*) : C_1^*$ and C_3^* are colliding in $n - r_f^*$ bits$\}$. The size of S is $D^2 \cdot 2^{r_f - r_f' - n - 1} = D \cdot 2^{r_f' - 1 - \mu}$. Hence, the time and memory complexities of this step are both $D \cdot 2^{r_f' - 1 - \mu}$.

E. Insert S into a hash table by $n - r_b^*$ inactive bits of P_1^* and $n - r_b^*$ inactive bits of P_3^*.

F. There are at most $2^{2(n - r_b^* - \mu)}$ possible values for the $2(n - r_b^*)$-bit index. For each index, we pick two distinct entries $(P_1^*, C_1^*, P_3^*, C_3^*)$, $(P_2^*, C_2^*, P_4^*, C_4^*)$ to generate the quartet. We will get

$$2 \cdot \binom{\frac{|S|}{2^{2(n - r_b^* - \mu)}}}{2} \cdot 2^{2(n - r_b^* - \mu)} = D^2 \cdot 2^{2r_b^*} \cdot 2^{2r_f^*} \cdot 2^{-2n-2}$$

quartets.

iii. Determine the key candidates involved in E_b and E_f and increase the corresponding counters. Denote the time complexity for processing one quartet as ϵ. Then the time complexity in this step is $D^2 \cdot 2^{2r_b^*} \cdot 2^{2r_f^*} \cdot 2^{-2n-2} \cdot \epsilon$.

(c) Select the top $2^{t + m_b + m_f - m_b' - m_f' - h}$ hits in the counters to be the candidates, which delivers a h-bit or higher advantage, where $0 < h \le t + m_b + m_f - m_b' - m_f'$.

(d) Guess the remaining $k - m_b - m_f$ unknown key bits according to the key schedule algorithm and exhaustively search over them to recover the correct key. The time complexity of this step is $2^{k + t - m_b' - m_f' - h}$.

Data Complexity. The data complexity is $D = y \cdot 2^{r_b} = \sqrt{s} 2^{n/2+1}/P$.

Memory Complexity. The memory complexity is $M = D + min\{D \cdot 2^{r_b^* - 1}, D \cdot 2^{r_f' - 1 - \mu}\} + 2^{t + m_b + m_f - m_b' - m_f'}$ for storing the data, the set S, and the key counters.

Time Complexity. The time complexity of collecting data is $T_0 = D$, the time complexity of doing partial encryption and decryption under guessed key bits is

$$T_1 = 2^{m_b' + m_f'} \cdot D = 2^{m_b' + m_f'} \cdot y \cdot 2^{r_b} = \sqrt{s} \cdot 2^{m_b' + m_f' + \frac{n}{2} + 1}/P,$$

the time complexity of generating set S is

$$T_2 = 2^{m_b' + m_f'} \cdot D \cdot min\{2^{r_b^* - 1}, 2^{r_f' - 1 - \mu}\}$$
$$= min\{\sqrt{s} \cdot 2^{m_b' + m_f' + r_b - r_b^* + \frac{n}{2}}/P, s \cdot 2^{m_b' + m_f' + r_f - r_f' + 1}/P^2\},$$

the time complexity of generating and processing quartet candidates is

$$T_3 = 2^{m_b' + m_f'} \cdot D^2 \cdot 2^{2r_b^*} \cdot 2^{2r_f^*} \cdot 2^{-2n-2} \cdot \epsilon = (s \cdot 2^{m_b' + m_f' - n + 2r_b + 2r_f - 2r_b' - 2r_f' + 1}/P^2) \cdot \epsilon,$$

and the time complexity of exhaustive search is $T_4 = 2^{m'_b + m'_f - t}$. $2^{k+t-m'_b - m'_f - h} = 2^{k-h}$, where $h \leq 2^{t+m_b+m_f-m'_b-m'_f}$. The overall time complexity is the sum of $T_i, i \in [0, 4]$.

On h. According to [Sel08], the success probability of differential analysis is

$$P_s = \int_{\frac{\sqrt{sS_N} - \Phi^{-1}(1-2^{-h})}{\sqrt{S_N+1}}}^{\infty} \phi(x)dx,$$

where S_N is the signal-to-noise ratio and $S_N = \frac{2^{-n} P^2}{2^{-2n}}$ in rectangle attacks as well as in boomerang attacks. In the algorithm, the parameter t not only gives much greater flexibility in choosing h, but also allows the previous rectangle key recovery algorithm to fit in easily regarding setting the key counters. We will discuss more about the relation with the previous algorithms in Sect. 4.

On ϵ. In the algorithm, m'_b bits of k_b and m'_f bits of k_f are guessed, respectively. With the guessed subkey bits, partial differential propagation over E_b (resp. E_f) can be ensured by properly selecting pairs. Now suppose input difference (resp. output difference) fall in a smaller space V_b^* (resp. V_f^*) where $r_b^* = |V_b^*|$ (resp. $r_f^* = |V_f^*|$). In step 3(d) of the algorithm, the subkey information is extracted from quartets with input difference in V_b^* and output difference in V_f^*. Then, ϵ is defined to be the time to process one such quartet.

Recall that a right quartet satisfies $E_b(P_1) \oplus E_b(P_2) = \alpha = E_b(P_3) \oplus E_b(P_4)$. Both pairs are encrypted by the same subkey, so a right quartet must agree on the remaining m_b^* bits of k_b. Under the guess of m'_b bits of k_b, there are $2^{r_b^*}$ possible input differences that lead to α difference after E_b. Since each pair suggests $2^{m_b^* - r_b^*}$ subkeys on average, both pairs agree on $2^{2(m_b^* - r_b^*)}/2^{m_b^*} = 2^{m_b^* - 2r_b^*}$ for E_b. Similarly, for E_f we get $2^{m_f^* - 2r_f^*}$ suggestions for the remaining m_f^* bits of k_f. Consequently, each quartet suggests $2^{m_b^* + m_f^* - 2r_b^* - 2r_f^*}$ possible subkeys.

There are different methods to deduce the remaining m_b^* bits of k_b suggested by these quartets. A recommended method is to precompute a hash table for all possible input pairs and the value of m_b^*-bit k_b that can lead to α difference. This table can be built with time complexity $2^{r_b^* + m_b^*}$ and indexed by the values of the pairs. The memory cost of this table is $2^{r_b^* + m_b^*}$ (rather than $2^{r_b^*}$ in [BDK01]). When processing a quartet, we can extract the subkey candidates suggested by both pairs by looking up the table twice. Do the same thing for E_f. Therefore, ϵ will be no more than $\max\{4, 2^{m_b^* - r_b^*} + 2^{m_f^* - r_f^*}\}$ memory accesses, provided that two lookup tables have been built with time and memory complexity of $2^{r_b^* + m_b^*} + 2^{r_f^* + m_f^*}$. If $2^{m_b^* - r_b^*} + 2^{m_f^* - r_f^*}$ is relatively large, ϵ can be lowered to no more than $\max\{2, 2^{m_b^* - 2r_b^*} + 2^{m_f^* - 2r_f^*}\}$ by using tables built for quartets. In this case, the memory cost increases to $2^{2r_b^* + m_b^*} + 2^{2r_f^* + m_f^*}$, which also means achieving the smallest ϵ at the cost of memory. This is specially profitable when $2^{2r_b^* + m_b^*} + 2^{2r_f^* + m_f^*}$ is not dominant for memory cost.

Note that sometimes the above method of processing quartets may not be applied directly. In certain cases, besides the r_b^* bits, some other non-active bits of pairs are needed to verify α difference after E_b, resulting in a larger time complexity for building a precomputation table as well as a larger memory cost. For the bottom part E_f, it is similar. As an example, this can be seen from rectangle attacks on SKINNY (*e.g.*, Fig. 7). In such cases, we suggest building lookup tables for smaller local operations. Consequently, ϵ can be equivalent to a few memory accesses.

Another method to determine the remaining subkey bits suggested by a quartet candidate is to guess and check. One can guess the remaining subkey bits and check if the quartet is a right one under the guess. Such a method does not require additional memory, whereas ϵ is an amount of partial encryptions or decrytions.

Minimizing the Time Complexity. As can be seen from the formulas of $T_i, i \in [0, 4]$, the overall time complexity depends on the number of guessed subkey bits $m_b' + m_f'$ and the number of filters $r_b' + r_f'$ obtained under these guessed subkey bits. In order to reduce the time complexity, a natural strategy is to guess those subkey bits which can lead to a large filter. If each subkey cell is equally profitable (*e.g.*, the attack on Serpent in Sect. 5.1), one can find by hand the subkey k_b' and k_f' to be guessed in the key recovery, so that the time complexity is minimized. However, it is not the case for many ciphers. For certain ciphers, not only the subkey cells are not equally profitable, but also the subkey cells are closely related through the key schedule. Finding the best parameters by hand is challenging. Moreover, given a set of parameters that permit an efficient key recovery, one may wonder whether it is optimal or not. Therefore, optimal rectangle attacks are possible only when the above key recovery algorithm is fed with a set of proper parameters.

3.3   Framework for Finding the Best Attacking Parameters

In this subsection, we present a framework which acts as a complement of our new key recovery algorithm. This framework finds the best attacking parameters for the rectangle attack. When we apply the parameters returned by this framework to our key recovery algorithm, the time complexity of the attack will be minimal.

Specifically, the framework takes as input a boomerang distinguisher with (α, δ, P^2), *i.e.*, the input difference and output difference, and its probability, and extended rounds (E_d, E_f), and returns (k_b', k_f') and the minimal time complexity. In essence, this is a optimization problem which can be solved with various tools. A similarity can be observed in finding optimal differential/linear trails [SHW+14, SWW21, KLT15], division property [HLM+20], meet-in-the-middle attack [SSD+18], etc. Therefore, tools like Mixed-Integer Linear Programming (MILP) and SAT which are widely used for solving these previously mentioned problems can be applied as well in this framework. Since we want to keep our framework generic and flexible, we will describe it as a template in a high level language. When it comes to a specific cipher, one can instantiate it and solve it with MILP solvers or SAT solvers.

Our framework has five modules:

Difference propagation. Model the differentials $\alpha' \xleftarrow{E_b^{-1}} \alpha$ and $\delta \xrightarrow{E_f} \delta'$, both of which propagate difference with probability 1. Compute r_b and r_f. Mark the state cell if its difference is fixed.

Value path. Mark the state cells whose values are needed for verifying α difference and δ difference. Alongside, mark the subkey k_b and k_f which are needed for the verification.

Guess-and-determine. Model the relation between the subkey bits and the internal state cells, *i.e.*, when certain subkey bits are guessed, the corresponding internal state cell can be determined. When a internal state cell resulting from some active cells is determined and should have a fixed difference, then a filter is reached. Model the number of filters $r_b' + r_f'$.

Key bridging.[3] Model the relation between subkey bits according to the key schedule algorithm. Model the number of *independent* guessed subkey bits $m_b' + m_f'$.

Objective function. Compute $T_i, i \in [0, 4]$ from $P, n, r_b, r_f, r_b', r_f', m_b'$ and m_f'. Set the objective function to $min \sum_0^4 T_i$.

Other constraints can be imposed alongside, such as constraints on memory. Given a rectangle distinguisher of a certain cipher, one can follow this framework to build a concrete model dedicated to this cipher and try different E_b and E_f to find a set of best parameters. Key information that can be extracted from these parameters include

- Subkey k_b' and k_f' which will be guessed;
- The number of independent key bits in k_b' and k_f', *i.e.*, $m_b' + m_f'$;
- The overall time complexity.

Feed these parameter to our key recovery algorithm, the rectangle key recovery will be optimized. For more details, one can refer to our source codes[4] which showcase the implementation of this framework for the attack on `Serpent`.

3.4   Extensions

In this subsection, we discuss possible extensions of our rectangle key recovery algorithm presented in Sect. 3.2. Details about the extensions listed below can be found in the full version of this paper [SZY+22].

When $r_b = n$. The algorithm in Sect. 3.2 applies only when $r_b < n$. However, it can be extended to the case when $r_b = n$ by changing the way of choosing plaintexts.

---

[3] "Key bridging" is borrowed from [DKS10a,DKS15] which originally connects two subkeys separated by several key mixing steps.

[4] https://drive.google.com/file/d/1gZpqtm4pg6ezZ4TrS9cRirnRz9YbqjgL/view? usp=sharing.

The Related-Key Setting. The algorithm in Sect. 3.2 is specifically targeted at the rectangle attack in the single-key setting. With small modifications, it can be adapted to the related-key setting for ciphers with a linear key schedule. This extension is particularly useful as many block ciphers, especially lightweight ones, employ a linear key schedule, *e.g.*, SKINNY [BJK+16a] and Deoxys-BC [JNPS16].

Boomerang Attack. An attacker can only choose plaintexts in rectangle attacks. However, in boomerang attacks, the attacker is allowed to choose plaintexts and ciphertexts adaptively. With this in mind, we also propose variants of our algorithm dedicated for boomerang attacks. We specifically consider the key recovery for $E = E_d \circ E_b$ and $E = E_f \circ E_d$. The algorithm for the latter case is presented as follows.

Boomerang Key Recovery for $E = E_f \circ E_d$. Similarly, we assume there exists a distinguisher of E_d, whose probability is P^2, input difference is α and output difference is δ. E_f is appended to E_d and partial subkey k'_f will be guessed.

1. Construct a set S_0 which is made up of y structures, each of 2^{r_f} ciphertexts. Let $D = y \cdot 2^{r_f}$. Query and collect two sets of data:

$$S_1 = \{(P_1, C_1)|P_1 = E^{-1}(C_1), C_1 \in S_0\},$$

$$S_2 = \{(P_2, C_2)|P_2 = P_1 \oplus \alpha, C_2 = E(P_2), P_1 \in S_1\}.$$

2. Split m'_f-bit k'_f into two parts: $G_L\|G_R$ where G_L has t bits, $0 \leq t \leq m'_f$.
3. Guess G_R:
   (a) Initialized a list of key counters for G_L and unguessed key bits of k_f.
   (b) Guess the t-bit G_L:
       i. For each data in S_1, S_2, do partial decryptions under k'_f. Let $C_1^* = Dec_{k'_f}(C_1)$ and $C_2^* = Dec_{k'_f}(C_2)$. Then the set of obtained C_1^* contains $y \cdot 2^{r_f}$ sub-structures, each of 2^{r_f} ciphertexts.
       ii. Construct a set as

$$S_{1,2} = \{(P_1, C_1^*, P_2, C_2^*)|P_2 = P_1 \oplus \alpha, C_2^* = Dec_{k'_f}(Enc(P_2))\}.$$

Insert $S_{1,2}$ into a hash table by $n - r_f^*$ inactive bits of C_1^* and $n - r_f^*$ inactive bits of C_2^*.
       iii. There are $y \cdot 2^{r_f}$ possible values for the $n - r_f^*$ bits of C_1^* and $2^{n-r_f^*}$ possible values for the $n - r_f^*$ bits of C_2^*. For each index, we pick two distinct entries (P_1, C_1^*, P_2, C_2^*) and (P_3, C_3^*, P_4, C_4^*) to generate the quartet. The number of quartet we will get is

$$\binom{\frac{|S_{1,2}|}{2^{n-r_f^*} \cdot y \cdot 2^{r_f}}}{2} \cdot 2^{n-r_f^*} \cdot y \cdot 2^{r_f} = D \cdot 2^{2r_f^*-n-1}.$$

       iv. Determine the key candidates involved in E_f and increase the corresponding counters. Denote the time complexity for processing one quartet as ϵ.

(c) Select the top $2^{t+m_f-m'_f-h}$ hits in the counters to be the candidates, $0 < h \le t + m_f - m'_f$, which delivers a h-bit or higher advantage.

(d) Guess the remaining $k - m_f$ unknown key bits according to the key schedule algorithm and exhaustively search over them to recover the correct key, where k is the key size.

Data Complexity. From y structures, we can form $y \cdot 2^{2r_f - 1}$ plaintext pairs. Among them, $y \cdot 2^{r_f - 1}$ pairs satisfy δ difference on average. Let s be the expected number of right quartets, so we have $y \cdot 2^{r_f - 1} \cdot P^2 = s$, $y = s \cdot 2^{1-r_f}/P^2$ and $D = y \cdot 2^{r_f} = 2s/P^2$. Therefore, the data complexity is $D_B = 2D = 4s/P^2$.

Memory Complexity. The memory complexity is $M = D_B + D + 2^{t+m_f-m'_f}$ to store the data, the set $S_{1,2}$ and the counters.

Time Complexity. The time complexity of collecting data is $T_0 = D_B$, the time complexity of doing partial encryption and decryption under guessed key bits is

$$T_1 = 2^{m'_f} \cdot D_B = 2^{m'_f} \cdot 2 \cdot y \cdot 2^{r_f} = s \cdot 2^{m'_f+2}/P^2,$$

the time complexity of generating set S is

$$T_2 = 2^{m'_f} \cdot D = s \cdot 2^{m'_f+1}/P^2,$$

the time complexity of generating and processing quartet candidates is

$$T_3 = 2^{m'_f} \cdot D \cdot 2^{2r_f^*} \cdot 2^{-n-1} \cdot \epsilon = s \cdot 2^{m'_f+2r_f-2r'_f-n}/P^2,$$

and the time complexity of exhaustive search is $T_4 = 2^{m'_f-t} \cdot 2^{k+t-m'_f-h} = 2^{k-h}$, where $h \le t + m_f - m'_f$.

4   Comparison with Related Works

Rectangle Key Recovery Algorithms in Previous Works. The rectangle attack was proposed by Biham, Dunkelman, and Keller in [BDK01] and has been applied to Serpent [ABK98]. Later, the same authors introduced a new rectangle key recovery algorithm in [BDK02] which improves the result on Serpent by reducing the time complexity. Since then, no much progress has been made until Zhao *et al.* proposed a new key recovery algorithm in [ZDM+20] which originally works for ciphers with a linear key schedule in the related-key setting, but it can be converted to the single-key setting trivially. Such an algorithm, when applied to SKINNY, outperforms the two previous key recovery algorithms. However, the algorithm presented in a very recent work [DQSW22] makes a step further on improving rectangle attacks on SKINNY. For convenience, we call these four rectangle key recovery algorithm in a chronological order by Algorithm 1, Algorithm

2, Algorithm 3, and Algorithm 4, respectively. As concluded in [DQSW22], these algorithms seem independent and perform differently for different parameters. Given a rectangle distinguisher, one can pick the algorithm with lowest complexity among them.

Similarities Between Our Algorithm and the Previous Algorithms. Our new algorithm reuses some techniques of the previous algorithms.

- Like Algorithm 2, we recommend using hash tables when generating pairs and quartets. It costs a certain amount of memory (not necessarily increases the overall memory complexity), but the time complexity is lowered.
- When constructing quartets, we apply the filters on both pairs simultaneously with the help of hash tables. This is also a strategy to trade memory with time which has been used in Algorithm 3 and 4.
- When processing a quartet, we make use of pre-computed tables so that the term ϵ appearing in the time complexity is as small as possible. This has been suggested in Algorithm 2 and we develop this technique in a more practical way.

Our New Algorithm Unifies All the Previous Rectangle Key Recovery Algorithms. All the previous four algorithms are distinct from each other by the number of guessed key bits. Figure 4 illustrates the comparison of our algorithm with the four previous algorithms.

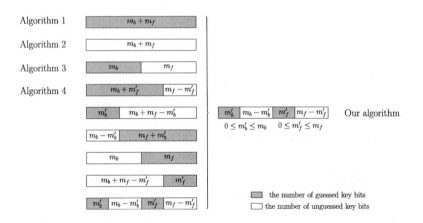

Fig. 4. Diagram of guessed key for different algorithms

Specifically, Algorithm 1 guesses the full $(m_b + m_f)$-bit subkey; the main refinement of Algorithm 2 is to generate quartets with birthday paradox without guessing key bits involved in E_b and E_f; Algorithm 3 guesses the m_b-bit key bits involved in E_b to generate quartets; Algorithm 4 extended Algorithm 3 by guessing additional key bits in E_f and exploiting the inner state bits as fast filters.

Our new algorithm supports any number of guessed key bits. Hence, it not only covers all the cases considered by the four previous algorithms, but also includes five types of new cases (see Fig. 4).

Any of the Previous Four Algorithms is a Special Case of Our Algorithm. We summarize the complexities of different algorithms in Table 2 using notations in this paper. Note the data complexity D remains the same and all the algorithms have to store the data and the subkey counters[5]. Some algorithm may need some extra memory. Therefore, we mainly focus on the comparison of the time complexity and the extra memory complexity.

From complexities listed in Table 2, we can see that Algorithm 1 to 4 are special cases of our algorithm by substituting the corresponding parameters–the exact number of guessed subkey bits and the number of resulted filters–for $m_b' + m_f'$ and r_b', r_f' in our formulas shown in the last big row of Table 2. Note $r_b^* = r_b - r_b', r_f^* = r_f - r_f'$. More specifically,

1. When replacing $m_b' = m_b, m_f' = m_f$ and setting $t = m_b + m_f$, we have Algorithm 1. Since $r_b^* = r_f^* = 0$, the time complexities T_2, T_3 disappear or can be neglected.
2. Algorithm 2 is the case of our algorithm with $m_b' = m_f' = 0, t = 0$ which constructs pairs on the bottom side for ciphertexts.
3. Algorithm 3 is the case of our algorithm with $m_b' = m_b, m_f' = 0$ which constructs pairs on the top side for plaintexts.
4. Algorithm 4 is the case of our algorithm with $m_b + m_f'$ guessed key bits which constructs pairs on the top side for plaintexts.

Table 2. Comparisons of different rectangle key recovery algorithms

Alg.	#Guessed bits	Extra memory	Time
1	$m_b + m_f$	0	$T_1 = 2^{m_b+m_f} \cdot D$
2	0	0	$T_2 = D^2 \cdot 2^{r_f-n-1} = \frac{D}{2} \cdot 2^{r_f-\mu}$
			$T_3 = D^2 \cdot 2^{2r_b+2r_f-2n-2} \cdot \epsilon_2$
3	m_b	$\frac{D}{2}$	$T_1 = 2^{m_b} \cdot D$
			$T_2 = 2^{m_b} \cdot \frac{D}{2}$
			$T_2 = 2^{m_b} \cdot D^2 \cdot 2^{2r_f-2n-2} \cdot \epsilon_3$
4	$m_b + m_f'$	$\frac{D}{2}$	$T_1 = 2^{m_b+m_f'} \cdot D$
			$T_2 = 2^{m_b+m_f'} \cdot \frac{D}{2}$
			$T_2 = 2^{m_b+m_f'} \cdot D^2 \cdot 2^{2r_f^*-2n-2} \cdot \epsilon_4$
This	$m_b' + m_f'$	$\frac{D}{2} \cdot min\{2^{r_b^*}, 2^{r_f^*-\mu}\}$	$T_1 = 2^{m_b'+m_f'} \cdot D$
			$T_2 = 2^{m_b'+m_f'} \cdot \frac{D}{2} \cdot min\{2^{r_b^*}, 2^{r_f^*-\mu}\}$
			$T_3 = 2^{m_b'+m_f'} \cdot D^2 \cdot 2^{2r_b^*+2r_f^*-2n-2} \cdot \epsilon$

---

[5] The key counters can be set flexibly. Thus the memory cost for them is elastic.

Application to Concrete Ciphers. Previously, the four previous key recovery algorithms are treated as separate ones. Given a rectangle distinguisher, one can compute the complexities for different algorithms and pick the algorithm with the lowest complexity. Now, with the new algorithm, we can work with this one only and the best parameters that allow to minimize the time complexity may likely lie outside the cases covered by the four previous algorithms. Section 5 includes a series of such examples.

5   Applications

In this section, we apply our new key recovery algorithm to four block ciphers using existing distinguishers: Serpent, CRAFT, SKINNY, and Deoxys-BC-256. We find that the best attacking parameters differ significantly from those which were used in previous works and even the number rounds in outer part E_b or E_f is different. Moreover, these new attacking parameters are not covered by the previous key recovery algorithms in many cases. Consequently, improved results on these ciphers are obtained.

5.1   Application to Serpent

We apply our new rectangle key recovery algorithm to Serpent [ABK98], which was the first target when the rectangle attack was proposed in 2001 [BDK01]. Serpent is a block cipher which ranked the second in the Advanced Encryption Standard (AES) finalist. It was an SP-network designed by Ross Anderson, Eli Biham, and Lars Knudsen, which has a block size of 128 bits and supports a key size of 128, 192 or 256 bits. Serpent iterates 32 rounds, and each round $i \in \{0, 1, ..., 31\}$ consists of three operations: key mixing, S-boxes and linear transformation. Suppose B_i represents the internal state before round i, K_i is the 128-bit subkey, and S_i denotes the application of S-box in round i. Let L be the linear transformation. Then the Serpent round function is defined as follows.

$$X_i = B_i \oplus K_i$$
$$Y_i = S_i(X_i)$$
$$B_{i+1} = L(Y_i), i = 0, \cdots, 30$$
$$B_{i+1} = Y_i \oplus K_{i+1}, i = 31$$

The internal state of Serpent can be seen as a 4×32 array, where each row is a 32-bit word. The S-boxes is applied to 4-bit columns. Serpent applies eight different 4-bit S-boxes, and these eight S-boxes are used four times. As our attack does not depend on the order of S-boxes, we omit the details here.

Distinguisher. We use the 8-round rectangle distinguisher of Serpent proposed by Biham et al. in [BDK01] to attack 10-round Serpent with E_b and

E_f consisting of round 0 and round 9 respectively. The probability of the distinguisher is $2^{-n}P^2 = 2^{-128-120.6}$, and other parameters of the attack are: $n = 128, m_b = r_b = 76, m_f = r_f = 20$.

Recently in [KT22], this distinguisher has been re-evaluated and a more accurate probability of $2^{-128-116.3}$ is reported. For a better comparison, we will mount key recovery attack with both probabilities of the distinguisher.

In the case of Serpent, a 4-bit key guess for an active S-box will lead to a 4-bit inner state filter for a pair of messages. That is, all the key nibbles corresponding to the active S-boxes of the first round and the last round are equivalently good for filtering data.

Parameters and Complexities. When we take the old probability, the best guessing parameters are $m'_f = r'_f = 20, m'_b = r'_b = 8$, which means guessing all the k_f and two nibbles of k_b. Note that, this type of guessing strategy is not covered in previous rectangle key recovery algorithms. The complexities are as follows.

- The data complexity is $D = y \cdot 2^{r_b} = \sqrt{s} \cdot 2^{n/2+1}/P = \sqrt{s} \cdot 2^{125.3}$.
- The memory complexity is $M = D + D^2 \cdot 2^{r'_f - n - 1} + 2^{t + m_b + m_f - m'_b - m'_f} = \sqrt{s} \cdot 2^{125.3} + s \cdot 2^{121.6} + 2^{t+68}$.
- The time complexity $T_1 = 2^{m'_b + m'_f} \cdot D = \sqrt{s} \cdot 2^{153.3}$;
- $T_2 = 2^{m'_b + m'_f} \cdot D^2 \cdot 2^{r'_f - n - 1} = s \cdot 2^{149.6}$;
- $T_3 = 2^{m'_b + m'_f} \cdot D^2 \cdot 2^{2r^*_b + 2r^*_f - 2n - 2} \cdot \epsilon = s \cdot 2^{28 + 250.6 + 2 \times 68 + 0 - 2 \times 128 - 2} \cdot \epsilon = s \cdot 2^{156.6} \cdot \epsilon$;
- $T_4 = 2^{k-h}, h < 68 + t$.

For each of the remaining quartets, it can be processed S-box by S-box, so ϵ takes about $1 + 2^{-4} + 2^{-8} + \cdots + 2^{-16*4} = 2^{0.09}$ memory accesses. Set $s = 4$, then the data, and memory complexities of our attack are both $2^{126.3}$. The time complexity besides the brute forcing part includes $2^{154.3}$ partial encryptions/decryptions and $2^{158.69}$ memory accesses. Assume a partial encryptions/decryptions is equivalent to 7 memory accesses as 7 S-boxes are involved. Then it needs $2^{159.11}$ memory accesses in total.

When we take the new probability, the guessing parameters $m'_f = r'_f = 20, m'_b = r'_b = 8$ are still the best. Another choice for these parameters is $m'_f = r'_f = 16, m'_b = r'_b = 12$ which leads to the same time complexity but a slightly higher memory complexity. Thus we choose the former one. Set $s = 4$, then the data, and memory complexities of our attack are both $2^{124.15}$. The time complexity besides the brute forcing part include $2^{152.15}$ partial encryptions/decryptions and $2^{154.39}$ memory accesses, which is about $2^{155.67}$ memory accesses in total.

The comparison with the previous rectangle attacks[6] based on the same distinguisher is presented in Table 3.

---

[6] In [DQSW22], a rectangle attack on 10-round Serpent was also given. However, the authors seem to mistake m_f, r_f for m_b, r_b. So we do not include their result in Table 3.

Table 3. Comparisons of key recovery attacks on 10-round Serpent where the time is measured by the number of memory accesses.

P^2	m_b, m_f	m_b', m_f'	Data	Memory	Time	Reference
$2^{-120.6}$	$76, 20$	$76,20$	$2^{126.8}$	2^{192}	2^{217}	[BDK01]
		$0,0$	$2^{126.3}$	$2^{126.3}$	$2^{173.8}$	[BDK02]
		$8,20$	$2^{126.3}$	$2^{126.3}$	$2^{159.11}$	This
$2^{-116.3}$	$76, 20$	$8,20$	$2^{124.15}$	$2^{124.15}$	$2^{155.67}$	This

5.2   Application to CRAFT

We apply our new rectangle key recovery algorithm to CRAFT in the single-key setting and obtain the first 19-round rectangle attack, which is one round more than the previous work in [HBS21].

Specification. CRAFT is a lightweight tweakable block cipher which was introduced by Beierle *et al.* [BLMR19]. It supports 64-bit plaintext, 128-bit key, and 64-bit tweak. Its round function is composed of involutory building blocks. The 64-bit input is arranged as a state of 4×4 nibbles. The state is then going through 32 rounds $\mathcal{R}_i, i \in 0, \cdots, 31$, to generate a 64-bit ciphertext. As depicted in Fig. 5, each round, excluding the last round, has five functions, *i.e.*, MixColumn (MC), AddRoundConstants (ARC), AddTweakey (ATK), PermuteNibbles (PN), and S-box (SB). The last round only includes MC, ARC and ATK, i.e., $\mathcal{R}_{31} = ATK_{31} \circ ARC_{31} \circ MC$, while for any $0 \leq i \leq 30$, $\mathcal{R}_i = SB \circ PN \circ ATK_i \circ ARC_i \circ MC$.

The tweakey schedule of CRAFT is rather simple. Given the secret key $K = K_0 \| K_1$ and the tweak $T \in \{0,1\}^{64}$, where $K_i \in \{0,1\}^{64}$, four round tweakeys $TK_0 = K_0 \oplus T$, $TK_1 = K_1 \oplus T$, $TK_2 = K_0 \oplus Q(T)$ and $TK_3 = K_1 \oplus Q(T)$ are generated, where Q is a nibble-wise permutation. Then at the round $\mathcal{R}_i$, $TK_{i\%4}$ is used as the subtweakey.

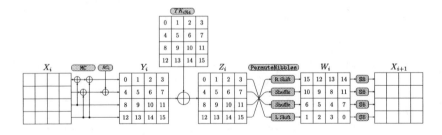

Fig. 5. A round of CRAFT

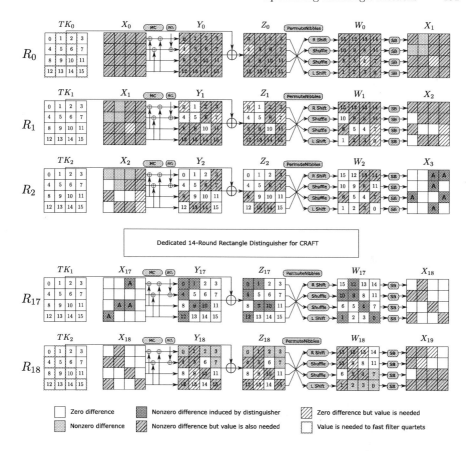

Fig. 6. A 19-round key recovery attack against CRAFT

Distinguisher. We use the 14-round rectangle distinguisher of CRAFT proposed by Hadipour *et al.* in [HBS21] to attack 19-round CRAFT with 3-round E_b and 2-round E_f, as shown in Fig. 6. The probability of the distinguisher is $2^{-n}P^2 = 2^{-64-55.85}$, and other parameters of the attack are: $n = 64, k = 128, m_b = 112, r_b = 60, m_f = r_f = 24$. The first three subtweakeys are TK_0, TK_1, and TK_2, respectively. The last subtweakey is TK_2. Note TK_2 shares the same key information with TK_0, and $k_b \cup k_f$ only contains $(16 + 12 + 6 - 6) \times 4 = 112$ information bits.

Parameters and Complexities. The best guessing parameters are $m_b' = 32, r_b' = 16, m_f = r_f' = 24$, and $|k_b' \cup k_f'| = 40$, which means guessing 10 cells of k_f and k_b to get 10 cells filters. The key cells to be guessed and the corresponding filters are highlighted with red squares in Fig. 6. Note that this type of guessing is not covered in previous rectangle key recovery attacks. The complexities of our new attack are as follows.

- The data complexity is $D = y \cdot 2^{r_b} = \sqrt{s} \cdot 2^{n/2+1}/P = \sqrt{s} \cdot 2^{60.92}$.
- The memory complexity is $M = D + D^2 \cdot 2^{r_f^* - n - 1} + 2^{m_b + m_f - m_b' - m_f'} = \sqrt{s} \cdot 2^{60.92} + s \cdot 2^{56.85} + 2^{t+72}$
- The time complexity $T_1 = 2^{m_b' + m_f'} \cdot D = \sqrt{s} \cdot 2^{100.92}$;
- $T_2 = 2^{m_b' + m_f'} \cdot D^2 \cdot 2^{r_f^* - n - 1} = s \cdot 2^{96.85}$;
- $T_3 = 2^{m_b' + m_f'} \cdot D^2 \cdot 2^{2r_b^* + 2r_f^* - 2n - 2} \cdot \epsilon = s \cdot 2^{40 + 121.85 + 2 \times 44 + 0 - 2 \times 64 - 2} \cdot \epsilon = s \cdot 2^{119.85} \cdot \epsilon$;
- $T_4 = 2^{k-h}, h < t + 72$.

Processing a candidate quartet to retrieve the rest of k_b and can be realized by looking up tables. The time unit ϵ can be equivalent to about 2 memory accesses which is around $2 \times \frac{1}{16} \times \frac{1}{19} = 2^{-7.24}$ encryption. The memory complexity for the look-up tables is about 2^{52} (For more details, see the full version [SZY+22]). If we set $s = 1$, $h = 28$ and $t = 0$, then the data, memory and time complexities of our attack are $2^{60.92}$, 2^{72}, and $2^{112.61}$, respectively. The success probability is about 74.59% which is computed by Selçuk's formula [Sel08].

The comparison with the previous rectangle attacks based on the same distinguisher is presented in Table 4.

Table 4. Comparisons of key recovery attacks on CRAFT

P^2	Rounds	m_b, m_f	m_b', m_f'	Data	Memory	Time	Reference
$2^{-55.85}$	$1 + 14 + 3$	$24, 84$	$24, 0$	$2^{60.92}$	2^{84}	$2^{101.7}$	[HBS21]
$2^{-55.85}$	$3 + 14 + 2$	$112, 24$	$32, 24$	$2^{60.92}$	2^{72}	$2^{112.61}$	This

5.3 Application to SKINNY

When we apply our new rectangle key recovery algorithm to SKINNY's distinguishers from [DQSW22], better attacks are obtained for three out of four distinguishers, and for the rest one, our attack matches with the one in [DQSW22]. Even though these distinguishers were searched dedicated for the key recovery algorithm in [DQSW22] (named Algorithm 4 in Sect. 4), we found that the best attacking parameters may be not covered by that key recovery algorithm.

Next, we give the detailed attack on 25-round SKINNY-64-128 and the attacks on 32-round SKINNY-128-384 and 26-round SKINNY-128-256 can be found in the full version [SZY+22].

Specification. SKINNY [BJK+16a] is a family of lightweight block ciphers which adopt the substitution-permutation network and elements of the TWEAKEY framework [JNP14]. Members of SKINNY are denoted by SKINNY-n-tk, where $n \in \{64, 128\}$ is the block size and $tk \in \{n, 2n, 3n\}$ is the tweakey size. The internal states of SKINNY are represented as 4×4 arrays of cells with each cell being a nibble in case of $n = 64$ bits and a byte in case of $n = 128$ bits. The tweakey state is seen as a group of z 4×4 arrays, where, $z = tk/n$. The arrays are marked as $TK1$, $(TK1, TK2)$ and $(TK1, TK2, TK3)$ for $z = 1, 2, 3$ respectively.

SKINNY iterates a round function for N_r rounds and each round consists of the following five steps.

1. SubCells (SC) - A 4-bit (resp. 8-bit) S-box is applied to all cells when n is 64 (resp. n is 128).
2. AddConstants (AC) - This step adds constants to the internal state.
3. AddRoundTweakey (ART) - The first two rows of the internal state absorb the first two rows of TK, where $TK = \bigoplus_{i=1}^{z} TK_i$.
4. ShiftRows (SR) - Each cell in row j is rotated to the right by j cells.
5. MixColumns (MC) - Each column of the internal state is multiplied by matrix M whose branch number is only 2.

The tweakey schedule of SKINNY is a linear algorithm. The tk-bit tweakey is first loaded into z 4×4 tweakey states. After each ART step, a cell-wised permutation P is applied to each tweakey state, where P is defined as: $P = [9, 15, 8, 13, 10, 14, 12, 11, 0, 1, 2, 3, 4, 5, 6, 7]$. Then cells in the first two rows of all tweakey states but TK_1 are individually updated using LFSRs. For complete details of the tweakeys scheduling algorithm, one can refer to [BJK+16a].

Distinguisher of SKINNY-64-128. We reuse the 18-round rectangle distinguisher of SKINNY-64-128 from [QDW+21, DQSW21] and apply our new rectangle key recovery algorithm to it. As a result, we obtain a new 25-round rectangle attack. The probability of the distinguisher is $2^{-n}P^2 = 2^{-64-55.34} = 2^{-119.34}$. Our key recovery extends the distinguisher by three rounds at the top and four rounds at the bottom, as shown in Fig. 7. The parameters for this attack are: $r_b = 8 \times 4 = 32, r_f = 12 \times 4 = 48, m_b = 10 \times 4 = 40$ and $m_f = 21 \times 4 = 84$. Due to the tweakey schedule, we can deduce $SKT_{22}[6, 1, 7, 2]$ from $STK_0[0, 5, 6, 7]$ and $STK_{24}[5, 0, 1, 4]$, and deduce $STK_{21}[6]$ from $STK_1[2]$ and $STK_{23}[5]$. Such that $k_b \cup k_f$ only contain $(31 - 5) \times 4 = 104$ information bits.

Parameters and Complexities. We apply the related-key version of our new algorithm to the above distinguisher. The best guessing parameters are $m_b' = 32, r_b' = 28$ and $m_f' = r_f' = 16$, which means guessing partial bits of k_b and k_f. This guessing strategy is not covered in previous rectangle key recovery algorithms. The complexities of our new attack are as follows.

- The data complexity is $D_R = 4 \cdot y \cdot 2^{r_b} = \sqrt{s} \cdot 2^{n/2+2}/P = \sqrt{s} \cdot 2^{61.67}$.
- The memory complexity is $M_R = D_R + D \cdot 2^{r_b^*} + 2^{t+m_b+m_f-m_b'-m_f'} = \sqrt{s} \cdot 2^{61.67} + \sqrt{s} \cdot 2^{63.67} + 2^{56+t}$
- The time complexity $T_1 = 2^{m_b'+m_f'} \cdot D_R = \sqrt{s} \cdot 2^{12 \times 4+61.67} = \sqrt{s} \cdot 2^{109.67}$;
- $T_2 = 2^{m_b'+m_f'} \cdot D \cdot 2^{r_b-r_b'} = \sqrt{s} \cdot 2^{12 \times 4+59.67+4} = \sqrt{s} \cdot 2^{111.67}$;
- $T_3 = 2^{m_b'+m_f'} \cdot D^2 \cdot 2^{2r_b^*+2r_f^*-2n} \cdot \epsilon = s \cdot 2^{12 \times 8+119.34+2 \times 4+2 \times 32-2 \times 64} \cdot \epsilon = s \cdot 2^{111.34} \cdot \epsilon$;
- $T_4 = 2^{128-h}, h < 56 + t$.

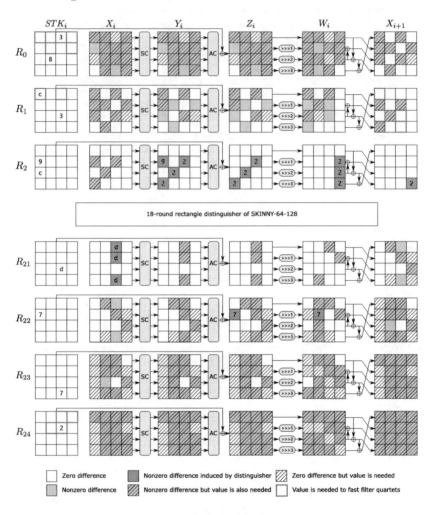

Fig. 7. A 25-round key recovery attack against SKINNY-64-128

Processing a candidate quartet to retrieve the rest of k_b and k_f can be realized by looking up tables about 35 times, which is around $35 \times \frac{1}{16} \times \frac{1}{25} = 2^{-3.51}$ encryption. The memory complexity of the looking-up tables is about 2^{48} (see the full version [SZY+22]). If we set $s = 1$, $h = 30$ and $t = 0$, then the data, memory and time complexities of our attack are $2^{61.67}$, $2^{63.67}$, and $2^{110.03}$, respectively. The success probability is about 75.81%.

The comparison with the previous rectangle attacks based on the same distinguisher is presented in Table 5.

Table 5. Comparisons of key recovery attacks on SKINNY-64-128

P^2	Rounds	m_b, m_f	m'_b, m'_f	Data	Memory	Time	Reference
$2^{-55.34}$	$2 + 18 + 5$	$12, 116$	$12, 40$	$2^{61.67}$	$2^{64.26}$	$2^{118.43}$	[DQSW22]
$2^{-55.34}$	$3 + 18 + 4$	$40, 84$	$32, 16$	$2^{61.67}$	$2^{63.67}$	$2^{110.03}$	This

5.4 Application to Deoxys-BC-256

We apply a variant of our new algorithm dedicated to boomerang attacks to Deoxys-BC-256 and obtain the first 11-round boomerang attack and also obtain an improved 11-round rectangle attack using the original algorithm. Next, we give details about the 11-round boomerang attack. For the 11-round rectangle attack, please refer to the full version [SZY+22].

Specification. Deoxys-BC is an AES-based tweakable block cipher [JNPS16], based on the tweakey framework [JNP14]. The Deoxys authenticated encryption scheme makes use of two versions of the cipher as its internal primitive: Deoxys-BC-256 and Deoxys-BC-384. Both versions are ad-hoc 128-bit tweakable block ciphers which besides the two standard inputs, a plaintext P (or a ciphertext C) and a key K, also take an additional input called a *tweak* T. The concatenation of the key and tweak states is called the *tweakey* state. For Deoxys-BC-256 the tweakey size is 256 bits.

Deoxys-BC is an AES-like design, *i.e.*, it is an iterative substitution-permutation network (SPN) that transforms the initial plaintext (viewed as a 4×4 matrix of bytes) using the AES round function, with the main differences with AES being the number of rounds and the round subkeys that are used every round. Deoxys-BC-256 has 14 rounds.

Similarly to the AES, one round of Deoxys-BC has the following four transformations applied to the internal state in the order specified below:

- AddRoundTweakey – XOR the 128-bit round subtweakey to the internal state.
- SubBytes – Apply the 8-bit AES S-box to each of the 16 bytes of the internal state.
- ShiftRows – Rotate the 4-byte i-th row left by $\rho[i]$ positions, where $\rho = (0, 1, 2, 3)$.
- MixColumns – Multiply the internal state by the 4×4 constant MDS matrix of AES.

After the last round, a final AddRoundTweakey operation is performed to produce the ciphertext.

We denote the concatenation of the key K and the tweak T as KT, i.e. $KT = K\|T$. The *tweakey* state is then divided into 128-bit words. More precisely, in Deoxys-BC-256 the size of KT is 256 bits with the first (most significant) 128 bits of KT being denoted W_2; the second word is denoted by W_1. Finally, we denote by STK_i the 128-bit *subtweakey* that is added to the state at round

i during the AddRoundTweakey operation. For Deoxys-BC-256, a subtweakey is defined as $STK_i = TK_i^1 \oplus TK_i^2 \oplus RC_i$. The 128-bit words TK_i^1, TK_i^2 are outputs produced by a special *tweakey schedule* algorithm, initialised with $TK_0^1 = W_1$ and $TK_0^2 = W_2$ for Deoxys-BC-256. The tweakey schedule algorithm is defined as $TK_{i+1}^1 = h(TK_i^1)$, $TK_{i+1}^2 = h(LFSR_2(TK_i^2))$, where the byte permutation h is defined as

$$\begin{pmatrix} 0 & 1 & 2 & 3 & 4 & 5 & 6 & 7 & 8 & 9 & 10 & 11 & 12 & 13 & 14 & 15 \\ 1 & 6 & 11 & 12 & 5 & 10 & 15 & 0 & 9 & 14 & 3 & 4 & 13 & 2 & 7 & 8 \end{pmatrix},$$

with the 16 bytes of a 128-bit tweakey word numbered by the usual AES byte ordering.

Boomerang Attack. We reuse the 9-round boomerang distinguisher of Deoxys-BC-256 proposed by Cid *et al.* [CHP+17,WP19] to attack 11-round boomerang Deoxys-BC-256 with 2-round E_f, as shown in Fig. 8. The probability of the distinguisher is $P^2 = 2^{-120.4}$, and other parameteres are: $n = 128, k = 256, m_b = r_b = 0, m_f = (16 + 10) \times 8 = 208, r_f = 16 \times 8 = 128$.

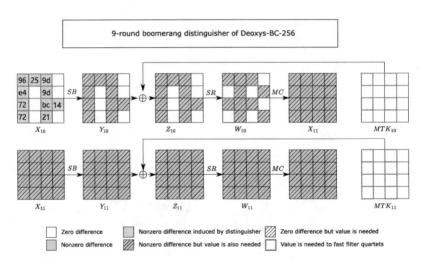

Fig. 8. Rectangle/Boomerang attack on 11-round reduced Deoxys-BC-256

The best guessing parameters are $m_f' = 12 \times 8 = 96$ and $r_f' = 8 \times 8 = 64$, which means guessing 8 bytes of k_f. The complexities of our new attack are as follows.

- The data complexity is $D_{RB} = 4s/P^2 = s \cdot 2^{122.4}$.
- The memory complexity is $M_{RB} = D_{RB} + D + 2^{m_f - m_f' + t} = s \cdot 2^{122.4} + s \cdot 2^{120.4} + 2^{112+t}$.
- The time complexity $T_1 = 2^{m_f'} \cdot D_{RB} = 2^{96} \cdot s \cdot 2^{122.4} = s \cdot 2^{218.4}$;

- $T_2 = 2^{m'_f} \cdot D = s \cdot 2^{216.4}$;
- $T_3 = 2^{m'_f} \cdot D \cdot 2^{2(r_f - r'_f)} \cdot 2^{-n} \cdot \epsilon = s \cdot 2^{96+120.4+2 \times 64 - 128} \cdot \epsilon = 2^{212.4} \cdot \epsilon$;
- $T_4 = 2^{256-h}, h < 112 + t$.

We consider the equivalent subtweakey $MTK_i = SR^{-1} \circ MC^{-1}(STK_i)$. To process a candidate quartet to retrieve the rest of k_f, we prepare some tables, which takes a memory complexity 2^{128}, so that ϵ is equivalent to about 1 memory accesses, equivalent to around $1 \times \frac{1}{16} \times \frac{1}{11} = 2^{-7.45}$ encryption. If we set $s = 1, h = 40$ and $t = 0$, then the data, memory and time complexities of our attack are $2^{122.4}, 2^{128}, 2^{218.65}$, respectively. The comparison with the previous boomerang attacks is presented in Table 6.

Table 6. Comparisons of key recovery attacks on Deoxys-BC-256

P^2	Rounds	m_b, m_f	m'_b, m'_f	Data	Memory	Time	Reference
$2^{-96.4}$	10	0,88	0,0	$2^{98.4}$	2^{88}	$2^{249.9}$	[ZDJ19]
$2^{-120.4}$	11	0,208	0,96	$2^{122.4}$	2^{128}	$2^{218.65}$	This

6   Concluding Remarks

In this paper, we propose a unified and generic rectangle key recovery algorithm as well as a framework for automatically finding the best attacking parameters. Combining both, we can find the optimal rectangle attack in terms of time complexity for a given distinguisher. We also extend the new algorithm to other related attacks, such as rectangle attacks in the related-key setting for ciphers with a linear key schedule and boomerang attacks in both the single-key and related-key setting. Applications to block ciphers Serpent, CRAFT, SKINNY and Deoxys-BC-256 show that the best rectangle or boomerang attacks are missed by the previous key recovery algorithms in many cases. Thus, better attacks can be obtained. Also, it is likely that previous rectangle attacks can be improved to some extent using the new key recovery algorithm.

Future Works. In this paper, we only apply the new rectangle key recovery algorithm to SPN ciphers. However, it should be noted that it is also applicable to Feistel ciphers. Our new key recovery algorithm is generic and does not exploit any property of the S-box as studied in [BCF+21]. It would be a potential future work to exploit properties of the S-box and find more fine-grained parameters for the new algorithm. To search rectangle distinguishers with the new key recovery algorithm taken into account is another topic of interest.

Acknowledgement. The authors would like to thank anonymous reviewers for their helpful comments and suggestions. The work of this paper was supported by the National Natural Science Foundation of China (Grants 62022036, 62132008, 62202460, 62172410, 61732021), the National Key Research and Development Program (No.

2022YFB2701900, No. 2018YFA0704704 and No. 2018YFB0803801). Jian Weng was supported by Major Program of Guangdong Basic and Applied Research Project under Grant No. 2019B030302008, National Natural Science Foundation of China under Grant No. 61825203, Guangdong Provincial Science and Technology Project under Grant No. 2021A0505030033, National Joint Engineering Research Center of Network Security Detection and Protection Technology, and Guangdong Key Laboratory of Data Security and Privacy Preserving.

References

[ABK98] Anderson, R., Biham, E., Knudsen, L.: Serpent: a proposal for the advanced encryption standard. NIST AES Proposal **174**, 1–23 (1998)

[BCF+21] Broll, M., Canale, F., Flórez-Gutiérrez, A., Leander, G., Naya-Plasencia, M.: Generic framework for key-guessing improvements. In: Tibouchi, M., Wang, H. (eds.) ASIACRYPT 2021, Part I. LNCS, vol. 13090, pp. 453–483. Springer, Cham (2021). https://doi.org/10.1007/978-3-030-92062-3_16

[BDK01] Biham, E., Dunkelman, O., Keller, N.: The rectangle attack — rectangling the serpent. In: Pfitzmann, B. (ed.) EUROCRYPT 2001. LNCS, vol. 2045, pp. 340–357. Springer, Heidelberg (2001). https://doi.org/10.1007/3-540-44987-6_21

[BDK02] Biham, E., Dunkelman, O., Keller, N.: New results on boomerang and rectangle attacks. In: Daemen, J., Rijmen, V. (eds.) FSE 2002. LNCS, vol. 2365, pp. 1–16. Springer, Heidelberg (2002). https://doi.org/10.1007/3-540-45661-9_1

[BJK+16a] Beierle, C., et al.: The SKINNY family of block ciphers and its low-latency variant MANTIS. In: Robshaw, M., Katz, J. (eds.) CRYPTO 2016, Part II. LNCS, vol. 9815, pp. 123–153. Springer, Heidelberg (2016). https://doi.org/10.1007/978-3-662-53008-5_5

[BK09] Biryukov, A., Khovratovich, D.: Related-key cryptanalysis of the full AES-192 and AES-256. In: Matsui, M. (ed.) ASIACRYPT 2009. LNCS, vol. 5912, pp. 1–18. Springer, Heidelberg (2009). https://doi.org/10.1007/978-3-642-10366-7_1

[BLMR19] Beierle, C., Leander, G., Moradi, A., Rasoolzadeh, S.: CRAFT: lightweight tweakable block cipher with efficient protection against DFA attacks. IACR Trans. Symmetric Cryptol. **2019**(1), 5–45 (2019)

[BS91] Biham, E., Shamir, A.: Differential cryptanalysis of DES-like cryptosystems. J. Cryptol. **4**(1), 3–72 (1991). https://doi.org/10.1007/BF00630563

[CHP+17] Cid, C., Huang, T., Peyrin, T., Sasaki, Y., Song, L.: A security analysis of Deoxys and its internal tweakable block ciphers. IACR Trans. Symmetric Cryptol. **2017**(3), 73–107 (2017)

[CHP+18] Cid, C., Huang, T., Peyrin, T., Sasaki, Yu., Song, L.: Boomerang connectivity table: a new cryptanalysis tool. In: Nielsen, J.B., Rijmen, V. (eds.) EUROCRYPT 2018. LNCS, vol. 10821, pp. 683–714. Springer, Cham (2018). https://doi.org/10.1007/978-3-319-78375-8_22

[DKS10a] Dunkelman, O., Keller, N., Shamir, A.: Improved single-key attacks on 8-round AES-192 and AES-256. In: Abe, M. (ed.) ASIACRYPT 2010. LNCS, vol. 6477, pp. 158–176. Springer, Heidelberg (2010). https://doi.org/10.1007/978-3-642-17373-8_10

[DKS10b] Dunkelman, O., Keller, N., Shamir, A.: A practical-time related-key attack on the KASUMI cryptosystem used in GSM and 3G telephony. In: Rabin, T. (ed.) CRYPTO 2010. LNCS, vol. 6223, pp. 393–410. Springer, Heidelberg (2010). https://doi.org/10.1007/978-3-642-14623-7_21

[DKS14] Dunkelman, O., Keller, N., Shamir, A.: A practical-time related-key attack on the KASUMI cryptosystem used in GSM and 3G telephony. J. Cryptol. **27**(4), 824–849 (2014)

[DKS15] Dunkelman, O., Keller, N., Shamir, A.: Improved single-key attacks on 8-round AES-192 and AES-256. J. Cryptol. **28**(3), 397–422 (2015)

[DQSW21] Dong, X., Qin, L., Sun, S., Wang, X.: Key guessing strategies for linear key-schedule algorithms in rectangle attacks. IACR Cryptol. ePrint Arch., p. 856 (2021)

[DQSW22] Dong, X., Qin, L., Sun, S., Wang, X.: Key guessing strategies for linear key-schedule algorithms in rectangle attacks. In: Dunkelman, O., Dziembowski, S. (eds.) EUROCRYPT 2022. LNCS, vol 13277, pp. 3-33. Springer, Cham (2022). https://doi.org/10.1007/978-3-031-07082-2_1

[HBS21] Hadipour, H., Bagheri, N., Song, L.: Improved rectangle attacks on SKINNY and CRAFT. IACR Trans. Sym. Cryptol., 140–198 (2021)

[HLM+20] Hao, Y., Leander, G., Meier, W., Todo, Y., Wang, Q.: Modeling for three-subset division property without unknown subset- improved cube attacks against Trivium and Grain-128AEAD. In: Canteaut, A., Ishai, Y. (eds.) EUROCRYPT 2020, Part I. LNCS, vol. 12105, pp. 466–495. Springer, Cham (2020). https://doi.org/10.1007/978-3-030-45721-1_17

[JNP14] Jean, J., Nikolić, I., Peyrin, T.: Tweaks and keys for block ciphers: the TWEAKEY framework. In: Sarkar, P., Iwata, T. (eds.) ASIACRYPT 2014, Part II. LNCS, vol. 8874, pp. 274–288. Springer, Heidelberg (2014). https://doi.org/10.1007/978-3-662-45608-8_15

[JNPS16] Jean, J., Nikolic, I., Peyrin, T., Seurin, Y.: Deoxys v1. 41. Submitted to CAESAR, 124 (2016)

[KKS00] Kelsey, J., Kohno, T., Schneier, B.: Amplified boomerang attacks against reduced-round MARS and serpent. In: Goos, G., Hartmanis, J., van Leeuwen, J., Schneier, B. (eds.) FSE 2000. LNCS, vol. 1978, pp. 75–93. Springer, Heidelberg (2001). https://doi.org/10.1007/3-540-44706-7_6

[KLT15] Kölbl, S., Leander, G., Tiessen, T.: Observations on the SIMON block cipher family. In: Gennaro, R., Robshaw, M. (eds.) CRYPTO 2015, Part I. LNCS, vol. 9215, pp. 161–185. Springer, Heidelberg (2015). https://doi.org/10.1007/978-3-662-47989-6_8

[KT22] Kidmose, A.B., Tiessen, T.: A formal analysis of boomerang probabilities. IACR Trans. Symmetric Cryptol. **2022**(1), 88–109 (2022)

[LGS17] Liu, G., Ghosh, M., Song, L.: Security analysis of SKINNY under related-tweakey settings. IACR Trans. Symmetric Cryptol. **2017**(3), 37–72 (2017)

[Mur11] Murphy, S.: The return of the cryptographic boomerang. IEEE Trans. Inf. Theory **57**(4), 2517–2521 (2011)

[QDW+21] Qin, L., Dong, X., Wang, X., Jia, K., Liu, Y.: Automated search oriented to key recovery on ciphers with linear key schedule applications to boomerangs in SKINNY and forkskinny. IACR Trans. Symmetric Cryptol. **2021**(2), 249–291 (2021)

[Sel08] Selçuk, A.A.: On probability of success in linear and differential cryptanalysis. J. Cryptol. **21**(1), 131–147 (2008)

[SHW+14] Sun, S., Hu, L., Wang, P., Qiao, K., Ma, X., Song, L.: Automatic security evaluation and (related-key) differential characteristic search: application to SIMON, PRESENT, LBlock, DES(L) and other bit-oriented block ciphers. In: Sarkar, P., Iwata, T. (eds.) ASIACRYPT 2014, Part I. LNCS, vol. 8873, pp. 158–178. Springer, Heidelberg (2014). https://doi.org/10.1007/978-3-662-45611-8_9

[SQH19] Song, L., Qin, X., Lei, H.: Boomerang connectivity table revisited: application to SKINNY and AES. IACR Trans. Symmetric Cryptol. **2019**(1), 118–141 (2019)

[SSD+18] Shi, D., Sun, S., Derbez, P., Todo, Y., Sun, B., Hu, L.: Programming the Demirci-Selçuk meet-in-the-middle attack with constraints. In: Peyrin, T., Galbraith, S. (eds.) ASIACRYPT 2018, Part II. LNCS, vol. 11273, pp. 3–34. Springer, Cham (2018). https://doi.org/10.1007/978-3-030-03329-3_1

[SWW21] Sun, L., Wang, W., Wang, M.: Accelerating the search of differential and linear characteristics with the SAT method. IACR Trans. Symmetric Cryptol. **2021**(1), 269–315 (2021)

[SZY+22] Song, L., et al.: Optimizing rectangle attacks: a unified and generic framework for key recovery. IACR Cryptol. ePrint Arch., p. 723 (2022)

[Wag99] Wagner, D.: The Boomerang attack. In: Knudsen, L. (ed.) FSE 1999. LNCS, vol. 1636, pp. 156–170. Springer, Heidelberg (1999). https://doi.org/10.1007/3-540-48519-8_12

[WP19] Wang, H., Peyrin, T.: Boomerang switch in multiple rounds. Application to AES variants and deoxys. IACR Trans. Symmetric Cryptol. **2019**(1), 142–169 (2019)

[ZDJ19] Zhao, B., Dong, X., Jia, K.: New related-tweakey boomerang and rectangle attacks on Deoxys-BC including BDT effect. IACR Trans. Symmetric Cryptol. **2019**(3), 121–151 (2019)

[ZDM+20] Zhao, B., Dong, X., Meier, W., Jia, K., Wang, G.: Generalized related-key rectangle attacks on block ciphers with linear key schedule: applications to SKINNY and GIFT. Des. Codes Crypt. **88**(6), 1103–1126 (2020). https://doi.org/10.1007/s10623-020-00730-1

Multiparty Computation

Random Sources in Private Computation

Geoffroy Couteau[1][(✉)] and Adi Rosén[2]

[1] CNRS, IRIF, Université Paris Cité, Paris, France
couteau@irif.fr
[2] CNRS, FILOFOCS, Tel Aviv, Israel
adiro@irif.fr

Abstract. We consider multi-party information-theoretic private computation. Such computation inherently requires the use of local randomness by the parties, and the question of minimizing the total number of random bits used for given private computations has received considerable attention in the literature, see, e.g., [5, 9, 14, 16, 17, 19, 21, 26].

In this work we are interested in another question: given a private computation, we ask how many of the players need to have access to a random source, and how many of them can be deterministic parties. We are further interested in the possible interplay between the number of random sources in the system and the total number of random bits necessary for the computation.

We give a number of results. We first show that, perhaps surprisingly, t players (rather than $t+1$) with access to a random source are sufficient for the information-theoretic t-private computation of any deterministic functionality over n players for any $t < n/2$; by a result of [16], this is best possible. This means that, counter intuitively, while private computation is impossible without randomness, it is possible to have a private computation even when the adversary can control *all* parties who can toss coins (and therefore sees all random coins). For randomized functionalities we show that $t+1$ random sources are necessary (and sufficient).

We then turn to the question of the possible interplay between the number of random sources and the necessary number of random bits. Since for only very few settings in private computation meaningful bounds on the number of necessary random bits are known, we consider the AND function, for which some such bounds are known. We give a new protocol to 1-privately compute the n-player AND function, which uses a single random source and 6 random bits tossed by that source. This improves, upon the currently best known results [18], at the same time the number of sources and the number of random bits ([18] gives a 2-source, 8-bits protocol). This result gives maybe some evidence that for 1-privacy, using the minimum necessary number of sources one can also achieve the necessary minimum number of random bits. We believe however that our protocol is of independent interest for the study of randomness in private computation.

© International Association for Cryptologic Research 2022
S. Agrawal and D. Lin (Eds.): ASIACRYPT 2022, LNCS 13791, pp. 443–473, 2022.
https://doi.org/10.1007/978-3-031-22963-3_15

1   Introduction

A multi-party *t-private* protocol for computing a function f is a distributed protocol that allows $n \geq 3$ players P_i, for $1 \leq i \leq n$, each possessing an individual secret input x_i, to jointly compute the value of $f(x)$ in a way that conceals, with respect to any coalition of at most t players, all information beyond what can be deduced from the value of f and their own inputs. Secure multi-party computation is a fundamental problem in cryptography. It has received intense attention, both in the computational and in the information-theoretic setting, starting with its introduction in the seminal works of Yao [27], and Goldreich, Micali, and Wigderson [12,13] (GMW). This is due to both its theoretical interest and its many applications (including, but not limited to, e-voting, auctions, private set intersections, privacy-preserving machine learning, and many more).

Information-Theoretic Secure Computation. In this work, we focus specifically on information-theoretic secure (private) computation, introduced in the seminal works of [4] and [7]. In this model, the protocol proceeds in rounds, where in each round each player sends a message to each other player, over a secure and authenticated point-to-point channel. The privacy property of such a protocol means, informally, that no coalition of at most t players can learn anything (in the information-theoretic sense) from the execution of the protocol, except what is implied by the value of $f(x)$ and the inputs of the player in the coalition. Private computation in this setting was the subject of considerable research, see e.g., [1,4,7,8,10,16,19,21] and references therein. In addition to its theoretical interest, this setting (and its variants) constitutes the foundation of many cryptographic applications, due (in part) to the existence of (efficient) compilers that can transform a generic representation of any function f (e.g., as a boolean circuit) into a secure protocol computing the same function f [4,7] with complexity proportional to the size of the representation.

Randomness in Secure Computation. It is a folklore result that the ability to sample random coins is necessary in order to perform private computations involving more than two players (except for the computation of very degenerate functions).[1] That is, the players must have access to (private) sources of unbiased, untemperable, independent random coins. Randomness is typically regarded as a scarce resource in the design of algorithms, and methods for saving random bits in various contexts have been the focus of a wide number of works (see, e.g., [23] and its many follow-ups, or [11,25] for surveys). In the context of information theoretic secure computation, a problem of fundamental interest is to understand how much randomness is required to securely compute a function. The design of randomness-efficient private protocols, and the quantification of the amount of randomness necessary to perform private computations of various functions and under various constraints has received considerable attention in the literature, see, e.g., [5,9,14,16,17,19,21,26].

---

[1] We remark that the two-party case, $n = 2$, is known to be qualitatively different [8].

On Random Sources in Secure Computation. In this work, we tackle the problem of randomness in secure computation from a new angle, which, to the best of our knowledge, was not investiagted in the past. The main motivation for reducing the randomness complexity of secure computation protocols is that producing high quality, unbiased, untemperable independent random coins is *expensive*: it requires an appropriate, well-calibrated device which can extract this randomness from well-chosen noisy sources. In addition, it is unfortunately common to generate randomness in a poor way, by reusing random strings several times, poorly seeding a pseudorandom generator, using an inappropriate randomness-generating functionalities in some computer languages or softwares etc. This is, of course, an extremely well understood issue in the cryptographic community: poor randomness generations has led to a number of broken implementations of cryptographic primitives, or insecure generations of cryptographic keys (e.g., [24] showed that the bad quality of the randomness used by major manufacturers of cryptographic hardware caused tens of millions of devices to use broken RSA keys. See also [22] for even more striking examples).

However, once a participant in a cryptographic protocol does have the means to generate randomness properly, then asking this participant to generate a lot of random coins does not necessarily incur a major additional cost. This suggests a natural, different question: rather than looking for bounds on the number of random bits that are necessary to privately compute given functions, or the interplay between the amount of randomness used and other complexity measures, is it possible to bound *how many* of the n players in a cryptographic protocol must have access to private random sources? While this question was, to the best of our knowledge, never studied before, we believe that it is of fundamental interest. From a theoretical point of view, given that secure computation is impossible with deterministic parties alone, it is a very natural question to understand how many of the parties must actually have the ability to generate unbiased random coins (we call such parties *sources*).

From a practical point of view, the question is also well motivated: if a secure computation protocol requires only a small number of (random) sources, then many other (cheaper) individuals that do not have the means or the capacity to produce high quality randomness can still be added to the system and participate in the secure computation.

1.1   Our Contributions

In this work, we seek to characterize the number k of players that must have access to a random source in a system of n players so that one can t-privately compute a (deterministic or randomized) functionality. Further, we are also interested in the question of the existence of a tradeoff between the number of players that have access to random sources, and the total number of random bits necessary for the private computation. Our main results are twofold.

A Full Characterization. We precisely characterize how many random sources are necessary and sufficient to t-privately compute an n-party functionality $\mathcal{F}$.

For the general case of randomized functionalities, we prove a simple lower bound: $t + 1$ sources are necessary. We also provide a matching upper bound, which follows from a simple tweak of the seminal BGW protocol [4]. Then, we turn our attention to the case of deterministic functionalities. Here, it follows from a lower bound of [16] that t random sources are necessary in general for t-private computation.

At first glance, it seems natural to believe that the lower bound of [16] is not tight in general. Indeed, if there are only t (fixed) parties that can generate randomness among all participants, and if the adversary can corrupt up to t parties, then the adversary can corrupt *all* participants which can generate randomness, and the protocol becomes entirely deterministic from the viewpoint of the adversary. Since secure computation is impossible with deterministic parties, we are tempted to conclude that such a protocol cannot be secure in general.

Our main technical result in this full characterization shows that, surprisingly, this intuition is flawed, and the lower bound of [16] is tight. Namely, we prove the following:

Theorem 1 (Informal). *For every deterministic n-party functionality $\mathcal{F}$, and every $t < n/2$, there exists a t-private protocol that securely computes $\mathcal{F}$ between n parties $P_1, \cdots, P_n$, if there is a size-t subset of the parties which have the ability to toss random coins.*

In other words: while secure computation is impossible without randomness, we show that secure computation is always possible using randomness, *even if the adversary is allowed to corrupt all parties that can produce randomness*. The proof of Theorem 1 is non-trivial; it relies on a careful combination of the GMW protocol (used as an outer protocol) and the BGW protocol (used as an inner protocol). At a very high level, the key idea is to *isolate* the t random sources, and to involve them solely in sub-computations that do not involve any actual input, letting the remaining parties perform the bulk of the sensitive computation, using random coins sent by these sources. Intuitively, we achieve the following dichotomy: either the adversary corrupts all sources, but in this case it cannot corrupt any of the parties that actually take part in the "sensitive part" of the computation; or the adversary corrupts at least one deterministic party, but then there is at least one uncorrupted source, which we leverage to generate random coins for all parties. The above intuition is relatively easy to instantiate when $t < n/3$; most of the complexity of our result stems from instantiating it for the optimal bound of $t < n/2$. Our complete characterization is summarized in Table 1.

Extension to UC Security and Statistical Security. For simplicity, all our protocols and lower bounds are discussed in the stand alone model, and with perfect security. However, all our constructions are proven secure using a black-box non-rewinding simulator. By a known result of [15], this implies that our protocols also enjoy perfect universal composability. Second, our lower bounds extend directly to the setting of statistically secure protocols; we actually directly prove

Table 1. Lower and upper bounds on the number of sources necessary for t-private computation of n-party functionalities. See Sect. 3 for discussions on defining the notion of the necessary number random sources.

	Deterministic functionalities	Randomized functionalities
Lower bound	t sources [16]	$t + 1$ sources (Sect. 3.1)
Upper bound	t sources (Sect. 4)	$t + 1$ sources (Sect. 3.2)

our lower bound with respect to statistical security in our proof of Theorem 7, and the proof of Theorem 6 in [16] extends also immediately to the setting of statistical privacy.

Extension to Adaptive Security. Our protocols achieve perfect selective security with straight-line black-box simulators. Therefore, it follows by known results [1, Section 8] that the protocols also enjoy adaptive simulation with respect to an *inefficient* simulator. Whether we can achieve the stronger notion of adaptive corruption with efficient simulation is an interesting open question.

Randomness Complexity of AND. In our second contribution, we turn to the question whether there is a tradeoff between the number of players that have access to a random source and the total number of random bits necessary for the private computation. The motivation for this question is that, in the constructions of our positive results, secure computation using an optimally small number of sources seems to require up to $\Theta(t)$ times more randomness compared to secure computation where all parties can toss coins (this is particularly visible in our simple upper bound for randomized functionalities). It is natural to wonder whether this is inherent: in order to reduce the number of sources, do we have to pay a price in randomness complexity? We put forward a conjecture stating that this is indeed the case for *complex* functionalities, i.e., n-party functionalities that do not have information-theoretic t-private protocols for $t \geq n/2$. Our conjecture states that, for such functionalities, a $\Theta(t)$ blowup in randomness complexity is necessary and sufficient to minimize the number of random sources. We view this conjecture as an interesting open question.

Then, in the course of getting a better understanding of the relation between randomness complexity and random sources, we turn our attention to a simple, yet very basic, concrete functionality: the n-party AND (it is very common in the literature on randomness complexity of secure computation to study the case of simple functionalities such as XOR [10,16,19,21] or AND [17], as they are basic functions). Here, the state of the art is the recent work of [17], that showed that 8 bits are sufficient to 1-privately compute the n-party AND functionality (the paper also shows that more than 1 bit is necessary). The upper bound of [17] uses two sources, and our question is whether we can match this upper bound using a *single* source or whether a private protocol with a single source will require more random bits.

Here, we again achieve a somewhat surprising result: we *improve* over the result of [17] in the two aspects at the time, i.e., we reduce both the number of sources and the number of random bits. Using a completely different protocol, we show that 6 bits tossed by a single source are sufficient to 1-privately compute the n-party AND functionality, for any $n \geq 3$.

2   Preliminaries

In this work, we consider perfectly secure protocols in the presence of semi-honest adversaries. More precisely, we focus on the *stand-alone* setting (security is argued for a single execution of the protocol in isolation), with *semi-honest* (perfect) security (the adversary sees the view of all corrupted parties, but all parties follow the specifications of the protocol) in a *static* corruption model (the adversary specifies the set of corrupted parties ahead of time).

Network Model. The parties interact over a synchronous network: the computation takes place in clearly defined rounds. All pairs of parties are connected via perfectly private and authenticated channels.

Notations. We let n denote the number of parties, and t denote the (maximum) number of corrupted parties. Let $[n]$ denote the set $\{1, \cdots, n\}$. We use the following notation for vectors, e.g., $\mathbf{x} = (x_1, \cdots, x_n)$; for any subset $C \subseteq [n]$, we write $\mathbf{x}_C$ for $(x_i)_{i \in C}$. Given a set S, we write $s \overset{\$}{\leftarrow} S$ to denote that s is sampled uniformly at random from S. Given a vector $\mathbf{x}$, we let $|\mathbf{x}|$ denote its length. An n-party deterministic functionality is a function $f : (\{0,1\}^*)^n \mapsto (\{0,1\}^*)^n$; we write $f_i(x_1, \cdots, x_n)$ to denote the i-th output of f on inputs $(x_1, \cdots, x_n)$, and $f_C(x_1, \cdots, x_n)$ to denote $(f(x_1, \cdots, x_n))_C$ for any $C \subseteq [n]$. For randomized functionality, every input vector $(x_1, \cdots, x_n)$ defines a *distribution* $f(x_1, \cdots, x_n)$ over the output space $(\{0,1\}^*)^n$. We say that the protocol computes the deterministic functionality $f : (\{0,1\}^*)^n \mapsto (\{0,1\}^*)^n$ (with perfect correctness) if, for every input $\mathbf{x} = (x_1, \cdots, x_n) \in (\{0,1\}^*)^n$, and for any outcome of all coin tosses, the output produced by each party P_i is always $f_i(\mathbf{x})$. When f is a randomized functionality, we say that a protocol computes f (with perfect correctness) if for every input $\mathbf{x} = (x_1, \cdots, x_n) \in (\{0,1\}^*)^n$, the distribution (over the randomness of the parties) of the joint outputs of the parties is exactly $f(x_1, \cdots, x_n)$. We write $\mathcal{D} \equiv \mathcal{D}'$ to denote that two distributions $\mathcal{D}$ and $\mathcal{D}'$ are identical. We sometime write distributions as $\{(a,b)\ :\ \text{sampling process}\}$ to denote a distribution over pairs (a,b) sampled according to the given sampling process. Given a probabilistic algorithm A, we slightly abuse notation and usually view $A(x)$ as the distribution corresponding to the output of A on input x.

2.1   Perfect Privacy

We first define the notion of a *view* of a player. The sets, functions, and random variables in the following definition are implicitly parametrized by a protocol π.

Definition 2 (View). *The view of party P_i (on a joint input $\mathbf{x}$ from all parties) at round $r \geq 1$, denoted $V_i^r(\mathbf{x})$, is the (joint) distribution of the sequence of messages received by P_i in rounds 1 to $r - 1$, and the sequence of the results of the coin tosses performed by P_i in rounds 1 to r.*

All the protocols we consider in this paper have deterministic upper bounds on the number of rounds. Hence we can also define the "final view" of the players after that upper bound is attained. We denote those without superscripts, i.e., $V_i(\mathbf{x})$.

Definition 3 (Output Distribution). *We let $O_i(\mathbf{x})$ denote the distribution of the output of P_i after an execution of the protocol with a joint input $\mathbf{x}$.*

Given a subset C of $[n]$, we write $V_C(\mathbf{x})$ to denote $(V_i(\mathbf{x}))_{i \in C}$ and $O_C(\mathbf{x})$ to denote $(O_i(\mathbf{x}))_{i \in C}$; we use $O(\mathbf{x})$ as a shorthand for $O_{[n]}(\mathbf{x})$.

Definition 4 (*t*-Privacy for deterministic functionalities [1]). *Let $f : (\{0,1\}^*)^n \mapsto (\{0,1\}^*)^n$ be an n-party deterministic functionality and let π be a protocol. We say that π is (perfectly) t-private if (1) π computes f with perfect correctness, and (2) there exists a probabilistic polynomial-time algorithm Sim such that for every $C \subset [n]$ of cardinality at most t and every $\mathbf{x} \in (\{0,1\}^*)^n$ where $|x_1| = \cdots = |x_n|$, it holds that $\mathsf{Sim}(C, \mathbf{x}_C, f_C(\mathbf{x})) \equiv V_C(\mathbf{x})$.*

While the above definition considers separately (with (1) and (2)) the issues of correctness and privacy, in the general case of randomized functionalities, the two notions are intertwined:

Definition 5 (*t*-Privacy for randomized functionalities ([1], def. 2.2)). *Let $f : (\{0,1\}^*)^n \mapsto (\{0,1\}^*)^n$ be an n-party randomized functionality and let π be a protocol. We say that π is (perfectly) t-private if (1) π computes f with perfect correctness, and (2) there exists a probabilistic polynomial-time algorithm Sim such that for every $C \subset [n]$ of cardinality at most t and every $\mathbf{x} \in (\{0,1\}^*)^n$ where $|x_1| = \cdots = |x_n|$, it holds that*

$$\{(v, y) \ : \ y \leftarrow f(\mathbf{x}), v \leftarrow \mathsf{Sim}(C, \mathbf{x}_C, y_C)\} \equiv (V_C(\mathbf{x}), O(\mathbf{x})),$$

where $(V_C(\mathbf{x}), O(\mathbf{x}))$ denotes the joint distribution of the corrupted parties' (final) views and the outputs of all parties in a run of the protocol on common input $\mathbf{x}$.

A simulator according to the above definitions is simply a machine that produces emulated views for all corrupted parties. However, it will be convenient when analyzing the security of our protocols to view the simulator Sim as an *interactive* machine, which pretends to play the role of the honest parties during an execution of the protocol, and interacts with the corrupted parties. Under this viewpoint, Sim receives as input $(C, \mathbf{x}_C, f_C(\mathbf{x}))$, but also the random tapes of all corrupted parties; this is w.l.o.g. since in the above definition, Sim will anyway sample these random coins itself when emulating the views.

3   On the Number of Random Sources in Private Computation

Parties participating in a private computation protocol may or may not have access to a random source. We call a party that has access to a random source a *source*, and assume that this party is given access to an arbitrarily long tape of independent unbiased random bits. Note that what we call a source is exactly the standard definition of a player in standard secure computation protocols. In contrast, players which do not have access to such a tape are called *deterministic parties*: the behavior of deterministic parties at any given time is entirely determined by a deterministic function of their input and the messages they received up to that time.

Static Versus Dynamic Measures. Note that our notions of source and deterministic parties is *static*: which parties can or cannot sample random bits is a priori fixed before the start of the protocol. In other words, if in at least one execution of a protocol π a given party has to sample a random coin, then that party is a source. Even if (say) only 10 distinct parties have to sample coins during any given execution of the protocol, but *which* of the parties sample coins vary over different executions, then we cannot say that π uses only 10 sources – it might be that *all* parties have to be sources. This static notion captures in a more realistic way the setting where some parties in a system have access to a high-quality random number generator, while others do not; the real-world meaning of the dynamic variant of the notion is less clear.

When one considers the static measure, another distinction is called for,

Universal Versus Non-universal Setting. Before we establish our main theorems, we formally define what we mean by a statement of the form "all n-party functionalities can be privately computed with s sources". This can be interpreted in two ways:

1. Fix s sources $(P_1, \cdots, P_s)$, and $n-s$ deterministic parties $(P_{s+1}, \cdots, P_n)$. For any n-party functionality $\mathcal{F}$ there is a protocol that uses the above parties and privately computes $\mathcal{F}$.
2. Fix an n-party functionality $\mathcal{F}$. Then there exists a choice of a subset S, $s = |S|$, of parties among $(P_1, \cdots, P_n)$ such that if $(P_i)_{i \in S}$ are sources, and the other parties are deterministic, then there exists a protocol that uses the above parties and privately computes $\mathcal{F}$.

We call a protocol of the first type *universal*, and a protocol of the second type *non-universal*. Universal protocols are more desirable, since we would like to capture settings where sources are defined by the availability of a good random number generator, and then one can privately compute *any* functionality in that system; we typically do not want the choice of the sources to depend on the specific functionality at hand. Looking ahead, our results will consider the static measure (as it better captures the situation in "realistic" systems), and will be proved with the best flavor: our upper bounds will be *universal* protocols, while our lower bounds hold even for *non-universal* protocols.

3.1 Lower Bounds

Theorem 6 (deterministic functionalities, lower bound). *For any number of parties n, there exists a deterministic n-party functionality $\mathcal{F}$ such that for any $t \leq n - 2$, any t-private n-party protocol computing $\mathcal{F}$ must have at least $s \geq t$ sources.*

The theorem follows directly from a result of Mansour and Kushilevitz [16] who showed that in order to t-privately compute the function xor, $t \leq n - 2$, at least t players with access to a local random source are necessary. Note that Mansour and Kushilevitz did not focus on the number of random sources in their work: their goal was to show that the *randomness complexity* of t-private computation of xor is at least t (that is, in any given execution of a t-private protocol computing xor, at least t random coins must be sampled). However, their proof proceeds by showing that in any given execution *at least t different parties* must sample at least one random bit, hence, as they note, their proof proves also that at least t players with access to a local random source are necessary to t-privately compute xor.

Theorem 7 (randomized functionalities, lower bound). *For any number of parties n, there exists a randomized n-party functionality $\mathcal{F}$ such that for any $t \leq n - 1$, any t-private n-party protocol computing $\mathcal{F}$ must have at least $s \geq t + 1$ sources.*

The proof follows the (natural) intuition that if all sources can be corrupted and the outputs of the honest parties depend on independent random coins, these random coins will not be independent of the view of the sources. In fact, the proof below also rules out any *statistically private* protocol for such functionalities, by showing that the statistical distance between the ideal distribution and the simulated distribution cannot be sub-constant.

Proof. Consider the following simple randomized functionality $\mathcal{F}$: on joint input $\mathbf{x}$, the output of each player is $\mathbf{x}$ together with a single bit chosen uniformly and independently at random. Assume that the number s of sources is at most t; since the functionality is symmetrical, let us, without loss of generality, call $P_1, \cdots, P_s$ the s sources, and $P_{s+1}, \cdots, P_n$ the remaining deterministic parties.

Let π be an arbitrary protocol computing $\mathcal{F}$ in the above setting, and Sim be any simulator. Let $C \leftarrow \{1, \cdots, s\}$; that is, the adversary corrupts exactly all the sources. Since all honest parties are deterministic, the only coins tossed during the entire protocol are tossed by corrupted parties. Since the entire joint input $\mathbf{x}$ is part of the output of each party (hence part of the view of the corrupted parties), there necessarily exists a *deterministic* function g such that $\{g(V) : V \leftarrow V_C(\mathbf{x})\} \equiv O(\mathbf{x})$. Now, given $y \leftarrow f(\mathbf{x})$, the input $(C, \mathbf{x}_C, y_C)$ to Sim depends solely on $\mathbf{x}$ and the independent random output bits defining the outputs of the corrupted parties, as defined by the functionality. Writing $((\mathbf{x}, b_1), \cdots, (\mathbf{x}, b_n)) \leftarrow f(\mathbf{x})$, the bits $(b_{s+1}, \cdots, b_n)$ are $n - s$ random bits independent of $(C, \mathbf{x}, y_C)$. Therefore,

$$\Pr[g(\mathsf{Sim}(C, \mathbf{x}_C, y_C)) = f(\mathbf{x})] \leq \frac{1}{2^{n-s}} \leq \frac{1}{2},$$

for any choice of randomness done by Sim. Therefore, the function g provides a simple distinguisher showing that the distributions $\{(v, y) : y \leftarrow f(\mathbf{x}), v \leftarrow \mathsf{Sim}(C, \mathbf{x}_C, y_C)\}$ and $(V_C(\mathbf{x}), O(\mathbf{x}))$ have (at least) a constant statistical distance. this concludes the proof.

3.2   Upper Bounds

In this section, we give the matching upper bounds for both deterministic and randomized functionalities. The upper bound for randomized functionalities follows from a simple and natural protocol; the protocol for deterministic functionalities is considerably more involved, and is the focus of Sect. 4.

Theorem 8 (deterministic functionalities, upper bound). *For any number of parties n and any $t < n/2$, there is a choice of t sources among the n players such that for any deterministic n-party functionality $\mathcal{F}$ there is a t-private protocol for $\mathcal{F}$ that works with those parties.*

Section 4 below is dedicated to the proof of Theorem 8.

Theorem 9 (randomized functionalities, upper bound). *For any number of parties n and any $t < n/2$, there is a choice of $t + 1$ sources among the n players such that for any (randomized) n-party functionality $\mathcal{F}$ there is a t-private protocol for $\mathcal{F}$ that works with those parties.*

The protocol for randomized functionalities captures the (correct, straightforward) intuition that if not all sources can be corrupted, then there is always at least one uncorrupted source which can distribute random coins to the deterministic parties. To formalize this intuition, we recall the seminal result of Ben-Or, Goldwasser, and Wigderson [4]:

Theorem 10 (BGW). *For any $t < n/2$ and any n-party (possibly randomized) functionality $\mathcal{F}$, there is a perfect t-private protocol for $\mathcal{F}$ (with communication and randomness proportional to the circuit size of $\mathcal{F}$).*

In the protocol guaranteed by the above theorem, all parties have access to their own random tape, and the size of the random tape is bounded by an a priori known polynomial in the circuit size of $\mathcal{F}$. Note that the BGW protocol also extends to securely computing randomized functionalities, and functionalities that provide different outputs to all parties [1]. In our case we have a fixed set of $t + 1$ parties which can toss random coins: they are called the *sources*, and are denoted $S_1, \cdots, S_{t+1}$; the remaining $n - t - 1$ parties, denoted $P_{t+2}, \cdots, P_n$, are deterministic. Given the functionality $\mathcal{F}$, let $B_{\mathcal{F}}$ be an upper bound on the maximum number of random coins tossed by any single party in the BGW protocol for computing $\mathcal{F}$ t-privately. The protocol to t-privately compute $\mathcal{F}$ as guaranteed by the theorem works as follows:

1. Each source S_i samples, for $j = t + 2$ to n, a random string $r_{i,j} \xleftarrow{\$} \{0,1\}^{B_{\mathcal{F}}}$ and sends it to P_j. Each party P_j sets $r_j = \bigoplus_{i=1}^{t+1} r_{i,j}$. In addition, each source S_i samples a random string $r_i \xleftarrow{\$} \{0,1\}^{B_{\mathcal{F}}}$.
2. All n parties run the BGW protocol for t-privately computing $\mathcal{F}$, where each player P_i, $i = 1$ to n, uses the tape r_i as their random source.
3. All parties output their output from the BGW protocol.

Correctness is straightforward, and t-privacy follows directly from the fact that from the viewpoint of any subset of t parties (random sources or deterministic), the random tape r_j used by any honest party P_j is perfectly distributed as a real random tape, since it is the XOR of $t + 1$ strings, at least one of which is guaranteed to be (random and) unknown to the corrupted parties.

4   Private Computation of Deterministic Functionalities

In this section, we prove that for every *deterministic* functionality $\mathcal{F}$: $(\{0,1\}^*)^n \mapsto (\{0,1\}^*)^n$, there exists a t-private n-party protocol which requires exactly t sources; these sources can be arbitrary players. Hence we show that for any deterministic functionality $\mathcal{F}$ there is a t-source *uniform* t-private protocol.

4.1   The GMW Protocol with Beaver Triples

To start we recall the seminal GMW protocol of Goldreich, Micali, and Wigderson [12], which we use in our construction. For our purpose, it will be more convenient to view GMW as an information-theoretic protocol in the *correlated randomness model* of Beaver [2,3], in which the parties have access to a trusted source of correlated random coins, in the form of random *Beaver triples*. Below, whenever we refer to *random (n out of n) shares* of a bit x, we mean the following: a string of n bits $x_1, \ldots, x_n$ sampled randomly conditioned on $\bigoplus_{i=1}^n x_i = x$. Given a value x, we write $\langle x \rangle$ as a more compact representation of the n-tuple $(x_1, \ldots, x_n)$ of shares of x.

Definition 11 (Beaver triple). *We say that n parties $(P_1, \ldots, P_n)$ receive a (random, n-party) Beaver triple if the parties receive random n out of n shares of a, b, and $a \cdot b$, where a and b are two independent random bits. That is, each party P_i receives a triple (a_i, b_i, c_i), where all triples are jointly sampled at random conditioned on $(\bigoplus_{i=1}^n a_i) \cdot (\bigoplus_{i=1}^n b_i) = \bigoplus_{i=1}^n c_i$.*

Theorem 12 (GMW + Beaver). *For any $t < n$, there exists a t-private information-theoretic secure n-party protocol in the correlated randomness model for computing any deterministic functionality $\mathcal{F} : (\{0,1\}^*)^n \mapsto (\{0,1\}^*)^n$ where,* *prior to the execution of the protocol, the parties can ask a trusted dealer for any number of random Beaver triples. Furthermore, no party needs to toss any additional random coin.*

The GMW Protocol. Let $P_1, \ldots, P_n$ be n parties with respective inputs $(x_1, \ldots, x_n)$, and let $C_{\mathcal{F}}$ be a boolean circuit with XOR and AND gates of fan-in 2 computing the functionality $\mathcal{F}$.[2] The parties will evaluate the circuit gate by gate, starting from the inputs and computing the value of a gate when the values of its two parent nodes (which are either input nodes or gates themselves) have been computed. The protocol maintains the following invariant: after evaluating a gate, each party P_i will hold an additive share v_i of the value v on this gate (i.e., $v = \bigoplus_{i=1}^{n} v_i$). Without loss of generality, we assume that the parties always hold shares of the inputs to a gate when evaluating it: if an input to the gate is an input bit b belonging to party P_i, we define the shares of $(P_1, \ldots, P_i, \ldots, P_n)$ to be $(0, \ldots, b, \ldots, 0)$.

- Evaluating an XOR gate $\mathsf{XOR}(u, v)$: the parties locally XOR their shares of u and v. No communication is required.
- Evaluating an AND gate $\mathsf{AND}(u, v)$: given $\langle u \rangle$ and $\langle v \rangle$ the parties must compute additive shares $\langle uv \rangle$ of $u \cdot v$. This is done using one invocation of the *secure multiplication* protocol defined below.
- Output: after evaluating an output gate whose output is assigned to a party P_i, all parties send their share of the output to P_i, who reconstructs the output.

Secure Multiplication. Let u, v be the inputs to the AND gate, and let (u_i, v_i) be P_i's share of the inputs, $1 \leq i \leq n$.

- *Beaver triple request.* All parties receive from the trusted dealer a random Beaver triple. Let (a_i, b_i, c_i) denote P_i's share of the triple.
- *Broadcast.* Each party P_i broadcasts $\alpha_i = u_i \oplus a_i$ and $\beta_i = v_i \oplus b_i$; all parties reconstruct $\alpha = \bigoplus_{i=1}^{n} \alpha_i = u \oplus a$ and $\beta = \bigoplus_{i=1}^{n} \beta_i = v \oplus b$.
- *Output.* Each party P_i outputs $\alpha \cdot v_i \oplus \beta \cdot a_i \oplus c_i$.

Security follows from the fact that the pairs u_i, v_i are uniformly random; correctness follows from the relation $\langle u \cdot v \rangle = (u \oplus a) \cdot \langle v \rangle + \langle a \rangle \cdot (v \oplus b) + \langle ab \rangle$.

In our main protocol, we will rely on the above version of the GMW protocol. It will be convenient to view it as follows: the GMW protocol involves *deterministic* parties in a model where all parties can request, upon need, a random Beaver triple in order to execute a secure multiplication.

---

[2] To be completely formal, since $\mathcal{F}$ can take inputs from $(\{0, 1\}^*)^n$, the circuit $C_{\mathcal{F}}$ must also depend on the input sizes $|x_1|, \ldots, |x_n|$, which means the parties have to reveal their input sizes to each other before the actual protocol starts. This does not contradict security, as privacy is only required to hold when $|x_1| = \ldots = |x_n|$; we ignore this technicality in the remainder of this paper.

4.2   Intuition Behind Our Protocol: Two Complementary Scenarios

We consider n parties wishing to t-privately compute a deterministic n-party functionality $\mathcal{F} : (\{0,1\}^*)^n \mapsto (\{0,1\}^*)^n$ on their private inputs, with exactly t sources $(S_1, \ldots, S_t)$, and $n - t$ deterministic parties, $(P_{t+1}, \ldots, P_n)$. We assume $t < n/2$. The first important observation is that the following two scenarios are mutually exclusive and cover all possible situations:

1. There is an honest majority among the $n - t$ the deterministic parties.
2. A majority of the $n - t$ deterministic parties is corrupted (*i.e.*, there are at least $\lceil (n - t)/2 \rceil$ corrupted deterministic parties). *But* in that case there is an honest majority among the t sources and there is at least one honest deterministic party.

Obviously the two scenarios are mutually exclusive and cover all possible situations. To see that in the second scenario there is still at least one honest deterministic party and there is an honest majority among the t sources, observe that $2t < n$ and hence $(n - t) - t > 0$. At the same time the number of corrupted sources is at most $t - (n - t)/2 < t/2$, hence there is an honest majority among the t sources.

Now, assume for a moment that the parties could somehow *know* in which scenario they are. In what follows we assume for simplicity that the functionality delivers the same output to all parties (the general case can be handled with standard techniques, as we will show in our full construction).

A Protocol for Scenario 1. If the parties know that the corruption pattern follows scenario 1 above, then we can *isolate the sources* and let the deterministic parties alone perform the computation as they have an honest majority among them. For simplicity, assume for now that the functionality output the same value to everyone. Since there is an honest majority among the deterministic parties, they can execute an appropriate BGW protocol among themselves, using random tapes sent by the sources (after the sources share their own inputs among the deterministic parties). During the entire protocol, the deterministic parties never send *anything* to the sources, except for the final output. Then, security follows from a simple case disjunction:

- If at least one source is honest, then the random tapes of the deterministic parties (obtained by XORing independent tapes received from each of the sources) are guaranteed to be uncorrupted, and security follows via the same argument as for the simple protocol from Sect. 3.2.
- Else, if all t sources are corrupted, then *all deterministic parties are honest*. In this case, security follows trivially from the fact that no corrupted party ever receives any message whatsoever, except the output itself.

More formally,

1. Each source S_i (for $i = 1$ to t) with input x_i computes $n - t$ random additive shares $(y_{i,j})_{t+1 \leq j \leq n}$ of x_i, and sends $y_{i,j}$ to party P_j for $j = t + 1$ to n.

Let $\mathcal{F}'$ be the following $(n-t)$-party functionality: on input $(x_j, y_{1,j}, \ldots, y_{t,j})$ of each party P_j, $\mathcal{F}'$ outputs $\mathcal{F}(\bigoplus_{j=1}^{n-t} x_{1,j}, \ldots, \bigoplus_{j=1}^{n-t} y_{t,j}, x_{t+1}, \ldots, x_n)$.

2. Each source S_i samples a random string $r_{i,j} \xleftarrow{\$} \{0,1\}^{B_{\mathcal{F}'}}$ and sends it to P_j for $i = 1$ to t and $j = t+1$ to n; Each party P_j sets $r_j \leftarrow \bigoplus_{i=1}^{t+1} r_{i,j}$.

3. The $n-t$ deterministic parties run the BGW protocol for securely computing $\mathcal{F}'$, where P_j uses r_j as its random tape to emulate the coin tosses in the BGW protocol.

4. The deterministic parties send the output of the BGW protocol to the t sources. All parties output this result.

Correctness follows from the fact that $\bigoplus_{j=1}^{n-t} y_{i,j} = x_i$, hence the output of $\mathcal{F}'$ is indeed $\mathcal{F}(x_1, \ldots, x_n)$. t-privacy follows immediately from the simple case disjunction outlined above. The general case, where different parties can receive different outputs, is easily handled with the standard reduction of multi-output secure computation to single-output secure computation: each party samples a random mask to mask its own output, and the parties jointly evaluate the single-output functionality that outputs (to everyone) the string of all outputs, each masked by the random mask of the corresponding party. Then, each party gets their own output (and nothing more) by removing their own mask.

A Protocol for Scenario 2. In scenario 2, we do not have anymore an honest majority among the $n - t$ deterministic parties (but there is still at least one honest party among the deterministic parties). However, this guarantees that there is now an honest majority among the *sources*. There are several solutions in this setting. We sketch one such solution: the deterministic parties can use the GMW protocol from Sect. 4.1, which tolerates up to all-but-one corruptions. The GMW protocol, in its version as described in Sect. 4.1, is deterministic, but the parties must request *random Beaver triples* from a trusted dealer. Here, we let the *sources* jointly emulate the trusted dealer: each time the deterministic parties ask for a random Beaver triple, the sources distributively generate and send to the parties (shares of) this triple. This distributed generation is performed among the sources using the BGW protocol. Since in this scenario a majority of the sources are honest, the Beaver triples are guaranteed to remain uncorrupted, and security follows from the security of the GMW protocol.

Our Goal: A Best of Both Worlds Protocol. In each of the two scenarios above, there is a secure protocol for computing $\mathcal{F}$; the trouble is, of course, that the parties do not know *in which* scenario they are. To solve this issue, our aim is, at a high level, to combine the two protocols above into a single *best of both worlds* protocol: a combined protocol which is guaranteed to be secure if at least *one* of the protocols is secure, which is always the case (as the two scenarios cover all possible situations). The idea of reconciling protocols with different security guarantees is not new: it originates in the work of Chaum [6]. Chaum's original motivation was the following: some protocols achieve *computational* security against $n-1$ corruptions, while others achieve *unconditional* security against $t < n/2$ corruptions (assuming secure point-to-point channels); however, no protocol achieves both at the same time. To overcome this limitation, Chaum introduced the idea of combining an *outer protocol*, computing the target functionality and an *inner protocol*, used by the parties to emulate some key sub-functionality required by the outer protocol. Crucially, the inner protocol is never invoked directly on private values held by the parties.

4.3   The Protocol

We represent in Fig. 1 and Fig. 2 a protocol which allows n players $(S_1, \ldots, S_t, P_{t+1}, \ldots, P_n)$, where only $(S_1, \ldots, S_t)$ can toss coins, to jointly and t-privately compute an arbitrary n-party deterministic functionality of their joint input. The protocol combines a GMW-based *outer protocol* with a BGW-based *inner protocol*. More precisely,

The Outer Protocol (Fig. 1). The outer protocol is essentially the protocol for *scenario 2* above: the sources $(S_1, \ldots, S_t)$ additively share their inputs among the deterministic parties $(P_{t+1}, \ldots, P_n)$, and the latter jointly run an instance of the GMW protocol to evaluate the original functionality to be computed, where the inputs are the inputs of the deterministic parties, and the shares of the inputs of the sources (now known to the deterministic parties). Each time the deterministic players need to receive a random Beaver triple, all players (sources and deterministic parties together) run the *inner protocol* in order to compute the shares of this triple to be given to the deterministic parties.

The Inner Protocol (Fig. 2). The inner protocol is the simple protocol of Sect. 3.2 (which is, in spirit, essentially the same as the protocol of scenario 1), applied to the specific functionality that distributes random shares of a random Beaver triple to the deterministic parties.

A Note on Input and Output Size. In the protocol, we assume that the length of the output of any participant is a priori known to all parties. This is without loss of generality since in the semi-honest model, we can always add a pre-initialization phase where all parties announce their input length to each other. Since t-privacy is only required to hold when all inputs are of the same length, this does not harm privacy. Then, all parties can compute an upper bound on the length of any output by computing $\kappa = \max_{i \in [n]} \max_{\mathbf{x}} |\mathcal{F}_i(\mathbf{x})|$, where the second maximum is taken over all possible inputs of the appropriate length. Finally, all outputs can be interpreted as elements of $\{0,1\}^\kappa$, by padding them with zeroes.

Outer Protocol $\Pi_{\mathcal{F}}$

Fix n participants $(S_1, \ldots, S_t, P_{t+1}, \ldots, P_n)$, where only the players S_i, $1 \leq i \leq t$ are sources.

Fix an n-party deterministic functionality $\mathcal{F} : (\{0,1\}^\ell)^n \mapsto (\{0,1\}^\kappa)^n$, and let the joint input to the players be $(x_1, \ldots, x_n) \in (\{0,1\}^\ell)^n$. Let κ be the length, known to everyone, of each participant's output.

Initialization. Each source S_i (for $i = 1$ to t) with input x_i computes $n - t$ random additive shares $(y_{i,j})_{t+1 \leq j \leq n}$ of x_i, samples $n - t$ random masks $m_{i,j} \xleftarrow{\$} \{0,1\}^\kappa$, $t + 1 \leq j \leq n$ and sends $(y_{i,j}, m_{i,j})$ to party P_j for $j = t+1$ to n. We call $m_i = \bigoplus_{j=t+1}^n m_{i,j}$ the *output mask* of S_i. We let $z_j = (x_j, y_{1,j}, \ldots, y_{t,j}, m_{1,j}, \ldots, m_{t,j})$ denote the *outer input* of party P_j for $j = t+1$ to n.

Execution. The outer protocol will first run an $(n - t)$-party "GMW + Beaver" protocol (as defined in Section 4.1), run on players $P_{t+1}, \ldots P_n$, and computing the $(n - t)$-party deterministic functionality $\mathcal{F}'$ defined below.

Each time that the "GMW + Beaver" protocol is supposed to request a Beaver triple from the trusted party, all parties run instead the inner protocol represented in Figure 2, which results in players $P_{t+1}, \ldots, P_n$ having what would have the trusted party give them. We note that in the GMW protocol the sequence of requests of the beaver triples is a function of the functionality being computed only (and not of the inputs or of previous random choices).

Functionality. The functionality $\mathcal{F}'$ is defined as follows: on input $(z_{t+1}, \ldots, z_n)$, where z_i is defined as above, let

$$(w_1, \ldots, w_n) = \mathcal{F}\left(\bigoplus_{j=t+1}^n y_{1,j}, \ldots, \bigoplus_{j=t+1}^n y_{t,j}, x_{t+1}, \ldots, x_n \right) ,$$

where all w_i are seen as elements in $\{0,1\}^\kappa$. Let

$$(m_1, \ldots, m_t) = \left(\bigoplus_{j=t+1}^n m_{1,j}, \ldots, \bigoplus_{j=t+1}^n m_{t,j} \right) .$$

The functionality $\mathcal{F}'$ outputs w_i to each party P_i for $i \geq t + 2$, and $(w_{t+1}, w_1 \oplus m_1, \ldots, w_t \oplus m_t)$ to P_{t+1}.

Output Phase. Once the execution of the protocol is completed, the deterministic parties first execute the output phase of the GMW protocol: for all $(i, j) \in [t+1, n]^2$, P_i sends its share of P_j's output to P_j. Then, P_{t+1} sends $w_i \oplus m_i$ to each source S_i, which unmasks w_i using their output mask m_i. Each deterministic party P_j outputs w_j and each source S_i outputs w_i.

Fig. 1. A t-private, t-sources, n-party protocol $\Pi_{\mathcal{F}}$ for any n-party deterministic functionality $\mathcal{F}$

Inner Protocol Π_{in}

Fix n participants $(S_1, \ldots, S_t, P_{t+1}, \ldots, P_n)$, where only the players S_i, $1 \leq i \leq t$ are sources.

Let $\mathcal{F}_{BT}$ be the n-party randomized functionality which, on any input to all parties, (ignores the input and) samples two independent unbiased random bits $(a, b) \xleftarrow{\$} \{0, 1\}^2$, and sets $(a_i, b_i, c_i)_{t+1 \leq i \leq n}$ to be uniformly random $(n - t)$ out of $(n - t)$ shares of $(a, b, a \cdot b)$. It outputs $\perp$ to each source S_i (for $i = 1$ to t) and (a_j, b_j, c_j) to each party P_j (for $j = t + 1$ to n). Let B_{BT} be an upper bound on the maximum number of coins tossed by any party during the t-private computation of $\mathcal{F}_{BT}$ by the BGW protocol.

1. **Tape sharing phase.** Each source S_k for $k = 1$ to t samples $n - t$ random strings $r_{k,\ell} \xleftarrow{\$} \{0, 1\}^{B_{BT}}$, $t + 1 \leq \ell \leq n$ and sends $r_{k,\ell}$ to P_ℓ. Each deterministic party P_ℓ sets $r_\ell \leftarrow \bigoplus_{k=1}^{t} r_{k,\ell}$. In addition each source S_k, for $k = 1$ to t, samples a random string $r_k \xleftarrow{\$} \{0, 1\}^{B_{BT}}$
2. **BGW phase** All n parties jointly run the BGW protocol for t-privately computing the n-party randomized functionality $\mathcal{F}_{BT}$, where they use the strings r_i, $1 \leq i \leq n$ as their random sources. All players use, e.g., 0 as their input (since $\mathcal{F}_{BT}$ ignores its input, any fixed input would do).
3. **Output** The output of each party is its output in the BGW protocol.

Fig. 2. The inner protocol Π_{in}

Security Analysis. The intuitive idea behind the security guarantee of our protocol is as follows. Observe that only the deterministic players receive messages that depend on the input of the functionality to be computed. Therefore, if the adversary does not corrupt any deterministic party then security is guaranteed. If, however, there are corrupted deterministic parties, then at least one source is uncorrupted. It follows that from the point of view of the adversary the randomness used in the BGW, inner, protocol is real randomness (provided by the at least one uncorrupted source), and the inner BGW protocol that is run on all players (to compute the Beaver triples) is secure since there is always an honest majority among all players. Since there is always at least one uncorrupted deterministic player (given the relation between n and t) we have that in this case (i.e., when there are corrupted deterministic players) the GMW + Beaver protocol is secure too. We note in passing that the correctness of our protocol is guaranteed since both the outer and the inner protocol are run on "honest-but-curious" players.

We now formally prove the security property of the protocol. Fix a functionality $\mathcal{F} : (\{0, 1\}^\ell)^n \mapsto (\{0, 1\}^\kappa)^n$ ($\mathcal{F}$ is deterministic). Let $C_S \subset [t]$ and $C_P \subset [n - t]$ denote the subsets of corrupted sources and corrupted deterministic parties, respectively. Since we consider a static corruption model, $C = (C_S, C_P)$

is known to the simulator. Let $\mathbf{x}$ be the joint input vector of the players. We describe a simulator Sim for the protocol defined above.

If no party is corrupted (i.e., $C_S = C_P = \{\emptyset\}$), the simulation is trivial. We assume now that at least one party is corrupted. On input $(C = (C_S, C_P), \mathbf{x}_C, \mathcal{F}_C(\mathbf{x}))$, Sim distinguishes between two cases: either $C_S \neq [t]$ (there is at least one uncorrupted source, some deterministic parties can be corrupted) or $C_S = [t]$ and $C_P = \{\emptyset\}$ (all sources are corrupted, and only them).

Case 1: $C_S \neq [t]$. Let $t' = |C_S| + |C_P| \leq t$ denote the number of corrupted parties. In the initialization phase, for every $i \in [t]\backslash C_S$ and every $j \in C_P$, Sim sends a uniformly random ℓ-bit string $y_{i,j}$ and a uniformly random κ-bit string $m_{i,j}$ to P_j on behalf of S_i. Sim also stores the input shares $(y_{i,j})_{t+1\leq j\leq n}$ and the outputs masks m_i of each corrupted source S_i (they can be computed from their inputs and random tapes, which Sim knows). Then, for every $j \in C_P$, Sim computes and stores the outer input $z_j = (x_{1,j}, \ldots, x_{t,j}, m_{1,j}, \ldots, m_{t,j})$ of P_j. Throughout the protocol, Sim maintains a local simulation of the shares held by each corrupted deterministic participant P_j for $j \in C_P$ of the value carried by each wire in the circuit.

When the parties evaluate an XOR gate, Sim simply updates its local simulation of the output wire shares of the corrupted parties, by locally XORing their shares of the input wires. Each time the $n - t$ deterministic parties evaluate an AND gate, Sim behaves as follows:

- *(Tape sharing phase)* For every $k \in [t]\backslash C_S$ and any $\ell \in C_P$, Sim samples a random string $r_{k,\ell}$ on behalf of S_k and sends it to P_ℓ.
- *Emulation of $\mathcal{F}_{\mathsf{BT}}$.* Sim locally emulates $\mathcal{F}_{\mathsf{BT}}$ as follows: it samples uniformly random triples (a_j, b_j, c_j) for every $j \in C_P$, and sets (a_j, b_j, c_j) to be the emulated output of $\mathcal{F}_{\mathsf{BT}}$ to P_j (note that the (a_j, b_j, c_j) are perfectly distributed as in the real execution from the viewpoint of all corrupted P_j, because $|C_P| \leq t < n - t$: there is at least one uncorrupted deterministic party). Then, Sim runs $\mathsf{SimBGW}(C, \mathbf{0}^{t'}, \mathsf{out}_C)$, where SimBGW is the perfect simulator for the BGW protocol, and out_C is equal to $\perp$ for all indices in C_S, and to (a_j, b_j, c_j) for each $j \in C_P$.
- *Secure multiplication.* Sim emulates the broadcast message of each honest deterministic party P_j by broadcasting two uniformly random bits (α_j, β_j) on their behalf.

Output Phase. At the end of the outer protocol, each party $P_i, t+1 \leq i \leq n$ holds a share $s_{i,j}$ of the output of P_j, and all shares held by corrupted deterministic parties are known to Sim. For every $j \in C_P\backslash\{t+1\}$, Sim sends $n - t - |C_P|$ uniformly random shares of $\mathcal{F}_j(\mathbf{x}) \oplus \bigoplus_{i\in C_p} s_{i,j}$ to P_j on behalf of each uncorrupted party P_k. Finally,

- If P_{t+1} is corrupted, Sim sends $n - t - |C_P|$ uniformly random shares of

$$(\mathcal{F}_{t+1}(\mathbf{x}), \mathcal{F}_1(\mathbf{x}) \oplus m_1, \ldots, \mathcal{F}_t(\mathbf{x}) \oplus m_t) \oplus \bigoplus_{i\in C_p} s_{i,1}$$

to P_1, on behalf of each uncorrupted party P_k.

– If P_{t+1} is honest, Sim sends $\mathcal{F}_i(\mathbf{x}) \oplus m_i$ to each corrupted source S_i on P_{t+1} behalf.

We now argue that Sim's emulation is perfect in Case 1. First, the simulation of the input sharing, mask sharing, and tape sharing phases are perfectly identical to an honest execution of the protocol. Second, since $C_S \neq [t]$, there exists at least one uncorrupted source. This guarantees that the string r_ℓ, used by each party P_ℓ as its random tape in (any given instance of) the BGW protocol, is a uniformly random string unknown to any corrupted party. Therefore, we can treat each participant in the BGW protocol as a probabilistic player in the analysis. Now, let (u, v) be the inputs to an AND gate, of which the deterministic parties hold shares; the shares of the corrupted parties are known to Sim. Let (u_j, v_j) denote P_j's share, for $j = t+1$ to n. Recall that the (a_j, b_j) part of the output of $\mathcal{F}_{\text{BT}}$ are uniformly random independent bits. Since Sim's messages (α_j, β_j) are uniformly random, so are $\alpha_j \oplus u_j$ and $\beta_j \oplus v_j$. By the t-privacy of BGW for randomized functionalities, the joint distribution of $\mathsf{SimBGW}(C, \mathbf{0}^{t'}, \text{out}_C)$ and all pairs $(\alpha_j \oplus u_j, \beta_j \oplus v_j)$ for each uncorrupted P_j are distributed perfectly as the joint distribution of the views of the corrupted parties in a real execution, together with the random outputs (a_j, b_j) of $\mathcal{F}_{\text{BT}}$ to all honest deterministic parties. Therefore, $\mathsf{SimBGW}(C, \mathbf{0}^{t'}, \text{out}_C)$ together with the simulated messages (α_j, β_j) is perfectly distributed as the corrupted parties' views together with the real messages $(\alpha_j, \beta_j) = (u_j \oplus a_j, v_j \oplus b_j)$.

It remains to argue that the simulation is perfect for the output phase as well. Consider a given output wire where P_j should receive the output, and assume without loss of generality that this wire goes out of an AND gate (since the parties can always add a dummy multiplication by 1 to any output gate). For simplicity, let us assume for now that $j \neq t+1$ (the case $j = t+1$ can be handled similarly). Let u, v be the inputs to this AND gate: it holds that $u \cdot v = \mathcal{F}_j(\mathbf{x}, \mathbf{y})$ (the case where $j = t+1$ is identical, except that $\mathcal{F}_{t+1}(\mathbf{x}, \mathbf{y})$ must be replaced by the longer output of P_{t+1}, which also includes the masked output of other players). Therefore, by the definition of $\mathcal{F}_{\text{BT}}$, the triples (a_k, b_k, c_k) are uniformly random triples conditioned on the c_k being random shares of $\mathcal{F}_{j+t}(\mathbf{x}, \mathbf{y}) \oplus \alpha \cdot v \oplus \beta \cdot u$, where α, β are the XOR of the messages α_k, β_k broadcast by all deterministic parties.

For each $k \in [t+1, n] \backslash C_P$, let us call γ_k the simulated random share of $\mathcal{F}_j(\mathbf{x}) \oplus \bigoplus_{i \in C_P} s_{i,j}$ sent by Sim on behalf of P_k. By construction, the sequence $(\gamma_k)_k$ and the sequence $(s_{i,j})_i$ jointly constitute uniformly random shares of $\mathcal{F}_j(\mathbf{x}) = u \cdot v$. Let us rewrite w_k the share of each party P_k for notational convenience (each w_k is either $s_{k,j}$ or γ_k, depending on whether P_k is corrupted or not). Then the (α_k, β_k, w_k) and the input shares (u_k, v_k) virtually define triples (a_k, b_k, c_k) as $(\alpha_k \oplus u_k, \beta_k \oplus v_k, w_k \oplus \alpha \cdot v_k \oplus \beta \cdot (\alpha_k \oplus u_k))$ which, by construction, are uniformly distributed as random Beaver triples. By the t-privacy of BGW for randomized functionalities, the joint distribution of $\mathsf{SimBGW}(C, \mathbf{0}^{t'}, \text{out}_C)$ together with all triples $(\alpha_k \oplus u_k, \beta_k \oplus v_k, w_k \oplus \alpha \cdot v_k \oplus \beta \cdot (\alpha_k \oplus u_k))$ is perfectly indistinguishable from the views of the corrupted parties in a real execution together with random Beaver triples (a_k, b_k, c_k). This implies that the joint distribution of $\mathsf{SimBGW}(C, \mathbf{0}^{t'}, \mathsf{out}_C)$ together with the simulated messages $(\alpha_k, \beta_k, \gamma_k)$ are perfectly distributed as in a real execution (with random Beaver triples (a_k, b_k, c_k) equal to $(\alpha_k \oplus u_k, \beta_k \oplus v_k, w_k \oplus \alpha \cdot v_k \oplus \beta \cdot (\alpha_k \oplus u_k)))$. This concludes the analysis for Case 1.

Case 2: $C_S = [t]$. In this case, the adversary corrupted all sources, and only them. Observe that all messages seen by the sources during the entire execution of the protocol are of two types:

- Messages exchanged during an execution of a BGW protocol for a secure multiplication. In all such instances, the inputs of the honest parties are never involved, since the BGW instances evaluate an input-independent randomized functionality.
- The output message, where each source S_i receives $w_i \oplus m_i$ from P_1, where m_i is a mask chosen by S_i and w_i is S_i's output in the protocol.

The simulation is therefore straightforward: during the entire execution of the protocol, Sim will just play honestly on behalf of the (deterministic) P_i's, and using inputs 0. Since the P_i only interact with the sources in input-independent protocols, this simulation is perfectly indistinguishable from the honest execution. Finally, Sim sends $w_i \oplus m_i$ to each source S_i at the end of the protocol on behalf of P_1, where w_i is $\mathcal{F}_i(\mathbf{x}, \mathbf{y})$ and m_i can be deterministically computed from the random tape of S_i (hence both are known to Sim). This concludes the analysis for Case 2.

5   On the Relation Between Randomness Complexity and the Number of Random Sources

In this section, we are interested in the relation between the randomness complexity of a perfect secure protocol for a given functionality, and the number of random sources that this protocol uses. The main question we ask is:

Does keeping the number of random sources to a minimum come at the cost of increasing the number of random bits necessary for the perfect secure computation?

To illustrate the question, consider the t-source protocol we described in Sect. 4. There is a natural variant of the protocol that uses n sources, but $\Omega(t)$ times less randomness: each time the parties jointly generate a Beaver triple using BGW (which are essentially the only steps that use randomness, besides the input sharing and output masking), the parties use their own random tape, instead of letting each of the $n - t$ deterministic parties aggregate (*i.e.*, XOR) t random tapes sent by each of the t sources. Ignoring the input sharing and output masking (for large enough functions, the Beaver triple generation dominates the cost), if the circuit has n_{AND} AND gates, this reduces the randomness complexity from $t \cdot (n - t + 1) \cdot B_{\mathsf{BT}} \cdot n_{\mathsf{AND}}$ bits to $n \cdot B_{\mathsf{BT}} \cdot n_{\mathsf{AND}}$ bits: a $\Omega(t)$ reduction. In the following, we put forth a conjecture stating that this factor t cost is essentially inherent.

5.1   A Preliminary Investigation

The randomness complexity of t-private n-party computation for the XOR functionality was studied in the work of [16]. Interestingly, this work achieves in particular the best known upper bound on the randomness complexity of t-private n-party XOR, and this upper bound is achieved using a minimal number of sources: exactly t. This seemingly contradicts the intuition that t-source private computation should require more randomness than private computation without limitations on the number of sources.

A Conjecture on Sources Versus Randomness. We warn the reader that what follows is a purely intuitive reasoning: our goal here is to develop an intuition about which conjecture can reasonably be expected. Intuitively, all known private computation protocols proceed, one way or another, by operating on random shares – this is how multiple parties can jointly manipulate private values. These shares do typically enjoy linear homomorphism: all linear functions can be computed on the shares, without any communication. This creates a crucial distinction between linear functions and nonlinear functions in secure computation: in the former, following an input-sharing phase, the protocol involves only local computation followed by a reconstruction of the final output. In contrast, for nonlinear function, there will necessarily be interactions where *intermediate values of the computation* are jointly manipulated and used to communicate.

Now, consider any t-source protocol for t-privately computing a nonlinear function. In this protocol, there necessarily exist parties that will be involved (*i.e.*, receive messages) in exchanges involving intermediate values of the computation – we call them *sensitive parties*, in the sense that they see messages where random coins are used to hide sensitive intermediate values. Assume that the adversary simultaneously corrupts some sources *and* one (or more) of the sensitive parties. Then, when a deterministic party sends a sensitive message to one of the sensitive parties, the randomness used to generate this message must be uncorrupted, and can only come from the sources. But the deterministic party cannot possibly know *which* of the sources are uncorrupted: it appears unavoidable, then, that the party must aggregate randomness for *all* t sources to obtain uncorrupted coins in this situation. Therefore, we expect that there should exists *nonlinear functions* where the $n - t$ deterministic parties will necessarily have to receive t coins from the sources for each coin they would have tossed themselves if they had the ability to. The above (informal) discussion clearly breaks down when we consider solely linear functions; for sufficiently complex functions, however, the t factor appears inherent.

Above, we did not precisely define what are *linear* and *nonlinear* functionalities. The informal conditions we stated, however, corresponds to the feature that partitions all Boolean functions into two classes: those that can be n-privately computed, and those that can only be t-privately computed for $t < n/2$ [8]. It also corresponds to the feature that typically distinguishes functionalities that admit n-party t-private protocols for $t \geq n/2$. For example, the subprotocol computing the AND gates in a circuit is the only component in the BGW protocol [4] that requires an honest majority, i.e., $t < n/2$; all other components handle linear parts of the circuit, and can have $t \geq n/2$ (this is discussed in details in [1]). Similarly, the (BGW-based) protocol used in our work to handle the AND gates is also precisely what requires a t-times randomness blowup. Hence, it seems plausible to expect that the functionalities for which the factor-t randomness blowup is inherent are the same functionalities for which private computation requires an honest majority. We state this in Conjecture 13. We view the proof of Conjecture 13 an interesting open question.

Conjecture 13. Let $\mathcal{F}$ be an n-party functionality that cannot be t-privately computed for $t \geq n/2$. For any $t < n/2$, let R_t be the randomness complexity of t-privately computing $\mathcal{F}$ (with any number of sources). Then the t-source randomness complexity of $\mathcal{F}$ is $\Theta(t \cdot R_t)$.

Results for the AND Functionality. Characterizing the minimal amount of randomness required for securely computing a functionality is non-trivial in general, and indeed, no such general characterization is known. We expect that relating the randomness complexity to the number of sources might be of comparable difficulty in general. Most previous works on randomness complexity focused on simple functionalities such as n-party XOR and n-party AND, as these are simple building blocks in other computations, and in order to make the problem tractable. Even for these simple functionalities randomness lower bounds are difficult to obtain, and in almost all known cases (with the exception of the 1-private computation of XOR, which can be done using a single random bit, and which is tight since private computation of XOR without randomness is impossible), the known upper bounds do not match the known lower bounds. Therefore, we focus on the following simpler question:

When t is a constant, is it possible to match the best known upper bound on the randomness complexity of simple functionalities such as n-party AND, using an optimally small number of random sources?

Note that t being a constant captures a setting where matching the best known randomness complexity would not contradict Conjecture 13. In particular, when $t = 1$, we ask: is it possible to 1-privately compute a functionality, using a single source, with a randomness complexity matching the best known multi-source randomness complexity for this functionality? The randomness complexity of the 1-private computation of the n-party AND functionality was investigated in a recent work [17]. Their upper bound uses 8 random bits to 1-privately compute AND (for any number of parties), and uses two random sources; they also give a lower bound stating that more than a single random bit is necessary to 1-privately compute AND. We obtain a non-trivial, and perhaps surprising result: we give a 6-bit 1-private protocol to compute AND (for any number of parties), which uses a single random source, thus improving the result of [17] both in the number of random bits and the number of sources. While this result is interesting in the context of understanding the relation between the number of sources and the randomness complexity, we view it as being mainly a result of independent interest on the randomness complexity of AND.

5.2   Randomness Upper Bound for Secure Computation of AND

For the n-party AND functionality, not much is known in the general case of t-privacy. A longstanding open question exists even in the case of 1-privacy, where there is still a considerable gap between the best known upper and lower bounds on the number of random bits required for the 1-private computation of AND. Here, the only known non-trivial lower bound was recently proven in [17]: More than one random bits are required for the 1-private computation of n-party AND. In the same work, the authors also improved the previously best known upper bound from 73 bits (implicit in [20]) to 8 bits.

The protocol of [17] requires two sources. In contrast, the 73-bit protocol of [20] requires a single source (which is optimal). It is therefore natural to wonder whether two sources are necessary to achieve a very low randomness complexity. Perhaps surprisingly, our result in this section indicates that it might not be the case: We give a 1-private protocol for n-party AND which uses 6 random bits, and a single source. Our result also tightens the gap between the best known lower and upper bounds on the randomness of AND in general, which is of independent interest.

Theorem 14. *For any $n \geq 3$, let $\mathcal{F}_{\mathsf{AND}n}$ be the following n-party functionality: on input of a single bit x_i to each party P_i, $\mathcal{F}_{\mathsf{AND}n}$ outputs $\bigwedge_{i=1}^{n} x_i$ to all parties.*

There exists an n-party perfect 1-private protocol for $\mathcal{F}_{\mathsf{AND}n}$ that uses a single source, and where that source tosses exactly 6 random coins.

A pictorial representation of the full protocol is given on Fig. 3 (initialization phase and main phase) and Fig. 4 (output phase). Before we proceed with the formal proof, we explain the intuition underlying the protocol. At its heart is a "transition protocol" (the main phase) which transitions from parties P_{i-1} and P_i having shares of $\bigwedge_{j=0}^{i-1} x_j$ to P_i and P_{i+1} having shares of $\bigwedge_{j=0}^{i} x_j$, while maintaining a carefully chosen invariant (described in the *main phase* below), and using exactly four random bits. Crucially, these four random bits can be reused for each step, with a cyclic shift of their roles (this will become clearer in the sequel). The output phase requires a final oblivious transfer to reconstruct the output, which requires 3 bits. One of the four bits of the main phase can actually be recycled for this purpose, hence only two "fresh" bits are required, leading to the 6 bits total cost.

The Main Phase. To simplify the exposition, we consider here $n + 1$ (and not n) parties, $(P_0, \cdots, P_n)$ (starting with index 0) each holding an input bit x_i. We will further assign a color code to the four random bits used during the main phase. During the main phase, the parties are placed on a line; for each $i \geq 1$ each party P_{i-1} will send messages solely to P_i and P_{i+1}. Fix three parties (P_{i-1}, P_i, P_{i+1}). The protocol will have in sequence the following invariant for all i between 1 and $n - 2$ (all sums are over $\mathbb{F}_2$):

- P_{i-1} and P_i hold a *mask* α_{i-1}, which is a random bit (from the viewpoint of P_j for $j \geq i$); let us call it the *blue bit*.

Fig. 3. Initialization phase and main phase of the 1-private protocol for the $(n + 1)$-AND functionality. Each party P_i has an input bit x_i. P_n receives the output $\prod_{j=1}^{n} x_j$. The protocol uses six random bits in total $(\alpha_0, R_1, \langle x_0 \rangle_0, \langle \alpha_0 x_0 \rangle_0, m_0, r)$, which are all generated by the single random source P_0. The color of a value indicates which of the six random bits masks it additively. All operations are over $\mathbb{F}_2$. (Color figure online)

- P_i and P_{i+1} hold a *rerandomizer* R_i, which is also a random bit (from the viewpoint of P_j for $j \geq i$), and which we call the *red bit*.
- P_{i-1} and P_i hold random additive shares of $\prod_{j=0}^{i-1} x_j$ (the AND of all inputs up to P_{i-1}). That is, P_{i-1} holds a random bit u_{i-1}, and P_i holds $u'_{i-1} = u_{i-1} + \prod_{j=0}^{i-1} x_j$. We call u_{i-1} and u'_{i-1} the *green bit* of P_{i-1} and P_i respectively.

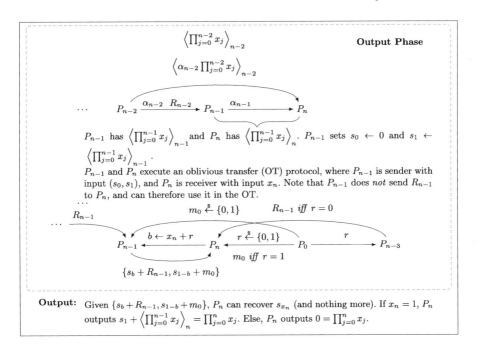

Fig. 4. Output phase of the 1-private protocol for the $(n+1)$-AND functionality. Each party P_i has an input bit x_i. P_n receives the output $\prod_{j=1}^{n} x_j$. The protocol uses six random bits in total $(\alpha_0, R_1, \langle x_0 \rangle_0, \langle \alpha_0 x_0 \rangle_0, m_0, r)$, which are all generated by the single random source P_0. The color of a value indicates which of the six random bits masks it additively. All operations are over $\mathbb{F}_2$. (Color figure online)

- In addition, P_{i-1} and P_i hold random additive shares of $\alpha_{i-1} \cdot \prod_{j=0}^{i-1} x_j$. That is, P_{i-1} holds a random bit v_{i-1}, and P_i holds $v'_{i-1} = v_{i-1} + \alpha_{i-1} \cdot \prod_{j=0}^{i-1} x_j$. We call v_{i-1} and v'_{i-1} the *orange bit* of P_{i-1} and P_i respectively. We use these notations and definitions to clarify that each share is a uniformly random bit from the viewpoint of the party that holds it, but the joint distribution (u_{i-1}, v_{i-1}) has a single bit of entropy.

It remains to explain how the parties communicate in order to transform the above situation to the corresponding situation (invariant) relative to P_i, P_{i+1} and P_{i+2}. Throughout this transition, the role of the blue bit remains identical, while the roles of the last three random bits will undergo a cyclic shift. The transition proceeds as follows:

- P_i defines the *new mask* α_i to be $\alpha_{i-1} + x_i$, and sends it to P_{i+1}. Observe that from the viewpoint of all parties $j \geq i+2$ (which we call "remaining parties" with respect to i), α_i is a uniform random bit (since x_i is masked by the uniform random "blue" bit α_{i-1}, about which they have no information). The bit α_i is defined as the new blue bit.

- P_{i-1} sends its two shares (that is, the green random bit u_{i-1} and the orange random bit v_{i-1}) to P_{i+1}.
- P_i computes $u_i = \alpha_i \cdot u'_{i-1} + v'_{i-1}$ and P_{i+1} computes $u'_i = \alpha_i \cdot u_{i-1} + v_{i-1}$. Observe that

$$u_i + u'_i = \alpha_i(u_{i-1} + u'_{i-1}) + v_{i-1} + v'_{i-1}$$
$$= (\alpha_{i-1} + x_i) \cdot \prod_{j=0}^{i-1} x_j + \alpha_{i-1} \cdot \prod_{j=0}^{i-1} x_j = \prod_{j=0}^{i} x_j,$$

hence u_i and u'_i do indeed form shares of $\prod_{j=0}^{i} x_j$. Furthermore, from the view point of the remaining parties with respect to i, these shares are indeed random, because u_i is additively masked with v'_{i-1} – that is, the *orange bit* of P_i. Therefore, we view the bits u_i and u'_i as the new *orange bit* of P_i and P_{i+1} respectively.

- P_i computes $v_i = \alpha_i \cdot (u'_{i-1} + v'_{i-1}) + R_i$ and P_{i+1} computes $v'_i = \alpha_i \cdot (u_{i-1} + v_{i-1}) + R_i$. Observe that

$$v_i + v'_i = \alpha_i(u_{i-1} + u'_{i-1} + v_{i-1} + v'_{i-1})$$
$$= (\alpha_{i-1} + x_i) \cdot (\prod_{j=0}^{i-1} x_j + \alpha_{i-1} \cdot \prod_{j=0}^{i-1} x_j)$$
$$= (\alpha_{i-1} + x_i) \cdot \prod_{j=0}^{i} x_j = \alpha_i \cdot \prod_{j=0}^{i} x_j,$$

hence v_i and v'_i do indeed form shares of $\alpha_i \cdot \prod_{j=0}^{i} x_j$. Furthermore, from the view point of the remaining parties with respect to i, these shares are indeed random, because v_i is additively masked with R_i – that is, the *red bit* of P_i (without R_{i-1}, which both parties add to their shares, the shares would be biased towards 0; the purpose of the rerandomizer R_i is precisely to rerandomize these shares). Therefore, we view v_i and v'_i as the new *red bit* of P_i and P_{i+1} respectively.

- It remains to set a new rerandomizer R_{i+1} bit to be used by P_{i+1} and P_{i+2}. Above, the blue, orange, and red bits have already been "used", hence we will recycle the green bit. Recall that P_{i+1} received P_{i-1}'s green random bit u_{i-1}, which is a uniformly random bit from the viewpoint of P_{i+1} and P_{i+2}. Therefore, P_{i+1} sets $R_{i+1} \leftarrow u_{i-1}$ and sends R_{i+1} to P_{i+2}.

The transition, and the invariant it maintains, are represented in Fig. 5.

Initialization Phase. The initialization phase sets up the invariant, for $i = 1$, in a relatively straightforward way. The source, P_0, samples the four random bits (the blue, green, orange, and red bits). It sets the first mask α_0 to be the blue bit, the first rerandomizer R_1 to be the red bit, and uses the green and orange bits to share its input x_0 as well as the value $\alpha_0 x_0$; that is, it sets the green bit

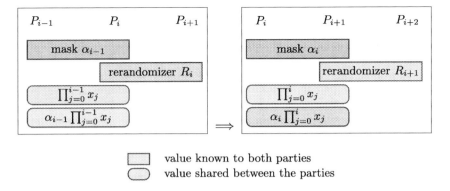

value known to both parties
value shared between the parties

Fig. 5. Pictural representation of the transition during the main phase. The color of a rectangle indicates which random bit has been used to randomize the value. Straight corners indicate values known to both parties, rounded corners indicate values shared between the parties. The transition shows the colors of the bottom three values being cycled upward, while the top color remains the same. (Color figure online)

to be $\langle x_0 \rangle_0$ and the red bit to be $\langle \alpha_0 x_0 \rangle_0$, and defines $\langle x_0 \rangle_1 \leftarrow x_0 + \langle x_0 \rangle_0$ and $\langle \alpha_0 x_0 \rangle_1 \leftarrow \alpha_0 x_0 + \langle \alpha_0 x_0 \rangle_0$. It sends $(\langle x_0 \rangle_1, \langle \alpha_0 x_0 \rangle_1)$ to P_1, together with α_0 and R_1. P_1 sends R_1 to P_2, and the first transition phase can begin (where P_0 will send the remaining shares $(\langle x_0 \rangle_0, \langle \alpha_0 x_0 \rangle_0)$ to P_2; observe that those are exactly the green and the orange random bits).

Output Phase. It remains to describe how the parties obtain the final output. Towards the end of the protocol, we slightly change the last (the $n - 1$'th) transition. Let us assume without loss of generality that the rerandomization bit R_{n-1} is the green bit; P_{n-1} does *not* send this rerandomization bit R_{n-1} (which P_{n-1} received from P_{n-3}) to P_n. Otherwise the $n - 1$'th transition remains the same and after its execution P_{n-1} and P_n hold random shares of $\prod_{j=0}^{n-1} x_j$.

The players P_{n-1} and P_n will then execute an information theoretic oblivious transfer protocol with the help of P_0 and P_{n-3}, where P_{n-1} will be the sender with inputs $s_0 = 0$ and its share of $\prod_{j=0}^{n-1} x_j$ (denoted s_1), and P_n will be the receiver, with input x_n. This way, P_n receives 0 if $x_n = 0$ and $\prod_{j=0}^{n-1} x_j$ otherwise; that is, P_n learns exactly $\prod_{j=0}^{n} x_j$.

The oblivious transfer proceeds as follows: the source P_0 generates two additional random bits (r, m_0). The bit r will be used to mask the *selection bit* x_n, and the two bits (m_0, R_{n-1}) will be used to mask the sender inputs (this is where we recycle R_{n-1}). P_0 sends $(r, r \cdot m_0)$ to P_n, and m_0 to P_{n-1}. Additionally, it sends r to P_{n-3}, who sends $R_{n-1} \cdot (1+r)$ to P_n. This way, P_n knows r and either R_{n-1} (if $r = 0$) or m_0 (if $r = 1$); this is exactly a random oblivious transfer correlation.

The actual oblivious transfer follows the standard information-theoretic oblivious transfer using a random oblivious transfer: P_n sends $b = x_n + r$ (its masked selection bit), and P_{n-1} replies with $(s_b + R_{n-1}, s_{1-b} + m_0)$. If $r = 0$, this pair is $(s_{x_n} + R_{n-1}, s_{1+x_n} + m_0)$ and P_n knows the mask R_{n-1}; otherwise, if $r = 1$, this pair is $(s_{1+x_n} + R_{n-1}, s_{x_n} + m_0)$ and P_n knows the mask m_0. Either way, P_n can extract and output $s_{x_n} = \prod_{j=0}^{n} x_j$. In total, two additional random bits were generated by P_0, bringing the total randomness complexity to six bits.

The Three-Party Case. Reading the above, it seems that the protocol requires at least four parties, since P_{n-3} to P_n are involved. However, P_{n-3} is involved solely because P_n should receive $R_{n-1} \cdot (1 + r)$, but P_0 might not know the value R_{n-1}. In the three party case, where $P_0 = P_{n-2}$, this is actually not an issue, because $R_1 = R_{n-1}$ is the first rerandomizer, generated by P_0 during the initialization. Therefore, in the three party case, we only need to slightly change the output phase by letting P_0 send $R_{n-1} \cdot (1 + r)$ directly to P_n, without involving P_{n-3} (who does not exist).

5.3 Security Analysis

Consider a static adversary corrupting a party P_i. We exhibit a simulator Sim which emulates the view of this corrupted party given i, x_i, and the output of the function, $\prod_{j=0}^{n} x_j$. First, if $\prod_{j=0}^{n} x_j = 1$, then the simulation is trivial, since Sim knows all inputs: Sim can simply honestly emulate the role of all honest parties. Therefore, we assume without loss of generality that $\prod_{j=0}^{n} x_j = 0$. The proof is somewhat different depending on which is the corrupted player, whether it is a "middle" player, one of the "end" players, or one of the two "starting" players.

Case 1: $i \notin \{0, 1, n-1, n\}$. This case corresponds to parties P_i which participate only in the main phase, except for $n - 3$, which receives an additional bit from P_0 in the output phase. We first prove the simulation of the views at the end of the main phase.

In the real protocol, each P_i receives exactly four bits by the end of the main phase:

- From player P_{i-1}: a mask α_{i-1} and a rerandomizer R_{i-1}; and
- From player P_{i-2}: P_{i-2}'s random share of $\prod_{j=0}^{i-2} x_j$ and of $\alpha_{i-2} \cdot \prod_{j=0}^{i-2} x_j$.

The simulation is straightforward: Sim samples and sends to P_i two random bits on behalf of P_{i-1} and two other random bits on behalf of P_{i-2}. It remains to show that this simulation is perfectly indistinguishable from a real protocol execution. For α_{i-1}, observe that by construction, $\alpha_{i-1} = \alpha_0 + \sum_{j=1}^{i-1} x_j$, where α_0 is a uniform random bit sampled by (the honest party) P_0; hence, the simulated α_{i-1} is distributed exactly as in the real protocol.

For the three remaining bits, the proof proceeds by induction on i, $i = 2$ being the base case. For $i = 2$, P_2 receives in the real protocol the red random bit from P_1 and the green and the orange random bits from P_0; i.e., in the real protocol, P_2 receives three independent random bits, as in the simulation.

Assume now that it has already been established that the simulation is correct for all players P_2 to P_{i-1}. Let (u, u') denote the two values sent by P_{i-3} to P_{i-1}

in the protocol, and let (v, v') be the two corresponding shares held by P_{i-2}. Let α_{i-3} be the mask received by P_{i-2}, and let (α_{i-2}, R_{i-2}) be the two bits sent by P_{i-2} to P_{i-1}. By the induction hypothesis, it holds that both the joint distribution of $(\alpha_{i-3}, u, v', R_{i-2})$ and the joint distribution of $(\alpha_{i-3}, v, v', R_{i-2})$ are each exactly the uniform distribution over $\{0, 1\}^4$. Then, observe that P_i receives in the real protocol the following:

- From P_{i-2}: $\alpha_{i-3}v + v'$ and $\alpha_{i-3}(v + v') + R_{i-2}$; and
- From P_{i-1}: α_{i-1} and $R_{i-1} = u$.

By the induction hypothesis, the joint distribution of $(\alpha_{i-3}v + v', \alpha_{i-3}(v+v') + R_{i-2}, u, \alpha_{i-1})$ is the uniform distribution over $\{0, 1\}^3$, which completes the induction step.

As to player number $n - 3$, in addition to the messages received during the main phase it receives a single additional independent (from all other messages) random bit from P_0. The simulation is trivial by sending on behalf of P_0 a fresh random bit.

Case 2: $i \in \{n - 1, n\}$. We now look at the parties that are involved in the output phase. The view of P_{n-1} in the protocol consists of (m_0, b), where m_0 is an independent random bit, and $b = x_n + r$, where r is an independent random bit. This is again perfectly simulated by sending a random bit m_0 on behalf of P_0 and a random bit b on behalf of P_n. Finally, the view of P_n is the following:

- P_n knows α_{n-1} and the two shares (u, u') of P_{n-2} (u, u' are P_{n-2}'s shares of $\prod_{i=0}^{n-2} x_i$ and $\alpha_{n-2} \cdot \prod_{i=0}^{n-2} x_i$ with P_{n-1});
- P_n receives $(r, r \cdot m_0, R_{n-1} \cdot (1 + r))$ from P_0 and P_{n-3};
- P_0 receives the two OT messages of P_{n-1}.

The two OT messages of P_{n-1} are equal to $(s_b + R_{n-1}, s_{1-b} + m_0)$, where $s_0 = 0$, and s_1 is P_{n-1}'s share of $\prod_{i=0}^{n-1} x_i$, the other share being, by construction, $\alpha_{n-1} \cdot u + u'$. We can open up the terms using $b = r + x_n$ and $s_1 = \prod_{i=0}^{n-1} x_i + \alpha_{n-1} \cdot u + u'$. Then, two cases can happen: (1) $r = 0$ or (2) $r = 1$.

Suppose that $r = 0$; then P_n got $(0, 0, R_{n-1})$ from P_0 and P_{n-3}. By construction, we have

$$s_b + R_{n-1} = bs_1 + R_{n-1} = x_n \cdot \left(\prod_{i=0}^{n-1} x_i + \alpha_{n-1}u + u' \right) + R_{n-1} = x_n \cdot (\alpha_{n-1}u + u') + R_{n-1},$$

where we use that $\prod_{i=0}^{n} x_i = 0$ by assumption. On the other hand, if $r = 1$, then P_n got $(1, m_0, 0)$ from P_0 and P_{n-3}, and by construction, we have

$$s_{1-b} + m_0 = (1 + b)s_1 + m_0 = x_n \cdot \left(\prod_{i=0}^{n-1} x_i + \alpha_{n-1}u + u' \right) + m_0 = x_n \cdot (\alpha_{n-1}u + u') + m_0,$$

using again the assumption. Now, to simulate, Sim will sample five random bits $(u, u', r, m_0, R_{n-1}) \xleftarrow{\$} \{0, 1\}^5$ and send (u, u') on behalf of P_2 and $(r, r \cdot m_0, R_{n-1} \cdot (1 + r))$ on behalf of P_0 and P_{n-3}. It remains to simulate the two OT messages.

If $r = 0$, then Sim will construct the $s_b + R_{n-1}$ term as $x_n \cdot (\alpha_{n-1}u + u') + R_{n-1}$, which is distributed exactly as in the protocol (recall that Sim knows the input x_n of the corrupted party). The remaining term, $s_{1-b} + m_0$, is simulated by sampling a uniformly random independent bit, which is a perfect simulation since P_n never received any information about m_0 (since it received $(0, 0, R_{n-1})$). If $r = 1$, Sim will construct the $s_b + m_0$ term as $x_n \cdot (\alpha_{n-1}u + u') + m_0$, which is distributed exactly as in the protocol, and simulate the $s_{1-b} + R_{n-1}$ term by a uniform random bit, which is a perfect simulation since P_{n-1} never received any information about the random masking bit R_{n-1}.

Case 3: $i \in \{0, 1\}$. It remains to deal with the first two parties, which is straightforward: in the real protocol P_1 receives four bits from P_0, two of which are truly random, and two of which are $(x_0, \alpha_0 x_0)$ masked by two more independent random bits. Sim can perfectly simulate this message by sending four random bits on behalf of P_0. P_0 never receives any message throughout the protocol (except the value of the function), hence privacy against P_0 holds trivially. This concludes the proof.

References

1. Asharov, G., Lindell, Y.: A full proof of the BGW protocol for perfectly secure multiparty computation. J. Cryptol. **30**(1), 58–151 (2017)
2. Beaver, D.: Efficient multiparty protocols using circuit randomization. In: Feigenbaum, J. (ed.) CRYPTO 1991. LNCS, vol. 576, pp. 420–432. Springer, Heidelberg (1992). https://doi.org/10.1007/3-540-46766-1_34
3. Beaver, D.: Precomputing oblivious transfer. In: Coppersmith, D. (ed.) CRYPTO 1995. LNCS, vol. 963, pp. 97–109. Springer, Heidelberg (1995). https://doi.org/10.1007/3-540-44750-4_8
4. Ben-Or, M., Goldwasser, S., Wigderson, A.: Completeness theorems for non-cryptographic fault-tolerant distributed computation (extended abstract). In: 20th ACM STOC, pp. 1–10. ACM Press (1988)
5. Blundo, C., De Santis, A., Persiano, G., Vaccaro, U.: Randomness complexity of private computation. Comput. Complex. **8**(2), 145–168 (1999)
6. Chaum, D.: The spymasters double-agent problem: multiparty computations secure unconditionally from minorities and cryptographically from majorities. In: Brassard, G. (ed.) CRYPTO 1989. LNCS, vol. 435, pp. 591–602. Springer, New York (1990). https://doi.org/10.1007/0-387-34805-0_52
7. Chaum, D., Crépeau, C., Damgård, I.: Multiparty unconditionally secure protocols (extended abstract). In: 20th ACM STOC, pp. 11–19. ACM Press (1988)
8. Chor, B., Kushilevitz, E.: A zero-one law for Boolean privacy. SIAM J. Discret. Math. **4**(1), 36–47 (1991)
9. Data, D., Prabhakaran, V.M., Prabhakaran, M.M.: Communication and randomness lower bounds for secure computation. IEEE Trans. Inf. Theory **62**(7), 3901–3929 (2016)
10. Gál, A., Rosén, A.: Lower bounds on the amount of randomness in private computation. In: 35th ACM STOC, pp. 659–666. ACM Press (2003)
11. Goldreich, O.: Foundations of Cryptography: Volume 2, Basic Applications. Cambridge University Press, Cambridge (2009)

12. Goldreich, O., Micali, S., Wigderson, A.: How to play any mental game or A completeness theorem for protocols with honest majority. In: Aho, A. (ed.) 19th ACM STOC, pp. 218–229. ACM Press (1987)

13. Goldreich, O., Micali, S., Wigderson, A.: How to prove all NP statements in zero-knowledge and a methodology of cryptographic protocol design (extended abstract). In: Odlyzko, A.M. (ed.) CRYPTO 1986. LNCS, vol. 263, pp. 171–185. Springer, Heidelberg (1987). https://doi.org/10.1007/3-540-47721-7_11

14. Jakoby, A., Liśkiewicz, M., Reischuk, R.: Private computations in networks: topology versus randomness. In: Alt, H., Habib, M. (eds.) STACS 2003. LNCS, vol. 2607, pp. 121–132. Springer, Heidelberg (2003). https://doi.org/10.1007/3-540-36494-3_12

15. Kushilevitz, E., Lindell, Y., Rabin, T.: Information-theoretically secure protocols and security under composition. In: Kleinberg, J.M. (ed.) 38th ACM STOC, pp. 109–118. ACM Press (2006)

16. Kushilevitz, E., Mansour, Y.: Randomness in private computations. In: Burns, J.E., Moses, Y. (eds.) 15th ACM PODC, pp. 181–190. ACM (1996)

17. Kushilevitz, E., Ostrovsky, R., Prouff, E., Rosén, A., Thillard, A., Vergnaud, D.: Lower and upper bounds on the randomness complexity of private computations of AND. In: Hofheinz, D., Rosen, A. (eds.) TCC 2019. LNCS, vol. 11892, pp. 386–406. Springer, Cham (2019). https://doi.org/10.1007/978-3-030-36033-7_15

18. Kushilevitz, E., Ostrovsky, R., Prouff, E., Rosén, A., Thillard, A., Vergnaud, D.: Lower and upper bounds on the randomness complexity of private computations of AND. SIAM J. Discret. Math. **35**(1), 465–484 (2021)

19. Kushilevitz, E., Ostrovsky, R., Rosén, A.: Amortizing randomness in private multi-party computations. In: Coan, B.A., Afek, Y. (eds.) 17th ACM PODC, pp. 81–90. ACM (1998)

20. Kushilevitz, E., Ostrovsky, R., Rosén, A.: Characterizing linear size circuits in terms of privacy. J. Comput. Syst. Sci. **58**(1), 129–136 (1999)

21. Kushilevitz, E., Rosén, A.: A randomness-rounds tradeoff in private computation. In: Desmedt, Y.G. (ed.) CRYPTO 1994. LNCS, vol. 839, pp. 397–410. Springer, Heidelberg (1994). https://doi.org/10.1007/3-540-48658-5_36

22. Lenstra, A.K., Hughes, J.P., Augier, M., Bos, J.W., Kleinjung, T., Wachter, C.: Ron was wrong, whit is right. IACR Cryptology ePrint Archive **2012**, 64 (2012)

23. Naor, J., Naor, M.: Small-bias probability spaces: efficient constructions and applications. SIAM J. Comput. **22**(4), 838–856 (1993)

24. Nemec, M., Sýs, M., Svenda, P., Klinec, D., Matyas, V.: The return of coppersmith's attack: practical factorization of widely used RSA moduli. In: Proceedings of the 2017 ACM SIGSAC Conference on Computer and Communications Security, CCS 2017, pp. 1631–1648 (2017)

25. Nisan, N., Ta-Shma, A.: Extracting randomness: a survey and new constructions. J. Comput. Syst. Sci. **58**(1), 148–173 (1999)

26. Rosén, A., Urrutia, F.: A new approach to multi-party peer-to-peer communication complexity. In: Blum, A. (ed.) ITCS 2019, vol. 124, pp. 64:1–64:19. LIPIcs (2019)

27. Yao, A.C.C.: How to generate and exchange secrets (extended abstract). In: 27th FOCS, pp. 162–167. IEEE Computer Society Press (1986)

Non-interactive Secure Computation of Inner-Product from LPN and LWE

Geoffroy Couteau[1]([✉]) and Maryam Zarezadeh[2]

[1] CNRS, IRIF, Université Paris Cité, Paris, France
couteau@irif.fr
[2] Barkhausen Institut, Dresden, Germany
maryam.zarezadeh@barkhauseninstitut.org

Abstract. We put forth a new cryptographic primitive for securely computing inner-products in a scalable, non-interactive fashion: any party can broadcast a public (computationally hiding) encoding of its input, and store a secret state. Given their secret state and the other party's public encoding, any pair of parties can *non-interactively* compute additive shares of the inner-product between the encoded vectors.

We give constructions of this primitive from a common template, which can be instantiated under either the LPN (with non-negligible correctness error) or the LWE (with negligible correctness error) assumptions. Our construction uses a novel twist on the standard non-interactive key exchange based on the Alekhnovich cryptosystem, which upgrades it to a non-interactive inner product protocol almost for free. In addition to being non-interactive, our constructions have linear communication (with constants smaller than all known alternatives) and small computation: using LPN or LWE with quasi-cyclic codes, we estimate that encoding a length-2^{20} vector over a 32-bit field takes less that 2 s on a standard laptop; decoding amounts to a single cheap inner-product.

We show how to remove the non-negligible error in our LPN instantiation using a one-time, logarithmic-communication preprocessing. Eventually, we show to upgrade its security to the malicious model using new sublinear-communication zero-knowledge proofs for low-noise LPN samples, which might be of independent interest.

1 Introduction

In this work, we put forth a new approach for non-interactive secure computation of inner products, one of the most basic and fundamental functionalities in secure computation. Our approach can be instantiated under either the learning parity with noise (LPN) or the learning with error (LWE) assumptions, two of the most important post-quantum assumptions. It builds upon a simple but powerful observation: a well-chosen tweak of the Alekhnovich key exchange [4] turns it into a non-interactive secure protocol for approximately computing inner products. Borrowing tools from the recent line of work on pseudorandom correlation generators [16–18], we show how to turn this into full fledged secure protocols for inner product, using a small preprocessing phase with communication

© International Association for Cryptologic Research 2022
S. Agrawal and D. Lin (Eds.): ASIACRYPT 2022, LNCS 13791, pp. 474–503, 2022.
https://doi.org/10.1007/978-3-031-22963-3_16

much smaller than the length of the vectors, both in the semi-honest and in the malicious setting.

1.1 Secure Inner-Product Made as Easy as Non-interactive Key Exchange

To better capture the attractive efficiency features of our protocols, we introduce the notion of *non-interactive inner product* (NIIP) protocols. At a high level, a NIIP specifies a pair of algorithm, Encode and Decode, where:

- Encode takes an input vector $\mathbf{x} \in \mathbb{F}^n$ over some field $\mathbb{F}$, and produces a pair $(\mathsf{pk_x}, \mathsf{sk_x})$. $\mathsf{pk_x}$ is the *public encoding*, and $\mathsf{sk_x}$ is the secret state. All parties can publicly reveal the encodings $\mathsf{pk_x}$, since they computationally hide their vectors $\mathbf{x}$.
- Decode takes as input a public encoding $\mathsf{pk_x}$, and a secret state $\mathsf{sk_y}$, and outputs a value z, such that the following holds: $z = \mathsf{Decode}(\mathsf{pk_x}, \mathsf{sk_y})$ and $z' = \mathsf{Decode}(\mathsf{pk_y}, \mathsf{sk_x})$ form *additive shares* of the inner product $\mathbf{x}^\mathsf{T} \cdot \mathbf{y} = z + z'$ over $\mathbb{F}$.

Therefore, an NIIP provides a very appealing way to compute inner products with a minimalistic interaction pattern: multiple parties can compute and publish encodings of their input ahead of time, locally keeping the secret state. Then, whenever two parties want to securely compute the inner product between their inputs, they can locally and non-interactively decode the other party's public encoding with their own secret state, and obtain additive shares of the output. One can compare this interaction pattern to the interaction pattern of non-interactive key exchange: after broadcasting their public keys, any two individuals from a network can locally compute a shared secret key. We achieve exactly the same interaction pattern, but for the significantly more "advanced" functionality of securely computing (shares of) inner products. We believe that this minimalistic interaction pattern makes our construction very appealing in many natural scenarios, and allow them to scale more efficiently to large networks of users (which is typically a bottleneck for secure computation).

LPN-Based Instantiation. Our primary instantiation of this approach relies on the learning parity with noise assumption. There, we only achieve correctness up to a vanishing (but non-negligible) error term ε, which is of the order of λ^2/n, where λ is a security parameter, and n is the vector dimension. Therefore, our protocol provides non-trivial correctness only for values of $n > \lambda^2$. We note that this is likely to be optimal: an NIIP with a much smaller correctness error would imply an LPN-based key exchange under LPN with noise rate higher than $\sqrt{n}$, which is a famous and long-standing open problem. Furthermore, we improve the protocol in two ways:

- Using an input-independent preprocessing phase with sublinear communication $O(\log n)$ (where the $O(\cdot)$ hides $\mathsf{poly}(\lambda)$ factors), the protocol can be made perfectly correct. This construction builds upon the recently introduced notion of pseudorandom correlation generators.

– By developing new types of zero-knowledge proofs with sublinear communication tailored to our protocol, we show how the security of our protocol can be enhanced from semi-honest to malicious, at a small cost. Our new zero-knowledge proofs, which demonstrate knowledge of a sparse vector in the kernel of a matrix with communication sublinear in the dimension (but linear in the sparsity), are of independent interest.

LWE-Based Instantiation. Our second instantiation is based on the learning with error assumption. There, we focus on the semi-honest setting, and directly achieve a full-fledged (negligible error) NIIP, without any preprocessing. This makes our protocol highly versatile in environments where it is desirable to minimize interactions. Furthermore, our LWE-based instantiation can be shown to provide information-theoretic security for one of the two parties.

1.2   Efficiency, Discussions and an Open Question

In addition to their optimal interaction pattern, our protocols have linear communication $O(n)$, with concrete small constants. Specifically, the constant is always smaller than 6, and can be asymptotically reduced to $2 + \epsilon$ for arbitrarily small ϵ when n grows (approaching the – optimal – cost of just exchanging the two vectors in the clear). In terms of computation, using relatively standard variants of LPN (or LWE) with a quasi-cyclic matrix, our protocols have $O(n \cdot \log n)$ computational complexity, where the cost is dominated by that of doing a matrix-vector multiplication with a quasi-cyclic matrix (this boils down to computing FFT's in dimension n). For $n \approx 10^7$, using the library of [24], the full matrix multiplication can be executed in less than 2 seconds on a personal laptop, according to the implementation of [17].

The LPN assumption with quasi-cyclic codes is relatively well studied [1,3, 17], and has been used in recent submissions to the post-quantum NIST competition [3,6,45]. There exist other candidate codes which lead to a much greater efficiency and are believed to provide secure variants of LPN; one standard such example is Alekhnovich assumption [4], which states that LPN remains hard when instantiated with a sparse code. However, our constructions require LPN to be simultaneously hard with respect to the code *and its dual code*. Intriguingly, to our knowledge, no code with fast encoding and fast dual encoding is known to provide (plausibly) secure LPN variants with respect to the code and its dual (for example, LPN with respect to the dual of sparse codes, which are LDPC codes, is easy due to the existence of efficient algorithms for LDPC codes). Hence, this raises an intriguing open question: *Are there linear-time encodable codes whose dual is also linear time encodable, such that both the code and its dual lead to hard LPN variants?* As we will discuss, this question is strongly related to the question of finding linear-time encodable codes where both the code and its dual are good codes (i.e., have linear minimum distance), a problem which seems to be still open in coding theory (but does not seem to have been studied much). A positive answer would provide a linear-time variant of the Alekhnovich cryptosystem, which would lead to significant improvements in LPN-based encryption. Furthermore, it would make our protocol strictly linear time as well. We believe that this question is therefore an important open question, whose study could open the road to strong efficiency improvements in LPN-based public-key cryptography.

1.3   Comparison to the State of the Art

Many methods from the literature can be used to securely compute inner products. We go through the main options here, and compare them to our result.

From OT/OLE. A first option is to use generic oblivious-transfer-based secure computation for inner product. This works especially well over $\mathbb{F}_2$, since the inner product between n bit vectors can be reduced to n oblivious transfers (OT). Using recent advances in silent OT extension [16–18], this can be done with asymptotic communication approaching three bits per oblivious transfer.

However, things become significantly more complicated over larger fields. To handle multiplications over a larger field $\mathbb{F}$, the standard OT-based method [36] induces a $\log |\mathbb{F}|$ overhead in the total number of OTs, which can quickly get prohibitive. A more efficient alternative is to build on recent advances in batch oblivious linear evaluation (OLE) over general fields, since an inner-product between length-n vectors over $\mathbb{F}$ can be reduced to a batch of n OLEs over $\mathbb{F}$. To our knowledge, the most efficient protocols for generating many OLEs are the work of [20], which constructs a "silent OLE extension" protocol assuming the hardness of *ring*-LPN over a fully-splitting ring, and the result of [10]. Being silent, the protocol of [20] achieves an asymptotically optimal communication of $2n + o(n)$ elements of $\mathbb{F}$, for a computational cost of $\tilde{O}(n)$ operations.

Our protocol achieves essentially the same asymptotic communication, and our computational complexity is also essentially on par with theirs. However, we improve on three core aspects:

- *Communication Pattern.* The protocol of [20] requires running a generic, interactive secure computation protocol to generate the seeds for the silent OLE extension, before running a local expansion and "derandomizing" the pseudorandom OLEs with additional interaction. In contrast, we achieve a minimal interaction pattern, where a single encoding of the input is broadcast simultaneously by all parties.
- *Underlying Assumption.* The protocol of [20] inherently requires a new "ring-LPN with fully splitting ring" assumption. In fact, their starting point is a construction based on a standard variant of LPN (LPN with quasi-cyclic codes, which we use here), which has *superquadratic* computational complexity $\tilde{O}(n^2)$. Then, their new assumption is introduced as a way to overcome this quadratic overhead. In contrast, we directly achieve quasilinear overhead, under the standard LPN assumption over quasi-cyclic codes.
- *Concrete Efficiency.* Measuring the concrete efficiency of [20] is relatively complex, but working out the parameters in the paper, the communication complexity of setting up the correlation is around $40 \cdot n$ for $n = 2^{20}$. For lower

values of n, it is much higher, and it drops quickly for higher values of n (e.g. around $3 \cdot n$ for $n = 2^{24}$). In contrast, our setup costs are minimal (e.g. around $0.7 \cdot n$ for $n = 2^{20}$) In practice, this means that this approach will start to outperform our protocol communication-wise only for $n > 2^{24}$.

As for the protocol of [10], their communication overhead is ∼33% larger than ours for short-ish vectors (from $6n$ to $8n$ elements of $\mathbb{F}$), and up to 4 times larger asymptotically (from $(2 + \varepsilon)n$ to $8n$ elements of $\mathbb{F}$). In addition, their construction requires a dedicated setup phase (while we only need a common random string). Their dedicated setup can be replaced with a PKI setup, at the cost of sacrificing further some efficiency. Other low-communication OLE protocols have been described in [47], but their concrete computational efficiency is significantly lower than that of [20].

From Homomorphic Encryption. Another standard solution is to rely on linearly homomorphic encryption, such as Paillier encryption [49]. In these solutions, one party encrypts its vector $\mathbf{x}$ and sends it to the other party, who homomorphically computes and sends back a rerandomized encryption of $\mathbf{x}^\mathsf{T} \cdot \mathbf{y}$, which the first party decrypts. For extremely large fields ($\log |\mathbb{F}| \gg 2048$), one can achieve the smallest communication across all known alternatives, with a communication of only $(n + o(n)) \log |\mathbb{F}|$ bits (i.e., essentially the cost of sending one of the two vectors in the clear), using a rate-1 homomorphic encryption scheme such as Damgård-Jurik [29]. However, this solution is not competitive with the previous approaches for any reasonable field sizes, communication-wise and computation-wise.

Using Ring-LWE-based linearly homomorphic encryption, a recent unpublished work [22] devised a carefully optimized semi-honest OLE protocol. By tailoring their protocol to inner products, we estimate that their protocol can achieve a communication comparable to our semi-honest protocol. This comes at the cost of using PKI setup and not having a non-interactive communication pattern as we do (furthermore, our protocol can be based on LWE rather than Ring-LWE).

1.4   Applications

Inner products are a fundamental operation in many standard privacy-preserving applications. In many of these applications, the non-interactive structure of our new protocol enables a very appealing realization of these applications in a multi-party setting. This includes for example biometric authentication [48] or pattern matching [38] (computing the Hamming distance between two strings can be non-interactively reduced to computing an inner product, since the Hamming distance between $\mathbf{x}$ and $\mathbf{y}$ is $\mathsf{HW}(\mathbf{x}) + \mathsf{HW}(\mathbf{y}) - 2 \cdot \mathbf{x}^\mathsf{T} \cdot \mathbf{y}$, where HW denotes the Hamming weight). With our non-interactive protocol, each user could publish a compact encoding associated to its fingerprint, and each authority could also have a list of public encodings of authorized fingerprints. Then, a user can authenticate himself with an authority with almost zero communication: the authority and the user locally compute shares of the Hamming distance, and the user reveal his share to the authority (a single field element). If the shares reconstruct to a value below the threshold, the authentication is successful.

Other applications can include distributed data mining and machine learning applications such as finding k-nearest neighbors (KNN) [55], rule mining [32], decision trees [52], support vector machine (SVM) classification [57], or privacy preserving neural network learning [8, 25].

Inner products are also used in secure similarity measure protocols such as secure multi-keyword searchable schemes [42], secure keyword similarity [43], similar document detection for plagiarism prevention, copyright protection and duplicate submission detection (where similar documents between two entities should be detected while keeping documents confidential [40, 46]), or secure profile proximity matching in social networks (e.g. in some applications, a user profile is defined as a vector of integers where attributes correspond to an interest; social proximity is defined as dot product of two user's vectors [26]. Similar methods are used in secure protocols for friend discovery in mobile social networks [33]). In many of these applications, the non-interactive nature of our protocols can allow to design scalable, multi-user variants.

2   Preliminaries

Throughout the paper, we denote the security parameter by λ. We use uppercase letters like M to denote matrices, bold lower-case letters like $\mathbf{v}$ to denote row vectors, and for column vectors we use the transpose $\mathbf{v}^{\mathsf{T}}$. We write $\mathbf{u}^{\mathsf{T}}||\mathbf{v}^{\mathsf{T}}$ two denote the horizontal concatenations of (horizontal) vectors, and $\mathbf{u}//\mathbf{v}$ to denote vertical concatenation. Eventually, we write $x \xleftarrow{\$} X$ (resp. $x \xleftarrow{\$} \mathcal{D}$) to denote that x is uniformly sampled from the set X (resp. randomly sampled according to distribution $\mathcal{D}$). For a finite set S, we denote the uniform distribution on S by $\mathbb{U}(S)$. We denote by Ber_τ the Bernoulli distribution with parameter τ, i.e., $e \sim \mathsf{Ber}_\tau$ means that the random variable e evaluates to 1 with probability τ and to 0 with probability $1 - \tau$. More generally, we write $\mathsf{Ber}_\tau(\mathbb{F})$ to denote the distribution that outputs a uniformly random element of $\mathbb{F}$ with probability τ, and 0 otherwise (note that with this definition, $\mathsf{Ber}_\tau(\mathbb{F}_2) = \mathsf{Ber}_{(1+\tau)/2}$; we ignore this slight discrepancy). We write $\mathcal{D}_0 \overset{c}{\approx} \mathcal{D}_1$ to denote that two (families of) distributions $\mathcal{D}_0$ and $\mathcal{D}_1$ are computationally indistinguishable. Eventually, we recall a standard lemma known in the LPN literature as the piling-up lemma:

Lemma 1 (Piling-up Lemma). *For any $0 < \tau < 1/2$ and random variables $(X_1, \cdots, X_n)$ i.i.d. to Ber_τ, it holds that $\Pr\left[\bigoplus_{i=1}^n X_i = 0\right] = (1 + (1 - 2\tau)^n)/2$.*

2.1   Learning Parity with Noise

The learning parity with noise (LPN) assumption with dimension k, m noisy samples, and noise rate τ states that it is infeasible to distinguish $(A, A \cdot \mathbf{s} + \mathbf{e})$ from random, where A is a random matrix in $\mathbb{F}_2^{m \times k}$, $\mathbf{s}$ is a random length-k

vector, and $\mathbf{e}$ is a length-m vector whose entries are sampled from Ber_τ. More generally, the LPN assumption can be formulated with respect to a family of linear codes over an arbitrary field $\mathbb{F}$, in which case it states that it is hard to distinguish a noisy codeword $A \cdot \mathbf{s} + \mathbf{e}$ from random (where A is a generator matrix for a random code from the family). Formally, given a dimension k, number of samples m, and field $\mathbb{F}$, let $\mathsf{Code}(m, k, \mathbb{F})$ be a probabilistic code generation algorithm that outputs a matrix $A \in \mathbb{F}^{m \times k}$ (A is viewed as the generator matrix of a linear code). Furthermore, we let $\mathsf{Code}^\perp(m, m - k, \mathbb{F})$ be a probabilistic code generation algorithm for the dual of Code, which outputs random *parity-check matrices* $B \in \mathbb{F}^{m \times m - k}$ for a random code $A \in \mathsf{Code}(m, k, \mathbb{F})$ (i.e., a full-rank matrix B such that $B^{\mathsf{T}} \cdot A = 0$; B is a generator for the dual of the code generated by A). We define the LPN assumption over $\mathbb{F}$ with respect to a code Code below.

Definition 2 (Learning Parity with Noise). *Fix a field* $\mathbb{F} = \mathbb{F}(\lambda)$, *dimension* $k = k(\lambda)$, *number of samples* $m = m(\lambda)$, *and noise rate* $\tau = \tau(\lambda)$. *The* $\mathsf{LPN}^m_{k,\tau}$ *assumption with respect to* Code *states that*

$$\{(A, \mathbf{b}) \mid A \xleftarrow{\$} \mathsf{Code}(m, k, \mathbb{F}), \mathbf{e} \xleftarrow{\$} \mathsf{Ber}_\tau(\mathbb{F})^m, \mathbf{s} \xleftarrow{\$} \mathbb{F}^k, \mathbf{b} \leftarrow A \cdot \mathbf{s} + \mathbf{e}\} \stackrel{c}{\approx}$$
$$\{(A, \mathbf{b}) \mid A \xleftarrow{\$} \mathsf{Code}(m, k, \mathbb{F}), \mathbf{b} \xleftarrow{\$} \mathbb{F}^m\}$$

The above LPN assumption has an equivalent dual formulation:

Definition 3 (Dual Learning Parity with Noise). *Fix a field* $\mathbb{F} = \mathbb{F}(\lambda)$, *dimension* $k = k(\lambda)$, *number of samples* $m = m(\lambda)$, *and noise rate* $\tau = \tau(\lambda)$. *The* $\mathsf{dual\text{-}LPN}^m_{k,\tau}$ *assumption with respect to* $\mathsf{Code}^\perp$ *states that*

$$\{(H, \mathbf{b}) \mid H \xleftarrow{\$} \mathsf{Code}^\perp(m, m - k, \mathbb{F}), \mathbf{e} \xleftarrow{\$} \mathsf{Ber}_\tau(\mathbb{F})^m, \mathbf{b} \leftarrow H^{\mathsf{T}} \cdot \mathbf{e}\} \stackrel{c}{\approx}$$
$$\{(H, \mathbf{b}) \mid H \xleftarrow{\$} \mathsf{Code}^\perp(m, m - k, \mathbb{F}), \mathbf{b} \xleftarrow{\$} \mathbb{F}^{m-k}\}$$

The following is standard:

Lemma 4. *For any* $\mathbb{F}, k, m, \tau$ *and code generation algorithm* Code, *the* $\mathsf{LPN}^m_{k,\tau}(\mathbb{F})$ *assumption with respect to* Code *and the* $\mathsf{dual\text{-}LPN}^m_{k,\tau}(\mathbb{F})$ *assumption with respect to* $\mathsf{Code}^\perp$ *are equivalent.*

Standard Codes and Noise Distributions. The classical LPN assumption is recovered by setting $\mathbb{F} = \mathbb{F}_2$ and Code to be the uniform distribution over $\mathbb{F}_2^{m \times k}$. However, the hardness of LPN is commonly assumed for other families of codes in the literature, such as sparse codes [4] (often called the "Alekhnovich assumption"), quasi-cyclic codes (used in several recent submissions to the NIST post-quantum competition [3,6,45]), Toeplitz matrices [35,44] and many more. All these variants of LPN generalize naturally to larger fields (and LPN is typically believed to be at least as hard, if not harder, over larger fields).

In addition, it is also relatively common to consider alternative noise distributions beyond the Bernoulli noise. The two most standard choices are exact noise (where the noise is sampled uniformly from the set of all $\tau \cdot m$-sparse vectors of $\mathbb{F}^m$) and regular noise (where the noise is a concatenation of $\tau \cdot m$ random unit vectors of length $1/\tau$). See [16, 18] for discussions about these alternative noise distributions. We will denote by $\mathsf{XN}_{\tau,m}(\mathbb{F})$ (for eXact Noise) the exact noise distribution, and by $\mathsf{RN}_{\tau,m}(\mathbb{F})$ (for Regular Noise) the regular noise distribution.

Security of LPN and Its Variants. Numerous attacks on LPN have been devised. Among the most standard attacks are Gaussian elimination, which solves LPN in time and sample complexity $\Theta(1/(1-\tau)^k)$ using $\Theta(k^2)$ memory, and its variants (e.g. pooled Gauss [34], and BKW [14]), and the Information Set Decoding attacks (introduced by Prange [50] and further improved in a long sequence of papers, see e.g. [12, 13]). In this work, we will be interested in variants of LPN with a very low number of samples (linear in the dimension) and a very low noise rate. This has several consequences: first, algorithms such as BKW (which require a very large number of samples) do not apply, and using a regular noise distribution has no known effect on security (in contrast, if the number of samples is at least quadratic in the dimension, attacks such as the Arora-Ge attack [7] can take advantage of the noise structure). Second, in the very low-noise regime, all improved variants of ISD become equivalent to the original (much simpler) algorithm of Prange.

We point out that increasing the field size beyond 2 is not known to reduce security (and actually seems to slightly *improve* security with respect to known attacks), and neither does using a different family of linear code, as long as they are good codes (i.e. a random code from the family has a linear minimum distance with high probability). A small exception to that are quasi-cyclic codes, where the strong structure allows for the DOOM attack [51], which slightly reduces security (but can be easily compensated by a small increase in the noise rate). We refer the reader to [16–18, 20] for more detailed discussions on the security of LPN with various types of noise distributions and code ensembles. As a rule of thumb, though: in our parameter setting, all known attacks will have a complexity of the form $2^{O(\tau \cdot m)}$. Hence, fixing the noise rate τ to λ/m for some fixed security parameter λ suffices to achieve exponential security (in λ) against all known attacks.

2.2   Learning with Errors

The learning with errors (LWE) assumption is a close variant of the LPN assumption. In essence, and using our generalized definition of LPN, the LWE assumption with dimension k, and m samples, is simply the LPN assumption over $\mathbb{Z}_q$ (for some large enough prime q) with respect to a different noise distribution, which trades *sparsity* for *small magnitude* – i.e., instead of being a distribution over vectors whose entries are mostly zero, the noise distribution samples vectors whose entries are *small in magnitude*. Multiple choices of such noise distributions are standard in the literature, including discrete Gaussian noise, or noise sampled uniformly from $[-B, B]$, where $B \ll q$ is a bound on the magnitude. We call 'LWE$_k^m(\mathbb{Z}_q, \chi)$ with respect to Code' the LWE assumption with dimension k, m samples, over $\mathbb{Z}_q$, with noise vector sampled from χ^m and matrix sampled from Code.

Rounding Lemma. Let $\lceil x \rfloor$ denotes the rounding of $x \in \mathbb{R}$ to the nearest integer. We recall the rounding lemma, from [21]:

Lemma 5 (Rounding of noisy shares). *Let (p, q) be two integers with $q/p \in \mathbb{N}$. Fix any $z \in \mathbb{Z}_p$, and (t_0, t_1) be two random elements of $\mathbb{Z}_q$ subject to $t_0 + t_1 = (q/p) \cdot z + e \bmod q$, where e is such that $q/(p \cdot |e|) \geq \lambda^{\omega(1)}$ (λ is a security parameter). Then with probability at least $1 - (|e| + 1) \cdot p/q \geq 1 - \lambda^{-\omega(1)}$, it holds that $R(t_0) + R(t_1) = z \bmod p$, where R is the deterministic rounding function $R : x \to \lceil (p/q) \cdot z \rfloor \bmod p$ and the probability is over the random choice of (t_0, t_1).*

3   Non-interactive Approximate Inner Product from LPN and LWE

In this section, we describe a general non-interactive protocol for securely computing the inner product between two vectors over $\mathbb{F}^n$, with ε correctness error (independent of the value of the inputs). Our general protocol can be instantiated either under the LPN assumption, in which case the error will be noticeable (but arbitrarily small), or under the LWE assumption (in which case the error can be made negligible). Our protocol enjoys an attractive *key exchange structure*: consider two parties Alice and Bob with respective inputs $(\mathbf{u}, \mathbf{v}) \in \mathbb{F}^n \times \mathbb{F}^n$. The protocol has the following interaction pattern:

- First, Alice and Bob broadcast *encodings* of their respective vectors $(\mathbf{u}, \mathbf{v})$, denoted $\mathsf{pk_u}$ and $\mathsf{pk_v}$, and locally keep a private state, which we denote by $\mathsf{sk_u}$ and $\mathsf{sk_v}$ respectively. The encodings have length $O(n)$ (the $O(\cdot)$ hides a small constant) and computationally hide the vector they encode.
- Second, Alice (resp. Bob) can locally compute $\alpha \leftarrow \mathsf{Decode}(\mathsf{pk_v}, \mathsf{sk_u})$ (resp. $\beta \leftarrow \mathsf{Decode}(\mathsf{pk_u}, \mathsf{sk_v})$), where Decode is some deterministic decoding algorithm. The values α and β form additive shares of a value $w \in \mathbb{F}$, where it holds that $w = \mathbf{u}^\mathsf{T} \cdot \mathbf{v}$ with probability at least ε (over the random coins of the encoding procedure).

We call a protocol with the above interaction pattern a *non-interactive approximate inner-product protocol* (NIAIP). We formalize this notion below.

3.1   Non-interactive Approximate Inner Product

Definition 6. *A non-interactive ε-approximate inner-product protocol (ε-NIAIP) over a field $\mathbb{F}$ is a tuple of probabilistic polynomial-time algorithms (Setup, Encode, Decode) such that Decode is deterministic, and*

- *Setup(1^λ) : on input the security parameter 1^λ in unary, outputs a common reference string (CRS) crs.*

- Encode($\mathsf{crs}, b, \mathbf{u}$) : *on input the CRS* crs, *a bit* b, $\mathbf{u} \in \mathbb{F}^n$, *outputs a pair* ($\mathsf{pk}_b, \mathsf{sk}_b$);
- Decode($\mathsf{crs}, \mathsf{pk}, \mathsf{sk}'$) : *on input the CRS* crs, *a public encoding* pk *and a secret state* sk', *outputs a value* $\gamma \in \mathbb{F}$.

Furthermore, an NIAIP *must satisfy two properties:*

- ε-**Correctness.** *For every common reference string* crs *in the domain of* $\mathsf{Setup}(1^\lambda)$ *and every pair* $(\mathbf{u}_0, \mathbf{u}_1) \in \mathbb{F}^n \times \mathbb{F}^n$ *of vectors, it holds that*

$$\Pr[\mathsf{Decode}(\mathsf{crs}, \mathsf{pk}_0, \mathsf{sk}_1) + \mathsf{Decode}(\mathsf{crs}, \mathsf{pk}_1, \mathsf{sk}_0) = \mathbf{u}_0^\mathsf{T} \cdot \mathbf{u}_1] \geq \varepsilon(\lambda, n),$$

  where the probability is taken over the joint random coins of both instances of Encode, $((\mathsf{pk}_b, \mathsf{sk}_b) \xleftarrow{\$} \mathsf{Encode}(\mathsf{crs}, b, \mathbf{u}_b))_{b \in \{0,1\}}$.
- **Indistinguishability.** *For every* $b \in \{0,1\}$, *the advantage of any (stateful) probabilistic polynomial-time (PPT) adversary* $\mathcal{A}$ *in distinguishing the following two experiments, parametrized by a bit* σ, *is negligible:*
  - $\mathcal{A}$ *receives* $\mathsf{crs} \xleftarrow{\$} \mathsf{Setup}(1^\lambda)$ *and outputs* $\mathbf{u} \in \mathbb{F}^n$.
  - *The challenger samples a pair* $(\mathsf{pk}_b, \mathsf{sk}_b) \xleftarrow{\$} \mathsf{Encode}(\mathsf{crs}, b, \mathbf{v})$, *where* $\mathbf{v}$ *is* 0^n *if* $\sigma = 0$, *and* $\mathbf{v} = \mathbf{u}$ *otherwise. The challenger sends* pk_b *to* $\mathcal{A}$.

A Note on Syntax. We note that in the above definition, the parties have fixed roles. In a multiparty setting, if all pairs of parties want to compute inner products, this means that they must publish two encodings of their input, one with role 0, and one with role 1. In many applications, however, it is natural to have "type-0" and "type-1" parties (e.g. clients and servers), such that secure computations tasks are only carried between a type-0 and a type-1 party.

3.2   A $(1 - \tau^2 m)$-NIAIP from LPN

We now proceed with the construction of an ε-NIAIP, from the learning parity with noise assumption. The construction is relatively simple in hindsight, and quite elegant; it is a natural twist on the Alekhnovich cryptosystem. The construction is parametrized by a field $\mathbb{F}$, and a vector length n. We let $k(n), m(n)$ denote respectively a dimension parameter and a number of samples, both to be specified later (but the reader can think of k and m as linear in n, e.g. $k = 2n$ and $m = 4n$), and $t = t(\lambda, n)$ denote a noise parameter (the reader can consider $t = \lambda$ to be a reasonable choice). Let Code be a probabilistic code generation algorithm. The construction is represented on Fig. 1.

Before we state the theorem, we introduce some notation: let $\mathsf{Code}_{\mathsf{right}}^\perp$ be the code generator that samples a random matrix $H \xleftarrow{\$} \mathsf{Code}^\perp(m, k + n, \mathbb{F})$ (hence $H \in \mathbb{F}^{m \times k + n}$) and outputs the matrix $H_{\mathsf{right}} \in \mathbb{F}^{m \times k}$ which contains the last k columns of H. Furthermore, we say that $\mathsf{Code}^\perp$ is a *nice code* if given H_{right}, there is an efficient algorithm to sample a random matrix H from $\mathsf{Code}^\perp(m, k + n, \mathbb{F})$

- Setup(1^λ) : sample $H \xleftarrow{\$} \mathsf{Code}^\perp(m, k+n, \mathbb{F})$ and output $\mathsf{crs} = H$.
- Encode($\mathsf{crs}, b, \mathbf{u}$) : parse crs as H and sample $\mathbf{r}_b \xleftarrow{\$} \mathsf{Ber}_\tau^m(\mathbb{F})$. If $b = 0$, output $\mathsf{pk}_0 \leftarrow (\mathbf{u}/\!\!/\mathbf{0}) - H^\mathsf{T} \cdot \mathbf{r}_0$ and $\mathsf{sk}_0 \leftarrow \mathbf{r}_0$. If $b = 1$, sample $\mathbf{s} \xleftarrow{\$} \mathbb{F}^k$, and output $\mathsf{pk}_1 \leftarrow H \cdot (\mathbf{u}/\!\!/\mathbf{s}) + \mathbf{r}_1$ and $\mathsf{sk}_1 \leftarrow (\mathbf{u}/\!\!/\mathbf{s})$.
- Decode($\mathsf{crs}, \mathsf{pk}, \mathsf{sk}'$) : output $\mathsf{pk}^\mathsf{T} \cdot \mathsf{sk}'$.

Fig. 1. A non-interactive approximate inner-product over $\mathbb{F}$ for vectors of length n

whose last k columns are exactly H_{right}[1]. We denote $H \xleftarrow{\$} \mathsf{Code}^\perp|_{H_{\mathsf{right}}}(m, k+n, \mathbb{F})$ this process.

Theorem 7. *Let* $\mathsf{Code}^\perp$ *be a nice code. Assume that the* $\mathsf{dual\text{-}LPN}_{m-(k+n),\tau}^m(\mathbb{F})$ *assumption with respect to* $\mathsf{Code}^\perp$, *and the (primal)* $\mathsf{LPN}_{k,\tau}^m(\mathbb{F})$ *assumption with respect to* $\mathsf{Code}_{\mathsf{right}}^\perp$ *both hold. Then the construction* (Setup, Encode, Decode) *on Fig. 1 is an* ε-NIAIP, *with* $\varepsilon \geq 1 - m\tau^2$.

Proof. We first prove ε-correctness. Observe that for any pair of inputs $(\mathbf{u}_0, \mathbf{u}_1) \in \mathbb{F}^n \times \mathbb{F}^n$ and every matrix $H \in \mathbb{F}^{m \times k+n}$, it holds that

$\mathsf{Decode}(\mathsf{crs}, \mathsf{pk}_0, \mathsf{sk}_1) + \mathsf{Decode}(\mathsf{crs}, \mathsf{pk}_1, \mathsf{sk}_0)$

$$= \mathsf{pk}_0^\mathsf{T} \cdot \mathsf{sk}_1 + \mathsf{pk}_1^\mathsf{T} \cdot \mathsf{sk}_0$$
$$= ((\mathbf{u}_0/\!\!/\mathbf{0}) - H^\mathsf{T} \cdot \mathbf{r}_0)^\mathsf{T} \cdot (\mathbf{u}_1/\!\!/\mathbf{s}) + (H \cdot (\mathbf{u}_1/\!\!/\mathbf{s}) + \mathbf{r}_1)^\mathsf{T} \cdot \mathbf{r}_0$$
$$= (\mathbf{u}_0^\mathsf{T}\|\mathbf{0}^\mathsf{T}) \cdot (\mathbf{u}_1/\!\!/\mathbf{s}) - \mathbf{r}_0^\mathsf{T} \cdot H \cdot (\mathbf{u}_1/\!\!/\mathbf{s}) + (\mathbf{u}_1/\!\!/\mathbf{s})^\mathsf{T} \cdot H^\mathsf{T} \cdot \mathbf{r}_0 + \mathbf{r}_1^\mathsf{T} \cdot \mathbf{r}_0$$
$$= \mathbf{u}_0^\mathsf{T} \cdot \mathbf{u}_1 - \mathbf{r}_0^\mathsf{T} \cdot H \cdot (\mathbf{u}_1/\!\!/\mathbf{s}) + (\mathbf{r}_0^\mathsf{T} \cdot H \cdot (\mathbf{u}_1/\!\!/\mathbf{s}))^\mathsf{T} + \mathbf{r}_1^\mathsf{T} \cdot \mathbf{r}_0$$
$$= \mathbf{u}_0^\mathsf{T} \cdot \mathbf{u}_1 + \mathbf{r}_1^\mathsf{T} \cdot \mathbf{r}_0 \text{ (since the transpose of a single field element is itself)}.$$

Now, since $\mathbf{r}_0$ and $\mathbf{r}_1$ are random Bernoulli noise vectors with rate τ, we have

$$\Pr[\mathbf{r}_1^\mathsf{T} \cdot \mathbf{r}_0 = 0] \geq 1 - m \cdot \tau^2,$$

since $\Pr[\mathbf{r}_1^\mathsf{T} \cdot \mathbf{r}_0 = 0] \geq \Pr[r_0^{(i)} \cdot r_1^{(i)} = 0 \forall i \leq m]$, which equal to $1 - \Pr[\exists i, r_0^{(i)} \cdot r_1^{(i)} = 1] \geq 1 - m\tau^2$, using a straightforward union bound and the fact that $\Pr[r_0^{(i)} \cdot r_1^{(i)} = 1] = \tau^2$ for any i.

We now prove indistinguishability, for $b = 0$ and $b = 1$. We proceed in a sequence of games of the form $G_{b,\sigma}^i$:

- Game $G_{0,0}^0$ is the initial game, with bits $b = 0$ and $\sigma = 0$. The challenger samples $H \xleftarrow{\$} \mathsf{Code}^\perp(m, k+n, \mathbb{F})$. Upon receiving $\mathbf{u} \in \mathbb{F}^n$ from $\mathcal{A}(\mathsf{crs})$, the challenger returns $\mathsf{pk}_0 \leftarrow 0^{k+n} - H^\mathsf{T} \cdot \mathbf{r}_0$, where $\mathbf{r}_0$ is a random Bernoulli noise.
- Game $G_{0,0}^1$: the challenger first receives a challenge, denoted $(H, \mathbf{c})$, for the $\mathsf{dual\text{-}LPN}_{m-(k+n),\tau}^m$ assumption with respect to $\mathsf{Code}^\perp$, where $\mathbf{c}$ is $H^\mathsf{T} \cdot \mathbf{e}$ for

----

[1] All known LPN-friendly codes satisfy this property.

some noise vector $\mathbf{e}$. Upon receiving $\mathbf{u} \in \mathbb{F}^n$ from $\mathcal{A}(\mathsf{crs})$, the challenger returns $\mathsf{pk}_0 \leftarrow 0^{k+n} - \mathbf{c}$. This game is perfectly indistinguishable from the previous one.

- Game $G_{0,0}^2$ is exactly as Game $G_{0,0}^1$, except that $\mathbf{c}$ is now a random vector from $\mathbb{F}^m$. Observe that distinguishing between $G_{0,0}^1$ and $G_{0,0}^2$ is exactly solving the dual-LPN$_{m-(k+n),\tau}^m$ assumption with respect to $\mathsf{Code}^\perp$.

- Game $G_{0,0}^3$: the challenger proceeds as in Game $G_{0,0}^2$, except that it outputs $\mathsf{pk}_0 \xleftarrow{\$} (\mathbf{u}/\!/0) - \mathbf{c}$. Since $\mathbf{c}$ is a uniformly random vector, this game is perfectly indistinguishable from the previous one.

- Game $G_{0,0}^4$: as the previous one, except that $\mathbf{c}$ is back to being of the form $H^\mathsf{T} \cdot \mathbf{e}$ for some noise vector $\mathbf{e}$. Distinguishing this game from $G_{0,0}^3$ is exactly solving the dual-LPN$_{m-(k+n),\tau}^m$ assumption with respect to $\mathsf{Code}^\perp$.

- Game $G_{0,1}^0$: this game is simply the initial game with bits $b = 0$ and $\sigma = 1$. Game $G_{0,1}^0$ is perfectly indistinguishable from $G_{0,0}^4$.

From the above, we conclude that the advantage of any polynomial time adversary in the indistinguishability experiment with $b = 0$ is at most twice its advantage against the dual-LPN$_{m-(k+n),\tau}^m(\mathbb{F})$ assumption with respect to $\mathsf{Code}^\perp$. We now address the case $b = 1$.

- Game $G_{1,0}^0$ is the initial game, with bits $b = 1$ and $\sigma = 0$. The challenger samples $H \xleftarrow{\$} \mathsf{Code}(m, k + n, \mathbb{F})$. Upon receiving $\mathbf{u} \in \mathbb{F}^n$ from $\mathcal{A}(\mathsf{crs})$, the challenger returns $\mathsf{pk}_1 \leftarrow H \cdot (0^n/\!/\mathbf{s}) + \mathbf{r}_1$, where $\mathbf{r}_1$ is a random Bernoulli noise and $\mathbf{s}$ is a random vector from $\mathbb{F}^k$.

- Game $G_{1,0}^1$: the challenger first receives a challenge, denoted $(H_{\mathsf{right}}, \mathbf{c})$, for the LPN$_{k,\tau}^m$ assumption with respect to $\mathsf{Code}_{\mathsf{right}}^\perp$, where $\mathbf{c}$ is $H_{\mathsf{right}} \cdot \mathbf{s} + \mathbf{e}$ for some random vector $\mathbf{s}$ and some noise vector $\mathbf{e}$. The challenger samples H as $H \xleftarrow{\$} \mathsf{Code}^\perp|_{H_{\mathsf{right}}}(m, k + n, \mathbb{F})$ (which is possible by definition since $\mathsf{Code}^\perp$ is a nice code). Let H_{left} be such that $H = H_{\mathsf{left}}\|H_{\mathsf{right}}$. Upon receiving $\mathbf{u} \in \mathbb{F}^n$ from $\mathcal{A}(H)$, the challenger returns $\mathsf{pk}_1 \leftarrow \mathbf{c}$. By construction of $\mathbf{c}$, since $H \cdot (0^n/\!/\mathbf{s}) = H_{\mathsf{right}} \cdot \mathbf{s}$, this game is perfectly indistinguishable from the previous one.

- Game $G_{1,0}^2$ is exactly as Game $G_{0,0}^1$, except that $\mathbf{c}$ is now a random vector from $\mathbb{F}^m$. Observe that distinguishing between $G_{0,0}^1$ and $G_{0,0}^2$ is exactly solving the LPN$_{k,\tau}^m$ assumption with respect to $\mathsf{Code}_{\mathsf{right}}^\perp$.

- Game $G_{1,0}^3$: the challenger proceeds as in Game $G_{0,0}^2$, except that it outputs $\mathsf{pk}_0 \xleftarrow{\$} H_{\mathsf{left}} \cdot \mathbf{u} + \mathbf{c}$. Since $\mathbf{c}$ is a uniformly random vector, this game is perfectly indistinguishable from the previous one.

- Game $G_{1,0}^4$: as the previous one, except that $\mathbf{c}$ is back to being of the form $H_{\mathsf{right}} \cdot \mathbf{s} + \mathbf{e}$. Distinguishing this game from $G_{0,0}^3$ is exactly solving the LPN$_{k,\tau}^m$ assumption with respect to Code.

- Game $G_{1,1}^0$: this game is simply the initial game with bits $b = 1$ and $\sigma = 1$. Since $H \cdot (\mathbf{u}/\!/\mathbf{s}) = H_{\mathsf{left}} \cdot \mathbf{u} + H_{\mathsf{right}} \cdot \mathbf{s}$, Game $G_{1,1}^0$ is perfectly indistinguishable from $G_{0,0}^4$.

From the above, we conclude that the advantage of any polynomial time adversary in the indistinguishability experiment with $b = 1$ is at most twice its advantage against the $\mathsf{LPN}^m_{k,\tau}(\mathbb{F})$ assumption with respect to $\mathsf{Code}^\perp_{\mathsf{right}}$. This concludes the proof.

3.3 Non-interactive Inner Product from LWE

A simple variant of our construction of non-interactive approximate inner-product leads to a construction under the learning with error (LWE) assumption. Unlike its LPN-based counterpart, this variant can actually achieve correctness exponentially close to 1.

Let $\mathbb{F}_p$ be the prime-order field over which we want to compute a non-interactive inner-product. Fix a bound B on the magnitude of the noise. Let $\mathbb{Z}_q$ be a ring, for some multiple q of p of size $q > (m \cdot B^2 + 1) \cdot p \cdot \lambda^{\omega(1)}$. The variant is described on Fig. 2. Eventually, we let χ denote a noise distribution. The exact choice of χ does not matter much, but we assume that all entries in a random sample from χ^m belong to $[-B, B]$ with overwhelming probability. Note that we follow an LPN-style description, by viewing the matrix of the LWE assumption as the generator matrix of some linear code over the ring $\mathbb{Z}_q$. While this is not so common in the LWE literature, this viewpoint allows for considerations on the choice of better codes to improve efficiency.

- $\mathsf{Setup}(1^\lambda)$: sample $H \xleftarrow{\$} \mathsf{Code}^\perp(m, k + n, \mathbb{Z}_q)$ and output $\mathsf{crs} = H$.
- $\mathsf{Encode}(\mathsf{crs}, b, \mathbf{u})$: parse crs as H and sample $\mathbf{r}_b \xleftarrow{\$} \chi^m$. If $b = 0$, output $\mathsf{pk}_0 \leftarrow (q/p) \cdot (\mathbf{u}/\!\!/0) - H^\mathsf{T} \cdot \mathbf{r}_0$ and $\mathsf{sk}_0 \leftarrow \mathbf{r}_0$. If $b = 1$, sample $\mathbf{s} \xleftarrow{\$} \mathbb{Z}_q^k$, and output $\mathsf{pk}_1 \leftarrow H \cdot (\mathbf{u}/\!\!/\mathbf{s}) + \mathbf{r}_1$ and $\mathsf{sk}_1 \leftarrow (\mathbf{u}/\!\!/\mathbf{s})$.
- $\mathsf{Decode}(\mathsf{crs}, \mathsf{pk}, \mathsf{sk}')$: output $\lceil (p/q) \cdot \mathsf{pk}^\mathsf{T} \cdot \mathsf{sk}' \rfloor \bmod p$.

Fig. 2. An LWE-based non-interactive inner-product over $\mathbb{F}_p$ for vectors of length n

Theorem 8. *Assuming the $\mathsf{LWE}^m_k(\mathbb{Z}_q, \chi)$ with respect to Code, the construction of Fig. 2 is an ε-NIAIP, with correctness ε negligibly close to 1.*

Proof. The protocol of Fig. 2 is identical to the LPN-based protocol of Fig. 1, up to two differences:

- $H^\mathsf{T} \cdot \mathbf{r}_0$ is used to mask $(q/p) \cdot (\mathbf{u}/\!\!/0)$ instead of $(\mathbf{u}/\!\!/0)$, and
- the output of Decode is fed to the *rounding procedure* R of the rounding lemma (Lemma 5) which, on input $x \in \mathbb{Z}_q$, outputs $R(x) = \lceil (p/q) \cdot x \rfloor \bmod p$.

Using the same analysis as for the correctness of the LPN-based protocol, if $(\mathsf{pk}_0, \mathsf{sk}_0)$ and $(\mathsf{pk}_1, \mathsf{sk}_1)$ are encodings of two inputs $(\mathbf{u}_0, \mathbf{u}_1) \in \mathbb{F}_p \times \mathbb{F}_p$, we have

$$\mathsf{pk}_0^\mathsf{T} \cdot \mathsf{sk}_1 + \mathsf{pk}_1^\mathsf{T} \cdot \mathsf{sk}_0 = (q/p) \cdot \mathbf{u}_0^\mathsf{T} \cdot \mathbf{u}_1 + \mathbf{r}_1^\mathsf{T} \cdot \mathbf{r}_0,$$

where $|\mathbf{r}_1^\mathsf{T} \cdot \mathbf{r}_0| \leq m \cdot B^2$. Let $e \leftarrow \mathbf{r}_1^\mathsf{T} \cdot \mathbf{r}_0$ denote the *output noise* and $z \leftarrow \mathbf{u}_0^\mathsf{T} \cdot \mathbf{u}_1$ denote the target output. The values $\mathsf{pk}_0^\mathsf{T} \cdot \mathsf{sk}_1$ and $\mathsf{pk}_1^\mathsf{T} \cdot \mathsf{sk}_0$ form random shares of $(q/p) \cdot z + e$ over $\mathbb{Z}_q$ with $|e| \leq m \cdot B^2$. Therefore, by the rounding lemma (Lemma 5), the outputs of Decode form additive shares of $z \in \mathbb{Z}_p$ with overwhelming probability. This concludes the proof of overwhelming correctness.

For security, the second part of the analysis is identical to the security analysis of the LPN-based protocol, and reduces to the $\mathsf{LWE}_k^m(\mathbb{Z}_q, \chi)$ assumption with respect to Code. The first part of the analysis, however, differs in a crucial way: a standard application of the leftover hash lemma shows that $H^\mathsf{T} \cdot \mathbf{r}_0$ is *statistically* close to a random vector. Therefore, the NIAIP actually enjoys statistical security for one of the two parties in the LWE setting. The rest of the game hops are identical – one must simply replace invocations of the dual LPN assumption by the statistical argument.

Like its LPN-based counterpart, this protocol leads to an NIAIP over an arbitrary prime order field (and can even be modified to give an inner product protocol over $\mathbb{Z}$); furthermore, it enjoys overwhelming correctness. However, as we will see later, it is possible to upgrade the correctness of the LPN-based NIAIP to perfect correctness, *and* its security to security against malicious adversaries, at a cost *sublinear* in n; this means that, asymptotically, the LPN-based protocol can be made perfectly correct and maliciously secure at negligible cost. In contrast, making the LWE-based protocol secure against malicious adversaries is more challenging, and we leave it to future work.

3.4   From NIAIP to Secure Computation of Inner Product

The natural usecase for NIAIP is to securely compute inner products: two parties $P_0, P1$ publish encodings of their respective inputs $\mathbf{u}$ and $\mathbf{v}$, locally compute shares of the inner product, and exchange their shares to reconstruct the output. An important technicality here is that the NIAIP indistinguishability notion does not directly imply security when revealing the share of P_0 to its opponent P_1. When correctness is overwhelming (as with our LWE-based instantiation), this is not an issue: given the output $\mathbf{u}^\mathsf{T} \cdot \mathbf{v}$ and the randomness of P_1, the simulator can compute P_1's share γ_1, and simulate the missing share as $\mathbf{u}^\mathsf{T} \cdot \mathbf{v} - \gamma_1$. Due to the overwhelming correctness, the simulation is indistinguishable from the honest protocol.

When using ε-NIAIP with non-negligible correctness error (as with our LPN-based instantiation), however, the *correctness error* translates to a *security loss* for the protocol: the simulation fails with probability $1 - \varepsilon$. Yet, this does not directly imply an attack on the protocol. In fact, for our LPN-based instantiation, we can get perfect simulation by giving the simulator the error term $\mathbf{r}_1^\mathsf{T} \cdot \mathbf{r}_0$. Concretely, this corresponds to allowing the adversary to learn a single sparse linear equation (given by $\mathbf{r}_1$) in the LPN noise vector $\mathbf{r}_0$. In turn, this means that the security reduces to an appropriate *LPN with leakage* assumption. Such variants of LPN are relatively standard, and can in particular be reduced to the standard LPN assumption, albeit with some loss [17, 20].

In an multiparty setting, where P_0 wants to compute the inner product of **u** with many other vectors, the leakage can be accumulated across corrupted parties. This translates to a larger loss for the assumption, and the LPN parameters must be adjusted to compensate, as a function of the maximum number of corrupted parties. An alternative solution is to first remove the error instead, using the sublinear-communication preprocessing phase described in Sect. 4.

3.5   Choosing the Parameters and the Code

Our non-interactive inner-product communicates $k + n + m$ bits ($k + n$ for pk_0 and m for pk_1). The security of our protocol relies on a relatively unusual set of parameters: we need to assume dual LPN with dimension $m - (k + n)$, m samples, noise rate τ with respect to the matrix H^T, as well as primal LPN with dimension k, m samples, noise rate τ with respect to the "right half" of H. We will discuss candidate choices for the underlying code afterwards. Regarding the parameters, we set $m - (k + n) = k$ to ensure that both assumptions achieve the same dimension and number of samples, in order to balance security. This implies $m = 2k + n$. From there, the choice of k induces a tradeoff between the noise rate (which must be kept low as the error probability of the protocol is $\tau^2 \cdot m$) and the communication of the protocol (which grows with k): picking a very large $k \gg n$ increase communication but achieves asymptotically a rate $1/2$ (as m approaches $2k$).

Concrete Parameters. For concrete instantiations, we consider a reasonable middle ground and set $k = n$ (hence $m = 3k$), leading to codes of rate $1/3$. This leads to a protocol with total communication $5n$ bits, only 2.5 times more than the communication of exchanging $\mathbf{u}_0$ and $\mathbf{u}_1$ in the clear. To estimate the concrete noise rate, we rely on the analysis of [16] which provides various formulas to compute lower bounds on the bit complexity of the most standard attacks on LPN. With a rate $1/3$ and using their formulas for the cost of ISD, Gaussian elimination, and low-weight parity-check attacks, we get the following (very close) approximation of the security level: choosing $\tau = \lambda/m$ provides $\lambda - 20$ bits of security (independently of the vector length n). Hence, for example, setting $\lambda = 100$ gives 80 bits of security, and an error probability of $\lambda^2/m = 0.3\%$ for vectors of length $n = 2^{20}$ (for smaller vectors, the error probability increases rapidly: e.g. around 10% for $n = 2^{15}$).

Asymptotic Parameters. Asymptotically, letting $m = 2k + n$ as before, the code rate is k/m for both codes. Let ε be an arbitrarily small constant, and set $k = \varepsilon \cdot n$ and $\tau = \lambda/m$ for a security parameter λ. The best known attack against LPN with code rate $k/m = O(1)$ and noise rate λ/m run in time $2^{O(\lambda)}$ (where the $O(\cdot)$ hides a $1/\varepsilon$ factor). With these parameters, the protocol communicates $3k + 2n = (2 + 3\varepsilon)n$ bits, which is arbitrarily close to the optimal communication of an *insecure* NIAIP that simply reveals the inputs in the clear. Settling for subexponential security in λ can further reduce communication to $2n + o(n)$.

Choosing the Code. It remains to discuss how to choose an appropriate code to instantiate the NIAIP. While the code has no impact on communication, it represents a tradeoff between computation and security. For example, using a uniformly random code leads to a security reduction to the most standard flavor of LPN, but comes at a huge computational cost: the computation scales as $O(n^2)$.

Some variants of LPN are conjectured to be secure with respect to *linear time encodable codes*, where the mapping $\mathbf{x} \to H \cdot \mathbf{x}$ can be computed in linear time (by the transposition principle [15,39], this also implies that the mapping $\mathbf{y} \to H^\intercal \cdot \mathbf{y}$ can be computed in linear time). This is for example the case of primal LPN instantiated with a sparse matrix H, with a constant number of nonzero entry per row, which corresponds to the Alekhnovich assumption [4]. Unfortunately, to our knowledge, for all known linear-time encodable code such that primal LPN is conjectured to hold with respect to H, the *dual assumption with respect to $H^\intercal$* turns out to be insecure. For sparse codes, typically, this is equivalent to the well-known fact that LDPC codes admit an efficient decoding algorithm.

Fortunately, if we settle for *quasi-linear time* encodable codes, we can circumvent the issue. For example, quasi-cyclic codes can be encoded in time $O(n \cdot \log n)$ using Fast Fourier Transform, and given a generator matrix H for a quasi-cyclic code, LPN is widely conjectured to hold both with respect to H_{right} in its primal form, and with respect to $H^\intercal$ in its dual form. Quasi-cyclic codes have been used in numerous recent works [1,3,17] as well as in submissions to the NIST post-quantum competition [3,6,45]. We note that, when using quasi-cyclic codes, one must account for the speedup given by the DOOM attack [51], which gives a $\sqrt{k}$ speedup for the attacker. To compensate for this attack, we must therefore aim at $\lambda + \log_2 k$ "pre-DOOM" bits of security, which can be done by increasing the noise rate from $(\lambda + 20)/m$ to $(\lambda + 20 + \log_2 k)/m$ with our concrete choice of parameters.

3.6 Open Problem: Finding a "Doubly Good" Linear Time Encodable Code

While the above provides a relatively satisfying solution, it remains an intriguing open question whether an appropriate choice of codes could possibly allow to achieve NIAIP with strictly linear computation. Following the recent analysis of LPN variants in [19,28], a core necessary requirement to achieve this is to find a linear-time encodable code such that both the code and its dual have *linear minimum distance* (in the dimension). Indeed, there exists efficient attacks on LPN with codes whose dual have low minimum dimension [5], and furthermore having linear minimum distance suffices to circumvent all known attacks against LPN [19,28]. However, although the question appears to be very natural, linear-time encodable code where both the code and its dual are good codes (i.e. exhibit linear minimum distance) have never been exhibited in the literature, and we raise their existence as an interesting theoretical (but also possibly practical, in light of our construction) open question.

4   Removing Correctness Errors via Sublinear Preprocessing

In this section, we show how to convert the LPN-based ε-NIAIP from the previous section into a two-party secure computation protocol for inner product, without correctness error. While the protocol is not an NIAIP anymore, all additional interactions take place during an input-independent preprocessing phase. Furthermore, the amount of computation and communication during this preprocessing phase is sublinear in n (more precisely, it will be of the form $\mathsf{poly}(\lambda) \cdot \log n$).

The ideal functionality $\mathcal{F}_{\mathsf{IP}}$ for secure computation of (shares of) an inner product over a field $\mathbb{F}$ is described on Fig. 4 (setting $\varepsilon = 1$). The intuition behind the protocol of this section is natural: the correctness error in the protocol of Fig. 1 is due to an additive term $\mathbf{r}_1^\mathsf{T} \cdot \mathbf{r}_0$ in the shares locally decoded by the parties. Since the $\mathbf{r}_b$ are sparse vectors, their inner product is zero with high probability $\approx 1 - \lambda^2/m$. To correct the error, the parties will distributively generate noise vectors $(\mathbf{r}_0, \mathbf{r}_1)$ together with additive shares of $\mathbf{r}_1^\mathsf{T} \cdot \mathbf{r}_0$. Crucially, this entire preprocessing requires communication and computation sublinear in the vector length n.

4.1   Picking the Right Noise Distribution

While the high level intuition is simple, the (asymptotic and concrete) efficiency of this approach turns out to be extremely sensitive to the noise distribution. In the previous section, we described the protocol using the standard Bernoulli noise distribution, since it allows for a reduction to the most common flavor of LPN. However, Bernoulli noise is a poor choice for allowing efficient preprocessing; using a regular noise distribution insteads allows for a considerably more efficient preprocessing, without harming security.

In a bit more details, setting $\tau = \lambda/m$, a vector $\mathbf{r}_b \overset{\$}{\leftarrow} \mathsf{Ber}_\tau(\mathbb{F})^m$ can be written as the sum of $\approx \lambda$ unit vectors. Therefore, securely computing (shares of) the inner product between two such vectors reduces to securely computing λ^2 products of elements of $\mathbb{F}$, and λ^2 secure equality tests between $\log m$-size bitstrings. This is already sublinear in $m = O(n)$, but the λ^2 overhead can incur a significant slowdown.

Instead, we sample $\mathbf{r}_0$ and $\mathbf{r}_1$ from the regular noise distribution: $\mathbf{r}_0$ and $\mathbf{r}_1$ are concatenations of λ random unit vectors. The corresponding variant of LPN, regular LPN, is not known to be any weaker than LPN in our regime of parameters. Let us introduce a few notations: we denote $\mathbf{r}_b = (\mathbf{r}_b^{(1)} /\!/ \cdots /\!/ \mathbf{r}_b^{(\lambda)})$ for $b = 0, 1$, where the $\mathbf{r}_b^{(i)}$ are unit vectors. Furthermore, we denote by $j_{b,i}$ and $r_{b,i}$ the position and the value of the nonzero entry in $\mathbf{r}_b^{(i)}$. then, we have

$$\mathbf{r}_1^\mathsf{T} \cdot \mathbf{r}_0 = \sum_{i=1}^{\lambda} (\mathbf{r}_1^{(i)})^\mathsf{T} \cdot \mathbf{r}_0^{(i)} = \sum_{i=1}^{\lambda} \mathsf{EQ}(j_{0,i}, j_{1,i}) \cdot (r_{0,i} r_{1,i}),$$

where $\mathsf{EQ}(x,y)$ returns 1 if $x = y$ and 0 otherwise. Therefore, securely distributing shares of $\mathbf{r}_1^\mathsf{T} \cdot \mathbf{r}_0$ reduces (mostly) to performing λ secure equality tests (for the $\mathsf{EQ}(j_{0,i}, j_{1,i})$ terms) between $\log(m/\lambda)$-bit strings, and secure products over $\mathbb{F}$ (for the $r_{0,i}r_{1,i}$ terms), which is quadratically reduced compared to the cost for Bernoulli noise.

4.2 The Protocol

We describe below a protocol for inner product, following our previous discussion. We use the following building blocks:

- $\mathcal{F}_{\mathsf{EQ}}$ is an ideal functionality parametrized by a domain $[k]$ which, given two inputs $(x,y) \in [k]^2$, outputs random shares b_A, b_B to Alice and Bob of $\mathsf{EQ}(x,y)$;
- $\mathcal{F}_{\mathsf{OLE}}$ is an ideal functionality parametrized by a field $\mathbb{F}$ which, given two inputs $(x,y) \in \mathbb{F}^2$, outputs random shares z_A, z_B of $x \cdot y$ to Alice and Bob.

The protocol in the $(\mathcal{F}_{\mathsf{EQ}}, \mathcal{F}_{\mathsf{OLE}})$-hybrid model is given on Fig. 3.

Protocol $\Pi_{\mathsf{IP}}^{\mathsf{sh}}$

- **Setup.** Let $\mathbb{F}$ be a prime order field. Sample $H \xleftarrow{\$} \mathsf{Code}^\perp(m, k+n, \mathbb{F})$ and output $\mathsf{crs} = H$.
- **Preprocessing.** Alice and Bob each sample random pairs $(j_{0,i}, r_{0,i}) \xleftarrow{\$} [m/\lambda] \times \mathbb{F}^*$ and $(j_{1,i}, r_{1,i}) \xleftarrow{\$} [m/\lambda] \times \mathbb{F}^*$ for $i = 1$ to λ. Let $\mathbf{r}_0, \mathbf{r}_1$ denote the corresponding regular noise vectors.
  - The parties call $\mathcal{F}_{\mathsf{EQ}}$ on inputs $(j_{0,i}, j_{1,i}) \in [m/\lambda]^2$ for $i = 1$ to λ. Let $(b_{0,i}, b_{1,i})$ denote Alice's and Bob's outputs. Let $c_{0,i} \leftarrow (-1)^{b_{0,i}}$ and $c_{1,i} \leftarrow (-1)^{b_{1,i}}$ for $i = 1$ to λ. Note that $c_{0,i} \cdot c_{1,i} = (-1)^{\mathsf{EQ}(j_{0,i}, j_{1,i})}$.
  - If $\mathbb{F} \neq \mathbb{F}_2$, the parties call $\mathcal{F}_{\mathsf{OLE}}$ over $\mathbb{F}$ twice, on inputs $(r_{0,i}, r_{1,i})$ and $(c_{0,i} \cdot r_{0,i}, c_{1,i} \cdot r_{1,i})$, for $i = 1$ to λ. Let $(\alpha_{0,i}, \alpha_{1,i})$ and $(\beta_{0,i}, \beta_{1,i})$ denote their respective outputs in each instance. Note that $\alpha_{0,i} + \alpha_{1,i} = r_{0,i} \cdot r_{1,i}$, and $\beta_{0,i} + \beta_{1,i} = c_{0,i}r_{0,i} \cdot c_{1,i}r_{1,i} = (-1)^{\mathsf{EQ}(j_{0,i}, j_{1,i})} \cdot r_{0,i}r_{1,i}$.
  - If $\mathbb{F} \neq \mathbb{F}_2$, the parties compute $z_0 = \sum_{i=1}^\lambda (\alpha_{0,i} - \beta_{0,i})/2$ and $z_1 = \sum_{i=1}^\lambda (\alpha_{1,i} - \beta_{1,i})/2$. Note that $z_0 + z_1 = \sum_{i=1}^\lambda r_{0,i}r_{1,i} \cdot (1 - (-1)^{\mathsf{EQ}(j_{0,i}, j_{1,i})})/2 = \sum_{i=1}^\lambda r_{0,i}r_{1,i} \cdot \mathsf{EQ}(j_{0,i}, j_{1,i}) = \mathbf{r}_0^\mathsf{T} \cdot \mathbf{r}_1$.
  - Else, if $\mathbb{F} = \mathbb{F}_2$, the parties set $(z_0, z_1) \leftarrow (\bigoplus_{i=1}^\lambda b_{0,i}, \bigoplus_{i=1}^\lambda b_{1,i})$. Note that $z_0 \oplus z_1 = \bigoplus_{i=1}^\lambda \mathsf{EQ}(j_{0,i}, j_{1,i}) = \mathbf{r}_0^\mathsf{T} \cdot \mathbf{r}_1$ (since $r_{0,i} = r_{1,i} = 1$ for all i when $\mathbb{F} = \mathbb{F}_2$).
- **Online Phase.** Let $(\mathbf{u}_0, \mathbf{u}_1)$ be the inputs of Alice and Bob.
  - Alice sends $\mathsf{pk}_0 \leftarrow (\mathbf{u}_0 /\!/ \mathbf{0}) - H^\mathsf{T} \cdot \mathbf{r}_0$ and sets $\mathsf{sk}_0 \leftarrow \mathbf{r}_0$, while Bob samples $\mathbf{s} \xleftarrow{\$} \mathbb{F}^k$, sends $\mathsf{pk}_1 \leftarrow H \cdot (\mathbf{u}_1 /\!/ \mathbf{s}) + \mathbf{r}_1$ and sets $\mathsf{sk}_1 \leftarrow (\mathbf{u}_1 /\!/ \mathbf{s})$.
  - Alice outputs $x_0 = \mathsf{pk}_1^\mathsf{T} \cdot \mathsf{sk}_0 - z_0$ and Bob outputs $x_1 = \mathsf{pk}_0^\mathsf{T} \cdot \mathsf{sk}_1 - z_1$.

Fig. 3. A non-interactive inner-product protocol with semi-honest security $\Pi_{\mathsf{IP}}^{\mathsf{sh}}$ over $\mathbb{F}$ for vectors of length n

Theorem 9. *Let* $\mathbb{F}$ *be a prime order field and* $\mathsf{Code}^{\perp}$ *be a nice code. Assume that the regular* $\mathsf{dual}\text{-}\mathsf{LPN}^{m}_{m-(k+n),\tau}(\mathbb{F})$ *assumption with respect to* $\mathsf{Code}^{\perp}$, *and the (primal) regular* $\mathsf{LPN}^{m}_{k,\tau}(\mathbb{F})$ *assumption with respect to* $\mathsf{Code}^{\perp}_{\mathsf{right}}$ *both hold. Then protocol on Fig. 3 securely realizes the inner product functionality* $\mathcal{F}_{\mathsf{IP}}(\mathbb{F}, n)$ *from Fig. 4 in the* $(\mathcal{F}_{\mathsf{EQ}}, \mathcal{F}_{\mathsf{OLE}})$*-hybrid model with semi-honest security and static corruption.*

Functionality $\mathcal{F}_{\mathsf{IP}}(\mathbb{F}, n,)$

The functionality $\mathcal{F}_{\mathsf{IP}}$ is parametrized by a field $\mathbb{F}$, and a vector length n. It interacts with two parties Alice and Bob, and an adversary $\mathcal{A}$. On input $(\mathsf{Input}, \mathbf{u} \in \mathbb{F}_q^n)$ from Alice and $(\mathsf{Input}, \mathbf{v} \in \mathbb{F}_q^n)$ from Bob, the functionality $\mathcal{F}_{\mathsf{IP}}$ proceeds as follows:

- If both parties are honest, sample $\alpha, \beta \in \mathbb{F}_q$ at random such that $\mathbf{u}^{\mathsf{T}} \cdot \mathbf{v} = \alpha + \beta$
- If Alice is corrupted, wait for a message $(\mathsf{Output}, \alpha \in \mathbb{F}_q)$ from $\mathcal{A}$ and set $\beta = \mathbf{u}^{\mathsf{T}} \cdot \mathbf{v} - \alpha$.
- If Bob is corrupted, wait for a message $(\mathsf{Output}, \beta \in \mathbb{F}_q)$ from the adversary and set $\alpha = \mathbf{u}^{\mathsf{T}} \cdot \mathbf{v} - \beta$.

The functionality outputs α to Alice and β to Bob, and then halts.

Fig. 4. Ideal functionality $\mathcal{F}_{\mathsf{IP}}$ for inner product between vectors over $\mathbb{F}^n$.

Proof. **Case 0: both parties are honest.** We first consider the case where no party is corrupted. Then, it follows by construction that $z_0 + z_1 = \mathbf{r}_0^{\mathsf{T}} \cdot \mathbf{r}_1$. Furthermore, we established previously in the proof of Theorem 7 that $\mathsf{pk}_1^{\mathsf{T}} \cdot \mathsf{sk}_0 + \mathsf{pk}_0^{\mathsf{T}} \cdot \mathsf{sk}_1 = \mathbf{u}_0^{\mathsf{T}} \cdot \mathbf{u}_1 + \mathbf{r}_0^{\mathsf{T}} \cdot \mathbf{r}_1$ (the online phase of the protocol is identical to an execution of Encode and Decode; only the distribution of $\mathbf{r}_0, \mathbf{r}_1$ changes). It follows that the outputs of Alice and Bob form additive shares of $\mathbf{u}_0^{\mathsf{T}} \cdot \mathbf{u}_1$ (with probability 1).

Case 1: Alice is Corrupted. Assume now that Alice is corrupted, with input $\mathbf{u}_0$. The simulator Sim activates $\mathcal{F}_{\mathsf{IP}}(\mathbb{F}, n)$ on behalf of Alice in the ideal world by sending $(\mathsf{Input}, \mathbf{u}_0)$. In the real world, it plays honestly the role of Bob in the preprocessing phase, emulates the answer of the functionalities $\mathcal{F}_{\mathsf{EQ}}$ and $\mathcal{F}_{\mathsf{OLE}}$ by returning either a random bit or a random element of $\mathbb{F}$, and stores the queries of Alice to the functionalities and the output z_0 that she computes from the answers to her queries. Sim extracts the $j_{0,i}$ from Alice's calls to $\mathcal{F}_{\mathsf{EQ}}$ and the $r_{0,i}$ from her calls to $\mathcal{F}_{\mathsf{OLE}}$, and reconstructs $\mathbf{r}_0 = \mathsf{sk}_0$. Sim emulates Bob in the online phase by sending $\mathsf{pk}_1 \xleftarrow{\$} \mathbb{F}^m$, and sets $x_0 \leftarrow \mathsf{pk}_1^{\mathsf{T}} \cdot \mathsf{sk}_0 - z_0$. Eventually, Sim sends (Output, x_0) to $\mathcal{F}_{\mathsf{IP}}(\mathbb{F}, n)$.

It remains to argue why the simulation is indistinguishable from an honest execution of the protocol. Observe that the behavior of Sim is perfectly indistinguishable to that of Bob, except that it sends $\mathsf{pk}_1 \xleftarrow{\$} \mathbb{F}^m$ instead of $\mathsf{pk}_1 \leftarrow H \cdot (\mathbf{u}_1 /\!/ \mathbf{s}) + \mathbf{r}_1$. Since the preprocessing phase does not leak any information about $\mathbf{r}_1$ (the answers of $\mathcal{F}_{\mathsf{EQ}}$ and $\mathcal{F}_{\mathsf{OLE}}$ to Alice being uniformly random by definition) and Sim does not need $\mathbf{r}_1$ to emulate these functionalities, the same sequence of games as in the proof of Theorem 7 shows that the advantage in distinguishing pk_1 from a uniformly random element in $\mathbb{F}^m$ is negligible under the (regular, primal) $\mathsf{LPN}^m_{k,\lambda/m}$ assumption with respect to Code.

Case 2: Bob is Corrupted. Assume now that Bob is corrupted, with input $\mathbf{u}_1$. Sim plays in the preprocessing phase and interacts with $\mathcal{F}_{\mathsf{IP}}(\mathbb{F}, n)$ in a symmetrical way, extracting the $(j_{1,i}, r_{1,i})$ and reconstructing the vector $\mathbf{r}_1$ and the value z_1. Sim emulates Alice in the online phase by sending $\mathsf{pk}_0 \stackrel{\$}{\leftarrow} \mathbb{F}^m$. Upon receiving pk_1 from Bob, Sim extracts $\mathsf{sk}_1 = (\mathbf{u}_1/\!\!/\mathbf{s})$ by solving $\mathsf{pk}_1 - \mathbf{r}_1 = H \cdot \mathbf{X}$ and parsing the solution $\mathbf{X}$ as $\mathsf{sk}_1 = (\mathbf{u}_1/\!\!/\mathbf{s})$ (which is guaranteed to be well-formed since Bob is semi honest). Eventually, Sim sets $x_1 \leftarrow \mathsf{pk}_0^\mathsf{T} \cdot \mathsf{sk}_1 - z_1$ and sends (Output, x_1) to $\mathcal{F}_{\mathsf{IP}}(\mathbb{F}, n)$.

As above, proving indistinguishability from an honest execution reduces to proving that $\mathsf{pk}_0 \stackrel{\$}{\leftarrow} \mathbb{F}^m$ is indistinguishable from setting $\mathsf{pk}_0 \leftarrow (\mathbf{u}_0/\!\!/\mathbf{0}) - H^\mathsf{T} \cdot \mathbf{r}_0$, which can be shown (since $\mathbf{r}_0$ is perfectly hidden from Bob), using the same sequence of games as in the proof of Theorem 7, to follow from the (regular) $\mathsf{dual\text{-}LPN}^m_{m-(k+n),\lambda/m}$ assumption with respect to Code.

4.3 Variant: Replacing λ Calls to $\mathcal{F}_{\mathsf{OLE}}$ by 2λ Calls to $\mathcal{F}_{\mathsf{OT}}$

Let $\mathcal{F}_{\mathsf{OT}}(\mathbb{F})$ be the oblivious transfer functionality over $\mathbb{F}$: on input $(s_0, s_1) \in \mathbb{F}^2$ from the sender and a bit b from the receiver, it outputs s_b to the receiver and nothing to the sender.

In the protocol of Fig. 3, the parties with shares $(b_{0,i}, b_{1,i})$ of $\mathsf{EQ}(j_{0,i}, j_{1,i})$ and values $(r_{0,i}, r_{1,i}) \in \mathbb{F}^2$ must compute additive shares of $(b_{0,i} \oplus b_{1,i}) \cdot r_{0,i} r_{1,i}$, which they do using two calls to $\mathcal{F}_{\mathsf{OLE}}$. We provide an alternative instantiation, which uses one call to $\mathcal{F}_{\mathsf{OLE}}$, and two additional calls to $\mathcal{F}_{\mathsf{OT}}$:

- Alice and Bob call $\mathcal{F}_{\mathsf{OLE}}$ on inputs $(r_{0,i}, r_{1,i}) \in \mathbb{F}^2$ and obtain additive shares $(\alpha_{0,i}, \alpha_{1,i})$ of their product.
- Alice and Bob perform two oblivious transfers in parallel. In the first OT, Alice plays the sender with inputs $(b_{0,i} \cdot \alpha_{0,i} + r_A, (1 - b_{0,i}) \cdot \alpha_{0,i} + r_A)$ for a random mask r_A, and Bob plays the receiver with input $b_{1,i}$. Concretely, Alice and Bob obtain this way shares of $(b_{0,i} \oplus b_{1,i}) \cdot \alpha_{0,i}$ (where Alice's share is r_A). In the other direction, Bob plays the role of the sender, using a random mask r_B, and Alice of the receiver with input $b_{0,i}$; Alice and Bob obtain additive shares of $(b_{0,i} \oplus b_{1,i}) \cdot \alpha_{1,i}$. Summing their shares, Alice and Bob do indeed obtain shares of $(b_{0,i} \oplus b_{1,i}) \cdot r_{0,i} r_{1,i}$.

4.4 Instantiating $\mathcal{F}_{\mathsf{EQ}}$ and $\mathcal{F}_{\mathsf{OLE}}$

With the above variant, the preprocessing boils down to λ invocations of $\mathcal{F}_{\mathsf{EQ}}$ on $\log(m/\lambda)$-bit strings, λ invocations of $\mathcal{F}_{\mathsf{OLE}}$ over $\mathbb{F}$, and 2λ invocations of $\mathcal{F}_{\mathsf{OT}}$ on $\log |\mathbb{F}|$-bit strings. There exists numerous options to implement the $\mathcal{F}_{\mathsf{EQ}}$ functionality. In our range of parameters, we estimate that the most efficient solution is the protocol of [27]. For equality test over ℓ-bit strings, it requires $\ell + o(\ell)$ oblivious transfers of $\log \ell$-bit strings, and $O(\log^* \ell)$ rounds of communication. Concretely, setting for example $\lambda = 120$ and $m = 3n$, for an inner product between string of length at most $n = 2^{20}$, the protocol of [27] can be instantiated either with 15 OTs of 16-bit strings and 14 OTs of bits in two rounds, or with 15 OTs of 16-bit strings, 4 OTs of 4-bit strings, and 2 OTs of bits, in three rounds (and no additional communication beyond the OTs). For $\mathcal{F}_{\mathsf{OLE}}$, the protocol of [36] requires $\log |\mathbb{F}|$ OTs per OLE over $\mathbb{F}$ (while recent OLE protocols such as [20] are much more efficient, their efficiency improvement "kicks in" only for a large enough number of OLE). With these choices of protocol, the full preprocessing boils down to $\lambda \cdot (\log(m/\lambda) + \log |\mathbb{F}| + 2)$ oblivious transfers.

Overall, setting $m = O(n)$, the communication of the preprocessing phase boils down to $O(\lambda \cdot (\log n + \log |\mathbb{F}|))$ oblivious transfer of small strings ($O(\log n)$-bit or $\log |\mathbb{F}|$-bit strings), which leads to a logarithmic communication in the vector length n. For example, using the standard instantiation for short string oblivious transfer [41], computing the inner product between two strings of length 2^{20} over a 32-bit field requires about $5 \cdot 10^5 \approx 0.5 \cdot n$ bits of communication, adding only a small overhead to the entire communication of the protocol. Using recent advances in silent OT extension [17,28], this overhead can be further reduced by a factor four.

5   Malicious Security

In this section, we enhance our protocol from Sect. 4 to withstand attacks from malicious adversaries.

5.1   Guaranteeing the Success of Extraction

In the malicious model, the parties may not follow the specifications of the protocol; in particular, they may not use their prescribed input. Therefore, to make the protocol from Fig. 3 secure against malicious behavior, the simulator must have a mean to extract the input of the corrupted party. When Alice is corrupted, since Sim emulates the preprocessing and stores her noise vector $\mathbf{r}_0$, the *effective input* $\mathbf{u}_0$ used by Alice can be extracted by computing $\mathsf{pk}_0 + H^\intercal \cdot \mathbf{r}_0$, and parsing it as $(\mathbf{u}_0 /\!/ \mathbf{0})$. However, the success of this extraction is only guaranteed if we can ensure that pk_0 will always be well-formed (i.e. the "bottom half" of pk_0 is of the form $M \cdot \mathbf{r}_0$ for a sparse $\mathbf{r}_0$, where M is the bottom half of $H^\intercal$). Similarly, if Bob is corrupted, Sim extracts $\mathbf{u}_1$ by solving the linear system $H \cdot \mathbf{X} = \mathsf{pk}_1 - \mathbf{r}_1$ to get $(\mathbf{u}_1 /\!/ \mathbf{s})$. However, this is an overdetermined system of equations which is not guaranteed to have a solution, and extraction will again succeed only if we can guarantee that pk_0 is well-formed (i.e., this system has a solution).

To guarantee the success of extraction, we let Alice and Bob add zero-knowledge proofs that their public keys $\mathsf{pk}_0, \mathsf{pk}_1$ are well-formed. With simple manipulations, it is easy to show that in both cases, this reduces to proving that a vector $\mathbf{v}$ is of the form $M \cdot \mathbf{e}$, where M is a public compressive matrix, and $\mathbf{e}$ is a secret sparse noise vector – i.e., this reduces to proving knowledge of a preimage in an instance of the syndrome decoding problem for the code with parity-check matrix M, which is a well-studied problem [2,23,53]. Unfortunately, existing solutions are prohibitively expensive in our setting: they require $O(\kappa \cdot m)$ communication, where κ is a statistical security parameter (which stems from parallel repetitions of an underlying zero-knowledge proof with constant soundness error, e.g. $2/3$ in Stern's scheme [53]) and m is the code dimension. Since our protocol operates in the high-dimension, low-noise setting, this causes a huge blowup to the total communication and computation.

5.2 A New Almost-Zero-Knowledge Proof for Low-Noise Syndrome Decoding

As a contribution of independent interest, we therefore design a new zero-knowledge proof system for the syndrome decoding problem, which is especially suited for instances with large dimension and low noise. For a syndrome decoding instance of dimension ℓ and a noise rate of λ/ℓ, our protocol boils down essentially to $O(\lambda \cdot \log \ell)$ actively secure oblivious transfers and λ OLE. On the downside, unlike Stern's protocol, our zero-knowledge proof is not an identification scheme: it is private coin and cannot be made non-interactive using the Fiat-Shamir heuristic.

Our approach follows the intuition underlying a recent line of work [9,11, 30,56] on efficient zero-knowledge proofs from pseudorandom correlation generators [16–18]. However, our goal is fundamentally different, since these works target linear communication zero-knowledge proofs for general (arithmetic) circuits; on the other hand, we construct a *sublinear communication* zero-knowledge proof for a specific problem.

Intuition. A recent line of work initiated in [16] has developed pseudorandom correlation generators (PCG) for the vector-OLE (VOLE) correlation. At a high level, a PCG for a VOLE correlation allows to distributively generate additive shares of $\Delta \cdot \mathbf{v}$, where Δ is a (chosen) element of $\mathbb{F}$ known to one of the parties, and $\mathbf{v}$ is a (long) pseudorandom vector over $\mathbb{F}$, known to the other party. We do not directly build on PCG, but observe that the main component in their construction is a protocol that relies on *puncturable pseudorandom functions* (PPRF) to distributively generate, with low communication, additive shares of $\Delta \cdot \mathbf{e}$ for a *sparse, regular* noise vector $\mathbf{e}$.

We rely on this PPRF-based protocol to authenticate the regular noise vector $\mathbf{e}$ (i.e., the witness of the prover) with low communication overhead, using an information-theoretic MAC Δ known to the verifier. Due to the regular structure of $\mathbf{e}$, this boils down to distributively generating and locally concatenating shares of $\Delta \cdot \mathbf{e}_i$ for $i = 1$ to λ, where the $\mathbf{e}_i$ are unit vectors (let j_i be the index of their nonzero entry, and e_i be the corresponding value). Such a protocol is called a *single point vector OLE*. We briefly recall how such shares are generated with sublinear communication:

– The verifier samples Δ, and a PRF key K for a PRF $\{\mathsf{PRF}_K : [\ell/\lambda] \mapsto \mathbb{F}\}_K$.
– The parties execute an interactive protocol to securely generate $K\{j_i\}$ (the key K punctured at j_i). Using variants of the Doerner-shelat protocol [31] on top of the GGM puncturable PRF [37], this requires $O(\log \ell)$ invocations of an oblivious transfer protocol.
– The prover obliviously receive the value $\mathsf{PRF}_K(j_i) + \Delta \cdot e_i$, using a single OLE over $\mathbb{F}$.
– In the malicious setting, when several instances are executed, additional consistency checks are required to guarantee that Δ remains the same across all executions. An efficient protocol for this task was given in [54], with minimal overhead compared to the semi-honest protocol.

Let $(\mathbf{q}_0, \mathbf{q}_1)$ denote the additive shares of $\Delta \cdot \mathbf{e}$ generated using the above protocol. To check that $\mathbf{v}$ is indeed of the form $M \cdot \mathbf{e}$, the verifier sends a random vector ρ to the prover, who replies with the value $\mathsf{ver}_0 = -\rho^{\mathsf{T}} \cdot (M \cdot \mathbf{q}_0) \in \mathbb{F}$. Then, the verifier sets $\mathsf{ver}_1 \leftarrow \rho^{\mathsf{T}} \cdot (M \cdot \mathbf{q}_1 - \Delta \cdot \mathbf{v})$ and check that $\mathsf{ver}_0 = \mathsf{ver}_1$.

Observe that $\mathsf{ver}_1 - \mathsf{ver}_0 = \rho^{\mathsf{T}} \cdot (M \cdot \mathbf{q}_1 - \Delta \cdot \mathbf{v} + M \cdot \mathbf{q}_0) = \rho^{\mathsf{T}} \cdot (M \cdot (\Delta \cdot \mathbf{e}) - \Delta \cdot \mathbf{v}) = 0$ if $M \cdot \mathbf{e} = \mathbf{v}$. Soundness will rely on the Schwarz-Zippel lemma to show that when $M \cdot \mathbf{e} \neq \mathbf{v}$, causing $\mathsf{ver}_0 = \mathsf{ver}_1$ is as hard as guessing Δ, which can happen only with probability $1/|\mathbb{F}|$ since Δ is perfectly hidden from the prover. This readily suffices when $\mathbb{F}$ is exponentially large. For smaller fields, we simply sample Δ from an appropriate extension field $\mathbb{F}'$ of $\mathbb{F}$ such that $|\mathbb{F}'| \geq 2^\kappa$ for some statistical security parameter κ; the rest of the protocol is identical, except that the parties must use a PRF from $[\ell/\lambda]$ to $\mathbb{F}'$, and execute the OLE's over $\mathbb{F}'$.

Zero-Knowledge Versus Almost-Zero-Knowledge. The above blueprint actually leads to a true zero-knowledge proof system with sublinear communication, when instantiated with a maliciously secure sublinear protocol for single point vector OLE. While it is possible to construct such protocols, recent works [17,54] have observed that one can achieve a much greater efficiency by slightly relaxing the single point VOLE functionality. In this relaxation, the verifier is allowed to learn roughly one bit of leakage about the noise vector $\mathbf{e}$. When instantiating our construction with the protocol of [54] (the state-of-the-art protocol of this line of work), the protocol we get is therefore not truly zero-knowledge. Nevertheless, it still suffices to construct a maliciously secure inner product protocol, which is our end goal, at the cost of relying on the *LPN with static leakage* assumption (first put forth in [17]), which states (informally) that LPN remains secure given one bit of leakage about the noise vector.

The Zero-Knowledge Proof. Since, for better efficiency, we do not achieve full-fledged zero-knowledge but only a relaxed version which suffices in our specific context, we do not provide here an isolated description of the zero-knowledge proof, and directly integrate it into our maliciously secure protocol. However, for the sake of completeness, we provide a description of the proof system in isolation (with and without the relaxation) in the full version of this paper.

5.3 Maliciously Secure Inner Product from LPN with Static Leakage

The full protocol, integrating the procedure for checking that pk_0 and pk_1 are well-formed, is described on Fig. 6, in the $\mathcal{F}_{\mathsf{pre}}^{\mathsf{mal}}$-hybrid model. These checks require the parties to have access to authenticated versions of the noise vectors $\mathbf{r}_0, \mathbf{r}_1$; this authentication procedure is executed in a preprocessing phase. The ideal functionality $\mathcal{F}_{\mathsf{pre}}^{\mathsf{mal}}$ describing the preprocessing phase is represented on Fig. 5. It follows closely the single-point vector-OLE functionality from [54], but enhances it to also distribute the inner product between pairs of single-point VOLEs. Similarly, our instantiation of this functionality will build upon the protocol of [54].

Functionality $\mathcal{F}_{\mathsf{pre}}^{\mathsf{mal}}(\mathbb{F}, \mathbb{F}', n)$

The functionality is parametrized by a field $\mathbb{F}$ and an extension field $\mathbb{F}'$ of $\mathbb{F}$, as well as a vector length n, which is assumed to be a power of 2.

Initialize. Upon receiving Input from Alice and Bob, sample $\Delta, \Delta' \xleftarrow{\$} \mathbb{F}'$ if both Alice and Bob are honest. Otherwise, if Bob is corrupted, receive Δ' from the adversary and sample $\Delta \xleftarrow{\$} \mathbb{F}'$; if Alice is corrupted, receive Δ from the adversary and sample $\Delta' \xleftarrow{\$} \mathbb{F}'$. Output Δ to Alice, Δ' to Bob, and ignore all subsequent Input commands.

Extend. Upon receiving $(\mathsf{Extend}, \mathbf{x})$ from Alice and $(\mathsf{Extend}, \mathbf{x}')$ from Bob, where $(\mathbf{x}, \mathbf{x}')$ are unit vectors over $\mathbb{F}^n$, do:

1. If Bob is honest, sample $\mathbf{y} \xleftarrow{\$} (\mathbb{F}')^n$. Otherwise, receive $\mathbf{y} \in (\mathbb{F}')^n$ from the adversary. Similarly, if Alice is honest, sample $\mathbf{y}' \xleftarrow{\$} (\mathbb{F}')^n$. Otherwise, receive $\mathbf{y}' \in (\mathbb{F}')^n$ from the adversary.
2. If Alice is honest, compute $\mathbf{z} \leftarrow \mathbf{y} + \Delta \cdot \mathbf{x}$. Otherwise, receive $\mathbf{z}$ from the adversary and recompute $\mathbf{y} \leftarrow \mathbf{z} - \Delta \cdot \mathbf{x}$. Similarly, if Bob is honest, compute $\mathbf{z}' \leftarrow \mathbf{y}' + \Delta' \cdot \mathbf{x}'$. Otherwise, receive $\mathbf{z}'$ from the adversary and recompute $\mathbf{y}' \leftarrow \mathbf{z}' - \Delta' \cdot \mathbf{x}'$.
3. If party $P \in \{A, B\}$, receive a set $I \subseteq [1, n]$ from the adversary. Let $j \in [1, n]$ be the index of the nonzero entry of $\mathbf{x}$ (if $P = B$) or $\mathbf{x}'$ (if $P = A$). If $j \in I$, send success to P and continue. Otherwise, send abort to both parties and abort.
4. If both parties are honest, set (w_0, w_1) to be random shares over $\mathbb{F}$ of $\mathbf{x}^\mathsf{T} \cdot \mathbf{x}'$. Otherwise, if Alice (resp. Bob) is corrupted, receive w_0 (resp. w_1) from the adversary, and set $w_1 \leftarrow \mathbf{x}^\mathsf{T} \cdot \mathbf{x}' - w_0$ (resp. $w_0 \leftarrow \mathbf{x}^\mathsf{T} \cdot \mathbf{x}' - w_1$).
5. Send $(\mathbf{z}, \mathbf{y}', w_0)$ to Alice and $(\mathbf{y}, \mathbf{z}', w_1)$ to Bob.

Global-key query. If party $P \in \{A, B\}$ is corrupted, receive $(\mathsf{guess}, \hat{\Delta})$ from the adversary with $\hat{\Delta} \in \mathbb{F}'$. If $\hat{\Delta} = \Delta$ and $P = A$, or if $\hat{\Delta} = \Delta'$ and $P = B$, send success to P and ignore any subsequent global-key query from P. Otherwise, send abort to both parties and abort.

Fig. 5. Ideal Functionality for the preprocessing step of maliciously secure inner product, parametrized by a field $\mathbb{F}$ with extension field $\mathbb{F}'$

Protocol $\Pi_{\mathsf{IP}}^{\mathsf{mal}}$

Let $\mathbb{F}'$ be the smallest extension field of $\mathbb{F}$ (possibly equal to $\mathbb{F}$) such that $|\mathbb{F}'| \geq 2^\kappa$, for a statistical security parameter κ. Fix parameters (k, m) as in the semi-honest protocol. Sample $H \xleftarrow{\$} \mathsf{Code}^{\perp}(m, k+n, \mathbb{F})$ and output $\mathsf{crs} = H \in \mathbb{F}^{m \times (k+n)}$.

Preprocessing. Alice and Bob send Input to $\mathcal{F}_{\mathsf{pre}}^{\mathsf{mal}}(\mathbb{F}, \mathbb{F}', m)$, and receive respective outputs $(\Delta, \Delta') \in \mathbb{F}' \times \mathbb{F}'$.

- Alice and Bob each sample random pairs $(j_{0,i}, r_{0,i}) \xleftarrow{\$} [m/\lambda] \times \mathbb{F}^*$ and $(j_{1,i}, r_{1,i}) \xleftarrow{\$} [m/\lambda] \times \mathbb{F}^*$ for $i = 1$ to λ. Let $\mathbf{r}_b = \mathbf{r}_b^{(1)} /\!/ \cdots /\!/ \mathbf{r}_b^{(\lambda)}$ for $b = 0, 1$ denote the corresponding regular noise vectors.
- Alice and Bob call the Extend command of $\mathcal{F}_{\mathsf{pre}}^{\mathsf{mal}}(\mathbb{F}, \mathbb{F}', m/\lambda)$ λ times, on respective inputs $(\mathbf{r}_0^{(i)}, \mathbf{r}_1^{(i)})$ for $i = 1$ to λ. Let $(\mathbf{z}_i, \mathbf{y}_i', w_{0,i})$ and $(\mathbf{z}_i', \mathbf{y}_i, w_{1,i})$ denote their outputs in the i-th instance respectively. Alice constructs $\mathbf{q}_0$ by concatenating all the $\mathbf{z}_i$, and $\mathbf{q}_0'$ by concatenating all the $\mathbf{y}_i'$. Similarly, Bob constructs $-\mathbf{q}_1$ by concatenating all the $\mathbf{z}_i'$, and $-\mathbf{q}_1'$ by concatenating all the $\mathbf{y}_i$. Eventually, Alice sets $z_0 \leftarrow \sum_i w_{0,i}$ and Bob sets $z_1 \leftarrow \sum_i w_{1,i}$. Note that by definition of $\mathcal{F}_{\mathsf{pre}}^{\mathsf{mal}}(\mathbb{F}, \mathbb{F}', m)$, it holds that $(\mathbf{q}_0, \mathbf{q}_1)$ form additive shares of $\Delta \cdot \mathbf{r}_1$, $(\mathbf{q}_0', \mathbf{q}_1')$ form additive shares of $\Delta' \cdot \mathbf{r}_0$, and (z_0, z_1) form additive shares of $\mathbf{r}_0^\mathsf{T} \mathbf{r}_1$.

Online Phase. Let $(\mathbf{u}_0, \mathbf{u}_1)$ be the inputs of Alice and Bob.

- Alice sends $\mathsf{pk}_0 \leftarrow (\mathbf{u}_0 /\!/ \mathbf{0}) - H^\mathsf{T} \cdot \mathbf{r}_0$ and sets $\mathsf{sk}_0 \leftarrow \mathbf{r}_0$, while Bob samples $\mathbf{s} \xleftarrow{\$} \mathbb{F}^k$, sends $\mathsf{pk}_1 \leftarrow H \cdot (\mathbf{u}_1 /\!/ \mathbf{s}) + \mathbf{r}_1$ and sets $\mathsf{sk}_1 \leftarrow (\mathbf{u}_1 /\!/ \mathbf{s})$. The following checks are performed in parallel:
- **Checking that pk_0 is well-formed:**
  - Let $M \in \mathbb{F}^{k \times m}$ be the last k rows of H^T. Note that the statement "there exists a vector $\mathbf{u}_0$ and a λ-regular vector $\mathbf{r}_0$ such that $\mathsf{pk}_0 = (\mathbf{u}_0 /\!/ \mathbf{0}) - H^\mathsf{T} \cdot \mathbf{r}_0$" is equivalent to "there exists a λ-regular vector $\mathbf{r}_0$ such that the last k coordinates of pk_0 are equal to $M \cdot \mathbf{r}_0$". Bob sends $K_0 \xleftarrow{\$} \{0,1\}^\lambda$ and both parties expand K_0 into $\rho_0 = (\mathsf{PRF}_{K_0}(0), \cdots, \mathsf{PRF}_{K_0}(k/\lambda)) \in (\mathbb{F}')^{1 \times k}$ using a PRF $\mathsf{PRF}: \{0,1\}^\lambda \mapsto \{0,1\}^\lambda$.
  - Alice sends $\mathsf{ver}_0 \leftarrow -\rho_0 \cdot (M \cdot \mathbf{q}_0')$. Bob aborts unless $\mathsf{ver}_0 = \rho_0 \cdot (M \cdot \mathbf{q}_1' - \Delta' \cdot \mathsf{pk}_0)$.
- **Checking that pk_1 is well-formed:**
  - Let $G \in \mathbb{F}^{(m-k-n) \times m}$ be a parity-check matrix of H. Note that the statement "there exists a vector $\mathbf{u}_1 /\!/ \mathbf{s}$ and a λ-regular vector $\mathbf{r}_0$ such that $\mathsf{pk}_1 = H \cdot (\mathbf{u}_1 /\!/ \mathbf{s}) + \mathbf{r}_1$" is equivalent to "there exists a λ-regular vector $\mathbf{r}_1$ such that $G \cdot \mathsf{pk}_1 = G \cdot \mathbf{r}_1$". Alice sends $K_1 \xleftarrow{\$} \{0,1\}^\lambda$ and both parties expand K_1 into $\rho_1 = (\mathsf{PRF}_{K_1}(0), \cdots, \mathsf{PRF}_{K_1}(k/\lambda)) \in (\mathbb{F}')^{1 \times (m-k-n)}$ using a PRF.
  - Bob sends $\mathsf{ver}_1' \leftarrow -\rho_1 \cdot (G \cdot \mathbf{q}_1)$. Alice aborts unless $\mathsf{ver}_1' = \rho_1 \cdot (G \cdot \mathbf{q}_0 - \Delta \cdot (G \cdot \mathsf{pk}_1))$.
- Alice outputs $x_0 = \mathsf{pk}_1^\mathsf{T} \cdot \mathsf{sk}_0 - z_0$ and Bob outputs $x_1 = \mathsf{pk}_0^\mathsf{T} \cdot \mathsf{sk}_1 - z_1$.

Fig. 6. A non-interactive inner-product protocol with malicious security $\Pi_{\mathsf{IP}}^{\mathsf{map}}$ over $\mathbb{F}$ for vectors of length n

5.4   Security Analysis

We first recall the LPN with static leakage assumption from [17,54]:

Definition 10 (Regular LPN with static leakage). *Fix a field* $\mathbb{F} = \mathbb{F}(\lambda)$, *dimension* $k = k(\lambda)$, *number of samples* $m = m(\lambda)$, *and noise rate* $\tau = \tau(\lambda)$. *The regular* $\mathsf{LPN}^m_{k,\tau}$ *assumption with static leakage with respect to* Code *holds if for every PPT algorithm* $\mathcal{A}$, *it holds that*

$$\left| \Pr[\mathsf{LPN\text{-}Succ}_{\mathcal{A}}(\lambda) = 1] - \frac{1}{2} \right| \leq \mathsf{negl}(\lambda),$$

where the experiment $\mathsf{LPN\text{-}Succ}_{\mathcal{A}}(\lambda)$ *is defined as follows:*

1. *Sample* $A \stackrel{\$}{\leftarrow} \mathsf{Code}(m, k, \mathbb{F}), \mathbf{s} \stackrel{\$}{\leftarrow} \mathbb{F}^k, \mathbf{e} \stackrel{\$}{\leftarrow} \mathsf{RN}_{\tau,m}(\mathbb{F})$, *and let* $(\alpha_1, \cdots, \alpha_{\tau m}) \in [1/\tau]^{\tau m}$ *denote the location of the nonzero entries of* $\mathbf{e}$. *Send* A *to* $\mathcal{A}$.
2. $\mathcal{A}$ *outputs* τm *subsets* $(I_1, \cdots, I_{\tau m})$ *of* $[1/\tau]$. *If* $\alpha_i \in I_i$ *for every* $i \leq \tau m$, *output* success *to* $\mathcal{A}$; *otherwise, abort the experiment and set the output to 0.*
3. *If the experiment did not abort, pick a random bit* $b \stackrel{\$}{\leftarrow} \{0,1\}$. *If* $b = 0$, *set* $\mathbf{u} \leftarrow A \cdot \mathbf{s} + \mathbf{e}$; *else, set* $\mathbf{u} \stackrel{\$}{\leftarrow} \mathbb{F}^m$. *Send* $\mathbf{u}$ *to* $\mathcal{A}$. *Output 1 if* $\mathcal{A}$ *answers with* b, *and 0 otherwise.*

We note that LPN with static leakage reduces to standard LPN assumption [17], but the reduction is not tight. Intuitively, the assumption allows the adversary to obtain one bit of leakage on $\mathbf{e}$ on average, which should reduce bit security by one bit at most. Since the reduction to LPN induces a much larger loss, we define this assumption as an independent assumption and use it with the same concrete parameter as for LPN.

On the Use of a PRF. The checks in the online phase require the parties to exchange long random strings ρ_0, ρ_1. To reduce communication, this is done by exchanging short keys, which the parties locally stretch into long pseudorandom strings by evaluating a PRF on a priori fixed inputs: $\rho_b \leftarrow (\mathsf{PRF}_{K_b}(0), \cdots, \mathsf{PRF}_{K_b}(k/\lambda))$, assuming that PRF has λ-bit outputs. It is a well-known result that any statistical test that succeeds with high probability for a random string, such as our application of the Schwarz-Zippel lemma, must succeed with comparable probability when evaluating a PRF on inputs fixed before the key was sampled, since any noticeable difference can be turned into an efficient distinguisher against the PRF.

Theorem 11. *Let* $\mathsf{Code}^\perp$ *be a nice code. Assume that the* $\mathsf{dual\text{-}LPN}^m_{m-(k+n),\tau}(\mathbb{F})$ *assumption with static leakage with respect to* $\mathsf{Code}^\perp$, *and the (primal)* $\mathsf{LPN}^m_{k,\tau}(\mathbb{F})$ *assumption with static leakage with respect to* $\mathsf{Code}^\perp_{\mathsf{right}}$ *both hold. Then the protocol* $\pi^{\mathsf{mal}}_{\mathsf{IP}}$ *securely computes the inner product functionality* $\mathcal{F}_{\mathsf{IP}}$ *with security against malicious adversaries in the* $\mathcal{F}^{\mathsf{mal}}_{\mathsf{pre}}$*-hybrid model.*

Due to lack of space, we defer the proof of Theorem 11 to the full version of this paper.

Efficiency. Compared to the semi-honest protocol, the online phase of Fig. 6 adds two rounds of interaction to the protocol, as well as 2λ bits (for exchanging the seeds) and two elements of $\mathbb{F}'$ (hence, the overall increase in communication is essentially negligible). Regarding computation, the cost of the check that pk_0 is well-formed is dominated by a multiplication by the matrix $M \cdot \mathbb{F}^{k \times m}$, which (setting $k = n$ for concreteness) is about twice faster than a multiplication by H. The cost of checking that pk_1 is well-formed is dominated by a multiplication by the parity-check matrix G of H for Bob (resp. two multiplications by G for Alice), which is about the same cost as a multiplication by H. Therefore, the computational cost of the maliciously secure protocol is about twice that of the semi-honest protocol.

Implementing the Malicious Preprocessing Functionality. Due to lack of space, we defer the discussion on how to implement the malicious preprocessing functionality to the full version of this paper.

References

1. Aguilar, C., Blazy, O., Deneuville, J.C., Gaborit, P., Zémor, G.: Efficient encryption from random quasi-cyclic codes. Cryptology ePrint Archive, Report 2016/1194 (2016). https://eprint.iacr.org/2016/1194
2. Aguilar, C., Gaborit, P., Schrek, J.: A new zero-knowledge code based identification scheme with reduced communication. In: 2011 IEEE Information Theory Workshop, pp. 648–652. IEEE (2011)
3. Aguilar-Melchor, C., Blazy, O., Deneuville, J.C., Gaborit, P., Zémor, G.: Efficient encryption from random quasi-cyclic codes. IEEE Trans. Inf. Theor. **64**(5), 3927–3943 (2018)
4. Alekhnovich, M.: More on average case vs approximation complexity. In: 44th FOCS, pp. 298–307. IEEE Computer Society Press, October 2003
5. Applebaum, B., Damgård, I., Ishai, Y., Nielsen, M., Zichron, L.: Secure arithmetic computation with constant computational overhead. In: Katz, J., Shacham, H. (eds.) CRYPTO 2017. LNCS, vol. 10401, pp. 223–254. Springer, Cham (2017). https://doi.org/10.1007/978-3-319-63688-7_8
6. Aragon, N., et al.: BIKE: bit flipping key encapsulation (2017)
7. Arora, S., Ge, R.: New algorithms for learning in presence of errors. In: Aceto, L., Henzinger, M., Sgall, J. (eds.) ICALP 2011. LNCS, vol. 6755, pp. 403–415. Springer, Heidelberg (2011). https://doi.org/10.1007/978-3-642-22006-7_34
8. Bansal, A., Chen, T., Zhong, S.: Privacy preserving back-propagation neural network learning over arbitrarily partitioned data. Neural Comput. Appl. **20**(1), 143–150 (2011)
9. Baum, C., Braun, L., Munch-Hansen, A., Scholl, P.: Appenzeller to brie: efficient zero-knowledge proofs for mixed-mode arithmetic and Z2k (2021)
10. Baum, C., Escudero, D., Pedrouzo-Ulloa, A., Scholl, P., Troncoso-Pastoriza, J.R.: Efficient protocols for oblivious linear function evaluation from ring-LWE. In: Galdi, C., Kolesnikov, V. (eds.) SCN 2020. LNCS, vol. 12238, pp. 130–149. Springer, Cham (2020). https://doi.org/10.1007/978-3-030-57990-6_7

11. Baum, C., Malozemoff, A.J., Rosen, M.B., Scholl, P.: Mac′n′Cheese: zero-knowledge proofs for boolean and arithmetic circuits with nested disjunctions. In: Malkin, T., Peikert, C. (eds.) CRYPTO 2021. LNCS, vol. 12828, pp. 92–122. Springer, Cham (2021). https://doi.org/10.1007/978-3-030-84259-8_4

12. Becker, A., Joux, A., May, A., Meurer, A.: Decoding random binary linear codes in $2^{n/20}$: how $1 + 1 = 0$ improves information set decoding. In: Pointcheval, D., Johansson, T. (eds.) EUROCRYPT 2012. LNCS, vol. 7237, pp. 520–536. Springer, Heidelberg (2012). https://doi.org/10.1007/978-3-642-29011-4_31

13. Bernstein, D.J., Lange, T., Peters, C.: Smaller decoding exponents: ball-collision decoding. In: Rogaway, P. (ed.) CRYPTO 2011. LNCS, vol. 6841, pp. 743–760. Springer, Heidelberg (2011). https://doi.org/10.1007/978-3-642-22792-9_42

14. Blum, A., Kalai, A., Wasserman, H.: Noise-tolerant learning, the parity problem, and the statistical query model. J. ACM (JACM) 50(4), 506–519 (2003)

15. Bordewijk, J.L.: Inter-reciprocity applied to electrical networks. Appl. Sci. Res. Sect. A 6(1), 1–74 (1957)

16. Boyle, E., Couteau, G., Gilboa, N., Ishai, Y.: Compressing vector OLE. In: Lie, D., Mannan, M., Backes, M., Wang, X. (eds.) ACM CCS 2018, pp. 896–912. ACM Press, October 2018

17. Boyle, E., et al.: Efficient two-round OT extension and silent non-interactive secure computation. In: Cavallaro, L., Kinder, J., Wang, X., Katz, J. (eds.) ACM CCS 2019, pp. 291–308. ACM Press, November 2019

18. Boyle, E., Couteau, G., Gilboa, N., Ishai, Y., Kohl, L., Scholl, P.: Efficient pseudo-random correlation generators: silent OT extension and more. In: Boldyreva, A., Micciancio, D. (eds.) CRYPTO 2019. LNCS, vol. 11694, pp. 489–518. Springer, Cham (2019). https://doi.org/10.1007/978-3-030-26954-8_16

19. Boyle, E., Couteau, G., Gilboa, N., Ishai, Y., Kohl, L., Scholl, P.: Correlated pseudorandom functions from variable-density LPN. In: 61st FOCS, pp. 1069–1080. IEEE Computer Society Press (2020)

20. Boyle, E., Couteau, G., Gilboa, N., Ishai, Y., Kohl, L., Scholl, P.: Efficient pseudorandom correlation generators from ring-LPN. In: Micciancio, D., Ristenpart, T. (eds.) CRYPTO 2020. LNCS, vol. 12171, pp. 387–416. Springer, Cham (2020). https://doi.org/10.1007/978-3-030-56880-1_14

21. Boyle, E., Kohl, L., Scholl, P.: Homomorphic secret sharing from lattices without FHE. In: Ishai, Y., Rijmen, V. (eds.) EUROCRYPT 2019. LNCS, vol. 11477, pp. 3–33. Springer, Cham (2019). https://doi.org/10.1007/978-3-030-17656-3_1

22. de Castro, L., Juvekar, C., Vaikuntanathan, V.: Fast vector oblivious linear evaluation from ring learning with errors. Cryptology ePrint Archive, Report 2020/685 (2020). https://eprint.iacr.org/2020/685

23. Cayrel, P.-L., Véron, P., El Yousfi Alaoui, S.M.: A zero-knowledge identification scheme based on the q-ary syndrome decoding problem. In: Biryukov, A., Gong, G., Stinson, D.R. (eds.) SAC 2010. LNCS, vol. 6544, pp. 171–186. Springer, Heidelberg (2011). https://doi.org/10.1007/978-3-642-19574-7_12

24. Chen, M.S., Cheng, C.M., Kuo, P.C., Li, W.D., Yang, B.Y.: Multiplying boolean polynomials with Frobenius Partitions in additive fast Fourier Transform. arXiv preprint arXiv:1803.11301 (2018)

25. Chen, T., Zhong, S.: Privacy-preserving backpropagation neural network learning. IEEE Trans. Neural Netw. 20(10), 1554–1564 (2009)

26. Cheng, Q., Gao, C.Z.: A cloud aided privacy-preserving profile matching scheme in mobile social networks. In: 2017 IEEE International Conference on Computational Science and Engineering (CSE) and IEEE International Conference on Embedded and Ubiquitous Computing (EUC), vol. 2, pp. 195–198. IEEE (2017)

27. Couteau, G.: New protocols for secure equality test and comparison. In: Preneel, B., Vercauteren, F. (eds.) ACNS 2018. LNCS, vol. 10892, pp. 303–320. Springer, Cham (2018). https://doi.org/10.1007/978-3-319-93387-0_16

28. Couteau, G., Rindal, P., Raghuraman, S.: Silver: silent VOLE and oblivious transfer from hardness of decoding structured LDPC codes. In: Malkin, T., Peikert, C. (eds.) CRYPTO 2021. LNCS, vol. 12827, pp. 502–534. Springer, Cham (2021). https://doi.org/10.1007/978-3-030-84252-9_17

29. Damgård, I., Jurik, M.: A length-flexible threshold cryptosystem with applications. In: Safavi-Naini, R., Seberry, J. (eds.) ACISP 2003. LNCS, vol. 2727, pp. 350–364. Springer, Heidelberg (2003). https://doi.org/10.1007/3-540-45067-X_30

30. Dittmer, S., Ishai, Y., Ostrovsky, R.: Line-point zero knowledge and its applications. In: 2nd Conference on Information-Theoretic Cryptography, ITC 2021. Schloss Dagstuhl-Leibniz-Zentrum für Informatik (2021)

31. Doerner, J., Shelat, A.: Scaling ORAM for secure computation. In: Thuraisingham, B.M., Evans, D., Malkin, T., Xu, D. (eds.) ACM CCS 2017, pp. 523–535. ACM Press, October/November 2017

32. Dong, C., Chen, L.: A fast secure dot product protocol with application to privacy preserving association rule mining. In: Tseng, V.S., Ho, T.B., Zhou, Z.-H., Chen, A.L.P., Kao, H.-Y. (eds.) PAKDD 2014. LNCS (LNAI), vol. 8443, pp. 606–617. Springer, Cham (2014). https://doi.org/10.1007/978-3-319-06608-0_50

33. Dong, W., Dave, V., Qiu, L., Zhang, Y.: Secure friend discovery in mobile social networks. In: 2011 Proceedings IEEE INFOCOM, pp. 1647–1655. IEEE (2011)

34. Esser, A., Kübler, R., May, A.: LPN decoded. In: Katz, J., Shacham, H. (eds.) CRYPTO 2017. LNCS, vol. 10402, pp. 486–514. Springer, Cham (2017). https://doi.org/10.1007/978-3-319-63715-0_17

35. Gilbert, H., Robshaw, M.J.B., Seurin, Y.: Good variants of HB$^+$ are hard to find. In: Tsudik, G. (ed.) FC 2008. LNCS, vol. 5143, pp. 156–170. Springer, Heidelberg (2008). https://doi.org/10.1007/978-3-540-85230-8_12

36. Gilboa, N.: Two party RSA key generation. In: Wiener, M. (ed.) CRYPTO 1999. LNCS, vol. 1666, pp. 116–129. Springer, Heidelberg (1999). https://doi.org/10.1007/3-540-48405-1_8

37. Goldreich, O., Goldwasser, S., Micali, S.: How to construct random functions (extended abstract). In: 25th FOCS, pp. 464–479. IEEE Computer Society Press, October 1984

38. Hazay, C., Toft, T.: Computationally secure pattern matching in the presence of malicious adversaries. In: Abe, M. (ed.) ASIACRYPT 2010. LNCS, vol. 6477, pp. 195–212. Springer, Heidelberg (2010). https://doi.org/10.1007/978-3-642-17373-8_12

39. Ishai, Y., Kushilevitz, E., Ostrovsky, R., Sahai, A.: Cryptography with constant computational overhead. In: Ladner, R.E., Dwork, C. (eds.) 40th ACM STOC, pp. 433–442. ACM Press, May 2008

40. Jiang, W., Samanthula, B.K.: N-gram based secure similar document detection. In: Li, Y. (ed.) DBSec 2011. LNCS, vol. 6818, pp. 239–246. Springer, Heidelberg (2011). https://doi.org/10.1007/978-3-642-22348-8_19

41. Kolesnikov, V., Kumaresan, R.: Improved OT extension for transferring short secrets. In: Canetti, R., Garay, J.A. (eds.) CRYPTO 2013. LNCS, vol. 8043, pp. 54–70. Springer, Heidelberg (2013). https://doi.org/10.1007/978-3-642-40084-1_4

42. Li, H., Li, H., Wei, K., Yin, S.L., Zhao, C.: A multi-keyword search algorithm based on polynomial function and safety inner-product method in secure cloud environment. J. Inf. Hiding Multimedia Sig. Process. **8**(2), 413–422 (2017)

43. Liu, Q., Peng, Y., Pei, S., Wu, J., Peng, T., Wang, G.: Prime inner product encoding for effective wildcard-based multi-keyword fuzzy search. IEEE Trans. Serv. Comput. **15**, 1799–1812 (2020)
44. Lyubashevsky, V., Masny, D.: Man-in-the-middle secure authentication schemes from LPN and Weak PRFs. In: Canetti, R., Garay, J.A. (eds.) CRYPTO 2013. LNCS, vol. 8043, pp. 308–325. Springer, Heidelberg (2013). https://doi.org/10.1007/978-3-642-40084-1_18
45. Melchor, C.A., et al.: Hamming quasi-cyclic (HQC). In: NIST PQC Round 2, pp. 4–13 (2018)
46. Murugesan, M., Jiang, W., Clifton, C., Si, L., Vaidya, J.: Efficient privacy-preserving similar document detection. VLDB J. **19**(4), 457–475 (2010)
47. Orlandi, C., Scholl, P., Yakoubov, S.: The rise of paillier: homomorphic secret sharing and public-key silent OT. In: Canteaut, A., Standaert, F.-X. (eds.) EUROCRYPT 2021. LNCS, vol. 12696, pp. 678–708. Springer, Cham (2021). https://doi.org/10.1007/978-3-030-77870-5_24
48. Osadchy, M., Pinkas, B., Jarrous, A., Moskovich, B.: SCiFI - a system for secure face identification. In: 2010 IEEE Symposium on Security and Privacy, pp. 239–254. IEEE (2010)
49. Paillier, P.: Public-key cryptosystems based on composite degree residuosity classes. In: Stern, J. (ed.) EUROCRYPT 1999. LNCS, vol. 1592, pp. 223–238. Springer, Heidelberg (1999). https://doi.org/10.1007/3-540-48910-X_16
50. Prange, E.: The use of information sets in decoding cyclic codes. IRE Trans. Inf. Theor. **8**(5), 5–9 (1962)
51. Sendrier, N.: Decoding one out of many. In: Yang, B.-Y. (ed.) PQCrypto 2011. LNCS, vol. 7071, pp. 51–67. Springer, Heidelberg (2011). https://doi.org/10.1007/978-3-642-25405-5_4
52. Shuguo, H., Ng, W.K.: Multi-party privacy-preserving decision trees for arbitrarily partitioned data. Int. J. Intell. Control Syst. **12**(4), 351–358 (2007)
53. Stern, J.: A new identification scheme based on syndrome decoding. In: Stinson, D.R. (ed.) CRYPTO 1993. LNCS, vol. 773, pp. 13–21. Springer, Heidelberg (1994). https://doi.org/10.1007/3-540-48329-2_2
54. Weng, C., Yang, K., Katz, J., Wang, X.: Wolverine: fast, scalable, and communication-efficient zero-knowledge proofs for boolean and arithmetic circuits. In: 2021 IEEE Symposium on Security and Privacy (SP), pp. 1074–1091. IEEE (2021)
55. Wong, W.K., Cheung, D.W.l., Kao, B., Mamoulis, N.: Secure KNN computation on encrypted databases. In: Proceedings of the 2009 ACM SIGMOD International Conference on Management of Data, pp. 139–152 (2009)
56. Yang, K., Sarkar, P., Weng, C., Wang, X.: Quicksilver: Efficient and affordable zero-knowledge proofs for circuits and polynomials over any field. IACR Cryptology ePrint Archive 2021/076 (2021)
57. Yu, H., Vaidya, J., Jiang, X.: Privacy-preserving SVM classification on vertically partitioned data. In: Ng, W.-K., Kitsuregawa, M., Li, J., Chang, K. (eds.) PAKDD 2006. LNCS (LNAI), vol. 3918, pp. 647–656. Springer, Heidelberg (2006). https://doi.org/10.1007/11731139_74

Efficient Adaptively-Secure Byzantine Agreement for Long Messages

Amey Bhangale[1], Chen-Da Liu-Zhang[2](✉) ⓘ, Julian Loss[3],
and Kartik Nayak[4] ⓘ

[1] UC Riverside, Riverside, USA
amey.bhangale@ucr.edu
[2] NTT Research, Sunnyvale, USA
chen-da.liuzhang@ntt-research.com
[3] CISPA Helmholtz Center, Saarbrücken, Germany
loss@cispa.de
[4] Duke University, Durham, USA
kartik@cs.duke.edu

Abstract. We investigate the communication complexity of Byzantine agreement protocols for long messages against an adaptive adversary. In this setting, prior n-party protocols either achieved a communication complexity of $O(nl \cdot \mathsf{poly}(\kappa))$ or $O(nl + n^2 \cdot \mathsf{poly}(\kappa))$ for l-bit long messages and security parameter κ. We improve the state of the art by presenting protocols with communication complexity $O(nl + n \cdot \mathsf{poly}(\kappa))$ in both the synchronous and asynchronous communication models. The synchronous protocol tolerates $t \leq (1 - \varepsilon)\frac{n}{2}$ corruptions and assumes a VRF setup, while the asynchronous protocol tolerates $t \leq (1 - \varepsilon)\frac{n}{3}$ corruptions under further cryptographic assumptions. Our protocols are very simple and combine subcommittee election with the recent approach of Nayak et al. (DISC '20). Surprisingly, the analysis of our protocols is *all but simple* and involves an interesting new application of Mc Diarmid's inequality to obtain *almost optimal* corruption thresholds.

Keywords: Adaptive adversary · Byzantine agreement · Long messages · Communication complexity

1 Introduction

Byzantine agreement (BA) is a fundamental problem in distributed computing. In a Byzantine agreement protocol consisting of n parties, each party starts with an input value, and at the end of the protocol, all honest (non-faulty) parties output a value. Byzantine agreement protocols guarantee that if all honest parties input the same value v, then they must output v; otherwise, they output

C.-D. Liu-Zhang—Work partially done while the author was at Carnegie Mellon University. Supported in part by the NSF award 1916939, DARPA SIEVE program, a gift from Ripple, a DoE NETL award, a JP Morgan Faculty Fellowship, a PNC center for financial services innovation award, and a Cylab seed funding award.

S. Agrawal and D. Lin (Eds.): ASIACRYPT 2022, LNCS 13791, pp. 504–525, 2022.
https://doi.org/10.1007/978-3-031-22963-3_17

any agreed upon value. Moreover, this holds even if some threshold t out of n parties are Byzantine (arbitrarily malicious).

Byzantine agreement and other consensus primitives form a core abstraction for many blockchains where consensus is required on large values among a large number of parties [6,21]. Moreover, due to the value of the transactions contained in these blockchains, they need to tolerate strong adaptive adversaries who are capable of corrupting any party based on the state of the protocols subject to the Byzantine threshold constraint. These requirements lead to the following natural question: *What is the lowest communication complexity possible for Byzantine agreement protocols on large values tolerating an adaptive adversary?*

This question has been partially answered in the literature. For instance, it has been shown that BA can be solved with $o(n^2)$ communication complexity against an adaptive adversary [1,6,11]. At a high level, these protocols take the approach of electing committees of size κ (where κ is a security parameter) and only the committee members send messages to all parties. This allows achieving a communication complexity of $O(n \cdot \mathsf{poly}(\kappa))$. However, this computation implicitly assumes inputs with a constant number of bits. If the inputs are of size l bits, the communication complexity is $O(nl \cdot \mathsf{poly}(\kappa))$.

A different line of work on extension protocols seeks to achieve the optimal communication complexity of $O(nl)$ for *long messages*. Currently, these works are only capable of considering messages that are very long, i.e., $l \gg n$ [9,10,16,19,22]. The best known protocols in this area achieve a communication complexity of $O(nl+\kappa n^2)$ [19] and the main goal of these works is to further reduce the latter term as much as possible. At a high level, these protocols take the approach of agreeing on the hash of an input value with $O(\kappa n^2)$ communication (κ is the size of a hash) assuming appropriate BA protocols for κ-sized inputs and then use erasure coding techniques to distribute the l-bit long blocks with communication $O(nl + \kappa n^2)$. In this work, we ask whether we can achieve the best of both approaches. In particular,

Does there exist a Byzantine agreement protocol for l bit values tolerating an adaptive adversary with $O(nl + n \cdot \mathsf{poly}(\kappa))$ communication complexity?

We answer this question positively. Surprisingly, the techniques from the two lines of work do not compose in a straightforward manner to achieve the desired communication complexity. In fact, Nayak et al. [19] present a lower bound of $\Omega(nl + A(\kappa) + n^2)$ where $A(\kappa)$ is the communication complexity of Byzantine agreement on κ bit inputs. However, the bound holds only for deterministic protocols. For the first time, we use randomization in the extension part (as well as the underlying protocol) to circumvent the lower bound and achieve $O(nl + n \cdot \mathsf{poly}(\kappa))$ complexity. We present two protocols one assuming synchronous network and another assuming asynchronous network, that achieve these guarantees.

In the following table, we show our improvements on both communication complexity and input range of l to reach optimality, with respect to the previous most efficient l-bit Byzantine agreement protocol due work by Nayak et al. [19] (Table 1).

Table 1. Comparison with state-of-the-art Byzantine agreement for l-bit messages.

Threshold	Model	Communication complexity	Input range l to reach optimality	Reference
$t < n/2$	sync.	$O(nl + n^2\kappa)$	$\Omega(\kappa n)$	[19]
		$O(nl + n \cdot \kappa^3)$	$\Omega(\kappa^3)$	**This work**
$t < n/3$	async.	$O(nl + n^2\kappa)$	$\Omega(\kappa n)$	[19]
		$O(nl + n \cdot \kappa^6)$	$\Omega(\kappa^6)$	**This work**

1.1   Simple Adaptively Secure BA Protocols for Long Messages

Our first result is a synchronous, adaptively secure BA protocol tolerating $t \leq (1 - \varepsilon) \cdot \frac{n}{2}$ Byzantine parties, for some arbitrary constant $\varepsilon > 0$. The second result is asynchronous and tolerates $t \leq (1 - \varepsilon) \cdot \frac{n}{3}$ corruptions.

Theorem (informal). *For all constants $\varepsilon > 0$, assuming appropriate cryptographic setup assumptions, there exists an adaptively secure synchronous Byzantine agreement protocol achieving a communication complexity of $O(nl + n \cdot \mathsf{poly}(\kappa))$ for l-bit values for*

1. *$t \leq (1 - \varepsilon) \cdot \frac{n}{2}$ Byzantine parties under a synchronous network, and*
2. *$t \leq (1 - \varepsilon) \cdot \frac{n}{3}$ Byzantine parties under an asynchronous network.*

We describe a very high-level intuition behind the synchronous protocol. Using an adaptively-secure subquadratic 1-bit BA protocol from [1], all parties can agree on a κ-bit accumulator value corresponding to one of the inputs with a communication of $O(\kappa^3 n)$. Thus the key challenge is to distribute the l-bit value to all parties with linear communication while tolerating an adaptive adversary. Typically, distributing a large value to n parties using erasure codes is performed in two steps. First, create n encoded shares of the value, one for each party, of size $O(\frac{l}{n})$, and send the shares to the respective parties. Then, each party sends its own share to all other parties. If every party receives sufficiently many shares (Byzantine parties may not send shares), they can reconstruct the l-bit value. Observe that the latter step incurs $\Omega(n^2)$ communication, thus dominating the $n \cdot \mathsf{poly}(\kappa)$ term of the desired communication complexity. To make this approach efficient, we have to find the right amount of shares to create and the right parties to share them with. If we naïvely create one share per party, we will need all parties to speak so that we can reconstruct the long message. Clearly, this results in poor communication complexity. On the other hand, if we share the messages with only a small committee C, an adaptive adversary can corrupt all the parties in C and prevent reconstruction of the long message.

To address these concerns, our solution relies on a "public" partition of parties into one of κ buckets such that each bucket holds n/κ parties. We then elect κ-sized committees at random (using the standard VRF approach for cryptographic sortition) to perform each of the two steps described earlier. In the first step, the value is encoded into κ shares of size $O(\frac{l}{\kappa})$ and the j-th share is sent to parties in bucket j. In the second step, the elected committee members from each of the κ buckets send their share to all parties. This incurs an $O(\kappa n \cdot \frac{l}{\kappa}) = O(ln)$ bits of communication. The crux of our argument lies in showing that when $t \leq (1 - \varepsilon) \cdot \frac{n}{2}$, sufficiently many buckets contain an honest party who is also elected as a committee member. Thus, the shares that these honest parties send are sufficient to reconstruct the initial value. If we elect parties to the committee C using the common approach of verifiable random functions, it is not possible to argue via standard Chernoff-type bounds that sufficiently many of the buckets will be covered by members of C. This is because the number of committee members across buckets are correlated and a rushing adaptive adversary can observe the number of committee members for any subset of the buckets before corrupting others. Instead, our argument relies on a subtle application of McDiarmid's inequality, which, to the best of our knowledge, has not been explored in this type of protocol. Our analysis shows that choosing a committee of (expected) size $O(\kappa)$ is enough for our purposes.

Using our insights from the synchronous setting, we also obtain a protocol for the asynchronous setting by substituting the 1-bit agreement protocol with the recent (asynchronous) BA construction of Blum et al. [3].

1.2   Related Work

Work Related to Extension Protocols. In the following, we denote as $\mathcal{A}(1), \mathcal{A}(\kappa)$ the communication complexity of a BA protocol with input domain of size 1 and κ bits, respectively. The problem of extending the domain of Byzantine agreement protocols is a well-studied one in the literature. To the best of our knowledge, the first work that considered this problem is that of Turpin and Coan [22] who showed how to reach agreement on messages from arbitrary domains given agreement on binary values in the corruption regime $t < n/3$ with synchrony. The problem has also been considered for other related primitives such as Byzantine broadcast [7,12] or reliable broadcast [4,19]. Previous works that focus on this problem are the works by Fitzi and Hirt [9], and that of Liang and Vaidya [16]. In the synchronous setting with $t < n/3$ and error-freeness, the protocol of Ganesh and Patra [10] previously provided the best known protocol which achieves $O(nl + n^2 \cdot \mathcal{A}(1))$ communication complexity. For the computational setting with $t < n/2$, the protocols of Ganesh and Patra [10] previously provided the best known solution achieving $O(nl + n\mathcal{A}(\kappa) + \kappa n^3)$. These complexities were recently further improved by the protocols of Nayak et al. [19] who gave protocols that achieve $O(nl + \mathcal{A}(\kappa) + n^2\kappa)$ communication complexity for the computational setting when $t < n/3$ or $t < n/2$. Nayak et al. also improved on error-free protocols in the $t < n/3$ setting, giving a protocol that achieves $O(nl + n\mathcal{A}(1) + n^3)$ communication complexity.

Our work improves over previous works on Byzantine agreement for long messages, both in the communication complexity as well as the input range of l to reach optimality for both the synchronous and asynchronous setting. However, our protocols require further tools. Compared to the protocol of Nayak et al.

[19], our synchronous protocol requires an additional setup for verifiable random functions [17], and our asynchronous protocol also requires several cryptographic assumptions, including non-interactive zero-knowledge, threshold fully-homomorphic encryption and anonymous public-key encryption.

Work Related to Adaptively Secure Sub-quadratic Communication Protocols. Dolev and Reischuk [8] first showed that deterministic Byzantine agreement protocols incur $\Omega(t^2)$ communication complexity when tolerating $t < n$ Byzantine faults. King et al. [13–15] presented the first Byzantine agreement protocols that can be solved with subquadratic communication complexity under inverse polynomial in n error probability. More recently, Algorand [6,11] showed constructions with $O(n \cdot \mathsf{poly}(\kappa))$ communication complexity for adaptively secure Byzantine agreement tolerating $t < (1 - \varepsilon)n/3$ Byzantine parties in the synchronous setting assuming memory erasures. This was further improved by Abraham et al. [1] in the synchronous and partially synchronous network setting tolerating $t < (1 - \varepsilon)n/2$ and $t < (1 - \varepsilon)n/3$ respectively without assuming memory erasures. Finally, Blum et al. [3] presented a subquadratic communication protocol in the asynchronous setting tolerating $t < (1 - \varepsilon)n/3$ faults. As discussed above, these protocols achieve subquadratic communication complexity, but fail to provide the asymptotically optimal complexity $O(nl)$ when l grows beyond n. Nonetheless, these protocols do serve as important building blocks in extension protocols such as the ones presented here (i.e., to agree efficiently on the short message shares).

2   Model and Preliminaries

We consider a setting with n parties $P_1, \ldots, P_n$ that have access to a complete network of pairwise authenticated channels. The adversary is adaptive, and can corrupt up to t parties at any point of the protocol execution in an arbitrary manner. However, we make two standard assumptions on the capability of the adversary (see, e.g., [3,5]). First, parties can perform an *atomic send operation*, i.e., they can send a message to any number of parties *simultaneously* and without the adversary corrupting them in between (different) sends. Second, the adversary cannot perform *after-the-fact* removal, i.e., cannot take back messages sent by parties while they were still honest.[1] We consider protocols in the synchronous and asynchronous network settings. In a synchronous network, we assume communication in lock-step rounds where messages sent by a party at the start of a round arrives at its destination by the end of that round. On the other hand, in an asynchronous network, messages are assumed to arrive at their destination eventually.

2.1   Definitions

Let us recap the definition of Byzantine agreement.

---

[1] In the absence of this assumption, no protocol (deterministic or randomized) can achieve $o(t^2)$ communication complexity as shown in Abraham et al. [1].

Definition 1 (Byzantine Agreement). *Let Π be a protocol executed by parties $P_1, \ldots, P_n$, where each party P_i starts with an input x_i and parties terminate upon generating output. We say that Π is an t-secure Byzantine agreement protocol if the following properties hold when up to t parties are corrupted:*

- *Validity: If all honest parties start with the same input x, then every honest party outputs x.*
- *Consistency: All honest parties output the same value.*

2.2 Primitives

Our protocols will make use of standard linear error correcting codes and cryptographic accumulators.

Linear Error Correcting Code. We use standard Reed-Solomon (RS) codes with parameters (κ, b). The codewords are elements in a Galois Field $GF(2^a)$ with $\kappa \leq 2^a - 1$. There are two algorithms:

- Encoding. Given inputs $m_1, \ldots, m_b$, the encoding function outputs κ codewords (a.k.a. shares) $(s_1, \ldots, s_\kappa)$ of length κ, such that any b codewords uniquely determine the input message and the other codewords.
- Decoding. Given κ codewords $(s_1, \ldots, s_\kappa)$, one can reconstruct the original message $(m_1, \ldots, m_b)$ even when $\kappa - b$ values are erased.

Looking ahead in our protocols, we will choose random committee subsets of κ parties out of the n parties, and we will set the parameter to b, to a lower bound on the number of honest parties in a committee.

Cryptographic Accumulators. We recall the definition of cryptographic accumulators [2]. Given a set of values, the primitive can produce an accumulated value and a witness for each element in the set. Then, given the accumulated value and a witness, one can verify that a particular element is in the set.

Definition 2. *A cryptographic accumulator consists of a tuple of algorithms* (Gen, Eval, CreateWit, Verify), *where:*

- Gen($1^\kappa, T$): *It takes a parameter κ and an accumulation threshold T and returns an accumulator key* ak.
- Eval(ak, $\mathcal{D}$): *It takes an accumulator key* ak *and a set of values to accumulate $\mathcal{D}$ and returns an accumulated value z for $\mathcal{D}$.*
- CreateWit(ak, z, d_i): *It takes an accumulator key* ak, *an accumulated value z for $\mathcal{D}$ and a value d_i, and returns $\perp$ if $d_i \notin \mathcal{D}$ or a witness w_i otherwise.*
- Verify(ak, z, w_i, d_i): *It takes an accumulator key, accumulated value z for $\mathcal{D}$, witness w_i, value d_i, and returns 1 if w_i is a witness for $d_i \in \mathcal{D}$ and 0 otherwise.*

We require our accumulator to satisfy standard collision-free properties [20].

2.3   Concentration Bounds I

We recall the Chernoff concentration bound.

Lemma 1 (Homogenous Chernoff Bound). *Let* $X_1, ..., X_n$ *be i.i.d. Bernoulli random variables with parameter* p. *Let* $X := \sum_i X_i$, *so* $\mu := E[X] = p \cdot n$. *Then, for* $\delta \in [0, 1]$,

$$\Pr[X \geq (1 + \delta) \cdot \mu] \leq e^{-\delta^2 \mu/(2+\delta)} \qquad and \qquad \Pr[X \leq (1 - \delta) \cdot \mu] \leq e^{-\delta^2 \mu/2}.$$

Let $\chi_{s,n}$ denote the distribution that samples a subset of the n parties, where each party is included independently with probability s/n. The following lemma will be useful in our analysis.

Corollary 1. *Fix* $\kappa \leq s \leq n$ *and* $\varepsilon > 0$, *and let* $t = (1-\varepsilon)n/2$ *be the number of corrupted parties. If* $C \leftarrow \chi_{s,n}$, *then* C *contains less than* $(1 - \frac{2}{3}\varepsilon)s/2$ *corrupted parties except with negligible probability.*

Proof. Let $H \subseteq [n]$ be the indices of the honest parties. Let X_j be the Bernoulli random variable indicating if $P_j \in C$, so $\Pr[X_j = 1] = s/n$. Define $Z := \sum_{j \notin H} X_j$. Then, since $E[Z] = t \cdot s/n = (1-\varepsilon)s/2$, setting $\delta = \frac{\varepsilon}{3(1-\varepsilon)}$ in Lemma 1 yields

$$\Pr\left[Z \geq (1 - \frac{2}{3}\varepsilon)s/2\right] \leq \mathtt{neg}(\kappa).$$

(Almost) the same proof yields:

Corollary 2. *Fix* $\kappa \leq s \leq n$ *and* $\varepsilon > 0$, *and let* $t = (1-\varepsilon)n/3$ *be the number of corrupted parties. If* $C \leftarrow \chi_{s,n}$, *then* C *contains less than* $(1 - \frac{2}{3}\varepsilon)s/3$ *corrupted parties except with negligible probability.*

Corollary 3. *Fix* $s \leq n$ *and* $0 < \varepsilon < 1$. *If* $C \leftarrow \chi_{s,n}$, *then* C *contains more than* $(1 - \varepsilon) \cdot s$ *many parties except with probability at most* $O(e^{-\varepsilon^2 s})$.

Proof. Let $H \subseteq [n]$ be the indices of the honest parties. Let X_j be the Bernoulli random variable indicating if $P_j \in C$, so $\Pr[X_j = 1] = s/n$. Define $Z := \sum_{j \notin H} X_j$. Then, since $E[Z] = s$, setting $\delta = \varepsilon$ in Lemma 1 yields

$$\Pr\left[Z \leq (1 - \varepsilon) \cdot s\right] \leq e^{\varepsilon^2 \cdot s/2}.$$

3   Balls and Buckets Analysis for Throwing ck Balls in k Buckets

Our protocols in subsequent sections rely on publicly partitioning n parties in κ distinct buckets and then electing $c\kappa$ out of the n parties uniformly at random. Some of the elected parties can be Byzantine; and our protocols require some properties on the number of distinct buckets containing honest elected parties. In this section, we present the technical inequality that will be used in our protocols in subsequent sections. We use the notation $[k]$ to denote the set $\{1, 2, \ldots, k\}$. We will start with the following concentration bound:

Theorem 1. *(McDiarmid's Inequality) Let $X_1, X_2, \ldots, X_n$ be independent random variables such that $X_j \in \mathcal{K}_j$, for some measurable set $\mathcal{K}_j$. Suppose $f : \prod_{j=1}^{n} \mathcal{K}_j \to R$ is 'Lipschitz' in the following sense: there exist $\sigma_1, \sigma_2 \ldots, \sigma_n \geq 0$ such that for each $1 \leq k \leq n$ and any two input sequences $x, x' \in \prod_j \mathcal{K}_j$, that differ only in the kth coordinate,*

$$|f(x) - f(x')| \leq \sigma_k.$$

Let $Y = f(X_1, X_2, \ldots, X_n)$. Then for any $\alpha > 0$,

$$\Pr[|Y - \mathbf{E}[Y]| \geq \alpha] \leq 2 \cdot \exp\left(-\frac{2\alpha^2}{\sum_{j=1}^{n} \sigma_j^2}\right).$$

The binomial distribution with parameters n and p is the discrete probability distribution of the number of successes in a sequence of n independent experiments, each asking a yes-no question, and each with its own Boolean-valued outcome: success (with probability p) or failure (with probability $1 - p$).

Let $c \geq 1$ and $k \geq 5$ be the parameters where k is the number of buckets and ck is the number of balls (committee members). Consider the following random experiment: We throw ck balls in k buckets independently and uniformly at random. Let b_i be the expected number of buckets with exactly i balls.

Let X_j^i be the indicator random variable that the jth bucket has exactly i balls. Thus, using linearity of expectation, we can write b_i as:

$$b_i = \sum_{j=1}^{k} \mathbf{E}[X_j^i].$$

We also have,

$$\mathbf{E}[X_j^i] = \binom{ck}{i} \cdot \left(\frac{1}{k}\right)^i \cdot \left(1 - \frac{1}{k}\right)^{ck-i}.$$

By linearity of expectation,

$$b_i = \sum_{j=1}^{k} \binom{ck}{i} \cdot \left(\frac{1}{k}\right)^i \cdot \left(1 - \frac{1}{k}\right)^{ck-i}$$

$$= k \cdot \binom{ck}{i} \cdot \left(\frac{1}{k}\right)^i \cdot \left(1 - \frac{1}{k}\right)^{ck-i}.$$

The following lemma shows that the number of buckets with exactly i balls is concentrated around b_i.

Lemma 2. *For $k \geq 2$ and $0 \leq i \leq c$,* $\Pr\left[\left|\begin{smallmatrix} number\ of\ buckets \\ with\ exactly\ i\ balls \end{smallmatrix} - b_i\right| \geq \varepsilon \cdot b_i\right] \leq$
$2\exp(-\frac{\varepsilon^2}{e^{5c}} \cdot k)$.

Proof. Suppose the k buckets are labeled with (distinct) numbers from $[k]$. Let $m = ck$ and define a function $f : [k]^{ck} \to R$ as follows.

$$f(a_1, a_2, \ldots, a_m) = |\{\ell \in [k] \mid \ell \text{ appears exactly } i \text{ times in } (a_1, a_2, \ldots, a_m)\}|.$$

We are interested in the random variable $Y = f(x_1, x_2, \ldots, x_m)$ where each x_j is distributed independently and uniformly in $[k]$. This is because we can think of x_j as the bucket number in which the jth ball lands. Therefore, $f(a_1, a_2, \ldots, a_m)$ is precisely the number of buckets that contain exactly i balls, when the jth ball goes into the bucket a_j for all $j \in [m]$.

It is clear that f is Lipschitz with a Lipschitz constant of 1, i.e., if you change only one input coordinate, then the function value changes by at most 1. Towards applying Theorem 1, we have $\sigma_j = 1$ for all $j \in [m]$ and hence $\sum_j \sigma_j^2 = m$. Note that

$$b_i = k \cdot \binom{ck}{i} \cdot \left(\frac{1}{k}\right)^i \cdot \left(1 - \frac{1}{k}\right)^{ck-i}$$

$$\geq k \cdot \left(\frac{ck}{i}\right)^i \cdot \left(\frac{1}{k}\right)^i \left(1 - \frac{1}{k}\right)^{ck}$$

$$\geq k \cdot \frac{c^i}{i^i} \left(1 - \frac{1}{k}\right)^{ck}$$

$$\geq k \cdot \frac{c^i}{i^i} \left(e^{-2\frac{1}{k}}\right)^{ck} \qquad \text{(Using } 1 - x \geq e^{-2x} \text{ for } x \in [0, \tfrac{1}{2}])$$

$$\geq \frac{c^i}{i^i e^{2c}} k.$$

Using McDiarmid's inequality 1,

$$\Pr[|Y - b_i| \geq \varepsilon \cdot b_i] \leq 2\exp\left(-\frac{2\varepsilon^2 b_i^2}{m}\right)$$

$$\leq 2\exp\left(-\frac{2\varepsilon^2 b_i^2}{ck}\right)$$

$$\leq 2\exp\left(-\frac{2\varepsilon^2 c^{2i}}{i^{2i} e^{4c} \cdot c} \cdot k\right) \qquad \text{(Using } b_i \geq \frac{c^i}{i^i e^{2c}} k)$$

$$\leq 2\exp\left(-\frac{\varepsilon^2}{e^{5c}} \cdot k\right). \qquad \text{(Using } i \leq c \text{ and } c \leq e^c)$$

We only need concentration for $i = 0, 1, \ldots, c - 1$ for the overall argument that follows next. Since each holds with probability $1 - \exp(-\varepsilon^2 k / e^{O(c)})$, by union bound, we have that the number of buckets with i balls is concentrated around its expectation for $i = 0, 1, \ldots, c - 1$ happens with probability at least $1 - c \cdot \exp(-\varepsilon^2 k / e^{O(c)})$.

Claim. Let $k \geq 5$ and $\tau \in (0, 1/2]$ be any constant. There exists a constant $0 \leq c_\tau \leq c$ such that the following two inequalities hold simultaneously. We have,

$$\sum_{i=0}^{c_\tau} b_i \leq \tau k \tag{1}$$

and

$$\sum_{i=1}^{c_\tau} i \cdot b_i \geq (\tau - o_c(1)) \cdot ck. \tag{2}$$

Proof. Let c_τ be the largest constant such that (1) holds. The sum $\sum_{i=0}^{c_\tau} b_i / k$ is the cumulative density of the binomial distribution with parameters ck and $\frac{1}{k}$ at c_τ. As the median of the binomial distribution with parameters ck and $\frac{1}{k}$ is c, we have $c_\tau \leq c$ for $\tau \in (0, 1/2]$. We will show that, for this constant c_τ, the inequality (2) holds.

$$
\begin{aligned}
\sum_{i=1}^{c_\tau} i \cdot b_i &= \sum_{i=0}^{c_\tau} i \cdot k \binom{ck}{i} \cdot \left(\frac{1}{k}\right)^i \cdot \left(1 - \frac{1}{k}\right)^{ck-i} \\
&= k \cdot \sum_{i=0}^{c_\tau} i \cdot \binom{ck}{i} \cdot \left(\frac{1}{k}\right)^i \cdot \left(1 - \frac{1}{k}\right)^{ck-i} \\
&= k \cdot \sum_{i=1}^{c_\tau} ck \cdot \binom{ck-1}{i-1} \cdot \left(\frac{1}{k}\right)^i \cdot \left(1 - \frac{1}{k}\right)^{ck-i} \qquad \left(k\binom{n}{k} = n\binom{n-1}{k-1}\right) \\
&= k \cdot ck \cdot \frac{1}{k} \cdot \sum_{i=1}^{c_\tau} \binom{ck-1}{i-1} \cdot \left(\frac{1}{k}\right)^{i-1} \cdot \left(1 - \frac{1}{k}\right)^{(ck-1)-(i-1)} \\
&= ck \cdot \sum_{i=0}^{c_\tau-1} \binom{ck-1}{i} \cdot \left(\frac{1}{k}\right)^i \cdot \left(1 - \frac{1}{k}\right)^{(ck-1)-i}. \qquad \text{(Setting } i \leftarrow i - 1\text{)}
\end{aligned}
$$

Now, the summation is precisely the cumulative density of the binomial distribution with parameters $ck - 1$ and $\frac{1}{k}$ at $c_\tau - 1$. We now rearrange the terms to get the cumulative density of the binomial distribution with parameters ck and $\frac{1}{k}$ at $c_\tau + 1$ in the summation. This way we can relate it to the constant τ.

$$\sum_{i=1}^{c_\tau} i \cdot b_i = ck \cdot \sum_{i=0}^{c_\tau - 1} \binom{ck-1}{i} \cdot \left(\frac{1}{k}\right)^i \cdot \left(1 - \frac{1}{k}\right)^{(ck-1)-i}$$

$$= ck \cdot \sum_{i=0}^{c_\tau - 1} \frac{\frac{ck-i}{ck}}{(1-1/k)} \binom{ck}{i} \cdot \left(\frac{1}{k}\right)^i \cdot \left(1 - \frac{1}{k}\right)^{ck-i}$$

$$\geq ck \cdot \sum_{i=0}^{c_\tau - 1} \binom{ck}{i} \cdot \left(\frac{1}{k}\right)^i \cdot \left(1 - \frac{1}{k}\right)^{ck-i}$$

$$= ck \cdot \sum_{i=0}^{c_\tau - 1} \frac{b_i}{k}$$

$$= ck \cdot \left(\left(\sum_{i=0}^{c_\tau + 1} \frac{b_i}{k}\right) - \frac{b_{c_\tau}}{k} - \frac{b_{c_\tau + 1}}{k}\right)$$

$$\geq ck \cdot \left(\tau - \frac{b_{c_\tau}}{k} - \frac{b_{c_\tau + 1}}{k}\right)$$

$$= ck \left(\tau - o_c(1)\right).$$

Here, in the first inequality, we used the fact that c_τ is at most c. The second inequality uses the fact that the constant c_τ is the largest constant that satisfies inequality (1) from the claim. Therefore, $\sum_{i=0}^{c_\tau + 1} \frac{b_i}{k} \geq \tau$.

For the final asymptotic, $\frac{b_{c_\tau}}{k} + \frac{b_{c_\tau + 1}}{k} = o_c(1)$, using the fact that the mode of a binomial distribution with parameters ck and $1/k$ is c, for any $0 \leq i \leq ck$

$$\frac{b_i}{k} \leq \frac{b_c}{k} = \binom{ck}{c} \left(\frac{1}{k}\right)^c \left(1 - \frac{1}{k}\right)^{ck-c}$$

$$\leq \frac{2^{ckH(1/k)}}{\sqrt{2\pi ck(1/k)(1 - 1/k)}} \left(\frac{1}{k}\right)^c \left(1 - \frac{1}{k}\right)^{ck-c}.$$

Here, $H(p) := p\log_2(1/p) + (1-p)\log_2(1/(1-p))$ is the binary entropy function and the last inequality uses Stirling's approximation. Using the bound $H(1/k) \leq (1/k)\log_2(2k)$ and the fact that $k \geq 5$,

$$\frac{b_i}{k} \leq \frac{2^{c\log_2(2k)}}{\sqrt{\pi c}} \left(\frac{1}{k}\right)^c \left(1 - \frac{1}{k}\right)^{ck-c}$$

$$\leq \frac{2^c}{\sqrt{\pi c}} \left(1 - \frac{1}{k}\right)^{ck-c}$$

$$\leq \frac{2^c}{\sqrt{\pi c}} e^{-c\left(1 - \frac{1}{k}\right)}. \qquad\qquad \text{(Using } 1 - x \leq e^{-x})$$

When $k \geq 5$, $e^{c\left(1-\frac{1}{k}\right)} > 2^c$ and hence $\frac{b_i}{k} \leq \frac{1}{\sqrt{\pi c}} = o_c(1)$.

Now, $c_\tau \leq c$ for every $\tau \in (0, 1/2]$. Using this, we combine Lemma 2 and Claim 3 along with a simple application of union bound and the fact that the sums are natural numbers, to get the following Corollary.

Corollary 4. *For all $\varepsilon > 0, c \geq 1, k \geq 5$ and $\tau \in (0, 1/2]$ there exists a constant $c_\tau \leq c$ such that the following holds. Suppose we throw ck balls in k buckets, each uniformly and independently at random. Let b'_i be the number of buckets with exactly i balls. Then the following two inequalities hold with probability at least $1 - 2 \cdot c \cdot \exp(-\frac{\varepsilon^2}{e^{5c}} \cdot k)$.*

1. $\sum_{i=0}^{c_\tau} b'_i \leq \lfloor (1 + \varepsilon)\tau k \rfloor$.
2. $\sum_{i=1}^{c_\tau} i \cdot b'_i \geq (1 - \varepsilon)(\tau - o_c(1)) \cdot ck$.

4 Adaptively Secure Synchronous Communication-Efficient Protocol for Long Messages

In this section, we describe an adaptively-secure communication-efficient protocols for long messages of size $l = O(\kappa)$. In particular, we will achieve a communication complexity of $ln + n \cdot \mathsf{poly}(\kappa)$ under the synchrony assumption while tolerating $t \leq (1 - \varepsilon)\frac{n}{2}$ faults.

4.1 Intuition

The $O(ln + \kappa n^2)$ Approach [19]**.** Let us start by recalling the extension protocol proposed by Nayak et al. [19] which achieves a communication complexity of $ln + \kappa n^2$ when $l \gg n$. The protocol splits the l-bit agreement task into two sub-goals. The first sub-goal is to identify whether all honest parties can agree on one of the honest inputs. The second sub-goal ensures parties share the l-bit value efficiently if they have decided to agree upon an honest input in the first sub-goal.

To achieve the first sub-goal, the protocol requires every party to create a cryptographic accumulator corresponding to their input values and run a κ-bit Byzantine agreement (BA) protocol to agree on the accumulated value. If the κ-bit BA protocol outputs the same value as their input, they engage in another 1-bit BA protocol with input 1. Otherwise, they input 0 to the 1-bit BA protocol. Finally, if the 1-bit BA protocol outputs 1, the parties proceed with the second sub-goal related to sharing the long inputs (described in the next paragraph). If the 1-bit BA protocol outputs 0, parties output $\perp$ and end the protocol. Observe that the κ-bit BA protocol ensures that parties have the same accumulated value as their output; however, the 1-bit BA protocol is the one which puts all parties in agreement on whether to engage in the "sharing" phase or not. If yes, it ensures that some honest party does have the input corresponding to the agreed-upon value (since otherwise, the 1-bit BA would output 0).

The second sub-goal relates to sharing the l-bit long input (for $l \gg n$) with every other party with communication complexity $O(ln)$. Observe that if all honest parties share this value with every party, trivially, we have a communication complexity of $O(ln^2)$. Moreover, we cannot rely on a single honest party (say a chosen leader) to share this value directly with other parties either. For one, we do not know which honest party has the input to be shared. Even if we did, a

Byzantine party can always claim to not have received this value from the honest leader. This cannot be distinguished from an honest party legitimately claiming to not receive the value from a Byzantine leader. To address this concern, Nayak et al. [19] rely on using erasure coding techniques instead. Each party that inputs 1 to the 1-bit BA protocol must have the same l-bit value (corresponding to the agreed-upon accumulated value). Thus, each such party can create appropriate (deterministic) n shares (using RS codes) with appropriate witnesses (cf. Definition 2) such that each share is of size $O(\frac{l}{n})$. We call this the *distribute* step of the protocol. The l-bit value can be reconstructed if a party receives a majority of distinct shares. Thus, when a party receives a share in the distribute step, using the witness, it verifies whether the share matches the agreed upon accumulated value. If yes, it shares this value with all other parties. This step is called the *reshare* step of the protocol. On receiving a majority of the shares, every party can reconstruct the l-bit value. The honest majority assumption ensures that all parties will be able to reconstruct the value; thus, no (Byzantine) party can claim to not have received it.

Observe that the BA protocol used in the first sub-goal requires a communication complexity of κn^2, which can be achieved using [18]. The communication complexity to achieve the second sub-goal is $O(\frac{l}{n} \cdot n^2) = O(ln)$ (sharing the witnesses along with the share to verify the correctness of shares incurs and additional $O(\kappa n^2)$ term, not described here in this intuition).

Towards $O(ln + n \cdot \mathsf{poly}(\kappa))$ Communication Complexity with Adaptive Security. We now describe our approach. At a high level, we maintain a similar structure and have similar sub-goals as that of Nayak et al. [19]. However, we need to achieve a better communication complexity while being adaptively secure which brings in several subtleties.

To achieve the first sub-goal, we rely on an underlying adaptively-secure BA protocol that has a communication complexity of $O(n \cdot \mathsf{poly}(\kappa))$ for κ and 1-bit inputs [1]. At a high-level, this protocol achieves a 1-bit sub-quadratic BA by selecting uniformly random and verifiable committees of size κ for each round of the execution. The parties in the committees send protocol messages to all other parties, who update their state based on the messages received. The committees are elected using verifiable random functions [17] which depends on the party's secret key; thus, adversary cannot predict whether a given party would be elected until the party sends a message to all other parties. Since this is a 1-bit BA protocol, for κ-bit BA we use κ independent instances of this protocol.

To achieve the second sub-goal of sharing the l-bit inputs, observe that the solution by [19] does not work in our scenario. In particular, in the reshare step, even if each party sends a 1-bit value to every other party, this trivially incurs a communication complexity of $O(n^2)$. When l is large, this is bounded by $O(ln)$; however, when l is small, e.g., $l < n$, this term is still quadratic. Thus, our goal is to achieve a communication complexity of $O(ln + n \cdot \mathsf{poly}(\kappa))$ even when $\kappa \leq l < n$ while achieving adaptive security. We take inspiration from the sharing technique used in [19] but attempt to constrain the number of parties

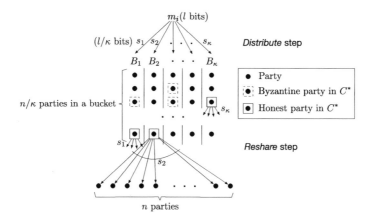

Fig. 1. Graphical representation of the distribute and reshare steps in our approach. The figure assumes party P_i is the only party engaging in the distribute step. In the distribute step, share s_j is shared with each of the parties in bucket B_j. In the reshare phase, a party in committee C^* and in bucket B_j shares share s_j with all the n parties. The figure does not show the process involved in the agreement of accumulated value and additional information such as witnesses shared by parties in the distribute and reshare step.

that can send messages in the distribute and reshare steps of the protocol using committee-based election techniques.

However, achieving this goal is riddled with challenges. First, in the distribute step, due to the adaptive security requirement, a party does not know which party will be in the committee in the reshare step. Second, in the distribute step, to respect the communication complexity requirement, parties can only share $\frac{l}{\kappa}$-sized shares with other parties, and not the entire l-bit message. Finally, the sharing must happen in such a way that sufficiently many honest parties in the reshare committee must have distinct shares so that the value can eventually be reconstructed by all parties.

Our solution relies on publicly partitioning the parties into κ different buckets $B_1, \ldots, B_\kappa$, e.g., based on their IDs. A visual sketch is depicted in Fig. 1. The input would be split into κ different shares $s_1, \ldots, s_\kappa$ of size $\frac{l}{\kappa}$ such that $(1-\varepsilon)\frac{\kappa}{2}$ distinct shares are sufficient to reconstruct the block ($\varepsilon > 0$, ε slack relates to the committee election in the reshare step).

During the distribute step, parties in bucket B_j would receive share s_j. In the reshare step, we elect an independent reshare committee C^* of size $O(\kappa)$. Thus, if a party belongs to C^* and is from bucket B_j, then this party shares s_j with all the parties. Note that due to the use of an accumulator, parties can verify the correctness of the shares relative to the (agreed-upon) accumulated value, and thus would ignore incorrect shares. If we can ensure that all parties receive $(1-\varepsilon)\frac{\kappa}{2}$ distinct shares to reconstruct the l-bit input, then we would achieve the goal with the desirable communication complexity.

The crux of the concern is that, there are only $O(\kappa)$ parties in C^*. Thus, in expectation, each bucket B_j has $O(1)$ parties who can potentially share s_j. Due to the stochasticity, some buckets may not have any parties elected. Moreover, in a round, we cannot expect parties in the committee C^* to send reshare messages at exactly the same instant. This difference in times can potentially be used by an adaptive adversary to adaptively corrupt parties such that sufficiently many distinct shares are not shared. In particular, based on the number parties elected in the first few buckets, the adversary can decide its corruption strategy for the remaining buckets. This disallows the use of standard Chernoff-type bounds which requires independence across buckets.

To address this, we instead rely on the balls and buckets analysis described in Sect. 3. In particular, we can present this abstraction as throwing $c\kappa$ balls (elected committee members in C^*) into κ buckets uniformly at random. The adversary has a corruption quota of slightly less than $\frac{c\kappa}{2}$ among the committee members. The goal is then to ensure that there exists a constant c such that $(1 - \varepsilon)\frac{\kappa}{2}$ distinct buckets have at least one honest committee member in C^*, so that these members are guaranteed to send the corresponding messages during the reshare step of the protocol. This is ensured in Corollary 4, which requires a careful analysis on the balls and buckets process via McDiarmid's inequality.

A final subtlety relates to the committee that should perform the distribute step. It turns out that due to the adaptive security and communication complexity requirement, the committee for the distribute step is the same as the parties that input 1 and participate in the first step of the 1-bit BA protocol (to achieve the first sub-goal). Intuitively, these are the parties which have access to the l-bit value corresponding to the agreed-upon accumulated value and are thus championing for all parties to agree upon the l-bit value. Thus, these parties *need* to send both these messages (the one in distribute step and the other in the first message for the 1-bit BA protocol) as a part of the same message; otherwise, the adaptive adversary can corrupt the parties after sending one of the two messages.

This completes the key intuition behind our protocol.

4.2   Protocol Description

As sketched above, our protocol makes use of several building blocks and setup.

Accumulator Setup. We assume a setup that chooses and distributes the accumulator keys.

Protocol Setup for Π_{sprBA}

Accumulators

Generate the accumulator key $\mathsf{ak} = \mathsf{Gen}(1^\kappa, \kappa)$ and give it to all parties.

Verifiable Random Functions. When describing our protocol, we assume that parties have available via a trusted setup efficient algorithms ComProve and ComVer that allow them to prove and verify membership of a committee, and we do not make this explicit in our protocol (this can typically be achieved via a VRF setup).

Short BA Protocols. We make use of the adaptively-secure sub-quadratic BA protocol of Abraham et al. [1] as a building block. for both the κ-valued BA, denoted as $\mathsf{BA}(\kappa)$, and the binary-valued BA, denoted $\mathsf{BA}(1)$. (Note that the protocol in [1] is binary, but one can simply run it κ many times in parallel to agree on a κ bit message.)

In the protocol [1], all parties participate in the protocol, and different subsets of parties speak at different rounds. More concretely, at each round i, a committee is chosen uniformly at random for each $b \in \{0,1\}$. Here, the committee is tied to the round number as well as the value b. Then, the committee members reveal themselves only when it is their turn to speak in the protocol. Intuitively, once members of the committee send their messages for round i, it is too late for the adversary to corrupt them, as they can not take back messages that were previously sent by honest parties.[2]

Finally, we would like to remark that the protocol in [1] has the property that if all honest parties in the first chosen committee have the same input value b, all honest parties output b. This property is in contrast to the standard notion of validity, which requires *all* honest parties to have the same input. Our protocol will make use of this in an essential way.

Reed-Solomon Codes. We will use two sub-protocols, Encode and Reconstruct, which are based on RS codes. We specify them relative to t_κ which in our protocol is set as $t_\kappa = (1 + \varepsilon)\frac{\kappa}{2}$.

- Encode(m). Given a message of size l, it divides the message into b blocks, and computes κ codewords $(s_1, \ldots, s_\kappa)$ using RS codes, such that even when t_κ values are erased, one can recover the original message.
- Reconstruct$(\mathcal{S}_i, \mathsf{ak}, z, t_\kappa)$ removes incorrect values s_j for each pair $(s_j, w_j) \in \mathcal{S}_i$ that cannot be verified by the witness w_j and accumulation value z. And then reconstructs the message using RS code, where at most t_κ values are removed.

Our protocol starts from a fixed (arbitrary) partition of the n parties into κ buckets $B_1, \ldots, B_\kappa$ of n/κ parties each. When describing our protocol, we will refer to C_i^b as the committee for the i-th round of an execution of $\mathsf{BA}(1)$ for the bit b. In our protocol specification, we make explicit the input value of *first* committee in $\mathsf{BA}(1)$, whereas the rest of the committees are implicit inside the protocol $\mathsf{BA}(1)$ and do not show up in the specification. Finally, we denote as C^* a special committee (also selected at random using ComProve) whose members are designated to perform the re-sharing step in our protocol.

---

[2] Observe that, since committee members are tied to the bit b, the newly corrupted members cannot equivocate unless they are in both committees. The likelihood of that event is negligible.

Protocol Π_{sprBA}

Let $t_\kappa = \lfloor (1+\varepsilon)\frac{\kappa}{2} \rfloor$. The protocol is described from the point of view of party P_i who holds an l-bit input message m_i.

1: Compute $\mathcal{D}_i := (s_1, \ldots, s_\kappa) = \mathsf{Encode}(m_i)$, the accumulation value $z_i = \mathsf{Eval}(\mathsf{ak}, \mathcal{D}_i)$. Input z_i to $\mathsf{BA}(\kappa)$.

2: When the above BA outputs z, if $z = z_i$ and $P_i \in C_1^1$, input 1 to $\mathsf{BA}(1)$. Moreover, distribute the long block as follows. Compute a witness $w_j = \mathsf{CreateWit}(\mathsf{ak}, z, s_j)$ for each share s_j in Step 1 and send the tuple (s_j, w_j) to each party $P_k \in B_j$. Otherwise, if $z \neq z_i$ and $P_i \in C_1^0$, input 0 to $\mathsf{BA}(1)$.

3: If the output of the above BA is 0, output $\perp$ and abort. Otherwise, if $P_i \in C^* \cap B_j$: For the set of tuples $\{(s_j, w_j)\}$ received in the previous step from parties in C_1^1, if there exists an (s_j, w_j) such that $\mathsf{Verify}(\mathsf{ak}, z, w_j, s_j) = 1$, then send (s_j, w_j) to all parties.

4: Let $\mathcal{S}_i := \{(s_j, w_j)\}$ be the set of messages received from the previous step from parties in C^*. If there are messages from parties belonging to at least $(1 - \varepsilon)\frac{\kappa}{2}$ different buckets, output the reconstructed value $\mathsf{Reconstruct}(\mathcal{S}_i, \mathsf{ak}, z, t_\kappa)$. Otherwise, output $\perp$.

The following theorem is proven via a sequence of lemmas.

Theorem 2. *Let $0 < \varepsilon < 1/6$. Assuming a setup for VRFs and accumulators, Π_{sprBA} is a synchronous Byzantine agreement protocol secure up to $t < (1 - 6\varepsilon)n/2$ adaptive corruptions. The communication complexity is $O(nl + \kappa^3 n)$ for l-bit input values.*

In the proofs, we will need that the sub-protocol $\mathsf{BA}(1)$ satisfies the following somewhat stronger *committee-based* notion of validity described in the lemma below.

Lemma 3. *If all honest parties in C_1^b input b to $\mathsf{BA}(1)$, and no honest party in C_1^{1-b} inputs $1 - b$ to $\mathsf{BA}(1)$, then the output of $\mathsf{BA}(1)$ is b.*

Proof. This follows from the fact that in protocol $\mathsf{BA}(1)$ only parties in the committee for the first round, which is C_1^b or C_1^{1-b}, speak and send their input to all other parties. Hence, if only honest parties in C_1^b input to $\mathsf{BA}(1)$ and no honest party from C_1^{1-b} inputs to $\mathsf{BA}(1)$, then it follows immediately from the validity proof given in [1] that the protocol should output b.

Lemma 4. *Π_{sprBA} satisfies validity for $t < (1 - 6\varepsilon)n/2$.*

Proof. If all honest parties have the same input message $m_i = m$, then all honest parties input the same accumulated value $z = z_i$ to $\mathsf{BA}(\kappa)$ in Step 1. By validity of $\mathsf{BA}(\kappa)$, all honest parties receive z as output. Hence, all honest parties in C_1^1 input 1 to $\mathsf{BA}(1)$ in Step 2 and distribute the shares of m. By Lemma 3, they receive 1 as output from $\mathsf{BA}(1)$.

Each honest party $P_j \in C^* \cap B_j$ receives a valid share s_j^i from each honest party $P_i \in C_1^1$, and forwards one of these shares to all parties. Parties are added to C^* uniformly at random, each with probability $c\kappa/n$, for constant c. Denote E_0 the event that fewer than $(1-\varepsilon)c\kappa$ parties are in C^* for $\varepsilon > 0$. By Corollary 3, we have that $\Pr[E_0]$ is negligible.

Whenever E_0 does not occur, we can map the process of distributing parties from C^* into buckets to the process of throwing $c\kappa$ or more balls at κ buckets. Moreover, the optimal strategy for the adversary to minimize the number of buckets in which an honest party sends a share is clearly to corrupt the buckets that contain smaller amount of parties from C^*.

Let us denote E_1 the event that $\frac{c\kappa}{2}(1-4\varepsilon)$ or more parties in C^* are corrupted. When $t < (1-6\varepsilon)n/2$, by Corollary 1, $\Pr[E_1]$ is negligible. Therefore, by a union bound, $\Pr[E_0 \cup E_1]$ is also negligible.

In the following, we condition on the event $\neg E_0 \wedge \neg E_1$ (which by the above occurs with overwhelming probability).

Let $c' = (1-\varepsilon)c$. By Corollary 4, and choosing $\tau = 1/2$, there is a constant $c'_{1/2}$ such that $\sum_{i=1}^{c'_{1/2}} i \cdot b_i \geq (1-\varepsilon)\left(1/2 - o_c(1)\right) \cdot c'\kappa \geq \frac{c'\kappa}{2}(1-2\varepsilon)$, where the last inequality holds as long as $o_c(1) \leq \frac{\varepsilon}{2(1-\varepsilon)}$. Substituting, $c' = (1-\varepsilon)c$, we have $\sum_{i=1}^{c'_{1/2}} i \cdot b_i \geq \frac{c\kappa}{2}(1-3\varepsilon)$. Therefore, the adversary can not corrupt all committee members in the buckets that contain up to $c'_{1/2}$ or less committee members. These amounts of buckets, t_κ, correspond to at most $\lfloor (1+\varepsilon)\kappa/2 \rfloor$ buckets, by Corollary 4.

Putting things together, at Step 4, at least honest parties from $\kappa - t_\kappa \geq (1-\varepsilon)\frac{\kappa}{2}$ buckets send a share, and thus every honest party receives at least that many valid shares. This way, all honest parties can reconstruct and output the long message m.

Lemma 5. Π_{sprBA} *satisfies consistency for* $t < (1-6\varepsilon)n/2$.

Proof. If $\mathsf{BA}(1)$ outputs 0, all honest parties output $\bot$. If $\mathsf{BA}(1)$ outputs 1, then by Lemma 3, there must exist an honest party $P_i \in C_1^1$ that input 1 to $\mathsf{BA}(1)$. First, this party P_i distributes its long messages m_i. Second, by Step 2 of the protocol, it must be the case that this honest party has received $z = z_i$. Using the consistency property of $\mathsf{BA}(\kappa)$, all honest parties must have delivered $z = z_i$. Thus, every honest party $P_j \in C^*$ obtains a valid tuple (s_j, w_j) from P_i and can verify its correctness using the accumulator value z and forward it. Hence, in Step 4, we can use the same argumentation as in the previous lemma to establish that at least $\kappa - t_\kappa$ honest parties in C^* send a share and every honest party can subsequently reconstruct m_i. Note that no other value can be reconstructed, because security of the accumulator and consistency of $\mathsf{BA}(\kappa)$ ensures that all honest parties share the same long message, and dishonest parties cannot compute valid pairs of share-witness different from those received by honest parties.

Communication Complexity. The most expensive steps in the protocol are the run of $\mathsf{BA}(\kappa)$ in Step 1 (which itself consists of κ parallel runs of $\mathsf{BA}(1)$) and the distribution of the long blocks in Step 2. The costs for Step 1 are bounded as $O(\kappa^3 \cdot n)$ since every run of BA(1) costs $O(\kappa^2 \cdot n)$. The costs for Step 2 are bounded by $O(l \cdot n + \kappa^2 n)$, given that each of $O(\kappa)$ parties send a message of length $\ell/\kappa + \kappa$ to all parties. Overall, we obtain a complexity of $O(n \cdot l + \kappa^3 \cdot n)$.

5   Adaptively Secure Asynchronous Communication-Efficient Protocol for Long Messages

We briefly recall the asynchronous adaptively-secure BA protocol of Blum et al. [3]. As for the previous protocol, the step of each round i is performed by a randomly chosen committee C_i, who reveals itself only when it is their turn to speak in the protocol. Again, we assume that parties are endowed (via some trusted setup) with efficient routines ComProve and ComVer that allow to prove and verify committee membership. The remaining accumulator setup is as for Π_{sprABA} and we also reuse the routines Encode and Reconstruct introduced in the previous section.

Again, we run two versions of the protocol, the first is for κ-valued messages and denoted as ABA(κ), the other for binary-valued messages, and denoted as ABA(1). Since the protocol in [3] is binary, we simply run it κ many times in parallel to agree on a κ bit message. As before, we choose the committees with expected size $c\kappa$. Note that in protocol [3], contrary to the synchronous case, the committees are not tied to a specific value.

Protocol Π_{sprABA}

Let $t_\kappa = \lfloor (1 + \varepsilon) \cdot \frac{\kappa}{3} \rfloor$. The protocol is described from the point of view of party P_i who holds an l-bit input message m_i.

1: Compute $\mathcal{D}_i := (s_1, \ldots, s_\kappa) = \mathsf{Encode}(m_i)$, the accumulation value $z_i = \mathsf{Eval}(\mathsf{ak}, \mathcal{D}_i)$. Input z_i to ABA(κ).

2: When the above BA outputs z, if $z = z_i$ and $P_i \in C_1$, input 1 to ABA(1). Moreover, distribute the long block as follows. Compute a witness $w_j = \mathsf{CreateWit}(\mathsf{ak}, z, s_j)$ for each share s_j in Step 1 and send the tuple (s_j, w_j) to each party $P_k \in B_j$. Otherwise, if $z \neq z_i$ and $P_i \in C_1$, input 0 to ABA(1).

3: If the output of the above BA is 0, output $\perp$ and abort. Otherwise, if $P_i \in C^* \cap B_j$: For the set of tuples $\{(s_j, w_j)\}$ received in the previous step from parties in C_1, if there exists an (s_j, w_j) such that $\mathsf{Verify}(\mathsf{ak}, z, w_j, s_j) = 1$, then send (s_j, w_j) to all parties.

4: Let $\mathcal{S}_i := \{(s_j, w_j)\}$ be the set of messages received from the previous step from parties in C^*. If there are messages from parties belonging to at least $\frac{2\kappa}{3} \cdot (1 - \varepsilon)$ different buckets, output the reconstructed value $\mathsf{Reconstruct}(\mathcal{S}_i, \mathsf{ak}, z, t_\kappa)$. Otherwise, output $\perp$.

We follow a very similar strategy as in the previous section. In our main theorem statement, we include the cryptographic setup required to run the protocol of Blum et al. [3] without going in to much details as to how they work. Roughly speaking, their protocol starts from an initial setup provided by a trusted dealer.

This initial setup allows parties to run a fixed number of multi-party computations (MPCs) and BAs with subquadratic communication complexity. The parties use these cheap (in terms of communication) MPCs to emulate the trusted dealer and refresh the setup for future cheap MPCs and BAs for any number of times. To run MPC with these complexities, their protocol requires strong setup assumptions including threshold fully homomorphic encryption, non-interactive zero knowledge, and anonymous public key encryption (where a ciphertext can not be linked to a public key without knowing the secret key).

Theorem 3. *Let $0 < \varepsilon < 1/4$. Assuming a setup for non-interactive zero-knowledge, threshold fully homomorphic encryption, and anonymous public key encryptions, Π_{sprABA} is an asynchronous Byzantine agreement protocol secure up to $t \le (1 - 6\varepsilon)n/3$ adaptive corruptions. The communication complexity is $O(nl + \kappa^6 n)$ for l-bit values.*

The proof of the following lemma is almost identical to that of Lemma 3.

Lemma 6. *If all honest parties in C_1 input b to $\mathsf{ABA}(1)$ then the output of $\mathsf{ABA}(1)$ is b.*

Lemma 7. *Π_{sprABA} satisfies validity if $t \le (1 - 6\varepsilon)n/3$ parties are corrupted.*

Proof. If all honest parties have the same input message $m_i = m$, then all honest parties input the same accumulated value $z = z_i$ to $\mathsf{ABA}(\kappa)$ in Step 1. By validity of $\mathsf{ABA}(\kappa)$, all honest parties receive z as output. Hence, all honest parties in C_1 input 1 to $\mathsf{ABA}(1)$ in Step 2 and distribute the shares of m. By Lemma 6, they receive 1 as output from $\mathsf{ABA}(1)$.

Each honest party $P_j \in C^* \cap B_j$ receives a valid share s_j^i from each honest party $P_i \in C_1$, and forwards one of these shares to all parties. Parties are added to C^* uniformly at random via ComProve with probability $c\kappa/n$. Denote E_0 the event that fewer than $(1 - \varepsilon)c\kappa$ parties are in C^*, for $\varepsilon > 0$.

Whenever E_0 does not occur, we can map the process of adding parties to C^* (via ComProve) to the process of throwing $c\kappa$ or more balls at κ buckets. By Corollary 3, we have that $\Pr[E_0]$ is negligible. Moreover, the optimal strategy for the adversary to minimize the number of buckets in which an honest party sends a share is clearly to corrupt the buckets that contain smaller amount of parties from C^*.

Let us denote E_1 the event that $\frac{c\kappa}{3}(1 - 4\varepsilon)$ or more parties in C^* are corrupted. By Corollary 2, $\Pr[E_1]$ is negligible. Therefore, by a union bound, $\Pr[E_0 \cup E_1]$ is also negligible.

In the following, we condition on the event $\neg E_0 \wedge \neg E_1$ (which by the above occurs with overwhelming probability).

Let $c' = (1 - \varepsilon)c$. By Corollary 4, and choosing $\tau = 1/3$, there is a constant $c'_{1/3}$ such that $\sum_{i=1}^{c'_{1/3}} i \cdot b_i \ge (1 - \varepsilon) \cdot (1/3 - o_c(1)) \cdot c'\kappa \ge \frac{c'\kappa}{3}(1 - 2\varepsilon)$, where the last inequality holds as long as $o_c(1) \le \frac{\varepsilon}{3(1-\varepsilon)}$. Therefore, the adversary can not corrupt all committee members in the buckets that contain up to $c'_{1/3}$

many committee members. These amounts of buckets correspond to at most $\lfloor(1+\varepsilon)\kappa/3\rfloor$ buckets, by Corollary 4.

Putting things together, at Step 4, at least $\kappa - t_\kappa \geq (1-\varepsilon)\frac{2\kappa}{3}$ honest parties in C^* send a share, and thus every honest party receives at least that many valid shares. This way, all honest parties can reconstruct and output the long message m.

The proof of the following lemma is identical as for the synchronous case.

Lemma 8. Π_{sprABA} *satisfies consistency if* $t \leq (1-6\varepsilon)n/3$ *parties are corrupted.*

Communication Complexity. The most expensive steps in the protocol are the run of $\mathsf{BA}(\kappa)$ in Step 1 (which itself consists of κ parallel runs of $\mathsf{BA}(1)$) and the distribution of the long blocks in Step 2. The costs for Step 1 are bounded as $O(\kappa^6 \cdot n)$ since every run of $\mathsf{BA}(1)$ costs $O(\kappa^5 \cdot n)$. The costs for Step 2 are bounded by $O(l \cdot n)$. Overall, we obtain a complexity of $O(n \cdot l + \kappa^6 \cdot n)$.

References

1. Abraham, I., et al.: Communication complexity of byzantine agreement, revisited. In: 38th ACM PODC, pp. 317–326. ACM (2019)
2. Barić, N., Pfitzmann, B.: Collision-free accumulators and fail-stop signature schemes without trees. In: Fumy, W. (ed.) EUROCRYPT 1997. LNCS, vol. 1233, pp. 480–494. Springer, Heidelberg (1997). https://doi.org/10.1007/3-540-69053-0_33
3. Blum, E., Katz, J., Liu-Zhang, C.-D., Loss, J.: Asynchronous Byzantine agreement with subquadratic communication. In: Pass, R., Pietrzak, K. (eds.) TCC 2020. LNCS, vol. 12550, pp. 353–380. Springer, Cham (2020). https://doi.org/10.1007/978-3-030-64375-1_13
4. Cachin, C., Tessaro, S.: Asynchronous verifiable information dispersal. In: IEEE Symposium on Reliable Distributed Systems (SRDS 2005), pp. 191–201. IEEE (2005)
5. Chan, T.-H.H., Pass, R., Shi, E.: Sublinear-round byzantine agreement under corrupt majority. In: Kiayias, A., Kohlweiss, M., Wallden, P., Zikas, V. (eds.) PKC 2020. LNCS, vol. 12111, pp. 246–265. Springer, Cham (2020). https://doi.org/10.1007/978-3-030-45388-6_9
6. Chen, J., Gorbunov, S., Micali, S., Vlachos, G.: ALGORAND AGREEMENT: super fast and partition resilient byzantine agreement. Cryptology ePrint Archive, Report 2018/377 (2018). https://eprint.iacr.org/2018/377
7. Chongchitmate, W., Ostrovsky, R.: Information-theoretic broadcast with dishonest majority for long messages. In: Beimel, A., Dziembowski, S. (eds.) TCC 2018. LNCS, vol. 11239, pp. 370–388. Springer, Cham (2018). https://doi.org/10.1007/978-3-030-03807-6_14
8. Dolev, D., Reischuk, R.: Bounds on information exchange for Byzantine agreement. In: Probert, R.L., Fischer, M.J., Santoro, N. (eds.) 1st ACM PODC, pp. 132–140. ACM, August 1982
9. Fitzi, M., Hirt, M.: Optimally efficient multi-valued Byzantine agreement. In: Ruppert, E., Malkhi, D. (eds.) 25th ACM PODC, pp. 163–168. ACM, July 2006

10. Ganesh, C., Patra, A.: Broadcast extensions with optimal communication and round complexity. In: Giakkoupis, G. (ed.) 35th ACM PODC, pp. 371–380. ACM, July 2016
11. Gilad, Y., Hemo, R., Micali, S., Vlachos, G., Zeldovich, N.: Algorand: scaling byzantine agreements for cryptocurrencies. Cryptology ePrint Archive, Report 2017/454 (2017). http://eprint.iacr.org/2017/454
12. Hirt, M., Raykov, P.: Multi-valued byzantine broadcast: the t < n case. In: Sarkar, P., Iwata, T. (eds.) ASIACRYPT 2014, Part II. LNCS, pp. 448–465. Springer, Heidelberg (2014). https://doi.org/10.1007/978-3-662-45608-8_24
13. King, V., Saia, J.: From almost everywhere to everywhere. In: DISC (2009)
14. King, V., Saia, J.: Breaking the $O(n^2)$ bit barrier: scalable byzantine agreement with an adaptive adversary. In: Richa, A.W., Guerraoui, R. (eds.) 29th ACM PODC, pp. 420–429. ACM, July 2010
15. King, V., Saia, J., Sanwalani, V., Vee, E.: Scalable leader election. In: 17th SODA, pp. 990–999. ACM-SIAM, January 2006
16. Liang, G., Vaidya, N.: Error-free multi-valued consensus with byzantine failures. In: Proceedings of the 30th Annual ACM SIGACT-SIGOPS Symposium on Principles of Distributed Computing (2011)
17. Micali, S., Rabin, M.O., Vadhan, S.P.: Verifiable random functions. In: 40th FOCS, pp. 120–130. IEEE Computer Society Press, October 1999
18. Momose, A., Ren, L.: Optimal communication complexity of authenticated byzantine agreement. In: 35th International Symposium on Distributed Computing (2021)
19. Nayak, K., Ren, L., Shi, E., Vaidya, N.H., Xiang, Z.: Improved extension protocols for byzantine broadcast and agreement. In: DISC (2020)
20. Nguyen, L.: Accumulators from bilinear pairings and applications. In: Menezes, A. (ed.) CT-RSA 2005. LNCS, vol. 3376, pp. 275–292. Springer, Heidelberg (2005). https://doi.org/10.1007/978-3-540-30574-3_19
21. The DFINITY Team: The internet computer for geeks. Cryptology ePrint Archive, Report 2022/087 (2022). https://ia.cr/2022/087
22. Turpin, R., Coan, B.A.: Extending binary Byzantine agreement to multivalued byzantine agreement. Inf. Process. Lett. **18**(2), 73–76 (1984)

Concurrently Composable
Non-interactive Secure Computation

Andrew Morgan[1(✉)] and Rafael Pass[2]

[1] Cornell University, Ithaca, USA
asmorgan@cs.cornell.edu
[2] Cornell Tech, New York, USA
rafael@cs.cornell.edu

Abstract. We consider the feasibility of non-interactive secure two-party computation (NISC) in the plain model satisfying the notion of superpolynomial-time simulation (SPS). While *stand-alone* secure SPS-NISC protocols are known from standard assumptions (Badrinarayanan et al., Asiacrypt 2017), it has remained an open problem to construct a *concurrently composable* SPS-NISC. Prior to our work, the best protocols require 5 rounds (Garg et al., Eurocrypt 2017), or 3 simultaneous-message rounds (Badrinarayanan et al., TCC 2017).

In this work, we demonstrate the first concurrently composable SPS-NISC. Our construction assumes the existence of:

– a non-interactive (weakly) CCA-secure commitment,
– a stand-alone secure SPS-NISC with subexponential security,

and satisfies the notion of "angel-based" UC security (i.e., UC with a superpolynomial-time helper) with perfect correctness.

We additionally demonstrate that both of the primitives we use (albeit only with polynomial security) are necessary for such concurrently composable SPS-NISC with perfect correctness. As such, our work identifies essentially *necessary* and *sufficient* primitives for concurrently composable SPS-NISC with perfect correctness in the plain model.

1 Introduction

Secure two-party computation is a primitive that allows two parties to compute the result $f(x, y)$ of a function f on their respective inputs x,y, while ensuring that nothing else is leaked. In this paper, we focus on secure two-party computation in the setting of minimal communication, where both players send just a *single message*. The first player, called the *receiver*, speaks first, and next the second player, called the *sender*, responds; finally, only the receiver recovers

R. Pass—Supported in part by NSF Award SATC-1704788, NSF Award RI-1703846, AFOSR Award FA9550-18-1-0267, and a JP Morgan Faculty Award. This material is based upon work supported by DARPA under Agreement No. HR00110C0086. Any opinions, findings and conclusions or recommendations expressed in this material are those of the author(s) and do not necessarily reflect the views of the United States Government or DARPA.

S. Agrawal and D. Lin (Eds.): ASIACRYPT 2022, LNCS 13791, pp. 526–555, 2022.
https://doi.org/10.1007/978-3-031-22963-3_18

the output $f(x, y)$ of the function. Such 2-round protocols are referred to as *non-interactive secure computation protocols (NISC)*[1].

Security of secure computation protocols is traditionally defined using the *simulation paradigm*, first introduced in [30] and extended in several later works [6,12,29,40]. Roughly speaking, security is defined by requiring that the "view" of any polynomial-time attacker can be simulated by a polynomial-time attacker that participates in an "idealized" version of the protocol where the parties only interact with a trusted party computing f. While this notion of "basic" simulation-based security is often adequate in cases where a protocol is run in isolation, there are several important properties of real-world security that are not considered by this definition. For instance, many protocols interact with other protocols, either through using them as components or sub-protocols or through existing in the same setting; intuitively, it is desirable that a definition of security should provide a guarantee that such a *composition* of multiple provably secure protocols is still secure. Some of the classical definitions of simulation-based security (e.g., [12,40]) in fact did guarantee such a notion of composability.

Concurrently Composable Secure Computation. All of the early definitions of simulation-based security, however, had a caveat; security was only considered when the protocol was executed in a *stand-alone setting* where only a single instance could be executed at a time. Realistically, protocols are often executed in a *concurrent* setting (originally formalized in [17,19,20]) where many instances of a protocol are executed, potentially simultaneously, between many different parties. An adversary in this model may control a large subset of the players, and furthermore is able to observe the results of ongoing interactions in order to adaptively influence future interactions by either reordering communication or changing the behavior of the corrupted parties. Ideally, we would want to be able to show that a protocol is *concurrently secure*, or that a notion analogous to simulation-based security holds even against a more powerful adversary in this multi-instance setting. As with composability, though, concurrent security is not implied by basic definitions of simulation-based security; while definitions such as those of [12,40] guaranteed composable security in a non-concurrent setting, the first definition to achieve both properties was that of *universally composable* (UC) security, first proposed in [13]. At a high level, UC security expands further on the simulation paradigm by considering an "external observer", or *environment*, which runs and observes interactions between an adversary and potentially many concurrent instances of a protocol Π. We say that Π *UC-realizes* some functionality f if the environment cannot distinguish between the "real" interaction and an "ideal" interaction between a polynomial-time simulator and the perfectly secure "idealized" version of the functionality f. Furthermore, if a protocol π UC-realizes some functionality g and Π uses π as a sub-protocol, the composability of UC guarantees that, since the environment cannot distinguish

---

[1] As is well-known, in this non-interactive setting, it is inherent that only one of the players can receive the output.

interactions with π from simulated interactions with the idealized g, we can effectively replace π with the idealized g when proving Π secure.

While UC security provides extremely strong guarantees, it also has correspondingly restrictive limitations on what can be proven secure. Even in the case of *two-party computation*, impossibility results exist showing that very few functionalities $f(x, y)$ can be computed UC-securely [15]—or, disregarding composability, even concurrently securely [38]—without introducing additional *trusted setup* assumptions.

The notion of *superpolynomial-time simulation* (SPS) [43], a relaxation of UC security which allows the simulator to run in superpolynomial time, has allowed for the construction of several protocols, both for two-party computation [3,41,43,47] and the more general case of *multi-party computation* [5,23,37], which are able to securely realize virtually all functionalities. While some definitions of SPS security provide the same concurrency guarantees as UC security, SPS security fails to uphold many of the desirable composability properties: the problem is that SPS security only requires that any polynomial time attacker can be simulated (in superpolynomial time), but to perform composition, we also need to simulate "simulated attackers", which run in superpolynomial time. The notion of *"angel-based" UC security* [45] and its generalization of *"UC-security with a superpolynomial-time helper"* [16] remedy this issue and provide for a composable notion of concurrent SPS-security: in these models, the simulation is polynomial-time but *both* the adversary and the simulator have access to a "helper" oracle (an "angel") which implements some specific superpolynomial-time functionality. Angel-based security is a strictly stronger notion than SPS security, and it retains all of the composability properties of standard UC security, with the important caveat that composability only holds with protocols that are secure with respect to the same oracle. Furthermore, secure computation protocols are feasible in the angel-based security model [16,31–33,39,45]; the most recent constructions have been based on the notion of "CCA-secure" commitments [16], which are commitment schemes that satisfy hiding in the presence of an adversaries that is given access to a "decommitment oracle".

On the Existence of Concurrently-Composable NISC. In this work, we consider the feasibility of concurently composable non-interactive (i.e., 2-round) secure computation protocols, NISCs. As is well known, even if we do not care about concurrency or composability, NISC protocols are not possible *in the plain model* (i.e., without any trusted set-up assumptions) using the standard notion of polynomial-time simulation [28]. On the other hand, if we consider the relaxed notion of SPS security, NISC protocols have been shown to be feasible based on standard assumptions in recent works [3,41,43]. (Indeed, enabling secure 2-round protocols was one of the original motivations behind the notion of SPS security [43].) These works, however, only consider *stand-alone* SPS security.

In fact, even if we require just *concurrent* SPS security (let alone both concurrent and composable), the question of what we can achieved remains open. The state of the art can be summarized as follows:

- [23] proposed the first concurrently secure constant-round protocol based on standard assumptions, and this bound was later reduced to 5 [24].
- [4] presented a three-round concurrently SPS-secure multi-party computation protocol for general functionalities, which can be reduced to two rounds for specific subclasses of functionalities; however, their protocol relies on the *simultaneous-message* model, and so it still requires five (or, for restricted functionalities, three) messages for two-party computation in the standard (synchronous) model.
- Other general two-round concurrently secure multi-party computation protocols (e.g., [7,8,25]) exist which require a common reference string (CRS) as "trusted setup".
- Two recent works (concurrent with and independent from this result) constructed two-round concurrently SPS-secure protocols without trusted setup in the simultaneous-message model (where all participants send a message at the same time in each round). [1] presented a two-round protocol for *two-sided* two-party computation (where both parties receive the output) satisfying concurrent SPS security, and [21] presented a two-round MPC protocol satisfying both concurrent and self-composable SPS security. In contrast to these works, we consider a *synchronous* model where only one participant may send a single message per round (i.e., non-interactive protocols), but we only consider one-sided functionalities.
- For the special case of zero-knowledge arguments of knowledge, [43] presented a 2-round protocol that satisfies concurrent SPS-security; but concurrent security only holds in the setting of "fixed", as opposed to "interchangeable", roles—that is, the attacker can corrupt either all provers, or all verifiers. (On a technical level, this notion of concurrency with "fixed roles" does not deal with *non-malleability* [17].)

Hence, prior work leaves open the question of whether, in the plain model, we can achieve a concurrently secure protocol even for *specific* two-party functionalities, such as zero-knowledge arguments of knowledge, in two *synchronous* (rather than simultaneous-message) rounds.

Meanwhile, for composable "angel-based" security in the plain model, the situation is even worse; the protocol proposed by [16] requires n^ϵ rounds, while [32] reduced this to logarithmic round complexity and [33] further reduced this to a constant. Thus, the literature leaves open the following fundamental problem:

Is concurrently composable NISC possible in the plain model, and if so, under what assumptions?

In fact, we are not aware of NISC protocols even for *specific functionalities* (e.g., zero-knowledge arguments of knowledge) that satisfy *any* "meaningful notion" of concurrent security with "interchangeable roles" (i.e., the adversary can corrupt the sender in some sessions and the receiver in others) even with respect to just *2 concurrent sessions!*[2]

---

[2] In particular, as far as we are aware, even getting a 2-round non-malleble SPS-zero-knowledge argument of knowledge was open.

1.1   Our Results

We solve both of the above questions by demonstrating the existence of a NISC protocol for *general* functionalities satisfying not only concurrent SPS security but also UC security with a superpolynomial-time helper. Our construction relies on the following building blocks:

– A *non-interactive CCA-secure commitment scheme* [9,16,35,42].
– A *stand-alone secure SPS-NISC* with subexponential security [3].

In fact, as we show, a relaxed version of CCA-secure commitments—which we refer to as *weakly CCA-secure commitments*—suffices; this notion differs from the standard notion of CCA security only in that the CCA oracle, given a commitment c, rather than returning both the value v committed to and the randomness r used in the commitment, instead returns just the value v (analogous to the definition of CCA security for encryption schemes [46]). Our main result, then, is as follows:

Theorem 1 (Informal). *Assume there exist a non-interactive weakly CCA-secure commitment scheme and a stand-alone subexponentially SPS-secure NISC protocol for general functionalities. Then there exists a NISC protocol for general functionalities (with perfect correctness) which achieves UC security with a superpolynomial-time helper (i.e., achieves angel-based security).*

We emphasize that before our result, it was not known how to even construct *non-malleable* 2-round protocols in the plain model (i.e., protocols secure under just *two different executions* where the adversary may play different roles) for *any* non-trivial functionality. Furthermore, we demonstrate that the two building blocks we rely on are also *necessary* for concurrently composable SPS-NISC with perfect correctness[3]:

Theorem 2 (Informal). *Assume the existence of a non-interactive NISC for general functionalities (with perfect correctness) satisfying UC security with a superpolynomial-time helper. Then, there exist both a non-interactive weakly CCA secure commitment scheme and a stand-alone secure SPS-NISC for general functionalities.*

Note that the only gap between the assumptions is that our feasibility result (Theorem 1) relies on the existence of a *subexponentially-secure* SPS-NISC, whereas Theorem 2 only shows that a *polynomially-secure* SPS-NISC is needed. But except for this (minor) gap, our work provides a full characterization of the necessary and sufficient primitives for NISC (with perfect correctness) satisfying UC security with a superpolynomial-time helper.

Thus, our work should be interpreted as showing that to upgrade a stand-alone secure NISC to become concurrently composable, the existence of weakly

---

[3] As usual, perfect correctness means that if both parties act honestly, then the protocol will output the correct result of the computation with probability 1.

CCA-secure commitments is both necessary and sufficient. Our work thus further motivates the importance of studying non-interactive CCA-secure commitments; furthermore, it highlights that perhaps the weaker notion of "weak" CCA security, introduced here, may be more natural than the stronger version used in earlier works.

On the Realizability of the Building Blocks. As just mentioned, our main results demonstrate that the two building blocks—non-interactive weakly CCA-secure commitments and stand-alone SPS-NISC—are both necessary and sufficient for constructing concurrently composable SPS-NISC. SPS-NISC with subexponential security can be constructed based on a variety of standard assumptions, such as subexponential hardness of the Decisional Diffie-Hellman, Quadratic Residuosity, or N^{th} Residuosity assumptions [3] or subexponential hardness of the Learning With Errors assumption [10].

Non-interactive CCA secure commitments, however, require more complex assumptions. They were first constructed in [42] based on adaptive one-way permutations; later, [35] presented such a scheme, albeit with only *uniform* security (i.e., security against uniform attackers) based on keyless collision-resistant hash functions, injective one-way functions, non-interactive witness-indistinguish-able arguments (NIWIs), and subexponentially-secure time-lock puzzles. Even more recently, [9] presented a scheme also satisfying non-uniform security by replacing the keyless collision-resistant hash function with a multi-collision-resistant keyless hash function; while their construction is only claimed to achieve "concurrent non-malleability" [36,44] (and not the stronger notion of CCA security), it seems that a relatively minor modification of their analysis (similar to the analysis in [35]) would show that their construction also achieves CCA security when all the underlying primitives satisfy subexponential security.

Overview. We give a technical overview of our main result in Sect. 2, provide definitions in Sect. 3, formally state Theorem 1 in Sect. 4. Due to space limitations, we have deferred the formal proof to the full version of our paper. In addition, we formalize and prove Theorem 2 in Sect. 5 (again, missing proofs for this section are provided in the full version.)

2 Technical Overview

In this section, we provide a high-level discussion of our security definition and our protocol. At a high level, UC security expands on the simulation paradigm by considering an "external observer", or *environment*, which runs and observes interactions between an adversary and potentially many concurrent instances of a protocol Π. We say that Π *UC-realizes* some functionality f if the environment cannot distinguish between the "real" interaction and an "ideal" interaction between a polynomial-time simulator and the perfectly secure "idealized" version of the functionality f. We will demonstrate a strong and composable notion of concurrent security using the *externalized UC model* [12,14], where we assume the adversary, the environment, and the simulator are strictly *polynomial-time* but have access to an "imaginary angel", or a global "helper" entity $\mathcal{H}$ that implements some superpolynomial-time functionality. (This notion was first considered in [45] for the case of non-interactive, stateless, angels) In our case (as in [16]) $\mathcal{H}$ will implement the CCA decommitment oracle $\mathcal{O}$ for a CCA secure commitment; while interacting with a party P, $\mathcal{H}$ will send a valid decommitment in response to any commitments made using that party's identity as the tag. (Since the adversary controls corrupted parties, this effectively means that $\mathcal{H}$ will decommit any commitments with a corrupted party's identifier, but none with an honest party's identifier). CCA security guarantees, then, that an adversary will never be able to break an honest party's commitment; on the other hand, the presence of the helper $\mathcal{H}$ makes it relatively easy for the simulator $\mathcal{S}$ we construct for the definition of UC security to extract information necessary for simulation from corrupted parties' commitments.

Aside from the commitment scheme, our protocol consists of two major subcomponents. First, in order to evaluate the functionality $f(x, y)$, we begin with a NISC protocol that satisfies *stand-alone* security with superpolynomial-time simulation. In order to build this into a protocol satisfying full UC security, however, we will need to leverage the CCA-secure commitment scheme in order to allow the simulator to extract the malicious party's input from their message; since the simulator is restricted to polynomial time (with access to the CCA helper $\mathcal{H}$), this cannot be done by simply leveraging the superpolynomial-time simulator of the underlying NISC. Instead, if both parties commit to their respective inputs and send the commitments alongside the messages of the underlying NISC, the simulator can easily use the CCA helper to extract the inputs from the commitments. This, however, presents another issue: namely, there must be a way to verify that a potentially malicious party commits to the correct input (i.e., the same one they provided to the NISC). For the case of a corrupted sender, this will require the other major component of our protocol: a 2-round zero-knowledge (ZK) interactive argument with SPS security; unsurprisingly, we remark that an appropriate such SPS-ZK protocol can be obtained from an SPS-NISC.

Towards intuitively describing our protocol, we now briefly describe how we deal with extracting from a malicious receiver and sender before presenting the complete protocol.

Dealing with a Malicious Receiver: Using "Interactive Witness Encryption". As suggested above, the first step towards extracting a malicious receiver's input x is to have the receiver commit to their input x and send the commitment c_x with their first-round message. This way, when the receiver is corrupted, the simulator can extract x using the decommitment helper $\mathcal{H}$. Of course, we require a way to verify that the commitment sent by the receiver is indeed a commitment to the correct value of x (i.e., the same as the receiver's input to the NISC which computes $f(x, y)$). We deal with this using a technique reminiscent of the recent non-concurrent NISC protocol of [41], by using the underlying NISC to implement an "interactive witness encryption scheme"[4]. The receiver will, in addition to their input x for f, input the randomness r_x used to generate the commitment c_x, as well as the corresponding decommitment d_x, to the NISC; the sender will input c_x in addition to y, and the NISC will return $f(x, y)$ *if and only if* (c_x, d_x) *is a valid commitment of x using randomness r_x*. Hence, if the receiver sends an invalid commitment to x to the sender, they receive $\perp$ from the NISC instead of the correct output; otherwise, if it is valid, the simulator can always extract the correct value of x from the commitment using $\mathcal{H}$.

Simulation with a Malicious Receiver: Using a "Two-Track" Functionality. The second key challenge in the corrupted-receiver case is to ensure that we can simulate the sender message of the underlying NISC protocol, since the simulator in this case does not know the sender's input y. To deal with this, we use an SPS-ZK argument to prove that the sender's NISC message is correctly generated, and we additionally add a *two-track* functionality for the underlying NISC and ZK argument to preserve simulatability. First, we add a trapdoor t, chosen at random and committed to by the receiver simultaneously with x. To ensure that the corrupted-receiver simulator can properly simulate the output of the NISC, we "fix" the output when the trapdoor is used; that is, we augment the NISC's functionality yet again to take inputs t' and z^* from the sender and output z^* if the sender provides t' which matches the receiver's trapdoor t. More explicitly, the sender can *program the output* of the computation in case it can recover the trapdoor t selected by the receiver.

The ZK argument will then prove that either (1) there exists a witness w_1 demonstrating that the sender's NISC message is correctly generated (with respect to their input y) given the receiver's first message, OR (2) there exists a witness w_2 which demonstrates that the sender's NISC message was generated using the trapdoor t and no input y (which, in particular, means that the NISC will output $\perp$ if the trapdoor is *incorrect*). The honest sender can provide a witness for statement (1), while the simulator in the malicious receiver case can decommit t using $\mathcal{H}$ to obtain the trapdoor and generate a witness for statement (2).

Dealing with a Malicious Sender: Using an "Argument of Knowledge". The above, however, is not quite sufficient to simulate for a corrupted sender as well; we furthermore need an *extractability*, or "argument of knowledge", property such that the sender not only proves that there exists such a witness but also demonstrates that it *knows* such a witness—in other words, such a witness should be extractable from the prover's message in superpolynomial time. This will be necessary to show that a corrupted sender cannot provide a valid witness

---

[4] Recall that *witness encryption* [22] is a primitive where a message m can be encrypted with a statement x so that anyone with a witness w to x can decrypt m, but m cannot be recovered if x is false. Here, we would like c_x to be the "statement" that the commitment is correctly generated, and the randomness r_x and decommitment d_x the "witness".

w_2 to the trapdoor without having recovered the correct trapdoor t and thus broken the security of the commitment scheme.

In our case, since the only extractor available to us is the decommitment oracle $\mathcal{H}$, we implement extractability by using a technique from [43] which adds a *commitment to the witness* to the statement of the proof. The sender provides a witness (w_1, w_2) and two commitments c_1 and c_2, and the proof accepts either if c_1 is a valid commitment to w_1 and w_1 is a valid witness to statement (1) above, or if the respective statement holds for c_2, w_2, and statement (2). This way, a corrupted sender must with overwhelming probability use a witness for statement (1) in its proof (implying that its NISC messages and commitment to y are correctly generated), as, otherwise, a commitment of a correct witness for statement (2) would reveal the trapdoor t when decommitted and thus clearly break CCA security of the commitment scheme. Finally, as w_1 includes y, the commitment c_1 also provides the necessary extractability for the corrupted sender's input y via the decommitment helper $\mathcal{H}$ in the corrupted-sender case.

2.1 Protocol Summary

With the intuition and components described above, we can summarize our full protocol Π for secure two-party computation of a functionality $f(\cdot, \cdot)$:

- The receiver, given input x, generates a random "trapdoor" t and does as follows:
  - Generates commitment c_x for $x||t$ (respectively), using randomness r_x.
  - Generates the first-round message zk_1 of a two-round SPS-ZK argument.
  - Generates the first-round message msg_1 of the underlying NISC protocol π, which will securely compute the functionality h described below, using (x, r_x, t) as its input.

  It sends $(\mathsf{msg}_1, \mathsf{zk}_1, c_x)$ to the sender.
- The sender, given input y and the receiver's first-round message $(\mathsf{msg}_1, \mathsf{zk}_1, c_x)$, does as follows:
  - Generates the second-round message msg_2 of the underlying NISC π, using $(c_x, y, \bot, \bot)$ as its input and r_{NISC} for randomness.
  - Using witness $w_1 = (r_{\mathsf{NISC}}, y)$ and letting c_1 and c_2 be commitments to w_1 and 0, respectively, generates the second-round message zk_2 of the ZK argument for statement $(\mathsf{msg}_1, \mathsf{msg}_2, c_x, c_1, c_2)$ proving that either:
    (1) there exists a witness $w_1 = (r_{\mathsf{NISC}}, y)$ that demonstrates that msg_2 was correctly and consistently generated with respect to the receiver's first message, the sender's input y, and the randomness r_{NISC}, and c_1 is a valid commitment to w_1, OR:
    (2) there exists a witness $w_2 = (r_{\mathsf{NISC}}, t, z^*)$ that demonstrates that msg_2 was generated using input $(c_x, \bot, t, z^*)$ (i.e., using the trapdoor instead of y), and c_2 is a valid commitment to w_2.

  It sends $(\mathsf{msg}_2, \mathsf{zk}_2, c_1, c_2)$ to the receiver.
- The receiver, given the sender's message $(\mathsf{msg}_2, \mathsf{zk}_2, c_1, c_2)$, does as follows:

- Verifies that zk_2 is an accepting proof with respect to the statement $(msg_1, msg_2, c_x, c_1, c_2)$. Terminates with output $\bot$ if not.
- Evaluates and returns the output z from the NISC π.

The functionality h for the inner NISC, on input (x, r_x, t) from the receiver and (c_x, y, t', z^*) from the sender, does the following:

- Verifies that c_x is correctly generated from $x \| t$ and the randomness r_x. Outputs $\bot$ if not.
- If the trapdoor t' given by the sender matches the receiver's trapdoor t, bypasses the computation of f and outputs the sender's input z^*.
- Otherwise, returns $f(x, y)$.

Correctness will follow from correctness of the underlying primitives and the fact that an honest sender and receiver will always generate c_x, msg_2, and zk_2 according to the protocol above; thus, if both parties are honest, the SPS-ZK proof from the sender will always accept and the receiver will always obtain $f(x, y)$ from evaluating GC.

In order to prove that Π $\mathcal{H}$-EUC-securely realizes the ideal two-party computation functionality $\mathcal{T}_f$, we need to prove that, for every polynomial-time environment $\mathcal{Z}$ and adversary $\mathcal{A}$ in the "real" execution of the protocol Π, there exists a polynomial-time simulator $\mathcal{S}$ in the "ideal" execution of the protocol $\Pi(\mathcal{T}_f)$ (where, instead of following the protocol, the receiver and sender send their respective inputs x and y to an instance of $\mathcal{T}_f$ and the receiver gets the output $f(x, y)$) such that $\mathcal{Z}$'s view is indistinguishable between the "real" execution using $\mathcal{A}$ and the "ideal" execution using $\mathcal{S}$. This property needs to hold even when the environment and adversary have access to a superpolynomial-time "helper" $\mathcal{H}$ implementing the CCA decommitment oracle. (Recall from above that the helper will provide a decommitment of any commitment whose tag corresponds to a corrupted party). Below, we provide a high-level sketch of the cases for simulating a corrupted sender and receiver.

2.2 Simulating for a Corrupted Receiver

When the receiver is corrupted, $\mathcal{S}$ first needs to extract the receiver's input x from their first message and send it to the ideal functionality; this is straightforward to do, since both x and the trapdoor t can be retrieved by running the decommitment helper $\mathcal{H}$ on the receiver's input c_x (and the committed values must be the same as the ones given to the NISC in order for the receiver to receive an output). However, $\mathcal{S}$ also needs to simulate the NISC message msg_2, the SPS-ZK proof zk_2, and the commitments c_1 and c_2 to send to the receiver without knowing the corresponding input y.

While one might be tempted to simply use the respective simulators from the definitions of security to simulate the messages for the SPS-ZK argument and the internal NISC, we cannot in fact run either of these simulators inside $\mathcal{S}$, since $\mathcal{S}$ is restricted to (helper-aided) polynomial time whereas, these simulators run in superpolynomial time. So, instead of using the simulators, these messages will be simulated by running the honest protocols using the trapdoor recovered from c_x. $\mathcal{S}$ can generate the NISC message msg_2 using the input $(c_x, \bot, t, z)$, where z is the output $f(x, y)$ returned from the ideal functionality $\mathcal{T}_f$. In addition, $\mathcal{S}$ can use the second track of the ZK argument with witness $w_2 = (r_{\mathsf{NISC}}, t, z)$, ensuring that it can generate both an accepting proof zk_2 and a NISC message that ensures the correct output ($z = f(x, y)$, contingent on the malicious receiver generating c_x correctly) without knowing the sender's input y.

In a sense, this alternative method of simulating the underlying NISC and ZK argument has interesting parallels to techniques in the context of *obfuscation*, where such two-track approaches are often used to go from indistinguishability-based security to simulation-based security; see e.g. [2,34]. We also note that a technique similar to ours (albeit implemented with garbled circuits rather than a NISC) was used in a very recent work to construct oblivious transfer from new assumptions [18].

Proving that these simulated messages are indistinguishable from the real ones follows through a series of hybrids and relies on complexity leveraging along with the simulation-based security of both primitives. First, in order to switch to the second track of the ZK argument, we need to ensure that the commitment c_2 commits to the trapdoor witness $(r_{\mathsf{NISC}}, t, z)$ rather than to 0. By CCA security of the commitment scheme, commitments of the two values are indistinguishable even by a party (the environment) with access to a decommitment oracle (in this case, the helper $\mathcal{H}$). Notice that, since the sender is honest, $\mathcal{H}$ will not provide the environment with decommitments to commitments generated with the sender's tag, which is precisely the property required of the oracle in the CCA security definition.

Next, we deal with switching to the second track of the SPS-ZK and, respectively, to inputting the trapdoor t to the NISC; we first switch the real proof zk_2 using w_1 to a simulated proof using the simulator for the ZK argument. Next, leveraging the fact that the simulated proof is indistinguishable for any msg_2 satisfying either condition of the ZK language (irrespective of *which* condition) and the fact that the simulator $\mathcal{S}'_R$ for the underlying NISC depends only on the adversary (and not on the specific inputs to the NISC), we can indistinguishably switch from the real NISC message using input $(c_x, y, \bot, \bot)$ to a simulated NISC message using $\mathcal{S}'_R$, and then from there to a real NISC message using the trapdoor input $(c_x, \bot, t, z)$. We then switch the simulated ZK proof back to a real ZK proof, this time using the trapdoor witness w_2; lastly, since the witness w_1 depends on y, we must switch the commitment c_1 for the (now unused) first track of the ZK to commit to 0, which will again follow from CCA security.

Complexity leveraging is required to prove indistinguishability between our hybrids, since we require a NISC secure against adversaries able to run the (superpolynomial-time) simulator of the ZK argument, and in turn a ZK argument secure against adversaries able to internally run the decommitment helper $\mathcal{H}$. Furthermore, while the intermediate hybrids clearly run in superpolynomial time, we note that the final simulator $\mathcal{S}$ will still run in polynomial time (with $\mathcal{H}$) and is hence still sufficient to prove the notion of "angel-based" UC security.

To summarize, the corrupted-receiver simulator $\mathcal{S}_R$ proceeds as follows:

- Receives the receiver's first-round message $(\mathsf{msg}_1, \mathsf{zk}_1, c_x)$.
- Uses the helper $\mathcal{H}$ to decommit c_x, receiving x^* and t.
- Sends x^* to the ideal functionality $\mathcal{T}_f$ and receives the output z.
- Generates the second-round message msg_2 of the underlying NISC π, using $(c_x, \bot, t, z)$ as its input and r_{NISC} for randomness.
- Using witness $w_2 = (r_{\mathsf{NISC}}, t, z)$ and letting c_1 and c_2 be commitments to 0 and w_2, respectively, generates the second-round message zk_2 of the ZK argument for the language described above and statement $(\mathsf{msg}_1, \mathsf{msg}_2, c_x, c_1, c_2)$.
- Sends $(\mathsf{msg}_2, \mathsf{zk}_2, c_1, c_2)$ to the receiver.

2.3 Simulating for a Corrupted Sender

When the sender is corrupted, $\mathcal{S}$ first needs to simulate the receiver's message $(\mathsf{msg}_1, \mathsf{zk}_1, c_x)$ to send to the sender; then, on receiving the sender's message $(\mathsf{msg}_2, \mathsf{zk}_2, c_1, c_2)$, $\mathcal{S}$ needs to either output $\bot$ (if the sender's message does not verify) or extract the sender's input y to send to the ideal functionality so that the honest receiver gets the correct output $f(x, y)$.

Simulating the first message without knowledge of x will require two changes: making c_x commit to $0\|t$ rather than to $x\|t$, and respectively changing the first NISC message to use 0 in place of the input x (since, as before, we cannot use a simulated NISC message due to simulation being superpolynomial-time).

We show indistinguishability through a series of hybrids similar to the corrupted receiver case. First, we can use simulation-based security to switch the real NISC message (with input x) to a simulated NISC message using the simulator $\mathcal{S}'_S$ for π. Next, the first message no longer depends on x, so we can leverage CCA security to indistinguishably switch c_x to commit to 0 instead. A minor subtlety with this step is that the polynomial-time adversary for CCA security cannot run the superpolynomial-time simulator $\mathcal{S}'_S$, so instead we leverage non-uniformity and provide the simulated first message of the NISC to the CCA security adversary as non-uniform advice. Finally, we can again leverage simulation-based security (and the input-independence of the simulator $\mathcal{S}'_S$) to switch from the simulated message to another real message using the input 0.

It remains to consider the receiver's output; the honest receiver will output the result from the ideal functionality in the ideal experiment, but we need to ensure that the receiver correctly outputs $\bot$ when the malicious sender provides invalid inputs in its second-round message. On receiving the sender's message $(\mathsf{msg}_2, \mathsf{zk}_2, c_1, c_2)$, the simulator will extract the malicious party's input by using the helper $\mathcal{H}$ to decommit c_1 (a commitment to the witness w_1, which contains y) and then verify the sender's message. If verification is successful, $\mathcal{S}$ will send the resulting value y^* to the ideal functionality (which will return the result to the honest receiver); if not, it will terminate with output $\bot$.

By soundness of the ZK argument, if $\mathcal{S}$ does not output $\bot$, then the sender is overwhelmingly likely to have provided a proof in zk_2 corresponding to a valid witness; furthermore, we can assert that this witness is overwhelmingly likely to be a witness $w_1 = (r_{\text{NISC}}, y)$ to part (1) of the ZK argument, since, if the sender could figure out an accepting witness $w_2 = (r_{\text{NISC}}, t, z^*)$ for part (2) with non-negligible probability, this would imply that an adversary could recover this by running a decommitment oracle on the commitment c_2 and subsequently use it to break CCA security of the commitment c_x (which contains t) sent by the receiver in the first round[5].

Given a valid witness to part (1), then, it must be the case that c_1 is a valid commitment to w_1 and that msg_2 is correctly generated with respect to the y given in w_1—so, on inputs corresponding to a valid commitment c_x of $x\|t$, the internal NISC π will output $f(x, y)$ for the same y the simulator receives by decommitting c_1. Hence, we can simulate the output by, if verification passes, having the receiver return the output from the ideal functionality (exactly as in the ideal interaction), which will always be $f(x, y)$ given the y extracted from c_1; the above argument shows that this strategy will produce an output identical to that of the internal NISC with overwhelming probability. Notably, this simulated output is now independent of the value of x used to generate the first-round message (and instead relies on the x sent to the ideal functionality by the honest receiver).

This gives us the completed corrupted-sender simulator $\mathcal{S}_S$, which proceeds as follows:

- Generates a random "trapdoor" t.
- Generates commitment c_x for $0\|t$ (respectively), using randomness r_x.
- Generates the first-round message zk_1 of a two-round ZK argument.
- Generates the first-round message msg_1 of the underlying NISC protocol π, which will securely compute the functionality h described below, using $(0, r_x, t)$ as its input.
- Sends $(\text{msg}_1, \text{zk}_1, c_x)$ to the sender.

- Receives the sender's message $(\text{msg}_2, \text{zk}_2, c_1, c_2)$.
- Verifies that zk_2 is an accepting proof with respect to the statement $(\text{msg}_1, \text{msg}_2, c_x, c_1, c_2)$. Terminates with output $\bot$ if not.
- Uses the helper $\mathcal{H}$ to recover w_1 (including y^*) from the commitment c_1.
- Verifies that w_1 is a valid witness for the statement $(\text{msg}_1, \text{msg}_2, c_x, c_1, c_2)$. If not, returns $\bot$.
- Sends y^* to the ideal functionality $\mathcal{T}_f$, which will return the output $f(x, y^*)$ to the receiver.

3   Definitions

3.1   Non-interactive Secure Computation

We start by defining *non-interactive secure computation* (NISC).

---

[5] In particular, notice that the commitments c_2 and c_x are generated by different parties and hence *using different tags*—hence, an adversary breaking CCA security with respect to c_x's tag is allowed to decommit c_2.

Definition 1 ([41], based on [3,27,48]). *A **non-interactive two-party computation protocol** for computing some functionality $f(\cdot,\cdot)$ (where f is computable by a polynomial-time Turing machine) is given by three PPT algorithms $(\mathsf{NISC}_1, \mathsf{NISC}_2, \mathsf{NISC}_3)$ defining an interaction between a sender S and a receiver R, where only R will receive the final output. The protocol will have common input 1^n (the security parameter); the receiver R will have input x, and the sender will have input y. The algorithms $(\mathsf{NISC}_1, \mathsf{NISC}_2, \mathsf{NISC}_3)$ are such that:*

- *$(\mathsf{msg}_1, \sigma) \leftarrow \mathsf{NISC}_1(1^n, x)$ generates R's message msg_1 and persistent state σ (which is not sent to S) given the security parameter n and R's input x.*
- *$\mathsf{msg}_2 \leftarrow \mathsf{NISC}_2(\mathsf{msg}_1, y)$ generates S's message msg_2 given S's input y and R's message msg_1.*
- *$\mathsf{out} \leftarrow \mathsf{NISC}_3(\sigma, \mathsf{msg}_2)$ generates R's output out given the state σ and S's message msg_2.*

We restrict our attentions to protocols satisfying perfect correctness:

- ***Correctness.** For any parameter $n \in \mathbb{N}$ and inputs x, y:*

$$Pr\left[(\mathsf{msg}_1, \sigma) \leftarrow \mathsf{NISC}_1(1^n, x) : \mathsf{NISC}_3(\sigma, \mathsf{NISC}_2(\mathsf{msg}_1, y)) = f(x, y)\right] = 1$$

Externalized Universally Composable Security. To define the notion of security proven in our main theorem, we use the framework of *universally composable security* [12,13], extended to include access to superpolynomial "helper functionalities" [14,16]. Specifically, we prove UC security in the presence of an external helper which allows the adversary to break the commitments of corrupted parties.

Model of Execution. We recall the discussion of UC security with external helper functionalities provided in [16]. Consider parties represented by polynomial-time interactive Turing machines [30]; the model contains a number of parties running instances of the protocol Π, as well as an *adversary* $\mathcal{A}$ and an *environment* $\mathcal{Z}$. The environment begins by invoking the adversary on an arbitrary input, and afterwards can proceed by invoking parties which participate in single instances of the protocol Π by providing them with their respective inputs, as well as a *session identifier* (which is unique for each instance of the protocol Π) and a *party identifier* (which is unique among the participants in each session). The environment can furthermore read the output of any party involved in some execution of Π, as well as any output provided by the adversary.

For the purposes of UC security, we will restrict our attention to environments which may only invoke a single session of the protocol Π—that is, any instances invoked must have the same session identifier. Concurrent and composable security (i.e., against more generalized environments) will follow from this via a *universal composition theorem*, which we will state later in this section.

The adversary, on the other hand, is able to control all communication between the various parties involved in executions of Π, and to furthermore modify the outputs of certain *corrupted* parties (which we here assume are decided non-adaptively, i.e., every party is either invoked as permanently corrupted or permanently uncorrupted). Uncorrupted parties will always act according to the protocol Π, and we assume that the adversary only delivers messages from uncorrupted parties that were actually intended to be sent (i.e., authenticated communication); the adversary can, on the other hand, deliver any message on behalf of a corrupted party. The adversary can also send messages to and receive them from the environment at any point.

We will furthermore assume a notion of security using an "imaginary angel" [45], which can be formalized in the *externalized UC* (EUC) setting [14]; both the corrupted parties and environment will have access to an external *helper functionality* $\mathcal{H}$, also defined as an interactive Turing machine—unlike the participants, adversary, or environment, however, $\mathcal{H}$ is not restricted to polynomial running time. $\mathcal{H}$ is persistent throughout the execution and is invoked by the environment immediately after the adversary is; furthermore, $\mathcal{H}$ must be immediately informed of the identity of all corrupted parties when parties are determined by the environment to be corrupted.

Finally, while honest players can only be invoked on a single session identifier, we allow the adversary to invoke $\mathcal{H}$ on behalf of corrupt parties using potentially *arbitrary* session identifiers; this is needed to prove the composition theorem.

The execution ends when the environment halts, and we assume the output to be the output of the environment. We let $\mathsf{Exec}_{\Pi,\mathcal{A},\mathcal{Z}}(1^n, z)$ denote the distribution of the environment's output, taken over the random tape given to $\mathcal{A}$, $\mathcal{Z}$, and all participants, in the execution above (with a single session of Π), where the environment originally gets as input security parameter 1^n and auxiliary input z. We say that Π *securely emulates* some other protocol Π' if, for any adversary $\mathcal{A}$, there exists a simulator $\mathcal{S}$ such that the environment $\mathcal{Z}$ is unable to tell the difference between the execution of Π with $\mathcal{A}$ and the execution of Π' with $\mathcal{S}$—that is, intuitively, the environment gains the same information in each of the two executions. Formally:

Definition 2 (based on [16]). *For some (superpolynomial-time) interactive Turing machine* $\mathcal{H}$, *we say a protocol* Π $\mathcal{H}$-***EUC-emulates*** *some protocol* Π' *if, for any polynomial-time adversary* $\mathcal{A}$, *there exists some simulated polynomial-time adversary* $\mathcal{S}$ *such that, for any non-uniform polynomial-time environment* $\mathcal{Z}$ *and polynomial-time distinguisher* D, *there exists negligible* $\nu(\cdot)$ *such that, for any* $n \in \mathbb{N}$ *and* $z \in \{0,1\}^*$:

$$|Pr[D(\mathsf{Exec}_{\Pi,\mathcal{A},\mathcal{Z}}(1^n, z)) = 1] - Pr[D(\mathsf{Exec}_{\Pi',\mathcal{S},\mathcal{Z}}(1^n, z)) = 1]| \leq \nu(n)$$

To prove that a protocol Π *securely realizes* an ideal functionality $\mathcal{T}$, we wish to show that it securely emulates an "ideal" protocol $\Pi(\mathcal{T})$ in which all parties send their respective inputs to an instance of $\mathcal{T}$ with the same session identifier and receive the respective output; note that the adversary does not receive the messages to or from each instance of $\mathcal{T}$.

Definition 3 (based on [16]). *For some (superpolynomial-time) interactive Turing machine* $\mathcal{H}$, *we say a protocol* Π $\mathcal{H}$-***EUC-realizes*** *some functionality* $\mathcal{T}$ *if it* $\mathcal{H}$-*EUC-emulates the protocol* $\Pi(\mathcal{T})$ *given above.*

In the case of two-party computation for functionality f, $\mathcal{T}$ will simply receive inputs x from the receiver and y from the sender and return $f(x,y)$ to the receiver:

Definition 4. *For some (superpolynomial-time) interactive Turing machine $\mathcal{H}$, we refer to a non-interactive two-party computation protocol Π for some functionality $f(\cdot,\cdot)$ as $\mathcal{H}$-**EUC-secure** if it $\mathcal{H}$-EUC-realizes the functionality $\mathcal{T}_f$, which, on input x from a receiver R and input y from a sender S, returns $f(x,y)$ to R.*

Remarks. Notice that, since $\mathcal{Z}$'s output is a (randomized) function of its view, it suffices to show that $\mathcal{Z}$'s view cannot be distinguished by any polynomial-time distinguisher D between the respective experiments. We can also without loss of generality assume that the environment $\mathcal{Z}$ in the real execution effectively runs the adversary $\mathcal{A}$ internally and forwards all of $\mathcal{A}$'s messages to and from other parties by using a "dummy adversary" $\mathcal{D}$ which simply forwards communication from $\mathcal{Z}$ to the respective party. This allows us to effectively view the environment $\mathcal{Z}$ and adversary $\mathcal{A}$ as a single entity.

Furthermore, observe that we use a *polynomial-time* simulator $\mathcal{S}$ in our definition of security. [28] shows that two-round secure computation protocols cannot be proven secure with standard polynomial-time simulation; hence, many protocols are proven secure using superpolynomial-time simulators (a technique originally proposed by [43,45]). Indeed, we note that, if $\mathcal{H}$ runs in time $T(\cdot)$, then a protocol that $\mathcal{H}$-EUC-realizes some functionality $\mathcal{T}$ with polynomial-time simulation will also UC-realize $\mathcal{T}$ with $\mathsf{poly}(T(\cdot))$-time simulation; hence, in a way, the simulator $\mathcal{S}$ we propose in our security definition can still be considered to do a superpolynomial-time amount of "work".

Universal Composition. The chief advantage of the UC security paradigm is the notion of *universal composition*; intuitively, if a protocol ρ UC-realizes (or, respectively, $\mathcal{H}$-EUC-realizes) an ideal functionality $\mathcal{T}$, then it is "composable" in the sense that any protocol that uses the functionality $\mathcal{T}$ as a primitive derives the same security guarantees from the protocol ρ as they would the ideal functionality.

More formally, given an ideal functionality $\mathcal{T}$, let us define a $\mathcal{T}$-*hybrid protocol* as one where the participating parties have access to an unbounded number of copies of the functionality $\mathcal{T}$ and may communicate directly with these copies as in an "ideal" execution (i.e., without communication being intercepted by the adversary). Each copy of $\mathcal{T}$ will have a unique session identifier, and their inputs and outputs are required to contain the respective identifier.

Then, if Π is a $\mathcal{T}$-hybrid protocol, and ρ is a protocol which realizes $\mathcal{T}$, then we can define a *composed protocol* Π^ρ by modifying Π so that the first message sent to $\mathcal{T}$ is instead an invocation of a new instance of ρ with the same session identifier and the respective message as input, and so that further messages are likewise relayed to the same instance of ρ instead, again with their contents as the respective input. Any output from an instance of ρ is substituted for the respective output of the corresponding instance of $\mathcal{T}$. The following powerful theorem, then, states the notion of composability intuitively described above.

Theorem 3 (Relativized Universal Composition [12,16]**).** *For some ideal functionality $\mathcal{T}$ and helper functionality $\mathcal{H}$, if Π is a $\mathcal{T}$-hybrid protocol, and ρ is a protocol that $\mathcal{H}$-EUC-realizes $\mathcal{T}$, then Π^ρ $\mathcal{H}$-EUC-emulates Π.*

Stand-Alone Security. As one of the key building blocks of our UC-secure protocol, we use a non-interactive secure computation protocol which satisfies the strictly weaker notion of *stand-alone security with superpolynomial-time simulation.* We recall the definition (as given in [41]) below:

- Consider a *real* experiment defined by an interaction between a sender S with input y and a receiver R with input x as follows:
  - R computes $(\mathsf{msg}_1, \sigma) \leftarrow \mathsf{NISC}_1(1^n, x)$, stores σ, and sends msg_1 to S.
  - S, on receiving msg_1, computes $\mathsf{msg}_2 \leftarrow \mathsf{NISC}_2(\mathsf{msg}_1, y)$ and sends msg_2 to R.
  - R, on receiving msg_2 computes $out \leftarrow \mathsf{NISC}_3(\sigma, \mathsf{msg}_2)$ and outputs out.

  In this interaction, one party $I \in \{S, R\}$ is defined as the *corrupted* party; we additionally define an *adversary*, or a polynomial-time machine $\mathcal{A}$, which receives the security parameter 1^n, an auxiliary input z, and the inputs of the corrupted party I, and sends messages (which it may determine arbitrarily) in place of I.

  Letting Π denote the protocol to be proven secure, we shall denote by $\mathsf{Out}_{\Pi,\mathcal{A},I}(1^n, x, y, z)$ the random variable, taken over all randomness used by the honest party and the adversary, whose output is given by the outputs of the honest receiver (if $I = S$) and the adversary (which may output an arbitrary function of its view).

- Consider also an *ideal* experiment defined by an interaction between a sender S, a receiver R, and a *trusted party* $\mathcal{T}_f$, as follows:
  - R sends x to $\mathcal{T}_f$, and S sends y to $\mathcal{T}_f$.
  - $\mathcal{T}_f$, on receiving x and y, computes $out = f(x, y)$ and returns it to R.
  - R, on receiving out, outputs it.

  As with the real experiment, we say that one party $I \in \{S, R\}$ is corrupted in that, as before, their behavior is controlled by an adversary $\mathcal{A}$. We shall denote by $\mathsf{Out}_{\Pi_f, \mathcal{A}, I}^{\mathcal{T}_f}(1^n, x, y, z)$ the random variable, once again taken over all randomness used by the honest party and the adversary, whose output is again given by the outputs of the honest receiver (if $I = S$) and the adversary.

Definition 5 ([41]**, based on** [3,27,43,45,48]**).** *Given a function $T(\cdot)$, a non-interactive two-party protocol $\Pi = (\mathsf{NISC}_1, \mathsf{NISC}_2, \mathsf{NISC}_3)$ between a sender S and a receiver R, and functionality $f(\cdot, \cdot)$ computable by a polynomial-time Turing machine, we say that Π **securely computes f with $T(\cdot)$-time simulation,** or that Π is a **non-interactive (stand-alone) secure computation protocol**

(with $T(\cdot)$-time simulation) for computing f, if Π is a non-interactive two-party computation protocol for computing f and, for any polynomial-time adversary $\mathcal{A}$ corrupting party $I \in \{S, R\}$, there exists a $T(n) \cdot poly(n)$-time simulator $\mathcal{S}$ such that, for any $T(n) \cdot poly(n)$-time algorithm $D : \{0,1\}^* \rightarrow \{0,1\}$, there exists negligible $\epsilon(\cdot)$ such that for any $n \in \mathbb{N}$ and any inputs $x, y \in \{0,1\}^n, z \in \{0,1\}^*$, we have:

$$\left| Pr[D(\mathsf{Out}_{\Pi,\mathcal{A},I}(1^n, x, y, z)) = 1] - Pr\left[D(\mathsf{Out}_{\Pi_f,\mathcal{S},I}^{T_f}(1^n, x, y, z)) = 1\right]\right| < \epsilon(n)$$

where the experiments and distributions Out are as defined above.

Furthermore, if Π securely computes f with $T(\cdot)$-time simulation for $T(n) = n^{\log^c(n)}$ for some constant c, we say that Π is **stand-alone secure with quasi-polynomial simulation**.

Badrinarayanan et al. [3] demonstrates that stand-alone secure NISC protocols with quasi-polynomial simulation exist assuming the existence of a notion of "weak OT", which in turn can be based on subexponential versions of standard assumptions [3,10]:

Theorem 4 ([3,10]). *Assuming subexponential hardness of any one of the Decisional Diffie-Hellman, Quadratic Residuosity, N^{th} Residuosity, or Learning With Errors assumptions, then for any constants $c < c'$ and any polynomial-time Turing-computable functionality $f(\cdot, \cdot)$ there exists a (subexponentially) stand-alone secure non-interactive two-party computation protocol with $T(\cdot)$-time security and $T'(\cdot)$-time simulation for $T(n) = n^{\log^c(n)}$ and $T'(n) = n^{\log^{c'}(n)}$.*

3.2   SPS-ZK Arguments

We proceed to recalling the definition of interactive arguments.

Definition 6 ([11,26,30]). *We refer to an interactive protocol (P, V) between a probabilistic prover P and a verifier V as an **interactive argument** for some language $\mathcal{L} \subseteq \{0,1\}^*$ if the following conditions hold:*

1. **Completeness.** *There exists a negligible function $\nu(\cdot)$ such that, for any $x \in \mathcal{L}$:*
$$Pr[\langle P, V \rangle(x) = \mathsf{Accept}] \geq 1 - \nu(|x|)$$

2. $T(\cdot)$-**time soundness.** *For any non-uniform probabilistic $T(\cdot)$-time prover P^* (not necessarily honest), there exists a negligible function $\nu(\cdot)$ such that, for any $x \notin \mathcal{L}$:*
$$Pr[\langle P^*, V \rangle(x) = \mathsf{Accept}] \leq \nu(|x|)$$

*Furthermore, if the above holds even if the statement $x \notin \mathcal{L}$ can be adaptively chosen by the cheating prover anytime prior to sending its last message, we call such a protocol ($T(\cdot)$-time) **adaptively sound**.*

We also require a notion of *zero-knowledge* [30] with superpolynomial simulation (SPS-ZK) [43], which states that the prover's witness w should be "hidden" from the verifier in the sense that proofs of a particular statement $x \in L$ should be simulatable in a manner independent of w:

Definition 7 ([43]). *We refer to an interactive argument for some NP language L (with witness relation R_L) as $T'(\cdot)$-**time simulatable zero-knowledge with** $T(\cdot)$-**time security** (or $(T(\cdot), T'(\cdot))$-simulatable zero-knowledge) if, for any $T(\cdot)$-time cheating verifier V^* (which can output an arbitrary function of its view), there exists a $T'(\cdot)$-time simulator* Sim *and negligible function $\nu(\cdot)$ such that, for any $T(\cdot)$-time non-uniform distinguisher D, given any statement $x \in L$, any witness $w \in R_L(x)$, and any auxiliary input $z \in \{0,1\}^*$, it holds that:*

$$|Pr[D(x, \langle P(w), V^*(z) \rangle(x)) = 1] - Pr[D(x, \mathsf{Sim}(x, z)) = 1]| \leq \nu(|x|)$$

Our construction will use a two-round adaptively sound zero-knowledge argument consisting of three polynomial-time algorithms, $(\mathsf{ZK}_1, \mathsf{ZK}_2, \mathsf{ZK}_3)$, defining the following interaction $\langle P, V \rangle$:

- V runs $(\mathsf{zk}_1, \sigma) \leftarrow \mathsf{ZK}_1(1^n)$, which takes as input the security parameter n and generates a first message zk_1 and persistent state σ.
- P runs $\mathsf{zk}_2 \leftarrow \mathsf{ZK}_2(\mathsf{wi}_1, x, w)$, which takes as input the first message wi_1, a statement x, and a witness w, and returns a second message zk_2.
- V runs $\{\mathsf{Accept}, \mathsf{Reject}\} \leftarrow \mathsf{ZK}_3(\mathsf{zk}_2, x, \sigma)$, which takes as input a second message zk_2, a statement x, and the persistent state σ, and returns Accept if zk_2 contains an accepting proof that $x \in L$ and Reject otherwise.

We observe that, in fact, this primitive is implied by the existence of a *standalone secure NISC* (see Definition 5).

Theorem 5. *For any constants $c < c'$, letting subexponential functions $T(n) = n^{\log^c(n)}$ and $T'(n) = n^{\log^{c'}(n)}$, then, if there exists a subexponentially standalone secure non-interactive two-party computation protocol for any polynomial-time Turing-computable functionality $f(\cdot, \cdot)$ with $T(\cdot)$-time security and $T'(\cdot)$-time simulation, then there exists a two-round interactive argument with $T(\cdot)$-time adaptive soundness and $(T(\cdot), T'(\cdot))$-simulatable zero-knowledge.*

The construction and its proof of security is straightforward, but for completeness we provide it in the full version.

3.3 Non-interactive CCA-Secure Commitments

Our construction will rely on non-interactive (single-message) tag-based commitment schemes satisfying the notion of CCA security [16,35,42].

Definition 8 (based on [35]). *A **non-interactive tag-based commitment scheme** (with $t(\cdot)$-bit tags) consists of a pair of polynomial-time algorithms* (Com, Open) *such that:*

- $c \leftarrow \mathsf{Com}(1^n, \mathsf{id}, v; r)$ *(alternately denoted* $\mathsf{Com}_{\mathsf{id}}(1^n, v; r)$*) takes as input an identifier (tag)* $\mathsf{id} \in \{0,1\}^{t(n)}$*, a value* v*, randomness* r*, and a security parameter* n*, and outputs a commitment* c*. We assume without loss of generality that the commitment* c *includes the respective tag* id*.*
- $\{\mathsf{Accept}, \mathsf{Reject}\} \leftarrow \mathsf{Open}(c, v, r)$ *takes as input a commitment* c*, a value* v*, and randomness* r*, and returns either* Accept *(if* c *is a valid commitment for* v *under randomness* r*) or* Reject *(if not).*

We consider commitment schemes having the following properties:

1. ***Correctness:*** *For any security parameter* $n \in \mathbb{N}$*, any* $v, r \in \{0,1\}^*$*, and any* $\mathsf{id} \in \{0,1\}^{t(n)}$*:*

$$\Pr[c \leftarrow \mathsf{Com}(1^n, \mathsf{id}, v; r) : \mathsf{Open}(c, v, r) = \mathsf{Accept}] = 1$$

2. ***Perfect binding (for sufficiently large inputs):*** *There exists* $n \in \mathbb{N}$ *such that, for any commitment string* c*, values* v, v' *with* $|v| \geq n$ *or* $|v'| \geq n$*, and randomness* r, r'*, if it is true that* $\mathsf{Open}(c, v, r) = \mathsf{Accept}$ *and* $\mathsf{Open}(c, v', r') = \mathsf{Accept}$*, then* $v = v'$*.*[6]

3. $T(\cdot)$***-time hiding:*** *For any* $T(\cdot)$*-time non-uniform distinguisher* D *and fixed polynomial* $p(\cdot)$*, there exists a negligible function* $\nu(\cdot)$ *such that, for any* $n \in \mathbb{N}$*, any* $\mathsf{id} \in \{0,1\}^{t(n)}$ *and any values* $v, v' \in \{0,1\}^{p(n)}$*:*

$$|\Pr[D(\mathsf{Com}(1^n, \mathsf{id}, v)) = 1] - \Pr[D(\mathsf{Com}(1^n, \mathsf{id}, v')) = 1]| \leq \nu(n)$$

For our construction, we require a strictly stronger property than just hiding: hiding should hold even against an adversary with access to a "decommitment oracle". This property is known as *CCA security* due to its similarity to the analogous notion for encryption schemes [46]. We introduce a weakening of CCA security, to which we shall refer as "weak CCA security", which is nonetheless sufficient for our proof of security, and, as we shall prove in Sect. 5, is *necessary* for our proof of security as well. We define this as follows:

Definition 9. *Let* $\mathcal{O}^*$ *be an oracle which, given a commitment* c*, returns a valid committed value* v—*that is, such that there exists some randomness* r *for which* $\mathsf{Open}(c, v, r) = \mathsf{Accept}$*.*

A tag-based commitment scheme $(\mathsf{Com}, \mathsf{Open})$ *is* $T(\cdot)$***-time weakly CCA-secure*** *with respect to* $\mathcal{O}^*$ *if, for any polynomial-time adversary* $\mathcal{A}$*, letting* $\mathsf{Exp}_b(\mathcal{O}^*, \mathcal{A}, n, z)$ *(for* $b \in \{0,1\}$*) denote* $\mathcal{A}$*'s output in the following interactive experiment:*

- $\mathcal{A}$*, on input* $(1^n, z)$*, is given oracle access to* $\mathcal{O}^*$*, and adaptively chooses values* v_0, v_1 *and tag* id*.*
- $\mathcal{A}$ *receives* $\mathsf{Com}(1^n, \mathsf{id}, v_b)$ *and returns an arbitrary output; however,* $\mathcal{A}$*'s output is replaced with* $\perp$ *if* $\mathcal{O}^*$ *was ever queried on any commitment* c *with tag* id*.*

---

[6] We remark that this property is stronger than statistical binding but weaker than fully perfect binding.

then, for any $T(\cdot)$-time distinguisher D, there exists negligible $\nu(\cdot)$ such that, for any $n \in \mathbb{N}$ and any $z \in \{0,1\}^*$, it holds that:

$$|\Pr[D(\mathsf{Exp}_0(\mathcal{O}^*, \mathcal{A}, n, z)) = 1] - \Pr[D(\mathsf{Exp}_1(\mathcal{O}^*, \mathcal{A}, n, z)) = 1]| \leq \nu(n)$$

We remark that the only difference from the "standard" notion of CCA security is that the CCA oracle, given a commitment c, rather than returning both the value v committed to and the randomness r used in the commitment, instead returns just the value v. This is similar to the definition of CCA security commonly used for encryption schemes [46].

4   Results

We state our main theorem and the respective protocol in this section.

Input: A commitment c, which without loss of generality contains identity id and was sent by party P in session S.
Output: A value v or the special symbol $\perp$.

Functionality:
1. Verify that $\mathsf{id} = (S, P)$ and return $\perp$ if not.
2. Otherwise, run the oracle $\mathcal{O}$ (from the definition of weak CCA security) to find a valid decommitment v (i.e., such that, for some randomness r $\mathsf{Open}(c, v, r) = \mathsf{Accept}$), and return it, or return $\perp$ if there is no valid decommitment (i.e., $\mathcal{O}$ returns $\perp$).

Fig. 1. Decommitment helper $\mathcal{H}$ for a weakly CCA-secure commitment scheme $(\mathsf{Com}, \mathsf{Open})$.)

Theorem 6. *If there exist superpolynomial-time functions $T_{\mathsf{Com}}(\cdot) = n^{\log^{c_0}(n)}$, $T_{\mathsf{ZK}}(\cdot) = n^{\log^{c_1}(n)}$, $T_{\mathsf{Sim}}(\cdot) = n^{\log^{c_2}(n)}$, and $T_\pi(\cdot) = n^{\log^{c_3}(n)}$ for constants $0 < c_0 < c_1 < c_2 < c_3$ so that there exist (1) a non-interactive weakly CCA-secure commitment scheme with respect to a $T_{\mathsf{Com}}(n)$-time oracle $\mathcal{O}$, (2) a non-interactive computation protocol for general polynomial-time Turing-computable functionalities satisfying $T_{\mathsf{ZK}}(\cdot)$-time stand-alone security and $T_{\mathsf{Sim}}(\cdot)$-time simulation, and (3) a non-interactive computation protocol for general polynomial-time Turing-computable functionalities satisfying $T_\pi(\cdot)$-time stand-alone security (and $T'(\cdot)$-time simulation for some $T'(\cdot) \gg T_\pi(\cdot)$), then, for any polynomial-time Turing-computable functionality $f(\cdot, \cdot)$, the protocol Π given in Fig. 2 for computing f is an $\mathcal{H}$-EUC-secure non-interactive secure computation protocol with respect to the helper $\mathcal{H}$ in Fig. 1.*

Let $T_{\mathsf{Com}}(\cdot), T_{\mathsf{ZK}}(\cdot), T_{\mathsf{Sim}}(\cdot), T_{\pi}(\cdot)$ be as given in the theorem. Π will use the following primitives:

- $(\mathsf{Com}, \mathsf{Open})$, a secure commitment scheme satisfying weak CCA security with respect to some oracle $\mathcal{O}$ having running time $T_{\mathsf{Com}}(n)$. This is primitive (1) given in the theorem.
- $(\mathsf{ZK}_1, \mathsf{ZK}_2, \mathsf{ZK}_3)$, a two-message interactive argument which satisfies $T_{\mathsf{ZK}}(n)$-time adaptive soundness and $(T_{\mathsf{ZK}}(\cdot), T_{\mathsf{Sim}}(\cdot))$-simulatable zero-knowledge (with respective $T_{\mathsf{Sim}}(\cdot)$-time simulator $\mathsf{Sim}_{\mathsf{ZK}}$). By Theorem 5, this can be constructed from the primitive (2) given in the theorem.
- $\pi = (\mathsf{NISC}_1, \mathsf{NISC}_2, \mathsf{NISC}_3)$, a *stand-alone secure* non-interactive two-party computation protocol for the functionality h given in Fig. 3 satisfying $T_{\pi}(\cdot)$-time security and $T'(\cdot)$-time simulation for some $T'(n) \gg T_{\pi}(n)$. This is implied by primitive (3) in the theorem.

We provide the complete proof, which constructs the polynomial-time simulator $\mathcal{S}$ (aided by $\mathcal{H}$) required for the definition of $\mathcal{H}$-EUC-security, in the full version.

5 Minimality of Assumptions

In this section, we prove that the protocol we construct in Theorem 6 can be constructed using nearly minimal assumptions—that is, that a NISC protocol satisfying externalized UC security implies both a (polynomial-time) stand-alone secure NISC protocol with superpolynomial-time simulation and weakly CCA-secure commitments. Thus, these primitives are not only sufficient but also *necessary* for the existence of an externalized UC-secure NISC. The only gap between the sufficient and necessary conditions is that Theorem 6 requires a stand-alone NISC having simulation-based security with respect to subexponential-time distinguishers, whereas one can only construct a polynomial-time secure stand-alone NISC from our definition of UC security.

Theorem 7. *Assume the existence of a protocol $\Pi = (\pi_1, \pi_2, \pi_3)$ for non-interactive computation of any polynomial-time Turing-computable functionality $f(\cdot, \cdot)$; further assume that Π satisfies the notion of UC security with respect to some superpolynomial-time helper $\mathcal{H}$. Then there exist both a stand-alone secure non-interactive two-party computation protocol (for any polynomial-time Turing-computable functionality $h(\cdot, \cdot)$) with superpolynomial-time simulation and a non-interactive weakly CCA-secure commitment scheme.*

Proof. The first implication is immediate; since stand-alone SPS security is strictly weaker than externalized UC security, any NISC protocol satisfying externalized UC security is already stand-alone secure with SPS.

So, it suffices to prove that externalized UC-secure NISC implies weakly CCA-secure commitments; formally, we prove the following:

Input: The receiver R (with identity P_R) and the sender S (with identity P_S) are given input $x, y \in \{0,1\}^n$, respectively, and both parties have common input 1^n and session ID id.

Output: R outputs $f(x, y)$.

Round 1: R proceeds as follows:

1. Generate trapdoor $t \leftarrow \{0,1\}^n$ and randomness $r_x \leftarrow \{0,1\}^*$.
2. Compute $c_x = \mathsf{Com}(1^n, (\mathsf{id}, P_R), x\|t; r_x)$.
3. Compute $(\mathsf{msg}_1, \sigma_{\mathsf{NISC}}) \leftarrow \mathsf{NISC}_1(1^n, (x, r_x, t))$, where the protocol $\pi = (\mathsf{NISC}_1, \mathsf{NISC}_2, \mathsf{NISC}_3)$ computes the functionality h given in Figure 3.
4. Compute $(\mathsf{zk}_1, \sigma_{\mathsf{ZK}}) \leftarrow \mathsf{ZK}_1(1^n)$.
5. Send $(\mathsf{msg}_1, \mathsf{zk}_1, c_x)$ to S.

Round 2: S proceeds as follows:

1. Generate randomness $r_1, r_2, r_{\mathsf{NISC}} \leftarrow \{0,1\}^*$.
2. Compute $\mathsf{msg}_2 = \mathsf{NISC}_2(\mathsf{msg}_1, (c_x, y, \perp, \perp); r_{\mathsf{NISC}})$.
3. Let $v = (\mathsf{msg}_1, \mathsf{msg}_2, c_x)$, $w_1 = (r_{\mathsf{NISC}}, y)$, and $w_2 = (\perp, \perp, \perp)$. Compute $c_1 = \mathsf{Com}(1^n, (\mathsf{id}, P_S), w_1; r_1)$ and $c_2 = \mathsf{Com}(1^n, (\mathsf{id}, P_S), 0; r_2)$.
4. Compute $\mathsf{zk}_2 \leftarrow \mathsf{ZK}_2(1^n, \mathsf{zk}_1, (v, c_1, c_2), (w_1, r_1, w_2, \perp))$ for the language L consisting of tuples (v, c_1, c_2), where $v = (\mathsf{msg}_1, \mathsf{msg}_2, c_x)$, such that there exists a witness (w_1, r_1, w_2, r_2) so that either:
   (a) $c_1 = \mathsf{Com}(1^n, (\mathsf{id}, P_S), w_1; r_1)$, and $w_1 = (r_{\mathsf{NISC}}, y)$ satisfies $\mathsf{msg}_2 = \mathsf{NISC}_2(\mathsf{msg}_1, (c_x, y, \perp, \perp); r_{\mathsf{NISC}})$.
   OR:
   (b) $c_2 = \mathsf{Com}(1^n, (\mathsf{id}, P_S), w_2; r_2)$, and $w_2 = (r_{\mathsf{NISC}}, t, z^*)$ satisfies $\mathsf{msg}_2 = \mathsf{NISC}_2(\mathsf{msg}_1, (c_x, \perp, t, z^*); r_{\mathsf{NISC}})$.
5. Send $(\mathsf{msg}_2, \mathsf{zk}_2, c_1, c_2)$ to R.

Output phase: R proceeds as follows:

1. Let $v = (\mathsf{msg}_1, \mathsf{msg}_2, c_x)$. If $\mathsf{ZK}_3(\mathsf{zk}_2, (v, c_1, c_2), \sigma_{\mathsf{ZK}}) \neq \mathsf{Accept}$, terminate with output $\perp$.
2. Compute $z = \mathsf{NISC}_3(\mathsf{msg}_2, \sigma_{\mathsf{NISC}})$. If $z = \perp$, terminate with output $\perp$; otherwise return z.

Fig. 2. Protocol Π for non-interactive secure computation.

Input: The receiver R has input (x, r_x, t), and the sender S has input (c_x, y, t', z^*)

Output: Either $f(x, y)$, z^*, or the special symbol $\perp$.

Functionality:

1. If $c_x \neq \mathsf{Com}(1^n, (\mathsf{id}, P_R), x\|t; r_x)$, return $\perp$.
2. If $t = t'$, then return z^*.
3. Otherwise, return $f(x, y)$ (or $\perp$ if either x or y is $\perp$).

Fig. 3. Functionality h used for the underlying 2PC protocol π.

Lemma 1. *Assume a protocol $\Pi = (\pi_1, \pi_2, \pi_3)$ for non-interactive computation of the functionality which, on inputs x and y, returns $f(x, y) = 1$ if $x = y$ and $f(x, y) = 0$ otherwise; further assume that Π satisfies the notion of UC security with a superpolynomial-time helper. Then there exists a commitment scheme $(\mathsf{Com}, \mathsf{Open})$ which satisfies correctness, perfect binding for sufficiently large inputs, and weak CCA security.*

Proof. We define the weakly CCA secure commitment scheme $(\mathsf{Com}, \mathsf{Open})$ as follows:

- $\mathsf{Com}(1^n, \mathsf{id}, x)$ generates random padding $p \leftarrow \{0, 1\}^n$ and outputs $c \leftarrow \pi_1(1^n, (\mathsf{id}, 1), x\|p)$ as well as the session identifier id.
  That is, c is the first (receiver's) message of a new instance of Π with receiver input x, padded by the random p, and session identifier id.
  Note: We shall assume throughout that the player identifiers in any instance of Π are equal to 1 for the sender and 2 for the receiver.
- $\mathsf{Open}(c, x, (p, r))$ outputs Reject if $c \neq \pi_1(1^n, (\mathsf{id}, 1), x\|p; r)$, and otherwise recovers the receiver's state σ after π_1 and outputs $b \leftarrow \pi_3(\pi_2(c, x), \sigma)$.
  That is, Open first verifies that the commitment c is validly generated with respect to the value x and the receiver's randomness; if not, it returns Reject. Otherwise, it returns the result (Accept if 1, Reject if 0) of running the sender of Π given the initial message c and sender's input x to produce a message m, and finally running the receiver of Π given m as the sender's message.

Correctness of $(\mathsf{Com}, \mathsf{Open})$ will follow directly from the correctness of Π. For the other two properties, we prove the following claims:

Claim 1. *For all sufficiently large input sizes $|x|$, $(\mathsf{Com}, \mathsf{Open})$ satisfies perfect binding.*

We defer some details to the full version, but provide a high-level summary of the argument here.

Essentially, perfect binding will follow from the correctness and security of Π. Fix the simulator $\mathcal{S}$ (and superpolynomial-time helper $\mathcal{H}$) given by the definition of $\mathcal{H}$-EUC security for Π as a secure implementation of the equality functionality, and assume for the sake of contradiction that there exists an infinite sequence of tuples (c, x, x') such that, for each such pair, $x \neq x'$ but there exist (p, r) and (p', r') for which $\mathsf{Open}(c, x, (p, r)) = \mathsf{Accept}$ and $\mathsf{Open}(c, x', (p', r')) = \mathsf{Accept}$ both with non-zero probability.

Then consider an environment $\mathcal{Z}$ which, on input x^*, will do as follows:

– Start an instance of Π with a corrupted receiver, session identifier id (and player identifiers 1 for the receiver and 2 for the sender), and input $x||p$ for the receiver and x^* for the sender.
– Substitute c for the receiver's first message to the honest sender, and receive the sender's response m.
– Run the standard final round π_3 of the receiver's protocol using m as the sender's message and r as the randomness to produce an output $\pi_3(m)|_r$.

If $x^* = x||p$, the output must be 1 by perfect correctness of Π in the real execution of this environment, so the same must hold with overwhelming probability in the ideal execution using $\mathcal{T}_f$. This in turn indicates that the simulator $\mathcal{S}$, when given c as the receiver's first message, extracts the output $x||p$ to send to the ideal functionality with overwhelming probability, as the ideal functionality must return 1 when comparing that output to the sender's input $x||p$.

However, if we consider a similar experiment to the above but using $x'||p'$ as the receiver's input rather than $x||p$ (and r' as the respective randomness), we can use the same logic to arrive at the conclusion that the input extracted by the simulator $\mathcal{S}$ from c and sent to the ideal functionality on behalf of the corrupted receiver is $x'||p'$ with overwhelming probability. Clearly, for sufficiently large $n \in \mathbb{N}$ (i.e., sufficiently large inputs x, x' in our infinite sequence of tuples (c, x, x')), this cannot be true simultaneously with the above fact; thus, by contradiction, $(\mathsf{Com}, \mathsf{Open})$ must satisfy perfect binding.

Claim 2. $(\mathsf{Com}, \mathsf{Open})$ *satisfies weak CCA security.*

Proof. Fix the simulator $\mathcal{S}$ and superpolynomial-time helper $\mathcal{H}$ implied by the definition of $\mathcal{H}$-EUC security of the protocol Π. Assume for the sake of contradiction that there exists an adversary $\mathcal{A}$ which can contradict the definition of weak CCA security (Definition 9). We first show that $\mathcal{A}$, which is by definition polynomial-time with oracle access to a weak CCA decommitment oracle $\mathcal{O}^*$, can also be effectively implemented in polynomial time with oracle access to the helper functionality $\mathcal{H}$.

Subclaim 1. *Any polynomial-time adversary $\mathcal{A}$ against weak CCA security with oracle access to the oracle $\mathcal{O}^*$ defined in Definition 9 can also be implemented in polynomial time using oracle access to the helper functionality $\mathcal{H}$ instead, with error at most negligible in the security parameter n of Π[7], and with the*

---

[7] We comment that, while the implementation of $\mathcal{O}^*$ does not decommit successfully with probability 1, decommitting with overwhelming probability is sufficient as it creates at most a negligible error in the adversary's output in the CCA security game.

additional property that $\mathcal{H}$ will never be queried using a session identifier sid *that is the same as the identifier used in $\mathcal{A}$'s challenge commitment.*

Proof. Consider replacing each of $\mathcal{A}$'s queries to $\mathcal{O}^*$ by the following process, which runs in polynomial time given oracle access to $\mathcal{H}$:

- Receive a commitment c to decommit, with tag id.
- Start a new instance of Π with a corrupted receiver and session identifier id (and player identifiers 1 for the receiver and 2 for the sender).
- Run the simulator $\mathcal{S}$ (which uses the helper $\mathcal{H}$) on the respective instance of Π, substituting c for the corrupted receiver's message. $\mathcal{S}$ will generate an input $x^*||p$ to send to the ideal functionality; return x^* to $\mathcal{A}$.

We claim that, if the above process does not generate correct responses to all oracle queries with overwhelming probability (i.e., $1 - \nu(n)$ for some negligible $\nu(\cdot)$), then there exists an environment $\mathcal{Z}$ able to distinguish between the real and simulated executions with non-negligible probability.

First, we consider a number of "hybrid" oracles $\mathcal{O}_0, \mathcal{O}_1, \ldots$, where in $\mathcal{O}_i$ the first i queries are answered by the true oracle $\mathcal{O}^*$ and all other queries are answered by the procedure above. Assume then for the sake of contradiction that there exists some fixed randomness r for the CCA security adversary such that, in the respective instance of the security game, the poly-time implementation of $\mathcal{O}^*$ gives at least one incorrect decommitment with some non-negligible probability $1/p(n)$. Then there necessarily exists some $i \in \mathbb{N}$ such that the oracle's outputs in $\mathcal{O}_i$ and $\mathcal{O}_{i-1}$ differ with non-negligible probability $1/q(n)$ (since the adversary in the CCA security game is restricted to at most a polynomial number of oracle queries).

We use this fact to construct our distinguishing environment $\mathcal{Z}$. Specifically, because of the above, there must exist $j \geq i$ for which the oracle's responses to the jth query differ between $\mathcal{O}_i$ and $\mathcal{O}_{i-1}$ with some non-negligible probability $1/q'(n)$; let $\mathcal{Z}$ receive as non-uniform advice the first such j, the jth query c, and the (padded) decommitment $x||p$ (which can be $\bot$ if c is an invalid commitment), which are determined by fixed randomness r and the responses from the true CCA oracle to the first $j - 1$ queries, and let it proceed as follows:

- Start a single instance of Π with a corrupted receiver, session identifier given by the tag of c (and player identifiers 1 for the receiver and 2 for the sender), and receiver and sender input both equal to $x||p$.
- Replace the receiver's first message with c, and return the output of the protocol.

By perfect correctness of Π, and the assumption that c is a valid first-round messages on input $x||p$, $\mathcal{Z}$ outputs 1 in the real interaction with probability 1; however, by our assumption that the responses to the jth oracle query in $\mathcal{O}_i$ and $\mathcal{O}_{i-1}$ differ with non-negligible probability $1/q'(n)$, we know that in the ideal interaction $\mathcal{S}$ must send some $x'||p' \neq x||p$ to the ideal functionality on behalf of the corrupted receiver with at least probability $1/q'(n)$. Therefore, since the honest sender's input to the ideal functionality is always $x\|p$, we observe that $\mathcal{Z}$ outputs 0 in the ideal interaction with probability $1/q'(n)$, thus contradicting security of Π by distinguishing the real and ideal interactions and completing our argument.

Lastly, we note that, during the $\mathcal{H}$-aided reimplementation of the adversary $\mathcal{A}$, $\mathcal{H}$ will never be queried using a session identifier sid that is the same as the identifier used in the challenge commitment. This follows from the restriction that the simulator $\mathcal{S}$ may never query $\mathcal{H}$ using an honest party's identifiers $(\mathsf{sid}, \mathsf{pid})$: the only corrupted parties are those with sid equal to the tags of the queried commitments, which by the definition of weak CCA security may never be identical to the tag of the challenge. □

In the full version, we also show the following, which together with the previous claim will provide a contradiction:

Subclaim 2. (Com, Open) *satisfies hiding against any polynomial-time adversary $\mathcal{A}$, even if the adversary is given oracle access to the helper functionality $\mathcal{H}$, as long as $\mathcal{A}$ never queries $\mathcal{H}$ using a session identifier* sid *that is the same as the identifier used in the challenge commitment.*

So, given an adversary $\mathcal{A}$ that contradicts weak CCA security using polynomial time and oracle access to the CCA oracle $\mathcal{O}^*$, Subclaim 1 implies that there is a reimplemented adversary $\mathcal{A}'$ that likewise contradicts weak CCA security and uses polynomial time and oracle access to the superpolynomial-time helper functionality $\mathcal{H}$ without invoking the helper using a session identifier equal to the tag of the challenge commitment. But this directly contradicts Subclaim 2, since weak CCA security without access to the CCA oracle is equivalent to hiding, and the subclaim shows that $\mathcal{A}'$ cannot break the hiding property of (Com, Open) without invoking $\mathcal{H}$ using the challenge commitment's tag. Therefore, by this contradiction, (Com, Open) satisfies weak CCA security, as desired. □

□

□

References

1. Abdolmaleki, B., Malavolta, G., Rahimi, A.: Two-Round Concurrently Secure Two-Party Computation. Cryptology ePrint Archive, Paper 2021/1357 (2021). https://eprint.iacr.org/2021/1357
2. Ananth, P., Brakerski, Z., Segev, G., Vaikuntanathan, V.: From selective to adaptive security in functional encryption. In: Gennaro, R., Robshaw, M. (eds.) CRYPTO 2015. LNCS, Part II, vol. 9216, pp. 657–677. Springer, Heidelberg (2015). https://doi.org/10.1007/978-3-662-48000-7_32
3. Badrinarayanan, S., Garg, S., Ishai, Y., Sahai, A., Wadia, A.: Two-message witness indistinguishability and secure computation in the plain model from new assumptions. In: Takagi, T., Peyrin, T. (eds.) ASIACRYPT 2017. LNCS, Part III, vol. 10626, pp. 275–303. Springer, Cham (2017). https://doi.org/10.1007/978-3-319-70700-6_10

4. Badrinarayanan, S., Goyal, V., Jain, A., Khurana, D., Sahai, A.: Round optimal concurrent MPC via strong simulation. In: Kalai, Y., Reyzin, L. (eds.) TCC 2017. LNCS, vol. 10677, pp. 743–775. Springer, Cham (2017). https://doi.org/10.1007/978-3-319-70500-2_25

5. Barak, B., Sahai, A.: How to play almost any mental game over the net - concurrent composition via super-polynomial simulation. In: 46th FOCS, pp. 543–552. IEEE Computer Society Press (2005). https://doi.org/10.1109/SFCS.2005.43

6. Beaver, D.: Foundations of secure interactive computing. In: Feigenbaum, J. (ed.) CRYPTO 1991. LNCS, vol. 576, pp. 377–391. Springer, Heidelberg (1992). https://doi.org/10.1007/3-540-46766-1_31

7. Benhamouda, F., Lin, H.: k-round multiparty computation from k-round oblivious transfer via garbled interactive circuits. In: Nielsen, J.B., Rijmen, V. (eds.) EUROCRYPT 2018. LNCS, Part II, vol. 10821, pp. 500–532. Springer, Cham (2018). https://doi.org/10.1007/978-3-319-78375-8_17

8. Benhamouda, F., Lin, H., Polychroniadou, A., Venkitasubramaniam, M.: Two-round adaptively secure multiparty computation from standard assumptions. In: Beimel, A., Dziembowski, S. (eds.) TCC 2018. LNCS, Part I, vol. 11239, pp. 175–205. Springer, Cham (2018). https://doi.org/10.1007/978-3-030-03807-6_7

9. Bitansky, N., Lin, H.: One-message zero knowledge and non-malleable commitments. In: Beimel, A., Dziembowski, S. (eds.) TCC 2018. LNCS, Part I, vol. 11239, pp. 209–234. Springer, Cham (2018). https://doi.org/10.1007/978-3-030-03807-6_8

10. Brakerski, Z., Döttling, N.: Two-message statistically sender-private OT from LWE. In: Beimel, A., Dziembowski, S. (eds.) TCC 2018. LNCS, Part II, vol. 11240, pp. 370–390. Springer, Cham (2018). https://doi.org/10.1007/978-3-030-03810-6_14

11. Brassard, G., Chaum, D., Crépeau, C.: Minimum disclosure proofs of knowledge. J. Comput. Syst. Sci. **37**(2), 156–189 (1988)

12. Canetti, R.: Security and composition of multiparty cryptographic protocols. J. Cryptol. **13**(1), 143–202 (2000). https://doi.org/10.1007/s001459910006

13. Canetti, R.: Universally composable security: a new paradigm for cryptographic protocols. In: 42nd FOCS, pp. 136–145. IEEE Computer Society Press (2001). https://doi.org/10.1109/SFCS.2001.959888

14. Canetti, R., Dodis, Y., Pass, R., Walfish, S.: Universally composable security with global setup. In: Vadhan, S.P. (ed.) TCC 2007. LNCS, vol. 4392, pp. 61–85. Springer, Heidelberg (2007). https://doi.org/10.1007/978-3-540-70936-7_4

15. Canetti, R., Kushilevitz, E., Lindell, Y.: On the limitations of universally composable two-party computation without set-up assumptions. In: Biham, E. (ed.) EUROCRYPT 2003. LNCS, vol. 2656, pp. 68–86. Springer, Heidelberg (2003). https://doi.org/10.1007/3-540-39200-9_5

16. Canetti, R., Lin, H., Pass, R.: Adaptive hardness and composable security in the plain model from standard assumptions. In: 51st FOCS, pp. 541–550. IEEE Computer Society Press (2010). https://doi.org/10.1109/FOCS.2010.86

17. Dolev, D., Dwork, C., Naor, M.: Non-malleable cryptography (1998)

18. Döttling, N., Garg, S., Hajiabadi, M., Masny, D., Wichs, D.: Two-round oblivious transfer from CDH or LPN. In: Canteaut, A., Ishai, Y. (eds.) EUROCRYPT 2020. LNCS, Part II, vol. 12106, pp. 768–797. Springer, Cham (2020). https://doi.org/10.1007/978-3-030-45724-2_26

19. Dwork, C., Naor, M., Sahai, A.: Concurrent zero-knowledge. In: 30th ACM STOC, pp. 409–418. ACM (1998). https://doi.org/10.1145/276698.276853

20. Feige, U.: Alternative Models for Zero-Knowledge Interactive Proofs. Ph.D. Thesis, Weizmann Institute of Science (1990)

21. Fernando, R., Jain, A., Komargodski, I.: Maliciously-Secure MrNISC in the Plain Model. Cryptology ePrint Archive, Paper 2021/1319 (2021). https://eprint.iacr.org/2021/1319

22. Garg, S., Gentry, C., Sahai, A., Waters, B.: Witness encryption and its applications. In: Boneh, D., Roughgarden, T., Feigenbaum, J. (eds.) 45th ACM STOC, pp. 467–476. ACM Press (2013). https://doi.org/10.1145/2488608.2488667

23. Garg, S., Goyal, V., Jain, A., Sahai, A.: Concurrently secure computation in constant rounds. In: Pointcheval, D., Johansson, T. (eds.) EUROCRYPT 2012. LNCS, vol. 7237, pp. 99–116. Springer, Heidelberg (2012). https://doi.org/10.1007/978-3-642-29011-4_8

24. Garg, S., Kiyoshima, S., Pandey, O.: On the exact round complexity of self-composable two-party computation. In: Coron, J.-S., Nielsen, J.B. (eds.) EUROCRYPT 2017. LNCS, Part II, vol. 10211, pp. 194–224. Springer, Cham (2017). https://doi.org/10.1007/978-3-319-56614-6_7

25. Garg, S., Srinivasan, A.: Two-round multiparty secure computation from minimal assumptions. In: Nielsen, J.B., Rijmen, V. (eds.) EUROCRYPT 2018. LNCS, Part II, vol. 10821, pp. 468–499. Springer, Cham (2018). https://doi.org/10.1007/978-3-319-78375-8_16

26. Goldreich, O.: Foundations of Cryptography: Basic Tools, vol. 1. Cambridge University Press, Cambridge (2001)

27. Goldreich, O., Micali, S., Wigderson, A.: How to play any mental game or A completeness theorem for protocols with honest majority. In: Aho, A., (ed.) 19th ACM STOC, pp. 218–229. ACM Press (1987). https://doi.org/10.1145/28395.28420

28. Goldreich, O., Oren, Y.: Definitions and properties of zero-knowledge proof systems. J. Cryptol. **7**(1), 1–32 (1994). https://doi.org/10.1007/BF00195207

29. Goldwasser, S., Levin, L.: Fair computation of general functions in presence of immoral majority. In: Menezes, A.J., Vanstone, S.A. (eds.) CRYPTO 1990. LNCS, vol. 537, pp. 77–93. Springer, Heidelberg (1991). https://doi.org/10.1007/3-540-38424-3_6

30. Goldwasser, S., Micali, S., Rackoff, C.: The knowledge complexity of interactive proof systems. SIAM J. Comput. **18**(1), 186–208 (1989)

31. Goyal, V., Lin, H., Pandey, O., Pass, R., Sahai, A.: Round-efficient concurrently composable secure computation via a robust extraction lemma. In: Dodis, Y., Nielsen, J.B. (eds.) TCC 2015. LNCS, Part I, vol. 9014, pp. 260–289. Springer, Heidelberg (2015). https://doi.org/10.1007/978-3-662-46494-6_12

32. Kiyoshima, S.: Round-efficient black-box construction of composable multi-party computation. In: Garay, J.A., Gennaro, R. (eds.) CRYPTO 2014. LNCS, Part II, vol. 8617, pp. 351–368. Springer, Heidelberg (2014). https://doi.org/10.1007/978-3-662-44381-1_20

33. Kiyoshima, S., Manabe, Y., Okamoto, T.: Constant-round black-box construction of composable multi-party computation protocol. In: Lindell, Y. (ed.) TCC 2014. LNCS, vol. 8349, pp. 343–367. Springer, Heidelberg (2014). https://doi.org/10.1007/978-3-642-54242-8_15

34. Lin, H., Pass, R., Seth, K., Telang, S.: Output-compressing randomized encodings and applications. In: Kushilevitz, E., Malkin, T. (eds.) TCC 2016. LNCS, Part I, vol. 9562, pp. 96–124. Springer, Heidelberg (2016). https://doi.org/10.1007/978-3-662-49096-9_5

35. Lin, H., Pass, R., Soni, P.: Two-round and non-interactive concurrent non-malleable commitments from time-lock puzzles. In: Umans, C., (ed.) 58th FOCS, pp. 576–587. IEEE (2017). https://doi.org/10.1109/FOCS.2017.59

36. Lin, H., Pass, R., Venkitasubramaniam, M.: Concurrent non-malleable commitments from any one-way function. In: Canetti, R. (ed.) TCC 2008. LNCS, vol. 4948, pp. 571–588. Springer, Heidelberg (2008). https://doi.org/10.1007/978-3-540-78524-8_31

37. Lin, H., Pass, R., Venkitasubramaniam, M.: A unified framework for concurrent security: universal composability from stand-alone non-malleability. In: Mitzenmacher, M., (ed.) 41st ACM STOC, pp. 179–188. ACM (2009). https://doi.org/10.1145/1536414.1536441

38. Lindell, Y.: Lower bounds for concurrent self composition. In: Naor, M. (ed.) TCC 2004. LNCS, vol. 2951, pp. 203–222. Springer, Heidelberg (2004). https://doi.org/10.1007/978-3-540-24638-1_12

39. Malkin, T., Moriarty, R., Yakovenko, N.: Generalized environmental security from number theoretic assumptions. In: Halevi, S., Rabin, T. (eds.) TCC 2006. LNCS, vol. 3876, pp. 343–359. Springer, Heidelberg (2006). https://doi.org/10.1007/11681878_18

40. Micali, S., Rogaway, P.: Secure computation. In: Feigenbaum, J. (ed.) CRYPTO 1991. LNCS, vol. 576, pp. 392–404. Springer, Heidelberg (1992). https://doi.org/10.1007/3-540-46766-1_32

41. Morgan, A., Pass, R., Polychroniadou, A.: Succinct non-interactive secure computation. In: Canteaut, A., Ishai, Y. (eds.) EUROCRYPT 2020. LNCS, Part II, vol. 12106, pp. 216–245. Springer, Cham (2020). https://doi.org/10.1007/978-3-030-45724-2_8

42. Pandey, O., Pass, R., Vaikuntanathan, V.: Adaptive one-way functions and applications. In: Wagner, D. (ed.) CRYPTO 2008. LNCS, vol. 5157, pp. 57–74. Springer, Heidelberg (2008). https://doi.org/10.1007/978-3-540-85174-5_4

43. Pass, R.: Simulation in quasi-polynomial time, and its application to protocol composition. In: Biham, E. (ed.) EUROCRYPT 2003. LNCS, vol. 2656, pp. 160–176. Springer, Heidelberg (2003). https://doi.org/10.1007/3-540-39200-9_10

44. Pass, R., Rosen, A.: Concurrent non-malleable commitments. In: 46th FOCS, pp. 563–572. IEEE (2005). https://doi.org/10.1109/SFCS.2005.27

45. Prabhakaran, M., Sahai, A.: New notions of security: Achieving universal composability without trusted setup. In: Babai, L. (ed.) 36th ACM STOC, pp. 242–251. ACM (2004). https://doi.org/10.1145/1007352.1007394

46. Rackoff, C., Simon, D.R.: Non-interactive zero-knowledge proof of knowledge and chosen ciphertext attack. In: Feigenbaum, J. (ed.) CRYPTO 1991. LNCS, vol. 576, pp. 433–444. Springer, Heidelberg (1992). https://doi.org/10.1007/3-540-46766-1_35

47. Schröder, D., Unruh, D.: Round optimal blind signatures. Cryptology ePrint Archive, Report 2011/264 (2011). https://eprint.iacr.org/2011/264

48. Yao, A.C.C.: Protocols for secure computations (extended abstract). In: 23rd FOCS, pp. 160–164. IEEE (1982). https://doi.org/10.1109/SFCS.1982.38

Attaining GOD Beyond Honest Majority with Friends and Foes

Aditya Hegde[1], Nishat Koti[2], Varsha Bhat Kukkala[2], Shravani Patil[2], Arpita Patra[2], and Protik Paul[2(✉)]

[1] Johns Hopkins University, Baltimore, USA
ahegde@cs.jhu.edu
[2] Indian Institute of Science, Bangalore, Bengaluru, India
{kotis,varshak,shravanip,arpita,protikpaul}@iisc.ac.in

Abstract. In the classical notion of multiparty computation (MPC), an honest party learning private inputs of others, either as a part of protocol specification or due to a malicious party's unspecified messages, is not considered a potential breach. Several works in the literature exploit this seemingly minor loophole to achieve the strongest security of guaranteed output delivery via a trusted third party, which nullifies the purpose of MPC. Alon et al. (CRYPTO 2020) presented the notion of *Friends and Foes* (FaF) security, which accounts for such undesired leakage towards honest parties by modelling them as semi-honest (friends) who do not collude with malicious parties (foes). With real-world applications in mind, it's more realistic to assume parties are semi-honest rather than completely honest, hence it is imperative to design efficient protocols conforming to the FaF security model.

Our contributions are not only motivated by the practical viewpoint, but also consider the theoretical aspects of FaF security. We prove the necessity of semi-honest oblivious transfer for FaF-secure protocols with optimal resiliency. On the practical side, we present QuadSquad, a ring-based 4PC protocol, which achieves fairness and GOD in the FaF model, with an optimal corruption of 1 malicious and 1 semi-honest party. Quad-Squad is, to the best of our knowledge, the first practically efficient FaF secure protocol with optimal resiliency. Its performance is comparable to the state-of-the-art dishonest majority protocols while improving the security guarantee from abort to fairness and GOD. Further, QuadSquad elevates the security by tackling a stronger adversarial model over the state-of-the-art honest-majority protocols, while offering a comparable performance for the input-dependent computation. We corroborate these claims by benchmarking the performance of QuadSquad. We consider the application of liquidity matching that deals with sensitive financial transaction data, where FaF security is apt. We design a range of FaF secure building blocks to securely realize liquidity matching as well as other popular applications such as privacy-preserving machine learning. Inclusion of these blocks makes QuadSquad a comprehensive framework.

Full version available at https://eprint.iacr.org/2022/1207.pdf

A. Hegde—Work done while at International Institute of Information Technology Bangalore.

S. Agrawal and D. Lin (Eds.): ASIACRYPT 2022, LNCS 13791, pp. 556–587, 2022.
https://doi.org/10.1007/978-3-031-22963-3_19

Keywords: Friends and Foes · Multiparty computation · Oblivious transfer

1 Introduction

The classical notion of multiparty computation (MPC) enables n mutually distrusting parties to compute a function over their private inputs, such that an adversary controlling up to t parties does not learn anything other than the output. Depending on its behaviour, the adversary can be categorized as *semi-honest* or *malicious*. A maliciously-secure MPC protocol may offer security guarantee with *abort, fairness* or *guaranteed output delivery (GOD)*. While security with abort may allow the adversary alone to receive the output (leaving out the honest parties), fairness makes sure either all or none receive the output. The strongest guarantee of GOD ensures that all honest participants receive the output irrespective of the adversarial behaviour. It is well known that honest majority is necessary to achieve GOD, whereas a dishonest majority setting can at best offer security with abort for general functionalities [28]. GOD is undoubtedly one of the most attractive features of an MPC protocol. Preventing repeated failures, it upholds the trust and interest of participants in the deployed protocol and saves a participant's valuable time and resources. Moreover, it also captures unforeseeable scenarios such as machine crashes and network delay.

It is well-known that the honest majority setting lends itself well for constructing efficient protocols for a large number of parties [1,2,18,33,45] and has been shown to be practical [6,64]. In this setting, MPC for a small number of parties [4,5,22,27,40,49,58,61,63,63] has gained popularity over the last few years due to applications such as financial data analysis [17] and privacy-preserving statistical studies [15] which typically involve 3 parties. This is corroborated by the popularity of MPC framework such as Sharemind [16] which works over 3 parties. In the literature, of all MPC protocols for a small population, several achieve the highest security guarantee of GOD [20,21,23,44,49,55,56]. In most of these protocols, when any malicious behaviour is detected, parties identify an *honest* party, referred to as Trusted Third Party (TTP) and make their inputs available to it in clear. Thereafter, TTP computes the desired function on parties' private inputs and returns the respective outputs. Such learning of inputs by an honest party is allowed in the traditional definition of security, although it nullifies the main purpose of MPC. In many real-world applications that deal with highly sensitive data, such as those in financial and healthcare sectors, information leak, even to an honest party, is unacceptable. Further, in the secure outsourced computation setting, where servers (typically run by reputed companies such as Amazon, Google, etc.) are hired to carry out the computation, it may be unacceptable to reveal private inputs to the server identified as a TTP.

Another issue that persists in traditionally secure MPC protocols is the following. The malicious adversary can potentially breach privacy of protocols by sending its view to some of the honest parties. However, traditional definitions do not acknowledge this view-leakage as an attack as honest parties are assumed to discard any non-protocol messages. In this way, traditional definition fails to account for the possibly curious nature of honest parties, which is a given in real-world scenarios. Consequently, many well-known protocols relying on threshold secret sharing (such as BGW [14]), satisfying traditional security against t malicious corruptions, immediately fall prey to this view-leakage attack. Indeed, an honest party on receiving the view of any t corrupt parties can learn the inputs of all the parties. Note that the traditional MPC protocols are vulnerable to this view-leakage attack which are not just restricted to GOD protocols but also protocols with weaker security notion of fairness. We emphasize that such a view-leakage attack is not irrational on the part of adversary's behaviour as it can be motivated by monetary incentives.

We showcase how reliance on a TTP and the view-leakage attack inherent in traditionally secure MPC is detrimental to data privacy in real-world applications via the example of liquidity matching. Consider a set of banks that have outstanding transactions that need to be settled among themselves. Liquidity matching enables settlement of inter-bank transactions while ensuring that each bank has sufficient liquidity. Here, liquidity means the balance of a bank, and matching requires that each bank, upon processing of the outstanding transactions, has non-negative balance. Since transactions comprise sensitive financial data, it is required to perform liquidity matching in a privacy-preserving manner. Hence, when designing MPC protocols for the same. It is imperative for the protocol to provide GOD, owing to the real-time nature of such transactions. That is, aborting the execution is not an acceptable option as it may lead to an indefinite delay in processing the transactions. The work of [7] has explored this application in the traditionally secure MPC setting. However, given the sensitive nature of the application, reliance on a TTP to attain GOD, and the view-leakage attack, render the traditionally secure MPC solution futile.

Inspired by the above compelling concerns of reliance on a TTP and view-leakage, [3] proposed a new MPC security definition, Friends & Foes (FaF). In this definition, an honest party's input is required to be safeguarded from quorums of other honest parties, in addition to the standard security against an adversary. This dual need is modelled through a decentralized adversary. Specifically, there is one malicious adversary that corrupts at most t out of n parties *(Foes)* and another semi-honest adversary, controlling at most h^* parties *(Friends)* out of the remaining $n - t$ parties. A protocol secure against such adversaries is said to be (t, h^*)-FaF secure. Technically, in the FaF model, not only should the views of t malicious parties, but also the views of every (disjoint) subset of h^* semi-honest parties, be simulatable separately. Moreover, FaF requires security to hold even when the malicious adversary sends its view to some of the other parties (semi-honest). Thus, FaF-security is a better fit for applications that deal with highly sensitive data, as in the case of liquidity matching.

Alon et al. showed in [3] that any functionality can be computed with fairness and GOD in the (t, h^*)-FaF model, iff $2t + h^* < n$ holds. Since protocols with a small number of parties are pragmatic, from the above condition it is evident that a minimum of 4 parties is necessary to achieve the desired level of FaF-security. This implies that $t = 1, h^* = 1$. While the sufficiency of $t = 1$ is well established in the literature [20,21,23,31,44,55,56,59,67], we trust that $h^* = 1$ also suffices for most practical purposes, assuming honest parties do not collude. Thus, we design protocols in the 4PC setting providing $(1,1)$-FaF security. It is worth noting that relying on a 4PC protocol with 2 malicious corruptions to achieve this goal is insufficient, since GOD is known to be impossible in this setting. On the other hand, although the 4 party honest-majority setting tackling a single corruption can offer GOD security, it is susceptible to the view-leakage attack.

Keeping practicality in mind, for the optimal 4PC setting considered, we describe the design choices made to attain an efficient protocol. To obtain a fast-response time as required for real-time applications, we operate in the preprocessing paradigm which has been extensively explored [9,34,35,54–56]. Here, the protocols are partitioned into two phases, a function dependent (input independent) *preprocessing phase* and an input dependent *online phase*. Following recent works [16,32,34,36] we build our protocols over 32 or 64 bit rings to leverage CPU optimizations. Further, to aid resource constrained clients in performing computationally intensive tasks, the paradigm of secure outsourced computation (SOC) has gained popularity. In this setting, clients can avail computationally powerful servers on a 'pay-per-use' basis from Cloud service providers. In this work, we provide secure protocols for performing computations in the 4-server SOC setting. The servers here are mapped to the parties of our 4PC.

When designing FaF-secure protocols in a given setting, it is both theoretically profound and practically important to know, whether information-theoretic security is possible to be achieved. If not, it is important to identify what cryptographic assumption is required. [3] shows impossibility of information-theoretic FaF-secure MPC with less than $2t+2h^*$ parties and presents a protocol relying on semi-honest oblivious transfer (OT) with at least $2t + h^* + 1$ parties. However, the necessity of OT in the latter setting was not known. We settle this question, showing the necessity of semi-honest OT. This proves the tightness of the protocol of [3] in terms of assumption, and implies that any 4PC in $(1,1)$-FaF setting requires semi-honest OT. This requirement puts FaF security closer to the dishonest majority setting where the same necessity holds [43,50], than the honest majority setting which is known to offer even the strongest security of GOD information-theoretically.

1.1 Related Work

We restrict the discussion to practically-efficient secret-sharing based (high throughput regime) MPC protocols over small population for arithmetic and Boolean world, since this is the regime of focus in this work.

In the honest-majority setting, we restrict to protocols achieving fairness and GOD over rings. The GOD protocol offering the best *overall* communication cost is that of [20]. [24,55,67], present 3PC protocols in the preprocessing paradigm, and thus have faster online phase than [20]. Of these, [55] elevates the security of the former two, from fairness to GOD. In the 4PC regime, [56] presents the best GOD protocol improving over the previously best-known fair protocol of [25] and GOD protocol of [21,55].

The work that comes closest to ours in terms of security achieved is that of Fantastic Four [31] which is devoid of function dependent preprocessing.

It attempts to offer a variant of GOD, referred to as *private robustness* without the honest party learning other parties' inputs. However, this work does not capture the behaviour of a malicious adversary which allows it to send its complete view to an honest party, thus falling short of satisfying the FaF security notion.

In the dishonest-majority setting, the study of practically-efficient protocols started with the work of [35] which was followed by [53,54]. This line of work culminated with [13] which has the fastest online phase. However, these protocols work over fields. The works that extend over rings are [30,65] and of these the latter is a better performer. In this regime, all the protocols work in preprocessing paradigm, where the common trend had been to generate Beaver multiplication triples [11] in the preprocessing and consume them in the online phase for multiplication. The majority of the works focus on bettering the preprocessing and choose either Oblivious Transfer (OT) [53] or Somewhat Homomorphic Encryption (SHE) [30,35,65] to enable triple generation.

1.2   Our Contribution

QuadSquad: A $(1,1)$-FaF Secure 4PC. We propose the first, efficient, $(1,1)$-FaF secure, 4PC protocol in the preprocessing paradigm, over rings (both $\mathbb{Z}_{2^\lambda}$ and $\mathbb{Z}_2$), that achieves fairness and GOD. Casting our protocol in the preprocessing paradigm allows us to obtain a fast online phase, with a cost comparable to the best-known dishonest as well as honest majority protocols. Furthermore, we achieve GOD, without incurring any additional overhead in the online phase, in comparison to our fair protocol. This is depicted in Table 1.

Here, with respect to honest-majority protocols, we compare Quad-Squad's multiplication with the best-known 4PC of Tetrad [56] which relies on a TTP, and the protocol of Fantastic Four [31] which offers *private robustness* without relying on a TTP. With respect to dishonest-majority protocols, we compare with the best-known OT-based protocol of MASCOT [53] since our protocol also relies on OTs in the preprocessing. While QuadSquad, [31] and [56] work over ring, [53] exploits field ($\mathbb{F}$) structure. Further, the protocol in [31] does not have a sepa-

Table 1. Comparison of mult of MASCOT, Fantastic Four and Tetrad with QuadSquad

Ref.	Preproc.	Online		Model	Security
	Comm.	Rounds	Comm.		
Tetrad ($\mathbb{Z}_{2^\lambda}$)	2	1	3	HM	GOD
Fantastic Four ($\mathbb{Z}_{2^\lambda}$)	NA	1	6	HM	GOD
MASCOT ($\mathbb{F}$)	7713	2	12	DM	abort
QuadSquad ($\mathbb{Z}_{2^\lambda}$)	1558	3	7	FaF	Fair
QuadSquad ($\mathbb{Z}_{2^\lambda}$)	3110	3	7	FaF	GOD

– The comm. complexity is given in terms of elements from $\mathbb{Z}_{2^\lambda}/\mathbb{F}$ (of size 2^{64}), as applicable. HM: Honest majority; DM: Dishonest majority.

rate preprocessing phase. We indicate this in Table 1 by "NA" (Not Applicable). As per the table, QuadSquad is comparable to both the honest-majority and dishonest-majority protocols in the online phase and outperforms [53] in the preprocessing. Our offer over [56], [31] is stronger security against an additional semi-honest corruption, with a comparable online cost. Our offer over [53] is the stronger guarantee of fairness/GOD with comparable online cost (and better preprocessing cost).

Necessity of OT. FaF is closer to dishonest majority (with 2 corruptions out of 4), and hence, public-key primitives are inevitable. We back this up by proving the necessity of OT. We prove the necessity of semi-honest OT for (t, h^*)-FaF (abort) secure protocol with $n \leq 2t + 2h^*$ (by constructing the former from the latter). The goal of this result is to justify that a protocol, including ours, in FaF-model will require public-key primitives. Given this, we use semi-honest OT, but restrict its use to preprocessing alone[1].

Building Blocks and Applications. We consider the application of liquidity matching where FaF security is more apt. We design a range of FaF secure building blocks to securely realize liquidity matching, as well as other popular applications such as privacy-preserving machine learning (PPML). The description of the building blocks appears in Table 2. Although these can be naively obtained by extending techniques from the literature, the resultant building blocks have a heavy communication overhead. We therefore go one step ahead and design customised building blocks which are efficient and help in improving the response time of these applications.

Table 2. Build blocks for various applications

Protocol	Input	Output	Description
$\llbracket \cdot \rrbracket\text{-Sh}^{\text{SOC}}$	v	$\llbracket v \rrbracket$	User $\llbracket \cdot \rrbracket$-shares input v with the servers
$\llbracket \cdot \rrbracket\text{-Rec}^{\text{SOC}}$	$\llbracket v \rrbracket$	v	Servers reconstruct v to U
BitExt	$\llbracket v \rrbracket$	$\llbracket \text{msb}(v) \rrbracket^{\text{B}}$	Extracts most significant bit of an arithmetic shared value v
Bit2A	$\llbracket b \rrbracket^{\text{B}}$	$\llbracket b \rrbracket$	Converts boolean sharing of a bit b to arithmetic sharing
BitInj	$\llbracket b \rrbracket^{\text{B}}, \llbracket v \rrbracket$	$\llbracket b \cdot v \rrbracket$	Outputs $\llbracket \cdot \rrbracket$-shares of $b \cdot v$, where bit b is $\llbracket \cdot \rrbracket^{\text{B}}$-shared and v is $\llbracket \cdot \rrbracket$-shared
DotPTr	$\{\llbracket x^s \rrbracket, \llbracket y^s \rrbracket\}_{s \in [n]}$	$\llbracket \sum_{s \in [n]} x^s \cdot y^s \rrbracket$	Outputs $\llbracket \cdot \rrbracket$-shares of dot product of $\llbracket \cdot \rrbracket$-shared vectors $\{x^s\}_{s \in n}, \{y^s\}_{s \in n}$

Benchmarks. We showcase the practicality of QuadSquad by benchmarking its MPC, as well as the performance of secure liquidity matching and PPML inference for two Neural Networks (NN). We implement and benchmark our 4PC protocol over a WAN network using the ring $\mathbb{Z}_{2^{64}}$, and report the latency, throughput and communication costs in the preprocessing and online phase. We observe that the throughput of our GOD protocol is comparable to that of the fair protocol, and has an overhead of up to $4.5\times$ in the online phase over [56] and [31]. This overhead indicates the cost to achieve the stronger notion of FaF-security. On the other hand, QuadSquad outperforms [53] by a factor of up to $4.5\times$ in the online phase. With respect to the applications, we observe a runtime of 6 and 10 s for the two NNs, and a runtime of 15 s for liquidity matching. The reported runtime for both applications is practical.

---

[1] As mentioned in Sect. 1.1, SHE offers an alternative to OT. However, relying on the heels of recent interesting work on OT [72] and the huge effort on improving OT in the last decade [19,52], we opt for OT based approach. Translating our approach in the SHE regime is left for future exploration.

1.3   Technical Highlights

In this section, we elaborate on the design choices of our protocol, the challenges involved and the approach taken to tackle them. One approach to achieving $(1, 1)$-FaF security in the 4PC setting is via a 4-party identifiable abort (IA) protocol, where upon detecting misbehaviour, the protocol can be re-run with a default input for the identified corrupt party. However, we deviate from this approach and choose dispute pair identification for achieving the desired security due to the following reasons. First, note that there is no customised 4PC IA protocol in the literature. Moreover, since the threshold of corruption in $(1, 1)$-FaF considering malicious as well as semi-honest parties corresponds to a dishonest majority, we have to consider IA protocols in the same setting to prevent susceptibility to view-leakage attack. This would inherently require us to consider generic n-party dishonest majority IA protocols, instantiated for the specific case of $n = 4$ and $t = 2$, which do not offer a practically efficient solution. Specifically, the state-of-the-art protocol in this setting [10] requires online communication of 24 elements per multiplication-gate, which is significantly higher than the online communication cost of our protocol. Designing a customised 4PC IA protocol is an orthogonal question which is left as an open problem.

Necessity of OT. To prove the necessity of semi-honest OT for a generic n-party (t, h^*)-FaF secure (abort) protocol with $t + h^* < n \leq 2t + 2h^*$, we construct the former from the latter. Recall that the necessity of $n > t + h^*$ for abort security and $n > 2t + h^*$ for GOD in the FaF model is known from [3]. Note that our proof holds up to $n \leq 2t + 2h^*$, which subsumes the optimal bound on n for the GOD setting. We show that an n-party (t, h^*)-FaF secure protocol π_f for computing the function $f((m_0, m_1), \bot, \ldots, \bot, b) = (\bot, \bot, \ldots, \bot, m_b)$, where $n \leq 2t + 2h^*$, can be used to construct a semi-honest OT. We give the formal proof in Sect. 3.

QuadSquad: Robust $(1, 1)$-**FaF Secure 4PC.** The core idea of our 4PC protocol lies in designing the sharing, reconstruction and multiplication primitives.

Sharing: To facilitate operating over rings and ensure privacy in FaF model with 1 malicious and 1 semi-honest party, we rely on Replicated Secret Sharing (RSS) with a threshold of 2. This requires 6 components where each pair of parties holds a common component. This is higher than the 4 components in RSS with threshold 1 and 3 which are typically used in honest and dishonest majority settings respectively. In QuadSquad, each party has only 3 components of a sharing which poses the challenge in ensuring an efficient reconstruction.

Reconstruction: Although a naive reconstruction towards all would require a communication of 12 elements, our protocol reduces this to an *amortized* cost of 7 elements. Both our sharing and reconstruction protocols extensively rely on primitives which leverage the honest behaviour of at least 3 parties to ensure dispute pair (DP) identification.

Multiplication: The higher number of components in our sharing semantics makes our multiplication protocol non-trivial. At a high level, the multiplication of 2 shared values results in 36 summands, which we broadly categorize into 3 types based on the number of parties which can locally compute each summand. We give separate treatment to each category, of which the summands that can be computed by a single party and those which cannot be computed by any party are of particular interest. The main challenge in the former is ensuring the correctness of a party's computation, for which we build upon the distributed Zero-Knowledge (ZK) protocol of [20]. The latter requires a new *distributed multiplication* protocol where two distinct pairs of parties hold the inputs to the multiplication and the goal is to additively share the product between the pairs. This primitive relies on OT. Here, the main challenge is ensuring the correctness of inputs to OT, for which we leverage the (semi) honest behaviour of at least 3 parties and the fact that every pair of parties holds a common component. Apart from several optimization techniques, the primary technical highlight in this part includes the new batch reconstruction and the distributed multiplication, both of which contribute to a highly efficient multiplication protocol.

Online: For efficiency, we follow the masked evaluation paradigm by tweaking RSS as follows. We share a value using a mask which is RSS shared and a masked value which is public. Circuit evaluation is then performed on the public masked values which are required to be reconstructed in the online phase [13, 44, 66].

Fair to GOD: In the optimistic run (where all parties behave honestly) of our 4PC protocol the function output is computed correctly. However, in case any malicious behaviour is detected during protocol execution, a dispute pair (DP) is identified which is assured to include the malicious party. The protocol that we obtain by terminating at the earliest point of dispute discovery, offers fairness. Note that the fair protocols existing in the literature [55, 56, 67] are susceptible to the view-leakage attack and thus are not FaF secure. Further, to extend the security guarantee to GOD without incurring additional communication overhead in the online phase, we follow the commonly used approach of segmented evaluation of a circuit. Specifically, we segment the circuit and execute the above protocol in a segment-by-segment manner. In case malicious behaviour is detected in any segment, as in our fair protocol, we identify a DP. Following this, for computation of the remaining segments, we resort to a single instance of a semi-honest 2PC which is executed by parties outside DP, which we refer to as the trusted pair (TP). We use the semi-honest 2PC in a black-box manner, and this can be instantiated with the state-of-the-art protocol. We use ABY2.0 [66], for this purpose, which is also designed in the preprocessing paradigm. To extend support for the online phase of [66], each pair of parties executes an instance of the preprocessing of [66], along with the preprocessing of QuadSquad. This ensures that in case DP is identified during the online phase, parties have the necessary preprocessed data for the 2PC.

Key Differences from Tetrad, Fantastic Four and MASCOT. The best known honest-majority 4PC given in Tetrad differs from our construction in many aspects starting with reliance on RSS with threshold 1. This ensures every party misses a single (as opposed to 3 for us) component, offering a very efficient reconstruction. They further utilize high redundancy (every component is held by 3 parties) and heavily rely on isolating one of the parties from most of the computation. This, together with the threshold of 1 guarantees that, in case malicious behaviour is detected during the computation, the isolated party is honest. This honest party is then elevated to a TTP. The protocol of [55] follows a similar approach for efficiency. In FaF-model, we fall short of the first and the latter paradigm fails due to the presence of an additional semi-honest party. Thus, our multiplication protocol involves all four parties and enforces different mechanisms to detect and handle malicious behaviour compared to the Tetrad protocol. Similar to [55,56], the efficiency of Fantastic Four can be attributed to the benefits of redundancy offered by RSS with threshold 1. Their work achieves a variant of GOD referred to as *private robustness* by first identifying a dispute pair in the execution involving all 4 parties, followed by reducing the computation to a 3-party malicious protocol. For this, their work eliminates one party from the dispute pair arbitrarily. Any malicious behaviour hereafter, asserts that the party from the dispute pair included in the 3PC is malicious. To achieve robustness, they execute a semi-honest 2-party protocol using the parties guaranteed to be honest. Although their approach circumvents revealing private inputs to a TTP for achieving robustness, it falls short of offering FaF-security. In particular, it is susceptible to the view-leakage attack in all the instances of its sub-protocols involving 2, 3 and 4 parties. Moreover, in [31], the switch from 4PC to 3PC upon identifying malicious behaviour is non-interactive. This can be attributed to the threshold of 1 which ensures that any three parties together possess all the components of the sharing. However, in our case, if any malicious behaviour is detected we fall back on a semi-honest 2PC. The sharing semantics of our protocol (required to prevent view-leakage attack) are such that a pair of parties does not hold all the shares. Hence we need additional interaction for converting from 4PC sharing to a 2PC sharing.

On the other hand, MASCOT [53] relies on RSS with threshold 3 (same as additive sharing). Though every party misses 3 shares like our case, riding on the advantage of shooting for a weaker guarantee of abort, they are able to leverage king-based approach [33] for reconstruction (only one party/king is enabled to reconstruct, which later sends the value to the rest) which only ensures detection, but falls short of recovery, from a malicious behaviour. [53] delegates checks to detect malicious behaviour to the end of the protocol whereas we need to verify correct behaviour at each step to ensure fairness/GOD.

Our work leaves open several interesting questions. We elaborate on these and the challenges involved therein in the full version of the paper.

2   Preliminaries

Setting and Security. We consider a set of four parties $\mathcal{P} = \{P_1, P_2, P_3, P_4\}$ which are connected by pair-wise private and authenticated channels in a synchronous network. The function to be computed is expressed as a circuit whose topology is public and is evaluated over a ring $\mathbb{Z}_{2^\lambda}$ of size 2^λ. Our protocols are designed in the FaF model with a static malicious adversary and a (different) semi-honest adversary each corrupting at most one (distinct) party. We make use of broadcast channel for simplicity of presentation, which can be instantiated using any protocol such as [38]. Our constructions achieve the strongest security guarantee of GOD, wherein parties receive the protocol output irrespective of the malicious adversary's strategy. We prove the security of our protocols in the ideal world/real world simulation paradigm. The security definitions and proofs appear in the full version of the paper.

In the SOC setting, the four servers execute our protocol. For client-server based computation, a client secret-shares its data with the servers. Servers perform the required operations on secret-shared data and obtain the secret-shared output. Finally, to provide the client's output, servers reconstruct the output towards it. The underlying assumption here is that the corrupt server can collude with a corrupt client. We consider computation over $\mathbb{Z}_{2^\lambda}$ and $\mathbb{Z}_{2^1}$. To deal with decimal values, we use Fixed-Point Arithmetic (FPA) [24,60,62,67] in which a value is represented as a λ-bit integer in signed 2's complement representation. The most significant bit (msb) denotes the sign bit, and d least significant bits are reserved for the fractional part. The λ-bit integer is then viewed as an element of $\mathbb{Z}_{2^\lambda}$, and operations are performed modulo 2^λ. We set $\lambda = 64, d = 13$, leaving $\lambda - d - 1$ bits for the integer part. Our protocols are cast in the preprocessing paradigm, wherein a protocol is divided into (a) function dependent (input independent) *preprocessing phase* and (b) input dependent *online phase*.

Notation 1. *Wherever necessary, we denote $\mathcal{P}$ by the unordered set $\{P_i, P_j, P_k, P_m\}$ and $\{P_i, P_{i+1}, P_{i+2}, P_{i+3}\}$. Note that $i, j, k, m \in [4]$ do not correspond to any fixed ordering, only constraint being $i \neq j \neq k \neq m$. Similarly for $i, i+1, i+2, i+3$, corresponding to a P_i, say P_2, $P_{i+1} = P_3$, $P_{i+2} = P_4$, $P_{i+3} = P_1$.*

Standard Building Blocks. Parties make use of a one-time key setup captured by functionality $\mathcal{F}_{\text{setup}}$, to establish pre-shared random keys for pseudo-random functions (PRF) among them. This functionality incurs a one-time cost, and thus can be instantiated using any FaF-secure protocol such as that of [3]. We make use of a *collision-resistant* hash function H and a commitment scheme Com.

Advanced Building Blocks. Here we discuss 4 primitives at a high-level: (a) 3-party joint message passing (jmp) from [55], with minor modifications (b) a related 4-party jmp primitive, (c) oblivious product evaluation (OPE) and (d) distributed zero-knowledge protocol.

3-Party Joint Message Passing (jmp3). The jmp primitive from [55] allows two parties P_i, P_j holding a common value v, to send it to a party P_k such that either P_k receives the correct v, or TTP is identified. For our purpose, we trivially modify their protocol to give out a dispute pair (DP) instead of a TTP to all the 4 parties. In [55], the jmp primitive is invoked for sending each value independently and the verification is amortized over many sends. Their protocol allows for such a decoupling due to its asymmetry and a pre-specified order of verification. For our protocol however, postponing verification causes security issues.

Specifically, batching the verification of different layers of the circuit together allows an adversary to follow a strategy which ensures that DP comprises of two (semi) honest parties. This is contrary to the requirement that DP must include the malicious party. To avoid this problem, we compress the send and verification of jmp so that an optimistic (no error) run takes one round and batch them together for many instances corresponding to a pair of senders. That is, a pair of parties, say P_i, P_j invoke jmp to send a vector $\overrightarrow{v}$ to P_k, and in parallel verification of correctness takes place. We call the modified variant as jmp3. It requires an amortized communication of 1 element.

4-Party Joint Message Passing (jmp4). jmp4 allows two parties P_i, P_j holding a common value v, to send it to the other two parties P_k, P_m such that, either both the parties receive the correct v or all the parties identify DP.

Notation 2. *We refer to the invocation of* jmp3(P_i, P_j, v, P_k) *as "P_i, P_j* jmp3-send v *to P_k" and* jmp4(P_i, P_j, v, P_k, P_m) *as "P_i, P_j* jmp4-send v *to P_k, P_m".*

Oblivious Product Evaluation (OPE). OPE (adapted from [53]) allows two parties holding $x \in \mathbb{Z}_{2^\lambda}$ and $y, z \in \mathbb{Z}_{2^\lambda}$ respectively, to compute an additive sharing of the product xy, such that one party holds $xy + z \in \mathbb{Z}_{2^\lambda}$ and the other holds $z \in \mathbb{Z}_{2^\lambda}$. We rely on techniques from [42,53] to obtain an OPE for λ-bit strings by running a total of λ 1-out-of-2 OTs on λ bits strings. In this work, we instantiate OTs using the protocol from Ferret [72], which incurs an (amortized) cost of 0.44 bits for generating one random correlated OT (amortized over batch generation of 10^7 correlated OTs). We can obtain an input-dependent OT (using techniques from [12,48]) at an additional cost of 2 elements and 1 bit. This results in a cost of $2\lambda + 1.44$ bits per OT. So an instantiation of OPE requires an amortised cost of $\lambda(2\lambda + 1.44)$ bits and 4 rounds. Note that we use OT in a black-box manner; thus, any improvement in OT, will improve the efficiency of our construction. Further, although OPE can be realised with oblivious linear evaluation (OLE), we opt for the approach of [53] due to better efficiency of OT. Hence, any improvements in OLE that surpasses OT can be translated to improving our protocol by replacing OPE with OLE.

Distributed Zero-knowledge (ZK). To verify a party P_i's correct behaviour, we extend the distributed zero-knowledge proofs introduced first in [18] offering *abort* security, and further optimized by Boyle *et al.* [20] to provide *robust* verification of degree-two relations. Such proofs involve a single prover and multiple verifiers, where the prover intends to prove the correctness of its (degree-two) computation over data which is *additively* distributed among the verifiers. In [20], the authors provide a distributed ZK protocol with sub-linear proof size, which is adapted for the verification of messages sent in a 3PC protocol with one corruption. Their ZK protocol extends in a straightforward manner to the 4-party case with one malicious corruption and one semi-honest corruption in the FaF model where a dispute pair is identified in case the verification fails. This is identical to extending the distributed ZK protocol to the case of 4 parties with 1 malicious corruption in the classical model and does not incur any overhead in our setting. Since the protocol in [20], and correspondingly ours, is constructed over fields, to support verification over rings, as in [20] verification operations are carried out on the extended ring $\mathbb{Z}_{2^\lambda}/f(x)$, which is the ring of all polynomials with coefficients in $\mathbb{Z}_{2^\lambda}$ modulo a polynomial f, of degree η, irreducible over $\mathbb{Z}_{2^1}$. Each element in $\mathbb{Z}_{2^\lambda}$ is lifted to a η-degree polynomial in $\mathbb{Z}_{2^\lambda}[x]/f(x)$ (which results in blowing up the communication by a factor η).

The details of the building blocks, including functionalities, protocols and proofs appear in the full version.

3 Necessity of Oblivious Transfer

Here, we show that semi-honest OT is necessary for a FaF-secure protocol. Our claim holds for $n \leq 2t + 2h^*$ which subsumes the case of n-party (t, h^*)-FaF security with optimal threshold of $t + h^* + 1$ and $2t + h^* + 1$ for abort and GOD [3] respectively, and the special case of 4-party $(1, 1)$-FaF security. The theorem and proof sketch are given below.

Theorem 3. *An n-party (t, h^*)-FaF secure (abort) protocol with $n \leq 2t + 2h^*$ implies 2-party semi-honest OT.*

Proof. Without loss of generality, we consider $n = 2t + 2h^*$. Let π_f be an n-party (t, h^*)-FaF secure abort protocol for computing the function $f((m_0, m_1), \perp, \ldots, \perp, b) = (\perp, \perp, \ldots, \perp, m_b)$. We construct a 2-party semi-honest OT protocol π_{OT} between a sender P_S with inputs (m_0, m_1) and a receiver P_R with input b using π_f. In π_{OT}, P_S emulates the role of $Q_S = \{P_1, P_2, \ldots P_{t+h^*}\}$ while P_R emulates the role of $Q_R = \{P_{t+h^*+1}, \ldots, P_n\}$ to run π_f. P_R outputs the same m_b as output by party P_n which it emulates while P_S outputs $\perp$. To prove the security of π_{OT}, we construct simulators $\mathcal{S}_S$ and $\mathcal{S}_R$ that generate the view of P_S and P_R respectively from their inputs.

Let P_S be corrupted by the semi-honest adversary $\mathcal{A}_{\mathsf{OT}}$ and let $H = \{P_1, \ldots, P_{h^*}\}$ and $I = Q_S \backslash H$. We now map $\mathcal{A}_{\mathsf{OT}}$ to an adversarial strategy against π_f as follows. Consider a malicious adversary $\mathcal{A}$ for π_f that corrupts parties in I but does not deviate from the protocol (since $\mathcal{A}_{\mathsf{OT}}$ is semi-honest). However, it sends the random tape, inputs and messages of all parties in I to every other party in H at the end of the protocol execution. Note that such an attack of leaking the view of the maliciously corrupted parties to the semi-honest adversary is valid in the FaF model. The semi-honest adversary $\mathcal{A}_{\mathcal{H}}$ for π_f runs $\mathcal{A}_{\mathsf{OT}}$ on the joint view of the parties in $I \cup H$ ($\mathcal{A}_{\mathcal{H}}$ receives the view of parties in I from $\mathcal{A}$) and outputs the same value as $\mathcal{A}_{\mathsf{OT}}$. Since $|I| = t$ and $|H| = h^*$, the security of π_f ensures that there exist simulators $\mathcal{S}_{\mathcal{A}}$ and $\mathcal{S}_{\mathcal{A}_{\mathcal{H}}}$ corresponding to the adversaries $\mathcal{A}$ and $\mathcal{A}_{\mathcal{H}}$. We construct the simulator $\mathcal{S}_S$ to run $\mathcal{S}_{\mathcal{A}}$ followed by $\mathcal{S}_{\mathcal{A}_{\mathcal{H}}}$ on P_S's input (m_0, m_1) and output the view generated by $\mathcal{S}_{\mathcal{A}_{\mathcal{H}}}$. Since $\mathcal{A}_{\mathcal{H}}$ receives the view of parties in I, the view generated by $\mathcal{S}_{\mathcal{A}_{\mathcal{H}}}$ includes the view of parties in $I \cup H$. Note that although $\mathcal{A}$ considered is malicious in π_f, it is emulated by a semi-honest adversary in the outer π_{OT} protocol and hence does not deviate from the protocol. Corresponding to such adversarial strategy of $\mathcal{A}$, the simulator $\mathcal{S}_{\mathcal{A}}$ may need to choose the input on behalf of $\mathcal{A}$. A simulator for a semi-honest adversary is not allowed to choose the input on behalf of the adversary, as discussed in [46]. However, since the parties in I controlled by the adversary $\mathcal{A}$ do not have inputs for f, this does not pose a problem in the proof and $\mathcal{S}_S$ can thus use $\mathcal{S}_\mathcal{A}$.

This proves the necessity of semi-honest-OT for (t, h^*)-FaF secure protocol where $t + h^* < n \leq 2t + 2h^*$. Moreover, the sufficiency of OT for the same is given in [3, Theorem 4.1]. The detailed constructions of the OT protocol, simulators and the corresponding indistinguishabilty argument appears in the full version.

Corollary 1. *An n-party (t, h^*)-FaF secure abort protocol with $n = t + h^* + 1$ implies 2-party semi-honest* OT.

Corollary 2. *An n-party (t, h^*)-FaF secure GOD protocol with $n = 2t + h^* + 1$ implies 2-party semi-honest* OT.

Both Corollary 1 and 2 follow directly from Theorem 3. For Corollary 1, the sender emulates $t + h^*$ parties and the receiver emulates 1 party. For the corrupt receiver we consider $I = \phi$ and $H = \{P_n\}$. For Corollary 2, the sender emulates $t + h^*$ parties and the receiver emulates $t + 1$ parties. For the corrupt receiver we consider $I = \{P_{t+h^*+1}, \ldots, P_{2t+h^*}\}$ and $H = \{P_n\}$.

4   Input Sharing and Reconstruction

To enforce security, we perform computation on secret-shared data. This section starts with the various sharing semantics we use, followed by a sharing and a reconstruction protocol for secret-shared computation. We further present an efficient batch reconstruction for a second type of sharing, which in turn, will act as the primary building block for our efficient (batch) multiplication protocol.

We begin with the motivation for the choice of our sharing semantics. As explained earlier, we rely on RSS with threshold 2 to tackle view-leakage attack where the semi-honest adversary may receive the view of the malicious adversary. Instead of using RSS directly, we slightly augment our sharing to RSS-share a random mask and make the masked secret available to all. This sharing style makes the online cost of a multiplication one reconstruction instead of two. If we use RSS directly for sharing a secret, then relying on the Beaver's multiplication triple technique [11], we would need reconstructing $x + \alpha_x$ and $y + \alpha_y$, where x, y are the inputs and α_x, α_y are the corresponding random masks. However, as per the latter sharing, we include the masked values $\beta_x = x + \alpha_x$, $\beta_y = y + \alpha_y$ along with RSS shares of α_x and α_y respectively in our sharing semantics. So the only reconstruction needed now is that of the masked valued of xy. This idea goes back to [66]. We now describe the sharing semantics.

1. $[\cdot]$-*sharing:* A value $v \in \mathbb{Z}_{2^\lambda}$ is said to be $[\cdot]$-shared (additively shared) among parties P_i, P_j, if P_i holds $[v]_i \in \mathbb{Z}_{2^\lambda}$ and P_j holds $[v]_j \in \mathbb{Z}_{2^\lambda}$ such that $v = [v]_i + [v]_j$.
2. $\langle \cdot \rangle$-*sharing:* A value $v \in \mathbb{Z}_{2^\lambda}$ is said to be $\langle \cdot \rangle$-shared among $\mathcal{P}$ if, each pair of parties (P_i, P_j), where $1 \leq i < j \leq 4$, holds $\langle v \rangle_{ij} \in \mathbb{Z}_{2^\lambda}$ such that

$v = \sum_{(i,j)} \langle v \rangle_{ij}$. This is equivalent to RSS of a value among 4 parties with threshold 2. Note that since $\langle v \rangle_{ij}$ represents the common share held by P_i, P_j, throughout the protocol we assume the invariant that $\langle v \rangle_{ij} = \langle v \rangle_{ji}$, for all $1 \le i < j \le 4$. $\langle v \rangle_i$ denotes P_i's share in the $\langle \cdot \rangle$-sharing of v.

3. $\llbracket \cdot \rrbracket$-*sharing:* A value $v \in \mathbb{Z}_{2^\lambda}$ is $\llbracket \cdot \rrbracket$-shared if
   - there exists $\alpha_v \in \mathbb{Z}_{2^\lambda}$ that is $\langle \cdot \rangle$-shared amongst $\mathcal{P}$ and
   - each $P_i \in \mathcal{P}$ holds $\beta_v = v + \alpha_v$.

   Note that the value α_v acts as the mask for v. We denote by $\llbracket v \rrbracket_i$, P_i's share in the $\llbracket \cdot \rrbracket$-sharing of v.

Note that all these sharings are linear i.e. given sharings of values $a_1, \ldots, a_m$ and public constants $c_1, \ldots, c_m$, sharing of $\sum_{i=1}^m c_i a_i$ can be computed non-interactively for an integer m.

4.1 $\llbracket \cdot \rrbracket$-sharing: Sharing and Reconstruction

Sharing. Protocol $\llbracket \cdot \rrbracket$-Sh either allows a party P_s to share a value v or ensures dispute pair (DP) detection. To generate $\llbracket v \rrbracket$, in the preprocessing phase, P_s together with every other party P_i, samples a random $\langle \alpha_v \rangle_{si} \in \mathbb{Z}_{2^\lambda}$, while P_s samples a random $\langle \alpha_v \rangle_{ij} \in \mathbb{Z}_{2^\lambda}$ with every pair of parties P_i, P_j. This allows P_s to learn α_v in clear. In the online phase, P_s computes $\beta_v = v + \alpha_v$ and sends it to P_t. Parties P_s, P_t then jmp4-send β_v to the rest. This step either allows the sharing to complete or identifies a DP. The protocol appears in Fig. 1.

Protocol $\llbracket \cdot \rrbracket$-Sh

- **Input, Output:** P_s has v. The parties output $\llbracket v \rrbracket$.
- **Primitives:** jmp4-send (§2).

Preprocessing: P_s together with (a) P_i, for each $P_i \in \mathcal{P} \backslash P_s$ samples random $\langle \alpha_v \rangle_{si} \in \mathbb{Z}_{2^\lambda}$; (b) $P_i, P_j \in \mathcal{P} \backslash P_s$, where $i \ne j$, samples random $\langle \alpha_v \rangle_{ij} \in \mathbb{Z}_{2^\lambda}$.

Online: P_s computes $\beta_v = v + \sum_{(i,j)} \langle \alpha_v \rangle_{ij}$ and sends it to P_t, where $s \ne t$. P_s, P_t jmp4-send β_v to $\mathcal{P} \backslash \{P_s, P_t\}$.

Fig. 1. $\llbracket \cdot \rrbracket$-sharing a value

Reconstruction. Protocol $\llbracket \cdot \rrbracket$-Rec allows parties to reconstruct v from $\llbracket v \rrbracket$ such that either v is obtained by all the parties or a DP is identified. As observed, a party misses three shares of $\langle \alpha_v \rangle$, which are needed for reconstructing v, each of which is held by two other parties. To reconstruct v towards a party P_s, in the preprocessing each pair (P_i, P_j) jmp3-send a commitment of their common share $\mathsf{Com}(\langle \alpha_v \rangle_{ij})$ to P_s. The common source of randomness (generated via the shared key setup) can be used for generating the commitments, so that it is identically generated by both the senders. Then in the online phase all the parties open the commitments sent during preprocessing. P_s first reconstructs α_v from consistent openings and then computes $v = \beta_v - \alpha_v$. Due to the use of jmp3, the preprocessing may fail, however once it is successful the online phase is robust. Hence, this reconstruction ensures fairness i.e. either all or none receive the output (in the latter case DP has been identified). In case the reconstruction protocol terminates with a dispute pair, to extend security to GOD, parties perform the circuit evaluation using a semi-honest 2PC protocol (Fig. 2).

Protocol $[\![\cdot]\!]$-Rec

- **Input, Output:** The parties input $[\![v]\!]$. The parties output v.
- **Primitives:** jmp4-send and Com (§2).

Preprocessing: Each $P_i, P_j, 1 \leq i < j \leq 4$ compute $\mathsf{Com}(\langle \alpha_v \rangle_{ij})$ and jmp4-send it to P_k, P_m.

Online: Each $P_i, P_j, 1 \leq i < j \leq 4$ open $\mathsf{Com}(\langle \alpha_v \rangle_{ij})$ to P_k and P_m. Each P_i accepts the opening consistent with the commitment received earlier and computes $v = \beta_v - \sum_{(i,j)} \langle \alpha_v \rangle_{ij}$.

Fig. 2. Reconstructing a $[\![\cdot]\!]$-shared value

4.2 $\langle \cdot \rangle$-sharing: Reconstruction

In our MPC protocol, for each multiplication gate we require to reconstruct a $\langle \cdot \rangle$-shared value in the online phase. Note that a party misses three shares of $\langle v \rangle$ needed for reconstruction, each of which is held by two other parties. For reconstructing v towards all the parties, naively, each pair can jmp4-send their common share to the other two parties. This requires 6 invocations of jmp4, thus a communication of 12 elements. Since reconstructing $\langle \cdot \rangle$-shared value is the only communication bottleneck in the online phase of our multiplication protocol, it is imperative to improve its efficiency.

Taking a step towards this, we allow two parties, say P_3, P_4 (w.l.o.g) to first reconstruct v and use jmp4-send to send it to the other two parties. Naively, the reconstruction towards P_3, P_4 requires 6 instances of jmp3-send, three per party to send its missing shares. To improve the communication cost further, we improve the cost of the second instance of the reconstruction of v (towards P_4 in our case), to 2 jmp3-send instances, leveraging the communication already done for the reconstruction towards P_3. This reduces the communication cost to 7 elements. Our protocol appears in Fig. 3.

Since jmp3 is defined for a vector of values, in $\langle \cdot \rangle$-Rec, parties execute reconstruction of multiple values together. The protocol is described for a single value. Extending it to a vector is straightforward. In our multiplication protocol, this translates to reconstruction of the output of all multiplication gates in a level of the circuit simultaneously.

Note that we can reconstruct v from $[\![v]\!]$ using $\langle \cdot \rangle$-Rec to reconstruct α_v. However, while $[\![\cdot]\!]$-Rec offers fairness, $\langle \cdot \rangle$-Rec does not. This implies if we use $\langle \cdot \rangle$-Rec for the final output, it is possible that the adversary gets the output while the honest parties do not. Further, when the computation is rerun in 2PC mode, the adversary can use a different input and obtain another evaluation, thus breaching security.

Protocol $\langle \cdot \rangle$-Rec

- **Input, Output:** The parties input $\langle v \rangle$. The parties output v.
- **Primitives:** jmp3-send and jmp4-send (§2).

Online:

- **(Reconstructing v to P_3.)** P_1, P_2 jmp3-send $\langle v \rangle_{12}$ to P_3. P_1, P_4 jmp3-send $\langle v \rangle_{14}$ to P_3. P_2, P_4 jmp3-send $\langle v \rangle_{24}$ to P_3.
- **(Reconstructing v to P_4.)** P_1, P_3 jmp3-send $\langle v \rangle_{13}$ to P_4. P_2, P_3 jmp3-send $\langle v \rangle_{12} + \langle v \rangle_{23}$ to P_4.
- **(Reconstructing v to P_1, P_2.)** P_3, P_4 jmp4-send $v = \sum_{(i,j)} \langle v \rangle_{ij}$ to P_1, P_2.

Fig. 3. Reconstructing a $\langle \cdot \rangle$-shared value

5 Multiplication

In this section, we present a multiplication protocol. Taking a top-down approach, we first present our multiplication protocol relying on a triple generation protocol in a black-box way. We then conclude with a triple generation protocol. To gain efficiency, several layers of amortisation are used. We mention them on the go and summarise at the end of the section.

5.1 Multiplication Protocol

The multiplication protocol (Fig. 4) allows parties to compute $[\![z]\!]$, given $[\![x]\!]$ and $[\![y]\!]$, where $z = x \cdot y$. We reduce this problem to that of reconstructing a $\langle \cdot \rangle$-shared value, assuming that parties have access to (a) $\langle \cdot \rangle$-sharing of a multiplication triple $(\alpha_x, \alpha_y, \alpha_x\alpha_y)$ for random α_x, α_y and (b) $\langle \cdot \rangle$-sharing of a random α_z. Both the requirements are input (i.e. x, y) independent and can be fulfilled during the preprocessing phase. The former requirement is obtained via a triple generation protocol tripGen (Fig. 6), discussed subsequently. The latter requirement can be achieved non-interactively using the shared key setup. The reduction works as follows. The random and independent secret α_z is taken as the mask for the $[\![\cdot]\!]$-sharing of product z. Since α_z is already $\langle \cdot \rangle$-shared, to complete $[\![z]\!]$, parties only need to obtain the masked value $\beta_z = z + \alpha_z$. Since β_z takes the following form $\beta_z = z + \alpha_z = xy + \alpha_z = (\beta_x - \alpha_x)(\beta_y - \alpha_y) + \alpha_z = \beta_x\beta_y - \beta_x\alpha_y - \beta_y\alpha_x + \alpha_x\alpha_y + \alpha_z$ and the parties hold $\langle\alpha_x\rangle$, $\langle\alpha_y\rangle$, $\langle\alpha_x\alpha_y\rangle$, $\langle\alpha_z\rangle$, and β_x,β_y in clear, the parties hold $\langle\beta_z\rangle$. Parties thus need to reconstruct β_z. To leverage the amortised cost of $\langle\cdot\rangle$-Rec, we batch many multiplications together. While for simplicity, we present the protocol in Fig. 4 for a single multiplication, our complexity analysis accounts for amortization.

Protocol mult

- **Input and Output:** The input is $[\![x]\!]$, $[\![y]\!]$ and the output is $[\![xy]\!]$.
- **Primitives:** tripGen (§5.2; Fig. 6) and $\langle\cdot\rangle$-Rec (§4.2; Fig. 3).

Preprocessing:
- Each P_i, P_j where $1 \le i < j \le 4$ sample random $\langle\alpha_z\rangle_{ij} \in \mathbb{Z}_{2^\lambda}$.
- Parties invoke tripGen with inputs $\langle\alpha_x\rangle, \langle\alpha_y\rangle$ to obtain $\langle\alpha_x\alpha_y\rangle$.

Online:
- Each P_i, P_j for $1 \le i < j \le 4$ and $(i,j) \ne (1,2)$ compute $\langle\beta_z\rangle_{ij}$ such that $\langle\beta_z\rangle_{ij} = -\beta_x\langle\alpha_y\rangle_{ij} - \beta_y\langle\alpha_x\rangle_{ij} + \langle\alpha_x\alpha_y\rangle_{ij} + \langle\alpha_z\rangle_{ij}$.
- P_1, P_2 compute $\langle\beta_z\rangle_{12} = \beta_x\beta_y - \beta_x\langle\alpha_y\rangle_{12} - \beta_y\langle\alpha_x\rangle_{12} + \langle\alpha_x\alpha_y\rangle_{12} + \langle\alpha_z\rangle_{12}$.
- Parties invoke $\langle\cdot\rangle$-Rec to obtain β_z.

Fig. 4. Multiplication protocol

5.2 Triple Generation Protocol

As a building block to our triple generation protocol, we first present a distributed multiplication protocol, where two distinct pairs of parties hold inputs to the multiplication and the goal is to additively share the product between the pairs. We build on this protocol to complete our triple generation.

Distributed Multiplication Protocol. Let P_i, P_j hold a and P_k, P_m hold b. The goal of a distributed multiplication is to allow P_i, P_j compute c^1 and P_k, P_m to compute c^2 such that $c^1 + c^2 = ab$. To achieve this, P_k and P_m locally sample c^2 (using one-time key setup) then parties engage in an instance of OPE (Sect. 2) where P_i, P_j and respectively P_k, P_m enact the receiver's and sender's role.

- P_i, P_j as the receivers input a and output either c^1 or DP.
- P_k, P_m as the senders input b, $-c^2$ and output either $\bot$ or DP.

Since the pair of receivers $\{P_i, P_j\}$ hold identical inputs and use a shared source of randomness, their corresponding messages in the underlying protocol for OPE realisation will be identical. They send their messages to the senders via an instance of jmp4. Recall that the jmp4 primitive ensures that a message commonly known to two sender parties is either communicated correctly to both the receiving parties, or a dispute pair DP is identified. In the former case, the pair of senders $\{P_k, P_m\}$, having the same input and receiver's message, will prepare identical sender messages as a part of OPE and communicate to the receivers via another instance of jmp4 primitive, resulting in either a successful communication of the sender message to the receivers $\{P_i, P_j\}$ or identification of DP. In the former case, OPE is concluded successfully. Note that the verification of jmp4 tackles any malicious behaviour, thus relying on semi-honest OPE suffices. Otherwise, DP is identified and the pair is guaranteed to include the malicious party. If fairness is the end goal, the protocol can terminate at this stage. Otherwise, it switches to an execution of a semi-honest 2PC (such as ABY2.0 [66]) with the parties outside DP to achieve the stronger guarantee of GOD.

Protocol disMult

- **Input and Output:** P_i, P_j hold a. P_k, P_m hold b. The first pair outputs c^1, the second pair c^2 such that $c^1 + c^2 = ab$. Otherwise the parties output DP.
- **Primitives:** OPE and jmp4 (§2).

- P_k and P_m locally sample a value c^2, using their shared key.
- P_i, P_j execute OPE with input a using jmp4 to send messages to P_k, P_m.
- P_k, P_m execute OPE with inputs $(b, -c^2)$ using jmp4 to send messages to P_i, P_j.

Fig. 5. Distributed multiplication protocol

Triple Generation Protocol. The triple generation protocol allows parties holding $\langle\alpha_x\rangle, \langle\alpha_y\rangle$ to generate $\langle\alpha_x\alpha_y\rangle$. We write the product $\alpha_x\alpha_y$ as below, consisting of 36 summands, categorizing them into three types as below and as shown in Table 3.

For the summands in type S_0, no single party holds the two constituent shares of α_x, α_y. For the summands in S_1, exactly one party holds the two constituent shares, and lastly for the summands in S_2, exactly two parties hold the two constituent shares. Note that there are 6 summands each, of the types S_0 and S_2 and 24 summands of type S_1. To generate $\langle\alpha_x\alpha_y\rangle$, we generate $\langle\cdot\rangle$-sharing of each summand of $\alpha_x\alpha_y$ and then sum them up to obtain $\langle\alpha_x\alpha_y\rangle$. The task of generating $\langle\cdot\rangle$-sharing for an individual summand differs based on the class it belongs to.

$$
\alpha_x \cdot \alpha_y = \sum_{\substack{(i,j) \\ 1\leq i < j \leq 4}} \langle\alpha_x\rangle_{ij} \cdot \sum_{\substack{(k,m) \\ 1\leq k < m \leq 4}} \langle\alpha_y\rangle_{km}
$$

$$
= \underbrace{\sum_{\substack{(i,j) \\ 1\leq i < j \leq 4}} \langle\alpha_x\rangle_{ij}\langle\alpha_y\rangle_{ij}}_{S_2} + \underbrace{\sum_{\substack{(i,j,k) \\ i,j,k\in[4]}} \langle\alpha_x\rangle_{ij}\langle\alpha_y\rangle_{ik}}_{S_1} + \underbrace{\sum_{\substack{(i,j),(k,m) \\ 1\leq i,k<j,m\leq 4}} \langle\alpha_x\rangle_{ij}\langle\alpha_y\rangle_{km}}_{S_0} \quad (1)
$$

Summands of S_2. Each summand in this type can be computed locally by 2 parties. For instance, $\langle\alpha_x\rangle_{ij}\langle\alpha_y\rangle_{ij}$ can be computed by P_i and P_j. Denoting $\langle\alpha_x\rangle_{ij}\langle\alpha_y\rangle_{ij}$ as τ_{ij}, $\langle\tau_{ij}\rangle$ is computed as follows:

$$P_i, P_j \text{ set } \langle \tau_{ij} \rangle_{ij} = \langle \alpha_{\mathsf{x}} \rangle_{ij} \langle \alpha_{\mathsf{y}} \rangle_{ij} \text{ and}$$
$$P_u, P_v \text{ set } \langle \tau_{ij} \rangle_{uv} = 0, \forall (u, v) \neq (i, j) \tag{2}$$

Summands of S_1. Each summand here can be computed locally by a single party. For instance, $\langle \alpha_{\mathsf{x}} \rangle_{ij} \langle \alpha_{\mathsf{y}} \rangle_{ik}$ can be computed by P_i alone. Then P_i's goal is to share this amongst the four parties so that one share is held by both P_i, P_k and the other by P_j, P_m. That is, for $\delta_i, \delta_i^1, \delta_i^2$ with $\delta_i = \delta_i^1 + \delta_i^2 = \langle \alpha_{\mathsf{x}} \rangle_{ij} \langle \alpha_{\mathsf{y}} \rangle_{ik}$, P_i, P_k intend to obtain δ_i^1 and P_j, P_m intend to obtain δ_i^2. The pairings $\{P_i, P_k\}$ and $\{P_j, P_m\}$ for various parties are done to balance the share count across the parties. We say that $\{P_i, P_k\}$ and respectively $\{P_j, P_m\}$ pair up for P_i's instance. Given this, $\langle \delta_i \rangle$ can be computed as (we set $k = i + 3$):

$$P_i, P_k \text{ set } \langle \delta_i \rangle_{ik} = \delta_i^1, \ P_j, P_m \text{ set } \langle \delta_i \rangle_{jm} = \delta_i^2$$
$$P_u, P_v \text{ set } \langle \delta_i \rangle_{uv} = 0, \text{ for all } (u, v) \neq (i, k), (j, m) \tag{3}$$

Now to achieve the above distribution of additive shares (δ_i^1, δ_i^2), P_i, P_j, P_m first locally sample δ_i^2 (using the shared key setup) and further, P_i computes and sends δ_i^1 to P_k. To keep P_i's misbehaviour in check, P_i is made to prove in zero-knowledge the correctness of its computation. With this high-level idea, we introduce two cost-cutting techniques.

Table 3. The summands of $\alpha_{\mathsf{x}} \cdot \alpha_{\mathsf{y}}$ with category $\{S_0, S_1, S_2\}$

	$\langle \alpha_{\mathsf{x}} \rangle_{12}$	$\langle \alpha_{\mathsf{x}} \rangle_{13}$	$\langle \alpha_{\mathsf{x}} \rangle_{14}$	$\langle \alpha_{\mathsf{x}} \rangle_{23}$	$\langle \alpha_{\mathsf{x}} \rangle_{24}$	$\langle \alpha_{\mathsf{x}} \rangle_{34}$
$\langle \alpha_{\mathsf{y}} \rangle_{12}$	S_2	S_1	S_1	S_1	S_1	S_0
$\langle \alpha_{\mathsf{y}} \rangle_{13}$	S_1	S_2	S_1	S_1	S_0	S_1
$\langle \alpha_{\mathsf{y}} \rangle_{14}$	S_1	S_1	S_2	S_0	S_1	S_1
$\langle \alpha_{\mathsf{y}} \rangle_{23}$	S_1	S_1	S_0	S_2	S_1	S_1
$\langle \alpha_{\mathsf{y}} \rangle_{24}$	S_1	S_0	S_1	S_1	S_2	S_1
$\langle \alpha_{\mathsf{y}} \rangle_{34}$	S_0	S_1	S_1	S_1	S_1	S_2

First, recall that there are 24 summands in S_1 and every P_i is capable of locally computing 6 of them. We combine the above procedure for 6 summands together. That is, δ_i^1, δ_i^2 are additive shares of $\delta_i = \sum_{(j,k)} \langle \alpha_{\mathsf{x}} \rangle_{ij} \langle \alpha_{\mathsf{y}} \rangle_{ik}$. This cuts our cost by $1/6$th. Next, leveraging the malicious-minority and non-collusion of the malicious and semi-honest adversaries (implied by FaF model), we customise disZK (Sect. 2) of [20] to prove that $\sum_{(j,k)} \langle \alpha_{\mathsf{x}} \rangle_{ij} \langle \alpha_{\mathsf{y}} \rangle_{ik} - \delta_i^1 - \delta_i^2 = 0$. As per the need of such ZK, each term in the statement is additively shared amongst P_j, P_k, P_m and is possessed in entirety by the prover P_i. For instance, $\langle \alpha_{\mathsf{x}} \rangle_{ij}$ is additively shared amongst P_j, P_k, P_m with P_j's share as $\langle \alpha_{\mathsf{x}} \rangle_{ij}$ and the shares of the rest set to 0. Similarly for other shares of α_{x} and α_{y}. δ_i^2 is additively shared amongst P_j, P_k, P_m with P_j's share as δ_i^2 and the shares of the rest set to 0. Lastly, δ_i^1 is additively shared amongst P_j, P_k, P_m with P_k's share as δ_i^1 and the shares of the rest set to 0. If the disZK is successful, then P_i, P_k output δ_i^1 and P_j, P_m output δ_i^2, using which $\langle \delta_i \rangle$ an be computed as above. Otherwise, the disZK returns a dispute pair. This is executed for every party's collection of S_1 summands.

Summands of S_0. No single party can compute the summands in this category. For instance, $\langle \alpha_{\mathsf{x}} \rangle_{ij} \langle \alpha_{\mathsf{y}} \rangle_{km}$ cannot be computed by any of the parties locally. We invoke the distributed multiplication protocol disMult (Fig. 5) for each such term, where the common input of $\{P_i, P_j\}$ and $\{P_k, P_m\}$ are $\langle \alpha_{\mathsf{x}} \rangle_{ij}$ and $\langle \alpha_{\mathsf{y}} \rangle_{km}$ respectively and their respective outputs are $\gamma_{ij,km}^1, \gamma_{ij,km}^2$, in case of success, or a dispute pair. Denoting $\gamma_{ij,km} = \gamma^1_{ij,km} + \gamma^2_{ij,km} = \langle \alpha_x \rangle_{ij} \langle \alpha_y \rangle_{km}$, the parties can now generate $\langle \gamma_{ij,km} \rangle$ as:

$$P_i, P_j \text{ set } \langle \gamma_{ij,km} \rangle_{ij} = \gamma^1_{ij,km}, \quad P_k, P_m \text{ set } \langle \gamma_{ij,km} \rangle_{km} = \gamma^2_{ij,km}$$
$$P_u, P_v \text{ set } \langle \gamma_{ij,km} \rangle_{uv} = 0, \text{ for all } (u,v) \neq (i,j), (k,m) \tag{4}$$

Protocol tripGen

- **Input and Output:** The parties input $\langle \alpha_x \rangle, \langle \alpha_y \rangle$. The output is $\langle \alpha_x \alpha_y \rangle$.
- **Primitives:** Protocol disMult (§5.2) and Protocol disZK (§2).

- For each of the 6 summands of the form $\langle \alpha_x \rangle_{ij} \langle \alpha_y \rangle_{km}$ for unordered pairs $\{P_i, P_j\}$ and $\{P_k, P_m\}$ in S_0, the parties execute disMult with the inputs of $\{P_i, P_j\}, \{P_k, P_m\}$ as $\langle \alpha_x \rangle_{ij}$ and $\langle \alpha_y \rangle_{km}$ respectively. The parties either output DP or $\{P_i, P_j\}, \{P_k, P_m\}$ output $\gamma^1_{ij,km}$ and $\gamma^2_{ij,km}$ respectively. In the latter case, parties compute $\langle \gamma_{ij,km} \rangle$ as shown in Equation 4.

- For every i, consider *all* the 6 summands of the form $\langle \alpha_x \rangle_{ij} \langle \alpha_y \rangle_{ik}$ for unordered pairs $\{P_i, P_j\}$ and $\{P_i, P_k\}$ in S_1.

  1. The parties P_i, P_j, P_m locally sample δ^2_i (using the shared key setup).
  2. P_i computes and sends $\delta^1_i = \sum_{(j,k)} \langle \alpha_x \rangle_{ij} \cdot \langle \alpha_y \rangle_{ik} - \delta^2_i$ to P_k.
  3. Parties invoke disZK to verify if $\sum_{(j,k)} \langle \alpha_x \rangle_{ij} \langle \alpha_y \rangle_{ik} - \delta^1_i - \delta^2_i = 0$. If disZK returns success, then P_i, P_j, P_k, P_m output $\langle \delta_i \rangle$ as shown in Equation 3. Otherwise, output the DP returned by disZK.

- For each of the 6 summands of S_2, of the form $\langle \alpha_x \rangle_{ij} \langle \alpha_y \rangle_{ij}$, parties compute $\langle \tau_{ij} \rangle$-sharing as shown in Equation 2.

- Every P_r for every $s \neq r$ computes

$$\langle \alpha_x \alpha_y \rangle_{rs} = \sum_{u,v:u \neq v} \langle \tau_{u,v} \rangle_{rs} + \sum_{1 \leq \ell \leq 4} \langle \delta_\ell \rangle_{rs} + \sum_{\substack{u,v:u \neq v \\ p,q:p \neq q}} \langle \gamma_{uv,pq} \rangle_{rs}$$

Fig. 6. Triple generation protocol

5.3 Summary

Amortizations. We summarise the various layers of amortization we use to get the best efficiency of our protocols. First, given a circuit with ℓ multiplication gates, the triple generation protocol creates $\langle \cdot \rangle$-sharing of ℓ triples at one go. All the summands of the form $\langle \alpha_x \rangle_{ij} \langle \alpha_y \rangle_{km}$ from S_0 category across all the ℓ instances use jmp4 for communication, whose verification is inherently batched for amortization. Next, the distributed ZK used for tackling the summands in S_1 can be used in an amortized sense as well. Recall that corresponding to a single triple generation, every P_i runs a single instance of distributed ZK to tackle 6 summands in its possession. However, we can extend this to accommodate 6ℓ summands across all the ℓ triples to achieve 40 bits of statistical security while working over a ring, by performing verification on the extended ring [1,20]. This means that we need to run overall 4 distributed ZK, one for every party. These cover all the amortizations done in the triple sharing protocol which constitutes the preprocessing of the multiplication protocol. The online phase of the multiplication protocol too exploits amortization of the batch $\langle \cdot \rangle$-reconstruction protocol. In the MPC protocol, we thus proceed level by level and execute all the multiplications placed in a level at one go.

Achieving Fairness. To obtain fairness, we can stop immediately after sensing a dispute. This means, in some cases, the effort needed for identifying a dispute pair, beyond sensing a dispute (which only says something is wrong and nothing beyond), can be slashed. For instance, in jmp4 parties can terminate immediately upon detecting conflict without identifying a dispute pair.

6 $(1,1)$-FaF Secure 4PC Protocol

Our complete protocol (4PC) realising the 4PC functionality ($\mathcal{F}_{\mathsf{4PC\text{-}FaF}}$) for evaluating a circuit in the $(1,1)$-FaF security model with fairness and GOD is described here as a composition of the protocols discussed so far. Formal details appear in the full version of the paper. Recall that our protocol is cast in the preprocessing paradigm. In the preprocessing phase, for each input gate u, parties execute the preprocessing of $[\![\cdot]\!]$-Sh to precompute $\langle \alpha_{\mathsf{u}} \rangle$. Further, for each multiplication gate with input wires u, v and output wire w, parties obtain $\langle \alpha_{\mathsf{w}} \rangle$ and $\langle \alpha_{\mathsf{u}} \alpha_{\mathsf{v}} \rangle$ by running the preprocessing of mult. This computation is done in parallel for all the multiplication gates. Finally, for each output gate of the circuit, parties execute the preprocessing phase of $[\![\cdot]\!]$-Rec. This completes the preprocessing.

In the online phase, parties evaluate the circuit gate-by-gate in a predetermined topological order. For each input gate u, they execute the online phase of $[\![\cdot]\!]$-Sh to obtain β_{u}. Addition gates are handled locally. For each multiplication gate with input wires u, v and output wire w, parties perform the online phase of mult to compute β_{w}. Finally, they reconstruct the value of an output wire w, using the online phase of $[\![\cdot]\!]$-Rec. As mentioned in Sect. 2, we batch the verification of all the parallel instances of jmp3 and jmp4 respectively for every pair of parties, and perform it with the send in the same round. In case of malicious behaviour in these instances, additionally at most 2 rounds are required to identify a dispute pair. The above protocol either succeeds or a dispute pair is identified, which includes the malicious party. This construction achieves fairness.

To attain GOD without incurring additional overhead in the online phase, we follow the approach of segmented evaluation described in [31]. Specifically, we divide the circuit into segments, and the protocol proceeds as described in a segment-by-segment manner with topological order. As in the case of our fair protocol, either the execution of a segment completes successfully, or a dispute pair is identified. In the latter case, the segment where the fault occurs and all the segments following it are evaluated using a semi-honest 2PC, which is executed by the parties outside the dispute pair. Using this approach, only the segment where the fault occurs incurs the cost of 2PC in addition to the cost of our fair protocol. Hence, this overhead which is limited to a single segment is insignificant. The cost of evaluating the subsequent segments is solely that of the semi-honest 2PC which we instantiate with [66]. Note that in segmented evaluation of the circuit, the output of a segment acts as the input to the following segment. Hence, rerunning the segment where malicious behaviour was detected requires the outputs from the prior segment with 4PC sharing semantics to be translated to 2PC sharing semantics. However, due to a threshold of 2 in the 4PC, no pair of parties hold all the components of sharing corresponding to any secret. This necessitates interaction among parties. Suppose S_m is the segment where malicious activity is detected and w.l.o.g. $\{P_3, P_4\}$ is identified as the dispute pair, which means the evaluation till segment S_{m-1} happened correctly. W.l.o.g let z be the output of the segment S_{m-1} which is also an input to the segment S_m. Since the evaluation of S_{m-1} was correct, all 4 parties have the correct $[\![\cdot]\!]$ sharing of z, which comprises of β_z and $\langle \alpha_z \rangle$. But to rerun S_m with $\{P_1, P_2\}$, they need the 2PC sharing of z. However, $\{P_1, P_2\}$ miss the $\langle \alpha_z \rangle_{34}$ component which is common to P_3, P_4 and hence cannot obtain the 2PC sharing of z locally. Making P_3, P_4 send this value to P_1 or P_2 or both does not suffice. Since either P_3 or P_4 is malicious, the malicious party can send a wrong value which will lead to an inconclusive state for $\{P_1, P_2\}$, failing to achieve the end goal of 2PC sharing. To address this problem, we resort to the same idea as that of $[\![\cdot]\!]$-Rec. That is, for each output wire z of all the segments, all pairs of parties P_i, P_j commit to their common share $\langle \alpha_z \rangle_{ij}$ in the preprocessing phase and jmp4-send the commitment to the other two parties. Now with the commitments established, parties in the dispute pair can send the opening corresponding to their respective commitments to the remaining two parties. In the above example, this corresponds to P_3, P_4 sending the opening of their commitments which contains $\langle \alpha_z \rangle_{34}$ to P_1, P_2. Following this, P_1, P_2 can decide the correct value of $\langle \alpha_z \rangle_{34}$ based on a valid opening, which is guaranteed to exist since one of P_3, P_4 is honest. Note that sending $\langle \alpha_z \rangle_{34}$ does not breach privacy since the malicious party can anyway send this value to other parties as a part of view-leakage, which is handled by our sharing semantics. Now P_1 sets its 2PC additive share $[\alpha_z]_1 = \langle \alpha_z \rangle_{12} + \langle \alpha_z \rangle_{13} + \langle \alpha_z \rangle_{14}$ and P_2 sets $[\alpha_z]_2 = \langle \alpha_z \rangle_{23} + \langle \alpha_z \rangle_{24} + \langle \alpha_z \rangle_{34}$, where $\alpha_z = [\alpha_z]_1 + [\alpha_z]_2$. Note that $(\beta_z, [\alpha_z]_1)$ and $(\beta_z, [\alpha_z]_2)$ is a valid 2PC sharing of z as per the semantics of [66]. However, as we describe below, this does not suffice.

Observe that the preprocessing of 2PC is performed along with the preprocessing of our 4PC protocol. Therefore, the value of mask corresponding to a wire z may differ in these two scenarios. To perform the 2PC execution of the circuit, we need to use the mask values selected during preprocessing for the 2PC. Let α'_z be the mask corresponding to wire z in the 2PC and $[\alpha'_z]_1$ and $[\alpha'_z]_2$ be the shares corresponding to P_1, P_2 respectively. Thus, the sharing of z requires to be updated according to α'_z, which essentially means updating the corresponding masked value, say β'_z such that $\beta'_z = z + \alpha'_z = (\beta_z - \alpha_z) + \alpha'_z$. Towards this, P_1 computes $v_1 = \beta_z - [\alpha_z]_1 + [\alpha'_z]_1$ and sends it to P_2. Similarly, P_2 computes $v_2 = [\alpha'_z]_2 - [\alpha_z]_2$ and sends it to P_1. Then P_1, P_2 locally obtain $\beta'_z = v_1 + v_2$ to complete the required 2PC sharing of z. Note that since both P_1, P_2 are (semi) honest, they send the correct values. Further, sending v_1 or v_2 does not breach privacy since they can learn these values from their own shares (for example, P_1 can compute v_2 given its shares $\beta_z, \beta'_z, [\alpha_z]_1, [\alpha'_z]_1$). The security of protocol 4PC as per the functionality $\mathcal{F}_{\mathsf{4PC\text{-}FaF}}$ is stated below.

Theorem 4. *Assuming collision resistant hash functions and semi-honest OT exists, protocol* 4PC *realizes* $\mathcal{F}_{\mathsf{4PC\text{-}FaF}}$ *with computational* $(1, 1)$-FaF *security.*

Security Against a Mixed Adversary. A closely related notion of security is that of a mixed adversary [8,26,37,39,41,47] which can simultaneously corrupt a subset of t parties maliciously and a disjoint subset of h^* parties in a semi-honest manner. In contrast to the FaF model, the adversary here is centralized. Consequently, the mixed security model allows the view of semi-honest parties to be available to the adversary while determining a strategy for the malicious parties. Although the mixed adversarial model might seem to subsume FaF, Alon et al. [3] showed that (t, h^*) mixed security does not necessarily imply (t, h^*)-FaF security. Given this, we constructed a 4PC protocol which is secure in the FaF model. However, we go a step beyond and show that our protocol is also secure against a $(1, 1)$-mixed adversary. For this, the crucial observation is that our protocol can withstand the scenario where the malicious adversary is provided with the view of semi-honest parties, which essentially captures the mixed adversarial model. Refer to the full version for details.

7   Applications and Benchmarks

This section focuses on evaluating the performance of QuadSquad. We first evaluate the performance of MPC and draw comparisons to concretely efficient traditional MPC protocols that come closest to our setting. We then establish the practicality of QuadSquad via the application of secure liquidity matching and PPML for neural network inference. We refer the readers to the full version for a detailed discussion on the benchmarking environment, secure protocols for the applications considered and analysis of performance bottlenecks. The source code of our implementation is available at quadsquad.

Environment. Benchmarks are performed over WAN using n1-standard-32 instances of Google Cloud, with machines located in East Australia (M_0), South Asia (M_1), South East Asia (M_2), and West Europe (M_3). The machines are equipped with 2.2 GHz Intel Xeon processors supporting hyper-threading and 128 GB RAM. Average bandwidth and round-trip time (rtt) between pair of machines was observed to be 180 Mbps and 158.31 ms respectively; though these values vary depending on the regions where the machines are located.

Software. We implement our protocol in C++17 using EMP toolkit [71]. Since we use OT as a black-box, it can be instantiated with any state-of-the-art OT protocol such as [29]. Since the public implementation of [29] is not available, we use EMP toolkit's Ferret OT [72]. We use the NTL library [68] for computation over ring extensions for disZK protocol. [53] and [31] are benchmarked in the MP-SPDZ [51] framework. Due to the unavailability of implementation of [56], we estimate its performance from microbenchmarks. We instantiate the collision resistant hash function with SHA256 and the PRF with AES-128 in counter mode. Computation is performed over $\mathbb{Z}_{2^{64}}$ for [31,56] and QuadSquad, and over $\mathbb{Z}_p$ for [53] where p is a 64-bit prime. We set the computational security parameter to $\kappa = 128$ and ensure statistical security of at least 2^{-40} for all the protocols. In particular, we set the degree of the polynomial modulus of the extended ring $\eta = 47$. We report the average value over 20 runs for each experiment.

Benchmarking Parameters. As a measure of performance, we report the online and overall (preprocessing + online) communication per party and latency for a single execution. To capture the combined effect of communication and round complexity, we additionally use *throughput* (tp) as a benchmark parameter, following prior works [56,60,67]. Here, tp denotes the number of operations (triples for 4PC preprocessing and multiplications for 4PC online protocol) that can be performed in one second.

7.1 Performance of 4PC QuadSquad

We compare the performance of our 4PC to Fantastic Four [31], Tetrad [56] and MASCOT [53]. We evaluate a circuit comprising 10^6 multiplication gates distributed over different depths. Recall that the online communication cost of our GOD protocol is similar to the fair protocol due to segment-wise evaluation. Hence, we only report the cost of the fair protocol for online comparison.

The performance of the online phase appears in Table 4. The latency of our protocol (fair and GOD) is up to 3.5× higher compared to honest majority protocol of [56] and the abort variant of [31]. This captures the overhead required to achieve the stronger notion of FaF-security. On

Table 4. Online costs for evaluating circuits with 10^6 mult gates over various depths. (**QS** denotes QuadSquad.)

Depth	Ref.	Online		
		Latency(s)	Comm. (MB)	tp
1	Fantastic Four	2.86	12.00	350066.51
	Tetrad	1.44	6.00	692947.87
	MASCOT	13.88	24.00	72023.80
	QS	2.94	14.00	340506.67
20	Fantastic Four	4.04	12.00	247286.04
	Tetrad	2.95	6.00	339321.20
	MASCOT	25.94	24.00	38554.22
	QS	7.42	14.00	134752.73
100	Fantastic Four	11.26	12.00	88771.32
	Tetrad	9.28	6.00	107764.43
	MASCOT	74.48	24.00	13425.63
	QS	30.92	14.00	32337.66
1000	Fantastic Four	87.82	12.00	11387.21
	Tetrad	80.52	6.00	12419.36
	MASCOT	289.69	24.00	3451.94
	QS	287.71	14.06	3475.69

the other hand, the dishonest majority protocol of [53] bears an overhead of 4.5× to 1.01× compared to ours.

The performance of the preprocessing depends only on the number of multiplication gates, not on the circuit depth. Hence, only the communication cost and throughput are reported in Table 5. [31] does not have preprocessing and is thus, not included. Further, unlike the online phase, Table 5 reports results for both fair and GOD variants independently since their performance in the preprocessing phase is different. The *communication* bottleneck in the preprocessing of QuadSquad is due to computing summands of S_0 which involves running six instances of disMult, while the *computational* bottleneck is due to computing the summands of S_1 which involves running four instances of disZK. We implement disZK using recursion as in [20] which ensures lower communication and computation costs at the expense of higher round complexity. Our benchmarks show that disMult always tends to have a higher latency than disZK and constitutes the performance bottleneck. Detailed discussion is provided in the full version.

The GOD variant requires running the preprocessing of [66] for every pair of parties which has an overhead of around 3 KB per multiplication gate per party. This approximately halves the throughput in the preprocessing phase when compared to the fair variant since the combined preprocessing across all [66] instances is akin to running six instances of disMult which in turn is the main bottleneck in fair preprocessing. With respect to throughput, [56] has the highest tp

Table 5. Preprocessing phase cost for generating a triple.

Ref.	Comm. (KB)	tp
Tetrad	0.004	958918.39
MASCOT	67.6	4548.64
QS (Fair)	3.115	8051.27
QS (GOD)	6.22	3934.01

owing to its low communication costs while the tp of QuadSquad Fair is around $1.8\times$ that of [53]. The tp of QuadSquad GOD is comparable to that of [53] despite a significantly lower communication cost because the implementation of [53] distributes the evaluation of OT instances across the available threads while our implementation runs it in a single thread to allow running the disZK protocol in parallel.

7.2 Applications

We consider applications of secure liquidity matching and PPML inference. Before describing these and evaluating their performance via QuadSquad, we describe the building blocks designed for the same.

Building Blocks. Each of these applications requires designing new building blocks, as described in Table 2. Specifically, we develop the following building blocks: sharing and reconstruction for SOC setting, dot product (DotP), dot product with truncation (DotPTr), conversion to arithmetic sharing from a Boolean shared bit (Bit2A), bit extraction to obtain Boolean sharing of the most significant bit (msb) from an arithmetic shared value (BitExt), bit injection to obtain arithmetic sharing of $b \cdot v$ from a Boolean sharing of a bit b and the arithmetic sharing of v (BitInj). Inclusion of these blocks makes QuadSquad a comprehensive framework. The details of the constructions and the complexity analysis are discussed in the full version.

Liquidity Matching. Secure liquidity matching involves executing a privacy-preserving variant of the **gridlock** algorithm. This algorithm identifies a set of transactions among banks which can be executed while ensuring that all the banks possess sufficient liquidity to process them. The gridlock algorithm can be considered for the following scenarios (i) the source and the destination banks of the transactions are open (non-private) (sodoGR), (ii) the source is open, but the

Table 6. Liquidity matching

#banks	#transactions	Online		Fair Total*		GOD Total*	
		Latency(s)	Comm. (KB)	Latency(s)	Comm. (MB)	Latency(s)	Comm. (MB)
256	50	5.23	21.28	9.46	4.75	10.35	14.56
	100	5.46	23.71	10.22	5.53	10.64	16.11
	250	5.70	32.04	10.56	7.87	11.06	20.77
	500	5.94	47.97	10.95	11.77	11.61	28.53
	1000	6.18	81.76	11.49	19.56	12.45	44.07
1024	50	5.70	74.41	10.72	7.98	12.17	44.91
	100	5.94	76.59	10.99	8.76	12.47	46.46
	250	6.18	83.36	11.32	11.10	12.89	51.13
	500	6.42	96.13	11.71	15.0	13.43	58.88
	1000	6.66	124.36	12.26	22.79	14.28	74.41

destination is hidden (secret) (sodsGR), and (iii) the source and the destination are hidden (ssdsGR). A secure realization for liquidity matching was provided in [7], albeit via traditionally secure MPC. Given the sensitive nature of financial data involved in liquidity matching, clearly, FaF-security is more apt. Hence, we focus on designing FaF-secure protocols for the same. Further, with respect to the three scenarios described above, note that in most practical cases hiding the transaction amount is sufficient. Hence, we consider only the sodoGR instance (details in the full version). However, we note that extending our techniques to the other two scenarios is also possible.

At a high level, the protocol is iterative where each iteration checks the feasibility of clearing a subset of transactions. The protocol terminates with a feasible set or reports a deadlock when no transactions can be cleared. Since the communication and computation costs are identical across all iterations, we benchmark the performance for a single iteration and report the costs in Table 6. We see similar trends as observed while evaluating the performance of MPC, where the GOD variant is on par with the fair variant with respect to the overall latency. Further, we observe that the latency of an iteration for both variants is within 15s even for a large number of banks and set of transactions.

PPML. For the application of PPML inference, we consider the popularly used [55,56,67,70] Neural Network (NN) architectures, given below.

- *FCNN:* Fully-Connected NN consists of two hidden layers, each with 128 nodes followed by an output layer of 10 nodes. ReLU is applied after each layer.
- *LeNet:* This NN consists of 2 convolutional layers and 2 fully connected layers, each followed by ReLU activation function. Moreover, the convolutional layers are followed by an average-pooling layer.

The inference task is performed over the publicly available MNIST [57] dataset which is a collection of 28×28 pixel, handwritten digit images with a label between 0 and 9 for each. We note that our techniques easily extend to securely

Table 7. NN inference where **QS** denotes QuadSquad.

Network	Ref.	Online			Total*	
		Latency (s)	Comm. (MB)	tp (queries/min)	Latency (s)	Comm. (MB)
FCN	Fantastic Four	48.06	27.71	43.75	48.06	27.71
FCN	Tetrad	1.66	0.006	47099.05	2.38	0.02
FCN	**QS Fair**	6.00	0.022	3176.65	29.77	371.15
FCN	**QS GOD**	6.00	0.022	3176.65	44.49	746.46
LeNet	Fantastic Four	220.17	134.28	84.22	220.17	134.28
LeNet	Tetrad	2.45	0.36	787.09	3.25	0.91
LeNet	**QS Fair**	10.36	1.27	64.24	308.89	7251.73
LeNet	**QS GOD**	10.36	1.27	64.24	607.53	14868.07

evaluating other NN architectures such as convolutional neural network (CNN) and VGG16 [69] used in other MPC-based PPML frameworks of [55,56,70].

We compare the performance of PPML inference via QuadSquad for the above mentioned NN with the honest majority protocols of [56] and [31]. PPML in the 4PC dishonest majority (malicious) setting has not been explored so far. The results of our experiments are summarised in Table 7. Note that the latency reported is obtained via a single instance of circuit evaluation, whereas the throughput is computed by running the inference on larger batches. Here, tp is the number of queries evaluated in a minute since inference over WAN requires more than a second to complete. Our fair and GOD variants have an overhead of 3x–4x in performance respectively. However we provide a stronger adversarial model compared to [56]. The numbers in Table 7 for [31] from MP-SPDZ [51] are unexpectedly high. We suspect that this anomaly is due to the preprocessing cost of [31]. However, the benchmarks seem consistent with those reported in [31] and pinpointing the exact cause is challenging due to the vast MP-SPDZ codebase. It is worth noting that the communication cost of [31] per query for larger batch sizes decreases to 0.93 MB per party for FCN and 0.46 MB per party for LeNet. The QuadSquad protocols have higher cost in the preprocessing phase from using more expensive primitives like OT and the feature dependent preprocessing phase for dot-product. However, the comparable online performance to [56] and [31] and the stronger security model make it a viable practical option despite the overhead in preprocessing.

Acknowledgements. Arpita Patra would like to acknowledge financial support from DST National Mission on Interdisciplinary Cyber-Physical Systems (NM-CPS) 2020–2025 and SERB MATRICS (Theoretical Sciences) Grant 2020–2023. Varsha Bhat Kukkala would like to acknowledge financial support from National Security Council, India. Nishat Koti would like to acknowledge support from Centre for Networked Intelligence (a Cisco CSR initiative) at the Indian Institute of Science, Bengaluru. Shravani Patil would like to acknowledge financial support from DST National Mission on Interdisciplinary Cyber-Physical Systems (NM-ICPS) 2020–2025. The authors would also like to acknowledge the support from Google Cloud for benchmarking.

References

1. Abspoel, M., Cramer, R., Damgård, I., Escudero, D., Yuan, C.: Efficient information-theoretic secure multiparty computation over $\mathbb{Z}/p^k\mathbb{Z}$ via galois rings. In: Hofheinz, D., Rosen, A. (eds.) TCC 2019. LNCS, vol. 11891, pp. 471–501. Springer, Cham (2019). https://doi.org/10.1007/978-3-030-36030-6_19
2. Abspoel, M., Dalskov, A., Escudero, D., Nof, A.: An efficient passive-to-active compiler for honest-majority MPC over rings. In: Sako, K., Tippenhauer, N.O. (eds.) ACNS 2021. LNCS, vol. 12727, pp. 122–152. Springer, Cham (2021). https://doi.org/10.1007/978-3-030-78375-4_6
3. Alon, B., Omri, E., Paskin-Cherniavsky, A.: MPC with friends and foes. In: Micciancio, D., Ristenpart, T. (eds.) CRYPTO 2020. LNCS, vol. 12171, pp. 677–706. Springer, Cham (2020). https://doi.org/10.1007/978-3-030-56880-1_24
4. Araki, T., et al.: Optimized honest-majority MPC for malicious adversaries - breaking the 1 billion-gate per second barrier. In: IEEE S&P (2017)
5. Araki, T., Furukawa, J., Lindell, Y., Nof, A., Ohara, K.: High-throughput semi-honest secure three-party computation with an honest majority. In: ACM CCS (2016)
6. Archer, D.W., et al.: From keys to databases-real-world applications of secure multi-party computation. Comput. J. (2018)
7. Atapoor, S., Smart, N.P., Alaoui, Y.T.: Private liquidity matching using MPC. IACR Cryptology ePrint Archive (2021)
8. Badrinarayanan, S., Jain, A., Manohar, N., Sahai, A.: Secure MPC: laziness leads to GOD. In: Moriai, S., Wang, H. (eds.) ASIACRYPT 2020. LNCS, vol. 12493, pp. 120–150. Springer, Cham (2020). https://doi.org/10.1007/978-3-030-64840-4_5
9. Baum, C., Damgård, I., Toft, T., Zakarias, R.: Better preprocessing for secure multiparty computation. In: Manulis, M., Sadeghi, A.-R., Schneider, S. (eds.) ACNS 2016. LNCS, vol. 9696, pp. 327–345. Springer, Cham (2016). https://doi.org/10.1007/978-3-319-39555-5_18
10. Baum, C., Orsini, E., Scholl, P.: Efficient secure multiparty computation with identifiable abort. In: Hirt, M., Smith, A. (eds.) TCC 2016. LNCS, vol. 9985, pp. 461–490. Springer, Heidelberg (2016). https://doi.org/10.1007/978-3-662-53641-4_18
11. Beaver, D.: Efficient multiparty protocols using circuit randomization. In: Feigenbaum, J. (ed.) CRYPTO 1991. LNCS, vol. 576, pp. 420–432. Springer, Heidelberg (1992). https://doi.org/10.1007/3-540-46766-1_34
12. Beaver, D.: Precomputing oblivious transfer. In: Coppersmith, D. (ed.) CRYPTO 1995. LNCS, vol. 963, pp. 97–109. Springer, Heidelberg (1995). https://doi.org/10.1007/3-540-44750-4_8
13. Ben-Efraim, A., Nielsen, M., Omri, E.: Turbospeedz: double your online SPDZ! Improving SPDZ using function dependent preprocessing. In: Deng, R.H., Gauthier-Umaña, V., Ochoa, M., Yung, M. (eds.) ACNS 2019. LNCS, vol. 11464, pp. 530–549. Springer, Cham (2019). https://doi.org/10.1007/978-3-030-21568-2_26
14. Ben-Or, M., Goldwasser, S., Wigderson, A.: Completeness theorems for non-cryptographic fault-tolerant distributed computation (extended abstract). In: STOC (1988)
15. Bogdanov, D., Kamm, L., Kubo, B., Rebane, R., Sokk, V., Talviste, R.: Students and taxes: a privacy-preserving social study using secure computation. IACR Cryptology ePrint Archive (2015)

16. Bogdanov, D., Laur, S., Willemson, J.: Sharemind: a framework for fast privacy-preserving computations. In: Jajodia, S., Lopez, J. (eds.) ESORICS 2008. LNCS, vol. 5283, pp. 192–206. Springer, Heidelberg (2008). https://doi.org/10.1007/978-3-540-88313-5_13

17. Bogdanov, D., Talviste, R., Willemson, J.: Deploying secure multi-party computation for financial data analysis - (short paper). In: Keromytis, A.D. (ed.) FC 2012. LNCS, vol. 7397, pp. 57–64. Springer, Heidelberg (2012). https://doi.org/10.1007/978-3-642-32946-3_5

18. Boneh, D., Boyle, E., Corrigan-Gibbs, H., Gilboa, N., Ishai, Y.: Zero-knowledge proofs on secret-shared data via fully linear PCPs. In: Boldyreva, A., Micciancio, D. (eds.) CRYPTO 2019. LNCS, vol. 11694, pp. 67–97. Springer, Cham (2019). https://doi.org/10.1007/978-3-030-26954-8_3

19. Boyle, E., Couteau, G., Gilboa, N., Ishai, Y., Kohl, L., Scholl, P.: Efficient pseudorandom correlation generators: silent OT extension and more. In: Boldyreva, A., Micciancio, D. (eds.) CRYPTO 2019. LNCS, vol. 11694, pp. 489–518. Springer, Cham (2019). https://doi.org/10.1007/978-3-030-26954-8_16

20. Boyle, E., Gilboa, N., Ishai, Y., Nof, A.: Practical fully secure three-party computation via sublinear distributed zero-knowledge proofs. In: ACM CCS (2019)

21. Byali, M., Chaudhari, H., Patra, A., Suresh, A.: FLASH: fast and robust framework for privacy-preserving machine learning. In: PETS (2020)

22. Byali, M., Hazay, C., Patra, A., Singla, S.: Fast actively secure five-party computation with security beyond abort. In: ACM CCS (2019)

23. Byali, M., Joseph, A., Patra, A., Ravi, D.: Fast secure computation for small population over the internet. In: ACM CCS (2018)

24. Chaudhari, H., Choudhury, A., Patra, A., Suresh, A.: ASTRA: high throughput 3PC over rings with application to secure prediction. In: ACM CCSW@CCS (2019)

25. Chaudhari, H., Rachuri, R., Suresh, A.: Trident: efficient 4PC framework for privacy preserving machine learning. In: NDSS (2020)

26. Chaum, D.: The spymasters double-agent problem: multiparty computations secure unconditionally from minorities and cryptographically from majorities. In: Brassard, G. (ed.) CRYPTO 1989. LNCS, vol. 435, pp. 591–602. Springer, New York (1990). https://doi.org/10.1007/0-387-34805-0_52

27. Chida, K., et al.: Fast large-scale honest-majority MPC for malicious adversaries. In: Shacham, H., Boldyreva, A. (eds.) CRYPTO 2018. LNCS, vol. 10993, pp. 34–64. Springer, Cham (2018). https://doi.org/10.1007/978-3-319-96878-0_2

28. Cleve, R.: Limits on the security of coin flips when half the processors are faulty (extended abstract). In: ACM STOC (1986)

29. Couteau, G., Rindal, P., Raghuraman, S.: Silver: silent VOLE and oblivious transfer from hardness of decoding structured LDPC codes. In: Malkin, T., Peikert, C. (eds.) CRYPTO 2021. LNCS, vol. 12827, pp. 502–534. Springer, Cham (2021). https://doi.org/10.1007/978-3-030-84252-9_17

30. Cramer, R., Damgård, I., Escudero, D., Scholl, P., Xing, C.: SPD$\mathbb{Z}_{2^k}$: efficient MPC mod 2^k for dishonest majority. In: Shacham, H., Boldyreva, A. (eds.) CRYPTO 2018. LNCS, vol. 10992, pp. 769–798. Springer, Cham (2018). https://doi.org/10.1007/978-3-319-96881-0_26

31. Dalskov, A., Escudero, D., Keller, M.: Fantastic four: honest-majority four-party secure computation with malicious security. In: USENIX Security (2021)

32. Damgård, I., Escudero, D., Frederiksen, T.K., Keller, M., Scholl, P., Volgushev, N.: New primitives for actively-secure MPC over rings with applications to private machine learning. In: IEEE S&P (2019)

33. Damgård, I., Nielsen, J.B.: Scalable and unconditionally secure multiparty computation. In: Menezes, A. (ed.) CRYPTO 2007. LNCS, vol. 4622, pp. 572–590. Springer, Heidelberg (2007). https://doi.org/10.1007/978-3-540-74143-5_32

34. Damgård, I., Orlandi, C., Simkin, M.: Yet another compiler for active security or: efficient MPC over arbitrary rings. In: Shacham, H., Boldyreva, A. (eds.) CRYPTO 2018. LNCS, vol. 10992, pp. 799–829. Springer, Cham (2018). https://doi.org/10.1007/978-3-319-96881-0_27

35. Damgård, I., Pastro, V., Smart, N., Zakarias, S.: Multiparty computation from somewhat homomorphic encryption. In: Safavi-Naini, R., Canetti, R. (eds.) CRYPTO 2012. LNCS, vol. 7417, pp. 643–662. Springer, Heidelberg (2012). https://doi.org/10.1007/978-3-642-32009-5_38

36. Demmler, D., Schneider, T., Zohner, M.: ABY - a framework for efficient mixed-protocol secure two-party computation. In: NDSS (2015)

37. Dolev, D., Dwork, C., Waarts, O., Yung, M.: Perfectly secure message transmission. J. ACM (JACM) (1993)

38. Dolev, D., Strong, H.R.: Authenticated algorithms for byzantine agreement. SIAM J. Comput. (1983)

39. Fitzi, M., Hirt, M., Maurer, U.: Trading correctness for privacy in unconditional multi-party computation. In: Krawczyk, H. (ed.) CRYPTO 1998. LNCS, vol. 1462, pp. 121–136. Springer, Heidelberg (1998). https://doi.org/10.1007/BFb0055724

40. Furukawa, J., Lindell, Y., Nof, A., Weinstein, O.: High-throughput secure three-party computation for malicious adversaries and an honest majority. In: Coron, J.-S., Nielsen, J.B. (eds.) EUROCRYPT 2017. LNCS, vol. 10211, pp. 225–255. Springer, Cham (2017). https://doi.org/10.1007/978-3-319-56614-6_8

41. Ghodosi, H., Pieprzyk, J.: Multi-party computation with omnipresent adversary. In: Jarecki, S., Tsudik, G. (eds.) PKC 2009. LNCS, vol. 5443, pp. 180–195. Springer, Heidelberg (2009). https://doi.org/10.1007/978-3-642-00468-1_11

42. Gilboa, N.: Two party RSA key generation. In: Wiener, M. (ed.) CRYPTO 1999. LNCS, vol. 1666, pp. 116–129. Springer, Heidelberg (1999). https://doi.org/10.1007/3-540-48405-1_8

43. Goldreich, O., Micali, S., Wigderson, A.: How to play any mental game or A completeness theorem for protocols with honest majority. In: STOC (1987)

44. Gordon, S.D., Ranellucci, S., Wang, X.: Secure computation with low communication from cross-checking. In: Peyrin, T., Galbraith, S. (eds.) ASIACRYPT 2018. LNCS, vol. 11274, pp. 59–85. Springer, Cham (2018). https://doi.org/10.1007/978-3-030-03332-3_3

45. Goyal, V., Song, Y., Zhu, C.: Guaranteed output delivery comes free in honest majority MPC. In: Micciancio, D., Ristenpart, T. (eds.) CRYPTO 2020. LNCS, vol. 12171, pp. 618–646. Springer, Cham (2020). https://doi.org/10.1007/978-3-030-56880-1_22

46. Hazay, C., Lindell, Y.: A note on the relation between the definitions of security for semi-honest and malicious adversaries. IACR Cryptology ePrint Archive (2010)

47. Hirt, M., Mularczyk, M.: Efficient MPC with a mixed adversary. In: LIPIcs (2020)

48. Ishai, Y., Kilian, J., Nissim, K., Petrank, E.: Extending oblivious transfers efficiently. In: Boneh, D. (ed.) CRYPTO 2003. LNCS, vol. 2729, pp. 145–161. Springer, Heidelberg (2003). https://doi.org/10.1007/978-3-540-45146-4_9

49. Ishai, Y., Kumaresan, R., Kushilevitz, E., Paskin-Cherniavsky, A.: Secure computation with minimal interaction, revisited. In: Gennaro, R., Robshaw, M. (eds.) CRYPTO 2015. LNCS, vol. 9216, pp. 359–378. Springer, Heidelberg (2015). https://doi.org/10.1007/978-3-662-48000-7_18

50. Ishai, Y., Prabhakaran, M., Sahai, A.: Founding cryptography on oblivious transfer – efficiently. In: Wagner, D. (ed.) CRYPTO 2008. LNCS, vol. 5157, pp. 572–591. Springer, Heidelberg (2008). https://doi.org/10.1007/978-3-540-85174-5_32

51. Keller, M.: MP-SPDZ: a versatile framework for multi-party computation. In: ACM CCS (2020)

52. Keller, M., Orsini, E., Scholl, P.: Actively secure OT extension with optimal overhead. In: Gennaro, R., Robshaw, M. (eds.) CRYPTO 2015. LNCS, vol. 9215, pp. 724–741. Springer, Heidelberg (2015). https://doi.org/10.1007/978-3-662-47989-6_35

53. Keller, M., Orsini, E., Scholl, P.: MASCOT: faster malicious arithmetic secure computation with oblivious transfer. In: ACM CCS (2016)

54. Keller, M., Pastro, V., Rotaru, D.: Overdrive: making SPDZ great again. In: Nielsen, J.B., Rijmen, V. (eds.) EUROCRYPT 2018. LNCS, vol. 10822, pp. 158–189. Springer, Cham (2018). https://doi.org/10.1007/978-3-319-78372-7_6

55. Koti, N., Pancholi, M., Patra, A., Suresh, A.: SWIFT: super-fast and robust privacy-preserving machine learning. In: USENIX Security (2021)

56. Koti, N., Patra, A., Rachuri, R., Suresh, A.: Tetrad: actively secure 4pc for secure training and inference. arXiv preprint arXiv:2106.02850 (2021)

57. LeCun, Y., Cortes, C.: MNIST handwritten digit database (2010). http://yann.lecun.com/exdb/mnist/

58. Lindell, Y., Nof, A.: A framework for constructing fast MPC over arithmetic circuits with malicious adversaries and an honest-majority. In: ACM CCS (2017)

59. Mazloom, S., Le, P.H., Ranellucci, S., Gordon, S.D.: Secure parallel computation on national scale volumes of data. In: USENIX Security (2020)

60. Mohassel, P., Rindal, P.: ABY^3: a mixed protocol framework for machine learning. In: ACM CCS (2018)

61. Mohassel, P., Rosulek, M., Zhang, Y.: Fast and secure three-party computation: the garbled circuit approach. In: ACM CCS (2015)

62. Mohassel, P., Zhang, Y.: SecureML: a system for scalable privacy-preserving machine learning. In: IEEE S&P (2017)

63. Nordholt, P.S., Veeningen, M.: Minimising communication in honest-majority MPC by batchwise multiplication verification. In: Preneel, B., Vercauteren, F. (eds.) ACNS 2018. LNCS, vol. 10892, pp. 321–339. Springer, Cham (2018). https://doi.org/10.1007/978-3-319-93387-0_17

64. Orlandi, C.: Is multiparty computation any good in practice? In: IEEE ICASSP (2011)

65. Orsini, E., Smart, N.P., Vercauteren, F.: Overdrive2k: efficient secure MPC over $\mathbb{Z}_{2^k}$ from somewhat homomorphic encryption. In: Jarecki, S. (ed.) CT-RSA 2020. LNCS, vol. 12006, pp. 254–283. Springer, Cham (2020). https://doi.org/10.1007/978-3-030-40186-3_12

66. Patra, A., Schneider, T., Suresh, A., Yalame, H.: Aby2. 0: improved mixed-protocol secure two-party computation. In: USENIX Security (2021)

67. Patra, A., Suresh, A.: BLAZE: blazing fast privacy-preserving machine learning. In: NDSS (2020)

68. Shoup, V.: NTL: a library for doing number theory (2021). https://libntl.org/

69. Simonyan, K., Zisserman, A.: Very deep convolutional networks for large-scale image recognition. arXiv preprint arXiv:1409.1556 (2014)

70. Wagh, S., Tople, S., Benhamouda, F., Kushilevitz, E., Mittal, P., Rabin, T.: Falcon: honest-majority maliciously secure framework for private deep learning. arXiv preprint (2020)
71. Wang, X., Malozemoff, A.J., Katz, J.: EMP-toolkit: efficient MultiParty computation toolkit (2016). https://github.com/emp-toolkit
72. Yang, K., Weng, C., Lan, X., Zhang, J., Wang, X.: Ferret: fast extension for correlated OT with small communication. In: ACM CCS (2020)

Towards Practical Topology-Hiding Computation

Shuaishuai Li[1,2]([⊠]) [iD]

[1] State Key Laboratory of Information Security, Institute of Information
Engineering, Chinese Academy of Sciences, Beijing 100093, China
lishuaishuai@iie.ac.cn
[2] School of Cyber Security, University of Chinese Academy of Sciences,
Beijing 100049, China

Abstract. Topology-hiding computation (THC) enables n parties to perform a secure multiparty computation (MPC) protocol in an incomplete communication graph while keeping the communication graph hidden. The work of Akavia et al. (CRYPTO 2017 and JoC 2020) shown that THC is feasible for any graph. In this work, we focus on the efficiency of THC and give improvements for various tasks including broadcast, sum and general computation. We mainly consider THC on undirected cycles, but we also give two results for THC on general graphs. All of our results are derived in the presence of a passive adversary statically corrupting any number of parties.

In the undirected cycles, the state-of-the-art topology-hiding broadcast (THB) protocol is the Akavia-Moran (AM) protocol of Akavia et al. (EUROCRYPT 2017). We give an optimization for the AM protocol such that the communication cost of broadcasting $O(\kappa)$ bits is reduced from $O(n^2\kappa^2)$ bits to $O(n^2\kappa)$ bits. We also consider the sum and general computation functionalities. Previous to our work, the only THC protocols realizing the sum and general computation functionalities are constructed by using THB to simulate point-to-point channels in an MPC protocol realizing the sum and general computation functionalities, respectively. By allowing the parties to know the exact value of the number of the parties (the AM protocol and our optimization only assume the parties know an upper bound of the number of the parties), we can derive more efficient THC protocols realizing these two functionalities. As a result, comparing with previous works, we reduce the communication cost by a factor of $O(n\kappa)$ for both the sum and general computation functionalities.

As we have mentioned, we also get two results for THC on general graphs. The state-of-the-art THB protocol for general graphs is the Akavia-LaVigne-Moran (ALM) protocol of Akavia et al. (CRYPTO 2017 and JoC 2020). Our result is that our optimization for the AM protocol also applies to the ALM protocol and can reduce its communication cost by a factor of $O(\kappa)$. Moreover, we optimize the fully-homomorphic encryption (FHE) based GTHC protocol of LaVigne et al. (TCC 2018) and reduce its communication cost from $O(n^8\kappa^2)$ FHE ciphertexts and $O(n^6\kappa)$ FHE public keys to $O(n^6\kappa)$ FHE ciphertexts and $O(n^5\kappa)$ FHE public keys.

S. Agrawal and D. Lin (Eds.): ASIACRYPT 2022, LNCS 13791, pp. 588–617, 2022.
https://doi.org/10.1007/978-3-031-22963-3_20

1   Introduction

The theory of secure multiparty computation (MPC) has drawn a great deal of attention since introduced by Yao [28] in 1982. In MPC, n parties $P_1, \ldots, P_n$ seek to compute some public function on their private inputs while keeping their inputs secret. There have been a great body of works to make MPC more and more general and efficient. However, most of these works assume that the communication graph is complete, meaning that every two parties can communicate directly, which is not always the case in real-world situations. For example, two parties may can not directly communicate with each other due to their long physical distance or other confidentiality reasons. For this reason, a line of works [8,9,17–19] considered designing MPC protocols over incomplete communication graph.

Moran et al. [25] considered a more complicated situation, where the communication graph is not only incomplete but also *sensitive*. They formalized the concept of topology-hiding computation (THC), which aims to design MPC protocols while keeping the graph topology hidden. There are many scenes, such as social networks, ISP networks, vehicle-to-vehicle communications, and other Internet of Things networks, where keeping the graph topology hidden is of great importance.

Motivated by building more efficient THC protocols, we consider the setting where the adversary may statically, passively corrupt up to at most $n - 1$ parties (only computational security is possible in such a setting). A series of works have resolved the feasibility question of THC in this setting. More concretely, the works of [21,25] built THC for graphs with logarithmic diameter[1]. Later, based on a special public-key encryption (PKE) scheme (aka PKCR encryption), the work of [3] built THC for several special graph classes that may have super-logarithmic diameter such as cycles, trees, and graphs with logarithmic circumference[2]. The feasibility of THC on any graph is established in the work of [1], which presented a construction of THC for *all* graphs by combining PKCR encryption and another novel technique called correlated random walks.

In this work, we focus on the efficiency of THC. In the undirected cycles, we follow the work of [3] and derive more efficient THC protocols for various tasks such as broadcast, sum and general computation (computing any circuit consists of addition and multiplication gates). We also extend some of our results and give several improvements for existing THC protocols on general graphs, including the topology-hiding broadcast (THB) protocol of [1] and the fully-homomorphic encryption (FHE) based general topology-hiding computation (GTHC) protocol of [22].

Other Related Works. There are also several works studying the feasibility of (computationally secure) THC in the fail-stop setting, where the adversary may instruct the corrupt parties to abort the protocol. The works of [6,22]

---

[1] The diameter of a graph is the greatest distance between two nodes in the graph.

[2] The circumference of a graph is the maximum length of a cycle in the graph.

showed how to construct THC protocols with small leakage. Some works studied the possibility of information-theoretic THC. [20] showed that information-theoretically secure MPC inherently leaks information about the graph topology to the adversary, which implies that information-theoretic THC on general graphs is impossible. A natural question is whether information-theoretic THC is possible for some subclasses of graphs, which is the main topic of [5]. Moreover, the work of [4] studied the feasibility of THC in different cryptographic setting: information-theoretic, given other cryptographic primitives such as key agreement and oblivious transfer. Finally, the work of [23] studied the feasibility of THC when assuming the network delay is not known (all other THC works assume the network delay has a known upper bound).

1.1   Our Contribution

As our first result, we give an optimization for the Akavia-Moran (AM) protocol (the state-of-the-art THB protocol for undirected cycles[3]) proposed by [3] and reduce its communication cost by a factor of $O(\kappa)$ in the amortized sense. Concretely, if one party wants to broadcast $O(\kappa)$ bits, the communication cost will be $O(n^2\kappa^2)$ bits using the AM protocol. Our optimization for the AM protocol can reduce the communication cost to $O(n^2\kappa)$ bits.

We then consider the sum and general computation functionalities. Before showing our results[4], we first clarify the state-of-the-art asymptotic communication complexity required for realizing these two functionalities, respectively. As noted in [3,21,25], given THB for some graph class and a PKE scheme, any functionality $\mathcal{F}$ can be topology-hidingly realized for the same graph class by using THB and PKE to simulate point-to-point channels in an MPC protocol realizing $\mathcal{F}$. Concretely, point-to-point channels are simulated as follows.

1. Each party uses THB to broadcast its public key in a setup phase.
2. To send a message x to P_j, P_i encrypts x using the public key of P_j and then uses THB to broadcast the resulting ciphertext.
3. Upon receiving the ciphertext, P_j can decrypt it to get x. Other parties know nothing about x because they do not know the decrypt key.

If the underlying PKE scheme satisfies that the ciphertext length is of the same order as the plaintext length (i.e., the ciphertext length is at most a positive constant multiple of the plaintext length)[5] and the underlying THB protocol is

---

[3] The original AM protocol is designed for directed cycles, and in particular, it assumes that all parties only know an upper-bound on n rather than the exact value of n. In this work, we extend this protocol to undirected cycles (which is direct) and moreover, we assume that all parties know the exact value of n. We remark that our optimization also works for the original AM protocol.

[4] Unlike the AM protocol and our optimization for the AM protocol, our THC protocols realizing sum and general computation functionalities rely on that the parties know the exact value of n.

[5] In fact, there are many PKE schemes, including the ElGamal [16] scheme and the Paillier [26] scheme, satisfy this property.

instantiated with the AM protocol, we can conclude that the state-of-the-art asymptotic communication complexity of topology-hidingly sending $O(\kappa)$ bits on a cycle is $O(n^2\kappa^2)$ bits (we do not count in the communication cost of step 1 because it can be executed once for all).

As we have said, the only topology-hiding protocols realizing the sum and general computation functionalities are constructed by using THB to simulate point-to-point channels in an MPC protocol realizing these two functionalities. We have clarified the state-of-the-art asymptotic communication complexity of simulating point-to-point channels, hence the left problem is to clarify the state-of-the-art asymptotic communication complexity[6] of realizing these two functionalities (without hiding the topology).

For the sum functionality, to the best of our knowledge, the state-of-the-art asymptotic communication complexity is $O(n\kappa)$ bits, which can be constructed from additively homomorphic encryption (which can be instantiated with the Paillier scheme [26]) as follows.

1. In the setup phase, each party samples a public key and broadcasts it. Let pk be the product of all the public keys.
2. P_1 encrypts its input x_1 with pk and sends the resulting ciphertext c_1 to P_2.
3. For $t = 2$ to $n - 1$, upon receiving the ciphertext c_{t-1}, P_t computes an encryption c_t of $\sum_{j=1}^{t} x_j$ by homomorphically adding x_t to c_{t-1} using the additive homomorphism. P_t sends c_t to P_{t+1}.
4. Upon receiving the ciphertext c_{n-1} from P_{n-1}, P_n computes an encryption c_n of $\sum_{j=1}^{n} x_j$ by homomorphically adding x_n to c_{n-1} using the additive homomorphism.
5. Finally, the parties execute a distributed decryption protocol to securely decrypt c_n.

The security of the above scheme is guaranteed by the semantic security of the underlying encryption scheme. If instantiating the additively homomorphic encryption scheme with the Paillier scheme, we argue that the communication cost of the above protocol will be $O(n\kappa)$ bits (we do not count in the communication cost of step 1 because it can be executed once for all), which can be derived from the following two points. Firstly, the ciphertext length of the Paillier scheme is of the same order as its plaintext length, which implies that the communication cost of step 2-4 is $O(n\kappa)$ bits. Secondly, we can find a distributed decryption protocol in [7] for Paillier ciphertexts with communication complexity $O(n\kappa)$ bits, which implies that the communication cost of step 5 can be $O(n\kappa)$ bits. Therefore, we conclude that the total communication cost is $O(n\kappa)$ bits.

Note that the state-of-the-art asymptotic communication complexity of sending or broadcasting $O(\kappa)$ bits is $O(n^2\kappa^2)$ bits, hence the state-of-the-art asymptotic communication complexity of topology-hidingly realizing the sum functionality is $O(n^3\kappa^2)$ bits. Our optimization for the AM protocol can reduce the

---

[6] Because the communication cost of sending a bitstring m is of the same order as that of broadcasting m, we refer to the communication complexity as the number of bits that are sent or broadcast.

communication cost to $O(n^3\kappa)$ bits. In this work, we give a new topology-hiding sum (THS) protocol which further reduces the communication cost to $O(n^2\kappa)$ bits.

Now we consider the general computation functionality which computes any circuit consisting of addition and multiplication gates. A THC protocol realizing the general computation functionality is called a GTHC protocol. To the best of our knowledge, in the presence of a passive adversary statically corrupting any number of parties, the state-of-the-art asymptotic communication complexity of MPC realizing the general computation functionality is $O((m+c)n\kappa)$ bits[7] where m and c are the number of inputs and multiplication gates in the circuit, which implies that the state-of-the-art asymptotic communication complexity of GTHC is $O((m+c)n^3\kappa^2)$ bits. Our optimization for the AM protocol can reduce the communication cost to $O((m+c)n^3\kappa)$ bits. In this work, we give a new GTHC protocol with communication complexity $O((m+c)n^2\kappa)$ bits.

Finally, we note that our optimization for the AM protocol also applies to the Akavia-LaVigne-Moran (ALM) protocol (the state-of-the-art THB protocol for general graphs) proposed by [1] and reduces its communication cost from $O(n^5\kappa^3)$ bits to $O(n^5\kappa^2)$ when the broadcast value is of length $O(\kappa)$ bits. Moreover, we consider the FHE-based GTHC protocol proposed by [22], which require the parties to communicate $O(n^8\kappa^2)$ FHE ciphertexts and $O(n^5\kappa)$ FHE public keys. We optimize this protocol such that the communication cost is reduced to $O(n^6\kappa)$ FHE ciphertexts and $O(n^5\kappa)$ FHE public keys.

We summarize our results by the following theorem.

Theorem 1. *There exist the following THC protocols in the presence of a passive adversary statically corrupting any number of parties:*

- *A THB protocol for undirected cycles with communication cost $O(n^2\kappa)$ bits while the broadcast value is of length $O(\kappa)$ bits.*
- *A THS protocol for undirected cycles with communication cost $O(n^2\kappa)$ bits while each input is of length $O(\kappa)$ bits.*
- *A GTHC protocol for undirected cycles with communication cost $O((m+c)n^2\kappa)$ bits while the underlying ring is of size $2^{O(\kappa)}$.*
- *A THB protocol for general graphs with communication cost $O(n^5\kappa^2)$ bits while the broadcast value is of length $O(\kappa)$ bits.*
- *A GTHC protocol for general graphs with communication cost $O(n^6\kappa)$ FHE ciphertexts and $O(n^5\kappa)$ FHE public keys.*

A comparison of our results to previous works is presented in Table 1.

1.2   Technical Overview

Before showing how to derive our protocols, we first revisit the AM and ALM protocols. Both of these two THB protocols are only for broadcasting a bit (a

---

[7] Both the arithmetic version of the protocol from [15] and the passive version of the protocol from [14] has communication complexity $O((m+c)n\kappa)$ bits.

Table 1. For all the THC protocols on undirected cycles and the THB protocol for general graphs, we always assume the input size is $O(\kappa)$ bits. The communication costs of the work of [3] for realizing the sum and general computation functionalities are computed as the communication costs of the constructions of THS and GTHC compiled black-box from the AM protocol (assume the parties know the exact value of n in the AM protocol). Additionally, we abbreviate 'FHE ciphertexts' by 'hcts' and 'FHE public keys' by 'hpks'.

Topology-hiding protocols	Communication complexity	References
THB for cycles	$O(n^2\kappa^2)$ bits	[3]
	$O(n^2\kappa)$ bits	Sect. 3
THS for cycles	$O(n^3\kappa^2)$ bits	[3]
	$O(n^2\kappa)$ bits	Sect. 4
GTHC for cycles	$O((m+c)n^3\kappa^2)$ bits	[3]
	$O((m+c)n^2\kappa)$ bits	Sect. 5
THB for general graphs	$O(n^5\kappa^3)$ bits	[1]
	$O(n^5\kappa^2)$ bits	Sect. 6
FHE-based GTHC for general graphs	$O(n^8\kappa^2)$ hcts $+ O(n^5\kappa)$ hpks	[22]
	$O(n^6\kappa)$ hcts $+ O(n^5\kappa)$ hpks	Sect. 6

bitstring can be broadcast bit-by-bit) and built by first presenting a topology-hiding OR protocol and then letting the broadcaster take the broadcast bit as input and each other party take 0 as input. We present them in the same framework, but with different parameters. The framework consists of two phases: an aggregate phase and a decrypt phase.

At the beginning of the aggregate phase, for each party P_i and each of its neighbor d, P_i samples a fresh public key and encrypts its input bit under this key, and sends the resulting ciphertext (together with the public key) to its neighbor d. At each following round, for each $i \in [n]$, P_i chooses a permutation σ of the set of its neighbors[8] and then for each of its neighbor d, P_i, upon receiving a ciphertext (together with a public key) from its neighbor d at the previous round, homomorphically OR's its own bit and adds a new public key layer to this ciphertext, and then sends the resulting ciphertext to its neighbor $\sigma(d)$. After T rounds[9], the parties execute the decrypt phase to decrypt the final ciphertexts. Concretely, each ciphertext is sent back through the same walk it traversed during the aggregate phase, and each party deletes its own public key layer in the reversed walk. Finally, each party derives a bit from each walk starting from itself and outputs the OR of these bits.

---

[8] The AM protocol uses the only non-identity permutation (i.e., each neighbor is mapped to the other neighbor). The ALM protocol uses a fresh random permutation.

[9] T equals $n-1$ in the AM protocol and $8n^3\kappa$ in the ALM protocol.

We can conclude that the communication cost is $4n(n-1) = O(n^2)$ cipher-texts and $2n(n-1) = O(n^2)$ public keys in the AM protocol and $4|E| \cdot 8n^3\kappa = O(n^5\kappa)^{10}$ ciphertexts and $2|E| \cdot 8n^3\kappa = O(n^5\kappa)$ public keys in the ALM proto-col. The results of [1,3,22] showed that the underlying encryption scheme can be instantiated with the ElGamal scheme [16], the Cock scheme [13] or the Regev scheme [27]. The ciphertext length will be at least $O(\kappa)$ bits if using the ElGa-mal or Cock scheme and $O(\kappa \log \kappa)$ bits if using the Regev scheme. Moreover, the public key length will be at least $O(\kappa)$ bits if using the ElGamal or Cock scheme and $O(\kappa \log^2 \kappa)$ bits if using the Regev scheme. Therefore, we know that the state-of-the-art communication complexity of the AM and ALM protocols are $O(n^2\kappa)$ and $O(n^5\kappa^2)$ bits, respectively. Note that both of these two protocols can only be used to broadcast a bit, and if we want to broadcast $O(\kappa)$ bits, then the communication cost of the AM and ALM protocols will be $O(n^2\kappa^2)$ and $O(n^5\kappa^3)$ bits, respectively.

THB for Undirected Cycles and General Graphs. The original AM pro-tocol [3] and ALM protocol [1] require the underlying PKE scheme to be OR-homomorphic. In the work of [2], the journal version of [1], the authors observe that designing topology-hiding OR protocol in fact does not require any homo-morphic property of the underlying encryption scheme. We restate this observa-tion:

> *To compute OR, upon receiving an encryption of a bit c, the computing party holding a bit b outputs an encryption of c if $b = 0$ and an encryption of 1 otherwise.*

In this observation, whether the computing party changes the encrypted bit depends on what its input is. Our novel idea is that if we only consider broadcast (instead of OR), then we can further extend this observation as follows:

> *To design broadcast, upon receiving an encryption of a bit c, the computing party holding a bit b outputs an encryption of c if the computing party is not the broadcaster (which guarantees that the bit encrypted will not be changed if it has been the broadcast bit) and an encryption of b otherwise (which guarantees that the bit encrypted will be the broadcast bit if it is not yet the broadcast bit).*

The main difference between our observation and the original observation is that in our observation, whether the computing party changes the encrypted bit depends on whether it is the broadcaster rather than what its input is. If the parties act as in our observation, then it is obvious that they can also get the broadcast value even if the broadcast value is not a bit value.

Let us explain how to drive our optimization for the AM and ALM protocols from our observation. In the original AM and ALM protocols, the underlying encryption scheme can be instantiated with the ElGamal scheme. However, to

---

[10] $|E|$ is the number of edges in the communication graph, which is no more than $C_n^2 = n(n-1)/2$.

encrypt bits, the actual ElGamal plaintext space is mapped to the set $\{0,1\}$ while the ciphertext length is still $O(\kappa)$ bits. Note that the ciphertext length of the ElGamal scheme is of the same order as its plaintext length (more precisely, an ElGamal ciphertext is twice the length of the corresponding plaintext), and with our novel observation, any value in the ElGamal plaintext space (instead of $\{0,1\}$ in the original AM and ALM protocols) can be the broadcast value, which can reduce the communication cost of the AM and ALM protocols by a factor of $O(\kappa)$ in the amortized sense.

THS for Undirected Cycles. Our THS protocol is based on a simple observation that each walk in the AM protocol passes through each party exactly once during the aggregate phase (which is not right in the original AM protocol where the parties only know an upper bound of n). If we let each party homomorphically add its input to each received ciphertext (assume the underlying encryption is additively homomorphic), then the final ciphertext of each walk is indeed an encryption of the sum of all the inputs. Because the standard ElGamal scheme does not have additive homomorphism, we instantiate the underlying encryption scheme with the scheme from [10] or [12]. Moreover, the ciphertext and public key lengths of both of these two schemes can be $O(\kappa)$ bits when the plaintext length is $O(\kappa)$ bits. Notice that the parties communicate $O(n^2)$ ciphertexts and $O(n^2)$ public keys as in the AM protocol, which leads to the claimed communication cost, i.e., $O(n^2\kappa)$ bits.

GTHC for Undirected Cycles. Our GTHC protocol also requires that the parties know the exact value of n. Concretely, we consider designing a GTHC protocol within the popular framework based on additive secret sharing. This framework consists of three phases: the input sharing phase, the circuit evaluation phase and the output recovery phase. In the input sharing phase, the parties generate additive sharings for the inputs. In the circuit evaluation phase, the parties perform a protocol to compute an additive sharing of the value of the computed function f (which is represented by an arithmetic circuit consisting of addition and multiplication gates) at the inputs. Finally, in the output recovery phase, the parties recover the output to the parties who are supposed to obtain the output. Because additive secret sharing is linearly homomorphic, the addition gates can be computed locally. Therefore, the key point for designing a GTHC protocol is how to compute a multiplication gate, i.e. how to securely compute an additive sharing of xy with x, y additively shared among the parties. Our starting point is that an additive sharing of xy can be computed by locally adding a public value $xy - r$ to an additive sharing of r where r is a random value. The additive sharing of r can be generated by letting each party P_i locally sample a random value r_i (set $r = \sum_{i \in [n]} r_i$). Now the goal is to publish the value $xy - r$. We present a topology-hiding protocol to achieve this goal in Sect. 5. We remark that the communication cost of this protocol is $O(n^2\kappa)$ bits, which implies the communication cost of computing a multiplication gate is $O(n^2\kappa)$ bits. Moreover, we use our THS protocol to execute the input sharing and output recovery phases such that the communication cost of sharing an input or recovering the output is $O(n^2\kappa)$ bits. Assume f has m inputs and c multiplication gates, then the total communication cost is $O((m+c)n^2\kappa)$ bits.

FHE-Based GTHC for General Graphs. The work of [22] gave a GTHC protocol based on FHE. We call this protocol the LZM^3T protocol. The main advantage of the LZM^3T protocol is its low round complexity, which amounts to the round complexity of the ALM protocol. However, if designing a GTHC protocol by compiling an MPC protocol π which realizes the general computation functionality from THB, then the round complexity of the resulting protocol will be k times that of the ALM protocol where k is the round complexity of π.

The LZM^3T protocol[11] is constructed by modifying the aggregate phase of the ALM protocol as follows. In the aggregate phase of the LZM^3T protocol, each party P_i *appends* the ciphertexts of its input x_i and its ID id_i to each received ciphertext. In such a way, at the end of the aggregate phase, each party P_i will receive $T = 8n^3\kappa$ pairs of ciphertexts $\{c_{t,b}\}_{t\in[T],b\in\{0,1\}}$ (together with the corresponding public key). Let $m_{t,b}$ be the decryption of $c_{t,b}$, then for each $t \in [T]$, there exists $i_t \in [n]$ such that $(m_{t,0}, m_{t,1}) = (x_{i_t}, id_{i_t})$. To compute a given function f, P_i compute an encryption of $f \circ \texttt{parse}$ on $(\{m_{t,b}\}_{t\in[T],b\in\{0,1\}})$, where $\texttt{parse}(\{m_{t,b}\}_{t\in[T],b\in\{0,1\}}) = (x_1,\ldots,x_n)$[12], using the full homomorphism of the underlying encryption. Finally, the parties execute the decrypt phase to decrypt the resulting ciphertexts. The LZM^3T has high communication cost because each party sends a ciphertext vector of length $O(t)$ at round t and the total rounds is $T = O(n^3\kappa)$, which yields at least $O((1 + 2 + \cdots + T) \cdot |E|) = O(T^2n^2) = O(n^8\kappa^2)$ ciphertexts communication during the aggregate phase. We optimize the aggregate phase such that $O(n^6\kappa)$ ciphertexts are sufficient[13].

Our idea is that in the aggregate phase, instead of appending an encryption of the input (together with an encryption of the ID) to each received ciphertext vector at each round, each party sends ciphertext vectors of length n at each round and for the i-th entry of the ciphertext vectors, the parties act exactly as in the optimized ALM protocol with P_i being the broadcaster and the input x_i of P_i being the broadcast value. This way, at the end of the aggregate phase, the last party in each walk will get a ciphertext vector of length n where the i-th entry is exactly an encryption of x_i. In particular, the ciphertexts in the same ciphertext vector are under the same public key, which allows the last

---

[11] The original protocol works in the fail-stop model where the adversary may instruct any party to abort the execution at any time, but we consider the passive version of this protocol.

[12] The function $\texttt{parse}$ may be derived as follows. For each $i \in [n]$, define the piecewise function h_i such that $h_i(a,b) = a$ if $b = id_i$ and $h_i(a,b) = 0$ if $b \neq id_i$. Then we set $y_i = (\sum_{t\in[T]} h_i(m_{t,0}, m_{t,1}))(\sum_{t\in[T]} m_{t,0}^{-1} h_i(m_{t,0}, m_{t,1}))^{-1}$ and $\texttt{parse} = (y_1,\ldots,y_n)$. Assume (x_i, id_i) appears in the multiset $\{(m_{t,0}, m_{t,1})\}_{t\in[T]}$ k times (the protocol guarantees that $k \geq 1$ with overwhelming probability), then $y_i = kx_i \cdot k^{-1} = x_i$. Therefore, $\texttt{parse}(\{m_{t,b}\}_{t\in[T],b\in\{0,1\}})$ equals $(x_1,\ldots,x_n)$ with overwhelming probability.

[13] More precisely, we reduce the communication cost from $O(n^8\kappa^2)$ ciphertexts and $O(n^5\kappa)$ public keys to $O(n^6\kappa)$ ciphertexts and $O(n^5\kappa)$ public keys.

party in each walk to compute an encryption of the given function using the full homomorphism of the underlying encryption. Finally, the decrypt phase is executed. It is obvious that our optimized aggregate phase only requires the parties to send $O(nT \cdot |E|) = O(n^6 \kappa)$ ciphertexts.

2   Preliminaries

Full Version of this Paper. Due to space constraints, we defer details like instantiation details, omitted proofs and functionalities, and some omitted protocols to the full version of this paper [24].

Notations. Let κ be the security parameter. For any positive integer m, $[m]$ denotes the set $\{1, \cdots, m\}$. We say a function $\varepsilon(\kappa)$ is negligible, denoted $\varepsilon(\kappa) = \mathsf{neg}(\kappa)$, if $\varepsilon(\kappa) = \kappa^{-\omega(1)}$. We say a function $\eta(\kappa)$ is overwhelming if $1 - \eta(\kappa)$ is negligible.

For any set A, let $|A|$ be the cardinality of A and $U(A)$ the uniform distribution over A. For a distribution D, let $x \leftarrow D$ denote the process of sampling x from D. For any two distributions X, Y, denote $\mathsf{SD}(X, Y)$ the statistical distance of X and Y. We say X and Y are identical, denoted $X \equiv Y$, if $\mathsf{SD}(X, Y) = 0$. We say X and Y are statistically indistinguishable, denoted $X \approx_s Y$, if $\mathsf{SD}(X, Y)$ is negligible. Finally, we say X and Y are computationally indistinguishable, denoted $X \approx_c Y$, if no efficient algorithm can distinguish them.

For any plaintext x and a public key pk, we denote $[\![x]\!]_{pk}$ an encryption of x under pk. If the public key is clear from the context, we will omit the public key and use $[\![x]\!]$ to represent an encryption of x under some public key.

2.1   Security Model

For all of our protocols, there are n parties $P_1, \ldots, P_n$ and the communication graph is modelled as an undirected graph $G = (V, E)$ where $V = [n]$ and $(i, j) \in E$ if and only if P_i and P_j can communicate with each other directly (we assume $(i, i) \notin E$ for every $i \in V$). We do not distinguish (i, j) and (j, i) because G is undirected. For any $i \in V$, the set $\mathcal{N}_i = \{j | (i, j) \in E\}$ represents the neighbors of P_i.

Adversarial Model. The adversary we consider in this work can statically corrupt any number of parties and moreover, it is passive and computationally bounded (PPT).

Communication Model. The concept of THC is formalized by [25], which gave the first (simulation-based) definition for topology hiding in the UC framework [11]. In the work of [1], a stronger variant of this definition is considered. In this work, we adopt this variant in our protocols.

In traditional UC model for MPC, the communication graph is assumed to be complete, i.e. each party can communicate directly with other parties. However, in the setting of THC, the communication graph is incomplete and private. To capture this, an ideal functionality $\mathcal{F}_{graph}$ is defined to describe what the parties can do in the communication graph and a special party P_{graph} is assumed to hold the communication graph. Concretely, $\mathcal{F}_{graph}$ consists of an initialization phase and a communication phase. In the initialization phase, $\mathcal{F}_{graph}$ receives the communication graph $G = (V, E)$ from P_{graph} and samples a label for each edge $e \in E$, and then send the labels of the edges in $\mathcal{N}_i$ to P_i for each $i \in [n]^{14}$. We note that in such a way, any two parties can tell whether they share an edge, but can not tell whether they share a neighbor. The communication phase provides secure communication between any party and its neighbors, which receives a message and an edge label from some party and sends the message to the other party holding this edge label. The formal description of $\mathcal{F}_{graph}$ is shown in Fig. 1.

Functionality $\mathcal{F}_{graph}$

The functionality involves $P_1, \ldots, P_n$ and a special party P_{graph} who takes an undirected graph $G = (V, E)$ as input.

- -

Initialization Phase.

1. Receive the graph $G = (V, E)$ from the party P_{graph}.
2. Choose a random injective function $\psi : E \to [n^2]$ to label each edge with a random element from $[n^2]$.
3. Send $\mathcal{L}_i = \{\psi(i, j) : j \in \mathcal{N}_i\}$ to P_i for each $i \in [n]$.

Communication Phase.

1. Receive from a party P_i a triple (i, h, m) which indicates P_i wants to send a message m to the neighbor on the edge labeled with h.
2. Find j such that $h = \psi(i, j)$. Send (h, m) to P_j where h tells P_j that m is sent by its neighbor on the edge labeled with h.

Fig. 1. The graph functionality $\mathcal{F}_{graph}$

Note that in the ideal world, the adversary has the information that P_{graph} sent the corrupted parties because the initialization phase is executed whenever a functionality $\mathcal{F}$ is realized. To capture this, the functionality $\mathcal{F}_{neigh}$ containing only the initialization phase of $\mathcal{F}_{graph}$ is defined. For any functionality $\mathcal{F}$, we use $\mathcal{F}_{neigh}||\mathcal{F}$ to represent composing $\mathcal{F}$ with $\mathcal{F}_{neigh}$. Now we give the security definition of THC in the UC model.

Definition 2. *We say that a protocol topology-hidingly realizes a functionality $\mathcal{F}$ if it UC-realizes $\mathcal{F}_{neigh}||\mathcal{F}$ in the $\mathcal{F}_{graph}$-hybrid model.*

---

[14] In the definition of [25], $\mathcal{F}_{graph}$ gives $\mathcal{N}_i$ to P_i, which gives any two parties the ability to tell whether they share a neighbor.

2.2   Privately Key-Commutative and Rerandomizable Encryption

The concept of privately key-commutative and rerandomizable (PKCR) encryption is introduced by [3]. Concretely, a PKCR encryption is a semantically secure PKE scheme (Keygen, Enc, Dec) with several additional properties. Denote $\mathcal{M}$ the plaintext space, $\mathcal{C}$ the ciphertext space, $\mathcal{PK}$ the public key space which forms an abelian group under the operation $\circledast$ and $\mathcal{SK}$ the secret key space. PKCR encryption requires the following properties.

– *Public-key rerandomizable*: For any $k \in \mathcal{PK}$, it holds that

$$\{k \circledast pk | (pk, sk) \leftarrow \texttt{Keygen}(1^\kappa)\} \approx_s \{pk | (pk, sk) \leftarrow \texttt{Keygen}(1^\kappa)\}.$$

– *Ciphertext rerandomizable*: There exists an efficient algorithm $\texttt{Rand} : \mathcal{C} \times \mathcal{PK} \rightarrow \mathcal{C}$ such that for any key pair (pk, sk) and any ciphertext $c = [\![x]\!]_{pk}$, it holds that
$$(x, pk, c, \texttt{Rand}(c, pk)) \approx_s (x, pk, c, \texttt{Enc}(x, pk))$$
and
$$\texttt{Dec}(\texttt{Rand}(c, pk), sk) = x.$$

– *Privately key-commutative*: There exist two efficient algorithms $\texttt{AddLayer} : \mathcal{C} \times \mathcal{PK} \times \mathcal{SK} \rightarrow \mathcal{C}$ and $\texttt{DelLayer} : \mathcal{C} \times \mathcal{PK} \times \mathcal{SK} \rightarrow \mathcal{C}$ such that for any two key pairs $(pk_1, sk_1), (pk_2, sk_2)$ and any ciphertext $c = [\![x]\!]_{pk_1}$, it holds that

$$\texttt{AddLayer}(c, pk_1, sk_2) \approx_s \texttt{Enc}(x, pk_1 \circledast pk_2)$$

and
$$\texttt{DelLayer}(c, pk_1, sk_2) \approx_s \texttt{Enc}(x, pk_1 \circledast pk_2^{-1}).$$

For the special case that (pk, sk) is a pair of keys, we let $\texttt{DelLayer}(c, pk, sk)$ output $\texttt{Dec}(c, sk)$ instead of $\texttt{Enc}(x, 1)$.

In this work, some of our protocols require the PKCR to be homomorphic, hence we introduce the following additional properties for PKCR.

Equipping PKCR with Homomorphism. Our THS protocol requires a PKCR with two additional properties.

– *Plaintext space forms a ring*: The plaintext space $\mathcal{M}$ is a ring $\mathcal{M}_r$ with the operations $+$ (addition) and $\cdot$ (multiplication).
– *Additively homomorphic*: There exists an efficient algorithm $\texttt{Add} : \mathcal{M}_r \times \mathcal{C} \times \mathcal{PK} \rightarrow \mathcal{C}$ such that for any plaintext $y \in \mathcal{M}_r$ and any ciphertext $c = [\![x]\!]_{pk}$, it holds that
$$\texttt{Add}(y, c, pk) \approx_s \texttt{Enc}(x + y, pk).$$

We call PKCR encryption with the above two properties additively homomorphic PKCR (ahPKCR) encryption.

Our GTHC protocol (for cycles) requires a stronger variant of ahPKCR, and we call this variant linearly homomorphic PKCR (lhPKCR) encryption. Concretely, lhPKCR requires a linear homomorphism described as follows.

– *Linearly homomorphic*: There exists an efficient algorithm $\texttt{Linear} : \mathcal{M}_r \times \mathcal{C}^2 \times \mathcal{PK} \to \mathcal{C}$ such that for any plaintext $a \in \mathcal{M}_r$ and any two ciphertexts $c_1 = [\![x]\!]_{pk}, c_2 = [\![y]\!]_{pk}$, it holds that

$$\texttt{Linear}(a, c_1, c_2, pk) \approx_s \texttt{Enc}(ax + y, pk).$$

Remark. The work of [3] has proved that the standard ElGamal scheme is a PKCR encryption. In the full version, we prove that both schemes from [10,12] are lhPKCR encryption. In this work, we also instantiate ahPKCR with one of these two schemes (lhPKCR encryption is also ahPKCR encryption).

3   Topology-Hiding Broadcast for Undirected Cycles

The AM protocol [3] is designed for broadcasting a bit, which we abbreviate by bit-THB. We seek to design a THB protocol which directly broadcasts a bitstring instead of a bit, we abbreviate this by string-THB. Notice that string-THB protocol can be simply constructed by just calling the AM protocol bit-by-bit. However, we seek to derive more efficient constructions than this naive way.

In this section, our main result is an optimization for the AM protocol, which will reduce its communication complexity by a factor of $O(\kappa)$ in the amortized sense. Throughout this section, we use the following public parameters.

– $(\texttt{Keygen}, \texttt{Enc}, \texttt{Dec}, \texttt{Rand}, \texttt{AddLayer}, \texttt{DelLayer})$ is a PKCR encryption scheme.
– $\mathcal{M}$ is the plaintext space and $\alpha \in \mathcal{M}$ is a dummy value known by all parties (e.g., α is the identity element if $\mathcal{M}$ is a group).

We aim to design a topology-hiding protocol to realize the broadcast functionality $\mathcal{F}_{bc}$ which receives a private input $x \in \mathcal{M}$ from one party and sends x to all parties. The formal description of $\mathcal{F}_{bc}$ can be seen in the full version.

3.1   The Protocol

Similar to the AM protocol, our protocol π_{bc} consists of an aggregate phase and a decrypt phase. In our protocol, each party names its two neighbors 0 and 1. At the beginning of the aggregate phase, for each party P_i and each of its neighbor b, P_i samples a fresh public key and encrypts α with this key, and sends the resulting ciphertext (together with the public key) to its neighbor b. At each following round, for each $i \in [n]$ and $b \in \{0, 1\}$, upon receiving a ciphertext (together with a public key k) from the neighbor b at the previous round, P_i

samples a fresh public key pk and then encrypts the broadcast value with the key $k \circledast pk$ if it is the broadcaster and adds the public key layer pk to the received ciphertext otherwise. Let c be the resulting ciphertext, then P_i sends c and $k \circledast pk$ to its neighbor $\bar{b} = 1 - b$. After $n - 1$ rounds, the parties execute a decrypt phase to decrypt the final ciphertexts (the decrypt phase is the same as in the AM protocol). Finally, the broadcaster outputs the broadcast value x and each other party outputs one of the decrypted values.

Protocol π_{bc}

Input: The broadcaster takes x as input. α is a dummy value known by all parties.

Output: All parties get x as output.

For each $i \in [n]$, P_i does the following.

1: Sample $(pk_{i \to b}^{(t)}, sk_{i \to b}^{(t)}) \leftarrow \text{Keygen}(1^\kappa)$ for each $t \in [n-1], b \in \{0,1\}$.
2: % **Aggregate Phase**
3: Compute $c_{i \to b}^{(1)} \leftarrow \text{Enc}(\alpha, pk_{i \to b}^{(1)})$ and set $k_{i \to b}^{(1)} = pk_{i \to b}^{(1)}$ for each $b \in \{0,1\}$.
4: Send $c_{i \to b}^{(1)}$ and $k_{i \to b}^{(1)}$ to neighbor b for each $b \in \{0,1\}$.
5: **for** $t = 1$ to $n - 2$ **do**
6:     For each $b \in \{0,1\}$, let $c_{i \leftarrow b}^{(t)}$ and $k_{i \leftarrow b}^{(t)}$ be the ciphertext and public key received from neighbor b at the previous round.
7:     Compute $k_{i \to b}^{(t+1)} = k_{i \leftarrow \bar{b}}^{(t)} \circledast pk_{i \to b}^{(t+1)}$ for each $b \in \{0,1\}$.
8:     **if** P_i is the broadcaster **then**
9:         Compute $c_{i \to b}^{(t+1)} \leftarrow \text{Enc}(x, k_{i \to b}^{(t+1)})$ for each $b \in \{0,1\}$.
10:     **else**
11:         Compute $c_{i \to b}^{(t+1)} \leftarrow \text{AddLayer}(c_{i \leftarrow \bar{b}}^{(t)}, k_{i \leftarrow \bar{b}}^{(t)}, sk_{i \to b}^{(t+1)})$ for each $b \in \{0,1\}$.
12:     **end if**
13:     Send $c_{i \to b}^{(t+1)}, k_{i \to b}^{(t+1)}$ to neighbor b for each $b \in \{0,1\}$.
14: **end for**
15: For each $b \in \{0,1\}$, let $c_{i \leftarrow b}^{(n-1)}$ and $k_{i \leftarrow b}^{(n-1)}$ be the ciphertext and public key received from neighbor b at the previous round.
16: **if** P_i is the broadcaster **then**
17:     Compute $e_{i \to b}^{(n-1)} \leftarrow \text{Enc}(x, k_{i \leftarrow b}^{(n-1)})$ for each $b \in \{0,1\}$.
18: **else**
19:     Compute $e_{i \to b}^{(n-1)} \leftarrow \text{Rand}(c_{i \leftarrow b}^{(n-1)}, k_{i \leftarrow b}^{(n-1)})$ for each $b \in \{0,1\}$.
20: **end if**
21: % **Decrypt Phase**
22: **for** $t = n - 1$ to 1 **do**
23:     Send $e_{i \to b}^{(t)}$ to neighbor b for each $b \in \{0,1\}$.
24:     **for** $b = 0$ to 1 **do**
25:         Let $e_{i \leftarrow b}^{(t)}$ be the ciphertext received from neighbor b at the previous round.
26:         Compute $e_{i \to \bar{b}}^{(t-1)} \leftarrow \text{DelLayer}(e_{i \leftarrow b}^{(t)}, k_{i \to b}^{(t)}, sk_{i \to b}^{(t)})$.
27:     **end for**
28: **end for**
29: **if** P_i is the broadcaster **then**
30:     **return** x.
31: **else**
32:     **return** $e_{i \to 0}^{(0)}$.
33: **end if**

Remark. In the full version of this paper, we discuss a naive idea to halve the round complexity of π_{bc}, which evidences that hiding the topology is a non-trivial cryptographic task.

3.2   Complexity Analysis

Claim 3. *If the underlying PKCR encryption scheme is instantiated with the ElGamal scheme [16], then the communication cost of π_{bc} is $O(n^2\kappa)$ bits while the broadcast value is of length $O(\kappa)$ bits.*

Proof. In the protocol π_{bc}, each party sends each of its two neighbors a single ciphertext and a public key at each round of the aggregate phase and a single ciphertext at each round of the decrypt phase. Let l_1 be the plaintext length of the underlying encryption scheme, l_2 the ciphertext length and l_3 the public key length. Because both the aggregate phase and the decrypt phase takes $n - 1$ rounds, the communication complexity of π_{bc} is $2n(n - 1)(2l_2 + l_3)$ bits. If instantiating the underlying PKCR encryption scheme with the ElGamal scheme [16] and setting $l_1 = O(\kappa)$, then we have $l_2 = 2l_1 = O(\kappa), l_3 = l_1 = O(\kappa)$. Namely, the communication cost of π_{bc} is $O(n^2\kappa)$ bits.   □

3.3   Security Proof

The following theorem states the security of the protocol π_{bc}, and we defer the formal proof to the full version.

Theorem 4. *If the underlying PKCR encryption scheme is semantically secure, then π_{bc} topology-hidingly realizes the functionality $\mathcal{F}_{bc}$ with passive security against any static adversary corrupting any number of parties.*

4   Topology-Hiding Sum for Undirected Cycles

In this section, we consider the sum functionality. As we have said, previous to this work, the only topology-hiding protocol realizing the sum functionality is constructed by using the AM protocol to simulate the pairwise channels in an MPC protocol realizing the sum functionality, which yields the state-of-the-art asymptotic communication complexity $O(n^3\kappa^2)$ bits. Our optimization for the AM protocol can reduce this communication cost to $O(n^3\kappa)$ bits. We give a new THS protocol which further reduces the communication cost to $O(n^2\kappa)$ bits.

Our starting point is to design THS without compiling black-box from THB, for which we need a PKCR encryption scheme with an additive homomorphism, i.e., an ahPKCR encryption scheme introduced in Sect. 2.2 (see the full version for more details about the instantiations of ahPKCR). Throughout this section, we use the following parameters.

- (Keygen, Enc, Dec, Rand, AddLayer, DelLayer, Add) is an ahPKCR encryption scheme.
- $\mathcal{M}_r$ is the plaintext space, which is a ring[15].

---

[15] $\mathcal{M}_r$ is $\mathbb{Z}_N$ for an RSA modulus N if using the scheme from [10] or $\mathbb{Z}_p$ for a large prime p if using the scheme from [12].

We aim to design a topology-hiding protocol to realize the sum functionality $\mathcal{F}_{sum}$ which receives a private input $x_i \in \mathcal{M}_r$ from P_i for each $i \in [n]$ and returns the sum $\sum_{i \in [n]} x_i$ to all parties. The formal description of $\mathcal{F}_{sum}$ can be seen in the full version.

4.1   The Protocol

Our protocol π_{sum} consists of an aggregate phase and a decrypt phase. In our protocol, each party names its two neighbors 0 and 1. At the beginning of the aggregate phase, for each party P_i and each of its neighbor b, P_i samples a fresh public key and encrypts its input x_i with this key, and sends the resulting ciphertext (together with the public key) to its neighbor b. At each following round, for each $i \in [n]$ and $b \in \{0, 1\}$, upon receiving a ciphertext (together with a public key k) from its neighbor b at the previous round, P_i homomorphically adds its input to the received ciphertext using the additive homomorphism of ahPKCR. Let c be the resulting ciphertext, then P_i adds a fresh public key layer pk to c and sends the resulting (layered) ciphertext and $k \circledast pk$ to its neighbor $\bar{b} = 1 - b$. After $n - 1$ rounds, the parties execute the decrypt phase to decrypt the final ciphertexts. Finally, each party outputs one of the decrypted values.

Protocol π_{sum}

Input: Each party P_i takes $x_i \in \mathcal{M}_r$ as input.
Output: All parties get $x = \sum_{i \in [n]} x_i$.

- -

For each $i \in [n]$, P_i does the following.
1: Sample $(pk_{i \to b}^{(t)}, sk_{i \to b}^{(t)}) \leftarrow \text{Keygen}(1^\kappa)$ for each $t \in [n-1], b \in \{0, 1\}$.
2: % **Aggregate Phase**
3: Compute $c_{i \to b}^{(1)} \leftarrow \text{Enc}(x_i, pk_{i \to b}^{(1)})$ and set $k_{i \to b}^{(1)} = pk_{i \to b}^{(1)}$ for each $b \in \{0, 1\}$.
4: Send $c_{i \to b}^{(1)}$ and $k_{i \to b}^{(1)}$ to neighbor b for each $b \in \{0, 1\}$.
5: **for** $t = 1$ to $n - 2$ **do**
6:     For each $b \in \{0, 1\}$, let $c_{i \leftarrow b}^{(t)}$ and $k_{i \leftarrow b}^{(t)}$ be the ciphertext and public key received from neighbor b at the previous round.
7:     Compute $k_{i \to b}^{(t+1)} = k_{i \leftarrow \bar{b}}^{(t)} \circledast pk_{i \to b}^{(t+1)}$ for each $b \in \{0, 1\}$.
8:     Compute $c_b \leftarrow \text{AddLayer}(c_{i \leftarrow \bar{b}}^{(t)}, k_{i \leftarrow \bar{b}}^{(t)}, sk_{i \to b}^{(t+1)})$ for each $b \in \{0, 1\}$.
9:     Compute $c_{i \to b}^{(t+1)} \leftarrow \text{Add}(x_i, c_b, k_{i \to b}^{(t+1)})$ for each $b \in \{0, 1\}$.
10:     Send $c_{i \to b}^{(t+1)}, k_{i \to b}^{(t+1)}$ to neighbor b for each $b \in \{0, 1\}$.
11: **end for**
12: For each $b \in \{0, 1\}$, let $c_{i \leftarrow b}^{(n-1)}$ and $k_{i \leftarrow b}^{(n-1)}$ be the ciphertext and public key received from neighbor b at the previous round.
13: Compute $e_{i \to b}^{(n-1)} \leftarrow \text{Add}(x_i, c_{i \leftarrow b}^{(n-1)}, k_{i \leftarrow b}^{(n-1)})$ for each $b \in \{0, 1\}$.
14: % **Decrypt Phase**
15: **for** $t = n - 1$ to 1 **do**
16:     Send $e_{i \to b}^{(t)}$ to neighbor b for each $b \in \{0, 1\}$.
17:     **for** $b = 0$ to 1 **do**
18:         Let $e_{i \leftarrow b}^{(t)}$ be the ciphertext received from neighbor b at the previous round.
19:         Compute $e_{i \to \bar{b}}^{(t-1)} \leftarrow \text{DelLayer}(e_{i \leftarrow b}^{(t)}, k_{i \to b}^{(t)}, sk_{i \to b}^{(t)})$.
20:     **end for**
21: **end for**
22: **return** $e_{i \to 0}^{(0)}$.

4.2 Complexity Analysis

Claim 5. *If the underlying ahPKCR encryption scheme is instantiated with the scheme from [10] or [12], then the communication cost of π_{sum} is $O(n^2\kappa)$ bits while each input is of length $O(\kappa)$ bits.*

Proof. In the protocol π_{sum}, each party sends each of its two neighbors a single ciphertext and a public key at each round of the aggregate phase and a single ciphertext at each round of the decrypt phase. Let l_1 be the plaintext length of the underlying encryption scheme, l_2 the ciphertext length and l_3 the public key length. Because both the aggregate phase and the decrypt phase takes $n-1$ rounds, the communication complexity of π_{sum} is $2n(n-1)(2l_2 + l_3)$ bits. If the underlying ahPKCR encryption scheme is instantiated with the scheme from [10] or [12], then we can set $l_1 = O(\kappa), l_2 = O(\kappa)$ and $l_3 = O(\kappa)$. Namely, the communication cost of π_{sum} is $O(n^2\kappa)$ bits while each input is of length $O(\kappa)$ bits. □

4.3 Security Proof

Theorem 6. *If the underlying ahPKCR encryption scheme is semantically secure, then π_{sum} topology-hidingly realizes the functionality $\mathcal{F}_{sum}$ with passive security against any static adversary corrupting any number of parties.*

We defer the proof to the full version.

5 General Topology-Hiding Computation for Undirected Cycles

In this section, we consider the general computation functionality which can compute any arithmetic circuit[16] consisting of addition and multiplication gates. As we have said, previous to this work, the only topology-hiding protocol realizing the general computation functionality is constructed by simulating the pairwise channels in an MPC protocol realizing the general computation functionality, which yields the state-of-the-art asymptotic communication complexity $O((m+c)n^3\kappa^2)$ bits where m and c are the number of inputs and multiplication gates in the circuit, respectively. Our optimization for the AM protocol can reduce the communication cost to $O((m+c)n^3\kappa)$ bits. We present a new GTHC protocol which further reduces the communication cost to $O((m+c)n^2\kappa)$ bits. Our GTHC protocol is designed in the popular MPC framework based on additive secret sharing. There are three phases in this framework: the input sharing phase, the circuit evaluation phase and the output recovery phase.

In the input sharing phase, the parties generate additive sharings for the inputs. In the circuit evaluation phase, the parties evaluate the circuit gate-by-gate. Throughout this phase, the parties maintain the invariant that for every

---

[16] In this work, we consider circuits over a ring of size $2^{O(\kappa)}$.

gate, the parties hold additive sharings of the values on the two input wires and get an additive sharing of the value on the output wire. Finally, in the output recovery phase, the parties recover the value on the output wire of the final gate.

We show how to use our THS protocol to deal with the input sharing and output recovery phases in Sect. 5.2. For the circuit evaluation phase, we know that addition gates can be done locally, so the only left problem is how to topology-hidingly (and efficiently) compute the multiplication gates. In Sect. 5.1, we give an efficient topology-hiding protocol to securely compute the multiplication gates.

Throughout this section, we need a lhPKCR encryption scheme introduced in Sect. 2.2 (see the full version for more details about the instantiations of lhPKCR) and use the following notations.

- $(\mathtt{Keygen}, \mathtt{Enc}, \mathtt{Dec}, \mathtt{Rand}, \mathtt{AddLayer}, \mathtt{DelLayer}, \mathtt{Linear})$ is a lhPKCR encryption scheme.
- $\mathcal{M}_r$ is the plaintext space of the lhPKCR scheme.
- For any plaintext $y \in \mathcal{M}_r$ and any ciphertext $c = [\![x]\!]_{pk}$, we define the function $\mathtt{Add}(y, c, pk)$ which outputs $\mathtt{Linear}(1, c, [\![y]\!]_{pk}, pk)$.

Additive Secret Sharing. An additive sharing of a secret value x is a vector $\langle x \rangle = (x_1, \ldots, x_n)$ where each party P_i holds a share x_i satisfying that any $n-1$ shares leak nothing about x. Additive secret sharing is linearly homomorphic, which means that for any public value c and any two additive sharings $\langle x \rangle = (x_1, \ldots, x_n), \langle y \rangle = (y_1, \ldots, y_n)$, we have

$$\langle x \rangle + \langle y \rangle = \langle x + y \rangle, c\langle x \rangle = \langle cx \rangle, c + \langle x \rangle = \langle c + x \rangle$$

where $c + \langle x \rangle = (c + x_1, x_2, \ldots, x_n)$.

5.1   Computing Multiplication Gates

In this section, we give a topology-hiding protocol to securely compute the multiplication gates. Concretely, we realize the functionality $\mathcal{F}_{mult}$ which receives additive sharings of x and y from the parties and sends an additive sharing of xy to the parties. We defer the formal description of $\mathcal{F}_{mult}$ to the full version.

Our starting point is that an additive sharing of xy can be computed as follows.

1. The parties generate an additive sharing $\langle r \rangle$ for a random value r where the share of P_i is r_i.
2. The parties execute a protocol to let all parties securely get the value $xy - r$.
3. The parties locally compute $\langle xy \rangle = xy - r + \langle r \rangle$.

It is easy to see that the above construction generates an additive sharing of xy. Notice that the generation of $\langle r \rangle$ can be done locally by letting each party sample a random value r_i and setting $r = \sum_{i \in [n]} r_i$. The left problem is how to securely publish the value $xy - r$. To solve this, we define and realize the mask functionality $\mathcal{F}_{mask}$ which receives private inputs $x_i, y_i, r_i \in \mathcal{M}_r$ from P_i for each $i \in [n]$ and returns the value $\sum_{i \in [n]} x_i \sum_{i \in [n]} y_i - \sum_{i \in [n]} r_i$ to all parties. The formal description of $\mathcal{F}_{mask}$ can be found in the full version.

5.1.1   The Protocol

Now we give a topology-hiding protocol π_{mask} which realizes the functionality $\mathcal{F}_{mask}$. This protocol consists of an aggregate phase and a decrypt phase. The aggregate phase can be viewed as two subphases and each takes $n-1$ rounds. In the first subphase, the parties act exactly as in the aggregate phase of our THS protocol: each party homomorphically adds its share of x to each received ciphertext using the homomorphism of lhPKCR. At the end of the first subphase, every party will get $[\![x]\!]$, an encryption of x, from each walk. Then the parties can execute the second subphase to compute encryptions of $xy-r$, which is based on two observations. The first observation is that $xy - r = \sum_{i\in[n]}(y_i x - r_i)$, which means that $[\![xy - r]\!]$ can be computed from $[\![y_1 x - r_1]\!], \ldots, [\![y_n x - r_n]\!]$ (under the same key) using the homomorphism of lhPKCR. The second observation is that every party P_i can compute $[\![y_i x - r_i]\!]$ from $[\![x]\!]$ using the homomorphism of lhPKCR.

We note that throughout the aggregate phase, each party adds a fresh public key layer to each received ciphertext at each round, which implies that each final ciphertext includes $2n - 2$ public key layers (because the aggregate phase takes $2n - 2$ rounds). Therefore, the parties execute the decrypt phase, which takes $2n - 2$ rounds, to decrypt the final ciphertexts. Due to lack of space, the formal description of π_{mask} is deferred to the full version.

Now we can present our protocol π_{mult} which realizes the functionality $\mathcal{F}_{mult}$ in the $\mathcal{F}_{mask}$-hybrid model.

Protocol π_{mult}

Input: The parties hold additive sharings $\langle x \rangle, \langle y \rangle$.
Output: The parties output $\langle xy \rangle$.

- -

1. Each party P_i samples a random value $r_i \leftarrow U(\mathcal{M}_r)$.
2. The parties invoke the functionality $\mathcal{F}_{mask}$ where each party P_i takes x_i, y_i and r_i as inputs. Let z be the output.
3. P_1 outputs $z + r_1$ and each other party P_i outputs r_i.

5.1.2   Complexity Analysis

Claim 7. *If the underlying lhPKCR encryption scheme is instantiated with the scheme from [10] or [12] and the functionality $\mathcal{F}_{mask}$ is realized by the protocol π_{mask}, then the communication cost of π_{mult} is $O(n^2 \kappa)$ bits while each input is of length $O(\kappa)$ bits.*

Proof. It is obvious that the communication complexity of π_{mult} is the same as that of π_{mask}. In the protocol π_{mask}, the aggregate phase takes $2n-2$ rounds, and where each party sends each of its two neighbors a ciphertext and a public key at each round of the first $n-1$ rounds and two ciphertexts and a public key at each round of the last $n-1$ rounds. The decrypt phase takes $2n-2$ rounds, and where each party sends each of its two neighbors a single ciphertext at each round. Let l_1 be the plaintext length of the underlying encryption scheme, l_2 the ciphertext length and l_3 the public key length, then the communication complexity is $2n(n-1)(5l_2 + 2l_3)$ bits. If instantiating the underlying lhPKCR encryption with the scheme from [10] or [12], we can set $l_1 = O(\kappa), l_2 = O(\kappa), l_3 = O(\kappa)$. Namely, the protocol π_{mult} has communication complexity $O(n^2\kappa)$ bits while each input is of length $O(\kappa)$ bits.   □

5.1.3   Security Proof

In this section, we first show that π_{mult} securely realizes the functionality $\mathcal{F}_{mult}$ in the $\mathcal{F}_{mask}$-hybrid model and then we show that π_{mask} securely realizes the functionality $\mathcal{F}_{mask}$.

Theorem 8. *Protocol π_{mult} topology-hidingly realizes the functionality $\mathcal{F}_{mult}$ in the $\mathcal{F}_{mask}$-hybrid model with passive security against any static adversary corrupting any number of parties.*

Proof. **Correctness.** The correctness of π_{mult} is guaranteed by the functionality $\mathcal{F}_{mask}$. Let $r = \sum_{i \in [n]} r_i$. The functionality $\mathcal{F}_{mask}$ guarantees that $z = xy - r$. At the end of π_{mult}, P_1 outputs $z_1 = z + r_1$ and each other party P_i outputs $z_i = r_i$. It holds that

$$\sum_{i \in [n]} z_i = z + r_1 + (r_2 + \cdots + r_n) = xy - r + r = xy.$$

Moreover, all r_is are random values, hence $\{z_i\}_{i \in [n]}$ is an additive sharing of xy.

Security. The security is obvious because the parties do not communicate with each other outside the invoking of $\mathcal{F}_{mask}$.   □

Theorem 9. *If the underlying lhPKCR encryption scheme is semantically secure, then π_{mask} topology-hidingly realizes the functionality $\mathcal{F}_{mask}$ with passive security against any static adversary corrupting any number of parties.*

Due to lack of space, we defer the proof to the full version.

5.2   General Topology-Hiding Computation

In this section, we present our GTHC protocol π_{mpc}, which consists of three phases: the input sharing phase, the circuit evaluation phase and the output recovery phase.

Input Sharing. The goal of input sharing is to generate additive sharings for the inputs. A subtle point is that we require that for any sharing $\langle x \rangle$ (assume x is the input of P_i), the adversary cannot know anything about the share of some party P_j if P_i and P_j are honest[17]. Now we consider a naive way with low

---

[17] If P_i is corrupt, we allow the adversary to know all the shares.

communication cost to share an input x: the input holder P_i shares x among its closed neighborhood (including itself and its two neighbors) and each other party shares 0 among its closed neighborhood, and then each party takes the sum of the share it kept and the shares received from each of their neighbors as its final share. In this process, for any party P_j who is not in the closed neighborhood of the input holder P_i (i.e., P_j is neither P_i nor a neighbor of P_i), if the adversary corrupts the two neighbors of P_j, then the adversary knows the share of P_j[18].

A simple way to share an input x is that the holder of x samples an additive sharing of x and then sends the shares to the parties by using THB to simulate the point-to-point communication, which yields $O(mn^3\kappa)$ bits communication because there are $O(mn)$ shares ($n-1$ shares should be sent for each input) and sending a share (of length κ bits) costs $O(n^2\kappa)$ bits communication. We adopt a more efficient way to share an input. Assume P_i wants to additively share its input x, then if we let each party P_j sample a share x_j, then the share of P_i is $x_i = x - \sum_{j \neq i} x_j$. Our goal is to let P_i get the value x_i while other parties know nothing about x_i. To do this, we let P_i sample a random value r and the parties execute the protocol π_{sum} where P_i takes $x + r$ as input and each other party P_j takes $-x_j$ as input. At the end of the protocol, the parties will get $y = x + r - \sum_{j \neq i} x_j = x_i + r$. It is obvious that the parties know nothing about x_i because r is uniformly random. On the other hand, P_i can compute $x_i = y - r$. Moreover, the communication cost equals exactly the communication cost of π_{sum}, i.e., $O(n^2\kappa)$ bits. Therefore, the communication cost of sharing m inputs will be $O(mn^2\kappa)$ bits.

Circuit Evaluation. Let $f : \mathcal{M}_r^m \to \mathcal{M}_r$ be the circuit to be computed and $s_1, \ldots, s_m$ are the inputs. The parties compute the circuit in a precomputed topological order. After the input sharing phase, the parties have gotten the additive sharings of the inputs. For each gate g with inputs x and y, the parties have additive sharings $\langle x \rangle$ and $\langle y \rangle$. If g is an addition gate, the parties locally compute $\langle x + y \rangle = \langle x \rangle + \langle y \rangle$. If g is a multiplication gate, the parties execute the protocol π_{mult} and our protocol guarantees that the outputs of the parties form an additive sharing of $\langle xy \rangle$. At the end of the computation, the parties output $\langle f(s_1, \ldots, s_m) \rangle$, an additive sharing of $f(s_1, \ldots, s_m)$. Because the communication cost of computing a multiplication gate is $O(n^2\kappa)$ bits, the total communication cost of this phase is $O(cn^2\kappa)$ bits where c is the number of the multiplication gates.

Output Recovery. Let f_i be the final share of P_i. Our protocol guarantees that $f(s_1, \ldots, s_m) = \sum_{i \in [n]} f_i$. If all parties want to get the value $f(s_1, \ldots, s_m)$, then a simple but inefficient way is that each party P_i uses our THB protocol to broadcast f_i, which will yield $O(n^3\kappa)$ bits communication. A more efficient way

---

[18] The share of P_j is of the form $x_j = a + b + c$ where a, b are two shares received from its two (corrupted) neighbors (hence the adversary knows a, b) and c is the share it kept. Note that P_j share 0 among its closed neighborhood, which means that the sum of the two shares it sent its two neighbors is $-c$, and hence the adversary knows the value of c. Finally, the adversary can get the share of P_j by computing $a + b + c$.

is that the parties execute our sum protocol π_{sum} where each party P_i takes f_i as input and the communication cost of this way is $O(n^2\kappa)$ bits.

If we only want one party P_j to get the output, then it can be realized by letting P_j add a random value r to its input and then subtract r from its output after the execution of the protocol π_{sum}.

The formal description of our GTHC protocol π_{mpc} is in the following.

Protocol π_{mpc}

Public parameters: $f : \mathcal{M}_r^m \to \mathcal{M}_r$ is a poly-size circuit over $\mathcal{M}_r$.
Input: The parties hold inputs $s_1, \ldots, s_m$.
Output: The parties output $f(s_1, \ldots, s_m)$.

- -

Input sharing. For each input s_i, the parties do the followings.

1. Let P_j be the input holder of s_i. To share s_i, P_j samples a random value $r \in \mathcal{M}_r$ and each other party P_k samples a random value $s_{i,k} \in \mathcal{M}_r$.

2. The parties execute π_{sum} where P_j takes $s_i + r$ as input and each other party P_k takes $-s_{i,k}$ as input. Let y be the output.

3. P_j computes $s_{i,j} = y - r$. The sharing of s_i is $\langle s_i \rangle = (s_{i,1}, \ldots, s_{i,n})$.

Circuit evaluation. For each gate g, the parties do the followings.

1. Let $\langle a \rangle = (a_1, \ldots, a_n), \langle b \rangle = (b_1, \ldots, b_n)$ be the two sharings on the input wires of g.

2. If g is an addition gate, the parties locally compute $\langle a + b \rangle = \langle a \rangle + \langle b \rangle$.

3. If g is a multiplication gate, the parties execute the protocol π_{mult} where each party P_i takes a_i, b_i as inputs. Let c_i be the output of P_i. The result is $\langle ab \rangle = (c_1, \ldots, c_n)$, an additive sharing of ab.

Output recovery. The parties do the followings.

1. Let $\langle f(s_1, \ldots, s_m) \rangle = (f_1, \ldots, f_n)$ be the final sharing.

2. If all parties wants to get the value $f(s_1, \ldots, s_m)$, the parties execute π_{sum} where each party P_i takes f_i as input.

3. If only one party P_j wants to get the output, then P_j samples a random value $r \in \mathcal{M}_r$. The parties execute π_{sum} where P_j takes $f_j + r$ as input and each other party P_i takes f_i as input. Let y be the output. P_j outputs $f = y - r$.

Complexity Analysis. We state the communication cost of π_{mpc} by the following claim.

Claim 10. *The communication complexity of π_{mpc} is $O((m + c)n^2\kappa)$ bits.*

Proof. Note that the communication costs of the input sharing, circuit evaluation and output recovery phases are $O(mn^2\kappa)$, $O(cn^2\kappa)$ and $O(n^2\kappa)$ bits, respectively. Therefore, the total communication cost of π_{mpc} is $O((m + c)n^2\kappa)$ bits.   □

Security Proof. The security of π_{mpc} is guaranteed by the security of π_{sum} and π_{mult} and we omit the details.

6   Topology-Hiding Computation on General Graphs

In this section, we give optimizations for two existing topology-hiding protocols on general graphs. Both of these two protocols rely on the random walk approach [1]. This approach relies on the following lemma [1], which states that in an undirected connected graph G, the probability that a random walk of length $8|V|^3\tau$ covers G is at least $1 - 2^{-\tau}$.

Lemma 11 ([1]). *Let $G = (V, E)$ be an undirected connected graph. Furthermore, let $\mathcal{W}(u, \tau)$ be a random variable whose value is the set of vertices covered by a random walk starting from u and taking $8|V|^3\tau$ steps. It holds that*

$$\Pr_{\mathcal{W}}[\mathcal{W}(u, \tau) = V] \geq 1 - 2^{-\tau}.$$

6.1   Topology-Hiding Broadcast for General Graphs

As we have said, our optimization for the AM protocol also applies to the ALM protocol [1]. We know the ALM protocol is the state-of-the-art THB protocol for general graphs. Our optimization reduces the communication cost of the ALM protocol by a factor of $O(\kappa)$ in the amortized sense. If the broadcast value is of length $O(\kappa)$ bits, then the communication cost of the ALM protocol will be $O(n^5\kappa^3)$ bits. With our optimization, the communication cost can be reduced to $O(n^5\kappa^2)$ bits. Throughout this section, we use the following public parameters.

- $(\mathsf{Keygen}, \mathsf{Enc}, \mathsf{Dec}, \mathsf{Rand}, \mathsf{AddLayer}, \mathsf{DelLayer})$ is a PKCR encryption scheme.
- $\mathcal{M}$ is the plaintext space and $\alpha \in \mathcal{M}$ is a dummy value known by all parties (e.g., α is the identity element if $\mathcal{M}$ is a group).

The Protocol. Our protocol π_{ggbc} consists of an aggregate phase and a decrypt phase. At the beginning of the aggregate phase, for each party P_i and each of its neighbor d, P_i samples a fresh public key and encrypts α under this key, and then sends the resulting ciphertext (together with the public key) to neighbor d. At each following round, for each $i \in [n]$ and each of its neighbor d, P_i, upon receiving a ciphertext c (together with a public key k) from its neighbor d at the previous round, samples a fresh public key pk and encrypts the broadcast value with the key $k \circledast pk$ if it is the broadcaster and adds the public key layer pk to the received ciphertext c otherwise, and then sends the resulting ciphertext to its neighbor $\sigma(d)$ (σ is a fresh random permutation of the set of the neighbors of P_i). After $T = 8n^3\kappa$ rounds, the parties execute a decrypt phase as in the ALM protocol to decrypt the final ciphertexts. Finally, the broadcaster outputs the broadcast value x and each other party outputs one of the decrypted values. Due to lack of space, we defer the formal description of π_{ggbc} to the full version.

Complexity Analysis. The following lemma states the communication cost of our protocol π_{ggbc}.

Claim 12. *If the underlying PKCR encryption scheme is instantiated with the ElGamal scheme, then the communication cost of π_{ggbc} is $O(n^5\kappa^2)$ bits while the broadcast value is of length $O(\kappa)$ bits.*

Proof. In the protocol π_{ggbc}, each party sends each of its neighbors a single ciphertext and a public key at each round of the aggregate phase and a single ciphertext at each round of the decrypt phase. Let l_1 be the plaintext length of the underlying encryption scheme, l_2 the ciphertext length and l_3 the public key length. Because both the aggregate phase and the decrypt phase takes $T = 8n^3\kappa$ rounds, the communication cost of π_{ggbc} is $T \cdot 2|E| \cdot (l_2 + l_3) + T \cdot 2|E| \cdot l_2 = O(n^5\kappa \cdot (l_2 + l_3))$ bits. If instantiating the underlying PKCR encryption scheme with the ElGamal scheme and setting $l_1 = O(\kappa)$, then we have $l_2 = 2l_1 = O(\kappa), l_3 = l_1 = O(\kappa)$. Namely, the communication cost of π_{ggbc} is $O(n^5\kappa^2)$ bits while the broadcast value is of length $O(\kappa)$ bits. □

Security Proof. We state the security of π_{ggbc} by the following theorem and defer the proof to the full version.

Theorem 13. *If the underlying PKCR encryption scheme is semantically secure, then π_{ggbc} topology-hidingly realizes the functionality $\mathcal{F}_{bc}$ with passive security against any static adversary corrupting any number of parties.*

6.2   General Topology-Hiding Computation for General Graphs

In [22], a GTHC protocol (we call it the LZM³T protocol) based on FHE is presented. The main advantage of the LZM³T protocol is its low round complexity, which amounts to the round complexity of the ALM protocol. However, if designing a GTHC protocol by compiling an MPC protocol π, which realizes the general computation functionality, from THB, then the round complexity of the resulting protocol will be k times that of the ALM protocol where k is the round complexity of π.

We first recall the LZM³T protocol, which consists of an aggregate phase and a decrypt phase. At each round of the aggregate phase, each party *appends* encryptions of its input and ID to each of the received ciphertext vectors (hence each ciphertext vector in round t is of length $O(t)$) and sends each neighbor one of the resulting ciphertext vector (together with the corresponding public key). At the end of the aggregate phase, each party receives ciphertext vectors containing encryptions of the inputs and then computes encryptions of the given function f. Finally, the party execute the decrypt phase, where each party sends each of its neighbors a single ciphertext, to decrypt the ciphertexts. We remark that the original LZM³T protocol is designed in the fail-stop model where the adversary may abort the protocol, but we consider its passive version in this work.

To clarify the communication cost of the LZM³T protocol, we note that the underlying encryption scheme of the LZM³T protocol is a so-called deeply fully-homomorphic public-key encryption (DFH-PKE) scheme (which can be viewed as an analogue of PKCR but offers full homomorphism). In the LZM³T protocol, DFH-PKE is instantiated with an FHE scheme and the public keys in different rounds of the LZM³T protocol are of different forms. Concretely, let $\mathcal{C}$ and $\mathcal{PK}$ be the ciphertext space and public key space of the FHE scheme, respectively, then during the aggregate phase of the LZM^3T protocol, the public keys sent at the first round are in $\mathcal{PK}$ and the public keys sent at each following round are in $\mathcal{PK} \times \mathcal{C}$ (the ciphertext space of DFH-PKE is always $\mathcal{C}$)[19]. Therefore, the communication cost of the LZM^3T protocol is $O(|E| + \sum_{t=2}^{T}(O(t)+1)|E| + T|E|) = O(T^2|E|) = O(n^8\kappa^2)$ FHE ciphertexts and $T|E| = O(n^5\kappa)$ FHE public keys.

In this section, we give an optimization for the LZM^3T protocol such that the communication cost is reduced to $O(n^6\kappa)$ FHE ciphertexts and $O(n^5\kappa)$ FHE public keys. The goal of the aggregate phase of the LZM^3T protocol is to collect encryptions of all the inputs. We give an optimized aggregate phase to achieve this goal. Concretely, instead of appending an encryption of the input (together with the ID) to each received ciphertext vector at each round, each party send ciphertext vectors of length n at each round and for the i-th entry of the ciphertext vectors, the parties act exactly as in our optimized THB protocol π_{ggbc} with P_i being the broadcaster and the input x_i of P_i being the broadcast value.

Complexity Analysis. Each party sends each of its neighbors n ciphertexts and a public key at each round of the aggregate phase, and a single ciphertext at each round of the decrypt phase. Recall that the public keys sent at the first round belong to $\mathcal{PK}$ and the public keys sent at each following round belong to $\mathcal{PK} \times \mathcal{C}$. Therefore, the total communication cost is $n|E| + (T-1)(n+1)|E| + T|E| = O(nT|E|) = O(n^6\kappa)$ FHE ciphertexts and $T|E| = O(n^5\kappa)$ FHE public keys.

Security Proof. The correctness of π_{ggbc} guarantees that the probability p_0 that the i-th entry of a final ciphertext vector at the end of the aggregate phase is an encryption of x_i is overwhelming. Hence, the probability p that for each $i \in [n]$, the i-th entry of a final ciphertext vector is an encryption of x_i satisfies that

$$p = p_0^n = (1 - \mathsf{neg}(\kappa))^n \geq 1 - n \cdot \mathsf{neg}(\kappa),$$

which is overwhelming because $n = \mathsf{poly}(\kappa)$. Furthermore, the full homomorphism of the underlying DFH-PKE scheme guarantees each ciphertext at the beginning of the decrypt phase is an encryption of $f(x_1, \ldots, x_n)$ with overwhelming probability. Therefore, at the end of the decrypt phase, each party get the value $f(x_1, \ldots, x_n)$ with overwhelming probability.

As for the security, the simulator just sends encryptions of 0 during the aggregate phase and encryptions of $f(x_1, \ldots, x_n)$ during the decrypt phase (the public keys are simulated with fresh public keys). The semantic security of the underlying DFH-PKE scheme guarantees that the ciphertexts and public keys in the real world are indistinguishable from the simulated ciphertexts and public keys, respectively.

We omit the details of the security proof because the proof will be much like the proof of Theorem 13 (DFH-PKE provides the required properties for the security proof similar to PKCR).

---

[19] We refer to [22, Appendix C] for more details about DFH-PKE and its instantiation.

Remark. Another advantage of our optimized protocol is that we only require the underlying scheme to homomorphically compute the given function, which means that if the given function contains only linear gates (addition, addition-by-constant and multiply-by-constant gates), then we only require the underlying scheme has linear homomorphism, i.e. a lhPKCR scheme is sufficient. However, the LZM^{3}T protocol requires the underlying scheme to homomorphically compute a much more complicated function than the given function (as we explained in Sect. 1.2), which makes it impossible to just use a lhPKCR scheme even the given function contains only linear gates.

7 Optimizations

In this section, we give several optimizations to obtain better concrete efficiency.

Improving the Concrete Efficiency Using Multi-ElGamal. All of our protocols use ElGamal-like schemes as the underlying PKCR schemes (the ciphertexts are of form (g^r, xh^r) or $(g^r, f^x h^r)$). We can extend the plaintext space of ElGamal-like schemes as follows to obtain better concrete efficiency. Concretely, to encrypt l messages $x_1, \ldots, x_l$, one samples l key pairs $(sk_1, pk_1), \ldots, (sk_l, pk_l)$ and random value r, and then compute the ciphertext as $(g^r, x_1 pk_1^r, \ldots, x_l pk_l^r)$ or $(g^r, f^{x_1} pk_1^r, \ldots, f^{x_l} pk_l^r)$. The ciphertext length of l messages is $l + 1$ group elements. However, if encrypting the l messages independently, then the total length of the resulting ciphertext is $2l$ group elements. The semantic security of such a multi-ElGamal scheme is also based on the DDH assumption in the underlying group.

Better Topology-Hiding Communication on Cycles. We give a more efficient topology-hiding realization for point-to-point communication on undirected cycles with knowing n. As we have said, point-to-point communication can be realized by compiling black-box from THB as follows.

1. Each party uses THB to broadcast its public key in a setup phase.
2. To send a message m to P_j, P_i encrypts m with the public key of P_j and then uses THB to broadcast the resulting ciphertext.
3. Upon receiving the ciphertext, P_j can decrypt it to get m. Other parties know nothing about m because they do not know the decrypt key.

If simulating point-to-point communication as above, then the communication cost of topology-hidingly sending a message m will equal the communication cost of topology-hidingly broadcasting a public key and a ciphertext of m (under some PKE scheme). Now we present a better way to realize point-to-point communication such that the communication cost of topology-hidingly sending a message m equals the communication cost of using our optimized THB protocol to broadcast m (rather than a public key and a ciphertext of m), which achieves better concrete efficiency.

Recall that our optimized THB protocol instantiates the underlying PKCR scheme with the ElGamal scheme. The plaintext space of the ElGamal scheme is a group and the ElGamal scheme is homomorphic under the group operation (the group operation is called multiplication), i.e., for any group elements x and y, $[\![xy]\!]_{pk}$ can be efficiently computed given $[\![x]\!]_{pk}$, y and pk. Now we modify our THS protocol as follows. The underlying scheme is replaced with the ElGamal scheme (instead of the scheme from [10] or [12]); each party homomorphically multiplies (instead of adds) its input to each received ciphertext using the homomorphism of ElGamal. It can be easily seen that at the end of the resulting protocol (we call the resulting protocol the product protocol), all parties get the product of all the inputs, and moreover, the communication cost of this resulting protocol equals the communication cost of our optimized THB protocol because both of these two protocols instantiate the underlying encryption scheme with the ElGamal scheme.

Now we show how to use the product protocol to realize point-to-point communication without additional communication cost.

1. To send a message x to P_j, the parties execute this product protocol, and where P_i takes x as input and P_j takes a random group element r as input, and each other party takes the identity group element as input.
2. At the end of the protocol, all parties get the value $y = xr$. P_j computes yr^{-1} as output.

The above execution is a secure realization for point-to-point communication because no parties know the value of x except P_i and P_j, which is guaranteed by the fact that only P_i and P_j know r and other parties know nothing about r (P_i can infer r from x and y).

8   Conclusion and Open Problem

In this work, we give efficient topology-hiding protocols realizing various functionalities, including the broadcast, sum and general computation functionalities. Our results show that when realizing these functionalities in undirected cycles, hiding the topology introduces at most multiplicative overhead of $O(n)$ in the asymptotic communication complexity. An open problem is that whether $O(n)$ is the optimal overhead.

Another direction is to extend our results to the fail-stop setting where the adversary may instruct the corrupted parties to abort the protocol. One of our results is an optimization for the ALM protocol. The work of [22] extended the ALM protocol to the fail-stop setting. A natural question is whether their method also applies to our optimized ALM protocol.

Acknowledgement. We are grateful for the helpful comments from the anonymous reviewers. This work was supported by the National Key Research and Development Program of China (No. 2020YFB1805402) and the National Natural Science Foundation of China (Grants No. 61872359 and No. 61936008).

References

1. Akavia, A., LaVigne, R., Moran, T.: Topology-hiding computation on all graphs. In: Advances in Cryptology - CRYPTO 2017–37th Annual International Cryptology Conference, Santa Barbara, CA, USA, 20–24 August 2017, Proceedings, Part I. pp. 447–467 (2017). https://doi.org/10.1007/978-3-319-63688-7_15
2. Akavia, A., LaVigne, R., Moran, T.: Topology-hiding computation on all graphs. J. Cryptol. **33**(1), 176–227 (2020). https://doi.org/10.1007/s00145-019-09318-y
3. Akavia, A., Moran, T.: Topology-hiding computation beyond logarithmic diameter. In: Advances in Cryptology - EUROCRYPT 2017–36th Annual International Conference on the Theory and Applications of Cryptographic Techniques, Paris, France, 30 April - 4 May 2017, Proceedings, Part III, pp. 609–637 (2017). https://doi.org/10.1007/978-3-319-56617-7_21
4. Ball, M., et al.: Topology-hiding communication from minimal assumptions. In: Theory of Cryptography - 18th International Conference, TCC 2020, Durham, NC, USA, 16–19 November 2020, Proceedings, Part II, pp. 473–501 (2020). https://doi.org/10.1007/978-3-030-64378-2_17
5. Ball, M., Boyle, E., Cohen, R., Malkin, T., Moran, T.: Is information-theoretic topology-hiding computation possible? In: Theory of Cryptography - 17th International Conference, TCC 2019, Nuremberg, Germany, 1–5 December 2019, Proceedings, Part I, pp. 502–530 (2019). https://doi.org/10.1007/978-3-030-36030-6_20
6. Ball, M., Boyle, E., Malkin, T., Moran, T.: Exploring the boundaries of topology-hiding computation. In: Advances in Cryptology - EUROCRYPT 2018–37th Annual nternational Conference on the Theory and Applications of Cryptographic Techniques, Tel Aviv, Israel, 29 April - 3 May, 2018 Proceedings, Part III, pp. 294–325 (2018). https://doi.org/10.1007/978-3-319-78372-7_10
7. Baum, C., Damgård, I., Toft, T., Zakarias, R.W.: Better preprocessing for secure multiparty computation. In: Applied Cryptography and Network Security - 14th International Conference, ACNS 2016, Guildford, UK, 19–22 June 2016. Proceedings. pp. 327–345 (2016). https://doi.org/10.1007/978-3-319-39555-5_18
8. Beimel, A., Gabizon, A., Ishai, Y., Kushilevitz, E., Meldgaard, S., Paskin-Cherniavsky, A.: Non-interactive secure multiparty computation. In: Advances in Cryptology - CRYPTO 2014–34th Annual Cryptology Conference, Santa Barbara, CA, USA, 17–21 August 2014, Proceedings, Part I, pp. 387–404 (2014). https://doi.org/10.1007/978-3-662-44381-1_22
9. Boyle, E., Cohen, R., Data, D., Hubácek, P.: Must the communication graph of MPC protocols be an expander? In: Advances in Cryptology - CRYPTO 2018–38th Annual International Cryptology Conference, Santa Barbara, CA, USA, 19–23 August 2018, Proceedings, Part III, pp. 243–272 (2018). https://doi.org/10.1007/978-3-319-96878-0_9
10. Bresson, E., Catalano, D., Pointcheval, D.: A simple public-key cryptosystem with a double trapdoor decryption mechanism and its applications. In: Advances in Cryptology - ASIACRYPT 2003, 9th International Conference on the Theory and Application of Cryptology and Information Security, Taipei, Taiwan, 30 November - 4 December 2003, Proceedings, pp. 37–54 (2003). https://doi.org/10.1007/978-3-540-40061-5_3
11. Canetti, R.: Universally composable security: a new paradigm for cryptographic protocols. In: 42nd Annual Symposium on Foundations of Computer Science, FOCS 2001, 14–17 October 2001, Las Vegas, Nevada, USA, pp. 136–145 (2001). https://doi.org/10.1109/SFCS.2001.959888

12. Castagnos, G., Laguillaumie, F.: Linearly homomorphic encryption from $$\mathsf{DDH}$$. In: Topics in Cryptology - CT-RSA 2015, The Cryptographer's Track at the RSA Conference 2015, San Francisco, CA, USA, 20-24 April 2015. Proceedings, pp. 487–505 (2015). https://doi.org/10.1007/978-3-319-16715-2_26

13. Cocks, C.C.: An identity based encryption scheme based on quadratic residues. In: Cryptography and Coding, 8th IMA International Conference, Cirencester, UK, 17-19 December 2001, Proceedings, pp. 360–363 (2001). https://doi.org/10.1007/3-540-45325-3_32

14. Cramer, R., Damgård, I., Nielsen, J.B.: Multiparty computation from threshold homomorphic encryption. In: Advances in Cryptology - EUROCRYPT 2001, International Conference on the Theory and Application of Cryptographic Techniques, Innsbruck, Austria, 6-10 May 2001, Proceeding, pp. 280–299 (2001). https://doi.org/10.1007/3-540-44987-6_18

15. Franklin, M.K., Haber, S.: Joint encryption and message-efficient secure computation. J. Cryptol. 9(4), 217–232 (1996). https://doi.org/10.1007/BF00189261

16. Gamal, T.E.: A public key cryptosystem and a signature scheme based on discrete logarithms. In: Advances in Cryptology, Proceedings of CRYPTO '84, Santa Barbara, California, USA, 19–22 August 1984, Proceedings, pp. 10–18 (1984). https://doi.org/10.1007/3-540-39568-7_2

17. Goldwasser, S., et al.: Multi-input functional encryption. In: Advances in Cryptology - EUROCRYPT 2014–33rd Annual International Conference on the Theory and Applications of Cryptographic Techniques, Copenhagen, Denmark, 11–15 May 2014. Proceedings, pp. 578–602 (2014). https://doi.org/10.1007/978-3-642-55220-5_32

18. Halevi, S., Ishai, Y., Jain, A., Kushilevitz, E., Rabin, T.: Secure multiparty computation with general interaction patterns. In: Proceedings of the 2016 ACM Conference on Innovations in Theoretical Computer Science, Cambridge, MA, USA, 14–16 January 2016, pp. 157–168 (2016). https://doi.org/10.1145/2840728.2840760

19. Halevi, S., Lindell, Y., Pinkas, B.: Secure computation on the web: computing without simultaneous interaction. In: Advances in Cryptology - CRYPTO 2011–31st Annual Cryptology Conference, Santa Barbara, CA, USA, 14–18 August 2011. Proceedings, pp. 132–150 (2011). https://doi.org/10.1007/978-3-642-22792-9_8

20. Hinkelmann, M., Jakoby, A.: Communications in unknown networks: preserving the secret of topology. Theor. Comput. Sci. 384(2-3), 184–200 (2007). https://doi.org/10.1016/j.tcs.2007.04.031

21. Hirt, M., Maurer, U., Tschudi, D., Zikas, V.: Network-hiding communication and applications to multi-party protocols. In: Advances in Cryptology - CRYPTO 2016–36th Annual International Cryptology Conference, Santa Barbara, CA, USA, 14–18 August 2016, Proceedings, Part II, pp. 335–365 (2016). https://doi.org/10.1007/978-3-662-53008-5_12

22. LaVigne, R., Zhang, C.L., Maurer, U., Moran, T., Mularczyk, M., Tschudi, D.: Topology-hiding computation beyond semi-honest adversaries. In: Theory of Cryptography - 16th International Conference, TCC 2018, Panaji, India, 11–14 November 2018, Proceedings, Part II, pp. 3–35 (2018). https://doi.org/10.1007/978-3-030-03810-6_1

23. LaVigne, R., Zhang, C.L., Maurer, U., Moran, T., Mularczyk, M., Tschudi, D.: Topology-hiding computation for networks with unknown delays. In: Public-Key Cryptography - PKC 2020–23rd IACR International Conference on Practice and Theory of Public-Key Cryptography, Edinburgh, UK, 4–7 May 2020, Proceedings, Part II, pp. 215–245 (2020). https://doi.org/10.1007/978-3-030-45388-6_8

24. Li, S.: Towards practical topology-hiding computation. Cryptology ePrint Archive, Paper 2022/1106 (2022). https://eprint.iacr.org/2022/1106

25. Moran, T., Orlov, I., Richelson, S.: Topology-hiding computation. In: Theory of Cryptography - 12th Theory of Cryptography Conference, TCC 2015, Warsaw, Poland, 23–25 March 2015, Proceedings, Part I, pp. 159–181 (2015). https://doi.org/10.1007/978-3-662-46494-6_8

26. Paillier, P.: Public-key cryptosystems based on composite degree residuosity classes. In: Advances in Cryptology - EUROCRYPT '99, International Conference on the Theory and Application of Cryptographic Techniques, Prague, Czech Republic, 2–6 May 1999, Proceeding, pp. 223–238 (1999). https://doi.org/10.1007/3-540-48910-X_16

27. Regev, O.: On lattices, learning with errors, random linear codes, and cryptography. J. ACM **56**(6), 1–40 (2009). https://doi.org/10.1145/1568318.1568324

28. Yao, A.C.: Protocols for secure computations (extended abstract). In: 23rd Annual Symposium on Foundations of Computer Science, Chicago, Illinois, USA, 3–5 November 1982, pp. 160–164 (1982). https://doi.org/10.1109/SFCS.1982.38

Real World Protocols

Key-Schedule Security for the TLS 1.3 Standard

Chris Brzuska[1]([⊠]), Antoine Delignat-Lavaud[2], Christoph Egger[3],
Cédric Fournet[2], Konrad Kohbrok[1], and Markulf Kohlweiss[4]

[1] Aalto University, Espoo, Finland
{chris.brzuska,konrad.kohbrok}@aalto.fi
[2] Microsoft Research Cambridge, Cambridge, UK
{antdl,fournet}@microsoft.com
[3] IRIF, Université Paris Cité, Paris, France
christoph.egger@alumni.fau.de
[4] University of Edinburgh, Edinburgh, UK
mkohlwei@ed.ac.uk

Abstract. Transport Layer Security (TLS) is the cryptographic backbone of secure communication on the Internet. In its latest version 1.3, the standardization process has taken formal analysis into account both due to the importance of the protocol and the experience with conceptual attacks against previous versions. To manage the complexity of TLS (the specification exceeds 100 pages), prior reduction-based analyses have focused on some protocol features and omitted others, e.g., included session resumption and omitted agile algorithms or vice versa.

This article is a major step towards analysing the TLS 1.3 key establishment protocol as specified at the end of its rigorous standardization process. Namely, we provide a full proof of the TLS *key schedule*, a core protocol component which produces output keys and internal keys of the key exchange protocol. In particular, our model supports all key derivations featured in the standard, including its negotiated modes and algorithms that combine an optional Diffie-Hellman exchange for forward secrecy with optional pre-shared keys supplied by the application or recursively established in prior sessions.

Technically, we rely on *state-separating proofs* (Asiacrypt '18) and introduce techniques to model large and complex derivation graphs. Our key schedule analysis techniques have been used subsequently to analyse the key schedule of Draft 11 of the MLS protocol (S&P '22) and to propose improvements.

Keywords: TLS 1.3 · Key schedule · Protocol analysis · State-separating proofs

1 Introduction

Transport Layer Security (TLS) is the most widely used authenticated secure channel protocol on the Internet, protecting the communications of billions of

© International Association for Cryptologic Research 2022
S. Agrawal and D. Lin (Eds.): ASIACRYPT 2022, LNCS 13791, pp. 621–650, 2022.
https://doi.org/10.1007/978-3-031-22963-3_21

users. Previous versions of TLS have suffered from impactful attacks against weaknesses in their design, including legacy algorithms (e.g. FREAK for export RSA [9], LogJam [2] for export Diffie-Hellman, WeakDH for ill-chosen groups, and exploits against Mantin biases of RC4 [21]); the RSA key encapsulation (e.g. the ROBOT [19] variant of Bleichenbacher's PKCS1 padding oracle); the fragile MAC-encode-encrypt construction leading to many variants of Vaudenay's padding oracles against CBC cipher suites (e.g. BEAST [38], Lucky13 [3]); the weak signature over nonces allowing protocol version downgrades (e.g. DROWN [5] and POODLE); attacks on other negotiated parameters [11], the key exchange logic (e.g. the cross-protocol attack of [49] and 3SHAKE [12]); exploitations of collisions on the hash transcript (e.g. SLOTH [15]). TLS 1.3 intends both to fix the weaknesses of previous versions and to improve the protocol performance, notably by lowering the latency of connection establishment from two roundtrips down to one, or even zero when resuming a connection.

Historically, the IETF process to adopt a standard involves an open consortium of contributors mostly coming from industry, with a bias towards early implementers. The TLS working group at the IETF acknowledged that this process puts too much emphasis on deployment and implementation concerns, and tends to address security issues reactively [51]. For TLS 1.3, it decided to address security upfront by welcoming feedback from various cryptographic efforts, including symbolic [29,30] and computational protocol models [34,35,48], both on paper and implemented in tools such as Tamarin or CryptoVerif. Early drafts of TLS 1.3 also drew much inspiration from Krawczyk's OPTLS protocol [47], which comes with a detailed security proof, although later versions diverged from it (in particular in the design of resumption). This proactive approach has certainly improved the overall design of TLS 1.3, and uncovered flaws along its 28 intermediate drafts. However, many of these efforts are incomplete (focusing, e.g., on fixed protocol configurations) or do not account for the final version published in RFC 8446, see Sect. 6 for a more detailed discussion of related work. Since final adoption, further questions have been raised about pre-shared keys, potential reflection attacks [37], and difficulties in separating resumption PSKs (produced internally by the key exchange) from external ones installed by the application. In short: we still miss provable security for the final Internet standard.

TLS can be decomposed into sub-protocols: the *record layer* manages the multiplexing, fragmentation, padding and encryption of data into packets (also called *records*) from three separate streams of handshake, alert, and application data. Incoming handshake messages are passed to the *handshake* sub-protocol, which in turn produces fresh record keys and outgoing handshake messages. Taking advantage of this well-understood modularity, other protocols re-use the TLS 1.3 handshake with different record layers: for instance, DTLS 1.3 is a variant based on UDP datagrams instead of TCP streams, while the IETF version of QUIC replaces the record layer with a much extended transport [42], adding features such as dynamic application streams and fine-grained flow control. Detailed security proofs for the TLS 1.3 record layer have been proposed by Patton et al. [52] (extending the work of Fischlin et al. [40] on stream-based channels),

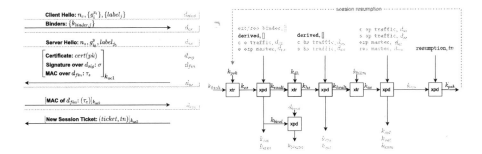

Fig. 1. Overview over the TLS 1.3 Handshake (left) and its key schedule (right). $[m]_k$ denotes encryption of message m under key k. k_{ae1} and τ_c are derived from k_{cht}, k_{ae2} and τ_s are derived from k_{sht}, and k_{ae3} is derived from k_{sat}. We color digests and keys in alternating pink and blue to clarify digest-key dependency. E.g., label c e traffic and digest d_{as} is used to derive k_{cet}. (Color figure online)

Badertscher et al. [6], and Bhargavan et al. [32], who also provide a verified reference implementation. Therefore, we defer to these works for the record layer, and focus on the handshake protocol.

1.1 TLS 1.3 Handshake and Key Schedule

The top of Fig. 1 gives an abstract view of the TLS 1.3 protocol message flow. In the client hello message, the client sends a nonce n_c, its Diffie-Hellman (DH) share g^x, a PSK *label* and a *binder* value for domain separation and session resumption. As a means of negotiation, the client may offer shares for different groups and different PSK options (thus the indices i, j in $g_i^{x_i}$, $label_j$, $binder_j$). The server communicates its choice of the DH group and the PSK when sending the server hello message which contains the server nonce n_s, its share $g_{i_0}^y$ (including the group description) and the label $label_{j_0}$ of the chosen PSK. The remaining messages consist of server certificate, signature $(C(pk), CV(\sigma))$, key confirmation messages in the forms of messages authentication codes (MACs) τ_s and τ_c computed over the transcript, and a *ticket* which is used on the client side to store a resumption key (later referred to as *resumption PSK*) derived from the key material of the current key exchange session.

The *key schedule* is the core part of the handshake that performs all key computations. It takes as main input PSK and DH key materials and, at each phase of the handshake, it derives keys, e.g., to encrypt client early traffic (k_{cet}), to compute the binder value (k_{binder}), to encrypt server handshake traffic (k_{sht}) and to encrypt client handshake traffic (k_{cht}).

The key schedule relies on the hashed key derivation function (HKDF) standard [45], which uses HMAC [7] to implement *extract* (xtr) and *expand* (xpd) operations. In addition, the key schedule makes calls to xpd to expand keys into further subkeys. The key schedule thus consists of a collection of xtr an xpd operations, organized in a graph. Each of the operations takes as input a *chaining* key and/or new key material, (k_{psk} in the xtr in the early phase and k_{dh} in the xtr in the in the handshake phase), together with the latest digest and auxiliary inputs such as a resumption status r and a ticket nonce tn.

In this article, we consider eight output keys of the TLS key schedule: k_{cet}, k_{eem}, k_{binder}, k_{cht}, k_{sht}, k_{cat}, k_{sat}, k_{eam}. They constitute a natural boundary, inasmuch as all other TLS keys and IVs are further derived from them in a transcript-independent manner.

1.2   Key Schedule Model and Key Exchange Model

We model the security of the key schedule as an indistinguishability game between a real and an ideal game. The real game allows the adversary to use their own dishonest application PSKs and Diffie-Hellman shares. In addition, it allows the adversary to instruct the game to sample honest PSKs and Diffie-Hellman shares. From these base keys, the adversary can then instruct the model to derive further keys. The adversary cannot see internal keys, but it can obtain the 8 output keys from the model. In turn, in the ideal game, the output keys are replaced by unique, random keys which are sampled independently from the input key material.

The interface of this model captures how the key exchange protocol uses the key schedule. The key exchange protocol should, indeed, not use the internal keys, but instead only use the output keys. Moreover, the final session keys are to be used only by the Record Layer to implement a secure channel. In a companion paper [25], we show that key exchange security of the TLS 1.3 handshake protocol reduces to the key schedule security established in this paper. Note that authentication is proved based on *keys* and does not capture binding between keys and identities, as needed, e.g., for reflection attacks [29].

Outline. We introduce our overall technical approach in Sect. 2. We define our assumptions for collision-resistance, pseudorandomness and pre-image resistance in Sect. 3. Section 4 defines syntax and security of the TLS key schedule. Section 5 states the main key schedule theorem and provides its proof. This article gives proof sketches of all lemmata, highlighting their conceptual insights. The complete proofs are provided in the full version [23]. Finally, Sect. 7 includes proposals for (late) changes to the TLS 1.3 standard.

2   Technical Approach

2.1   Handles

Complex derivation steps make it crucial to maintain administrative *handles* in the model state, both for internal bookkeeping and security modeling as well as for communication with the adversary. Namely, to instruct the model to perform further computations on keys, the adversary can point to the keys to be used via handles. Such handles are particularly important for honest keys, i.e., honest psks, honest Diffie-Hellman shares and honest internal keys derived via xtr and xpd from honest base keys, because the model cannot provide the adversary with the actual values of these secrets.

Our model constructs handles as nested data records where each nesting step keeps track of the inputs which were used to compute the associated key. We have base handles for PSKs and DH secrets, including handles for dummy zero values to be used in noDH and noPSK mode as well as base handles for a fixed $0salt$ and fixed $0ikm$.

$$
\begin{array}{ll}
\mathsf{dh}\langle\mathsf{sort}(X,Y)\rangle & \text{Diffie-Hellman secret} \\
h = \mathsf{psk}\langle ctr, alg\rangle & \text{application PSK} \\
\mathsf{noDH}\langle alg\rangle & \text{fixed } 0^{\mathsf{len}(alg)} \text{ Diffie-Hellman secret} \\
\mathsf{noPSK}\langle alg\rangle & \text{fixed } 0^{\mathsf{len}(alg)} \text{ PSK} \\
0salt & \text{fixed } 0 \text{ salt} \\
0ikm\langle alg\rangle & \text{fixed } 0^{\mathsf{len}(alg)} \text{ initial key material (IKM)}
\end{array}
$$

The model then inductively applies the following constructors to build all other handles from the base handles:

$$\mathsf{xtr}\langle name, left\ parent\ handle, right\ parent\ handle\rangle.$$

$$\mathsf{xpd}\langle name, label, parent\ handle, other\ arguments\rangle.$$

For example, given a handle to the early master secret h_{es}, the handle h_{cet} to the client early transport secret is defined as

$$h_{cet} = \mathsf{xpd}\langle cet, \mathtt{c\ e\ traffic}, h_{es}, t_{es}\rangle$$

where t_{es} is the transcript of the protocol messages exchanged so far, and 'c e traffic' is the constant byte string label prescribed in the RFC [53] for this derivation step.

Agility. Our model is *agile*, i.e., it supports multiple algorithms. Thus, we tag the handles $h = \mathsf{psk}\langle ctr, alg\rangle$, $\mathsf{noPSK}\langle alg\rangle$ and $0ikm\langle alg\rangle$ with the algorithm alg for which the keys are intended. Jumping ahead, we note that we also tag *keys* with their intended algorithm so that in the key derivation

$$k_{cet} = \mathsf{xpd}(k_{es}, \mathtt{c\ e\ traffic}, d_{es}),$$

the agile xpd function can retrieve the correct hash algorithm alg to use within hmac from the key's tag. We write $\mathsf{alg}(h_{cet})$ for the algorithm descriptor of h_{cet} and $\mathsf{tag}_h(k)$ for key k tagged with this algorithm.

Length. The handle determines the algorithm, and the algorithm determines the length of keys and outputs of a hash-algorithm alg. For convenience, we write $\mathsf{len}(h_{cet})$ as an alias for $\mathsf{len}(\mathsf{alg}(h_{cet}))$.

Note that we introduced handles $0ikm\langle alg\rangle$ for the dummy key value $0^{\mathsf{len}(alg)}$ as well as $0salt$ for the 1-bit-long 0-key. This is because hmac pads keys with zeroes up to their block length and thus, storing multiple zero values would introduce redundancy in the model without a correspondence in real-life.

Name and Level. In addition to the algorithm and its key length, the handle determines the key name (*cet*) and a *level.* The level is the number of resumptions the handle records, counting from 0 and adding one for each node with a **resumption** label. We write $\text{level}(h_{cet})$ for this level. We will often need to refer to the *parent* names of a particular key (name) n, and write the pair of parent names as $\text{prntn}(n)$. In the case of xpd, the key is only derived from one key and thus, in this case, $\text{prntn}(n) = (n_1, \bot)$. Conversely, we refer by $\text{chldrnn}(n_1)$ to the set of all key names which are derived from n_1. In particular, if $\text{prntn}(n) = (n_1, \bot)$, then $n \in \text{chldrnn}(n_1)$. We refer to all names which share a parent with n as $\text{sblngn}(n)$.

Handshake Mode. Jumping ahead, we note that we use handle data also to communicate the handshake mode to the key schedule model. A $\text{noDH}\langle alg \rangle$ Diffie-Hellman handle signals a psk_ke mode, while a $\text{noPSK}\langle alg \rangle$ PSK handle signals a dh_ke mode.

2.2 Application Key Registration and Honesty

Honesty of a handle is a crucial concept to model that the key associated with the handle, when returned to the adversary, looks pseudorandom. Honesty is inductively computed, starting from the base keys: All zero keys have dishonest handles. Handles of application PSKs are honest if their key was sampled by the security model and dishonest if their key was sampled by the security model. Diffie-Hellman handles are honest if both shares are honest. Derived handles are honest if and only if at least one of their input handles are honest. Considering the derivation graph (cf. right side of Fig, 1), we obtain that the h_{esalt} handles and the handles which appear *before* have the same honesty as the last PSK handle, while the handles after h_{esalt} are honest if the last PSK handle was honest *or* the last Diffie-Hellman handle was honest.

2.3 State-Separating Proofs (SSPs)

In the following we use the the pseudorandomness game $\text{Gxpd}_{n,\ell}^0$ for the xpd function (depicted in Fig. 2) as a running example to introduce core concepts. As is common in cryptography, security is modeled as an interaction between an adversary $\mathcal{A}$ (which can be thought of

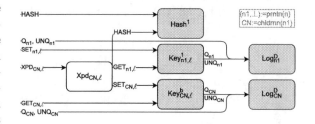

Fig. 2. Game $\text{Gxpd}_{n,\ell}^b$ for $b \in \{0,1\}$

as sitting left of the picture) and a program which we call the *game.* This interaction happens via so-called *oracles*—which we describe in pseudo-code—corresponding to the arrows from the left side of the picture. The task of the adversary consists in *distinguishing* two variants of the game G^0 and G^1 with identical interfaces and we measure the success probability of any such adversary $\mathcal{A}$ and call it *advantage*.

Definition 1 (Advantage). *For adversary $\mathcal{A}$, we define the advantage*

$$\mathsf{Adv}(\mathcal{A}; G^0, G^1) := \left| \Pr\left[1 = \mathcal{A} \to G^0\right] - \Pr\left[1 = \mathcal{A} \to G^1\right] \right|.$$

In particular, for the pseudorandomness game $\mathsf{Gxpd}^b_{n,\ell}$ for xpd, the analogous definition is as follows.

Definition 2 (XPD). *For adversary $\mathcal{A}$, we define the* xpd *pseudorandomness advantage* $\mathsf{Adv}(\mathcal{A}, \mathsf{Gxpd}^0_{n,\ell}, \mathsf{Gxpd}^1_{n,\ell})$ *as*

$$\left| \Pr\left[1 = \mathcal{A} \to \mathsf{Gxpd}^0_{n,\ell}\right] - \Pr\left[1 = \mathcal{A} \to \mathsf{Gxpd}^1_{n,\ell}\right] \right|,$$

where Fig. 2 defines $\mathsf{Gxpd}^0_{n,\ell}$.

The graphs specifying such a security game suggest a natural flow downwards. While we discuss the details of the game later in this section, one can extract a conceptual picture already from the graph alone. Concretely the intended usage (by the adversary) of $\mathsf{Gxpd}^b_{n,\ell}$ consists on first registering input values using the $\mathsf{SET}_{n_1,\ell}$ oracle, executing key derivation using the $\mathsf{XPD}_{CN,\ell}$ oracle and finally retrieving and testing the output using the $\mathsf{GET}_{n,\ell}$ oracle. In addition, the adversary gets access to auxiliary oracles, namely the HASH oracle modeling a cryptographic hash function as well as the Q and UNQ oracles.[1] Finally, $\mathsf{Gxpd}^b_{n,\ell}$ is structured in individual components which we call *packages*.

Definition 3 (Package). *A package M consists of a set of oracles $[\to \mathsf{M}] = \{\mathsf{O1}, .., \mathsf{Ot}\}$, specified by pseudo-code and operating on a set of state variables Σ, specified on the top of each package description. All other variables used by oracles are temporary and their values are forgotten after each call. The oracles of M may depend on oracles $[\mathsf{M} \to] = \{\mathsf{O'1}, .., \mathsf{O't'}\}$, i.e., make calls to oracles in $[\mathsf{M} \to]$. We say that a package M is stateless if $\Sigma = \emptyset$. We say that a package M is a game if $[\mathsf{M} \to] = \emptyset$.*

While some oracles of a package are exposed to the adversary, others are used only internally within the game. A monolithic version of a game such as $\mathsf{Gxpd}^b_{n,\ell}$ can be obtained by *inlining* all internal oracle calls. With the concept of packages we can now discuss the individual parts of $\mathsf{Gxpd}^b_{n,\ell}$. $\mathsf{Xpd}_{CN,\ell}$ is a parallel composition of $\mathsf{Xpd}_{n,\ell}$ for all children of n_1 exposing the oracles $\mathsf{XPD}_{n,\ell}$ for $n \in CN$, we write $\mathsf{XPD}_{CN,\ell}$ as shorthand for these oracles. The $\mathsf{Xpd}_{CN,\ell}$ packages are the only stateless packages in the game, indicated by the white color as opposed to the gray of stateful packages (Fig. 2).

---

[1] These two oracles in particular are necessary for composition: Note that the main oracles the adversary interacts with are subscripted by a name n and a level ℓ while the Q and UNQ oracles only take the name n as subscript. We will share the same Q and UNQ oracles between many instances of $\mathsf{Gxpd}^b_{n,\ell}$ and therefore need to allow reductions access to these oracles.

The $\mathrm{XPD}_{n,\ell}$ oracle of package $\mathrm{Xpd}_{n,\ell}$ (Fig. 3) computes a new handle $h \leftarrow \mathsf{xpd}\langle n, label, h_1, args\rangle$ alongside a new key $k \leftarrow \mathsf{xpd}(k_1, (label, d))$ based on the parent handle h_1, the arguments (e.g. transcript) and the bit r indicating whether this is a resumption session. The evaluation also includes a *label* which depends on the name of the package as well as the resumption bit. Note that the oracle only receives the *handle* of the input key from the adversary and only returns the newly constructed *handle* of the newly derived key. Concrete secrets are passed to $\mathsf{Key}_{n,\ell}^b$ packages using the GET and SET oracles. Here we can distinguish the upper $\mathsf{Key}_{n_1,\ell}^1$ package and the lower $\mathsf{Key}_{CN,\ell}^b$ packages (for all n in CN). We defer discussion about the Q and UNQ oracle calls to the description of the Log package.

The upper $\mathsf{Key}_{n_1,\ell}^1$ package offers oracle $\mathrm{SET}_{n_1,\ell}(h, hon, k)$ to the adversary which allows it to register a key. The oracle first verifies that the handle h matches the name n and level ℓ of this key package and—modeling algorithmic agility—verifies that the algorithm tag matches the value of the key, and else, assert throws an *abort*. As this is an ideal key package (indicated by superscript $^{b=1}$) for honest keys, instead of using the value provided by the adversary a fresh value is sampled—as indicated by using $\leftarrow_{\$}$ in contrast to $\leftarrow$ used for assignments. Finally the key is stored in this package's state and the handle returned to the caller. The GET oracle simply restores algorithm tagging on the key value and returns it to the caller (in this case the Xpd package). The lower $\mathsf{Key}_{CN,\ell}^b$ packages work the other way round in that they expose the GET oracle to the adversary while the SET oracle is used by Xpd. We encode the distinguishing task for the adversary in the $\mathsf{Key}_{CN,\ell}^b$ package: In $\mathrm{Gxpd}_{n,\ell}^0$ ($b = 0$), the keys returned from the GET oracle of the $\mathsf{Key}_{CN,\ell}^0$ is honestly computed based on the input keys while in the ideal game $\mathrm{Gxpd}_{n,\ell}^1$ the values of honest keys are sampled in the Key package ignoring the value computed by Xpd.

Finally, queries Q_n and UNQ_n to the Log_n package (Fig. 4) model collisions. The Q query simply returns if a *handle* is re-used while UNQ concerns itself with collisions between keys via an abort pattern and a mapping method. In slightly nonstandard notation, we use existential quantors here to express searching for *indices* into tables. The pattern models conditions on states where the game aborts (i.e. terminates and outputs a special symbol), cf. Sect. 5.3 for their use.

$\underline{\mathbf{Xpd}_{n,\ell}}$

Parameters

n : name

ℓ : level

$\mathsf{prntn} : N \to (N_\perp \times N_\perp)$

$\mathsf{label} : N \times \{0,1\} \to \{0,1\}^{96}$

State

no state

$\underline{\mathrm{XPD}_{n,\ell}(h_1, r, args)}$

$n_1, \_ \leftarrow \mathsf{prntn}(n)$

$label \leftarrow \mathsf{label}(n, r)$

$h \leftarrow \mathsf{xpd}\langle n, label, h_1, args\rangle$

$(k_1, hon) \leftarrow \mathrm{GET}_{n_1,\ell}(h_1)$

if $n = psk$:

$\quad \ell \leftarrow \ell + 1$

$\quad k \leftarrow \mathsf{xpd}(k_1, (label, args))$

else

$\quad alg \leftarrow \mathsf{alg}(h_1)$

$\quad d \leftarrow \mathsf{HASH}(\mathbf{tag}_{alg}(args))$

$\quad k \leftarrow \mathsf{xpd}(k_1, (label, d))$

$h \leftarrow \mathrm{SET}_{n,\ell}(h, hon, k)$

return h

Fig. 3. Xpd package

$\mathsf{Key}^b_{n,\ell}$

Parameters	State
n : name	$K_{n,\ell}$: Keytable
ℓ : level	

$\underline{\mathsf{SET}_{n,\ell}(h, hon, k^\star)}$

assert $\mathsf{name}(h) = n$
assert $\mathsf{level}(h) = \ell$
assert $\mathsf{alg}(k^\star) = \mathsf{alg}(h)$
$k \leftarrow \mathsf{untag}(k^\star)$
assert $\mathsf{len}(h) = |k|$
if $\mathsf{Q}_n(h) \neq \bot$: **return** $\mathsf{Q}_n(h)$
if $b \wedge hon$:
  $k \leftarrow\!\!{\scriptstyle\$}\; \{0,1\}^{\mathsf{len}(h)}$
$h' \leftarrow \mathsf{UNQ}_n(h, hon, k)$
if $h' \neq h$: **return** h'
$K_{n,\ell}[h] \leftarrow (k, hon)$
return h

$\underline{\mathsf{GET}_{n,\ell}(h)}$

assert $K_{n,\ell}[h] \neq \bot$
$(k^\star, hon) \leftarrow K_{n,\ell}[h]$
$k \leftarrow \mathsf{tag}_h(k^\star)$
return (k, hon)

$\mathsf{Log}^{P,map}_n$

Parameters
n : name

State

L_n : Log

$\underline{\mathsf{Q}_n(h)}$

if $L_n[h] = \bot$: **return** $\bot$
else
  $(h', \_, \_) \leftarrow L_n[h]$
  return h'

$\underline{\mathsf{UNQ}_n(h, hon, k)}$

if $(\exists\, h' : L_n[h'] = (h', hon', k)$
      $\wedge\, \mathsf{level}(h) = r \wedge \mathsf{level}(h^\star) = r')$:
  if $map(r, hon, r', hon'\, \mathsf{J}_n[k])$:
    $L_n[h] \leftarrow (h', hon, k)$
    $\mathsf{J}_n[k] \leftarrow 1$
    return h'
if $(\exists\, h^\star : L_n[h^\star] = (h', hon', k)$
      $\wedge\, \mathsf{level}(h) = r \wedge \mathsf{level}(h^\star) = r')$:
  $P(r, hon, r', hon')$
$L_n[h] \leftarrow (h, hon, k)$
return h

P	the command $P(r, hon, r', hon')$ is
Z	$\emptyset$
A	**if** $hon = hon' = 0 \wedge r = r' = 0$: **throw** *abort*
D	**if** $hon = hon' = 0$: **throw** *abort*
R	**if** $hon = hon' = 0$: **throw** *abort* **else throw** *win*
F	**throw** *abort*

---

map	the command $map(r, hon, r', hon', \mathsf{J}_n[k])$ is
0	0
1	$hon = hon' = 0 \wedge r \neq r' \wedge 0 \in \{r, r'\} \wedge \mathsf{J}_n[k] \neq 1$
∞	$hon = hon' = 0$

Fig. 4. Code for the Key and Log. In addition we use Nkey for a single key package that answers queries for all levels from the same table and 0key for a NKey package which consistently answers with the constant all-zeros key.

We use the **throw** notation here to allow special symbols in addition to *abort* which is also used by assert. In the game $\text{Gxpd}_{n,\ell}^b$, the D pattern aborts on collisions between dishonest keys. The F and R pattern abort if there is a collision between key values, regardless of their honesty, and they return different abort messages. Z does not abort at all, and A aborts upon a collision of two dishonest level 0 keys (which we use to constrain the adversary's psk registrations in the key schedule model).

Mapping methods filter certain collisions (preventing an *abort* event. ∞ allows collisions between Diffie-Hellman secrets (the adversary can construct colliding values via $X^zY = XY^z$) and the 1 method allows the adversary to register a dishonest application PSK colliding with an dishonest resumption PSK. The mapping methods are only used in the proof and not in the security model.

3   Assumptions

3.1   Collision-Resistance

Figure 5 defines the collision-resistance game $\text{Gcr}^{\text{f-}alg,b}$ for a given function f-alg, where $f \in \{\text{hash}, \text{xtr}, \text{xpd}\}$ and $alg \in \mathcal{H}$ which TLS 1.3 currently defines as

$$\mathcal{H} = \{\text{sha256}, \text{sha384}, \text{sha512}\}$$

(see FIPS 180-2). The HASH oracle takes as input a text t from the domain of f-alg and returns its digest d. If that text t has not been queried before, the digest is stored in table H at index t. In the ideal game ($b = 1$), the oracle first checks whether d already occurs in H, and if so, throws an abort. Hence, the adversary can distinguish between the real and the ideal game if and only if it can submit two different texts with the same digest. Our definition generalizes to n-ary functions by letting the text t be the tuple of their arguments.

$\underline{\text{Gcr}^{\text{f-}alg,b}}$

$\underline{\text{HASH}(t)}$

assert $t \in dom(\text{f-}alg)$
$d \leftarrow \text{f-}alg(t)$
if $H[t] = \bot$:
    if $b \wedge d \in range(H)$:
        throw *abort*
    $H[t] \leftarrow d$
return d

Fig. 5. $\text{Gcr}^{\text{f-}alg,b}$ code.

Definition 4 (Collision-Resistance). *For an adversary $\mathcal{A}$, a function $f \in \{\text{hash}, \text{xtr}, \text{xpd}\}$ and algorithm $alg \in \mathcal{H}$, define collision-resistance advantage* $\text{Adv}(\mathcal{A}, \text{Gcr}^{\text{f-}alg,0}, \text{Gcr}^{\text{f-}alg,1})$ *is*

$$\left| \Pr\left[1 = \mathcal{A} \to \text{Gcr}^{\text{f-}alg,0}\right] - \Pr\left[1 = \mathcal{A} \to \text{Gcr}^{\text{f-}alg,1}\right] \right|.$$

Agile Collision-Resistance. It is convenient to define the *agile* collision-resistance game $\text{Gacr}^{f,b}$ as well, where $f \in \{\text{hash}, \text{xtr}, \text{xpd}\}$ takes *tagged* inputs, i.e., hash takes a single input, tagged with the algorithm to use, xpd takes three inputs $(k, label, args)$, where k is tagged, and xtr takes inputs (k_1, k_2) where one is tagged, and if both are tagged, they are tagged consistently. The adversary can then make queries to HASH with values in the domain of the *agile* functions. We write $\text{Hash}^b := \text{Gacr}^{\text{hash},b}$. See Sect. 2.1 for further discussion of tagging.

3.2 Pseudorandomness of xpd

For most key names n, Definition 2 already captures pseudorandomness of xpd. We now cover two special cases.

XPD to Derive PSK. For $n = psk$ (cf. Fig. 6a), the *layer* index increases from ℓ to $\ell + 1$. Thus, the $\mathsf{XPD}_{psk,\ell}$ oracle reads keys via $\mathsf{GET}_{rm,\ell}$ queries, but writes keys using the level $\ell + 1$ query $\mathsf{SET}_{psk,\ell+1}$. Another difference in $\mathsf{Gxpd}^b_{psk,\ell}$ compared to the general $\mathsf{Gxpd}^b_{n,\ell}$ is that the lower Log^{D1}_{psk} package uses a $D1$ pattern for logging which ignores level 0 $\mathsf{UNQ}_{psk}(h, hon, k)$ queries with $hon = 0$ whenever there already exists a dishonest handle h' for key value k at level 0. Since $\mathsf{XPD}_{psk,\ell}$ writes only on level $\ell + 1 > 0$, this difference in logging does not affect the strength of the assumption, but it makes the assumption code align with the key schedule game, cf. Sect. 4.1. Finally, for deriving the psk, no hash-operation is performed.

Definition 5 (XPD for psk). *For an adversary $\mathcal{A}$, we define the* xpd *pseudo-randomness advantage for psk derivation* $\mathsf{Adv}(\mathcal{A}, \mathsf{Gxpd}^0_{psk,\ell}, \mathsf{Gxpd}^1_{psk,\ell})$ *as*

$$\left| \Pr\left[1 = \mathcal{A} \to \mathsf{Gxpd}^0_{psk,\ell}\right] - \Pr\left[1 = \mathcal{A} \to \mathsf{Gxpd}^1_{psk,\ell}\right] \right|$$

XPD to Derive Esalt. For $n = esalt$, the lower Log^R_{esalt} package uses an R pattern instead of a D pattern, sending abort messages whenever the same key value k is registered as an *esalt* under two distinct handles h and h' (across all levels and regardless of honesty). Note that the adversary could simulate the R pattern itself (by retrieving all keys and checking for equality) and thus, the R pattern only *weakens* the adversary since it can no longer query the game after triggering an R abort and since the adversary does not learn the value of the collision which caused the abort.

Definition 6 (XPD for esalt). *For an adversary $\mathcal{A}$, we define the* xpd *pseudorandomness advantage for esalt derivation* $\mathsf{Adv}(\mathcal{A}, \mathsf{Gxpd}^0_{esalt,\ell}, \mathsf{Gxpd}^1_{esalt,\ell})$ *as*

$$\left| \Pr\left[1 = \mathcal{A} \to \mathsf{Gxpd}^0_{esalt,\ell}\right] - \Pr\left[1 = \mathcal{A} \to \mathsf{Gxpd}^1_{esalt,\ell}\right] \right|.$$

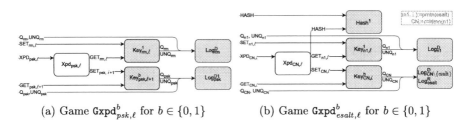

(a) Game $\mathsf{Gxpd}^b_{psk,\ell}$ for $b \in \{0,1\}$ (b) Game $\mathsf{Gxpd}^b_{esalt,\ell}$ for $b \in \{0,1\}$

Fig. 6. xpd assumptions

$\underline{\mathbf{Xtr}^b_{n,\ell}}$

Parameters

n : name

ℓ : level

b : bit

$\mathsf{prntn} : N \rightarrow (N_\perp \times N_\perp)$

$\mathsf{label} : N \times \{0,1\} \rightarrow \{0,1\}^{96}$

State

no state

$\mathbf{XTR}_{n,\ell}(h_1, h_2)$

$n_1, n_2 \leftarrow \mathsf{prntn}(n)$

if $\mathsf{alg}(h_1) \neq \perp \wedge \mathsf{alg}(h_2) \neq \perp$:

    assert $\mathsf{alg}(h_1) = \mathsf{alg}(h_2)$

$h \leftarrow \mathsf{xtr}\langle n, h_1, h_2 \rangle$

$(k_1, hon_1) \leftarrow \mathsf{GET}_{n_1,\ell}(h_1)$

$(k_2, hon_2) \leftarrow \mathsf{GET}_{n_2,\ell}(h_2)$

$k \leftarrow \mathsf{xtr}(k_1, k_2)$

$hon \leftarrow hon_1 \vee hon_2$

if $b \wedge hon_2$:

    $k^* \leftarrow_\$ \{0,1\}^{\mathsf{len}(k)}$

    $k \leftarrow \mathsf{tag}_{\mathsf{alg}(k)}(k^*)$

    $h \leftarrow \mathsf{SET}_{n,\ell}(h, hon, k)$

return h

(a) Code of Xtr

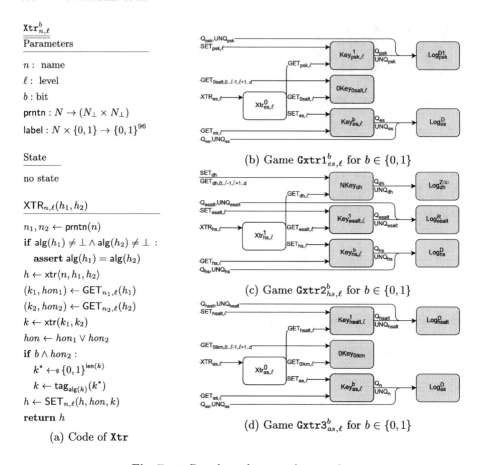

(b) Game $\mathbf{Gxtr1}^b_{es,\ell}$ for $b \in \{0,1\}$

(c) Game $\mathbf{Gxtr2}^b_{hs,\ell}$ for $b \in \{0,1\}$

(d) Game $\mathbf{Gxtr3}^b_{as,\ell}$ for $b \in \{0,1\}$

Fig. 7. xtr Pseudorandomness Assumption

3.3   Pseudorandomness of xtr

The TLS 1.3 key schedule performs three xtr operations (cf. Fig. 1), and the modeling is analogous to the XPD assumptions, except that for the early secret *es*, xtr security relies on the *psk* which is the *right* input to xtr, and for the application secret *as*, xtr security relies on *esalt* which is the *left* input to xtr. The derivation of the handshake secret *hs* is a special case, because its security is an *OR* of the honesty of its left and right input. We here state the xtr security assumption required for *hs* security based on its *left* input *esalt* and turn to the security based in its right input (the Diffie-Hellman (DH) secret) shortly. Note that the security of *esalt* will be applied *after* the security of the DH secret and thus, the bit b in the $\mathbf{Xtr}^b_{hs,\ell}$ is already set to 1 and samples output keys uniformly at random whenever the Diffe-Hellman secret is honest. The security of *esalt* thus only increases security for those keys where the Diffie-Hellman secret is dishonest.

Definition 7 (XTR advantages). *For adversary $\mathcal{A}$, level $\ell \in \mathbb{N}_0$, we define the* xtr *pseudorandomness advantage for* es *as* $\mathsf{Adv}(\mathcal{A}, \mathtt{Gxtr1}^0_{es,\ell}, \mathtt{Gxtr1}^1_{es,\ell})$, *the pseudorandomness advantage for* hs *as* $\mathsf{Adv}(\mathcal{A}, \mathtt{Gxtr2}^0_{hs,\ell}, \mathtt{Gxtr2}^1_{hs,\ell})$ *and the pseudorandomness advantage for as as* $\mathsf{Adv}(\mathcal{A}, \mathtt{Gxtr3}^0_{as,\ell}, \mathtt{Gxtr3}^1_{as,\ell})$, *where Fig. 7b–7d define the games* $\mathtt{Gxtr1}^b_{es}$, $\mathtt{Gxtr2}^b_{hs}$ *and* $\mathtt{Gxtr}^b_{as}$ *and Definition 1 defines advantage.*

3.4 Salted ODH

Our salted oracle Diffie-Hellman assumption (SODH) is a stronger variant of the oracle Diffie-Hellman assumption introduced by Abdalla et al. [1] and the PRF oracle Diffie-Hellman assumption studied by Brendel et al. [20]. Most importantly, SODH is an *agile*, i.e., it requires pseudorandomness of the derived keys even when the adversary can see hash-values of the same Diffie-Hellman secret under *different* hash-functions and different, possibly adversarially chosen salts. In practice, different salts can emerge from disagreement between server and client

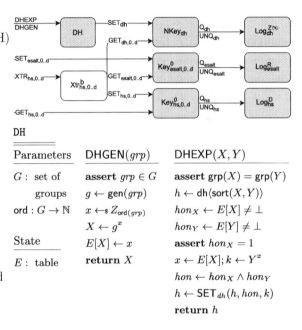

Fig. 8. Game $\mathtt{Gsodh}^b$ (top), package $\mathtt{Dh}$ (bottom)

about the PSK to use since the early salt *esalt* (and possibly also the *alg*) changes when the PSK changes (see Fig. 1). The $\mathtt{Gsodh}^b$ game (cf. Fig. 8) allows the adversary to generate honest Diffie-Hellman shares via XTR, to combine them (or an honest and a dishonest share) into a Diffie-Hellman secret via DHEXP and to derive keys from them via $\mathsf{XTR}_{n,\ell}$ for an arbitrary level $\ell \in \{0,..,d\}$. Oracle $\mathsf{GET}_{n,\ell}$ then allows to retrieve the derived keys. Note that pseudorandomness is modeled, this time, by a bit in the $\mathsf{Xtr}^b_{n,\ell}$ package (Fig. 7a).

Definition 8 (SODH). *For an adversary $\mathcal{A}$, we define the Salted Oracle Diffie Hellman (SODH) advantage* $\mathsf{Adv}(\mathcal{A}, \mathtt{Gsodh}^0, \mathtt{Gsodh}^1) :=$

$$\left| \Pr\left[1 = \mathcal{A} \to \mathtt{Gsodh}^0\right] - \Pr\left[1 = \mathcal{A} \to \mathtt{Gsodh}^1\right]\right|,$$

3.5 Pre-image Resistance for xpd

Pseudorandomness and collision resistance of xpd also imply that it is hard to find pre-images for *honest* output keys. We prove this implication in the full version of this article [23, Lemma E.7] and in this conference version rely on pre-image resistance as a separate assumption for convenience.

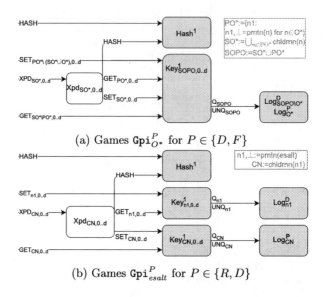

(a) Games $\mathtt{Gpi}_{O*}^{P}$ for $P \in \{D, F\}$

(b) Games $\mathtt{Gpi}_{esalt}^{P}$ for $P \in \{R, D\}$

Fig. 9. Pre-image resistance assumptions

Definition 9 (Pre-image resistance advantages). *For an adversary $\mathcal{A}$ and level $\ell \in \mathbb{N}_0$ we define the pre-image resistance advantage for deriving keys in O^* (a set to be specified later)* $\mathsf{Adv}(\mathcal{A}, \mathtt{Gpi}_{O*}^{D}, \mathtt{Gpi}_{O*}^{F}) :=$

$$\left| \Pr\left[1 = \mathcal{A} \to \mathtt{Gpi}_{O*}^{D}\right] - \Pr\left[1 = \mathcal{A} \to \mathtt{Gpi}_{O*}^{F}\right] \right|,$$

the pre-image resistance advantage for deriving keys with the same parent as esalt by $\mathsf{Adv}(\mathcal{A}, \mathtt{Gpi}_{esalt}^{D}, \mathtt{Gpi}_{esalt}^{F}) :=$

$$\left| \Pr\left[1 = \mathcal{A} \to \mathtt{Gpi}_{esalt}^{D}\right] - \Pr\left[1 = \mathcal{A} \to \mathtt{Gpi}_{esalt}^{F}\right] \right|.$$

Figure 9b and Fig. 9b define $\mathtt{Gpi}_{O*}^{P}$ and $\mathtt{Gpi}_{esalt}^{P}$.

Our modular assumptions for xpd and xtr are agile, multi-instance security assumptions with registration of dishonest keys. They reduce to their non-agile, single-instance, monolithically written counterparts with a security loss equal to the number of honest keys. Since TLS 1.3 currently only supports hash-algorithms of different length, indeed, our agile assumptions for xtr and xpd reduce to *non-agile* assumptions. In turn, we can only reduce our modular agile SODH assumption to an *agile* monolithic SODH assumption, because TLS 1.3 indeed requires such a strong, agile SODH assumption (cf. Sect. 3.4 and Sect. 7) for further discussion. See full version [23, Appendix E] for the reduction proofs.

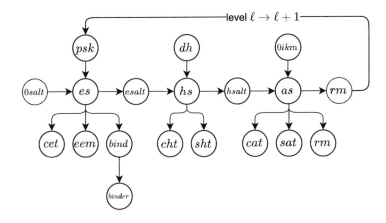

Fig. 10. Parent names prntn in TLS 1.3

4 Key Schedule

We reason about the TLS 1.3 key schedule in terms of its three elementary operations extract (xtr), expand (xpd) and computation of Diffie-Hellman secrets. This section first introduces an abstract key schedule syntax and refines it to capture TLS 1.3 as part of a bigger class of *TLS-like* key schedules. We then define key schedule security and state our theorem for all TLS-like key schedules.

4.1 Key Schedule Syntax

Our formalization interprets the key schedule as a directed graph where nodes describe *key names* (cf. Fig. 10 for the case of TLS 1.3). In addition to the set of names N and the graph description (encoded as prntn function, cf. Sect. 2.1), a key schedule has a function label which maps the name and a resumption bit to a derivation label. We conveniently model hmac operations by using xpd with *empty label* as an alias for hmac. By sound cryptographic practice, a key should be either used for xpd or for hmac but not both, so if a node has an empty label, it is not allowed to have siblings. Similarly, xtr operations only yield a single child, and the multiple children of xpd operations are derived using distinct labels.

Definition 10 (Key Schedule Syntax). *A key schedule* $ks = (N, \mathsf{label}, \mathsf{prntn})$ *consists of a set of names* N *and two functions*

$$\mathsf{label} : \qquad\qquad N \times \{0,1\} \to \{0,1\}^{96} \cup \{\bot\}$$
$$\mathsf{prntn} : \qquad\qquad N \to (N \cup \bot) \times (N \cup \bot)$$

with the previously described restrictions.

Figure 10 describes the prntn function of the TLS 1.3 key schedule as a graph. Stating and proving our theorem in terms of the concrete TLS key schedule would require listing and treating each xpd operation individually. Instead, we prove our theorem for all *TLS-like* key schedules (of which the TLS key schedule is an instance). We consider a key schedule as *TLS-like* if it aligns with TLS in terms of base keys and xtr operations and treats the *psk* name as the main root from which all keys except for the base keys can be reached. Moreover, a TLS-like key schedule only has a single loop. This loop contains the edge from *rm* to *psk* and models resumptions. This edge has the special property of increasing the associated level as the *psk* is computed in an earlier session to be used in a later key schedule session. As such the cycle does not contradict an ordering on key computations.

Definition 11 (TLS-like Key Schedule Syntax). *A key schedule ks = $(N, \mathsf{label}, \mathsf{prntn})$ is TLS-like if its prntn graph satisfies the above restrictions, its set of names N contains at least the names $0salt, psk, es, esalt, dh, hs, hsalt, 0ikm, as, rm$ and the prntn function maps $0salt$, dh and $0ikm$ to $(\perp, \perp)$, maps es, hs and as according to Fig. 10, maps psk to $(rm, \perp)$ and each of the remaining names n to some pair $(n_1, \perp)$ with $n_1 \neq \perp$.*

We use several subsets of N which we summarize in Table 1.

4.2   Key Schedule Security Model

Our key schedule security model captures that the key schedule produces keys which are pseudorandom and unique. We formulate security as indistinguishability between a real and an ideal game where the real game implements the actual key schedule derivations, while in the ideal game, output keys are unique, and honest keys are sampled uniformly at random. Concretely, we follow a simulation approach (somewhat similar to the Canetti and Krawczyk [26] approach to key exchange), where the ideal game is defined as a composition of a simulator $\mathcal{S}$ and an ideal functionality. The simulator instructs the ideal functionality to produce output keys of certain length, however the *value* of the output keys is sampled independently from the simulator. As we require that no adversary can distinguish these two settings this captures security: The protocol determines when an output key becomes available and which type of key but no information about the concrete value is disclosed in the protocol (as the simulator does not have such information).

Concretely, in our ideal game $\mathsf{Gks}^1(\mathcal{S})$ (Fig. 11b), the simulator $\mathcal{S}$ is a parameter and the $\mathsf{Key}^1_{O^*, 0..d}$ and Log_{O^*} packages (cf. Sect. 2.3) constitute the ideal functionality. Namely, the $\mathsf{Key}^1_{O^*, 0..d}$ package samples a uniformly random key for handles which correspond to honest keys with a name $n \in O^*$ and some level $0 \leq \ell \leq d$. The Log_{O^*} package, in turn, ensures that each handle corresponds to a *different* key, modeling key uniqueness for both honest and dishonest keys.

Similarly, we describe the real execution of the key schedule as a game Gks^0, written in pseudocode. Following the SSP methodology outlined in Sect. 2.3, we split the pseudocode of the game Gks^0 into several packages most of which (Xpd, Xtr, DH, Key, and Log) have been introduced before and Check is described in

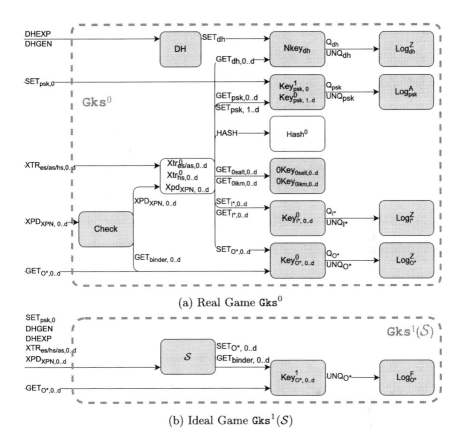

(a) Real Game Gks^0

(b) Ideal Game $\text{Gks}^1(\mathcal{S})$

Fig. 11. Key schedule security games with internal keys I^*, output keys O^* and XPN, the set of key names produced by xpd. We write OK_n as an abbreviation for $\text{Nk}_n \rightarrow \text{L}_n^Z$. We initialize K and Nk_n with suitable 0 values (cf. Sect. 2.1).

Table 1. Notation

N	The set of all (key) names
N^*	$N \setminus \{psk, dh\}$
I^*	The set of internal keys $\{n \in N^* \mid \text{chldrnn}(n) = \emptyset\}$
O^*:	The set of output keys $\{n \in N^* \mid \text{chldrnn}(n) = \emptyset\}$
O:	$O^* \cup \{psk\}$
S:	The set of separation points (Definition 13)
XPN:	The set of expand names $\{n \in N : \text{prntn}(n) = (\_, \perp)\}$
XPR:	The set of representatives (Sect. 4.3)

Sect. 4.3. Figure 11a depicts the composed game Gks^0—recall that this graph is not merely an illustration, it is part of the formal definition of Gks^0.

The game Gks^0 exposes $\mathsf{SET}_{psk,0}$ and DHGEN oracles which sample honest Diffie-Hellman shares, honest application PSKs and enable the adversary to register dishonest application PSKs with a chosen value. The XTR and XPD oracles trigger key derivations. Finally, the adversary can access output keys via the GET oracle on the (real) key package $\mathsf{Key}^0_{O^*,0..d}$.

Definition 12 (Key Schedule Advantage). *For a key schedule* $ks = (N, \mathsf{label}, \mathsf{prntn})$, *a natural number* d, *a simulator* $\mathcal{S}$ *and an adversary* $\mathcal{A}$ *which makes queries for at most* d *levels we define the advantage* $\mathsf{Adv}(\mathcal{A}, \mathsf{Gks}^0, \mathsf{Gks}^1(\mathcal{S})) :=$

$$\left| \Pr\left[1 = \mathcal{A} \to \mathsf{Gks}^0\right] - \Pr\left[1 = \mathcal{A} \to \mathsf{Gks}^1(\mathcal{S})\right] \right|,$$

where Fig. 11b defines $\mathsf{Gks}^1(\mathcal{S})$ *and Fig. 11a defines* Gks^0.

4.3 Front-End Checks

The Check package acts as a restriction on the adversary since the **assert** conditions in the Check code force the adversary to use the correct Diffie-Hellman shares and binder value in its transcript when the transcript is included in a derivation step. In terms of composability, the **assert** conditions in Check force the key exchange to call the key schedule with consistent values, i.e., derive the Diffie-Hellman secret from a pair of shares that is included in the transcript and not from an unrelated pair of shares. The TLS 1.3 specification ensures these innocent conditions, and requiring them formally means that the proof breaks down when session memory in TLS 1.3 is unsafely implemented.

In addition to enforcing the use of consistent shares in the transcript, the XPD oracle of the Check package (Fig. 12) ensures that the resumption flag is consistent with the level of the PSK; and that the binder tag included in the transcript of later stages (at the end of the last ClientHello message) is the same that was computed and checked in the early stage. The transcript is not included into all xpd derivations, but only once on the path from psk to output key, and Check only filters queries on these particular derivation steps.

Check

$\mathsf{XPD}_{n,\ell}(h_1, r, args)$

if $n = bind$:

    if $r = 0$, **assert** $\mathsf{level}(h_1) = 0$

    if $r = 1$, **assert** $\mathsf{level}(h_1) > 0$

elseif $n \in S \cap early$:

    $binder \leftarrow \mathsf{BinderArgs}(args)$

    $h_{bndr} \leftarrow \mathsf{BinderHand}(h_1, args)$

    $(k, \_) \leftarrow \mathsf{GET}_{binder,\ell}(h_{bndr})$

    assert $binder = k$

elseif $n \in S$:

    $X, Y \leftarrow \mathsf{DhArgs}(args)$

    $h_{dh} \leftarrow \mathsf{DhHand}(h_1)$

    assert $h_{dh} = \mathsf{dh}\langle \mathsf{sort}(X, Y) \rangle$

    $binder \leftarrow \mathsf{BinderArgs}(args)$

    $h_{bndr} \leftarrow \mathsf{BinderHand}(h_1, args)$

    $(k, \_) \leftarrow \mathsf{GET}_{binder,\ell}(h_{bndr})$

    assert $binder = k$

$h \leftarrow \mathsf{XPD}_{n,\ell}(h_1, r, args)$

return h

Fig. 12. Code of Check

Since including the transcript ensures domain separation between different protocol runs and derivation pathes, we refer to the derivation steps which include the transcript as a *separation point*.

Definition 13 (Separation Points). *For a key schedule* $ks = (N, \mathsf{label},$ $\mathsf{prntn})$, *we call* $S \subseteq N$ *a set of separation points, if it satisfies the following two requirements:*

- $\forall\, n \in O$: *the path from* psk *to* n *contains an* $n' \in S$.
- *If there exists a path from* dh *to an* $n \in O$, *then it contains an* $n' \in S$.

In addition, for each xpd operation, we choose one representative child. I.e., $XPR \subseteq N$ is a *representative set* for ks if $psk, esalt \in XPR$ and for each name $n \in N$ with only a single parent (these are the xpd nodes), either n or exactly one sibling of n is contained in XPR.

5 Key Schedule Theorem

Theorem 1. *Let* ks *be a TLS-like key schedule with representative set* XPR *and separation points* S. *Let* $d \in \mathbb{N}$. *There is an efficient simulator* $\mathcal{S}$ *such that for all adversaries* $\mathcal{A}$ *which make queries for at most* d *resumption levels,*

$$\mathsf{Adv}(\mathcal{A}, \mathsf{Gks}^0, \mathsf{Gks}^1(\mathcal{S})) \le \mathsf{Adv}(\mathcal{A} \to \mathcal{R}_{cr}^{main}, \mathsf{Gacr}^{hash,b})$$

$$+ \sum_{j \in \{Z,D\}, \mathsf{f} \in \{\mathsf{xtr},\mathsf{xpd}\}} \mathsf{Adv}(\mathcal{A} \to \mathcal{R}_{j,\mathsf{f}}^{main}, \mathsf{Gacr}^{\mathsf{f},b})$$

$$+ \max_{i \in \{0,1\}} \Big[\mathsf{Adv}(\mathcal{A}_i \to \mathcal{R}_{sodh}^{main}, \mathsf{Gsodh}^b)$$

$$\sum_{\ell=0}^{d-1} \Big(\mathsf{Adv}(\mathcal{A}_i \to \mathcal{R}_{es,\ell}^{main}, \mathsf{Gxtr}_{es,\ell}^b)$$

$$+ \mathsf{Adv}(\mathcal{A}_i \to \mathcal{R}_{hs,\ell}^{main}, \mathsf{Gxtr}_{hs,\ell}^b)$$

$$+ \mathsf{Adv}(\mathcal{A}_i \to \mathcal{R}_{as,\ell}^{main}, \mathsf{Gxtr}_{as,\ell}^b)$$

$$+ \sum_{n \in XPR} \Big(\mathsf{Adv}(\mathcal{A}_i \to \mathcal{R}_{n,\ell}^{main}, \mathsf{Gxpd}_{n,\ell}^b) \Big) \Big)$$

$$+ \mathsf{Adv}(\mathcal{A}_i \to \mathcal{R}_{esalt,pi}^{main}, \mathsf{Gpi}_{esalt}^b)$$

$$+ \mathsf{Adv}(\mathcal{A}_i \to \mathcal{R}_{O^*,pi}^{main}, \mathsf{Gpi}_{O^*}^b) \Big],$$

where $\mathcal{A}_i$ *behaves as* $\mathcal{A}$ *except that it returns bit* i *on a so-called win abort (cf. [23, Lemma D.4]);* $\mathcal{R}_*^{main} := \mathcal{R}^{ch\text{-}map} \to \mathcal{R}_*$ *when replacing* $*$ *by* cr, (Z,f), (D,f), $sodh$, es, hs, as, n, O^*, pi *or* $esalt$, pi, *the simulator* $\mathcal{S}$ *is marked in grey in [23, Fig. 26b], [23, Fig. 32a] defines* $\mathcal{R}_{sodh}$, *[23, Fig. 34a] defines* $\mathcal{R}_{es,\ell}$, $\mathcal{R}_{hs,\ell}$ *and* $\mathcal{R}_{as,\ell}$ *are defined analogously, and [23, Fig. 34b] defines* $\mathcal{R}_{n,\ell}$ *for* $n \in XPR$, $0 \le \ell \le d$, *[23, Fig. 32c] defines* $\mathcal{R}_{esalt,pi}$ *and [23, Fig. 32d] defines* $\mathcal{R}_{O^*,pi}$.

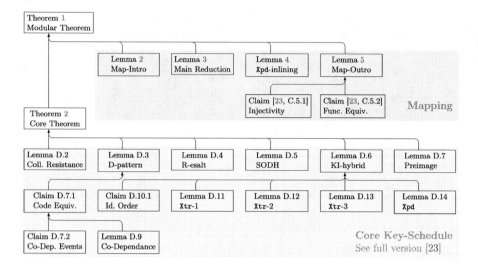

Fig. 13. Proof structure

5.1 Proof Technique

A recurrent proof technique which we use are *reductions*, written in SSP style. As usually, we want to show that if there is an adversary $\mathcal{A}$ which successfully distinguishes between two games G^0_{big} and G^1_{big}, then based on $\mathcal{A}$, we can construct an adversary $\mathcal{B}$ of similar complexity as $\mathcal{A}$ which successfully distinguishes between two games G^0_{sml} and G^1_{sml}. Our reductions will have the following form.

Lemma 1 (Reduction Technique). *If we can define a reduction $\mathcal{R}$ such that*

$$\mathsf{G}^0_{big} \overset{code}{\equiv} \mathcal{R} \to \mathsf{G}^0_{sml} \quad (1) \qquad and \qquad \mathsf{G}^1_{big} \overset{code}{\equiv} \mathcal{R} \to \mathsf{G}^1_{sml} \quad (2)$$

then

$$\mathsf{Adv}(\mathcal{A}; \mathsf{G}^0_{big}, \mathsf{G}^1_{big}) = \mathsf{Adv}(\mathcal{B}; \mathsf{G}^0_{sml}, \mathsf{G}^1_{sml}), \quad (3)$$

where

$$\mathcal{B} := \mathcal{A} \to \mathcal{R}. \quad (4)$$

Proof. Assuming Eq. 1, 2 and 4, we deduce Eq. 3 as follows:

$$\mathsf{Adv}(\mathcal{A}, \mathsf{G}^0_{big}, \mathsf{G}^1_{big})$$

$$\overset{def.}{=} \left| \Pr\left[1 = \mathcal{A} \to \mathsf{G}^0_{big}\right] - \Pr\left[1 = \mathcal{A} \to \mathcal{R} \to \mathsf{G}^1_{big}\right] \right|$$

$$\overset{Eq. 1\&2}{=} \left| \Pr\left[1 = \mathcal{A} \to (\mathcal{R} \to \mathsf{G}^0_{sml})\right] - \Pr\left[1 = \mathcal{A} \to (\mathcal{R} \to \mathsf{G}^1_{sml})\right] \right|$$

$$= \left| \Pr\left[1 = (\mathcal{A} \to \mathcal{R}) \to \mathsf{G}^0_{sml})\right] - \Pr\left[1 = (\mathcal{A} \to \mathcal{R}) \to \mathsf{G}^1_{sml}\right] \right|$$

$$\overset{def.}{=} \mathsf{Adv}(\mathcal{A} \to \mathcal{R}, \mathsf{G}^0_{sml}, \mathsf{G}^1_{sml}) \overset{Eq. 4}{=} \mathsf{Adv}(\mathcal{B}, \mathsf{G}^0_{sml}, \mathsf{G}^1_{sml})$$

Map

$\mathsf{SET}_{\mathrm{psk},0}(h, hon, k)$

$h' \leftarrow \mathsf{SET}_{\mathrm{psk},0}(h,$
$\qquad\qquad hon, k)$
$M_{\mathrm{psk}}[h] \leftarrow h'$
return h

$\mathsf{GET}_{n \in O^*, \ell}(h)$

assert $M_{n,\ell}[h] \neq \perp$
$h' \leftarrow M_{n,\ell}[h]$
return
$\qquad \mathsf{GET}_{n, \mathsf{level}(h')}(h')$

$\mathsf{XPD}_{n \in XPN, \ell}(h_1, r, args)$

$i_1, \_ \leftarrow \mathsf{prntidx}(n, \ell)$
assert $M_{i_1}[h_1] \neq \perp$
$label \leftarrow \mathsf{label}(n, r)$
$\ell_1 \leftarrow \mathsf{level}(M_{i_1}[h_1])$
$h \leftarrow \mathsf{xpd}\langle n, label, h_1, args\rangle$

$h' \leftarrow \mathsf{XPD}_{n,\ell_1}\!\left(\dfrac{M_{i_1}[h_1],}{r, args}\right)$

if $n = psk$: $\ell \leftarrow \ell + 1$
$M_{n,\ell}[h] \leftarrow h'$
return h

$\mathsf{DHGEN}()$

return $\mathsf{DHGEN}()$

$\mathsf{DHEXP}(X, Y)$

$h \leftarrow \mathsf{dh}\langle \mathsf{sort}(X, Y)\rangle$
$h' \leftarrow \mathsf{DHEXP}(X, Y)$
if $M_{dh}[h] = \perp$:
$\qquad M_{dh}[h] \leftarrow h'$
return h

$\mathsf{XTR}_{n \in \{es, hs, as\}, \ell}(h_1, h_2)$

$i_1, i_2 \leftarrow \mathsf{prntidx}(n, \ell)$
assert $M_{i_1}[h_1] \neq \perp$
assert $M_{i_2}[h_2] \neq \perp$
$\ell' \overset{\mathrm{choose}}{\leftarrow} \mathsf{level}(M_{i_1}[h_1]),$
$\qquad\qquad \mathsf{level}(M_{i_2}[h_2])$
$h \leftarrow \mathsf{xtr}\langle n, h_1, h_2\rangle$

$h' \leftarrow \mathsf{XTR}_{n,\ell'}\!\left(\dfrac{M_{i_1}[h_1],}{M_{i_2}[h_2]}\right)$

$M_{n,\ell}[h] \leftarrow h'$
return h

Fig. 14. Oracles of Map. Here, $\ell \in \{0 \ldots d\}$. $\ell' \overset{\mathrm{choose}}{\leftarrow} \mathsf{level}(M_{n_1}[h_1]), \mathsf{level}(M_{n_2}[h_2])$ assigns to ℓ' the value $\mathsf{level}(M_{n_1}[h_1])$ if it is not $\perp$ and $\mathsf{level}(M_{n_2}[h_2])$, else.

Importantly, throughout this article, we define reductions graphically as composition of previously defined packages so that the reduction *re-uses* code, as opposed to the usual technique which introduces new code for a reduction. As a result, we can argue Eqs. 1 and 2 graphically. E.g., in [23, Fig. 31a] we highlight the reduction in gray and observe that the only change from Fig. 15a is the collision resistance assumption—the $\mathsf{G}^b_{\mathrm{sml}}$ in this case. Observing the graph of Gks^0 (cf. Fig. 11a) closely and comparing it with the graphs of the assumptions introduced in Sect. 3, one can identify that the assumptions are almost sub-graphs of Gks^0, and by an appropriately chosen sequence of reduction arguments, the graphs of the assumptions will appear as actual subgraphs.

5.2 Proof of Theorem 1

We need to show the indistinguishability of the real game Gks^0 and the ideal game $\mathsf{Gks}^1(\mathcal{S})$. [23, Fig. 25a] depicts the real game Gks^0 (cf. Fig. 11a), with slightly different graph layouting. [23, Fig. 26b] depicts the ideal game $\mathsf{Gks}^1(\mathcal{S})$ (cf. Fig. 11b) where the simulator $\mathcal{S}$ is described in concrete code. To show the indistinguishability between Gks^0 ([23, Fig. 25a]) and $\mathsf{Gks}^1(\mathcal{S})$ ([23, Fig. 26b]), we make 4 *game hops*, depicted as the sequence of the five games depicted in [23, Fig. 25a], [23, Fig. 25b], [23, Fig. 25c], [23, Fig. 26a] and [23, Fig. 26b]. We now describe each of the game hops and state the corresponding lemma, see Fig. 13 for a proof overview.

First, recall that the key schedule security model stores keys in a redundant fashion (a) due to possible equal values of a dishonest resumption psk ($\mathsf{level}(h) > 0$) and an adversarially registered application psk ($\mathsf{level}(h) = 0$) and (b) due to the equal values of the (dishonest) DH keys corresponding to (X^a, Y) and (X, Y^a).

Lemma 2 introduces a Map package (see [23, Fig. 25b] for the game and the left column of Fig. 14 for the code of Map) to remove the redundantly stored keys—note that the Log^{A1}_{psk} and the $\mathsf{Log}^{Z\infty}_{dh}$ package now use the $map = 1$ and the $map = \infty$ code of Log (see Fig. 4 for its code). As a result, any adversary playing against Gcore^0 (defined in [23, Fig. 25b]) cannot create (this particular) redundancy anymore since the $\text{Key}_{psk,\ell}$ and DHKey_{dh} packages do not store the key again when the mapping code is triggered. We defer the proof of code equality proof of Lemma 2 to the full version [23]. It relies on proving the invariant that whenever Gks^0 stores key k with honesty hon under handle h, then game Gks^{0Map} stores key k with honesty hon under the mapped handle $h' = M[h]$. The proof proceeds by induction over the oracle calls.

Lemma 2 (Map-Intro). *For all adversaries $\mathcal{A}$ which make queries for at most d resumption levels,*

$$\Pr\left[1 = \mathcal{A} \to \text{Gks}^0\right] = \Pr\left[1 = \mathcal{A} \to \text{Gks}^{0Map}\right].$$

In particular $\text{Gks}^0 \overset{func}{\equiv} \text{Gks}^{0Map}$.

Lemma 3 then reduces the indistinguishability of Gks^{0Map} ([23, Fig. 25b]) and Gks^{1Map} ([23, Fig. 25c]) to the indistinguishability of Gcore^0 and $\text{Gcore}^1(\mathcal{S}^{core})$ using reduction R^{core}. The indistinguishability of Gcore^0 and $\text{Gcore}^1(\mathcal{S}^{core})$ will be established in Theorem 2 in Appendix 5.3 and contains the main technical argument of this article.

Lemma 3 (Main). *For all PPT adversaries $\mathcal{A}$ which make queries for at most d resumption levels,*

$$\text{Adv}(\mathcal{A}, \text{Gks}^{0Map}, \text{Gks}^{1Map})$$
$$=\text{Adv}(\mathcal{A} \to \mathcal{R}^{ch\text{-}map}, \text{Gcore}^0, \text{Gcore}^1(\mathcal{S}^{core})),$$

where [23, Fig. 25b] defines Gks^{0Map}, [23, Fig. 25c] defines Gks^{1Map}, $\mathcal{R}^{ch\text{-}map}$ and $\mathcal{S}^{core}$ are marked in grey in [23, Fig. 25c], and Fig. 15a and Fig. 15b define Gcore^0 and $\text{Gcore}^1(\mathcal{S}^{core})$, respectively.

Proof. The proof of Lemma 3 is an instance of Lemma 1 with $\text{G}^0_{\text{big}} = \text{Gks}^{0Map}$, $\text{G}^1_{\text{big}} = \text{Gks}^{1Map}$, $\text{G}^0_{\text{sml}} = \text{Gcore}^0$, $\text{G}^1_{\text{sml}} = \text{Gcore}^1(\mathcal{S}^{core})$ and $\mathcal{R} = \mathcal{R}^{ch\text{-}map}$.

By Lemma 1, it suffices to show that

$$\text{Gks}^{0Map} \overset{code}{\equiv} \mathcal{R}^{ch\text{-}map} \to \text{Gcore}^0 \tag{5}$$

$$\text{Gks}^{1Map} \overset{code}{\equiv} \mathcal{R}^{ch\text{-}map} \to \text{Gcore}^1(\mathcal{S}^{core}) \tag{6}$$

Equation 5 follows by definition, since [23, Fig. 25b] defines Gks^{0Map} as the composition of $\mathcal{R}^{ch\text{-}map}$ and Gcore^0. Similarly, for Eq. 6, [23, Fig. 25c]

In Lemma 4, we inline the $\text{Xpd}_{n,0..d}$ code into Map for $n \in O^*$ and call the result Map-Xpd (see [23, Fig. 25c] and [23, Fig. 26a] for the two games). The proof is a simple inlining argument and included into the full version [23] for completeness.

Lemma 4 (Xpd-Inlining). *For all PPT adversaries $\mathcal{A}$ which make queries for at most d resumption levels,*

$$\Pr\left[1 = \mathcal{A} \to \text{Gks}^{1Map}\right] = \Pr\left[1 = \mathcal{A} \to \text{Gks}^{Mapxpd}\right].$$

In particular $\text{Gks}^{1Map} \overset{code}{\equiv} \text{Gks}^{Mapxpd}$.

Finally, Lemma 5 establishes the (perfect) indistinguishability of $\mathsf{Gks}^{\mathsf{Map\text{-}Xpd}}$ and $\mathsf{Gks}^1(\mathcal{S})$. The proof of Lemma 5, essentially, removes or rather *inverts* the mapping on the output keys in order to recover the ideal functionality. Inverting the handle mapping, however, requires that it is *injective*. Conceptually, it is also clear that injectivity of the handle mapping needs to play a role in the proof: We prove uniqueness of output keys which means that equal keys imply equal handles. The injectivity proof ensures that the mapping did not introduce additional collisions and that the proof of Theorem 2 indeed suffices to establish the uniqueness of output keys in $\mathsf{Gks}^1(\mathcal{S})$.

Lemma 5 (Map-Outro). *For all PPT adversaries $\mathcal{A}$ which make queries for at most d resumption levels,*

$$\Pr\left[1 = \mathcal{A} \to \mathsf{Gks}^{Mapxpd}\right] = \Pr\left[1 = \mathcal{A} \to \mathsf{Gks}^1(\mathcal{S})\right].$$

In particular, $\mathsf{Gks}^{Mapxpd} \stackrel{func}{\equiv} \mathsf{Gks}^1(\mathcal{S})$.

In summary, Lemma 3 is the core argument, Lemma 2 is proven via a mechanical invariant proof, Lemma 5 is proven via a conceptually interesting invariant proof and Lemma 4 is a straightforward inlining argument.

Theorem 1 directly follows from Lemma 2–Lemma 5 and Theorem 2 (stated in Sect. 5.3).

$$\mathsf{Adv}(\mathcal{A}, \mathsf{Gks}^0, \mathsf{Gks}^1(\mathcal{S})) \stackrel{\mathrm{Lm.}\ 2}{=} \mathsf{Adv}(\mathcal{A}, \mathsf{Gks}^{0\mathrm{Map}}, \mathsf{Gks}^1(\mathcal{S}))$$

$$\stackrel{\mathrm{Lm.}\ 5}{=} \mathsf{Adv}(\mathcal{A}, \mathsf{Gks}^{0\mathrm{Map}}, \mathsf{Gks}^{\mathrm{Mapxpd}})$$

$$\stackrel{\mathrm{Lm.}\ 4}{=} \mathsf{Adv}(\mathcal{A}, \mathsf{Gks}^{0\mathrm{Map}}, \mathsf{Gks}^{1\mathrm{Map}})$$

$$\stackrel{\mathrm{Lm.}\ 3}{=} \mathsf{Adv}(\mathcal{A} \to \mathcal{R}^{\mathrm{ch\text{-}map}}, \mathsf{Gks}^{0\mathrm{core}}, \mathsf{Gks}^{1\mathrm{core}}(\mathcal{S}^{\mathrm{core}}))$$

$$\stackrel{\mathrm{Th.}\ 2}{\leq} \mathsf{Adv}(\mathcal{A} \to \mathcal{R}^{\mathrm{main}}_{\mathrm{cr}}, \mathsf{Gacr}^{\mathrm{hash},b})$$

$$+ \sum_{j \in \{Z,D\}, \mathsf{f} \in \{\mathsf{xtr}, \mathsf{xpd}\}} \mathsf{Adv}(\mathcal{A} \to \mathcal{R}^{\mathrm{main}}_{j,\mathsf{f}}, \mathsf{Gacr}^{\mathrm{hash},b})$$

$$+ \max_{i \in \{0,1\}} \mathsf{Adv}(\mathcal{A}_i \to \mathcal{R}^{\mathrm{main}}_{\mathrm{sodh}}, \mathsf{Gsodh}^b)$$

$$+ \mathsf{Adv}(\mathcal{A}_i \to \mathcal{R}^{\mathrm{main}}_{esalt,pi}, \mathsf{Gpi}^b_{esalt})$$

$$+ \mathsf{Adv}(\mathcal{A}_i \to \mathcal{R}^{\mathrm{main}}_{O^*,pi}, \mathsf{Gpi}^b_{O^*})$$

$$+ \sum_{\ell=0}^{d-1} \left(\mathsf{Adv}(\mathcal{A}_i \to \mathcal{R}^{\mathrm{main}}_{es,\ell}, \mathsf{Gxtr}^b_{es,\ell}) \right.$$

$$+ \mathsf{Adv}(\mathcal{A}_i \to \mathcal{R}^{\mathrm{main}}_{hs,\ell}, \mathsf{Gxtr}^b_{hs,\ell})$$

$$+ \mathsf{Adv}(\mathcal{A}_i \to \mathcal{R}^{\mathrm{main}}_{as}, \mathsf{Gxtr}^b_{as,\ell})$$

$$+ \sum_{n \in XPR} \left(\mathsf{Adv}(\mathcal{A}_i \to \mathcal{R}^{\mathrm{main}}_{n,\ell}, \mathsf{Gxpd}^b_{n,\ell}) \right) \bigg),$$

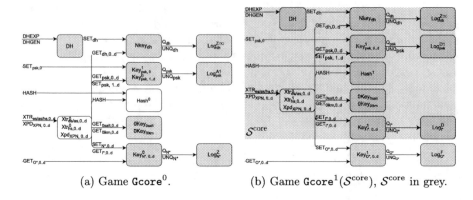

(a) Game Gcore^0.   (b) Game Gcore$^1(\mathcal{S}^{\mathrm{core}})$, $\mathcal{S}^{\mathrm{core}}$ in grey.

Fig. 15. Games for Theorem 2

where XPR is the representative set required by the theorem, $\mathcal{R}_*^{\mathrm{main}} :=$ $\mathcal{R}^{\mathrm{ch\text{-}map}} \to \mathcal{R}_*$ when replacing $*$ by cr, (Z,f), (D,f) sodh, es, hs, as, n, O^*, pi or $esalt$, pi.

5.3 Core Key Schedule Theorem

It remains to show that the *core* key schedule game Gcore^0 without the Map and Check package in front (Fig. 15a is indistinguishable from an ideal game Gcore$^1(\mathcal{S}^{\mathrm{core}})$ which consists of an ideal functionality with a simulator $\mathcal{S}^{\mathrm{core}}$ (Fig. 15b). The proof of Theorem 2 can be found in the full version [23, Appendix D]

Theorem 2 (Core). *Let ks be a TLS-like key schedule with XPR. Let d be an integer. Let $\mathcal{S}^{core}$ be the efficient simulator defined in [23, Fig. 26b]. Then, for all adversaries $\mathcal{A}$ which make queries for at most d resumption levels, we have that*

$$\mathsf{Adv}(\mathcal{A}, \mathtt{Gcore}^0, \mathtt{Gcore}^1(\mathcal{S}^{core}))$$

$$\leq \sum_{\mathcal{R} \in \{\mathcal{R}_{cr}, \mathcal{R}_Z, \mathcal{R}_D\}} \mathsf{Adv}(\mathcal{A} \to \mathcal{R}, \mathtt{Gacr}^b)$$

$$+ \max_{i \in \{0,1\}} \mathsf{Adv}(\mathcal{A}_i \to \mathcal{R}_{sodh}, \mathtt{Gsodh}^b)$$

$$+ \mathsf{Adv}(\mathcal{A}_i \to \mathcal{R}_{esalt,pi}, \mathtt{Gpi}^b_{esalt})$$

$$+ \mathsf{Adv}(\mathcal{A}_i \to \mathcal{R}_{O^*,pi}, \mathtt{Gpi}^b_{O^*})$$

$$+ \sum_{\ell=0}^{d-1} \Big(\mathsf{Adv}(\mathcal{A}_i \to \mathcal{R}_{es,\ell}, \mathtt{Gxtr}^b_{es,\ell})$$

$$+ \mathsf{Adv}(\mathcal{A}_i \to \mathcal{R}_{hs,\ell}, \mathtt{Gxtr}^b_{hs,\ell})$$

$$+ \mathsf{Adv}(\mathcal{A}_i \to \mathcal{R}_{as,\ell}, \mathtt{Gxtr}^b_{as,\ell})$$

$$+ \sum_{n \in XPR} \big(\mathsf{Adv}(\mathcal{A}_i \to \mathcal{R}_{n,\ell}, \mathtt{Gxpd}^b_{n,\ell}) \big) \Big),$$

where XPR is the required representation set (cf. Table 1), Fig. 15a defines $\mathtt{Gcore}^0$ *and Fig. 15b defines* $\mathtt{Gcore}^1(\mathcal{S}^{core})$, *[23, Fig. 31a] defines* $\mathcal{R}_{cr}^{\rightarrow}$, *[23, Fig. 32a] defines* $\mathcal{R}_{sodh}$, *[23, Fig. 34a] defines* $\mathcal{R}_{es,\ell}$, $\mathcal{R}_{hs,\ell}$ *and* $\mathcal{R}_{as,\ell}$ *are defined analogously, and* $\mathcal{R}_{n,\ell}$ *for* $n \in XPR$ *and* $0 \leq \ell \leq d$ *is defined in [23, Fig. 34b],* $\mathcal{R}_{esalt,pi}$ *is defined in [23, Fig. 32c] and* $\mathcal{R}_{O^*,pi}$ *is defined in [23, Fig. 32d].*

6 Related Work

The following discussion focuses on attacker capabilities and security guarantees, and glosses over the exact encoding into security games and the use of multiple keys and stages.

Dowling et al. [34–36] present a multi-stage security model of draft-05, draft-10, and the final version of the standard. Their multi-stage model considers psk_ke, dh_ke, and psk_dhe_ke modes in isolation. Li et al. [48] adapt the multi-stage security model to also capture the recursive nature of the TLS 1.3 key schedule, by accounting for the re-use of resumption secrets between different modes (psk_ke, psk_dhe_ke, and the now removed semi-static share 0-RTT).

Cremers et al. [29,30] investigate the security of draft-10 and draft-21, using the automated Tamarin prover (in the symbolic model). Their work investigates the proposed post-handshake client authentication and finds an attack that exploited a missing binding between PSKs and transcripts that led to the addition of binders to the standard. To our knowledge ours is the first reduction proof that models the additional security afforded by binder values.

Bhargavan et al. [10] also model TLS 1.3, decomposed into 3 separate pieces: dh_ke 1-RTT handshake, the 0-RTT handshake, and the record protocol. They verify these models using both ProVerif [18] and CryptoVerif [16]. A limitation of their model is the informal way in which the separate guarantees for the three components are combined to justify the overall security of the protocol.

Blanchet [17] introduces a new proof modularization framework in CryptoVerif, which bears significant similarities with the state-separating proof framework [24] that our work is based on. The work also updates some of the model from draft-18 to draft-28; however, the model still assumes that all pre-shared keys are derived from resumption secrets and does not capture adaptively-created dishonest application PSKs, or the security of PSK binders.

Many other works focus on analysing certain properties of the TLS 1.3 handshake protocol. For instance, Arfaou et al. [4] specifically analyse the privacy of the TLS 1.3 psk_ke, dh_ke, and psk_dhe_ke handshakes. Fischlin et. al. [41] analyse the draft-06 TLS 1.3 handshake, and show that its modes achieve key confirmation in isolation. Fischlin et. al. [39] considers replay attacks against various drafts of TLS 1.3 0-RTT handshakes such as draft-14's psk_ke mode, similarly considering versions and modes in isolation. Other relevant papers on TLS handshake analysis are [27,37,46].

The idea of analyzing a key schedule (rather than a key exchange protocol) is conceptually similar to the SIGMA-I pattern of Krawczyk [44] and Krawczyk and Wee [47]. These works prove a reduction from key exchange security to key schedule security analogously to our companion paper [25].

Recent work also looked at the tightness of TLS 1.3 security proofs [31,33]. Besides natural birthday bounds for collision resistance, our reductions avoid the common quadratic loss in the number of sessions. We remark however, that tightness was not the principal focus of our analysis.

Subsequent work to the present article [22] uses our methodology, e.g., our recursive handle structure and the style of encoding security guarantees in Log packages to analyse the key schedule security of the Messaging Layer Security (MLS) protocol whose conclusions were integrated into the IETF standard, e.g., [28]. In the present paper, in addition to key techniques which were picked up by [22], we introduce a plethora of techniques to tackle *indirect* domain separation by late hashing of Diffie-Hellman shares and binders such as the notion of separation points and the Check component introduced in Sect. 4.3. In a similar way, the additional mapping step (Lemma 2, 4 and 5) handle redundancy not present in MLS. See Sect. 7 for simplifications of the TLS protocol which would allow for a much simpler analysis than the one presented in this article.

7   Lessons Learned and Afterthoughts on the Key Schedule

We now discuss changes to the key schedule that would improve its security and simplify its analysis and may be of independent interest for other protocols.

Simplify SODH. The salted Diffie-Hellman computation extracts entropy from the DH secret and mixes it with the PSK-derived salt (which is under adversarial influence). A separate DH extraction, preferably hashing the (sorted) public shares together with the secret, followed by a dual PRF, would enable a proof based on the simpler and better understood Oracle Diffie-Hellman assumption. The hashing of shares would also remove the need to map DH secrets (currently computable from multiple pairs of shares), and would enable the use of a more abstract functionality such as a CCA-secure KEM (as in TLS 1.2 [14]). These changes would thus also ease the integration of post-quantum secure primitives.

Eliminate PSK Mapping. Similarly, *directly* applying domain-separation for computations based on application and resumption PSKs via distinct labels would remove the need to map PSKs and argue via inclusion of binders at separation points indirectly. Both proposals follow the same design pattern: first sanitize input key materials to prevent malleability (DH secrets) and collisions (dishonest resumption PSKs and adversarially-chosen application PSKs).

Avoid Agile Assumptions. Our development supports multiple hash algorithms without requiring any hash-agile assumptions, by observing that the hash functions currently used by TLS 1.3 have pairwise-distinct digest lengths. This is brittle, e.g. adding support for SHA3 with the same lengths as SHA2 would require to formally account for cross-algorithm collisions. This may be prevented by tagging the outputs of all extractors and KDFs with hash algorithms. Similarly, we may avoid the current need for agile (S)ODH assumptions by tagging group elements with both a group descriptor and a single extraction algorithm.

Prevent PSK Reflections. Drucker and Gueron note that TLS 1.3 is subject to reflection attacks due to its symmetric use of PSKs [37]. Hence, in our model, the same PSK handle may either be used by two parties, as intended, or by the same party acting both as a client and as a server. This is a security risk, inasmuch as applications may embed identity information in PSK identifiers to benefit from their early authentication. It may also enable key synchronization attacks and other variants of key compromise impersonation [13] when identities are also symmetrical. When using PSKs, the standard unfortunately forbids certificate-based authentication, which would otherwise provide more detailed, role-specific identity information. At the key schedule level, it may be possible to enforce better separation by tagging PSK identifiers with roles.

Enforce Stronger Modularity. Applied cryptographers often complain that, in TLS 1.2, the subtle interleaving of the handshake with the record layer hinders its analysis based on the well-established Bellare-Rogaway [8] security model [43]. While TLS 1.3 tries to enforce cleaner separation between handshake and record keys, it still fails in some important places. Notably, the handshake traffic secrets, meant to be released to the record layer (be it TLS, DTLS, or QUIC) are also used by the handshake to derive finished keys. Similarly, some handshake messages are encrypted under keys derived from application traffic secrets (e.g. New Session Ticket, carrying resumption PSKs, late client authentication, and key updates). This complicates the modeling of data stream security, as application data may be interleaved with handshake messages (e.g. the same QUIC packet may contain both data and session tickets). To prevent such issues, and many others, we suggest the RFC documents more explicitly its application interface and, in particular, recommends not to derive keys from keys released to the record layer.

References

1. Abdalla, M., Bellare, M., Rogaway, P.: The oracle diffie-hellman assumptions and an analysis of DHIES. In: Naccache, D. (ed.) CT-RSA 2001. LNCS, vol. 2020, pp. 143–158. Springer, Heidelberg (2001). https://doi.org/10.1007/3-540-45353-9_12
2. Adrian, D., et al.: Imperfect forward secrecy: how Diffie-Hellman fails in practice. In: ACM CCS 2015, pp. 5–17. ACM Press (2015). https://doi.org/10.1145/2810103.2813707
3. AlFardan, N.J., Paterson, K.G.: Lucky thirteen: breaking the TLS and DTLS record protocols. In: 2013 S&P, pp. 526–540. IEEE (2013). https://doi.org/10.1109/SP.2013.42
4. Arfaoui, G., Bultel, X., Fouque, P.A., Nedelcu, A., Onete, C.: The privacy of the TLS 1.3 protocol. PoPETs **2019**(4), 190–210 (2019). https://doi.org/10.2478/popets-2019-0065

5. Aviram, N., et al.: DROWN: breaking TLS using SSLv2. In: USENIX Security 2016, pp. 689–706. USENIX (2016)
6. Badertscher, C., Matt, C., Maurer, U., Rogaway, P., Tackmann, B.: Augmented secure channels and the goal of the TLS 1.3 record layer. In: Au, M.-H., Miyaji, A. (eds.) ProvSec 2015. LNCS, vol. 9451, pp. 85–104. Springer, Cham (2015). https://doi.org/10.1007/978-3-319-26059-4_5
7. Bellare, M.: New proofs for NMAC and HMAC: security without collision resistance. J. Cryptol. **28**(4), 844–878 (2014). https://doi.org/10.1007/s00145-014-9185-x
8. Bellare, M., Rogaway, P.: Entity authentication and key distribution. In: Stinson, D.R. (ed.) CRYPTO 1993. LNCS, vol. 773, pp. 232–249. Springer, Heidelberg (1994). https://doi.org/10.1007/3-540-48329-2_21
9. Beurdouche, B., et al.: A messy state of the union: taming the composite state machines of TLS. In: 2015 S&P, pp. 535–552. IEEE (2015). https://doi.org/10.1109/SP.2015.39
10. Bhargavan, K., Blanchet, B., Kobeissi, N.: Verified models and reference implementations for the TLS 1.3 standard candidate. In: 2017 S&P, pp. 483–502. IEEE (2017). https://doi.org/10.1109/SP.2017.26
11. Bhargavan, K., Brzuska, C., Fournet, C., Green, M., Kohlweiss, M., Zanella-Béguelin, S.: Downgrade resilience in key-exchange protocols. In: 2016 S&P, pp. 506–525. IEEE (2016). https://doi.org/10.1109/SP.2016.37
12. Bhargavan, K., Delignat-Lavaud, A., Fournet, C., Pironti, A., Strub, P.Y.: Triple handshakes and cookie cutters: Breaking and fixing authentication over tls. In: IEEE Symposium on Security & Privacy (Oakland) (2014). `pubs/triple-handshakes-and-cookie-cutters-sp14.pdf`
13. Bhargavan, K., Delignat-Lavaud, A., Pironti, A.: Verified contributive channel bindings for compound authentication. In: NDSS 2015. ISOC (2015)
14. Bhargavan, K., Fournet, C., Kohlweiss, M., Pironti, A., Strub, P.-Y., Zanella-Béguelin, S.: Proving the TLS handshake secure (as it is). In: Garay, J.A., Gennaro, R. (eds.) CRYPTO 2014. LNCS, vol. 8617, pp. 235–255. Springer, Heidelberg (2014). https://doi.org/10.1007/978-3-662-44381-1_14
15. Bhargavan, K., Leurent, G.: Transcript collision attacks: breaking authentication in TLS, IKE and SSH. In: NDSS 2016. ISOC (2016)
16. Blanchet, B.: CryptoVerif: computationally sound mechanized prover for cryptographic protocols. In: Formal Protocol Verification, vol. 117, p. 156 (2007)
17. Blanchet, B.: Composition theorems for CryptoVerif and application to TLS 1.3. In: CSF, pp. 16–30 (2018). https://doi.org/10.1109/CSF.2018.00009
18. Blanchet, B., Smyth, B., Cheval, V., Sylvestre, M.: ProVerif 2.00: automatic cryptographic protocol verifier. User Manual (2018)
19. Böck, H., Somorovsky, J., Young, C.: Return of bleichenbacher's oracle threat (ROBOT). In: USENIX Security 2018, pp. 817–849. USENIX (2018)
20. Brendel, J., Fischlin, M., Günther, F., Janson, C.: PRF-ODH: relations, instantiations, and impossibility results. In: Katz, J., Shacham, H. (eds.) CRYPTO 2017. LNCS, vol. 10403, pp. 651–681. Springer, Cham (2017). https://doi.org/10.1007/978-3-319-63697-9_22
21. Bricout, R., Murphy, S., Paterson, K.G., van der Merwe, T.: Analysing and exploiting the mantin biases in RC4. Cryptology ePrint Archive, Report 2016/063 (2016). http://eprint.iacr.org/2016/063
22. Brzuska, C., Cornelissen, E., Kohbrok, K.: Security analysis of the mls key derivation. In: 2022 IEEE Symposium on Security and Privacy, pp. 595–613. IEEE Computer Society, Los Alamitos (2022). https://doi.org/10.1109/SP46214.2022.00035

23. Brzuska, C., Delignat-Lavaud, A., Egger, C., Fournet, C., Kohbrok, K., Kohlweiss, M.: Key-schedule security for the TLS 1.3 standard. Cryptology ePrint Archive, Report 2021/467 (2021). https://eprint.iacr.org/2021/467
24. Brzuska, C., Delignat-Lavaud, A., Fournet, C., Kohbrok, K., Kohlweiss, M.: State separation for code-based game-playing proofs. In: ASIACRYPT 2018, Part III. LNCS, vol. 11274, pp. 222–249. Springer, Heidelberg (Dec 2018). https://doi.org/10.1007/978-3-030-03332-3_9
25. Brzuska, C., Egger, C.: Key exchange to key schedule reduction for TLS 1.3 (2022). preprint
26. Canetti, R., Krawczyk, H.: Universally composable notions of key exchange and secure channels. In: Knudsen, L.R. (ed.) EUROCRYPT 2002. LNCS, vol. 2332, pp. 337–351. Springer, Heidelberg (2002). https://doi.org/10.1007/3-540-46035-7_22
27. Chen, S., Jero, S., Jagielski, M., Boldyreva, A., Nita-Rotaru, C.: Secure communication channel establishment: TLS 1.3 (over TCP Fast Open) vs. QUIC. In: Sako, K., Schneider, S., Ryan, P.Y.A. (eds.) ESORICS 2019. LNCS, vol. 11735, pp. 404–426. Springer, Cham (2019). https://doi.org/10.1007/978-3-030-29959-0_20
28. Cornelissen, E.: Pull request 453: Use the GroupContext to derive the joiner_secret. https://github.com/mlswg/mls-protocol/pull/453
29. Cremers, C., Horvat, M., Hoyland, J., Scott, S., van der Merwe, T.: A comprehensive symbolic analysis of TLS 1.3. In: ACM CCS 2017, pp. 1773–1788. ACM Press (2017)
30. Cremers, C., Horvat, M., Scott, S., van der Merwe, T.: Automated analysis and verification of TLS 1.3: 0-RTT, resumption and delayed authentication. In: 2016 S&P, pp. 470–485. IEEE (2016). https://doi.org/10.1109/SP.2016.35
31. Davis, H., Günther, F.: Tighter proofs for the SIGMA and TLS 1.3 key exchange protocols. In: Sako, K., Tippenhauer, N.O. (eds.) ACNS 2021. LNCS, vol. 12727, pp. 448–479. Springer, Cham (2021). https://doi.org/10.1007/978-3-030-78375-4_18
32. Delignat-Lavaud, A., et al.: Implementing and proving the TLS 1.3 record layer. In: IEEE Security & Privacy. IEEE (2017)
33. Diemert, D., Jager, T.: On the tight security of TLS 1.3: theoretically sound cryptographic parameters for real-world deployments. J. Cryptol. **34**(3), 1–57 (2021). https://doi.org/10.1007/s00145-021-09388-x
34. Dowling, B., Fischlin, M., Günther, F., Stebila, D.: A cryptographic analysis of the TLS 1.3 handshake protocol candidates. In: ACM CCS 2015, pp. 1197–1210. ACM Press (2015). https://doi.org/10.1145/2810103.2813653
35. Dowling, B., Fischlin, M., Günther, F., Stebila, D.: A cryptographic analysis of the TLS 1.3 draft-10 full and pre-shared key handshake protocol. Cryptology ePrint Archive, Report 2016/081 (2016). http://eprint.iacr.org/2016/081
36. Dowling, B., Fischlin, M., Günther, F., Stebila, D.: A cryptographic analysis of the TLS 1.3 handshake protocol. J. Cryptol. **34**(4), 1–69 (2021). https://doi.org/10.1007/s00145-021-09384-1
37. Drucker, N., Gueron, S.: Selfie: reflections on TLS 1.3 with PSK. J. Cryptol. **34**(3), 1–18 (2021). https://doi.org/10.1007/s00145-021-09387-y
38. Duong, T., Rizzo, J.: Here come the ⊕ ninjas (2011). http://nerdoholic.org/uploads/dergln/beast_part2/ssl_jun21.pdf
39. Fischlin, M., Günther, F.: Replay attacks on zero round-trip time: the case of the TLS 1.3 handshake candidates. In: 2017 IEEE European Symposium on Security and Privacy (EuroS&P), pp. 60–75. IEEE (2017)

40. Fischlin, M., Günther, F., Marson, G.A., Paterson, K.G.: Data is a stream: security of stream-based channels. In: Gennaro, R., Robshaw, M. (eds.) CRYPTO 2015. LNCS, vol. 9216, pp. 545–564. Springer, Heidelberg (2015). https://doi.org/10.1007/978-3-662-48000-7_27

41. Fischlin, M., Günther, F., Schmidt, B., Warinschi, B.: Key confirmation in key exchange: a formal treatment and implications for TLS 1.3. In: 2016 S&P, pp. 452–469. IEEE (2016). https://doi.org/10.1109/SP.2016.34

42. Iyengar, J., Thomson, M.: QUIC. IETF draft (2019)

43. Jager, T., Kohlar, F., Schäge, S., Schwenk, J.: Authenticated confidential channel establishment and the security of TLS-DHE. J. Cryptol. 30(4), 1276–1324 (2017). https://doi.org/10.1007/s00145-016-9248-2

44. Krawczyk, H.: SIGMA: the "SIGn-and-MAc" approach to authenticated diffie-hellman and its use in the IKE protocols. In: Boneh, D. (ed.) CRYPTO 2003. LNCS, vol. 2729, pp. 400–425. Springer, Heidelberg (2003). https://doi.org/10.1007/978-3-540-45146-4_24

45. Krawczyk, H.: Cryptographic extraction and key derivation: the HKDF scheme. In: Rabin, T. (ed.) CRYPTO 2010. LNCS, vol. 6223, pp. 631–648. Springer, Heidelberg (2010). https://doi.org/10.1007/978-3-642-14623-7_34

46. Krawczyk, H.: A unilateral-to-mutual authentication compiler for key exchange (with applications to client authentication in TLS 1.3). In: ACM CCS 2016, pp. 1438–1450. ACM Press (2016). https://doi.org/10.1145/2976749.2978325

47. Krawczyk, H., Wee, H.: The OPTLS protocol and TLS 1.3. Cryptology ePrint Archive, Report 2015/978 (2015). http://eprint.iacr.org/2015/978

48. Li, X., Xu, J., Zhang, Z., Feng, D., Hu, H.: Multiple handshakes security of TLS 1.3 candidates. In: 2016 S&P, pp. 486–505. IEEE (2016). https://doi.org/10.1109/SP.2016.36

49. Mavrogiannopoulos, N., Vercauteren, F., Velichkov, V., Preneel, B.: A cross-protocol attack on the TLS protocol. In: ACM CCS 2012, pp. 62–72. ACM Press (2012). https://doi.org/10.1145/2382196.2382206

50. Möller, B., Duong, T., Kotowicz, K.: This poodle bites: exploiting the SSL 3.0 fallback (2014). https://www.openssl.org/~bodo/ssl-poodle.pdf

51. Paterson, K.G., van der Merwe, T.: Reactive and proactive standardisation of TLS. In: Security Standardisation Research, pp. 160–186 (2016)

52. Patton, C., Shrimpton, T.: Partially specified channels: the TLS 1.3 record layer without elision. Cryptology ePrint Archive, Report 2018/634 (2018)

53. Rescorla, E.: The Transport Layer Security (TLS) Protocol Version 1.3 (2018). https://tools.ietf.org/html/rfc8446

YOLO YOSO: Fast and Simple Encryption and Secret Sharing in the YOSO Model

Ignacio Cascudo[1(✉)] ⓘ, Bernardo David[2], Lydia Garms[1,3], and Anders Konring[2]

[1] IMDEA Software Institute, Madrid, Spain
ignacio.cascudo@imdea.org
[2] IT University of Copenhagen, Copenhagen, Denmark
bernardo@bmdavid.com, konr@itu.dk
[3] Keyless Technologies Limited, London, UK
lydia.garms@keyless.io

Abstract. Achieving adaptive (or proactive) security in cryptographic protocols is notoriously difficult due to the adversary's power to dynamically corrupt parties as the execution progresses. Inspired by the work of Benhamouda *et al.* in TCC 2020, Gentry *et al.* in CRYPTO 2021 introduced the YOSO (You Only Speak Once) model for constructing adaptively (or proactively) secure protocols in massively distributed settings (*e.g.* blockchains). In this model, instead of having all parties execute an entire protocol, smaller *anonymous committees* are randomly chosen to execute each individual round of the protocol. After playing their role, parties encrypt protocol messages towards the next anonymous committee and erase their internal state before publishing their ciphertexts. However, a big challenge remains in realizing YOSO protocols: *efficiently* encrypting messages towards anonymous parties selected at random without learning their identities, while proving the encrypted messages are valid with respect to the protocol. In particular, the protocols of Benhamouda *et al.* and of Gentry *et al.* require showing ciphertexts contain valid shares of secret states. We propose concretely efficient methods for encrypting a protocol's secret state towards a random anonymous committee. We start by proposing a very simple and efficient scheme for encrypting messages towards randomly and anonymously selected parties. We then show constructions of publicly

I. Cascudo—Supported by the Spanish Government under the project SecuRing (ref. PID2019-110873RJ-I00/MCIN/AEI/10.13039/501100011033), by the Madrid Government as part of the program S2018/TCS-4339 (BLOQUES-CM) co-funded by EIE Funds of the European Union, and by a research grant from Nomadic Labs and the Tezos Foundation.

B. David—Supported by the Concordium Foundation and by the Independent Research Fund Denmark (IRFD) grants number 9040-00399B (TrA^{2}C), 9131-00075B (PUMA) and 0165-00079B.

L. Garms—Supported by a research grant from Nomadic Labs and the Tezos Foundation.

A. Konring—Supported by the IRFD grant number 9040-00399B (TrA^{2}C).

S. Agrawal and D. Lin (Eds.): ASIACRYPT 2022, LNCS 13791, pp. 651–680, 2022.
https://doi.org/10.1007/978-3-031-22963-3_22

verifiable secret (re-)sharing (PVSS) schemes with concretely efficient proofs of (re-)share validity that can be generically instantiated from encryption schemes with certain linear homomorphic properties. In addition, we introduce a new PVSS with proof of sharing consisting of just two field elements, which as far as we know is the first achieving this, and may be of independent interest. Finally, we show that our PVSS schemes can be efficiently realized from our encryption scheme.

1   Introduction

Cryptographic protocols traditionally rely on secure channels among parties whose identities are publicly known. However, while knowing parties' identities makes it easy to construct secure channels, it also makes it easy for an adaptive (or mobile) adversary to corrupt parties as a protocol execution proceeds. Recently, an elegant solution for this problem has been suggested [1,12]: instead of keeping secret state throughout the execution, parties periodically transfer their state to randomly selected anonymous parties, potentially after computing on this state (as is the case of MPC).

YOSO Model: We say protocols with the aforementioned property are in the YOSO (*i.e.* You Only Speak Once) model, since parties are only required to act in a protocol execution when selected at random, which potentially only happens once. The YOSO model is especially interesting in massively distributed settings (*e.g.* blockchains), where a huge number of parties are potentially involved but it is desirable to have only smaller committees execute a protocol for the sake of efficiency. Using small committees saves computation and communication, and since the identity of parties in the committee currently holding secret states is not known, an adversary cannot do better than corrupt random parties. Recent work [17] improves the work of [12] by achieving guaranteed output delivery in a constant number of rounds without relying on trusted setup.

Role Assignment: At the core of protocols in the YOSO model is a scheme for encrypting messages towards *roles* rather than parties. A party randomly selected to perform a role can decrypt the messages sent to that role. This allows for executing traditional secret sharing [1] or MPC [12] protocols among roles that are performed by different parties as the execution proceeds. Besides passing confidential messages among parties assigned to certain roles, it is also paramount to allow parties to authenticate outgoing messages on behalf of the role they have just performed. This task has been modeled [12] and realized [1,14] as a functionality that outputs public keys for a random subset of anonymous parties in such a way that these parties can both decrypt messages encrypted under these keys and prove they were the rightful receivers. However, existing methods for role assignment [1,5,14] are still based on powerful primitives (*e.g.* FHE), incur too high costs and, most importantly, are incompatible with efficient techniques for publicly proving that encrypted secret shares are valid.

In this work we design schemes for role assignment that are not only efficient in sending messages to parties selected in the future but also amenable to the currently best techniques for publicly proving that encrypted messages are valid shares of a secret state, which is central to protocols in the YOSO model.

1.1 Related Works

Keeping Secrets: The seminal solution of [1] starts by selecting an auxiliary committee via an anonymous lottery (*e.g.* based on a VRF). Each party in this committee generates an ephemeral key pair and publishes the ephemeral public key and an encryption of the ephemeral secret key under the long-term public key of a party they choose at random. Encrypting towards an anonymous party can be done by encrypting under its ephemeral public key. However, since corrupted parties in the auxiliary committee will always choose other corrupted parties while the honest parties choose at random, this method needs a corruption ratio of $1/4$ of the parties in order to arrive at an honest majority committee.

RPIR: The constraint on corruption ratio of [1] was subsequently solved in [14] via random-index private information retrieval (RPIR). RPIR allows a client to retrieve a random index from a database in such a way that the servers holding the database do not learn what index was retrieved. The solution of [14] consists in running a RPIR protocol with a database holding the public keys of all parties and having parties in a committee execute the client using MPC, outputting re-randomized versions of the public keys output by RPIR. While this solution allows for working in an honest majority scenario and achieves better asymptotic efficiency than [1], the concrete complexity is still quite high.

Encryption to the Future: A different approach is taken in [5], which constructs a primitive called Encryption to the Future (ETF). Instead of having committees actively participate in selecting future committees and help them receive their messages, ETF allows for non-interactively encrypting towards the winner of a lottery that is executed as part of an underlying blockchain ledger. Also, it allows for a party to prove it was the winner of this lottery (*i.e.* the receiver of a ciphertext) without exposing whether it won future lotteries. Although this solution can be constructed from simple tools like garbled circuits and oblivious transfer (after a setup phase), each encryption still requires communication and computational complexities linear in the total number of parties.

The ETF construction of [5] relies on a relaxation of Witness Encryption called Witness Encryption over Commitments (cWE), where one can encrypt a message towards the holder of an opening of a commitment to a valid witness of an NP relation. More specifically, we are interested in the case of Encryption to the Current Winner (ECW), where the data needed to determine the party selected to perform a role is already in the underlying blockchain (but still does not reveal who the party is). In order to realize ECW, each party commits to a witness of a predicate showing they win a lottery for the current parameter. A party encrypting towards a role simply encrypts the message towards the party who has such a committed witness to winning the lottery for a current parameter. A party who wins can decrypt the message encrypted towards the role using their witness. They can perform *Authentication from the Past* (AfP) on a message by doing a signature of knowledge on that message using their lottery winning witness.

The ETF constructions of [5] suffer from a major drawback: every encryption towards an anonymously selected party has communication complexity $O(n\kappa)$ where n is the *total* number of parties and κ is the security parameter. Even if preprocessing is allowed, these constructions still require the sender to publish n cWE ciphertexts or to have the eligible receivers perform a round of anonymous broadcast that is only usable for a single encryption. On the other hand, the AfP constructions only have $O(\kappa)$ communication complexity.

PVSS Compatibility: A drawback in current role assignment [1,5,14] is that they are not amenable to publicly verifiable secret (re)sharing. Both in YOSO proactive secret sharing [1] and YOSO MPC [12], the committees executing each round of the protocol do not simply send unstructured messages but shares of a secret that must be verified. While this can be done via generic non-interactive zero knowledge proofs of encrypted shares validity, such a solution incurs very high computational and communication costs.

Publicly Verifiable Secret Sharing (PVSS): An integral part of YOSO protocols is having each committee perform PVSS towards the next committee. A PVSS scheme allows for any party to check that an encrypted share vector is valid. A number of PVSS constructions are known [2,11,16,20–22] that different techniques for proving that a vector of encrypted shares are valid shares of a given secret. Recently, the SCRAPE [6] and ALBATROSS [7] PVSS schemes have significantly improved on the complexity of such schemes by making the share validity check and reconstructions procedures cheaper than previous works. While these works are based on number theoretical assumptions, a recent work has shown how to efficiently build PVSS from lattice based assumptions [13]. These works are not fit for the YOSO model because they require the parties to know the identities (or rather the public keys) of the parties receiving the shares when checking share validity, precluding (re)sharing towards anonymous parties. A key part of this work is that we explore the fact that the share validity check of SCRAPE can be modified to work regardless of the public keys used to encrypt the shares.

1.2   Our Contributions

In this work we address the issue of constructing simple ECW schemes amenable to efficient publicly verifiable secret (re)sharing (PVSS) protocols. Our contributions are summarized as follows:

Simple Encryption to Future (ECW): We construct a simple ECW scheme based on a mixnet and an additively homomorphic public key encryption scheme. Our scheme requires a setup phase where a mixnet is used but this setup can be either done once and reused for multiple times (using our reusable AFP) or preprocessed so that future encryptions can be done non-interactively. Our ECW ciphertexts have size linear *only in the number of parties who open them*.

Reusable Private Authentication from the Past (AFP): We show how to reuse our ECW setup even when a party performs multiple rounds of AFP, *i.e.* proving that it was selected to decrypt a given ECW ciphertext. This scheme guarantees that the adversary cannot predict which parties can decrypt future ECW ciphertexts while keeping the setup constant size.

Generic Efficient PVSS: We construct a generic PVSS protocol with efficient proofs of encrypted shares validity from any IND-CPA additively homomorphic encryption scheme with an efficient proof of decryption correctness without any generic zero knowledge proofs, which we call HEPVSS. This general result sheds new light on the construction on efficient PVSS schemes.

New PVSS with Minimal Overhead: Moreover, we introduce a new PVSS construction named DHPVSS with *constant-size proof of sharing correctness* which, as far as we know, is the first PVSS to achieve this. More precisely, the PVSS communicates only the n encrypted shares (which are one group element each) and two field elements for the proof. This may be of independent interest for other applications, such as randomness beacons.

Efficient PVSS for Anonymous Committees based on ECW: We instantiate our PVSS constructions based on our ECW and AFP schemes along with a protocol for resharing a secret towards a future random anonymous committee. This allows for parties to keep a secret alive, which is a core component of YOSO MPC.

1.3   Our Techniques

In this section we highlight the main technical components of our contributions. We remark that our main goal is providing simple constructions that yield efficient instantiations of PVSS towards anonymous committees along with efficient AfP schemes allowing parties to prove they received shares sent to a given role.

Encryption to the Future. We introduce a simple ECW protocol where each party chooses a key pair in the system and then a mixnet is used to anonymize them. We can then define a simple lottery predicate that selects one of these keys. The winner of the lottery can trivially know that they have won this lottery. By combining this with an IND-CPA encryption scheme that encrypts a message under that key, we can obtain IND-CPA ECW. Using a homomorphic encryption scheme we can also encrypt to multiple lottery winners and prove that the same message is received by all of them.

Authentication from the Past

The Easy Way: An easy way of obtaining reusable ECW setup is to repeat the lottery setup and obtain multiple anonymized keys for each party. Then, any party can use a new anonymized public key for each AFP tag. This ensures that the AFP scheme can be executed a bounded number times before lottery winners can be linked to specific public keys in the setup and ciphertexts starts betraying their receivers.

The Reusable Way: In the full version of this paper [8], we show that a party can prove membership in a given committee without needing to reveal its role in this committee. This is done by signing a message with a ring signature [19] where the secret key corresponds to a public key in the committee. These signatures hide the identity of the party. Moreover, we require the signature to be linkable [18], so that no two parties can claim the same secret key. Using this and an anonymous channel, we can construct an AfP that can be used multiple times without linking a party P_i to its setup public key. More interestingly, we also present a protocol that leverages the presence of a dealer (which could be a party that encrypted the message to that committee) to reduce the size of these proofs of membership to constant (for the parties making the claims). This uses Camenisch-Lysyanskaya signatures [4], where the dealer signs the public keys of the committee, and the parties can then "complete" one of these signatures without revealing which one. We introduce a simple linkable version of these signatures.

PVSS. We introduce two constructions for PVSS. The first, HEPVSS, is based on a generic encryption scheme which enjoys certain linearity properties with respect to encryption and decryption, and has the advantage that the security of the PVSS can be based on IND-CPA security of the scheme. The homomorphic properties of the scheme allow for simple proofs of sharing correctness and reconstruction. While we are only aware of El Gamal scheme satisfying the notion of the homomorphic properties we need, we hope that a relaxed version of this abstraction allows to capture other encryption schemes with homomorphic properties such as latticed-based assumptions or Paillier in future work. In our second scheme DHPVSS, we introduce the idea of providing the dealer with an additional key pair for share distribution. This idea is powerful in combination with a technique used in SCRAPE to prove that encrypted shares lie on a polynomial of the right degree. The novelty is that, while in SCRAPE this needed an additional discrete logarithm equality (DLEQ) proof *for each share*, our new scheme requires *a single DLEQ proof*. This reduces the sharing correctness proof to only two $\mathbb{Z}_p$-elements while each encrypted shares is still one group element.

We also introduce PVSS resharing protocols for both constructions, where a committee, among which a secret is PVSSed, can create shares of the same secret for the next committee, in a publicly verifiable way.

PVSS Towards Anonymous Committees. Finally, we show that we can replace standard encryption and authentication in our PVSS protocols by ECW and AFP and thereby obtain PVSS toward anonymous committees.

2   Preliminaries

2.1   Sigma-Protocols

At several points of this paper we will require non-interactive zero knowledge arguments of knowledge, where most of our statements are instances of a general structure where we want to prove knowledge of preimage of some element via a *vector-space homomorphism* f: that is, let $\mathbb{F}$ be a finite field, $\mathcal{W}$ and $\mathcal{X}$ be $\mathbb{F}$-vector spaces, and $f : \mathcal{W} \to \mathcal{X}$ be a vector space homomorphism. Let

$$R_{\mathsf{Pre}} = \{(w, x) \in \mathcal{W} \times \mathcal{X} : x = f(w)\}.$$

The standard (Schnorr-like) Σ-protocol Π_{Pre} for R_{Pre} is in Fig. 1. It is easy to see it is a zero knowledge proof of knowledge with soundness error $1/|\mathbb{F}|$.

Generic Σ-protocol $\Pi_{\mathsf{Pre}}(w; x, f)$

Proof of knowledge of witness w for x with respect to the relation $R_{\mathsf{Pre}} = \{(w, x) \in \mathcal{W} \times \mathcal{X} : x = f(w)\}$.
Public parameters: Finite field $\mathbb{F}$, vector spaces $\mathcal{W}, \mathcal{X}$ over $\mathbb{F}$, vector space homomorphism $f : \mathcal{W} \to \mathcal{X}$, $x \in \mathcal{X}$.
Protocol:
1. The prover samples $r \leftarrow_{\$} \mathcal{W}$, sends $a = f(r)$ to the verifier.
2. The verifier samples $e \leftarrow_{\$} \mathbb{F}$, sends it to the sender.
3. The prover sends $z \leftarrow r + e \cdot w$ to the verifier.
4. The verifier accepts if $z \in \mathcal{W}$ and $f(z) = a + e \cdot x$.

Fig. 1. Generic Σ-protocol for knowledge of homomorphism-preimage

A non-interactive zero-knowledge (NIZK) proof of knowledge in the random oracle model is obtained by applying the Fiat-Shamir transform (Fig. 2).

Generic non-interactive argument of knowledge $\Pi_{\mathsf{NI-Pre}}(w; x, f)$

Non-interactive argument of knowledge of witness for x for the relation $R_{\mathsf{Pre}} = \{(w, x) \in \mathcal{W} \times \mathcal{X} : x = f(w)\}$ in the random oracle model.
Public parameters: Finite field $\mathbb{F}$, vector spaces $\mathcal{W}, \mathcal{X}$ over $\mathbb{F}$, vector space homomorphism $f : \mathcal{W} \to \mathcal{X}$, $x \in \mathcal{X}$, random oracle $\mathcal{H} : \{0,1\}^* \to \mathbb{F}$. Let $pp = (\mathbb{F}, \mathcal{W}, \mathcal{X}, \mathcal{H})$.
$\Pi_{\mathsf{NI-Pre}}.\mathsf{Prove}(w; pp, x, f)$:
    $r \leftarrow_{\$} \mathcal{W}$, $a \leftarrow f(r)$, $e \leftarrow \mathcal{H}(x, a)$, $z \leftarrow r + e \cdot w$, **return** $\pi \leftarrow (e, z)$
$\Pi_{\mathsf{NI-Pre}}.\mathsf{Verify}(pp, x, f, \pi)$:
    Parse $\pi = (e, z)$ and **return accept** if and only if $z \in \mathcal{W}$ and $e = \mathcal{H}(x, f(z) - e \cdot x)$.

Fig. 2. Generic non-interactive argument of knowledge of homomorphism-preimage

Cyclic Group Homomorphism Preimage, DL Knowledge and DLEQ Knowledge Proofs. Some useful examples of homomorphism-preimage relations R_{Pre} are given by discrete logarithm and discrete logarithm equality. Indeed, a cyclic group $\mathbb{G}$ of prime order p has a vector space structure over the field $\mathbb{Z}_p$, and a group homomorphism $f : \mathbb{G} \to \mathbb{G}'$ between groups of order p is also a $\mathbb{Z}_p$-vector homomorphism.[1] Let G be a generator of $\mathbb{G}$. Given $X \in \mathbb{G}$, a discrete logarithm DL proof of knowledge $\mathsf{DL}(w; G, X)$ asserts knowledge of $w \in \mathbb{Z}_p$ with $X = w \cdot G$ (we denote this as $w = \mathsf{DL}_G(X)$). In the language above this is provided by $\Pi_{\mathsf{NI-Pre}}(w; (X), f_G)$ with $f_G(w) = w \cdot G$. This is the non-interactive version of the well known Schnorr proof.

Similarly, let G, H be elements in $\mathbb{G}$. Given $X, Y \in \mathbb{G}$ the discrete logarithm equality proof $\mathsf{DLEQ}(w; G, X, H, Y)$ is a non-interactive proof of knowledge of $w \in \mathbb{Z}_p$ with $w = \mathsf{DL}_G(X) = \mathsf{DL}_H(Y)$, which can be obtained by using $\Pi_{\mathsf{NI-Pre}}(w; (X, Y), f_{(G,H)})$, where $f_{G,H}(w) := (w \cdot G, w \cdot H)$.

2.2 $\mathbb{Z}_p$-linear Homomorphic Encryption

The results in this paper require encryption schemes with certain homomorphic properties, that allow for simple proofs of plaintext knowledge. These properties are attained by El Gamal encryption scheme.

Definition 1 ($\mathbb{Z}_p$-linearly homomorphic encryption scheme). *Let $\mathcal{E} = (\mathcal{E}.\mathsf{Gen}, \mathcal{E}.\mathsf{Enc}, \mathcal{E}.\mathsf{Dec})$ be a public key encryption scheme, and let p be a prime number. We say $\mathcal{E}$ is $\mathbb{Z}_p$-linearly homomorphic ($\mathbb{Z}_p$-LHE) if the plaintext space $(\mathfrak{P}, \boxplus_{\mathfrak{P}})$, randomness space $(\mathfrak{R}, \boxplus_{\mathfrak{R}})$, ciphertext space $(\mathfrak{C}, \boxplus_{\mathfrak{C}})$ each have a $\mathbb{Z}_p$-vector space structure and for all public keys pk output by $\mathcal{E}.\mathsf{Gen}$, $\mathcal{E}.\mathsf{Enc}_{\mathsf{pk}} : \mathfrak{P} \times \mathfrak{R} \to \mathfrak{C}$ is a $\mathbb{Z}_p$-vector space homomorphism, i.e. for all $m_1, m_2 \in \mathfrak{C}$, $\rho_1, \rho_2 \in \mathfrak{R}$,*

$$\mathcal{E}.\mathsf{Enc}_{\mathsf{pk}}(m_1; \rho_1) \boxplus_{\mathfrak{C}} \mathcal{E}.\mathsf{Enc}_{\mathsf{pk}}(m_2; \rho_2) = \mathcal{E}.\mathsf{Enc}_{\mathsf{pk}}(m_1 \boxplus_{\mathfrak{P}} m_2; \rho_1 \boxplus_{\mathfrak{R}} \rho_2).$$

Remark 1. $\mathbb{Z}_p$-linear homomorphic encryption schemes have simple NIZK of plaintext (and randomness) knowledge, implied by Fig. 2 by taking $\mathcal{W} = \mathfrak{P} \times \mathfrak{R}$, $\mathcal{X} = \mathfrak{C}$ and the proof $\Pi_{\mathsf{NI-Pre}}((m, \rho); c, \mathcal{E}.\mathsf{Enc}_{\mathsf{pk}})$ for the relation $R_{\mathsf{Enc}} = \{((m, \rho), c) \in \mathcal{W} \times \mathcal{X} : c = \mathcal{E}.\mathsf{Enc}_{\mathsf{pk}}(m; \rho)\}$.

Proofs of Decryption Correctness. We also need proofs of decryption correctness which keep the secret key hidden, i.e. NIZK proofs for the relation

$$R_{\mathcal{E}, \mathsf{Dec}} = \{(\mathsf{sk}; (\mathsf{pk}, m, c)) : (\mathsf{pk}, \mathsf{sk}) \text{ is a valid key-pair for } \mathcal{E} \text{ and } m = \mathcal{E}.\mathsf{Dec}_{\mathsf{sk}}(c)\}.$$

If the prover knows the randomness under which the message was encrypted, the proving algorithm $\mathcal{E}.\mathsf{ProveDec}(\mathsf{sk}; (\mathsf{pk}, m, c))$ can simply output that randomness $\pi \in \mathfrak{R}$; the verification $\mathcal{E}.\mathsf{VerifyDec}(\mathsf{pk}, m, c, \pi)$ accepts if $\mathsf{Enc}_{\mathsf{pk}}(m; \pi) = c$.

Unfortunately El Gamal encryption scheme does not allow a decryptor to retrieve the randomness under which a message has been encrypted. Instead, a proof of correctness of decryption for El Gamal can be constructed from the following property of this scheme, which we call $\mathbb{Z}_p$-linear decryption.

---

[1] This extends to direct products of groups of order p, i.e. $\mathcal{W} = \mathbb{G}_1 \times \cdots \times \mathbb{G}_m$, $\mathcal{X} = \mathbb{G}'_1 \times \cdots \times \mathbb{G}'_n$ and $f = (f_1, \ldots, f_m) : \mathcal{W} \to \mathcal{X}$ where $f_i : \mathbb{G}_i \to \mathcal{X}$ are all group homomorphisms.

Definition 2. *Let $\mathcal{E} = (\mathsf{Gen}, \mathsf{Enc}, \mathsf{Dec})$ be a $\mathbb{Z}_p$-linearly homomorphic encryption scheme and denote $\mathcal{PK}$ and $\mathcal{SK}$ the sets of public and secret keys respectively. $\mathcal{E}$ has $\mathbb{Z}_p$-linear decryption if:*

- *$\mathcal{PK}$ and $\mathcal{SK}$ are $\mathbb{Z}_p$-vector spaces.*
- *There exists a $\mathbb{Z}_p$-linear homomorphism $F : \mathcal{SK} \to \mathcal{PK}$ such that $\mathsf{pk} = F(\mathsf{sk})$ for all $(\mathsf{pk}, \mathsf{sk})$ outputted by Gen.*
- *For all $c \in \mathfrak{C}$, the function $D_c(\mathsf{sk}) := \mathsf{Dec}_{\mathsf{sk}}(c)$ is $\mathbb{Z}_p$-linear in sk, i.e. for all $\mathsf{sk}_1, \mathsf{sk}_2 \in \mathcal{SK}$, it holds that $D_c(\mathsf{sk}_1 \boxplus_{\mathcal{SK}} \mathsf{sk}_2) = D_c(\mathsf{sk}_1) \boxplus_{\mathfrak{P}} D_c(\mathsf{sk}_2)$.*

In this case we have the algorithms $(\mathcal{E}.\mathsf{ProveDec}, \mathcal{E}.\mathsf{VerifyDec})$ that constitute a NIZK proof for $R_{\mathcal{E},\mathsf{Dec}}$:

Algorithm 1. $\mathcal{E}.\mathsf{ProveDec}(\mathsf{sk}, (\mathsf{pk}, m, c))$	**Algorithm 2.** $\mathcal{E}.\mathsf{VerifyDec}(\mathsf{pk}, m, c, \pi)$
$\mathcal{W} \leftarrow \mathcal{SK}, \mathcal{X} \leftarrow \mathcal{PK} \times \mathfrak{P} \times \mathfrak{C},$	$\mathcal{W} \leftarrow \mathcal{SK}, \mathcal{X} \leftarrow \mathcal{PK} \times \mathfrak{P} \times \mathfrak{C}$
$pp \leftarrow (\mathbb{Z}_p, \mathcal{W}, \mathcal{X}, \mathcal{H})$	$pp \leftarrow (\mathbb{Z}_p, \mathcal{W}, \mathcal{X}, \mathcal{H})$
$w \leftarrow \mathsf{sk}, \ x \leftarrow (\mathsf{pk}, m), \ f(\cdot) \leftarrow (F(\cdot), D_c(\cdot))$	$x \leftarrow (\mathsf{pk}, m), f(\cdot) \leftarrow (F(\cdot), D_c(\cdot))$
return $\pi \leftarrow \Pi_{\mathsf{NI-Pre}}.\mathsf{Prove}(w; pp, x, f)$	**return** $\Pi_{\mathsf{NI-Pre}}.\mathsf{Verify}(pp, x, f)$

The El Gamal decryption function as usually described is not linear but affine, but we can easily fix this by e.g. defining $\mathsf{sk}^* = (\mathsf{sk}_1^*, \mathsf{sk}_2^*) = (1, \mathsf{sk}) \in \mathbb{Z}_p^2$ and letting $\mathsf{Dec}_{\mathsf{sk}^*}(C_1, C_2) := C_2 \cdot \mathsf{sk}_1^* - C_1 \cdot \mathsf{sk}_2^*$. Then $D_C(\mathsf{sk}^*)$ is clearly a $\mathbb{Z}_p$-linear function.

2.3   Shamir Secret Sharing on Groups of Order p

The well known degree-t Shamir scheme allows to split a secret $s \in \mathbb{Z}_p$ in n shares (where $0 \le t < n < p$) in such a way that any set of $t + 1$ shares give full information about the secret s while any set of t give no information on s.

Here we will consider situations where the secret is an element $S = sG$ of a group $\mathbb{G}$ of order p with generator G, but the dealer does not know s (and hence cannot apply the usual Shamir sharing using s as secret). On the other hand, it is enough that the shares allow to reconstruct S and not s. We define Shamir secret sharing in a group of order p as shown in Fig. 3. (Shamir secret sharing scheme over $\mathbb{Z}_p$ is retrieved by setting $\mathbb{G} = (\mathbb{Z}_p, +), G = 1$). We denote by $\mathbb{Z}_p[X]_{\le t}$ the set of polynomials in $\mathbb{Z}_p[X]$ of degree at most t.

2.4   The SCRAPE Test

In SCRAPE [6], a technique for checking correctness of Shamir sharing in publicly verifiable secret sharing was introduced. Letting aside the details on how the technique works there, we are interested in the following fact, which in turn comes from well known results in coding theory[2].

---

[2] Specifically from the fact that the dual of a Reed-Solomon code is a generalized Reed-Solomon code of a certain form.

Shamir secret sharing on a group $\mathbb{G}$ of order p

Public parameters: Let $pp = (\mathbb{G}, G, p, t, n, \{\alpha_i : i \in [0, n]\})$, where $\mathbb{G}$ is a group of prime order p with generator G, $0 \leq t < n < p$ are integers, and $\alpha_0, \alpha_1, \ldots, \alpha_n \in \mathbb{Z}_p$ are pairwise distinct.

GShamir.Share(pp, S), where pp as above, and $S \in \mathbb{G}$:

$\quad m(X) \leftarrow_\$ \{m(X) \in \mathbb{Z}_p[X]_{\leq t} : m(\alpha_0) = 0\}$

$\quad$ for $i \in [n]$, $A_i \leftarrow S + m(\alpha_i) \cdot G$

$\quad$ **return** $(A_1, \ldots, A_n)$

GShamir.Rec$(pp, I, (A_i)_{i \in I})$, where $I \subseteq [n], |I| = t+1$ and $(A_i)_{i \in I} \in \mathbb{G}^{t+1}$:

$\quad$ **return** $S' \leftarrow \sum_{i \in I} \lambda_{i,I} A_i$, where, for $i \in I$, $\lambda_{i,I} := \prod_{j \in I, j \neq i} \frac{\alpha_0 - \alpha_j}{\alpha_i - \alpha_j}$

Fig. 3. Shamir sharing on a group of order p

Theorem 1 (SCRAPE dual-code test). *Let $1 \leq t < n$ be integers. Let p be a prime number with $p \geq n$. Let $\alpha_1, \ldots, \alpha_n$ be pairwise different points in $\mathbb{Z}_p$. Define the coefficients $v_i = \prod_{j \in [n] \setminus \{i\}} (\alpha_i - \alpha_j)^{-1}$. Let*

$$C = \{(m(\alpha_1), \ldots, m(\alpha_n)) : \ m(X) \in \mathbb{Z}_p[X]_{\leq t}\}.$$

Then for every vector $(\sigma_1, \ldots, \sigma_n)$ in $\mathbb{Z}_p^n$,

$$(\sigma_1, \ldots, \sigma_n) \in C \quad \Leftrightarrow \quad \sum_{i=1}^n v_i \cdot m^*(\alpha_i) \cdot \sigma_i = 0, \quad \forall m^* \in \mathbb{Z}_p[X]_{\leq n-t-2}.$$

2.5 Mix Networks (Mixnets)

In this paper we use a mixnet to anonymize a set of public encryption keys, each generated (with their corresponding secret keys) by a party in the system. Let $\mathcal{P}$ be the set of all parties generating these keys. In the coming sections we will assume such a mixnet and that the output is subsequently be written to a blockchain. The output is a set of shuffled keys $\mathsf{pk}_{\mathsf{Anon},j} : j \in [n]$, for which each party knows the index that corresponds to their public key, but nothing else about the permutation. Denote this permutation $\psi : \mathcal{P} \to [n]$, i.e. party ID_i knows $j = \psi(i)$ and the corresponding key-pair.

We will use the fact that a party can encrypt a message under the public key $\mathsf{pk}_{\mathsf{Anon},j}$. It is clear that party $ID_{\psi^{-1}(j)}$ can decrypt the message, while the rest of the parties (even the sender) remain oblivious about the identity of the receiver. Notice that this setup can be instantiated via a verifiable mixnet (*e.g.* [3]).

2.6 Encryption to the Future

We use the model for Encryption to the Future (EtF) from [5], which defines this primitive with respect to a blockchain ledger that has an built-in lottery mechanism. Before presenting the definition of EtF and related concepts, we recall the model for blockchain ledgers from [15], which is used to state the definitions of [5] and that captures properties of natural Proof-of-Stake (PoS) based protocols such as [10]. We present a summary of the framework in the full version of the paper [8] and discuss below the main properties we will use in the EtF definitions.

Blockchain Structure. A genesis block $B_0 = (\mathsf{Sig.pk}_1, \mathsf{aux}_1, \mathsf{stake}_1), \ldots, \mathsf{Sig.pk}_n, \mathsf{aux}_n, \mathsf{stake}_n)$, aux associates each party P_i to a signature scheme public key $\mathsf{Sig.pk}_i$, an amount of stake stake_i and auxiliary information aux_i (*i.e.* any other relevant information required by the blockchain protocol). As in [10], we assume that the genesis block is generated by an initialization functionality $\mathcal{F}_{\mathsf{INIT}}$ that registers all parties' $\mathsf{Sig.pk}_i$, aux_i when the execution starts and assigns stake_i for P_i. Within the execution model of [15], $\mathcal{F}_{\mathsf{INIT}}$ is executed by the environment (as defined in the full version of the paper [8]). A blockchain $\mathbf{B}$ relative to a genesis block B_0 is a sequence of blocks $B_1, \ldots, B_n$ associated with a strictly increasing sequence of slots $\mathsf{sl}_1, \ldots, \mathsf{sl}_m$ such that $B_i = (\mathsf{sl}_j, H(B_{i-1}), \mathsf{d}, \mathsf{aux})$, where sl_j indicates the time slot that B_i occupies, $H(B_{i-1})$ is a collision resistant hash of the previous block, d is data and aux is auxiliary information required by the blockchain protocol (*e.g.* a proof that the block is valid for slot sl_j). We denote by $\mathbf{B}^{\lceil \ell}$ the chain (sequence of blocks) $\mathbf{B}$ where the last ℓ blocks have been removed and if $\ell \geq |\mathbf{B}|$ then $\mathbf{B}^{\lceil \ell} = \epsilon$. Also, if $\mathbf{B}_1$ is a prefix of $\mathbf{B}_2$ we write $\mathbf{B}_1 \preceq \mathbf{B}_2$. For the sake of simplicity, we identify each party P_i participating in the protocol by its public key $\mathsf{Sig.pk}_i$.

Evolving Blockchains. In an EtF scheme, the future is defined with respect to a future state of the underlying blockchain. In particular, we want to make sure that the initial chain $\mathbf{B}$ has "correctly" evolved into the final chain $\tilde{\mathbf{B}}$. Otherwise, the adversary can easily simulate a blockchain where it wins a future lottery and finds itself with the ability to decrypt. Fortunately, the *Distinguishable Forking* property from [15] allows us to distinguish a sufficiently long chain in an honest execution from a fork generated by the adversary by looking at the combined amount of stake proven in such a sequence of blocks. This property is used to construct a predicate called $\mathsf{evolved}(\cdot, \cdot)$. First, let $\Gamma^V = (\mathsf{UpdateState}^V, \mathsf{GetRecords}, \mathsf{Broadcast})$ be a blockchain protocol with validity predicate V and where the $(\alpha, \beta, \ell_1, \ell_2)$-*distinguishable forking* property holds. And let $\mathbf{B} \leftarrow \mathsf{GetRecords}(1^\lambda, \mathsf{st})$ and $\tilde{\mathbf{B}} \leftarrow \mathsf{GetRecords}(1^\lambda, \tilde{\mathsf{st}})$.

Definition 3 (Evolved Predicate). *An evolved predicate is a polynomial time function* $\mathsf{evolved}$ *that takes as input blockchains* $\mathbf{B}$ *and* $\tilde{\mathbf{B}}$

$$\mathsf{evolved}(\mathbf{B}, \tilde{\mathbf{B}}) \in \{0, 1\}.$$

It outputs 1 if and only if $\mathbf{B} = \tilde{\mathbf{B}}$ *or the following holds (i)* $V(\mathbf{B}) = V(\tilde{\mathbf{B}}) = 1$; *(ii)* $\mathbf{B}$ *and* $\tilde{\mathbf{B}}$ *are consistent i.e.* $\mathbf{B}^{\lceil \kappa} \preceq \tilde{\mathbf{B}}$ *where* κ *is the common prefix parameter; (iii) Let* $\ell' = |\tilde{\mathbf{B}}| - |\mathbf{B}|$ *then it holds that* $\ell' \geq \ell_1 + \ell_2$ *and* $\mathsf{u\text{-}stakefrac}(\tilde{\mathbf{B}}, \ell' - \ell_1) > \beta$.

Blockchain Lotteries. The vast majority of PoS-based blockchain protocols has an inbuilt lottery scheme for selecting parties to generate blocks. In this lottery any party can win the right to generate a block for a certain slot with a probability proportional to its relative stake in the system. In the model from [5], a party can decrypt an EtF ciphertext if it wins this lottery. It can be useful to conduct multiple independent lotteries for the same slot sl, which is associated to a set of roles $P_1, \ldots, P_n$. Depending on the lottery mechanism, each pair (sl, P_i) may yield zero, one or multiple winners. A party with access to the blockchain can locally determine whether it is the lottery winner for a given role by executing a procedure using its lottery witness $\mathsf{sk}_{L,i}$ related to $(\mathsf{Sig.pk}_i, \mathsf{aux}_i, \mathsf{stake}_i)$, which may also give the party a proof of winning for others to verify. The definition below from [5] details what it means for a party to win a lottery.

Definition 4 (Lottery Predicate). *A lottery predicate is a polynomial time function* lottery *that takes as input a blockchain* **B**, *a slot* sl, *a role* P *and a lottery witness* $\mathsf{sk}_{L,i}$ *and outputs 1 if and only if the party owning* $\mathsf{sk}_{L,i}$ *won the lottery for the role* P *in slot* sl *with respect to the blockchain* **B**.
Formally, we write lottery$(\mathbf{B}, \mathsf{sl}, \mathsf{P}, \mathsf{sk}_{L,i}) \in \{0, 1\}$.

It is natural to establish the set of lottery winning keys $\mathcal{W}_{\mathbf{B}, \mathsf{sl}, \mathsf{P}}$ for parameters $(\mathbf{B}, \mathsf{sl}, \mathsf{P})$. This is the set of eligible keys satisfying the lottery predicate.

Modelling EtF. We are now ready to present the model of [5] for encryption to the future winner of a lottery (*i.e.* EtF). The blocks of an underlying blockchain ledger and their relative positions in the chain are used to specify points in time. Intuitively, this notion allows for creating ciphertexts that can only be decrypted by a party that is selected to perform a certain role R at a future slot sl according to a lottery scheme associated with a blockchain protocol (*i.e.* a party that has a lottery secret key $\mathsf{sk}_{L,i}$ such that lottery$(\tilde{\mathbf{B}}, \mathsf{sl}, \mathsf{P}, \mathsf{sk}_{L,i}) = 1$).

Definition 5 (Encryption to the Future). *A pair of PPT algorithms* $\mathcal{E} = (\mathsf{Enc}, \mathsf{Dec})$ *in the context of a blockchain* Γ^V *is an EtF-scheme with evolved predicate* evolved *and a lottery predicate* lottery. *The algorithms work as follows*

Encryption. ct $\leftarrow$ Enc$(\mathbf{B}, \mathsf{sl}, \mathsf{P}, m)$ *takes as input an initial blockchain* **B**, *a slot* sl, *a role* P *and a message* m. *It outputs a ciphertext* ct *- an encryption to the future.*

Decryption. $m/\bot \leftarrow$ Dec$(\tilde{\mathbf{B}}, \mathsf{ct}, \mathsf{sk})$ *takes as input a blockchain state* $\tilde{\mathbf{B}}$, *a ciphertext* ct *and a secret key* sk *and outputs the original message* m *or* $\bot$.

Correctness. An EtF-scheme is said to be correct if for honest parties i and j, there exists a negligible function μ *such that*

$$
\left| \Pr \left[\begin{array}{l} \mathsf{view} \leftarrow EXEC^{\Gamma}(\mathcal{A}, \mathcal{Z}, 1^{\lambda}) \\ \mathbf{B} = \mathsf{GetRecords}(\mathsf{view}_i) \\ \tilde{\mathbf{B}} = \mathsf{GetRecords}(\mathsf{view}_j) \\ \mathsf{ct} \leftarrow \mathsf{Enc}(\mathbf{B}, \mathsf{sl}, \mathsf{P}, m) \\ \mathsf{evolved}(\mathbf{B}, \tilde{\mathbf{B}}) = 1 \\ \mathsf{lottery}(\tilde{\mathbf{B}}, \mathsf{sl}, \mathsf{P}, \mathsf{sk}) = 1 \end{array} : \mathsf{Dec}(\tilde{\mathbf{B}}, \mathsf{ct}, \mathsf{sk}) = m \right] - 1 \right| \leq \mu(\lambda).
$$

Security. Security is defined with a game $\text{Game}^{\text{IND-CPA}}_{\Gamma,\mathcal{A},\mathcal{Z},\mathcal{E}}$ described in Algorithm 3, where a challenger $\mathcal{C}$ and an adversary $\mathcal{A}$ execute an underlying blockchain protocol with an environment $\mathcal{Z}$ as described in the full version of the paper [8]. In this game, $\mathcal{A}$ chooses a blockchain $\mathbf{B}$, a role P for the slot sl and two messages m_0 and m_1 and sends it all to $\mathcal{C}$, who chooses a random bit b and encrypts the message m_b with the parameters it received and sends ct to $\mathcal{A}$. $\mathcal{A}$ continues to execute the blockchain until an evolved blockchain $\tilde{\mathbf{B}}$ is obtained and outputs a bit b'. If the adversary is a lottery winner for the challenge role P in slot sl, the game outputs a random bit. If the adversary is not a lottery winner for the challenge role P in slot sl, the game outputs $b \oplus b'$. The reason for outputting a random guess in the game when the challenge role is corrupted is as follows. Normally the output of the IND-CPA game is $b \oplus b'$ and we require it to be 1 with probability $1/2$. This models that the guess b' is independent of b. This, of course, cannot be the case when the challenge role is corrupted. We therefore output a random guess in these cases. After this, any bias of the output away from $1/2$ still comes from b' being dependent on b.

Algorithm 3. $\text{Game}^{\text{IND-CPA}}_{\Gamma,\mathcal{A},\mathcal{Z},\mathcal{E}}$

$\mathsf{view}^r \leftarrow \mathsf{EXEC}^\Gamma_r(\mathcal{A}, \mathcal{Z}, 1^\lambda)$ ▷ $\mathcal{A}$ executes Γ with $\mathcal{Z}$ until round r
$(\mathbf{B}, \mathsf{sl}, \mathsf{P}, m_0, m_1) \leftarrow \mathcal{A}(\mathsf{view}^r_\mathcal{A})$ ▷ $\mathcal{A}$ outputs challenge parameters
$b \leftarrow_\$ \{0,1\}$
$\mathsf{ct} \leftarrow \mathsf{Enc}(\mathbf{B}, \mathsf{sl}, \mathsf{P}, m_b)$
$\mathsf{st} \leftarrow \mathcal{A}(\mathsf{view}^r_\mathcal{A}, \mathsf{ct})$ ▷ $\mathcal{A}$ receives challenge ct
$\mathsf{view}^{\tilde{r}} \leftarrow \mathsf{EXEC}^\Gamma_{(\mathsf{view}^r, \tilde{r})}(\mathcal{A}, \mathcal{Z}, 1^\lambda)$ ▷ Execute from view^r until round $\tilde{r}$
$(\tilde{\mathbf{B}}, b') \leftarrow \mathcal{A}(\mathsf{view}^{\tilde{r}}_\mathcal{A}, \mathsf{st})$
if $\mathsf{evolved}(\mathbf{B}, \tilde{\mathbf{B}}) = 1$ **then**   ▷ $\tilde{\mathbf{B}}$ is a valid evolution of $\mathbf{B}$
     if $sk^\mathcal{A}_{L,j} \notin \mathcal{W}_{\tilde{\mathbf{B}},\mathsf{sl},\mathsf{P}}$ **then**   ▷ $\mathcal{A}$ does not win role P
         return $b \oplus b'$
     end if
end if
return $\hat{b} \leftarrow_\$ \{0,1\}$

Definition 6 (IND-CPA Secure EtF). *An EtF-scheme $\mathcal{E} = (\mathsf{Enc}, \mathsf{Dec})$ in the context of a blockchain protocol Γ executed by PPT machines $\mathcal{A}$ and $\mathcal{Z}$ is said to be IND-CPA secure if, for any $\mathcal{A}$ and $\mathcal{Z}$, there exists a negligible function μ such that for $\lambda \in \mathbb{N}$:*

$$\left| 2 \cdot \Pr\left[\text{Game}^{\text{IND-CPA}}_{\Gamma,\mathcal{A},\mathcal{Z},\mathcal{E}} = 1 \right] - 1 \right| \le \mu(\lambda).$$

ECW as a Special Case of EtF. In this work, we focus on a special class of EtF called ECW where the underlying lottery is always conducted with respect to the current blockchain state. This has the following consequences

1. $\mathbf{B} = \tilde{\mathbf{B}}$ means that $\mathsf{evolved}(\mathbf{B}, \tilde{\mathbf{B}}) = 1$ is trivially true.
2. The winner of role P in slot sl is already defined in $\mathbf{B}$.

Notice that in ECW there is no need for checking if the blockchain has 'correctly' evolved and all lottery parameters (*e.g.* stake distribution and randomness extracted from the blockchain) are static. Hence, when constructing an ECW scheme, the lottery winner is already decided at encryption time. While an ECW is simpler to realize than a more general EtF, it is shown in [5] that ECW can be used to instantiate YOSO MPC and then be transformed into EtF given an identity based encryption scheme.

Authentication from the Past (AfP). When the winner of a role S sends a message m to a future role R then it is typically also needed that R can be sure that the message m came from a party P which, indeed, won the role S. This concept is formalized as an AfP scheme as follows.

Definition 7 (Authentication from the Past). *A pair of PPT algorithms* $\mathcal{U} = (\mathsf{Sign}, \mathsf{Ver})$ *is a scheme for authenticating messages as a winner of a lottery in the past in the context of blockchain Γ with lottery predicate* lottery *such that:*

Authenticate. $\sigma \leftarrow \mathsf{AfP.Sign}(\mathbf{B}, \mathsf{sl}, \mathsf{S}, \mathsf{sk}, m)$ *Takes As Input A Blockchain* $\mathbf{B}$*, a slot* sl*, a role* S *and a message* m*. It outputs a signature* σ *that authenticates the message* m*.*
Verify. $\{0,1\} \leftarrow \mathsf{AfP.Ver}(\tilde{\mathbf{B}}, \mathsf{sl}, \mathsf{S}, \sigma, m)$ *uses the blockchain* $\tilde{\mathbf{B}}$ *to ensure that* σ *is a signature on* m *produced by the secret key winning the lottery for slot* sl *and role* S*.*

Furthermore, an AfP-scheme has the following properties:

Correctness.

$$\left| \Pr \left[\begin{array}{l} \mathsf{view} \leftarrow \mathit{EXEC}^{\Gamma}(\mathcal{A}, \mathcal{Z}, 1^{\lambda}) \\ \mathbf{B} = \mathsf{GetRecords}(\mathsf{view}_i) \\ \tilde{\mathbf{B}} = \mathsf{GetRecords}(\mathsf{view}_j) \\ \sigma \leftarrow \mathsf{AfP.Sign}(\mathbf{B}, \mathsf{sl}, \mathsf{S}, \mathsf{sk}, m) \\ \mathsf{lottery}(\mathbf{B}, \mathsf{sl}, \mathsf{S}, \mathsf{sk}) = 1 \\ \mathsf{lottery}(\tilde{\mathbf{B}}, \mathsf{sl}, \mathsf{S}, \mathsf{sk}) = 1 \end{array} : \mathsf{AfP.Ver}(\tilde{\mathbf{B}}, \mathsf{sl}, \mathsf{S}, \sigma, m) = 1 \right] - 1 \right| \leq \mu(\lambda)$$

In other words, an AfP on a message from an honest party with a view of the blockchain $\mathbf{B}$ *can attest to the fact that the sender won the role* S *in slot* sl*. If another party, with blockchain* $\tilde{\mathbf{B}}$ *agrees, then the verification algorithm will output 1.*

Security. *The EUF-CMA game detailed in 4 is used to define the security of an AfP scheme. In this game, the adversary has access to a signing oracle* $\mathcal{O}_{\mathsf{AfP}}$ *which it can query with a slot* sl*, a role* S *and a message* m_i*, obtaining AfP signatures* $\sigma_i = \mathsf{AfP.Sign}(\mathbf{B}, \mathsf{sl}, \mathsf{S}, \mathsf{sk}_j, m_i)$ *where* $\mathsf{sk}_j \in \mathcal{W}_{\mathbf{B}, \mathsf{sl}, \mathsf{S}}$ *i.e.* $\mathsf{lottery}(\mathbf{B}, \mathsf{sl}, \mathsf{S}, \mathsf{sk}_j) = 1$*. The oracle maintains the list of queries* $\mathcal{Q}_{\mathsf{AfP}}$*. Formally, an AfP-scheme* $\mathcal{U}$ *is said to be EUF-CMA secure in the context of a* blockchain protocol Γ executed by PPT machines $\mathcal{A}$ and $\mathcal{Z}$ if there exists a negligible function μ such that for $\lambda \in \mathbb{N}$:

$$\Pr\left[\mathrm{Game}_{\Gamma,\mathcal{A},\mathcal{Z},\mathcal{U}}^{\mathsf{EUF\text{-}CMA}} = 1\right] \leq \mu(\lambda)$$

Algorithm 4. $\mathrm{Game}_{\Gamma,\mathcal{A},\mathcal{Z},\mathcal{U}}^{\mathsf{EUF\text{-}CMA}}$

$\mathsf{view} \leftarrow \mathsf{EXEC}^{\Gamma}(\mathcal{A}, \mathcal{Z}, 1^{\lambda})$ $\triangleright$ $\mathcal{A}$ executes Γ with $\mathcal{Z}$

$(\mathbf{B}, \mathsf{sl}, \mathsf{S}, m', \sigma') \leftarrow \mathcal{A}^{\mathcal{O}_{\mathsf{AfP}}}(\mathsf{view}_{\mathcal{A}})$

if $(m' \in \mathcal{Q}_{\mathsf{AfP}}) \vee (\mathsf{sk}_{L,j}^{\mathcal{A}} \in \mathcal{W}_{\mathbf{B},\mathsf{sl},\mathsf{S}})$ **then** $\triangleright$ $\mathcal{A}^{\mathcal{O}_{\mathsf{AfP}}}$ won or queried illegal m'

    return 0

end if

$\mathsf{view}^{\tilde{r}} \leftarrow \mathsf{EXEC}_{(\mathsf{view}^r, \tilde{r})}^{\Gamma}(\mathcal{A}, \mathcal{Z}, 1^{\lambda})$ $\triangleright$ Execute from view^r until round $\tilde{r}$

$\tilde{\mathbf{B}} \leftarrow \mathsf{GetRecords}(\mathsf{view}_i^{\tilde{r}})$

if $\mathsf{evolved}(\mathbf{B}, \tilde{\mathbf{B}}) = 1$ **then**

    if $\mathsf{Ver}(\mathbf{B}, \mathsf{sl}, \mathsf{S}, \sigma', m') = 1$ **then** $\triangleright$ $\mathcal{A}$ successfully forged an AfP

        return 1

    end if

end if

return 0

AfP Privacy. The specific privacy property we seek is that an adversary, observing AfP tags from honest parties, cannot use this information to enhance its chances in predicting the winners of lotteries for roles for which an AfP tag has not been published.

Definition 8 (AfP Privacy). *An AfP scheme $\mathcal{U}$ with corresponding lottery predicate* lottery *is private if a PPT adversary is unable to distinguish between the scenarios defined in 5 and 6 with more than negligible probability in the security parameter.*

Scenario 0 ($b = 0$) *In this scenario (5) the adversary is first running the blockchain Γ together with the environment $\mathcal{Z}$. At round r the adversary is allowed to interact with the oracle $\mathcal{O}_{\mathsf{AfP}}$ as described in 7. The adversary then continues the execution until round $\tilde{r}$ where it outputs a bit b'.*

Scenario 1 ($b = 1$) *This scenario (6) is identical to scenario 0 but instead of interacting with $\mathcal{O}_{\mathsf{AfP}}$, the adversary interacts with a simulator $\mathcal{S}$.*

Algorithm 5. $b = 0$	**Algorithm 6.** $b = 1$
$\mathsf{view}^r \leftarrow \mathsf{EXEC}_r^{\Gamma}(\mathcal{A}, \mathcal{Z}, 1^{\lambda})$	$\mathsf{view}^r \leftarrow \mathsf{EXEC}_r^{\Gamma}(\mathcal{A}, \mathcal{Z}, 1^{\lambda})$
$\mathcal{A}^{\mathcal{O}_{\mathsf{AfP}}}(\mathsf{view}_{\mathcal{A}}^r)$	$\mathcal{A}^{\mathcal{S}}(\mathsf{view}_{\mathcal{A}}^r)$
$\mathsf{view}^{\tilde{r}} \leftarrow \mathsf{EXEC}_{(\mathsf{view}^r, \tilde{r})}^{\Gamma}(\mathcal{A}, \mathcal{Z}, 1^{\lambda})$	$\mathsf{view}^{\tilde{r}} \leftarrow \mathsf{EXEC}_{(\mathsf{view}^r, \tilde{r})}^{\Gamma}(\mathcal{A}, \mathcal{Z}, 1^{\lambda})$
return $b' \leftarrow \mathcal{A}^{\mathcal{O}_{\mathsf{AfP}}}(\mathsf{view}_{\mathcal{A}}^{\tilde{r}})$	**return** $b' \leftarrow \mathcal{A}^{\mathcal{S}}(\mathsf{view}_{\mathcal{A}}^{\tilde{r}})$

We let $\text{Game}^{\text{ID-PRIV}}_{\Gamma,\mathcal{A},\mathcal{Z},\mathcal{U},\mathcal{E}}$ denote the game where a coinflip decides whether the adversary is executed in scenario 0 or scenario 1. We say that the adversary wins the game (i.e. $\text{Game}^{\text{ID-PRIV}}_{\Gamma,\mathcal{A},\mathcal{Z},\mathcal{U},\mathcal{E}} = 1$) iff $b' = b$. Finally, an AfP scheme $\mathcal{U}$ is called private in the context of the blockchain Γ and underlying lottery predicate lottery if the following holds for a negligible function μ.

$$\Pr\left[\text{Game}^{\text{ID-PRIV}}_{\Gamma,\mathcal{A},\mathcal{Z},\mathcal{U},\mathcal{E}} = 1\right] \leq 1/2 + \mu(\lambda)$$

3   ECW Based on $\mathbb{Z}_p$-Linearly Homomorphic Encryption

This section presents an ECW protocol based on a $\mathbb{Z}_p$-linearly homomorphic encryption scheme described in Sect. 2.2 and a mixnet (Sect. 2.5). Together with the ECW, we introduce an AfP scheme - a mechanism that allows a committee member to authenticate messages. The two schemes will be the backbone of the anonymous PVSS presented in Sect. 6. Before presenting the actual ECW and AfP protocols, we introduce the underlying lottery predicate that will be the cornerstone in our two schemes.

3.1   Lottery Predicate

We assume a running blockchain (we give a precise description in the full version) and a function param that has access to the blockchain state. During the setup, each party samples an encryption key pair $(\text{sk}_{\mathcal{E},i}, \text{pk}_{\mathcal{E},i})$ and inputs $\text{pk}_{\mathcal{E},i}$ to the mixnet (Sect. 2.5). The output of the mixnet is a tuple $\{(j, \text{pk}_{\text{Anon},j}) : j \in [n]\}$ which is written on the blockchain and accessible to every party through param function. The function param takes as input the blockchain $\mathbf{B}$ and the slot sl and outputs a tuple $(\{(j, \text{pk}_{\text{Anon},j})\}_{j\in[n]}, \eta) \leftarrow \text{param}(\mathbf{B}, \text{sl})$. Here, $(j, \text{pk}_{\text{Anon},j})$ is equal to $(\psi(i), \text{pk}_{\mathcal{E},i})$ for the permutation ψ defined by the mixnet. Finally, η is the public randomness from the blockchain corresponding to $\mathbf{B}$ and sl. Not, that only the owner of $\text{sk}_{\mathcal{E},i}$ knows j such that $\text{pk}_{\text{Anon},j} = \text{pk}_{\mathcal{E},i}$. Let $\mathcal{H} : \{0,1\}^* \rightarrow [n]$ be a hash function that outputs a number that points to a specific index in the list of public keys. The lottery predicate lottery is detailed below.

Algorithm 7. lottery$(\mathbf{B}, \text{sl}, \mathsf{P}, \text{sk}_{L,i})$

$(\{(j, \text{pk}_{\text{Anon},j})\}_{j\in[n]}, \eta) \leftarrow \text{param}(\mathbf{B}, \text{sl})$
$(\text{pk}_{\mathcal{E},i}, \text{sk}_{\mathcal{E},i}) \leftarrow \text{sk}_{L,i}$
$k \leftarrow \mathcal{H}(\text{sl}\|\mathsf{P}\|\eta)$
return 1 iff $\text{pk}_{\mathcal{E},i} = \text{pk}_{\text{Anon},k}$

It is easy to see that the lottery described above associates a *single* party (from the set of eligible parties) with the role P. Furthermore, the party can locally check if it won the lottery by checking that the output of the hash function points to its own public key in the permuted set. Crucially, the party winning the lottery can stay covert since no other party can link the winning lottery key to the owner of the corresponding secret key. These properties will be useful when we want to encrypt shares towards an anonymous committee.

3.2 ECW Protocol

This section introduces a ECW protocol (Fig. 4) based on the lottery predicate presented in Sect. 3.1. We note that ECW is just a restricted version of EtF where the lottery is conducted wrt. the *current* blockchain $\mathbf{B}$ and slot sl. Thus, all definitions in Sect. 2.6 applies to ECW schemes too.

ECW Protocol

Public parameters: A prime p, a $\mathbb{Z}_p$-linearly homomorphic encryption scheme $\mathcal{E} = (\mathcal{E}.\mathsf{Gen}, \mathcal{E}.\mathsf{Enc}, \mathcal{E}.\mathsf{Dec})$ with notation as in Section 2.2 and a lottery as described in Section 3.1.

Set-up:
1. Every party runs $\mathcal{E}.\mathsf{Gen}()$ obtaining a key pair $(\mathsf{sk}_{\mathcal{E},i}, \mathsf{pk}_{\mathcal{E},i})$.
2. Each party inputs $\mathsf{pk}_{\mathcal{E},i}$ to the mixnet. The output of the mixnet is a tuple $\{(j, \mathsf{pk}_{\mathsf{Anon},j}) : j \in [n]\}$ which is written on the blockchain and accessible to every party when using the **param** function.

Encryption protocol: Input $(\mathbf{B}, \mathsf{sl}, \mathsf{P})$ and $m \in \mathfrak{P}$.
1. Run $\mathsf{param}(\mathbf{B}, \mathsf{sl})$ and obtain $(\{(l, \mathsf{pk}_{\mathsf{Anon},l})\}_{l \in [n]}, \eta)$.
2. Obtain random index by $k \leftarrow \mathcal{H}(\mathsf{sl}\|\mathsf{P}\|\eta)$.
3. Choose ρ in $\mathfrak{R}$ and set $c = \mathcal{E}.\mathsf{Enc}_{\mathsf{pk}_{\mathsf{Anon},k}}(m, \rho)$.
4. Sender outputs c.

Decryption protocol: Input for party i is $\mathbf{B}, \mathsf{sk}_{L,i}$ and c.
1. Checks that $\mathsf{lottery}(\mathbf{B}, \mathsf{sl}, \mathsf{P}, \mathsf{sk}_{L,i}) = 1$.
2. Outputs $m = \mathcal{E}.\mathsf{Dec}_{\mathsf{sk}_{\mathsf{Anon},i}}(c)$.

Fig. 4. ECW protocol

Theorem 2 (IND-CPA ECW). *Let $\mathcal{E}$ be an IND-CPA secure $\mathbb{Z}_p$-linearly homomorphic encryption scheme. The construction in Fig. 4 with lottery predicate as in Sect. 3.1 is an IND-CPA secure ECW (as in Definition 6).*

(See proof sketch in full version [8])

3.3 AfP Protocol

In this section we present our AfP protocol. It is described in Fig. 5 and is based on a Signature of Knowledge (SoK) [9]. A SoK scheme is a pair of algorithms (SoK.sign, SoK.verify) and is defined in context of a relation R. We consider statements of the form $x = (\mathbf{B}, \mathsf{sl}, \mathsf{P})$ and witnesses $w = \mathsf{sk}$. We say that $R(x = (\mathbf{B}, \mathsf{sl}, \mathsf{P}), w = \mathsf{sk}) = 1$ iff $\mathsf{lottery}(\mathbf{B}, \mathsf{sl}, \mathsf{P}, \mathsf{sk}) = 1$. A signature is produced by running $\sigma \leftarrow \mathsf{SoK.sign}(x, w, m)$. And it can be verified by checking that the output of $\mathsf{SoK.verify}(x, \sigma, m)$ is 1. Our AfP uses the SoK to sign m under the knowledge of $\mathsf{sk}_{L,i}$ such that $\mathsf{lottery}(\mathbf{B}, \mathsf{sl}, \mathsf{P}, \mathsf{sk}_{L,i}) = 1$. This will exactly attest that the message m was sent by the winner of the lottery for P. An instantiation of this AfP protocol could use DL proofs (Sect. 2.1).

AfP Protocol

Public parameters and **Set-up** as described in Figure 4 plus additional setup for the SoK scheme $\mathsf{SoK} = (\mathsf{SoK.sign}, \mathsf{SoK.verify})$.

Authentication protocol: Input for party i is $(\mathbf{B}, \mathsf{sl}, \mathsf{P})$ and $m \in \mathfrak{P}$.

1. Checks that $\mathsf{lottery}(\mathbf{B}, \mathsf{sl}, \mathsf{P}, \mathsf{sk}_{L,i}) = 1$.
2. Constructs an SoK on the message m of knowledge of $\mathsf{sk}_{L,i}$ such that $\mathsf{lottery}(\mathbf{B}, \mathsf{sl}, \mathsf{P}, \mathsf{sk}_{L,i}) = 1$ resulting in $\sigma \leftarrow \mathsf{SoK.sign}((\mathbf{B}, \mathsf{sl}, \mathsf{P}), \mathsf{sk}_{L,i})$.
3. Sender outputs $\sigma \leftarrow \sigma_{\mathsf{SoK}}$.

Verification protocol: Input is $(\mathbf{B}, \mathsf{sl}, \mathsf{P}, \sigma, m)$

1. Parses σ as the SoK signature σ_{SoK}.
2. Verifies that σ_{SoK} is a valid SoK on the message m proving knowledge of $\mathsf{sk}_{L,i}$. I.e. it runs $b \leftarrow \mathsf{SoK.verify}((\mathbf{B}, \mathsf{sl}, \mathsf{P}), \sigma_{\mathsf{SoK}}, m)$.
3. Verifier outputs b.

Fig. 5. AfP protocol

Theorem 3 (EUF-CMA AfP). *Let $\mathcal{E}$ be an IND-CPA secure and $\mathbb{Z}_p$-linearly homomorphic encryption scheme and let SoK be a simulatable and extractable SoK scheme. The construction in Fig. 5 with lottery predicate as in Sect. 3.1 is EUF-CMA AfP as defined in Definition 7.*

(See proof sketch in full version [8])

AfP Privacy. The privacy property of an AfP scheme says that no adversary can distinguish between interacting with an AfP oracle $\mathcal{O}_{\mathsf{AfP}}$ and a simulator $\mathcal{S}$ during a blockchain execution. Intuitively, this provides the guarantee that observing other AfP tags does not enhance an adversary's chance of guessing future lottery winners.

Theorem 4 (AfP Privacy). *Assume $\mathcal{E}$, lottery and SoK scheme as in 3. The construction in Fig. 5 has AfP privacy as in Definition 8.*

(See proof sketch in full version [8])

An AfP based on the setup presented in Fig. 4 will not provide a good foundation for YOSO-MPC or even just a proactive secret sharing scheme. The reason is, that as soon as a party ID_i publishes an AfP tag, any other party can verify that ID_i won the lottery and, thus, link the identity of ID_i to the public key $\mathsf{pk}_{\mathsf{Anon},\psi(i)}$ from the output of the mixnet. This will ruin the setup for this party when future lotteries are conducted. More importantly, a powerful adversary is able to identify any subsequent ECW ciphertexts towards this party and can design its corruption strategy accordingly. What we want is a new ephemeral public key $\mathsf{pk}_{\mathsf{Anon},\psi(i)}$ for each party and for each slot sl in the blockchain execution where an AfP is produced. Note that a new lottery setup is necessary for each slot sl even though different parties are producing AfP tags in different slots. The reason is that observing *any* AfP tag, inadvertently, skews the probability distribution and helps the adversary in guessing future lottery winner.

A simple way to solve the above issue is to repeat the lottery setup and obtain multiple vectors of the format $\{(j, \mathsf{pk}_{\mathsf{Anon},j}) : j \in [n]\}$. Then, any party can use a new anonymized public key for each AfP tag. We describe this property as *bounded* AfP privacy. Bounded AfP privacy ensures that the AfP scheme can be executed a bounded number times before lottery winners can be linked to specific public keys in the setup and ECW ciphertexts starts betraying their receivers. Note that the idea of generating multiple lottery setups in batches (preprocessing) can result in more efficient protocols. But it has the downside that, while using the preprocessed public keys, the number of parties in the system is static. In Sect. 6 we look at how to use the ECW and AfP in an anonymous PVSS protocol where we want encrypt towards multiple parties. In such a setting we can use linkable ring signatures (see full version [8]) to prove membership in a committee without directly revealing our public key in the setup.

3.4   AfP with Reusable Setup

In the full version [8], we describe an efficient NIZK that allows for a party ID_i to prove knowledge of a lottery secret key $\mathsf{sk}_{L,i}$ such that $\mathsf{lottery}(\mathbf{B}, \mathsf{sl}, \mathsf{P}_j, \mathsf{sk}_{L,i}) = 1$ for $\mathsf{P}_j \in \{\mathsf{P}_1, \ldots, \mathsf{P}_n\}$ without revealing P_j. Using this NIZK and an anonymous channel, we can construct an AfP that can be used multiple times without linking a party P_i to its setup public key. In order to generate an AfP on message m on behalf of role P in slot sl, P_i with $\mathsf{sk}_{L,i}$ such that $\mathsf{lottery}(\mathbf{B}, \mathsf{sl}, \mathsf{P}, \mathsf{sk}_{L,i}) = 1$ first generates a NIZK π proving knowledge of $\mathsf{sk}_{L,i}$ such that $\mathsf{lottery}(\mathbf{B}, \mathsf{sl}, \mathsf{P}_j, \mathsf{sk}_{L,i}) = 1$ for $\mathsf{P}_j \in \{\mathsf{P}_1, \ldots, \mathsf{P}_n\}$. Now P_i generates an SoK σ on the message m of knowledge of a valid proof π for the aforementioned statement. ID_i publishes σ through an anonymous channel, avoiding its identity to be linked to the set $\{\mathsf{P}_1, \ldots, \mathsf{P}_n\}$. The security and privacy guarantees for this AfP follow in a straightforward way from our previous analysis. While using this construction has a clear extra cost in relation to our simple AfP, we show in the full version [8] how to efficiently perform such a reusable setup AfP on a set of ciphertexts, which is useful for our resharing application.

4   Publicly Verifiable Secret Sharing

4.1   Model

We define a publicly verifiable secret sharing (PVSS) scheme with t privacy and $t+1$-reconstruction, based on the models provided in [6,16,20,21]. The goal is for a dealer to share a secret $S \in \mathbb{G}$ to a set of n parties $\mathcal{P} = \{P_1, \cdots, P_n\}$, so that $t + 1$ shares will be needed to reconstruct the secret and no information will be revealed from t shares. We require public verifiability for correctness of sharing by the dealer, and for reconstruction of the secret by a set of $t + 1$ parties. Due to this requirement, the protocol is entirely carried out using a public ledger.

We provide the syntax below. A modification we introduce with respect to the usual model is that we include asymmetric key pairs for dealers and an additional initial round where the parties can broadcast an ephemeral public key. This will allow for more efficient constructions as we will see in Sect. 4.3.

Setup

- Setup(1^λ) outputs public parameters pp.
- DKeyGen(pp), performed by the dealer, outputs a key pair $(\mathsf{pk}_D, \mathsf{sk}_D)$.
- KeyGen(pp, id_i), performed by i-th share receiver, outputs a key-pair $(\mathsf{pk}_i, \mathsf{sk}_i)$.
- VerifyKey(pp, id, pk), performed by a public verifier, outputs $0/1$ (as a verdict on whether pk is valid).

Distribution

- Dist($pp, \mathsf{pk}_D, \mathsf{sk}_D, \{\mathsf{pk}_i : i \in [n]\}, S$) performed by the dealer, and where $S \in \mathbb{G}$ is a secret, outputs encrypted shares $C_i : i \in [n]$ and a proof $\mathsf{Pf}_{\mathsf{Sh}}$ of sharing correctness.

Verification

- Verify($pp, \mathsf{pk}_D, \{(\mathsf{pk}_i, C_i) : i \in [n]\}, \mathsf{Pf}_{\mathsf{Sh}}$) performed by the public verifier outputs $0/1$ (as a verdict on whether the sharing is valid).

Reconstruction

- DecShare($pp, \mathsf{pk}_D, \mathsf{pk}_i, \mathsf{sk}_i, C_i$), performed by a share receiver, outputs a decrypted share A_i and a proof $\mathsf{Pf}_{\mathsf{Dec}_i}$ of correct decryption.
- VerifyDec($pp, \mathsf{pk}_D, C_i, A_i, \mathsf{Pf}_{\mathsf{Dec}_i}$) outputs $0/1$ (as a verdict on whether A_i is a valid decryption of C_i).
- Rec($pp, \{A_i : i \in \mathcal{T}\}$) for some $\mathcal{T} \subseteq [n]$ of size $t + 1$ outputs a secret S. We will only apply this algorithm to inputs where $\mathcal{T}$ is of size $t+1$ and such that all A_i have passed the verification check.

We let $\mathcal{PK}_D$ and $\mathcal{PK}$ contain all key pairs output by DKeyGen and KeyGen respectively. For non–deterministic algorithms we sometimes explicitly reference the randomness r input. For example, Dist($pp, \mathsf{pk}_D, sk_D, \{\mathsf{pk}_i : i \in [n]\}, S; r$). One of our constructions will not require pk_D, sk_D and consequently DKeyGen. In that case we omit these arguments from the inputs to the other algorithms.

We require a PVSS to satisfy correctness, verifiability and IND1-secrecy. We give these definitions in the full version of this paper.

4.2 HEPVSS: Generic PVSS from $\mathbb{Z}_p$-LHE Scheme

We present in Fig. 6 our construction for a PVSS scheme HEPVSS based on a $\mathbb{Z}_p$-LHE scheme with proof of correct decryption. This construction does not require the dealer to hold a key pair or parties to prove honest generation of keys and therefore we remove this from the syntax. Moreover, because the dealer does not have a key pair, here we do not require the public keys pk_i to be ephemeral.

The construction is relatively straightforward: the dealer construct the (group) Shamir sharing of the secret, and encrypts the shares using the $\mathbb{Z}_p$-LHE scheme, resulting in ciphertexts C_i. The sharing correctness proof needs to assert, not only that each C_i is individually a correct encryption, but also that the underlying plaintext messages are evaluations of a polynomial of degree at most t. Here we use the fact that the set of polynomials of degree at most t is a vector space, and the map that sends a polynomial to its evaluation in some point is linear, so we can capture the above statement in terms of knowledge of preimage of a certain linear map. For the proofs of security (correctness, indistinguishability of secrets and verifiability) we refer to the full version.

4.3 DHPVSS: A PVSS with Constant-Size Sharing Correctness Proof

We now give an optimized construction of a PVSS with a proof of sharing correctness consisting of just two field elements. The PVSS scheme, which we call DHPVSS, has IND1-secrecy under the DDH assumption.

We explain the idea of the construction next: Let $A_i = a_i \cdot G$ be (purportedly) group Shamir shares for a secret $S \in \mathbb{G}$. A SCRAPE check (Theorem 1) consists on the verification $\sum_{i=1}^n v_i \cdot m^*(\alpha_i) \cdot a_i \stackrel{?}{=} 0$, or alternatively

$$\sum_{i=1}^n v_i \cdot m^*(\alpha_i) \cdot A_i \stackrel{?}{=} O,$$

for O the identity element of $\mathbb{G}$. Here v_i are fixed coefficients dependent on the α_i and $m^*(X)$ is sampled uniformly at random from $\mathbb{Z}_p[X]_{\leq n-t-2}$. If it is not true that all a_i are of the form $m(\alpha_i)$ for some polynomial $m(X) \in \mathbb{Z}_p[X]_{\leq t}$, then the check succeeds with probability at most $1/p$.

In [6], the encrypted shares were $C_i = a_i \cdot \mathsf{pk}_i$. Because these are in different bases the check above cannot be directly applied on the C_i, and then the strategy consisted on sending additional elements $a_i \cdot H$ (for some group generator H), proving that the underlying a_i's are the same, and carrying out the check on these $a_i \cdot H$. All this introduces overhead which is linear in n.

Instead, in DHPVSS, the dealer has a key-pair $(\mathsf{sk}_D, \mathsf{pk}_D)$, with $\mathsf{pk}_D = \mathsf{sk}_D \cdot G$, and encrypts A_i as $C_i = A_i + \mathsf{sk}_D \cdot E_i$, where $E_i = \mathsf{sk}_i \cdot G$ is an ephemeral public key of the i-th party. Note that $\mathsf{sk}_D \cdot E_i$ can be seen as a shared Diffie-Hellman key between dealer and the i-th party or, alternatively, C_i can be seen as an El-Gamal encryption of A_i under E_i with randomness sk_D.

Algorithms for Public Verifiable Secret Sharing Scheme HEPVSS

HEPVSS.Setup($1^\lambda, t, n$):

    $(\mathbb{G}, G, p, \mathcal{E}) \leftarrow_\$ \mathcal{G}(1^\lambda)$. Choose pairwise distinct $\alpha_0, \alpha_1, \cdots \alpha_n \in \mathbb{Z}_p$

    return $pp = (\mathbb{G}, G, p, t, n, \{\alpha_i : i \in [0, n]\}, \mathcal{E})$

HEPVSS.KeyGen(pp, id):

    return $(\mathsf{sk}, \mathsf{pk}) \leftarrow_\$ \mathcal{E}.\mathsf{Gen}(1^\lambda)$

HEPVSS.Dist($pp, \{\mathsf{pk}_i : i \in [n]\}, S$):

    Parse pp as $(\mathbb{G}, G, p, n, \{\alpha_i : i \in [0, n]\}, \mathcal{E}) := (pp_{\mathsf{Sh}}, \mathcal{E})$

    $(\{A_i : i \in [n]\}, m(X)) \leftarrow \mathsf{GShamir}(pp_{\mathsf{Sh}}, S)$

    for $i \in [n]$ **do**

        $\rho_i \leftarrow_\$ \mathfrak{R}, \ C_i \leftarrow \mathcal{E}.\mathsf{Enc}_{\mathsf{pk}_i}(A_i, \rho_i)$

    end for

    $\mathcal{W} \leftarrow \mathbb{G} \times \mathbb{Z}_p[X]_{\leq t} \times \mathfrak{R}^n, \quad \mathcal{X} \leftarrow \{0\} \times \mathfrak{C}^n, \quad pp_\pi \leftarrow (\mathbb{Z}_p, \mathcal{W}, \mathcal{X}, \mathcal{H})$

    $w \leftarrow (S, m(X), \rho_1, \ldots, \rho_n), \quad x \leftarrow (0, C_1, \ldots, C_n)$

    Let f given by

        $f(w) := (m(\alpha_0), \mathcal{E}.\mathsf{Enc}_{\mathsf{pk}_1}(S + m(\alpha_1) \cdot G; \rho_1), \ldots, \mathcal{E}.\mathsf{Enc}_{\mathsf{pk}_n}(S + m(\alpha_n) \cdot G; \rho_n))$

    $\mathsf{Pf}_{\mathsf{Sh}} \leftarrow \Pi_{\mathsf{NI-Pre}}.\mathsf{Prove}(w; pp_\pi, x, f)$

    return $(\{C_i : i \in [n]\}, \mathsf{Pf}_{\mathsf{Sh}})$

HEPVSS.Verify($pp, \{(\mathsf{pk}_i, C_i) : i \in [n]\}, \mathsf{Pf}_{\mathsf{Sh}}$):

    return $\Pi_{\mathsf{NI-Pre}}.\mathsf{Verify}(pp_\pi, x, f, \mathsf{Pf}_{\mathsf{Sh}})$, with $\mathcal{W}, \mathcal{X}, pp_\pi, x, f$ as in HEPVSS.Dist

HEPVSS.DecShare($pp, \mathsf{pk}, \mathsf{sk}, C$):

    $A \leftarrow \mathsf{Dec}_{\mathsf{sk}}(C), \ \mathsf{Pf}_{\mathsf{Dec}} \leftarrow \mathcal{E}.\mathsf{ProveDec}(A, C, \mathsf{pk})$

    return $(A, \mathsf{Pf}_{\mathsf{Dec}})$

HEPVSS.VerifyDec($pp, \mathsf{pk}_i, A_i, C_i, \mathsf{Pf}_{\mathsf{Dec}i}$):

    return $\mathcal{E}.\mathsf{VerifyDec}(A_i, C_i, \mathsf{pk}_i, \mathsf{Pf}_{\mathsf{Dec}i})$

HEPVSS.Rec($pp, \{A_i : i \in \mathcal{T}\}$):

    return $\mathsf{GShamir}.\mathsf{Rec}(pp, \{A_i : i \in \mathcal{T}\})$

Fig. 6. Algorithms for HEPVSS

The advantage is that now $\sum_{i=1}^n v_i \cdot m^*(\alpha_i) \cdot A_i \overset{?}{=} O$ is equivalent to

$$\sum_{i=1}^n v_i \cdot m^*(\alpha_i) \cdot C_i \overset{?}{=} \mathsf{sk}_D \cdot \left(\sum_{i=1}^n v_i \cdot m^*(\alpha_i) \cdot E_i \right),$$

which is *one single* DLEQ proof $\mathsf{DLEQ}(\mathsf{sk}_D; G, \mathsf{pk}_D, U, V)$ for *publicly computable*

$$U = \sum_{i=1}^n v_i \cdot m^*(\alpha_i) \cdot E_i, \quad V = \sum_{i=1}^n v_i \cdot m^*(\alpha_i) \cdot C_i.$$

One detail is that, as opposed to the PVSS in [6] (where $m^*(X)$ was locally sampled by the verifier), the prover needs to know $m^*(X)$ so this is sampled via a random oracle. The algorithms can be found in Fig. 7 and Fig. 8.

Algorithms for PVSS scheme DHPVSS, Setup and Distribution

DHPVSS.Setup($1^\lambda, t, n$):

  $(\mathbb{G}, G, p) \leftarrow_\$ \mathcal{G}(1^\lambda)$. Choose pairwise distinct $\alpha_0, \alpha_1, \cdots \alpha_n \in \mathbb{Z}_p$

  $\forall i \in [n] \quad v_i \leftarrow \prod_{j \in [n] \setminus \{i\}} (\alpha_i - \alpha_j)^{-1}$

  return $pp = (\mathbb{G}, G, p, t, n, \alpha_0, \{(\alpha_i, v_i) : i \in [n]\})$

DHPVSS.DKeyGen(pp):

  $\mathsf{sk}_D \leftarrow_\$ \mathbb{Z}_p^*, \mathsf{pk}_D \leftarrow \mathsf{sk}_D \cdot G$

  return $(\mathsf{pk}_D, \mathsf{sk}_D)$

DHPVSS.KeyGen(pp, id):

  $\mathsf{sk} \leftarrow_\$ \mathbb{Z}_p^*, E \leftarrow \mathsf{sk} \cdot G, \Omega \leftarrow \mathsf{DL}(\mathsf{sk}; G, E, id), \mathsf{pk} \leftarrow (E, \Omega)$

  return $(\mathsf{pk}, \mathsf{sk})$

DHPVSS.VerifyKey(pp, id, pk):

  parse pk as (E, Ω)

  return accept iff Ω is valid w.r.t G, E, id

DHPVSS.Dist($pp, \mathsf{pk}_D, \mathsf{sk}_D, \{\mathsf{pk}_i : i \in [n]\}, S$):

  parse pk_i as (E_i, Ω_i), pp as $(\mathbb{G}, G, p, t, n, \alpha_0, \{(\alpha_i, v_i) : i \in [n]\})$

  $pp_{\mathsf{Sh}} \leftarrow (\mathbb{G}, G, p, t, n, \{\alpha_i : i \in [0, n]\})$

  $(\{A_i\}_{i \in [n]}, m(X)) \leftarrow \mathsf{GShamir.Share}(pp_{\mathsf{Sh}}, S)$

  $\forall i \in [n], C_i \leftarrow \mathsf{sk}_D \cdot E_i + A_i$

  $m^* \leftarrow \mathcal{H}(\mathsf{pk}_D, \{(\mathsf{pk}_i, C_i) : i \in [n]\})$ (for a RO $\mathcal{H} : \{0,1\}^* \rightarrow \mathbb{Z}_p[X]_{\leq n-t-2}$)

  $V \leftarrow \sum_{i=1}^n v_i \cdot m^*(\alpha_i) \cdot C_i, U \leftarrow \sum_{i=1}^n v_i \cdot m^*(\alpha_i) \cdot E_i$

  $\mathsf{Pf}_{\mathsf{Sh}} \leftarrow \mathsf{DLEQ}(\mathsf{sk}_D; G, \mathsf{pk}_D, U, V)$

  return $(\{C_i : i \in [n]\}, \mathsf{Pf}_{\mathsf{Sh}})$

Fig. 7. Algorithms for PVSS scheme DHPVSS, setup and distribution

Security. We prove that DHPVSS satisfies correctness, indistinguishability of secrets and verifiability in the full version.

Communication Complexity Comparison. The communication complexity of DHPVSS.Dist is $(n + 2) \log p$ bits. In contrast, HEPVSS.Dist instantiated with El Gamal is of $(3n + 3) \log p$ bits. Secret distribution in SCRAPE [6] requires $(3n+1) \log p$ bits, which was reduced to $(n+t+2) \log p$ bits in ALBATROSS [7]. Therefore DHPVSS.Dist obtains an additive saving of $t \log p$ bits with respect to the best previous alternative. The communication of both DHPVSS.DecShare and HEPVSS.DecShare is $3 \log p$ bits. The share decryption complexities in [6] and [7] are similar to ours. More details can be found in the full version of this paper.

5   PVSS Resharing

In this section we introduce protocols that allow a committee $\mathcal{C}_r$ of size n_r, among which a secret has been PVSSed with an underlying t_r-threshold Shamir scheme,

---

Algorithms for PVSS scheme DHPVSS, Verification and Reconstruction

DHPVSS.Verify($pp, \mathsf{pk}_D, \{(\mathsf{pk}_i, C_i) : i \in [n]\}, \mathsf{Pf_{Sh}}$):

    parse pk_i as (E_i, Ω_i), pp as $(\mathbb{G}, G, p, t, n, \{(\alpha_i, v_i) : i \in [n]\})$

    $m^* \leftarrow \mathcal{H}(\mathsf{pk}_D, \{(\mathsf{pk}_i, C_i) : i \in [n]\})$

    $V \leftarrow \sum_{i=1}^n v_i m^*(\alpha_i) \cdot C_i, U \leftarrow \sum_{i=1}^n v_i m^*(\alpha_i) \cdot E_i$

    return accept iff $\mathsf{Pf_{Sh}}$ is valid w.r.t G, pk_D, U, V

DHPVSS.DecShare($pp, \mathsf{pk}_D, \mathsf{pk}, \mathsf{sk}, C$):

    parse pk as (E, Ω)

    $A' \leftarrow C - \mathsf{sk} \cdot \mathsf{pk}_D$

    $\mathsf{Pf_{Dec}} \leftarrow \mathsf{DLEQ}(\mathsf{sk}; G, E, \mathsf{pk}_D, C - A')$

    return $(A', \mathsf{Pf_{Dec}})$

DHPVSS.VerifyDec($pp, \mathsf{pk}_D, \mathsf{pk}_i, C_i, A_i, \mathsf{Pf}_{\mathsf{Dec}i}$):

    parse pk_i as (E_i, Ω_i)

    return accept iff $\mathsf{Pf}_{\mathsf{Dec}i}$ is valid w.r.t $G, E_i, \mathsf{pk}_D, C_i - A_i$

DHPVSS.Rec($pp, \{A_i : i \in \mathcal{T}\}$):

    return GShamir.Rec($pp, \{A_i : i \in \mathcal{T}\}$)

Fig. 8. Algorithms for PVSS scheme DHPVSS, verification and reconstruction

to create a PVSS of the same secret for the next committee $\mathcal{C}_{r+1}$ of size n_{r+1} and with threshold t_{r+1}. By design, the protocols will keep the secret hidden from any adversary corrupting at most t_r parties from $\mathcal{C}_r$ and t_{r+1} from $\mathcal{C}_{r+1}$, and will be correct as long as there are $t_r + 1$ honest parties in $\mathcal{C}_r$. In particular, this can be used by a party P to transmit a message to a committee in the future, by keeping this secret being reshared among successive committees and setting the last Shamir threshold to be 0.

Suppose for now that the secret sharing scheme were for secrets over $\mathbb{Z}_p$. Each party in $\mathcal{C}_r$ would hold $\sigma_\ell = m_r(\alpha_\ell)$ where m_r is the sharing polynomial for that round, of degree t_r. A subcommittee L_r of $t_r + 1$ parties in $\mathcal{C}_r$ can then reshare the secret by PVSSing their shares among $\mathcal{C}_{r+1}$ with Shamir scheme of degree t_{r+1}. The parties in $\mathcal{C}_{r+1}$ then compute the sum of the received shares weighted by coefficients $\lambda_{\ell, L_r} := \prod_{j \in L_r, j \neq \ell} \frac{\alpha_0 - \alpha_j}{\alpha_\ell - \alpha_j}$. Indeed, if we denote $[\sigma_\ell]$ the vector of shares sent by P_ℓ in L_r, then $\sum_{\ell \in L_r} \lambda_{\ell, L_r}[\sigma_\ell] = \sum_{\ell \in L_r} \lambda_{\ell, L_r}[m(\alpha_\ell)] = [\sum_{\ell \in L_r} \lambda_{\ell, L_r} m(\alpha_\ell)] = [m(\alpha_0)]$.

In our situation, each party $\mathsf{P}_{r,i}$ in $\mathcal{C}_r$ has instead a group element as share, and needs to PVSS it among $\mathcal{C}_{r+1}$ using the algorithm Dist from previous section. However, the proof in Dist only guarantees that the distributed shares are consistent with some secret. Here we require in addition that this secret is the shared that the party has received previously.

To be more precise, in round r, each party $\mathsf{P}_{r,i}$ in committee $\mathcal{C}_r$ has $A_{r,i}$ as share and in addition the encryption $C_{r,i} = \mathcal{E}.\mathsf{Enc}_{\mathsf{pk}_{r,i}}(A_{r,i})$ of $A_{r,i}$ is public. $\mathsf{P}_{r,i}$ now needs to create shares of $A_{r,i}$ for the committee $\mathcal{C}_{r+1}$. Let $A_{i \to j}$ be the share that will be sent to $\mathsf{P}_{r+1,j}$. This will be encrypted as $C_{i \to j} = \mathcal{E}.\mathsf{Enc}_{\mathsf{pk}_{r+1,j}}(A_{i \to j})$

and $P_{r,i}$ must prove that $C_{i \to j}$ are encryptions of a correct sharing whose secret is indeed the plaintext of $C_{r,i}$.

When a subset L_r of $\mathcal{C}_r$ of $t_r + 1$ parties have correctly reshared, each $P_{r+1,j}$ sets $A_{r+1,j} = \sum_{\ell \in L_r} \lambda_{\ell,L_r} A_{\ell \to j}$ as their share and the corresponding public ciphertext $C_{r+1,j} = \sum_{\ell \in L_r} \lambda_{\ell,L_r} C_{\ell \to j}$ can be locally computed by everyone.

5.1   Resharing for HEPVSS

In the case of HEPVSS, the additional proof that the reshared value is the one corresponding to the public ciphertext can be integrated easily in HEPVSS.Dist if the encryption scheme has $\mathbb{Z}_p$-linear decryption. We give the construction and more details in the full version [8].

5.2   Resharing for DHPVSS

In the case of DHPVSS, the situation is slightly more complicated due to the fact that the encryption of shares involves a key from the dealer. Here there are different dealers, i.e. the final share of each party in $\mathcal{C}_{r+1}$ is a linear combination of shares sent by the parties in L_r. Thanks to the fact that the encryption is also a linear operation with respect to the public key of the sender, we can define a public key for committee L_r. Indeed, if we call pk_{D_ℓ} the public key of $P_{r,\ell}$ when acting as sender, then $\mathsf{pk}_{D,L_r} := \sum_{\ell \in L_r} \lambda_{\ell,L_r} \cdot \mathsf{pk}_{D_\ell}$. Then we want to make sure that the output encryption for $P_{r+1,j}$ is $C_{r+1,j} = \mathsf{sk}_{r+1,j} \cdot \mathsf{pk}_{D,L_r} + \sum_{\ell \in L_r} \lambda_{\ell,L_r} A_{\ell \to j}$.

At the beginning of the resharing, each party $P_{r,i}$ in committee $\mathcal{C}_r$ has as share $A_{r,i} = C_{r,i} - \mathsf{sk}_i \cdot \mathsf{pk}_{D,L_{r-1}}$ where sk_i is the secret key for decrypting shares, and needs to create shares $A_{i \to j}$ of $A_{r,i}$ and encrypt them using the public keys $\mathsf{pk}_{[n_{r+1}]} = \{\mathsf{pk}_j : j \in [n_{r+1}]\}$ of the parties of the next round and its own secret key sk_{D_i} (i.e. this party will create $C_{[n_{r+1}]} = \{C_{i \to j} : j \in [n_{r+1}]\}$ with $C_{i \to j} = \mathsf{sk}_{D_i} \cdot \mathsf{pk}_j + A_{i \to j}$) and prove their validity. In conclusion we need a proof for the following relation

$$
\begin{aligned}
R_{\mathsf{DHPVSS,Reshare}} = \{&(m(X), \mathsf{sk}_i, \mathsf{sk}_{D_i}); (pp, \mathsf{pk}_i, \mathsf{pk}_{D_i}, \mathsf{pk}_{D,L_{r-1}}, \mathsf{pk}_{[n_{r+1}]}, C_{r,i}, C_{[n_{r+1}]}) : \\
& \mathsf{pk}_i = \mathsf{sk}_i \cdot G, \ \mathsf{pk}_{D_i} = \mathsf{sk}_{D_i} \cdot G, \ m(X) \in \mathbb{Z}_p[X]_{\le t}, \ m(\beta_0) = 0, \\
& \text{and } \forall j \in [n_{r+1}], \ C_{i \to j} = \mathsf{sk}_{D_i} \cdot \mathsf{pk}_j + A_{i \to j}, \\
& \text{where } A_{i \to j} = (C_{r,i} - \mathsf{sk}_i \cdot \mathsf{pk}_{D,L_{r-1}}) + m(\beta_j) \cdot G\}
\end{aligned}
$$

However, we also want to use the SCRAPE technique to reduce the size of the witness and hence of the proof. Note that if we set $U_j = C_{i \to j} - \mathsf{sk}_{D_i} \cdot \mathsf{pk}_j - C_{r,i} + \mathsf{sk}_i \cdot \mathsf{pk}_{D,L_{r-1}}$ for all $j \in [n_{r+1}]$ and $U_0 = O$, we want to make sure that for all $j \in [0, n_{r+1}]$, $U_j = m(\beta_j) \cdot G$ for a polynomial of degree $\le t$ (in addition to the conditions $\mathsf{pk}_i = \mathsf{sk}_i \cdot G$ and $\mathsf{pk}_{D_i} = \mathsf{sk}_{D_i} \cdot G$).

For $j \in [0, n]$, let $v'_j = \prod_{k \in [0,n] \setminus \{j\}} (\beta_j - \beta_k)^{-1}$. Observe these are not exactly the same coefficients as in the description of DHPVSS in Sect. 4.3 because they include the evaluation point β_0. By Theorem 1, we want to prove $\sum_{j=0}^{n} v_i' \cdot m^*(\beta_j) \cdot U_j = O$, for a random polynomial m^* of degree $n - t - 1$ (note here we apply Theorem 1 to a code of length $n + 1$, rather than n).

Observe $\sum_{j=0}^{n} v_j' \cdot m^*(\beta_j) \cdot U_j = U' - \mathsf{sk}_{D_i} \cdot V' + \mathsf{sk}_i \cdot W'$ for publicly computable

$$U' := \sum_{j=1}^{n} v_j' \cdot m^*(\beta_j) \cdot (C_{i \to j} - C_{\mathsf{r},i}), \quad V' := \sum_{j=1}^{n} v_j' \cdot m^*(\beta_j) \cdot \mathsf{pk}_j, \text{ and}$$

$$W' := \sum_{j=1}^{n} v_j' \cdot m^*(\beta_j) \cdot \mathsf{pk}_{D, L_{\mathsf{r}-1}},$$

and therefore $P_{\mathsf{r},i}$ needs a proof of knowledge for

$$R'_{\mathsf{DHPVSS,Reshare},m^*} = \{(\mathsf{sk}_i, \mathsf{sk}_{D_i}); (\mathsf{pk}_i, \mathsf{pk}_{D_i}, U', V', W') :$$
$$\mathsf{pk}_i = \mathsf{sk}_i \cdot G, \quad \mathsf{pk}_{D_i} = \mathsf{sk}_{D_i} \cdot G, \quad U' = \mathsf{sk}_{D_i} \cdot V' - \mathsf{sk}_i \cdot W'\}$$

where we remark that now the witness only contains two elements but on the other hand relation depends on a polynomial $m^*(X)$ that has been sampled uniformly at random among polynomials of degree at most $n - t - 1$. This leads to the protocol for PVSS resharing in Fig. 9.

6   Anonymous PVSS via ECW and AfP

In this section, we show how to construct PVSS (and re-sharing) for anonymous committees by instantiating our previous PVSS constructions using our ECW and AfP schemes. We start by showing how our previous protocols can be adapted to work with ECW and AfP instead of standard encryption and authentication. We then show how the optimizations in the DDH based constructions via the SCRAPE trick carry over to our anonymous setting if we instantiate our ECW and AfP schemes from similar assumptions. The protocols we construct in this section work in the YOSO model supporting up to $t < n/2$ corrupted parties and can be used as efficient building blocks for the protocols of [1,12].

In the previous sections, we have constructed both a PVSS scheme (Sect. 4.2) and a PVSS re-sharing scheme (Sect. 5.1) based on $\mathbb{Z}_p$-linear encryption schemes (as defined in Sect. 2.2). Despite being efficient, these constructions are not fit for the YOSO model because they require the dealer to know the public keys of the parties who will receive shares, consequently revealing their identities. In order to solve this issue, we show that these protocols can also be instantiated with the ECW scheme of Sect. 3 even though they were designed to be instantiated with a $\mathbb{Z}_p$-linear encryption scheme. The core idea is that our ECW preserves all the properties of the underlying $\mathbb{Z}_p$-linear encryption scheme while adding the ability to encrypt towards a role rather than towards a party who owns a public key.

Protocol for DHPVSS resharing

Participants: $\mathcal{C}_r = \{P_{r,1}, \ldots, P_{r,n_r}\}$ and $\mathcal{C}_{r+1} = \{P_{r+1,1}, \ldots, P_{r+1,n_{r+1}}\}$.

Public information: A group $\mathbb{G}$ of prime order p, with generator G. "Sender" key pairs $(\mathsf{sk}_{D_i}, \mathsf{pk}_{D_i} = \mathsf{sk}_{D_i} \cdot G)$ for every party $P_{r,i} \in \mathcal{C}_r$, a "sender committee" public key $\mathsf{pk}_{D,L_{r-1}}$, and "receiver" key pairs $(\mathsf{sk}_{r,i}, \mathsf{pk}_{r,i} = \mathsf{sk}_{r,i} \cdot G)$ for $P_{r,i}$, where $r = \mathsf{r}, \mathsf{r}+1$, and $1 \le i \le n_r$; thresholds t_r, t_{r+1}. Evaluation points $(\alpha_0, \alpha_1, \ldots, \alpha_{n_r})$, $(\beta_0, \beta_1, \ldots, \beta_{n_{r+1}})$. Random oracles $\mathcal{H} : \{0,1\}^* \to \mathbb{Z}_p[X]_{\le n-t-1}$, $\mathcal{H}' : \{0,1\}^* \to \mathbb{Z}_p$. Let $\mathcal{W} \leftarrow \mathbb{Z}_p^2$, $\mathcal{X} \leftarrow \mathbb{G}^3$, and $pp_\pi \leftarrow (\mathbb{Z}_p, \mathcal{W}, \mathcal{X}, \mathcal{H}')$.

Input: Public ciphertexts $C_{\mathsf{r},i} = \mathsf{sk}_{\mathsf{r},i} \cdot \mathsf{pk}_{D,L_{r-1}} + A_{\mathsf{r},i}$ such that $A_{\mathsf{r},i} = h_{\mathsf{r}}(\alpha_i) \cdot G$ for some polynomial h_{r} of degree $\le t_{\mathsf{r}}$.

Output: A public key $\mathsf{pk}_{D,L_{\mathsf{r}}}$ for a subset L_{r} of $\mathcal{C}_{\mathsf{r}}$, of size $t_{\mathsf{r}} + 1$. Public output ciphertexts $(C_{\mathsf{r}+1,1}, \ldots, C_{\mathsf{r}+1,n_{\mathsf{r}+1}})$ and a proof π that, for all $j = 1, \ldots, n_{\mathsf{r}+1}$, $C_{\mathsf{r}+1,j} = \mathsf{sk}_{\mathsf{r}+1,j} \mathsf{pk}_{D,L_{\mathsf{r}}} + A_{\mathsf{r}+1,j}$ such that $A_{\mathsf{r}+1,j} = h_{\mathsf{r}+1}(\beta_j) \cdot G$ for some polynomial $h_{\mathsf{r}+1}$ of degree $\le t_{\mathsf{r}+1}$ and $h_{\mathsf{r}+1}(\beta_0) = h_{\mathsf{r}}(\alpha_0)$.

Protocol:

1. Let $pp_{\mathsf{Sh},\mathsf{r}+1} = (\mathbb{G}, G, p, t_{\mathsf{r}+1}, n_{\mathsf{r}+1}, \{\beta_j : j \in [0, n_{\mathsf{r}+1}]\})$.
2. Resharing: For $i = 1, \ldots, n_{\mathsf{r}}$, $P_{\mathsf{r},i}$ does the following:
   (a) $A_{\mathsf{r},i} \leftarrow C_{\mathsf{r},i} - \mathsf{sk}_{\mathsf{r},i} \cdot \mathsf{pk}_{D,L_{r-1}}$.
   (b) $(\{A_{i \to j} : j \in [n_{\mathsf{r}+1}]\}, m_i(X)) \leftarrow \mathsf{GShamir.Share}(pp_{\mathsf{Sh},\mathsf{r}+1}, A_{\mathsf{r},i})$.
   (c) For $j \in [n_{\mathsf{r}+1}]$, $C_{i \to j} \leftarrow \mathsf{sk}_{D_i} \cdot \mathsf{pk}_{\mathsf{r}+1,j} + A_{i \to j}$.
   (d) $m_i^*(X) \leftarrow \mathcal{H}(\{C_{\mathsf{r},i} : i \in [n_{\mathsf{r}}]\}, \mathsf{pk}_{D,L_{r-1}})$.
   (e) $U_i' \leftarrow \sum_{j=1}^n v_j' \cdot m_i^*(\beta_j) \cdot (C_{i \to j} - C_{\mathsf{r},i})$, $\quad V_i' \leftarrow \sum_{j=1}^n v_j' \cdot m_i^*(\beta_j) \cdot \mathsf{pk}_{\mathsf{r}+1,j}$, $W_i' \leftarrow (\sum_{j=1}^n v_j' \cdot m_i^*(\beta_j)) \cdot \mathsf{pk}_{D,L_{r-1}}$.
   (f) $\pi_{\mathsf{r},i} \leftarrow \Pi_{\mathsf{NI-Pre}}.\mathsf{Prove}((\mathsf{sk}_{\mathsf{r},i}, \mathsf{sk}_{D_i}); pp_\pi, (\mathsf{pk}_{\mathsf{r},i}, \mathsf{pk}_{D_i}, U_i'), f_i)$,
      where $f_i(\mathsf{sk}_{\mathsf{r},i}, \mathsf{sk}_{D_i}) := (\mathsf{sk}_{\mathsf{r},i} \cdot G, \mathsf{sk}_{D_i} \cdot G, \mathsf{sk}_{D_i} \cdot V_i' - \mathsf{sk}_{\mathsf{r},i} \cdot W_i')$.
   (g) Output $\{C_{i \to j} : j \in [n_{\mathsf{r}+1}]\}, \pi_{\mathsf{r},i}$.
3. Reconstruction of next share encryptions: each party in $\mathcal{P}$ locally constructs the encryptions of the shares for the following round as follows:
   (a) For each $i \in \mathcal{C}_{\mathsf{r}}$:
      i. Compute U_i' and f_i as above (from public information and $P_{\mathsf{r},i}$'s output $\{C_{i \to j} : j \in [n_{\mathsf{r}+1}]\}$).
      ii. Compute $\Pi_{\mathsf{NI-Pre}}.\mathsf{Verify}(pp_\pi, (\mathsf{pk}_{\mathsf{r},i}, \mathsf{pk}_{D_i}, U_i'), f_i, \pi_{\mathsf{r},i})$.
   (b) Define L_{r} the set of $t + 1$ first indices for which the above proofs accept.
   (c) For $j \in [n_{\mathsf{r}+1}]$, $C_{\mathsf{r}+1,j} \leftarrow \sum_{\ell \in L_{\mathsf{r}}} \lambda_{\ell,L} \cdot C_{\ell \to j}$.
   (d) $\mathsf{pk}_{D,L_{\mathsf{r}}} \leftarrow \sum_{\ell \in L_{\mathsf{r}}} \lambda_{\ell,L_{\mathsf{r}}} \cdot \mathsf{pk}_{D_\ell}$.
   (e) Output $(\{C_{\mathsf{r}+1,j} : j \in [n_{\mathsf{r}+1}]\}, (\pi_{\mathsf{r},\ell})_{\ell \in L_{\mathsf{r}}}, \mathsf{pk}_{D,L_{\mathsf{r}}})$.

Fig. 9. Protocol for DHPVSS resharing

6.1   Constructing **HEPVSS** with ECW

We modify HEPVSS to use our ECW scheme $\mathcal{E} = (\mathsf{Enc}, \mathsf{Dec})$ for lottery predicate $\mathsf{lottery}(\mathbf{B}, \mathsf{sl}, \mathsf{P}, \mathsf{sk}_{L,i})$ from Sect. 3 instead of a $\mathbb{Z}_p$-linear encryption scheme. We make the following modifications to the HEPVSS algorithms in Fig. 6, :

– **Communication:** All messages are posted to the underlying blockchain ledger used by the ECW scheme $\mathcal{E}$.
– HEPVSS.Setup($1^\lambda, t, n$): Besides the original setup parameters, we assume that n distinct role identifiers $\mathsf{P}_1, \ldots, \mathsf{P}_n$ are available and that an underlying blockchain protocol Γ is executed.
– HEPVSS.KeyGen(pp, id): Instead of publishing pk_i, each party P_i provides pk_i as input to the mixnet assumed as setup for $\mathsf{lottery}(\mathbf{B}, \mathsf{sl}, \mathsf{P}, \mathsf{sk}_{L,i})$ and associated ECW scheme $\mathcal{E}$. The mixnet output $\{(j, \mathsf{pk}_{\mathsf{Anon},j})\}_{j \in [n]}$ is assumed to be available on the underlying blockchain and accessible as

$$(\{(j, \mathsf{pk}_{\mathsf{Anon},j})\}_{j \in [n]}, \eta) \leftarrow \mathsf{param}(\mathbf{B}, \mathsf{sl}).$$

Party P_i sets $\mathsf{sk}_{L,i} \leftarrow (\mathsf{pk}_{\mathcal{E},i}, \mathsf{sk}_{\mathcal{E},i})$.
– HEPVSS.Dist($pp, \{\mathsf{pk}_i : i \in [n]\}, S$): Instead of computing $C_i \leftarrow \mathcal{E}.\mathsf{Enc}_{\mathsf{pk}_i}(A_i, \rho_i)$, the dealer computes $C_i \leftarrow \mathsf{Enc}(\mathbf{B}, \mathsf{sl}, \mathsf{P}_i, A_i)$ using randomness ρ_i. Notice that this is equivalent to computing $C_i \leftarrow \mathcal{E}.\mathsf{Enc}_{\mathsf{pk}_{\mathsf{Anon},j}}(A_i, \rho_i)$ for a j such that $\mathsf{lottery}(\mathbf{B}, \mathsf{sl}, \mathsf{P}_i, \mathsf{sk}_{L,j}) = 1$. Hence, $\mathsf{Pf}_{\mathsf{Sh}}$ can still be computed via the same procedure. The dealer publishes

$$(\{C_i : i \in [n]\}, \{\mathsf{pk}_{\mathsf{Anon},j} : i \in [n]\}, \mathsf{Pf}_{\mathsf{Sh}}).$$

Notice that the public key $\mathsf{pk}_{\mathsf{Anon},j}$ used to generate each C_i is publicly known due to the structure of the lottery scheme.
– HEPVSS.Verify($pp, \{(\mathsf{pk}_i, C_i) : i \in [n]\}, \mathsf{Pf}_{\mathsf{Sh}}$): No modification is needed, since $(\{C_i : i \in [n]\}, \{\mathsf{pk}_{\mathsf{Anon},j} : i \in [n]\}, \mathsf{Pf}_{\mathsf{Sh}})$ has the same structure as in the original protocol.
– HEPVSS.DecShare($pp, \mathsf{pk}_j, \mathsf{sk}_{L,j}, C_i$): Party P_j checks that its lottery witness $\mathsf{sk}_{L,j}$ is such that $\mathsf{lottery}(\mathbf{B}, \mathsf{sl}, \mathsf{P}_i, \mathsf{sk}_{L,j}) = 1$ and, if yes, computes $A_i \leftarrow \mathsf{Dec}(\tilde{\mathbf{B}}, C_i, \mathsf{sk}_{L,j})$. Proof $\mathsf{Pf}_{\mathsf{Dec}}$ is generated as in the original protocol. Notice that this procedure is also equivalent to generating an AfP $\mathsf{Pf}_{\mathsf{Dec}} \leftarrow \mathsf{AfP}.\mathsf{Sign}(\tilde{\mathbf{B}}, \mathsf{sl}, \mathsf{P}_i, \mathsf{sk}_{L,j}, A_i)$.
– HEPVSS.VerifyDec($pp, \mathsf{pk}_i, A_i, C_i, \mathsf{Pf}_{\mathsf{Dec}_i}$): Proof $\mathsf{Pf}_{\mathsf{Dec}}$ is checked as in the original protocol. Notice that this procedure is also equivalent to generating an AfP $\{0, 1\} \leftarrow \mathsf{AfP}.\mathsf{Ver}(\tilde{\mathbf{B}}, \mathsf{sl}, \mathsf{P}_i, \mathsf{Pf}_{\mathsf{Dec}}, A_i)$.
– HEPVSS.Rec($pp, \{A_i : i \in \mathcal{T}\}$): No modification is needed.

Due to the properties of the ECW scheme and the underlying lottery scheme, shares are encrypted towards parties randomly chosen to perform each role P_i whose identity remains unknown during the share distribution and verification phases. In case a reconstruction happens, parties executing each role reveal themselves by proving correctness of decrypted shares, which constitutes an AfP since it involved proving knowledge of $\mathsf{sk}_{L,j}$ such that $\mathsf{lottery}(\mathbf{B}, \mathsf{sl}, \mathsf{P}_i, \mathsf{sk}_{L,j}) = 1$.

6.2   Constructing Resharing for **HEPVSS** with **ECW**

In the context of resharing, the parties selected to execute roles $P_1, \ldots, P_n$ in slot sl_r wish to publicly verifiable reshare the secret whose shares they received towards roles $P'_1, \ldots, P'_{n'}$ in a future slot sl_{r+1}. In practice, this means that the resharing information will be received by a new randomly selected set of anonymous parties performing these roles in the future. Once again we explore the fact that our ECW inherits the properties of the underlying $\mathbb{Z}_p$-linear encryption scheme to modify the resharing protocol for **HEPVSS** (Sect. 5.1) to work with ECW. We show how to obtain an ECW based (and thus anonymous) resharing protocol in the full version of the paper [8].

6.3   Efficient DDH-Based Instantiation via **DHPVSS**

The most efficient instantiations of our techniques are obtained when using a variant of the El Gamal encryption scheme together with the SCRAPE share validity check. In order to enjoy the efficiency improvement, we show our ECW is also compatible with these optimizations in the full version of the paper [8].

References

1. Benhamouda, F., et al.: Can a public blockchain keep a secret? In: Pass, R., Pietrzak, K. (eds.) TCC 2020. LNCS, vol. 12550, pp. 260–290. Springer, Cham (2020). https://doi.org/10.1007/978-3-030-64375-1_10
2. Boudot, F., Traoré, J.: Efficient publicly verifiable secret sharing schemes with fast or delayed recovery. In: Varadharajan, V., Mu, Y. (eds.) ICICS 1999. LNCS, vol. 1726, pp. 87–102. Springer, Heidelberg (1999). https://doi.org/10.1007/978-3-540-47942-0_8
3. Boyle, E., Klein, S., Rosen, A., Segev, G.: Securing Abe's mix-net against malicious verifiers via witness indistinguishability. In: Catalano, D., De Prisco, R. (eds.) SCN 2018. LNCS, vol. 11035, pp. 274–291. Springer, Cham (2018). https://doi.org/10.1007/978-3-319-98113-0_15
4. Camenisch, J., Lysyanskaya, A.: Signature schemes and anonymous credentials from bilinear maps. In: Franklin, M. (ed.) CRYPTO 2004. LNCS, vol. 3152, pp. 56–72. Springer, Heidelberg (2004). https://doi.org/10.1007/978-3-540-28628-8_4
5. Campanelli, M., David, B., Khoshakhlagh, H., Konring, A., Nielsen, J.B.: Encryption to the future: a paradigm for sending secret messages to future (anonymous) committees. Cryptology ePrint Archive, Report 2021/1423 (2021). https://eprint.iacr.org/2021/1423
6. Cascudo, I., David, B.: SCRAPE: scalable randomness attested by public entities. In: Gollmann, D., Miyaji, A., Kikuchi, H. (eds.) ACNS 2017. LNCS, vol. 10355, pp. 537–556. Springer, Cham (2017). https://doi.org/10.1007/978-3-319-61204-1_27
7. Cascudo, I., David, B.: ALBATROSS: publicly AttestabLe BATched randomness based on secret sharing. In: Moriai, S., Wang, H. (eds.) ASIACRYPT 2020. LNCS, vol. 12493, pp. 311–341. Springer, Cham (2020). https://doi.org/10.1007/978-3-030-64840-4_11
8. Cascudo, I., David, B., Garms, L., Konring, A.: YOLO YOSO: fast and simple encryption and secret sharing in the YOSO model. Cryptology ePrint, Report 2022/242 (2022). https://eprint.iacr.org/2022/242

9. Chase, M., Lysyanskaya, A.: On signatures of knowledge. In: Dwork, C. (ed.) CRYPTO 2006. LNCS, vol. 4117, pp. 78–96. Springer, Heidelberg (2006). https://doi.org/10.1007/11818175_5

10. David, B., Gaži, P., Kiayias, A., Russell, A.: Ouroboros Praos: an adaptively-secure, semi-synchronous proof-of-stake blockchain. In: Nielsen, J.B., Rijmen, V. (eds.) EUROCRYPT 2018. LNCS, vol. 10821, pp. 66–98. Springer, Cham (2018). https://doi.org/10.1007/978-3-319-78375-8_3

11. Fujisaki, E., Okamoto, T.: A practical and provably secure scheme for publicly verifiable secret sharing and its applications. In: Nyberg, K. (ed.) EUROCRYPT 1998. LNCS, vol. 1403, pp. 32–46. Springer, Heidelberg (1998). https://doi.org/10.1007/BFb0054115

12. Gentry, C., et al.: YOSO: you only speak once - secure MPC with stateless ephemeral roles. In: Malkin, T., Peikert, C. (eds.) CRYPTO 2021. LNCS, vol. 12826, pp. 64–93. Springer, Cham (2021). https://doi.org/10.1007/978-3-030-84245-1_3

13. Gentry, C., Halevi, S., Lyubashevsky, V.: Practical non-interactive publicly verifiable secret sharing with thousands of parties. Cryptology ePrint Archive, Report 2021/1397 (2021). https://eprint.iacr.org/2021/1397

14. Gentry, C., Halevi, S., Magri, B., Nielsen, J.B., Yakoubov, S.: Random-index PIR and applications. In: Nissim, K., Waters, B. (eds.) TCC 2021. LNCS, vol. 13044, pp. 32–61. Springer, Cham (2021). https://doi.org/10.1007/978-3-030-90456-2_2

15. Goyal, R., Goyal, V.: Overcoming cryptographic impossibility results using blockchains. In: Kalai, Y., Reyzin, L. (eds.) TCC 2017. LNCS, vol. 10677, pp. 529–561. Springer, Cham (2017). https://doi.org/10.1007/978-3-319-70500-2_18

16. Heidarvand, S., Villar, J.L.: Public verifiability from pairings in secret sharing schemes. In: Avanzi, R.M., Keliher, L., Sica, F. (eds.) SAC 2008. LNCS, vol. 5381, pp. 294–308. Springer, Heidelberg (2009). https://doi.org/10.1007/978-3-642-04159-4_19

17. Kolby, S., Ravi, D., Yakoubov, S.: Towards efficient YOSO MPC without setup. Cryptology ePrint Archive, Report 2022/187 (2022). https://eprint.iacr.org/2022/187

18. Liu, J.K., Wei, V.K., Wong, D.S.: Linkable spontaneous anonymous group signature for ad hoc groups. In: Wang, H., Pieprzyk, J., Varadharajan, V. (eds.) ACISP 2004. LNCS, vol. 3108, pp. 325–335. Springer, Heidelberg (2004). https://doi.org/10.1007/978-3-540-27800-9_28

19. Rivest, R.L., Shamir, A., Tauman, Y.: How to leak a secret. In: Boyd, C. (ed.) ASIACRYPT 2001. LNCS, vol. 2248, pp. 552–565. Springer, Heidelberg (2001). https://doi.org/10.1007/3-540-45682-1_32

20. Ruiz, A., Villar, J.L.: Publicly verifiable secret sharing from Paillier's cryptosystem. In: Western European Workshop on Research in Cryptology 2005 (2005)

21. Schoenmakers, B.: A simple publicly verifiable secret sharing scheme and its application to electronic voting. In: Wiener, M. (ed.) CRYPTO 1999. LNCS, vol. 1666, pp. 148–164. Springer, Heidelberg (1999). https://doi.org/10.1007/3-540-48405-1_10

22. Stadler, M.: Publicly verifiable secret sharing. In: Maurer, U. (ed.) EUROCRYPT 1996. LNCS, vol. 1070, pp. 190–199. Springer, Heidelberg (1996). https://doi.org/10.1007/3-540-68339-9_17

State Machine Replication Under Changing Network Conditions

Andreea B. Alexandru[1]($\boxtimes$) , Erica Blum[1] , Jonathan Katz[1] ,
and Julian Loss[2]

[1] University of Maryland, College Park, USA
{aandreea,erblum}@umd.edu, jkatz@cs.umd.edu
[2] CISPA Helmholtz Center for Information Security, Saarbrücken, Germany
loss@cispa.de

Abstract. Protocols for state machine replication (SMR) are typically designed for synchronous or asynchronous networks, with a lower corruption threshold in the latter case. Recent *network-agnostic* protocols are secure when run in either a synchronous or an asynchronous network. We propose two new constructions of network-agnostic SMR protocols that improve on existing protocols in terms of either the adversarial model or communication complexity:
1. an *adaptively secure* protocol with optimal corruption thresholds and quadratic amortized communication complexity per transaction;
2. a statically secure protocol with near-optimal corruption thresholds and *linear* amortized communication complexity per transaction.

We further explore SMR protocols run in a network that may change between synchronous and asynchronous arbitrarily often; parties can be uncorrupted (as in the proactive model), and the protocol should remain secure as long as the appropriate corruption thresholds are maintained. We show that purely asynchronous proactive secret sharing is impossible without some form of synchronization between the parties, ruling out a natural approach to proactively secure network-agnostic SMR protocols. Motivated by this negative result, we consider a model where the adversary is limited in the total number of parties it can corrupt over the duration of the protocol and show, in this setting, that our SMR protocols remain secure even under arbitrarily changing network conditions.

Keywords: State machine replication · Consensus · Proactive security

1 Introduction

Protocols for *state machine replication (SMR)* allow a set of parties $P_1, \ldots, P_n$ to agree on a continuously growing, ordered log of transactions. SMR protocols

A. B. Alexandru, E. Blum and J. Katz—Work supported in part by NSF award #1837517.

J. Loss—Part of this work was done while the author was a postdoctoral researcher at the University of Maryland and at the Carnegie Mellon University.

S. Agrawal and D. Lin (Eds.): ASIACRYPT 2022, LNCS 13791, pp. 681–710, 2022.
https://doi.org/10.1007/978-3-031-22963-3_23

enable the evolving state of a distributed system to be replicated across multiple parties, even when some of them are malicious. SMR lies at the core of many distributed applications and has recently received considerable attention in the context of blockchain protocols. Most of the literature focuses on protocols that are secure in either the *synchronous* or the *asynchronous* model. SMR protocols in the synchronous model can tolerate $t < n/2$ corrupted parties (or $t < n$ corrupted parties if external validity is not required [34]), but may fail if the synchrony assumption is violated. On the other hand, asynchronous protocols are secure under arbitrary network conditions, but do not exist when $t \geq n/3$.

Recent work of Blum, Katz, and Loss [7] introduced the *network-agnostic* model in which a single protocol is required to be secure regardless of whether it is run in a synchronous or an asynchronous network, for different corruption thresholds. In subsequent work [8], they show that for any thresholds $t_a \leq t_s$ with $2t_s + t_a < n$, there is an SMR protocol that tolerates t_a corrupted parties if the network is asynchronous and simultaneously tolerates t_s corrupted parties if the network is synchronous. A major benefit of network-agnostic protocols over classical ones is that t_a, t_s can be chosen arbitrarily subject to the above constraints. This allows a protocol designer to flexibly choose t_a, t_s so as to minimize the probability of failure based on assumed properties of the environment.

Although network-agnostic protocols have recently received significant attention [5,7–9,17,29], several open questions regarding network-agnostic SMR remain. For one, existing results are primarily concerned with feasibility rather than efficiency; this is especially true when considering protocols secure against an adaptive adversary who can choose which parties to corrupt during the execution of the protocol. Perhaps the most significant limitation of prior work is that it either requires the network to be synchronous for the lifetime of the protocol, or else guarantees security only if the attacker never exceeds the corruption threshold of t_a. Providing a more elegant treatment of networks that can change arbitrarily often between synchronous and asynchronous was left as an explicit open question in prior work.

1.1 Challenges and State-of-the-Art

We begin with a brief overview of network-agnostic SMR, and then explain how existing solutions (do not) deal with the issues raised above.

Network-Agnostic SMR. The goal of an SMR protocol is to impose order on transactions that arrive in parties' buffers in an arbitrary fashion. An SMR protocol must ensure *consistency*, which means that all parties agree on the order in which transactions are committed to some log, and *liveness*, which means that any transactions in the buffers of honest parties are eventually appended to the log. SMR is significantly more challenging than the related problem of Byzantine agreement, where parties agree on only a single value.

A network-agnostic SMR protocol must remain secure if the network is synchronous and there are at most t_s corruptions, or if the network is asynchronous and there are at most t_a corruptions. As a key building block for SMR in this setting, Blum et al. [8] introduced a novel protocol for asynchronous common subset (ACS) that allows parties to agree on a subset of $n - t_a$ inputs in the presence of t_a corrupted parties in an asynchronous network. Their protocol has the property that if all honest parties supply *the same input* B to the protocol, then honest parties include B in their output even when t_s parties are corrupted. This facilitates the following strategy: parties first attempt to agree on an input B using a synchronous protocol. If the network is synchronous, this step will succeed even in the presence of t_s corrupted parties; thus, parties all use the same input B to ACS which outputs this block even if there are t_s corrupted parties. On the other hand, if the network is asynchronous, t_a-security of ACS ensures that all parties can agree on B without relying on the synchronous protocol.

Problems with Existing Solutions. Blum et al. [8] present two SMR protocols, Tardigrade and Upgrade. Tardigrade is secure against an adaptive adversary and requires $O(n^4)$ bits of communication for n transactions. Upgrade gives a more efficient alternative against a static adversary that requires only $O(n^3)$ bits of communication for n^2 transactions. However, Upgrade relies on random subcommittees to execute the most expensive steps of the protocol. Such protocols are not adaptively secure and require very large committees in order to provide meaningful corruption bounds. This arguably offsets the communication improvements made by Upgrade, as it only offers an asymptotic improvement if the total number of parties in the system is in the order of hundreds of thousands.

Moreover, their work only considers non-switching networks, i.e., the network is either synchronous or asynchronous for the entire duration of the protocol. Thus, if at any point in the lifetime of the protocol the adversary surpasses t_a corrupted parties, their protocols might be insecure if the network is ever asynchronous. We are interested in a more flexible model that tolerates repeated transitions of the network between synchronous and asynchronous behavior, and even in the presence of an adaptive, mobile adversary.

1.2   Our Contributions

We study protocols in a more realistic model where network conditions can arbitrarily change over time, and parties can also recover from corruptions. Such recovery is necessary if we want to allow more than t_a corruptions when the network is synchronous, but then restrict the adversary to fewer than t_a corruptions when the network becomes asynchronous.

Modeling Recovery from Key Exposure. Modeling parties that are temporarily corrupted (sometimes referred to in the literature as *transient faults*) is non-trivial when parties have long-term keys. To model the process of uncorruption, we endow parties with a mechanism to forcibly "flush out" the adversary. (This could be achieved, for example, by having parties restart their computer in safe mode at the onset of a new protocol epoch.) The adaptive adversary can then choose to re-corrupt those parties or new ones. However, without additional measures in place, the internal state of the previously corrupted parties (including their long-term secret keys) remains known to the adversary. Proactive secret sharing is the main technique to refresh parties' keys for threshold signatures and related primitives commonly used in communication-efficient randomized SMR protocols. We prove that without further restrictions, secure proactive secret sharing protocols in the pure asynchronous and network-agnostic setting are impossible. While this may seem to be a folklore result, modeling and proving such a result is non-trivial. One of our contributions is to formalize this result and provide a rigorous proof.

To address the above impossibility in the context of SMR protocols, we consider a model in which the attacker is limited to corrupting a set S of at most t_s parties *for the lifetime of the protocol.* (It may corrupt this entire set of parties when the network is synchronous, and must uncorrupt at least $t_s - t_a$ of them when the network becomes asynchronous.) Since transient corruptions are rarely considered in the context of SMR, limiting the total number of faults to t_s seems like a reasonable assumption which is in line with most of the existing literature.

Practical Network-Agnostic SMR. We propose two new efficient protocols for SMR, Update and Upstate.

Update is adaptively secure for optimal corruption thresholds and has $O(n^3)$ communication complexity for committing a block of $O(n)$. This is an $O(n)$ improvement over Tardigrade [8], which requires $O(n^4)$ communication to commit blocks of $O(n)$ transactions. We obtain the improvement by carefully applying error-correcting codes in a new ACS protocol.

Upstate is statically secure for near-optimal corruption thresholds and has $O(n^2)$ communication complexity to commit blocks of $O(n)$ transactions. Upstate achieves its improved communication complexity by using committees. Upstate compares favorably to Upgrade [8]: while Upgrade requires $O(n^3)$ communication to commit blocks of $O(n^2)$ transactions, Upstate commits blocks of $O(n)$ transactions and requires $O(n^2)$ communication.

SMR Tolerating Key Exposure. We show that our protocols are also secure when the network can transition between synchronous and asynchronous behavior and the adversary can be mobile across epochs, but is limited to corrupting at most t_s unique parties. Adding reboots at the beginning of each protocol epoch to flush the adversary out helps Update and Upstate to withstand the key exposures caused by the adversary's mobility. Security in this case follows naturally from the structure of network-agnostic protocols. In order to be secure under a higher number of corruptions during the synchronous phase, some parts of the protocol have to use high thresholds for message collection. Although the adversary can know up to t_s keys/key shares during an asynchronous phase following a transition from a synchronous phase, it can only actively corrupt t_a parties and is not able to break security even if it forges or erases keys.

Open Questions. We leave open the question of designing an adaptively secure SMR protocol in our setting with quadratic communication complexity per committed block. We also leave open to explore communication-efficient proactive network-agnostic SMR protocols that bypass the impossibility result of network-agnostic proactive secret sharing. We remark that although our protocols use threshold cryptosystems to boost efficiency and censorship resilience, these may not be necessary. Thus, it is plausible that a solution for key refresh could be achieved without limiting the adversary to corrupting a set of t_s parties. One could then hope to use a network-agnostic ACS protocol to agree on a new list of valid public keys obtained from distributed key generation.

1.3 Related Work

Network-agnostic protocols were introduced by Blum et al. in the context of Byzantine agreement [7], and were later extended to multi-party computation [9] and SMR [8]. The latter presents two network-agnostic SMR protocols. Tardigrade achieves total communication $O(n^4 + n^3\ell)$ against adaptive adversaries, for n the number of parties and ℓ the block size. Upgrade uses committees to achieve total communication $O(n^3 + n\ell)$ against static adversaries (but tolerates fewer corruptions). Appan et al. [5] proposed a protocol for network-agnostic perfectly secure multi-party computation; their protocol uses a novel network-agnostic perfectly secure verifiable secret sharing protocol.

Since our protocols need to support both synchronous and asynchronous networks, and asynchronous SMR protocols are less communication efficient compared to their synchronous counterparts [2,3], we focus here on asynchronous SMR protocols tolerating $t < n/3$ corruptions. Canonical constructions for SMR and atomic broadcast are based on multi-value validated asynchronous Byzantine agreement or asynchronous common subset [11,15,21,24,28] with cubic communication complexity for input sizes linear in n. Only a few existing protocols in the asynchronous setting tolerate *adaptive* corruptions. EPIC [25] and DAG-Rider [23] achieve adaptive security with cubic total communication complexity; Dumbo2 [21] can be modified to achieve adaptive security by using the MVBA from [26]. Neither can be easily adapted to the network-agnostic setting.

A final group of related works concerns secret sharing and distributed key generation (DKG) where parties may crash and then recover or where the set of participants may change. In the *proactive model* [31], the adversary can be mobile across the corrupted parties over time. *Proactive secret sharing* (PSS) was introduced by Herzberg et al. [22]. Canetti et al. [12] and Frankel et al. [16] gave solutions for synchronous DKG against adaptive proactive adversaries using verifiable secret sharing schemes. Benhamouda et al. [6] introduced a secret-sharing protocol for passing secrets from one anonymous committee to another, while Groth [20] proposed a DKG scheme based on publicly verifiable secret sharing that allows refreshing key shares to a new committee. In the asynchronous case, Cachin et al. [10] presented a proactive refresh protocol assuming clock ticks that define epochs, based on [13] which recovers state in an SMR protocol. Schulze et al. [33] proposed a mobile PSS protocol in a partially synchronous network. Recently, several works [27,32,35] have proposed more efficient dynamic/mobile PSS protocols assuming eventual synchrony, short periods of synchrony at the end of an epoch, or synchronized epochs. Subsequent to our work, Yurek et al. [36] constructed an asynchronous dynamic PSS protocol (circumventing our impossibility result) but with respect to different definitions than ours.

A related notion of security in the presence of exposed parties was considered in [19], which studied synchronous authenticated broadcast with both corrupted parties and parties who are honest but whose keys have been exposed.

Paper Organization. We describe our model in Sect. 2, and provide definitions in Sect. 3. In Sect. 4, we present an ACS protocol that uses error-correcting codes in order to achieve $O(n^3)$ communication against an adaptive adversary, and prove its special properties. This ACS protocol is used as a building block in the Update SMR protocol presented in Sect. 5, which achieves optimal corruption thresholds in a network-agnostic setting. In Sect. 6, we describe an asymptotically more efficient SMR protocol, Upstate, that is secure under near optimal thresholds against a static adversary. In Sect. 7, we prove that under a restricted adversarial model, the SMR protocols discussed so far remain secure under arbitrary network transitions. In Sect. 8, we model and provide an impossibility proof for proactive asynchronous verifiable secret sharing. This result motivates our restricted mobile adversarial model.

2   Model

Network. We consider n parties $P_1, \ldots, P_n$ that are connected via pairwise authenticated channels and have access to a public key infrastructure. During the protocol's execution, transactions are delivered to parties' local buffers. We are not concerned with how these transactions originate; in practice, there is an external mechanism where clients gossip these transactions in the network.

When the network is *synchronous*, messages between parties are delivered with a finite, known delay Δ, and the local clocks of the parties are synchronized. When the network is *asynchronous*, messages between parties are eventually delivered to their intended recipient, but may be adversarially delayed or reordered. The local clocks of parties are only assumed to be monotonically increasing and are not necessarily synchronized anymore. If an asynchronous phase is followed by a synchronous phase, all messages sent during the asynchronous phase of the network are delivered by the beginning of the synchronous phase. Transitions between synchronous and asynchronous behaviors can happen arbitrarily.

An SMR protocol operates in logical intervals called *epochs*, which are measured and incremented locally. Another concept is that of a *round of communication*. In the synchronous setting, a round r refers to the time between $(r-1)\Delta$ and $r\Delta$. In the asynchronous case, the round number will describe some particular send actions that are performed by a party.

We assume that parties perform *atomic send operations*, i.e., parties can send a message to multiple parties simultaneously in such a way that the adversary cannot corrupt them in between individual sends. Moreover, we assume that the adversary cannot perform *after the fact removal*, i.e., the adversary cannot indefinitely prevent a message from being delivered once it is sent by an honest party, even if the adversary corrupts it at some point after the send action.

Threat Model. We consider a *Byzantine fault* model, in which some fraction of the parties may be corrupted by an adversary. The adversary controls the local computations, messages, and current state of any corrupted party, and can coordinate the actions of all corrupted parties. Uncorrupted parties are called *honest*. For any honestly-initiated communication, the adversary receives the epoch τ, the sender identity S, the receiver identity R and the message m (which can be encrypted, in which case the adversary does not see its contents). The adversary determines when to deliver each message.

We assume that the adversary is (t_a, t_s)-limited, i.e., for some fixed thresholds t_s, t_a $(t_a \leq t_s)$, up to $t_s < n/2$ parties may be corrupted if the network is synchronous and up to $t_a < n/3$ parties may be corrupted if the network is asynchronous. (The optimal trade-off between t_s, t_a is known to be $2t_s + t_a < n$ [8]). In Sects. 4–5 we consider an *adaptive and rushing* adversary that adaptively corrupts parties over the course of a protocol execution; in Sect. 6, we consider a *static* adversary who corrupts parties prior to the start of an epoch.

Further, we address a mobile adversary. In Sect. 8, we consider an *epoch-wise mobile adaptive adversary* that can move freely between parties from epoch to epoch as long as it does not exceed more than t_s adaptive corruptions in the synchronous case and t_a adaptive corruptions in the asynchronous case at a given moment in time or in a given epoch. In Sect. 7, we consider a slightly different adversary who adaptively corrupts at most t_s parties *over the lifetime of the protocol*, and is only permitted to move between those t_s parties between epochs. We will explicitly mention the adversary's capabilities in each section.

Reboot. To enable protocols to withstand network changes, we assume a reboot mechanism that causes a party to restart its device, thereby flushing out the adversary. Reboots occur at specified times during the protocols, not necessarily simultaneously. The adversary can immediately corrupt a party after rebooting, as long as it does not exceed the allowed threshold at that time. The restart is performed via code written in untamperable memory. Importantly, rebooting does not remove the previous state of a corrupted party from the adversary's view; in particular, the adversary still knows the secret state of a party, including any secret keys that were held by that party during corruption. Furthermore, the internal state of a corrupted party that has restarted may have been arbitrarily modified by the adversary. For clarity, we call a party *actively corrupted* when the adversary actively controls that party's behavior and *passively corrupted* or *exposed* if the party was uncorrupted either by the adversary or by reboot.

Keys. Every party P_i holds a private key sk_i of a threshold signature scheme with individual public signature key pk_i and public key pk. Further, every party P_i holds a private key dk_i of a threshold encryption scheme with individual public verification key vk_i and public key ek. The threshold for both schemes is $t_s + 1$. We assume a trusted dealer that generates $PK = (pk_1, \ldots, pk_n, pk, vk_1, \ldots, vk_n, ek)$ and $sk_1, \ldots, sk_n, dk_1, \ldots, dk_n$ and outputs a signature and encryption private keys sk_i, dk_i and the public key PK to each party P_i.

A party P_i can use its signature key sk_i to generate a signature share σ_i on a message m. The signature share σ_i can be verified using the message m and the public verification key pk_i, and is called *valid* if the verification is successful. As a shorthand notation for legibility, we use $\langle m \rangle_i$ for a threshold signature σ_i

of message m under secret key sk_i. A set of $t_s + 1$ valid signature shares on the same message m can be used to compute a signature σ for that message, which can be verified using the public key pk and m.

A party P_i can encrypt a message m using the public encryption key ek to generate a ciphertext c, and can use its decryption key dk_i to obtain a decryption share c_i of c. A decryption share c_i can be verified with respect to c, ek and vk_i and is called *correct* if the verification is successful. A set of $t_s + 1$ correct decryption shares can be used to obtain the decryption m of the ciphertext c.

We assume adaptively secure idealized threshold signature scheme and threshold encryption scheme. For a parameter κ, a signature share and a full signature have length $O(\kappa)$. We implicitly assume that parties use domain separation when constructing signatures to ensure only local context validity. An encryption of a message m of length $|m|$ has length $|m| + O(\kappa)$, and a decryption share has length $O(\kappa)$; these criteria can be met using standard KEM/DEM mechanisms.

3 Preliminaries

State machine replication protocols enable a set of parties to emulate a single server by agreeing on an ever-growing, ordered log of transactions.[1] Given that SMR protocols usually continue indefinitely, we opt for a definition that clearly states how the logs are constructed and committed, and their relation order depending on epochs. A party maintains an ever-growing append-only log consisting of *blocks* of transactions: $blocks_i = (block_i[1], block_i[2], \ldots)$, where the notation $block_i[e]$ refers to the block output by party P_i in epoch e. Each $block_i[e]$ is initialized with a special character $\perp$ and populated by a set of transactions by P_i in epoch e. A party's epoch number is incremented after it outputs a block.

Definition 1 (State Machine Replication (SMR)). *Let Π be a protocol executed by n parties $P_1, \ldots, P_n$. Let pp be some public parameters (e.g., PKI). Parties receive transactions as input, locally maintain arrays blocks, and output blocks and a publicly verifiable proof $\pi_i[e]$ for each $block_i[e]$ in blocks. Π is a secure SMR protocol tolerating t corruptions if the following properties hold:*

- *(t-Consistency) If an honest party outputs a block B in epoch e then all honest parties output B in epoch e.*
- *(t-Completeness) Every honest party outputs a block in all epochs.*
- *(t-Liveness) If a transaction tx is input to at least $n - t$ honest parties, then all honest parties eventually output a block containing tx.*
- *(t-External validity) If an honest party outputs (B, π), then for a fixed public Boolean function Verify it holds that $\mathsf{Verify}(pp, B, \pi) = 1$.*

Definition 2 (Binary Byzantine Agreement (BA)). *Let Π be a protocol executed by n parties $P_1, \ldots, P_n$, where each party P_i begins holding input $x_i \in \{0, 1\}$ and parties terminate upon generating output. Π is a secure BA protocol tolerating t corruptions if the following properties hold:*

---

[1] Following [29], we distinguish between SMR and atomic broadcast in that the former explicitly requires an externally verifiable proof of output validity.

- *(t-Validity)* If every honest party's input is equal to the same value x, then every honest party outputs x.
- *(t-Consistency)* All honest parties output the same message x.
- *(t-Termination)* Every honest party eventually terminates with output x.

Definition 3 (Asynchronous Common Subset (ACS)). *Let Π be a protocol executed by n parties $P_1, \ldots, P_n$, where each party P_i begins holding input $x_i \in \{0,1\}^*$ and parties output sets of cardinality at most n. Π is a secure ACS protocol tolerating t corruptions if the following properties hold:*

- *(t-Validity)* If every honest party's input is equal to the same value x, then every honest party outputs the value $\{x\}$.
- *(t-Validity with termination)* If every honest party's input is equal to the same value x, then every honest party outputs the value $\{x\}$ and terminates.
- *(t-Consistency)* If an honest party outputs S, all honest parties output S.
- *(t-Set quality)* If an honest party outputs a set S, then S contains the input of at least one honest party.
- *(t-Termination)* Every honest party generates output and terminates.

Block agreement (introduced in [8]) is a validated agreement on objects called *pre-blocks*. A pre-block is a vector of length n where the ith entry is either $\perp$ or a message with a valid signature attached. The *quality* of a pre-block is defined as the number of entries that are not $\perp$; a *k-quality pre-block* has quality at least k.

Definition 4 (Block Agreement (BLA)). *Let Π be a protocol executed by n parties $P_1, \ldots, P_n$, where each party P_i begins holding input $x_i \in \{0,1\}^*$ and terminates upon generating output. Π is a secure BLA protocol tolerating t corruptions if the following properties hold:*

- *(t-Validity)* If every honest party has input an $(n-t)$-quality pre-block, then every honest party outputs an $(n-t)$-quality pre-block.
- *(t-Consistency)* Every honest party outputs the same pre-block B.

Next, we briefly introduce some standard cryptographic primitives we use.

Threshold Signature Schemes. A (t,n)-threshold signature scheme is a signature scheme allowing $t+1$ parties out of n to compute a signature on a message, with up to $t < n$ corruptions. It is *non-interactive* if parties can non-interactively compute signature shares that can be combined in the signature on a message, using protocols TS.Setup, TS.KeyGen, TS.Sign, TS.ShVer, TS.Verify for setup, key generation, partial signing, share verification and signature verification. The desired properties are correctness, security (unforgeability under chosen-message attack) and robustness (any number $\geq t+1$ of signature shares can be combined to yield a signature) against a probabilistic polynomial-time adversary.

Linear Error Correcting Codes. We adopt from [30] the description of error correcting codes, in particular, the Reed-Solomon (RS) code. An (n,b)-RS code encodes b data symbols into codewords of n symbols, and can decode the codewords to recover the original data.

Given inputs $m_1, \ldots, m_b$, the encoding function ENC computes codewords $s_1, \ldots, s_n$. Knowledge of any b elements of the codeword uniquely determines the input message and the remaining of the codeword.

The decoding function DEC computes $(m_1, \ldots, m_b)$, and is capable of tolerating up to c errors and d erasures in codewords $(s_1, \ldots, s_n)$, if and only if $n - b \geq 2c + d$.

Committee Election. A first method to elect a committee uses threshold signatures to produce an unpredictable coin. The coin is used to determine an ordering of parties by computing the hash $H(\mathsf{coin}, i)$ and to order the parties accordingly. To elect a size κ committee, one simply takes the first κ parties in the ordering. The second method, known as *cryptographic sortition*, uses verifiable random functions (VRF) to allow each party to individually determine whether they are part of a committee, and then prove their membership to others [1,18]. During the protocol, parties are elected to a committee if and only if the output of the VRF on a specific string is less than a parameter b.

Throughout the paper, we deal with several security parameters. The signature size and the hash output size depend on a parameter that ensures computational security. The committee sizes depend on a parameter that ensures a negligible failure probability. To streamline notation, we denote all these by κ.

4   Asynchronous Common Subset

The flow of the ACS protocol is outlined in Fig. 1 and its concrete steps are shown in Fig. 3. Each party $P_1, \ldots, P_n$, starts with an input of size ℓ and splits it into b blocks. These b blocks are then encoded into n codewords of size ℓ/b using a linear error correcting code. Each party P_i forms a message containing the j-th codeword and a hash of the input, signs it and sends it to party P_j. Upon receiving a validly signed message, each party multicasts it, along with the associated signature which will serve as a proof of the codeword validity. We refer to this procedure of input distribution as INDI, and present it in Fig. 2. INDI is performed before the agreement on whose messages to output, and ensures that all parties are eventually able to reconstruct the selected inputs despite an adaptive adversary.

Upon receiving $n - t_s$ messages containing codewords, parties attempt to reconstruct the input. Instructions related to reconstruction (referred to as RECON) are shown in Fig. 2. Upon reconstructing a valid input from some party P_j, parties multicast a signed vote message. Upon receiving $t_s + 1$ votes for P_j, parties assemble a certificate of validity for the reconstructed value of P_j, which consists of $t_s + 1$ signatures on h_j, used to form a full signature. The parties multicast a commit message carrying this certificate and the combined signature. We note that recently, Das et al. [14] proposed an asynchronous reliable broadcast protocol using error correcting codes (but without digital signatures) that is related to this step. Finally, upon receiving a unique commit message for party P_j, parties input 1 to the corresponding BA_j instance. We implicitly assume that if honest parties receive conflicting commit messages, they do not input 1 to the respective BA.

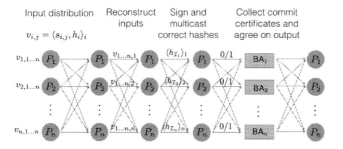

Fig. 1. Diagram of the steps in the Π_{ACS} protocol. BA stands for Byzantine Agreement. $\mathcal{I}_i$ is the set of indices j for which party P_i reconstructed the initial message of party P_j.

INDI(x)

1. Encode x using ENC into codewords $s_{i,1} \dots, s_{i,n}$. Compute $h_i := H(x)$.
2. For $j \in [n]$, compute $\varphi_{i,j} := \mathsf{TS.Sign}(\mathsf{PK}, \mathsf{sk}_i, (s_{i,j}, h_i))$. Set $v_{i,j} := (s_{i,j}, h_i, \varphi_{i,j})$. Send $v_{i,j}$ to party P_j.
3. Upon receiving a valid $v_{j,i} = (s_{j,i}, h_j, \varphi_{j,i})$, multicast $\langle v_{j,i} \rangle_i$.
4. Output the received set of $\{\langle v_{j,k} \rangle_k\}$ for P_j from P_k.

RECON($\{\langle v_{j,k} \rangle_k\}$)

1. Parse $v_{j,k}$ as $(s_{j,k}, h_j, \varphi_{j,k})$ and ignore the ones with invalid signatures (either from P_j or from P_k). Let K be the set of remaining messages.
2. If there exists a subset $K' \subseteq K$ such that $|K'| \geq n - t_s$ and all contained messages $v_{j,k}$ have the same value h_j, compute $x = \mathsf{DEC}(\{s_{j,k}\}_{k \in K'})$.
3. If $H(x) = h$, output x. Else, output $\perp$.

Fig. 2. Input distribution and reconstruction from the perspective of party $P_{i \in \{1,\dots,n\}}$.

Protocol Π_{Term} (Fig. 4) assembles an output certificate that allows parties to output and terminate (OC 0), ensuring no honest parties are "left behind".

Across the protocols, we use PK as the public keys output by TS.KeyGen and sk_i the secret key associated to P_i. For simplicity, in Π_{ACS} and the corresponding functionalities, we use $\varphi_{i,j}$ as both the signature of P_i over $s_{i,j}$, and over h_i, sent to party P_j. In this section (and all sections but Sect. 7), we use a binary BA protocol with t_a-validity, t_a-consistency, and t_a-termination in the presence of $t_a < n/3$ adaptive corruptions, and communication complexity of $O(n^2)$.

Encoding and Reconstruction. ENC and DEC are associated to a (n, b)-RS code (Sect. 3). In the reconstruct procedure RECON, before feeding the codewords into the DEC algorithm, parties first check that the corresponding signatures are correct. Then, parties check whether at least $n - t_s$ of the messages

$$\Pi_{\mathsf{ACS}}(x_i)$$

1. Run INDI(x) and store $\{\langle v_{j,k}\rangle_k\}$ for P_j as they are received from P_k.
2. Input $\{\langle v_{j,k}\rangle_k\}$ to RECON. If RECON outputs x_j, multicast a vote $\mathsf{vote}_i := \langle \mathsf{vote}, \langle h_j \rangle_i, \varphi_{j,i} \rangle_i$.
3. Upon receiving $t_s + 1$ valid votes from distinct P_k on j, combine the threshold signatures into a full signature and form a certificate $c_j := (\mathsf{commit}, \langle h_j \rangle)$ and send it to all parties.
4. Upon receiving a commit certificate c_j for the input of a party P_j, forward it to all parties.
5. Upon receiving a commit certificate for party P_j input 1 to BA_j. After outputting 1 in at least $n - t_a$ BA instances, input 0 for the rest.
6. Set $\mathcal{S}$ to be the set of indices of the BA instances that delivered 1.
7. Output according to the following output conditions:

OC 0. If P_i has received a valid certificate $(\mathsf{output}, \tilde{c}, x, h)$, multicast $(\mathsf{output}, \tilde{c}, x, h)$. Output x and terminate.
OC 1. Else if P_i (i) has obtained $n - t_s$ certificates $(\mathsf{commit}, \langle h_j \rangle)$ and (ii) reconstructed inputs x_j such that $h_j = H(x_j)$ of distinct P_j, all have the same value x, then input (x_j, h_j) to Π_{Term}.
OC 2. Else if P_i has (i) $|\mathcal{S}| \geq n - t_a$, (ii) all n BA instances have terminated, (iii) P_i has obtained certificate $(\mathsf{commit}, \langle h_j \rangle)$ for $j \in \mathcal{S}$, (iv) reconstructed input x_j such that $h_j = H(x_j)$ and such that a strict majority of $\{x_j\}_{j \in \mathcal{S}}$ has value x, then input (x_j, h_j) to Π_{Term}.
OC 3. Else if P_i has (i) $|\mathcal{S}| \geq n - t_a$, (ii) all n BA instances have terminated, (iii) P_i has obtained certificates $(\mathsf{commit}, \langle h_j \rangle)$ and (iv) reconstructed input x_j such that $h_j = H(x_j)$ for all $j \in \mathcal{S}$, then output $S = \bigcup_{j \in \mathcal{S}} x_j$ and terminate.

Fig. 3. ACS protocol from the perspective of party $P_{i \in \{1,\dots,n\}}$.

$$\Pi_{\mathsf{Term}}(x, h)$$

1. Multicast $\langle x, h \rangle_i$.
2. Upon receiving at least $t_s + 1$ valid signature shares $\langle x, H(x) \rangle_i$ from distinct parties, aggregate the signature shares into an output certificate $\tilde{c}$ for x and multicast $(\mathsf{output}, \tilde{c}, x, H(x))$. Output x and terminate.
3. Upon receiving a valid output certificate $\tilde{c}$ for x, multicast $(\mathsf{output}, \tilde{c}, x, h)$. Output x and terminate.

Fig. 4. Termination helper protocol from the perspective of party $P_{i \in \{1,\dots,n\}}$.

have the same associated hash value. If an honest party has not managed to reconstruct an input yet, it waits for more messages, then calls RECON again. Thus, each party feeds at least $n - t_s$ valid codewords in DEC. The (n, b)-RS code allows a party to split an input in b blocks and encode them into n codewords. In order to tolerate d erasures, it must be possible to reconstruct the b blocks from $n - d$ correct codewords. Furthermore, to tolerate c errors among $n - d$ codewords, it must hold that $n - b \geq 2c + d$.

If we let b be equal to t_s, we can tolerate either $t_s + t_a$ erasures, or tolerate t_a errors along with $t_s - t_a$ erasures (since $n > 2t_s + t_a$). This means we need to wait for $n - t_s + t_a$ codewords in total in order to guarantee correct reconstruction in the asynchronous case when t_a parties are corrupted. Thus, a gain in communication efficiency, obtained from using codewords to achieve agreement on length κ hashes instead of length ℓ inputs and from not multicasting the reconstructed output, leads to potentially having to wait for $n - t_s + t_a$ messages in order to reconstruct the correct output if the adversary delivered t_a bad codewords.

If we let b be equal to t_a, we can tolerate either t_s errors and no erasures, or $2t_s$ erasures. This corresponds to the synchronous case when t_s parties are corrupted, and honest parties receive all messages that were sent after at most Δ time. Therefore, if an honest party only receives $n - t_s$ codewords, they are all correct. However, we will show below that there is no need to tolerate t_s errors in the synchronous case. Briefly, we can use extra information—the hash value—in order to detect an incorrect reconstruction, and there will be sufficiently many inputs of the honest parties correctly reconstructed in order to achieve termination. Therefore it suffices to let $b = t_s$ throughout.

Lemma 1. *Suppose there are at most t_a corruptions. Given a certificate* (commit, $\langle h \rangle$) *for a party P, all honest parties can eventually reconstruct the same output in a run of Π_{ACS}.*

Proof. If P is honest, then all honest parties will eventually receive $n - t_s$ valid codewords of the true input (since we assume unforgeable signatures), allowing them to correctly reconstruct x.

Assume P is dishonest. To obtain a valid commit certificate on P's hash $\langle h \rangle$, $t_s - t_a + 1$ honest parties need to have seen $n - t_s$ valid messages, all with the same $h = H(x)$. Of these $n - t_s$ messages, t_a could have been sent by corrupted parties in the multicast round. In the worst case, in the first round when P sent codewords, it could have sent only $n - t_s - t_a$ codewords (but all valid) to distinct honest parties. Eventually, all honest parties receive the $n - t_s - t_a$ codewords and can reconstruct the same input x if the code tolerates $t_s + t_a$ erasures.

On the other hand, the adversary might send t_a malicious codewords which will prevent correct reconstruction from $n - t_s$ codewords. However, assuming H is a collision-resistant hash function, except with negligible probability, there do not exist inputs $x \neq x'$ reconstructed by different sets of codewords such that $h = H(x) = H(x')$. Therefore, if after inputting $n - t_s$ codewords to RECON and not obtaining a valid output with respect to h, the honest parties wait until they receive sufficient codewords in order to be able to correctly reconstruct.

As stated above, each input of size ℓ is split into to $b = t_s$ blocks: $n - t_s > t_a + t_s = 2t_a + t_s - t_a$. This means that the code can tolerate either $t_a + t_s$ erasures, or $t_s - t_a$ erasures and t_a errors if parties wait for $n - t_s + t_a$ messages to honest parties. $\qquad\square$

Lemma 2. *If there are at most t_a corruptions, there cannot be two valid certificates* (commit, $\langle h \rangle$), (commit, $\langle h' \rangle$), *associated with P, and $h \neq h'$.*

Proof. If P is honest, then all honest parties eventually receive $n - t_s$ valid messages containing codewords and the same hash h of the true input, so they can correctly reconstruct x. Therefore, assuming unforgeable signatures, no valid commit message (commit, $\langle h' \rangle$) for $h' \neq h$ can exist.

Now suppose P is dishonest. Since there is a certificate (commit, $\langle h \rangle$) constructed from at least $t_s + 1$ signatures, and $t_s + 1 > t_a$, at least one honest party P_j signed h. This implies P_j reconstructed an input x such that $h = H(x)$ and saw $n - t_s$ distinct valid messages $v_{*,l} = (s_{*,l}, h)$. At most t_a messages could have originated from malicious parties, so $n - t_s - t_a > t_s + 1$ were messages that honest parties relayed honestly. Assume there is a different honest party P_i that participated in a different commit certificate on h' for P. Then that party also saw $n - t_s$ distinct valid messages $v_{*,l'} = (s_{*,l'}, h')$, out of which $n - t_s - t_a > t_s + 1$ were messages that honest parties relayed honestly. These sets of honest parties should not intersect, so $2(n - t_s - t_a) < n - t_a$, but this contradicts our assumption that $n > 2t_s + t_a$.   □

Note that if the network is synchronous and $t_s = \lfloor n/2 \rfloor, t_a = 0$, different honest parties could receive commit certificates on different hashes of the same malicious party (honest parties always multicast the received certificates). In such a case, honest parties detect equivocation and do not input 1 in the associated BA. However, if the network is asynchronous equivocation is not necessarily detected. Nevertheless, as we see below, validity will still hold.

Lemma 3. Π_{ACS} *satisfies* t_s*-validity with termination.*

Proof. Suppose all honest parties have the same input x and up to t_s parties are corrupted. At most $t_s < \lfloor \frac{n-t_a}{2} \rfloor + 1 < n - t_s$ reconstructed values can be different than x, so there cannot exist an output certificate on a value $x' \neq x$ even if two honest parties accept different commit certificates for the same corrupted party.

Honest parties will eventually be able to obtain valid commit certificates for the inputs of at least $n - t_s$ honest parties, and therefore (by assumption) eventually obtain at least $n - t_s$ valid certificates for x. At this point, if an honest party has not yet output, it will input $\{x\}$ to Π_{Term} (in OC 1). If at least $t_s + 1$ parties call Π_{Term} via OC 1, then eventually, each party will receive an honest output certificate on $\{x\}$, output and terminate. Below we handle the case in which some honest parties output before the above conditions were satisfied.

Assume party P output before the above could occur. If P called Π_{Term} via OC 2, then despite t_s corruptions that could break security of the t_a-secure BA, it saw x' reconstructed in a strict majority of valid values associated with $n - t_a$ BA terminated instances. Any set of BA instances constituting a strict majority must contain at least one instance corresponding to honest party, since $\lfloor \frac{n-t_a}{2} \rfloor + 1 > t_s + 1$, and so $\{x'\} = \{x\}$ by assumption. Furthermore, in this case P would have input (x, h) to Π_{Term}, and so all parties eventually receive an output certificate on $\{x\}$. Since $n - t_s > \lfloor \frac{n-t_a}{2} \rfloor + 1$, and honest parties' inputs can always eventually be reconstructed, each honest party will be eventually able to output due to OC 0, even if it was not able to finish the reconstruction of the corrupted parties' inputs.

Finally, if P output S as a result of OC 3, then P did not observe a strict majority of BA instances in S corresponding to the same value. By assumption, the honest parties have the same input x, so this implies a strict majority of values S correspond to corrupted parties. However, this contradicts the assumption that only t_s parties are corrupted, because $\lfloor \frac{|S|}{2} \rfloor \geq t_s$. Therefore, no honest party outputs via OC 3 when all honest parties have the same input.   □

Lemma 4. Π_{ACS} *satisfies* t_a-*set quality.*

Proof. Suppose an honest party P_i output a set S.

If P_i output $S = \{x\}$ due to OC 0, then P_i must have obtained a valid output certificate of at least t_s+1 signatures on x, which requires that at least one honest party (call it P_j) input (x,h) to $\Pi_{\mathsf{Term}}(x,h)$ in OC 1 or OC 2. Consider each case. If P_j input (x,h) due to OC 1, then it gathered a valid certificate on at least $n-t_s$ values equal to x. At least $n-t_s-t_a \geq t_s+1$ of the parties associated to these values are honest, so RECON returns their correct original input value. Otherwise, if P_j input (x,h) due to OC 2, then it output 1 in at least $n-t_a$ BA instances and it saw a strict majority of the reconstructed corresponding inputs reconstruct to the value x. Because $n \geq n - t_s + \lfloor \frac{n-t_a}{2} \rfloor + 1$, x was input by some honest party. Thus, in either case some honest party input x.

If P output S due to OC 3, then it output 1 in at least $n - t_a$ BA instances but without the majority condition satisfied. At least one of these instances corresponds to an honest party, so S contains some honest party's input.   □

Lemma 5. Π_{ACS} *is* t_a-*terminating.*

Proof. Assume no honest party has output yet. Eventually, all honest parties will obtain at least $n - t_a$ valid commit certificates, since there are at least $n - t_a$ honest parties. Moreover, by Lemma 2, even on malicious inputs, honest parties cannot obtain multiple valid certificates. By the t_a-terminating property of BA, all parties terminate all n BA instances eventually. By the t_a-consistency of BA, all honest parties will agree on the set S of BA instances that output 1. Finally, by Lemma 1, all honest parties reconstruct the same inputs associated to S. This allows some honest party to output and terminate.

It remains to show that once some honest party P_i has terminated, all honest parties eventually terminate. If P_i output due to OC 0 (implying it received a valid output certificate from OC 1 or OC 2), then eventually all honest parties receive the certificate multicast by P_i and terminate (if they have not already).

If P_i output due to condition OC 3, then it must have terminated all BA instances, obtained commit certificates and reconstructed all inputs corresponding to $S = \{i|\mathsf{BA}_i \text{ output } 1\}$ for some $|S| \geq n - t_a$. Then, t_a-termination and consistency of BA ensure that each other honest party P_j eventually observes parts (i) and (ii) of OC 3 to be true. Furthermore, each honest party eventually reconstructs each $\{x_j\}_{j \in S}$ and receives the certificates needed to terminate, since P_i must have sent these certificates to all other parties during ACS.   □

Lemma 6. Π_{ACS} *satisfies* t_a*-consistency.*

Proof. Assume an honest party P_i has output S. By Lemma 5, each other honest party eventually outputs some set S'. It remains to show that for each possible combination of output conditions, $S = S'$.

Suppose $S = \{x\}$ was output via OC 0, i.e., upon receiving a valid output certificate. There are two subcases.

First, suppose P_j output $S' = \{x'\}$ via OC 0. The existence of an output certificate for x implies that there exists an honest party P who contributed a share via either OC 1 or OC 2; likewise, some honest party P' contributed a share for x'. If both P and P' contributed shares via OC 1, then quorum intersection among the two sets of $n - t_s$ certificates implies $x = x'$. If (say) P and P' contributed shares by OC 1 and OC 2, respectively, then any set of $n - t_s$ BA instances and any set of $\lfloor \frac{n-t_a}{2} \rfloor + 1$ BA instances must intersect at an honest party, and so $x = x'$. Finally, if both P and P' contributed shares via OC 2, then they agree on $\mathcal{S}$, and once again $x = x'$.

Second, suppose towards a contradiction that P_j output $S = \cup_{j \in \mathcal{S}} x_j$ for reconstructed values x_j via OC 3. Of those $n - t_a$ values, at most t_s can have a value $x' \neq x$. But this means that P_j saw at least $n - t_a - t_s \geq t_s + 1$ reconstructed values equal to x, in which case the order of else-if clauses would have caused P_j to output via OC 2, a contradiction.

Third, say P_i outputs S as a result of OC 3. The case in which P_j output $\{x'\}$ via OC 0 is equivalent to the second subcase above. Suppose P_j also output a set S' via OC 3. Both P_i and P_j must have seen all BA instances terminate and agree on the set of BA instances $\mathcal{S}$ that output 1. By Lemma 1, we have $S' = S$. □

Communication Complexity. The Π_{ACS} protocol has a communication complexity of $O(n^2 \ell + \kappa n^3)$ per input of size ℓ.

5   The Update SMR Protocol

In this section, we consider an adaptive adversary without mobility, which can actively corrupt at most t_s parties if the network is synchronous, and can corrupt at most t_a parties if the network is asynchronous, in any given epoch. Protocol 5 describes our construction for a network-agnostic SMR protocol.

Apart from the ACS protocol described in Sect. 4, we also use a block agreement protocol (BLA), whose role is to make parties agree on the input to ACS if the network is synchronous. Honest parties input $(n - t_s)$-quality pre-blocks of length L to the BLA and ignore any pre-blocks with quality less than $n - t_s$.

We use the adaptively secure BLA protocol from [8], which we call Π_{BLA}. The protocol has a total complexity of $O(\kappa n^3 + \kappa n^2 L)$ per pre-block of size L. Π_{BLA} has R inner rounds and guarantees t_s-validity, t_s-consistency and t_s-termination in a synchronous network when up to t_s parties are corrupted. We cannot guarantee these in an asynchronous network. However, even if the network is asynchronous, any honest party who terminates Π_{BLA} does so with output that is a valid $n - t_s$-quality pre-block.

The logical flow of the network-agnostic SMR is the following. In every epoch, each honest party first selects a random sample of L/n transactions from its buffer of transactions. The selected transactions are then threshold encrypted. Next, the parties multicast their encrypted samples and start to assemble a $(n - t_s)$-quality pre-block. If an honest party succeeds in assembling such a pre-block within the allotted time, it inputs it to Π_{BLA}, which is guaranteed to terminate with consistent output B^* if the network is synchronous. Regardless, honest parties will then input either B^* if obtained from Π_{BLA} or a $(n - t_s)$-quality pre-block to Π_{ACS}. Recall that Π_{ACS} is guaranteed to terminate regardless of the network condition. Lastly, honest parties participate in constructing the final block: they jointly decrypt the output value of Π_{ACS}, populate the block with the unique transactions, assemble a validity certificate on the hash of the obtained block, and remove the posted transactions from their buffer.

We consider that epoch e starts for a party at time $T_e = \mu(e-1)$ as measured by the local clock. The parameter μ is a spacing parameter that should be heuristically tuned by the network designers to improve throughput, i.e., not have too much overlap or separation between epochs. If the network is synchronous, then epochs start at the same time for all parties. If the network is asynchronous, parties might start the epochs at different times and might not output a block until they have to start the next epoch. We implicitly assume parties can distinguish between messages from different epochs, e.g. by tagging messages with e.

Below we give our main results on Update. The proofs use the results on Π_{ACS} and Π_{BLA} discussed so far, and are provided in the full version [4].

Condition $(*)$. Assume $t_a \leq t_s$, $2t_s + t_a < n$, and $t_a \leq n/3$, $t_s \leq n/2$.

Theorem 1. *Under condition* $(*)$, Π_{SMR} *is (1)* t_s*-consistent and* t_s*-complete if the network is synchronous and (2)* t_a*-consistent and* t_a*-complete if the network is asynchronous.*

Theorem 2. *Under condition* $(*)$, Π_{SMR} *is (1)* t_s*-externally valid if the network is synchronous and (2)* t_a*-externally valid if the network is asynchronous.*

Theorem 3. *Under condition* $(*)$, Π_{SMR} *is (1)* t_s*-live if the network is synchronous and (2)* t_a*-live if the network is asynchronous.*

Communication Complexity. In Π_{SMR}, the parties select a batch of L/n transactions, construct a pre-block of size $O(L|\mathsf{tx}|)$, and input the pre-block to Π_{BLA}. If Π_{BLA} outputs, it also outputs a pre-block of size $O(L|\mathsf{tx}|)$. The input to Π_{ACS} is of size $O(L|\mathsf{tx}|)$, and if the network is synchronous, the output is of size $O(L|\mathsf{tx}|)$. Conversely, if the network is asynchronous, the output is of size $O(nL|\mathsf{tx}|)$. Since the transactions were randomly selected from honest parties' buffers, with high probability there will be $O(nL)$ transactions in the output block after decryption, assuming that throughput is not limited by a lack of transactions.

Step 1 of Π_{SMR} incurs $O(nL|\mathsf{tx}| + n^2\kappa)$ total communication. In step 2, Π_{BLA} incurs $O(\kappa n^3 + \kappa n^2 L|\mathsf{tx}|)$ total communication and Π_{ACS} incurs $O(\kappa n^3 + n^2 L|\mathsf{tx}|)$

$$\Pi_{\mathsf{SMR}}$$

Step 1. Proposal selection.
1.1 At time $T_e = \mu(e-1)$: Set $B_i^e := (\bot, \ldots, \bot)$ an empty pre-block of size n, and set $\mathsf{ready}_e = \mathsf{false}$.
1.2 Let x_i be a threshold encryption of a random selection of L/n transactions without replacement from the first L transactions in the party's buffer. Multicast x_i.
1.3 Upon receiving a validly signed message x_j, if $B_i^e[j] = \bot$, set $B_i^e[j] := x_j$.
1.4 Upon assembling a $(n - t_s)$-quality pre-block B_i^e, set $\mathsf{ready}_e = \mathsf{true}$.

Step 2. Agreement.
2.1 At time $T_e + \Delta$: If $\mathsf{ready}_e = \mathsf{true}$, pass B_i^e as input to Π_{BLA}^e. If Π_{BLA}^e terminates, let B^* be the output.
2.2 At time $T_e + (5R+1)\Delta$: Terminate Π_{BLA}^e if not already terminated.
2.3 Pass B^* or wait until $\mathsf{ready}_e = \mathsf{true}$ and pass B_i^e as input to Π_{ACS}^e.
2.4 Receive $S = \{B_j^*\}_{j \in \mathcal{S}}$, where $\mathcal{S} \subset \{1, \ldots, n\}$ from Π_{ACS}^e.

Step 3. Output and public verification.
3.1 On input $S = \{B_j^*\}_{j \in \mathcal{S}}$, for each $j \in \mathcal{S}$, do:
- Jointly decrypt the values in $S = \{x_j\}_{j \in \mathcal{S}}$.
- Create a block by sorting $\bigcup_{j \in \mathcal{S}} x_j$ in canonical order.
- Hash and sign block, then multicast $\langle H(\mathsf{block}) \rangle_i$.
3.2 On receiving $t_s + 1$ distinct valid signatures $\langle h \rangle_j$ s.t. $h = H(\mathsf{block})$, do:
- Assemble π as $\langle h \rangle$ and proof of correct decryption of S.
- Remove the transactions in block from the buffer and output (block, π).
3.3 Update $e \leftarrow e + 1$.

Fig. 5. Update SMR protocol with adaptive security for party $P_{i \in \{1, \ldots, n\}}$.

total communication. Finally, in step 3, the parties assemble an output block and then multicast the signatures of the hash of the block to construct a proof, incurring $O(\kappa n^2)$ communication.

Summing over all steps, we see that Update incurs a total communication of $O(\kappa n^3 + \kappa n^2 L |\mathsf{tx}|)$. Choosing a proposal sample size L that is $O(n)$ yields an asymptotic total communication of $O(\kappa n^3)$ per block of transactions and an amortized communication complexity of $O(\kappa n^2)$ per transaction.

6   The Upstate SMR Protocol

We consider a static adversary that is able to corrupt up to $\hat{t}_a = (1-\epsilon)t_a$ parties in the asynchronous case and up to $\hat{t}_s = (1-\epsilon)t_s$ parties in the synchronous case, for a small $\epsilon > 0$. Informally, the ϵ slack in the corruption thresholds ensures that with high probability the fraction of corruptions in a smaller committee chosen at random is close to the fraction of corruptions in the pool of n parties.

Figure 6 describes the input selection mechanism INSE^κ that handles input encoding and primary committee election. The input of size $\ell = L/\kappa$ is split as before into b blocks, which are then encoded into n codewords of size ℓ/b (Sect. 3).

$$\mathsf{INSE}^\kappa(e, x_i)$$

1. Encode x_i using ENC into codewords $s_{i,1} \ldots, s_{i,n}$.
2. Compute $h_i := H(x_i)$ and signature $\sigma_i := \mathsf{TS.Sign}(\mathsf{PK}, \mathsf{sk}_i, e)$.
3. Set $v_{i,j} := (s_{i,j}, h_i, \sigma_i)$. For $j \in \{1, \ldots, n\}$, send $(v_{i,j}, \varphi_{i,j})$ to party P_j, where $\varphi_{i,j} := \mathsf{TS.Sign}(\mathsf{PK}, \mathsf{sk}_i, v_{i,j})$.
4. Upon receiving $n - \hat{t}_s$ messages $v_{j,i} = (s_{j,i}, h_j, \sigma_j)$, select $\hat{t}_s + 1$ signatures σ_j and compute coin from them.
5. For each $j \in \{1, \ldots, n\}$, compute $\bar{h}_j := H(\mathsf{coin}, j)$ and select the first κ values to populate the primary committee index set $\mathcal{C}$.
6. For each $j \in \mathcal{C}$, multicast the codeword $s_{j,i}$ and $\varphi_{j,i}$ received from P_j.
7. For each member j in $\mathcal{C}$, output the received $\{s_{j,k}, \varphi_{j,k}, h_j\}$, from P_k.

Fig. 6. Input selection—input encoding and primary committee election—from the perspective of party $P_{i \in \{1, \ldots, n\}}$ in epoch e.

Each party sends the i-th codeword with a hash and a threshold signature over the epoch number to party P_i. Combining $\hat{t}_s + 1$ threshold signatures yields an unpredictable value that is used to select a committee of κ parties whose inputs will form the output.

Protocol 7 describes our construction for a network-agnostic committee-based SMR protocol. At the start of each epoch, parties choose a random sample of L/κ transactions from their buffers. The parties then run an input selection procedure, called INSE, to select κ committee members. Inputs from committee members are gathered into pre-blocks, which are passed to committee-based versions of BLA and ACS in the same way as in Update. Because the committee is of size κ, the pre-blocks are $(1 - t_s/n)\kappa$-quality. The committee-based ACS and BLA protocols are described at the end of the section, with additional details in the full version of the paper [4]. After running BLA and ACS, the parties construct the final block by jointly decrypting the output value of $\varPi^\kappa_{\mathsf{ACS}}$.

Condition (**). Assume $t_a \leq t_s$, $2t_s + t_a < n$, $t_a \leq n/3$, $t_s \leq n/2$ and $\hat{t}_a := (1 - \epsilon)t_a$, $\hat{t}_s := (1 - \epsilon)t_s$ for $\epsilon > 0$.

Theorem 4. *Under condition* (**) *except with negligible probability,* $\varPi^\kappa_{\mathsf{SMR}}$ *is (1) $\hat{t}_s$-consistent, $\hat{t}_s$-complete, $\hat{t}_s$-externally valid and $\hat{t}_s$-live if the network is synchronous and (2) $\hat{t}_a$-consistent, $\hat{t}_a$-complete, $\hat{t}_a$-externally valid and $\hat{t}_a$-live if the network is asynchronous.*

The proof follows along the same lines as the proofs of Theorems 1–3, using the properties of the committee-based protocols $\varPi^\kappa_{\mathsf{ACS}}$ and $\varPi^\kappa_{\mathsf{BLA}}$.

Committee-Based Asynchronous Common Subset. We now present an ACS protocol $\varPi^\kappa_{\mathsf{ACS}}$ in a network-agnostic setting with static corruptions.

An overview of the protocol appears in Fig. 8 and the concrete steps are shown in Fig. 9. Inputs of size ℓ are passed to the input selection procedure INSE (Fig. 6), which determines the *primary committee* $\mathcal{C}$. Next, each party multicasts

$$\Pi_{\mathsf{SMR}}^{\kappa}$$

Step 1. Proposal selection.

1.1 At time $T_e = \mu(e-1)$: Set $B_i^e := (\bot, \ldots, \bot)$ an empty pre-block of size κ, and set $\mathsf{ready}_e = \mathsf{false}$.

1.2 Let x_i be a threshold encryption of a random selection of L/κ transactions without replacement from the first L in the party's buffer.

1.3 Run $\mathsf{INSE}(e, x_i)$ and store $\mathcal{C}$ and $\{s_{j,i}, \varphi_{j,i}, h_j\}_{j \in \mathcal{C}}$, as they are received.

1.4 Upon receiving $n - \hat{t}_s$ codewords of x_j, if (1) $h_j = H(x_j)$ and $B_i^e[j'] = \bot$, set $B_i^e[j'] := x_j$, where j' is the lexicographic order of P_j in $\mathcal{C}$.

1.5 Upon assembling a $(1 - t_s/n)\kappa$-quality pre-block B_i^e, set $\mathsf{ready}_e = \mathsf{true}$.

Step 2. Agreement.

2.1 At time $T_e + 2\Delta$: If $\mathsf{ready}_e = \mathsf{true}$, pass B_i^e as input to $\Pi_{\mathsf{BLA}}^{\kappa,e}$. If $\Pi_{\mathsf{BLA}}^{\kappa,e}$ terminates, let B^* be the output.

2.2 At time $T_e + (7R + 2)\Delta$: Terminate $\Pi_{\mathsf{BLA}}^{\kappa,e}$ if not already terminated.

2.3 Pass B^* or wait until $\mathsf{ready}_e = \mathsf{true}$ and pass B_i^e as input to $\Pi_{\mathsf{ACS}}^{\kappa,e}$.

2.4 Receive $S = \{B_j^*\}_{j \in \mathcal{S}}$, where $\mathcal{S} \subset \{1, \ldots, n\}$ from $\Pi_{\mathsf{ACS}}^{\kappa,e}$.

Step 3. Output and public verification.

3.1 Run Step 3 from **Update** Π_{SMR}.

Fig. 7. SMR protocol with adaptive security for party $P_{i \in \{1, \ldots, n\}}$.

the codewords they received from the members of the primary committee. To reduce communication, one *secondary* committee is elected for each member of the primary committee. The secondary committee is responsible for constructing certificates of correctness for the reconstructed values of the primary committee. The secondary committees are self-elected as described in Sect. 3. Finally, parties agree on which primary committee members' values to output by running κ parallel BA instances.

Inputs are split into $b = \hat{t}_s$ blocks using an error correcting code that tolerates either $\hat{t}_s$ erasures or $\hat{t}_a$ errors and $\hat{t}_s - \hat{t}_a$ erasures. For simplicity, in $\Pi_{\mathsf{ACS}}^{\kappa}$, we use $\varphi_{i,j}$ as both the signature of P_i over $s_{i,j}$ and over h_i, sent to P_j. Across the protocols, H denotes a collision-resistant hash function and b a bound ensuring committees of size κ in expectation.

Lemma 7. $\Pi_{\mathsf{ACS}}^{\kappa}$ is $\hat{t}_a$-consistent, $\hat{t}_a$-terminating, has $\hat{t}_s$-validity with termination and $\hat{t}_a$-set quality except with negligible probability.

Committee-Based Block Agreement Protocol. Throughout the remainder of the section, we consider a network that is synchronous with up to $\hat{t}_s = (1-\epsilon)t_s$ corruptions, such that with high probability a committee of size κ will have up to $t_s\kappa/n$ corrupted members. Honest parties are assumed to input $(1 - t_s/n)\kappa$-quality pre-blocks of total length κ to the block agreement protocol.

We construct a protocol BLA^{κ}, based on the BA protocol from [1,2] and the block agreement protocol from [8], with several changes to achieve security against adaptive adversaries at a quadratic communication per pre-block. The

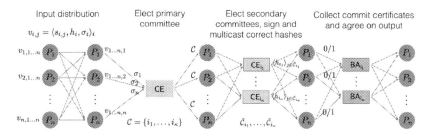

Fig. 8. Diagram of the steps in the Π_{ACS}^{κ} protocol. CE stands for committee election and BA for Byzantine Agreement.

$$\Pi_{ACS}^{\kappa,e}(x_i)$$

1. Run $\mathsf{INSE}^{\kappa}(e, x_i)$ and store $\mathcal{C}$ and $\{\{s_{j,k}\}, h_j, \{\varphi_{j,k}\}\}_{j \in \mathcal{C}}$, as they are received from P_k.
2. For each $j \in \mathcal{C}$, elect a secondary committee $\bar{\mathcal{C}}_j$ of size $O(\kappa)$ as follows:
   - Self-elect: if $\mathsf{VRF}_{\mathsf{sk}_i}(i, j, e, \mathsf{coin}) < \mathsf{b}$ then compute proof ξ_i for $P_i \in \bar{\mathcal{C}}_j$.
   - If $P_i \in \bar{\mathcal{C}}_j$, input $\{\langle v_{j,k} \rangle_k\}$ to RECON. If RECON outputs x_j, multicast a vote $\mathsf{vote}_i = (\mathsf{vote}, \langle h_j \rangle_i, \varphi_{j,i}, \xi_i)$.
3. For $j \in \mathcal{C}$, upon receiving $t_s \kappa/n + 1$ valid votes from distinct P_k in $\bar{\mathcal{C}}_j$, form a certificate $c_j := (\mathsf{commit}, \langle h_j \rangle)$ and send it to all parties.
4. Upon receiving a commit certificate c_j for the input of party P_j, forward it to all parties.
5. Upon receiving a commit certificate c_j on for party P_j, input 1 to BA_j. After outputting 1 in at least $(1 - t_a/n)\kappa$ BAs, input 0 for the rest.
6. Set $\mathcal{S}$ to be the set of indices of the BA instances that delivered 1.
7. Output according to step 7 in Π_{ACS}, where the set in OC 1 has size $(1 - t_s/n)\kappa$ and the sets in OC 2 and OC 3 have size $(1 - t_a/n)\kappa$.

Fig. 9. ACS protocol from the perspective of party $P_{i \in \{1, \dots, n\}}$ in epoch e.

high-level idea is to elect a leader who proposes an input among the ones sent by the parties, such that honest parties will commit on the same value. In our protocol, the proposal of inputs is performed before the leader election. Due to the forward secure signatures, the adversary cannot later corrupt the leader and cause them to equivocate. The construction is given in the full version [4].

Parties encode their pre-blocks into codewords and distribute them, along with the hash, for future reconstruction and verification. The protocol is run for multiple rounds, and a leader is elected at each round. The parties commit on a value when they receive sufficient votes on that value, prioritizing votes with higher round numbers. In each round, a different committee is tasked with assembling a certificate. In a given round, only votes from the current committee are considered valid. Π_{BLA}^{κ} makes calls to a graded consensus protocol Π_{GC}^{κ}, which makes a call to a Propose protocol $\Pi_{Propose}^{\kappa}$.

Communication Complexity. $\Pi_{\mathsf{ACS}}^{\kappa}$ has communication complexity $O(\kappa n \ell + \kappa^2 n^2)$ communication and $\Pi_{\mathsf{BLA}}^{\kappa}$ has communication complexity $O(R\kappa^2 n^2 + \kappa n \ell)$, per input of size ℓ. In $\Pi_{\mathsf{SMR}}^{\kappa}$, $\Pi_{\mathsf{BLA}}^{\kappa}$ and $\Pi_{\mathsf{ACS}}^{\kappa}$ are run on pre-blocks of size $O(L|\mathsf{tx}|)$. If the network is synchronous, the output is of size $O(L|\mathsf{tx}|)$, while if the network is asynchronous, the output is of size $O(\kappa L|\mathsf{tx}|)$. After decryption, since the transactions were randomly selected from honest parties buffers, with high probability, there will be $O(\kappa L)$ transactions in the output block.

For simplicity, we omit the $|\mathsf{tx}|$ factor in the following paragraph. $\Pi_{\mathsf{SMR}}^{\kappa}$ incurs $O(n^2 L/(\kappa b) + n^2 \kappa)$ total communication for step 1.3 and $O(n^2 \kappa L/b + n^2 \kappa^2)$ total communication in step 1.4. In step 2, $\Pi_{\mathsf{BLA}}^{\kappa}$ incurs $O(R\kappa^2 n^2 + \kappa n^2 L/b + \kappa n L)$ total communication and $\Pi_{\mathsf{ACS}}^{\kappa}$ incurs $O(\kappa n^2 L/b + \kappa n L + \kappa^2 n^2)$ total communication.

Since $b = \hat{t}_s = O(n)$, Upstate incurs a total communication of $O(R\kappa^2 n^2 + \kappa n L|\mathsf{tx}|)$. This allows us to select a proposal sample size of $L = O(R\kappa n)$ and obtain a total communication of $O(R\kappa^2 n^2)$ per transaction and an amortized communication complexity of $O(\kappa n)$ per block L.

7   SMR Under Arbitrary Network Changes

We now consider a network that can arbitrarily transition between synchronous and asynchronous behaviors and a *constrained epoch-mobile adaptive adversary*, who can corrupt at most t_s unique parties over the duration of the protocol, and can move between those t_s parties from epoch to epoch, as long as it does not exceed the t_a or t_s limit in any epoch or at any moment in time. In this model, parties' local machines may reboot to flush the adversary out. Importantly, the state of the parties is not removed from the adversary's view after uncorruptions.

Adding a reboot step at the beginning of each epoch to the network-agnostic protocols discussed so far, Update and Upstate, as well as Tardigrade, results in protocols that are secure under arbitrary network changes, as long as rebooting ensures that $n > 2t_s + t_a$, $t_a \leq t_s$, with at most $t_s - t_a$ exposed keys in the asynchronous case, in the restricted epoch-mobile model. For simplicity, we assume the reboot is instantaneous; otherwise we can adjust the timings of the steps.

Theorem 5. *Protocols* Update, Upstate, *and* Tardigrade *[8] with reboots are secure under arbitrary network changes against a constrained epoch-mobile adaptive adversary, where* $n > 2t_s + t_a$, $t_a \leq t_s$.

We prove the first part of Theorem 5 below, after some technical observations. Proofs of the rest of Theorem 5 and of the Lemmata are given the full version [4].

Throughout, we use threshold cryptographic primitives with a threshold of $t_s + 1$. Although the adversary has access to up to t_s keys/key shares, it cannot create full signatures or certificates on its own because these require at least $t_s + 1$ valid contributions; likewise, it cannot decrypt independently of the honest parties. Moreover, while forming commit or output certificates, honest parties only sign messages that they locally verified, such as a hash value whose associate input was correctly reconstructed, or the output of the Π_{ACS} protocol.

In all protocols in this section, we use the binary BA protocol from [7], which is also designed for a network-agnostic setting with $n > 2t_s + t_a$. It is signature-free, apart from a threshold cryptosystem with high threshold of $t_s + 1$ to compute the common coin and ensure termination. This ensures that even with t_s key exposures (but only t_a active corruptions), the protocol remains t_a-valid, t_a-consistent and t_a-terminating against an adaptive adversary.

Lemma 8. *In a Π_{ACS} execution, if there are at most t_a corruptions and $t_s - t_a$ exposed parties, then at least $n - t_a$ BA instances will terminate with output 1.*

Lemma 9. *Suppose there are at most t_a corruptions and $t_s - t_a$ exposed parties during an execution of Π_{ACS}. Given a certificate for a party P, $(\mathsf{commit}, \langle h \rangle)$, all honest parties eventually reconstruct the same output.*

Lemma 10. *If there are at most t_a corruptions, there cannot be two valid certificates $(\mathsf{commit}, \langle h \rangle)$, $(\mathsf{commit}, \langle h' \rangle)$ associated with P such that $h \neq h'$.*

Proof. (Theorem 5, Update) When the network is only synchronous or only asynchronous, or there is a single asynchronous to synchronous transition, the proof follows directly from the security proof of Update in Sect. 5.

Suppose the network has undergone a transition from synchronous to asynchronous. The adversary actively controls at most t_a parties, but may have exposed up to t_s parties. This means that each pre-block created by an actively corrupted party may contain up to t_s validly signed adversarial ciphertexts. However, exposed parties still act honestly, so each pre-block created by an honest party contains at most t_a malicious ciphertexts. Because pre-block entries are received directly from the corresponding party, an honest party's $(n - t_s)$-quality pre-block will have at least $n - t_s - t_a$ honestly created and signed ciphertexts.

In the following, we first examine the security of the building blocks and then the security of the overall protocol.

ACS. In Π_{ACS}, parties need to be able to reconstruct all values corresponding to the at least $n - t_a$ BA instances that terminated with output 1. The use of codewords makes the analysis slightly subtler, since the adversary can forge valid but bad codewords and distribute them in the multicast round of INDI as if they originated from the exposed parties. By Lemma 8, at least $n - t_a$ BA instances will still terminate, despite exposures. Coupled with Lemmata 9 and 10, which show there cannot be conflicting certificates and all honest parties are able to eventually correctly reconstruct the same input, it follows that Π_{ACS} achieves t_a-termination, t_a-set quality and t_a-consistency. Finally, t_s-validity with termination has the same proof as in Lemma 3.

BLA. There is a Leader mechanism in Π_{BLA} [8], that is obtained using a strict majority of parties. Hence it is still unpredictable in the presence of t_s exposed parties. The property required of Π_{BLA} in the asynchronous case is the following: if an honest party does output in Π_{BLA}, its output is a $(n - t_s)$-quality pre-block. Honest parties only validate and multicast $(n - t_s)$-quality blocks, so this property still holds.

SMR. A corrupted party can forge the signature of an exposed party when assembling its own $(n - t_s)$-quality pre-block. Therefore, up to t_a pre-blocks input to Π_{BLA} could have only $n - 2t_s$ entries originating from honest parties. If such a block is output by Π_{BLA}, then the same holds for the output of Π_{ACS}.

By t_a-consistency and t_a-validity with termination of Π_{ACS}, all honest parties output the same set of pre-blocks. As a result, at least $n - t_a > t_s$ parties contribute valid decryption shares, and so every honest party is able to reconstruct the same block. Therefore, Update SMR is t_a-consistent and t_a-complete.

Next, we argue that t_a-liveness holds. If an adversarial pre-block is output by ACS, only $n - 2t_s$ honest parties are guaranteed to remove L/n transactions in a given epoch. Thus, the presence of key exposures increases the number of epochs needed for tx to move to the front of sufficiently many honest parties' buffers (see [4]). However, this still happens and ensures that tx is eventually output, but the probability increases with the number of epochs.

External validity follows from consistency of Π_{ACS}, since a threshold of $t_s + 1$ is used in the validity certificates over the block hashes.

Finally, the adversary cannot break the liveness of the protocol by erasing threshold key shares of the corrupted parties: any $t_s + 1$ shares can be used to reconstruct, so in order to prevent reconstruction, the adversary would need to erase at least $n - t_s - t_a$ shares. But this would require the adversary to corrupt more than t_s parties over the duration of the protocol, since $2t_s + t_a < n$. We conclude that security is preserved even across multiple network transitions. □

8   Asynchronous Proactive Secret Sharing

We first consider an asynchronous network in the presence of a mobile adaptive adversary. At the end, we extend the analysis to changing network conditions.

In each epoch, the adversary is limited to t_a corruptions, but those t_a corruptions need not target the same parties in each epoch. Thus, over multiple epochs, the adversary could have controlled more than $t_a + 1$ different parties. While a party is corrupted, its current epoch is considered to be undefined, since it can behave arbitrarily. Upon becoming uncorrupted, a party's local epoch number is considered to be the epoch in which it was originally corrupted. We refer to the parties that are not corrupted as *honest* (in that epoch).

Here, we use an additional assumption of secure (authenticated private) channels, implemented using a pairwise shared key inaccessible to the adversary, e.g., stored in secure hardware. We show that even with secure channels, it is impossible to have a proactive asynchronous protocol without making any assumption on epoch length (as in [10] where epochs are defined to take place between clock ticks) but with epochs determined by a successful reshare of the secret (as in [33] but where the network is partially synchronous). While Cachin et al. [10] briefly remark upon this impossibility before making the assumption of clock ticks and "asynchronous proactive channels", we fully model and prove this result.

Definition 5. *A (t_a+1)-out-of-n proactive verifiable secret sharing scheme with reshare is defined by an algorithm* Share *and protocols* Reshare, Reconstruct *that satisfy the following:*

- Share *takes as input a secret $s \in \mathbb{F}$ and outputs shares $(s_1^{(0)}, \ldots, s_n^{(0)})$. Party P_i, $i = 1, \ldots, n$ is given $s_i^{(0)}$ and sets its epoch number to 0.*
- Reshare *is an interactive protocol run by a subset of parties $\mathcal{S}$ of size at least $n - t_a$ that takes as input an epoch number τ, a set of shares associated to that epoch number consisting of the share of each of the parties in $\mathcal{S}$: $(s_{i_1}^{(\tau)}, \ldots, s_{i_{|S|}}^{(\tau)})$ and outputs to every party P_i, $i \in [n]$ a new share $s_i^{(\tau+1)}$ or an error symbol $\perp$. A party P_i that receives output from* Reshare *with associated epoch τ sets its epoch number to $\tau + 1$.*
- Reconstruct *is an interactive protocol run by a subset of parties $\mathcal{S}$ of size at least $n - t_a$, that takes as input a epoch number τ, a set of shares $(s_{i_1}^{(\tau)}, \ldots, s_{i_{|S|}}^{(\tau)})$ and outputs to all parties either a value $s' \in \mathbb{F}$ or an error symbol $\perp$.*

An honest party is said to *complete* Share, Reshare, *or* Reconstruct *in epoch τ* when they generate the corresponding output from the algorithm in epoch τ.

We give a standard privacy game between a challenger and an adversary $\mathcal{A}$ where the goal of the adversary is to learn the secret in the full version of the paper [4]. The advantage of the adversary is denoted by $\mathsf{Adv}(\mathcal{A})$.

Definition 6. *A proactive verifiable secret sharing scheme with reshare is secure against a t_a-limited adversary if it satisfies the following:*

- *(Privacy):* $\mathsf{Adv}(\mathcal{A})$ *is negligible.*
- *(Correctness): For any $s \in \mathbb{F}$, conditioned on the adversary eventually delivering all messages between honest parties, it holds that: if during any epoch τ, a set $\mathcal{S}$ of least $n - t_a$ honest parties locally call* Reconstruct *on epoch number τ and local shares associated with τ, they obtain the initially shared secret:* Reconstruct$(\tau, \{s_i^{(\tau)}\}_{i \in \mathcal{S}}) =$ Reconstruct(Share(s)). *Furthermore, all parties in $\mathcal{S}$ proceed to epoch $\tau + 1$.*
- *(Liveness): For any epoch number $\tau \geq 0$, if an honest party has reached epoch τ, i.e., has obtained output from the* Reshare *protocol associated to epoch $\tau - 1$, then all honest parties will eventually reach a epoch number $\tau' \geq \tau$, provided the adversary delivers all messages sent between honest parties so far and the responses triggered by these messages.*

In verifiable secret sharing, in order to achieve correctness, Share, Reshare and Reconstruct need to implicitly have validation procedures of the inputs. We asked for at least $n - t_a$ instead of $t_a + 1$ parties to participate in Reconstruct to guarantee success against t_a malicious parties who could submit t_a invalid shares. Nevertheless, $t_a + 1$ valid shares are sufficient to reconstruct the secret.

Theorem 6. *There does not exist a secure asynchronous (t_a+1)-out-of-n proactive verifiable secret sharing scheme with reshare.*

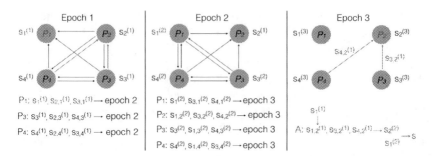

Fig. 10. We denote by $s_{j,i}^{(\tau)}$ the intermediate share obtained by party P_i from party P_j in epoch τ. P_j can construct its share for the next epoch $s_j^{(\tau+1)}$ from $n - t_a$ values $s_{j,i}^{(\tau)}$. The red quantities are in the view of the adversary. The red edges represent delayed messages from epoch 1 delivered in epoch 3. (Color figure online)

Proof. We show that an adversary can break privacy by amassing shares corresponding to $t_a + 1$ parties in a single epoch. Then, we prove that protocols which avoid the prior attack do not satisfy liveness. For simplicity we first consider the case of non-interactive reshare protocols, and then handle the general case.

Non-interactive Reshare Protocol. Consider $n = 4$ and $t_a = 1$. This counterexample is depicted in Fig. 10 and can be extended to arbitrary n and corruption threshold $t_a < n/3$.

The adversary corrupts party P_1 in epoch 1. At this point in time, the adversary knows the state of P_1, which includes the share $s_1^{(1)}$. Each honest party locally initiates the Reshare protocol at the onset of epoch 1. The adversary instructs P_1 not to deliver any message and delivers all the following messages: from P_2 to all other parties, from P_3 only to P_1 and P_4, and from P_4 only to P_1 and P_3. The parties P_3, P_4 thus obtain sufficient information to construct their shares $s_1^{(2)}, s_3^{(2)}, s_4^{(2)}$ and advance to epoch 2. However, P_2 remains in epoch 1. The adversary uncorrupts party P_1 after Reshare was completed. At this point in time, the view of the adversary includes $s_1^{(1)}$ and the intermediate shares for $s_1^{(2)}$. The adversary allows P_1 to also advance to epoch 2.

At the onset of epoch 2, each honest party locally initiates the Reshare protocol. The adversary delivers all messages between parties. This enables all parties to obtain their corresponding share $s_1^{(3)}, s_2^{(3)}, s_3^{(3)}, s_4^{(3)}$, and advance to epoch 3.

At the onset of epoch 3, the adversary corrupts party P_2 and delivers the messages originated in epoch 1 from P_3 and P_4 destined to P_2. The adversary now has 3 messages, counting $s_1^{(1)}$, and is able to obtain $s_2^{(2)}$. Hence, it reconstructs s from two correct shares in epoch 2: $s_1^{(2)}, s_2^{(2)}$, without corrupting more than $t_a = 1$ party per epoch.

Restarting and flushing the adversary out does not prevent this attack, since there is no synchronizing signal instructing a corrupted party to restart before the first Reshare is completed. This could be addressed using erasures and/or interaction; however, we show that protocols that avoid this attack are not live.

Interactive Reshare Protocols. Consider a generic interactive Reshare protocol where two parties, P_i and P_j, start an epoch with $s_i^{(\tau)}$ and $s_j^{(\tau)}$, respectively. After r rounds of communication, P_i obtains $s_{j,i}^{(\tau)}$ and P_j obtains $s_{i,j}^{(\tau)}$.

If only one of the r messages is useful for computing the new share, then the previous attack still applies. If more than one of the r messages are needed for computing the new share, and honest parties erase their previous state when transitioning to a new epoch (implying they do not respond to messages originated from previous epochs), then the above attack does not break privacy. But such an interactive asynchronous protocol where parties can only advance to the next epoch after repeated interactions does not achieve liveness, as shown next.

Consider now that the adversary delays all messages destined to P_1, hence keeping it in epoch 1, while allowing the rest of the parties to progress an arbitrarily large number of epochs τ. At this point, the adversary delivers all messages that were sent so far, including the messages originated at P_1 as response to the received messages. However, since obtaining the output of any Reshare requires interaction and the other honest parties do not respond to messages originated in previous epochs in order to preserve privacy, a party P_1 cannot reach a subsequent epoch based only on the messages sent so far, breaking liveness.   □

The attack above hinges on the fact that a party can still retrieve in epoch $\tau' > \tau$ the contents of a message sent to it in epoch τ. Both privacy and liveness would be maintained if parties had access to "setup-free asynchronous forward-secure channels" with the following properties: (1) A message sent in epoch τ can only be read in epoch τ; (2) At the onset of epoch $\tau + 1$, the sender and receiver on that channel have access to the new secret and public key, respectively, i.e., the adversary does not control the delivery of this information (it should not be interactive); (3) Messages in different epochs are encrypted with different keys.

Secure co-processors using forward secure encryption are not sufficient to implement this kind of channel. Say a party P_1 was delayed and is still in epoch τ, and all other parties advanced to epoch $\tau' > \tau$, updating their channel keys. But when honest parties start a new Reshare, they cannot use the key associated to P_1's epoch τ, because an adversary corrupting P_1 in epoch τ would learn shares from epoch τ' and break privacy. These are points (1) and (3). So until the adversary delivers the messages from epoch τ, P_1 is stuck, but this does not break liveness if the protocol is non-interactive. If point (2) is satisfied, the other parties need to already have the public key in the channel for epoch $\tau + 1$, otherwise the impossibility proof for interactive protocols would apply. But a forward secure with unique public key allows a ciphertext encrypted at epoch $\tau + 1$ to be decrypted at epoch τ, so privacy is broken.

Note that in [10], the transition between epochs is *external*, triggered by a clock tick, and can happen even if a party did not complete the Reshare protocol in the current epoch. This allows parties to rely on the clock tick event to set new channel keys in a synchronized way.

To circumvent the result in Theorem 6, Yurek et al. [36] considered high reconstruction thresholds and defined local epochs such that a party can decide to not pass to a subsequent epoch even if it has all shares to do so, unlike our definition based on completing a Reshare. Briefly, the impossibility does not hold because (i) a party decides to progress to the next epoch after receiving at least $n - t_a$ epoch τ messages (while in epoch τ), forcing the adversary to deliver at least these many messages to every party per epoch; (ii) combined with a high reconstruction threshold of $n - t_a$, the t_a shares held by the adversary in epoch τ and the at most t_a messages it could have delayed are not sufficient to reconstruct $s^{(\tau)}$, as $n - t_a > 2t_a$. We also mention that the constructions in [36] assume every party has Paillier key pairs that are not refreshed after corruptions.

Proactive Secret Sharing Under Network Changes. We again consider a network that can arbitrarily switch between synchronous and asynchronous cases and $n > 2t_s + t_a$, $t_a \leq n/3$, $t_s \leq n/2$. Note that in this setting, the Reconstruct threshold is at least $t_s + 1$ and the Reshare threshold is $n - t_s$ in order to satisfy privacy in case the network is synchronous.

Corollary 1. *There does not exist a secure (t_s, t_a)-proactive verifiable secret sharing scheme with reshare under arbitrary network transitions.*

Proof. Assume the network is in an asynchronous state, so the adversary can corrupt up to t_a parties in the same local epoch. The arguments in the proof of Theorem 6 still hold. For the privacy attack, the adversary delays the messages in epoch τ towards $t_s - t_a + 1$ honest parties, until the epoch(s) it corrupts these parties (if $t_s \geq 2t_a$, it needs more epochs to corrupt all $t_s - t_a + 1$ parties), while allowing the rest of the parties to complete the refresh in all epochs, i.e., deliver and receive at least $n - t_s$ share messages. For the interactive liveness attack, the adversary can still cause the parties to be arbitrarily far apart.   □

We remark that the clock ticks used in Π_{SMR} (Sect. 5) to start an epoch are not the same as the ones assumed in [10]. In our model, the epoch started at T_e does not necessarily finish by T_{e+1}, and can continue in the background, so liveness could be lost if all parties would erase their key shares at T_{e+1}.

References

1. Abraham, I., et al.: Communication complexity of byzantine agreement, revisited. In: Robinson, P., Ellen, F. (eds.) 38th ACM PODC, pp. 317–326. ACM, July 2019
2. Abraham, I., Devadas, S., Dolev, D., Nayak, K., Ren, L.: Synchronous byzantine agreement with expected $O(1)$ rounds, expected $O(n^2)$ communication, and optimal resilience. In: Goldberg, I., Moore, T. (eds.) FC 2019. LNCS, vol. 11598, pp. 320–334. Springer, Cham (2019). https://doi.org/10.1007/978-3-030-32101-7_20
3. Abraham, I., Malkhi, D., Nayak, K., Ren, L., Yin, M.: Sync HotStuff: simple and practical synchronous state machine replication. In: 2020 IEEE Symposium on Security and Privacy, pp. 106–118. IEEE Computer Society Press, May 2020
4. Alexandru, A.B., Blum, E., Katz, J., Loss, J.: State machine replication under changing network conditions. Cryptology ePrint Archive, Report 2022/698 (2022). https://eprint.iacr.org/2022/698
5. Appan, A., Chandramouli, A., Choudhury, A.: Perfectly-secure synchronous MPC with asynchronous fallback guarantees. Cryptology ePrint Archive, Report 2022/109 (2022). https://eprint.iacr.org/2022/109

6. Benhamouda, F., et al.: Can a public blockchain keep a secret? In: Pass, R., Pietrzak, K. (eds.) TCC 2020. LNCS, vol. 12550, pp. 260–290. Springer, Cham (2020). https://doi.org/10.1007/978-3-030-64375-1_10

7. Blum, E., Katz, J., Loss, J.: Synchronous consensus with optimal asynchronous fallback guarantees. In: Hofheinz, D., Rosen, A. (eds.) TCC 2019. LNCS, vol. 11891, pp. 131–150. Springer, Cham (2019). https://doi.org/10.1007/978-3-030-36030-6_6

8. Blum, E., Katz, J., Loss, J.: TARDIGRADE: an atomic broadcast protocol for arbitrary network conditions. In: Tibouchi, M., Wang, H. (eds.) ASIACRYPT 2021. LNCS, vol. 13091, pp. 547–572. Springer, Cham (2021). https://doi.org/10.1007/978-3-030-92075-3_19

9. Blum, E., Liu-Zhang, C.-D., Loss, J.: Always have a backup plan: fully secure synchronous MPC with asynchronous fallback. In: Micciancio, D., Ristenpart, T. (eds.) CRYPTO 2020. LNCS, vol. 12171, pp. 707–731. Springer, Cham (2020). https://doi.org/10.1007/978-3-030-56880-1_25

10. Cachin, C., Kursawe, K., Lysyanskaya, A., Strobl, R.: Asynchronous verifiable secret sharing and proactive cryptosystems. In: Atluri, V. (ed.) ACM CCS 2002, pp. 88–97. ACM Press, November 2002

11. Cachin, C., Poritz, J.A.: Secure intrusion-tolerant replication on the internet. In: Proceedings International Conference on Dependable Systems and Networks, pp. 167–176. IEEE (2002)

12. Canetti, R., Gennaro, R., Jarecki, S., Krawczyk, H., Rabin, T.: Adaptive security for threshold cryptosystems. In: Wiener, M. (ed.) CRYPTO 1999. LNCS, vol. 1666, pp. 98–116. Springer, Heidelberg (1999). https://doi.org/10.1007/3-540-48405-1_7

13. Castro, M., Liskov, B.: Proactive recovery in a Byzantine-Fault-Tolerant system. In: 4th Symposium on Operating Systems Design and Implementation (2000)

14. Das, S., Xiang, Z., Ren, L.: Balanced quadratic reliable broadcast and improved asynchronous verifiable information dispersal. Cryptology ePrint Archive, Report 2022/052 (2022). https://eprint.iacr.org/2022/052

15. Duan, S., Reiter, M.K., Zhang, H.: BEAT: asynchronous BFT made practical. In: Lie, D., Mannan, M., Backes, M., Wang, X. (eds.) ACM CCS 2018, pp. 2028–2041. ACM Press, October 2018

16. Frankel, Y., MacKenzie, P., Yung, M.: Adaptively-secure optimal-resilience proactive RSA. In: Lam, K.-Y., Okamoto, E., Xing, C. (eds.) ASIACRYPT 1999. LNCS, vol. 1716, pp. 180–194. Springer, Heidelberg (1999). https://doi.org/10.1007/978-3-540-48000-6_15

17. Ghinea, D., Liu-Zhang, C.-D., Wattenhofer, R.: Optimal synchronous approximate agreement with asynchronous fallback. Cryptology ePrint Archive, Report 2022/354 (2022). https://eprint.iacr.org/2022/354

18. Gilad, Y., Hemo, R., Micali, S., Vlachos, G., Zeldovich, N.: Algorand: scaling byzantine agreements for cryptocurrencies. In: Proceedings of the 26th Symposium on Operating Systems Principles, New York, NY, USA, pp. 51–68. ACM (2017)

19. Gordon, S.D., Katz, J., Kumaresan, R., Yerukhimovich, A.: Authenticated broadcast with a partially compromised public-key infrastructure. Inf. Comput. 234, 17–25 (2014)

20. Groth, J.: Non-interactive distributed key generation and key resharing. Cryptology ePrint Archive, Report 2021/339 (2021). https://eprint.iacr.org/2021/339

21. Guo, B., Lu, Z., Tang, Q., Xu, J., Zhang, Z.: Dumbo: faster asynchronous BFT protocols. In: Ligatti, J., Ou, X., Katz, J., Vigna, G. (eds.) ACM CCS 2020, pp. 803–818. ACM Press, November 2020

22. Herzberg, A., Jarecki, S., Krawczyk, H., Yung, M.: Proactive secret sharing or: how to cope with perpetual leakage. In: Coppersmith, D. (ed.) CRYPTO 1995. LNCS, vol. 963, pp. 339–352. Springer, Heidelberg (1995). https://doi.org/10.1007/3-540-44750-4_27

23. Keidar, I., Kokoris-Kogias, E., Naor, O., Spiegelman, A.: All you need is DAG. In: Proceedings of the 2021 ACM Symposium on Principles of Distributed Computing, pp. 165–175 (2021)

24. Kursawe, K., Shoup, V.: Optimistic asynchronous atomic broadcast. In: Caires, L., Italiano, G.F., Monteiro, L., Palamidessi, C., Yung, M. (eds.) ICALP 2005. LNCS, vol. 3580, pp. 204–215. Springer, Heidelberg (2005). https://doi.org/10.1007/11523468_17

25. Liu, C., Duan, S., Zhang, H.: EPIC: efficient asynchronous BFT with adaptive security. In: International Conference on Dependable Systems and Networks (DSN), pp. 437–451. IEEE (2020)

26. Lu, Y., Lu, Z., Tang, Q., Wang, G.: Dumbo-MVBA: optimal multi-valued validated asynchronous byzantine agreement, revisited. In: Emek, Y., Cachin, C. (eds.) 39th ACM PODC, pp. 129–138. ACM, August 2020

27. Maram, S.K.D., et al.: CHURP: dynamic-committee proactive secret sharing. In: Cavallaro, L., Kinder, J., Wang, X., Katz, J. (eds.) ACM CCS 2019, pp. 2369–2386. ACM Press, November 2019

28. Miller, A., Xia, Y., Croman, K., Shi, E., Song, D.: The honey badger of BFT protocols. In: Weippl, E.R., Katzenbeisser, S., Kruegel, C., Myers, A.C., Halevi, S. (eds.) ACM CCS 2016, pp. 31–42. ACM Press, October 2016

29. Momose, A., Ren, L.: Multi-threshold byzantine fault tolerance. In: Vigna, G., Shi, E. (eds.) ACM CCS 2021, pp. 1686–1699. ACM Press, November 2021

30. Nayak, K., Ren, L., Shi, E., Vaidya, N.H., Xiang, Z.: Improved extension protocols for byzantine broadcast and agreement. In: 34th International Symposium on Distributed Computing. Schloss Dagstuhl-Leibniz-Zentrum für Informatik (2020)

31. Ostrovsky, R., Yung, M.: How to withstand mobile virus attacks (extended abstract). In: Logrippo, L. (ed.) 10th ACM PODC, pp. 51–59. ACM, August 1991

32. Rambaud, M., Urban, A.: Asynchronous dynamic proactive secret sharing under honest majority: refreshing without a consistent view on shares. Cryptology ePrint Archive, Report 2022/619 (2022). https://eprint.iacr.org/2022/619

33. Schultz, D.A., Liskov, B., Liskov, M.: Mobile proactive secret sharing. In: Proceedings of the 27th ACM Symposium on Principles of Distributed Computing, p. 458 (2008)

34. Shi, E.: Foundations of distributed consensus and blockchains. Book manuscript (2020)

35. Vassantlal, R., Alchieri, E., Ferreira, B., Bessani, A.: Cobra: dynamic proactive secret sharing for confidential BFT services. In: Symposium on Security and Privacy (SP), pp. 1528–1528. IEEE Computer Society (2022)

36. Yurek, T., Xiang, Z., Xia, Y., Miller, A.: Long live the honey badger: robust asynchronous DPSS and its applications. Cryptology ePrint Archive, Report 2022/971 (2022). https://eprint.iacr.org/2022/971

Blockchains and Cryptocurrencies

Non-interactive Mimblewimble Transactions, Revisited

Georg Fuchsbauer[1(✉)] and Michele Orrù[2]

[1] TU Wien, Vienna, Austria
`georg.fuchsbauer@tuwien.ac.at`
[2] UC Berkeley, Berkeley, USA
`michele.orru@berkeley.edu`

Abstract. Mimblewimble is a cryptocurrency protocol that promises to overcome notorious blockchain scalability issues and provides user privacy. For a long time its wider adoption has been hindered by the lack of non-interactive transactions, that is, payments for which only the sender needs to be online. Yu proposed a way of adding non-interactive transactions to stealth addresses to Mimblewimble, but this turned out to be flawed. Building on Yu and integrating ideas from Burkett, we give a fixed scheme and provide a rigorous security analysis strenghtening the previous security model from Eurocrypt'19. Our protocol is considered for implementation by MimbleWimbleCoin and a variant is now deployed as MimbleWimble Extension Blocks (MWEB) in Litecoin.

1 Introduction

Mimblewimble (MW) is a cryptocurrency protocol that addresses the problem of ever-growing blockchain data that needs to be stored by full nodes in the system. While in all other cryptocurrencies, such as Bitcoin, the full transaction history must be kept for ever,[1] in MW, coins can be deleted after having been spent while *maintaining public verifiability of the ledger*. Instead of growing linearly (like Bitcoin [Nak08], whose blockchain is now > 400 GB)[2], MW-based currencies only need to store the currently existing coins (the *UTXO set*) plus some small data per transaction.

Mimblewimble achieves this by cleverly combining three ideas that were initially envisioned for Bitcoin: (1) *Confidential transactions* [Max15] hide the transacted amount by only including *commitments* to the amounts of the inputs and outputs and giving proofs that the sum of the input values equals that of the output values, showing the transaction is "balanced". Thus, no transaction creates fresh money (apart from *coinbase transactions*, which create money explicitly). Confidential transactions are now implemented e.g. in Monero.[3]

---

[1] An exception are recent proposals building on more speculative technology such as recursive zk-SNARKs; cf. https://minaprotocol.com/lightweight-blockchain.

[2] https://www.blockchain.com/charts/blocks-size.

[3] https://www.getmonero.org/resources/moneropedia/stealthaddress.html.

© International Association for Cryptologic Research 2022
S. Agrawal and D. Lin (Eds.): ASIACRYPT 2022, LNCS 13791, pp. 713–744, 2022.
https://doi.org/10.1007/978-3-031-22963-3_24

(2) *CoinJoin* [Max13a] is the idea of merging (or *aggregating*) several transactions into one big transaction, in a way that makes it impossible to associate the inputs and outputs of the original transactions. In Bitcoin, this can only be done by having the creators of the transactions interact in order to merge them before being included in the blockchain. In contrast, in MW merging can be done a posteriori without involving the original creators. The result is that in a MW blockchain all transactions are merged into one huge transaction, and there is no information about which inputs led to which outputs.

(3) *Transaction cut-through* [Max13b] is the idea that if a transaction spends an output (which corresponds to a "coin" in the system) txo_1 and creates txo_2, which is then spent by another transaction creating txo_3, then this should be equivalent to a "cut-through" transaction spending txo_1 and creating txo_3. While in Bitcoin this could only be done for "unconfirmed transactions", i.e., ones not yet included in any block, MW allows cut-through to be done after confirmation, which is what enables MW's space-efficiency improvements. As every spent coin is removed, the result is that the huge transaction representing a MW ledger only has inputs that are the coinbase transactions and outputs that are the unspent coins. In addition, this greatly improves user privacy, as the blockchain reveals neither the transacted amounts nor the transaction graph defining how coins are being transferred (in Bitcoin all this can be inferred from the blockchain).

The main shortcoming of Mimblewimble is that the sender and the receiver(s) of a transaction need to compute the transaction in an interactive protocol. It is thus not possible for a sender to simply transfer money to a destination address without any involvement of the owner of that address, which is the standard setting in all major cryptocurrencies.

Mimblewimble (MW) was first proposed by an anonymous author in 2016 [Jed16]. After being initially investigated by Poelstra [Poe16], a formal model and an analysis of MW were provided by Fuchsbauer, Orrù and Seurin (FOS) [FOS19] in 2019. In 2020, Burkett [Bur20] proposed an extension of Mimblewimble supporting non-interactive transactions, later refined by Yu [Yu20]. We will refer to this extension as MW-Yu. In this work, we first asses the security of MW-Yu [Yu20, §2.1] and describe discovered vulnerabilities. We then fix the scheme, also integrating an idea from a more recent proposal from Burkett [Bur21] and give security proofs that our scheme satisfies (an appropriate adaptation of) the rigorous FOS [FOS19] security model for *aggregate cash systems*.

MimbleWimbleCoin plans to implement the protocol by year-end 2022.[4] A variant of our protocol is used in the *MimbleWimble Extension Blocks* (MWEB), which are now supported by Litecoin (one of the top cryptocurrencies with a market capitalization of > 4 billion USD).[5]

The Mimblewimble Protocol. MW uses a group $\mathbb{G}$ (which we denote additively) of prime order p with two generators G and H. As with confidential

---

[4] https://www.mwc.mw/mimble-wimble-coin-articles/mimblewimble-non-interactive-transactions-review.

[5] https://blog.litecoin.org/litecoin-core-v0-212-release-282f5405aa11 and https://twitter.com/DavidBurkett38/status/1555100039822954496.

transactions [Max15], a *coin* is a Pedersen commitment $C = \mathsf{Cmt}(v, q) := vH + qG$ to its value v using some randomness $q \in \mathbb{Z}_p$, together with a so-called *range proof* π guaranteeing that v is contained in some interval of admissible values. In MW, knowledge of the opening q of the commitment enables spending the coin. Similarly to Bitcoin, a transaction in MW contains a list of input coins $C \in \mathbb{G}^n$ and output coins $\hat{C} \in \mathbb{G}^{\hat{n}}$, where

$$C_i = v_i H + q_i G \text{ for } i \in [n] \text{ and } \hat{C}_i = \hat{v}_i H + \hat{q}_i G \text{ for } i \in [\hat{n}] .$$

Leaving fees and coinbase (a.k.a. *minting*) transactions aside, a transaction is *balanced* if and only if $\sum \hat{v} - \sum v = 0$ (where for a vector $v = (v_1, \ldots, v_n)$, we let $\sum v := \sum_{i=1}^{n} v_i$). For coins as defined above, this is equivalent to

$$\sum \hat{C} - \sum C = \left(\sum \hat{q} - \sum q \right) G ,$$

a quantity called the *kernel excess* $E \in \mathbb{G}$ in MW. If the transaction is balanced, then knowledge of the openings $\hat{q}$ and q of all involved coins implies knowledge of the discrete logarithm $\log E$ (to base G) of the excess E. Intuitively, if the producer of the transaction proves knowledge of $\log E$ then, together with the binding property of Pedersen commitments, this should guarantee that the transaction is balanced. In MW this is done by generating a signature σ under public key E, using its discrete logarithm $\sum \hat{q} - \sum q$ as the signing key.

FOS [FOS19] prove that when using Schnorr signatures (and assuming the range proofs are *simulation-extractable*; cf. Sect. 5), balancedness follows from the hardness of computing discrete logarithms in $\mathbb{G}$ in the random-oracle model. They also show that as long as a user owning a coin C in the ledger keeps the opening private, no one can steal C (i.e., create a transaction that spends C).

Transactions in Mimblewimble can easily be merged non-interactively, in a similar way to CoinJoin [Max13a]. Consider two transactions $\mathsf{tx}_1 = (\hat{C}_1, C_1, \pi_1, E_1, \sigma_1)$ and $\mathsf{tx}_2 = (\hat{C}_2, C_2, \pi_2, E_2, \sigma_2)$. The *aggregate transaction* tx is defined as the concatenation of inputs and outputs, that is, (letting "$\|$" concatenation)

$$\mathsf{tx} = \left(\hat{C}_1 \| \hat{C}_2, C_1 \| C_2, \pi_1 \| \pi_2, E_1 \| E_2, \sigma_1 \| \sigma_2 \right) .$$

A transaction $\mathsf{tx} = (C, \hat{C}, \pi, E, \sigma)$ is valid if all π's and σ's verify and if

$$\sum \hat{C} - \sum C = \sum E . \tag{0}$$

As outputs in one transaction that also appear as inputs in the other cancel out in Eq. (0) for tx, they can simply be removed from the input and output list (together with their range proofs), while validity of tx will be maintained. This has been called *transaction cut-through* in the literature [Max13b]. In MW, the ledger is defined as the cut-through of the aggregation of all transactions. Since every spent coin (a.k.a. "transaction output", TXO) is removed by cut-through, the outputs in the ledger are precisely the *unspent TXOs* (UTXO), representing the current state of the ledger. FOS [FOS19] further remarked that if the used signature scheme supports aggregation, then $\sigma_1 \| \sigma_2$ can be replaced by their aggregation to save further space. Then the only trace of a transaction whose outputs have been spent in the ledger is the value E.

Even if the lists of inputs and outputs in an aggregate transaction tx are shuffled, one can still link inputs and outputs come from the same component transaction, as tx will contain an excess value E that equals the difference between the sum of the outputs and inputs of the original transaction. This can be prevented by using *kernel offsets* [Dev20b], where E is replaced by $E + tG$ for a random $t \leftarrow_{\$} \mathbb{Z}_p$ and t is included in the transaction; the aggregate of two transactions with (E_1, t_1) and (E_2, t_2) will then contain $(E_1 \| E_2, t_1 + t_2)$. A consequence of kernel offsets is that, given an aggregated transaction, nothing can be deduced about which inputs and outputs belonged to the same original transaction. This is implied by our notion of *transaction privacy* (Sect. 6.6), which we prove our scheme to satisfy.

Our analysis concerns the application layer, and we do not provide network-level privacy guarantees. Network adversaries that observe transactions being broadcast, or traffic analysis in general, constitute an entirely different problem that we consider outside the security of the Mimblewimble protocol per se. In practice, protocols like Dandelion [VFV17] and Tor[6] can help mitigating attacks at the network level. See for instance their adoption in Grin[7].

Non-interactive Transactions. Most implementations of MW create new transactions via an *interactive* protocol between sender and receiver in order to produce the Schnorr signature σ under a secret key that depends on the openings of the sender's and the receiver's coins.[8] FOS [FOS19] proposed a transaction protocol, where the sender creates all output coins, so that she can compute σ on her own. She then sends the receiver (through a separate private channel) the transaction along with the secret key associated to one of the output coins. The latter creates a transaction spending this coin, merges it with the received transaction and broadcasts the aggregate transaction to the miners. The downside of this approach is that there is a window of time in which both sender and receiver can spend a coin, which can lead to deniability issues for payments.

In 2020, Yu [Yu20] posted on ePrint an extension of MW for achieving non-interactive transactions by adding *stealth addresses* [vS13, Tod14]. Each user has a *wallet* (or stealth address) $(A, B) \in \mathbb{G}^2$. Given a destination wallet, a sender can derive a one-time address, unique for every transaction, to which she sends the money. These one-time addresses are unlinkable to the wallet they correspond to, yet the owner of the wallet is (the only one) able to derive the secret key for it. In detail, the sender chooses a uniform element $r \leftarrow_{\$} \mathbb{Z}_p$ and defines the one-time key for stealth address $(A = aG, B = bG)$ as $P = \mathrm{H}(rA) \cdot G + B$, where

---

[6] https://www.torproject.org/.

[7] https://docs.grin.mw/wiki/miscellaneous/dandelion/.

[8] In GRIN this is documented in the grin-wallet documentation: https://raw.githubusercontent.com/mimblewimble/grin-wallet/master/doc/transaction/basic-transaction-wf.png.

In BEAM, this is documented in the developer documentation: https://github.com/BeamMW/beam/wiki/Cryptographic-primitives.

H is a cryptographic hash function. Being provided $R := rG$, the owner of (A, B) can derive the secret key $\log P$ as $\mathrm{H}(aR) + b$.

Integrating stealth addresses into MW is not straightforward, as the currency does not provide addresses for sending money. Yu's proposal [Yu20], built on top of Burkett's [Bur20], received multiple feedbacks from the community, and was further updated with notes describing possible attacks and countermeasures. In essence, the idea is to extend an output (C, π) in MW by a one-time key P chosen by the sender for a destination address, as well as an ephemeral key R that allows the receiver to compute the secret key for P. To prevent the value P from being modified (which would mean stealing it from the receiver), a signature ρ on P under signature-verification key R (of which the sender knows the logarithm) is added. An output is thus of the form $(C, \pi, R, \rho, P, \chi)$.

Moreover, the mechanism for letting the receiver derive the secret key for P can also be used to let the receiver obtain the opening of the commitment C (Yu [Yu20, §2.1.1] does this by setting $q = \mathrm{H}(\mathrm{H}(rA)G + B)$). Note that knowing the so-called "view key" (a, B) of stealth address (aG, B), one can derive from R both P (and thus check if the payment is for that address) and q (and thus check if C commits to a given amount).

Usually in cryptocurrencies, when spending an output linked to a key P, the transaction is signed with the secret key of P. In Mimblewimble however, aggregation of transactions should hide which inputs and outputs come from the same component transaction. Yu therefore proposes to use logarithms of the values P in the inputs and the values $\hat{R}$ in the outputs to "authenticate" the spending, similarly to how the openings of the input coins authenticate the output coins via Eq. (0) in MW. Namely by proving knowledge of the logarithm of $\sum \hat{R} - \sum P$.

Yu proposes to simply arrange the $\hat{R}$ values so that the above results in the excess E (defined as $\sum \hat{C} - \sum C$). However, this is only possible if one of the outputs $\hat{C}_i$ goes back to the sender (who can choose the corresponding value $\hat{q}_i$ arbitrarily); for all other coins, $\hat{R}_j$ (together with the stealth address) defines $\hat{q}_j$, which defines E, for which $\hat{R}_j$ has to be chosen, which is infeasible. We therefore modify the scheme and introduce a *stealth excess* $X := \sum \hat{R} - \sum P$, under which we add (as for E) a signature to the transaction. Our scheme then supports transactions for which all outputs are sent to destination addresses. At the time of writing, the core proposal in [Yu20, §2.1] is still affected by further issues. The ones known before our analysis are the following:

- As illustrated in [Yu20, §2.9.1], MW-YU is susceptible to a rogue-key attack [Yu20, §2.9.3]. A fix was also proposed, which requires the addition of one signature per transaction input, namely a signature proving knowledge of the logarithm of P. The security and correctness analysis of this proposed change are not detailed further.
- Mixing NIT with non-NIT transactions, as envisaged in [Yu20], leads to correctness issues within the balance equations.[9] No argument for why the

---

[9] https://forum.mwc.mw/t/non-interactive-transaction-and-stealth-address/32.

security is preserved is given, especially w.r.t. [Yu20, Eq. ②]. (We do not considered "mixed transactions" in our scheme.)

A major drawback of Yu's and our scheme (and MWEB) is the lack of support for transaction cut-through. Since an output is associated with a value $\hat{R}_i$ and an input is associated with a value P_j, if an output is spent via an input in an aggregated transaction, these values do not cancel out, and removing them would thus change the stealth excess $\sum \hat{R} - \sum P$ (we discuss this in detail in Sect. 4.3). We note that in practice, nodes would only store and check validity of the most recent excesses and perform cut-trough for coins that have been spent in the past beyond a so-called *horizon* (cf. [Bur21, §4]). Cut-through enables attacks by miners who could change outputs of transactions (and violate *transaction-binding*, see below), which is only relevant for *recent* transactions; once they are in a block beyond the horizon, they are "protected" by the consensus mechanism (a security layer that is outside of our model).

Differences to MWEB. The variant used by Litecoin [Bur21] differs in how exactly the secrets for an output are derived from a stealth address (A, B): In our scheme, from a Diffie-Hellman (DH) share $R = rG$, we derive $(k, q) := \mathrm{H}(rA)$, which defines the one-time address as $P := kG + B$ and the coin as $C := vH + qG$. Outputs in [Bur21] have an additional element K_e (in addition to K_s, which corresponds to our R) used as the Diffie-Hellman share (deriving its randomness from $\log K_s$). A symmetric key, derived from the DH-shared key, is then used to encrypt v and derive q. Our variant is arguably simpler, which facilitates our formal analysis.

Our Contributions

Scheme. We propose a new protocol for non-interactive transactions, greatly inspired by Yu [Yu20] and using an idea by Burkett [Bur21] to overcome one of the found issues. Our protocol is a variant of what is now already being used by Litecoin in its MimbleWimble Extension Blocks. In Sect. 4 we discuss further issues that emerged after the publication of [Yu20].

Model. We then analyze our protocol in a strengthening of the model proposed in [FOS19], which did not protect against a malleability attack by miners (discussed below). We only consider non-interactive transactions, which greatly simplifies the security notions. We define security experiments that capture the following attacks:

(i)   creating money other than via coinbase transactions *(inflation resistance)*
(ii) spending someone else's output in the ledger *(theft prevention)*
(iii) stealing money from a transaction not yet merged with the ledger *(transaction-binding)*
(iv) breaking privacy by learning anything about the transacted amounts, the destination addresses or the relations of the inputs and outputs in an aggregated transaction *(transaction privacy)*

Inflation resistance and *theft* prevention are straightforward adaptations of the notions from [FOS19, Def. 10 and 11]. *Transaction privacy* is stronger than FOS's privacy notion [FOS19, Def. 12], which only guarantees that amounts are hidden (FOS's scheme does not use kernel offsets, which means one can "disaggregate" transactions). To concisely capture all anonymity, privacy and confidentiality guarantees, we define a simulation-based notion requiring that a transaction can be simulated without knowledge of any information that transactions are supposed to hide.

We introduce *transaction-binding*, a notion that protects users against malicious miners by guaranteeing that no outputs can be removed from a transaction. In particular, after a transaction tx that spends some output txo was broadcast, no one can create a transaction tx′ that spends txo but does *not* include *all* outputs of tx. We note that *theft resistance* [FOS19, Def. 11] (which deals with interactive transactions) only guarantees the following: a user that engages in a protocol with the adversary spending value in C and creating change C' for herself is guaranteed that C' are included in the ledger as soon as any of C is spent.

Proof. We prove the security of our protocol by following the provable-security methodology and giving security reductions of the different security notions to standard computational hardness assumptions in idealized models.

In our security proofs, we assume that the *discrete logarithm problem* is hard in the underlying group $\mathbb{G}$ and for transaction privacy we additionally make the *decisional Diffie-Hellman (DDH) assumption*. Our main building block is a *zero-knowledge* proof system for proving knowledge of discrete logarithms that satisfies *strong simulation-extractability* (defined in Sect. 5).

We show that the Schnorr signature scheme, and a variant thereof, which we use to improve efficiency of our scheme, satisfy these notions in an idealized model, namely the combination of the *algebraic group model* [FKL18] and the *random oracle model* without making any computational assumptions. Finally, we assume that the used range proofs are merely proofs of knowledge[10] and do not require that they are simulation-extractable as in previous analyses [FOS19].

2   Preliminaries

Let ε denote the empty string, and $[a]$ the set $\{1, \ldots, a\}$ (for some $a \in \mathbb{N}$). We assume the existence of a group $\mathbb{G}$ of prime order p and two "nothing-up-my-sleeve" generators $G, H \in \mathbb{G}$ (that is, the discrete logarithm of H to base G is not known to anyone). The length of the prime p is the security parameter λ. (A typical choice could be the group Secp256k1 and hence $\lambda = 256$.) For $X \in \mathbb{G}$, we let $\log X$ denote the discrete logarithm of X to base G, that is $\log X = x$ with $X = xG$.

---

[10] This is in some sense minimal, since for Pedersen commitments the language (see Sect. 2) is trivial; cf. Sect. 6.1.

Proofs of Possession. We consider a cryptographic hash function which we model as a random oracle and denote by $H(\cdot)$. We use (key-prefixed) Schnorr signatures, which are unforgeable under the DL assumption in the random oracle model (ROM), and whose security has been extensively studied in the past literature [PS00, Seu12]. Here we interpret Schnorr signatures as (zero-knowledge) proofs of knowledge of the secret key, that is, if $X = xG \in \mathbb{G}$ is the public key then a Schnorr signature is a proof of knowledge of $x = \log X$.

We generalize this to a proof of knowledge of two logarithms that has the same size as a Schnorr signature. Interpreting knowledge of $\log X$ as "possessing" X, we call the proof system PoP for "proof of possession". More formally, PoP is a proof system for the following NP-relation (whose statements contains a part m, sometimes called a "tag"), defined w.r.t. a group description $(p, \mathbb{G}, G)$:

$$\left\{ \left((X, Y, m), (x, y) \right) \ : \ X = xG \ \wedge \ Y = yG \ \wedge \ m \in \{0, 1\}^* \right\} .$$

A proof for a statement $(X, Y, m) \in \mathbb{G}^2 \times \{0, 1\}^*$ is computed via PoP.P using the witness (x, y) by picking a uniform $r \leftarrow_\$ \mathbb{Z}_p$, defining $R := rG$, computing $(c, d) := H(X, Y, m, R)$ and returning a proof $(R, s) \in \mathbb{G} \times \mathbb{Z}_p$ with $s := r + c \cdot x + d \cdot y \bmod p$. The verification algorithm PoP.V$((X, Y, m), (R, s))$ computes $(c, d) := H(X, Y, m, R)$ and checks whether $sG = R + c \cdot X + d \cdot Y$ (see also Fig. 2, page 18).

The system PoP can also be used to prove knowledge of a witness $x \in \mathbb{Z}_p$ for statements $(X = xG, m)$ by using Schnorr signing and verification (defined like above but setting $y := 0$). A proof of possession of X with tag m is thus a Schnorr signature on m under public key X. We use PoP proofs for different *types* of values (proofs ψ for (P, D), proofs σ for excesses (E, X) and proofs ρ for R). We assume that these are "domain-separated", which can easily be achieved by including the type in the tag of the statement. We also assume that random oracles H used elsewhere in the scheme (e.g. to derive the value q) are domain-separated from H used for PoP.

In the full version we show that in the *algebraic group model* [FKL18] combined with the ROM, the proof system PoP is a *strongly simulation-sound zero-knowledge proof of knowledge* of logarithms, a property that will be central in the security analysis of our protocol. *Zero-knowledge* means that there exists a simulator (which here controls the random oracle) that can simulate proofs for any statements without being given a witness that are indistinguishable from honestly generated proofs. *Proof of knowledge* (PoK) means that there exists an extractor that from any prover (which here is assumed to be algebraic; see Sect. 5) that produces a valid proof ψ for a statement (X, m) (or (X, Y, m)) can extract the witness $\log X$ (or $(\log X, \log Y)$). Proofs are *simulation-sound* (also called *simulation-extractable* (SE) for PoKs) if a witness can be extracted from a prover even if the prover can obtain simulated proofs ψ_i for statements (X_i, m_i) of its choice (except the one it is proving). For *strong* SE the only restriction is that the pair $((X, m), \psi)$ must be different from all query/response pairs $((X_i, m_i), \psi_i)$.

Pedersen Commitments. We employ Pedersen commitments, which are homomorphic w.r.t. the committed values and the used randomness. A value $v \in \mathbb{Z}_p$ is committed by sampling $q \leftarrow_\$ \mathbb{Z}_p$ and setting

$$C = \mathsf{Cmt}(v, r) := vH + qG \ .$$

A commitment is opened by sending $(v$ and$)$ q and testing $C \stackrel{?}{=} vH + qG$. Pedersen commitments are perfectly hiding (i.e., no information about the value is leaked) and computationally binding (i.e., under the discrete logarithm (DL) assumption, no adversary can change their mind about a committed value, that is, find a commitment and two openings $v \neq v'$ to it).

Range Proofs. We require a proof system for statements on commitments, in particular for the NP language defined by the following relation asserting that a committed value is contained in an admissible interval:

$$\left\{ \big(C, (v, r)\big) \ : \ C = \mathsf{Cmt}(v, r) \wedge v \in [0, v_{\max}] \right\}$$

We assume a zero-knowledge proof system RaP for proofs of knowledge of a witness (v, r) for a statement C such that $0 \le v \le v_{\max}$. (Note that we do not assume RaP to be simulation-sound [FOS19, Def. 8], whereas FOS required this in their proof of theft prevention. Our scheme could thus be potentially instantiated with a more efficient range proof system than theirs.) We denote the prover algorithm by $\pi \leftarrow \mathsf{RaP.P}(C, (v, r))$ and the verifier by $b \leftarrow \mathsf{RaP.V}(C, \pi)$. A typical choice of proof system for RaP are Bulletproofs [BBB+18], which do not introduce any new trust assumption (as its parameters are random group elements, as for Pedersen commitments).

3   Proposal for MW with Non-interactive Transactions

We start with presenting the scheme and then discuss the reason for our design choices, such as adding *stealth excesses* (Sect. 4.1) and *doubling keys* (which prevent a sub-exponential-time attack; Sect. 4.2).

3.1   Data Structures

A **stealth address** is a pair $(A = aG, B = bG) \in \mathbb{G}^2$, for which we call $(a, B) \in \mathbb{Z}_p \times \mathbb{G}$ the **view key** and $(a, b) \in \mathbb{Z}_p^2$ the **spend key**.

A **transaction** in MW-NIT is composed of (see also Fig. 1):

- A list of **outputs**: tuples of the form $txo = (\hat{C}, \hat{\pi}, \hat{R}, \hat{\rho}, \hat{P}, \hat{\chi})$, each implicitly associated to an **output address** (A, B), composed of:
  - an **ephemeral key** $\hat{R} = \hat{r}G \in \mathbb{G}$, chosen by the sender, which defines two keys as:
    $$(\hat{k}, \hat{q}) := \mathrm{H}(\hat{r}A)$$
    (note that $(\hat{k}, \hat{q})$ can be computed from the view key and $\hat{R}$, as $\hat{r}A = a\hat{R}$)

inputs	outputs	inputs	outputs
$txo_1 \leftarrow P_1, D_1, \psi_1$	$\hat{C}_1, \hat{\pi}_1, \hat{R}_1, \hat{\rho}_1, \hat{P}_1, \chi_1$	$txo_1 \leftarrow P_1, D_1, \psi_1$	$\hat{C}_1, \hat{\pi}_1, \hat{R}_1, \hat{\rho}_1, \hat{P}_1, \chi_1$
$txo_2 \leftarrow P_2, D_2, \psi_2$	$\hat{C}_2, \hat{\pi}_2, \hat{R}_2, \hat{\rho}_2, \hat{P}_2, \chi_2$	$txo_2 \leftarrow P_2, D_2, \psi_2$	$\hat{C}_2, \hat{\pi}_2, \hat{R}_2, \hat{\rho}_2, \hat{P}_2, \chi_2$
$\vdots$	$\vdots$	$\vdots$	$\vdots$
	s, f, t, y, E, X, σ		$\mathbf{ct}, s, f, t, y, \boldsymbol{E}, \boldsymbol{X}, \sigma$

Fig. 1. Left: Visualization of a (simple) MW-NIT transaction. Inputs consist of a value P_i contained in a previous transaction output, a "doubling key" D_i and a proof of possession (PoP) ψ_i of P_i and D_i. Outputs consist of a commitment $\hat{C}_i$ to their value, an associated range proof $\hat{\pi}_i$, an ephemeral key $\hat{R}_i$, a signature (or PoP) $\hat{\rho}_i$ under $\hat{R}_i$, the one-time address $\hat{P}_i$ and an epoch χ_i. The kernel consists of the supply s, the fee f, the offsets t and y and the PoP σ of E and X. The excess E and the stealth excess X can be computed as in (1) and (2). **Right:** Visualization of an aggregated MW-NIT transaction. It additionally contains a cut-through list $\mathbf{ct}$, and lists of excesses, stealth excesses and corresponding PoPs.

- a **commitment** $\hat{C} := v\hat{H} + \hat{q}G$ to the coin value $\hat{v}$, using randomness $\hat{q}$
- a **range proof** $\hat{\pi}$ proving knowledge of an opening (v, q) of $\hat{C}$, with $v \in [0, v_{\max}]$
- a **one-time output public key** $\hat{P} \in \mathbb{G}$, computed from $\hat{k}$ as $\hat{P} := \hat{B} + kG$ (note that the *spend* key is required to compute $\log \hat{P}$)
- a **proof of possession** $\hat{\rho}$ of $\hat{R}$ with tag $\hat{C}\|\hat{\pi}\|\hat{P}\|\hat{\chi}$
- an **epoch** $\hat{\chi}$ in which the output was created
- A list of **inputs** of the form (P, D, ψ) where
  - $P \in \mathbb{G}$ is the one-time **public key** of the transaction output being spent (each value P is only allowed once in the ledger)
  - $D \in \mathbb{G}$ is the one-time **doubling key**, chosen by the sender, that "doubles" P
  - ψ is a **proof of possession** of P and D with tag the transaction output being spent
- The **kernel**, which is composed of:
  - the **supply** $s \in [0, v_{\max}]$, indicating the amount of money created in the transaction
  - the **fee** $f \in [0, v_{\max}]$, indicating the fee paid for the current transaction
  - the **offset** $t \in \mathbb{Z}_p$
  - the **excess** $E \in \mathbb{G}$, defined as the difference between the commitments in the outputs (including the fee) and the inputs (including the supply), shifted by the offset. If C_i is the i-th input commitment, that is, the value contained in the output in which P_i appears, then

$$E := \sum \hat{C} + fH - \sum C - sH - tG , \qquad (1)$$

which can be seen as $E := E' - tG$ in terms of the *true excess* $E' := \sum \hat{C} + fH - \sum C - sH$

- the **stealth offset** $y \in \mathbb{Z}_p$
- the **stealth excess** $X \in \mathbb{G}$, defined as the difference between the ephemeral keys $\hat{R}_i$ from the outputs and the doubling one-time keys D_i from the inputs, shifted by the stealth offset y

$$X := \sum \hat{R} - \sum D - yG \tag{2}$$

- a **proof of possession** σ of E and X (with empty tag ε)

A (simple, i.e., non-aggregated; see below) transaction is thus of the form:

$$\mathrm{tx} = \big((P, D, \psi), (\hat{C}, \hat{\pi}, \hat{R}, \hat{\rho}, \hat{P}, \hat{\chi}), (s, f, t, y, \sigma)\big)$$

3.2   Transaction Creation

Consider a transaction output $\mathrm{txo} = (C, \pi, R, \rho, P, \chi)$ spent to an address (A', B').

- Given the corresponding view key (a', B'), one can compute the shared keys k and q (the opening for the commitment C) as:

$$(k, q) := \mathrm{H}(a'R) .$$

- Given the corresponding spend key (a', b'), one can compute the secret key for P as $\log P = b' + k$.

To create a transaction that, in an epoch $\hat{\chi}$, spends transaction outputs txo_i of values v_i from one-time keys P_i, for $i \in [n]$, and creates outputs of values $\{\hat{v}_i\}_{i \in [\hat{n}]}$ for destination addresses $\{(A_i, B_i)\}_{i \in [\hat{n}]}$, creating an amount s of new money and paying f in fees so that $\hat{\mathbf{v}} \in [0, v_{\max}]^{\hat{n}}$ and $\sum \hat{\mathbf{v}} + f = \sum v + s$, do the following:

- for each input index $i \in [n]$:
  - compute all values q_i and $p_i := \log P_i$, for $i \in [n]$, as described above
  - select a random $d_i \leftarrow_{\$} \mathbb{Z}_p$ and set $D_i := d_i G$
  - compute a proof of possession

$$\psi_i \leftarrow \mathsf{PoP.P}((P_i, D_i, \mathrm{txo}_i), (p_i, d_i))$$

- for each output index $i \in [\hat{n}]$:
  - select a random ephemeral key $\hat{r}_i \leftarrow_{\$} \mathbb{Z}_p$ and set $\hat{R}_i := \hat{r}_i G$
  - compute the shared secrets for the destination address (A_i, B_i)

$$(\hat{k}_i, \hat{q}_i) := \mathrm{H}(\hat{r}_i A_i) \tag{3}$$

and from them compute the output commitment and the one-time key

$$\hat{C}_i := \hat{v}_i H + \hat{q}_i G \tag{4}$$
$$\hat{P}_i := \hat{B}_i + \hat{k}_i G \tag{5}$$

- compute a range proof $\hat{\pi}_i \leftarrow \mathsf{RaP.P}(\hat{C}_i, (\hat{v}_i, \hat{q}_i))$
- compute a proof of possession of the output ephemeral key

$$\hat{\rho}_i \leftarrow \mathsf{PoP.P}((\hat{R}_i, \hat{C}_i \| \hat{\pi}_i \| \hat{P}_i \| \hat{\chi}), \hat{r}_i) \tag{6}$$

– sample uniformly at random $t \leftarrow_\$ \mathbb{Z}_p$ and compute (where E is as in (1))

$$e := \sum \hat{q} - \sum q - t = \log E$$

– sample uniformly at random $y \leftarrow_\$ \mathbb{Z}_p$ and compute (where X is as in (2))

$$x := \sum \hat{r} - \sum d - y = \log X$$

– compute a proof of possession of E and X with empty tag:

$$\sigma \leftarrow \mathsf{PoP.P}((E, X, \varepsilon), (e, x))$$

The final transaction is

$$\mathsf{tx} := \big((P_i, D_i, \psi_i)_{i \in [n]}, \ (\hat{C}_i, \hat{\pi}_i, \hat{R}_i, \hat{\rho}_i, \hat{P}_i, \hat{\chi})_{i \in [\hat{n}]}, \ (s, f, t, y, \sigma)\big) \ . \tag{7}$$

3.3 Transaction Aggregation

Aggregate transactions are essentially concatenations of the composing transactions. In contrast to Jedusor's [Jed16] and FOS' [FOS19] protocols, *MW-NIT does not perform any cut-through*, as this is insecure, as we show in Sect. 4.3. Outputs of one transaction that are spent as inputs of another one in the aggregation are therefore kept in a *cut-through list* $\mathbf{ct}$, which stores the concatenation of the output and the input spending the latter.

While simple transactions do not (need to) contain the (stealth) excesses (displayed in light gray in Fig. 1), aggregate transactions (also displayed in Fig. 1) contain lists of excesses $\mathbf{E}$, stealth excesses $\mathbf{X}$ and associated proofs $\boldsymbol{\sigma}$. An aggregated transaction is thus of the form

$$\big((P_i, D_i, \psi_i)_{i \in [n]}, (\hat{C}_i, \hat{\pi}_i, \hat{R}_i, \hat{\rho}_i, \hat{P}_i, \hat{\chi}_i)_{i \in [\hat{n}]}, (\mathbf{ct}, s, f, t, y, (E_i, X_i, \sigma_i)_{i \in [\bar{n}]})\big) \tag{8}$$

where $\mathbf{ct} := \big(C'_i, \pi'_i, R'_i, \rho'_i, P'_i, \chi'_i, P'_i, D'_i, \psi'_i\big)_{i \in [n']}$. A simple transaction (7) can be cast as (8) by setting $\mathbf{ct} := ()$, $\bar{n} = 1$ and computing E and X as in Eqs. (1) and 2. Given transactions tx_1 and tx_2, assuming w.l.o.g. that they are of the form (8), compute their aggregation tx as follows:

– define $\mathbf{txi}$ as the concatenation of the inputs of tx_1 and tx_2, and $\mathbf{txo}$ as the concatenation of their outputs, $\mathbf{ct}$ as the concatenation of their cut-through lists and and $\mathbf{ker}$ as the concatenation of lists of excesses, stealth excesses and associated signatures σ.
– if the same value P appears in two entries of $\mathbf{txi}$, or if the same value P appears in two entries of $\mathbf{txo}$, then abort
– if a value P appears in an entry of $\mathbf{txi}$ and in an entry of $\mathbf{txo}$, remove the two entries from their resp. lists, concatenate the entries and add them to $\mathbf{ct}$

- sort each list **txi**, **txo** and **ct** (lexicographically) and sort **ker** by the E values (required to hide which inputs and outputs comes from which transaction)
- compute the aggregated supply, fee, offset, and stealth offset (from the supplies s_i, etc., of tx_i):

$$s := s_1 + s_2 \qquad f := f_1 + f_2 \qquad t := t_1 + t_2 \qquad y := y_1 + y_2$$

- return $\text{tx} := (\textbf{txi}, \textbf{txo}, (\textbf{ct}, s, f, t, y, \textbf{ker}))$.

3.4 Output Verification

We define when a view key (a, B) accepts a transaction output. Given an amount v and an output $txo = (\hat{C}, \hat{\pi}, \hat{R}, \hat{\rho}, \hat{P}, \hat{\chi})$, compute $(k, q) := \text{H}(a\hat{R})$, and accept the output if txo has never been previously received in epoch $\hat{\chi}$ $\hat{C} = vH + qG$ and $\hat{P} = B + kG$.

3.5 Transaction Verification

Simple Transactions. A transaction

$$\text{tx} = \left((P_i, D_i, \psi_i)_{i \in [n]}, \ (\hat{C}_i, \hat{\pi}_i, \hat{R}_i, \hat{\rho}_i, \hat{P}_i, \hat{\chi}_i)_{i \in [\hat{n}]}, \ (s, f, t, y, \sigma)\right),$$

is valid w.r.t. a list of (previous) outputs **txo** with $txo_i = (C_i, \pi_i, R_i, \rho_i, P_i, \chi_i)$ if the P_i values in the inputs of tx and **txo** coincide and if the following hold:

(i) all input proofs are valid: for all $i \in [n]$: $\text{PoP.V}((P_i, D_i, txo_i), \psi_i) = \textbf{true}$
(ii) all range proofs are valid: for all $i \in [\hat{n}]$: $\text{RaP.V}(\hat{C}_i, \hat{\pi}) = \textbf{true}$
(iii) all PoPs of $\hat{R}$ are valid: for all $i \in [\hat{n}]$: $\text{PoP.V}(\hat{R}_i, \hat{C}_i \| \hat{\pi}_i \| \hat{P}_i \| \hat{\chi}_i, \hat{\rho}_i) = \textbf{true}$
(iv) the excess proof of possession is valid: $\text{PoP.V}((E, X, \varepsilon), \sigma) = \textbf{true}$, for

$$E := \sum \hat{C} - \sum C + (f - s)H - tG \tag{9}$$
$$X := \sum \hat{R} - \sum D - yG \tag{10}$$

Aggregate Transactions. An aggregate transaction as in (8)

$$\text{tx} = \left(\textbf{txi}, \widehat{\textbf{txo}}, (\textbf{ct}, s, f, t, y, E, X, \sigma)\right)$$

with $\textbf{txi} = (P_i, D_i, \psi_i)_{i \in [n]}$, $\widehat{\textbf{txo}} = (\hat{C}_i, \hat{\pi}_i, \hat{R}_i, \hat{\rho}_i, \hat{P}_i, \hat{\chi}_i)_{i \in [\hat{n}]}$, $\textbf{ct} := (\overline{\textbf{txo}} \| \overline{\textbf{txi}}) = (\overline{txo}_i \| \overline{txi}_i)_{i \in [\bar{n}]}$ is verified w.r.t. previous outputs **txo** as follows:

Check that **in**, $\widehat{\textbf{txo}}$ and **ct** are sorted lexicographically, then re-arrange the cut-through terms: set the outputs being spent and the inputs spending them, as well as the freshly created outputs, as

$$\textbf{txo}^* := \textbf{txo} \| \overline{\textbf{txo}} = (C_i, \pi_i, R_i, \rho_i, P_i, \chi_i)_i$$
$$\textbf{txi}^* := \textbf{txi} \| \overline{\textbf{txi}} = (P_i, D_i, \psi_i)_i$$
$$\widehat{\textbf{txo}}^* := \widehat{\textbf{txo}} \| \overline{\textbf{txo}} = (\hat{C}_i, \hat{\pi}_i, \hat{R}_i, \hat{\rho}_i, \hat{P}_i, \hat{\chi}_i)_i$$

(Note that the last n' elements of $\mathbf{txo}^*$ and $\widehat{\mathbf{txo}}^*$ are equal but denoted differently). Verify the transaction $(\mathbf{in}^*, \widehat{\mathbf{txo}}^*, (s, f, t, y, \boldsymbol{E}, \boldsymbol{X}, \boldsymbol{\sigma}))$ w.r.t. $\mathbf{txo}^*$: check (i)–(iii) as for simple transactions, and the following instead of (iv):

(iv′) for all $i \in [\bar{n}] : \mathsf{PoP.V}((E_i, X_i, \varepsilon), \sigma_i) = \mathbf{true}$

(v′) additionally, the following "balance equations" are checked:

$$\sum \boldsymbol{E} = \sum \hat{\boldsymbol{C}} - \sum \boldsymbol{C} + (f - s)H - tG \tag{11}$$

$$\sum \boldsymbol{X} = \sum \hat{\boldsymbol{R}} - \sum \boldsymbol{D} - yG \tag{12}$$

(Note that in (11) it suffices to sum the $\hat{\boldsymbol{C}}$ up to $\hat{n}$ and the $\boldsymbol{C}$ up to n, as the remaining terms from $\mathbf{ct}$ cancel out.)

3.6   Inclusion of Transactions in the Ledger

A ledger Λ is simply an aggregated transaction of the form (8) without any inputs (as the inputs of any transaction added Λ must spend existing outputs, these are thus moved to the cut-through list.

A transaction tx of the form (7) or (8) is included in Λ by aggregating Λ and tx to Λ', checking that Λ' has no inputs (thus all inputs of tx were spent/cut-through) and checking validity of Λ' w.r.t. an empty list $\mathbf{txo}$, as defined in Sect. 3.5. If any of the checks fail, return $\bot$, otherwise Λ'. (If Λ is known to be valid, it suffices to identify, for every transaction input (P_j, D_j, ψ_j), the ledger output txo_{i_j} containing P_j, and check validity of tx is w.r.t. $txo_{i_1}, \ldots, txo_{i_n}^*$.)

4   Fallacies in the Initial Proposal

We list below the main attacks found in Yu's scheme, and which motivated the design choices for our scheme in Sect. 3. Originally [Yu20, §2.2.2], transactions did not include the values D_i, nor the stealth excess X with the respective offset y. Instead, a valid transaction had to satisfy

$$E + tG = \sum \hat{\boldsymbol{R}} - \sum \boldsymbol{P} \ , \tag{13}$$

(in our notation) [Yu20, Eq. ②] instead of Eq. (10), and ψ and σ only proved knowledge of the discrete logarithms of P and E, respectively.

4.1   Correctness

Equation (13) can be achieved if one of the outputs, say the i-th, goes back to the creator of the transaction (e.g., because it is a "change output"). She can just set $\hat{R}_i := E + tG + \sum \boldsymbol{P} - \sum_{j \neq i} \hat{R}_j$ (for which she knows $\log \hat{R}_i$) and then sample q_i uniformly. However, it is infeasible to create a transaction whose outputs are all linked to destination addresses, e.g., a transaction with a single output: $\hat{R}$ (together with the address) determines the coin opening q, which defines the value E; but (re-)defining $\hat{R}$ so that (13) holds would lead to a new value E.

(In Yu's notation [Yu20, Eq. ②], the value r_o depends on q, which in turn is computed from r_o.)

In order not to restrict the format of transactions (and because it allows us to prove the scheme secure), we introduced stealth excesses X, which along with the proof of possession σ accounts for the "excess" in stealth addresses. We also introduce a *stealth offset* to preserve privacy of aggregated transactions.

4.2   The Feed-Me Attack

It turns out that merely adding a stealth excess leads to an attack (against *transaction-binding*, see Sect. 6.5), which was first found by @south_lagoon77, alias kurt.[11] Consider the scheme in Sect. 3 but without any D values, which are replaced by the corresponding P values in the equations; in particular, the balance equation for one-time keys Eq. (10) is replaced by:

$$X = \sum \hat{R} - \sum P - y^* G. \tag{10*}$$

To explain the attack, it suffices to focus on non-aggregated transactions. Consider Alice, an honest user with address (aG, B), that creates two transactions tx_1 and tx_2, both with one input and one output, transferring respectively v_1 to Bob and $v_2 > v_1$ to Charlie:

$$(C_1, \dots) = txo_1 \quad \leftarrow \quad \boxed{P_1, \psi_1 \mid \dots, \hat{R}_1, \hat{\rho}_1, \dots}_{t_1, y_1, E_1, X_1, \dots} \tag{tx_1}$$

$$(C_2, \dots) = txo_2 \quad \leftarrow \quad \boxed{P_2, \psi_2 \mid \dots, \hat{R}_2, \hat{\rho}_2, \dots}_{t_2, y_2, E_2, X_2, \dots} \tag{tx_2}$$

Both transaction are broadcast to the miners. A malicious miner can now forge a new transaction, transferring the amount $v_2 - v_1$ to himself, as follows:

$$txo_2 \quad \leftarrow \quad \boxed{P_2, \psi_2 \mid \dots, \hat{R}_1, \hat{\rho}_1, \dots \| \dots R^*, \rho^*, \dots}_{t_1, y^*, E_1, X_1, \dots} \tag{tx^*}$$

It combines the input of tx_2 and the output and the excesses from tx_1. A second output is computed "honestly", choosing $r^* \leftarrow_\$ \mathbb{Z}_p$, setting $R^* = r^* G$ and signing any P value (knowing $\log P$) via ρ^*. The miner also creates the corresponding coin C^*, so tx^* satisfies Eq. (9), by setting $C^* := \mathsf{Cmt}(v_2 - v_1, q_2 - q_1)$, where q_1 and q_2 are the openings of C_1 and C_2 (which the miner can either obtain by knowing Alice's view key, or *by having sent the outputs that are now being spent by* tx_1 *and* tx_2 *to Alice in the first place*.) Finally, the miner needs to compute y^* so that tx^* satisfies Eq. (10*), that is, $y^* G = R^* + \hat{R}_1 - P_2 - X_1$. By validity of tx_1, again from (10*), we get $0 = -\hat{R}_1 + P_1 + y_1 G + X_1$ and by adding the two equations:

$$y^* G = R^* + P_1 - P_2 + y_1 G. \tag{14}$$

---

[11] See: https://twitter.com/davidburkett38/status/1466460568525713413.

The crucial observation now is that if the miner knows the values k_1 and k_2 that define P_1 and P_2, resp. (which it can either obtain by knowing Alice's view key or by being the creator of the outputs spent by tx_1 and tx_2), then it knows the discrete logarithm of $P_1 - P_2 = (k_1 - k_2)G$, as the value B from Alice's address *cancels out*. The miner can thus compute y^* satisfying (14), thus completing the forged transaction tx^* that transfers the value $v_2 - v_1$ to the miner's address.

Fixes. To prevent this attack, our first fix was to derive the one-time key multiplicatively, as $P_i = k_i B$ in Eq. (5). The term $P_1 - P_2$ then becomes $(k_1 - k_2)B$, which is non-zero with overwhelming probability and therefore it becomes hard to compute y^*. More generally, as long as the adversary cannot find distinct hash function outputs $k_{1,1}, \ldots, k_{1,n_0}, k_{2,1}, \ldots, k_{2,n_1}$ in Eq. (3) so that

$$\sum k_1 - \sum k_2 = 0 \, , \tag{15}$$

this variant of the scheme (without the D values) satisfies transaction binding.

However, Wagner's *k-list tree algorithm* [Wag02] can be used to find such values in sub-exponential time. In order to be protected against active adversaries ready to invest substantial computing power, a user therefore would need to limit the number of its pending transactions at any point in time (which could degrade scalability of the system). To overcome this downside, we follow Burkett's approach [Bur21] and introduce an additional group element D in every transaction input which replaces P in the balance equation (10*), yielding (12). Since the D_i's are chosen by the creator of the transaction (whereas the P_i's are chosen by the previous spender, who in *Feed-Me* types of attacks is malicious), the values corresponding to the $k_{i,j}$ above are random, and thus the probability that (15) holds is negligible.

Since the D values are chosen by the honest user, the adversary in the Feed-Me attack does not know $\log(D_1 - D_2)$ (after replacing P values by D values in (14)), so we just reverted to the original format $P := B + kG$ for one-time keys and prove this variant secure.

4.3   On Transaction Cut-Through

Suppose that, in an aggregate transaction, an output $(C, \pi, R, \rho, P, \chi)$ of one transaction is spent as input (P, D, ψ) of another transaction. One may wonder if, as with original MW, cut-through can be applied, that is, remove the spent output and the input referring to it from the aggregate transaction.

While validity of the coin-balance equation (11) would be maintained, this is not the case for the "address equation" (12). One may thus consider (as Yu does [Yu20, §2.1.1] for (sufficiently old parts of) the ledger) adding a value Z defined as the difference of the sum of all removed $\hat{R}$ values and all removed $\hat{D}$ values to the aggregated transaction. The check in Eq. 12 would be replaced by $\sum \hat{R} - \sum D + Z = \sum X + yG$, where the sums are only over the indices that have not been removed in the outputs ($\sum \hat{R}$) and the inputs ($\sum D$).

However, since Z is not bound to anything, this scheme would be insecure. Consider a miner that collects transactions and aggregates them. Then she simply replaces one of the remaining $\hat{R}$ values by a value of which she knows the discrete logarithm, puts a new $\hat{P}$ value, produces a corresponding proof $\hat{\rho}$ and defines Z as $\sum \boldsymbol{X} + yG + \sum \boldsymbol{D}$ minus the sum of the $\hat{\boldsymbol{R}}$ values including her own. This results in a valid transaction of which the miner now owns one of the outputs (assuming the miner knows the view key of the stealth address it stole the coin from; otherwise it made the coin unspendable by its owner).

We suspect that Yu assumed all R and P values remain for each (possibly aggregated) transaction when included in the blockchain, since in [Yu20, Eq. ③], it says "$SUM(R - P')_{spent\ at\ height}$", which suggests that all these values need to be present. In addition, we note that simply removing cut-through inputs or outputs would make Equations ③ and ④ incorrect.

Example. Consider two 1-input/1-output transactions tx_1 and tx_2 (assume that all supplies and fees are 0).

$$txo_1 \quad \leftarrow \quad \boxed{P_1, D_1, \psi_1 \mid C_2, \pi_2, R_2, \rho_2, P_2, \chi_2}_{t_2, y_2, E_2, X_2, \sigma_2} \qquad (\mathsf{tx}_2)$$

$$\leftarrow \quad \boxed{P_2, D_2, \psi_2 \mid C_3, \pi_3, R_3, \rho_3, P_3, \chi_3}_{t_3, y_3, E_3, X_3, \sigma_3} \qquad (\mathsf{tx}_3)$$

where tx_2 spends some output txo_1, creating one output, which is then spent by tx_3 (in particular, we have $\mathsf{PoP.V}((P_2, D_2, \mathsf{tx}_2.\mathsf{out}), \psi_2) = \mathbf{true}$). Suppose tx_2 and tx_3 could be merged as

$$txo_1 \leftarrow \boxed{P_1, D_1, \psi_1 \mid C_3, \pi_3, R_3, \rho_3, P_3, \chi_3}_{t_2+t_3, y_2+y_3, (E_2, E_3), (X_2, X_3), (\sigma_2, \sigma_3), Z}$$

which is valid if ψ_1 and ρ_3 (and π_3), as well as σ_2, σ_3, are valid on their respective messages, and the following holds:

$$C_3 - C_1 = E_2 + E_3 + (t_2 + t_3)G$$
$$R_3 - D_1 + Z = X_2 + X_1 + (y_2 + y_3)G$$

Then a miner could simply choose r^*, p^*, χ_3^* set $R_3^* := r^*G$, $P_3^* := p^*G$, create ρ_3^* honestly, define $Z^* := X_2 + X_3 + (y_2 + y_3)G - R_3^* + P_1$ and create the following (valid!) transaction, for which she knows the temporary spending key p^*:

$$txo_1 \leftarrow \boxed{P_1, D_1, \psi_1 \mid C_3, \pi_3, R_3^*, \rho_3, P_3^*, \chi_3^*}_{t_2+t_3, y_2+y_3, (E_2, E_3), (X_2, X_3), (\sigma_2, \sigma_3), Z^*}$$

In the full version we also show that in addition to R and D, also both values ρ and ψ of spent transaction must be kept, as each removal leads to an attack.

4.4   Replay Attacks

Yu [Yu20, §2.9.2] explains a replay attack for MW that is a result of non-interactive transactions: the adversary pays Alice via some output txo, which

PoP.Setup(1^λ)	PoP.P$\big(par, (X, Y, m), (x, y)\big)$	PoP.V$\big(par, (X, Y, m), \psi\big)$
$(p, \mathbb{G}, G) \leftarrow \mathsf{GrGen}(1^\lambda)$	$(p, \mathbb{G}, G, \mathrm{H}) := par$	$(p, \mathbb{G}, G, \mathrm{H}) := par$
fix $\mathrm{H} \colon \{0,1\}^* \to \mathbb{Z}_p^2$	$r \leftarrow\!\!\$\ \mathbb{Z}_p \,;\ R := rG$	$(R, s) := \psi$
return $(p, \mathbb{G}, G, \mathrm{H})$	$(c, d) := \mathrm{H}(X, Y, m, R)$	$(c, d) := \mathrm{H}(X, Y, m, R)$
	$s := r + cx + dy \bmod p$	**return**
	return $\psi := (R, s)$	$(sG = R + cX + dY)$

Fig. 2. Batch Schnorr zero-knowledge simulation-extractable proof of knowledge of two logarithms PoP[GrGen] w.r.t. a group generator GrGen.

Alice later spends. Then the adversary pays her again, creating the exact same output; if Alice accepts it, the adversary can replay Alice's previous spend, making her lose the money.

A simple fix for replay attacks is requiring users to store all outputs ever received and never accept the same output a second time. A more viable method is using time stamps (named *epochs* and denoted χ in our notation), which Yu introduces in order to prevent rogue-key attacks. "Each *Input* must attach its own proof for [P_i], as a second proof for the coin ownership" [Yu20, §2.9.3].

While it is not specified which message is signed, it is crucial that the entire output specifically including the time stamp (and not just C) is signed. Otherwise, the above attack still works, as the adversary can change the time stamp in the replayed transaction (so the user accepts it) and recompute ρ, and send it to the user again. If the proof contained in the user's spendings did not authenticate the time stamp (or ρ), then the previous spend would still be valid on the replayed transaction. This is why in MW-NIT we define ψ as a proof that involves the *entire* output.

Epochs. If the user only accepts outputs that correspond to the current epoch, she only needs to compare a new output to those received in the same epoch; she can therefore delete all outputs from previous epochs. The duration of an epoch is a global parameter of the system, where short time intervals minimizes data storage, while larger intervals yield better privacy (as there are more transactions per epoch).

5   Simulation-Extractability of Schnorr Signatures

Before analyzing our scheme, we introduce and analyze its main building block. Key-prefixed Schnorr signatures can be reinterpreted as zero-knowledge proofs of knowledge of the secret key, with the statement also containing the message. To improve efficiency, we generalize this to a "batch" version that enables proving knowledge of the logarithms of two group elements, that is, proofs for the NP language defined w.r.t. a group description $(p, \mathbb{G}, G)$ by the following relation:

$$\big\{ \big((X, Y, m), (x, y)\big) \,:\, X = xG \wedge Y = yG \wedge m \in \{0,1\}^* \big\} \,. \tag{16}$$

The proof system PoP is defined in Fig. 2. We also use it to prove statements (X, m) with witness x by using standard Schnorr signatures, that is, PoP.P runs Sch.Sign and PoP.V runs Sch.Ver. The witness relation for PoP is thus the union of (16) and $\{((X, m), x) : X = xG\}$.

We show that PoP satisfies *strong simulation extractability* in the *algebraic group model* [FKL18] (see below) and the random oracle model (a tion of models also used in [FPS20] to show tight security of Schnorr signatures under the discrete-logarithm assumption).

Simulation-Extractability. Strong simulation extractability for the above language means that from any adversary that returns a proof ψ^* for a statement (X^*, Y^*, m^*), the witness $(\log X^*, \log Y^*)$ can be extracted; and this holds even if the adversary gets access to an oracle that on inputs (X_i, Y_i, m_i) returns simulated proofs ψ_i for these statements. The only restriction is that the returned pair $((X^*, Y^*, m^*), \psi^*)$ must be different from all query/response pairs $((X_i, Y_i, m_i), \psi_i)$. Thus, forging a fresh proof ψ^* on a queried statement is considered a break of *strong* simulation-extractability if the extractor fails to extract a witness from ψ^*. (Note that this notion is stronger than forms of related-key-attack security for signature schemes (like UNF-CRO as defined and used in [FOS19]), where the adversary can only query signatures under keys for which it knows the difference in secret keys w.r.t. the challenge key.)

The Algebraic Group Model. In the algebraic group model (AGM) [FKL18], adversaries are assumed to return a *representation* of any group element that they return. This means that, after having received input group elements $Z_1, \ldots, Z_n$, whenever the adversary returns a group element X, it must also return coefficients $\zeta_1, \ldots, \zeta_n$ so that $X = \sum \zeta_i Z_i$.

All our security proofs (except for the privacy notion) are reductions of solving the discrete logarithm (DL) problem to breaking the analyzed security notion of our scheme MW-NIT, assuming that PoP satisfies (strong) simulation-extractability (SE) in the AGM. The reduction thus receives a DL challenge Z and simulates the security game to an adversary $\mathcal{A}$, which we assume is algebraic. To leverage SE of PoP *in the AGM*, the reduction must construct an *algebraic* SE adversary, that is, one that accompanies each group-element output by their representations. However, the reduction can only return representations in basis (G, Z), its own group-element inputs. In particular, the reduction will run the adversary on some group elements $X_1, \ldots, X_n$, which it produces from its inputs G and Z in an "algebraic" way (i.e., knowing representations in basis (G, Z)). The adversary's group-element outputs will thus be in basis $X_1, \ldots, X_n$, which the reduction can then translate into the basis (G, Z).

For our reductions make use of simulation extractability, we must therefore strengthen the notion and consider auxiliary inputs. In the SE game, the adversary receives, besides a description of the underlying group, with generator G, and possible proof system parameters, an "auxiliary" uniform group element Z. At the end of its execution, the algebraic adversary must accompany each group element queried to the simulation oracle and output to the challenger (in particular, group elements in the statements (X_i, Y_i, m) for which the extractor must extract the witness) by a representation in basis (G, Z).

Security of PoP. Extending the techniques for showing tight security of Schnorr signatures in the AGM+ROM [FPS20], we show that in this model our proof system PoP is SE with auxiliary inputs, which also extends to standard Schnorr signatures. The proof can be found in the full version.

Claim 1. *In the AGM and the ROM, the proof system* PoP *in Fig. 2 is strongly simulation-extractable with auxiliary group-element input.*

Corollary 1. *In the AGM and the ROM, Schnorr signatures are proofs of secret keys that are strongly simulation-extractable with auxiliary group-element input.*

6   Security Analysis of MW-NIT

6.1   Assumptions

In our security analysis of the protocol from Sect. 3, we assume that range proofs in RaP prove knowledge of the committed value v and the opening q. (Note that for the employed Pedersen commitment, a proof of language membership, that is not "of knowledge" is vacuous, as for any C there always exists an opening e.g. $(v = 0, q = \log C)$.) We thus assume that there exists an extractor that from (an adversary outputting) a range proof π for $C \in \mathbb{G}$ can extract the values $v \in [0, v_{\max}]$ and $q \in \mathbb{Z}_p$.

We assume the existence of strongly simulation-sound (sSS) zero-knowledge (zk) proofs of knowledge (PoK) of the discrete logarithm of group elements with tags. In the full version, we show that in the combination of the random-oracle model and the algebraic group model [FKL18], Schnorr signatures are *adaptive* sSS zk-PoKs of the logarithm of the public key, for which the message acts as a tag. We furthermore extended this to proofs of knowledge of two logarithms, so that the proofs are of the same size as Schnorr signatures.

Finally, we assume that the discrete logarithm (DL) problem is hard in the group underlying the system, and for transaction privacy that the decisional Diffie-Hellman (DDH) assumption holds.

6.2   Syntax

We briefly review the syntax of an *aggregate cash system* [FOS19] and describe the adaptations required to capture addresses and non-interactive transactions.

Running $(pp, \Lambda) \leftarrow \mathsf{Setup}(1^\lambda, v_{\max})$ on input the security parameter λ in unary and a maximal coin value $v_{\max}$ creates the public parameters and an empty ledger. A *ledger* Λ specifies a *supply* $\Lambda.\mathsf{sply}$ (also denoted s) representing the value stored in Λ and a list of *transaction outputs* (TXOs) $\Lambda.\mathsf{out}$. Users create addresses (or "wallets") by running $(pk, vk, sk) \leftarrow \mathsf{KeyGen}(pp)$, which returns a public key (*address*), a *view key* and a *spending key sk*.

A *transaction* tx has three attributes: a *supply* tx.sply specifying the amount of money it creates, a list tx.in of *inputs* and a list tx.out of *outputs* txo_i. A transaction is created by running tx $\leftarrow$ Send$(pp, (\mathbf{txo}, \mathbf{v}, \mathbf{sk}), (\hat{\mathbf{v}}, \mathbf{pk}, \chi), s, f)$ on vectors of transaction outputs $\mathbf{txo} = (txo_i)_i$, corresponding values $\mathbf{v} = (v_i)_i$ and spending keys $\mathbf{sk} = (sk_i)_i$, and vectors of output values $\hat{\mathbf{v}}$, destination addresses $\mathbf{pk}$, and epochs χ, as well as a supply s and a fee f. To aggregate transactions $\mathsf{tx}_1, \ldots, \mathsf{tx}_n$, run tx $\leftarrow$ Agg$(pp, (\mathsf{tx}_1, \ldots, \mathsf{tx}_n))$ (which returns $\perp$ if they are incompatible, e.g. having an input in common).

Using a vector of view keys $\mathbf{vk}$ and a list of values $\hat{\mathbf{v}}$, one obtains the list of outputs of a transaction tx belonging to these keys by running $\mathbf{txo} \leftarrow$ Rcv$(pp, \mathsf{tx}, \hat{\mathbf{v}}, \mathbf{vk})$. If tx does not spend $\hat{v}_i \in \hat{\mathbf{v}}$ to $vk_i \in \mathbf{vk}$, then $txo_i \in \mathbf{txo}$ is set to $\perp$. Finally, $\Lambda' \leftarrow$ Ldgr$(pp, \Lambda, \mathsf{tx})$ returns an updated ledger Λ' including tx if it is valid and spends outputs present in the ledger, otherwise $\Lambda' := \perp$;

Correctness. We require the following straightforward correctness condition. Let $(pk_j, vk_j, sk_j)_j$ be key triples generated by KeyGen, and for $k \in [n]$ let tx'_k be a transaction, $\mathbf{v}'_k$ a vector of elements in $[0, v_{\max}]$, $\mathbf{vk}'_k \subseteq (vk_j)_j$ and let $\mathbf{sk}'_k$ be the corresponding spending keys (that is, if $\mathbf{vk}'_k = (vk_{j_i})_i$ for some j_i, then $\mathbf{sk}'_k = (sk_{j_i})_i$). For all $k \in [n]$, define $\mathbf{txo}_k \leftarrow$ Rcv$(pp, \mathsf{tx}'_k, \mathbf{v}'_k, \mathbf{vk}'_k)$.

Let indices i_j be so that $txo_{i_j} \neq \perp$ (where we let $(txo_\iota)_\iota := \mathbf{txo}_1 \| \ldots \| \mathbf{txo}_n$), let $\hat{\mathbf{v}} \in [0, v_{\max}]^*$, $\hat{\mathbf{pk}} \subseteq (pk_j)_j$, and s and f such that $\sum v'_{i_j} = \sum \hat{v}_i + f - s$. Then for tx $\leftarrow$ Send$(pp, ((txo_{i_j})_j, (v'_{i_j})_j, (sk'_{i_j})_j), (\hat{\mathbf{v}}, \hat{\mathbf{pk}}, \chi), s, f)$ and $\mathbf{txo} \leftarrow$ Rcv$(pp, \mathsf{tx}, \hat{\mathbf{v}}, \hat{\mathbf{vk}})$ where $\hat{\mathbf{vk}}$ corresponds to $\hat{\mathbf{pk}}$, we have $\perp \notin \mathbf{txo}$, that is, all outputs are accepted.

Comparison to FOS. The syntax of Send and Rcv differs from the one in [FOS19] due to the inclusion of addresses (as well as fees and epochs) and transactions being non-interactive. We moreover simplified notation by merging their algorithm Mint, used for creating money, with Send (which is now non-interactive and takes a supply as input). That is, Mint$(pp, \hat{\mathbf{v}}, \mathbf{pk}, \chi)$ is an alias for Send$(pp, (), (\hat{\mathbf{v}}, \mathbf{pk}, \chi), \sum \hat{\mathbf{v}}, 0)$.

6.3   Inflation Resistance

Definition. Informally, inflation resistance guarantees that the only way to create money in an *aggregate cash system*, such as Mimblewimble, is explicitly via the supply contained in transactions. The notion is defined by the following game, adapted from [FOS19, Def. 10] and formalized in Fig. 3.

The adversary is given the system parameters (for MW-NIT they contain the elements G and H and potential parameters for the range proof), and its task is to produce a (valid) ledger and a transaction tx^* (accepted by the ledger) that spends an amount that exceeds the supply of the ledger (plus its own supply).

Game $\mathrm{INFL}_{\mathsf{CASH},\mathcal{A}}(\lambda, v_{\max})$

$(pp, \Lambda) \leftarrow \mathsf{Setup}(1^\lambda, v_{\max})$

$(\Lambda^*, \mathsf{tx}^*, \hat{\mathbf{v}}, \mathbf{vk}) \leftarrow \mathcal{A}(pp, \Lambda)$

return $(\bot \notin \mathsf{Rcv}(pp, \mathsf{tx}^*, \hat{\mathbf{v}}, \mathbf{vk})$ // view keys accept outputs of tx^*

    and $\mathsf{Ldgr}(pp, \Lambda^*, \mathsf{tx}^*) \neq \bot$ // tx^* is accepted by the ledger

    and $\Lambda^*.\mathsf{sply} < \sum \hat{\mathbf{v}} + \mathsf{tx}^*.\mathsf{fees} - \mathsf{tx}^*.\mathsf{sply})$ // ... and spends more than there is

Fig. 3. Game for inflation resistance $\mathrm{INFL}_{\mathsf{CASH},\mathcal{A}}(\lambda, v_{\max})$.

In addition to the output amounts $\hat{\mathbf{v}}$ of tx^*, the adversary must also return view keys, which accept the outputs of tx^*. Letting s denote the ledger supply, s^* the supply and f^* the fee of tx^*, the adversary wins if

$$s < \sum \hat{\mathbf{v}} + f^* - s^* . \tag{17}$$

In the full version we give a proof of the following theorem. It follows closely that of [FOS19, Theorem 13] for MW-FOS, since a ledger (or transaction) in MW-NIT contains an MW-FOS ledger (or transaction). While FOS did not consider fees and kernel offsets, these can be added to the argument.

Theorem 1. *If the range-proof system* RaP *and the proof-of-possession system* PoP *are extractable and if the discrete-logarithm assumption holds in the underlying group, then MW-NIT satisfies inflation resistance.*

6.4   Theft Resistance

We define two notions that protect users from losing money. The first one is an adaptation of the notion from [FOS19] to a scheme with non-interactive transactions. It guarantees that outputs in the ledger belonging to a user can only be spent by that user.

The main difference between MW-FOS and MW-NIT is that the former relies on the coin keys (the opening of the commitments) being kept secret, while in MW-NIT, the spender knows (and defines) the openings of the receivers' commitments.[12] In MW-NIT, the security relies on the secrecy of the "*spend key*" for the user's stealth address. We assume that the *view key* is known to the adversary (as delegating scanning for transactions should not endanger the security of these transactions).

Definition. Resistance to theft means that for any output belonging to a user in the ledger (that is, it was accepted by the user's view key), no matter how it was received (e.g., sent by the adversary), as long as the output has never

---

[12] Note that this is unavoidable for non-interactive transactions: knowing the (sum of) the receivers' keys is necessary to compute the excess proof σ.

Game $\mathrm{STEAL}_{\mathsf{CASH},\mathcal{A}}(\lambda, v_{\max})$	Oracle KEYGEN()
$(pp, \Lambda) \leftarrow \mathsf{Setup}(1^\lambda, v_{\max})$	$j := j + 1$
$Hon, Archv := ()\ ;\ j := 0$	$(pk_j, vk_j, sk_j) \leftarrow \mathsf{KeyGen}(pp)$
$\mathcal{A}^{\text{KEYGEN,SEND,LEDGER}}(pp, \Lambda)$	$\mathbf{return}\ (j, vk_j, pk_j)$
$\mathbf{return}\ (Hon \not\subseteq \Lambda.\mathsf{out})$	

Oracle SEND$((\mathbf{txo}, \mathbf{v}, I), (\hat{\mathbf{v}}, \mathbf{pk}, \boldsymbol{\chi}), s, f)$	Oracle LEDGER$(\mathsf{tx}, \hat{v}, I)$
$\mathbf{if}\ \mathbf{txo} \not\subseteq Hon\ \mathbf{then\ return}\ \bot$	$\Lambda' := \mathsf{Ldgr}(pp, \Lambda, \mathsf{tx})$
$\mathsf{tx} \leftarrow \mathsf{Send}\big(pp, (\mathbf{txo}, \mathbf{v}, (sk_i)_{i \in I}),$	$\mathbf{if}\ \Lambda' = \bot\ \mathbf{then\ return}\ \bot$
$\hspace{3.5em}(\hat{\mathbf{v}}, \mathbf{pk}, \boldsymbol{\chi}), s, f\big)$	$\mathbf{else}\ \Lambda := \Lambda'$
$\mathbf{if}\ \mathsf{tx} = \bot\ \mathbf{then\ return}\ \bot$	$/\!/$ Check for new honest outputs in tx:
$Hon := Hon - \mathbf{txo}\ /\!/$ remove spent outputs	$\mathbf{txo} \leftarrow \mathsf{Rcv}(pp, \mathsf{tx}, \hat{v}, (vk_i)_{i \in I})$
$\mathbf{return}\ \mathsf{tx}$	$\mathbf{for}\ i \in [\![\lVert\mathbf{txo}\rVert]\!]:$
	$\quad \mathbf{if}\ txo_i \neq \bot\ \mathbf{and}\ txo_i \notin Archv$
	$\qquad Hon := Hon \,\|\, txo_i$
	$\qquad Archv := Archv \,\|\, txo_i$
	$\mathbf{return}\ \Lambda$

Fig. 4. Game for theft resistance $\mathrm{STEAL}_{\mathsf{CASH},\mathcal{A}}(\lambda, v_{\max})$

been spent before and the user keeps her spend key safe, no one except her can spend it (even if her view key is publicly known). This is formalized via the game in Fig. 4, which is an adaptation of [FOS19, Fig. 8]. Honest users are simulated by the experiment and the adversary can create new users by calling KEYGEN; the adversary can make users spend outputs they own (stored in the list Hon) by calling SEND; moreover it can submit any transactions to the ledger using it oracle LEDGER. If the transaction contains outputs that are accepted by honest users, it adds these to Hon. As users are not supposed to accept outputs they have already owned (cf. Sect. 4.4), the experiment stores all outputs ever received in a list $Archv$. The adversary wins the game if it spends any of the honest user's outputs, that is, if some output in Hon is not in the ledger.

Remark. Note that the game in Fig. 4 for a scheme with non-interactive transactions is a lot simpler than [FOS19, Fig. 8], which had to take care of the interactive spending protocol. In particular, the definition of the coins an honest user owns in [FOS19] is cumbersome, whereas for non-interactive transactions, anything accepted by the honest user's view key (and not previously owned) is considered belonging to her. Note also that we do not require an oracle MINT, since the adversary can run SEND with an empty input list.

Theorem 2. *If* PoP *is a simulation-sound proof of knowledge of discrete logarithms (cf. Sect. 5) and the DL assumption holds in the underlying group, then* MW-NIT *satisfies theft-resistance.*

Proof. Consider a user owning an output $txo = (C, \pi, R, \rho, P, \chi)$ with amount v in the ledger, that is, txo is accepted (see Sect. 3.4) by her stealth address $(A = aG, B)$, meaning $P = B + kG$ where $(k, q) = H(aR)$. Spending this coin requires proving possession of P with tag txo, but an honest user, unless she spends that output, never proves possession of P with tag txo.

We formally use a theft to break the DL assumption assuming simulation-extractability of PoP. The reduction receives a DL challenge $B^* \in \mathbb{G}$, chooses $a^* \leftarrow_{\$} \mathbb{Z}_p$, sets a random honest user's stealth address to $(A^* := a^*G, B^*)$ and gives the adversary the view key (a^*, B^*).

Whenever the user is asked to spend an output $txo' = (C', \pi', R', \rho', P', \chi')$ belonging to the user, the reduction computes the transaction as specified, choosing a doubling key $D' := d'G$ for a $d' \leftarrow_{\$} \mathbb{Z}_p$. As it does not know the logarithm of P' (since this requires knowledge of $\log B^*$), it runs the zero-knowledge simulator for a proof of possession ψ for (P', D') with tag txo'. (Note that the reduction is algebraic w.r.t. its DL challenge B^*, in that it can give representations of all queried elements in basis (G, B^*), in particular $P' = B^* + k'G$, $D' = d'G$.)

Assume an output $txo = (C, \pi, R, \rho, P, \chi)$ belonging to the user is spent by the adversary. (If the adversary attacked a different user, the reduction aborts.) Then the corresponding transaction input must contain a proof ψ^* of possession of (P, D^*) with tag txo for some D^* (for which the reduction can derive a representation in basis (G, B^*) from the algebraic adversary's representation). By the definition of the security game, the honest user has never spent txo before. This means that the reduction has never queried a simulated proof for (P, D^*, txo). Therefore, by simulation-extractability in the AGM, the reduction can extract $p = \log P$, and since $P = B^* + kG$, for a value k known to the reduction, it can compute the solution $p - k$ to its DL challenge B^*.   □

6.5   Transaction-Binding

While the previous notion states that once a user owns an output in the ledger it cannot be purloined, we also need to guarantee that nothing can be "stolen" from a transaction *before* it is even added to the ledger (this protects against malicious miners, for example). In particular, if a user produces a transaction tx then no one should be able to create a transaction that contains *one* of the inputs of tx while not containing *all* its outputs (since transactions can be aggregated, further inputs and outputs could have been added to the original transaction). Thus, while *theft-resistance* protects the outputs of a transaction, *transaction-binding* in some sense protects the inputs.

Definition. We define transaction-binding via the following game, formalized in Fig. 5. The experiment simulates all honest users, which the adversary can create by calling KEYGEN, which creates a new address, for which the adversary receives the view key. The adversary can instruct honest users to spend outputs to addresses of the adversary's choice, and the experiment computes the corresponding transaction using the users' spending keys and gives it to the adversary. The adversary's goal is to create a transaction tx* which *spends the*

```
┌─────────────────────────────────────────────────────────────────────────────┐
│  Game TXBND_CASH,A(λ, v_max)                                                  │
├─────────────────────────────────────────────────────────────────────────────┤
│  (pp, Λ) ← Setup(1^λ, v_max)                                                  │
│  j := 0;  HTxs := ()   // honest transactions                                 │
│  (Λ, tx*, v̂, I) ← A^KEYGEN,SEND(pp)                                           │
│  Λ* := Ldgr(pp, Λ, tx*)                                                        │
│  return (∃ tx ∈ HTxs : Ldgr(pp, Λ, tx) ≠ ⊥        // tx accepted by Λ...       │
│         and Λ* ≠ ⊥ and Ldgr(pp, Λ*, tx) = ⊥       // ...but not after tx* was added │
│         and ⊥ ∉ Rcv(pp, tx, v̂, (vk_i)_{i∈I})      // tx sends values v̂ to vk... │
│         and ⊥ ∈ Rcv(pp, tx*, v̂, (vk_i)_{i∈I}))    // ...but tx* does not       │
│                                                                               │
│                                                                               │
│  Oracle KEYGEN()            Oracle SEND((txo, v, I), (v̂, pk, χ), s, f)        │
│  ───────────────            ─────────────────────────────────────────────     │
│  j := j + 1                 tx ← Send(pp, (txo, v, (sk_i)_{i∈I}), (v̂, pk, χ), s, f) │
│  (pk_j, vk_j, sk_j) ← KeyGen(pp)   if tx = ⊥ then return ⊥                    │
│  return (j, vk_j, pk_j)     HTxs := HTxs || tx                                 │
│                             return tx                                          │
└─────────────────────────────────────────────────────────────────────────────┘
```

Fig. 5. Game for transaction-binding $\text{TXBND}_{\text{CASH},A}(\lambda, v_{\max})$.

same input as an honest transaction tx, but *does not contain all the outputs of* tx *that belong to honest users.*

We formalize this by having the adversary return a ledger Λ that must accept the attacked honest transaction tx, but after tx* is included in Λ, the latter does not accept tx anymore (thus tx and tx* have an input in common); the adversary also returns values and indices of honest users, so that their view keys accept tx but do not accept tx* (thus one of the outputs of tx is missing in tx*).

Remark. While it might seem restrictive that only stealing outputs of honest users is considered a break of the notion, it is not. In aggregate cash systems like Mimblewimble (with cut-through), an adversary can always "steal" outputs it owns from any transaction tx: simply create a transaction that spends these outputs and then merge it with tx; the result is a transaction in which some of the outputs have been replaced by new ones. We do thus not consider this an attack and transaction-binding gives no guarantees against it.

The following is proved in the full version; we give proof intuition below.

Theorem 3. *If* PoP *is a strongly simulation-sound proof of knowledge of discrete logarithms (cf. Sect. 5) and the DL assumption holds in the underlying group, then MW-NIT satisfies transaction-binding.*

Proof Intuition. As this is the most complex notion to analyze, we start with some intuition in a simplified scenario. Consider an adversary that sends Alice a transaction with one output $txo = (C, \pi, R, \rho, P, \chi)$ and that Alice creates a transaction

$$\mathsf{tx} = \big((P, D, \psi), (\hat{C}, \hat{\pi}, \hat{R}, \hat{\rho}, \hat{P}, \hat{\chi}), (s, f, t, y, \sigma)\big)$$

that spends txo to Bob. Moreover, assume this is the only transaction Alice makes. The adversary's goal is now to create a "forged" transaction $\mathsf{tx}^* = ((P, D^*, \psi^*), txo^*, (s^*, f^*, t^*, y^*, \sigma^*))$ that has P as its input, but with a different (single) output $txo^* = (C^*, \pi^*, R^*, \rho^*, P^*, \chi^*)$. We show that conditions (I)–(III) must hold with overwhelming probability, by reducing the DL problem to it, assuming strong simulation-extractability (SE) of the proofs of possession. In (IV) we show that even then the game can only be won with negligible probability.

(I) $D = D^*$. Assume this is not the case. Under SE of PoP, this can be used to break DL by simulating the game as in the proof of theft-resistance. Given a DL challenge B, the reduction embeds it into Alice's wallet (aG, B) for $a \leftarrow_\$ \mathbb{Z}_p$. It computes tx as prescribed, except that it simulates the proof ψ (as its witness depends on $\log B$). When the adversary outputs a transaction with input (P, D^*, ψ^*), it can extract the witness (p, d^*) from ψ^*, as the only simulated proof was for a different statement (P, D). Since $P = B + kG$, where k is computed from (aG, B) according to (3), the reduction can return $\log B = p - k$.

(II) $R^* \neq \hat{R}$. Assume $R^* = \hat{R}$. Since txo^* must be different, either the tag $C^* \| \pi^* \| P^* \| \chi^*$ for ρ^*, or ρ^* itself is different. As the statement/proof pair is different from the one created by Alice, one can extract $\log R^*$ by strong simulation extractability ("strong", since possibly only the proof differs). Given a DL challenge $\hat{R}$, the reduction embeds it in the output of tx. Not knowing $\log \hat{R}$, the reduction can still compute $(\hat{k}, \hat{q}) = H(a'\hat{R})$ using Bob's view key (a', B') (recall that Bob must be honest). From this, the reduction computes $\hat{C}$, $\hat{\pi}$ and $\hat{P}$. The proofs $\hat{\rho}$ and σ, whose witnesses depend on $\log \hat{R}$, are simulated. If the adversary returns a transaction tx^* with $R^* = \hat{R}$, then from ρ^* the reduction can extract $\log \hat{R}$ (since the tag or ρ^* must be different), solving the DL challenge.

(III) $X^* \neq X$, that is, the stealth excess of tx^* is different from that of tx. Assume $X^* = X$. Then from their definitions in (2) we get $R^* - D - y^*G = \hat{R} - D - yG$, where we used $D^* = D$ from (I). Thus $\hat{R} = R^* + (y - y^*)G$. Since ρ^* proves knowledge of $\log R^*$, this means the adversary must also know $\log \hat{R}$.
Formally, as in case (II), the reduction embeds a DL challenge as $\hat{R}$ and simulates the proofs $\hat{\rho}$ and $\hat{\sigma}$ to compute tx. If the adversary's forgery violates (III), then from ρ^* the reduction can extract $r^* = \log R^*$ (since, by (II), ρ^* is for $R^* \neq \hat{R}$, and the simulated proof $\hat{\rho}$ was for $\hat{R}$) and thus compute the solution $r^* + y - y^*$.

(IV) Finally, we show that the adversary cannot win the game when (I)–(III) hold either. From (I) and (2), we have $X^* := R^* - D - y^*G$. Since σ^*

contained in tx^* proves knowledge of $x^* := \log X^*$ (since $X^* \neq X$ by (III)) and ρ^* proves knowledge of $r^* := \log R^*$ (since $R^* \neq \hat{R}$ by (II)), this means that the adversary must know $\log D = r^* - y^* - x^*$.

The reduction embeds its DL challenge as D, the value in the input of tx, and simulates proofs ψ and σ (whose DL depend on $\log D$). The rest of tx is computed as prescribed. If the adversary is successful, then from ρ^* the reduction extracts r^* (no ρ proofs were ever simulated), and from σ^* the reduction extracts x^* (the simulated proof σ was under $X \neq X^*$) and computes $d := r^* - y^* - x^*$ as above.

While the above provides some intuition, the actual proof which can be found in the full version, is more complex by considering the "complete" scenario:

- Alice may create other transactions, of which parts may be reused in tx^*.
- The transaction tx^* could be an aggregated transaction, and in its stealth-excess list, parts can be reused from transactions by Alice.

6.6   Transaction Privacy

This section considers an attacker that passively observes blocks and attempts to recover information about the transaction graph or the transacted amounts. In Jedusor's original proposal [Jed16], no guarantee of privacy was given besides hiding transaction amounts, and this was reflected in prior definitions [FOS19, Def. 12]. In particular, in the initial version of Mimblewimble one can "disaggregate" transactions [Dev20a], that is, link inputs and outputs that come from the same original transaction. As a consequence, one could infer how money was being spent across the network.

GRIN introduced *transaction offsets*, which enable stronger anonymity guarantees by preventing disaggregation. To reflect this, we present a stronger privacy notion than the one provided in [FOS19], which is tailored to non-interactive transactions. We stress that our analysis is limited to the cryptographic properties of the scheme and it does not provide network-level privacy guarantees.

Definition. Our scheme provides three basic anonymity guarantees:

- a transaction hides the amounts in its inputs and outputs, as well as
- the destination addresses of the outputs (and inputs), *except to the receivers of the transaction*;
- in an aggregated transaction, it is not possible to tell which inputs and outputs belonged to the same component transaction *except for what can be deduced via the receiver's keys and the epochs of the outputs*.

The above are implied by the following simulation-based definition, formalized in Fig. 6. The adversary has access to an oracle that creates honest users and a challenge oracle that produces and aggregates transactions, taking input:

- lists $\mathbf{ref}_i = (ref_{i,j})_j$, for $i \in [\ell]$, where $ref_{i,j}$ is either a tuple $(txo_{i,j}, v_{i,j}, sk_{i,j})$ or an identifier $id_{i,j}$ of a previously generated output, within the same or a previous oracle call ($\mathbf{ref}_i$ thus specifies the inputs of the i-th transaction)

Game $\text{TXPRV}_{\text{CASH},\mathcal{A}}(\lambda, v_{\max})$

$b \leftarrow\!\!\$ \{0,1\}$

$Pks, Txos := ()$ // hash tables

$(pp, \Lambda) \leftarrow \text{Setup}(1^\lambda, v_{\max})$

$b' \leftarrow \mathcal{A}^{\text{Tx}_b}(pp, \Lambda)$

return $(b = b')$

$\text{Tx}_0((\mathbf{ref}_i, (\hat{\mathbf{id}}_i, (\hat{\mathbf{v}}_i, \hat{\mathbf{pk}}_i, \hat{\chi}_i)), s_i, f_i))_{i \in [\ell]}$

if $\exists (i,j) \neq (i',j') : \hat{id}_{i,j} = \hat{id}_{i',j'}$ **or**

   $Txos(\hat{id}_{i,j}) \neq \bot$ **then abort**

for $i \in [\ell]$ // get ref's to previous txo's

   $\mathbf{in}_i := \text{GET}_0(\mathbf{ref}_i)$

   $\text{tx}_i \leftarrow \text{Send}(pp, \mathbf{in}_i, (\hat{\mathbf{v}}_i, \hat{\mathbf{pk}}_i, \hat{\chi}_i), s_i, f_i)$

   // store outputs for honest users in $Txos$

   $\text{UPDTXOS}(\text{tx}_i, (\hat{\mathbf{id}}_i, (\hat{\mathbf{v}}_i, \hat{\mathbf{pk}}_i)))$

$\text{tx} \leftarrow \text{Agg}(pp, \text{tx}_1, \ldots, \text{tx}_\ell)$

return tx

Subprocedure $\text{GET}_b(\mathbf{ref}_i)$

$\mathbf{in} := ()$

for $j \in [|\mathbf{ref}_i|]$

   if $ref_{i,j} =: id$ // $ref_{i,j}$ is an id

      if $Txos(id) = (txo, v, sk) \neq \bot$

         if $b = 0 : \mathbf{in} := \mathbf{in} \,\|\, (txo, v, sk)$

         if $b = 1 : \mathbf{in} := \mathbf{in} \,\|\, txo$

      else

         if $b = 0 :$ **abort**

         if $b = 1 : \mathbf{in} := \mathbf{in} \,\|\, id$

   if $ref_{i,j} =: (txo, v, sk)$

      $\mathbf{in} := \mathbf{in} \,\|\, (txo, v, sk)$

return in

Oracle $\text{KEYGEN}()$

$(pk, vk, sk) \leftarrow \text{KeyGen}(pp)$

// add values to table Pks

$Pks(pk) := (sk, vk)$

return pk

$\text{Tx}_1((\mathbf{ref}_i, (\hat{\mathbf{id}}_i, (\hat{\mathbf{v}}_i, \hat{\mathbf{pk}}_i, \hat{\chi}_i)), s_i, f_i))_{i \in [\ell]}$

if $\exists (i,j) \neq (i',j') : \hat{id}_{i,j} = \hat{id}_{i',j'}$ **or**

   $Txos(\hat{id}_{i,j}) \neq \bot$ **then abort**

for $i \in [\ell]$

   $\mathbf{in}_i := \text{GET}_1(\mathbf{ref}_i)$

   if $\exists id \in \mathbf{in}_i : id \notin \hat{\mathbf{id}}_1 \,\|\, \ldots \,\|\, \hat{\mathbf{id}}_{i-1}$

   abort   // id not a previous output

foreach (i,j) // remove honest keys...

   if $Pks(\hat{pk}_{i,j}) = \bot$ // ... and values

      $out_{i,j} := (\hat{id}_{i,j}, (\hat{v}_{i,j}, \hat{pk}_{i,j}, \hat{\chi}_{i,j}))$

   else $out_{i,j} := (\hat{id}_{i,j}, (\bot, \bot, \hat{\chi}_{i,j}))$

$\mathbf{in}' := \text{Sort}(\mathbf{in}) ; \mathbf{out}' := \text{Sort}(\mathbf{out})$

$s := \sum_i s_i ; f := \sum_i f_i$

$\text{tx} \leftarrow \text{Sim}(\mathbf{in}', \mathbf{out}', s, f, \ell)$

for $i \in [\ell]$

   $\text{UPDTXOS}(\text{tx}, (\hat{\mathbf{id}}_i, (\hat{\mathbf{v}}_i, \hat{\mathbf{pk}}_i)))$

return tx

Subproc. $\text{UPDTXOS}(\text{tx}_i, (\hat{\mathbf{id}}_i, (\hat{\mathbf{v}}_i, \hat{\mathbf{pk}}_i)))$

for $j \in [|\hat{\mathbf{id}}_i|]$

   if $(\hat{sk}_{i,j}, \hat{vk}_{i,j}) := Pks(\hat{pk}_{i,j}) \neq \bot$

      $txo_{i,j} \leftarrow \text{Rcv}(pp, \text{tx}_i, \hat{v}_{i,j}, \hat{vk}_{i,j})$

      $Txos(\hat{id}_{i,j}) := (txo_{i,j}, \hat{v}_{i,j}, \hat{sk}_{i,j})$

Fig. 6. Game for transaction privacy $\text{TXPRV}_{\text{CASH},\mathcal{A}}(\lambda, v_{\max})$

- lists $(\mathbf{id}_i, (\hat{\mathbf{v}}_i, \hat{\mathbf{pk}}_i, \hat{\chi}_i))$, where $id_{i,j}$ serves as the unique identifier of the corresponding triple value/address/epoch (this specifies the outputs of the i-th transaction)
- supplies s_i and fees f_i

Consider transactions tx_i produced by Send on input the i-th elements of the above lists, and tx, produced by Agg on the tx_i's. Transaction privacy requires that tx is indistinguishable from a transaction created by a *simulator* Sim, which is only given:

- a list $\mathbf{in}$ of length the total number of inputs, whose elements are either an output txo_i or an identifier id_i where $id_i \in \hat{\mathbf{id}}$ from $\hat{\mathbf{id}}$ below (that is, it points to an output of a component transaction); in particular, it does not receive values nor keys
- a list $(\hat{\mathbf{id}}, (\hat{\mathbf{v}}, \hat{\mathbf{pk}}, \hat{\boldsymbol{\chi}}))$ of output identifiers and triples which are either for adversarial keys or which are $(\perp, \perp, \hat{\chi}_i)$ if the output is for an honest user
- the total supply and fee $s, f \in [0, v_{\max}]$ and the number of transactions ℓ.

Theorem 4. *If the proof systems* RaP *and* PoP *are zero-knowledge and if DDH is hard in* $\mathbb{G}$, *then MW-NIT satisfies transaction privacy in the random oracle model.*

Proof. We first define the simulator. The simulator Sim takes as input: a list $\mathbf{in}$ of length n, whose elements are of the form txo_i or id_i; an $\hat{n}$-element list for the outputs with identifiers $\hat{\mathbf{id}}$ and elements the form $(\hat{v}_i, \hat{pk}_i), \hat{\chi}_i)$ or $(\perp, \perp, \chi_i)$ together with their identifiers; total supply and fees s, f and the number of transactions ℓ.

Let $I_{\mathsf{id}} \subseteq n$ denote the set of indices for which $in_i = id_i$, that is, the references to outputs of the transaction to be simulated (which will thus be cut through); for $i \in [n] \setminus I_{\mathsf{id}}$, the entries in_i are explicit output.

- for each output index $i \in [\hat{n}]$ for which $(\hat{v}_i, \hat{pk}_i) \neq (\perp, \perp)$, sample $\hat{r}_i \leftarrow_{\$} \mathbb{Z}_p$ and from them compute $\hat{R}_i = \hat{r}_i G$ and $\hat{P}_i$ (using $\hat{pk}_i = (\hat{A}_i, \hat{B}_i)$) and $\hat{C}_i$ (using $\hat{v}_i$) as prescribed in Send.
- for each $i \in [\hat{n}]$ with $(\hat{v}_i, \hat{pk}_i) = (\perp, \perp)$, pick random values $\hat{C}_i, \hat{R}_i, \hat{P}_i \leftarrow_{\$} \mathbb{G}$
- for each $i \in [\hat{n}]$, simulate the range proofs $\hat{\pi}_i$ for statements $\hat{C}_i$, and the proofs ρ_i for $\hat{R}_i$ with tag $\hat{C}_i \| \hat{\pi}_i \| \hat{P}_i \| \chi_i$. Let $txo_i := (\hat{C}_i, \hat{\pi}_i, \hat{R}_i, \hat{\rho}_i, \hat{P}_i, \hat{\chi}_i)$.
- for each input index $i \in [n]$, pick a random value $D_i \leftarrow_{\$} \mathbb{G}$
- for each $i \in I_{\mathsf{id}}$, let k_i be such that $in_i = id_{k_i} \in \hat{\mathbf{id}}$ (if there is none, abort); simulate ψ_i for the statement $(\hat{P}_{k_i}, D_i, txo_{k_i})$ where $\hat{P}_{k_i}, txo_{k_i}$ are defined above; let $I_{\mathsf{ct}} := \{k_i\}_{i \in I_{\mathsf{id}}}$ be the indices of the cut-through outputs
- for each $i \in [n] \setminus I_{\mathsf{id}}$, with $in_i =: (C_i, \pi_i, R_i, \rho_i, P_i, \chi_i)$, simulate the proof ψ_i for the statement (P_i, D_i, in_i)
- the input list of tx is $(P_i, D_i, \psi_i)_{i \in [n] \setminus I_{\mathsf{id}}}$, ordered lexicographically
- the output list of tx is $\mathbf{txo} = (txo_i)_{i \in [\hat{n}] \setminus I_{\mathsf{ct}}}$, ordered lexicographically
- the cut-through list $\mathbf{ct}$ are the (ordered) elements $(txo_{k_i}, \hat{P}_{k_i}, D_i, \psi_i)_{i \in I_{\mathsf{id}}}$
- pick random values $E_2, \ldots, E_\ell, X_2, \ldots, X_\ell \leftarrow_{\$} \mathbb{G}$, as well as $t, y \leftarrow_{\$} \mathbb{Z}_p$
- set $E_1 := \sum \hat{C} - \sum C + (f - s)H - tG - \sum_{i=2}^{\ell} E_i$
  and $X_1 := \sum \hat{R} - \sum D - yG - \sum_{i=2}^{\ell} X_i$ (note that we could have $\ell = 1$)
  For $i \in [\ell]$: simulate σ_i for (E_i, X_i) with tag ε
- set $\mathsf{tx.sply} := s$ and $\mathsf{tx.fees} = f$

We start with a real transaction and consider a sequence of hybrid games that turns it into a simulated transaction.

H_0 In the "real" game, the component transactions are created as described (in Sect. 3.2) using the spending keys; they are then aggregated (Sect. 3.3).

H_1 In the first hybrid, all RaP proofs π and PoP proofs (cf. Sect. 5) ψ, ρ and σ_i are simulated. By the zero-knowledge property of both primitives, this change is indistinguishable from the honest computation of the range proofs and the proofs of possession.

H_2 For every output for an address that was generated by the address oracle, in the generation of the key shares in Eq. (3), the argument $\hat{r}_{i,j} A_{i,j}$ of the hash function is replaced by a random value $Z_{i,j} \leftarrow_{\$} \mathbb{G}$. This is indistinguishable by the DDH assumption, noting that all $\hat{R}_{i,j}$ and $A_{i,j}$ for such outputs are created by the reduction and their logarithms are never used in the simulation of the game (the former because $\rho_{i,j}$ and σ_i are simulated; the latter because $\psi_{i,j}$ is simulated and the address oracle does not reveal any secret keys).

H_3 The game aborts if the adversary at some point queries $Z_{i,j}$ for some i, j to the random oracle. Since the adversary has no information on $Z_{i,j}$, the probability of aborting is negligible. Note that in H_3, the values $\hat{k}_{i,j}$ and $\hat{q}_{i,j}$ are uniformly random and independent.

Now that we have showed that the adversary's return value can only change negligibly between H_0 and H_3, it remains to argue that a transaction generated in H_3 is distributed equivalently to a transaction computed by the simulator.

In a call to TX_0, let I_{ex} be the set of indices (i, j) for which $ref_{i,j}$ is an explicit input (and not an id) and let I_{adv} be the set of indices (i, j) for which $\hat{pk}_{i,j}$ was not generated by the oracle KEYGEN. In a transaction produced in H_3, for honest outputs, the coin openings $\hat{q}_{i,j}$, for $(i, j) \notin I_{adv}$, are uniformly random and independent. Thus, by the definition of $E_1, \ldots, E_\ell$, we have that for fixed values $(C_{i,j})_{(i,j) \in I_{ex}}$ (i.e., the inputs defined by the adversary) and $(\hat{C}_{i,j})_{(i,j) \in I_{adv}}$ (i.e., outputs for adversarial addresses), and $s := \sum s_i$ and $f := \sum f_i$, the tuple $\left((\hat{C}_{i,j})_{(i,j) \notin I_{adv}}, (E_i)_{i=1}^\ell, \sum t_i \right)$ is uniformly random conditioned on $\sum E_i = \sum \sum \hat{C}_{i,j} - \sum \sum C_{i,j} + (f - s)H - (\sum t_i)G$. This is exactly how the simulator produces these values.

Since for honest outputs the values $\hat{k}_{i,j}$, for $(i, j) \notin I_{adv}$, are uniformly random and independent, the corresponding values $\hat{P}_{i,j}$ are uniform and independent, as the simulator produces them. Finally, by the definition of the values $D_{i,j}$, $\hat{R}_{i,j}$ and X_i, the tuple $\left((D_i)_{i=1}^n, (\hat{R}_i)_{i=n^*+1}^{\hat{n}}, (X_i)_{i=1}^\ell, \sum y_i \right)$ is uniformly random conditioned on $\sum X_i = \sum \sum \hat{R}_{i,j} - \sum \sum D_{i,j} - (\sum y_i)G$. Again, this is how the simulator generates these values. Finally, in a transaction produced in H_3, all RaP and PoP proofs are simulated, which is how the simulator generates them, and the outputs/input pairs in the cut-through list of the simulator are those that Agg would put there. $\qquad\square$

Acknowledgements. The first author is supported by the Vienna Science and Technology Fund (WWTF) through project VRG18-002. We would like to thank MWC and David Burkett for the fruitful collaboration; we are also grateful to the anonymous reviewers for their helpful comments.

References

[BBB+18] Bünz, B., Bootle, J., Boneh, D., Poelstra, A., Wuille, P., Maxwell, G.: Bulletproofs: short proofs for confidential transactions and more. In: IEEE S&P 2018, pp. 315–334. IEEE (2018)

[Bur20] Burkett, D.: Offline transactions in Mimblewimble (2020). https://gist. github.com/DavidBurkett/32e33835b03f9101666690b7d6185203

[Bur21] Burkett, D.: One-sided transactions in Mimblewimble (consensus layer) (2021). https://github.com/DavidBurkett/lips/blob/master/lip-0004. mediawiki

[Dev20a] Grin Developers: Grin documentation: Intro (2020). https://github.com/ mimblewimble/grin/blob/master/doc/intro.md

[Dev20b] Grin Developers. Grin documentation: Mimblewimble (2020). https://docs. grin.mw/wiki/introduction/mimblewimble/mimblewimble/#kernel-offsets

[FKL18] Fuchsbauer, G., Kiltz, E., Loss, J.: The algebraic group model and its applications. In: Shacham, H., Boldyreva, A. (eds.) CRYPTO 2018, Part II. LNCS, vol. 10992, pp. 33–62. Springer, Cham (2018). https://doi.org/10. 1007/978-3-319-96881-0_2

[FOS19] Fuchsbauer, G., Orrù, M., Seurin, Y.: Aggregate cash systems: a cryptographic investigation of mimblewimble. In: Ishai, Y., Rijmen, V. (eds.) EUROCRYPT 2019, Part I. LNCS, vol. 11476, pp. 657–689. Springer, Cham (2019). https://doi.org/10.1007/978-3-030-17653-2_22

[FPS20] Fuchsbauer, G., Plouviez, A., Seurin, Y.: Blind Schnorr signatures and signed ElGamal encryption in the algebraic group model. In: Canteaut, A., Ishai, Y. (eds.) EUROCRYPT 2020, Part II. LNCS, vol. 12106, pp. 63–95. Springer, Cham (2020). https://doi.org/10.1007/978-3-030-45724-2_3

[Jed16] Jedusor, T.E.: Mimblewimble (2016). https://download.wpsoftware.net/ bitcoin/wizardry/mimblewimble.txt

[Max13a] Maxwell, G.: CoinJoin: Bitcoin privacy for the real world, August 2013. BitcoinTalk post. https://bitcointalk.org/index.php?topic=279249.0

[Max13b] Maxwell, G.: Transaction cut-through, August 2013. BitcoinTalk post. https://bitcointalk.org/index.php?topic=281848.0

[Max15] Maxwell, G.: Confidential Transactions (2015). https://people.xiph.org/ ~greg/confidential_values.txt

[Nak08] Nakamoto, S.: Bitcoin: a peer-to-peer electronic cash system (2008). http:// bitcoin.org/bitcoin.pdf

[Poe16] Poelstra, A.: Mimblewimble (2016). https://download.wpsoftware.net/ bitcoin/wizardry/mimblewimble.pdf

[PS00] Pointcheval, D., Stern, J.: Security arguments for digital signatures and blind signatures. J. Cryptol. **13**(3), 361–396 (2000)

[Seu12] Seurin, Y.: On the exact security of schnorr-type signatures in the random oracle model. In: Pointcheval, D., Johansson, T. (eds.) EUROCRYPT 2012. LNCS, vol. 7237, pp. 554–571. Springer, Heidelberg (2012). https://doi.org/ 10.1007/978-3-642-29011-4_33

[Tod14] Todd, P.: Stealth addresses (2014). http://www.mail-archive.com/bitcoin-development@lists.sourceforge.net/msg03613.html

[VFV17] Bojja Venkatakrishnan, S., Fanti, G.C., Viswanath, P.: Dandelion: redesigning the bitcoin network for anonymity. CoRR, abs/1701.04439 (2017)

[vS13]   van Saberhagen, N.: CryptoNote v 2.0 (2013). https://cryptonote.org/whitepaper.pdf

[Wag02] Wagner, D.: A generalized birthday problem. In: Yung, M. (ed.) CRYPTO 2002. LNCS, vol. 2442, pp. 288–304. Springer, Heidelberg (2002). https://doi.org/10.1007/3-540-45708-9_19

[Yu20]   Yu, G.: Mimblewimble non-interactive transaction scheme. Cryptology ePrint Archive, Report 2020/1064 (2020). https://ia.cr/2020/1064

A Universally Composable Non-interactive Aggregate Cash System

Yanxue Jia[1] , Shi-Feng Sun[1(✉)] , Hong-Sheng Zhou[2] , and Dawu Gu[1(✉)]

[1] Shanghai Jiao Tong University, Shanghai, China
{jiayanxue,shifeng.sun,dwgu}@sjtu.edu.cn
[2] Virginia Commonwealth University, Richmond, USA
hszhou@vcu.edu

Abstract. Mimblewimble is a privacy-preserving cryptocurrency, providing the functionality of transaction aggregation. Once certain coins have been spent in Mimblewimble, they can be deleted from the UTXO set. This is desirable: now storage can be saved and computation cost can be reduced. Fuchsbauer et al. (EUROCRYPT 2019) abstracted Mimblewimble as an Aggregate Cash System (ACS) and provided security analysis via game-based definitions.

In this paper, we revisit the ACS, and focus on *Non-interactive* ACS, denoted as NiACS. We for the first time propose a simulation-based security definition and formalize an ideal functionality for NiACS. Then, we construct a NiACS protocol in a hybrid model which can securely realize the ideal NiACS functionality in the Universal Composition (UC) framework. In addition, we propose a building block, which is a variant of the ElGamal encryption scheme that may be of independent interest. Finally, we show how to instantiate our protocol, and obtain the first NiACS system with UC security.

1 Introduction

Decentralized cryptocurrencies like Bitcoin have attracted huge attention in the past decade. While these cryptocurrencies have multiple advantages over the traditional electronic payment systems, we must note that these benefits are at the expense of transaction-privacy or user-anonymity [6, 32]: users' transaction data in the distributed ledgers of the cryptocurrency systems are public, and thus can be traced. Many strategies have been taken to improve the privacy (e.g., using a fresh pseudonymous address for each payment). Unfortunately, it has been demonstrated that the expected user-anonymity can still be lost: an attacker could deanonymize the transactions on the ledger by clustering and analyzing the transaction graph [36, 40].

Motivated by these security concerns, extensive efforts have been devoted to develop privacy-preserving techniques for improving the amount confidentiality and user anonymity of cryptocurrencies. Typically, homomorphic commitments are used to ensure the confidentiality of the amounts in transactions. To enable user anonymity, there exist two design paradigms:

© International Association for Cryptologic Research 2022
S. Agrawal and D. Lin (Eds.): ASIACRYPT 2022, LNCS 13791, pp. 745–773, 2022.
https://doi.org/10.1007/978-3-031-22963-3_25

(i) First, anonymity sets are introduced to hide the identities of the users. Good examples include Monero [37], Zcash [8] and Quisquis [19]. Unfortunately, as mentioned in [19], the information that which coins have been spent in Monero/Zcash is not allowed to be revealed, and thus the already spent coins cannot be eliminated from the cryptocurrency systems; as a consequence, the size of UTXO sets in these systems will grow constantly. Then Quisquis [19] was proposed to solve this problem but at the price of introducing a complicated mechanism: the users have to have their wallets to "watch on" the blockchain so that certain information (e.g., wallet address or public key) in their wallets can be properly updated. Moreover, Quisquis suffers from the so-called "front-running" attacks as pointed out in [11].

(ii) To achieve anonymity, coins of a transaction can be mixed with those of other transactions; this is called CoinJoin. Now, the coins that have been spent can be deleted from the UTXO set; In this way, the size of UTXO set will be significantly reduced. We note that, many systems (e.g., CoinShuffle [41] and Mixcoin [10]) under this design paradigm focus on anonymity but not considering the confidentiality of the amounts in transactions. It is worth mentioning that the anonymity of cryptocurrencies under this design paradigm may be weakened, when some parties are designated for receiving and mixing transactions. Still, it has attracted much attention thanks to its potential for high performance.

Mimblewimble. A new cryptocurrency dubbed Mimblewimble, which follows the second paradigm and considers confidentiality, was proposed by an anonymous author in [26] and further improved by Poelstra [39]. A nice feature Mimblewimble additionally enjoys is that, when multiple transactions are aggregated and the corresponding coins are mixed, it allows cut-through[1] while maintaining the verifiability of the aggregate transaction. This feature can reduce storage and benefit new users to verify the system. To formally analyze the security of Mimblewimble, Fuchsbauer et al. [21] abstracted it as an Aggregate Cash System (ACS) and formalized its security via a series of games. Specifically, they proposed three game-based security properties: *inflation-resistance* ensures that coins can only be supplied by legitimate ways (e.g., coinbase transactions), *theft-resistance* guarantees that no one can spend coins without the corresponding spending keys, and *transaction indistinguishability* requires that the amount should be hidden and change coins and output coins be indistinguishable. The work [21] by Fuchsbauer et al. is significant for the formal security analysis of Mimblewimble, but their definition is still subject to the following limitations:

– First, we point out that the security games proposed in [21] are not "succinct" enough. For example the theft-resistance property definition is strongly correlated with their construction. More concretely, to define theft-resistance

---

[1] A basic property of the UTXO model is that a sequence of two transactions, the first one spending an output out_1 and creating out_2, followed by the second one spending out_2 and creating out_3, is equivalent to a single cut-through transaction spending out_1 and creating out_3.

property, a notion of *pre-transaction* has been introduced. However, this *pre-transaction* is part of their protocol construction. This indicates that their theft-resistance property definition is not general enough: their definition only allows *pre-transaction* dependent protocols, and does not allow other natural constructions.

– Second, Fuchsbauer et al. [21] did not define the unlinkability of inputs and outputs, which is an important security property of ACS. More specifically, this property means that, when a transaction is mixed with others, anyone *not involved in these transactions* cannot identify which inputs and/or outputs belong to the same transaction. Note that if a party can obtain the individual transactions before aggregation, then she/he must be aware of the linkability of the inputs and outputs; we thus do not consider the unlinkability[2] against the parties who are continuously monitoring the network, or parties who are responsible for aggregating transactions.

– While game-based definitions are useful for capturing the security properties of ACS as in [21], it is more desirable to investigate the security properties in the real/ideal simulation paradigm: First, following the game-based definition approach, typically we are not clear if the list of security properties that we formalized are sufficient; often certain natural security properties are missed. Second, following the real/ideal simulation paradigm, "The security guarantees achieved are easily understood (because the ideal model is easily understood) [34]." In addition, simulation-based definitions allow sequential or even universal composability, enabling modular design and analysis. Please see Lindell's tutorials [34,35] for a more careful elaboration.

In addition, a transaction in ACS has to be generated jointly by the sender and receiver (see Sect. 2.2 for more details). In practice, however, it is not easy to guarantee that both the sender and receiver are always online at the same time. For example, it may be difficult for an online retailer to keep his wallet online all the time to receive irregular payments. A better way is that the retailer publishes an account for receiving payments on the sales website, and the buyers can complete payments at any time without the retailer's cooperation. Beam [1] and MWC [3], the two representative projects based on ACS, have made efforts to mitigate the problem to some extent, but do not solve it completely.

1.1   Contributions

In this work, we focus on mitigating the above limitations by proposing an Aggregate Cash System supporting non-interactive payments, denoted as NiACS, and defining its security in the real/ideal simulation paradigm. Our contributions are summarized below:

---

[2] In practice, Grin and Beam enhance unlinkability by leveraging Dandelion relay protocol [18] that aggregates transactions during the propagation. However, their approach still cannot realize *complete* unlinkability, since someone on the network will always be able to see an unaggregated transaction.

We first define an ideal functionality $\mathcal{F}_{\text{NiACS}}$, which captures the core features of NiACS but does not depend on the concrete design of NiACS. Our ideal functionality $\mathcal{F}_{\text{NiACS}}$ captures the *inflation-resistance, theft-resistance*, and *transaction indistinguishability* properties in [21]; in addition our functionality $\mathcal{F}_{\text{NiACS}}$ captures *unlinkability*, which is a very important security property for privacy-preserving cryptocurrencies. We remark that, the *unlinkability* has not been formalized in [21].

Our ideal functionality $\mathcal{F}_{\text{NiACS}}$ is *not* introduced for formalizing security properties for *interactive* ACS. However, to capture interactive payments, we can redefine the ideal functionality; for example, we can let the functionality inform the receiver before dealing with a transaction, and this is missing in the current functionality $\mathcal{F}_{\text{NiACS}}$.

Furthermore, we propose a NiACS protocol Π_{NiACS} that UC-realizes $\mathcal{F}_{\text{NiACS}}$ in a hybrid model. In contrast to Mimblewimble, our design can support non-interactive payments. That is, the sender is able to generate a valid transaction by himself, and the receiver can directly obtain private information of output coins from the transaction without out-of-band communication over a private channel. Particularly, to avoid the out-of-band communication, we propose a new variant of ElGamal encryption, the ciphertext of which includes a Pedersen commitment and its openings (i.e., randomness and value) can be obtained readily by the holder of the decryption key. Moreover, we present a concrete instantiation of our NiACS protocol, thus obtaining the first NiACS with UC security.

1.2 Related Work

Over the past decade, extensive efforts have been made to achieve provably secure privacy-preserving cryptocurrencies [8,10,19,26,37]. For example, Ring Confidential Transaction (RingCT), the core protocol of Monero, was first formally analyzed by Sun et al. [42], which was further refined by subsequent works [17,33,45]. In addition, Zcash was proposed along with formal security properties by Ben-Sasson et al. [8]. However, Garman et al. [23] pointed out that the security properties defined in [8] is incomplete and complex, and adversary can leverage these weaknesses to break the security. Moreover, Garman et al. [23] gave a simulation-based definition to avoid the weaknesses. More recently, more and more works have focused on the simulation-based definitions for Blockchain protocols. Badertscher et al. abstracted Bitcoin as a ledger functionality in [7]. Kerber et al. [28] gave a private ledger functionality and designed a privacy-preserving proof-of-stake (PoS) blockchain protocol that can securely realize the private ledger functionality in the UC setting.

Mimblewimble was first proposed by [26] and then improved further by Poelstra [39]. Mimblewimble is simple to implement and has been used in three open-source cryptocurrency projects, i.e., Beam [1], Grin [2], and MWC [3]. However, no formal security analysis has been given for these works until the work by Fuchsbauer et al. [21]. In particular, Fuchsbauer et al. [21] abstracted Mimblewimble as ACS and defined its security properties for the first time.

However, these security properties are incomplete and complex. In particular, unlinkability is an important property of Mimblewimble, but not formally defined in [21]. Besides, they proposed a new one-round interactive ACS that has been implemented in MWC [3]. Later, Yu [44] leveraged one-time addresses to achieve non-interactive payments for Mimblewimble, but without formal analysis.

In a concurrent and independent work, Fuchsbauer et al. [22] pointed out and fixed the flaws in the proposal by [44], and formally analyzed their own modified scheme based on game-based definitions. Fuchsbauer et al. [22] and Yu [44] share the same initial idea of achieving non-interactive transactions with us, but there are many differences between their construction and ours. In particular, Fuchsbauer et al. [22] added a new type of excess $X := \prod \hat{R}_i / \prod D_i$, called "stealth excess", where $\hat{R}_i$ is used to "transmit" the secret key of a one-time address and D_i is a one-time doubling key used to prevent feed-me attack. For a coin, when it is in an output list, it will be associated with $\hat{R}_i$; when it is in an input list, it will be associated with D_i. Since $\hat{R}_i \neq D_i$, if the coin is cut through, the stealth excess cannot be verified. Therefore, their scheme cannot support *cut-through*. In contrast, our transactions only include one type of excess, namely the original excess in Mimblewimble, and thus our construction still supports cut-through. Note that cut-through is an important feature of Mimblewimble as it can save the on-chain storage cost. In addition, we for the first time define a simulation-based security model for NiACS, while Fuchsbauer et al. [22] still follows a game-based security model, which is not suitable for complex execution environments.

2 Technical Overview

To overcome the security and practicality issues mentioned before, we first define an ideal functionality for ACS supporting non-interactive payments, denoted by $\mathcal{F}_{\mathsf{NiACS}}$. Compared to the game-based security definition proposed in [21], $\mathcal{F}_{\mathsf{NiACS}}$ is more general and comprehensive. Furthermore, we propose a new non-interactive payment system, dubbed Π_{NiACS}, that securely realizes $\mathcal{F}_{\mathsf{NiACS}}$. Before showing the high-level idea of our design, we first briefly introduce how to define an ideal functionality that captures the desirable security of NiACS.

2.1 Non-interactive Aggregate Cash System Functionality

As ACS is essentially a privacy-preserving ledger, we attempt to define its ideal functionality with the abstraction $\mathcal{F}_{\mathsf{Ledger}}$ of the most basic ledger Bitcoin [7,29] as the starting point. At a high level, the ledger functionality defined in [29] is the same as that defined in [7]. More concretely, anyone can submit a transaction to $\mathcal{F}_{\mathsf{Ledger}}$, then $\mathcal{F}_{\mathsf{Ledger}}$ will validate the transaction by a predicate Validate. If the transaction is valid, it will be added into a buffer. Periodically, the transactions in the buffer will be moved to state in the form of a block, where the state refers to the ledger state and the transactions in the state cannot be changed. Moreover, anyone is allowed to read the content of state. In a nutshell, $\mathcal{F}_{\mathsf{Ledger}}$ defines the basic interfaces of a ledger, including submitting transactions, maintaining ledger, and reading ledger.

Compared to the basic ledger, ACS additionally protects *privacy* (payment amount confidentiality, sender anonymity and receiver anonymity) and allows *aggregation* of transactions before packing. Therefore, to define the ideal functionality of ACS, we need to further specify the content of a transaction and add interfaces for aggregation. In addition, in this work, we focus on ACS supporting non-interactive payments, and thus we denote the ideal functionality as $\mathcal{F}_{\text{NiACS}}$.

To preserve privacy, a transaction cannot contain the identifiers of relevant parties and the amount of each coin, but a transaction needs to specify which coins are spent or created. Therefore, for each coin, we define an identifier cid that is pseudorandom and does not reveal its amount and owner, and for each party, $\mathcal{F}_{\text{NiACS}}$ maintains a list of coins that are possessed by the party. When a party called user wants to transfer some coins, he inputs $(\{\text{cid}_i\}, \{\hat{P}_j, \hat{v}_j\})$ to $\mathcal{F}_{\text{NiACS}}$ where $\{\text{cid}_i\}$ is an identifier list of the coins to be spent, $\hat{P}_j$ is a receiver who will receive a coin of amount $\hat{v}_j$. If all the coins identified by $\{\text{cid}_i\}$ are owned by the party, and the sum of the amounts is enough, $\mathcal{F}_{\text{NiACS}}$ will notify the adversary (namely, simulator) $\mathcal{S}$ to generate a coin identifier $\hat{\text{cid}}_j$ for each output coin whose owner is $\hat{P}_j$ and amount is $\hat{v}_j$. At this point, $\mathcal{F}_{\text{NiACS}}$ generates a transaction $\mathsf{TX} := (\{\text{cid}_i\}, \{\hat{\text{cid}}_j\})$ according to the party's payment request. We can see that $\mathcal{F}_{\text{NiACS}}$ generates the transaction without the participation of any receiver, which means that the functionality captures the *non-interactive payments*. Moreover, it is the transaction that will be added to state, not the payment request. Therefore, when other parties obtain state by reading the ledger, regarding the transaction, they can only see the identifiers in $\{\text{cid}_i\}$ and $\{\hat{\text{cid}}_j\}$ but learn nothing about the owners and the amounts. However, if parties can get the individual transaction, they can learn the linkability of the coins in it, which will weaken the sender anonymity. The aggregation explained below helps to break the linkability.

As mentioned before, unlike in Bitcoin, a transaction in NiACS will be aggregated with other transactions before being packed into a block. Thus, the coins of a transaction are mixed with coins in other transactions such that the linkability of input and output coins is broken. More specifically, in $\mathcal{F}_{\text{NiACS}}$, we add a role called aggregator who is responsible for aggregating transactions. Once a transaction TX is generated, $\mathcal{F}_{\text{NiACS}}$ sends it to the parties who act as aggregators. Then, an aggregator will aggregate the transactions to a "large" transaction, which will be added to buffer and eventually moved to state. For example, given two transactions $\mathsf{TX}_1 := (\{\text{cid}_i^1\}, \{\hat{\text{cid}}_j^1\})$ and $\mathsf{TX}_2 := (\{\text{cid}_i^2\}, \{\hat{\text{cid}}_j^2\})$, an aggregator can generate an aggregate transaction $\mathsf{TX}_1 + \mathsf{TX}_2 := (\{\text{cid}_i^1\} \cup \{\text{cid}_i^2\}, \{\hat{\text{cid}}_j^1\} \cup \{\hat{\text{cid}}_j^2\})$ and submit it to $\mathcal{F}_{\text{NiACS}}$. When others get the aggregate transaction, they cannot identify which coins belong to a transaction as the coin identifiers are independent and pseudorandom. In addition, a user is allowed to spend the output coins of an unconfirmed transaction with an elevated fee, as described in [4]. Therefore, cut-through can occur when the transactions are aggregated.

To sum up, we define $\mathcal{F}_{\text{NiACS}}$ by adding privacy protection and aggregation features to the basic ledger functionality $\mathcal{F}_{\text{Ledger}}$. In $\mathcal{F}_{\text{NiACS}}$, a transaction only contains pseudorandom and independent coin identifiers, and thus anyone cannot learn the amounts and participants. In addition, there are aggregators responsible for aggregating transactions and submitting the aggregate transactions to the ledger. Through aggregation, some coins can be cut through, which can reduce the storage of the ledger. Moreover, a transaction is stored in the ledger after being mixed with other transactions such that the linkability of the input coins and output coins is hidden, which further enhances sender anonymity.

Next we proceed to introduce the high-level idea of our design Π_{NiACS}. Since our design is inspired by Mimblewimble [21,39], before continuing we first briefly recall the main idea of Mimblewimble.

2.2   Recall Mimblewimble

Mimblewimble [21,39] is an interactive payment system with support for transaction aggregation. Briefly, a coin in Mimblewimble is a Pedersen commitment $\mathsf{cm} := g^r h^v$, where v is the amount of this coin, and it is spent with only the randomness r (usually called spending key)[3]. A transaction here consists of an input list, an output list, and a kernel, as shown in Fig. 1; the concept of kernel is firstly introduced in Mimblewimble, which plays a crucial role in guaranteeing the validity of the transaction. Particularly, the input (resp. output) list includes the spent (resp. newly created) coins, and the kernel contains the contents used for proving the balance of the transaction and the ownership of the spent coins. To illustrate how the validity of transactions is guaranteed, we take a concrete example as below.

Let TX_1 be a transaction including 2 input coins $\{\mathsf{cm}_1^1, \mathsf{cm}_2^1\}$ and 3 output coins $\{\hat{\mathsf{cm}}_1^1, \hat{\mathsf{cm}}_2^1, \hat{\mathsf{cm}}_3^1\}$[4]. Besides, an item called *excess* $E_1 := \prod_{j=1}^3 \hat{\mathsf{cm}}_j^1 / \prod_{i=1}^2 \mathsf{cm}_i^1$ is contained in its kernel. Obviously, if the transaction is balanced, E_1 is a commitment to 0. To show the balance of this transaction, the sender generates a proof that E_1 is a commitment to 0 as shown in Fig. 1; essentially, this is realized by invoking a zero-knowledge ideal functionality $\mathcal{F}_{\mathsf{NIZK}}^{\mathsf{zero}}$, and the witness is the randomness of E_1. However, the randomness of E_1 is derived from the randomnesses of both the input commitments $\{\mathsf{cm}_i^1\}_{i \in [2]}$ and output commitments $\{\hat{\mathsf{cm}}_j^1\}_{j \in [3]}$, and the randomnesses of output commitments are only known to the receiver, so the sender has to generate the proof interactively with the receiver. Moreover, since the ownership of the coin in Mimblewimble is equivalent to the knowledge of the opening of the commitment, the proof also implies that the input coins are indeed spent by the owner.

Further to break the linkability of inputs and outputs in a transaction, Mimblewimble adopts the idea of CoinJoin, that is, to aggregate different transactions into a "large" one. As indicated in [21], however, it is not hard to find out the input and output coins of a transaction from the aggregate transaction by solving

---

[3] In contrast, the coin in other cryptocurrencies like Zcash is spent with the opening of the commitment and a secret key associated with the address recording the coin.

[4] Note that for each output coin $\hat{\mathsf{cm}}_i^1$, there is also a range proof to guarantee that the committed value is valid (i.e., $v \in [0, v_{\mathsf{max}}]$), but we ignore it here for simplicity.

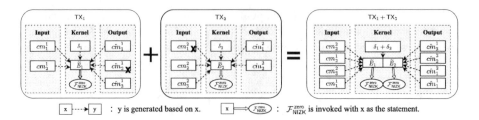

Fig. 1. The transaction and aggregation process of Mimblewimble ($\hat{cm}_2^1 = cm_1^2$).

a simple subset sum problem based on the excess. To solve this problem, an offset is added to blind the excess, e.g., the final excess in the kernel of TX_1 becomes $\tilde{E}_1 := E_1 \cdot g^\delta$. Next we take the example given in Fig. 1 to explain the aggregation process: The initial input (resp. output) list of the aggregate transaction $TX_1 + TX_2$ is the union of input (resp. output) lists of TX_1 and TX_2 in random order. If some coins in TX_2's input list are also in TX_1's output list, then the coins (together with the associated range proofs) are removed from the input and output lists of $TX_1 + TX_2$, which is the so-called *cut-through*. More concretely, $\hat{cm}_2^1$ in TX_1 is equal to cm_1^2 in TX_2, so in $TX_1 + TX_2$, cm_1^2 and $\hat{cm}_2^1$ are removed from input list and output list of the aggregate transaction, respectively. The kernel of $TX_1 + TX_2$ is the union of the TX_1's kernel and TX_2's kernel, except that the offset of $TX_1 + TX_2$ is $\delta_1 + \delta_2$.

From the above, we can see that proving the excess being a commitment to 0 is the main reason of making Mimblewimble interactive. Next, we show how to surround this obstacle and design a NiACS that securely realizes the proposed ideal functionality $\mathcal{F}_{\mathsf{NiACS}}$.

2.3   Our Non-interactive Aggregate Cash System Π_{NiACS}

Recall that in Mimblewimble each coin is spent with the randomness of its commitment as the spending key, and the output coins of each transaction have to be created by the receiver. Therefore, the sender knows nothing about the randomness of each output coin, and he has to interact with the receiver for proving that the excess is a commitment to 0. To realize non-interactive payments, a natural choice is to let the sender create the output coins. Using this approach, the sender can generate the proof of balance by himself, but the associated randomness can never be used as the spending key of the coin. Hence, our essential idea is to verify the balance of the transaction and the ownership of the input coins separately. To this end, we introduce an address for each coin in our Π_{NiACS}, then the secret key corresponding to the address is used to spend the associated coin while the randomness of the associated commitment is used only to prove balance. Following this way, the interaction between the sender and receiver can be avoided, but *the first challenging task we face is to bind a coin and an address*.

In fact, the combination of commitments and addresses have been employed previously to achieve privacy-preserving cryptocurrencies (e.g., Monero [37] and

Zcash [8]). Among them, a signature for each transaction is usually generated for preventing it from being tampered with. In our design, however, distinct transactions will be mixed or aggregated to hide the relations of input coins and output coins (namely, linkability). Then when verifying the aggregate transaction, the verifiers need to pick out the individual transaction to verify the signature, which will break the unlinkability. Therefore, it is not easy to bind a coin and an address while supporting transaction aggregation.

Bind an Address and a Coin. As discussed before, binding a coin to an address through a signature on the whole transaction will break the unlinkability. Therefore, a natural idea is to bind each coin and the associated address through a separate signature. However, the question is how to generate such a signature?

Fortunately, we observe that in our Π_{NiACS}, the randomnesses of commitments do not act as the spending keys anymore, and the sender knows the randomnesses of all output coins as they are generated by the sender himself rather than the receiver. Moreover, the proof of the excess being a commitment to 0 leaks nothing about the randomnesses of the coins, due to the zero-knowledge property. Hence, our idea is to use the randomness of each commitment as the signing key to sign the corresponding address, which can be achieved by leveraging the primitive named signature of knowledge [15].

More specifically, signature of knowledge extends the traditional notion of digital signature to the notion that allows one to issue signatures on behalf of any NP statement, which can be interpreted as follows: "A person in possession of a witness w to the statement $x \in \mathcal{L}$ has signed message m." An instance of signature of knowledge can be related to a language. In the confidential transaction, for each commitment, a range proof is generated to prove that the committed value is within a specific range $[0, v_{\max}]$. Therefore, we can define the language $\mathcal{L}_{\mathsf{range}} := \{\mathsf{cm} \mid \exists\, r, v \text{ s.t. } \mathsf{cm} = g^r h^v \wedge v \in [0, v_{\max}]\}$, and only the one knowing the opening (r, v) of cm can sign an address by invoking $\mathcal{F}_{\mathsf{SoK}}^{\mathsf{range}}$.

To guarantee the validity of transactions, *the second challenge is to prove the balance of each transaction as well as the knowledge of spending keys (i.e., the ownership of input coins).* Regarding the former, it can be proved in the same way as Mimblewimble. Therefore, the main challenge is to prove the ownership of the input coins.

Prove the Ownership of Input Coins. A natural solution is to provide a zero-knowledge proof that the sender knows the corresponding secret key of the address. However, an independent proof can be stolen and used in other transactions. A common approach for avoiding this problem is to bind the address and the transaction through a signature of knowledge (i.e., sign the transaction using the secret key), but as discussed before, signing the whole transaction will break the unlinkability. Therefore, what we essentially need is to bind the address to an "abstract" of the transaction that does not reveal the relation of the inputs and outputs. We observe that an excess in Mimblewimble is abstracted from all input and output coins of a transaction, and that it reveals nothing about the relation between the inputs and outputs, due to the added offset. Thus, we bind the address of each coin to the transaction via signing its excess with the associated spending key. Then the same excess will be signed n times if the transaction includes n input coins. In this case, when the transaction is aggregated with others, any party can learn that these input coins belong to the same transaction, which may reveal partial information about the linkability. To avoid this leakage, our key idea is to randomly split the excess into n parts, and then to sign each part with a separate spending key. Using this approach, the sender can prove the knowledge of spending keys while preventing the proofs from being stolen and used in other transactions. Similarly, this can be realized through the signature of knowledge functionality, where the witness is the spending key and the message is a part of the excess.

Following the above way, the sender can generate a valid transaction in a non-interactive way, but the receiver cannot spend the received coins as she does not know the private information (i.e., openings of commitments). Therefore, *the third challenge is how to send the private information to the receiver.*

Send Private Information to Receiver. A natural approach is to send the value and randomness to the receiver through a private communication channel. In this way, the sender and receiver must interact at least once per transaction, which defeats our purpose of achieving non-interactive payments. Another way is to encrypt the private information with the receiver's public key and send the ciphertext along with each output coin. This will avoid the interaction between the sender and receiver, but results in a significant increase of transaction size. Inspired by the recent work due to Chen et al. [16], we propose a novel way of encrypting the private information while mitigating the transaction expansion.

In particular, Chen et al. [16] proposed a twisted ElGamal encryption to transfer values privately (from sender to receiver) as follows. Roughly, the sender encrypts a value v into a ciphertext in the form of $(pk^r, g^r h^v)$, where $pk = g^{sk}$ and sk is known by the receiver and r is randomly chosen by the sender, and includes the ciphertext in the transaction; as $g^r h^v$ is in fact a Pedersen commitment, we write the ciphertext as (X, cm) for simplicity. After receiving the ciphertext, the receiver can then recover v by computing $\mathsf{cm}/X^{\frac{1}{sk}}$. Note that the value is in a certain range, and thus the receiver can get v from h^v. Unfortunately, the receiver cannot get the randomness r, so she cannot spend the coin cm. To overcome this problem, they proposed to spend the coin in an alternative way. More specifically, after recovering the amount v from $C := (X, \mathsf{cm})$, the receiver generates a new coin $C' := (X', \mathsf{cm}')$ with the equivalent amount as C. Further, the receiver provides a proof through a Σ-protocol to prove that the messages in cm and cm' are identical.

At the first glance, their approach works in our design as well. Unfortunately, we find it does not support cut-through. Particularly, we assume that a coin cm created in transaction TX_c is spent in transaction TX_s through a new coin cm' with the equivalent amount. Note that in TX_c, it is cm that is used to generate the excess $E_c := \mathsf{cm} \cdot E_c^* \cdot g^{\delta_c}$, where E_c^* denotes the excess of other coins excluding cm and δ_c denotes the offset. In contrast, it is cm' that is used to generate the excess $E_s := E_s^*/\mathsf{cm}' \cdot g^{\delta_s}$ of TX_s, where E_s^* is the excess of other commitments than cm' and δ_s is the offset. Now we can see that if the two transactions are aggregated and the coin is cut through, then the excess of the aggregate transaction should be $E_s^* \cdot E_c^* \cdot g^{\delta_s + \delta_c}$ according to our design.

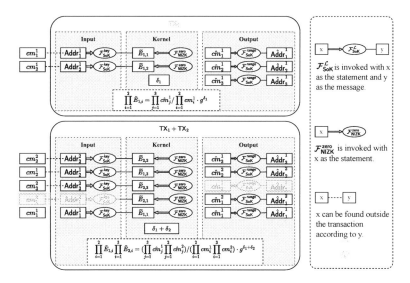

Fig. 2. The transaction and aggregation process of Π_{NiACS} ($\hat{\mathsf{cm}}_2^1 = \mathsf{cm}_1^2$).

Following the above approach, however, $E_s \cdot E_c = E_s^* \cdot E_c^* \cdot \frac{\mathsf{cm}}{\mathsf{cm}'} \cdot g^{\delta_s + \delta_c}$, which is not equal to $E_s^* \cdot E_c^* \cdot g^{\delta_s + \delta_c}$ as $\frac{\mathsf{cm}}{\mathsf{cm}'} \neq 1$. Therefore, the approach by Chen et al. fails to work in our design.

To tackle the above problem, our essential idea is to enable the receiver to recover both the value and the randomness directly from the coin cm. To this end, we propose a new variant of ElGamal by generating the ciphertext as $(pk^r, g^{H(g^r)}h^v)$, where the randomness of the commitment is chosen through a random oracle $H(\cdot)$. In this way, the receiver holding sk can easily recover g^r and thus get $H(g^r)$.

To this point, we obtain our NiACS protocol Π_{NiACS}. Following the above ideas, the transaction and aggregation process in our design are as shown in Fig. 2. More details are shown in Sect. 4.

3   Simulation-Based Security for NiACS

In this section, we propose a simulation-based security definition for NiACS through an ideal functionality $\mathcal{F}_{\mathsf{NiACS}}$.

As $\mathcal{F}_{\mathsf{NiACS}}$ is essentially a ledger that records aggregate transactions rather than individual ones. Therefore, we define $\mathcal{F}_{\mathsf{NiACS}}$ starting from the basic ledger

---

Algorithm 1. State Update

1: **procedure** EXTENDSTATE(, , buffer, T, counter)
2:     Send $\langle$CLOCKREAD, sid$\rangle$ to $\mathcal{G}_{\mathsf{Clock}}$ and receive $\langle$CLOCKREAD, sid, $\tau\rangle$ from $\mathcal{G}_{\mathsf{Clock}}$;
3:     **if** $|\tau - \mathsf{T} \cdot \mathsf{counter}| > \mathsf{T}$ **then**
4:         := $||$Blockify(τ, buffer);
5:         buffer := ε;
6:         counter := counter $+ 1$;
7:         Send $\langle$CLOCKUPDATE, sid$\rangle$ to $\mathcal{G}_{\mathsf{Clock}}$.

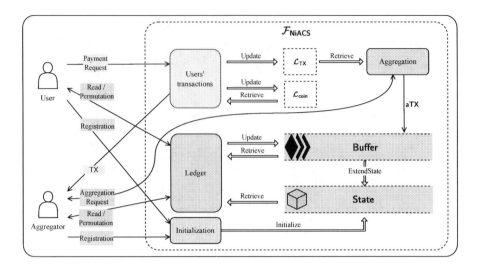

Fig. 3. Overview of ideal functionality $\mathcal{F}_{\mathsf{NiACS}}$.

functionality $\mathcal{F}_{\mathsf{Ledger}}$ formalized by Kiayias et al. [29] and follow their parameters. Prior to introducing our functionality $\mathcal{F}_{\mathsf{NiACS}}$, we first recall the parameters used later: buffer is to contain the valid transactions that have not been confirmed, state is the state of ledger containing confirmed transactions, the constant T denotes the time interval between generating blocks, and counter is to keep track of the number of state updates. In addition, the state is updated by EXTEND-STATE shown in Algorithm 1, where the function Blockify(τ, buffer) is used to organize the transactions in buffer into a block and τ is a time obtained from a global clock ideal functionality $\mathcal{G}_{\mathsf{Clock}}$.

Now we proceed to introduce our functionality $\mathcal{F}_{\mathsf{NiACS}}$ as shown in Fig. 3. Roughly speaking, $\mathcal{F}_{\mathsf{NiACS}}$ consists of four parts: *Initialization, Users' transactions, Aggregation, and Ledger*. In initialization part, parties register on the ledger while stating their roles (user/aggregator), and users need to state their initial amounts. The registration information will be recorded into the genesis block. After the system is bootstrapped, the parties can also register. Here, for simplicity, we assume that parties only register at the beginning. In users' transactions part, users can submit payment requests to $\mathcal{F}_{\mathsf{NiACS}}$, and if a payment request is valid, $\mathcal{F}_{\mathsf{NiACS}}$ will generate the corresponding transaction and send it to the aggregators. In aggregation part, aggregators can send aggregation requests to $\mathcal{F}_{\mathsf{NiACS}}$, and if an aggregation request is valid, $\mathcal{F}_{\mathsf{NiACS}}$ will aggregate corresponding transactions and return the aggregate transaction to the aggregator. In ledger part, any party can read the ledger. Moreover, the adversary can (1) directly submit transactions without being aggregated to ledger, and (2) permute the buffer, which reflects his influence on the delivery. Next, we introduce each part of $\mathcal{F}_{\mathsf{NiACS}}$ in detail.

Initialization. In Fig. 4, we describe the initialization process. $\mathcal{F}_{\mathsf{NiACS}}$ first initializes state $:= \epsilon$, buffer $:= \epsilon$ and counter $:= 0$. Besides, $\mathcal{F}_{\mathsf{NiACS}}$ initializes

---

Functionality $\mathcal{F}_{\text{NiACS}}$: Initialization

The functionality is parameterized with variables $\mathcal{L}_{\text{coin}}$, $\mathcal{L}_{\text{TX}}$, $\mathcal{L}_{\mathcal{A}}$, state, buffer, counter and a constant T. Initially, $\mathcal{L}_{\text{coin}} := \emptyset$, $\mathcal{L}_{\text{TX}} := \emptyset$, $\mathcal{L}_{\mathcal{A}} := \emptyset$, state $:= \varepsilon$, buffer $:= \varepsilon$ and counter $:= 0$. Upon receiving a message $\langle \text{CORRUPT}, \text{sid}, P_t \rangle$ from adversary $\mathcal{S}$, add P_t to $\mathcal{L}_{\mathcal{A}}$.

Initialization: Upon receiving a message $\langle \text{REGISTRATION}, \text{sid}, \text{Infor}_{\text{reg}}, P_k \rangle$ from P_k, do:

1: **if** There is $(P_k, \cdot, \cdot)$ in buffer **then** Ignore the message;
2: **else**
3:      Parse $\text{Infor}_{\text{reg}} := (\text{role}, v_k)$ where role $\in \{\text{user}, \text{aggregator}\}$;
4:      **if** role $=$ user $\wedge v_k \in [0, v_{\max}]$ **then**
5:          Send $\langle \text{REGISTRATION}, \text{sid}, \text{user}, v_k, P_k \rangle$ to adversary $\mathcal{S}$;
6:          **if** Receive message $\langle \text{REGISTRATED}, \text{sid}, (P_k, \text{user}), \text{cid}_k \rangle$ from $\mathcal{S}$ **then**
7:              Add $(\text{cid}_k, v_k, P_k, P_k)$ to $\mathcal{L}_{\text{coin}}$;
8:              buffer $:=$ buffer$||(P_k, \text{user}, (\text{cid}_k, v_k))$;
9:      **else if** role $=$ aggregator $\wedge v_k = \perp$ **then**
10:         Send $\langle \text{REGISTRATION}, \text{sid}, \text{aggregator}, \perp, P_k \rangle$ to adversary $\mathcal{S}$;
11:         **if** Receive message $\langle \text{REGISTRATED}, \text{sid}, (P_k, \text{aggregator}), \perp \rangle$ from $\mathcal{S}$ **then**
12:             buffer $:=$ buffer$||(P_k, \text{aggregator}, \perp)$;
13:     Upon receiving $\langle \text{INITIALIZED}, \text{sid} \rangle$ from $\mathcal{S}$, (state, buffer, counter) $:=$
        $\text{EXTENDSTATE}(\text{state}, \text{buffer}, \text{T}, \text{counter})$, send $\langle \text{INITIALIZED}, \text{sid}, \text{cid}_k / \perp \rangle$ to P_k.

Fig. 4. Ideal functionality of NiACS (Initialization).

three lists, $\mathcal{L}_{\text{coin}}$, $\mathcal{L}_{\text{TX}}$ and $\mathcal{L}_{\mathcal{A}}$ for recording coins, transactions and corrupted parties, respectively. At the beginning, $\mathcal{F}_{\text{NiACS}}$ will be notified which parties are corrupted by receiving the message $\langle \text{CORRUPT}, \text{sid}, P_t \rangle$ from adversary $\mathcal{S}$. Then P_t will be recorded in $\mathcal{L}_{\mathcal{A}}$. For registration, a party P_k will send the registration information to $\mathcal{F}_{\text{NiACS}}$. In the registration information, P_k needs to declare his role. If P_k acts as a user, he needs to declare his initial amount. Once receiving a registration message $\langle \text{REGISTRATION}, \text{sid}, \text{Infor}_{\text{reg}}, P_k \rangle$ from P_k, $\mathcal{F}_{\text{NiACS}}$ first checks if the party has registered before. If so, $\mathcal{F}_{\text{NiACS}}$ ignores the message. Note that a party can only register as one role. If the party wants to register as a user and the corresponding initial amount v_k is in a valid range, $\mathcal{F}_{\text{NiACS}}$ sends $\langle \text{REGISTRATION}, \text{sid}, \text{user}, v_k, P_k \rangle$ to adversary $\mathcal{S}$. Then $\mathcal{S}$ will generate a coin identifier cid_k for the initial coin, and send a message $\langle \text{REGISTRATED}, \text{sid}, (P_k, \text{user}), \text{cid}_k \rangle$ to $\mathcal{F}_{\text{NiACS}}$. At this point, the initial coin of P_k is created, and $\mathcal{F}_{\text{NiACS}}$ will add the coin $(\text{cid}_k, v_k, P_k, P_k)$ into $\mathcal{L}_{\text{coin}}$ in the format of (identifier, value, owner, creator) and adds $(P_k, \text{user}, (\text{cid}_k, v_k))$ into buffer. If P_k is registered as an aggregator, after receiving the agreement from $\mathcal{S}$, $\mathcal{F}_{\text{NiACS}}$ adds $(P_k, \text{aggregator}, \perp)$ into buffer. We allow the adversary to decide when the registration is finished, and thus once receiving $\langle \text{INITIALIZED}, \text{sid} \rangle$ from $\mathcal{S}$, $\mathcal{F}_{\text{NiACS}}$ executes EXTENDSTATE to get the genesis state. $\mathcal{F}_{\text{NiACS}}$ returns $\langle \text{INITIALIZED}, \text{sid}, \text{cid}_k \rangle$ to inform P_k of successful registration.

Users' Transactions. In Fig. 5, we describe the process of a user submitting a transaction. A user P_k forwards a payment request $\langle \text{SUBMIT}, \text{sid}, P_k, \mathcal{L}_{\text{Agg}}, \{\text{cid}_i\}, \{(\hat{P}_j, \hat{v}_j)\} \rangle$ to $\mathcal{F}_{\text{NiACS}}$ to initiate the process of generating a transaction. In the payment request, $\mathcal{L}_{\text{Agg}}$[5] is a list of aggregators who

---

[5] Environment $\mathcal{Z}$ can abstract the situation that a party can send a transaction to different aggregator sets at different times, by assigning different aggregator lists for a transaction.

Functionality $\mathcal{F}_{\mathsf{NiACS}}$: Users' transactions

Upon receiving a message $\langle\textsc{Submit}, \mathsf{sid}, P_k, \mathcal{L}_{\mathsf{Agg}}, \{\mathsf{cid}_i\}, \{(\hat{P}_j, \hat{v}_j)\}\rangle$ from P_k, do the following:

1: $(\mathsf{state}, \mathsf{buffer}, \mathsf{counter}) := \textsc{ExtendState}(\mathsf{state}, \mathsf{buffer}, \mathsf{T}, \mathsf{counter})$;
2: Set $\mathsf{Info} := (\{\mathsf{cid}_i\}, \{(\hat{P}_j, \hat{v}_j)\})$, and retrieve $(\mathsf{TX}, \mathcal{L}^*_{\mathsf{Agg}}, \mathsf{Info})$ from $\mathcal{L}_{\mathsf{TX}}$ according to Info;
3: **if** there is no $(\mathsf{TX}, \mathcal{L}^*_{\mathsf{Agg}}, \mathsf{Info})$ in $\mathcal{L}_{\mathsf{TX}}$ **then**
4:      **for** each cid_i **do**
5:          Retrieve $(\mathsf{cid}_i, v_i, P_i, \cdot)$ from $\mathcal{L}_{\mathsf{coin}}$;
6:          **if** $P_i \neq \bot$ **then**
7:              **if** $P_k \neq P_i \vee \mathsf{cid}_i \notin \mathsf{state}||\mathsf{buffer}$ **then** Ignore the message;
8:          **else**
9:              **if** $P_k \notin \mathcal{L}_{\mathcal{A}} \vee \mathsf{cid}_i \notin \mathsf{state}||\mathsf{buffer}$ **then** Ignore the message;
10:     **if** $\sum_i v_i \neq \sum_j \hat{v}_j \vee \exists j, s.t., \hat{v}_j \notin [0, v_{\mathsf{max}}]$ **then** Ignore the message;
11:     **for** each j **do**
12:         **if** $P_k \in \mathcal{L}_{\mathcal{A}} \vee \hat{P}_j \in \mathcal{L}_{\mathcal{A}}$ **then** Send $\langle\textsc{RequestID}, \mathsf{sid}, (\hat{P}_j, \hat{v}_j)\rangle$ to $\mathcal{S}$;
13:         **else** Send $\langle\textsc{RequestID}, \mathsf{sid}, \bot\rangle$ to $\mathcal{S}$;
14:         Receive $\langle\textsc{ResponseID}, \mathsf{sid}, \hat{\mathsf{cid}}_j\rangle$ from $\mathcal{S}$;
15:         Add $(\hat{\mathsf{cid}}_j, \hat{v}_j, \hat{P}_j, P_k)$ to $\mathcal{L}_{\mathsf{coin}}$;
16:     Send $\langle\textsc{ResponseID}, \mathsf{sid}, \{\hat{\mathsf{cid}}_j\}\rangle$ to P_k;
17:     Generate $\mathsf{TX} := (\{\mathsf{cid}_i\}, \{\hat{\mathsf{cid}}_j\})$;
18:     $\mathcal{L}^*_{\mathsf{Agg}} := \emptyset$;
19:     **for** each $\mathsf{Agg}_t \in \mathcal{L}_{\mathsf{Agg}}$ **do**
20:         **if** Agg_t is an aggregator **then**
21:             **if** $P_k \in \mathcal{L}_{\mathcal{A}}$ **then**
22:                 Send $\langle\textsc{SendTX}, \mathsf{sid}, \mathsf{TX}, P_k, \mathsf{Agg}_t\rangle$ to $\mathcal{S}$;
23:             **else**
24:                 Send $\langle\textsc{SendTX}, \mathsf{sid}, \bot, P_k, \mathsf{Agg}_t\rangle$ to $\mathcal{S}$;
25:         **if** Receive $\langle\textsc{SendTX}, \mathsf{sid}, P_k, \mathsf{Agg}_t, \mathsf{OK}\rangle$ from $\mathcal{S}$ **then**
26:             Send $\langle\textsc{ReceivedTX}, \mathsf{sid}, \mathsf{TX}\rangle$ to Agg_t;
27:             Add Agg_t to $\mathcal{L}^*_{\mathsf{Agg}}$;
28:     Write $(\mathsf{TX}, \mathcal{L}^*_{\mathsf{Agg}}, \mathsf{Info})$ to $\mathcal{L}_{\mathsf{TX}}$;
29: **else**
30:     **for** each $\mathsf{Agg}_t \in \mathcal{L}_{\mathsf{Agg}}/\mathcal{L}^*_{\mathsf{Agg}}$ **do**
31:         **if** Agg_t is an aggregator **then**
32:             **if** $P_k \in \mathcal{L}_{\mathcal{A}}$ **then**
33:                 Send $\langle\textsc{SendTX}, \mathsf{sid}, \mathsf{TX}, P_k, \mathsf{Agg}_t\rangle$ to $\mathcal{S}$;
34:             **else**
35:                 Send $\langle\textsc{SendTX}, \mathsf{sid}, \bot, P_k, \mathsf{Agg}_t\rangle$ to $\mathcal{S}$;
36:         **if** Receive $\langle\textsc{SendTX}, \mathsf{sid}, P_k, \mathsf{Agg}_t, \mathsf{OK}\rangle$ from $\mathcal{S}$ **then**
37:             Send $\langle\textsc{ReceivedTX}, \mathsf{sid}, \mathsf{TX}\rangle$ to Agg_t;
38:             Add Agg_t to $\mathcal{L}^*_{\mathsf{Agg}}$;
39:     Rewrite $(\mathsf{TX}, \mathcal{L}^*_{\mathsf{Agg}}, \mathsf{Info})$ to $\mathcal{L}_{\mathsf{TX}}$;

Fig. 5. Ideal functionality of NiACS (Users' transactions).

can receive the transaction and aggregate it, $\{\mathsf{cid}_i\}$ is the set of coins to be spent, and $\{(\hat{P}_j, \hat{v}_j)\}$ is the set of receivers and the corresponding values. Upon receiving a payment request, $\mathcal{F}_{\mathsf{NiACS}}$ will perform the following three steps:

- *Transaction validation*: $\mathcal{F}_{\mathsf{NiACS}}$ first needs to get the current state and check if P_k can spend all the coins in $\{\mathsf{cid}_i\}$. More specifically, for each cid_i, $\mathcal{F}_{\mathsf{NiACS}}$ retrieves $(\mathsf{cid}_i, v_i, P_i, \cdot)$ from $\mathcal{L}_{\mathsf{coin}}$ and checks if $P_i = P_k$. If so, P_k can spend this coin. Note that it is possible that $P_i = \bot$, which means that the coin is generated by a corrupted party and has no designated owner. In this case, any corrupted party in $\mathcal{L}_{\mathcal{A}}$ can spend this coin. For all i, if P_k can indeed spend coin cid_i and all these coins are in state, $\mathcal{F}_{\mathsf{NiACS}}$ further checks if all the output values are valid (i.e., $\hat{v}_j \in [0, v_{\mathsf{max}}]$ for all j) and the transaction is balanced (i.e., $\sum_i v_i = \sum_j \hat{v}_j$). If all above verifications pass, $\mathcal{F}_{\mathsf{NiACS}}$ will generate new coins for the receivers as below.

- *Creating new coins*: $\mathcal{F}_{\mathsf{NiACS}}$ sends a message to request $\mathcal{S}$ to generate the identifiers of new coins. Since the adversary $\mathcal{S}$ knows the values/amounts of coins generated or received by corrupted parties, $\mathcal{F}_{\mathsf{NiACS}}$ will send $\langle \mathrm{REQUESTID}, \mathsf{sid}, (\hat{P}_j, \hat{v}_j) \rangle$ to the adversary if the sender P_k or a receiver $\hat{P}_j$ is corrupted. Otherwise, $\mathcal{F}_{\mathsf{NiACS}}$ will send $\langle \mathrm{REQUESTID}, \mathsf{sid}, \perp \rangle$ to capture that both the receiver and the amount of the coin are hidden from $\mathcal{S}$. Upon receiving the response $\langle \mathrm{RESPONSEID}, \mathsf{sid}, \hat{\mathsf{cid}}_j \rangle$ from $\mathcal{S}$, where $\hat{\mathsf{cid}}_j$ is the identifier of the new coin, $\mathcal{F}_{\mathsf{NiACS}}$ records $(\hat{\mathsf{cid}}_j, \hat{v}_j, \hat{P}_j, P_k)$ in $\mathcal{L}_{\mathsf{coin}}$. After getting the identifiers of all the new coins, $\mathcal{F}_{\mathsf{NiACS}}$ represents the transaction as $\mathsf{TX} := (\{\mathsf{cid}_i\}, \{\hat{\mathsf{cid}}_j\})$, which will be sent to the designated aggregators in $\mathcal{L}_{\mathsf{Agg}}$ as below.

- *Sending* TX *to aggregators*: Although an aggregator list $\mathcal{L}_{\mathsf{Agg}}$ for a transaction TX is assigned in the input message, whether or not an aggregator can receive the transaction TX is eventually determined by the adversary $\mathcal{S}$, so the set of aggregators who indeed receive the transaction is a subset of the assigned aggregators. When receiving a transaction for the first time, $\mathcal{F}_{\mathsf{NiACS}}$ initializes a list $\mathcal{L}_{\mathsf{Agg}}^*$ to record the aggregators who will finally receive the transaction. For each aggregator Agg_t in $\mathcal{L}_{\mathsf{Agg}}$, $\mathcal{F}_{\mathsf{NiACS}}$ will ask $\mathcal{S}$ if Agg_t can receive the transaction through a message $\langle \mathrm{SENDTX}, \mathsf{sid}, \mathsf{TX}, P_k, \mathsf{Agg}_t \rangle$. Note that if the sender P_k is corrupted, $\mathcal{S}$ can know which transaction is required to be sent to an aggregator, so $\mathsf{TX} \neq \perp$. But when the sender is honest, $\mathcal{S}$ cannot know the information about the transaction, and thus $\mathsf{TX} = \perp$. Upon receiving $\langle \mathrm{SENDTX}, \mathsf{sid}, P_k, \mathsf{Agg}_t, \mathrm{OK} \rangle$, $\mathcal{F}_{\mathsf{NiACS}}$ will send $\langle \mathrm{RECEIVEDTX}, \mathsf{sid}, \mathsf{TX} \rangle$ to Agg_t and add Agg_t to $\mathcal{L}_{\mathsf{Agg}}^*$. After sending the transaction to the allowed aggregators, $\mathcal{F}_{\mathsf{NiACS}}$ needs to record the transaction into $\mathcal{L}_{\mathsf{TX}}$, including its transaction identifier TX, aggregators receiving the transaction $\mathcal{L}_{\mathsf{Agg}}^*$ and its details $(\{\mathsf{cid}_i\}, \{(\hat{P}_j, \hat{v}_j)\})$. In addition, P_k can repeatedly input the same transaction, but with different aggregator lists. In this case, $\mathcal{F}_{\mathsf{NiACS}}$ only sends the transaction to the new aggregators in $\mathcal{L}_{\mathsf{Agg}}/\mathcal{L}_{\mathsf{Agg}}^*$.

Aggregation. In Fig. 6, we show how $\mathcal{F}_{\mathsf{NiACS}}$ aggregates certain transactions and puts the aggregate transactions into buffer. An aggregator Agg_k can ask $\mathcal{F}_{\mathsf{NiACS}}$ to aggregate the transactions in $\{\mathsf{TX}_t\}$ and put the aggregate transaction into the ledger by submitting an aggregation request $\langle \mathrm{AGGREGATE}, \mathsf{sid}, \{\mathsf{TX}_t\} \rangle$. Upon receiving the request, $\mathcal{F}_{\mathsf{NiACS}}$ initializes three empty lists $\mathcal{L}_{\mathsf{inp}}$, $\mathcal{L}_{\mathsf{outp}}$ and $\mathcal{L}_{\mathsf{cut}}$. $\mathcal{L}_{\mathsf{inp}}$ and $\mathcal{L}_{\mathsf{outp}}$ are used to record the identifiers of spent coins and created coins in the aggregate transaction, respectively. For each transaction TX_t in $\{\mathsf{TX}_t\}$, $\mathcal{F}_{\mathsf{NiACS}}$ first checks if the aggregator Agg_k indeed received the transaction according to the records in $\mathcal{L}_{\mathsf{TX}}$. If not, $\mathcal{F}_{\mathsf{NiACS}}$ will ignore the transaction TX_t, otherwise parses TX_t as $(\{\mathsf{cid}_i\}, \{\hat{\mathsf{cid}}_j\})$ and adds all identifiers in $\{\mathsf{cid}_i\}$ and $\{\hat{\mathsf{cid}}_j\}$ to $\mathcal{L}_{\mathsf{inp}}$ and $\mathcal{L}_{\mathsf{outp}}$ respectively. At this point, the transactions in $\{\mathsf{TX}_t\}$ received by the aggregator Agg_k have been aggregated into $(\mathcal{L}_{\mathsf{inp}}, \mathcal{L}_{\mathsf{outp}})$. Then cut-through proceeds as follows: For each spent coin $\mathsf{cid}_i \in \mathcal{L}_{\mathsf{inp}}$, $\mathcal{F}_{\mathsf{NiACS}}$ checks if it belongs to $\mathcal{L}_{\mathsf{outp}}$, if so, cid_i will be removed from $\mathcal{L}_{\mathsf{inp}}$ and $\mathcal{L}_{\mathsf{outp}}$. Obviously, if a cut happens on a coin that is created or received by a corrupted party, the adversary $\mathcal{S}$ will

---

Functionality $\mathcal{F}_{\mathsf{NiACS}}$: Aggregation

Upon receiving a message $\langle \textsc{Aggregate}, \mathsf{sid}, \{\mathsf{TX}_t\} \rangle$ from an aggregator Agg_k, do:

1: $(\mathsf{state}, \mathsf{buffer}, \mathsf{counter}) := \textsc{ExtendState}(\mathsf{state}, \mathsf{buffer}, \mathsf{T}, \mathsf{counter})$;
2: Initialize $\mathcal{L}_{\mathsf{inp}} := \emptyset$, $\mathcal{L}_{\mathsf{outp}} := \emptyset$, $\mathcal{L}_{\mathsf{cut}} := \emptyset$, $c := 0$;
3: **for** each TX_t **do**
4:     Retrieve $(\mathsf{TX}_t, \mathcal{L}^*_{\mathsf{Agg},t}, \mathsf{Info}_t)$ from $\mathcal{L}_{\mathsf{TX}}$;
5:     **if** $\mathsf{Agg}_k \in \mathcal{L}^*_{\mathsf{Agg},t}$ **then**
6:         Parse $\mathsf{TX}_t := (\{\mathsf{cid}_i\}, \{\hat{\mathsf{cid}}_j\})$;
7:         Add all $\{\hat{\mathsf{cid}}_j\}$ to $\mathcal{L}_{\mathsf{outp}}$;
8:         **for** each cid_i **do**
9:             **if** $\mathsf{cid}_i \notin \mathcal{L}_{\mathsf{outp}}$ **then** Add cid_i to $\mathcal{L}_{\mathsf{inp}}$;
10:            **else**
11:                Remove cid_i from $\mathcal{L}_{\mathsf{outp}}$;
12:                $c := c + 1$;
13:                Retrieve $(\mathsf{cid}_i, v_i, P_i, P_k)$ from $\mathcal{L}_{\mathsf{coin}}$;
14:                **if** $P_i \in \mathcal{L}_{\mathcal{A}} \vee P_k \in \mathcal{L}_{\mathcal{A}}$ **then** Add cid_i into $\mathcal{L}_{\mathsf{cut}}$;
15: $\mathsf{aTX} := (\mathcal{L}_{\mathsf{inp}}, \mathcal{L}_{\mathsf{outp}})$;
16: **if** all $\mathsf{cid}_i \in \mathcal{L}_{\mathsf{inp}}$ are in $\mathsf{state} || \mathsf{buffer}$ **then**
17:     $\mathsf{buffer} := \mathsf{buffer} || \mathsf{aTX}$;
18:     Send $\langle \textsc{AggTX}, \mathsf{sid}, \mathsf{aTX} \rangle$ to Agg_k and $\langle \textsc{AggTX}, \mathsf{sid}, \mathsf{Agg}_k, \mathsf{aTX}, c, \mathcal{L}_{\mathsf{cut}} \rangle$ to $\mathcal{S}$;

Fig. 6. Ideal functionality of NiACS (Aggregation).

Functionality $\mathcal{F}_{\mathsf{NiACS}}$: Ledger

Upon receiving a message $\langle \textsc{SubmitToLedger}, \mathsf{sid}, \{\mathsf{cid}_i\}, \{(\hat{\mathsf{cid}}_j, \hat{P}_j, \hat{v}_j)\} \rangle$ from adversary $\mathcal{S}$ (on behalf of a corrupted user or a corrupted aggregator), do the following:

1: $(\mathsf{state}, \mathsf{buffer}, \mathsf{counter}) := \textsc{ExtendState}(\mathsf{state}, \mathsf{buffer}, \mathsf{T}, \mathsf{counter})$;
2: **for** each cid_i **do**
3:     Retrieve $(\mathsf{cid}_i, v_i, P_i, \cdot)$ from $\mathcal{L}_{\mathsf{coin}}$;
4:     **if** $(P_i \neq \bot \wedge P_i \notin \mathcal{L}_{\mathcal{A}}) \vee \mathsf{cid}_i \notin \mathsf{state} || \mathsf{buffer}$ **then** Ignore the message;
5: **if** $\sum_i v_i \neq \sum_j \hat{v}_j \vee \exists j, s.t., \hat{v}_j \notin [0, v_{\mathsf{max}}]$ **then** Ignore the message;
6: **for** each j **do**
7:     Add $(\hat{\mathsf{cid}}_j, \hat{v}_j, \hat{P}_j, \bot)$ to $\mathcal{L}_{\mathsf{coin}}$;
8: Generate $\mathsf{TX} := (\{\mathsf{cid}_i\}, \{\hat{\mathsf{cid}}_j\})$;
9: $\mathsf{buffer} := \mathsf{buffer} || \mathsf{TX}$;

Upon receiving a message $\langle \textsc{Read}, \mathsf{sid} \rangle$ from a party P_k or adversary $\mathcal{S}$, do the following:

1: $(\mathsf{state}, \mathsf{buffer}, \mathsf{counter}) := \textsc{ExtendState}(\mathsf{state}, \mathsf{buffer}, \mathsf{T}, \mathsf{counter})$;
2: **if** $P_k \in \mathcal{L}_{\mathcal{A}}$ or the requester is $\mathcal{S}$ **then**
3:     Send $\langle \textsc{Read}, \mathsf{sid}, (\mathsf{state}, \mathsf{buffer}) \rangle$ to the requestor;
4: **else**
5:     Send $\langle \textsc{Read}, \mathsf{sid}, \mathsf{state} \rangle$ to the requestor;

Upon receiving a message $\langle \textsc{Permute}, \mathsf{sid}, \pi \rangle$ from adversary $\mathcal{S}$, apply the permutation π on the elements of buffer;

Fig. 7. Ideal functionality of NiACS (Ledger).

be aware of it. Thus, $\mathcal{F}_{\mathsf{NiACS}}$ uses $\mathcal{L}_{\mathsf{cut}}$ to record these coins. We allow $\mathcal{S}$ to know how many coins (related to honest parties and corrupted parties) are cut, and denotes the number as a variable c. After executing the above process, $\mathcal{L}_{\mathsf{inp}}$ and $\mathcal{L}_{\mathsf{outp}}$ constitute the aggregate transaction aTX. Finally, if all the input coins of aTX are in state, $\mathcal{F}_{\mathsf{NiACS}}$ adds aTX into buffer and sends $\langle \textsc{AggTX}, \mathsf{sid}, \mathsf{aTX} \rangle$ and $\langle \textsc{AggTX}, \mathsf{sid}, \mathsf{Agg}_k, \mathsf{aTX}, c, \mathcal{L}_{\mathsf{cut}} \rangle$ to Agg_k and $\mathcal{S}$, respectively.

Ledger. For the basic interfaces of a ledger, we follow the ledger functionality defined in [29]. To be self-contained, we show the ledger functionality in Fig. 7. More specifically, we follow their definition in the following three aspects: (1) The abstraction of consensus layer: $\mathcal{F}_{\text{NiACS}}$ executes the procedure EXTENDSTATE shown in Algorithm 1 to extend the state, which is an abstract of consensus layer; (2) The way of parties and adversary reading the ledger: for an honest party, $\mathcal{F}_{\text{NiACS}}$ only provides state, but for a corrupted party, $\mathcal{F}_{\text{NiACS}}$ give state and buffer; (3) Allowing adversary to permute buffer: to abstract the case where adversary can delay the delivery of transactions in the network, $\mathcal{F}_{\text{NiACS}}$ receives a permutation π from the adversary, and apply the permutation on buffer.

In addition, we allow the adversary $\mathcal{S}$ to directly submit transactions to the ledger. Note that in the ledger functionality defined in [29], both honest and corrupted parties can directly submit transactions to the ledger. Whereas, in our NiACS, each honest sender's transaction first needs to be aggregated and then submitted to the ledger by the designated aggregators. Therefore, honest parties who intend to protect privacy will not directly submit transactions to the ledger.

Security Properties Captured By our Definition. Informally, our ideal functionality $\mathcal{F}_{\text{NiACS}}$ captures the following security properties: *inflation-resistance, theft-resistance, transaction indistinguishability, and unlinkability.* More specifically, $\mathcal{F}_{\text{NiACS}}$ requires parties to register the initial amounts and spend the coins with enough value, which implies inflation-resistance. For each coin, $\mathcal{F}_{\text{NiACS}}$ records its owner and only allows the owner to spend the coin, which means theft-resistance. A transaction consists of an input list and an output list, each containing multiple coin identifiers cid. Since the coin identifiers are pseudorandom, the transaction amount is hidden and change coins and output coins are indistinguishable obviously, which provides transaction indistinguishability. Moreover, the transactions contained in the state of the ledger is in an aggregate form, so the irrelevant parties cannot learn which coins belong to the same transaction, i.e., unlinkability.

4   Our Non-interactive Aggregate Cash System

In this section, we present the details of our protocol Π_{NiACS}. First, we propose a new variant of ElGamal encryption that is important for realizing non-interactive payments. Then, we introduce the ideal functionalities and auxiliary algorithms used through our design. At last, we present our protocol based on these functionalities, auxiliary algorithms, and the variant of ElGamal encryption.

4.1   New Variant of ElGamal Encryption

Inspired by the twisted ElGamal encryption [16], we propose a new variant of ElGamal encryption scheme shown in Fig. 8. The ciphertext is of the form $\left(pk^r, g^{H(g^r)}h^m\right)$ for a message $m \in \mathbb{Z}_p$. Therefore, the receiver can recover both the randomness $H(g^r)$ and the message m by using the secret key sk, which plays a crucial role for our design. We remark that, as shown in [11,16,19], the encrypted message m can be efficiently recovered from h^m when the message space is small, e.g., by brute-force enumeration as in [11,19], or Shanks's algorithm as in [16]. We show the security of our new variant of ElGamal encryption by Theorem 1, and please find the proof in the full version.

Setup(1^λ): runs $(\mathbb{G}, g, p) \leftarrow \mathsf{GroupGen}(1^\lambda)$, picks $h \xleftarrow{\$} \mathbb{G}^*$, chooses a hash function $H : \mathbb{G} \mapsto \mathbb{Z}_p$, and outputs $pp := (\mathbb{G}, g, h, p, H)$ as the global public parameters.

KeyGen(pp): chooses $sk \xleftarrow{\$} \mathbb{Z}_p$, computes $pk := g^{sk}$, and outputs a key pair (sk, pk).

Enc(pk, m): chooses $r \xleftarrow{\$} \mathbb{Z}_p$, computes $X := pk^r$, $\alpha := H(g^r)$, $Y := g^\alpha h^m$, and outputs the ciphertext $C := (X, Y)$.

Dec(sk, C): parses $C := (X, Y)$, computes $\alpha := H(X^{\frac{1}{sk}})$, $h^m := \frac{Y}{g^\alpha}$, recovers m from h^m.

Fig. 8. New variant of ElGamal.

Theorem 1. *Assuming that the Divisible Computational Diffie-Hellman (DCDH) problem is hard[6], the proposed encryption scheme is IND-CPA secure in the random oracle model.*

4.2 Ideal Functionalities and Auxiliary Algorithms

We design our protocol in a hybrid model. To ease the understanding of our protocol, we first recall the subroutine ideal functionalities invoked in our design and represent some specific processes as auxiliary algorithms. We give the details of these functionalities and auxiliary algorithms in the full version.

Ideal Functionalities. The ideal functionalities used throughout our design can be divided into two categories; the first is used for transaction layer, while the second is for consensus layer. For the former, it is summarized in Table 1. For the latter, we note that the functionality $\mathcal{F}_{\mathsf{NiACS}}$ defined in Sect. 3 is a private ledger, and thus can be seen as a "private" version of $\mathcal{F}_{\mathsf{Ledger}}$ defined in [29]. Therefore, we focus on designing privacy-preserving transaction layer while assuming there is a secure consensus layer. In this work, we design our protocol $\mathit{\Pi}_{\mathsf{NiACS}}$ by leveraging the functionality $\mathcal{F}_{\mathsf{Ledger}}$.

Auxiliary Algorithms. For the auxiliary algorithms, we divide them into two categories: one-time addresses and construction of transactions.

One-Time Addresses. In our system, each user has a permanent address $\mathsf{Addr} := g^{\mathsf{Key}}$, where $\mathsf{Key} \xleftarrow{\$} \mathbb{Z}_p$ is the associated secret key and g is a generator of the cyclic group $\mathbb{G}$ with order p. We use one-time address to hide the identity of a user in the real world. One-time addresses/secret keys are generated as follows:

---

[6] Informally, the DCDH assumption means that, given a tuple (g, g^a, g^b), where g is a generator of a cyclic group $\mathbb{G}$ with prime order p and $a, b \xleftarrow{\$} \mathbb{Z}_p$, the probability of computing $g^{a/b}$ is negligible.

- GenOTAddr is to generate a one-time address and its auxiliary string for a user with permanent address Addr. It takes Addr as input, and outputs a one-time address pk and corresponding auxiliary string R.
- GenOTKey is to generate a one-time spending key. It takes a permanent address/key pair (Addr, Key) and a one-time address/auxiliary string (pk, R) as input, if (pk, R) is derived from (Addr, Key), outputs the one-time secret key sk, otherwise outputs $\perp$.

Table 1. Ideal functionalities and descriptions

$\mathcal{F}_{\mathsf{NIZK}}^{\mathsf{addr}}$	Non-interactive zero-knowledge for language $\mathcal{L}_{\mathsf{addr}} := \{(pk, R) \mid \exists\ (\mathsf{Addr}, r),$ s.t. $pk = \mathsf{Addr}^{H(\mathsf{Addr}^r)}, R = g^r\}$, which is used to prove that the one-time address pk and its auxiliary string R are correctly generated
$\mathcal{F}_{\mathsf{NIZK}}^{\mathsf{zero}}$	Non-interactive zero-knowledge for language $\mathcal{L}_{\mathsf{zero}} := \{\mathsf{cm} \mid \exists\ r,$ s.t. $\mathsf{cm} = g^r h^0\}$, which is used to prove that each excess part is a commitment to 0
$\mathcal{F}_{\mathsf{NIZK}}^{\mathsf{enc}}$	Non-interactive zero-knowledge for language $\mathcal{L}_{\mathsf{enc}} := \{(pk, (X, \mathsf{cm})) \mid \exists\ (r, v),$ s.t. $X = pk^r, \mathsf{cm} = g^{H(g^r)} h^v\}$, which is used to prove that the amount v is correctly encrypted
$\mathcal{F}_{\mathsf{SoK}}^{\mathsf{range}}$	Signature of knowledge for language $\mathcal{L}_{\mathsf{range}} := \{\mathsf{cm} \mid \exists\ (r, v),$ s.t. $\mathsf{cm} = g^r h^v \wedge v \in [0, v_{\mathsf{max}}]\}$, which is used to prove that the amount of each coin is within a valid range and to sign an address
$\mathcal{F}_{\mathsf{SoK}}^{\mathsf{key}}$	Signature of knowledge for language $\mathcal{L}_{\mathsf{key}} := \{pk \mid \exists\ sk,$ s.t. $pk = g^{sk}\}$, which is used to prove the knowledge of a spending key and to sign an excess part
$\mathcal{F}_{\mathsf{SMT}}$	Secure message transmission is for users to send transactions to aggregators

Construction of Transactions. The remaining algorithms are used to generate and verify transactions as follows:

- GenExcess is to generate the excess and offset. It takes as input all the commitments and their openings in both the input and output lists (i.e., $\{\mathsf{cm}_i, (\alpha_i, v_i)\}$ and $\{\hat{\mathsf{cm}}_j, (\hat{\alpha}_j, \hat{v}_j)\}$), then chooses an offset δ and computes the final excess $\tilde{E}$ and its randomness $\tilde{e}$. After that, it splits the excess $\tilde{E}$ into n parts, s.t., $\tilde{E} = \tilde{E}_1 \cdot \tilde{E}_2 \cdots \tilde{E}_n$, and outputs $(\{\tilde{E}_i, \tilde{e}_i\}, \delta)$.
- GenOutput and VerOutput are to generate and verify the output coins, respectively. For each output, GenOutput takes $(\hat{v}_j, \mathsf{Addr}_j)$ as input, then generates and outputs a one-time address $\hat{\mathsf{cid}}_j := (\hat{pk}_j, \hat{R}_j)$, a proof $\hat{\pi}_j^{\mathsf{addr}}$ that the one-time address is correctly generated, a ciphertext $(\hat{X}_j, \hat{\mathsf{cm}}_j)$ of v_j, a proof $\hat{\pi}_j^{\mathsf{enc}}$ that $(\hat{X}_j, \hat{\mathsf{cm}}_j)$ is correctly generated, a signature $\hat{\sigma}_j^{\mathsf{range}}$ on $(\hat{pk}_j, \hat{R}_j)$ and the randomness $\hat{\alpha}_j$ of $\hat{\mathsf{cm}}_j$. VerOutput takes $(\hat{\mathsf{cid}}_j, \hat{\pi}_j^{\mathsf{addr}}, (\hat{X}_j, \hat{\mathsf{cm}}_j), \hat{\pi}_j^{\mathsf{enc}}, \hat{\sigma}_j^{\mathsf{range}})$ as input, then outputs 1 if $\hat{\pi}_j^{\mathsf{addr}}, \hat{\pi}_j^{\mathsf{enc}}$ and $\hat{\sigma}_j^{\mathsf{range}}$ are valid, and 0 otherwise.

- GENINPUT and VERINPUT are used to generate and verify the proof of spending key for each input coin, respectively. GENINPUT takes as inputs a partial excess $\tilde{E}_i$ and the associated randomness $\tilde{e}_i$, a coin identifier cid_i (i.e., one-time address) and the corresponding one-time spending key sk_i, then outputs a proof $\tilde{\pi}_i^{\mathsf{zero}}$ that $\tilde{E}_i$ is a commitment to 0 and a signature σ_i^{key} that proves the knowledge of sk_i and binds the input coin to $\tilde{E}_i$. VERINPUT takes $(\mathrm{cid}_i, (\tilde{E}_i, \tilde{\pi}_i^{\mathsf{zero}}), \sigma_i^{\mathsf{key}})$ as input, and outputs 1 if both $\tilde{\pi}_i^{\mathsf{zero}}$ and σ_i^{key} are valid, otherwise returns 0.
- AGGREGATE is to aggregate a valid individual transaction TX with an (aggregate) transaction $(\mathcal{L}_I, \mathcal{L}_O, \mathcal{L}_K, \Delta)$. It takes as input a transaction TX, an input list $\mathcal{L}_I$, an output list $\mathcal{L}_O$, a kernel list $\mathcal{L}_K$ and Δ, then outputs a new aggregate transaction $(\mathcal{L}_I, \mathcal{L}_O, \mathcal{L}_K, \Delta)$.

4.3   Description of Π_{NiACS}

Given the above ideal functionalities and auxiliary algorithms, we show the specification of our Π_{NiACS} in Fig. 9, Fig. 10, Fig. 11 and Fig. 12. Please refer to the full version for the detailed description.

Protocol Π_{NiACS}: Initialization

A party P_k, upon receiving message $\langle \text{REGISTRATION}, \mathsf{sid}, \mathsf{Infor}_{\mathsf{reg}}, P_k \rangle$ from $\mathcal{Z}$, does the following:

1: Parse $\mathsf{Infor}_{\mathsf{reg}} := (\mathsf{role}, v_k)$;
2: **if** $\mathsf{role} = \mathsf{user} \wedge v_k \in [0, v_{\mathsf{max}}]$ **then**
3:     $\mathsf{Key}_k \xleftarrow{\$} \mathbb{Z}_p$, $\mathsf{Addr}_k := g^{\mathsf{Key}_k}$;
4:     $(pk_k, R_k) := \text{GENOTADDR}(\mathsf{sid}, \mathsf{ssid}, \mathsf{Addr}_k)$, and set $\mathsf{cid}_k := (pk_k, R_k)$;
5:     Randomly choose $\alpha_k \xleftarrow{\$} \mathbb{Z}_p$, and compute $\mathsf{cm}_k := g^{\alpha_k} h^{v_k}$;
6:     $\mathsf{Initcoin} := (\mathsf{Addr}_k, (\mathsf{cid}_k, \mathsf{cm}_k), (\alpha_k, v_k))$;
7:     Invoke $\mathcal{F}_{\mathsf{Ledger}}$ with $\langle \text{REGISTRATION}, \mathsf{sid}, (P_k, \mathsf{user}, \mathsf{Initcoin}) \rangle$;
8:     Upon receiving $\langle \text{INITIALIZED}, \mathsf{sid} \rangle$ from $\mathcal{F}_{\mathsf{Ledger}}$, output $\langle \text{INITIALIZED}, \mathsf{sid}, \mathsf{cid}_k \rangle$ to $\mathcal{Z}$;
9: **else if** $\mathsf{role} = \mathsf{aggregator} \wedge v_k = \bot$ **then**
10:     Invoke $\mathcal{F}_{\mathsf{Ledger}}$ with $\langle \text{REGISTRATION}, \mathsf{sid}, (P_k, \mathsf{aggregator}, \bot) \rangle$;
11:     Upon receiving $\langle \text{INITIALIZED}, \mathsf{sid} \rangle$ from $\mathcal{F}_{\mathsf{Ledger}}$, output $\langle \text{INITIALIZED}, \mathsf{sid} \rangle$ to $\mathcal{Z}$;
12: **else**   Ignore the message;

Fig. 9. Our Π_{NiACS} supporting non-interactive payments (Initialization).

Protocol Π_{NiACS}: Users' transactions

A party P_k with permanent address and key $(\text{Addr}, \text{Key})$, upon receiving a message $\langle \text{Submit}, \text{sid}, P_k, \mathcal{L}_{\text{Agg}}, \{\text{cid}_i\}, \{(\hat{P}_j, \hat{v}_j)\} \rangle$ from $\mathcal{Z}$, does the following:

1: Invoke $\mathcal{F}_{\text{Ledger}}$ with $\langle \text{Read}, \text{sid} \rangle$, get $\langle \text{Read}, \text{sid}, \text{state} \rangle$ (A corrupted P_k will also get buffer);
2: Initialize $\text{in} := 0$, $\text{out} := \sum_j \hat{v}_j$, $\mathcal{I} := \emptyset$, $\mathcal{I}' := \emptyset$;
3: **for** each cid_i **do**
4:     **if** There is no cid_i in state **then** Ignore the message;
5:     **else**
6:         Retrieve $(\text{cid}_i, (X_i, \text{cm}_i))$ from state;
7:         $sk_i := \text{GenOTKey}(\text{sid}, \text{ssid}, \text{Addr}, \text{Key}, \text{cid}_i)$;
8:         **if** $sk_i = \bot$ **then** Ignore the message;
9:         **else**
10:            $(\alpha_i, v_i) := \text{Dec}(sk_i; (X_i, \text{cm}_i))$;
11:            **if** $v_i \notin [0, v_{\max}]$ **then** Ignore the message;
12:            **else** $\text{in} := \text{in} + v_i$;
13: **if** $\text{in} = \text{out}$ **then**
14:     **for** each j **do**
15:         Retrieve $(\hat{P}_j, \hat{\text{Addr}}_j)$ from state;
16:         $((\hat{\text{cid}}_j, \hat{\pi}_j^{\text{addr}}, (\hat{X}_j, \hat{\text{cm}}_j), \hat{\pi}_j^{\text{enc}}, \hat{\sigma}_j^{\text{range}}), \hat{\alpha}_j) := \text{GenOutput}(\text{sid}, \text{ssid}, (\hat{v}_j, \hat{\text{Addr}}_j))$;
17:     $(\{\bar{E}_i, \bar{e}_i\}, \delta) := \text{GenExcess}(\{\text{cm}_i, \alpha_i, v_i\}, \{\hat{\text{cm}}_j, \hat{\alpha}_j, \hat{v}_j\})$;
18:     **for** each i **do**
19:         $(\pi_i^{\text{zero}}, \sigma_i^{\text{key}}) := \text{GenInput}(\text{sid}, \text{ssid}, sk_i, \text{cid}_i, \bar{E}_i, \bar{e}_i)$;
20:     Set $\text{TX} := (\{(\text{cid}_i, \sigma_i^{\text{key}})\}, \{(\hat{\text{cid}}_j, \hat{\pi}_j^{\text{addr}}, (\hat{X}_j, \hat{\text{cm}}_j), \hat{\pi}_j^{\text{enc}}, \hat{\sigma}_j^{\text{range}})\}, \{(\bar{E}_i, \pi_i^{\text{zero}})\}, \delta)$;
21:     **for** each $\text{Agg}_t \in \mathcal{L}_{\text{Agg}}$ **do**
22:         Invoke $\mathcal{F}_{\text{SMT}}$ with $\langle \text{Send}, \text{sid}, \text{ssid}, \text{TX}, P_k, \text{Agg}_t \rangle$;
23:     Output $\langle \text{ResponseID}, \text{sid}, \{\hat{\text{cid}}_j\} \rangle$ to $\mathcal{Z}$;
24: **else** Ignore the message.

Fig. 10. Our Π_{NiACS} supporting non-interactive payments (Users' transactions).

Initialization. Figure 9 shows the initialization process of Π_{NiACS}. Steps 1–6 show the initialization process of a user, including generating permanent address/key and initial coin, and submitting the initial information to $\mathcal{F}_{\text{Ledger}}$. Steps 7–8 show the initialization process of an aggregator, i.e., registering the role to $\mathcal{F}_{\text{Ledger}}$.

Users' Transactions. In Fig. 10, we describe how a user constructs a transfer transaction. In steps 3–13, the user checks if the transfer request from $\mathcal{Z}$ is valid. If so, the user generates the transaction by invoking GenOutput, GenExcess and GenInput as shown in steps 14–20. At last, the user sends the transaction to the designated aggregators through $\mathcal{F}_{\text{SMT}}$ as shown in steps 21–22.

Aggregation. Figure 11 shows the process of aggregation. In steps 2–14, the aggregator checks if the transactions received from $\mathcal{F}_{\text{SMT}}$ are valid by verifying the kernel and invoking VerInput and VerOutput, and records the valid transactions. Then the aggregator aggregates the valid transactions specified by $\mathcal{Z}$ through executing Aggregate and submits the aggregate transaction to $\mathcal{F}_{\text{Ledger}}$, as shown in steps 16–21. Note that the aggregator just outputs the coin identifiers in (aggregate) transactions to $\mathcal{Z}$, rather than the real-world (aggregate) transactions. Therefore, the aggregator executes Clean to extract the coin identifiers from (aggregate) transactions.

Protocol Π_{NiACS}: Aggregation

An aggregator Agg_t, upon receiving $\langle \text{SENT}, \mathsf{sid}, \mathsf{ssid}, \mathsf{TX}, P_k, \mathsf{Agg}_t \rangle$ from $\mathcal{F}_{\mathsf{SMT}}$ where $\mathsf{TX} := (\{(\mathsf{cid}_i, \sigma_i^{\mathsf{key}})\}, \{(\hat{\mathsf{cid}}_j, \hat{\pi}_j^{\mathsf{addr}}, (\hat{X}_j, \hat{\mathsf{cm}}_j), \hat{\pi}_j^{\mathsf{enc}}, \hat{\sigma}_j^{\mathsf{range}})\}, \{(\bar{E}_i, \bar{\pi}_i^{\mathsf{zero}})\}, \delta)$, does the following:

1: Invoke $\mathcal{F}_{\mathsf{Ledger}}$ with $\langle \text{READ}, \mathsf{sid} \rangle$, get $\langle \text{READ}, \mathsf{sid}, \mathsf{state} \rangle$;
2: **for** each cid_i **do**
3:     **if** cid_i is in state **then** Retrieve $(\mathsf{cid}_i, (X_i, \mathsf{cm}_i))$ from state;
4:     **else** Ignore the message;
5: **if** $\prod_j \hat{\mathsf{cm}}_j / \prod_i \mathsf{cm}_i \cdot g^\delta = \prod_i \bar{E}_i$ **then**
6:     **for** each $\bar{E}_i$ **do**
7:         **if** VERINPUT$(\mathsf{sid}, \mathsf{ssid}, (\mathsf{cid}_i, (\bar{E}_i, \bar{\pi}_i^{\mathsf{zero}}), \sigma_i^{\mathsf{key}})){=}0$ **then**
8:             Ignore the message;
9:     **for** each $\hat{\mathsf{cm}}_j$ **do**
10:         **if** VEROUTPUT$(\mathsf{sid}, \mathsf{ssid}, (\hat{\mathsf{cid}}_j, \hat{\pi}_j^{\mathsf{addr}}, (\hat{X}_j, \hat{\mathsf{cm}}_j), \hat{\pi}_j^{\mathsf{enc}}, \hat{\sigma}_j^{\mathsf{range}})){=}0$ **then**
11:             Ignore the message;
12: **else** Ignore the message;
13: Generate $\mathsf{TX}^* := (\{\mathsf{cid}_i\}, \{\hat{\mathsf{cid}}_j\})$;
14: Add $(\mathsf{TX}^*, \mathsf{TX})$ into $\mathcal{L}_{\mathsf{TX}}$;
15: Output $\langle \text{RECEIVEDTX}, \mathsf{sid}, \mathsf{TX}^* \rangle$ to $\mathcal{Z}$;

Upon receiving a message $\langle \text{AGGREGATE}, \mathsf{sid}, \{\mathsf{TX}_t^*\} \rangle$ from $\mathcal{Z}$, do the following:

16: Initialize $\mathcal{L}_I := \emptyset$, $\mathcal{L}_O := \emptyset$, $\mathcal{L}_K := \emptyset$ and $\Delta := 0$;
17: **for** each TX_t^* **do**
18:     Retrieve the transaction TX_t from $\mathcal{L}_{\mathsf{TX}}$;
19:     $(\mathcal{L}_I, \mathcal{L}_O, \mathcal{L}_K, \Delta) := \text{AGGREGATE}(\mathsf{TX}_t, \mathcal{L}_I, \mathcal{L}_O, \mathcal{L}_K, \Delta)$;
20: Set $\mathsf{aTX} := (\mathcal{L}_I, \mathcal{L}_O, \mathcal{L}_K, \Delta)$, and $\mathsf{aTX}^* := \text{CLEAN}(\mathsf{aTX})$;
21: Invoke $\mathcal{F}_{\mathsf{Ledger}}$ with $\langle \text{SUBMIT}, \mathsf{sid}, \mathsf{aTX} \rangle$;
22: Output $\langle \text{AGGTX}, \mathsf{sid}, \mathsf{aTX}^* \rangle$ to $\mathcal{Z}$;

Fig. 11. Our Π_{NiACS} supporting non-interactive payments (Aggregation).

Protocol Π_{NiACS}: Ledger

A party P_k, upon receiving a message $\langle \text{READ}, \mathsf{sid} \rangle$ from $\mathcal{Z}$, do the following:

1: Invoke $\mathcal{F}_{\mathsf{Ledger}}$ with $\langle \text{READ}, \mathsf{sid} \rangle$;
2: **if** P_k is uncorrupted **then**
3:     Receive $\langle \text{READ}, \mathsf{sid}, \mathsf{state} \rangle$ from $\mathcal{F}_{\mathsf{Ledger}}$;
4:     Set $\mathsf{state}^* := \text{CLEAN}(\mathsf{state})$;
5:     Output $\langle \text{READ}, \mathsf{sid}, \mathsf{state}^* \rangle$ to $\mathcal{Z}$;
6: **else**
7:     Receive $\langle \text{READ}, \mathsf{sid}, (\mathsf{state}, \mathsf{buffer}) \rangle$ from $\mathcal{F}_{\mathsf{Ledger}}$;
8:     Set $\mathsf{state}^* := \text{CLEAN}(\mathsf{state})$, $\mathsf{buffer}^* := \text{CLEAN}(\mathsf{buffer})$;
9:     Output $\langle \text{READ}, \mathsf{sid}, (\mathsf{state}^*, \mathsf{buffer}^*) \rangle$ to $\mathcal{Z}$;

Adversary $\mathcal{A}$, upon receiving a message $\langle \text{PERMUTE}, \mathsf{sid}, \pi \rangle$ from $\mathcal{Z}$, do the following:

10: Forward $\langle \text{PERMUTE}, \mathsf{sid}, \pi \rangle$ to $\mathcal{F}_{\mathsf{Ledger}}$.

Fig. 12. Our Π_{NiACS} supporting non-interactive payments (Ledger).

Ledger. In Fig. 12, we describe the part related to reading and maintaining ledger. Steps 2–5 show how the honest party obtains state. Besides state, a corrupted party can also obtain buffer and permute it as shown in steps 7–10. Likewise, the party just outputs the coin identifiers in state or buffer to $\mathcal{Z}$. Therefore, the aggregator executes CLEAN to extract the coin identifiers from state or buffer.

4.4   Security

Next we show the security of Π_{NiACS} against the static adversaries by Theorem 2. Please refer to the full version for the proof.

Theorem 2. *Assuming that DCDH problem is hard, the protocol Π_{NiACS} UC-realizes $\mathcal{F}_{\mathsf{NiACS}}$ in the $\{\mathcal{F}_{\mathsf{NIZK}}, \mathcal{F}_{\mathsf{SoK}}, \mathcal{F}_{\mathsf{SMT}}, \mathcal{F}_{\mathsf{Ledger}}, \mathcal{F}_{\mathsf{RO}}\}$-hybrid model, in the presence of static malicious adversaries.*

5   Instantiations

In the previous section, we describe our protocol Π_{NiACS} and prove it can UC-realize $\mathcal{F}_{\mathsf{NiACS}}$ in a hybrid model. In this section, we describe how to realize the subroutine ideal functionalities $\mathcal{F}_{\mathsf{NIZK}}$ and $\mathcal{F}_{\mathsf{SoK}}$ used in our Π_{NiACS}, which dominate the cost of our protocol. Next, we will describe the sub-protocols to achieve $\mathcal{F}_{\mathsf{NIZK}}$ and $\mathcal{F}_{\mathsf{SoK}}$ in the stand-alone setting and the UC setting.

Stand-Alone Setting. Recall our Π_{NiACS}, $\mathcal{F}_{\mathsf{NIZK}}^{\mathsf{zero}}$ is used to prove that an excess part $\tilde{E}_i$ is a commitment to 0, namely $E_i := g^{e_i}$, and $\mathcal{F}_{\mathsf{SoK}}^{\mathsf{key}}$ is used to prove the knowledge of secret key sk to a public key $pk := g^{sk}$ while signing an address. We can see that the languages in the two functionalities can be summarized as $\mathcal{L}_{\mathsf{DLOG}} := \{X \mid \exists\, x,\ \text{s.t.}\ X = g^x\}$. Therefore, $\mathcal{F}_{\mathsf{NIZK}}^{\mathsf{zero}}$ and $\mathcal{F}_{\mathsf{SoK}}^{\mathsf{key}}$ can be securely realized based on the Σ-protocol for proving knowledge of a discrete logarithm shown in Fig. 13. More specifically, for $\mathcal{F}_{\mathsf{NIZK}}^{\mathsf{zero}}$, X is the excess part, and x is the corresponding discrete logarithm. By using Fiat-Shamir transform [20], the interactive protocol in Fig. 13 can be converted into a non-interactive one where the challenge c is generated by a random oracle with (X, R) as the input. In practice, the random oracle will be instantiated by a hash function. Obviously, when X is pk and x is sk, the protocol in Fig. 13 can be used to prove the knowledge of a spending key, and can also be transformed to a non-interactive protocol by using Fiat-Shamir transform. At this point, we obtain a protocol for zero-knowledge proof of spending key. Next, we need to transform it into a protocol for signature of knowledge. Much work (e.g., [5,14]) has proved that the Fiat-Shamir transform can also be used to convert a public-coin proof of

Prover $(X = g^x, x)$		Verifier (X)
$r \xleftarrow{\$} \mathbb{Z}_p, R := g^r$	$\xrightarrow{\quad R \quad}$	$c \xleftarrow{\$} \mathbb{Z}_p$
	$\xleftarrow{\quad c \quad}$	
$z := c \cdot x + r$	$\xrightarrow{\quad z \quad}$	if $g^z = X^c R,\ b := 1$ else, $b := 0$

Fig. 13. Interactive Zero-knowledge proof of a discrete logarithm.

knowledge into a signature scheme by taking the message to be signed as the part of input to random oracle. More concretely, in our protocol, the excess part $\tilde{E}_i$ will be input to the random oracle along with (X, R). Therefore, we obtain the protocol that can securely realize $\mathcal{F}_{\mathsf{SoK}}^{\mathsf{key}}$.

Like other privacy-preserving cryptocurrencies, we also leverage Bulletproof [12] to generate range proofs. As mentioned in [12], Bulletproof is a public-coin proof of knowledge, and thus Bulletproof can also be converted into a non-interactive scheme by using Fiat-Shamir transform. Similarly, based on Bulletproof, we can obtain the protocol to securely realize $\mathcal{F}_{\mathsf{SoK}}^{\mathsf{range}}$ by taking the message to be signed (i.e., the address of each output coin in our Π_{NiACS}) as the part of input to random oracle.

The new variant of ElGamal proposed in this work can allow the receiver to obtain the value and randomness of a commitment by decryption, but the ciphertext needs to be generated using a hash function. Likewise, the one-time address and its auxiliary string are generated by using hash function. Hence, we cannot use Σ-protocol to realize $\mathcal{F}_{\mathsf{NIZK}}^{\mathsf{enc}}$ and $\mathcal{F}_{\mathsf{NIZK}}^{\mathsf{addr}}$. We need to use the general-purpose zk-SNARK [9,25,38,43].

UC Setting. The above protocols only securely realize the corresponding ideal functionalities in the stand-alone setting. Next, we discuss how to transform the above protocols to achieve UC security.

As for the Σ-protocol, we can use the compiler proposed by Camenisch et al. [13] to transform them to realize UC-security. The known practical instantiations (e.g., [9,25,38,43]) for SNARK also do not UC-realize $\mathcal{F}_{\mathsf{NIZK}}$ as they cannot satisfy Black-Box Simulation Extractability. Like other works, e.g. Hawk [31], Gyges [27], Ouroboros Crypsinous [28], we can also leverage the C∅C∅ framework proposed by Kosba et al. [30] to achieve Black-Box Simulation Extractability (namely, SSE-NIZK) in the standard CRS model.

6   Performance Analysis

In this section, we first give a performance estimation of our Π_{NiACS} where $\mathcal{F}_{\mathsf{NIZK}}$ and $\mathcal{F}_{\mathsf{SoK}}$ are achieved in the stand-alone setting. Then, we compare our Π_{NiACS} with Mimblewimble [39] and the work by Fuchsbauer et al. [22].

Table 2. Performance estimation and comparison.

	Spending time	Verifying time	TX size
[39]	$(2m+2) \cdot \exp + H + m \cdot T_{\text{range}}^{\text{P}}$	$3 \cdot \exp + H + m \cdot T_{\text{range}}^{\text{V}}$	$(m+n+2) \cdot |\mathbb{G}| + 2 \cdot |\mathbb{Z}_p|$ $+ m \cdot |\pi^{\text{range}}|$
[22]	$(4n+6m+3) \cdot \exp$ $+(2n+3m+1) \cdot H+$ $m \cdot (T_{\text{range}}^{\text{P}} + T_{\text{addr}}^{\text{P}} + T_{\text{enc}}^{\text{P}})$	$(3n+5) \cdot \exp + (n+1) \cdot H+$ $m \cdot (T_{\text{range}}^{\text{V}} + T_{\text{addr}}^{\text{V}} + T_{\text{enc}}^{\text{V}})$	$(3n+4m+3) \cdot |\mathbb{G}|$ $+(n+m+3) \cdot |\mathbb{Z}_p|$ $+ m \cdot (|\pi^{\text{range}}| + |\pi^{\text{addr}}| + |\pi^{\text{enc}}|)$
Π_{NiACS}	$(4n+7m+1) \cdot \exp$ $+(3n+2m) \cdot H+$ $m \cdot (T_{\text{range}}^{\text{P}} + T_{\text{addr}}^{\text{P}} + T_{\text{enc}}^{\text{P}})$	$(4n+1) \cdot \exp + 2n \cdot H+$ $m \cdot (T_{\text{range}}^{\text{V}} + T_{\text{addr}}^{\text{V}} + T_{\text{enc}}^{\text{V}})$	$(5n+4m) \cdot |\mathbb{G}|$ $+(2n+1) \cdot |\mathbb{Z}_p|$ $+ m \cdot (|\pi^{\text{range}}| + |\pi^{\text{addr}}| + |\pi^{\text{enc}}|)$

n: the number of input coins; m: the number of output coins; $\exp$: an exponentiation operation in group $\mathbb{G}$ with prime order p; H: a hash function; $|\mathbb{G}|$: the length of element in group $\mathbb{G}$; $|\mathbb{Z}_p|$: the length of element in $\mathbb{Z}_p$; $T_{\text{x}}^{\text{P/V}}$: the time to generate/verify a proof for language $\mathcal{L}_{\text{x}}$ ($\text{x} \in \{\text{range}, \text{addr}, \text{enc}\}$); $|\pi^{\text{x}}|$: the length of proof for language $\mathcal{L}_{\text{x}}$ ($\text{x} \in \{\text{range}, \text{addr}, \text{enc}\}$); The costs marked in blue are not necessary against rational adversaries; The costs marked in gray are not actually mentioned in [22], but they are necessary against malicious adversaries.

6.1 Performance Estimation

According to the instantiations described above, we give a performance estimation in Table 2. More specifically, according to the results shown in [12], the proving time $T_{\text{range}}^{\text{P}}$ for range $[0, 2^{64}]$ is 29ms while the verification time $T_{\text{range}}^{\text{V}}$ is 3.9ms. The range proof size π^{range} is 675 bytes. For the languages $\mathcal{L}_{\text{addr}} := \{(pk, R) \mid \exists (\text{Addr}, r)\}$ and $\mathcal{L}_{\text{enc}} := \{(pk, (X, \text{cm})) \mid \exists (r, v), \text{ s.t. } X = pk^r, \text{cm} = g^{H(g^r)} h^v\}$, we use the scheme in [25], a general-purpose zk-SNARK, to generate the proofs, and thus the proof sizes $|\pi_{\text{addr}}|$ and $|\pi_{\text{enc}}|$ are both $2\mathbb{G}_1 + \mathbb{G}_2$. The corresponding proving time ($T_{\text{addr}}^{\text{P}}$ and $T_{\text{enc}}^{\text{P}}$) and verification time ($T_{\text{addr}}^{\text{V}}$ and $T_{\text{enc}}^{\text{V}}$) mainly depend on the number of constraints. Concretely, we implement the hash function in $\mathcal{L}_{\text{addr}}$ and $\mathcal{L}_{\text{enc}}$ by using MiMCHash-256. The number of constraints required by $\mathcal{L}_{\text{addr}}$ and $\mathcal{L}_{\text{enc}}$ is $11,742$ and $14,799$, respectively[7]. Moreover, in practice, the proofs for $\mathcal{L}_{\text{addr}}$ and $\mathcal{L}_{\text{enc}}$ are not necessary as explained below, and we mark the corresponding costs in blue.

In the security analysis in Sect. 4.4, we assume that the adversary will have malicious behaviors arbitrarily. However, it is reasonable to assume that the adversary is rational in practice. As mentioned in [24], a rational adversary is expected to act in a utility-maximizing way. The costs marked in blue are related to $\mathcal{F}_{\text{NIZK}}^{\text{addr}}$ and $\mathcal{F}_{\text{NIZK}}^{\text{enc}}$, which are used to ensure that the one-time address and ciphertext are correctly generated for the receiver, respectively. The receiver in practice can identify if the one-time address and ciphertext are valid without the proofs, and if not, the receiver can abort the deal (e.g., refuse to send the goods), and thus can not be harmed. Moreover, the sender cannot benefit from it. Therefore, a rational adversary will not carry out this malicious behavior. Obviously, the receiver can identify if a one-time address is valid by invoking

---

[7] If zk-SNARK is transformed to SSE-NIZK by using the framework in [30], the number of constraints required by $\mathcal{L}_{\text{addr}}$ and $\mathcal{L}_{\text{enc}}$ will increase to about $71,742$ and $74,799$, respectively.

GENOTKEY. Next, we will explain how the receiver identifies whether a ciphertext is generated correctly.

If a transaction containing ciphertext (X^*, Y) can be confirmed, Y must be a valid commitment due to our design, i.e., $Y = g^\alpha h^v$. If X^* associated with Y is generated correctly, denoted as X, the receiver can recover (α, v) by computing $\alpha := H(X^{\frac{1}{sk}}), h^v := Y/g^\alpha$ and recovering v from h^v where $v \in [0, 2^{64}]$. Otherwise, i.e., $X^* = X' \neq X$, the receiver will obtain $\alpha' = H(X'^{\frac{1}{sk}}) \neq \alpha$ and $h^{v'} = Y/g^{\alpha'} = g^{\alpha-\alpha'} h^v$. Due to the random oracle, $h^{v'}$ is randomly distributed and so the probability of $v' \in [0, 2^{64}]$ is $\frac{2^{64}}{2^{256}}$, which is negligible. Therefore, the receiver can recognize the invalid ciphertext by checking if $v \in [0, 2^{64}]$.

6.2   Comparison

We also give the performance estimations of Mimblewimble [39] and the non-interactive solution proposed independently and concurrently by Fuchsbauer et al. [22] in Table 2. It can be seen that both our work and Fuchsbauer et al. [22] degrade performance to achieve non-interaction, and the performances of the two non-interactive solutions are comparable. As for our work, besides introducing addresses and related proofs, the main reason leading to a higher cost is that our protocol needs to split the excess into multiple parts. Similarly, Fuchsbauer et al. [22] also introduce addresses and related proofs. Although they do not split the excess, they add a doubling key for each one-time address, thus resulting in the comparable additional cost. In a nutshell, the two non-interactive solutions are more suitable for the scenarios where non-interaction is strongly desirable. Nevertheless, designing a non-interaction version without degrading performance is still a challenging problem.

Acknowledgements. We would like to thank the anonymous reviewers for their insightful suggestions and comments. This work was supported in part by the National Key Research and Development Project 2020YFA0712300 and the National Natural Science Foundation of China (Grant No. 62272294). Hong-Sheng Zhou acknowledges support by NSF grant CNS-1801470, a Google Faculty Research Award and a research gift from Ergo Platform.

References

1. Beam documentation. https://documentation.beam.mw/
2. Grin documentation. https://docs.grin.mw/wiki/transactions/contracts/
3. Mwc documentation. https://www.mwc.mw/docs
4. Solving unconfirmed bitcoin transactions in electrum. https://data-dive.com/unconfirmed-bitcoin-transactions-electrum
5. Abdalla, M., An, J.H., Bellare, M., Namprempre, C.: From identification to signatures via the fiat-shamir transform: minimizing assumptions for security and forward-security. In: Knudsen, L.R. (ed.) EUROCRYPT 2002. LNCS, vol. 2332, pp. 418–433. Springer, Heidelberg (2002). https://doi.org/10.1007/3-540-46035-7_28

6. Androulaki, E., Karame, G.O., Roeschlin, M., Scherer, T., Capkun, S.: Evaluating user privacy in bitcoin. In: Sadeghi, A.-R. (ed.) FC 2013. LNCS, vol. 7859, pp. 34–51. Springer, Heidelberg (2013). https://doi.org/10.1007/978-3-642-39884-1_4

7. Badertscher, C., Maurer, U., Tschudi, D., Zikas, V.: Bitcoin as a transaction ledger: a composable treatment. In: Katz, J., Shacham, H. (eds.) CRYPTO 2017. LNCS, vol. 10401, pp. 324–356. Springer, Cham (2017). https://doi.org/10.1007/978-3-319-63688-7_11

8. Ben-Sasson, E., et al.: Zerocash: decentralized anonymous payments from bitcoin. In: 2014 IEEE Symposium on Security and Privacy, pp. 459–474. IEEE Computer Society Press (2014). https://doi.org/10.1109/SP.2014.36

9. Ben-Sasson, E., Chiesa, A., Genkin, D., Tromer, E., Virza, M.: SNARKs for C: verifying program executions succinctly and in zero knowledge. In: Canetti, R., Garay, J.A. (eds.) CRYPTO 2013. LNCS, vol. 8043, pp. 90–108. Springer, Heidelberg (2013). https://doi.org/10.1007/978-3-642-40084-1_6

10. Bonneau, J., Narayanan, A., Miller, A., Clark, J., Kroll, J.A., Felten, E.W.: Mixcoin: anonymity for bitcoin with accountable mixes. In: Christin, N., Safavi-Naini, R. (eds.) FC 2014. LNCS, vol. 8437, pp. 486–504. Springer, Heidelberg (2014). https://doi.org/10.1007/978-3-662-45472-5_31

11. Bünz, B., Agrawal, S., Zamani, M., Boneh, D.: Zether: towards privacy in a smart contract world. In: Bonneau, J., Heninger, N. (eds.) FC 2020. LNCS, vol. 12059, pp. 423–443. Springer, Cham (2020). https://doi.org/10.1007/978-3-030-51280-4_23

12. Bünz, B., Bootle, J., Boneh, D., Poelstra, A., Wuille, P., Maxwell, G.: Bulletproofs: short proofs for confidential transactions and more. In: 2018 IEEE Symposium on Security and Privacy, pp. 315–334. IEEE Computer Society Press (2018). https://doi.org/10.1109/SP.2018.00020

13. Camenisch, J., Krenn, S., Shoup, V.: A framework for practical universally composable zero-knowledge protocols. In: Lee, D.H., Wang, X. (eds.) ASIACRYPT 2011. LNCS, vol. 7073, pp. 449–467. Springer, Heidelberg (2011). https://doi.org/10.1007/978-3-642-25385-0_24

14. Camenisch, J., Stadler, M.: Efficient group signature schemes for large groups. In: Kaliski, B.S. (ed.) CRYPTO 1997. LNCS, vol. 1294, pp. 410–424. Springer, Heidelberg (1997). https://doi.org/10.1007/BFb0052252

15. Chase, M., Lysyanskaya, A.: On signatures of knowledge. In: Dwork, C. (ed.) CRYPTO 2006. LNCS, vol. 4117, pp. 78–96. Springer, Heidelberg (2006). https://doi.org/10.1007/11818175_5

16. Chen, Yu., Ma, X., Tang, C., Au, M.H.: PGC: decentralized confidential payment system with auditability. In: Chen, L., Li, N., Liang, K., Schneider, S. (eds.) ESORICS 2020. LNCS, vol. 12308, pp. 591–610. Springer, Cham (2020). https://doi.org/10.1007/978-3-030-58951-6_29

17. Esgin, M.F., Zhao, R.K., Steinfeld, R., Liu, J.K., Liu, D.: MatRiCT: efficient, scalable and post-quantum blockchain confidential transactions protocol. In: Cavallaro, L., Kinder, J., Wang, X., Katz, J. (eds.) ACM CCS 2019, pp. 567–584. ACM Press (2019). https://doi.org/10.1145/3319535.3354200

18. Fanti, G., et al.: Dandelion++: lightweight cryptocurrency networking with formal anonymity guarantees (2018)

19. Fauzi, P., Meiklejohn, S., Mercer, R., Orlandi, C.: Quisquis: a new design for anonymous cryptocurrencies. In: Galbraith, S.D., Moriai, S. (eds.) ASIACRYPT 2019. LNCS, vol. 11921, pp. 649–678. Springer, Cham (2019). https://doi.org/10.1007/978-3-030-34578-5_23

20. Fiat, A., Shamir, A.: How to prove yourself: practical solutions to identification and signature problems. In: Odlyzko, A.M. (ed.) CRYPTO 1986. LNCS, vol. 263, pp. 186–194. Springer, Heidelberg (1987). https://doi.org/10.1007/3-540-47721-7_12

21. Fuchsbauer, G., Orrù, M., Seurin, Y.: Aggregate cash systems: a cryptographic investigation of mimblewimble. In: Ishai, Y., Rijmen, V. (eds.) EUROCRYPT 2019. LNCS, vol. 11476, pp. 657–689. Springer, Cham (2019). https://doi.org/10.1007/978-3-030-17653-2_22

22. Fuchsbauer, G., Orrù, M.: Non-interactive mimblewimble transactions, revisited. Cryptology ePrint Archive, Paper 2022/265 (2022). https://eprint.iacr.org/2022/265

23. Garman, C., Green, M., Miers, I.: Accountable privacy for decentralized anonymous payments. In: Grossklags, J., Preneel, B. (eds.) FC 2016. LNCS, vol. 9603, pp. 81–98. Springer, Heidelberg (2017). https://doi.org/10.1007/978-3-662-54970-4_5

24. Groce, A., Katz, J., Thiruvengadam, A., Zikas, V.: Byzantine agreement with a rational adversary. In: Czumaj, A., Mehlhorn, K., Pitts, A., Wattenhofer, R. (eds.) ICALP 2012. LNCS, vol. 7392, pp. 561–572. Springer, Heidelberg (2012). https://doi.org/10.1007/978-3-642-31585-5_50

25. Groth, J.: On the size of pairing-based non-interactive arguments. In: Fischlin, M., Coron, J.-S. (eds.) EUROCRYPT 2016. LNCS, vol. 9666, pp. 305–326. Springer, Heidelberg (2016). https://doi.org/10.1007/978-3-662-49896-5_11

26. Jedusor, T.E.: Mimblewimble (2016). https://download.wpsoftware.net/bitcoin/wizardry/mimblewimble.txt

27. Juels, A., Kosba, A.E., Shi, E.: The ring of Gyges: investigating the future of criminal smart contracts. In: Weippl, E.R., Katzenbeisser, S., Kruegel, C., Myers, A.C., Halevi, S. (eds.) ACM CCS 2016, pp. 283–295. ACM Press (2016). https://doi.org/10.1145/2976749.2978362

28. Kerber, T., Kiayias, A., Kohlweiss, M., Zikas, V.: Ouroboros crypsinous: privacy-preserving proof-of-stake. In: 2019 IEEE Symposium on Security and Privacy, pp. 157–174. IEEE Computer Society Press (2019). https://doi.org/10.1109/SP.2019.00063

29. Kiayias, A., Zhou, H.-S., Zikas, V.: Fair and robust multi-party computation using a global transaction ledger. In: Fischlin, M., Coron, J.-S. (eds.) EUROCRYPT 2016. LNCS, vol. 9666, pp. 705–734. Springer, Heidelberg (2016). https://doi.org/10.1007/978-3-662-49896-5_25

30. Kosba, A., et al.: How to use SNARKs in universally composable protocols. Cryptology ePrint Archive, Report 2015/1093 (2015). http://eprint.iacr.org/2015/1093

31. Kosba, A.E., Miller, A., Shi, E., Wen, Z., Papamanthou, C.: Hawk: the blockchain model of cryptography and privacy-preserving smart contracts. In: 2016 IEEE Symposium on Security and Privacy, pp. 839–858. IEEE Computer Society Press (2016). https://doi.org/10.1109/SP.2016.55

32. Koshy, P., Koshy, D., McDaniel, P.: An analysis of anonymity in bitcoin using P2P network traffic. In: Christin, N., Safavi-Naini, R. (eds.) FC 2014. LNCS, vol. 8437, pp. 469–485. Springer, Heidelberg (2014). https://doi.org/10.1007/978-3-662-45472-5_30

33. Lai, R.W.F., Ronge, V., Ruffing, T., Schröder, D., Thyagarajan, S.A.K., Wang, J.: Omniring: scaling private payments without trusted setup. In: Cavallaro, L., Kinder, J., Wang, X., Katz, J. (eds.) ACM CCS 2019, pp. 31–48. ACM Press (2019). https://doi.org/10.1145/3319535.3345655

34. Lindell, Y.: Tutorial on secure multi-party computation (2003). http://www.cs.biu.ac.il/lindell/research-statements/tutorial-secure-computation.ppt

35. Lindell, Y.: Survey: secure composition of multiparty protocols (2005). http://www.cs.biu.ac.il/lindell/research-statements/survey-composition-40-min-05.ppt
36. Meiklejohn, S., et al.: A fistful of bitcoins: characterizing payments among men with no names. Commun. ACM **59**(4), 86–93 (2016). https://doi.org/10.1145/2896384, https://doi.org/10.1145/2896384
37. Noether, S.: Ring signature confidential transactions for monero. Cryptology ePrint Archive, Report 2015/1098 (2015). http://eprint.iacr.org/2015/1098
38. Parno, B., Howell, J., Gentry, C., Raykova, M.: Pinocchio: nearly practical verifiable computation. In: 2013 IEEE Symposium on Security and Privacy, pp. 238–252. IEEE Computer Society Press (2013). https://doi.org/10.1109/SP.2013.47
39. Poelstra, A.: Mimblewimble (2016). https://download.wpsoftware.net/bitcoin/wizardry/mimblewimble.pdf
40. Ron, D., Shamir, A.: Quantitative analysis of the full bitcoin transaction graph. In: Sadeghi, A.-R. (ed.) FC 2013. LNCS, vol. 7859, pp. 6–24. Springer, Heidelberg (2013). https://doi.org/10.1007/978-3-642-39884-1_2
41. Ruffing, T., Moreno-Sanchez, P., Kate, A.: CoinShuffle: practical decentralized coin mixing for bitcoin. In: Kutyłowski, M., Vaidya, J. (eds.) ESORICS 2014. LNCS, vol. 8713, pp. 345–364. Springer, Cham (2014). https://doi.org/10.1007/978-3-319-11212-1_20
42. Sun, S.-F., Au, M.H., Liu, J.K., Yuen, T.H.: RingCT 2.0: a compact accumulator-based (linkable ring signature) protocol for blockchain cryptocurrency monero. In: Foley, S.N., Gollmann, D., Snekkenes, E. (eds.) ESORICS 2017. LNCS, vol. 10493, pp. 456–474. Springer, Cham (2017). https://doi.org/10.1007/978-3-319-66399-9_25
43. Wahby, R.S., Setty, S.T.V., Ren, Z., Blumberg, A.J., Walfish, M.: Efficient RAM and control flow in verifiable outsourced computation. In: NDSS 2015. The Internet Society (2015)
44. Yu, G.: Mimblewimble non-interactive transaction scheme. Cryptology ePrint Archive, Paper 2020/1064 (2020). https://eprint.iacr.org/2020/1064
45. Yuen, T.H., et al.: RingCT 3.0 for blockchain confidential transaction: shorter size and stronger security. In: Bonneau, J., Heninger, N. (eds.) FC 2020. LNCS, vol. 12059, pp. 464–483. Springer, Cham (2020). https://doi.org/10.1007/978-3-030-51280-4_25

Practical Provably Secure Flooding
for Blockchains

Chen-Da Liu-Zhang[1] [ID], Christian Matt[2] [ID], Ueli Maurer[3], Guilherme Rito[3] [ID], and Søren Eller Thomsen[4]([✉]) [ID]

[1] NTT Research, Sunnyvale, USA
chen-da.liuzhang@ntt-research.com
[2] Concordium, Zurich, Switzerland
cm@concordium.com
[3] Department of Computer Science, ETH Zurich, Zurich, Switzerland
{maurer,gteixeir}@inf.ethz.ch
[4] Concordium Blockchain Research Center, Aarhus University, Aarhus, Denmark
sethomsen@cs.au.dk

Abstract. In recent years, permisionless blockchains have received a lot of attention both from industry and academia, where substantial effort has been spent to develop consensus protocols that are secure under the assumption that less than half (or a third) of a given resource (e.g., stake or computing power) is controlled by corrupted parties. The security proofs of these consensus protocols usually assume the availability of a network functionality guaranteeing that a block sent by an honest party is received by all honest parties within some bounded time. To obtain an overall protocol that is secure under the same corruption assumption, it is therefore necessary to combine the consensus protocol with a network protocol that achieves this property under that assumption. In practice, however, the underlying network is typically implemented by flooding protocols that are not proven to be secure in the setting where a fraction of the considered total weight can be corrupted. This has led to many so-called eclipse attacks on existing protocols and tailor-made fixes against specific attacks.

To close this apparent gap, we present the first practical flooding protocol that provably delivers sent messages to all honest parties after a logarithmic number of steps. We prove security in the setting where all parties are publicly assigned a positive weight and the adversary can corrupt parties accumulating up to a constant fraction of the total weight. This can directly be used in the proof-of-stake setting, but is not limited to it. To prove the security of our protocol, we combine known results about the diameter of Erdős–Rényi graphs with reductions between different types of random graphs. We further show that the efficiency of our protocol is asymptotically optimal.

The practicality of our protocol is supported by extensive simulations for different numbers of parties, weight distributions, and corruption strategies. The simulations confirm our theoretical results and show that messages are delivered quickly regardless of the weight distribution, whereas protocols that are oblivious of the parties' weights completely

© International Association for Cryptologic Research 2022
S. Agrawal and D. Lin (Eds.): ASIACRYPT 2022, LNCS 13791, pp. 774–805, 2022.
https://doi.org/10.1007/978-3-031-22963-3_26

fail if the weights are unevenly distributed. Furthermore, the average message complexity per party of our protocol is within a small constant factor of such a protocol.

Keywords: Flooding networks · Peer-to-peer networks · Blockchain · Network layer · Multicast

1 Introduction

1.1 Motivation

Since Nakamoto proposed the first decentralized permisionless blockchain protocol [32], a significant line of works has been done. In such protocols, one considers a setting where different parties are weighted according to how much of a resource they own (mining power, stake, space, etc.), and security relies on the fact that a certain fraction of the total weight (typically more than the majority, or two thirds) is owned by the honest parties.

Current blockchain protocols typically are proven secure assuming the availability of a *multicast* network, which allows each party to distribute a value among the parties within some delivery time Δ (see e.g. [3,12,14–16,20,34,36]). However, very little attention has been devoted to the construction of provably secure multicast networks themselves.

In practice, the multicast network is typically implemented via a message-diffusion mechanism, where in order for a party P to distribute a message, P sends the message to a subset of its neighbors, who then forward the message to their neighbors and so on. The idea is that if the graph induced by the honest parties is connected, the message will reach all the honest parties, and if the graph has low diameter, it will reach all honest parties after only a few iterations. Indeed, there have been works that study how to randomly select the neighbors so that the induced graph remains connected with small diameter after removing corrupted nodes (see e.g. [24,30,37]).

Unfortunately, to the best of our knowledge, currently analyzed diffusion mechanisms do not consider weighted parties, and therefore can only be proven secure when a certain constant fraction of the parties is honest (in particular it is not enough to assume a fraction of the total weight is owned by honest parties). This means that when such a message diffusion mechanism is used to build a blockchain, the overall protocol relies on *both* the constant-honest-fraction-of-weight assumption *and* the constant-honest-fraction-of-parties assumption.

Note that for a fixed weight distribution, a bound on the corrupted weight also implies a bound on the number of parties that can be corrupted, where this maximum is achieved by greedily corrupting parties with the least weight first. Hence, current multicast protocols could in principle also be used assuming only a bound on the corrupted weight. However, the message complexity of such protocols is inversely proportional to the guaranteed honesty ratio. That is, to still guarantee security under more corrupted parties, the remaining parties have

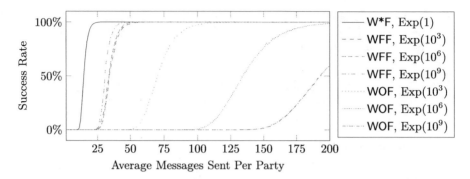

Fig. 1. Comparison of our WFF protocol with a weight oblivious protocol WOF that chooses a fix number of random neighbors independently of their weight. The simulations are for $n = 1024$ parties with exponential weight distributions $\text{Exp}(r)$ where the heaviest party's weight is r times the lightest party's weight. Note that for $\text{Exp}(1)$, WFF and WOF are identical. For each setting, we consider a 50% corruption threshold, and a greedy corruption strategy where lighter parties are corrupted first. Each simulation was repeated 10 000 times and the success rate measures how often all parties received a single sent message.

to send to more neighbors. In particular, this means that in many of the current weight distributions where there are very few people owning a large fraction of the total weight, but thousands of parties owning a tiny little fraction of the weight, the incurred concrete message complexity to achieve security significantly blows up (see an example in Fig. 1, where even for large sizes of neighborhood sizes, the protocol fails).

The need for a practically efficient multicast network secure solely relying on the constant-honest-fraction-of-weight assumption is therefore apparent.

1.2   Our Contributions

In this work, we investigate provably secure protocols that implement a multicast network for the weighted setting, relying solely on the constant-honest-fraction-of-weight assumption. Additionally, we are interested in protocols that are concretely efficient. In short, we explore the following natural questions:

Is there a provably secure multicast protocol in the weighted setting, assuming only a constant fraction of honest weight? And if so, is there a practically efficient one?

We answer both of these questions in the affirmative by presenting the first multicast protocol WFF (weighted fan-out flooding) that relies solely on the constant-honest-fraction-of-weight assumption, and evaluate its practical efficiency by performing various simulations. More concretely, we prove the following theorem:

Theorem 1 (Informal). *Let κ be a security parameter, n be the number of parties, and $\gamma \in [0,1]$ be the fraction of the total weight that is guaranteed to belong to honest parties. Further, let $\delta_{Channel}$ be an upper bound on the delays of the underlying point-to-point channels. Then, WFF is a secure flooding protocol with maximal delay $\Delta := \left(7 \cdot \log\left(\frac{6n}{\log(n)+\kappa}\right)+2\right) \cdot \delta_{Channel}$ and message complexity $2n \cdot \frac{\log(n)+\kappa}{\gamma}$.*

Note that the maximum delay and the message complexity in the theorem are independent of the weight distribution. By naturally assigning the weights to corresponding stake quantities, the achieved guarantees match those required in previous proof-of-stake blockchain protocols (see e.g. [12,15,16]), and therefore our protocol can be used to build a blockchain protocol from point-to-point channels without the need for any additional assumption apart from those needed in the blockchain protocol itself.

Asymptotic Optimality and Practicality. Our protocol has the property that 1) parties accumulating large amounts of weight need to send to more parties, and 2) the number of parties that each party sends to increases logarithmically in the total number of parties. We prove that both properties are inherent for secure flooding protocols, meaning that Theorem 1 is asymptotically optimal. Concretely, for the first point, if a small set S (say, of constant size) accumulates more than a γ-fraction of the weight, then this set necessarily needs to send at least to a linear number $\Theta(n)$ of parties.

This means it is undesirable to have parties with very small weight and also to have parties with a huge weight. A simple way to mitigate this in practice is to exclude parties with less than $W_{\min}$ weight and cap the maximal weight to $W_{\max}$. This means if we use the flooding for a proof-of-stake blockchain, that parties with a huge amount of stake need to split their stake over several nodes such that none has more than $W_{\max}$ weight. Parties with very little stake can still obtain data from other nodes by requesting data from them periodically. We discuss this further below.

Simulations. We use simulations to evaluate the practicality of our provably secure protocol. The simulations confirm our theoretical results and also show that our protocol is practical: Messages are diffused quickly to all parties with high success probability even when weights are unevenly distributed. On the other hand, as our simulations also show, prior protocols—oblivious of the parties' weights—fail completely for neighborhood sizes for which our provably secure protocol succeeds (see Fig. 1). This in particular means that our protocol achieves the necessary security guarantees considerably fewer number of messages than current (weight-oblivious) protocols.

1.3 Model and Assumptions

Network and Corruption Model. We assume all parties have access to an underlying network that allows them to establish point-to-point channels to other parties. We further assume each party p is publicly assigned a weight $W_p > 0$ and an adversary can corrupt parties accumulating at most a constant fraction $1 - \gamma$ of the total weight. For simplicity, we consider static corruptions in our proofs, but using the techniques from [30], all our results can be extended to security against delayed adaptive adversaries (adversaries for which there is a delay from the time they decide to corrupt a party until the party is effectively controlled by the adversary). Intuitively, if a corruption takes longer than the duration from the earliest point in time an adversary can learn the neighbors of a party till the neighbors are guaranteed to have resent the message to other parties, then adaptivity does not help the adversary prevent delivery of any messages. However, there is significant overhead involved in proving this because the adversary can still dynamically decide how many parties are left to guarantee delivery for. This is why we only present proofs for a static adversary and refer to [30] for techniques for how to prove such statement.

Realising Public Weights from Resource Assumptions. Proof-of-stake blockchains rely on a constant fraction of the stake being honest (typically more than $1/2$ [14,15] or more than $2/3$ [12]). Furthermore, a blockchain itself provides a ledger accessible by all parties describing how much stake each party owns. Hence, it is immediate how to assign weights to parties by simply accessing the ledger in order to instantiate the weights for our protocols.

To achieve a weight distribution for blockchain protocols that rely on a constant fraction of the computational resources being honest [20,34–36] one can make use of the techniques for committee selection for such setting [35,36]. The idea behind this is that for long fragments of a chain with high chain-quality, the distribution of block creators is similar to the distribution of computational resources among parties. Hence, this distribution translates directly to a weight distribution publicly available to all parties. For techniques to achieve a high chain-quality, see [34].

Delivery to Zero-Weight Parties. While we assume that all parties have positive weight and parties with zero weight cannot contribute to the security of the protocol, it is still desirable in practice to allow such parties to obtain the state of the system. This can be achieved, e.g., by letting such parties fetch missing data from other nodes. We discuss some options in the full version of this work [26].

Static Versus Dynamic Weight. For simplicity, we consider for this paper the static-weight setting, in which the weight of all parties remains fixed. When weight is instantiated with the stake in a proof-of-stake, this might appear unrealistic. This is, however, not a real limitation of our protocol when combined with such a blockchain. For example in [15], to prove their protocol secure for a dynamic stake, the authors divide time into epochs where the stake used for producing blocks remains unchanged and additionally make assumptions on the speed that stake can between epochs. In their proofs, they note that all parties agree on the stake distribution in a previous epoch. We note that our proofs only rely on the weight being static for the propagation of a single message, and the time it takes to propagate a message is very small compared to such epochs.

Practicality of Complete Network. We note that the assumption that any two parties can establish a point-to-point connection between each other is indeed a reasonable assumption, e.g., in the proof-of-stake setting: Parties who want to participate in the protocol first need to register their node, see, e.g., [6]. This registration process can include the node's IP address and further required information that allows other nodes to establish a connection with that node.

1.4   Technical Overview

Flooding Protocol Skeleton. Our protocol follows the basic structure of previous flooding protocols: When a party p receive a message m for the first time, p samples a set of neighbors N from the party set $\mathcal{P}$, according to some probability distribution $\mathcal{N}_p$. The party then forwards the message m to all parties in N. The crucial variable of this protocol is the distribution $\mathcal{N}_p$, i.e., how parties select their peers.

Remark 1. In most practical blockchain implementations, parties do not resample their peers for every message, but keep the connections over an extended period of time [22,29]. We note that our protocol can also be used in such a fashion and all our results can be translated to such a setting. The reason for resampling peers often is that against a delayed adaptive adversary [30], security can only be guaranteed if the corruption delay is longer than the time peers keep their connections. Hence, resampling more often provides better security guarantees.

Dependency of Neighborhood Selection on Weight Distribution. It is clear that to achieve efficient results, one must make use of the overall weight distribution to decide whether a party p_i forwards the message to party p_j. What is perhaps less clear, is what the required *amount* of dependency is. We here argue intuitively that the neighborhood selection must depend (at least) on both the weights of p_i and p_j: Consider a weight distribution where p_i's weight is overwhelming, and there are many parties with very little weight (including p_j). In this case, the adversary has corruption budget to corrupt all parties except for p_i and p_j. Therefore, in order to guarantee that an honest p_j receives the message, p_i must send to that party with probability 1. Consequently, the neighborhood selection distribution $\mathcal{N}_{p_i}$ must depend on p_i's weight. It follows via an analogous argument that p_i must send to p_j if the latter's weight is overwhelming. Hence, the probability to choose p_j in $\mathcal{N}_p$ must also depend on p_j's weight.

A Simple Inefficient Solution. From the above observations, we see that the neighborhood distribution must depend on both the weights W_i of p_i and W_j of p_j. A simple idea is to let each party p_i internally emulate W_{p_i} parties, and then run a traditional unweighted flooding protocol among $W = \sum_p W_p$ nodes, where two nodes are connected with some probability ρ. By properties of Erdős–Rényi graphs, this leads to a secure flooding protocol [30]. Note that the probability that a node from p_i is connected to a node from p_j depends on both weights W_{p_i} and W_{p_j}, namely $1 - (1 - \rho)^{W_{p_i} \cdot W_{p_j}}$.

However, the resulting protocol is highly inefficient, since it has a message complexity that depends on the total sum of the weights W, rather than the number of parties. Note that in current proof-of-stake systems, the total stake is in the order of billions, so any dependency on the total weight is highly undesirable.

Scaling Invariance. The simple protocol from above not only is inefficient if the total weight is large, it also has the undesirable property that the efficiency depends on the "unit" of the weight: If we multiply everybody's weight by 100, the overall number of messages increases substantially, even though this scaling has no effect on the possible corruptions. We thus postulate that practical protocols should be invariant under such weight scalings.

A simple fix seems to be to normalize the weight distribution by dividing every party's weight by the weight of the lightest party. This, however, introduces two issues: First, since the number of internally emulated nodes must be an integer, this division leads to rounding issues, with implications for the security argument. Secondly, introducing an additional extremely light party now has a massive impact on the efficiency, even though this additional party does not substantially change the possible corruptions.

A First Theoretical Protocol. Our first technical theoretical contribution is a new simple way to choose the neighbors in the flooding protocol. More precisely, we generalize the approach above and show that it is actually enough to emulate a number of nodes that is proportional to the total number of parties (rather than the total weight).

For that, we introduce the notion of an emulation-function $\mathrm{E} : \mathcal{P} \to \mathbb{N} \setminus \{0\}$. According to the emulation function, we let each party p internally emulate $\mathrm{E}(p) \geq 1$ different nodes, in a graph consisting of $n_{\mathrm{E}} := \sum_p \mathrm{E}(p)$ nodes. As explained above, the basic idea is to create an Erdős–Rényi graph on the emulated graph with n_{E} nodes and edge-probability ρ. Then, we say that a party p_i forwards the message to p_j if *any* of the emulated nodes from p_i is connected to *any* of the emulated nodes from p_j. This means that the probability that p_i forwards the message to p_j is $1 - (1 - \rho)^{\mathrm{E}(p_i) \cdot \mathrm{E}(p_j)}$.

We then consider the emulation function $\mathrm{E}(p) = \lceil \alpha_p \cdot n \rceil$, where α_p is p's fraction of the total weight. That is, we let each party emulate a number of nodes proportional to the number of parties scaled by the party's relative weight. Note that the ceiling ensure that each party emulates at least one node. We then prove that by choosing ρ appropriately such that the unweighted subgraph emulated by honest parties remains connected with low diameter, we obtain a flooding protocol with message complexity $O((\log(n) + \kappa) \cdot n \cdot \gamma^{-1})$ and time complexity $O(\log(n) \cdot \delta_{\mathrm{Channel}})$.

A Practical Protocol. Although the method described above is intuitive and gives us asymptotically good complexities, it is very far from being practical. In particular, the protocol requires every party to locally flip $\Omega(n)$ coins for each message. Similar to current protocols deployed in practice, we would like to have a protocol that instead chooses a *fixed* set of neighbors (possibly dependent on the weight distribution, but nothing else), and provide provable security for it.

We propose a protocol where each party p chooses to send to $K = k \cdot E(p) = k \cdot \lceil \alpha_p \cdot n \rceil$ distinct parties (for a parameter k), according to a weighted sampling without replacement [7]. More precisely, p chooses K parties, where the probability to choose a certain tuple[1] of parties $(q_1, \ldots, q_K)$ (among the set of parties $\mathcal{P} \setminus \{p\}$) is

$$\Pr[(q_1, \ldots, q_K)] = \prod_{i=1}^{K} \frac{E(q_i)}{n_E - E(p) - E(q_1) - \cdots - E(q_{i-1})}.$$

We show that this practical protocol has the same asymptotic guarantees as the first protocol above.

Importance of Emulation Function. Even though that this protocol is so simple that it can be described in a few lines, it is by no means trivial. In fact, it is crucial for the correctness of the protocol that the emulation function is used to determine both the number of neighbors *and* the distribution of these neighbors.

To see that it is crucial to use the emulation function to decide how many neighbors each party should choose, consider a small change to the protocol, namely send to $K = k \cdot \alpha_p \cdot n$ parties (instead of $K = k \cdot E(p)$). Now, consider a sender p with a small fraction of the total weight α_p, and let us estimate the parameter k to ensure that this p sends to at least one honest party. As any party potentially could be corrupt it must be that p sends to more than just one neighbor. Hence, it must be that $k > \frac{1}{\alpha_p \cdot n}$, just to ensure this very minimal requirement. A rough bound on the message complexity of such protocol would be $\sum_{p'} k \cdot \alpha_{p'} \cdot n > \frac{1}{\alpha_p}$, which is impractical if α_p is small.

To see that it is crucial to weigh the selection of neighbors with the emulation function, we consider another small change to the protocol, namely to select parties weighted by their weight instead of the emulation function. Now, consider a weight distribution where just one party p has a very small fraction of the total weight and all others having roughly equal weight. Note, that for any party choosing less than n neighbors the probability that p is chosen as a neighbor becomes arbitrarily small for a decreasing α_p. Hence, to ensure that p receives a message this would induce a quadratic message complexity which is impractical.

Security Proof. Proving security of such a protocol in the weighted setting directly is non-trivial for two reasons: First, the choices of whether to send to a neighbor or not are not independent. Secondly, the fact that the choices are

---

[1] The probability to choose the unordered neighborhood set $N = \{q_1, \ldots, q_K\}$ is the sum over the probabilities of all permuted tuples.

according to an arbitrary weight distribution makes the analysis considerably harder than traditional graph-theoretic results that consider the non-weighted setting. Instead of providing a direct graph-theoretic analysis, we give a security proof via a sequence of intermediate protocols, essentially relating the success probability of the first protocol above based on Erdős–Rényi graphs to the practical protocol. This leads to Theorem 1. Due to space constraints, many proofs are left out of this version. We refer to the full version of this paper [26] for these.

1.5   Current State of the Art and Related Work

Flooding Networks in a Byzantine Setting. [24] was the first to relate probabilistic gossiping to the connectivity of the induced graph. They considered $(1 - \gamma) \cdot n$ out of n parties failing and showed that each party needs to forward a message with probability $\rho > \frac{\log(n)+\kappa}{\gamma \cdot n}$ to any other party to ensure that messages are delivered to all non-failing parties with a probability overwhelming in κ.

[30] observed that against an adversary capable of adaptively corrupting up to t parties, any flooding network where each party sends to less than t neighbors is inherently insecure (an adversary can simply corrupt all neighbors of a sender). To mitigate this problem and achieve a protocol secure against a Byzantine adaptive adversary, [30] formalized the notion of a delayed adversary (informally introduced by [35]) for which there is a delay from the time the adversary decides to corrupt a party until the party is effectively controlled by the adversary. In this setting, they showed that against an adversary delayed for the time it takes to send a message plus the time it takes to resend a message, it is sufficient to on average send to $\Omega((\log(n) + \kappa) \cdot \gamma^{-1})$ neighbors to achieve a flooding protocol that with an overwhelming probability in κ has $O(\log(n))$ round complexity for n parties with at most $(1 - \gamma) \cdot n$ of the parties being corrupted. In this work, we match the theoretical performance of their flooding protocol with a practical protocol that only relies a γ fraction of the weight remaining honest, which is more relevant in the blockchain setting.

Kadcast [37] is a recent flooding protocol specifically designed for blockchains. Interestingly, they claim that structured networks are inherently more efficient than unstructured networks and propose a structured protocol with $O(\log n)$ neighbors and $O(\log n)$ steps to propagate a message, which is similar to what we achieve using an unstructured network. It is unclear how their protocol performs under Byzantine failures. Further, we note that structured networks are inherently vulnerable to attacks by adaptive adversaries.

A different line of work [27,28,31] considers how to propagate updates in a database using gossip where at most t of the processors may be corrupted. The setting is however different from ours as they assume that at least t honest parties get the update as input initially, and only updates input to some honest processor can be accepted by the other processors.

Probabilistic communication have also been used to improve the communication complexity for both multi-party-computation (MPC) [9] and Byzantine broadcast [39]. In [9], communication between honest parties is assumed to be hidden from the adversary. This is exploited by constructing a random communication network with an average polylogarithmic degree based on Erdős–Rényi graphs. They thereby achieve a MPC protocol with low communication locality that is secure against a fully adaptive adversary. [39] combines the classic broadcast protocol by Dolev and Strong [17] with gossiping based upon Erdős–Rényi-graphs to obtain the first broadcast algorithm with a sub-cubic communication complexity for a dishonest majority. Using similar techniques and assuming a trusted setup they also achieve an asymptotically optimal communication complexity for parallel broadcast.

A different line of work considers the problems of MPC and Agreement on incomplete communication networks [10,11,18,21,23,25,40]. To circumvent complexity bounds for fully adaptive adversaries, the seminal work of [18] introduced the problem of *almost-everywhere agreement* as a relaxation of agreement where not all nodes are required to be consistent, but a small number of nodes are allowed to be inconsistent. Since then, the relaxation has also been extended to MPC [21], and different aspects of solutions to this problem have been continuously improved [10,11,23,25,40]. Notably, [25] used probabilistic communication to increase the number of consistent parties, and [11] used Erdős–Rényi graphs with a diameter of 2 to obtain a construction secure not only against adaptive corruptions but also an adversary allowed to adaptively remove some communication links. In our work nodes are also of bounded degree, but contrary to this line of work we work in a slightly weaker adversarial model which allows us to ensure correctness for *all* parties.

Attacks on the Network Layers of Blockchains. Attacks on network layers of blockchains are not only a theoretical concern. In fact, several works [5,22,29,38] have shown that it has been possible to launch eclipsing attacks[2] against nodes in the Bitcoin network and the Ethereum network.

Bitcoin's peer-to-peer network works by letting each node in the network maintain 8 outgoing connections and up to 117 incoming connections. This is clearly insecure when considering a resource-constrained adversary instead of a traditional adversary (as the probability of only connecting to adversarial nodes can be arbitrarily high). Additional to this inherent insecurity, [22] showed how to eclipse a node that is already a part of an existing honest network by exploiting a bias in the way a peer selects its outgoing connections. They launched such an attack with only 4600 bots and achieved 85% success probability to actually eclipse a targeted node.

By default, a node in the Ethereum peer-to-peer network selects 13 outgoing connections contrary to the 8 that is the default in Bitcoin. Hence, one might be led to believe that it is more difficult to eclipse an Ethereum node than a Bitcoin node. However, in a Ethereum neighbors are selected using a distance measure that is based on nodes' public keys. Exploiting that in a prior version

---

[2] An attack where an adversary tricks an honest party into talking only with adversarial parties. It is thereby possible for the adversary to manipulate the honest node in various ways.

of the Ethereum client a single computer was allowed to run several nodes, [29] showed that just a single computer can be used to mount an attack by creating multiple carefully selected public keys.

[5] showed that BGP-Hijacking can also be used to eclipse Bitcoin nodes. However, we note that such attack is immediately observable as an adversary will need to announce a false BGP prefix publicly. In [38], it was shown that a stealthier version of such an attack in can also be launched against a Bitcoin node by additionally influencing how a bitcoin node selects its outgoing connections. We note that such attacks are attacks on the infrastructure of the internet, and therefore fall outside the scope of our model.

We note that the attacks presented in [22,29,38] all rely on exploiting the heuristics used to select outgoing connections for nodes in the peer-to-peer network. Hence, such attacks would not have been possible if, instead of heuristics a provably secure protocol (such as the one presented in this work) had been deployed.

Detecting Eclipse Attacks. As a way of mitigating attacks on the network layer a line of work considers the possibility of detecting eclipse attacks [4,41,44]. [41] provide a method for using supervised learning to detect eclipsing attacks based on the metadata in packages. We note that this method is only as good as its data set for training, and hence cannot be used to detect attacks in general. A different approach is to try to detect eclipse attacks based on the absence of new blocks [4,44]. However, this method has the drawback that it becomes arbitrarily slow as the fraction of resources controlled by an adversary approaches 50%, and even for small values, it takes upwards of 3 hours to detect. Finally, it has been considered to detect eclipse attacks using an additional overlay gossip protocol [4]. However, contrary to this work this is not *proven* to work but rather demonstrated to work empirically.

Consequences of Eclipse Attacks. If a party is eclipsed it is immediate that security proofs that rely on guaranteed message delivery no longer apply. Several works have shown that eclipse attacks do not only invalidate the security proofs but actually invalidate the actual security of blockchain protocols [22,33,43]. Eclipsing can be used to invalidate the total order that blockchain provides and thereby allow double-spend attacks [22], amplify the rewards from selfish mining [33], and dramatically speed up "stake-bleeding"-attacks [43].

The Generals' Scuttlebutt: Byzantine-Resilient Gossip Protocols [13]. Concurrent with and independent of our work, [13] considered the problem of designing a message diffusion mechanism based on the majority of honest stake assumption. The main focus of that paper is to design a network protocol specifically for the Ouroboros Praos consensus protocol [15]. To mitigate a specific denial-of-service attack possible in that protocol (and related proof-of-stake protocols), the authors propose a mechanism that relies on long-lived connections between parties to synchronize chains instead of generically diffusing messages. A consequence of these long-lived connections between parties is that an adaptive adversary can eclipse a set of honest parties. Because their ideal functionality allows such eclipsing, the functionality is different from the assumed functionality of [15] (and thereby the functionality implemented in this work), and the authors argue in [13] that security of [15] can be proven using this new functionality. In contrast to that, the focus of our work is to realize the flooding functionality without eclipsing assumed by most existing blockchain protocols. Hence, while some techniques are similar, the results of [13] are mostly orthogonal to our work.

2   Notation and Model

2.1   Notation

We will use κ to denote the security parameter of our protocols. We will write $A \overset{\$}{\leftarrow} \mathcal{D}$ to sample the value A from the distribution $\mathcal{D}$ and use the infix notation $\sim$ to denote that two random variables are distributed identically. We will let $\mathcal{B}(n, \rho)$ denote the binomial distribution with parameters n and ρ, and $\mathcal{U}(A)$ denote the uniform distribution on a set A. We denote by $\log x$ the natural logarithm of x. In our proofs we will write RHS and LHS to refer to respectively the right hand side and left hand side of (in)equalities.

Graphs. We use standard notation for graphs and let $G = (\mathcal{V}, E)$ be a graph with nodes $\mathcal{V}$ and edges E. An edge can be either directed in which case we will write (v, z) to denote the edge from v to z, or undirected in which case we will write $\{v, z\}$ to denote the edge between the two nodes. We write $\mathtt{dist}(v, z)$ to denote the shortest distance between two nodes v and z. Further, we use the shorthand notation $\mathtt{MaxDist}(G, v) \triangleq \max_{z \in \mathcal{V}} \mathtt{dist}(v, z)$ for the maximum distance from v to any node in a graph $G = (\mathcal{V}, E)$, and the following notation $\mathtt{Diam}(G) \triangleq \max_{v \in \mathcal{V}} \mathtt{MaxDist}(G, v)$ for the diameter of a graph G.

We also define Erdős–Rényi graphs and digraphs.

Definition 1 (Erdős–Rényi (di)graphs). *An Erdős–Rényi (di)graph is an (di)graph $G = (\mathcal{V}, E)$ where all possible edges are present with an independent probability ρ. That is for any $v, z \in \mathcal{V}$, we have $\Pr[\{v, z\} \in E] = \rho$ for Erdős–Rényi graphs and $\Pr[(v, z) \in E] = \rho$ for digraphs. To sample such a graph G with $|\mathcal{V}| = \eta$, we write $G \overset{\$}{\leftarrow} \mathcal{G}_{\mathrm{ER}}(\eta, \rho)$ and for the directed case $G \overset{\$}{\leftarrow} \mathcal{G}_{\overrightarrow{\mathrm{ER}}}(\eta, \rho)$.*

2.2   Parties, Weight, Adversary and Communication Network

We let $\mathcal{P}$ denote the static set of parties for which our protocols will work. For convenience we let $n := |\mathcal{P}|$ and let $\mathcal{H} \subseteq \mathcal{P}$ be the set of parties that are honest.

We assume that a public weight is assigned to each party. We let W_p denote the weight assigned to party p, and let $\alpha_p := \frac{W_p}{\sum_{p \in \mathcal{P}} W_p}$ i.e., the fraction of the total weight assigned to party p.

We allow an adversary to corrupt any subset of the parties such that the remaining set of honest parties together constitutes more than a $\gamma \in (0, 1]$ fraction of the total weight. Formally, we assume that $\sum_{p \in \mathcal{H}} \alpha_p \geq \gamma$, and that all parties have a non-zero positive weight i.e. $\forall p \in \mathcal{P}, W_p > 0$.[3] We will refer to this assumption as the honest weight assumption. For simplicity, we consider a static adversary, although our results also hold against a so-called delayed-adaptive adversary [30], where the corruptions can be adaptively chosen but only happen after a certain amount of time.

Parties $\mathcal{P}$ have access to a complete network of point-to-point authenticated channels that guarantee delivery within a bounded delay. Concretely, we assume that all channels ensure delivery within δ_{Channel} time.

3   Weighted Flooding

In this section we present a practical and provably secure flooding protocol WFF (weighted fan-out flooding) that only relies on the honest weight assumption. Before doing so we first present our definition of a flooding protocol in Sect. 3.1. Then, in Sect. 3.2 we present a generic skeleton for flooding protocols that is parameterized by the way parties selects their neighbors, instantiate this skeleton in order to obtain our practical protocol (WFF), and prove that it is sufficient to consider the way neighbors are selected in order to derive security of a protocol. We use this skeleton to define our theoretical flooding protocol that is secure based upon each party emulating a number of nodes proportional to their weight in an Erdős–Rényi graph (Sect. 3.3). Finally, in Sect. 3.4 we use two intermediary protocols in order to derive the security of WFF from our theoretical protocol. All proofs can be found in the full version [26].

3.1   Properties of Flooding Protocols

Below we give our property based definition of a flooding protocol.[4]

Definition 2. *Let Π be a protocol executed by parties $\mathcal{P}$, where each party $p \in \mathcal{P}$ can input a message at any time, and as a consequence all parties get a message as output. We say that Π is a Δ-flooding protocol if the two properties hold with a probability overwhelming in the security parameter κ for each message m:*

1) If m is input by an honest party for the first time at time τ, then by time $\tau + \Delta$ it is ensured that all other honest parties output m.

---

[3] For a discussion of the necessity of the zero-weight requirement see Sect. 4 and for methods to anyway achieve delivery to such zero-weight parties we refer to the full version of this work [26].

[4] Note that for protocols with no secrecy (each event is leaked to the adversary), and for functionalities that give the adversary full control while respecting these properties a simulation-based security notion is directly implied by the property-based definition. For flooding networks, this technique is used in the proofs in [30].

2) If m is output by an honest *party at time* τ, *then by time* $\tau + \Delta$ *it is ensured that all honest parties output m.*

Note that this definition subsumes the assumptions that many blockchain protocols rely on [12,15,16,20,34,36]. To the best of our knowledge only [16] relies on both Properties 1) and 2), whereas the other works only rely solely on Property 1). However, as Property 2) essentially comes for free for the type of protocols we consider (each party will forward everything they receive and thereby act as if they themselves send the message) we have chosen to include it in our definition. Furthermore, because of this structure of our protocols, it is sufficient to bound the probability of Property 1) in order to show that our protocols are in fact flooding protocols according to the definition. For our proofs and lemma statements, it is, therefore, useful to define notation for the predicate that a message input to an honest party for the first time is delivered respecting the delivery bound for a flooding protocol, which is what we encapsulate in the predicate below.

Definition 3 (Timely delivery). *For a message m that is input for the first time at an honest party at time* τ *we say that m is* Δ-timely-delivered *if all honest parties have output m no later than time* $\tau + \Delta$. *We let* $\texttt{Timely}_m(\Delta)$ *denote the induced predicate.*

Similarly, for a message m that is input for the first time at an honest party, we define the *message complexity* as the number of messages sent by honest parties until all honest parties output m. Looking ahead, since our protocols only consist of forwarding the initial message m, the total message complexity is simply $|m|$ times the message complexity.

Mitigating Denial-of-Service Attacks. It is immediate that any protocol that lives up to the definition of a flooding protocol, as given above, is open to denial-of-service attacks. An adversary can simply flood arbitrary messages until the bandwidth is exceeded. This is possible because the definition requires *all* messages to be forwarded. To prevent such attacks, it is natural to consider a notion of validity and only require the delivery guarantees to apply for "valid" messages. Concretely, one could let each party $p \in \mathcal{P}$ have an updatable local predicate $\texttt{Valid}_p$ and only require that messages that are considered valid by all parties for Δ after being input/output for the first time should be propagated.

For clarity of presentation, we have left this out of our definition and protocols. However, we note that it is easy to accommodate our protocols to such notion by letting each party check if a message is valid before propagating it. We note that with such modification, all our proofs and lemmas still hold for messages that are considered valid by all parties for at least Δ after they are input/output.

3.2   A Skeleton for Flooding Protocols

We now present a skeleton for our flooding algorithm. The structure of the protocol is very similar to the protocols proposed in [30], but contrary to their protocols our protocol takes an additional parameter $\mathcal{N}$, which is an algorithm that allows each party to sample a set of neighbors. We refer to this parameter as the *neighborhood selection algorithm*.

The protocol accepts two commands: One for sending and one for checking which messages have been received. Once a send command is issued to a party, the party will forward the message to a set of neighbors that are determined using the neighborhood selection algorithm. Furthermore, once a message is received on a point-to-point channel the receiver checks if the message has already been relayed and if not it forwards the message to a set of neighbors that is again selected using the neighborhood selection algorithm.

Protocol $\pi_{\text{Flood}}(\mathcal{N})$

We use $\mathcal{N}_p$ to denote the neighborhood distribution of party p. Each party $p_i \in \mathcal{P}$ keeps track of a set of relayed messages $\texttt{Relayed}_i$ which will also be used to keep track of which messages party p_i has received.

Initialize: Initially, each party p_i sets $\texttt{Relayed}_i := \varnothing$.

Send: When p_i receives $(\textit{Send}, m)$, they sample a set of neighbors $N \overset{\$}{\leftarrow} \mathcal{N}_p$ and forwards the message to all parties in N. Finally, they set $\texttt{Relayed}_i := \texttt{Relayed}_i \cup \{m\}$.

Get Messages: When p_i receives $(\textit{GetMessages})$ they return $\texttt{Relayed}_i$.

When party p_i receives message m on a point-to-point channel where $m \notin \texttt{Relayed}_i$, p_i continues as if they had received $(\textit{Send}, m)$. Otherwise, m is ignored.

Looking ahead and as an example of a neighborhood selection algorithm we present our practical and provably secure neighborhood selection algorithm.

A Practical Neighborhood Selection Algorithm. Our algorithm WFS(E, k) (abbreviation for "Weighted Fan-out Selection") takes two parameters: a function $\text{E} : \mathcal{P} \to \mathbb{N}$ that allows to take stake into account when deciding how many neighbors each party should select and a parameter k that scales this number.

The idea of the algorithm is that each party p chooses $K := k \cdot \text{E}(p)$ number of neighbors (excluding themselves). The neighbors are chosen according to weighted sampling without replacement [7] where each party again is being weighted with E. More precisely, party p chooses K neighbors from $\mathcal{P} \setminus \{p\}$, and the probability to choose the tuple of neighbors $(q_1, \ldots, q_K)$ is defined as:

$$\Pr[(q_1, \ldots, q_K)] = \prod_{i=1}^{K} \frac{\text{E}(q_i)}{\sum_{q \in \mathcal{P} \setminus \{p, q_1, \ldots, q_{i-1}\}} \text{E}(q)}.$$

The probability to choose a certain neighborhood set $\{q_1, \ldots, q_K\}$ is then the sum over the probabilities over all the permuted tuples. We denote by $\mathcal{W}(K, \text{E}, p)$ the resulting distribution.

Algorithm $\mathsf{WFS}_p(\mathrm{E}, k)$

1: Let $N := \varnothing$.
2: Set $K := k \cdot \mathrm{E}(p)$.
3: Sample $N \overset{\$}{\leftarrow} \mathcal{W}(K, \mathrm{E}, p)$.
4: **return** N.

Our final protocol is the protocol obtained by instantiating the flooding skeleton π_{Flood} with the neighborhood selection algorithm WFS that again is to be instantiated with the function $\mathrm{E}(p) := \lceil \alpha_p \cdot n \rceil$. We name this protocol the *weighted fan-out flooding* protocol and use the abbreviation $\mathsf{WFF}(k) := \pi_{\mathrm{Flood}}(\mathsf{WFS}(\mathrm{E}, k))$ for $\mathrm{E}(p) := \lceil \alpha_p \cdot n \rceil$. In Sects. 3.3 and 3.4 it will become apparent why this exact choice of function is advantageous and ensures a secure protocol, but for now we simply state our final theorem which states that WFF is in fact a flooding protocol with a logarithmic round complexity and a low message complexity.

Theorem 2. *Let* $\Delta := \left(7 \cdot \log\left(\frac{6n}{\log(n) + \kappa} \right) + 2 \right) \cdot \delta_{Channel}$. *Then* $\mathsf{WFF}\left(\frac{\log(n) + \kappa}{\gamma} \right)$ *is a* Δ*-flooding protocol with message complexity less than* $2n \cdot \frac{\log(n) + \kappa}{\gamma}$.

The Honest Sending Process. To prove security of WFF we will relate the security of WFF to a series of other protocol which will all take the structure of π_{Flood} but use different neighborhood selection algorithms. Hence, we would like to be able to relate the security of the overall flooding protocol to just the neighborhood selection algorithm used. To do so we first define a random process for creating a graph where each honest party is a node, given a family of neighborhood selection algorithms $\mathcal{N}$, a starting party p, and a distance λ. The intuition is that this process mimics the worst-case behavior of the adversary during a sending process starting from party p. However, separating this into a process without adversarial influence allows us to relate probabilistic experiments without taking into account the choices of an adversary which could have a strategy that depends on parts of the outcome of the experiments.

Definition 4. *Let* $\mathcal{N}$ *be a family of neighborhood selection algorithms, let* $p \in \mathcal{H}$, *and let* $\lambda \in \mathbb{N}$ *be a distance. We let the* honest sending process, $\mathsf{HSP}(p, \mathcal{N}, \lambda)$, *be a random process that returns a directed graph* $G = (\mathcal{V}, E)$ *defined by the following random procedure:*

1. *Initially,* $E := \varnothing$. *Furthermore, we keep track of set* Flipped $:= \varnothing$ *that consists of nodes that have already had their outgoing edges decided, and a first-in-first-out queue* ToBeFlipped $:= \{(p, 0)\}$ *of nodes and their distance from* p *that are to have their edges decided.*
2. *The process proceeds with the following until* ToBeFlipped $== \varnothing$.
   (a) *Take out the first element of* ToBeFlipped *and let it be denoted by* (p', i).

(b) Let $N \xleftarrow{\$} \mathcal{N}_{p'}$ and set $N := N \cap \mathcal{H}$.

(c) Update the set of edges $E := E \cup \{(p', p'') \mid p'' \in N\}$ and let Flipped := Flipped $\cup \{p'\}$.

(d) If $i + 1 < \lambda$, for all $p'' \in N\backslash$Flipped add $(p'', i + 1)$ to ToBeFlipped.

3. Finally, return $G = (\mathcal{H}, E)$.

Next, we are interested in bounding the probability that a message is delivered within the time guaranteed by the flooding algorithm in terms of the probability that there is a low distance to all parties from the sender. We show that the probability that π_{Flood} ensures timely delivery for a message is lower-bounded by the probability that the honest sending process results in a graph where the sender can reach all other honest nodes within a certain number of steps.

Lemma 1. *Let $\mathcal{N}$ be a family of neighborhood selection algorithms, let $p \in \mathcal{H}$, and let $\lambda \in \mathbb{N}$ be a distance. Further, let m be a message that is input to p for the first time during the execution of $\pi_{Flood}(\mathcal{N})$ and let $G \xleftarrow{\$} HSP(p, \mathcal{N}, \lambda)$. Then,*

$$\Pr[\text{MaxDist}(G, p) \le \lambda] \le \Pr[\text{Timely}_m(\lambda \cdot \delta_{Channel})]. \tag{1}$$

Proof Idea. We observe the random experiment arising from delivering the message m in the protocol and construct a new graph where each honest party corresponds to a node and we include a directed edge from one party to another if a message is sent and delivered before time $\lambda \cdot \delta_{\text{Channel}}$. In this graph, we observe that if the distance is at most λ from the sender to any party then the message was delivered timely. We then define how to use this experiment to define the HSP experiment by copying a subset of the edges from this new graph to the honest sending graph and thereby ensuring that any path in the graph from the honest sending process will also be in this new graph.   □

Lemma 1 ensures that it is sufficient to consider neighborhood selection algorithms and prove that graphs constructed via the honest sending process has a low distance from the sender to all other parties.

3.3 A Theoretical Protocol: Emulating Nodes in Erdős–Rényi Graphs

Our central idea for achieving a flooding network that relies on the honest weight assumption is to let each party emulate a number of nodes proportional to their weight in a hypothetical Erdős–Rényi graph. We will refer to this hypothetical graph as the *emulated graph*. Now, our idea is that if there is an edge between an emulated node v and another emulated node z corresponds to that the party emulating node v should forward the message to the party emulating z. Our goal is now to ensure each honest party emulates at least one node and that the emulated graph has a low diameter, as this will result in that all parties will receive the message quickly.

Concretely, we introduce a function $\text{E} : \mathcal{P} \rightarrow \mathbb{N}\backslash\{0\}$ which for each party determines how many nodes this party should act as in the emulated graph.

We refer to this function as the *emulation function*.[5] For such emulation function we define notation for the number of emulated nodes $n_E \triangleq \sum_{p \in \mathcal{P}} E(p)$ and the number of honest nodes that are emulated $h_E \triangleq \sum_{p \in \mathcal{H}} E(p)$.

Before looking at how to choose an emulation function, let us present how the idea leads to a very simple algorithm for selecting neighbors by letting the emulated graph take the form of an Erdős–Rényi graph. We let ρ denote the probability that there should be an edge between any two nodes in the emulated graph. The probability that party p_i should forward a message to party p_j is:

$$\Pr[p_i \text{ should forward a message to } p_j]$$
$$:= \Pr[\text{exists edge from any of } p_i\text{'s emulated nodes to any of } p_j\text{'s}]$$
$$= 1 - \Pr[\text{there are no edges between any of } p_i \text{ and } p_j\text{'s emulated nodes}]$$
$$= 1 - (1 - \Pr[\text{there is an edge between any two emulated nodes})^{E(p_i) \cdot E(p_j)}$$
$$= 1 - (1 - \rho)^{E(p_i) \cdot E(p_j)}.$$
$$(2)$$

This gives rise to the following family of neighbor selection algorithms indexed by a party $p \in \mathcal{P}$ and parameterized by an emulation function E and an edge probability ρ.

Algorithm ER-Emulation$_p(E, \rho)$

1: Let $N := \varnothing$.
2: Let $P := \mathcal{P} \setminus p$.
3: **while** $P \neq \varnothing$ **do**
4:     Pick $r \in P$.
5:     Sample $c \xleftarrow{\$} \mathcal{U}([0, 1])$.
6:     **if** $c \leq 1 - (1 - \rho)^{E(p) \cdot E(r)}$ **then**
7:         Update $N := N \cup \{r\}$.
8:     Update $P := P \setminus \{r\}$.
9: **return** N.

Relating Erdős–Rényi Graphs and the Honest Sending Process. We now formalize the intuition that given that an emulated graph is "well connected" then the graph from the honest sending process is also "well connected". In particular, we relate the probability that the distance in a directed Erdős–Rényi graph is large to the probability that the distance from the sender is large in the honest sending process.

Lemma 2. *Let $\rho \in [0, 1]$, let $\lambda \in \mathbb{N}$, let $p \in \mathcal{H}$, and let $E : \mathcal{P} \to \mathbb{N} \setminus \{0\}$ be an emulation function. Further, let $G_1 \xleftarrow{\$} HSP(p, \text{ER-Emulation}(E, \rho), \lambda)$ and let $G_2 \xleftarrow{\$} \mathcal{G}_{\overrightarrow{ER}}(h_E, \rho)$. Then for any node $v \in V$ we have,*

---

[5] For a function to be an emulation function, we require that all parties should emulate at least 1 node, which is why the codomain of the function is defined to be $\mathbb{N} \setminus \{0\}$.

$$\Pr[\texttt{MaxDist}(G_2, v) \leq \lambda] \leq \Pr[\texttt{MaxDist}(G_1, p) \leq \lambda]. \qquad (3)$$

Proof Idea. We use Eq. (2) and a mapping between the nodes of G_2 and the honest parties to define both graph distributions in terms of the same random experiment. We then observe that the edges that are relevant for the distance from v in G_2 are also included in G_1. □

Next, we show that the probability that a particular node can reach all other nodes within a certain distance in a directed Erdős–Rényi graph is lower-bounded by the probability that an undirected Erdős–Rényi graph has a high diameter.

Lemma 3. *Let $\rho \in [0, 1]$, let $\lambda \in \mathbb{N}$ and let $\eta \in \mathbb{N}$. Further, let $G_1 = (\mathcal{V}_1, E_1) \xleftarrow{\$}$ $\mathcal{G}_{\overrightarrow{\text{ER}}}(\eta, \rho)$ and let $G_2 = (\mathcal{V}_2, E_2) \xleftarrow{\$} \mathcal{G}_{\text{ER}}(\eta, \rho)$. Then for any node $v \in \mathcal{V}_1$ we have,*

$$\Pr[\texttt{Diam}(G_2) \leq \lambda] \leq \Pr[\texttt{MaxDist}(G_1, v) \leq \lambda]. \qquad (4)$$

Proof Idea. We define a coupling between the two graphs such that the edges that are relevant for the distance from v in G_1 are ensured to have undirected counterparts included in G_2. Hence, any path starting from v in G_2 translates to a similar path in G_1. □

Choosing a Good Emulation Function. Let us now turn our attention to how to select a good emulation function. Before looking at a concrete function, let us consider what properties constitute a good emulation function. The only property of the emulation function that we have used so far is that all parties should emulate at least 1 node.[6] However, there are additional things that we want from a useful emulation function:

1. It should ensure a low distance from any sender in the graph resulting from the honest sending process.
2. The message complexity of the protocol should be as small as possible.

Lemmas 2 and 3 bounds the probability that the honest sending process results in a graph with some nodes not reachable within the sender in terms of the probability that an Erdős–Rényi graph (of size identical to the number of honest emulated nodes) has a large diameter. Furthermore, looking ahead we will instantiate $\rho \approx \frac{\log(h_{\text{E}}) + \kappa}{h_{\text{E}}}$ to obtain an Erdős–Rényi graph that has a diameter logarithmic in h_{E} unless with a probability that is negligible in κ. Unfortunately, h_{E} will not be known at the time of instantiation, so we will have to instantiate ρ with a lower bound on h_{E} in the denominator and similarly an upper bound in the denominator. For this discussion, let us use n_{E} as an upper bound.

The expected number of neighbors for a party is linear in ρ. To see this let $N \xleftarrow{\$} \texttt{ER-Emulation}_p(\text{E}, \rho)$ and let us estimate the expected size of N using Bernoulli's inequality:

---

[6] This property was used in the proof of Lemma 2.

$$E[|N|] = \sum_{r \in \mathcal{P} \setminus \{p\}} 1 - (1-\rho)^{E(p) \cdot E(r)} \leq \sum_{r \in \mathcal{P} \setminus \{p\}} \rho \cdot E(p) \cdot E(r) \leq \rho \cdot E(p) \cdot n_E. \quad (5)$$

Hence, for ρ chosen according to the above, a bound on the expected message complexity will be

$$O\left((\log(n_E) + \kappa) \cdot \frac{n_E^2}{h_E}\right). \quad (6)$$

Our approach for finding a good emulation function has thus been to search for an emulation function which makes this value as small as possible. As result of this approach we choose the emulation function to be $E(p) := \lceil \alpha_p \cdot n \rceil$. For this emulation function above we can derive the following bounds using only the honest weight assumption:

$$h_E = \sum_{p \in \mathcal{H}} E(p) \geq \sum_{p \in \mathcal{H}} \alpha_p \cdot n \geq \gamma \cdot n, \quad (7)$$

and

$$n_E = \sum_{p \in \mathcal{P}} E(p) \leq \sum_{p \in \mathcal{P}} (\alpha_p \cdot n + 1) = 2 \cdot n. \quad (8)$$

By plugging the bounds from Eqs. (7) and (8) into Eq. (6) we acquire an expected message complexity that is upper bounded by $O\left((\log(n) + \kappa) \cdot \frac{n}{\gamma}\right)$ when parameters are instantiated to obtain a logarithmic diameter of the graph. If we instead of assuming a constant fraction of honest weight assumed a constant fraction of honest parties, we could let $E(p) := 1$, which would result in $n_E := 1$ and thereby a protocol identical to the one proposed in [30]. By using the same analysis as above we would then be able to bound the expected message complexity by $O\left((\log(n) + \kappa) \cdot \frac{n}{\gamma}\right)$. Interestingly, the bound on the message complexity for the weighted section would only be a factor of ≈ 4 larger than the corresponding bound for the non-weighted setting.

Proving Security of Our Theoretical Flooding Protocol. We now state and prove that the probability that $\pi_{\text{Flood}}(\text{ER-Emulation}(E, \rho))$ protocol does not ensure timely delivery is negligible for certain choices of E and ρ. To prove this, we make use of probabilistic bounds on the diameter of undirected Erdős–Rényi graphs from the full version of [30]. As a first step, we bound the probability that the distance of the honest sending process using the neighborhood selection algorithm ER-Emulation(E, ρ) has a large distance from the sender.

Lemma 4. *Let* $E(p) := \lceil \alpha_p \cdot n \rceil$, *let* $d \in [7, \infty]$, *and let* $\rho := \frac{d}{\gamma \cdot n}$. *Further, let* $p \in \mathcal{H}$ *and* $G \xleftarrow{\$} HSP(p, \text{ER-Emulation}(E, \rho), ((7 \cdot \log(\frac{n}{d}) + 2)))$. *Then*

$$\Pr\left[\text{MaxDist}(G, p) \leq \left(7 \cdot \log\left(\frac{n}{d}\right) + 2\right)\right]$$
$$\geq 1 - \left(2 \cdot n \cdot \left(e^{-\frac{d}{18}} + \left(6 \cdot \log\left(\frac{n}{d}\right) + 1\right) \cdot e^{-\frac{7 \cdot d}{108}}\right) + e^{-\gamma \cdot n \cdot \left(\frac{d}{9} - 2\right)}\right). \quad (9)$$

Proof Idea. We use Eqs.(7) and (8) to bound the size of the emulated graph in the honest sending process and apply Lemmas 2 and 3 to reduce the probability to the probability that an Erdős–Rényi graph has a low diameter. The bound then follows by instantiating Lemma 3 in the full version of [30].   □

A direct corollary of Lemmas 1 and 4 is that the probability that the protocol $\pi_{\text{Flood}}(\text{ER-Emulation}(\text{E}, \rho))$ ensures timely delivery is lower bounded by Eq. (9) when choosing E and ρ as discussed above.

3.4   Security of WFF

In the previous section we proved that ER-Emulation induces a secure protocol. Unfortunately, it is not a practical neighborhood selection algorithm, as it requires each party to do n coin-flips per message that is sent and forwarded. In this section, we introduce two intermediate algorithms in order to prove WFF secure (Fast-ER-Emulation and Practical-ER-Emulation) by doing gradual changes to ER-Emulation, until we finally arrive at the algorithm WFS which is both practical, simple, and similar to algorithms deployed in practice (except that this algorithm maintains its complexity even for weighted corruptions).

Intermediary Neighborhood Selection Algorithms. We first introduce the algorithm Fast-ER-Emulation, which is distributed identically to ER-Emulation, but is more practical. The algorithm exploits that another way of creating an Erdős–Rényi graph is to first decide how many edges each node should have using the binomial distribution and then select these neighbors at random.

Below we will abuse notation slightly and write $\text{E}(P)$ to denote the set of emulated nodes for a set of parties $P \subseteq \mathcal{P}$ and an emulation function E,[7]

$$\text{E}(P) \triangleq \{p_i \mid p \in P \wedge i \in \{1, 2, \ldots, \text{E}(p)\}\}.$$

Algorithm Fast-ER-Emulation$_p(\text{E}, \rho)$

1: Let $N := \varnothing$.
2: **for** $i := 0$; $i < \text{E}(p)$; $i{+}{+}$ **do**
3:     Sample $k \xleftarrow{\$} \mathcal{B}\left(|\text{E}(\mathcal{P} \setminus \{p\})|, \rho\right)$.
4:     Let A be k nodes sampled from $\text{E}(\mathcal{P} \setminus \{p\})$ without replacement.
5:     Set $N := N \cup \{p' \mid p'_j \in A \wedge j \in \mathbb{N}\}$.
6: **return** N.

We now show Fast-ER-Emulation and ER-Emulation are identically distributed.

---
[7] This set may be different from the actual set of nodes that will be emulated in an execution of the protocol as dishonest parties might choose to deviate from the protocol. However, it is still useful to define the set in order to define honest behavior.

Lemma 5. *Let $\rho \in [0,1]$, let $\lambda \in \mathbb{N}$, let $p \in \mathcal{H}$, and let $\mathrm{E} : \mathcal{P} \to \mathbb{N} \setminus \{0\}$ be an emulation function. If $G_1 \xleftarrow{\$} HSP(p, \text{ER-Emulation}(\mathrm{E}, \rho), \lambda)$ and $G_2 \xleftarrow{\$} HSP(p, \text{Fast-ER-Emulation}(\mathrm{E}, \rho), \lambda)$ then $G_1 \sim G_2$.*

Proof Idea. We show that the graphs are distributed identically by showing that their respective neighborhood selection algorithms are distributed identically. This is shown by showing that for both distributions each edge between emulated nodes appears with independent probability ρ. □

A problem of Fast-ER-Emulation is that each party p needs to make $\mathrm{E}(p)$ number of draws from the binomial distribution. One way to avoid this is to make a single random draw for the number of nodes all emulated nodes should send to and then afterward choose this number of nodes uniformly without replacement. Below we present the algorithm Practical-ER-Emulation, which does exactly that.

Algorithm Practical-ER-Emulation$_p(\mathrm{E}, \rho)$

1: Let $N := \varnothing$.
2: Sample $k \xleftarrow{\$} \mathcal{B}\left(\mathrm{E}(p) \cdot |\mathrm{E}(\mathcal{P} \setminus \{p\})|, \rho\right)$.
3: Let A be k nodes sampled from $\mathrm{E}(\mathcal{P} \setminus \{p\})$ without replacement.
4: Set $N := \{p \mid p_i \in A \wedge i \in \mathbb{N}\}$.
5: **return** N.

Practical-ER-Emulation is not distributed identically to Fast-ER-Emulation, as there is a smaller expected overlap between the selected emulated nodes. However, it still holds that the graph resulting from the honest sending process based upon Practical-ER-Emulation has a higher chance of having a low distance from the sender than the graph resulting from the honest sending process based upon Fast-ER-Emulation. We make this intuition formal in the lemma below.

Lemma 6. *Let $\rho \in [0,1]$, let $\lambda \in \mathbb{N}$, let $p \in \mathcal{H}$, and let $\mathrm{E} : \mathcal{P} \to \mathbb{N} \setminus \{0\}$ be an emulation function. If $G_1 \xleftarrow{\$} HSP(p, \text{Fast-ER-Emulation}(\mathrm{E}, \rho), \lambda)$ and $G_2 \xleftarrow{\$} HSP(p, \text{Practical-ER-Emulation}(\mathrm{E}, \rho), \lambda)$ then*

$$\Pr[\text{MaxDist}(G_1, p) \leq \lambda] \leq \Pr[\text{MaxDist}(G_2, p) \leq \lambda]. \tag{10}$$

Proof Idea. We define a coupling between the two graphs by defining a coupling between their respective neighborhood selection algorithms and ensuring that the set of neighbors sampled by Practical-ER-Emulation is a superset of the neighbors of those sampled by Fast-ER-Emulation. We define the coupling using rejection sampling and ensure that any neighbor that is rejected when sampling neighbors for Fast-ER-Emulation will also be rejected when sampling neighbors for Practical-ER-Emulation. □

Note that Lemmas 1 and 4 to 6 together imply that the probability that $\pi_{\text{Flood}}(\text{Fast-ER-Emulation}(\mathrm{E}, \rho))$ and $\pi_{\text{Flood}}(\text{Practical-ER-Emulation}(\mathrm{E}, \rho))$ do not ensure timely delivery is negligible for a certain choice of E and ρ. Note that Practical-ER-Emulation is very similar to WFS. The main difference is that in Practical-ER-Emulation the number of neighbors is sampled according to the binomial distribution whereas WFS chooses a fixed number of neighbors. We use this observation to relate the probability that the graph constructed by the honest sending process of Practical-ER-Emulation has a low distance from the sender to the probability that the honest sending process of WFS has a low distance from the sender.

Lemma 7. *Let $\rho \in [0,1]$, let $\epsilon \in [0,1]$ let $\lambda \in \mathbb{N}$, let $p \in \mathcal{H}$, let $k \geq \lceil (1 + \epsilon) \cdot n_E \cdot \rho \rceil$, and let* $\mathsf{E} : \mathcal{P} \to \mathbb{N} \setminus \{0\}$ *be an emulation function. If $G_1 \xleftarrow{\$} \mathsf{HSP}(p, \mathsf{Practical\text{-}ER\text{-}Emulation}(\mathsf{E}, \rho), \lambda)$ and $G_2 \xleftarrow{\$} \mathsf{HSP}(p, \mathsf{WFS}(\mathsf{E}, k), \lambda)$ then*

$$\Pr[\mathtt{MaxDist}(G_1, p) \leq \lambda] - |\mathcal{H}| \cdot e^{-\frac{\epsilon^2 \cdot (n-1) \cdot \rho}{3}} \leq \Pr[\mathtt{MaxDist}(G_2, p) \leq \lambda]. \quad (11)$$

Proof Idea. Similarly to the proof of Lemma 6, we define a coupling between the two graphs by defining a coupling between their neighborhood selection algorithms using rejection sampling. However, in this coupling the invariant that the edges sampled by WFS are a superset of those of Practical-ER-Emulation is only maintained when no party samples more than k neighbors in Practical-ER-Emulation. We bound the probability that this happens using a Chernoff bound. □

We now provide a corollary that bounds the concrete probability that a message that is input via WFF is delivered timely.

Corollary 1. *Let $k \in \mathbb{N}$ such that $k \geq \frac{42}{\gamma}$. If m is a message that is input to some honest party in* $\mathsf{WFF}(k)$ *then*

$$\Pr\left[\mathtt{Timely}_m \left(\left(7 \cdot \log\left(\frac{n \cdot 6}{k \cdot \gamma} \right) + 2 \right) \cdot \delta_{Channel} \right) \right] \geq 1 - n \cdot e^{-\frac{(n-1) \cdot k}{n \cdot 24}}$$
$$- e^{-\gamma \cdot n \cdot \left(\frac{k \cdot \gamma}{54} - 2 \right)} - \left(2 \cdot n \cdot \left(e^{-\frac{k \cdot \gamma}{108}} + \left(6 \cdot \log\left(\frac{n \cdot 6}{k \cdot \gamma} \right) + 1 \right) \cdot e^{-\frac{7 \cdot k \cdot \gamma}{648}} \right) \right). \quad (12)$$

Proof Idea. We bound the size of the emulated graph and apply Lemmas 1 and 4 to 7. □

As observed earlier, it is sufficient to bound the probability that a message is timely delivered in order to bound the probability that any of the two properties of a flooding protocol is achieved. Further, note that a party p sends at most $k \cdot \mathsf{E}(p)$ messages when a message is forwarded. Hence, the message complexity is bounded by $\sum_{p \in \mathcal{H}} k \cdot \mathsf{E}(p) \leq 2 \cdot k \cdot n$. Therefore, the security of WFF (and thereby Theorem 2) follows directly from this corollary.

4   Asymptotic Optimality and Practical Considerations

Our results from Sect. 3.2 show that the protocol $\mathsf{WFF}(k)$ provides provably secure flooding. With respect to efficiency, the results show that there are two possible drawbacks: First, the emulation function $\mathbf{E}(p) = \lceil \alpha_p \cdot n \rceil$ forces parties with very high weight to send to many parties, which lead to bandwidth issues. Secondly, Theorem 2 shows that in our protocol, the number of parties each node has to send to increases logarithmically in the total number of nodes. In this section, we show that both properties are inherent for "flooding protocols".

4.1 Workload of Heavy Parties

It is easy to see that in at least in extreme cases, very heavy parties have to send to a lot of other parties: If there is a single party that has the majority of the total weight, it could be that only this party and an additional one are honest. Since the heavy party is the only one that can be relied upon for message delivery, it needs to send to all other parties. The following lemma generalizes this idea to less extreme settings.

Lemma 8. *For any protocol Π that guarantees delivery to all honest parties, and for any subset $S \subseteq \mathcal{P}$ such that $\sum_{p \in S} \alpha_p \geq \gamma$, we have with overwhelming probability that*

$$\sum_{p \in S} \mathtt{degree}_{\Pi}(p) \geq |\mathcal{P} \backslash S|. \tag{13}$$

Proof. Let S be any such set. By the honesty assumption it could be that there is exactly one honest party in $\mathcal{P} \backslash S$. To guarantee delivery to this party, some party in S must send to it. Since it cannot be distinguished which party in $\mathcal{P} \backslash S$ is honest, the parties in S must send to all parties in $\mathcal{P} \backslash S$. □

Another consequence of Lemma 8 is that having a huge number of nodes with very little weight also increases the workload for all other nodes, as shown below.

Corollary 2. *Assume there is a large set $T \subseteq \mathcal{P}$ of parties with combined relative weight $\leq 1 - \gamma$ and $|T| \geq n - \epsilon$ for some constant $\epsilon > 0$, and define $S := \mathcal{P} \backslash T$. Then, the average degree of the parties in S must be at least $\frac{n-\epsilon}{\epsilon} \in \Omega(n)$ with overwhelming probability.*

Proof. Since $\sum_{p \in S} \alpha_p = 1 - \sum_{p \in T} \alpha_p \geq \gamma$, Lemma 8 implies that the average degree of the parties in S is at least $\frac{|\mathcal{P} \backslash S|}{|S|}$ with overwhelming probability. By assumption, we have $\frac{|\mathcal{P} \backslash S|}{|S|} = \frac{|T|}{n - |T|} \geq \frac{n-\epsilon}{\epsilon} \in \Omega(n)$. □

Limiting the Workload. As we have seen above, having very heavy or many very light parties necessarily yields a large number of outgoing connections for some of the nodes. This is not only undesirable but may also become prohibitive in practice due to limited network bandwidth. If the flooding is deployed, say for a proof-of-stake blockchain, this can be mitigated by putting a lower and an upper limit on the amount of stake for actively participating nodes. This implies that people holding a lot of stake need to split their stake over several nodes (which is anyway beneficial for decentralization if they are run in different locations), and people with too little stake need to, e.g., delegate their stake to another node if supported by the blockchain. The latter can still passively participate by fetching data from other nodes. We discuss how zero-weight parties can fetch in the full version of this work [26].

4.2   Logarithmic Growth of Message Complexity

It is well known that Erdős–Rényi graphs are connected with high probability if and only if edges are included with probability larger than $\frac{\log n}{n}$ [8, Theorem 7.3]. This means the expected degree of a node must be larger than $\log n$ to obtain a connected graph, even without considering corruptions. Since our proofs in Sect. 3 depart from Erdős–Rényi graphs, one cannot hope to prove a better message complexity with our proof techniques.

On the other hand, our final protocol $\mathsf{WFF}(k)$ does not choose neighbors in the way Erdős–Rényi graphs are constructed, but more closely correspond to so-called directed k-out graphs, which have also been considered in the literature. Those are directed graphs where for each node v independently, k uniformly random other nodes are sampled and directed edges from v to the k sampled nodes are added. It is known that such graphs are connected with probability approaching 1 for $n \to \infty$ already for constant $k = 2$ [19]. Hence, at least without corruptions, $O(n)$ overall message complexity should be enough for our protocol. When considering corruptions, however, a result by Yagan and Makowski [42] implies that $\log n$ connections for each node are necessary, as we show below. This shows that $\mathsf{WFF}(k)$ and Theorem 2 are asymptotically optimal, at least for the special case in which all parties have the same weight.

Lemma 9. *For any flooding protocol in which all honest parties send to k uniformly chosen nodes and delivery to all honest nodes is guaranteed with probability $\geq 1/2$ where up to a $(1 - \gamma)$ fraction of nodes can be corrupted, we have for sufficiently large n that*

$$k \geq \frac{\log n}{\gamma + 1/n - \log(1 - \gamma - 1/n)}.$$

Proof. Yagan and Makowski [42] have considered the setting in which for each of the n nodes p_i, k distinct random other nodes are sampled and undirected edges between p_i and all k sampled nodes are added to a graph. They then consider the subgraph H consisting of the first $\lfloor \gamma' n \rfloor$ nodes for some constant $\gamma' \in (0,1)$ and show in [42, Theorem 3.2] that

$$k < \frac{\log n}{\gamma' - \log(1 - \gamma')} \implies \lim_{n \to \infty} \Pr[H \text{ contains isolated node}] = 1.$$

To translate this to our setting, first note that corrupting at most $\lfloor (1 - \gamma)n \rfloor$ nodes from the end to leave the first $\lfloor \gamma n + 1 \rfloor$ parties honest is a valid adversarial strategy. To be compatible with the result above, we can set $\gamma' := \gamma + 1/n$. Further note that a node p being isolated in H has the same probability as an honest node not sending to any other honest node and no honest node sending to that one in a flooding protocol. In that case, if p is the sender in the flooding protocol, no honest node will receive the message, and if some other node is the sender, p will not receive the message. Hence, the flooding protocol will fail to deliver the message to all honest nodes in both cases. This implies that, for sufficiently large n, flooding protocols with $k < \frac{\log n}{\gamma + 1/n - \log(1 - \gamma - 1/n)}$ fail to deliver messages with high probability. $\square$

5   Performance Evaluation via Simulations

In order to show that our protocol WFF performs well in practice, we perform various benchmarks with varying weight distributions and adversarial strategies. The source code, and a description of how to run the benchmarks, can be found at https://github.com/guilhermemtr/Weighted-Flooding-Simulator.[8]

5.1   Scope of Simulations

Weight Distributions. We consider weight distributions covering scenarios where parties have similar weights as well as scenarios with different weights. More concretely, we consider:

- The constant distribution (Const), characterized by the number of parties n. In this distribution all parties have equal weights and is therefore equal to the non-weighted setting. This serves as a baseline for our simulations.
- The exponential distribution (Exp), characterized by the number of parties n and the weight ratio r between the heaviest party and the lightest party. It corresponds to the (perhaps more realistic) exponential weight distribution— wherein the weights of parties form an exponential curve. More concretely, for $i \in \{1, \ldots, n-1\}$, the weight of p_{i+1} is $r^{-(n-1)}$ times the weight of p_i.
- The few heavy distribution (FH), characterized by the number of parties n, the weight ratio r between the heaviest and lightest party, and the number of heavy parties c. It corresponds to the distribution where $n - c$ parties have constant weight, and the other c parties have r times more weight. This weight distribution is meant to capture extreme scenarios.

Sender. In order to ensure that our protocol performs well *independently* of the weight of the sender, for the exponential distribution, we consider three choices for the sender: heaviest, lightest and median-weight party, and for the few heavy weight distribution, we consider both a heavy and a light party as the sender.

Corruption Strategies. Given that parties in our protocol simply forward a message to their neighbors, we consider the worst behavior that prevents message propagation, i.e. corrupted parties simply do not send. We consider adversaries

---

[8] All simulations were performed on the ETH Zurich Euler cluster, but there are no hindrances to running them on less powerful computers.

that can corrupt up to 50% of the total weight. To ensure that our protocol performs well independently of how adversaries spend their corruption budget, we consider adversaries that greedily corrupt as many parties as possible, following one of the strategies below:

- Random corruption (Rand) where the adversary corrupts parties uniformly at random.
- Light-First corruption (Light) where the adversary corrupts parties by their weight in increasing order, starting by the lighter ones.
- Heavy-First corruption (Heavy) where the adversary corrupts parties by their weight in decreasing order, starting from the heavier ones.

As one might note, for the constant weight distribution the corruption strategy is irrelevant. For this reason, for the constant weight distribution we only consider the random corruption strategy.

5.2   Methodology

To obtain statistical confidence, we make 10 000 runs for each parameter configuration (e.g. weight distribution, adversary strategy, choice of sender, number of parties, etc.). All runs are executed independently.

In the evaluations, a run is considered successful if the sender's message is delivered to *all* (honest and dishonest) parties. As one might note, this contrasts with the timely predicate (see Definition 3), which only requires a message to be delivered to all honest parties. Thus, the success rate metric we consider for the evaluations is actually a lower bound on the real success rate of our protocol. The rationale behind this definition is as follows: consider an adversary that corrupts a set C of parties; if the adversary would alternatively pick some party $p \in C$, and corrupt $C \setminus \{p\}$, then the protocol would have to guarantee that every honest party, including p still gets the message. Since p is now honest, it seems a harder requirement to make p now also receive the message. This justifies our choice of making adversaries corrupt as many parties as possible.

When counting successful runs, we do not take latency into account. The reason for this is that all our simulations have in common that once they succeed, they have a very low latency.[9] Further details on this and plots of the actual latency can be found in the full version of this paper [26].

To ensure our protocol performs well *independently* of the sender's weight, we take the worst result among the sender choices (for each weight distribution).

5.3   Simulations and Results

Comparison Against Weight-Oblivious Protocols. To compare the performance of WFF and a weight oblivious protocol, we measured the success rate for WFF(k)

---

[9] The maximum latency observed in any of our simulations is $9 \cdot \delta_{\text{Channel}}$ for any succeeding run.

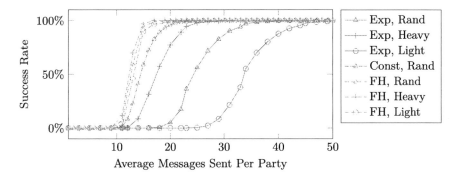

Fig. 2. Success rate of WFF protocol for different weight distributions and corruption strategies, depending on the average number of messages sent per party, for $n = 1024$ parties, a 50% corruption threshold, a ratio of 10^6 between heaviest and lightest parties and $c = 10$ heavy parties for FH.

and a weight oblivious protocol WOF $:= \pi_{\text{Flood}}(\text{WFS}(\text{E}, k))$ with $\text{E}(p) := 1$ for different exponential weight distribution (with changing ratios between the heaviest and lightest party).[10] The results can be found in Fig. 1. The plot shows that our protocol (WFF) achieves 100% success rate at a much lower number of transmitted messages than the weight-oblivious one (WOF). Only exception is when the weight ratio between the heaviest and the lightest parties is 1, the exponential weight distribution is the same as the constant weight distribution, and hence the protocols become identical. Note, that while the WFF protocol achieves practical security with low message complexity regardless of the ratio between the heaviest and lightest party, the message complexity of WOF in order to achieve a 100% success rate, increases drastically as the ratio increases.

Performance for Changing Weight Distributions. In Sect. 3.2, we bounded the message complexity of WFF by $\frac{2 \cdot n \cdot (\log(n) + \kappa)}{\gamma}$ (see Theorem 2), and in Sect. 4.2 we showed that this number of messages is inherent for the constant weight distribution (see Lemma 9), implying that WFF is optimal up to a constant factor for this distribution. Although the obtained upper-bound is independent of the weight, since it is tight only for the constant weight distribution, it could be that WFF performs poorly for other distributions. To show this is not the case, we measured the success rate for sending a single message in WFF(k) as a function of the message complexity (induced by adjusting k) for different weight distributions and corruption strategies. See Fig. 2.

Unsurprisingly, the adversarial strategy inducing the highest cost is corrupting as many light nodes as possible. This fits the intuition from Sect. 3.3: By corrupting as many light nodes as possible, an adversary can get a slight advantage in terms of the number of emulated nodes that they control because the

---

[10] The protocol WOF $:= \pi_{\text{Flood}}(\text{WFS}(\text{E}, k))$ for $\text{E}(p) := 1$ corresponds to the protocol where each party simply selects k parties uniformly at random as their neighbors without taking weight into account.

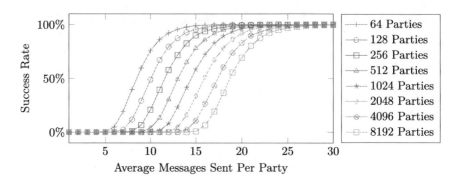

Fig. 3. Scalability of WFF protocol. We consider the constant weight distribution, and the random corruption strategy, with a 50% corruption threshold.

ceiling embedded in the emulation function has a proportionally larger effect on such nodes. Furthermore, note that for the constant weight distribution $\mathsf{WFF}(k)$ simply selects k neighbors uniformly at random and at least $\lceil \gamma \cdot n \rceil$ of the parties remains honest. Hence, this corresponds to the performance that can be expected by additionally assuming that a certain fraction of the parties remains honest and use flooding protocols tailored to this setting. We emphasize that our protocol only induces marginally larger (within a small constant factor) message complexity for all the considered weight distributions and corruption strategies. This aligns with Sect. 3.3, where our bound on the message complexity for the weighted setting was only worse by a factor of 4 compared to the bound that relied on a constant fraction of honest parties. Therefore, security for our protocol in the weighted setting comes at a much lower cost comparatively.

Scalability. A key feature of flooding protocols is their scalability. To benchmark the scalability of our proposed protocol WFF, we measured, for different numbers of parties, the success rate of the protocol depending on the average number of messages each party sends (again induced by varying k). For simplicity, we chose to only include the constant weight distribution (the performance for varying weight distributions is plotted in Fig. 2). The results can be found in Fig. 3. From the plot, it is clear that the message complexity (normalized by the number of parties) of our protocol only increases logarithmically in the number of parties, and hence this once again confirms our theory from Sect. 3.4.

By the time of writing, there are around 12k running Bitcoin nodes [1] and roughly 8k nodes in the Ethereum network [2]. Extrapolating from Figs. 2 and 3, it seems that independently of the stake distribution, WFF can realize a secure flooding network with an average number of connections per message of just ∼55 for such number of nodes. We conclude that this is within the realm of the number of connections existing widely used implementations maintain by default. Note, however, that the workload is not distributed evenly among nodes in WFF, as heavier nodes need to maintain more connections. In Sect. 4, we showed that this is inherent for this type of protocol in the weighted setting.

Acknowledgements. The work was in part done while Chen-Da Liu-Zhang was at Carnegie Mellon University and Søren Eller Thomsen was at Purdue University. Chen-Da Liu-Zhang was supported in part by the NSF award 1916939, DARPA SIEVE program, a gift from Ripple, a DoE NETL award, a JP Morgan Faculty Fellowship, a PNC center for financial services innovation award, and a Cylab seed funding award.

References

1. Bitnodes.io (2022). https://bitnodes.io/. Accessed 16 Sept 2022
2. ethernodes.org (2022). https://ethernodes.org/. Accessed 16 Sept 2022
3. Abraham, I., Malkhi, D., Nayak, K., Ren, L., Yin, M.: Sync HotStuff: simple and practical synchronous state machine replication. In: IEEE Symposium on Security and Privacy, pp. 106–118. IEEE (2020)
4. Alangot, B., Reijsbergen, D., Venugopalan, S., Szalachowski, P., Yeo, K.S.: Decentralized and lightweight approach to detect eclipse attacks on proof of work blockchains. IEEE Trans. Netw. Serv. Manag. **18**(2), 1659–1672 (2021)
5. Apostolaki, M., Zohar, A., Vanbever, L.: Hijacking bitcoin: Routing attacks on cryptocurrencies. In: IEEE Symposium on Security and Privacy, pp. 375–392. IEEE (2017)
6. Badertscher, C., Gaži, P., Kiayias, A., Russell, A., Zikas, V.: Ouroboros genesis: composable proof-of-stake blockchains with dynamic availability. In: Proceedings of the 2018 ACM SIGSAC Conference on Computer and Communications Security, CCS 2018, pp. 913–930. ACM (2018). https://doi.org/10.1145/3243734.3243848
7. Ben-Hamou, A., Peres, Y., Salez, J.: Weighted sampling without replacement. Braz. J. Probab. Stat. **32**(3), 657–669 (2018). https://www.jstor.org/stable/26496522
8. Bollobás, B.: Random Graphs. Cambridge Studies in Advanced Mathematics, 2nd edn. Cambridge University Press (2001). https://doi.org/10.1017/CBO9780511814068
9. Chandran, N., Chongchitmate, W., Garay, J.A., Goldwasser, S., Ostrovsky, R., Zikas, V.: The hidden graph model: communication locality and optimal resiliency with adaptive faults. In: ITCS, pp. 153–162. ACM (2015)
10. Chandran, N., Garay, J., Ostrovsky, R.: Improved fault tolerance and secure computation on sparse networks. In: Abramsky, S., Gavoille, C., Kirchner, C., Meyer auf der Heide, F., Spirakis, P.G. (eds.) ICALP 2010. LNCS, vol. 6199, pp. 249–260. Springer, Heidelberg (2010). https://doi.org/10.1007/978-3-642-14162-1_21
11. Chandran, N., Garay, J.A., Ostrovsky, R.: Almost-everywhere secure computation with edge corruptions. J. Cryptol. **28**(4), 745–768 (2015)
12. Chen, J., Micali, S.: Algorand: a secure and efficient distributed ledger. Theor. Comput. Sci. **777**, 155–183 (2019)
13. Coretti, S., Kiayias, A., Moore, C., Russell, A.: The generals' scuttlebutt: byzantine-resilient gossip protocols. Cryptology ePrint Archive, Report 2022/541 (2022). https://ia.cr/2022/541
14. Daian, P., Pass, R., Shi, E.: Snow White: robustly reconfigurable consensus and applications to provably secure proof of stake. In: Goldberg, I., Moore, T. (eds.) FC 2019. LNCS, vol. 11598, pp. 23–41. Springer, Cham (2019). https://doi.org/10.1007/978-3-030-32101-7_2
15. David, B., Gaži, P., Kiayias, A., Russell, A.: Ouroboros praos: an adaptively-secure, semi-synchronous proof-of-stake blockchain. In: Nielsen, J.B., Rijmen, V. (eds.) EUROCRYPT 2018. LNCS, vol. 10821, pp. 66–98. Springer, Cham (2018). https://doi.org/10.1007/978-3-319-78375-8_3

16. Dinsdale-Young, T., Magri, B., Matt, C., Nielsen, J.B., Tschudi, D.: Afgjort: a partially synchronous finality layer for blockchains. In: Galdi, C., Kolesnikov, V. (eds.) SCN 2020. LNCS, vol. 12238, pp. 24–44. Springer, Cham (2020). https://doi.org/10.1007/978-3-030-57990-6_2

17. Dolev, D., Strong, H.R.: Authenticated algorithms for byzantine agreement. SIAM J. Comput. **12**(4), 656–666 (1983)

18. Dwork, C., Peleg, D., Pippenger, N., Upfal, E.: Fault tolerance in networks of bounded degree. SIAM J. Comput. **17**(5), 975–988 (1988)

19. Fenner, T.I., Frieze, A.M.: On the connectivity of random m-orientable graphs and digraphs. Combinatorica **2**(4), 347–359 (1982). https://doi.org/10.1007/BF02579431

20. Garay, J., Kiayias, A., Leonardos, N.: The bitcoin backbone protocol: analysis and applications. In: Oswald, E., Fischlin, M. (eds.) EUROCRYPT 2015. LNCS, vol. 9057, pp. 281–310. Springer, Heidelberg (2015). https://doi.org/10.1007/978-3-662-46803-6_10

21. Garay, J.A., Ostrovsky, R.: Almost-everywhere secure computation. In: Smart, N. (ed.) EUROCRYPT 2008. LNCS, vol. 4965, pp. 307–323. Springer, Heidelberg (2008). https://doi.org/10.1007/978-3-540-78967-3_18

22. Heilman, E., Kendler, A., Zohar, A., Goldberg, S.: Eclipse attacks on bitcoin's peer-to-peer network. In: USENIX Security Symposium, pp. 129–144. USENIX Association (2015)

23. Jayanti, S., Raghuraman, S., Vyas, N.: Efficient constructions for almost-everywhere secure computation. In: Canteaut, A., Ishai, Y. (eds.) EUROCRYPT 2020. LNCS, vol. 12106, pp. 159–183. Springer, Cham (2020). https://doi.org/10.1007/978-3-030-45724-2_6

24. Kermarrec, A., Massoulié, L., Ganesh, A.J.: Probabilistic reliable dissemination in large-scale systems. IEEE Trans. Parallel Distrib. Syst. **14**(3), 248–258 (2003)

25. King, V., Saia, J., Sanwalani, V., Vee, E.: Towards secure and scalable computation in peer-to-peer networks. In: FOCS, pp. 87–98. IEEE (2006)

26. Liu-Zhang, C.D., Matt, C., Maurer, U., Rito, G., Thomsen, S.E.: Practical provably secure flooding for blockchains. Cryptology ePrint Archive, Paper 2022/608 (2022). https://eprint.iacr.org/2022/608

27. Malkhi, D., Mansour, Y., Reiter, M.K.: On diffusing updates in a byzantine environment. In: SRDS, pp. 134–143. IEEE (1999)

28. Malkhi, D., Pavlov, E., Sella, Y.: Optimal unconditional information diffusion. In: Welch, J. (ed.) DISC 2001. LNCS, vol. 2180, pp. 63–77. Springer, Heidelberg (2001). https://doi.org/10.1007/3-540-45414-4_5

29. Marcus, Y., Heilman, E., Goldberg, S.: Low-resource eclipse attacks on ethereum's peer-to-peer network (2018). https://eprint.iacr.org/2018/236

30. Matt, C., Nielsen, J.B., Thomsen, S.E.: Formalizing delayed adaptive corruptions and the security of flooding networks. In: Advances in Cryptology - CRYPTO 2022. Springer (2022, to appear)

31. Minsky, Y., Schneider, F.B.: Tolerating malicious gossip. Distrib. Comput. **16**(1), 49–68 (2003)

32. Nakamoto, S.: Bitcoin: a peer-to-peer electronic cash system. Decentralized Bus. Rev. 21260 (2008)

33. Nayak, K., Kumar, S., Miller, A., Shi, E.: Stubborn mining: generalizing selfish mining and combining with an eclipse attack. In: EuroS&P, pp. 305–320. IEEE (2016)

34. Pass, R., Shi, E.: FruitChains: a fair blockchain. In: PODC, pp. 315–324. ACM (2017)

35. Pass, R., Shi, E.: Hybrid consensus: efficient consensus in the permissionless model. In: DISC. LIPIcs, vol. 91, pp. 39:1–39:16. Schloss Dagstuhl - Leibniz-Zentrum für Informatik (2017)

36. Pass, R., Shi, E.: **Thunderella**: blockchains with optimistic instant confirmation. In: Nielsen, J.B., Rijmen, V. (eds.) EUROCRYPT 2018. LNCS, vol. 10821, pp. 3–33. Springer, Cham (2018). https://doi.org/10.1007/978-3-319-78375-8_1

37. Rohrer, E., Tschorsch, F.: Kadcast: a structured approach to broadcast in blockchain networks. In: Proceedings of the 1st ACM Conference on Advances in Financial Technologies, AFT 2019, pp. 199–213. ACM (2019). https://doi.org/10.1145/3318041.3355469

38. Tran, M., Choi, I., Moon, G.J., Vu, A.V., Kang, M.S.: A stealthier partitioning attack against bitcoin peer-to-peer network. In: IEEE Symposium on Security and Privacy, pp. 894–909. IEEE (2020)

39. Tsimos, G., Loss, J., Papamanthou, C.: Gossiping for communication-efficient broadcast. Cryptology ePrint Archive, Report 2020/894 (2020). https://ia.cr/2020/894

40. Upfal, E.: Tolerating a linear number of faults in networks of bounded degree. Inf. Comput. **115**(2), 312–320 (1994)

41. Xu, G., et al.: Am I eclipsed? A smart detector of eclipse attacks for ethereum. Comput. Secur. **88**, 101604 (2020)

42. Yagan, O., Makowski, A.M.: On the scalability of the random pairwise key predistribution scheme: gradual deployment and key ring sizes. Perform. Eval. **70**(7–8), 493–512 (2013). https://doi.org/10.1016/j.peva.2013.03.001

43. Zhang, S., Lee, J.: Eclipse-based stake-bleeding attacks in POS blockchain systems. In: BSCI, pp. 67–72. ACM (2019)

44. Zheng, H., Tran, T., Arden, O.: Total eclipse of the enclave: detecting eclipse attacks from inside tees. In: IEEE ICBC, pp. 1–5. IEEE (2021)

SNACKs: Leveraging Proofs of Sequential Work for Blockchain Light Clients

Hamza Abusalah[1($\boxtimes$)], Georg Fuchsbauer[2], Peter Gaži[3], and Karen Klein[4]

[1] IMDEA Software Institute, Madrid, Spain
hamza.abusalah@imdea.org
[2] TU Wien, Vienna, Austria
georg.fuchsbauer@tuwien.ac.at
[3] IOG, Chennai, India
peter.gazi@iohk.io
[4] ETH Zurich, Zürich, Switzerland
karen.klein@inf.ethz.ch

Abstract. The success of blockchains has led to ever-growing ledgers that are stored by all participating *full nodes*. In contrast, *light clients* only store small amounts of blockchain-related data and rely on the mediation of full nodes when interacting with the ledger. A broader adoption of blockchains calls for protocols that make this interaction trustless.

We revisit the design of light-client blockchain protocols from the perspective of classical proof-system theory, and explain the role that proofs of sequential work (PoSWs) can play in it. To this end, we define a new primitive called *succinct non-interactive argument of chain knowledge (SNACK)*, a non-interactive proof system that provides clear security guarantees to a verifier (a light client) even when interacting only with a single dishonest prover (a full node). We show how augmenting any blockchain with any *graph-labeling PoSW* (GL-PoSW) enables SNACK proofs for this blockchain. We also provide a unified and extended definition of GL-PoSWs covering all existing constructions, and describe two new variants. We then show how SNACKs can be used to construct light-client protocols, and highlight some deficiencies of existing designs, along with mitigations. Finally, we introduce *incremental SNACKs* which could potentially provide a new approach to *light mining*.

Keywords: Blockchains · Light clients · Proofs of sequential work

1 Introduction

Since the appearance of the seminal Bitcoin whitepaper [Nak08] and the subsequent launch of its implementation maintaining the Bitcoin ledger, blockchain technology has witnessed enormous growth in adoption.

However, this remarkable success also uncovered some of the deficiencies of the original Bitcoin protocol and its derivatives. Their objective is to maintain

© International Association for Cryptologic Research 2022
S. Agrawal and D. Lin (Eds.): ASIACRYPT 2022, LNCS 13791, pp. 806–836, 2022.
https://doi.org/10.1007/978-3-031-22963-3_27

an append-only ledger of transactions that records the full financial (or computational) history of the system, and the size of this ledger therefore grows with speed proportional to the use of the system. For example, the Bitcoin and Ethereum blockchains both consist of hundreds of gigabytes. This makes maintain the full blockchain unattractive for ordinary users, and the requirement to do so would be prohibitive to a wider adoption of these systems.

Light-Client Blockchain Protocols. The above development results in an urgent need for solutions that enable interaction with the blockchain for so-called *light clients*[1] that do not store the entire blockchain. This interaction is typically mediated by so-called *full nodes* that store the full blockchain state. This mediation should be *trustless* in that the light client is provided security guarantees without having to assume the honesty of the full node(s) it interacts with.

Trustless light-client protocols can power a variety of applications within the blockchain ecosystem. The basic one is *bootstrapping*, where a light client, holding only an authentic copy of the genesis block, tries to obtain a reliable picture of the current ledger state (or a commitment to it), that would then enable further interaction with the ledger such as verifying *transaction inclusion* or even contributing to extending the chain (called *light mining* [KLZ21]). Interestingly, light-client techniques also find applications in *cross-chain communication protocols* [BCD+14, GKZ19, KZ19], where the goal is to communicate the occurrence of an event on a source chain to an independent target chain: here the (validator of the) target chain plays the role of a light client for the source chain, seeking to verify the occurrence of that event without validating the entire source chain.

The need for light-client protocols was already predicted in the Bitcoin whitepaper, where so-called *simplified payment verification (SPV)* is proposed: the light client downloads only the block headers (which contain the proof-of-work solutions) from a full node; these suffice to trustlessly verify the amount of work invested to produce that chain; inclusion of individual transactions can then be verified by specifically asking for the openings of the respective Merkle-tree commitments contained in the block headers. Alas, while practically helpful, SPV still requires storage and communication linear in the length of the blockchain and hence provides no asymptotic improvement. On the other end of the spectrum are solutions based on *succinct non-interactive arguments of knowledge (SNARKs)* [GGPR13] that provide impressive asymptotic improvements, but often suffer from unfavorable concrete efficiency, reliance on a trusted setup, or on novel hardness assumptions.

NIPoPoWs. Given the initial success of proof-of-work (PoW) blockchains, there has been significant effort towards developing practical light-client protocols for PoW, aiming at *sublinear* (in the length of the blockchain) communication, while relying only on basic and efficient cryptographic building blocks, and requiring no additional trust assumptions. This has led to two main constructions:

---

[1] The term *light node* or *light client* is sometimes used solely to refer to nodes adopting SPV (see below); we mean by it any node that does not store the full blockchain.

superblock-based non-interactive proofs of proof-of-work (NIPoPoWs) [KMZ20] and FlyClient [BKLZ20]. In greater detail, [KMZ20] provides a definition of the NIPoPoW primitive and an instantiation based on so-called superblocks: blocks that contain a PoW that is "stronger than needed", as it would remain valid also against a more restrictive difficulty threshold. Their technique is leveraged to enable light mining [KLZ21]; unfortunately, the approach only guarantees succinctness of the provided proofs if the adversary is limited to $1/3$ of the total hash rate in the system and is only analyzed in the static-difficulty setting. On the other hand, FlyClient also instantiates the NIPoPoW primitive, is proven secure for any sub-$1/2$ adversary, provides significantly better efficiency, and is analyzed also in the variable-difficulty setting.

It appears natural that underlying any of these light-client protocols must be a classical two-party proof system which allows a *prover*, representing a full node, to convince a *verifier*, the light client, of its knowledge of a blockchain that it commits to. However, the protocols [KMZ20,BKLZ20] are not interpreted in this way: they were designed in a model where a light client is assumed to be connected to *multiple* provers, and the soundness guarantees are formulated only under the assumption that at least one of them is honest. This might appear unsatisfying, given that an inspection of the actual protocols would suggest that a modular interpretation with the above-discussed two-party building block playing the central role would be possible.

Proofs of Sequential Work. The incompleteness of the provided picture is further underscored by the structure of the FlyClient protocol, which is strongly reminiscent (as the authors themselves observe) to a seemingly unrelated primitive, a *proof of sequential work (PoSW)* [MMV13]. A PoSW is a proof system in which a prover, given a statement χ and a parameter n, computes a proof that convinces the verifier that n sequential computational steps have been performed since χ was received. The authors of [BKLZ20] indeed remark that their construction resembles the PoSW of Cohen and Pietrzak [CP18], but the exact relationship, as well as potential opportunities for further generalizations and alternative constructions, remain—to the best of our knowledge—unstudied.

Our Contributions. In this paper, we set out to fill the above-described gaps in the theory underlying light-client protocols. Our main goals are to allow basing the development of these protocols on the classical theory of proof systems, and to explain the role that proofs of sequential work can play in their design. Our contributions can be summarized as follows:

1. We define a new general primitive called *succinct non-interactive argument of chain knowledge (SNACK)*, which is a non-interactive proof system for a specific NP language, formally capturing the above intuition.
2. To construct SNACKs from so-called *graph-labeling* proofs of sequential work (GL-PoSW), we unify existing definitions, add *knowledge-soundness* as a new property, and give two constructions rooted in previous work achieving it.
3. We show how to augment any blockchain with any knowledge-sound GL-PoSW and construct a SNACK system for the augmented chain.

4. We show how SNACKs can be used to construct light-client blockchain protocols, and compare them to existing solutions.

5. We present a novel *void-commitment attack* against a naive class of designs of bootstrapping protocols, and show how to mitigate this attack.

6. We define *incremental* SNACKs, which could allow for constructions of light miners with better resilience than existing proposals.

1. Defining SNACKs. Consider a family $\Gamma = (\Gamma_n)_{n \in \mathbb{N}}$ of weighted directed acyclic graphs (DAGs), that is, the vertices of each DAG are attributed non-negative weights summing to 1. Consider *labels* associated to the vertices and let R be a relation defined on the labels of the vertices, which formalizes some "validity" requirement. (The DAG will represent a blockchain, with edges capturing validation dependencies.) Let Com be a commitment scheme. We define a *chain commitment language* $\mathcal{L}_{\Gamma,R,\mathsf{Com}}$ that consists of pairs (ϕ, n) where ϕ is a Com-commitment to the labels of Γ_n that are valid with respect to R.

We then consider an interactive proof system for $\mathcal{L}_{\Gamma,R,\mathsf{Com}}$ called an *argument of chain knowledge (ACK)*, which satisfies a relaxation of knowledge soundness called α-*knowledge soundness*: any prover that convinces a verifier of a statement (ϕ, n) must know a path in Γ_n of weight at least α and being valid w.r.t. R. We focus on *succinct* and *non-interactive* arguments, i.e., SNACKs.

2. Knowledge-sound PoSW schemes. All known PoSW constructions [MMV13, CP18, AKK+19, DLM19] (except for the subclass of the much stronger and less efficient *verifiable delay functions* [BBBF18]) are based on a random-oracle-induced labeling of a particular DAG G. We provide a unifying definition capturing all existing such *graph-labeling* PoSWs, for which we consider an arbitrary weight distribution on the vertices of G, which will define the distribution for challenge sampling (while prior constructions always sample uniformly). Furthermore, we define a notion of knowledge soundness for GL-PoSW, which will prove useful for constructing SNACKs from GL-PoSWs: knowledge soundness of the SNACK will follow from that of the underlying GL-PoSW.

We propose two knowledge-sound GL-PoSW schemes: The first is based on the PoSW scheme from [AKK+19], the second is a slight modification of the PoSW scheme from [CP18] which is better suited to our SNACK applications (by allowing weight on *all* vertices as opposed to only the leaves as in [CP18]).

3. Constructing SNACKs for blockchains. A blockchain can be viewed as a path with potential extra edges representing additional validation dependencies between blocks, so that block validity can be determined by a relation R applied to the block and its parents in this DAG. By adding extra (short) fixed-size data to each block, we show how to bind this blockchain DAG to the DAG of a GL-PoSW whose sequential computation can be efficiently verified (see Fig. 1).

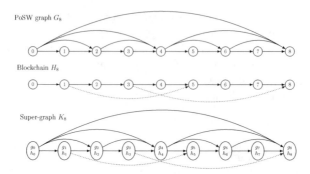

Fig. 1. Graph H_8 represents the dependency relations in the blockchain, G_8 is the chain graph underlying our PoSW scheme based on [AKK+19]; K_8 represents the graph structure underlying the augmented blockchain. A label $k_i = (g_i, h_i)$ of K_8 consists of a blockchain block h_i and a PoSW-related label g_i, which is typically small, e.g. 256 bits, and consists of a hash the labels of the parents of vertex i in K_8. The "proof" in h_i, e.g. PoW in Bitcoin, must depend on all parent labels in K_8 as well as g_i.

The augmented blockchain then gives rise to a SNACK system for a validity relation $\tilde{R}$, which beyond checking the original block validity via R, also verifies the consistency of the added PoSW data. A proof in this SNACK scheme convinces the verifier that the prover *knows* blocks of a certain weight in a blockchain that are (i) valid and (ii) have been mined sequentially (since they lie on a path)—a crucial guarantee in light-client protocols, as discussed next.

4. *SNACKS in the real world.* Our treatment so far has been fully independent of the actual Sybil-protection mechanism (e.g., proofs of work/stake/space) of the underlying blockchain. However, the implications and usefulness of the sequentiality guaranteed by a SNACK highly depend on this mechanism. For example, in a proof-of-work (PoW) blockchain, it is costly to generate blocks and thus the guarantee of a sequentially-generated set of blocks is valuable, because an adversary controlling only a minority of the computational power cannot generate the longest such sequence. In contrast, in the proof-of-stake setting, sequentiality is a weak guarantee, as generating a block requires a mere digital signature and long sequences can be readily created. Hence, our main focus is on applying SNACKs in the PoW setting, which was the only setting considered in [KMZ20, BKLZ20]. Nonetheless, we believe that our approach has much wider applicability, for instance, to blockchains combining proofs of space [DFKP15, AAC+17] with verifiable delay functions [BBBF18] such as Chia [CP19]. We leave this question to follow-up work.

SNACKs can be employed for bootstrapping in the presence of at least one honest prover: the light client simply obtains proofs from all provers and picks the heaviest successful one. However, SNACKs also allow for applications where there is only a single prover. For instance, if a verifier V knows, for application-specific reasons, (an estimate of) the current length of a blockchain, then V only has to check a single SNACK proof evidencing that the prover knows a path of roughly the correct length satisfying the SNACK guarantees of validity and sequentiality. This proof is then enough to convince the verifier that the prover holds the right blockchain (maybe up to a short suffix).

5. *The Void-Commitment Attack and preventing it.* Surprisingly, however, we observe that the above approach turns out insufficient for a typical bootstrapping scenario where the obtained chain commitment is meant to serve as a self-sufficient, universal anchor of trust in future interactions with other full nodes. We describe a simple attack, called the *void-commitment attack*, that allows the attacker to trick the light client into accepting a chain commitment that will turn out completely useless in future interactions with any honest full node. To the best of our knowledge, this attack has not been observed before.

We show how to remedy the attack by instead letting the prover establish a commitment to some *stable common prefix* of all honestly held chains, one that is then universally understood by all honest full nodes, which appears significantly more desirable in practice. Towards formalizing this, we introduce a security definition of *secure common-prefix bootstrapping* and prove that our final protocol achieves this notion. Our proof is based on an adversary-limiting assumption in the spirit of (c, L)-adversaries assumed in [BKLZ20]. However, we observe that their original (somewhat informal) assumption is insufficient for formal reasoning in any convincingly general model, and we hence present its formalization that addresses several of the original deficiencies (e.g., assuming that all competing chains—"forks"—must be of the same length).

6. *Incremental SNACKs.* A powerful extension of PoSWs, called *incremental PoSWs* [DLM19], allows to extend an existing PoSW by additional sequential computation into a new PoSW covering the full computation. We add this property to our formalism of GL-PoSWs and SNACKs. We observe that using an incremental GL-PoSW to construct a SNACK system on top of a blockchain whose underlying chain graph is simple (i.e., corresponds to a path) leads to an incremental SNACK. To date, the only existing construction of an incremental GL-PoSW [DLM19] is defined for a uniform challenge distribution, while our applications of SNACKs require different distributions. We leave it as an exciting open problem to construct incremental GL-PoSW for arbitrary weight functions.

This approach could allow for constructing *light miners* in the sense of [KLZ21] without having to assume a sub-1/3-adversary—a clear improvement over [KLZ21]. Pursuing this idea is outside of our current scope and we leave it to future work.

Further Notes on Related Work. The superblock-based approach to light clients [KMZ20,KLZ21] draws inspiration from the interactive protocol of

[KLS16], and has led to an exciting line of follow-up work [KKZ19,KPZ20, DKKZ20].

FlyClient [BKLZ20] is closely related to our generic SNACK construction when instantiated with the PoSW from [CP18]; we conjecture that FlyClient satisfies the guarantees of a SNACK, and discuss the relationship further in Sect. 6. It employs an elegant technique (variable-difficulty Merkle mountain ranges) to cope with the variable-difficulty setting. This is a strong indication that our generic design can also be tweaked to handle variable difficulty. We leave this as an interesting open problem, remarking that the possibility of using general weight functions could prove useful here. However, FlyClient does not support incremental proofs (and hence cannot be used for light mining).

While our concrete constructions do not outperform FlyClient efficiency-wise, we put some of the intuitions of FlyClient on more solid formal footing, generalize their construction, and propose extensions (such as incrementality). In particular, we formalize the concept and the security of light-client protocols, which we believe is lacking in FlyClient, as well as the concept of a commitment to the chain serving as anchor of trust for verifiers. While FlyClient leaves some room for interpretation (particularly relevant for the void commitment attack), we clearly specify our protocol and give a rigorous security analysis.

Regarding SNARK-based constructions, the light-client protocol Plumo [VGS+21] is designed for the BFT-based consensus of the Celo blockchain. While it achieves impressive concrete succinctness among SNARK-based proposals, it is still best suited for incremental proofs and requires heavier cryptographic tools, most importantly, a trusted setup. Mina (formerly Coda) [BMRS20] employs SNARKs for a significantly more ambitious goal of providing a constant-size blockchain.

2   Notation and Basic Definitions

General. We let $\mathbb{N}$ denote the set $\{1, 2, \ldots\}$ and set $\mathbb{N}_0 := \mathbb{N} \cup \{0\}$. For integers i, j such that $i \leq j$, we let $[i : j] := \{i, i+1, \ldots, j\}$, $[n] := [1 : n]$, and $[n]_0 := [0 : n]$. We let ε denote the empty string; for strings a and b we denote their concatenation by $a\|b$. For a distribution $\mathcal{D}$, we denote by $d \xleftarrow{\$} \mathcal{D}$ sampling d according to $\mathcal{D}$ (for a set $\mathcal{D}$, the uniform distribution is implied).

DAGs and Chain Graphs. For a directed acyclic graph (DAG) $G = (V, E)$ on $n + 1$ vertices, we always number its vertices $V = [n]_0$ in topological order and often write G_n to make this explicit. For $v \in [n]_0$, we denote the parent vertices of v in G by $\mathrm{parents}_G(v)$, and their number (i.e., the indegree of v) by $\deg_G(v)$; thus, $\mathrm{parents}_G(v) = (v_1, \ldots, v_{\deg_G(v)})$. We also let $\deg(G) := \max_{v \in V}\{\deg_G(v)\}$. We drop the subscript G when G is clear from the context. For convenience , we assume that the tuple $\mathrm{parents}(v)$ is given in reverse topological order.

Let $(G_n = ([n]_0, E_n))_{n \geq 0}$ be a family of DAGs. We make the assumption that for each $n \geq 0$, G_n is obtained from G_{n+1} by removing the vertex $n + 1$ and its adjacent edges. We also assume that $\deg(G_n) \in \mathrm{polylog}(n)$.

Definition 1 (Chain graph). *Let* $G_n = ([n]_0, E_n)$ *be a DAG. We call* G_n *a chain graph if* $E_n \supseteq \{(i-1, i) : i \in [n]\}$. *A chain graph* $G_n = ([n]_0, E_n)$ *is called simple if* $E_n = \{(i-1, i) : i \in [n]\}$, *i.e., it forms a path.*

Graph Labeling and Weighted DAGs. The following notion of weighted DAGs will be convenient when we define proof of sequential work (PoSW) schemes with arbitrary, not just uniform, sampling distributions.

Definition 2 (Weighted DAGs). *We call* $\Gamma_n = (G_n, \Omega_n)$ *a weighted DAG if* $G_n = ([n]_0, E_n)$ *is a DAG and* $\Omega_n : [n]_0 \to [0,1]$ *is a function such that* $\Omega_n([n]_0) = 1$, *where for* $S \subseteq [n]_0$ *we let* $\Omega_n(S) = \sum_{s \in S} \Omega_n(s)$.

In this work, we leverage the fact that the validity of (the headers of) a blockchain can be checked "locally", e.g., in Bitcoin, assuming fixed difficulty, (the header of) the i-th block h_i is valid if it contains the hash of the previous block h_{i-1} and a valid proof of work. We represent these dependencies by a chain graph which contains an edge $i \to j$ if block h_i is required to check the validity of h_j (in fixed-difficulty Bitcoin the graph is thus a simple chain graph).

Validity is captured by a relation R_ψ, where ψ is the genesis block of the blockchain, and h_i is valid if $R_\psi(i, h_i, (h_{\iota_1}, \ldots, h_{\iota_q})) = 1$, where $h_{\iota_1}, \ldots, h_{\iota_q}$ are h_i's parent blocks. We emphasize that we consider "SPV" or "header" validity, which is the standard desideratum for blockchains adopted by light clients, and in particular does not verify the validity of contained transactions.

Definition 3 (Labeled DAGs and blockchain validity). *Let* $G_n = ([n]_0, E_n)$ *be a DAG. A (graph) labeling of* G_n *is a mapping* $L : [n]_0 \to \{0,1\}^*$. *(This naturally extends to labelings of subgraphs of* G_n.) *A (block-)chain is a labeled chain graph.[2] For a polynomial-time (PT) relation* R_ψ, *a blockchain* (G_n, L) *with genesis block* $L(0) = \psi$ *is* R_ψ*-valid if for all* $i \in [n]$: $R_\psi\big(i, L(i), (L(j))_{j \in \text{parents}_G(i)}\big) = 1$.

We define the notion of *oracle-based* graph labelings, which will later be used by graph-labeling proof of sequential work (GL-PoSW) schemes, where the prover computes the labels of a given graph, sends a commitment to them to the verifier and is then challenged to open some of them. An oracle-based labeling of a graph G defines the labels of the sources of G as the oracle evaluation on the empty string; the label of any other vertex is defined as the evaluation on the labels of the parents of the vertex. In our applications to blockchains the vertices are the blocks and their labels represent blockchain data. We therefore consider an "augmented" definition allowing to include arbitrary data in the labels.

Definition 4 (Oracle-based graph labeling). *Let* $G_n = ([n]_0, E_n)$ *be a DAG and* $\tau = (\tau_i)_{i \in [n]_0}$ *be a tuple of oracles, with each* $\tau_i : \{0,1\}^* \to \{0,1\}^\lambda$. *For any* $X = (x_0, \ldots, x_n) \in (\{0,1\}^*)^{n+1}$ *the* X-*augmented* τ-*labeling* $L^\tau : [n]_0 \to \{0,1\}^*$ *of* G_n *is recursively defined as*

---

[2] We use the words *chain* and *blockchain* as synonyms throughout the paper.

$$L^\tau(i) := \begin{cases} \tau_i(\varepsilon) \| x_i & \text{if parents}(i) = \emptyset, \\ \tau_i\big(L^\tau(\text{parents}(i))\big) \| x_i & \text{otherwise,} \end{cases} \tag{1}$$

where $L^\tau(\text{parents}(i)) := L^\tau(i_1) \| \cdots \| L^\tau(i_k)$ for $(i_1, \dots, i_k) := \text{parents}(i)$. If $X = (\varepsilon, \dots, \varepsilon)$, we call L^τ the τ-labeling of G_n.

Vector Commitment (VC) Schemes. A VC scheme Com lets one commitment to message vectors m and give short openings for (subsets of) components of m. It has four algorithms: The parameters cp are computed via setup; a vector is committed to via $(\phi, \text{aux}) \leftarrow \text{commit}(cp, (m_1, \dots, m_n))$, which returns a commitment ϕ and aux. To give an opening ρ of ϕ to m_i at position i, run $\text{open}(cp, \phi, \text{aux}, m_i, i)$. The opening is verified by running $\text{ver}(cp, \phi, m_i, i, \rho)$, which returns a bit. (We generalize this to opening a set I of indices via $\text{ver}(cp, \phi, (m_i)_{i \in I}, I, \rho)$.) The scheme must be *position-binding*, meaning no adversary can compute a commitment ϕ and two openings ρ, ρ' for $m_i \neq m_i'$ that both verify at position i. (See the full version [AFGK22] for a formal definition.)

3   Defining SNACKs

In this section we introduce our main primitive of a *succinct non-interactive argument of chain knowledge (SNACK)*. Intuitively, it is an argument system for an NP language $\mathcal{L}_{\Gamma, R, \text{Com}}$ that is parameterized by a family of weighted DAGs $\Gamma = (\Gamma_n)_{n \geq 0}$ with $\Gamma_n = (G_n = ([n]_0, E_n), \Omega_n)$, a polynomial-time relation $R \subseteq \mathbb{N}_0 \times (\{0, 1\}^*)^2$, and a vector commitment scheme Com.

An element $(\phi, n) \in \mathcal{L}_{\Gamma, R, \text{Com}}$ consists of a Com commitment ϕ to a labeling of G_n that is *valid* as defined by R, which checks every label w.r.t. the labels of its parents (Definition 3). Looking ahead, R will serve two purposes: in GL-PoSW schemes, R checks the validity of an oracle-based graph labeling, and in our SNACK systems for *augmented* blockchains, whose vertex labels include a GL-PoSW label, R additionally verifies blockchain validity.

A SNACK proof for a statement (ϕ, n) proves knowledge of an R-valid labeling of Γ_n as well as an opening of ϕ to this labeling. This is formalized by requiring that from a prover computing a valid proof such a labeling and an opening can be *extracted*. To enable more efficient schemes, we only require extraction of labels that lie on a path P that has a certain weight, as measured by Ω_n. We call SNACK system α-*knowledge-sound*[3], if it guarantees that from a valid proof for (ϕ, n) a labeled path of weight at least $\alpha \in (0, 1]$ can be extracted, Setting $\alpha = 1$ recovers standard knowledge soundness.

Analogously to SNARKs, we require succinctness of SNACKs, that is, proofs are of size poly-logarithmic in n and efficient to generate and verify.

Valid Paths in a Weighted DAG. To make the above formal, we need to adapt the definition of a valid labeling of a graph G to paths P in G. In a path,

---

[3] This is akin to f-extractability [BCKL08] of proof systems, which relaxes knowledge soundness by only requiring extraction of a partial witness (or a function thereof).

a vertex might have a parent in G that is not part of P, still the relation R expects a label for it. We therefore define a valid path as containing, for every $v \in P$, a "witness" p_v, which is the set of purported parent labels, which must be accepted by R. We require p_v to be in accord with the labeling of P, that is, if a parent u of v lies on P then p_v must contain the label of u.

Definition 5 (Valid paths). *Let $G_n = ([n]_0, E_n)$ be a DAG, and $R \subseteq \mathbb{N}_0 \times (\{0,1\}^*)^2$ a relation. Furthermore, let P be a path in G_n, L_P a labeling of P, and $(p_v)_{v \in P} \in (\{0,1\}^*)^{|P|}$ a $|P|$-tuple of bitstrings with $p_v = (p_v[1], \ldots, p_v[\deg(v)])$. We say that $(P, L_P, (p_v)_{v \in P})$ is an R-valid path in G_n if for all $v \in P$ with $(v_1, \ldots, v_{\deg(v)}) := \mathrm{parents}(v)$, we have*

$$R(v, L_P(v), p_v) = 1 \ and \ \forall i \in [\deg(v)] \ if \ v_i \in P \ then \ p_v[i] = L_P(v_i) . \quad (2)$$

For a weighted DAG $\Gamma_n = (G_n = ([n]_0, E_n), \Omega_n)$, we say that $(P, L_P, (p_v)_{v \in P})$ is (α, R)-valid in Γ_n if in addition $\Omega_n(P) \geq \alpha$.

For blockchains we typically require $0 \in P$, so R_ψ verifies the genesis block.

Chain Commitment Languages. We formally define the language $\mathcal{L}_{\Gamma,R,\mathsf{Com}}$ for a SNACK proof system, where a statement $\eta = (\phi, n)$ consists of a Com commitment ϕ to an R-valid labeling of the graph G_n. The labeling together with an opening of ϕ constitutes a witness w for η. We parameterize the language (akin languages parameterized by a group [GS08]), where parameters *prm* are generated (formally by an algorithm G) during a setup phase. This allows us to capture SNACKs with instantiations of Com for which (position-)binding only holds under honestly generated parameters *cp*; it also allows us to include the salt χ defining a random oracle τ for τ-labelings in PoSW schemes, and to include the genesis block ψ of a blockchain, both of which are assumed to have been generated independently of the adversary. (Below these are subsumed into parameters σ on which the relation R can depend.)

Formally, $\mathcal{L}_{\Gamma,R,\mathsf{Com}}$ is defined via a parameter-dependent ternary polynomial-time (PT) relation $\mathcal{R}$ over tuples (prm, η, w) as the statements η for which there exists a witness such that $\mathcal{R}(prm, \eta, w) = 1$. For standard NP relations, $prm = \varepsilon$.

Definition 6 (Chain commitment language). *Let $\Gamma = (\Gamma_n)_{n \geq 0}$ be a family of weighted DAGs and Com a vector commitment scheme. We define*

$$\mathcal{R}_{\Gamma,R,\mathsf{Com}}^{(\alpha)} := \left\{ \begin{array}{l} (prm = (\sigma, cp), \eta = (\phi, n), \\ w = (P, L_P, (p_v)_{v \in P}, \rho)) \end{array} : \begin{array}{l} (P, L_P, (p_v)_{v \in P}) \ is \ (\alpha, R)\text{-}valid \\ \wedge \ \mathsf{Com.ver}(cp, \phi, L_P, P, \rho) = 1 \end{array} \right\} \quad (3)$$

where $R \subseteq \mathbb{N}_0 \times (\{0,1\}^*)^2$ is a PT relation that depends on σ. We let $\mathcal{R}_{\Gamma,R,\mathsf{Com}} := \mathcal{R}_{\Gamma,R,\mathsf{Com}}^{(1)}$ and $\mathcal{L}_{\Gamma,R,\mathsf{Com}}$ denote the language defined by $\mathcal{R}_{\Gamma,R,\mathsf{Com}}$.

We now define the SNACK system which is the central primitive we are interested in. The generality of the SNACK definition stems from leaving the specification of both the underlying relation R and Com open.

Definition 7 (SNACK). *A tuple of PPT algorithms* (P, V) *is a succinct non-interactive argument of chain knowledge (SNACK) for the language* $\mathcal{L}_{\Gamma,R,\mathsf{Com}}$ *with parameter generator* G *from Definition 6 if the following properties hold:*

Completeness: *For all* $\lambda \in \mathbb{N}$, $\mathrm{prm} \leftarrow \mathsf{G}(1^\lambda)$, $\eta, w \in \{0,1\}^*$ *with* $(\mathrm{prm}, \eta, w) \in \mathcal{R}_{\Gamma,R,\mathsf{Com}}$: $\Pr\left[\pi \leftarrow \mathsf{P}(\mathrm{prm}, \eta, w) : \mathsf{V}(\mathrm{prm}, \eta, \pi) = 1\right] = 1$.

(α, ϵ)**-Knowledge soundness:** *For every PPT prover* $\tilde{\mathsf{P}}$ *there exists a PPT extractor* E *such that*

$$\Pr\left[\begin{array}{l} \mathrm{prm} \leftarrow \mathsf{G}(1^\lambda); r \xleftarrow{\$} \{0,1\}^{\mathrm{poly}(\lambda)} \\ (\eta, \pi) := \tilde{\mathsf{P}}(\mathrm{prm}; r); \\ w' \leftarrow \mathsf{E}(\mathrm{prm}, r) \end{array} : \begin{array}{l} \mathsf{V}(\mathrm{prm}, \eta, \pi) = 1 \,\wedge \\ \mathcal{R}^{(\alpha)}_{\Gamma,R,\mathsf{Com}}(\mathrm{prm}, \eta, w') = 0 \end{array}\right] \le \epsilon(\lambda) \ , \tag{4}$$

with $\mathcal{R}^{(\alpha)}_{\Gamma,R,\mathsf{Com}}$ *from* (3). *We say that* (P, V) *has universal* (α, ϵ)*-knowledge soundness if there exists a single extractor* $\mathsf{E}^{\tilde{\mathsf{P}}}$ *with oracle access to* $\tilde{\mathsf{P}}$ *that satisfies* (4) *for all PPT provers* $\tilde{\mathsf{P}}$.

Succinctness: *For all* $\mathrm{prm} \leftarrow \mathsf{G}(1^\lambda)$, $(\mathrm{prm}, \eta, w) \in \mathcal{R}_{\Gamma,R,\mathsf{Com}}$ *and* $\pi \leftarrow \mathsf{P}(n, t$ $\eta, w)$, *we have* $|\pi| \le \mathrm{poly}(\lambda, \log n)$, P *runs in time* $\mathrm{poly}(\lambda, n)$, *and* V *runs in time* $\mathrm{poly}(\lambda, \log n)$.

We remark that the SNACKs we construct in Sect. 5 have universal extractors in the random oracle model. Note that we could have first defined an (interactive) *argument of chain knowledge (ACK)* without requiring succinctness. A SNACK (as required for our applications) then is any succinct non-interactive ACK.

4   Graph-Labeling Proofs of Sequential Work

Intuitively, proofs of sequential work (PoSW) are proof systems in which a prover, upon receiving a statement χ and a parameter n, convinces a verifier that n sequential computational steps have passed since χ was received. We define *augmented graph-labeling* PoSWs, a special class of PoSWs that covers all recent and efficient constructions [MMV13, CP18, AKK+19, DLM19]. Our definition does however not cover the number-theoretic constructions of *verifiable delay functions* [BBBF18, Pie19, Wes19], which are PoSWs in which statements have unique proofs. This is not required for our applications; moreover, known constructions are far less efficient than graph-labeling (GL) PoSWs.

4.1   Defining Graph-Labeling PoSW

All random-oracle-aided PoSW constructions [MMV13, CP18, AKK+19, DLM19] follow the same blueprint; they are defined and constructed interactively and then turned non-interactive using the Fiat-Shamir transformation [FS87].[4] A graph-labeling PoSW scheme is parameterized by a family of weighted DAGs

---

[4] The PoSW of [DLM19] is defined and constructed non-interactively by employing an on-the-fly sampling technique.

$\Gamma = (\Gamma_n)_{n \in \mathbb{N}}$. Let $\Gamma_n = (G_n = ([n]_0, E_n), \Omega_n)$ be a DAG from this family with weight distribution $\Omega_n \colon [n]_0 \to [0,1]$ with $\Omega([n]_0) = 1$. The prover P, upon receiving a statement χ from the verifier V, uses χ to instantiate a sequence of oracles $\tau = (\tau_i)_{i \in [n]_0}$. In all constructions except [AKK+19], τ_i is defined by salting a random oracle $\mathcal{O}$ as $\tau_i(\cdot) := \mathcal{O}(\chi, i, \cdot)$; the construction from [AKK+19] uses χ to sample random permutations. Next, P computes a τ-labeling L (Definition 4) of Γ_n and produces a commitment ϕ_L to L using a vector commitment scheme. Finally, P and V run an interactive protocol in which V essentially checks that the responses of P to a challenge set $S \subset [n]_0$ sampled according to Ω_n are in accord with ϕ. See Fig. 2 for the syntax to formally define PoSW in Definition 9.

Our definition of graph-labeling PoSW generalizes existing definitions in several ways, which are particularly useful for constructing SNACKs from PoSWs: First, while previous work only considered challenges sampled uniformly at random, we allow for arbitrary sampling distributions Ω_n. Second, we extend the security guarantees of PoSW by requiring *knowledge* soundness, which will be necessary when constructing SNACKs from PoSW. Existing PoSW schemes implicitly satisfy a form of knowledge soundness, and we make this explicit. Finally, we allow the prover to embed *arbitrary* additional data, as augmentation, into the computation. While this doesn't seem useful for classical applications of PoSW, it will be a crucial property for our later application to SNACKs.

In defining graph-labeling PoSW, we require proofs to be short and verification to be fast, as for SNARK systems. Unlike general-purpose SNARKs however, we require practically efficient provers and no setup assumptions.

Towards generalizing PoSW to arbitrary weight functions, we define the weight of a sequence of parallel oracle queries to $\tau = (\tau_i)_{i \in [n]_0}$. A parallel query is a set of simultaneous queries to oracles τ_i, i.e. a tuple $((x_1, i_1), \ldots, (x_m, i_m))$ which is answered by $(\tau_{i_1}(x_1), \ldots, \tau_{i_m}(x_m))$. The weight of a sequence of parallel queries is the sum of the respective "heaviest" nodes in each parallel query.

Definition 8 (Sequential weight). *Let $Q = (Q_1, \ldots, Q_\ell)$ be a sequence of parallel queries to an oracle $\tau = (\tau_i)_{i \in [n]_0}$. We define the* sequential weight *of Q with respect to a weight function $\Omega_n \colon [n]_0 \to [0,1]$ as*

$$\Omega_{seq}(Q) := \sum_{i=1}^{\ell} \max\{\Omega_n(j) : Q_i \text{ contains a query to } \tau_j\} \ .$$

Note that if Ω_n is uniform, i.e., $\forall i \in [n]_0 : \Omega_n(i) = \frac{1}{n+1}$, then $\Omega_{seq}(Q) = \frac{\ell}{n+1}$.

We write $(out_A, out_B) \leftarrow \langle A(in_A) \leftrightarrow B(in_B) \rangle$ to denote an execution of interactive algorithms A, taking input in_A and outputting out_A, and B, taking input in_B and outputting out_B. We write $A(in_A; r)$ to make A's randomness explicit. We now define augmented graph-labeling PoSW.

Definition 9 (Augmented GL-PoSW). *Let $\Gamma = (\Gamma_n = (G_n, \Omega_n))_{n \in \mathbb{N}}$ be a family of weighted DAGs such that for all n, G_n has a unique sink n. A pair of PPT algorithms $(P := (P_0, P_1), V := (V_0, V_1, V_2))$, with access to an oracle $\tau = (\tau_i)_{i \in \mathbb{N}_0}$ is an augmented (oracle-based) graph-labeling proof of sequential* work (GL-PoSW) *if it instantiates the template described in Fig. 2 by specifying a vector commitment scheme* Com = (setup, commit, open, ver) *and the subroutines* PoSW.label, PoSW.open *and* PoSW.ver; *and it satisfies the following properties:*

Completeness: *For all* $n, \lambda \in \mathbb{N}$ *it holds that*

$$\Pr\left[(out_P, out_V) \leftarrow \langle P(1^n) \leftrightarrow V(1^\lambda, n)\rangle : out_V = 1\right] = 1 \ .$$

(α, ϵ)-**Soundness:** *For all* $\lambda \in \mathbb{N}$ *and every PPT adversary* $(\tilde{P}', \tilde{P} = (\tilde{P}_0, \tilde{P}_1))$ *s.t.* $\tilde{P}$ *makes a sequence* Q *of parallel queries to* $\tau = (\tau_j(\cdot))_{j \in [n]_0}$ *of sequential weight* $\Omega_{seq}(Q) < \alpha$, *it holds that*

$$\Pr\left[\begin{array}{cc} (n, st) \leftarrow \tilde{P}'(1^\lambda) & \\ (out_{\tilde{P}}, out_V) \leftarrow \langle \tilde{P}(st) \leftrightarrow V(1^\lambda, n)\rangle & : \ out_V = 1 \end{array}\right] \leq \epsilon(\lambda) \ .$$

Succinctness: *The size of the transcript* $|\langle P(1^n) \leftrightarrow V(1^\lambda, n)\rangle|$ *as a function of* λ *and* n *is upper-bounded by* $\mathrm{poly}(\lambda, \log n)$. *The running time of* P *is* $\mathrm{poly}(\lambda, n)$ *and that of* V *is* $\mathrm{poly}(\lambda, \log n)$.

We say that (P, V) *is* (α, ϵ)-*knowledge-sound we additionally have:*

(α, ϵ)-**Knowledge soundness:** *There exists a PPT extractor* E *such that for every PPT adversary* $(\tilde{P}', \tilde{P} = (\tilde{P}_0, \tilde{P}_1))$ *we have*

$$\Pr\left[\begin{array}{cc} r \xleftarrow{\$} \{0,1\}^{\mathrm{poly}(\lambda)}; \ (n, st) := \tilde{P}'(1^\lambda; r) & out_V = 1 \ \wedge \\ (out_{\tilde{P}}, out_V) \leftarrow \langle \tilde{P}(st; r) \leftrightarrow V(1^\lambda, n)\rangle & : \ \mathcal{R}_{\Gamma, R, \mathsf{Com}}^{(\alpha)}\left(prm, (out_{\tilde{P}_0}, n),\right. \\ w' \leftarrow E^{\tilde{P}}(1^\lambda, r) & w') = 0 \end{array}\right] \leq \epsilon(\lambda),$$

where prm *is as sampled by* V_0, $out_{\tilde{P}_0}$ *is the output* ϕ_L *of* $\tilde{P}_0$ *and relation* $\mathcal{R}_{\Gamma, R, \mathsf{Com}}^{(\alpha)}$ *is as in* (3) *with* $R := R_\chi$ *defined as*

$$R(i, L(i), p_i) = 1 \quad iff \quad L(i) = \tau_i(p_i) \| x_i \ for \ some \ x_i \in \{0,1\}^* \ . \tag{5}$$

In the full version [AFGK22] we prove that every knowledge-sound GL-PoSW is indeed a sound PoSW.

Theorem 1. *Every* (α, ϵ)-*knowledge-sound graph-labeling PoSW is* (α, ϵ')-*sound (cf. Definition 9) with* $\epsilon' := \epsilon + (q^2 + 1)/2^\lambda$, *where* q *is an upper bound on the number of the adversary's oracle queries.*

The following lemma now directly follows from the respective definitions.

Lemma 1. *Let* (P, V) *be an (interactive)* (α, ϵ)-*knowledge-sound graph-labeling PoSW based on a family of weighted DAGs* Γ *and a commitment scheme* Com. *Then applying the Fiat-Shamir transformation [FS87] to* (P, V) *results in a SNACK system for the language* $\mathcal{L}_{\Gamma, R, \mathsf{Com}}$, *when* R *is defined as in* (5).

Verifier V = (V_0, V_1, V_2):
Stage V_0: On input $(1^\lambda, n)$:

1. $\chi \xleftarrow{\$} \{0,1\}^\lambda$
2. $cp \leftarrow$ Com.setup(1^λ)
3. **send** $prm := (\chi, cp)$ **to** P_0

Stage V_1: On input ϕ_L:

1. $\forall i \in [t]$ **do** $\iota_i \xleftarrow{\$} \Omega_n$
2. **send** $\iota = (\iota_i)_{i=1}^t$ **to** P_1

Stage V_2: On input $(\gamma_i = (o_i, \rho_i))_{i=1}^t$:

1. $\forall i \in [t]$ **do**
   (a) $b_i^{(1)} :=$ PoSW.ver(χ, ι_i, o_i)
   (b) $b_i^{(2)} :=$ Com.ver$(cp, \phi_L, L(\iota_i), \iota_i, \rho_i)$
2. **output** $\bigwedge_{i=1}^t (b_i^{(1)} \wedge b_i^{(2)})$

Prover P = (P_0, P_1) :
Stage P_0: On input 1^n and $prm := (\chi, cp)$:

1. $L :=$ PoSW.label$(\chi, 1^n)$
   Use χ to sample oracles $\tau := (\tau_i(\cdot))_{i \in [n]_0}$
   and compute a (possibly augmented) τ-labeling L of G_n satisfying Def. 4.
2. $(\phi_L, \text{aux}) \leftarrow$ Com.commit(cp, L)
3. **send** ϕ_L **to** V_1

Stage P_1: On input $\iota = (\iota_i)_{i=1}^t$:

1. $\forall i \in [t]$ **do**
   (a) $o_i \leftarrow$ PoSW.open$(\chi, cp, \phi_L, \text{aux}, L, \iota_i)$
   We assume that o_i contains $L(\iota_i)$
   (b) $\rho_i \leftarrow$ Com.open$(cp, \phi_L, \text{aux}, L(\iota_i), \iota_i)$
   (c) $\gamma_i := (o_i, \rho_i)$
2. **send** $(\gamma_1, \ldots, \gamma_t)$ **to** V_2

Fig. 2. The template of a GL-PoSW, parametrized by $(\Gamma_n)_{n \in \mathbb{N}}$, a VC scheme Com and the number of challenges t. Note that explicitly requiring P_1 to compute ρ_i doesn't prevent P_1 from opening the commitment also at other indices as part of PoSW.open.

All the constructions of graph-labeling PoSWs we consider here use the following very simple commitment scheme for the graph labeling L: The prover commits to the labels of a graph which were derived through a graph-labeling computation (cf. Definition 4). While the verifier could simply recompute the labels to check consistency of a label $L(i)$, for certain graph structures the following scheme will allow for much more efficient verification. Intuitively, the idea is to check consistency of the labels of a randomly sampled subgraph.

To formalize consistency of labels in this context, we need the following definition of consistent strings, which is stronger than prior definitions in the literature [MMV13, CP18, AKK+19]. We associate to each vertex i a value $y_i := p_i \| x_i$, where p_i represents the (augmented) labels of the *parents* of i and x_i some potential augmentation of i. In order to also reason about the label of the last node, we introduce a dummy child, that is, we add vertex $n+1$ and an edge $(n, n+1)$.

Definition 10 (Consistent strings). *Let $\tau = (\tau_i)_{i \in [n]_0}$ be a tuple of oracles, with $\tau_i : \{0,1\}^* \to \{0,1\}^\lambda$. For a DAG $G_n = ([n]_0, E_n)$, let $G_n^+ = ([n+1]_0, E_n^+)$ with $E_n^+ = E_n \cup \{(n, n+1)\}$. Furthermore, $\forall i \in [n+1]_0$ let $\deg(i)$ be the number of parents of i in G_n^+ and $y_i := p_i \| x_i \in \{0,1\}^*$ where $p_i := p_i[1] \| \ldots \| p_i[\deg(i)]$. We say y_i is* consistent *with $y_{i'}$ w.r.t. G_n , and denote it by $y_i \prec y_{i'}$ if $(i, i') \in E_n^+$ and if i is the j-th parent of i' in G_n^+ (in reverse topological order), then the j-th block in the decomposition of $y_{i'}$ is equal to $\tau_i(p_i) \| x_i$, i.e., $p_{i'}[j] = \tau_i(p_i) \| x_i$.*

Below we give a specific vector commitment scheme called SPC, which will also be used in our constructions of graph-labeling PoSW.

Construction 1 (Shortest Path Commitment). *Let* $G = (G_n = ([n]_0, E_n))_{n \in \mathbb{N}}$ *be a DAG family such that for all* n, G_n *has a unique sink* n, *and let* $\tau := (\tau_i)_{i \in \mathbb{N}_0}$ *be a tuple of oracles with* $\tau_i : \{0,1\}^* \to \{0,1\}^\lambda$. *We construct a* τ-*based vector commitment* $\mathsf{SPC} = (\mathsf{setup}, \mathsf{commit}, \mathsf{open}, \mathsf{ver})$ *for universe* $\mathcal{U} = \{0,1\}^*$ *and message space* $\mathcal{M} = (\mathcal{M}_n)_{n \in \mathbb{N}}$ *where* $\mathcal{M}_n \subseteq \mathcal{U}^n$ *consists of the labels of nodes* $[n-1]_0$ *of all valid* X-*augmented* τ-*labelings of* G_n *using* $L := L^\tau$ *as per Definition 4.*

- $cp \leftarrow \mathsf{setup}(1^\lambda)$: *On input* 1^λ, *output empty public parameters* $cp := \varepsilon$.
- $(\phi_L, \mathrm{aux}) \leftarrow \mathsf{commit}(cp, L)$: *On input* $L \in \mathcal{M}^n$, *output the commitment* $\phi_L := \tau_n(L(\mathrm{parents}(n)))$ *(i.e. the first part of the label* $L(n)$*) and auxiliary information* $\mathrm{aux} := L$.
- $\rho \leftarrow \mathsf{open}(cp, \phi_L, \mathrm{aux}, L(i), i)$: *Let* $\mathrm{path}(i) \subseteq G_n$ *be the first shortest path from* i *to* n *in* G_n *with respect to the lexicographical ordering.[5] For all nodes* j *in* $\mathrm{path}(i)$ *output the labels of all parents of* j, *i.e.,* $\rho := \big(L(\mathrm{parents}(j)), x_j\big)_{j \in \mathrm{path}(i)}$.
- $\mathsf{ver}(cp, \phi_L, L(i), i, \rho) \in \{0,1\}$: *For* $\mathrm{path}(i) = (i_0, \ldots, i_l = n)$ *parse* $\rho = (\rho_{i_0}, \ldots, \rho_{i_l})$ *and* ρ_{i_j} *as* (p_{i_j}, x_{i_j}), *and check for all* $j \in [l]$ *whether* $\rho_{i_{j-1}} \prec \rho_{i_j}$ *according to Definition 10; output 1 iff all these checks pass and* $\tau_n(p_{i_l}) = \phi_L$.

4.2 Constructing Graph-Labeling PoSWs

In this section we construct a GL-PoSW scheme, which can be seen as a variant of the skiplist-based PoSW construction [AKK+19], where for efficiency reasons we replace random permutations by a hash function modeled as a random oracle. In the full version [AFGK22] we give a new knowledge-sound GL-PoSW scheme, which is an adaptation of the scheme from [CP18].

For simplicity of exposition, we consider the PoSW construction with empty augmentation. The augmented counterpart appears in the SNACK construction in Sect. 5, where the blockchain data is the augmentation data.

A Graph-Labeling PoSW Based on Skiplists. To define the PoSW construction we specify the unspecified parts in the blueprint in Fig. 2, namely a weighted DAG family $(G_n, \Omega_n)_{n \in \mathbb{N}}$ and algorithms $\mathsf{PoSW.label}, \mathsf{PoSW.open}, \mathsf{PoSW.ver}, \mathsf{Com}$.

Construction 2. *Let* $G_n = ([n]_0, E_n)$ *be a DAG with edge set*

$$E_n = \big\{(i,j) \in [n]_0^2 : \exists k \geq 0 \text{ s.t. } (j-i) = 2^k \wedge 2^k | i\big\}$$

(cf. Fig. 3). Let $\Omega_n : [n]_0 \to [0,1]$ *be an arbitrary weight function, and let* $\mathcal{H} : \{0,1\}^* \to \{0,1\}^\lambda$ *be a hash function which we model as a random oracle.*

- $L := \mathsf{PoSW.label}(\chi)$: *Sample oracles* $\tau_i(\cdot) := \mathcal{H}(\chi, i, \cdot)$ *and output an augmented* τ-*based labeling* $L := L^\tau$ *of* G_n *as per Definition 4.*

---

[5] Note that such a path exists since G_n has a unique sink.

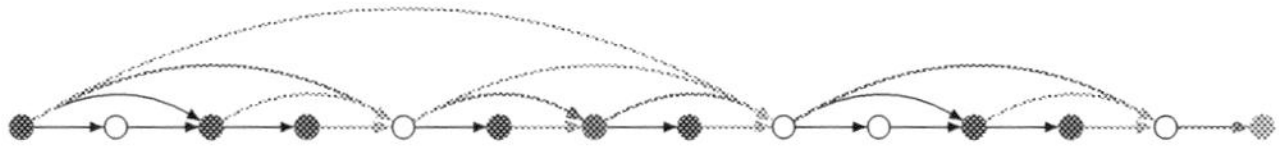

Fig. 3. Illustration of Construction 2. The label of the last node (green) serves as the commitment. On input a challenge (red node), P opens all the nodes (blue) that are required to verify the shortest path (red edges) from source to sink which passes through the challenge node. To verify, V evaulates the opening (red and orange edges). (Color figure online)

- Com *is defined by* SPC *(Construction 1). Hence* $(\phi_L, \text{aux}) \leftarrow$ SPC.commit (cp, L) *where* $cp := \varepsilon$ *is empty.*
- $o_i \leftarrow$ PoSW.open$(\chi, cp, \phi_L, \text{aux}, L, \iota_i)$: *For each challenge* ι_i, *send the labels of all parents of the (unique) shortest path from 0 to* ι_i *in* G_n: *Let* $\text{path}'(\iota_i)$ *denote the shortest path in* G *which starts at 0 , ends at n and goes through* ι_i . *For each node in* $\text{path}'(\iota_i)$ *output the labels of all its parents, i.e.* $o_i := \big(L(\text{parents}(j))\big)_{j \in \text{path}'(\iota_i)}.$
- $b_i^{(1)} \leftarrow$ PoSW.ver(χ, ι_i, o_i): *Check the consistency of* $\text{path}'(\iota_i)$: *For* $\text{path}'(\iota_i) = (i_0 = 0, \dots, i_l = n)$ *parse* $o_i = (\nu_{i_0}, \dots, \nu_{i_l})$ *and check for all* $i, j \in [l]$ *with* $(i, j) \in E_n$ *whether* $\nu_i \prec \nu_j$ *according to Definition 10; output 1 iff all checks pass.*

We remark that we could optimize PoSW.open and PoSW.ver in Construction 2 by removing the redundant output/checks that are already done by Com.open and Com.ver, but for readability's sake, we keep the current exposition.

In the full version [AFGK22] we prove that Construction 2 is a knowledge-sound GL-PoSW as per Definition 9 for arbitrary weight function Ω_n. The proof closely resembles that of [AKK+19] by replacing the random permutations by random oracles and additionally taking into account non-uniform weights.

Theorem 2. *Let* $\alpha \in (0, 1]$. *The scheme from Construction 2 with parameter t and arbitrary* Ω_n *is an* (α, ϵ)-*knowledge-sound augmented GL-PoSW with* $\epsilon := \alpha^t + 3 \cdot q^2/2^\lambda$, *where q is an upper bound on the adversary's oracle queries.*

5   Constructing SNACKs from GL-PoSWs

We now show how to augment any blockchain with the computation of any (knowledge-sound) GL-PoSW scheme. This will then allow us to build a SNACK system for an augmented chain commitment language $\mathcal{L}_{\Gamma, R_\sigma, \text{Com}}$, where R_σ is a PT relation that checks the validity of blocks in the (augmented) blockchain, whose genesis block is σ, as well as the consistency of the infused PoSW-related data. An accepting proof for a statement (ϕ, n) convinces a verifier that the prover *knows* a certain number of blocks (committed to by ϕ), in an augmented blockchain of length n with genesis block σ, and furthermore these blocks are (1) valid and (2) mined sequentially.

Augmented Blockchains. We augment an existing blockchain by intertwining the computation of the PoSW and the mining of the blockchain. More concretely, let $\Gamma_n = (G_n = ([n]_0, E_G), \Omega_n)$ be the underlying weighted DAG of a graph-labeling PoSW scheme (PoSW.P, PoSW.V) adhering to Fig. 2 with $\Omega_n : [n]_0 \rightarrow [0, 1]$ s.t. $\Omega_n([n]_0) = 1$. We furthermore assume that G_n is a chain graph as per Definition 1. Recall that the PoSW computation mainly involves computing labels of vertices by using an oracle $\tau := (\tau_i(\cdot))_{i \in [n]_0}$.

Now consider a blockchain with underlying chain graph $H_n = ([n]_0, E_H)$ and associated validity relation R_ψ. Recall (Definition 3) that a blockchain with genesis block $h_0 := \psi$ and a PT relation R_ψ is valid if and only if for every vertex $i \in [n]$, its label h_i, and its parents' labels $h_{i_1}, \ldots, h_{i_p}$, it holds

$$R_\psi(i, h_i, (h_{i_1}, \ldots, h_{i_p})) = 1 \ . \tag{6}$$

For example, in fixed-difficulty Bitcoin, the i-th block h_i has a single parent h_{i-1} and R_ψ checks whether h_i contains a valid proof of work w.r.t. h_i and h_{i-1}.

We combine the respective chain graphs G_n and H_n underlying the PoSW scheme and the blockchain to an *augmented* chain graph K_n (see Fig. 1):

$$K_n := ([n]_0, E_K) \quad \text{with} \quad E_K := E_G \cup E_H \ . \tag{7}$$

We obtain an *augmented blockchain* by labeling the chain graph K_n using algorithms Init and Mine, as formalized in Fig. 4. In particular, from an initial genesis block ψ, we define in Init, an augmented genesis block $\sigma := L_K(0)$ which contains, in addition to ψ, PoSW-related data such as χ and cp. For a vertex $i \in [n]$, algorithm Mine computes $L_K(i)$ by alternating in computing PoSW labels ℓ_i and blockchain-specific labels h_i. The computation of ℓ_i is defined as for the underlying PoSW scheme, except that the extra incoming edges inherited from the graph H_n are considered in the computation of ℓ_i. Additionally, the label ℓ_i is extended to $g_i := (\ell_i, \phi_i)$ by a commitment ϕ_i to all labels $((g_j, h_j))_{j \in [i-1]_0} \| \ell_i$. The label h_i is computed the way miners in the original blockchain protocol generate blocks. Finally, the augmented label of the ith vertex is defined as $L_K(i) := k_i = (g_i, h_i)$.

In Line 4, Mine computes a proof π_i for the block, which is inherited from the underlying blockchain, for which a block $h_i := (i, d_i, \pi_i)$ was valid if $R_\psi(i, h_i, L_H(\text{parents}_H(i))) = 1$. For example, in Bitcoin, π_i is a PoW, computed based on (i, d_i) as well as the L_H-label (i.e., the corresponding block) of the single H-parent vertex in Bitcoin's chain graph H_n. In the augmented blockchain, we augment the validity relation R_ψ and define $\tilde{R}_\psi$ which still considers the same graph structure H but takes *augmented* labels as input; hence (6) becomes:

$$\tilde{R}_\psi(i, L_K(i), L_K(\text{parents}_H(i))) = 1 \ . \tag{8}$$

For example, for the augmented Bitcoin, the PoW π_i is now computed based on (i, d_i, g_i) as well as the single parent block $L_K(\text{parents}_H(i))$.

This overriding allows us to include PoSW labels g_i into the relation and make blockchain-specific labels h_i, or in particular the proofs π_i they contain,

Algorithm Init:	Algorithm Mine:
On input 1^λ and ψ:[10]	On input $((k_j := (g_j, h_j))_{j \in [i-1]_0}, d_i)$:
1. $\chi \xleftarrow{\$} \{0,1\}^\lambda$	1. $\ell_i := \tau_i(L_K(\text{parents}_K(i)))$
2. $\ell_0 := \tau_0(\varepsilon)$	2. $(\phi_i, \text{aux}_i) \leftarrow \text{Com.commit}(cp, (k_j)_{j \in [i-1]_0} \| \ell_i)$
3. $cp \leftarrow \text{Com.setup}(1^\lambda)$	3. $g_i := (\ell_i, \phi_i)$
4. $(\phi_0, \text{aux}_0) \leftarrow \text{Com.commit}(cp, \ell_0)$	4. Compute π_i s.t.
5. $g_0 := (\ell_0, \phi_0)$	$\quad \tilde{R}_\psi\big(i, (g_i, h_i := (i, d_i, \pi_i)), \ L_K(\text{parents}_H(i))\big) = 1$
6. $h_0 := (0, d_0 := \psi \| \chi \| cp, \pi_0 := \varepsilon)$	5. $\textbf{return } (L_K(i) := k_i := (g_i, h_i), \text{aux}_i)$
7. $\textbf{return } (\sigma := L_K(0) := k_0 := (g_0, h_0), \text{aux}_0)$	

Fig. 4. The mining algorithm Mine for augmented blockchains.

depend on the PoSW labels g_i's in a way that allows us to translate the PoSW sequentiality guarantees on g_i's to h_i's, or in particular π_i's. We elaborate more on the sequentiality guarantees towards the end of this section.

As the ith augmented block contains both blockchain-specific data h_i and PoSW-specific data g_i, we define an augmented validity relation that checks the validity of (a) the blockchain-specific data using $\tilde{R}_\psi$ and (b) the PoSW data as defined in (5), more concretely we define

$$R_\sigma(i, L_K(i), L_K(\text{parents}_K(i))) = 1 \Leftrightarrow \tag{9}$$
$$\tilde{R}_\psi(i, L_K(i), L_K(\text{parents}_H(i))) = 1 \ \wedge \ \exists x_i \text{ s.t. } L_K(i) = \tau_i(L_K(\text{parents}_K(i))) \| x_i \ .$$

In order to verify that $L_K(0)$ indeed contains the blockchain genesis block ψ on which R_σ depends, we include 0 in the sequence of challenges ι.

Arguments of Knowledge for Augmented Blockchains. We construct a SNACK system $\Pi = (\text{SNACK.P}, \text{SNACK.V})$ for the language $\mathcal{L}_{\Gamma, R_\sigma, \text{Com}}$ as in Definition 6 with R_σ being as in (9). In our construction, the parameter generator G would simply output $prm := \sigma$ that defines R_σ.

As a first step in constructing a SNACK for $\mathcal{L}_{\Gamma, R_\sigma, \text{Com}}$, we construct a succinct *interactive* argument system of chain knowledge (ACK) (P, V) for the language $\mathcal{L}_{\Gamma, R_\sigma, \text{Com}}$, which is formally depicted in Fig. 6. The idea is to use the challenge/response phase of the underlying PoSW scheme, still with respect to the family $(G_n, \Omega_n)_{n \in \mathbb{N}}$, but with respect to the labeling L_K. Recall that in a PoSW scheme $(\text{PoSW.P}, \text{PoSW.V})$, the verifier PoSW.V runs Com.ver and PoSW.ver, where the latter operates w.r.t. the graph structure of G. However, in our augmentation, we added edges from H to this graph (resulting in K), which is why we extend PoSW.ver to PoSW.ver$_K$ to take this into account. Analogously, we define PoSW.open$_K$. Both algorithms are given in Fig. 5 and are used as subroutines in Fig. 6. Similarly, if Com.ver is defined w.r.t. some graph structure (e.g. shortest path in case of SPC or Merkle commitment), then this graph structure stays unchanged, but we require augmented labels and potentially also additional labels of H-parents (of the path).

Algorithm PoSW.ver$_K$:

On input (χ, ι_i, o_i):

1. Run $b_i := \mathsf{PoSW.ver}(\chi, \iota_i, o_i)$ modified as follows: whenever it queries $\tau_j(L_K(\mathrm{parents}_G(j)))$ for some j, issue query $\tau_j(L_K(\mathrm{parents}_K(j)))$ instead.
   (Missing labels are provided in $o_i^{(2)}$.)

2. **return** b_i

Algorithm PoSW.open$_K$:

On input $(\chi, cp, \phi_n, \mathsf{aux}_n, L_K, \iota_i)$:

1. $o_i^{(1)} \leftarrow \mathsf{PoSW.open}(\chi, cp, \phi_n, \mathsf{aux}_n, L_K, \iota_i)$
   (PoSW.open acts based on edges E_G.)

2. $\mathcal{J} := \{ j \in [n]_0 : L_K(\mathrm{parents}_G(j))$ appear in $o_i^{(1)} \}$

3. $o_i^{(2)} := \{ (j, L_K(\mathrm{parents}_H(j))) \}_{j \in \mathcal{J}}$

4. **return** $o_i := (o_i^{(1)}, o_i^{(2)})$

Fig. 5. PoSW.open$_K$ and PoSW.ver$_K$ defined based on PoSW.open and PoSW.ver.

Remark 1 (On cp, ϕ_i and aux_i). *All known GL-PoSW (see Sect. 4), including ours use the* SPC *commitment from Construction 1 with* $cp = \varepsilon$. *Moreover, if* $(\mathsf{PoSW.P}, \mathsf{PoSW.V})$ *is instantiated with say Construction 2, then* $cp = \varepsilon, \phi_i = \ell_i$ *and* $\mathsf{aux}_i = \varepsilon$. *This means that the only additional data stored in each block of the blockchain due to our augmentation is a label* ℓ_i .

In the following theorem we show that the Fiat-Shamir transform of this argument system is a SNACK system. As the underlying PoSW schemes support arbitrary weight functions Ω_n, so does our SNACK system.

Theorem 3. *Let* $(\mathsf{SNACK.P}, \mathsf{SNACK.V})$ *be the non-interactive version of* $(\mathsf{ACK.P}, \mathsf{ACK.V})$ *from Fig. 6, then in the random oracle model,* $(\mathsf{SNACK.P}, \mathsf{SNACK.V})$ *is an* (α, ϵ)-*knowledge-sound SNACK for* $\mathcal{L}_{\Gamma, R_\sigma, \mathsf{Com}}$, *as in Definition 6 and* R_σ *as in* (9), *if* $(\mathsf{PoSW.P}, \mathsf{PoSW.V})$ *is an* (α, ϵ)-*knowledge-sound* τ-*based graph-labeling PoSW as in Definition 9 with* Com *being its underlying commitment scheme,* $(G_n = ([n]_0, E_G), \Omega_n)_{n \in \mathbb{N}}$ *its weighted graph family, and* τ *modeled as a random oracle.*

Verifier ACK.V = $(\mathsf{V}_1, \mathsf{V}_2)$

Stage V_1: On input η:

1. $\forall i \in [t]$ **do** $\iota_i \xleftarrow{\$} \Omega_n$
2. $\iota_0 := 0$
3. **send** $\iota := (\iota_i)_{i=0}^t$ to P

Stage V_2: On input $\gamma = (o_i, \rho_i)_{i=0}^t$:

1. $\forall i \in [t]_0$ **do:**
   (a) $b_i^{(1)} := \mathsf{PoSW.ver}_K(\chi, \iota_i, o_i)$
   (b) $b_i^{(2)} := R_\sigma(\iota_i, L_K(\iota_i), p_i)$
   (c) $b_i^{(3)} := \mathsf{Com.ver}(cp, \phi, L_K(\iota_i), \iota_i, \rho_i)$
2. **output** $\bigwedge_{i=0}^t b_i^{(1)} \wedge b_i^{(2)} \wedge b_i^{(3)}$

Prover ACK.P:

On input $(\eta, (L_K(j))_{j \in [n]_0}, \mathsf{aux}_n)$ and ι:

1. **parse** η as $\eta = (cp, \phi, n)$
2. $\forall i \in [t]_0$ **do:**
   (a) $o_i \leftarrow \mathsf{PoSW.open}_K(\chi, cp, \phi, \mathsf{aux}_n, (L_K(j))_{j \in [n]_0}, \iota_i)$
   We assume o_i contains $L_K(\iota_i)$ and $p_i := L_K(\mathrm{parents}_K(\iota_i))$
   (b) $\rho_i \leftarrow \mathsf{Com.open}(cp, \phi, \mathsf{aux}_n, L_K(\iota_i), \iota_i)$
   (c) $\gamma_i := (o_i, \rho_i)$
3. **send** $\gamma := (\gamma_i)_{i=0}^t$ to V_2

Fig. 6. The interactive proof system ACK which underlies our SNACK construction.

To prove the theorem, we use $\Pi := (\mathsf{ACK.P}, \mathsf{ACK.V})$ and Alg. Mine (Fig. 4) to build an augmented PoSW whose knowledge-soundness implies that of the SNACK. We obtain a (non-interactive) $(\mathsf{SNACK.P}, \mathsf{SNACK.V})$ by applying the Fiat-Shamir transform [FS87] to Π. The proof is in the full version [AFGK22].

Sequentiality of π_i's. By (α, ϵ)-knowledge soundness of $(\mathsf{SNACK.P}, \mathsf{SNACK.V})$ from Theorem 3, with probability at least $1 - \epsilon$, we can extract from any prover $\tilde{\mathsf{P}}$ that convinces SNACK.V of the validity of (ϕ, n), an (α, R)-valid path $(P, L_P, (p_v)_{v \in P})$ in Γ_n and an opening ρ of L_P w.r.t. ϕ. For concreteness, let $L_P = (k_{i_j} = (g_{i_j}, h_{i_j}))_{j \in [m]}$. By sequentiality of the underlying $(\mathsf{PoSW.P}, \mathsf{PoSW.V})$, it follows that $(g_{i_j})_{j \in [m]}$ was computed sequentially. However, for the corresponding proofs $(\pi_{i_j})_{j \in [m]}$ in $(h_{i_j})_{j \in [m]}$, it was not explicitly required by Mine (see Fig. 4) that π_{i_j} is computed *after* its corresponding, and sequentially computed, g_{i_j}. Therefore, in principle, all of these $(\pi_{i_j})_{j \in [m]}$ could have been computed in parallel by $\tilde{\mathsf{P}}$ *before* $\tilde{\mathsf{P}}$ started the sequential computation of $(g_{i_j})_{j \in [m]}$. This shows that while a SNACK system guarantees sequentiality on the augmented graph K_n via the sequentiality on G_n, this sequentiality does not necessarily translate to sequentiality on H_n, and guaranteeing sequentiality on H_n is what most applications of a SNACK system rely on (see Sect. 6).

This issue is however easy to resolve in any blockchain: To ensure that the proofs $(\pi_{i_j})_{j \in [m]}$ in $(h_{i_j})_{j \in [m]}$ were computed sequentially, it suffices for the blockchain mining protocol Mine to ensure the following:

Assumption: For all $j \in [n]$ it holds that π_j must have been computed after g_j.

Then the sequentiality of $(\pi_{i_j})_{j \in [m]}$ directly follows from the sequentiality of $(g_{i_j})_{j \in [m]}$: now that π_{i_j} is computed after g_{i_j}, one could think of this as an edge from g_{i_j} to π_{i_j}, and as g_{i_j} is computed after $k_{i_{j-1}} = (g_{i_{j-1}}, h_{i_{j-1}})$, a path that goes through $(g_{i_1}, \ldots, g_{i_m})$ translates to a path that goes through $(g_{i_1}, \pi_{i_1}, \ldots, g_{i_m}, \pi_{i_m})$, hence ensuring sequentiality of the proofs.

The above assumption is trivially satisfied by any blockchain which has immutability as one of its defining properties: a block in the chain cannot be modified without modifying all subsequent blocks. For example, in Bitcoin, where $h_j = (j, d_j, \pi_j)$, as assumed in Mine, contains a valid PoW π_j with respect to d_j where d_j is implicitly assumed to contain the hash of the previous block. Simply including g_j in d_j ensures that π_j is computed after g_j.

6   Applications to Blockchain Light Clients

We now describe how SNACKs can be applied in the design of light-client blockchain protocols. Informally speaking, the goal of such protocols is to allow a light client, who only knows the genesis block, to *bootstrap* by obtaining a commitment to a chain that is, except for some unreliable suffix, matching the chains being held by honest full nodes. Others can then prove statements about the honest chain w.r.t. this commitment, and the light client does not need to trust the provers. The commitment thus serves as an anchor of trust.

We start by defining some vocabulary that allows us to make this intuition precise. We consider a long-term execution of a blockchain ledger protocol Π by a set of parties called *full nodes*. At a particular time t, we call a party *honest* if it is uncorrupted by the adversary (and hence follows Π), it is online and fully synchronized with the state of the protocol Π.[6] A chain is called *honest* at time t if it is held by some honest party executing the full protocol, i.e., a full node. We call an honest chain *maximal* if it has maximal length among all honest chains. Note that several different maximal chains might exist for any t, but they share the same length which we call the *honest length* at time t. We call an honest party *synchronized* at time t if it is holding a maximal chain.

General Assumptions. The κ-*common-prefix* property [GKL15, PSs17] mandates that any two chains C_1, C_2 that are honest at times $t_1 \leq t_2$ satisfy $C_1^{\lceil \kappa} \preceq C_2$, where $(\cdot)^{\lceil \kappa}$ denotes removing the last κ blocks of a chain and $\preceq$ is the prefix relation. (This property has become a standard requirement for Nakamoto-style blockchain protocols: together with *chain growth* and *chain quality*, it implies consistency and liveness of the produced ledger [GKL15, PSs17].) It has been shown to be achieved, except with an error negligible in κ, by Nakamoto-style protocols across various Sybil-protection mechanisms: proof of work [GKL15, PSs17, BMTZ17], proof of stake [KRDO17, DPS19, DGKR18, BGK+18], and proof of space [CP19]. We will assume that the considered blockchain protocol Π satisfies κ-common prefix for some κ so that the probability of this assumption being violated is acceptably small. We refrain from mentioning this error explicitly in our statements to maintain readability.

We assume that the execution of the protocol Π results in a family of chain graphs $\{K_n = ([n]_0, E_n)\}_{n \geq 0}$, meaning that at any point in the execution of Π, any blockchain with n blocks produced by Π has its chain-graph structure determined by K_n (cf. Definition 1). (Thus the chain-graph structure is independent of the data contained in the blocks.) Recall that for every $n \geq 0$, K_n is assumed to be obtained from K_{n+1} by removing vertex $n + 1$ and adjacent edges.

Forking Adversaries. In our analysis we need to assume some limitation on an adversary's ability to create an alternative chain that "forks away" from any currently honest chain at some significant depth and achieve (at least) the honest length, even if it contains some fraction of invalid blocks. This type of assumption was first described in [BKLZ20], who explicitly allow the adversary to include (a limited fraction of) *invalid* blocks in its fork. Below we discuss how we formalize the spirit of their assumption for our setting in Definition 11, while overcoming some shortcomings of the original formulation.

First, in their context of a PoW chain, an invalid block may contain an incorrect proof of work, but every block must still contain a correct hash of its predecessor. (If this was not required, the assumption would be false, as the adversary could simply glue parts of the honest blockchain together.) We capture validity of blocks by an abstract relation R, without assuming anything about

---

[6] Such honest parties are called *alert* in [PS17, BGK+18]; we will not maintain this distinction and will always assume honest parties to be alert.

"invalid" blocks. As we consider blockchains whose underlying graph structure is an arbitrary (rather than simple) chain graph, we employ the notion of R-valid paths as per Definition 5 to formally define forks. Our assumption requires that an adversary that creates a (valid) path that forks away from the honest blockchain sufficiently deep (as specified by a parameter ℓ) can only include in its path a c-fraction of blocks after the forking point. Note that in a typical PoW blockchain, any such adversary could also create the blocks not lying on its path by ignoring the PoW but including a correct hash; this would then also violate the assumption in [BKLZ20]. From this perspective, our assumption is *weaker* than that of [BKLZ20], as the adversary has to achieve a c-fraction of valid blocks *along a path*, but it is *stronger* in that the adversary need not produce blocks (with valid hashes) outside of its path.

Furthermore, the original assumption [BKLZ20] does not consider adversaries that create a fork (potentially containing invalid blocks) whose length exceeds the honest length n_h. As we show, such adversaries can be used to break light-client protocols in the sense of the precise security definition (Definition 12) we give. Our assumption will thus also contain a limit on the adversary's power of *extending* chains. Intuitively, this does not make the assumption stronger, since if the last block of the adversary's fork is at position $n^* > n_h$, then the adversary's task is harder, as it needs to include more blocks in its path so a c-fraction of its (now longer) fork is valid. A definitional subtlety arises when $n^* \geq n_h + \ell - \kappa$, meaning that a fork of length ℓ could start beyond the stable prefix of the honest chains, which ends at $s_h := n_h - \kappa$. If the adversary's chain agrees with the honest prefix, then "forking from the honest chains" is not well-defined, as honest chains can differ after s_h. In this case we consider the forking point f to be the adversary's last block before s_h. (This is captured by Case (2) in Definition 11 below.)

One might wonder if forking from an honest chain at some point $f' > s_h$ could give the adversary an advantage, as the c-fraction is now measured between $f < f'$ and n^*. However, a similar situation could also arise before s_h, in which case it is subject to Case (1) in Definition 11 (which corresponds to the original assumption [BKLZ20]): there might be an (honest) orphaned fork of length $\kappa' \leq \kappa$ (these are not excluded by κ-common-prefix) forking at $n_h - \ell$ and the adversary can try to extend it. To achieve a c-fraction in $[n_h - \ell + 1 : n_h]$, the adversary thus needs to mine $c\ell - \kappa'$ blocks while the honest miners only mine $\ell - \kappa'$ blocks. Arguably, a Case (2) fork is harder to compute: consider an adversary that extends an instable honest chain after $s_h + \kappa'$. Then to achieve a c-fraction of blocks in $[s_h + 1, n_h + \ell - \kappa]$ (the optimal choices of forking point f in Definition 11 and n^*), the adversary has to mine $c\ell - \kappa'$ while the honest miners only mine $\kappa - \kappa'$ blocks (thus in less time than in the Case (1) example before).

Definition 11 ($((c, \ell)$-forks and (c, ℓ, ϵ_F)-adversaries). *Let Π be a blockchain protocol with validity relation R and chain graph $(K_n)_{n \geq 0}$, satisfying κ-common prefix. Let $c \in (0, 1]$, $\ell \in \mathbb{N}$ with $\ell > \kappa$. Fix some time t in the execution of Π*

and let n_h be the honest length at time t and $L_h \colon [s_h]_0 \to \{0,1\}^*$ be the labeling of the honest stable prefix, with $s_h := n_h - \kappa$.

- An ℓ-fork is an R-valid (Definition 5) path $\big(P = (i_0 = 0, \ldots, i_q = n^*), L, (p_v)_{v \in P}\big)$ in K_{n^*}, such that $n^* \geq n_h$ and either
  (1) for some $j \in [q] \colon i_j \leq s_h$ and $n^* \geq i_j + \ell - 1$, and we have:
  $$L(i_{j-1}) = L_h(i_{j-1}) \text{ and } L(i_j) \neq L_h(i_j).$$
  (2) or $n^* \geq s_h + \ell$ and for all $i_j \leq s_h \colon L(i_j) = L_h(i_j)$.
- A (c, ℓ)-fork is an ℓ-fork $(P, L_P, (p_v)_{v \in P})$ for which P contains at least a c-fraction of the blocks after the forking point f, i.e.,

$$\big|P \cap [f + 1 : n^*]\big| \geq c \cdot (n^* - f) \;,$$

where $f := i_{j-1}$ in Case (1) and $f := \max\{i_j : i_j \leq s_h\}$ in Case (2).
- A (c, ℓ, ϵ_F)-adversary against Π is an adversary whose probability of producing a (c, ℓ)-fork at any point throughout the execution of Π is at most ϵ_F.

Observe that for $c = 1$, the adversary's goal collapses to an ℓ-common-prefix violation. For PoW, one can rely on existing bounds such as [GRR21]. For general c, the connection between the assumption of (c, ℓ, ϵ_F)-adversaries (or the original assumption in [BKLZ20]) and more basic blockchain assumptions remains open.

Our Results. The high-level idea of our protocols is that any blockchain commitment suggested by a prover for adoption by a light client needs to be accompanied by a SNACK proof parametrized in such a way that no (c, ℓ, ϵ_F)-adversary would be able to produce this SNACK for a chain that does not share the necessary common prefix with honest chains, as this would require the prover (by SNACK knowledge soundness) to construct a valid path that is beyond the capabilities of any such restricted adversary.

As a warm-up, in Sect. 6.1 we present a naive SNACK-based protocol for light-client bootstrapping in the multi-prover setting. The light client obtains (concise) information from several full nodes, and, informally speaking, if at least one of them is (honest and) synchronized then the light client will end up holding a commitment to a chain of honest length. (If *all* provers are malicious, the client might adopt a commitment to a chain arbitrarily violating the common-prefix property or the maximal-length requirement.) This is analogous to the guarantees provided by the FlyClient protocol [BKLZ20].

We also present a simple variant of our first protocol for settings where the light client can be assumed to know an approximation of the current honest length (e.g. derived from the time passed since the client's previous bootstrapping). This protocol provides meaningful guarantees even when run with a single (potentially malicious) prover.

We don't formally analyze these two protocols, as their security guarantees described informally above turn out to be insufficient for the most common practical setting. To illustrate this, in Sect. 6.2 we describe an attack against the bootstrapping approach taken by both our proposals as well as a naive use of previous work, the *void-commitment attack*. It consists of an adversary producing

---

On input tuples $(\phi_i, n_i, \pi_i)_{i \in [N]}$ the light client does the following:

1. For all tuples, ordered by decreasing values of n_i:
   (a) let α_i and Ω_i be as discussed in the text
   (b) check if π_i is a valid proof for the statement (ϕ_i, n_i) for an (α_i, ϵ)-knowledge-sound SNACK system for $\mathcal{L}_{\Gamma, R, \mathsf{Com}}$ with weight function Ω_i
   (c) if π_i verifies then stop and return $(\phi, n) := (\phi_i, n_i)$
2. Return $\bot$.

Fig. 7. Protocol 1: A Naive Light-Client Bootstrapping Protocol (informal).

a private chain almost identical to some maximal honest chain, and luring the light client into accepting a commitment to his chain. The obtained commitment is then useless in future interactions if the adversary keeps the opening secret.

Motivated by this attack, in Sect. 6.3 we first define *secure bootstrapping* (Definition 12): a light client is guaranteed to obtain a commitment to a *stable common prefix* of all honest chains, which can serve as an anchor of trust. Anyone holding an honest chain can then prove properties about its stable prefix to the light client. We then propose our final SNACK-based protocol (Fig. 9) and prove that it satisfies secure bootstrapping. We do so via a technical result (Theorem 4) that allows us to reason about the limitations of (c, ℓ, ϵ_F)-adversaries in creating forks with (α, R)-valid paths and hence producing valid SNACKs.

SNACK-Compatible Blockchains and Commitments. As our protocols rely on a SNACK system, we assume the blockchain in question admits such a system. GL-PoSW-augmented blockchains as presented in Sect. 5 are one example. We let K_n for $n \in \mathbb{N}$ denote the DAG (technically a *chain graph* as in Definition 1) of such a blockchain of length n and let R be the relation that defines validity of its blocks. (In the construction in Sect. 5 this corresponds to R_σ from Eq. (9).) We let Com be the commitment scheme for which the light client should obtain a commitment to the chain. Together, these define the language $\mathcal{L}_{\Gamma, R, \mathsf{Com}}$ for the SNACK system, where $\Gamma := (K_n, \Omega_n)_{n \geq 0}$ and Ω_n which we will define. In addition, we assume the following:

Assumption: Every block (header) of the blockchain contains a Com-commitment to all the previous blocks.

When considering the SPC commitment (Construction 1) in GL-PoSW-augmented blockchains, this assumption trivially holds: the commitment contained in a block is simply the τ-evaluation (the "hash") of the parent labels (blocks). The assumption is also true for "FlyClient-compatible" blockchains, whose block headers need to contain *Merkle mountain range commitments* [BKLZ20].

Further note that in our (and [BKLZ20]) approaches to light-client protocols the commitment provided by a prover cannot be independent of the blockchain: otherwise, a malicious prover could modify (and thereby invalidate) a single block in (the stable prefix of) an honest chain, commit to the altered chain and later prove properties of the modified block to any verifier holding the commitment. As this modified blockchain does *not* constitute a (c, ℓ)-fork (neither w.r.t. Definition 11 nor the original assumption [BKLZ20]), the light-client protocol cannot protect against it. (In particular, the adversary can still compute a SNACK by proving knowledge of a (heavy) path that does not go through the node.)

6.1 Naive Bootstrapping Protocols

In Protocol 1, the "naive" protocol, the light client receives from each of N full nodes a commitment ϕ_i to a purported blockchain of length n_i and a SNACK proof π_i for the statement (ϕ_i, n_i). It outputs (one of) the commitment(s) for the maximal value n that is accompanied by a valid SNACK proof (see Fig. 7).

The SNACK proofs are parametrized (via α_i and Ω_i) based on the proclaimed value of n_i so that they prove knowledge of a path which, assuming (c, ℓ, ϵ_F)-adversaries (Definition 11), must share the necessary common prefix with the honest blockchain. This can be quantified precisely, and we provide parameters for our final protocol in Theorem 4. The intuition behind the design of Protocol 1 is not flawed, and in fact, the same reasoning (expressed more concretely and implicitly using a specific SNACK) lies behind FlyClient. We omit the detailed treatment for Protocol 1 as its main purpose is to motivate the subsequent attack.

Protocol 1 does have some use cases, for example if the prover convincing the light client is the entity that later proves statements about the honest chain. Another application is obtaining an estimate of the honest length in the multiprover setting (by simply outputting the length n_i of the accepted tuple).

Assuming the light client knows the current honest length n_h, a simple variant of Protocol 1, presented in Fig. 8, can then be run with a *single prover*. It guarantees that either the client again obtains a commitment to an honest-length chain or she learns that the prover is malicious or lagging behind and hence should not be trusted. In fact, also imprecise estimates of n_h (such as those obtained from Protocol 1) can be leveraged in a similar way.

6.2 The Void-Commitment Attack

The following attack applies to Protocols 1 and 2, as well as a naive use of the FlyClient protocol. We stress that the attack does not contradict security claims in previous work (or the informal argument given in Sect. 6.1), but rather highlights that despite these claims, protocols following the structure described in Sect. 6.1 fall short of solving a class of important practical use cases.

The attack works as follows: an adversary A first obtains from an honest full node some maximal honest chain; let h be (the header of) its terminating block. A then mines a new block h' on top of h, which it will however keep secret. It then participates as prover in one of the mentioned protocols following its specification, but using its chain terminating with h'. If A's commitment is adopted by the light client then the latter will hold a commitment to a chain to which only A knows an opening, which will be of no use for "bootstrapping" applications that would involve interactions with other full nodes.

Note that even if the protocol is run with honest full nodes only, the light client may still end up with a similarly unusable commitment if the prover's chain will eventually lose the "longest-chain race" and not become part of the prefix of future honest chains. This observation extends to the FlyClient protocol if used naively: if the light client only keeps the last block and the contained commitment as its output from the bootstrapping (rather than the full ℓ-suffix), further interactions with other full nodes would suffer from the above attack.

6.3 A Light-Client Protocol for Common-Prefix Commitment

We now show that, using SNACKs, the original intuitive goal can still be achieved: (a) obtain a commitment guaranteed to be to (a relevant part of) an honest-length chain; (b) anyone, not only the commitment provider, can use it to prove statements about the ledger state. While it would be desirable to guarantee a commitment to the stable prefix $[s_h]_0$ with $s_h = n_h - \kappa$ of the honest chain, this cannot be achieved when only making the assumption of (c, ℓ, ϵ_F)-adversaries: the latter only precludes forks of length ℓ, so a (c, ℓ, ϵ_F)-adversary could create a differing block at position $s_h + 1$. But then it could also insert a "malicious" commitment there (cf. our discussion before Sect. 6.1). In order to fix the commitment to the honest chain, we therefore place it at latest at position $n_h - \ell + 1$.

Definition 12 (Secure common-prefix bootstrapping). *For $\kappa, \ell \in \mathbb{N}$, let Π be a blockchain protocol satisfying κ-common prefix for $\kappa < \ell$ for which each block contains a commitment to its predecessors. Fix some time t and let n_h be the honest length at time t and $(h_0, \ldots, h_{s_h})$ be the (headers of the) stable prefix of the honest chain. A light client securely ℓ-common-prefix bootstraps (ℓ-CP bootstraps) at time t if for some $m \in [n_h - \ell : s_h - 1]$ it ends up holding the commitment ϕ to $(h_0, \ldots, h_m)$ contained in h_{m+1}.*

In Protocol 3 in Fig. 9, instead of committing to the entire chain, the full nodes commit to the (stable) prefix of the honest chain of length $n - \ell$, and use a SNACK to prove knowledge of a heavy chain contained in the commitment. Now to ensure that the commitment is actually to the stable prefix, we require the provers to show that they know an extension by ℓ blocks of what was committed.

On input the honest length n_h and a tuple (ϕ, n, π), if $n < n_h$, return $\bot$. Else:

1. let α_n and Ω_n be as discussed in the text;
2. if π is valid for (ϕ, n) for an (α_n, ϵ)-knowledge-sound SNACK system for $\mathcal{L}_{\Gamma, R, \mathsf{Com}}$ with weight function Ω_n then return ϕ;
3. else return $\bot$.

Fig. 8. Protocol 2: Single-Prover Bootstrapping with Length (informal).

Let Π be blockchain protocol with validity relation R, chain graph $(K_n)_{n \geq 0}$ and parameters prm. On input N tuples of the form $\left(\phi, n, \pi, (k_i)_{i=n-\ell+1}^n, (\iota_j, k_{\iota_j}, \rho_{\iota_j})_{j=1}^q\right)$ for some $q \leq \ell \cdot \deg(K_n)$, ordered by decreasing values of n, check for each tuple the following:

(a) Let $m := n - \ell$; check whether ϕ is contained in k_{m+1}

(b) $\mathsf{SNACK.V}\big(prm, (\phi, m), \pi\big) \overset{?}{=} 1$, where SNACK is (α_m, ϵ)-knowledge-sound for $\mathcal{L}_{(K_m, \Omega_m)_{m \geq 0}, R, \mathsf{Com}}$ with α_m and Ω_m as in Theorem 4

(c) For all $i \in [m+1 : n] : R(i, k_i, (k_j)_{j \in \mathrm{parents}(i)}) \overset{?}{=} 1$

(d) For all $j \in [1 : q] : \mathsf{Com.ver}(cp, \phi, k_{\iota_j}, \iota_j, \rho_{\iota_j}) \overset{?}{=} 1$

(e) If all checks verify, return (ϕ, n)

Return $\perp$

Fig. 9. Light-Client Protocol 3: Multi-Prover Bootstrapping Common Commitment

For simplicity, the provers simply send (the headers of) these blocks and give commitment openings to the blocks that are necessary to check their validity. (To further optimize we could only check samples from the last ℓ blocks.)

We next define appropriate values α_m, Ω_m for the SNACK scheme used in our light-client Protocol 3, which will guarantee secure ℓ-CP bootstrapping.

Theorem 4. *Let Π be a blockchain protocol with underlying graph $(K_n)_{n \geq 0}$ satisfying κ-common prefix. Let $c \in (0, 1]$ and $\ell \in \mathbb{N}$ with $\ell > \kappa$. For $m \in \mathbb{N}$ define α_m and $\Omega_m \colon [m]_0 \to [0, 1]$ as*

$$\alpha_m := 1 - \left(\log_c \left(\tfrac{\ell - 1}{m + \ell} \right) \right)^{-1}$$

$$\Omega_m(i) := S \cdot \frac{1}{m + \ell - i} \ \text{for } 0 \leq i \leq m \qquad \text{where } S := \left(\textstyle\sum_{j=0}^m \frac{1}{m + \ell - j} \right)^{-1}. \tag{10}$$

Then, except with probability at most ϵ_F, no (c, ℓ, ϵ_F)-adversary can create an ℓ-fork $(P, L_P, (p_v)_{v \in P})$ in K_{n^*} where P starts at 0 and ends at n^*, such that, with $m^* := n^* - \ell$:

- *P contains the last ℓ blocks, i.e., $[m^* + 1 : n^*] \subseteq P$, and*
- *P has weight at least α_{m^*} w.r.t. Ω_{m^*}, i.e., $\Omega_{m^*}(P \cap [m^*]_0) \geq \alpha_{m^*}$.*

We give a proof overview and defer the proof to the full version [AFGK22]. Let K_n be the blockchain graph and $m := n - \ell$. Initially, we keep α_m indeterminate and define a weight function Ω_m on K_m, which is inspired by the sampling distribution of the FlyClient protocol [BKLZ20]. We then give the adversary's optimal strategy, which, given the constraints on its resources, maximizes the weight of its chain. Finally, we set α_m large enough, so that the optimal (and thus every) chain produced by a (c, ℓ, ϵ_F)-adversary has weight less than α_m.

A (c, ℓ, ϵ_F)-adversary, whose goal is to produce an ℓ-fork at time t that contains all the last ℓ blocks, is limited to choosing a point f (see Definition 11), after which it forks from some existing chain, and some length $n^* \geq n_h$, where n_h denotes the honest length at time t, and deciding which blocks after f to include in its path. (We do not make any assumptions on the blockchain graph and assume any sequence of blocks is a path.) By assumption, after the forking point there can be at most $c(n^* - f)$ valid blocks.

We will use an increasing weight distribution Ω_m, that is, later blocks in K_m weigh more. So to maximize the weight of its path, the adversary must put all its blocks just preceding the last ℓ blocks. Specifically, we adopt the hyperbolically increasing function from [BKLZ20], which assigns to the i-th block weight proportional to $\frac{1}{m+\ell-i}$. For any forking point f, the weight of the $(1-c)$-fraction of the blocks after f (which the adversary must skip) is the same, so all forking points are "equally bad".

Theorem 4 now allows us to prove that Protocol 3 provides a light client for ℓ-CP bootstrapping secure against (c, ℓ, ϵ_F)-adversaries.

Corollary 1 (Security of Protocol 3). *Let $\kappa, \ell \in \mathbb{N}$ with $\ell > \kappa$ and let Π be a blockchain protocol with validity relation R and graph family $(K_n)_{n \geq 0}$ that satisfies κ-common prefix. Assume the honest length $n_h > \ell$ and consider a light client running Protocol 3 (Fig. 9) with N full nodes, at least one of which is (honest and) synchronized and all others are controlled by a (c, ℓ, ϵ_F)-adversary. Let (ϕ^*, n^*) be the output of the light client. For $m \geq 0$, let α_m and Ω_m be as in Theorem 4. If Com is ϵ_C-position-binding and SNACK an $(\alpha_{n^*-\ell}, \epsilon)$-knowledge-sound for language $\mathcal{L}_{\Gamma,R,\mathsf{Com}}$ where $\Gamma := (\Gamma_m = (K_m, \Omega_m))_{m \geq 0}$, then the client securely ℓ-CP-bootstraps except with probability $\epsilon + \epsilon_C + \epsilon_F$.*

We give a proof sketch and defer the formal proof to the full version. Assume a (c, ℓ, ϵ_F)-adversary that prevents the light client from bootstrapping and let (ϕ, n) be its output. We have $n \geq n_h$, the maximum honest length, since otherwise an honest miner would have convinced the light client.

By (α_m, ϵ)-knowledge soundness, for $m := n - \ell$, of the SNACK sent by the adversary, we can extract an R-valid path in K_m of weight at least α_m. We extend it by the sent blocks $k_{m+1}, \ldots, k_n$ to a path P in K_n, which satisfies the two requirements at the end of Theorem 4. Moreover, P is R-valid, since position-binding of Com guarantees that the sent parent labels $k_{\iota_1}, \ldots, k_{\iota_q}$ conform to those of the extracted path.

Let $s_h := n_h - \kappa$ denote the length of the honest stable prefix. Finally, P is an ℓ-fork, since either $n \geq s_h + \ell$ and it agrees with the stable prefix of the honest chain (fork of Type (2) in Definition 11), or it forks off earlier, at latest at $m + 1$ (since ϕ contained in block $m + 1$ must be different from the commitment contained in the honest prefix for the client not to bootstrap), meaning it is a fork of Type (1). By Theorem 4, no (c, ℓ, ϵ_F)-adversary can create such a fork, which proves Corollary 1.

In the full version [AFGK22], we show that when using the SNACK based on (our variant of) the PoSW from [CP18], Protocol 3 achieves virtually the same efficiency as FlyClient [BKLZ20].

Acknowledgements. The first two authors are supported by the Vienna Science and Technology Fund (WWTF) through project VRG18-002. The first author has also received funding in part from the European Research Council (ERC) under the European Union's Horizon 2020 research and innovation program under project PIC-OCRYPT (grant agreement No. 101001283), the Spanish Government under projects SCUM (ref. RTI2018-102043-B-I00), the Madrid Regional Government under project BLOQUES (ref. S2018/TCS-4339), and a research grant from Nomadic Labs and the Tezos Foundation. The last author is supported in part by ERC CoG grant 724307 and conducted part of this work at ISTA, funded by the ERC under the European Union's Horizon 2020 research and innovation programme (682815 - TOCNeT).

References

[AAC+17] Abusalah, H., Alwen, J., Cohen, B., Khilko, D., Pietrzak, K., Reyzin, L.: Beyond Hellman's time-memory trade-offs with applications to proofs of space. In: Takagi, T., Peyrin, T. (eds.) ASIACRYPT 2017. Part II, volume 10625 of LNCS, pp. 357–379. Springer, Heidelberg (2017). https://doi.org/10.1007/978-3-319-70697-9_13

[AFGK22] Abusalah, H., Fuchsbauer, G., Gaži, P., Klein, K.: SNACKs: Leveraging proofs of sequential work for blockchain light clients. Cryptology ePrint Archive, Report 2022/240 (2022). https://eprint.iacr.org/2022/240

[AKK+19] Abusalah, H., Kamath, C., Klein, K., Pietrzak, K., Walter, M.: Reversible proofs of sequential work. In: Ishai, Y., Rijmen, V. (eds.) EUROCRYPT 2019. Part II, volume 11477 of LNCS, pp. 277–291. Springer, Heidelberg (2019). https://doi.org/10.1007/978-3-030-17656-3_10

[BBBF18] Boneh, D., Bonneau, J., Bünz, B., Fisch, B.: Verifiable delay functions. In: Shacham, H., Boldyreva, A. (eds.) CRYPTO 2018. Part I, volume 10991 of LNCS, pp. 757–788. Springer, Heidelberg (2018). https://doi.org/10.1007/978-3-319-96884-1_25

[BCD+14] Back, A., et al.: Enabling Blockchain Innovations with Pegged Sidechains (2014). https://blockstream.com/sidechains.pdf. Accessed 16 Aug 2019

[BCKL08] Belenkiy, M., Chase, M., Kohlweiss, M., Lysyanskaya, A.: P-signatures and noninteractive anonymous credentials. In: Canetti, R. (ed.) TCC 2008. LNCS, vol. 4948, pp. 356–374. Springer, Heidelberg (2008). https://doi.org/10.1007/978-3-540-78524-8_20

[BGK+18] Badertscher, C., Gazi, P., Kiayias, A., Russell, A., Zikas, V.: Ouroboros genesis: composable proof-of-stake blockchains with dynamic availability. In: Lie, D., Mannan, M., Backes, M., Wang, X., (eds.), ACM CCS 2018, pp. 913–930. ACM Press (2018)

[BKLZ20] Bünz, B., Kiffer, L., Luu, L., Zamani, M.: FlyClient: super-light clients for cryptocurrencies. In: 2020 IEEE Symposium on Security and Privacy, pp. 928–946. IEEE (2020)

[BMRS20] Bonneau, J., Meckler, I., Rao, V., Shapiro, E.: Coda: decentralized cryptocurrency at scale. Cryptology ePrint Archive, Report 2020/352 (2020). https://eprint.iacr.org/2020/352

[BMTZ17] Badertscher, C., Maurer, U., Tschudi, D., Zikas, V.: Bitcoin as a transaction ledger: a composable treatment. In: Katz, J., Shacham, H. (eds.) CRYPTO 2017. Part I, volume 10401 of LNCS, pp. 324–356. Springer, Heidelberg (2017). https://doi.org/10.1007/978-3-319-63688-7_11

[CP18] Cohen, B., Pietrzak, K.: Simple proofs of sequential work. In: Nielsen, J.B., Rijmen, V. (eds.) EUROCRYPT 2018. LNCS, vol. 10821, pp. 451–467. Springer, Cham (2018). https://doi.org/10.1007/978-3-319-78375-8_15

[CP19] Cohen, B., Pietrzak, K.: The Chia Network blockchain (2019). https://www.chia.net/assets/ChiaGreenPaper.pdf

[DFKP15] Dziembowski, S., Faust, S., Kolmogorov, V., Pietrzak, K.: Proofs of space. In: Gennaro, R., Robshaw, M. (eds.) CRYPTO 2015. LNCS, vol. 9216, pp. 585–605. Springer, Heidelberg (2015). https://doi.org/10.1007/978-3-662-48000-7_29

[DGKR18] David, B., Gaži, P., Kiayias, A., Russell, A.: Ouroboros praos: an adaptively-secure, semi-synchronous proof-of-stake blockchain. In: Nielsen, J.B., Rijmen, V. (eds.) EUROCRYPT 2018. LNCS, vol. 10821, pp. 66–98. Springer, Cham (2018). https://doi.org/10.1007/978-3-319-78375-8_3

[DKKZ20] Daveas, S., Karantias, K., Kiayias, A., Zindros, D.: A gas-efficient superlight bitcoin client in solidity. Cryptology ePrint Archive, Report 2020/927 (2020). https://eprint.iacr.org/2020/927

[DLM19] Döttling, N., Lai, R.W.F., Malavolta, G.: Incremental proofs of sequential work. In: Ishai, Y., Rijmen, V. (eds.) EUROCRYPT 2019. LNCS, vol. 11477, pp. 292–323. Springer, Cham (2019). https://doi.org/10.1007/978-3-030-17656-3_11

[DPS19] Daian, P., Pass, R., Shi, E.: Snow white: robustly reconfigurable consensus and applications to provably secure proof of stake. In: Goldberg, I., Moore, T. (eds.) FC 2019. LNCS, vol. 11598, pp. 23–41. Springer, Heidelberg (2019). https://doi.org/10.1007/978-3-030-32101-7_2

[FS87] Fiat, A., Shamir, A.: How to prove yourself: practical solutions to identification and signature problems. In: Odlyzko, A.M. (ed.) CRYPTO'86. LNCS, vol. 263, pp. 186–194. Springer, Heidelberg (1987). https://doi.org/10.1007/3-540-47721-7_12

[GGPR13] Gennaro, R., Gentry, C., Parno, B., Raykova, M.: Quadratic span programs and succinct NIZKs without PCPs. In: Johansson, T., Nguyen, P.Q. (eds.) EUROCRYPT 2013. LNCS, vol. 7881, pp. 626–645. Springer, Heidelberg (2013). https://doi.org/10.1007/978-3-642-38348-9_37

[GKL15] Garay, J., Kiayias, A., Leonardos, N.: The bitcoin backbone protocol: analysis and applications. In: Oswald, E., Fischlin, M. (eds.) EUROCRYPT 2015. LNCS, vol. 9057, pp. 281–310. Springer, Heidelberg (2015). https://doi.org/10.1007/978-3-662-46803-6_10

[GKZ19] Gazi, P., Kiayias, A., Zindros, D.: Proof-of-stake sidechains. In: 2019 IEEE Symposium on Security and Privacy, pp. 139–156. IEEE (2019)

[GRR21] Gaži, P., Ren, L., Russell, A.: Practical settlement bounds for proof-of-work blockchains. Cryptology ePrint Archive, Report 2021/805 (2021). https://eprint.iacr.org/2021/805

[GS08] Groth, J., Sahai, A.: Efficient non-interactive proof systems for bilinear groups. In: Smart, N.P. (ed.) EUROCRYPT 2008. LNCS, vol. 4965, pp. 415–432. Springer, Heidelberg (2008). https://doi.org/10.1007/978-3-540-78967-3_24

[KKZ19] Karantias, K., Kiayias, A., Zindros, D.: Compact storage of superblocks for NIPoPoW applications. In: Pardalos, P., Kotsireas, I., Guo, Y., Knottenbelt, W. (eds.) Mathematical Research for Blockchain Economy. SPBE, pp. 77–91. Springer, Cham (2020). https://doi.org/10.1007/978-3-030-37110-4_6

[KLS16] Kiayias, A., Lamprou, N., Stouka, A.-P.: Proofs of proofs of work with sublinear complexity. In: Clark, J., Meiklejohn, S., Ryan, P.Y.A., Wallach, D., Brenner, M., Rohloff, K. (eds.) FC 2016. LNCS, vol. 9604, pp. 61–78. Springer, Heidelberg (2016). https://doi.org/10.1007/978-3-662-53357-4_5

[KLZ21] Kiayias, A., Leonardos, N., Zindros, D.: Mining in logarithmic space. In: Vigna, G., Shi, E., (eds.), ACM CCS 2021, pp. 3487–3501. ACM Press (2021)

[KMZ20] Kiayias, A., Miller, A., Zindros, D.: Non-interactive proofs of proof-of-work. In: Bonneau, J., Heninger, N. (eds.) FC 2020. LNCS, vol. 12059, pp. 505–522. Springer, Heidelberg (2020). https://doi.org/10.1007/978-3-030-51280-4_27

[KPZ20] Kiayias, A., Polydouri, A., Zindros, D.: The velvet path to superlight blockchain clients. Cryptology ePrint Archive, Report 2020/1122 (2020). https://eprint.iacr.org/2020/1122

[KRDO17] Kiayias, A., Russell, A., David, B., Oliynykov, R.: Ouroboros: a provably secure proof-of-stake blockchain protocol. In: Katz, J., Shacham, H. (eds.) CRYPTO 2017. Part I, volume 10401 of LNCS, pp. 357–388. Springer, Heidelberg (2017). https://doi.org/10.1007/978-3-319-63688-7_12

[KZ19] Kiayias, A., Zindros, D.: Proof-of-work sidechains. In: Bracciali, A., Clark, J., Pintore, F., Rønne, P.B., Sala, M. (eds.) FC 2019 Workshops. LNCS, vol. 11599, pp. 21–34. Springer, Heidelberg (2019). https://doi.org/10.1007/978-3-030-43725-1_3

[MMV13] Mahmoody, M., Moran, T., Vadhan, S.: Publicly verifiable proofs of sequential work. In: Robert, D., Kleinberg, J., editor, ITCS 2013, pp. 373–388. ACM (2013)

[Nak08] Nakamoto, S.: Bitcoin: A Peer-to-Peer Electronic Cash System (2008). https://bitcoin.org/bitcoin.pdf. Accessed 19 June 2018

[Pie19] Pietrzak, K.: Simple verifiable delay functions. In Blum, A., editor, ITCS 2019, vol. 124, pp. 60:1–60:15. LIPIcs (2019)

[PS17] Pass, R., Shi, E.: The sleepy model of consensus. In: Takagi, T., Peyrin, T. (eds.) ASIACRYPT 2017. Part II, volume 10625 of LNCS, pp. 380–409. Springer, Heidelberg (2017). https://doi.org/10.1007/978-3-319-70697-9_14

[PSs17] Pass, R., Seeman, L., Shelat, A.: Analysis of the blockchain protocol in asynchronous networks. In: Coron, J.-S., Nielsen, J.B. (eds.) EUROCRYPT 2017. LNCS, vol. 10211, pp. 643–673. Springer, Cham (2017). https://doi.org/10.1007/978-3-319-56614-6_22

[VGS+21] Vesely, P., et al.: Plumo: An ultralight blockchain client. Cryptology ePrint Archive, Report 2021/1361 (2021). https://eprint.iacr.org/2021/1361

[Wes19] Wesolowski, B.: Efficient verifiable delay functions. In: Ishai, Y., Rijmen, V. (eds.) EUROCRYPT 2019. Part III, volume 11478 of LNCS, pp. 379–407. Springer, Heidelberg (2019). https://doi.org/10.1007/978-3-030-17659-4_13

Author Index

Printed in the United States
by Baker & Taylor Publisher Services